ISBN: 0-538-01780-5

Library of Congress Catalog Card Number: 83-60939

2 3 4 5 6 K 7 6 5 4

Printed in the United States of America

REVARD PFEFFER
463-45-5275
1710 Logansport #306
560-1895

INTERMEDIATE ACCOUNT

Comprehensive Volume

Eighth Edition

Jay M. Smith, Jr., PhD, CPA
Professor of Accounting
School of Accountancy
Graduate School of Management
Brigham Young University

K. Fred Skousen, PhD, CPA
Director, School of Accountancy
Professor of Accounting
Graduate School of Management
Brigham Young University

A78

Published by
SOUTH-WESTERN PUBLISHING

CINCINNATI WEST CHICAGO, ILL. DALLAS PELHAM MANOR, N.Y.

PREFACE

The seventh edition of *Intermediate Accounting* was a significant revision of this widely accepted textbook. The response to the changes from both accounting educators and students has been very positive. Our objective of making this text the most teachable intermediate text on the market is still foremost in our minds in the revisions and refinements incorporated in the eighth edition. No major organizational changes were considered necessary to the many changes in the last edition. The 25 chapters are divided into 5 logically related parts. Each chapter contains four types of end-of-chapter materials: questions, discussion cases, exercises, and problems. A brief description of the content precedes each discussion case, exercise, and problem. Sufficient material is included for each chapter to permit varying assignments from class to class.

Since the publication of the seventh edition, the FASB has issued several new accounting standards. With few exceptions, these standards have dealt with specialized industry accounting issues. Because we have decided to be selective in our treatment of financial accounting topics, very few of these specialized areas are included in this edition. The few standards that have affected the text coverage have been interspersed throughout the text with the same conciseness and clarity used in previous editions. Appendix C provides a listing of all APB and FASB pronouncements to mid-1983 and the chapter references where the standard is discussed.

In addition to the issued standards, the FASB has been wrestling with many difficult conceptual and implementation issues that are still in various stages of investigation. These include the conceptual issues of revenue and expense recognition, current value and constant dollar information and its usefulness, pension reporting, income tax allocation, and reporting cash flows. We have added to this edition material related to these current study areas to provide students with an awareness of the complex issues still on the FASB agenda. These are long-term projects that have no quick and easy solutions. Differences of opinion among educators and practitioners are sincere and strong. We have tried to include these differing views in a way that should stimulate students' thinking and help them to realize the dynamic nature of the accounting profession.

In some areas, such as pensions (Chapter 16) and current values for personal financial statements (Chapter 24), new appendices have been added to the chapter for selective assignment to students. In other cases, such as income tax allocation (Chapter 20) and revenue recognition (Chapter 19), the text material has been expanded to clearly identify the issues being discussed. We believe these topics should be addressed in the classroom, and that time should be allowed for student involvement with these difficult and challenging issues. To assist students in grasping these issues, several new and updated discussion cases have been added to the chapters involved in these discussion areas.

In addition to work being done by the FASB, the Internal Revenue Service and the U.S. Congress have had some impact on topics in this text. New tax laws designed to stimulate the economy were passed in both 1981 and 1982. Some of the provisions in the new laws, such as the Investment Tax Credit (Chapter 20), directly affect the coverage of *Intermediate Accounting*. We have selectively updated material to describe the most current tax requirements.

Following is a brief description of the most significant changes in the eighth edition:

- Chapter 2—Changed illustration from manufacturing company to merchandising company.
- Chapter 3—Updated conceptual framework material; added Concepts Statement No. 3, "Elements of Financial Statements of Business Enterprises."
- Chapter 5—Expanded early discussion of funds statement with increased emphasis on cash flows.
- Chapter 11—Introduced and discussed implication of ACRS as substitute for accelerated depreciation on the tax return.
- Chapter 16—Added appendix covering the preliminary views of major changes in pension accounting.
- Chapter 20—Updated for 1981 and 1982 income tax laws.
- Chapter 23—Introduced T-accounts in development of funds statement.
- Chapter 24—Added new appendix on personal financial statements and their use of current values.

The annual newsletter is now arranged by chapters to permit instructors to update the text with new developments between editions. Each newsletter is indexed to permit an easy identification of changes that we feel should be made as the subject is taught.

The authors wish to thank the Financial Accounting Standards Board, the American Institute of Certified Public Accountants, the Securities and Exchange Commission, and the American Accounting Association for permission to quote from their various publications and pronouncements.

Jay M. Smith, Jr.
K. Fred Skousen

ABOUT THE AUTHORS

Jay M. Smith, Jr., PhD, CPA, is Professor of Accounting at the School of Accountancy, Brigham Young University. He holds a bachelor's and a master's degree from BYU and a PhD from Stanford University. He has twenty-six years of teaching experience at BYU, Stanford University, the University of Minnesota where he served as department chairman for four years, and at the University of Hawaii. He has received several awards and recognitions in accounting, including fellowships from the Danforth and Sloan Foundations, the Distinguished Faculty Award from the BYU School of Management, and several teaching excellence awards. Professor Smith has written extensively in accounting journals and has been involved in several research projects, including work done on grants from the Ford Foundation, Peat, Marwick, Mitchell & Co., and Arthur Andersen & Co. He served as editor of the Education Research Department of the Accounting Review from 1976 to 1978, as secretary to the Auditing Section of the American Accounting Association, and as a member of the editorial board for the Auditing Section's journal. He is a member of the American Institute of CPAs, the Utah Association of CPAs, and the American Accounting Association and has served on numerous committees of these organizations.

K. Fred Skousen, PhD, CPA, is Professor of Accounting and Director of the School of Accountancy at Brigham Young University. He holds a bachelor's degree from BYU and the master's and PhD degrees from the University of Illinois. Professor Skousen has taught at the University of Illinois, the University of Minnesota, the University of California at Berkeley, and the University of Missouri. He received Distinguished Faculty Awards at the University of Minnesota and at BYU and was recognized as the National Beta Alpha Psi Academic Accountant of the Year in 1979. Professor Skousen is the author or co-author of numerous articles, research reports, and books. He served as Director of Research and a member of the Executive Committee of the American Accounting Association and is a member of the American Institute of CPAs, the Accounting Research Association, and the Utah Association of CPAs. He is currently serving on the Board of Directors of the UACPA and on Council for the AICPA. Dr. Skousen has also served as a consultant to the Controller General of the United States, the Federal Trade Commission, the California Society of CPAs, and several large companies. He was a Faculty Resident on the staff of the Securities and Exchange Commission and a Faculty Fellow with Price Waterhouse and Co.

CONTENTS

Part 2 Assets

Part 1 Overview of Accounting and Its Theoretical Foundation

1 THE ACCOUNTING PROFESSION

CHAPTER OBJECTIVES

Describe the nature of accounting and the various opportunities available to students with an accounting background.

Identify the key historical events that have affected the growth and development of accounting.

Describe the public accounting profession and its entry requirements.

Identify and describe the organizations that exercise the greatest influence on the accounting profession.

Encourage students to prepare themselves for the many challenges facing accountants.

This text centers upon the accounting profession, one of society's youngest and most exciting professions. Traditionally, the term "professional" has been used to designate a doctor, dentist, or lawyer—members of old and established professions. Increasingly, however, students are discovering the challenges and opportunities of accounting. To help students understand more fully the profession of accounting, this introductory chapter will focus on (1) the different types of accountants and their attributes, (2) the historical development of the profession, and (3) the organizations that exercise significant influence on members of the accounting profession.

WHAT IS ACCOUNTING?

As indicated in the following quotation, the objective of accounting is to provide information that can be used in making economic decisions.

> Accounting is a service activity. Its function is to provide quantitative information, primarily financial in nature, about economic entities that is intended to be useful in making economic decisions—in making reasoned choices among alternative courses of action.[1]

Several important concepts are included in this definition of accounting. Accounting is a **service activity**. It is intended to fulfill a **useful** function in our society by offering to provide service to various segments of the economic community involved directly or indirectly with business entities. It is primarily concerned with **quantitative financial information** describing the activities of a business, rather than qualitative, judgmental evaluations of those activities. The output of the accounting system is intended to serve as an aid to users who must make **economic decisions** among alternative actions available to them.

Economists and environmentalists remind us that we live in a world with limited resources. We must use our natural resources, our labor, and our financial wealth wisely so as to maximize their benefits to society. The better the accounting system that measures the cost of using these resources, the better the decisions that can be made for allocating them. To the extent that accounting information meets these needs, the accounting system is fulfilling its major purpose. As the needs of society and environmental conditions change, the techniques, concepts, and to some extent even the basic objectives of accounting must also change.

Management Accounting and Financial Accounting

A distinction is commonly made between management (or managerial) accounting and financial accounting. **Management accounting** is primarily concerned with information used for management decision making within the entity. Accurate and timely information is essential to management in making short-term operating decisions and long-term resource allocation decisions. Do we make this product or another one? Do we build a new production plant or expand existing facilities? Do we increase prices or cut costs?

The information required by management for making both short- and long-term decisions should be supplied by a well-integrated management information system. The type and amount of information generated by any particular system is determined by the needs and desires of management.

---

[1] *Statements of the Accounting Principles Board, No. 4,* "Basic Concepts and Accounting Principles Underlying Financial Statements of Business Enterprises" (New York: American Institute of Certified Public Accountants, 1970), par. 40.

Although general guidelines exist for these management information systems, specific details vary widely among industries and among entities within the same industry.

More businesses have failed because of poor management decisions, often based on inadequate accounting information, than because of inferior technology or products. The critical need for trained management accountants is especially evident when economic conditions are unstable and demand a rapid analysis of the impact of external factors on a company's well-being.

The other area of accounting, and the one this text is primarily concerned with, is financial accounting. In contrast with management accounting, **financial accounting** focuses on the information needs of users outside the entity. The primary external users of financial information include creditors, investors, government agencies, and the general public. These groups are interested in the financial activities of an entity but are not directly involved in its operations. They must rely upon those managing the enterprise to provide a stewardship report of their activities in the form of financial statements. They are not in a position to obtain directly the information they desire.

Most external users are interested in more than one entity and need to compare the financial statements of two or more entities in order to evaluate their relative efficiencies. These users may wish to make choices among reporting entities. Examples of these choices include investing decisions by stockholders, lending decisions by banks and other credit institutions, and employment decisions by employees. Essentially, these are all resource allocation decisions. In order to permit comparisons of financial statements, a consistent and comparable pattern must be followed in summarizing and reporting information to external users. The development of principles and procedures to promote uniformity, consistency, and quality in financial reporting is the subject matter of financial accounting.

The Accounting Profession

The accounting profession may be subdivided into two major segments: public accounting and internal accounting. The **public accountant** functions as an independent expert and performs services for many clients. The **internal accountant** may have similar training and perform duties similar to those of a public accountant, but works for a single entity, generally in a staff position. The two major segments of the profession can be further subdivided as follows:

Public Accounting	Internal Accounting
External auditor	Financial or general accountant
Tax specialist	Cost accountant
Management consultant	Internal auditor
	Tax accountant
	Systems analyst

Public Accounting. The term "public accounting" is generally equated with the services provided by **certified public accountants (CPAs)**. Public accounting firms offer various services to clients, primarily auditing, tax, and management consulting services. In addition, these firms provide accounting services, such as preparation of financial statements, for some "small business" clients.

Auditing is the dominant activity in larger public accounting firms. The **external (independent) auditor** examines the financial statements of a client and expresses an opinion as to the fairness of the statements and their adherence to generally accepted accounting principles. The auditor must be knowledgeable in accounting and must also possess skills in evaluating evidence that supports the amounts reported in the financial statements prepared by the client. The financial statements of all publicly held companies must be examined by an external auditor. Many privately held companies also engage public accounting firms to audit their financial statements, since audited statements are frequently required to obtain credit and in some cases to provide assurance to stockholders who are not actively involved in management.

In contrast with lawyers, the auditor does not serve solely as an advocate for the client who pays for the services. An auditor has a professional obligation to protect the interests of society as an independent expert. External users of financial statements must rely on the auditor's opinion as to the fairness of management's representations in the financial statements. This relationship between the external auditor, the client, and society is unique to the accounting profession.

Tax specialists in public accounting firms prepare tax returns and assist clients in tax planning and in resolving tax problems. CPAs also function as **management consultants**, offering advice to clients in such areas as systems design, organization, personnel, finance, internal control, and employee benefits. These services are frequently referred to as **management advisory services (MAS)**.

CPAs in large public accounting firms typically specialize in auditing, tax, or MAS. The degree of specialization decreases as firm size decreases. The nature of public accounting firms and the requirements for becoming a CPA are discussed in detail later in the chapter.

Internal Accounting. A team of internal accountants is generally necessary to provide the data required for both internal and external reporting. The **financial or general accountant** is primarily concerned with the recording and summarizing of financial accounting information and the preparation of financial statements. **Cost accountants** are responsible for analyzing detailed cost information and preparing various reports for use by management.

Internal auditors review the work performed by accountants and others within the enterprise and report their findings to management. Although internal auditors are employees of the enterprise, they must be independent with respect to the employees whose work they review. Thus, internal auditors generally report to a high level of management. External auditors frequently rely to some extent on the work performed by internal auditors.

Internal **tax accountants** may be employed to prepare tax returns and advise management in matters relating to taxation. A company may also employ **systems analysts** who design and monitor information systems.

HISTORICAL DEVELOPMENT OF ACCOUNTING

Accounting has been called "the language of business." Its development has closely paralleled the needs arising from reporting increasingly complex business and economic transactions. Among the earliest accounting records were those kept as part of the feudal system during the early middle ages. Lords of the manors collected taxes from their subjects, and used the proceeds to further the work of the estate and to meet their personal needs. A report of stewardship was prepared by the more conscientious of the lords for review by their subjects. Another activity during this period that involved the accountant's skills was the maintaining of voyage records for those involved with trade between countries. These records were usually maintained for a single voyage, at the end of which the records were closed, and the profit or loss was calculated. Banking institutions, which arose in the 11th and 12th centuries in the Italian states, often lent money to finance such voyages. These various business activities required a record of income and outgo, especially when the spoils were divided at the end of the voyage.

Because many of these business ventures originated in the European countries bordering on the Mediterranean Sea, such as Spain, Portugal, Italy, and Greece, it is not surprising that one of the earliest treatises in accounting was written by an Italian monk, Luca Paciolo. He was really a mathematician who used his analytical skills to describe the system of double-entry accounting, which had been evolving for decades. The work was first published in 1494 and carried the title *Summa de Arithmetica Geometria Proportioni et Proportionalita*.

Accounting did not progress rapidly as a discipline until business began to grow in size, and until a need arose to distinguish more clearly between the ownership of the entity and its operation. The Industrial Revolution had its birth in England, and it was there that the increased need for accounting developed. In 1845, the first Companies Act was passed permitting a business to be organized as a company with the status of a legal entity. These companies could borrow money, issue stock, pay debts, and carry on activities in the same manner as an individual. This new organizational form permitted the pooling of capital by many individuals to acquire the economic resources necessary to produce newly invented goods or to expand operations. Since many different individuals provided financial resources to carry out these business functions, a need arose to account to these investors and creditors for the use of their resources. This accounting took the form of financial reports that summarized the increase or decrease in resources over a period of time and the current status of the resources. In the United States, this concept of separate legal entities became popular as states such as New

York, Vermont, and Massachusetts passed corporation laws and created new entities with the same attributes as their English counterparts.

As the Industrial Revolution took hold in the United States, companies grew in size. Large personal fortunes were invested in corporations, marking the beginnings of Standard Oil, American Telephone and Telegraph, Ford Motor Company, and other twentieth-century industrial giants. Accounting systems became even more important following the adoption in 1913 of the Sixteenth Amendment to the U. S. Constitution giving the federal government the power to tax income. This placed added emphasis upon the concept of income to measure the ability of individuals and corporations to supply resources to the government for expanded social and defense needs.

A serious problem emerged as the need for accounting increased. Because the discipline had grown so rapidly, and because business activities were changing at an ever-increasing pace, accounting procedures had to be developed without extended debate or discussion. Accountants developed methods that seemed to meet the needs of their respective companies, resulting in diverse procedures among companies in accounting for similar activities. The comparability of the resulting financial reports, therefore, was often questionable. Management could manipulate the records and produce significantly different results depending upon the desired objective. During the 1920s, the differences led to financial statements that were often inflated in value. Market values of stocks rose higher than the underlying real values warranted until the entire structure collapsed in the Great Depression of the early 1930s. The government of the United States, under the leadership of President Franklin D. Roosevelt, vigorously attacked the depression, and among other things, created the Securities and Exchange Commission (SEC). This new agency was given a responsibility to protect the interests of stock investors by preventing a recurrence of the conditions that led to the stock market crash in 1929. In 1933, Congress passed the Securities Act and in 1934, the Securities Exchange Act. The broad power granted to the SEC by Congress will be more fully discussed in a separate section. The emergence of the SEC forced the accounting profession to unite and to become more diligent in developing accounting principles and ethics to govern the profession. The SEC required independent audits of companies that came under its jurisdiction. This was a great boost to the field of auditing, and has resulted in a tremendous increase in the number of certified public accountants who fill the role of external auditor.

World War II brought a pause in the growth of the profession, but the prosperity that followed the war and the introduction of electronic data processing equipment into business systems created needs for increasingly sophisticated accounting systems. New high-technology industries such as television, aerospace, electronics, and synthetic fibers required systems that could organize vast amounts of accounting data into financial reports needed to meet varied users' needs. More responsibility was forced onto the professional accountants by the courts as class-action civil suits and even criminal suits were brought against accountants who were accused of being negligent in performing their functions.

In the late 1970s, several Congressional committees studied the profession, and even proposed legislation to further control accounting and overcome perceived weaknesses in it. These included the Metcalf Committee, a Senate committee that published a mammoth report in 1977 called the *Accounting Establishment*, and the Moss Committee, a House of Representatives committee that drafted and introduced legislation to regulate the accounting profession. Because of these activities, several changes were made within the structure of the accounting profession to answer some of the criticism of the congressional committees. The SEC was asked to report annually to Congress to evaluate the progress of the profession. The SEC annual reports have generally been positive, and the attempt to regulate the profession externally has been abandoned by Congress, at least for the present. The profession, however, recognizes a need to continually strive to improve the quality of its work if it wishes to retain the right of self-regulation.

This brief review of accounting history demonstrates clearly how accounting in the United States has changed to keep pace with a rapidly changing economy. Similar changes have occurred in other countries, and more international co-operation in accounting is taking place each year. With the past as a guide, it can be assumed that there are many exciting challenges ahead for those who are part of the accounting profession. The organizations that have been and will continue to be instrumental in helping direct these changes are identified and discussed later in the chapter.

PUBLIC ACCOUNTING

Members of certain professions—notably medicine and law—are charged with an especially high degree of public responsibility. Characteristics of such a profession include the licensing of members and a restriction on entry into the profession based upon such variables as education, experience, and the passing of a qualifying examination. Public accounting acquired these characteristics early in its development. England and its related countries in the British Empire identified its professionals as "Chartered Accountants" (CAs), and in the United States the designation became "Certified Public Accountant" (CPA).

The CPA Certificate

Public accounting developed rapidly in response to the need to add a degree of credibility to the financial statements being issued to investors and other users. The first CPA certificate was issued by the State of New York in 1896. It followed the pattern developed in England where the first CA certificate was issued in 1854. The establishment of laws providing for public accounting certification quickly spread to other states. By 1908, there were sixteen states issuing CPA certificates, and by 1925, all states and territories had provisions to control entry into public accounting. Requirements for certification varied, but typically included passing a written examination and obtaining experience in public accounting for a specified period of time.

Unlike the situation in England, the authority to regulate professions developed by states rather than by a central government agency. Upon meeting the certification requirements of a particular state, an individual could practice as a CPA, but only in that state. As the mobility of CPAs increased, and as CPA firms expanded from local offices to become regional, national, and international in scope, it became increasingly necessary to grant CPAs reciprocity across state lines without taking another written examination. This led to the states uniting with the profession to give a uniform CPA examination in all states and territories. The first uniform examination was given in 1917 in three states. This grew to 30 states by 1936, and in 1952, the last state adopted the uniform examination making it effective throughout the United States. This process differs from both the legal and medical professions that require separate examinations in each state.

The CPA examination is given over a 2½ day period the first week of May and the first week of November. It is given simultaneously in hundreds of locations throughout the country. Grading usually takes about three months, and is done uniformly under the direction of the American Institute of Certified Public Accountants (AICPA), the national professional body that has been given the authority to prepare and control the CPA examination. The examination contains four sections: (1) Accounting Practice, two parts, (2) Accounting Theory, (3) Auditing, and (4) Business Law. Some states add a fifth section dealing with ethics. The nationwide average pass rate on each section is about 30 percent; however, only about 10 to 15 percent of the first-time candidates pass the entire examination in one sitting. Most states permit a candidate to "conditionally pass" sections of the examination. This means that if the other sections are passed within a certain time period, the certificate will be granted without retaking the previously passed sections. Pass rates are affected greatly by the preparation of the students, including educational background and experience. For serious candidates and those with advanced degrees in accounting, the pass rate is considerably higher than the above averages indicate.

The various states have still maintained the right to specify the experience and education requirements necessary for professional certification. These vary from no experience to three years' experience under the direction of a CPA, and from no specific education to a master's degree in accounting. After meeting a state's initial requirements for professional entry, annual dues must be paid to the state to maintain a valid certificate. Many states also require that CPAs meet certain continuing education requirements to retain the right to practice. Because each of these requirements is governed by state statutes, it is difficult to bring them into uniformity. The AICPA has recommended that certain minimum guidelines for professional education be met, both for entry and for continuing education, but achieving the desired uniformity is a slow process.

As indicated in the table below, the number of professional accountants holding the CPA certificate has increased dramatically over the past ten years. Over 60,000 individuals sit for the examination each time it is offered. Although other accounting certificates have been introduced in the United States in the past fifteen years, namely the Certified Management Accountant (CMA) certificate and the Certified Internal Auditor (CIA) certificate, the CPA is still the most universally accepted evidence of professional accounting competence. Intermediate accounting is especially valuable in preparing candidates for the accounting practice and accounting theory sections of the examination.

Year	Individuals Holding CPA Certificate (estimated)	Individuals Holding Membership in AICPA
1950	38,000	16,000
1960	70,000	38,000
1970	114,000	75,000
1973	146,000	95,000
1975	172,000	112,000
1977	200,000	130,000
1979	230,000	150,000
1982	250,000	184,000

Development of International CPA Firms

Because of the importance of personal liability for professional conduct, professional firms are generally organized as either a proprietorship or a partnership. Only recently have state laws been changed to permit "professional corporations." These special corporations provide for many of the benefits of corporate structure, but still retain the personal liability of the professionals involved. As the accounting profession developed, the partnership form of organization became the most common. Over time, a relatively few partnerships have become dominant in the United States. Each has spread its influence internationally and is now recognized as an international organization. Each of these firms has many offices, with offices in foreign countries often operated through a foreign national partner or affiliate firm.

Some of the large accounting firms had their beginnings in England in the late 1800s and came to the United States as part of the shift in emphasis to the United States as the Industrial Revolution crossed the ocean. As business on this side of the Atlantic Ocean became prominent, these firms changed their headquarters to the United States and became recognized as primarily American firms with international affiliations. Other firms originated in the United States and grew domestically first, then spread internationally. The chart on page 10 identifies the largest accounting firms and includes some pertinent data concerning them. World-wide revenues for these firms range from approximately $60 million to over $1 billion annually.

Selected Data on Large CPA Firms

Name of Firm	Location of National Office	Date Organized	Number of Partners (1981)
Alexander Grant & Co.	Chicago	1924	350
Arthur Andersen & Co.	Chicago	1913	1,400
Arthur Young & Company	New York	1894	1,944
Coopers & Lybrand	New York	1898	2,010
Deloitte Haskins & Sells	New York	1895	2,000
Ernst & Whinney	Cleveland	1903	1,600
Fox and Company	Denver	1900	270
Klynveld Main Goerdler	New York	1903	500
Laventhol and Horwath	Philadelphia	1915	235
Peat, Marwick, Mitchell & Co.	New York	1897	1,931
Price Waterhouse & Co.	New York	1850	1,613
Seidman & Seidman	New York	1910	150
Touche, Ross & Co.	New York	1900	1,979

Much of the criticism of the accounting profession by Congress and governmental bodies such as the Federal Trade Commission (FTC) has been directed to the monopoly position occupied by the larger CPA firms. However, members of these firms emphasize that large firms are highly competitive with one another. Members of the large firms also correctly emphasize that many of their clients are very large multinational companies, and that only an accounting firm with similar size and scope of operations can provide the type of services needed by these entities.

A definite ordering of professionals within CPA firms has become traditional. New members of the firm are generally hired directly from college and begin as staff accountants. They progress through positions of senior staff, manager, and partner if they remain with the firm. Responsibilities increase as the professional advances in the firm. Most partners reach their position within ten to fifteen years after being hired. Although salaries vary, it is not unusual for a partner to earn well in excess of $100,000 per year.

Regional and Local Public Accounting Firms

Although almost all large publicly held corporations are audited by a few large CPA firms, there are many small businesses and nonprofit entities that are serviced by regional and local CPA firms, including a large number of sole practitioners. In these firms, most of the work is centered in the tax and systems planning areas, with some accounting or record keeping being performed. The role of auditing becomes less important as firm size decreases. A CPA in a small firm is expected to be something of an accounting generalist as opposed to the more specialized positions of CPAs in large regional and national firms. Not only do CPAs in these larger firms specialize in audit, tax, or MAS, they also tend to specialize in certain industries.

A vital role is played by the smaller public accounting firms. The thousands of small entities in the U. S. are crucial to the nation's economy, and the accountants who serve these entities enjoy challenging and rewarding careers.

ORGANIZATIONS INFLUENCING AND REGULATING THE PROFESSION

An auditor's opinion on the financial statements is recognized as a label of credibility. In order to preserve this credibility, the accounting profession has found it necessary to establish regulations for members within the profession and to establish standards and principles to govern the work performed. Various organizations exercise influence over this regulation. The major organizations involved include the American Institute of Certified Public Accountants (AICPA), state boards and state societies or associations of accountants, the Financial Accounting Standards Board (FASB), the Securities and Exchange Commission (SEC), and the American Accounting Association (AAA).

American Institute of Certified Public Accountants (AICPA)

The **American Institute of Certified Public Accountants** is the professional organization of practicing certified public accountants in the United States. The organization was formed in 1887 and was originally named the American Institute of Accountants. A monthly publication, the *Journal of Accountancy*, was first issued by the Institute in 1905, providing a means of communication concerning the problems of accounting and the challenges and responsibilities faced by the profession.

One of the major functions of the AICPA is to assist the states in the regulation of those entering the profession by administering and grading the Uniform CPA Examination. Other responsibilities include establishing and enforcing rules of professional conduct (professional ethics), establishing standards of auditing practice, representing and speaking for the members of the profession to government, education, and the business community, and, in the past, establishing generally accepted accounting principles. This latter responsibility has been assumed by the Financial Accounting Standards Board (FASB), an entity organized separately from the AICPA. Only CPAs may belong to the Institute; membership, however, is voluntary. At the present time, about 75 percent of CPAs belong to the Institute (see page 9).

Although membership in the AICPA has been traditionally individual, the influence of the firm is often felt through the individual's participation in Institute activities. Because of this influence, and because the duties and responsibilities of members in large firms often differ from those in medium and small firms, the AICPA has instituted a firm membership in one of two sections: (1) the **SEC practice firms** section for firms that have clients subject to SEC registration and reporting requirements, and (2) the **private companies practice firms** section for those firms that do not have SEC clients. The SEC practice firms are subject to more stringent regulation than the private companies practice firms, although a high quality of performance is expected of all firms. A firm may belong to both sections, and most of the larger firms do. The regulation of firms and establishment of these divisions was one of the actions taken by the AICPA to satisfy the government committees that were critical of the profession. It has resulted in more attention being paid to the needs and problems of smaller private entities as opposed to those of large public companies.

State Boards and State Societies or Associations

There are two groups within the states that assume responsibility for the professional activities of certified public accountants: (1) state boards and (2) state societies or associations. The members of a **state board of accountancy** are normally appointed by the governor of the state. The state board is responsible for determining and regulating the admission requirements of new members into the profession. This responsibility includes administering the examination and evaluating the candidate's education and experience prior to the issuance of a certificate. Once a state board has approved issuance of a certificate, it must further determine that the appropriate regulations governing the use of the certificate are followed by those who are recognized as CPAs. These boards, therefore, have the power to issue and to revoke the CPA certificate.

The **state societies or associations of certified public accountants** are responsible for meeting the professional organizational needs of the members in each state. State societies are presently independent organizations; however, they maintain close relationships with the staff of the AICPA. National committee assignments of the Institute, for example, are generally initiated by the state societies. Several state societies are also instituting continuing education requirements, often utilizing AICPA course offerings as one means of satisfying these requirements. While not all states have adopted mandatory continuing education requirements, there is a definite trend in that direction.

Neither the Institute nor the state societies can issue or revoke a certificate. They may admit and suspend members from their respective organizations based upon their own rules and regulations; however, they cannot prevent one from using the "CPA" designation.

Financial Accounting Standards Board (FASB)

In 1973, the **Financial Accounting Standards Board** was organized and given the private sector responsibility for establishing standards of financial accounting and reporting. The Board is an independent organization consisting of seven salaried, full-time members drawn from professional accounting and business. The headquarters of the Board is in Stamford, Connecticut. The Board has its own research staff and an annual budget in excess of 8 million dollars. Its major function is to study accounting issues and produce **Statements of Financial Accounting Standards** and **Statements of Financial Accounting Concepts.** Prior to issuing these statements, the Board typically appoints a task force of technical experts who study the existing literature and prepare and distribute a **discussion memorandum** that identifies the principal issues involved with a given accounting topic. The memorandum usually includes a discussion of the various points of view as to the resolution of the issues, but does not come to a specific conclusion. An extensive bibliography is usually included. Readers of the discussion memorandum are invited to comment either in writing or orally at a public hearing. Sometimes a topic is not defined well enough to issue a discussion memorandum, and the FASB issues a preliminary document identified as an "Invitation to Comment." The topic is briefly discussed in the document, and readers are encouraged to send their comments to the FASB for more definite formulation of specific issues.

After a discussion memorandum has been issued and comments from interested parties have been evaluated, the Board issues an **exposure draft** of a Statement which includes specific recommendations for financial accounting and reporting. Reaction to the exposure draft is requested from the accounting and business community, and after this input is received and analyzed, the Board issues a final Statement. The time frame for the FASB's standard-setting process varies, but in some cases may be in excess of two years.

Statements of *standards* are recognized by the profession as representing the generally accepted position of the profession, and must be followed unless circumstances warrant an exception to the standard. When exceptions to **generally accepted accounting principles (GAAP)** are necessary, the accountant must clearly disclose the nature of and reason for the deviation in the financial statements. Failure to include the disclosure is a violation of Rule 203 of the professional Code of Ethics issued by the AICPA. Statements of *concepts* do not establish accounting principles within the meaning of Rule 203, but "are intended to set forth objectives and fundamentals that will be the basis for development of financial accounting and reporting standards."[2]

The FASB is continually called upon to clarify and interpret its standards. In response to these requests, the Board issues interpretations of standards. **Interpretations** are reviewed and approved by the Board in the same manner as standards and have the same authority as standards. Thus, failure to follow an FASB Interpretation is a departure from GAAP. The FASB authorized its staff to issue **Technical Bulletins** to provide guidance on a timely basis concerning the application of accounting principles. They do not establish new financial accounting and reporting standards or amend existing standards. Although the Board does not approve the technical bulletins, members of the Board are kept informed of the matters proposed for bulletins and are given the opportunity to review proposed bulletins prior to issuance.

Prior to the formation of the FASB, accounting principles were established under the direction of the AICPA. From 1939–1959, principles were formed by the *Committee on Accounting Procedures* (*CAP*). Their pro-

---

[2] *Statement of Financial Accounting Concepts No.* 3, "Elements of Financial Statements of Business Enterprises" (Stamford: Financial Accounting Standards Board, 1979), p. i.

nouncements were known as *Accounting Research Bulletins* (*ARBs*). From 1959 to 1973, principles were formed by the *Accounting Principles Board* (*APB*) and issued as *Opinions*. Pronouncements of a conceptual nature were also issued by the APB. These *APB Statements*, like the FASB's Statements of Concepts, did not establish accounting principles. Dissatisfaction with the part-time nature of these boards, their failure to react quickly to some issues, and the lack of broad representation on the boards because of their direct relationship to the AICPA, led to the formation in 1972 of a special AICPA committee headed by a former commissioner of the SEC. This committee recommended the organization that became known as the Financial Accounting Standards Board.

The FASB is organized independently from the AICPA, although the AICPA does continue to have a major impact through its funding an involvement in the organizational structure. The Board is directly controlled by the Financial Accounting Foundation, composed of nine trustees appointed by a Board of Electors comprised of members from the six sponsoring institutions, which are:

(1) American Accounting Association (academe)
(2) American Institute of Certified Public Accountants (public accounting)
(3) Financial Analysts Federation (investors and investment advisors)
(4) Financial Executives Institute (corporate executives)
(5) National Association of Accountants (management accountants)
(6) Securities Industry Associates (investment bankers)

In addition, there is a trustee-at-large who is endorsed by the principal national associations in the banking industry. The Foundation has the responsibility of appointing members of the FASB, of appointing a Financial Accounting Standards Advisory Council of at least twenty members (usually about forty members have been appointed), of raising funds necessary to support the Board, and of periodically reviewing and revising the organizational structure. Approximately half of the funding comes from industry and the financial community; the other half from the public accounting profession. No single annual contribution of more than $50,000 can be accepted under the Foundation by-laws.

Securities and Exchange Commission (SEC)

The **Securities and Exchange Commission** was created by an act of Congress in 1934. Its primary role is to regulate the issuance and trading of securities by corporations to the general public. The Commission's intent is not to prevent the trading of speculative securities, but to insist that investors have adequate information. Thus, the SEC's objective is to insure *full and fair disclosure* of all material facts concerning securities offered for public investment. The SEC may use its statutory authority to prescribe accounting and reporting requirements for all companies falling under its jurisdiction. This includes most major companies in the United States.

The regulations of the SEC require independent audits of annual financial statements. The SEC reviews both the reports and the supporting verification to ascertain compliance with the law. The principal governing acts of the SEC are the Securities Act of 1933 and the Securities Exchange Act of 1934. Although the SEC has the power to issue regulations declaring how corporations should report financial affairs to shareholders, it has, for the most part, relied upon the accounting profession, through the AICPA and FASB, to perform this function.[3]

The reporting requirements of the SEC are found in Regulation S-K and Regulation S-X. The Commission also issues pronouncements or "releases" on specific accounting and auditing matters. For many years, the SEC issued a single series of pronouncements entitled *Accounting Series Releases (ASRs)*. In 1982, the Commission announced plans to codify certain ASRs and instituted two new series of pronouncements: (1) *Financial Reporting Releases (FRRs)*, which replaced non-enforcement-related ASRs and (2) *Accounting and Auditing Enforcement Releases (AAERs)*, which replaced enforcement-related ASRs. The staff of the SEC issues *SEC Staff Bulletins*, which are unofficial interpretations that provide guidance in the application of SEC reporting requirements.

Congress has urged the SEC to take a more active role in the regulation of the accounting profession and requires an annual report from the SEC as to its evaluation of the profession. The first of these reports was issued in 1978. In the 1979 report, the SEC concluded:

> The Commission remains unconvinced that comprehensive direct governmental regulation of accounting or accountants would afford the public either increased protection or a more meaningful basis for confidence in the work of public accountants.[4]

The SEC has reiterated this position in subsequent reports.

American Accounting Association (AAA)

The **American Accounting Association** was known as the American Association of University Instructors in Accounting from 1918 until 1935, when its name was changed to its present designation. The AAA is primarily an organization for accounting educators, although others are admitted to membership. A quarterly journal, the *Accounting Review*, is sponsored by the AAA. Articles in the *Accounting Review* generally discuss matters of accounting theory as compared with articles in the *Journal of Accountancy* that are primarily concerned with matters of accounting practice. AAA committee reports and discussions of these reports are available to AAA members upon request. Selected research projects are published by the AAA in the accounting research monograph series.

---

[3]For additional information on the nature and workings of the SEC, see K. Fred Skousen, *An Introduction to the SEC*, Third Edition (Cincinnati: South-Western Publishing Co., 1983).

[4]Report to Congress of the SEC on Accounting Regulation, 1979.

Although the AAA has a permanent executive secretary, its officers and committees rotate each year among the members. The AAA does not claim to serve as a majority voice for accounting educators. Its major role is to serve as a forum within which individual educators can express their views either individually or in specially appointed committees. Another important objective is to encourage and support research activity designed to add new understanding in the field of accounting.

Special-interest sections have developed within the AAA, and members of the Association may join one or more of these sections. The largest of these are the tax and auditing sections, each having over 1,000 members and its own quarterly journal. Other sections include management advisory services, international accounting, public sector, and management accounting.

Other Organizations

Although the aforementioned groups have traditionally exercised the most direct influence upon the regulation of accountants and the establishment of accounting principles, the influence of other groups has also been felt. The **Financial Executives Institute (FEI)**, formerly the Controllers' Institute, is a national organization composed of financial executives employed by large corporations. The FEI membership includes treasurers, controllers, and financial vice-presidents. The FEI publishes a monthly journal, *The Financial Executive*, and has sponsored several research projects relating to financial reporting problems. These research projects have covered a variety of topics including the manner in which a company operating in a number of industries should report the financial progress attained by different company segments, the effect of price-level adjustments upon managerial decisions, the concept of materiality in financial reporting, and the accounting problems of multinational companies.

Another influential group is the **National Association of Accountants (NAA)**. This organization is more concerned with the use of accounting information within the enterprise than with external reporting, and thus has directed its research primarily toward cost accounting and information systems. Its monthly publication, *Management Accounting*, has traditionally dealt mainly with problems involving information systems and the use of accounting data within the business organization. Because a firm's information system can provide information for both internal and external users, the NAA is concerned about the relationship of accounting principles for internal reporting to those for external reporting.

Several societies of financial analysts have been formed. The most prominent of these groups is the **Financial Analysts Federation**. Admittance to this group is based upon a qualifying examination. Because financial analysts are a major user of external accounting reports, they are very much concerned with the present status of financial reporting. Members of this group have often been critical of corporate financial reporting practices and have continued to request increased disclosure of pertinent financial data.

ATTRIBUTES OF PROFESSIONAL ACCOUNTANTS

A decision to pursue a particular career should be based on an understanding of the nature of the work involved. Accounting can be very rewarding, but at times very demanding. In addition to the requisite technical skills, a successful accountant or auditor must possess certain personal attributes and, perhaps most important of all, a genuine interest in performing the work.

Among the many important attributes a person who provides accounting services must have are the following: (1) an **analytical** mind, one that can look at many detailed parts and generalize to an evaluation of the whole; (2) an **orderly** mind, one that can organize many complex business transactions and summarize them into meaningful reports for the benefit of one or more users; and (3) a **quick** and **efficient** mind, one that can rapidly see the interrelationships of data.

In addition to these intellectual qualities, a successful accountant must relate well with people and be able to communicate clearly, both orally and in writing. In many ways, an accountant must be a salesperson who can convince others of the importance of accounting reports. It is in this "people" area that many accountants fail to meet the needs of the profession. Students who possess a combination of these intellectual and social qualities are likely to find accounting very rewarding.

Accountants work under varying degrees of pressure. Deadlines are important, as financial decisions often must be made quickly and accurately. CPAs often must meet client deadlines for issuing new securities or satisfying demands of investors and creditors. Because of this pressure, hours are frequently long, especially as deadlines approach. Accountants are primarily selling their time and must develop the skill to work rapidly, but with accuracy.

CHALLENGES FOR THE PROFESSION

The profession of accounting is still experiencing growing pains. As the requirements for knowledge increase, students must be willing to stay longer in school preparing for professional entry, and be willing to continue the educational process throughout their careers. The larger public accounting firms have extensive training programs. It is not unusual for professionals in these firms to spend one or more months a year in formal training sessions.

Accountants face many challenges in the 1980s. The proliferation of accounting standards has placed a heavy burden on small private businesses who must meet the same accounting requirements as the large public companies. This has led some accountants to argue that there is an accounting standards overload and that relief is needed for the smaller entities and the accountants who serve them.[5] The question of whether there should be a

---

[5]Gerald W. Hepp and Thomas W. McRae, "Accounting Standards Overload: Relief Is Needed," *Journal of Accountancy* (May, 1982), pp. 52–62.

modification of the generally accepted accounting principles for these smaller firms is under study by the profession. Some of the standards have become burdensome even for the larger public companies, and these standards need to be reviewed in the light of the FASB's conceptual framework, as discussed in Chapter 3.

Many technical areas, such as foreign exchange rate changes and accounting for the oil and gas industry, have world-wide political and economic implications. As the economies of the world continue to become more interrelated and the international impact of business decisions becomes increasingly widespread, accountants must be willing to devote their talents to reporting events as they transpire in a clear and orderly fashion to facilitate the economic and political decision-making process.

This first chapter is designed to help students understand the overall profession of accounting and the many opportunities and challenges of the profession. Regardless of the final direction an accounting student takes, intermediate accounting is basic to the development of the expertise required for any area within the profession.

QUESTIONS

1. What is the major function of accounting in our society?
2. Distinguish between management accounting and financial accounting.
3. Identify the major activities of (a) public accountants and (b) internal accountants.
4. Describe the role of the external auditor.
5. How did the development of the corporate form of organization affect the need for accounting?
6. Why is comparability of financial statements among companies important?
7. What are the requirements an accountant must meet to be a CPA?
8. What factors have led to the development of large international CPA partnerships?
9. How does the mix of accounting work differ between the few large national and international CPA firms and the thousands of smaller regional and local firms?
10. What is the principal function of the AICPA, and how does the Institute relate to the state boards and state societies or associations?
11. How is the FASB organized and supported?
12. Briefly describe the FASB's standard-setting process.
13. How does the SEC influence the accounting profession?
14. What attributes are most critical to becoming a competent professional accountant?
15. Why is accounting considered an exacting profession?

DISCUSSION CASES

case 1-1 (Should I be an accountant?) Three college students, Eric Denna, Russell Snow, and Cynthia Murri, are considering a career in accounting. They met at a careers day exhibit and began discussing their perceptions of what an accounting career would be like. To Eric, accounting was a field in which he could use his great love for mathematics. "I have always done well in math classes, and see accounting as nothing more than applied mathematics. Anything to avoid taking more English." Russell saw the field differently. To him, an accountant has to be able to communicate clearly to others and in an organized way. "I really get a bang out of convincing people to see things my way. Accounting provides the facts that make presentations more persuasive." Cynthia thought that accounting offered many different opportunities and that the demand for accountants was so great that almost any combination of intellectual and social abilities would be successful. "I like the idea of being able to become an expert in some aspect of accounting, and thus name my price." After some discussion, they decided to meet with an accounting professor for more information. Professor Cameron agreed to the meeting. As Professor Cameron, how would you react to these points of view?

case 1-2 (How large is too large?) The existence of a relatively few large CPA firms that service virtually all of the major industrial and financial firms and thus dominate the accounting profession, has led to criticism through the years. In a staff study for Senator Metcalf and his Subcommittee on Reporting, Accounting, and Management, the following assertion was made:

> The AICPA has developed prestige because of its size, resources, management, and the professional reputation of CPAs for objectivity, which has been accepted by the public and governmental authorities until recent years. Analysis of AICPA activities reveals that the organization primarily promotes the perceived interest of the large national accounting firms. Those interests are generally sympathetic to the management interests of large corporate clients which are primary sources of revenue for large accounting firms. (p. 129, 1976 report)

What dangers do you see from this concentration of power? What advantages are present because of the emergence of a few large firms?

case 1-3 (The missing financial records) In 1983, Robert Parsons began a new business providing landscaping and yard maintenance services to businesses and individual homes. The business grew rapidly and several employees were hired. The additional employees required additional equipment and larger purchases of supplies and materials. To help finance the expansion, Parsons brought in a partner, John Sabin. Together they obtained a $50,000 loan from the bank to assist in their expansion needs. Neither Parsons nor Sabin has any business or accounting background. Their records consist of a checkbook with check stubs showing amounts but no explanations, and a receipts book used when customers pay for the services rendered. Usual terms are cash upon completion of the work, although credit is granted to some customers. No accounts receivable records are maintained; however, a daily log of jobs worked on by employees is kept for salary purposes.

The bank has called and requested a copy of the statements for the year 1984. In desperation, the partners look in the phone book and call Annette Burton, a local CPA. They explain their problem and ask for help. Is this situation one in which a CPA can help? How can financial statements be prepared when records are as incomplete as those presented in this case?

case 1-4 (Is the accounting profession recession-proof?) A Wall Street Journal article in May, 1982, was titled "Business is Good for Accountants Despite Slump." This article was written at a time when the United States was in a recession, some industries even in a depression, and the number of entities going bankrupt was increasing. Why is the profession of accounting somewhat "recession-proof" when compared with other professions and trades?

case 1-5 (SEC: A necessary evil?) Susan Dean and Steven Peterson were selected to present a case in competition with students from other universities dealing with the need for a government agency oversight responsibility to monitor the quality of accounting in the private sector. Draft an outline showing the points you think Susan and Steve should make.

2 REVIEW OF THE ACCOUNTING PROCESS

CHAPTER OBJECTIVES

Review the steps normally followed in accumulating and summarizing accounting data.

Describe and illustrate the use of a work sheet to facilitate the summarizing process.

Explain the nature of single-entry accounting systems and illustrate the preparation of financial statements from single-entry data.

Certain procedures must be established by every business unit to provide the data to be reported on the financial statements. These procedures are collectively referred to as the **accounting process** or the **accounting cycle.**

OVERVIEW OF THE ACCOUNTING PROCESS

The accounting process consists of two interrelated parts: (1) the **recording phase** and (2) the **summarizing phase.** During the fiscal period, transactions are recorded in the various books of record as they occur. At the end of the fiscal period, the recorded data are brought up to date through adjustments. The adjusted data are then summarized, and the financial statements are prepared. There is an overlapping of the two phases since the recording of transactions is an ongoing activity which does not cease at the end of an accounting period, but continues uninterrupted while events of the preceding period are being summarized. The recording and summarizing phases of the accounting process are reviewed and illustrated in this chapter using data from Porter Inc., a hypothetical merchandising company. The underlying accounting concepts and principles, the form, and the content of the basic financial statements are discussed and illustrated in Chapters 3, 4, and 5.[1]

The accounting process, illustrated below, generally includes the following steps in well-defined sequence:

Recording Phase

1. *Appropriate business documents are prepared or received.* This documentation provides the basis for making an initial record of each transaction.
2. *Transactions are recorded.* Based upon the supporting documents from Step 1, each transaction is recorded in chronological order in books of original entry (journals).
3. *Transactions are posted.* Each transaction, as classified and recorded in the journals, is posted to the appropriate accounts in the general and subsidiary ledgers.

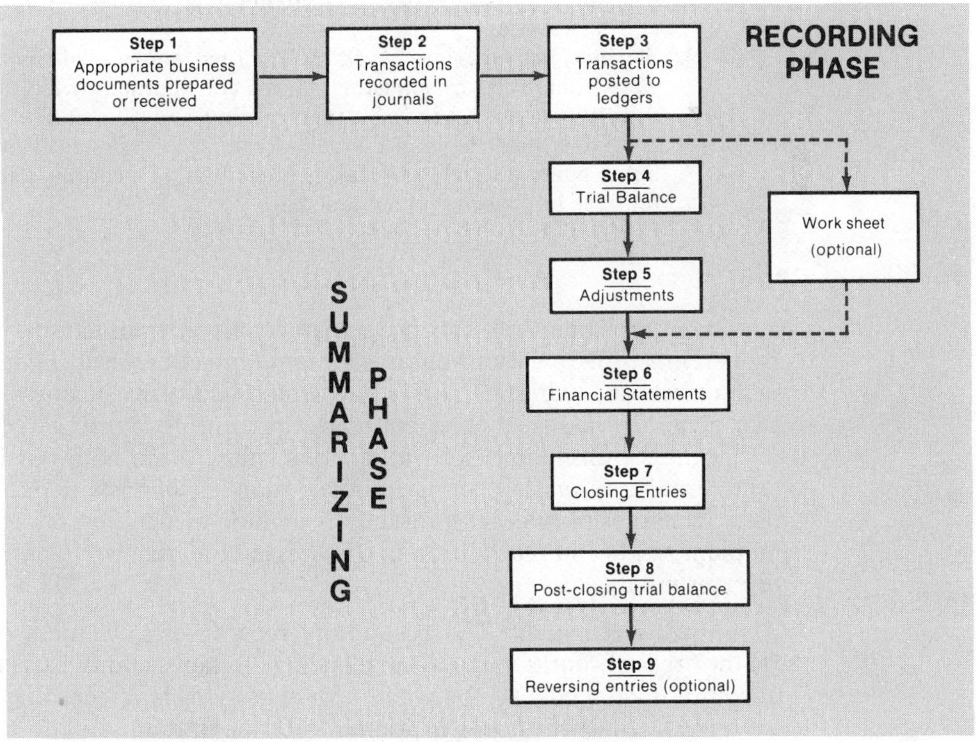

The Accounting Process

[1]Appendix B provides an illustrated set of financial statements from the 1982 annual report of General Mills, Inc.

Summarizing Phase

4. *A trial balance of the accounts in the general ledger is taken.* The trial balance, usually prepared on a work sheet, provides a summary of the information as classified in the ledger, as well as a general check on the accuracy of recording and posting.
5. *The data required to bring the accounts up to date are compiled.* Before financial statements can be prepared, all accountable information that has not been recorded must be determined. Often adjustments are first made on a work sheet, and may be formally recorded and posted at any time prior to closing (Step 7). If a work sheet is not used, the adjusting entries must be posted at this point so the accounts are current prior to the preparation of financial statements.
6. *Financial statements are prepared.* Statements summarizing operations and showing the financial position and changes in financial position are prepared from the information on the work sheet or directly from the adjusted accounts.
7. *Temporary accounts are closed.* Balances in the *nominal (temporary) accounts* and, in the case of a periodic inventory system, balances in the inventory accounts are closed into appropriate summary accounts. As determined in summary accounts, the results of operations are transferred to the appropriate owners' equity accounts.
8. *A post-closing trial balance is taken.* A trial balance is taken to determine the equality of the debits and credits after posting the adjusting and closing entries.
9. *Selected accounts are reversed.* Accrued and prepaid balances that were established by adjusting entries are returned to the nominal accounts that are to be used in recording and summarizing activities involving these items in the new period. This last step is not required but is often desirable as a means of facilitating recording and adjusting routines in the succeeding period.

Recording Phase

Accurate statements can be prepared only if transactions have been properly recorded. A **transaction** is an event or action resulting in a change in the assets, the liabilities, and/or the owners' equity of a business. There are two general classes of transactions requiring accounting recognition: (1) *business transactions,* or transactions entered into with outsiders; and (2) *internal transactions,* or accountable transfers of costs within the business. Examples of internal transactions include recognition of depreciation on plant assets and recognition of a decrease in market value of inventories or investments.

Accounting Records. The **accounting records** of a business consist of: (1) the original source materials evidencing the transactions, called *business* or *source documents;* (2) the records for classifying and recording the transactions, known as the *books of original entry* or *journals;* and (3) the records for summarizing the effects of transactions upon individual asset, liability, and owners' equity accounts, known as the *ledgers.*

12/19/85
JACKIE HELD
JOE VISITED
IN LIBRARY
DRUNK
ON CHAMPAGN

CHAPTER 2 / *Review of the Accounting Process* **23**

The manner in which the accounting records are organized and employed within a business is referred to as its **accounting system.** The exact form the accounting records take depends on the complexity and degree of mechanization of the system. The various recording routines in each system are developed to meet the special needs of the business unit. Recording processes must be designed to provide accurate information on a timely and efficient basis, and at the same time they must serve as effective controls in preventing mistakes and guarding against dishonesty.

Business Documents. Normally a business document prepared or received is the first record of each transaction. Such a document offers detailed information concerning the transaction and also fixes responsibility by naming the parties involved. The business documents provide support for the data to be recorded in the books of original entry. Copies of *sales invoices* or *cash register tapes,* for example, are the evidence in support of the sales record; *purchase invoices* support the purchase or invoice record; *debit* and *credit memorandums* support adjustments in debtor and creditor balances; *check stubs* or *duplicate checks* provide data concerning cash disbursements; the corporation *minutes book* supports entries authorized by action of the board of directors; *journal vouchers* prepared and approved by appropriate officers are a source of data for adjustments or corrections that are to be reported in the accounts. Documents underlying each recorded transaction provide a means of verifying the accounting records and thus form a vital part of the information and control system.

Books of Original Entry. Transactions are analyzed from the information provided on business documents. They are then recorded in chronological order in the appropriate books of original entry, the **journals.** Transactions are analyzed in terms of accounts to be maintained for (1) assets, (2) liabilities, (3) owners' equity, (4) revenues, and (5) expenses. Classes (4) and (5) are nominal or temporary owners' equity accounts summarizing income data for the current period. The analysis is expressed in terms of **debit** and **credit** relationships. Asset and expense accounts have left-hand or debit balances and are decreased by entries on the right-hand or credit side. Liabilities, owners' equity, and revenue accounts have credit balances and are decreased by entries on the debit side.

Although it would be possible to record every transaction in a single journal, this is rarely done. Whenever a number of transactions of the same character take place, special journals may be designed in which the transactions can be conveniently entered and summarized. Special journals eliminate much of the repetitive work involved in recording routine transactions. In addition, they permit the recording function to be divided among accounting personnel, each individual being responsible for a separate record. This specialization often results in greater efficiency as well as a higher degree of control.

Some examples of special journals are the *sales journal,* the *purchases journal,* the *cash receipts journal,* the *cash disbursements journal,* the *payroll register,* and the *voucher register.* Some of these journals are used by

Porter Inc. and are illustrated later in this chapter. Regardless of the number and nature of special journals, certain transactions cannot appropriately be recorded in the special journals and are recorded in the *general journal*.

Sales on account are recorded in the sales journal. The subsequent collections on account, as well as other transactions involving the receipt of cash, are recorded in the cash receipts journal. Merchandise purchases on account are entered in the purchases journal. Subsequent payments on account, as well as other transactions involving the payment of cash, are recorded in the cash disbursements journal or in the *check register*. A *payroll record* may be employed to accumulate payroll information, including special payroll withholdings for taxes and other purposes.

Column headings in the various journals specify the accounts to be debited or credited; account titles and explanations may therefore be omitted in recording routine transactions. A Sundry column is usually provided for transactions that are relatively infrequent, and account titles are specially designated in recording such transactions.

The use of special columns facilitates recording and also serves to summarize the effects of a number of transactions upon individual account balances. The subsequent transfer of information from the journals is thus simplified, as this process is performed with the aggregates of many transactions rather than with separate data for each transaction. Certain data must be transferred individually—data affecting individual accounts receivable and accounts payable and data reported in the Sundry columns—but the volume of transcription is substantially reduced.

Transactions not occurring frequently enough to justify a special journal are recorded in the general journal. The general journal provides debit and credit columns and space for designating account titles; thus, it can be used in recording any transaction. A particular business unit may not need certain special journals, but it must have a general journal.

The Voucher System. A relatively large organization ordinarily provides for the control of purchases and cash disbursements through adoption of some form of a **voucher system.** With the use of a voucher system, checks may be drawn only upon a written authorization in the form of a *voucher* approved by some responsible official.

A voucher is prepared, not only in support of each payment to be made for goods and services purchased on account, but also for all other transactions calling for payment by check, including cash purchases, retirement of debt, replenishment of petty cash funds, payrolls, and dividends. The voucher identifies the person authorizing the expenditure, explains the nature of the transaction, and names the accounts affected by the transaction. Vouchers related to purchase invoices should be compared with receiving reports. Upon verification, the voucher and the related business documents are submitted to the appropriate official for final approval. Upon approval, the voucher is numbered and recorded in a *voucher register*. The voucher register is a book of original entry and takes the place of a purchases journal. Charges on each voucher are classified and summarized in appropriate Debit columns, and the amount to be paid is listed in an Accounts Payable or

Vouchers Payable column. After a voucher is entered in the register, it is placed in an unpaid vouchers file together with its supporting documents.

Checks are written in payment of individual vouchers. The checks are recorded in a check register as debits to Accounts Payable or Vouchers Payable and credits to Cash. Charges to the various asset, liability, or expense accounts, having been recognized when the payable was recorded in the voucher register, need not be listed in the payments record. When a check is issued, payment of the voucher is reported in the voucher register by entering the check number and the payment date. Paid vouchers and invoices are removed from the unpaid vouchers file, marked "paid," and placed in a separate paid vouchers file. The balance of the payable account, after the credit for total vouchers issued and the debit for total vouchers paid, should be equal to the sum of the unpaid vouchers as reported in the voucher register and as found in the unpaid vouchers file. The voucher register, while representing a journal, also provides the detail in support of the accounts or vouchers payable total. Thus, the need for a separate record reporting the individual payable accounts is eliminated.

Posting to the Ledger Accounts. Information as reported on a business document and analyzed, classified, and summarized in terms of debits and credits in the journals is transferred to accounts in the ledger. This transfer is referred to as **posting.** The accounts then summarize the full effects of the transactions upon assets, liabilities, owners' equity, revenues, and expenses, and are used for preparing the financial statements.

Accounts are sometimes referred to as real (or permanent) accounts and nominal (or temporary) accounts. The balance sheet accounts are referred to as **real accounts;** the income statement accounts and the dividends account are referred to as **nominal accounts.** If during the course of the accounting period a balance sheet or an income statement account balance represents both real and nominal elements, it may be described as a **mixed account.** For example, the store supplies account before adjustment is composed of two elements: (1) the store supplies used, and (2) the store supplies still on hand. There is no need to analyze mixed accounts until financial statements are prepared. At this time the real and nominal portions of each mixed account must be determined.

When accounts are set up to record subtractions from related accounts reporting positive balances, such accounts are termed **contra accounts** (or offset accounts). Allowance for Doubtful Accounts is a contra account to Accounts Receivable. Sales Returns and Allowances is a contra account to Sales. Certain accounts relate to others but must be added rather than subtracted on the statements and are referred to as **adjunct accounts.** Examples of these are Freight In that is added to the Purchases balance and Additional Paid-In Capital that is added to the Capital Stock balance.

The real and nominal accounts required by a business unit vary depending upon the nature of the business, its properties and activities, the information to be provided on the financial statements, and the controls to be employed in carrying out the accounting functions. The accounts to be maintained by a particular business are usually expressed in the form of a

chart of accounts. This chart lists the accounts in systematic form with identifying numbers or symbols that are to form the framework for summarizing business operations.

It is often desirable to establish separate ledgers for detailed information in support of balance sheet or income statement items. The **general ledger** carries summaries of all accounts appearing on the financial statements, while separate **subsidiary ledgers** afford additional detail in support of general ledger balances. For example, a single accounts receivable account is usually carried in the general ledger, and individual customers' accounts are shown in a subsidiary *accounts receivable ledger;* the capital stock account in the general ledger is normally supported by individual stockholders' accounts in a subsidiary *stockholders ledger;* selling and general and administrative expenses may be summarized in a single general ledger account, individual expenses being carried in a subsidiary *expense ledger*. The general ledger account that summarizes the detailed information reported elsewhere is known as a **control account.** The accounts receivable account from a general ledger and excerpts from the corresponding accounts receivable subsidiary ledger are shown below.

GENERAL LEDGER

Account **Accounts Receivable** Account No. **116**

Date		Item	Post. Ref.	Debit	Credit	Balance Debit	Balance Credit
1984							
Oct.	1	Balance	√			5,260	
	13		J18		25	5,235	
	28		J18		65	5,170	

ACCOUNTS RECEIVABLE LEDGER

Name **Allen Company**
Address **436 Monroe St., Danville, California 94526**

Date		Item	Post. Ref.	Debit	Credit	Balance
1984						
Oct.	10		S35	750		750
	13		J18		25	725

Name **King & Co.**
Address **48 Converse Rd., Los Angeles, California 90036**

Date		Item	Post. Ref.	Debit	Credit	Balance
1984						
Oct.	24		S35	1,502		1,502
	28		J18		65	1,437

Whenever possible, individual postings to subsidiary accounts are made directly from the business document evidencing the transaction. This practice saves time and avoids errors that might arise in summarizing and transferring this information. A business document also provides the basis for the journal entry authorizing the postings to the control account in the general ledger. In many instances business documents themselves are used to represent a book of original entry. When this is done, business documents are assembled and summarized, and the summaries are transferred directly to the appropriate control accounts as well as to the other accounts affected in the general ledger. Whatever the procedure may be, if postings to the subsidiary records and to the control accounts are made accurately, the sum of the detail in a subsidiary record will agree with the balance in the control account. A reconciliation of each subsidiary record with its related control account should be made periodically, and any discrepancies found should be investigated and corrected.

The use of subsidiary records results in a number of advantages: (1) the number of accounts in the general ledger is reduced, thus making the general ledger more useful as a basis for preparing reports; (2) errors in the general ledger are minimized because of fewer accounts and fewer postings; (3) the accuracy of the posting to a large number of subsidiary accounts may be tested by comparing the total of the balances of the accounts with the balance of one account in the general ledger; (4) totals relating to various items are readily obtained; (5) specialization of accounting duties and individual accounting responsibilities is made possible; and (6) daily posting is facilitated for accounts that must be kept up to date, such as customer and creditor accounts.

Illustration of Journals and Posting. Porter Inc. maintains the following books of original entry: sales journal, cash receipts journal, voucher register, cash disbursements journal, and general journal. The format of a particular journal must satisfy the needs of the individual business unit. Those presented for the Porter Inc. are illustrative only.

Sales Journal. The sales journal as summarized at the end of the month appears as follows:

SALES JOURNAL

Cash Sales Dr.	Accts. Rec. Dr.	Date		Description	Sales Cr.
	2,100		31	Sales on account for day.........	2,100
2,250			31	Cash sales for day...............	2,250
9,800	40,150		31	Total............................	49,950
(√)	(116)				(41)

One entry is made to record the sales on account for each day. Accounts Receivable is debited; Sales is credited. Debits are posted to the individual customers' accounts in the accounts receivable ledger directly from the sales invoices.

One entry is also made for the cash sales for each day. Cash Sales is debited and Sales is credited. The Cash Sales column is used so that all sales transactions are included in the sales journal. An entry crediting Cash Sales is also made in the cash receipts journal.

The numbers in parentheses at the bottom of the journal refer to the accounts to which the totals are posted. The (√) under the Cash Sales column is explained in the following section.

Cash Receipts Journal. The cash receipts journal appears as follows:

CASH RECEIPTS JOURNAL

Cash Dr.	Sales Disc. Dr.	Date	Description	Post. Ref.	Sundry Cr.	Cash Sales Cr.	Accts. Rec. Cr.
8,565		31	Notes receivable	113	8,500		
			Interest revenue......	72	65		
1,960	40	31	Collection on accounts	√			2,000
2,250		31	Cash sales...........	√		2,250	
151,550	395	31	Total................		106,245	9,800	35,900
(111)	(42)				(√)	(√)	(116)

One entry is made each day for the total amount collected on accounts receivable. In this entry Cash and Sales Discounts are debited and Accounts Receivable is credited. Credits are posted to the individual customers' accounts in the accounts receivable subsidiary ledger from a separate list of receipts on account maintained by the cashier.

In order to maintain the cash receipts journal as a complete record of all cash received, an entry crediting Cash Sales is made each day. An entry debiting Cash Sales is also made in the sales journal as explained earlier. To avoid double posting of the transaction, the total of the Cash Sales Dr. column in the sales journal and the total of the Cash Sales Cr. column in the cash receipts journal are checked (√) and are not posted. As a result, the debit to Cash for cash sales is posted from the cash receipts journal as a part of the total of the Cash Dr. column, and the credit to Sales for cash sales is posted from the sales journal as a part of the total of the Sales Cr. column. A (√) under the Sundry column indicates that the amounts in this column are posted individually and not in total. In the illustration, $8,500 was posted to Notes Receivable (account number 113), and $65 was posted to Interest Revenue (account number 72).

Voucher Register. The voucher register takes the place of a purchases journal, providing a record of all authorized payments to be made by check. The voucher register appears on the following page. For illustrative purposes, separate debit columns are provided for two accounts—Purchases and Payroll. Other items are recorded in the Sundry Dr. column. Additional separate columns could be added for other items, such as advertising, if desired. The total amount of each column is posted to the corresponding account, with the exception of the Sundry Dr. and Cr. columns which are posted individually.

VOUCHER REGISTER

Date	Vou. No.	Payee	Paid Date	Paid Ck. No.	Accounts Payable Cr.	Purchases Dr.	Payroll Dr.	Account	Sundry Post. Ref.	Sundry Amount Dr.	Sundry Amount Cr.
31	7132	Security National Bank	12/31	3106	9,120			Notes Payable	211	9,120	
31	7133	Payroll	12/31	3107	1,640		2,130	FICA Tax Payable	215		90
								Income Tax Payable	214		400
31	7134	Far Fabrications			3,290	3,290					
31	7135	Midland Inc.			1,500	1,500					
31	7136	Nyland Supply Co.			5,550	5,550					
31		Total			55,375	24,930	2,130			33,645	5,330
					(213)	(51)	(620)			(√)	(√)

Cash Disbursements Journal. The cash disbursements journal is illustrated below. It accounts for all of the checks issued during the period. Checks are issued only in payment of properly approved vouchers. The payee is designated together with the number of the voucher authorizing the payment. The cash disbursements record when prepared in this form is frequently called a *check register.*

CASH DISBURSEMENTS JOURNAL

Date	Check No.	Account Debited	Vou. No.	Accounts Payable Dr.	Purchase Discounts Cr.	Cash Cr.
31	3106	Security National Bank	7132	9,120		9,120
31	3107	Payroll	7133	1,640		1,640
31	3108	Pat Bunnell	7005	1,500	30	1,470
31		Total		61,160	275	60,885
				(213)	(52)	(111)

General Journal. The general journal, with illustrative entries for the month of December, appears on the following page. This general journal is prepared in three-column form. A pair of columns is provided for the entries that are to be made to the general ledger accounts. A "detail" column is provided for the individual debits and credits to subsidiary records that accompany entries affecting general ledger control accounts.

From Manual Operations to Electronic Data Processing. As an organization grows in size and complexity, the recording and summarizing process becomes more involved, and means are sought for improving efficiency and

JOURNAL

Date		Description	Post. Ref.	Detail	Debit	Credit
1984						
Dec.	1	Notes Receivable	113		8,000	
		Accounts Receivable............	116			8,000
		M. E. Scott	AR	8,000		
		Received note from customer.				
	13	Allowance for Doubtful Accounts. .	117		1,270	
		Accounts Receivable............	116			1,270
		W. G. Haag......................	AR	1,270		
		To write off uncollectible account.				
	31	Payroll Taxes Expense	625		250	
		FICA Tax Payable	215			250
		To record employer's FICA tax for month.				

reducing costs. Some enterprises may find that a system involving primarily manual operations is adequate in meeting their needs. Others may find that information processing needs can be handled effectively only through mechanical devices or electronic data processing (EDP) equipment.

In a manual accounting system all operations are performed by hand. Original source materials—invoices, checks, and other business documents—are written out, and the data they contain are transferred by hand to the journals, the ledgers, and eventually to the financial statements.

As the volume of record keeping expands, mechanical equipment may be added to the system. Machines to supplement manual operations often include posting machines, accounting machines, and billing machines. By using special papers, these machines are able to prepare original documents and journal and ledger records at one time, thus saving the work of transferring data. They also can perform a few routine arithmetic operations, such as adding journal columns and computing ledger balances.

Companies requiring great speed and accuracy in processing large amounts of accounting data may utilize an electronic computer system capable of storing and recalling data, performing many mathematical functions, and making certain routine decisions based on mathematical comparisons. These systems normally include various other machines that can "read" data from magnetic tapes or punched cards and print information in a variety of forms, all under the control of the computer.

Modern computer systems have great capabilities. The individual steps of recording, classifying, and summarizing may be combined into one process. The information traditionally recorded in journals and ledgers may be stored in memory banks or on computer discs and recalled as needed. On-line, real-time systems have the capability of continuous updating of all relevant files. This makes it possible for reports to be produced on a much more timely basis.

Despite their tremendous capabilities, electronic systems cannot replace skilled accountants. In fact, their presence places increased demands on the accountant in directing the operations of the system to assure the use of appropriate procedures. Although all arithmetical operations can be assumed to be done accurately by the computer, the validity of the output data depends upon the adequacy of the instructions given it. Unlike a human accountant, a computer cannot think for itself but must be given explicit instructions in performing each operation. This has certain advantages in that the accountant can be sure every direction will be carried out precisely. On the other hand, this places a great responsibility on the accountant to anticipate any unusual situations requiring special consideration or judgment. Particular techniques must also be developed for checking and verifying data recorded in electronic form.

The remainder of this chapter is concerned with the summarizing activities required in preparing periodic financial statements. The exact manner in which these activities are carried out will vary according to the degree of automation of the particular accounting system. Although the computer can be programmed to report information in any desired format, the input to and output from computer systems differ considerably in form from that of manual and machine systems. Despite such differences, all accounting systems are designed to serve the same information processing function.

Throughout this text, a manual accounting system is used to facilitate the illustration of concepts and procedures. In actual practice, most companies of any substantial size use some type of computer system. The advent of microcomputers has put EDP within the reach of many smaller companies that previously had to rely on manual or mechanized systems.

Summarizing Phase

The accounting routine at the close of the fiscal period is frequently referred to as the *periodic summary*. The steps in the process were outlined earlier, and they are described in more detail in the following sections.

Preparing a Trial Balance. After all transactions for the period have been posted to the ledger accounts, the balance for each account is determined. Every account will have either a debit, credit, or zero balance. A **trial balance** is a list of each account balance and it, therefore, indicates whether the debits equal the credits. Thus, a trial balance provides a check on the accuracy of recording and posting.

Compiling Adjusting Data. Division of the life of a business into periods of arbitrary length creates many problems for the accountant who must summarize the financial operations for the designated period and report on the financial position at the end of that period. Transactions during the period have been recorded in *real* and *nominal* accounts. At the end of the period, accounts with mixed balances require adjustment. At this time, too, other financial data, not recognized currently, must be entered in the accounts to bring the books up to date. This requires analysis of individual accounts and various source documents.

In order to illustrate this part of the accounting process, the adjusting data for Porter Inc. are presented in the following sections. The data are classified according to the typical areas requiring updating at the end of a designated time period, in this case the year 1984. The adjusting data must be combined with the information on the trial balance in bringing the accounts up to date. The trial balance for Porter Inc. appears in the first two amount columns of the work sheet on pages 36 and 37. The accounts listed in the trial balance do not reflect the following information:[2]

Asset Depreciation and Cost Amortization:

(a) Buildings and equipment depreciation, 10% per year.
(b) Office furniture and fixtures depreciation, 20% per year.
(c) Goodwill amortization for the year, $2,900.

Doubtful Accounts:

(d) The allowance for doubtful accounts is to be increased by $1,100.

Accrued Expenses:

(e) Salaries and wages, $2,150.
(f) Interest on bonds payable, $5,000.

Accrued Revenues:

(g) Interest on notes receivable, $250.

Prepaid Expenses:

(h) Prepaid insurance, $3,800.

Deferred Revenues:

(i) Rent received in advance, $475.

Provision for Income Tax:

(j) Provision of $8,000 to be made for federal and state income taxes.

Inventory:

(k) A periodic inventory system is used; the ending inventory balance is $51,000.

Asset Depreciation and Cost Amortization. Charges to operations for the use of buildings and equipment and intangible assets must be recorded at the end of the period. In recording asset depreciation or amortization, operations are charged with a portion of the asset cost, and the carrying value of the asset is reduced by that amount. A reduction in an asset for depreciation is usually recorded by a credit to a contra account. Adjustments at the end of the year for depreciation and amortization for Porter Inc. are as follows:

(a) Depreciation Expense—Buildings and Equipment	15,600	
Accumulated Depreciation—Buildings and Equipment		15,600
To record depreciation on buildings and equipment.		
(b) Depreciation Expense—Office Furniture and Fixtures	3,800	
Accumulated Depreciation—Office Furniture and Fixtures		3,800
To record depreciation on office furniture and fixtures.		
(c) Amortization of Goodwill	2,900	
Goodwill		2,900
To record amortization of goodwill.		

[2]The data are coded to correspond to the letters given on the work sheet on pages 36 and 37.

Doubtful Accounts. Provision is ordinarily made for the probable expense resulting from failure to collect receivables. In recognizing the probable expense arising from the policy of granting credit to customers, operations are charged with the estimated expense, and receivables are reduced by means of a contra account. When there is positive evidence that receivables are uncollectible, receivables are written off against the contra account. To illustrate, the adjustment for Porter Inc. at the end of the year assumes the allowance account is to be increased by $1,100. The adjustment is as follows:

(d) Doubtful Accounts Expense..........................	1,100	
Allowance for Doubtful Accounts....................		1,100
To provide for doubtful accounts.		

Accrued Expenses. During the period, certain expenses may have been incurred although payment is not to be made until a subsequent period. At the end of the period, it is necessary to determine and record the expenses not yet recognized. In recording an accrued expense, an expense account is debited and a liability account is credited. The adjusting entries to record accrued expenses for Porter Inc. are:

(e) Salaries and Wages Expense.........................	2,150	
Salaries and Wages Payable		2,150
To record accrued salaries and wages.		
(f) Interest Expense....................................	5,000	
Interest Payable		5,000
To record accrued interest on bonds.		

At the beginning of the new period, adjustments for accrued expenses may be reversed to make it possible to record expense payments during the new period in the usual manner. The nature of reversing entries is explained more fully later in the chapter.

Accrued Revenues. During the period, certain amounts may have been earned although collection is not to be made until a subsequent period. At the end of the period, it is necessary to determine and record the earnings not yet recognized. In recording accrued revenues, an asset account is debited and a revenue account is credited. The illustrative entry recognizing the accrued revenues for Porter Inc. is as follows:

(g) Interest Receivable.................................	250	
Interest Revenue..................................		250
To record accrued interest on notes receivable.		

Prepaid Expenses. During the period, charges may have been recorded on the books for commodities or services that are not to be received or used up currently. At the end of the period, it is necessary to determine the portions of such charges that are applicable to subsequent periods and hence require recognition as assets.

The method of adjusting for prepaid expenses depends upon how the expenditures were originally entered in the accounts. The charges for the commodities or services may have been recorded as debits to (1) an expense account or (2) an asset account.

Original Debit to an Expense Account. If an expense account was originally debited, the adjusting entry requires that an asset account be debited for the expense applicable to the future period and the expense account be credited. The expense account then remains with a debit balance representing the amount applicable to the current period. The adjusting entry may be reversed at the beginning of the new period as explained later in the chapter.

Original Debit to an Asset Account. If an asset account was originally debited, the adjusting entry requires that an expense account be debited for the amount applicable to the current period and the asset account be credited. The asset account remains with a debit balance that shows the amount applicable to future periods. In this instance, no reversing entry is needed. An adjusting entry for prepaid insurance for Porter Inc. illustrates this situation as follows:

(h) Insurance Expense	4,200	
Prepaid Insurance		4,200
To record expired insurance ($8,000 − $3,800 = $4,200).		

Since the asset account Prepaid Insurance was originally debited, the amount of the prepayment must be reduced to reflect only the $3,800 that remains unexpired.

Deferred Revenues. Payments may be received from customers prior to the delivery of goods or services. Amounts received in advance are recorded by debiting an asset account, usually Cash, and crediting either a revenue account or a liability account. At the end of the period, it is necessary to determine the amount of revenue to be deferred to future periods. The method of adjusting for deferred revenues depends on whether the initial receipts for undelivered goods or services were recorded as credits to (1) a revenue account or (2) a liability account.

Original Credit to a Revenue Account. If a revenue account was originally credited, this account is debited and a liability account is credited for the revenue applicable to a future period. The revenue account remains with a credit balance representing the earnings applicable to the current period. Again, this adjustment may be reversed as explained later.

Assuming the credit was made originally to the revenue account, the entry to record rent received in advance for Porter Inc. is as follows:

(i) Rent Revenue	475	
Rent Received in Advance		475
To record rent received in advance.		

Original Credit to a Liability Account. If a liability account was originally credited, this account is debited and a revenue account is credited for the amount applicable to the current period. The liability account remains with a credit balance that shows the amount applicable to future periods. In this instance, no reversing entry is needed.

Provision for Income Tax. When a corporation reports earnings, provision must be made for federal and state income taxes. Income Tax is debited and Income Tax Payable is credited. The entry to record estimated tax payable for Porter Inc. is as follows:

(j) Income Tax..	8,000	
Income Tax Payable................................		8,000
To record estimated income tax payable.		

Preparing a Work Sheet. The adjusting data must be combined with the information on the trial balance to bring the accounts up to date. This may be done and the financial statements developed through the preparation of a **work sheet.** In the construction of a work sheet, trial balance data are listed in the first pair of amount columns. The adjusting entries are listed in the second pair of columns. Sometimes a third pair of columns is included to show the trial balance after adjustment. Account balances as adjusted are carried to the appropriate statement columns. A work sheet for a merchandising enterprise will include a pair of columns for the income statement accounts and for the balance sheet accounts. Two columns for retained earnings may be placed between the Income Statement and Balance Sheet columns if sufficient transactions warrant it. A similar work sheet form may be used for a manufacturing enterprise except that a set of Manufacturing Schedule columns may be added. There are no columns for the statement of changes in financial position, because this statement contains a rearrangement of information included in the balance sheet and income statement. A discussion of the preparation of the statement of changes in financial position is deferred to Chapter 23.

The work sheet for Porter Inc. is shown on pages 36 and 37. All adjustments previously illustrated are included. The simple procedure for reporting the ending inventory balance should be noted. The beginning balance is transferred as a debit to the Income Statement columns, while the ending balance is entered directly as a credit in the Income Statement columns and as a debit in the Balance Sheet columns. An alternative procedure is to adjust the inventory balance in the Adjustments columns by crediting the beginning balance and debiting the ending balance. Corresponding amounts are closed through Cost of Goods Sold or Income Summary to the Income Statement columns, and the ending inventory balance is transferred to the Balance Sheet columns.

Preparing Financial Statements. The **financial statements** are prepared using the work sheet as the basic source of data for the presentations. The basic financial statements are illustrated in Chapters 4 and 5. They include the balance sheet, the income statement, and the statement of changes in financial position.

Adjusting and Closing the Inventory Accounts. When the periodic inventory method is used, physical inventories must be taken at the end of the

Porter
Work
For Year Ended

	Account Title	Trial Balance Debit	Trial Balance Credit	Adjustments Debit	Adjustments Credit	
1	Cash	83,110				1
2	Notes Receivable	28,000				2
3	Accounts Receivable	106,500				3
4	Allowance for Doubtful Accounts		1,610		(d) 1,100	4
5	Inventory	45,000				5
6	Prepaid Insurance	8,000			(h) 4,200	6
7	Land	114,000				7
8	Buildings and Equipment	156,000				8
9	Accum. Depr.—Buildings and Equipment		38,600		(a) 15,600	9
10	Office Furniture and Fixtures	19,000				10
11	Accum. Depr.—Office Furniture and Fixtures		3,200		(b) 3,800	11
12	Goodwill	55,400			(c) 2,900	12
13	Accounts Payable		37,910			13
14	Payroll Taxes Payable		5,130			14
15	Dividends Payable		3,400			15
16	8% First-Mortgage Bonds		140,000			16
17	Common Stock, $20 par		150,000			17
18	Additional Paid-In Capital		50,000			18
19	Retained Earnings		139,350			19
20	Dividends	13,600				20
21	Sales		583,000			21
22	Sales Discounts	3,500				22
23	Purchases	157,500				23
24	Purchase Discounts		3,290			24
25	Freight In	5,100				25
26	Salaries and Wages Expense	162,450		(e) 2,150		26
27	Heat, Light, and Power	27,480				27
28	Payroll Taxes Expense	13,300				28
29	Sales, Salaries, and Commissions	31,000				29
30	Advertising Expense	13,200				30
31	Administrative Salaries	87,300				31
32	Miscellaneous General Expense	14,700				32
33	Interest Revenue		1,100		(g) 250	33
34	Rent Revenue		2,550	(i) 475		34
35	Interest Expense	15,000		(f) 5,000		35
36	Doubtful Accounts Expense			(d) 1,100		36
37	Depr. Exp.—Buildings and Equipment			(a) 15,600		37
38	Depr. Exp.—Office Furniture and Fixtures			(b) 3,800		38
39	Amortization of Goodwill			(c) 2,900		39
40	Salaries and Wages Payable				(e) 2,150	40
41	Interest Payable				(f) 5,000	41
42	Insurance Expense			(h) 4,200		42
43	Interest Receivable			(g) 250		43
44	Rent Received in Advance				(i) 475	44
45	Income Tax			(j) 8,000		45
46	Income Tax Payable				(j) 8,000	46
47		1,159,140	1,159,140	43,475	43,475	47
48	Net Income					48
49						49

Inc.
Sheet
December 31, 1984

	Income Statement		Balance Sheet		
	Debit	Credit	Debit	Credit	
1			83,110		1
2			28,000		2
3			106,500		3
4				2,710	4
5	45,000	(k) 51,000	(k) 51,000		5
6			3,800		6
7			114,000		7
8			156,000		8
9				54,200	9
10			19,000		10
11				7,000	11
12			52,500		12
13				37,910	13
14				5,130	14
15				3,400	15
16				140,000	16
17				150,000	17
18				50,000	18
19				139,350	19
20			13,600		20
21		583,000			21
22	3,500				22
23	157,500				23
24		3,290			24
25	5,100				25
26	164,600				26
27	27,480				27
28	13,300				28
29	31,000				29
30	13,200				30
31	87,300				31
32	14,700				32
33		1,350			33
34		2,075			34
35	20,000				35
36	1,100				36
37	15,600				37
38	3,800				38
39	2,900				39
40				2,150	40
41				5,000	41
42	4,200				42
43			250		43
44				475	44
45	8,000				45
46				8,000	46
47	618,280	640,715	627,760	605,325	47
48	22,435			22,435	48
49	640,715	640,715	627,760	627,760	49

period to determine the inventory to be reported on the balance sheet and the cost of goods sold to be reported on the income statement. When perpetual or book inventories are maintained, the ending inventory and the cost of goods sold balances appear in the ledger and an adjustment is not required. The closing procedures for merchandising companies are described in the following paragraphs. Accounting for inventories of manufacturers is explained in Chapter 8.

Periodic (Physical) Inventories. When using the periodic inventory method, all purchases of merchandise during a period are recorded in a purchases account. At the end of the period, before adjustments are made, the inventory account shows the beginning inventory balance. The ending balance, based on a physical count, is established in the inventory account by an adjusting entry or through the closing process.

Using a closing procedure and Porter Inc. as an example, the following entry would be made:

Inventory (Ending)	51,000	
Inventory (Beginning)		45,000
Income Summary		6,000

With this procedure, cost of goods sold appears only as a calculated figure on the income statement; it does not appear in the accounts. An advantage to the approach used here is that all amounts required for preparing an income statement are summarized in the Income Statement columns of the work sheet (see pages 36 and 37).

Perpetual Inventories. When a perpetual inventory is maintained, a separate purchases account is not used. The inventory account is debited whenever goods are acquired. When a sale takes place, two entries are required: (1) the sale is recorded in the usual manner, and (2) the merchandise sold is recorded by a debit to Cost of Goods Sold and a credit to the inventory account. Subsidiary records for inventory items are normally maintained. Detailed increases and decreases in the various inventory items are reported in the subsidiary accounts, and the costs of goods purchased and sold are summarized in the inventory control account. At the end of the period, the inventory account reflects the inventory on hand; the cost of goods sold account is closed into Income Summary.

Closing the Nominal Accounts. Adjusting entries, which are usually prepared on the work sheet, must be formally recorded in the general journal and posted to the ledger to bring the accounts up to date prior to closing. The procedures for adjusting and closing the inventory account were described in the preceding sections. In addition, all nominal account balances are closed to Income Summary. The balance in the income summary account is closed to an owners' equity account. If a work sheet is prepared, the balances in the Income Statement columns provide the data for closing entries. The closing entries for Porter Inc. are presented on the following page.

Closing Entries

1984			
Dec. 31	Sales	583,000	
	Interest Revenue	1,350	
	Rent Revenue	2,075	
	Sales Discount		3,500
	Income Summary		582,925
	To close revenue accounts into Income Summary.		
	Income Summary	560,490	
	Inventory	51,000	
	Purchase Discounts	3,290	
	Inventory		45,000
	Purchases		157,500
	Freight In		5,100
	Salary and Wages Expense		164,600
	Heat, Light, and Power		27,480
	Payroll Taxes Expense		13,300
	Sales, Salaries, and Commissions		31,000
	Advertising Expense		13,200
	Administrative Salaries		87,300
	Miscellaneous General Expense		14,700
	Interest Expense		20,000
	Doubtful Accounts Expense		1,100
	Depreciation Expense—Buildings and Equipment		15,600
	Depreciation Expense—Office Furniture and Fixtures		3,800
	Amortization of Goodwill		2,900
	Insurance Expense		4,200
	Income Tax		8,000
	To close beginning inventory and expense accounts into Income Summary and record ending inventory.		
	Income Summary	22,435	
	Retained Earnings		22,435
	To transfer the balance in Income Summary to Retained Earnings.		
	Retained Earnings	13,600	
	Dividends		13,600
	To close Dividends into Retained Earnings.		

Preparing a Post-Closing Trial Balance. After the closing entries are recorded in the general journal and posted to the ledger accounts, a post-closing trial balance is prepared to verify the equality of the debits and credits. The post-closing trial balance for Porter Inc. is presented on page 40.

Reversing the Accounts. At the beginning of a new period, the adjusting entries for accrued expenses, accrued revenues, prepaid expenses when the original debit was to an expense account, and deferred revenues when the original credit was to a revenue account may be reversed. **Reversing entries** are not necessary, but they make it possible to record the expense payments or revenue receipts in the new period in the usual manner. If a reversing entry is not made, for example, for accrued expenses, the expense payments would

Porter Inc.
Post-Closing Trial Balance
December 31, 1984

Cash	83,110	
Notes Receivable	28,000	
Accounts Receivable	106,500	
Allowance for Doubtful Accounts		2,710
Interest Receivable	250	
Inventory	51,000	
Prepaid Insurance	3,800	
Land	114,000	
Buildings and Equipment	156,000	
Accumulated Depreciation—Buildings and Equipment		54,200
Office Furniture and Fixtures	19,000	
Accumulated Depreciation—Office Furniture and Fixtures		7,000
Goodwill	52,500	
Accounts Payable		37,910
Income Tax Payable		8,000
Payroll Taxes Payable		5,130
Salaries and Wages Payable		2,150
Interest Payable		5,000
Dividends Payable		3,400
8% First-Mortgage Bonds		140,000
Rent Received in Advance		475
Common Stock, $20 par		150,000
Additional Paid-In Capital		50,000
Retained Earnings		148,185
	614,160	614,160

have to be analyzed as to (1) the amount representing payment of the accrued liability, and (2) the amount representing the expense of the current period. Alternatively, the accrued and deferred accounts could be left unadjusted until the close of the subsequent reporting period when they would be adjusted to their correct balances.

The adjustments establishing accrued and prepaid balances for Porter Inc. were illustrated earlier in the chapter. The appropriate reversing entries are shown below.

Reversing Entries

1985			
Jan. 1	Salaries and Wages Payable	2,150	
	Salaries and Wages Expense		2,150
	Interest Payable	5,000	
	Interest Expense		5,000
	Interest Revenue	250	
	Interest Receivable		250
	Rent Received in Advance	475	
	Rent Revenue		475

To illustrate accounting for an accrued expense when (1) reversing entries are made and (2) reversing entries are not made, assume that accrued salaries on December 31, 1984, are $350 and on December 31, 1985, are $500. Payment of salaries for the period ending January 4, 1985, is $1,000. Adjustments are made and the books are closed annually on December 31.

The possible entries are shown below:

	(1) Assuming Liability Account Is Reversed	(2) Assuming Liability Account Is Not Reversed: (a) Transaction in Next Period Is Analyzed.	(2) Assuming Liability Account Is Not Reversed: (b) Transaction in Next Period Is Not Analyzed. Adjustment at Close of Next Reporting Period.
December 31, 1984 Adjusting entry to record accrued salaries.	Salaries .... 350 Salaries Payable 350	Salaries ...... 350 Salaries Payable 350	Salaries ...... 350 Salaries Payable 350
December 31, 1984 Closing entry to transfer expense to the income summary account.	Income Summary.......... xxx Salaries xxx	Income Summary ..... xxx Salaries xxx	Income Summary ..... xxx Salaries xxx
January 1, 1985 Reversing entry to transfer balance to the account that will be charged when payment is made.	Salaries Payable .... 350 Salaries 350	No entry	No entry
January 4, 1985 Payment of salaries for period ending January 4, 1985.	Salaries .... 1,000 Cash 1,000	Salaries Payable ..... 350 Salaries ...... 650 Cash 1,000	Salaries ...... 1,000 Cash 1,000
December 31, 1985 Adjusting entry to record accrued salaries.	Salaries .... 500 Salaries Payable 500	Salaries ...... 500 Salaries Payable 500	Salaries ...... 150 Salaries Payable 150

SINGLE-ENTRY SYSTEMS — A SPECIAL CASE

The procedures just described leading to the preparation of financial statements are those required in a **double-entry system.** This is the characteristic system employed in accounting practice and requires analysis of each transaction in terms of debits and credits. Any set of procedures that does not provide for the analysis of each transaction in terms of double entry is referred to as a **single-entry system.**

Single-entry systems differ widely depending on the needs of the organization and the originality of the people maintaining the system. Records found in a single-entry system may vary from a narrative of transactions recorded in a single journal, called a *daybook,* to a relatively complete set of journals and a ledger providing accounts for all significant items.

Single-entry procedures are frequently found in organizations whose activities do not warrant the employment of a bookkeeper. Such organizations might include unincorporated retail businesses, professional and service units, and nonprofit organizations. Persons acting in a fiduciary capacity, such as estate executors and trust custodians, may also limit their record keeping to single-entry procedures. When double-entry records are not maintained, a professional accountant is normally engaged at different intervals to prepare financial statements, tax returns, and any other required reports on an accrual basis.

Records in Single-Entry Systems

All variations of single-entry systems encountered in practice cannot be described here. A characteristic single-entry system consists of the following records: (1) a daybook or general journal, (2) a cashbook, and (3) ledger accounts showing debtor and creditor balances.

Single-entry procedures commonly take the following form. A cashbook is maintained showing all the transactions affecting cash. Instead of naming accounts to be debited or credited as a result of cash receipts and disbursements, a description of the transaction is offered and a column for the amount of cash is provided. Transactions not shown in the cashbook are recorded in a daybook in descriptive form. Whenever the account of a debtor, a creditor, or the owner is affected, attention is directed to the need for posting by indicating "dr" or "cr" before the amount. Offsetting debits or credits are not shown since accounts in the ledger are maintained only for customers, creditors, and the owner. At the end of the period, reports may be limited to summaries of customer and creditor balances. Of course, because it is single entry, there is no direct way of knowing if the balances are correct.

Preparation of Financial Statements from Single-Entry Records

When records do not offer a complete summary of transactions, the preparation of accurate financial statements raises a number of special problems. These are discussed in the following sections.

Preparation of the Balance Sheet. When the ledger consists of account balances for customers and creditors only, the preparation of the balance sheet calls for reference to a number of different sources. Cash is reported at the balance shown in the cashbook after this figure has been reconciled with the totals of cash on hand and on deposit with the bank. Receivables and payables are summarized from the accounts maintained with debtors and creditors. Merchandise and supplies balances are found by taking physical inventories. Past statements, cash records, and other documents are reviewed in determining the book values of depreciable assets. Other assets and liabilities, including accrued and prepaid items, are determined by a review of the records, including invoices, documents, and other available sources offering evidence or information concerning transactions of the past, present, and future. The owner's capital balance in a double-entry system represents an amount arrived at by combining beginning capital, additional investments and withdrawals, and revenue and expense account balances; in single-entry, capital is simply the difference between the total reported for assets less the total reported for liabilities.

Determination of the Net Income or Loss from Comparative Balance Sheet Data and Cash Summary. In the absence of revenue and expense accounts, net income may be calculated by the single-entry method. The owner's capital at the beginning of the period is subtracted from owner's capital at the end of the period. The difference is then increased for any withdrawals and decreased for any investments made by the owner during the period. Beginning and ending owner's capital balances are taken from the balance sheets prepared at the end of the previous period and at the end of the current period. Investments and withdrawals are ascertained from owner's capital and drawing accounts maintained in the ledger, or in the absence of these, from the cashbook and other memorandum records.

To illustrate the determination of net income or loss, assume the owner's capital is reported on comparative balance sheets as follows: January 1, $20,000; December 31, $30,000. In the absence of investments or withdrawals by the owner, it must be concluded that the net income for the year was $10,000. However, assume the owner has invested $2,500 and has withdrawn $9,000 during the year. Net income is then computed as follows:

Owner's capital, December 31		$30,000
Owner's capital, January 1		20,000
Net increase in owner's capital		$10,000
Add excess of owner's withdrawals over investments:		
Withdrawals	$9,000	
Investments	2,500	6,500
Net income for the year		$16,500

Preparation of the Income Statement. A summary of the net income or loss calculated from comparative capital balances is generally inadequate. The owner needs a detailed statement of operations disclosing sales, cost of goods sold, operating expenses, and miscellaneous revenue and expense items to evaluate past success or failure and to plan future activities. Creditors may insist upon such statements. In addition, revenue and expense data must be itemized for income tax purposes.

An itemized income statement can be prepared by (1) rewriting transactions in double-entry form or (2) computing the individual revenue and expense balances by reference to cash receipts and disbursements and the changes in asset and liability balances. Obviously, little or nothing is saved by the adoption of a single-entry system if transactions are rewritten in double-entry form and posted to accounts. When the second procedure is followed, an analysis of all cash receipts and disbursements is required, unless this is already provided by special analysis columns in the cash journals. Cash receipts must be classified as: (1) receipts for goods sold for cash, (2) receipts of other revenue items, (3) collections on customers' accounts, (4) proceeds from the sale of assets other than merchandise, (5) amounts borrowed, and (6) investments by the owner. Cash payments must be classifed as (1) payments for mechandise purchased for cash, (2) payments of other expense items, (3) payments on trade creditors' accounts, (4) payments for the purchase of assets other than merchandise, (5) loans paid off, and (6) withdrawals by the owner. These data, together with the data provided by the balance sheet, are used in the preparation of the income statement on an accrual basis. Obviously, the accuracy of the income statement will depend on the accuracy of the information used in computing revenue and expense items. The procedures followed in computing revenue and expense balances on an accrual basis are illustrated in the following sections.

Sales. The amount to be reported for sales consists of the total of cash sales and sales on account. Sales are computed from the cash receipts analysis and comparative balance sheet data as follows:

Cash sales		$ 7,500
Sales on account:		
Notes and accounts receivable at the end of the period	$1,500	
Collections on notes and accounts receivable during the period	3,000	
	$4,500	
Deduct notes and accounts receivable at the beginning of the period	2,000	2,500
Sales for the period		$10,000

Notes and accounts receivable in the foregoing tabulation are limited to those arising from sales of merchandise.

The computation of gross sales is complicated if sales discounts and returns and allowances exist, or if accounts thought to be uncollectible are written off. For example, assume sales data as follows:

Data from cash records:	
Cash sales	$10,000
Collections on accounts receivable arising from sales	42,000
Data from balance sheets:	
Accounts receivable at the beginning of the period	$14,300
Accounts receivable at the end of the period	12,500
Supplementary data from special analysis of records:	
Accounts written off during the period	$ 600
Sales discounts allowed customers during the period	850
Sales returns and allowances during the period	300

The supplementary data indicate that uncollectible accounts of $600, sales discounts of $850, and sales returns and allowances of $300 are to be recognized. These amounts must be added to cash collections in arriving at gross sales, for there must have been sales equivalent to the reductions in accounts receivable from these sources. Gross sales for the period are computed as follows:

Cash sales		$10,000
Sales on account:		
Accounts receivable at the end of the period	$12,500	
Collections on accounts receivable	42,000	
Accounts receivable written off	600	
Accounts receivable reduced by discounts	850	
Accounts receivable reduced by sales returns and allowances	300	
	$56,250	
Deduct accounts receivable at the beginning of the period	14,300	41,950
Gross sales for the period		$51,950

Failure to recognize uncollectible accounts, sales discounts, and sales returns and allowances will be counterbalanced by an understatement in gross sales. Although the omissions will have no effect on the net income balance, revenue and expense balances will not be stated accurately.

Cost of Goods Sold. The inventory balance shown on the balance sheet prepared at the end of the preceding fiscal period is reported on the income statement as the beginning inventory.

The amount to be reported for purchases consists of the total of cash purchases and purchases on account. Purchases are computed from the cash payments analysis and comparative balance sheet data as follows:

Cash purchases		$1,500
Purchases on account:		
Notes and accounts payable at the end of the period	$2,500	
Payments on notes and accounts payable during the period	5,000	
	$7,500	
Deduct notes and accounts payable at the beginning of the period	3,500	4,000
Purchases for the period		$5,500

Notes and accounts payable in the foregoing tabulation are limited to those arising from purchases of merchandise.

The inventory balance shown on the balance sheet at the end of the current period is reported on the income statement as the ending inventory. In the first year complete statements are prepared, an estimate of the beginning inventory must be made.

When purchase discounts and purchase returns and allowances reduce accounts payable, the computation of purchases follows the same procedure as for gross sales. The purchases balance is increased by the total purchase discounts and purchase returns and allowances since there must have been purchases equivalent to the reductions in the accounts payable from these sources.

Expense Items. An expense balance is computed from the analysis of cash payments and comparative balance sheet data. The computation of an expense item is made as follows:

Cash payments representing expense		$1,000
Add amounts not included in cash payments but to be charged to current period:		
Amount prepaid at the beginning of the period	$250	
Amount accrued at the end of the period	150	400
		$1,400
Deduct amounts included in payments but not to be charged to current period:		
Amount prepaid at the end of the period	$200	
Amount accrued at the beginning of the period	100	300
Expense for the period		$1,100

The charge for depreciation or amortization to be recognized on the income statement may be made by special analysis of balance sheet as well as cash data, if the balance sheet reflects depreciation in the asset balances. For example, assume no acquisition or disposal of property during the period and beginning and ending store furniture balances of $30,000 and $28,500 respectively. Depreciation is reported at $1,500, the net decrease in the asset account. Assume, however, the following information is assembled at the end of a fiscal period:

Data from cash records:	
Payments for store furniture, including payments on notes arising from acquisition of store furniture	$ 2,500
Data from balance sheets:	
Store furniture at the beginning of the period	$ 9,000
Store furniture at the end of the period	10,850
Installment notes payable arising from acquisition of store furniture	4,000

The charge for depreciation for the period is computed as follows:

Balance of store furniture at the beginning of the period		$ 9,000
Add acquisitions of store furniture:		
Cash paid on acquisition of store furniture	$2,500	
Amount owed at the end of the period on acquisition of store furniture	4,000	6,500
Balance of store furniture before depreciation		$15,500
Deduct balance of store furniture at the end of the period		10,850
Depreciation of store furniture for period		$ 4,650

The charge for depreciation developed from the cash records and balance sheet data should be confirmed by computations based upon the individual property items held. The inability to confirm depreciation may indicate that property balances are not reported accurately on the balance sheet. The following analysis is made to support the charge calculated above.

Property	Date Acquired	Cost	Accumulated Depreciation— Prior Years	Remaining Cost	Estimated Life	Remaining Life from Beginning of Year	Depreciation Current Year
Store furniture	4/1/80	$24,000	$15,000	$ 9,000	6 yrs.	2¼ yrs.	$4,000
Store furniture	7/1/84	6,500	....	6,500	5 yrs.	....	650 (½ yr.)
		$30,500	$15,000	$15,500			$4,650

Other Revenue Items. Other revenue balances are computed from the analysis of cash receipts and comparative balance sheet data as shown at the top of the next page.

A comprehensive illustration of preparing financial statements from single-entry records is provided as an appendix to this chapter. In addition to the statements discussed and illustrated in this chapter, a statement of changes in financial position could also be prepared. This statement is discussed in depth in Chapter 23.

Cash receipts representing revenue		$ 800
Add amounts not included in cash receipts but to be credited to current period:		
Amount prepaid at the beginning of the period	$300	
Amount accrued at the end of the period	50	350
		$1,150
Deduct amounts included in receipts but not to be credited to current period:		
Amount prepaid at the end of the period	$225	
Amount accrued at the beginning of the period	175	400
Other revenue for the period		$ 750

Changing from Single Entry to Double Entry

The management of a business may find that single-entry procedures fail to meet its needs and may decide to change to double entry. Single-entry records may be converted to double entry by first drawing up a balance sheet as of the date of change. This statement is used as the basis for a journal entry establishing all asset, asset valuation, liability, and capital accounts. If additional accounts are to be added to a ledger already in use, accounts are opened and balances recorded for those items not included. If new books are to be used, accounts are opened and balances are recorded for all the items reported in the opening journal entry.

Use of Single-Entry Systems

Single entry is described here because it represents a special type of system that accountants are likely to encounter when called upon to prepare financial statements, audit books and records, and prepare government information reports and income tax returns, especially when dealing with small businesses.

Among the advantages of single-entry systems are the following:

(1) Record keeping is simplified and the cost of maintaining records is minimal.
(2) Individuals sometimes use formal financial statements only for tax returns and occasional borrowing. When needed for these purposes, financial statements can be prepared from the single-entry records as demonstrated in this chapter.

Among the disadvantages of single-entry procedures are the following factors:

(1) A trial balance offering a check on the mathematical accuracy of posting is not available.
(2) Preparation of the balance sheet from miscellaneous sources and memoranda may result in omissions and misstatements.
(3) Detailed analysis of transactions is necessary in arriving at a summary of operations. Misstatements of assets and liabilities, particularly failures to report assets at properly depreciated or amortized balances, affect revenue

and expense balances and may result in material misstatement of net income or loss.

(4) There is failure to provide a centralized and coordinated accounting system subject to internal control and available for satisfactory and convenient audit by public accountants and Internal Revenue agents.

FROM TRANSACTIONS TO STATEMENTS

The usual procedures for recording transactions and the sequence of events leading to the preparation of financial statements have been briefly reviewed in this chapter. The treatment applied to these transactions and events was referred to as the accounting process.

The accounting process includes the functions of analyzing, classifying, recording, summarizing, and reporting. It includes the successive steps that constitute the accounting cycle. It starts with the first written record of the transactions of an entity and concludes with the final summarized financial statements.

The significance of the accounting process in our economic society and its applicability to every business unit, regardless of size, must be appreciated. Although the procedures may be modified to meet special conditions, and may be effected through a variety of manual or computer systems, the process reviewed here is fundamental to the accounting for all enterprises.

APPENDIX

PREPARATION OF FINANCIAL STATEMENTS FROM SINGLE-ENTRY RECORDS ILLUSTRATED

The following example illustrates the preparation from single-entry records of (1) a balance sheet, (2) a summary of net income by analysis of capital changes, and (3) an income statement reporting revenue and expense detail. S & P Enterprises does not maintain double-entry records. Balance sheet data, an analysis of cash receipts and disbursements, and supplementary data required in the development of financial statements from the single-entry data are assembled at the end of 1984 as follows:

Comparative Balance Sheet Data

	December 31, 1984	January 1, 1984
Assets		
Cash	$ 5,200	$ 3,200
Notes receivable	3,000	2,500
Accounts receivable	4,500	6,000
Interest receivable	50	150
Inventory	24,600	20,000
Supplies on hand	600	400
Prepaid miscellaneous expense	—	100
Long-term investments	2,200	9,700
Furniture and fixtures (cost less accumulated depreciation)	8,325	5,800
Total assets	$48,475	$47,850
Liabilities		
Accounts payable	$ 9,000	$ 7,500
Salaries payable	250	200
Miscellaneous expense payable	150	—
Unearned rent revenue	125	150
Total liabilities	$ 9,525	$ 7,850

Supplementary data developed from an analysis of business documents include the following:

(1) Purchase discounts of $600 were received on the payment of creditor invoices during the year. Sales returns and allowances amounted to $1,480.

(2) Furniture and fixtures were acquired during the year for cash, $3,500. Depreciation is recognized at 10% per year; one half of the normal rate is used for current acquisitions.

Analysis of Cash Receipts and Disbursements

Cash balance, January 1, 1984		$ 3,200
Receipts:		
Cash sales	$ 9,200	
Accounts receivable arising from sales	42,000	
Notes receivable arising from sales	6,000	
From rental of store space	1,750	
From interest and dividends	400	
From sales of investments, cost $7,500	6,250	65,600
		$68,800
Disbursements:		
Accounts payable arising from purchases	$40,000	
For salaries	4,200	
For rent	4,400	
For supplies	1,000	
Acquisition of furniture and fixtures	3,500	
For miscellaneous expense	1,500	
Owner's withdrawals	9,000	63,600
Cash balance, December 31, 1984		$ 5,200

A balance sheet as of December 31, 1984, prepared from the foregoing data, is illustrated on the next page.

S & P Enterprises
Balance Sheet
December 31, 1984

Assets			Liabilities and Owner's Equity		
Current assets:			Current liabilities:		
Cash	$ 5,200		Accounts payable	$9,000	
Notes receivable	3,000		Salaries payable	250	
Accounts receivable	4,500		Miscellaneous expense payable	150	
Interest receivable	50		Unearned rent revenue	125	$ 9,525
Inventory	24,600				
Supplies on hand	600	$37,950			
Long-term investments		2,200			
Furniture and fixtures (cost less accumulated depreciation)		8,325	Owner's equity: Scott Peterson, capital		38,950
Total assets		$48,475	Total liabilities and owner's equity		$48,475

The net income or loss can be calculated from the comparative balance sheet data and a summary of the investments and withdrawals by the owner (as provided by the cash records) shown below.

S & P Enterprises
Summary of Changes in Owner's Equity
For Year Ended December 31, 1984

Scott Peterson, capital, December 31, 1984	$38,950
Scott Peterson, capital, January 1, 1984 (assets, $47,850, less liabilities, $7,850)	40,000
Net decrease in owner's equity	$ (1,050)
Withdrawals by owner during year	9,000
Net income for year	$ 7,950

An income statement with revenue and expense detail is shown on the next page. Schedules in support of the balances reported on the income statement are as follows:

(A) Computation of sales:		
Cash sales		$ 9,200
Sales on account:		
Notes and accounts receivable, December 31	$ 7,500	
Collections on notes and accounts receivable	48,000	
(A-1) Notes and accounts receivable reduced by sales returns and allowances	1,480	
	$56,980	
Deduct notes and accounts receivable, January 1	8,500	48,480
Gross sales for the year		$57,680

S & P Enterprises
Income Statement
For Year Ended December 31, 1984

Revenue from sales:				
Sales		(A)	$57,680	
Less sales returns and allowances		(A-1)	1,480	$56,200
Cost of goods sold:				
Inventory, January 1, 1984			$20,000	
Purchases	(B) $42,100			
Less purchase discounts	(B-1) 600		41,500	
Merchandise available for sale			$61,500	
Less Inventory, December 31, 1984			24,600	36,900
Gross profit on sales				$19,300
Operating expenses:				
Salaries		(C)	$ 4,250	
Rent expense		(D)	4,400	
Supplies expense		(E)	800	
Depreciation expense—furniture and fixtures		(F)	975	
Miscellaneous expense		(G)	1,750	12,175
Operating income				$ 7,125
Other revenue and expense items:				
Interest and dividend revenue		(H)	$ 300	
Rent revenue		(I)	1,775	
Loss on sale of investments		(J)	(1,250)	825
Net income				$ 7,950

(B) Computation of purchases:

Purchases on account:	
Accounts payable, December 31	$ 9,000
Payments on accounts payable	40,000
(B-1) Discounts allowed on accounts payable	600
	$49,600
Deduct accounts payable, January 1	7,500
Purchases for the year	$42,100

Computation of operating expenses:

(C) Salaries:

Payments for salaries	$ 4,200
Add salaries payable, December 31	250
	$ 4,450
Deduct salaries payable, January 1	200
Salaries for the year	$ 4,250

(D) Rent expense:

Payments for rent	$ 4,400

(E) Supplies expense:

Payments for supplies	$ 1,000
Add supplies on hand, January 1	400
	$ 1,400
Deduct supplies on hand, December 31	600
Supplies used during the year	$ 800

(F) Depreciation expense—furniture and fixtures:

Balance of furniture and fixtures, January 1	$ 5,800
Add cash paid on acquisition of furniture and fixtures	3,500
Balance of furniture and fixtures before depreciation	$ 9,300
Deduct balance of furniture and fixtures, Dec. 31	8,325
Depreciation of furniture and fixtures for the year	$ 975

Depreciation charge is substantiated as follows:

Property	Date Acquired	Cost	Accumulated Depreciation—Prior Years	Remaining Cost	Estimated Life	Remaining Life from Beginning of Year	Depreciation Current Year
Furniture and fixtures	1980	$ 6,000	$2,100	$3,900	10 years	6½ years	$600
Furniture and fixtures	1983	2,000	100	1,900	10 years	9½ years	200
Furniture and fixtures	1984	3,500	......	3,500	10 years	....	175 (½ yr.)
		$11,500	$2,200	$9,300			$975

(G) Miscellaneous expense:

Miscellaneous expense payments	$ 1,500
Add: Prepaid miscellaneous expense, January 1	100
Miscellaneous expense payable, December 31	150
Miscellaneous expense for the year	$ 1,750

(H) Computation of interest and dividend revenue:

Interest and dividend receipts	$ 400
Add interest receivable, December 31	50
	$ 450
Deduct interest receivable, January 1	150
Total interest and dividend revenue for the year	$ 300

(I) Computation of rent revenue:

Rent receipts	$ 1,750
Add unearned rent revenue, January 1	150
	$ 1,900
Deduct unearned rent revenue, December 31	125
Total rent revenue for the year	$ 1,775

(J) Computation of loss on sale of investments:

Cost of investments sold	$ 7,500
Proceeds from sale	6,250
Loss on sale of investments	$ 1,250

The use of a work sheet for the preparation of a balance sheet and income statement in the previous example is illustrated on pages 54 and 55. Opening balances are listed in the first pair of columns. Summaries of the transactions for the year appear in the second pair of columns. Cash receipts and disbursements are summarized first, followed by entries to adjust the balance sheet accounts to the proper ending balances. This approach produces the same results as the separate schedules developed on pages 50 to 52. Data on the work sheet should be traced to the statements presented on pages 49 to 51.

In the preceding example, a balance sheet was prepared first. The income statement was then drawn up from special schedules that developed revenue and expense balances. These procedures are convenient under simple circumstances. However, when the preparation of the financial statements involves a number of special analyses and computations and when certain difficulties are anticipated, work sheets will be useful in assembling the financial data.

QUESTIONS

1. Distinguish between the recording and summarizing phases of the accounting process.
2. List and describe the procedures in the accounting process. Why is each step necessary?
3. Distinguish between: (a) real and nominal accounts, (b) general journal and special journals, (c) general ledger and subsidiary ledgers.
4. What advantages are provided through the use of: (a) special journals, (b) subsidiary ledgers, and (c) the voucher system?
5. The Tantor Co. maintains a sales journal, a voucher register, a cash receipts journal, a cash disbursements journal, and a general journal. For each account listed below, indicate the most common journal sources of debits and credits.

Cash
Marketable Securities
Notes Receivable
Accounts Receivable
Allowance for Doubtful Accounts
Merchandise Inventory
Land and Buildings
Accumulated Depreciation
Notes Payable
Vouchers Payable
Capital Stock
Retained Earnings
Sales
Sales Discounts
Purchases
Freight In
Purchase Returns and Allowances
Purchase Discounts
Salaries
Depreciation

6. As Beechnut Mining Company's independent certified public accountant, you find that the company accountant posts adjusting and closing entries directly to the ledger without formal entries in the general journal. How would you evaluate this procedure in your report to management?
7. Explain the nature and the purpose of (a) adjusting entries, (b) closing entries, and (c) reversing entries.
8. Give three common examples of contra accounts; explain why contra accounts are used.
9. What are the major advantages of electronic data processing as compared with manual processing of accounting data?
10. One of your clients overheard a computer manufacturer sales representative saying the computer will make the accountant obsolete. How would you respond to this comment?
11. What are the implications of electronic data processing for the accountant?
12. Payment of insurance in advance may be recorded in either (a) an expense account or (b) an asset account. Which method would you recommend? What periodic entries are required under each method?
13. Describe the nature and purpose of a work sheet.
14. What effect, if any, does the use of a work sheet have on the sequence of the summarizing phase of the accounting process?
15. Distinguish between the closing procedures followed by a merchandising enterprise using a periodic (physical) inventory system and one using a perpetual inventory system.

S & P
Work
For Year Ended

	Account Title	Balance Sheet January 1, 1984 Debit	Balance Sheet January 1, 1984 Credit	Transactions 1984 Debit	Transactions 1984 Credit	
1	Cash	3,200		(a) 65,600	(b) 63,600	1
2	Notes Receivable	2,500		(d) 6,500	(a) 6,000	2
3	Accounts Receivable	6,000		(d) 41,980	(a) 42,000	3
4					(c) 1,480	4
5	Interest Receivable	150			(e) 100	5
6	Inventory	20,000				6
7	Supplies on Hand	400		(f) 200		7
8	Prepaid Miscellaneous Expense	100			(g) 100	8
9	Long-Term Investments	9,700			(a) 7,500	9
10	Furniture and Fixtures (cost less					10
11	accumulated depreciation)	5,800		(b) 3,500	(h) 975	11
12	Accounts Payable		7,500	(b) 40,000	(j) 42,100	12
13				(i) 600		13
14	Salaries Payable		200		(k) 50	14
15	Unearned Rent Revenue		150	(l) 25		15
16	Scott Peterson, Capital		40,000			16
17		47,850	47,850			17
18						18
19						19
20	Sales				(a) 9,200	20
21					(d) 48,480	21
22	Sales Returns and Allowances			(c) 1,480		22
23	Purchases			(j) 42,100		23
24	Purchase Discounts				(i) 600	24
25	Salaries			(b) 4,200		25
26				(k) 50		26
27	Rent Expense			(b) 4,400		27
28	Supplies Expense			(b) 1,000	(f) 200	28
29	Depr. Exp.—Furniture and Fixtures			(h) 975		29
30	Miscellaneous Expense Payable				(m) 150	30
31	Miscellaneous Expense			(g) 100		31
32				(b) 1,500		32
33				(m) 150		33
34	Interest and Dividend Revenue			(e) 100	(a) 400	34
35	Rent Revenue				(a) 1,750	35
36					(l) 25	36
37	Loss on Sale of Investments			(a) 1,250		37
38	Scott Peterson, Drawing			(b) 9,000		38
39						39
40				224,710	224,710	40
41	Net Income					41
42						42
43						43
44						44
45	Scott Peterson, Capital, Dec. 31, 1984					45
46						46

Explanation of transactions and adjustments:
(a) To record cash receipts.
(b) To record cash disbursements.
(c) To record sales returns and allowances.
(d) To establish notes and accounts receivable balances at end of year.
(e) To establish interest receivable balance at end of year.
(f) To establish supplies on hand balance at end of year.

Enterprises
Sheet
December 31, 1984

	Income Statement 1984		Capital December 31, 1984		Balance Sheet December 31, 1984		
	Debit	Credit	Debit	Credit	Debit	Credit	
1					5,200		1
2					3,000		2
3							3
4					4,500		4
5					50		5
6	20,000	24,600			24,600		6
7					600		7
8							8
9					2,200		9
10							10
11					8,325		11
12							12
13						9,000	13
14						250	14
15						125	15
16				40,000			16
17							17
18							18
19							19
20							20
21		57,680					21
22	1,480						22
23	42,100						23
24		600					24
25							25
26	4,250						26
27	4,400						27
28	800						28
29	975						29
30						150	30
31							31
32							32
33	1,750						33
34		300					34
35							35
36		1,775					36
37	1,250						37
38			9,000				38
39							39
40	77,005	84,955					40
41	7,950			7,950			41
42	84,955	84,955					42
43							43
44			9,000	47,950			44
45			38,950			38,950	45
46			47,950	47,950	48,475	48,475	46

(g) To eliminate prepaid miscellaneous expense.
(h) To record depreciation.
(i) To record discounts on purchases.
(j) To establish accounts payable balance at end of year.
(k) To establish salaries payable balance at end of year.
(l) To establish unearned rent revenue balance at end of year.
(m) To establish miscellaneous expense payable balance at end of year.

16. The accountant for the S. A. Beckham Store after completing all adjustments except for the merchandise inventory, makes the following entry to close the beginning inventory, to set up the ending inventory, to close all nominal accounts, and to report the net result of operations in the capital account.

Inventory (December 31, 1984)	22,500	
Sales	250,000	
Purchase Discounts	2,500	
Inventory (January 1, 1984)		25,000
Purchases		175,000
Selling Expense		25,000
General and Administrative Expense		18,750
Interest Expense		1,875
S. A. Beckham, Capital		29,375

(a) Would you regard this procedure as being acceptable? (b) What alternate procedure could you have followed in adjusting and closing the accounts?

17. Distinguish between single-entry and double-entry procedures.

18. What are the sources of information for balance sheet items when the single-entry plan is followed?

19. Distinguish between the manner in which an owner's capital balance is computed in a double-entry system as compared with a single-entry system.

20. State how each of the following items is computed in preparing an income statement when single-entry procedures are followed and the accrual basis is used in reporting net income:

(a) Sales
(b) Purchases
(c) Depreciation on equipment
(d) Sales salaries
(e) Insurance expense
(f) Interest revenue
(g) Rent revenue
(h) Taxes

21. In developing the sales balance, the owner of a business recognizes cash collections from customers and the change in the receivables balance but ignores the write-off of uncollectible accounts. Indicate the effects, if any, that such omissions will have on net income.

22. Greater accuracy is achieved in financial statements prepared from double-entry data as compared with single-entry data. Do you agree? Explain.

EXERCISES

exercise 2-1 (Journal entries—perpetual inventory)

The Almond Supply Company, a merchandising firm, engaged in the following transactions during April, 1984. Almond Supply Company records inventory on the perpetual system.

In a perpetual system you (D) inventory when you get it & (C) it when you sale it

1984

Apr. 1 Purchased building and land for $50,000 in cash and a $250,000 mortgage payable over 30 years. The land was appraised at $100,000 and the building at $300,000.

4 Sold merchandise to the Edmunds Corporation for $4,500; terms 2/10, n/30, FOB shipping point. Edmunds paid $75 freight on the goods. The merchandise cost $2,790.

5 Received inventory costing $7,500; terms, n/30.

7 Received payment from Edmunds for goods shipped April 4.

15 The payroll for the first half of April was $8,000. (Ignore payroll taxes.)

18 Traded in a truck that cost $3,000 with a net book value of $500 for a nonsimilar machine with a fair market value of $4,350. A trade-in allowance of $400 is allowed on the truck.

Apr. 22 Declared a dividend at $.58 per share on the common stock. Common stock outstanding is 45,500 shares.

Record the above transactions in general journal form.

exercise 2-2 (Special journals)

Using sales and cash receipts journals as illustrated previously in the text, record the following transactions:

(a) A sale on account is made to J. A. Fairchild for $3,600.
(b) A check for $3,528 is received from Fairchild representing payment of the invoice less a sales discount of $72.
(c) Cash sales for the day are $5,260.
(d) Cash of $4,800 is received on a 60-day, 12% note for this amount issued to the bank.
(e) A dividend check for $320 is received on shares of stock owned.

exercise 2-3 (Adjusting and reversing entries)

In analyzing the accounts of J. E. Ledbetter, the adjusting data listed below are determined on December 31, the end of an annual fiscal period.

(a) The prepaid insurance account shows a debit of $2,700, representing the cost of a 3-year fire insurance policy dated July 1.
(b) On October 1, Rent Revenue was credited for $3,600, representing revenue from subrental for a 4-month period beginning on that date.
(c) Purchase of advertising materials for $2,400 during the year was recorded in the advertising expense account. On December 31 advertising materials of $525 are on hand.
(d) On November 1, $2,250 was paid as rent for a 6-month period beginning on that date. The rent expense account was debited.
(e) Miscellaneous Office Expense was debited for office supplies of $1,350 purchased during the year. On December 31 office supplies of $285 are on hand.
(f) Interest of $195 is accrued on notes payable.

(1) Give the adjusting entry for each item. (2) What reversing entries would be appropriate? (3) What sources would provide the information for each adjustment?

exercise 2-4 (Computing accrued income statement amounts)

The following information is taken from the records of Mario's Tune-up Shop:

	Balance January 1, 1984	Balance December 31, 1984	Transactions During 1984
Accruals:			
Interest receivable	$ 540	$ 650	
Wages payable	1,100	1,150	
Interest payable	800	950	
Cash receipts and payments:			
Interest on notes receivable			$ 1,240
Wages			64,000
Interest on notes payable			930

Compute the interest revenue, the wages expense, and the interest expense for the year.

exercise 2-5 (Adjusting entries)

Upon inspecting the books and records for Stanley Builders Supply Co. for the year ended December 31, 1984, you find the following data. What entries are required to bring the accounts up to date?

(a) A receivable of $225 from H. R. Thomas is determined to be uncollectible. The company maintains no allowance for such losses.

(b) A creditor, the Tanner Co., has just been awarded damages of $1,600 as a result of breach of contract during the current year by Stanley Builders Supply. Nothing appears on the books in connection with this matter.
(c) A fire destroyed part of a branch office. Furniture and fixtures that cost $8,500 and had a book value of $6,500 at the time of the fire were completely destroyed. The insurance company has agreed to pay $5,000 under the provision of the fire insurance policy. Ignore income tax consequences.
(d) Advances of $1,000 to salespersons have been recorded as sales salaries.
(e) Machinery at the end of the year shows a balance of $17,250. It is discovered that additions to this account during the year totaled $4,000, but of this amount $2,250 should have been recorded as repairs. Depreciation is to be recorded at 10% on machinery owned throughout the year, but at one half this rate on machinery purchased or sold during the year. (Round to nearest dollar)

exercise 2-6 (Adjusting and closing entries)

Accounts of Solar Heating Co. at the end of the first year of operations show the following balances:

Cash	$ 34,000	
Investments	40,000	
Land	80,000	
Buildings	160,000	
Machinery	100,000	
Accounts Payable		$ 60,000
Common Stock		300,000
Premium on Common Stock		30,000
Sales		600,000
Purchases	280,000	
Sales Commissions	200,000	
General Operating Expenses	104,000	
Investment Revenue		8,000
	$998,000	$998,000

The end of the year physical inventory is $60,000. Prepaid operating expenses are $3,000 and sales commissions payable are $6,000. Investment revenue receivable is $2,000. Depreciation for the year on buildings is $4,000 and on machinery, $5,000. Federal and state income taxes for the year are estimated at $25,000. Give the entries to adjust and close the books.

exercise 2-7 (Adjusting entries)

Account balances before and after adjustment on December 31 follow. Give the adjustment that was made for each account.

	Before Adjustment		After Adjustment	
Account Title	Debit	Credit	Debit	Credit
(a) Inventory	$67,000		$76,000	
(b) Allowance for Doubtful Accounts	3,500			$14,000
(c) Accumulated Depreciation		$36,000		43,000
(d) Sales Salaries	64,400		65,900	
(e) Income Tax	11,000		12,700	
(f) Royalty Revenue		18,000		23,000
(g) Interest Revenue		1,300		1,750

exercise 2-8 (Adjusting and reversing entries)

On May 16, 1984, Brenda Sycamore paid insurance for a three-year period beginning June 1. She recorded the payment as follows:

Prepaid Insurance	504	
Cash		504

(1) What adjustment is required on December 31? What reversing entry, if any, would you make?
(2) What nominal account could be debited instead of Prepaid Insurance? What adjustment would then be necessary? What reversing entry, if any, would you make?

exercise 2-9 (Adjusting entries)

The data listed below were obtained from an analysis of the accounts of Noble Distributor Company as of March 31, 1984, in preparation of the annual report. Noble records current transactions in nominal accounts and does not reverse adjusting entries. What are the appropriate adjusting entries?

(a) Prepaid Insurance has a balance of $14,100. Noble has the following policies in force.

Policy	Date	Term	Cost	Coverage
A	1/1/84	2 years	$ 3,600	Shop equipment
B	12/1/83	6 months	1,800	Delivery equipment
C	7/1/83	3 years	12,000	Buildings

(b) Subscriptions Received in Advance has a balance of $56,250. The following subscriptions were included in the balance.

Inception	Amount	Term
July 1, 1983	$27,000	1 year
October 1, 1983	22,200	1 year
January 1, 1984	28,800	1 year
April 1, 1984	20,700	1 year

(c) Interest Payable has a balance of $825. Noble owes a 10%, 90-day note for $45,000 dated March 1, 1984.
(d) Supplies Inventory has a balance of $2,190. An inventory of supplies revealed a total of $1,410.
(e) Salaries Payable has a balance of $9,750. The payroll for the 5-day workweek ended April 3, totaled $11,250.

exercise 2-10 (Closing the books)

An accountant for Jolley, Inc., a merchandising enterprise, has just finished posting all the year-end adjusting entries to the ledger accounts and now wishes to close the ledger balances in preparation for the new period.

For each of the accounts listed below, indicate whether the year-end balance should be: (1) carried forward to the new period, (2) closed by debiting the account, or (3) closed by crediting the account.

(a) Cash	(k) Accounts Payable
(b) Sales	(l) Accounts Receivable
(c) Dividends	(m) Prepaid Insurance
(d) Inventory (Beginning)	(n) Interest Receivable
(e) Selling Expenses	(o) Sales Discounts
(f) Capital Stock	(p) Freight In
(g) Income Summary	(q) Interest Revenue
(h) Wages Expense	(r) Supplies on Hand
(i) Dividends Payable	(s) Retained Earnings
(j) Purchases	(t) Accumulated Depreciation

exercise 2-11 (Closing entries)

The Lennon's Tannery shows a credit balance in the income summary account of $129,600 after the revenue and expense items have been transferred to this account at the end of a fiscal year. Give the remaining entries to close the books, assuming:

(a) The business is a sole proprietorship: the owner, D. H. Lennon, has made withdrawals of $36,000 during the year and this is reported in a drawing account.

(b) The business is a partnership: the owners, D. H. Lennon and B. L. Oster, share profits 5:3; they have made withdrawals of $48,000 and $38,400 respectively, and these amounts are reported in drawing accounts.
(c) The business is a corporation: the ledger reports additional paid-in capital, $800,000, and retained earnings, $200,000; dividends during the year of $56,000 were charged to a dividends account.

exercise 2-12 (Account analysis—unearned service fees)

Service fee collections in 1984 are $43,500; service fee revenue reported on the income statement is $40,800. The balance sheet prepared at the beginning of the year reported service fees receivable, $1,800, and unearned service fees, $1,350; the balance sheet at the end of the year reported service fees receivable, $2,280. What is the amount of unearned service fees at the end of the year?

exercise 2-13 (Account analysis—sales salaries expense)

Sales salaries are reported on the income statement for 1984 at $19,260. Balance sheet data relating to sales salaries are as follows:

	January 1, 1984	December 31, 1984
Prepaid salaries (advances to sales agents)	$ 450	$ 180
Salaries payable	1,260	1,350

How much cash was paid during 1984 for sales salaries expense?

exercise 2-14 (Account analysis—gross sales)

Total accounts receivable for the Bako Company were as follows: on January 1, $6,000; on January 31, $6,300. In January, $9,500 was collected on accounts, $600 was received for cash sales, accounts receivable of $700 were written off as uncollectible, and allowances on sales of $100 were made. What amount should be reported for gross sales on the income statement for January?

exercise 2-15 (Determining income from equity account analysis)

On November 1, the capital of D. T. Conners was $8,500 and on November 30 the capital was $12,187. During the month, Conners withdrew merchandise costing $500 and on November 25 paid a $4,000 note payable of the business with interest at 10% for three months with a check drawn on a personal checking account. What was Conners' net income or loss for the month of November?

exercise 2-16 (Determining income from equity account analysis)

An analysis of the records of J. L. Kane disclosed changes in account balances for 1984 and the supplementary data listed below. From these data, calculate the net income or loss for 1984.

Cash	$ 2,400 decrease
Accounts receivable	1,500 increase
Merchandise inventory	$15,500 increase
Accounts payable	2,100 increase

During the year, Kane borrowed $20,000 in notes from the bank and paid off notes of $15,000 and interest of $750. Interest of $250 is accrued as of December 31, 1984. There was no interest payable at the end of 1983.

In 1984, Kane also transferred certain marketable securities to the business and these were sold for $5,300 to finance the purchase of merchandise.

Kane made weekly withdrawals in 1984 of $250.

PROBLEMS

problem 2-1 (Using special journals)

Beesley Distributing, Inc., a fruit wholesaler, records business transactions in the following books of original entry: general journal (GJ); voucher register (VR); check register (CKR); sales journal (SJ); and cash receipts journal (CRJ). Beesley uses a voucher system. At the close of business on April 18, Beesley recorded and filed the following business documents:

(a) Sales invoices for sales on account totaling $4,600.
(b) The day's cash register tape showing receipts for cash sales at $700.
(c) A list of cash received on various customer accounts totaling $2,930. Sales discounts taken were $30.
(d) The telephone bill for $60 payable in one week.
(e) Vendors' invoices for $5,000 worth of fruit received.
(f) Check stub for payment of last week's purchases from All-Growers Farms, $5,940. Terms of 1/10, n/30 were taken.
(g) Check stub for repayment of a $10,000, 90-day note to Mercantile Bank, $10,300.
(h) A letter notifying Beesley that Littex Markets, a customer, has declared bankruptcy. All creditors will receive 10 cents on every dollar due. Littex owes Beesley $1,300.

Instructions:

(1) Indicate the books of original entry in which Beesley recorded each of the business documents. (Use the designated abbreviations.)
(2) Record the debits and credits for each entry as though only a general journal were used. Use account titles implied by the voucher system.

problem 2-2 (Using special journals)

A fire destroyed Fong Company's journals. However, the general ledger and accounts receivable subsidiary ledger were saved. An inspection of the ledgers reveals the following information:

General Ledger

Cash (11)

May 1 Bal.	7,500		
31	7,165		

Sales (41)

		May 31	8,925

Sales Discounts (42)

May 3	25		

Accounts Receivable (12)

May 1 Bal.	2,925	May 31	4,425
31	6,160		

Accounts Receivable Ledger

A

May 1 Bal.	275		
5	1,500		

B

May 1 Bal.	1,200	May 13	1,200
5	375		

C

May 2	935		

D

May 1 Bal.	1,450	May 11	725

E

May 2	2,500	May 3	2,500
12	850		

Fong's credit policy is 1/10, n/30.

Instructions:

Reconstruct the sales and cash receipts journals from the information given. Assume a Cash Sales column is used in the journals.

problem 2-3 (Adjusting and reversing entries)

The trial balance of Kohler's Diamonds, shows, among other items, the following balances on December 31, 1984, the end of a fiscal year:

Accounts Receivable	225,000	
9% Century City Bonds	150,000	
Land	275,000	
Buildings	300,000	
Accumulated Depreciation—Buildings		173,250
8% First-Mortgage Bonds Payable		300,000
Rent Revenue		71,500
Office Expense	7,500	

The following facts are ascertained on this date upon inspection of the company's records.

(a) It is estimated that approximately 2% of accounts receivable may prove uncollectible.
(b) Interest is receivable semiannually on the Century City bonds on March 1 and September 1.
(c) Buildings are depreciated at 5% a year; however, there were building additions of $50,000 during the year. The company computes depreciation on asset acquisitions during the year at one half the annual rate.
(d) Interest on the first-mortgage bonds is payable semiannually on February 1 and August 1.
(e) Rent revenue includes $3,750 that was received on November 1, representing rent on part of the buildings for the period November 1, 1984, to October 31, 1985.
(f) Office supplies of $2,000 are on hand on December 31. Purchases of office supplies were debited to the office expense account.

Instructions:

(1) Prepare the journal entries to adjust the books on December 31, 1984.
(2) Give the reversing entries that may appropriately be made at the beginning of 1985.

problem 2-4 (Adjusting entries)

The bookkeeper for the Sandie Corp. is preparing an income statement for the year ended December 31, 1984, reporting income from operations as $88,720. Accounts have not yet been closed, and a review of the books disclosed the need for the following adjustments:

(a) The account, Office Expense, shows the cost of all purchases of office supplies for the year. At the end of 1984 there are supplies of $480 on hand.
(b) The allowance for doubtful accounts shows a debit balance of $160. It is estimated that 3% of the accounts receivable as of December 31 will prove uncollectible. The accounts receivable balance on this date is $23,280.
(c) The ledger shows a balance for accrued salaries and wages of $1,440 as of December 31, 1983, which was left unchanged during 1984. No recognition was made in the accounts at the end of 1984 for accrued salaries and wages which amounted to $1,560.
(d) The ledger shows a balance for interest receivable of $300 as of December 31, 1983, which was left unchanged during 1984. No recognition was made in the accounts at the end of 1984 for accrued interest which amounted to $352.

(e) The prepaid insurance account was debited during the year for amounts paid for insurance and shows a balance of $960 at the end of 1984. The unexpired portions of the policies on December 31, 1984, total $448.
(f) A portion of a building was subleased for three months, November 1, 1984, to February 1, 1985. Unearned Rent Revenue was credited for $960 and no adjustment was made in this account at the end of 1984.
(g) The interest expense account was debited for all interest charges incurred during the year and shows a balance of $1,500. However, of this amount, $400 represents a discount on a 60-day note payable due January 30, 1985.
(h) Provision for income tax for 1984 is to be computed at a 40% rate.

Instructions: Give the entries that are required on December 31, 1984, to bring the books up to date. (Round to nearest dollar, and in recording income tax, provide a schedule to show how the corrected income subject to tax was determined.)

problem 2-5 (Transactions based on adjusting entries)

The accountant for Besner Plumbing made the following adjusting entries on December 31, 1984:

(a) Prepaid Rent	600	
Rent Expense		600
(b) Advertising Materials Inventory	1,000	
Advertising Expense		1,000
(c) Interest Revenue	250	
Unearned Revenue		250
(d) Office Supplies Inventory	500	
Office Expense		500
(e) Prepaid Insurance	525	
Insurance Expense		525

Further information is provided as follows:

(a) Rent is paid every October 1.
(b) Advertising materials are paid at one time (June 1) and are used evenly throughout the year.
(c) Interest is received every March 1.
(d) Office supplies are purchased every July 1 and used evenly throughout the year.
(e) Yearly insurance premium is payable each August 1.

Instructions: For each adjusting entry, indicate the original transaction entry that was made.

problem 2-6 (Adjusting entries)

The bookkeeper for the Irwin Wholesale Electric Co. prepares no reversing entries and records all revenue and expense items in nominal accounts during the period. The following balances, among others, are listed on the trial balance at the end of the fiscal period, December 31, 1984, before accounts have been adjusted:

Accounts Receivable	$152,000
Allowance for Doubtful Accounts (credit balance)	1,000
Interest Receivable	2,800
Discounts on Notes Payable	300
Prepaid Real Estate and Personal Property Tax	1,800
Salaries and Wages Payable	4,000
Discounts on Notes Receivable	2,800
Unearned Rent Revenue	1,500

Inspection of the company's records reveals the following as of December 31, 1984.

(a) Uncollectible accounts are estimated at 3% of the accounts receivable balance.
(b) The accrued interest on investments totals $2,400.
(c) The company borrows cash by discounting its own notes at the bank. Discounts on notes payable at the end of 1984 are $1,600.
(d) Prepaid real estate and personal property taxes are $1,800, the same as at the end of 1983.
(e) Accrued salaries and wages are $4,300.
(f) The company accepts notes from the customers giving its customers credit for the face of the note less a charge for interest. At the end of each period, any interest applicable to the succeeding period is reported as a discount. Discounts on notes receivable at the end of 1984 are $1,500.
(g) Part of the company's properties had been sublet on September 15, 1983, at a rental of $3,000 per month. The arrangement was terminated at the end of one year.

Instructions: Give the adjusting entries required to bring the books up to date.

problem 2-7 (Preparation of work sheet, adjusting and closing entries)

Account balances taken from the ledger of the Farley Development Company on December 31, 1984, are as follows:

Accounts Payable	$ 36,000	Land	$69,600
Accounts Receivable	67,200	Long-Term Investments	12,600
Advertising Expense	4,800	Mortgage Payable	48,000
Accumulated Depreciation— Buildings	19,800	Notes Payable—Short Term	15,000
		Office Expense	16,080
Allowance for Doubtful Accounts	1,380	Purchases	138,480
Buildings	72,000	Purchase Discounts	1,140
Capital Stock, $10 par	180,000	Retained Earnings, Dec. 31, 1983	14,040
Cash	24,000	Sales	246,000
Dividends	14,400	Sales Discounts	5,400
Freight In	3,600	Sales Returns	3,360
Insurance Expense	1,440	Selling Expense	49,440
Interest Expense	2,640	Supplies Expense	4,200
Interest Revenue	660	Taxes—Real Estate, Payroll, and Other	7,980
Inventory, Dec. 31, 1983	64,800		

Adjustments on December 31 are required as follows:

(a) The inventory on hand is $90,720.
(b) The allowance for doubtful accounts is to be increased to a balance of $3,000.
(c) Buildings are depreciated at the rate of 5% per year.
(d) Accrued selling expenses are $3,840.
(e) There are supplies of $780 on hand.
(f) Prepaid insurance relating to 1985 and 1986 totals $720.
(g) Accrued interest on long-term investments is $240.
(h) Accrued real estate, payroll, and other taxes are $900.
(i) Accrued interest on the mortgage is $480.
(j) Income tax is estimated to be 40% of the income before income tax.

Instructions:

(1) Prepare an eight-column work sheet.
(2) Prepare adjusting, closing, and reversing entries.

problem 2-8 (Preparation of work sheet, adjusting and closing entries)

The following account balances are taken from the general ledger of the Whitni Corporation on December 31, 1984, the end of its fiscal year. The corporation was organized January 2, 1978:

Cash on Hand and in Banks	$ 36,125	Sales Discounts	$ 7,000
Notes Receivable	18,500	Purchases	330,000
Accounts Receivable	56,000	Freight In	8,800
Allowance for Doubtful Accounts	650	Purchase Returns and Allowances	3,000
Inventory, January 1, 1984	82,500	Purchase Discounts	3,400
Office Supplies	6,200	Maintenance and Repairs of Buildings	6,300
Land	20,000	Heat, Light, and Power	11,000
Buildings	147,600	Taxes	10,200
Accumulated Depreciation—Buildings	18,000	Sales Salaries	35,000
Office Furniture and Fixtures	15,000	Sales Commissions	12,300
Accumulated Depreciation—		Travel Expense	8,500
Office Furniture and Fixtures	9,000	Advertising Expense	23,125
Notes Payable	20,000	Officers Salaries	25,000
Accounts Payable	45,700	Office Salaries	14,000
Common Stock, $100 par	100,000	Insurance Expense	8,500
Additional Paid-in Capital	10,000	Postage, Telephone, and Telegraph	1,400
Retained Earnings	125,000	Miscellaneous Office Expense	1,500
Sales	560,000	Interest Revenue	800
Sales Returns and Allowances	10,000	Interest Expense	1,000

Data for adjustments at December 31, 1984, are as follows:

(a) Inventories:
Merchandise inventory, $88,500; office supplies, $1,000.

(b) Depreciation and Amortization (to nearest month for additions):
Office furniture and fixtures, 10%
Buildings, 4%. Additions to the buildings costing $50,000 were completed June 30, 1984.

(c) The allowance for doubtful accounts is to be increased to a balance of $3,200.

(d) Accrued expenses:
Sales salaries, $400.
Interest on notes payable, $50.
Property tax, $2,000.

(e) Prepaid expenses: insurance, $2,500.

(f) Accrued revenue: interest on notes receivable, $500.

(g) The following information is also to be recorded:
(1) On December 30, the board of directors declared a quarterly dividend of $1.50 per share on common stock, payable January 25, 1985, to stockholders of record January 15, 1985.
(2) Income tax for 1984 is estimated at $13,000.
(3) The only charges to Retained Earnings during the year resulted from the declaration of the regular quarterly dividends.

Instructions:

(1) Prepare an eight-column work sheet. There should be a pair of columns each for trial balance, adjustments, income statement, and balance sheet.
(2) Prepare all the journal entries necessary to give effect to the foregoing information and to adjust and close the books of the corporation.
(3) Prepare the reversing entries that may appropriately be made.

problem 2-9 (Single-entry conversion)

The following information is obtained from single-entry records of Craig Jackson.

	March 31	January 1
Notes receivable	$ 3,600	$ 4,500
Accounts receivable	26,400	13,500
Interest receivable	240	300
Inventory	3,000	11,400
Prepaid operating expenses	660	750
Store equipment (net)	9,000	9,750
Notes payable	3,600	3,000
Accounts payable	7,500	10,500
Interest payable	150	90
Operating expenses payable	1,500	810

The cashbook shows the following:

Balance, January 1		$ 4,500
Receipts: Accounts receivable	$10,800	
Notes receivable	4,500	
Interest revenue	600	
Investment by Jackson	1,800	17,700
		$22,200
Payments: Accounts payable	$15,600	
Notes payable	2,400	
Interest expense	450	
Operating expenses	5,100	23,550
Balance, March 31—bank overdraft		$ (1,350)

Instructions:

(1) Compute the net income or loss for the three-month period by considering the changes in the owner's capital.

(2) Prepare an income statement for the three-month period accompanied by schedules in support of revenue and expense balances.

problem 2-10 (Single-entry conversion)

Balance sheets for the Fugal Hardware Stores prepared in 1984 report the following balances:

Assets	June 30	January 1
Cash	$ 84,500	$ 33,000
Notes receivable	21,000	20,000
Accounts receivable	95,000	74,000
Inventory	150,000	160,000
Prepaid expenses	10,000	12,000
Long-term investments (at cost)	10,000	40,000
Buildings and equipment (net)	120,000	100,000
	$490,500	$439,000
Liabilities and Stockholders' Equity		
Notes payable	$ 58,000	$ 75,000
Accounts payable	75,000	60,000
Interest payable	900	—
Expenses payable	3,000	2,000
Bonds payable	—	50,000
Common stock, $100 par	130,000	100,000
Premium on common stock	150,000	100,000
Retained earnings	73,600	52,000
	$490,500	$439,000

An analysis of cash receipts and disbursements discloses the following:

Receipts		Disbursements	
Capital stock	$ 80,000	Trade creditors—notes and accounts	$210,000
Trade debtors—notes and accounts	230,000	Expenses	70,000
Cash sales	65,000	Dividends	40,000
Notes receivable discounted:		Equipment	28,000
Face value, $20,000, proceeds	19,500	Bonds	50,000
12% note issued to bank, dated March 31, 1984	30,000		
Sale of investments	25,000		

Instructions:

(1) Prepare an income statement supported by schedules showing computations of revenue and expense balances for the six-month period ended June 30, 1984.
(2) Prove the net income or loss determined in part (1) by preparing a retained earnings statement.

problem 2-11 (Work sheet and financial statements)

Knight & Lesser operate a retail store, sharing profits equally. The following is a balance sheet for the partnership on January 1, 1984.

Knight & Lesser
Balance Sheet
January 1, 1984

Assets		Liabilities and Owners' Equity	
Cash	$ 260	Accounts payable	$ 4,900
Notes receivable	1,500	Expenses payable	260
Accounts receivable	6,500	Knight, capital	8,900
Interest receivable	40	Lesser, capital	4,700
Inventory	7,000		
Prepaid expenses	260		
Furniture and fixtures	3,200		
Total assets	$18,760	Total liabilities and owners' equity	$18,760

On December 31, 1984, asset and liability balances are:

Assets		Liabilities	
Notes receivable	$ 1,500	Cash overdraft	$ 200
Accounts receivable	7,650	Notes payable	2,500
Interest receivable	50	Accounts payable	12,100
Inventory	10,000	Expenses payable	200
Prepaid expense	300		$15,000
Furniture and fixtures	5,000		
	$24,500		

Cash receipts and disbursements for the year were:

Receipts			Disbursements		
Investment by Knight		$ 800	Withdrawals by Knight ($225 monthly)		$ 2,700
Cash sales		4,450	Withdrawals by Lesser ($225 monthly)		2,700
Receipts on accounts and notes	$30,000		On accounts payable	$22,300	
Less discounts	400	29,600	Less discounts	1,500	20,800
Interest on notes		80	Purchase of store fixtures on July 1, 1984		2,200
Amount borrowed from bank on October 1; issued $2,500, 8% note due in one year		2,500	Operating expenses		9,490
		$37,430			$37,890

Interest of $50 on the note payable is included in the expenses payable total of $200 as of December 31.

Doubtful accounts written off during the year totaled $300.

Sales returns and allowances during the year were $600.

Instructions:

(1) Prepare a work sheet for the preparation of a balance sheet and an income statement.
(2) Prepare for the year ended December 31, 1984, (a) a balance sheet and (b) an income statement accompanied by a statement of changes in the partners' capitals.

problem 2-12 (Computation of cash collections)

The following data are relative to the operation of the Garden Homes, Inc., during 1984.

Gross potential rents	$211,688
Vacancies	42,609
Space occupied by corporation for own use	4,925
Prepaid rent:	
Beginning of period	302
End of period	984
Delinquent rent:	
Beginning of period	377
End of period	79
Deposits (tenants)	100
Refund to tenants	20
Uncollectible rents	80

Instructions: Prepare a schedule showing cash collections related to rent for the year.

(AICPA adapted)

*problem 2-13 (Single-entry work sheet)

The Braxton Printing Company is a proprietorship owned by R. L. Braxton, who does not take the time to keep detailed accounting records. Braxton purchased the business on January 1, 1984. He asks you to prepare interim financial statements for the six months ended June 30, 1985, and he provides the following schedule:

	June 30, 1985	December 31, 1984
Cash	$ 2,039	$ 1,650
Note receivable	600	—
Accounts receivable	1,700	1,300
Supplies inventory	3,140	2,370
Prepaid insurance	264	315
Equipment (original cost)	10,200	8,600*
Total assets	$17,943	$14,235
Accounts payable	$ 1,100	$ 890
Expenses payable	70	55
Total liabilities	$ 1,170	$ 945

*As of January 1, 1984.

You are able to accumulate the following information.

(a) The schedule for December 31, 1984, was taken from the financial statements you prepared for Braxton as of that date.
(b) The cash balance of $2,039 was taken from the bank statement. The client's checkbook reveals the following:

Deposits:

Collections from customers	$45,025
Sale of equipment	400
Loan from bank ($2,000, 4-month note due September 30, 1985)	1,960
	$47,385

*Relates to Appendix

Withdrawals:	
Payments to suppliers	$25,496
Insurance premiums	264
Employee's salary	3,200
Payment on Braxton's income tax	1,300
Purchase of equipment	1,600
Withdrawn by Braxton as salary	12,400
Miscellaneous expenses, including prepaid rent, $300	2,736
	$46,996

(c) A check for $450 was received from a customer on June 30, 1985, and mailed to the bank on that day. The payment was deducted from the accounts receivable as of June 30 but not recorded in the checkbook or by the bank until July 2.

(d) Braxton excluded from accounts receivable $150 that he says is uncollectible. He estimates that the cost of this sale was $120.

(e) The note receivable is non-interest-bearing and is due on September 1, 1985. It was accepted on May 1, 1985, from a delinquent account receivable.

(f) Printing equipment that was included in the original purchase price at $1,000 was sold for $400 on March 31. New equipment costing $1,600 was installed on April 1. All equipment has an estimated life of 10 years. Disregard salvage value of assets.

(g) Braxton hired an assistant on April 1, 1985, at a salary of $13,200 per year. (Disregard any payroll taxes.)

(h) An examination of insurance policies reveals the following:

Policy	Acquired	Term	Premium	Unexpired December 31, 1984
#2479	Jan. 1, 1984	3 years	$360	$240
C2160	June 1, 1984	1 year	180	75
831	April 1, 1985	1 year	72	
C2380	June 1, 1985	1 year	192	
			$804	$315

(i) Actual expenses payable are miscellaneous public utility charges which you compute to be $70 at June 30. The $300 item at June 30 is an extra month's rent that Braxton paid in error. He listed the item when the landlord advised him of the overpayment.

Instructions: Prepare a work sheet showing the account balances on December 31, 1984, the adjustments required in reporting revenue and expenses on an accrual basis for the six months ended June 30, 1985, the results of operations for the six months ended June 30, 1985, and the financial position at June 30, 1985. Formal journal entries and financial statements are not required.

(AICPA adapted)

3 THE CONCEPTUAL FRAMEWORK OF ACCOUNTING

CHAPTER OBJECTIVES

Explain the need for a conceptual framework.

Identify the major components of the FASB conceptual framework.

Discuss the objectives of financial reporting.

Discuss the qualitative characteristics of accounting information.

Define the elements of financial statements of business enterprises.

Consider the nature of the traditional accounting model.

In Chapter 1 accounting was identified as a service activity designed to provide useful information, primarily financial in nature, for decision-making purposes. The accounting process was reviewed in Chapter 2, detailing the means by which entity transactions were measured and communicated. It is important to note that the accounting process generates information for a variety of potential users. Managers are the major "internal" users of the information produced by the accounting process. They use accounting information, as well as other data, in making a number of decisions concerning the operations of the business. "External" users of accounting information include owners, lenders, suppliers, potential investors and creditors, employees, financial analysts, representatives of labor unions and government agencies, and the general public. These external users are generally not directly involved in the daily management of the business and must rely to a significant extent on the periodic financial reports supplied by management to provide the information they need to make investment, lending, and other decisions. The objective of this text is primarily to consider external financial reporting requirements. This chapter explores the conceptual framework of accounting as a basis for understanding the theory and practice of financial reporting. The major accounting issues and current accounting practice are described in the remaining chapters of the text.

NEED FOR A CONCEPTUAL FRAMEWORK

As pointed out in Chapter 1, accounting has evolved to meet the needs of business in measuring and communicating the results of enterprise activity. As business has grown in size and complexity, so has accounting. A major factor in the growth and complexity of business was the introduction of the corporate form of organization, which encourages a broad base of ownership. The development of corporations has also increased the need for external financial reporting because the owners of business entities—the stockholders—are seldom the managers of those entities and need periodic reports to evaluate a company's financial position and results of operations and thus management's performance.

Accounting for large and complex organizations presents many challenges to accountants, such as establishing adequate accounting controls and ensuring the proper recording and classification of the thousands of transactions that occur yearly. From an external reporting viewpoint, another extremely important challenge is selecting the most appropriate methods for reporting enterprise activity. Often, there are several justifiable reporting alternatives for a particular transaction. Therefore, accountants are continually required to use their judgment in selecting from among reporting alternatives the one that most accurately reflects the financial position and results of operations for the entity given the specific circumstances involved. If businesses and their activities were identical, reporting alternatives could be eliminated. However, businesses are different. Even within a particular industry, companies are not organized in exactly the same way, they do not produce identical products or provide identical services, and their accounting systems and the reports generated therefrom are not uniform. Thus, accountants must exercise professional judgment in fulfilling their roles as suppliers of useful information for decision makers.

For some time, accountants and business executives have agreed that a broad framework of financial accounting and reporting concepts is needed to assist those charged with the responsibility of financial reporting.[1] Such a framework should provide guidelines for proper reporting under particular circumstances. It should assist accountants and others in selecting from among reporting alternatives the method that best represents the economic

---

[1]See the appendix to this chapter for a brief chronology of attempts to establish a framework for generally accepted accounting principles.

reality of the situation and should, therefore, result in reporting the most useful information for decision making purposes.

A conceptual framework of generally accepted accounting principles will not solve all accounting or reporting problems, however. A conceptual framework should provide guidance and offer a standard or frame of reference. But it will not eliminate the need for judgment in terms of, for example, what information should be supplied, what specific method of reporting would be most appropriate under the circumstances, and in what form the information should be presented.

When the Financial Accounting Standards Board was established, it responded to this need for a general framework by undertaking a comprehensive project to develop a "conceptual framework for financial accounting and reporting." This project has been described as an attempt to establish a constitution for accounting. The completed framework should provide both support and guidance for individual financial accounting standards. Because of its potential impact on future accounting practice, all students interested in accounting should be aware of the components of the FASB conceptual framework and should monitor the progress of this important project.

COMPONENTS OF THE FASB CONCEPTUAL FRAMEWORK: AN OVERVIEW

The conceptual framework project was one of the original FASB agenda items. It is viewed as a long-term, continuing project to be developed in stages. Because of its significant potential impact on many aspects of financial reporting, and therefore its controversial nature, progress must be deliberate. The project has high priority and receives a large share of FASB resources. Currently, there are nine major components of the framework project, in varying stages of completion, that deal with accounting and reporting for business enterprises.[2] These components, and the related documents that have been prepared or issued by the FASB, are listed at the top of the next page. Each of the framework components is discussed briefly in the following sections.

Objectives of Financial Reporting by Business Enterprises

The starting point for the conceptual framework was determined to be the objectives of financial reporting. Study on this topic produced the first of a series of planned publications from the conceptual framework project. The results of this phase of the project were published in November, 1978, as *Statement of Financial Accounting Concepts No. 1*, "Objectives of Financial Reporting by Business Enterprises."[3] The objectives are discussed in some detail later in the chapter.

---

[2]Financial reporting by nonbusiness enterprises is being considered by the FASB as a separate phase of the framework project.

[3]In conjunction with this phase of the project, the FASB has also published *Statement of Financial Accounting Concepts No. 4*, "Objectives of Financial Reporting by Nonbusiness Organizations," December 1980.

Framework Component	Related Documents
(1) Objectives of financial reporting by business enterprises	Statement of Financial Accounting Concepts No. 1 (1978)
(2) Qualitative characteristics of accounting information	Statement of Financial Accounting Concepts No. 2 (1980)
(3) Elements of financial statements of business enterprises	Statement of Financial Accounting Concepts No. 3 (1980)
(4) Accounting recognition criteria	Research reports
(5) Measurement	Statement of Financial Accounting Standards No. 33 (1979)
(6) Reporting income (7) Reporting cash flows (8) Reporting financial position	Combined Exposure Draft (1981)
(9) Financial statements and other means of financial reporting	Invitation to Comment (1980)

Qualitative Characteristics of Accounting Information

This part of the project was intended to identify and clarify qualitative characteristics of information that should be considered in adopting reporting standards for both business and nonbusiness enterprises. Results of this phase should be useful to standard-setting bodies, such as the FASB, and also to preparers, auditors, and users of financial statements in understanding and applying accounting standards. These results were published in May, 1980, as *Statement of Financial Accounting Concepts No. 2*, "Qualitative Characteristics of Accounting Information," and its main points are discussed later in the chapter.

Elements of Financial Statements of Business Enterprises

This phase of the conceptual framework resulted in definitions for the main elements of the general purpose financial statements: assets, liabilities, equity, investments by owners, distributions to owners, comprehensive income, revenues, expenses, gains, and losses. The definitions developed by the FASB were published as *Statement of Financial Accounting Concepts No. 3*, "Elements of Financial Statements of Business Enterprises," in December, 1980. These definitions are presented in a later section of this chapter and are incorporated throughout the text.

Accounting Recognition Criteria

This component was added to the framework project in 1979. The intent is to develop criteria for accounting recognition of the elements of financial statements. Logically, this phase follows identification of the elements of financial statements mentioned earlier. Now that the elements have been identified and defined, the recognition criteria can be determined. This is considered the most difficult part of the framework. To date several research reports dealing with this topic have been prepared. Specific revenue recognition problems are covered in Chapter 19.

Measurement

This part of the framework is specifically concerned with the effects of changing prices on business enterprises. Historically, accountants have ignored the fact that the dollar, which is the common measuring unit in the United States, is unstable, i.e., its purchasing power fluctuates as general price levels change. Further, accountants have measured the results of transactions in terms of "historical cost," the exchange price at the date of a transaction; they have not reported current values, the exchange prices at dates subsequent to the transaction date. Thus, accountants have traditionally not measured and reported the impact of either general or specific price changes on business entities.

After considerable study, the FASB has issued Statement of Financial Accounting Standards No. 33 which requires most large companies to disclose supplementary information concerning the impact of both specific and general price changes on a business entity. The nature of these requirements and the issues involved in reporting price changes are discussed at length in Chapter 24.

Reporting Income, Cash Flows, and Financial Position

In November, 1981, the FASB issued an exposure draft, "Income, Cash Flows, and Financial Position," addressing three components of the conceptual framework. After evaluating the comments received on the exposure draft, the Board decided that "further development of concepts for reporting income should be concurrent with the development of concepts for measurement and recognition."[4] The Board further decided to postpone issuance of a concepts statement on cash flows and financial position until concepts for reporting income have been developed. Issues relating to these three components are briefly described in the following paragraphs.

Reporting Income. This phase of the study is designed to determine the kinds of income information that should be furnished based on the objectives of financial reporting. The results of this phase may dramatically change the format currently used for the income statement. A significant part of this phase of the study is to identify useful criteria for classifying revenues, gains, expenses, and losses. The issues involved in reporting income are discussed in several chapters, especially Chapter 4 and Chapters 19 through 22.

---

[4] *FASB Status Report,* No. 139 (January 13, 1983), p. 5.

Reporting Funds Flow. This part of the framework project will reconsider APB Opinion No. 19 concerning the statement of changes in financial position (funds statement). The objective is to determine the appropriate information to be reported about an enterprise's flow of funds and its liquidity position. The funds statement is discussed in Chapters 5 and 23.

Reporting Financial Position. This component of the framework, as well as the two preceding components, deals primarily with the display of key relationships. In this case the primary relationships are those dealing collectively with the overall financial position of a company—its liquidity and solvency—and individually with its assets, liabilities, and owners' equity. Recent economic conditions have caused managers, investors, and creditors to place renewed emphasis on balance sheet relationships, increasing the significance of this component of the conceptual framework. Several chapters in the text, especially Chapter 5, deal with the theoretical and practical problems of reporting financial position.

Financial Statements and Other Means of Financial Reporting

The objective of this component of the conceptual framework is to determine where the information specified by the objectives of financial reporting should be disclosed—in the financial statements themselves or elsewhere. It is also concerned with who should disclose what information—should there be uniform disclosures for all business enterprises or selected disclosures for particular enterprises? A position paper designated as an "Invitation to Comment," has been developed to explain the criteria that the FASB might use in making the preceding distinctions. Included in that document is the illustration reproduced on the following page, showing an information reporting spectrum.

Definition, Recognition, Measurement, and Display

In considering the individual components of the conceptual framework, the interrelationships become apparent. Decisions concerning one part of the framework have influenced, and will continue to influence, other parts. However, the Board has clearly indicated that certain aspects must be considered independently—definition, recognition, measurement, and display.[5] These four distinct aspects and their related components are illustrated on the following page.

To show the distinctness of each of these aspects of the framework, consider the problem of reporting a particular asset on the balance sheet. The item must first qualify as an asset, i.e., it must possess the characteristics of an asset as defined by the FASB. However, it must also meet the criteria for recognition and have attributes that are capable of reliable measurement or estimation. If an item qualifies as an asset, meets the criteria for recognition,

[5]See *Statement of Financial Accounting Concepts No. 3,* "Elements of Financial Statements of Business Enterprises" (Stamford: Financial Accounting Standards Board, December 1980), par. 16–17.

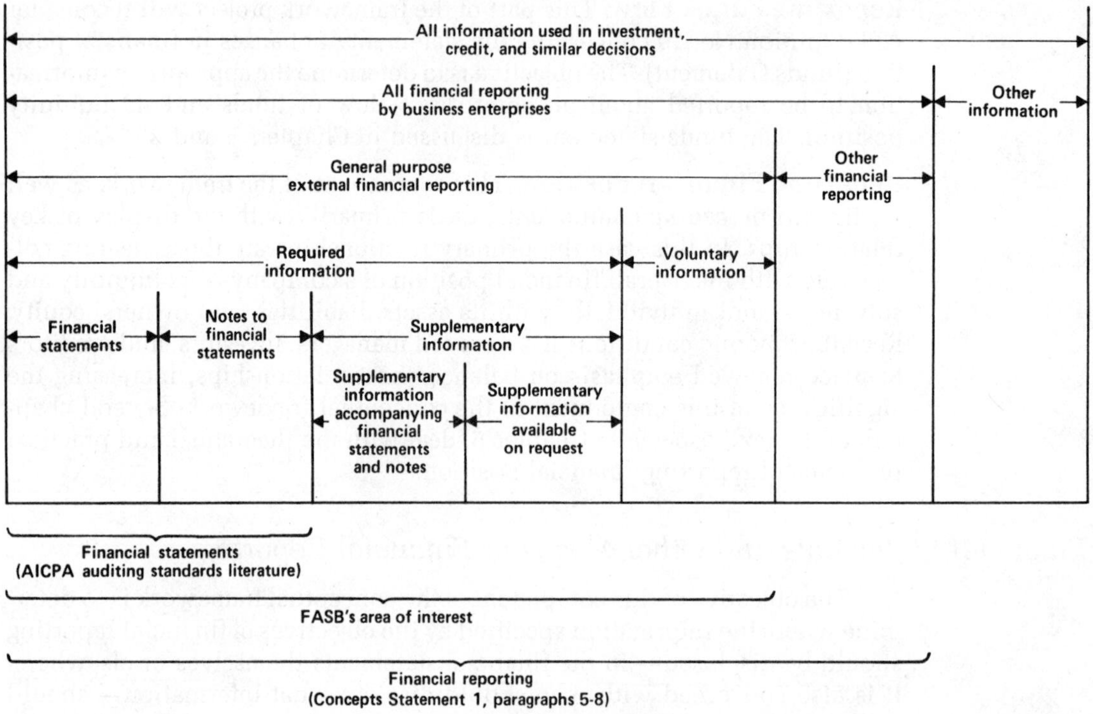

Source: FASB *Invitation to Comment,* "Financial Statements and Other Means of Financial Reporting," (May, 1980, p. 2.)

Information Spectrum

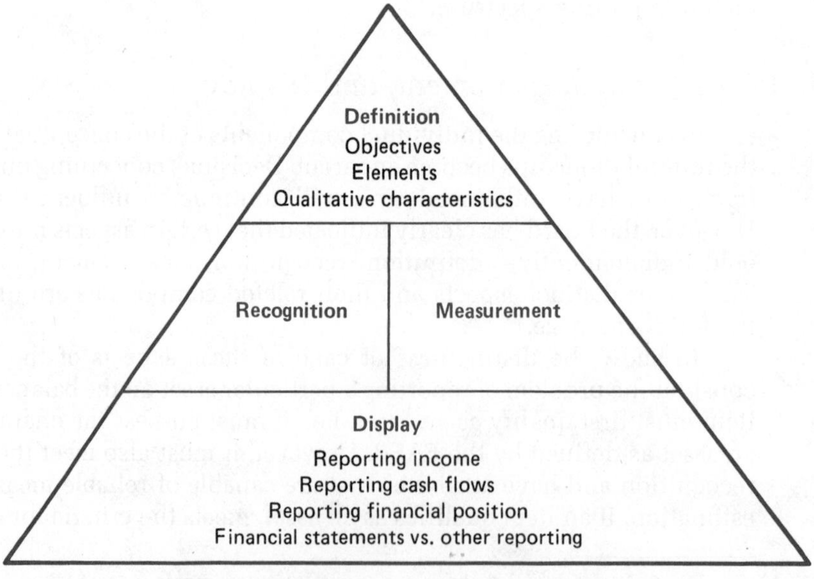

Major Aspects and Related Components of Conceptual Framework

and is measurable, then it can be determined how best to display or report the asset on the balance sheet. Some items may qualify as elements of financial statements in terms of definition, but may not be reported on the statements because of recognition or measurement problems. The most appropriate means of reporting, the display aspect, is yet another independent consideration.

OBJECTIVES OF FINANCIAL REPORTING

In discussing the first component of the framework, the objectives of financial reporting, four points should be made initially. First, the objectives of financial reporting are important and were given number one priority by the FASB because they determine the purposes and overall direction of accounting. Without identifying the goals for financial reporting, e.g., who needs what kind of information and for what reasons, accountants cannot determine the recognition criteria needed, which measurements are useful, or how best to report accounting information. The objectives presented in this section are those of the FASB as summarized and adapted from Statement of Financial Accounting Concepts No. 1.[6] Because the FASB is the primary standard-setting body for accounting in the private sector, the FASB objectives should be considered carefully. However, it should also be recognized that another group might identify somewhat different objectives for financial reporting. The objectives, as well as the other components of the conceptual framework, should therefore not be interpreted as "universal truths."

A second and related point is that the objectives of financial reporting are not immutable but are directly connected with the needs of those for whom the information is intended and must be considered in their environmental context. Financial reporting is not an end in itself but is directed toward satisfying the need for useful information in making business and economic decisions. Thus, the objectives of financial reporting may change in response to changes in the information needs of decision makers and in the economic, legal, political, and social aspects of the total business environment.

Third, the objectives of financial reporting are intended to be broad in nature. Financial reporting encompasses not only disclosures in financial statements, which are a primary means of communicating information to external parties, but also other information provided by the accounting system concerning an enterprise's resources, obligations, and earning ability. The objectives must be broadly based to satisfy a variety of user needs. Thus, they are objectives for general purpose financial reporting, attempting to satisfy the common interests of various potential users rather than to meet the specific needs of any selected group.

---

[6]*Statement of Financial Accounting Concepts No. 1,* "Objectives of Financial Reporting by Business Enterprises" (Stamford: Financial Accounting Standards Board, November 1978).

A fourth point is that the objectives of financial reporting are primarily directed toward the needs of those external users of accounting data who lack the authority to prescribe the information they desire. For example, the Internal Revenue Service or the Securities and Exchange Commission can require selected information from individuals and companies; investors and creditors must rely to a significant extent on the information contained in the periodic financial reports supplied by management, and, therefore, are the major users toward which financial reporting is directed.

Information for Decison Making

As already pointed out, the overall objective of financial reporting is to provide information for decision-making purposes. The FASB states:

> Financial reporting should provide information that is useful to present and potential investors and creditors and other users in making rational investment, credit, and similar decisions. The information should be comprehensible to those who have a reasonable understanding of business and economic activities and are willing to study the information with reasonable diligence.[7]

The emphasis in this overall objective is on investors and creditors as the primary external users because in satisfying their needs, most other general-purpose needs of external users will be met. This objective also recognizes a fairly sophisticated user of financial reports, one who has a reasonable understanding of accounting and business.

Assessing Cash Flow Prospects

The major concern of investors and creditors is in assessing future cash flows. Investment and lending decisions are made with the expectation of eventually increasing cash resources. An investor hopes to recover the initial investment, receive a return on that investment in the form of cash dividends, and ultimately sell the investment for more than it cost. Creditors seek to recover their cash outlays by repayments of the loans and to increase cash resources from interest payments. In making decisions, investors and creditors must consider the amounts, timing, and uncertainty (risk) of these prospective cash flows.

A company is similar to an investor in desiring to recover its investment plus receive a return on that investment. A company invests cash in noncash resources in order to produce a product or service for which it will receive cash inflows, with the amounts returned hopefully in excess of the amounts invested. To the extent a company is successful in generating favorable cash flows, it can pay dividends and interest, and the market prices of its securities will increase. Thus, the expected cash flows to investors and creditors are directly related to the expected cash flows of business enterprises. This relationship is captured in another key objective of financial reporting:

---

[7] *Ibid.*, par. 34.

> ...financial reporting should provide information to help investors, creditors, and others assess the amounts, timing, and uncertainty of prospective net cash inflows to the related enterprise.[8]

Information About Enterprise Resources and Claims Against Resources

Financial accounting does not purport to measure directly the value of a business. However, financial reporting should provide information that clearly identifies entity resources (assets) and the claims against those resources—creditor claims (liabilities) and ownership interests (owners' equity). By highlighting the relationships between assets, liabilities, and owners' equity items, investors, creditors, and others should be able to determine the financial strengths and weaknesses of an enterprise and assess its position of liquidity and solvency. Such information will help users determine the financial status of a company which, in turn, should provide insight into the prospects of future cash flows. It may also help individuals estimate the overall value of a business. To be complete, financial reports must disclose the significant changes in resources and claims against resources arising from transactions, events, and circumstances.

Information About Enterprise Performance and Earnings

The FASB states that "the primary focus of financial reporting is information about an enterprise's performance provided by measures of earnings and its components."[9] There are several aspects of this important objective. Clearly, investors and creditors are mostly concerned with expectations of future enterprise performance. However, to a large degree, they rely on evaluations of past performance as measures of future performance. The FASB concludes that information about enterprise earnings, measured by accrual accounting, generally provides a better indicator of enterprise performance than does information about current cash receipts and disbursements. However, the FASB recognizes that investors and creditors primarily want information about earnings as an indicator of future cash-flow potential.

Investors and creditors use reported earnings and information concerning the components of earnings in a variety of ways. For example, earnings may be interpreted by users of financial statements as an overall measure of managerial effectiveness, as a predictor of future earnings and long-term "earning power," and as an indicator of the risk of investing or lending. The information may be used to establish new predictions, confirm previous expectations, or change past evaluations.

Information About How Funds Are Obtained and Used

Notwithstanding the emphasis on earnings, another objective of financial reporting is to:

---

[8] *Ibid.*, par. 37.
[9] *Ibid.*, par. 43.

> ...provide information about how an enterprise obtains and spends cash, about its borrowing and repayment of borrowing, about its capital transactions, including cash dividends and other distributions of enterprise resources to owners, and about other factors that may affect an enterprise's liquidity or solvency.[10]

Much of the information to satisfy this objective is provided in the Statement of Changes in Financial Position, although information about earnings and economic resources and claims against resources may also be useful in evaluating the liquidity and solvency of a firm.

Additional Objectives

Although the objectives of financial reporting are aimed primarily at the needs of external users, financial reporting should also provide information that allows managers and directors to make decisions that are in the best interest of the owners. A related objective is that sufficient information should be provided to allow the owners to assess how well management has discharged its stewardship responsibility over the entrusted resources. This requires an additional objective—that financial reporting include explanations and interpretations to help users understand the financial information provided.

In summary, if the objectives discussed in the preceding paragraphs are fully attained, the FASB believes those who make economic decisions will have better information upon which to evaluate alternative courses of action and the expected returns, costs, and risks of each. The result should be a more efficient allocation of scarce resources among competing uses by individuals, enterprises, markets, and the government.

QUALITATIVE CHARACTERISTICS OF ACCOUNTING INFORMATION

Individuals who are charged with a responsibility for financial reporting should continually seek to provide the best, i.e., most useful, information possible within reasonable cost constraints. The problem is very complex because of the many choices among acceptable reporting alternatives. The key aspects of definition, recognition, measurement, and display are again apparent. For example, what items should be capitalized as assets or reported as liabilities? Which revenues and costs should be assigned to a particular reporting period and on what basis? What are the attributes to be measured: historical costs, current values, or net realizable values? At what level of aggregation or disaggregation should information be presented? Where should specific information be disclosed—in the financial statements, in the notes to the financial statements, or perhaps not at all? These and similar choices must be made by policy makers, such as members of the FASB or SEC; by managements as they fulfill their stewardship roles; and by accountants as they assist management in reporting on a company's activities.

---

[10] *Ibid.*, par. 49.

To assist in choosing among financial accounting and reporting alternatives, several criteria have been established by the FASB. These criteria relate to the qualitative characteristics of accounting information. The illustration below presents a hierarchy of these qualities and will be used as a frame of reference in discussing them.[11]

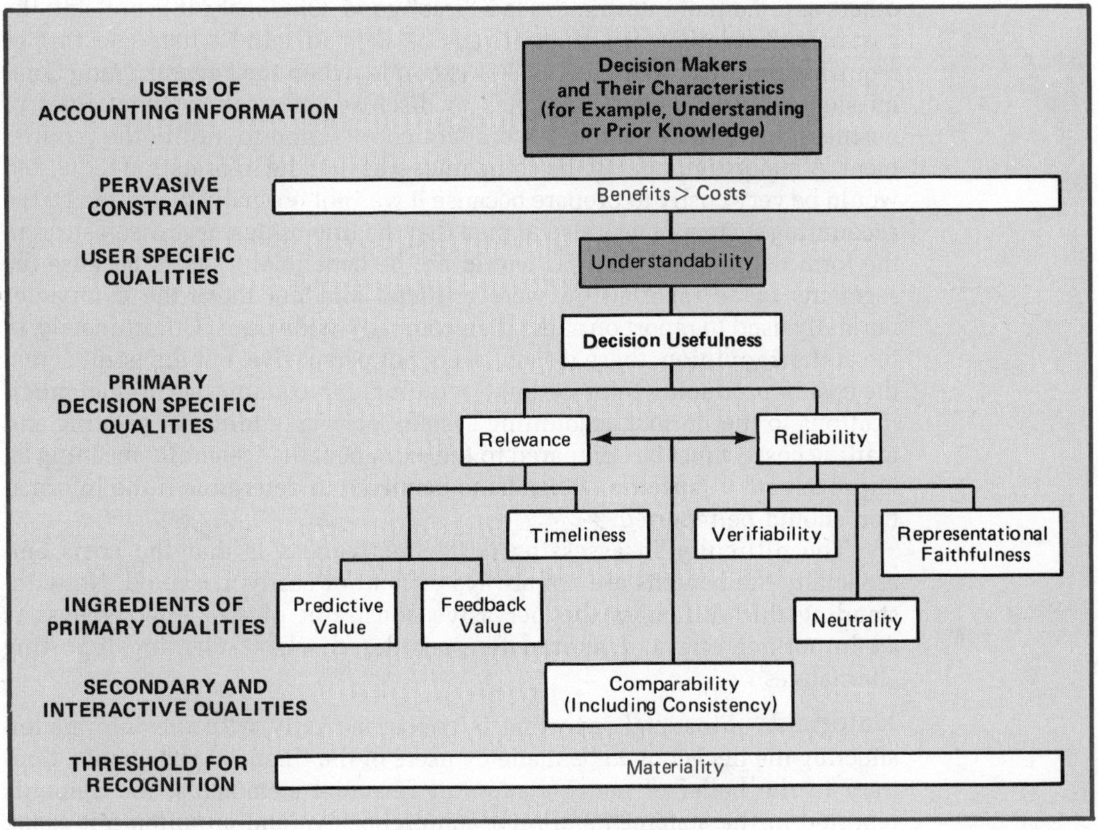

A Hierarchy of Accounting Qualities

The quality of **decision usefulness** is central to the hierarchy. All other characteristics are viewed in terms of their contribution to the usefulness of information for decision making.

Cost Effectiveness and Materiality

In satisfying the informational qualities identified in the illustration, there are two characteristics that affect all other informational qualities: (1) cost effectiveness and (2) materiality. **Cost effectiveness** is a pervasive

[11] The hierarchy presented in the illustration is from Figure 1 of *Statement of Financial Accounting Concepts No. 2*, "Qualitative Characteristics of Accounting Information" (Stamford: Financial Accounting Standards Board, May, 1980), page 15.

constraint suggesting that the benefits of information must exceed the costs of supplying information. The other characteristic, **materiality**, deals with the threshold for recognition.

Cost Effectiveness. Information is like other commodities in that it must be worth more than it costs to be desirable. Too often government regulators and others assume that information is a "free" good. Obviously, it is not, and the cost-benefit relationship must always be kept in mind when selecting or requiring reporting alternatives. For example, when the Federal Trade Commission required large companies to disclose information about lines of business, a group of companies brought court action to nullify the requirement. A major argument of the companies was that the information requested would be very costly to prepare because it was not normally generated by the accounting system. It was also argued that the line-of-business disclosures in the form required by the FTC would not be beneficial to users because the segments to be reported on were artificial and not those the companies normally used to report on a less than company-wide basis. Unfortunately, in the authors' opinion, these reasons were not persuasive, but the point is that the cost of producing information (including, for example, additional modifications to the normal accounting system, or even additional printing and mailing costs) must be compared to the extra benefits (generally meaning an improvement in specific decisions to be made) to determine if the information should be reported.

The difficulty in assessing cost effectiveness is that the costs and especially the benefits are not always evident or easily measured. Notwithstanding this difficulty, the pervasive constraint of cost effectiveness is an important one and should be considered when selecting reporting alternatives.

Materiality. Financial reporting is concerned only with the information affecting the decisions to be made by users of the financial statements. Contrary to the belief of many readers of financial statements, the amounts reported in the statements are not comprehensive and are often not exact. For many decisions such completeness and exactness are not required. There is, of course, a point at which disclosures become relevant, when information that is incomplete or inexact does affect a decision. This point defines the boundary between information that is material and information that is immaterial.

Materiality is an overriding concept related to but distinguishable from the primary qualities of relevance and reliability. Materiality determines the threshold for recognition of accounting items and is primarily quantitative in nature. It is directed toward the specific question, is the item large enough or the degree of accuracy precise enough to influence the decision of a user of the information? Of course, the degree of influence caused by the size of the item also depends on the nature of the item and the circumstances in which judgment must be made. Certain information may be relevant to a decision, e.g., whether overtime is paid on a particular job. However, if the amount of overtime is negligible, that bit of information will have little or no influence on a decision to accept the job. Under those circumstances, information about overtime pay would be immaterial. Thus, relevance and materiality are both related to the concept of information usefulness. However, relevance is directed toward the *nature* of the information while materiality focuses on the *size* of a judgment item in a given set of circumstances.

At the present time, there are few guidelines to assist the preparers of financial reports in applying the concept of materiality. Where guidelines do exist, they are not uniform. For example, 10 percent is the materiality guideline for disclosing segment data for diversified companies, 3 percent is considered material in determining the significance of dilution for earnings per share computations, and there is a zero materiality threshold in the area of foreign corrupt practices. Managers and accountants must therefore exercise judgment in determining whether a failure to disclose certain data will affect the decisions of the users of financial statements.

Past court cases also help determine what is material by providing examples of where the lack of disclosure of certain information in the financial statements has been considered a material misstatement. The failure to disclose proper inventory values or pending sales of large amounts of assets, the failure to disclose the imminence of a highly profitable transaction or to disclose a significant downward readjustment of reported earnings are a few examples.[12]

In summary, the following point should be kept in mind in making judgments concerning materiality:

> The omission or misstatement of an item in a financial report is material if, in the light of surrounding circumstances, the magnitude of the item is such that it is probable that the judgment of a reasonable person relying upon the report would have been changed or influenced by the inclusion or correction of the item.[13]

User-Specific Qualities

The hierarchy previously illustrated distinguishes user-specific qualities such as **understandability** from qualities inherent in accounting information or decision-specific qualities. The quality of understandability is essential to decision usefulness because information cannot be useful to decision makers if it is not understood, even though the information may be relevant and reliable. The understandability of information depends on both user characteristics and the inherent characteristics of the information presented. Hence, understandability can be evaluated only with respect to specific classes of decision makers. As indicated earlier, financial reporting is directed toward those users who have a reasonable understanding of business and economic activities and who are willing to study the information provided with reasonable diligence.

---

[12]For additional examples of quantitative materiality considerations, see Appendix C of FASB Statement of Concepts No. 2.

[13]*Statement of Financial Accounting Concepts No. 2,* "Qualitative Characteristics of Accounting Information" (Stamford: Financial Accounting Standards Board, May, 1980), par. 132.

Primary Decision-Specific Qualities

In the following statement, the FASB identified **relevance** and **reliability** as the primary qualities inherent in useful accounting information:

> The qualities that distinguish "better" (more useful) information from "inferior" (less useful) information are primarily the qualities of relevance and reliability, with some other characteristics that those qualities imply.[14]

Relevance. The relevance of information may be judged only in relation to its intended use. If information is not relevant to the needs of decision makers, it is useless regardless of how well it meets other criteria. The objective of relevance, then, is to select methods of measuring and reporting that will aid those individuals who rely on financial statements to make decisions. Many critics of financial statements have argued that traditionally prepared statements are irrelevant to many decisions that must be made. An increasing amount of research is being conducted to evaluate this criticism. What information is required by those who must make a decision? How can current practice be changed to improve the relevance, and thus the usefulness, of accounting information?

The FASB defines relevant information as that which will "make a difference." Information may confirm expectations or change them. In either case, a decision maker's assessment of the probability of occurrence of some event is affected by the information. If the decision maker's assessment is not affected by certain information, that information is not relevant and therefore not useful to the decision maker. Thus, the FASB relates relevance to the predictive or confirmation value of information. If a user can better predict future consequences based on information about past events and transactions, then such information is relevant.[15]

As shown in the illustration on page 81, two key ingredients of relevant information are its **feedback value** and **predictive value.** Information provides feedback on past actions that helps confirm or correct earlier expectations. Such information can then be used to help predict future outcomes. Normally relevant information provides both feedback and predictive value at the same time. Knowledge of previous activities and consequences generally improves a decison maker's ability to predict the results of similar future actions. As stated by the FASB, "Without a knowledge of the past, the basis for prediction will usually be lacking. Without an interest in the future, knowledge of the past is sterile."[16]

Timeliness is another key ingredient of relevance, relating directly to decision usefulness. Information furnished after a decision has been made is of no value. All accounting systems should be established to provide information to users in a timely manner. In meeting this criterion, financial statements must be prepared prior to the time an accountant can be absolutely certain as to the results of an entity's operations. The entity is an ongoing

---

[14] *Ibid.*, par. 15.
[15] *Ibid.*, par. 46–50.
[16] *Ibid.*, par. 51.

enterprise with many interacting activities. Thus, any attempt to measure the success of an entity at some point in time before its dissolution must rely heavily on estimates. Decisions by investors, creditors, governmental authorities, managers, and others rely on these estimates. By convention, the year has been established as the normal period for reporting. Annual statements, as well as statements covering shorter intervals, such as quarters, have been provided by entities to satisfy the needs of those requiring financial information.

It is evident that the degree of relevance of information will vary for different users depending on their particular needs and circumstances. Therefore, trade-offs exist among the desirable qualities of useful information, including reliability and the other qualities yet to be discussed. As stated by the FASB:

> In the last analysis each decision maker judges what accounting information is useful, and that judgment is influenced by factors such as the decisions to be made, the methods of decision making used, the information already possessed or obtainable from other sources, and the decision maker's capacity (alone or with professional help) to process the information.[17]

Reliability. The second primary quality of accounting information is reliability. Accounting information is reliable if users can depend on it to represent the economic conditions or events that it purports to represent.[18] Reliability does not mean absolute accuracy. Obviously, there are degrees of reliability. Information that is based on judgments and includes estimates and approximations cannot be totally accurate, but it should be reliable. The objective, then, is to present the type of information in which users can have confidence. To accomplish this objective, information must contain the key ingredients of reliability: **verifiability** and **representational faithfulness.**

Verification implies consensus. Accountants seek to base their findings on facts that are determined objectively and that can be verified by other trained accountants. The FASB indicates that "verifiable financial accounting information provides results that would be substantially duplicated by independent measurers using the same measurement methods."[19]

All accounting measurements, however, cannot be completely free from subjective opinions and judgments. Cash receipts and disbursements can be adequately supported by vouchers, and cash on hand is determined by count; full support and verification for this element and its changes are available. Findings here can be readily verified. Purchases of goods and services, as well as sales, are also generally well supported by evidence and are subject to verification. There are a number of areas in accounting, however, where determinations must be based in part on judgment, estimate, and other subjective factors. The recognition of depreciation is an example. But the degree of estimate can be minimized by the attempt to develop evidence lending objective support to conclusions. Verifiable determinations are encouraged

---

[17] *Ibid.*, par. 36.
[18] *Ibid.*, par. 62.
[19] *Ibid.*, par. 82.

as a means of reducing possible error, bias, or intentional distortion, and achieving an accounting that can be accepted with confidence.

Two kinds of bias are possible in accounting information: **measurer bias** and **measurement bias.** Verifiability protects primarily against measurer bias. Representational faithfulness deals mostly with measurement bias. That is, does the measurement show what it purports to show. The measurements reported on the balance sheet, for example, have been criticized because they do not reflect the value of a company. However, that has not been their purpose. If the purpose of balance sheet measurements is accepted in its traditional context of reporting on the financial status of a company as measured by historical costs based on past transactions, then such information can be said to exhibit the quality of representational faithfulness. The information may be rejected as not measuring the right thing, that is, as not being relevant, but the information would be reliable in the sense of not having measurement bias.

Secondary and Interactive Qualities

There are at least three additional qualities that directly influence accounting information. Listed in the order they are discussed, these concepts are: (1) neutrality, (2) comparability, and (3) consistency.

Neutrality. Financial statements should not be biased in favor of one group to the detriment of another. This may seem in conflict with the primary quality of relevance; however, the presumption of the FASB is that external financial reports are general purpose statements that should meet the common needs of a wide variety of users. Specialized needs must be met in other ways.

The concept of neutrality is similar to the all-encompassing principle of "fairness." It is also directly related to other informational criteria, especially reliability. As stated by the FASB,

> To be neutral, accounting information must report economic activity as faithfully as possible, without coloring the image it communicates for the purpose of influencing behavior in *some particular direction.*[20]

Comparability. The essence of comparability is that information becomes much more useful when it can be related to a benchmark or standard, that is, when it is compared to another firm or to similar information for the same firm but for other equivalent periods of time. Thus, comparability may be regarded as intracomparability, or comparability within a single enterprise, and intercomparability, or comparability between enterprises. The comparability within a single firm relates more to consistency, which is discussed in the next section.

Financial reports should provide information permitting a comparison of one company with another. This requires that like things be accounted for in the same manner on the financial statements. Basic similarities and differ-

---

[20] *Ibid.*, par. 100.

ences in the activities of companies should be clearly apparent from the financial statements. They should not be influenced by selection and use of different accounting methods.

One of the greatest unsolved problems in accounting is the present acceptance of alternative accounting methods under situations that do not appear to be sufficiently different to warrant different practices. Much current research in accounting is directed toward identifying circumstances justifying the use of a given method of accounting. If this research is successful, alternative methods can be eliminated where circumstances are found to be the same. In the meantime, current practice requires disclosure of the accounting methods used, as well as the impact of changes in methods when a change can be justified. There is also pressure on accountants to indicate the "preferability" of one accounting method over another. Although the disclosures currently made do not generally provide enough information for a user to convert the published financial information from one accounting method to another, they do provide information that can assist the user in determining the degree of intercompany comparability.

Consistency. Consistency is an important ingredient of intracomparability and useful accounting information. In view of the number of reporting alternatives, such as the different procedures for cost allocation in measuring depreciation, the different approaches for pricing inventories in developing cost of goods sold, and the different forms and classifications for the presentation of operating and financial data, the methods adopted should be consistently employed if there is to be continuity and comparability in the accounting presentations. In analyzing statements, one constantly seeks to identify and evaluate the changes and trends within the enterprise. Conclusions concerning financial position and operations may be materially in error if, for example, accelerated depreciation is applied against the revenue of one year and straight-line depreciation against the revenue of the next year, or if securities are reported under long-term investments in one year and under current assets in the following year. Consistency in the application of accounting procedures is also recognized as a means of ensuring integrity in financial reporting; the use of alternate procedures in succeeding periods opens the doors to manipulation of net income and asset and equity measurements.

This is not to suggest that methods once adopted should not be changed. A continuing analysis of the business activities, as well as changing conditions, may suggest changes in accounting methods and presentations leading to more informative statements. These changes should be incorporated in the accounting system and statements. But the financial statements should be accompanied by a clear explanation of the nature of the changes and their effects, where they are material, so current reporting can be properly interpreted and related to past reporting.

Both consistency and comparability are concepts relating to the relationships of two or more accounting numbers rather than to the informational quality of the number itself, as is true with the primary qualities of relevance and reliability.

ELEMENTS OF FINANCIAL STATEMENTS

In Statement of Financial Accounting Concepts No. 3, the FASB has established definitions for the ten basic elements of financial statements of business enterprises. These elements comprise the building blocks upon which financial statements are constructed. The elements are interrelated and collectively report the performance and status of an enterprise. For reference purposes, the FASB definitions of the ten basic elements are listed below. These definitions and the issues surrounding them are discussed in detail as they are introduced in later chapters.

Assets are probable future economic benefits obtained or controlled by a particular entity as a result of past transactions or events.

Liabilities are probable future sacrifices of economic benefits arising from present obligations of a particular entity to transfer assets or provide services to other entities in the future as a result of past transactions or events.

Equity is the residual interest in the assets of an entity that remains after deducting its liabilities. In a business enterprise, the equity is the ownership interest.

Investments by owners are increases in net assets of a particular enterprise resulting from transfers to it from other entities of something of value to obtain or increase ownership interests (or equity) in it. Assets are most commonly received as investments by owners, but that which is received may also include services or satisfaction or conversion of liabilities of the enterprise.

Distributions to owners are decreases in net assets of a particular enterprise resulting from transferring assets, rendering services, or incurring liabilities by the enterprise to owners. Distributions to owners decrease ownership interests (or equity) in an enterprise.

Comprehensive income is the change in equity (net assets) of an entity during a period from transactions and other events and circumstances from nonowner sources. It includes all changes in equity during a period except those resulting from investments by owners and distributions to owners.

Revenues are inflows or other enhancements of assets of an entity or settlements of its liabilities (or a combination of both) during a period from delivering or producing goods, rendering services, or other activities that constitute the entity's ongoing major or central operations.

Expenses are outflows or other using up of assets or incurrences of liabilities (or a combination of both) during a period from delivering or producing goods, rendering services, or carrying out other activities that constitute the entity's ongoing major or central operations.

Gains are increases in equity (net assets) from peripheral or incidental transactions of an entity and from all other transactions and other events and circumstances affecting the entity during a period except those that result from revenues or investments by owners.

Losses are decreases in equity (net assets) from peripheral or incidental transactions of an entity and from all other transactions and other events and circumstances affecting the entity during a period except those that result from expenses or distributions to owners.[21]

NATURE OF THE ACCOUNTING MODEL: AN UNRESOLVED ISSUE

Perhaps one of the most important issues to be resolved by the conceptual framework is the nature of the accounting model to be used for financial reporting. The traditional accounting model is comprised of several basic features. First, the business enterprise is viewed as a specific **economic entity** separate and distinct from its owners and any other business unit. It is the entity and its activities that receive the focus of attention for accounting purposes.

Second, in the absence of evidence to the contrary, the entity is viewed as a **going concern.** This continuity assumption provides support for the preparation of a balance sheet reporting costs assignable to future activities rather than realizable values that would attach to properties in the event of voluntary liquidation or forced sale. This same assumption calls for the preparation of an income statement reporting only such portions of revenues and costs as are allocable to current activities.

Third, only **past transactions and events** affecting an entity are accounted for. Such transactions and events provide the basis for accounting entries, and any changes in resources and equity values are generally not recorded until a transaction has taken place.

A fourth and related point is that accounting, as it is practiced today, is founded on the **cost valuation principle.** The amount of money or the monetary value of other assets exchanged in an arm's-length transaction is the amount used as the basis for recording the transaction. Cost represents a value regarded as definite and immediately determinable, and thus also satisfies the criteria of verifiability and neutrality. The use of historical costs is supported as a means of closing the doors to possible error, bias, or even intentional misstatement, and achieving an accounting that can be accepted with confidence.

Fifth, transactions are measured in **monetary units,** and, in the United States at least, the dollar is used as the measuring unit. As mentioned earlier, value changes in the dollar have historically been ignored. Accounting systems are designed to account for the use of given units of money, that is, their inflow and their outflow. Thus, accounting systems tend to produce statements that summarize stewardship functions of management. Changes in the value of the monetary unit are not significant when a historical cost principle is adopted that regards only the accounting for original dollars as important. However, many accountants feel uncomfortable about the relevance of accounting information that is insensitive to changes in the value of the measuring unit. Although all accounts shown on the balance sheet are labeled dollars, they are not dollars of equal purchasing power. These various dollars

---

[21] *Statement of Financial Accounting Concepts No. 3, op. cit.,* pp. xi–xii.

are added together as though the monetary units are equivalent. But when the value of the dollar fluctuates greatly over time, such an assumption obviously loses its validity.

Sixth, it is assumed that accounting information is needed on a timely basis and so the life of a business entity is divided into specific **accounting periods.** For each time period an income measure is determined on an **accrual basis.** This means that revenues are recognized as earned, not necessarily when cash is received; and expenses are recognized when incurred, not necessarily when cash is paid.

Revenues for a period are generally determined by application of the concept of **revenue recognition.** Expenses for a period are determined by association with specific revenues or a particular time period. This association process is frequently referred to as the **matching** process. The revenue recognition and matching concepts are discussed in Chapters 4 and 19.

Another concept often associated with the traditional accounting model is **conservatism.** This means that when there is genuine doubt concerning which of two or more reporting alternatives should be selected, business is best served by adopting a conservative approach, that is, by choosing the alternative with the least favorable effect on owners' equity. However, conservatism does not mean deliberate and arbitrary understatement of net assets and earnings. Conservatism should be used to deal with uncertainties when a degree of skepticism is warranted. A common example of accounting practice is reporting inventories at the lower of cost or market values. Thus, the concept of conservatism is a useful one, but one that should be applied carefully and used only as a moderating and refining influence to the accounting process as a whole.

Many of the above assumptions and features of the accounting model are being questioned. If the conceptual framework relaxes these assumptions or otherwise changes the accounting model, financial reporting will be affected. Students should not only pay attention to the unresolved and controversial issues that will be discussed throughout the text, but they should also be prepared to monitor and keep pace with the changes that will occur in accounting in the future.

Establishing a conceptual framework for accounting is an ongoing project. It is certainly not an easy task nor will its completion necessarily provide solutions to all accounting problems. The FASB has made commendable progress, but much remains to be done. Even some of the work already accomplished is being, and will continue to be, reconsidered and revised to correct weaknesses. Nevertheless, progress is being made. Meeting user needs for financial information in an increasingly complex environment will continue to be a major problem for accounting professionals. Increasing governmental regulation of business and accounting is another challenge to be faced. Furthermore, accountants are being asked to assume additional responsibilities, e.g., the detection of fraud and the reporting of the social impact of enterprise activity. These responsibilities must be performed in a manner that will maintain high professional standards and thus avoid legal difficulties.

The challenges facing the accounting profession are significant. They provide an exciting opportunity for future accountants to make important contributions to their profession and to society. Resolution of problems may not be easy, but it will be rewarding and will certainly make a career in accounting interesting.

APPENDIX

CHRONOLOGY OF ATTEMPTS TO ESTABLISH GENERALLY ACCEPTED ACCOUNTING PRINCIPLES

Attempts to establish an authoritative set of generally accepted accounting principles began in the early 1900's. Among the leaders in such attempts were accounting educators, as individuals and collectively as a part of the American Accounting Association (AAA). As a result of this activity and interest, the Executive Committee of the AAA issued the first of several publications dealing with accounting principles in June, 1936, as a "Tentative Statement of Accounting Principles Affecting Corporate Reports." The latest in this series was published by the AAA in 1966 under the title "A Statement of Basic Accounting Theory."

During this period from 1936 to 1966, there were additional publications by the AAA and by the American Institute of Certified Public Accountants (AICPA). Among the most prominent were: "A Statement of Accounting Principles," by Sanders, Hatfield, and Moore (1938); "An Introduction to Corporate Accounting Standards," by Paton and Littleton (1940); Accounting Research Study (ARS) No. 1, "The Basic Postulates of Accounting," by Moonitz (1961); and Accounting Research Study No. 3, "A Tentative Set of Broad Accounting Principles for Business Enterprises," by Sprouse and Moonitz (1962).

In 1970 the Accounting Principles Board (APB) published its Statement No. 4, "Basic Concepts and Accounting Principles Underlying Financial Statements of Business Enterprises." There were two main purposes of this statement: (1) to provide a basis for understanding the broad fundamentals of financial accounting, and (2) to help guide the future development of financial accounting.[22] The statement was intended to be primarily descriptive of current practice. This was in contrast to ARS Nos. 1 and 3, which were

[22]*Statement of the Accounting Principles Board No. 4,* "Basic Concepts and Accounting Principles Underlying Financial Statements of Business Enterprises" (New York: American Institute of Certified Public Accountants, October, 1970), par. 2.

primarily prescriptive and were judged to be too radically different from existing practice to be accepted at the time they were issued. However, it is interesting to note that many of the principles proposed by Sprouse and Moonitz in ARS Nos. 1 and 3 are now becoming accepted.

Statement No. 4 identified the objectives of financial statements and the basic features and elements of financial accounting. In effect, it tried to capture the existing framework of accounting. It divided generally accepted accounting principles into three levels: *pervasive principles* dealing with recognition and measurement of events; *broad operating principles* relating to the selection, measurement, and presentation on financial statements; and *detailed principles,* which are included in the specific rules and procedures to be applied to particular circumstances.

In 1973 the AICPA published a report from a special study group, chaired by Robert M. Trueblood, concerning the "Objectives of Financial Statements." This report was the result of 18 months of study by some of the most knowledgeable accountants in the United States. It was an attempt to clarify and make more specific the objectives of financial statements. The objectives had been stated previously, in Statement No. 4 and elsewhere in the literature, but not in sufficient detail to provide guidance for financial reporting. The Trueblood committee, as it is often referred to, identified 12 objectives that tried to answer the questions: Who needs financial statements? What information do they need? How much of the needed information can be provided by accounting? and, What framework is required to provide the needed information?[23]

When the Financial Accounting Standards Board (FASB) was established in 1973, one of the first items placed on its agenda was its conceptual framework project. As indicated in the chapter, members of the FASB are devoting considerable time and energy to various facets of this project. As the FASB proceeds with their task of establishing a conceptual framework for accounting, they will continue to be aided by the past efforts of those who have previously attempted to establish generally accepted accounting principles.

QUESTIONS

1. Who are the primary "internal" and "external" users of accounting information?
2. What impact has the corporate form of business had on financial reporting?
3. Why is judgment required for accountants in fulfilling their role as suppliers of information?
4. The conceptual framework project is receiving a large share of the FASB's resources. What is the project expected to accomplish? What is it not likely to do?
5. List the nine components that currently comprise the FASB conceptual framework.

[23]*Report of the Study Group on the Objectives of Financial Statements,* "Objectives of Financial Statements" (New York: American Institute of Certified Public Accountants, October, 1973).

6. Why are definition, recognition, measurement, and display considered separate and distinct aspects of the conceptual framework?
7. Identify the major objectives of financial reporting as specified by the FASB.
8. Identify and describe the two criteria that impact on all the other informational qualities.
9. Why is it so difficult to measure the cost effectiveness of accounting information?
10. What is the current materiality standard in accounting?
11. Distinguish between the primary informational qualities of relevance and reliability.
12. What characteristics directly affect the relevance of information? Explain.
13. Does reliability mean absolute accuracy? Explain.
14. Two types of bias may exist in accounting information. What are they and to which of the qualities of accounting information do they relate?
15. Define comparability. How does comparability differ from uniformity?
16. Of what value is consistency in financial reporting?
17. List and define the ten basic elements of financial statements.
18. Identify and describe the basic features of the traditional accounting model.
19. What impact might the FASB conceptual framework have on the accounting model?

DISCUSSION CASES

case 3-1 (The continuing attempt to establish a conceptual framework) As a student of accounting, you have noticed that a substantial portion of the literature deals with establishing a comprehensive set of concepts upon which accounting principles can be based. This is currently the case and has been for the past 50 years. Yet, in discussions with colleagues and friends, you have to admit that the accounting profession still cannot point to an authoritative set of accounting concepts and principles that are universally accepted within the business community. As you think about this problem, at least three questions come to mind: (1) Why have accountants not been able to develop a conceptual framework? (2) Is an overall conceptual framework of accounting even needed? and (3) What are the members of the FASB doing differently, if anything, so that they might expect to succeed in establishing a conceptual framework for accounting where others have failed? Discuss possible answers to these questions.

case 3-2 (Are CPAs merely shiny-pants bookkeepers?) During the 1960's, a great corporate merger movement occurred in the United States. Companies expanded their operations by adding other companies to their organization. Often, they were in completely unrelated fields. Accounting for these mergers often encouraged even more mergers because it sometimes enabled companies that were starting to look weak financially to merge with a company with positive financial statements, and thus postpone the disclosure of poor management to statement users. In an attempt to clarify the accounting rules and to eliminate financial statement manipulation that did not truly present the entity's financial status, the Accounting Principles Board proposed a change in accounting for mergers.

One of the business executives heavily involved in merger activity commented publicly that the Board had no right to issue such pronouncements. If the accounting requirement were changed, the executive argued, merger activity would decline and economic growth in our economy would stagnate. This would not be for society's best interest as a whole. Referring to the accountants on the Board as nothing more than "shiny-pants bookkeepers," the executive issued a strong statement against the Board recommendation.

Assume that the accounting rules would have limited merger activity and thus reduced economic growth, should this result affect the decision by an accounting body as to how transactions should be recorded and reported? Should the impact on society be the most important consideration for an accounting principle?

case 3-3 (Definition, recognition, measurement, and display considerations in financial reporting) In September of 1979, the SEC adopted amendments to Regulation S-X, requiring separate disclosure of redeemable preferred stock. In taking such action, the SEC noted an increase in the use of complex securities—such as preferred stocks subject to mandatory redemption requirements—that exhibit both debt and equity characteristics. The question recently considered by FASB was whether or not such securities should be classified as liabilities rather than as equity securities. How might the FASB's distinctions among the definitional, recognition, measurement, and display aspects of their conceptual framework assist in resolving this or similar issues?

case 3-4 (External reporting: the difficult task of satisfying diverse informational needs) Teri Green has recently been promoted. She is now the chief financial officer of Teltrex, Inc., and has primary responsibility for the external reporting function. During the past three weeks, Green has met with Jeff Thalman, the senior vice president of Westmore First National Bank where Teltrex has a $1,000,000 line of credit; Susan David, a financial analyst for Stubbs, Jones, and McConkie, a brokerage firm; and Brian Ellis, who is something of a corporate gadfly and who owns 2 percent of Teltrex's outstanding common stock. Each of these individuals has commented on Teltrex's last year's annual report, pointing out deficiencies and suggesting additional information they would like to see presented in this year's annual report. From Green's point of view, explain the nature of general purpose financial statements and indicate the informational qualities of the accounting data that she must be concerned with in fulfilling Teltrex's external reporting responsibility.

EXERCISES

exercise 3-1 (Qualitative characteristics of accounting information)

Identify the qualitative characteristics most likely violated by each of the following situations. (Briefly support your answers.)

(a) A prospective purchaser of a company receives only the conventional financial statements.
(b) An investor examines the published annual reports of all companies in the steel industry for the purpose of investing in the most profitable one.
(c) A company uses the prefix "reserve" for a contra asset, a liability, and a retained earnings appropriation.
(d) A company reports all of its land, buildings, and equipment on the basis of a recent appraisal.
(e) Management elects to change its method of inventory valuation in order to overcome an unprofitable year from operations. This change enables the company to report a gradual growth in earnings.

exercise 3-2 (Applications of accounting characteristics and concepts)

For each situation listed, indicate by letters the appropriate qualitative characteristic(s) or accounting concept(s) applied. A letter may be used more than once, and more than one characteristic or concept may apply to a particular situation.

(a) Understandability
(b) Verifiability
(c) Timeliness
(d) Representational faithfulness
(e) Neutrality
(f) Relevance
(g) Going concern
(h) Economic entity
(i) Historical cost
(j) Quantifiability
(k) Materiality
(l) Comparability
(m) Conservatism

(1) Goodwill is only recorded in the accounts when it arises from the purchase of another entity at a price higher than the fair market value of the purchased entity's tangible assets.
(2) Marketable securities are valued at the lower of cost or market.
(3) All payments out of petty cash are debited to Miscellaneous Expense.
(4) Plant assets are classified separately as land or buildings, with an accumulated depreciation account for buildings.
(5) Periodic payments of $1,500 per month for services of H. Hay, who is the sole proprietor of the company, are reported as withdrawals.
(6) Small tools used by a large manufacturing firm are recorded as expenses when purchased.
(7) Marketable securities are recorded at cost.
(8) A retail store estimates inventory, rather than taking a complete physical count, for purposes of preparing monthly financial statements.
(9) A note describing the company's possible liability in a lawsuit is included with the financial statements even though no formal liability exists at the balance sheet date.
(10) Depreciation on plant assets is consistently computed each year by the straight-line method.

exercise 3-3 (Theoretical support for corrected balance sheet)

G. Peay prepared the following balance sheet for Peay Inc. as of December 31, 1984. Review each item listed, and considering the additional data given, prepare a corrected, properly classified balance sheet. Where a change is made in reporting an item, disclose in a separate note the theoretical support for your suggested change. Record any offsetting adjustments in the retained earnings account, except for possible contributed capital changes.

Assets		Liabilities and Owner's Equity	
Cash	$ 30,000	Accounts payable	$ 85,000
Marketable securities	55,000	Taxes payable	65,000
Notes receivable	40,000	Notes payable	120,000
Accounts receivable	130,000	Mortgage payable	273,000
Inventories	195,000	Capital stock	300,000
Land and buildings	520,000	Retained earnings	140,000
Accumulated depreciation—buildings	(27,000)		
Goodwill	40,000		
	$983,000		$983,000

Additional data:
(a) Cash includes a bank checking account of $20,000, current checks and money orders on hand of $5,000, and $5,000 in checks that could not be cashed. Peay feels the latter will probably not be recovered.
(b) Marketable securities are listed at year-end market values. They were purchased early in 1984 for $46,800.
(c) Peay estimates that all receivables are collectible except for a three-year-old past due note of $8,000. Past collection experience indicates that two percent of current notes and accounts prove uncollectible.
(d) Land and buildings are recorded at initial cost. At date of acquisition, land was valued at $70,000 and buildings at $450,000. Building depreciation has been correctly recorded.
(e) Goodwill was recorded when Peay received an offer of $50,000 more for the business than the recorded asset values.

(continued)

(f) Of the notes payable, $30,000 will be due in 1985 with the remainder coming due in 1986 and 1987.
(g) The mortgage is payable in annual payments of $19,500.
(h) The capital stock has a par value of $100 per share; 2,500 shares are issued and outstanding.

exercise 3-4 (Theoretical support for corrected income statement)

A. Hoyle prepared the following income statement for the calendar year 1984:

Revenues	$80,000
Expenses	50,000
Net income.	$30,000

An examination of the records reveals the following:

(a) Hoyle is the sole proprietor.
(b) Business operations include:
1. A catering service
2. An equipment rental shop
3. Rental of a part of Hoyle's home for small receptions.
(c) Revenues included:

1. Catering service sales	$50,000
2. Equipment rentals	12,500
3. Reception rental space.	17,500
	$80,000

(d) Expenses consisted of:

1. Cost of goods sold (catering)	$15,000
2. Other costs (catering).	11,500
3. Depreciation—equipment rented	1,500
4. Repairs and other costs—equipment rented	2,500
5. Depreciation, $2,000; cleaning, $4,500; and miscellaneous costs, $1,000—reception rental space	7,500
6. Living expenses—family	12,000
	$50,000

Indicate what changes, if any, you would make in the income statement format and amount of Hoyle's income for 1984 and give theoretical support for your conclusions.

4 THE INCOME STATEMENT

CHAPTER OBJECTIVES

Explain the importance of measuring and reporting income and its components.

Describe the economic approach and the transaction approach to income determination.

Discuss the impact of changing prices on the measurement and reporting of income.

Describe and illustrate the content and form of the income statement.

Describe and illustrate the reporting of changes in retained earnings.

Accounting systems are designed to provide a variety of reports and analyses for internal and external use. Traditionally, the information made available for external use has been reported in a set of financial statements consisting of: (1) an **income statement** presenting the results of operations of an entity for a reporting period; (2) a **balance sheet** reporting the financial position of a business at a certain date; and (3) a **statement of changes in financial position** (funds statement) describing the changes in enterprise resources over the reporting period. The three primary statements are referred to as general-purpose financial statements because they are intended for use by a wide variety of external users. Although there has been some discussion as to the need for special purpose statements directed to specific external users, there has been no significant movement toward this in practice.

Sometimes a **retained earnings statement** is provided, or combined with the income statement, showing the changes in retained earnings for the period. When there are changes other than those affecting retained earnings that impact on total owners' equity, a supplemental **statement of changes in owners' equity** may be presented to provide a complete reconciliation of the beginning and ending equity balances.

This chapter focuses on the importance of measuring and reporting income and the nature and content of the income statement. The retained earnings statement is also described and illustrated. The balance sheet is discussed in Chapter 5. The statement of changes in financial position is introduced in Chapter 5, but covered in detail in Chapter 23. The statement of changes in owners' equity is discussed and illustrated in Chapter 18.

IMPORTANCE OF MEASURING AND REPORTING INCOME

The **income statement**, alternately titled the *earnings statement*, the *statement of profit and loss*, or the *statement of operations*, summarizes business activities for a given period and reports the net income or loss resulting from operations and from certain other defined activities.

The measuring and reporting of business income and its components is generally regarded as one of the most important responsibilities of accountants. Reference is made to the income statement by many different groups who need to evaluate the results of business activities. As discussed in Chapter 3, information on past income may be used as a measure of overall managerial performance and as an indicator of future income potential. Information about income may also be useful in determining the worth of a business, for it is business income that ultimately validates asset values. Proper measurement of income promotes the flow of capital to the most profitable and presumably the most efficient enterprises, providing for optimal allocation of scarce economic resources.

The current emphasis on the income statement may be attributed primarily to (1) the information needs of investors and creditors, (2) an increase in the internal use of accounting information, and (3) the pervasive influence of the tax laws on business entities.

Needs of Investors and Creditors

As indicated by the FASB in Statement of Financial Accounting Concepts No. 1, the primary objective of financial reporting is to provide information useful for decision making.[1] The types of information to be supplied are therefore dependent on the needs of users and their particular decisions.

Investors and creditors are considered to be among the most important external users of financial information. In today's business world, most in-

[1] *Statement of Financial Accounting Concepts No. 1*, "Objectives of Financial Reporting by Business Enterprises" (Stamford: Financial Accounting Standards Board, 1978).

vestors and creditors have very little direct contact with the companies in which they have holdings. Although they can attend annual stockholders' meetings, very few of them actually do. Instead, they rely on information published in financial statements, newspapers, and the financial press as a basis for evaluating management's performance and the company's ability to generate favorable cash flows in the future. Specifically, investors and creditors, and those who advise or represent them, must assess the amounts, timing, and uncertainty of prospective cash receipts. Such receipts take the form of dividends or interest and the proceeds from the sale of stock or the redemption or maturity of securities and loans.

While recognizing the importance of future cash flow prospects, the FASB has stated that accrual accounting provides a better indication of enterprise performance than information about current cash receipts and disbursements.[2] Thus, the income statement reports income and its components on an accrual basis. In the future, however, additional cash flow information, perhaps even on a projected basis, may be required.

Increased Internal Use of Accounting Information

Not only has there been increased interest in the income statement by outside users, but the same can also be said for the primary internal user—management. Years ago, proprietors often could acquire an intuitive feel as to how well things were going in an enterprise; but, today, in most situations, the complexity of modern business makes this impossible. Managements of large and growing corporate enterprises, dealing in many different product areas, need to have profitability information to answer questions relating to past, present, and projected programs. Questions arise such as: How effective was our past advertising policy? Should we make or buy certain component parts for our end-line products? Should we add to our product lines? Information systems within the enterprise must provide answers to these and related questions and often do so in the context of some version of an income report.

Income Tax Laws

Since 1913 when the 16th amendment to the Constitution was passed, taxes on income at both national and state levels have become increasingly significant. To comply with income tax laws, every business entity must have some system for the measurement of income. However, generally accepted accounting principles are not based on the tax law. Income measurement for tax purposes is related to governmental regulatory, social, and financial objectives and responsibilities. Income determination according to generally accepted accounting principles, however, is related primarily to the decision-making needs of investors, creditors, and managers. These differing objectives create many differences between taxable income and "book" in-

---

[2] *Ibid.*, par. 44.

come, which must be accounted for and reconciled. The emphasis in this text is on proper reporting for financial accounting purposes and not on what may be appropriate or desirable for tax purposes. Significant differences between accounting for tax purposes and for financial accounting purposes are noted, however, where appropriate.

NATURE OF INCOME

With increasing attention being given to reporting income, it is only natural that certain questions have been raised: What purpose should the measurement of income serve in our economy? How can it best serve this purpose? Is the accountant's function limited to that of a historian reporting on the past? Or should accountants try to provide the best guide for estimating future income potential? All of these questions are appropriate; however, all of the answers may not be provided by the same income statement, and some purposes are being better satisfied than others by present accounting methods.

At least part of the reason why the measurement of income has presented problems to accountants is the lack of a precise definition of **income**. Another important factor is the need to exercise judgment on a great many matters in arriving at such a measurement. Thus, considerable research has been directed toward the subject of income determination. Two primary approaches to income measurement have been predominant: the **economic approach** and the **transaction approach**.

Economic Approach ✗

A business entity commences activities in the attempt to increase its **net assets** (total assets − total liabilities) through profitable operations. This increase in net assets, referred to by many economists as a change in the *wealth* or *well-offness* of the entity, represents the *income* of the firm. Thus, the **economic approach** to the determination of income is to value the net assets of an entity at two different times and compute the change that has occurred. If the change is positive, after adjustment for any investment or withdrawal of assets by the owners, there has been income. If the change is negative, there has been a loss. Because income is determined by comparing the value of net assets at two different times, this method is sometimes referred to as the **valuation method**.

The valuation method is most commonly used by economists in their discussion of income. One of the most-quoted economists in accounting literature, J. R. Hicks, defined income as the maximum value that an entity can distribute during a period and still expect to be as well-off at the end of the period as it was at the beginning of the period.[3] The problem inherent in this concept of income is in defining the **value of net assets**. Is it the historical

[3]J. R. Hicks, *Value and Capital*, 2d ed. (Oxford University Press, 1946).

cost of the net assets reduced by some amount for their use? Is it the current value of the net assets determined by replacement or market values? Is it the historical cost of the net assets adjusted for the change in price levels since original acquisitions? All of these, as well as other concepts, may be regarded as satisfying the general term, value of net assets. Another question that must be resolved is what is to be included in net assets. Should intangible items, such as goodwill, patents, and leaseholds be included in assets? Should the value of employees be reported as an asset? Should estimated payments relating to warranties and pensions be included in liabilities?

For many years economists, and recently some accountants, have approached these difficult questions by attempting to define net assets in terms of the present value of the future cash benefits that net assets are expected to provide. Advocates of this approach maintain that to measure the true economic income of a firm, we should determine the amounts of future cash flows at different points in time. Then, with the use of appropriate discount rates, the present worth of these streams of future benefits could be determined. Net assets thus computed could be compared at different time intervals in arriving at an income measure that would show increased (or decreased) well-offness.

Although this concept has some theoretical merit, it has had minor influence upon practice primarily because of the measurement problems involved. We live in an uncertain world with limited knowledge of future cash flows. Expectations as to these future flows vary among those individuals with interest in the company. Also, with limited knowledge of the future, what should be accepted as the appropriate discount rates to apply to cash flows in arriving at asset values? Because of these and other uncertainties, accountants have turned to more direct ways of defining income.

Transaction Approach ★

The method of income determination that has proved most acceptable to accountants is the **transaction approach**, also sometimes referred to as the matching method. This approach measures the results of enterprise transactions and involves the determination of the amount of revenue earned by an entity during a given period and the amount of expenses applicable to that revenue. The difference between these two items is recognized as **net income**. If users were willing to wait until the end of the life of a business unit for the full results of its operations, it would be an easy matter to compute the total revenues and total expenses of the business and the resulting net income or net loss. However, users of income statements, seeking to judge the progress of an entity, need periodic measurements of business profitability. In fact, users seem increasingly interested in receiving financial statements more frequently than at the traditional annual intervals. To satisfy this need, interim statements are also provided by most large companies. Thus, the element of timing, both for revenue and expense, becomes ever more significant. Rather than concentrating on asset valuations, the center of attention is thus transferred to a discussion of **revenue recognition** and **expense**

recognition. It should be noted, however, that because the financial statements are fundamentally interrelated, the point in time at which revenues and expenses are recognized is also the time when changes in amounts of net assets are recognized.

Revenue Recognition. **Revenues** are defined by the FASB as "inflows or other enhancements of assets of an entity or settlements of its liabilities (or a combination of both) during a period from delivering or producing goods, rendering services, or other activities that constitute the entity's ongoing major or central operations."[4] Generally, revenues are derived from activities such as selling products, rendering services, or permitting others to use enterprise resources in exchange for interest, rent, royalties, or similar fees. Proceeds from the disposal of resources such as plant and equipment or long-term investments should not be included in revenues; however, if such assets are sold at a gain, the resulting increase in net assets should be reported as a separate component of income. Assets acquired by purchase, proceeds from borrowing, and capital contributions do not give rise to revenue.

Although the above description of revenues defines the activities that produce revenue, it does not specify the time period in which revenue should be recorded and recognized in the income statement. A general **revenue recognition rule** has evolved stating that revenue should be recorded when two conditions are met: (1) the earnings process is complete or virtually so; and (2) an exchange has taken place. These criteria have led to the conventional recognition of revenue at a specific point in the earnings process—when assets are sold or services are rendered. However, some accountants would argue that an exchange does not necessarily have to occur for recognition of revenue. What is critical is that objective measurement is possible, whether or not an exchange has taken place, in addition to the earnings process being substantially complete. There are sufficient deviations from the general rule to justify a closer look into the nature of revenue recognition.

The nature and duration of the earnings process or revenue-producing cycle vary among industries and among individual entities. The beginning point is not well defined, but assume that it begins with the development of proposals for a certain product by an individual or by the research and development department of a business unit. From the idea stage, the future product is carefully described in plans and engineering specifications. Bills of material are prepared, a production schedule is agreed upon, and raw materials are ordered, delivered, and placed into production. Labor and factory overhead are added to the raw materials as the product proceeds through the manufacturing process. Once completed, the product is transferred to the finished goods warehouse. The product is listed in company catalogs and promoted in advertising campaigns, and moves through the company's distribution system to the final sale. Frequently sales are on a credit basis, and, after a period of time, collections are made on the accounts.

---

[4] *Statement of Financial Accounting Concepts No. 3*, "Elements of Financial Statements of Business Enterprises" (Stamford: Financial Accounting Standards Board, 1980), par. 63.

The product may be sold with a warranty for necessary repairs or replacements. The cycle thus extends from the original idea to the end of the warranty period. All these steps are involved in the recognition of sales revenue. If there is a failure at any step, revenue may be seriously curtailed or possibly completely eliminated. And yet, there is only one aggregate revenue amount for the entire cycle, the selling price of the goods. The question then is: When should revenue be recognized?

Answers to the question of when revenue should be recognized can be divided into two broad categories: (1) at one specific point in the cycle, or (2) at two or more points in the cycle.[5] The prevailing practice provides for recognition of revenue at one specific point in the cycle. Of course, determining the specific point presents a problem. Applying the previously mentioned guidelines, revenue from the sale of products is recognized at the **point of sale**, usually interpreted to mean the time of delivery to customers. It is felt that prior to the sale, there has not been an arm's-length determination of the market value of the goods. This makes any objective measure of revenue subject to dispute. In addition, most accountants feel that the **critical event** is the sale of an item, and that the earnings process is not complete until the sales commitment has been substantially fulfilled. The same guidelines dictate that revenue from services is recognized *when services have been performed and are billable*, and that revenue from permitting others to use enterprise resources is recognized *as resources are used or as time passes.*

There are three notable exceptions to the general rule. One exception to the general rule of recognizing revenue at the point of sale is found, for example, when market values are firmly established and the marketability of a given product is assured. Revenue in such instances is recognized at the **point of completed production**. Farm products with assured sales prices meet these criteria. In other cases, when uncertainty exists as to the collectibility of a receivable arising from the sale of goods or services, recognition of revenue may be deferred to the **point of actual cash collection**. The *installment sales method* of accounting is an example of the application of this practice. Although the installment sales method of deferring revenue beyond the point of sale is accepted as an alternate method for purposes of income taxation, it is not generally accepted for financial statement purposes "unless the circumstances are such that the collection of the sale price is not reasonably assured."[6]

The third exception is when revenue is recognized at two or more points in the cycle. Although conceptually one can maintain that revenue is being earned continuously throughout the cycle, the measurement of revenue on a continuous basis may be impractical. It also raises special questions, such as: Should revenue of an equal amount be assigned to each phase of the cycle?

---

[5]This subject was considered by a special AAA Committee on Realization which was established in 1964 and published its conclusions in 1966. Some of their comments on the point of revenue recognition are included in this section. *Accounting Review* (Evanston, Illinois: American Accounting Association, April 1965), pp. 312-322.

[6]*Opinions of the Accounting Principles Board, No. 10*, "Omnibus Opinion—1966" (New York: American Institute of Certified Public Accountants, 1967), par. 12.

Or should revenue be recognized in proportion to the costs incurred in each phase of the cycle? In certain cases, however, the production phase of the cycle extends over more than one accounting period and some allocation of revenue over the periods involved is considered essential to meaningful statements. Construction contracts for buildings, roads, and dams requiring several periods to complete are often of this nature. The **percentage-of-completion** method of accounting is used to meet these special conditions. This method requires a firm contract for sale prior to construction and an ability to estimate with reasonable accuracy the costs remaining to be incurred on the project. Portions of the total estimated revenue are recognized as the project progresses.

Thus, revenue recognition occurs at certain specifically defined points in the revenue-producing cycle. Generally, the recognition criteria are met and revenues are recorded at the point of sale. However, earlier or later recognition may be required due to the circumstances mentioned. Prior to revenue recognition, valuations are stated in terms of cost. After the recognition criteria are satisfied, use is made of *estimated or actual realizable values*. Discussion will certainly continue within the accounting profession as to the validity and acceptability of alternative points of revenue recognition. However, regardless of the point of revenue recognition selected, the relationship that has been defined between revenues and expenses will still hold. Issues related to revenue recognition are discussed more completely in Chapter 19.

Expense Recognition. Expenses may be defined as "outflows or other using up of assets or incurrences of liabilities (or a combination of both) during a period from delivering or producing goods, rendering services, or carrying out other activities that constitute the entity's ongoing major or central operations."[7] Some expenses may be directly associated with revenues as, for example, cost of goods sold. Other expenses are associated indirectly with revenue by assignment to particular periods of time during which the revenues have been recognized. Still other costs are not charged currently to the income statement because they relate to future revenues and, therefore, are shown as assets on the balance sheet. When the future service potential has expired, the costs are then associated with current revenues and reported as expenses. Expenses do not include repayment of borrowing, expenditures to acquire assets, distributions to owners (including the acquisition of treasury stock), or corrections of errors dealing with expenses of prior periods.

A primary difficulty in income determination is the decision as to how various expenses are, in fact, to be associated with revenues. It has not been possible to prescribe exact rules for *association* or *matching*.[8] Certain guidelines for the matching of expenses with revenues in arriving at net income or loss have evolved through time. When an accountant is faced with an absence of guidelines, judgment must be exercised. Three **expense**

---

[7] *Statement of Financial Accounting Concepts No. 3, op. cit.*, par. 65.

[8] Recent accounting pronouncements have been more specific in establishing guidelines for making these associations. Critics of this trend have stated their fear that accounting may become a set of rigid rules if such a trend continues.

matching principles have been noted as being of special significance: (1) associating cause and effect; (2) systematic and rational allocation; and (3) immediate recognition.[9]

Associating Cause and Effect. Some costs can be associated directly with specific revenues. When this association is possible, the cost is recognized as an expense of the period in which the revenue is recognized. Thus, if an inventory item on hand at the end of a period represents a source of future revenue under the point of sale principle, the cost of producing the item is deferred to a future period and it is reported as an asset. Certain costs, such as labor and materials, usually can be directly related to the cost of producing the inventory item. Other costs, such as factory overhead, may be assumed to be associated with an inventory item on some logical basis such as the number of labor hours or the number of machine hours required to produce the item. Judgment plays an increasingly important part as the association becomes less direct.

Care must be taken to assure that proper recognition is made of all costs already incurred, as well as those yet to be incurred relative to any revenues currently recognized.

Systematic and Rational Allocation. In the absence of a direct cause and effect relationship, a different basis for expense recognition is commonly used. Here an attempt is made to associate costs in a systematic and rational manner with the products or the periods benefited. In arriving at period expense recognition, estimates must be made of the timing pattern of the benefits received from the individual costs and systematic allocation methods developed. The methods adopted should appear reasonable to an unbiased observer and should be followed consistently.

Some of the costs allocated to a period become expenses immediately and are associated with current revenues. Other costs *attach* to inventories and other assets on some logical basis and thus are associated with future revenues by being deferred as assets. Examples of costs that are associated with periods in a systematic way include costs of buildings and equipment, insurance, and taxes.

Immediate Recognition. Those costs that cannot be related to revenues either by associating cause and effect or by systematic and rational allocation, must be recognized as expenses of the current period. In some instances, prior period adjustments must be made, generally to correct past errors. These adjustments are discussed in Chapter 18. Most costs, however, are recognized as expenses in the period when no discernable future revenues can be associated with them.

Changes in Estimates. In reporting periodic revenues and in attempting to properly match those expenses incurred to generate current period revenues, accountants must continually make judgments. The numbers reported in the

---

[9]*Statements of the Accounting Principles Board, No. 4*, "Basic Concepts and Accounting Principles Underlying Financial Statements of Business Enterprises" (New York: American Institute of Certified Public Accountants, 1970).

financial statements reflect these judgments and are based on estimates of such factors as the number of years of useful life for depreciable assets, the amount of gas or oil to be produced, the amount of uncollectible accounts expected, or the amount of warranty liability to be recorded on the books. These and other estimates are made using the best available information at the statement date. However, conditions may change subsequently, and the estimates may need to be revised. Naturally, if either revenue or expense amounts are changed, the income statement is affected. The question is whether the previously reported income measures should be revised or whether the changes should impact only on the current and future periods.

The APB stated in Opinion No. 20 that adjustments in estimates should be made either in the current period or in the current and future periods. No retroactive adjustment or pro forma statements are to be prepared for a change in estimate.[10] These adjustments are felt to be part of the normal accounting process and not a change of past periods.

To illustrate, assume that for the past three years Mapleton Hardware Inc. has estimated that 3 percent of its accounts receivable sales would be uncollectible. However, recent experience has shown that about 4 percent of credit sales have actually been uncollectible. Company management should change its current and future provision for uncollectible accounts to the 4 percent guideline but should not, according to APB Opinion No. 20, retroactively adjust the reported income figures for the past three years. If the amount of the change is material, separate disclosure should be made concerning the change in estimate in the notes to the financial statements.

Gains and Losses. The FASB uses the terms **gains** and **losses** to reflect the increases and decreases in net assets resulting from peripheral or incidental activities of an entity.[11] As indicated earlier, gains from the sale of assets other than inventory are distinguished from revenues from normal operating activities. Similarly, losses from disposal of such assets are to be distinguished from expenses. While similar in some respects to revenues and expenses, gains and losses should be reported separately but as a part of income from continuing operations.

There are two primary differences in the classification and recognition of revenues and expenses versus gains and losses. The principal distinction is between an enterprise's ongoing major or central operations and its peripheral or incidental transactions and activities. Of course, this distinction depends on the type of enterprise and activities involved. The sale of a delivery truck by the management of a pizza restaurant would probably be classified as a peripheral transaction and a gain or loss recognized. The sale of a delivery truck by a car dealer would probably be considered as an ongoing central activity, with the proceeds being recognized as revenue and the cost of the delivery truck as an expense (cost of goods sold).

---

[10] *Opinions of the Accounting Principles Board, No. 20*, "Accounting Changes" (New York: American Institute of Certified Public Accountants, 1971), par 31.

[11] *Statement of Financial Accounting Concepts No. 3, op. cit.*, pars. 67-68.

The second difference is that revenues and expenses are reported at gross amounts, with expenses being subtracted from revenues to show the net amount of profit. Gains and losses are reported as separate items of income, usually at their net amounts. These classification and display differences are illustrated in the income statement on page 112.

Effects of Changing Prices

As indicated in Chapter 3, accountants have traditionally ignored the impact of changing prices on financial statements. Thus, income has been measured by matching historical costs against recognized revenues, with none of the amounts being adjusted for the effects of inflation. Recognizing that the users of financial statements need to have an understanding of the impact of changing prices on a business enterprise, the FASB issued Statement No. 33, "Financial Reporting and Changing Prices."[12]

This statement, which applies primarily to certain large, publicly-held companies, requires disclosure of selected information on a supplemental basis. It does not affect the nature of the basic financial statements; income is still to be measured and reported on a historical cost basis, using the recognition and matching principles. The supplemental information to be disclosed reflects both general price changes (the impact of inflation) and specific price changes of selected items, primarily inventories and plant assets. Price-level adjusted information must be disclosed for such items as income from continuing operations, gains and losses in purchasing power, and net assets at year-end. This and other selected information is to be reported for the current fiscal year and each of the preceding four years. The supplemental information must be included in any published annual report that contains the primary financial statements, although the information can be presented in several different formats.

Discussion of the details of these requirements and the mechanics of adjusting for price changes is deferred to Chapter 24. The main point to note here is that the accounting profession, in recognition of the needs of investors and creditors, now requires additional information concerning the components of income that reflect the impact of changing prices. Even though additional effort is required to prepare and interpret such information, the potential benefits for increased understanding of the results of enterprise activity seem to be well worth the effort.

REPORTING INCOME—THE INCOME STATEMENT

The importance of the revenue-expense relationships and the significance attached to the income of an entity by various users, especially investors and creditors, have been described in the first part of this chapter. In view of the importance attached to income measurement, the question con-

[12] *Statements of Financial Accounting Standards, No. 33*, "Financial Reporting and Changing Prices," (Stamford: Financial Accounting Standards Board, 1979).

tinually arises, How can the components of income be presented on the income statement in the most informative and useful manner?

Reporting Results of Operations on an All-Inclusive Basis

Historically, there have been two generally accepted forms for income statement presentation, and the selection of the form reflected the manner in which the business unit preferred to recognize unusual items. One form, referred to as the **current operating performance income statement**, provided for reporting only normal and recurring operating items; other components, such as unusual and nonrecurring items and prior period adjustments, were recorded directly in retained earnings and reported on an accompanying statement that summarized all the changes in retained earnings for the period. An alternative form, known as the **all-inclusive income statement**, provided for the presentation of unusual and nonrecurring items on the face of the income statement after normal operating items. In employing the first form, the final amount was generally designated as net income; in the second form, the final amount was designated by some as net income and by others as net income after extraordinary items. Because both of these income statement forms were being used in practice, there was a lack of consistency in the reporting by enterprises and thus a real danger of misinterpretation of the results of operations by statement users.

With the issuance of Accounting Principles Board Opinion No. 9, "Reporting the Results of Operations," a modified all-inclusive concept of income presentation was adopted. Both ordinary operations and extraordinary items are to be presented on the income statement, but as separate and distinct categories. Applicable income tax amounts are associated with the separate categories. In effect, all items of income are to be recognized on the income statement with the exception of certain prior period adjustments.

The Concept of Comprehensive Income

The FASB has continued to adopt the all-inclusive concept of reporting income. In Statement of Financial Accounting Concepts No. 3, the FASB defines **comprehensive income** as the total change in equity during a period, except any changes resulting from investments by owners and any distributions to owners. Thus, comprehensive income is a measure of the change in net assets during a period arising from transactions and other events and circumstances from nonowner sources.[13] In practice, the terms **net income** and **net earnings** are frequently used to denote the change in net assets from nonowner sources. The FASB did not define the term "earnings" in Concepts Statement No. 3, but stated that the term was being reserved for possible future use as a separate component of comprehensive income.

The FASB is currently reviewing the entire area of income reporting. It is felt that there is not sufficient disclosure and emphasis on the effects of

[13] *Statement of Financial Accounting Concepts No. 3, op. cit.*, pars. 56-58.

unusual events or transactions and on the economic changes that affect the relationships between recurring revenues and expenses. While a suggested format for reporting the various income components has not yet been specified, there does seem to be a consensus that a distinction should be made between the ongoing central activities of a business and its peripheral and incidental transactions and events.

Content of the Income Statement

The income statement generally consists of a series of sections developing the net income for the period. As mentioned earlier, all elements of income, except for prior period adjustments, are to be included. Major categories included within the normal operations section are: (1) revenues from the sale of goods and services; (2) cost of goods sold and expenses of providing services; (3) operating expenses; (4) other revenue and expense items; (5) gains and losses; and (6) income tax relative to income from normal operations. Depending on individual circumstances, additional sections in the income statement would report other income components all shown net of their tax effect. Illustrative statements are presented on pages 112 and 113.

Sales. **Revenue from sales** reports the total sales to customers for the period. This total should not include additions to billings for sales and excise taxes that the business is required to collect on behalf of the government. These billing increases are properly recognized as current liabilities. Sales returns and allowances and sales discounts should be subtracted from gross sales in arriving at net sales revenue. When the sales price is increased to cover the cost of freight to the customer and the customer is billed accordingly, freight charges paid by the company should also be subtracted from sales in arriving at net sales. Freight charges not absorbed by the buyer are recognized as selling expenses.

Cost of Goods Sold. When merchandise is acquired from outsiders, the cost of goods relating to sales of the period must be determined. As illustrated on page 112, **cost of goods available for sale** is first determined. This is the sum of the beginning inventory, purchases, and all other buying, freight, and storage costs relating to the acquisition of goods. A net purchases balance is developed by subtracting purchase returns and allowances and purchase discounts from gross purchases. **Cost of goods sold** is calculated by subtracting the ending inventory from the cost of goods available for sale.

When the goods are manufactured by the seller, the **cost of goods manufactured** must first be calculated. Cost of goods manufactured replaces purchases in the summary just described. The determination of cost of goods manufactured begins with the cost of goods in process at the beginning of the period. To this is added the cost of materials put into production, the cost of labor applied to material conversions, and all the other costs for services and facilities utilized in manufacturing, including factory supervision, indirect labor, depreciation and other costs relating to factory buildings and equipment, factory supplies used, patent amortization, and factory light, heat, and power. The total thus obtained represents the cost of goods completed and goods still in production. The goods in process inventory at the end of the period is subtracted from this total in arriving at the cost of the goods finished and made available for sale.

In practice, the distinction between those costs included in inventory as production costs and those classified as selling and administrative expenses is not always clear nor consistently applied among firms. This can result in differing income measures because some costs are included as part of the inventory while others are not.

Operating Expenses. Operating expenses are generally reported in two categories: (1) selling expenses and (2) general and administrative expenses. **Selling expenses** include such items as sales salaries and commissions and related payroll taxes, advertising and store displays, store supplies used, depreciation of store furniture and equipment, and delivery expenses. **General and administrative expenses** include officers' and office salaries and related payroll taxes, office supplies used, depreciation of office furniture and fixtures, telephone, postage, business licenses and fees, legal and accounting services, contributions, and similar items. Charges related to the use of buildings, such as rent, depreciation, taxes, insurance, light, heat, and power, should be allocated in some equitable manner to manufacturing activities and to selling and general and administrative activities. In the case of the merchandising concern, charges relating to buildings are generally reported in full in the general and administrative category.

As explained in detail in Chapter 7, credit sales usually result in an operating expense reported as Doubtful Accounts Expense or Bad Debt Expense. This expense may be classified as a selling expense or as a general and administrative expense, depending on departmental responsibility within the organization. Since this expense often is the result of the general credit policy of an enterprise, it is classified under general and administrative expenses in this text.

Other Revenues and Expenses. This category includes items identified with financial management and miscellaneous recurring activities. Other revenues include interest and dividend revenues and revenues from rentals, royalties, and service fees. Other expenses include interest expense and expenses related to the miscellaneous revenue items reported.

Gains and Losses. As discussed previously, gains and losses are distinguished from revenues and expenses and are reported as a separate component of income from continuing operations. Gains and losses are usually reported at their net amounts.

Income Tax Relative to Income from Continuing Operations. The income tax expense relating to continuing operations is reported as a separate item and is deducted to arrive at income from continuing operations. Income tax allocation procedures are frequently required due to differences between "book" income and taxable income. These procedures are discussed in detail in Chapter 20. In reporting the tax, the components included in its determination should be disclosed. Parenthetical remarks or notes in the income statement may be considered appropriate in defining the nature and purpose of the allocations.

Below-the-Line Items. Certain components of income are sometimes referred to as **below-the-line items**, i.e., the components disclosed after income from continuing operations. Three such items are: (1) discontinued operations, (2) the effects of a change in accounting principle, and (3) extraordinary items. These special items relate to unusual events and thus are not reported frequently. However, when reported, these items should be disclosed as separate components of income and displayed below income from continuing operations net of the applicable income taxes. These components of income are explained in Chapter 21. For illustrative purposes, an extraordinary item is included in the income statement on page 112.

Earnings per Share. On the income statement for a corporation, net income is followed by a special presentation of earnings per share for the period in accordance with APB Opinion No. 15.[14] Earnings per share is computed by dividing income from continuing operations, and any other major category of income subsequently disclosed, by the weighted average number of shares of common stock outstanding. For example, the Barnsby Corporation income statement illustrated on page 112 shows earnings per share of $.60 for income from continuing operations and $.04 for the extraordinary gain, or a total of $.64 for net income. These figures were derived by dividing each income component by 50,000 shares of common stock outstanding during the period.

APB Opinion No. 15 also requires the presentation of additional earnings-per-share information if there is a potential dilution of earnings due to the existence of convertible securities or stock options or warrants. This subject is discussed in detail in Chapter 22.

Form of the Income Statement

The income statement traditionally has been prepared in either multiple-step or single-step form. An example of an income statement in multiple-step form is presented on page 112 and in single-step form on page 113.

In the **multiple-step form,** the ordinary operations are first summarized and designated as "Income from continuing operations before income tax." The income tax related to ordinary operations is computed and deducted. The title of the remaining figure varies depending on whether there are other components of income to be disclosed. The illustrations in this chapter assume only one other income item — an extraordinary gain. A more comprehensive illustration of reporting income is presented in Chapter 21.

An income statement prepared in **single-step form** does not contain separate sections for cost of goods sold, operating expenses, other revenues and expenses, gains and losses, and income tax. All ordinary revenues and

[14] *Opinions of the Accounting Principles Board, No. 15*, "Earnings per Share" (New York: American Institute of Certified Public Accountants, 1969).

Barnsby Corporation
Income Statement
For Year Ended December 31, 1984

Revenue from sales:				
Sales			$510,000	
Less: Sales returns and allowances		$ 7,500		
Sales discounts		2,500	10,000	$500,000
Cost of goods sold:				
Inventory, January 1, 1984			$ 95,000	
Purchases		$320,000		
Freight in		15,000		
Delivered cost of purchases		$335,000		
Less: Purchase returns and allowances	$1,000			
Purchase discounts	4,000	5,000	330,000	
Goods available for sale			$425,000	
Less inventory, December 31, 1984			125,000	300,000
Gross profit on sales				$200,000
Operating expenses:				
Selling Expenses:				
Sales salaries		$ 30,000		
Advertising expense		15,000		
Depreciation expense—selling and delivery equipment		5,000		
Miscellaneous selling expense		10,000	$ 60,000	
General and administrative expenses:				
Officers' and office salaries		$ 48,000		
Taxes and insurance		20,000		
Miscellaneous supplies expense		5,000		
Depreciation expense—office furniture and fixtures		5,000		
Doubtful accounts expense		2,500		
Amortization expense		10,600		
Miscellaneous general expense		4,400	95,500	155,500
Operating income				$ 44,500
Other revenues and expenses:				
Interest revenue		$ 3,000		
Dividend revenue		5,000	$ 8,000	
Interest expense			(7,500)	500
Gains and losses:				
Gain on sale of investment				5,000
Income from continuing operations before income tax				$ 50,000
Income tax				20,000
Income from continuing operations				$ 30,000
Extraordinary gain (less applicable income tax of $1,200)				1,800
Net income				$ 31,800
Earnings per common share (50,000 shares outstanding):				
Income from continuing operations				$.60
Extraordinary gain				.04
Net income				$.64

Multiple-Step Statement

Barnsby Corporation Income Statement For Year Ended December 31, 1984		
Revenues and gains:		
Net sales	$500,000	
Other revenues—interest and dividends	8,000	
Gain on sale of investments	5,000	$513,000
Expenses:		
Cost of goods sold	$300,000	
Selling expenses	60,000	
General and administrative expenses	95,500	
Interest expense	7,500	
Income tax	20,000	483,000
Income from continuing operations		$ 30,000
Extraordinary gain (less applicable income tax of $1,200)		1,800
Net income		$ 31,800
Earnings per common share (50,000 shares outstanding):		
Income from continuing operations		$ .60
Extraordinary gain		.04
Net income		$ .64

Single-Step Income Statement

gains and expenses and losses are listed and summarized, without disclosing gross profit, operating income, or pretax income. The single-step form is in reality a modified single-step form if there are below-the-line items to be disclosed separately.

Many accountants have raised objections to the multiple-step income statement form. They point out that the various income designations have no universal meaning and may prove a source of confusion to the reader. Quoting such designations in the absence of a complete income statement may prove ambiguous or actually misleading. They further maintain that multiple-step presentation implies certain cost priorities and an order for cost recoveries. But there is no such order and there can be no earnings unless all costs are recovered. These accountants support the single-step form that minimizes sectional labeling. However, recent accounting pronouncements seem to be moving toward greater sectionalization of the income statement through separate identification of each significant income component. Such disclosures should help investors and creditors in assessing the amounts and timing of future cash flows.

The above income statement is a *condensed* single-step income statement, with much of the revenue and expense detail omitted. Whether prepared in multiple-step or single-step form, the income statement is frequently condensed and simply reports totals for certain classes of items, such as cost of goods sold, selling expenses, general expenses, other revenues and expenses, and gains and losses. Additional detail may be provided by the use of supporting schedules and explanatory notes as illustrated in General Mills' income statement in Appendix B. Notes to the financial statements are further discussed and illustrated in Chapter 5.

The use of condensed income statements by large units engaged in a number of diversified activities has been severely criticized. Income statements prepared in condensed form may tend to disguise the important trends operating within the individual segments of a diversified company. Because of this, the FASB, in Statement No. 14, and the Securities and Exchange Commission both require disclosure of sales and profit information by major segments of a company. This issue is further explored in Chapter 21.

When goods are manufactured by the seller, the cost of the goods manufactured must be determined before the cost of goods sold can be computed. If a summary of cost of goods manufactured is to accompany the financial statements, it should be presented as a schedule in support of the amount reported on the income statement. Assuming the goods available for sale in the example on page 112 were obtained by manufacture rather than by purchase, cost of goods sold on the income statement would be presented as shown below. The supporting schedule follows.

Cost of goods sold:		
Finished goods inventory, January 1, 1984	$ 40,000	
Add cost of goods manufactured per schedule	310,000	
Goods available for sale	$350,000	
Less finished goods inventory, December 31, 1984	50,000	$300,000

Barnsby Corporation
Schedule of Cost of Goods Manufactured
For Year Ended December 31, 1984

Direct materials:				
Raw materials inventory, January 1, 1984			$ 30,000	
Purchases		$105,000		
Freight in		10,000		
Delivered cost of raw materials		$115,000		
Less: Purchase returns and allowances	$1,000			
Purchase discounts	4,000	5,000	110,000	
Total cost of raw materials available for use			$140,000	
Less raw materials inventory, December 31, 1984			40,000	
Raw materials used in production				$100,000
Direct labor				140,000
Factory overhead:				
Indirect labor			$ 20,000	
Factory supervision			14,500	
Depreciation expense—factory buildings and equipment			12,000	
Light, heat, and power			10,000	
Factory supplies expense			8,500	
Miscellaneous factory overhead			15,000	80,000
Total manufacturing costs				$320,000
Add goods in process inventory, January 1, 1984				25,000
				$345,000
Less goods in process inventory, December 31, 1984				35,000
Cost of goods manufactured				$310,000

Schedule of Cost of Goods Manufactured

Frequently, only the cost of goods sold is reported on the income statement. If a schedule of the cost of goods sold is to be provided, it should summarize the cost of goods manufactured as well as the change in finished goods inventories. Instead of reporting beginning and ending inventories, it is possible simply to report inventory variations for the period in arriving at the cost of materials used, cost of goods manufactured, or cost of goods sold. For example, an increase in the finished goods inventory would be subtracted from the cost of goods manufactured in arriving at the cost of goods sold; a decrease in the finished goods inventory would be added to the cost of goods manufactured in arriving at the cost of goods sold.

REPORTING CHANGES IN RETAINED EARNINGS

In the case of a corporation, if transactions affecting the stockholders' equity have been limited to changes in retained earnings, a **retained earnings statement** is prepared. This statement reports the beginning balance for retained earnings, any prior period adjustments shown net of tax to arrive at the adjusted retained earnings at the beginning of the period, earnings for the period, dividend declarations, and the ending retained earnings balance. Prior period adjustments are made primarily for corrections of errors in the financial statements of earlier periods. A retained earnings statement to accompany the income statement prepared on page 112 follows.

Barnsby Corporation
Retained Earnings Statement
For Year Ended December 31, 1984

Retained earnings, January 1, 1984	$149,000
Deduct prior period adjustment—correction of inventory overstatement, net of income tax refund of $9,000	9,000
Adjusted retained earnings, January 1, 1984	$140,000
Add net income per income statement	31,800
	$171,800
Deduct dividends declared	20,000
Retained earnings, December 31, 1984	$151,800

Retained Earnings Statement

The income statement and retained earnings statement may be prepared in *combined* form. In preparing the combined statement, net income data are first listed and summarized. The amount of net income for the period is then combined with the retained earnings balance at the beginning of the period or the adjusted balance due to prior period adjustments. This total is adjusted for dividend declarations in arriving at the retained earnings balance at the end of the period. Data can be presented in either multiple-step or single-step form. The combined statement listing data in single-step form can be prepared in the following form (details for revenues, gains, and expenses have been omitted).

Barnsby Corporation Income and Retained Earnings Statement For Year Ended December 31, 1984		
Revenues and gains		$514,800
Expenses		483,000
Net income		$ 31,800
Adjusted retained earnings, January 1, 1984:		
Retained earnings, January 1, 1984	$149,000	
Deduct prior period adjustment—correction of inventory overstatement, net of income tax refund of $9,000	9,000	140,000
		$171,800
Deduct dividends declared		20,000
Retained earnings, December 31, 1984		$151,800

Combined Income and Retained Earnings Statement

The income statement is certainly one of the most important statements prepared for the general use of creditors, investors, and others. The data reported provide a measure of a firm's past profitability and assist the user in assessing prospective future cash flows, either in the form of dividends, interest and repayment of loans, or appreciation in net asset values. There is currently considerable interest in the measurement and reporting of income. This may lead the FASB to dramatically revise currently accepted accounting practice in this area.

QUESTIONS

1. Which accounting statements are considered general purpose financial statements?
2. Why is the measurement of business income considered to be one of the most important responsibilities of accountants?
3. What specific reasons can you offer for the historical importance of the income statement?
4. Why is the net income figure computed on the basis of generally accepted accounting principles often not the same as taxable income computed from IRS directives?
5. An article in a financial journal was titled "What are Earnings? The Growing Creditability Gap." What do you think was meant by this title?
6. What are the major differences between the economic and transaction approaches to income determination?

7. What concepts of the "value of net assets" might be applied in the economic approach to income determination?
8. What two conditions must normally be met for revenue to be recognized? At what point in the revenue cycle are these conditions usually met?
9. What are three specific exceptions to the general rule of revenue recognition?
10. Why is the process of matching costs with revenues in income determination so difficult.
11. Do you think matching expenses with revenues is more difficult to apply in a machine assembly plant than in a CPA firm? Why?
12. What guidelines are used to match costs with revenues in determining income?
13. How are revenues and expenses different from gains and losses?
14. Why are changes in estimates to be reported only in current and future periods and not retroactively adjusted?
15. How has the accounting profession responded to the need for recognizing the impact of changing prices?
16. What is comprehensive income?
17. What criticism of the income statement might be met by distinguishing among the various components of income?
18. (a) What objections can be made to the mutliple-step income statement? (b) What objections can be made to the single-step income statement?
19. What information not found in the income statement or the balance sheet is disclosed in the retained earnings statement?

DISCUSSION CASES

case 4-1 (How to hit targeted earnings without really trying) The Temas Computer Specialist Co. was under investigation by the SEC for practices that leveled income fluctuations from year to year. This "smoothing" was accomplished by sending bills prior to the date a service assignment was completed or by delaying billings on services completed when a reduced income figure was desired. Practices such as these were conducted by Temas' managers to meet strictly specified company earnings goals from which their compensation was determined. What accounting and other issues are involved in this case?

case 4-2 (When should revenue be recognized?) You are engaged as a consultant to Graybull Corporation, a manufacturer of farm implements. Graybull sells its products to dealers who in turn sell them to local farmers. As an inducement to carry sufficient inventory, the dealers are not required to pay for merchandise received until 30 days after a sale to a customer. In addition, dealers are permitted to return unsold merchandise at any time within nine months from the time it is received. The dealers hold the title to the merchandise while it is in their hands. In some years Graybull has had very little merchandise returned; in other years returns have amounted to 25% of the shipments. Bad debts have traditionally been low. No interest is charged dealers on their account balances. At what point would you recommend Graybull recognize the revenue from sales to its dealers?

case 4-3 (Revenue recognition) J. McNiven is a Kansas farmer whose main crop is wheat. At harvest time, McNiven delivers the wheat to a grain elevator and receives a warehouse receipt for it. Later, sometimes several months later, the wheat is sold. The decision to sell the wheat is based on the need for cash and on the forecast of the future wheat market. At what point in time should McNiven recognize revenue from the wheat crop?

case 4-4 (Deferring initial operating losses) Small loan companies often experience losses in the operation of newly opened branch loan offices. Such results can usually be anticipated by management prior to making a decision on expansion. It has been recommended that the operating losses of newly opened branches should be reported as deferred charges during the first twelve months of operation or until the first profitable month occurs. Such deferred charges would then be amortized over a five-year period. Would you support this recommendation?

case 4-5 (Matching expenses) Kwik-Bild Corporation sells and erects shell houses. These are frame structures completely finished on the outside but unfinished on the inside except for flooring, partition studding, and ceiling joists. Shell houses are sold chiefly to customers who are handy with tools and who have time to do the interior wiring, plumbing, wall completion and finishing, and other work necessary to make the shell houses livable dwellings.

Kwik-Bild buys shell houses from a manufacturer in unassembled packages consisting of all lumber, roofing, doors, windows and similar materials necessary to complete a shell house. Upon commencing operations in a new area, Kwik-Bild buys or leases land as a site for its local warehouse, field office, and display houses. Sample display houses are erected at a total cost of from $12,000 to $15,000 including the cost of the unassembled packages. The chief element of cost of the display houses is the unassembled packages, since erection is a short low-cost operation. Old sample models are torn down or altered into new models every three to seven years. Sample display houses have little salvage value because dismantling and moving costs amount to nearly as much as the cost of an unassembled package.

A choice must be made between (a) expensing the costs of sample display houses in the period in which the expenditure is made, and (b) spreading the costs over more than one period. Discuss the advantages of each method. Would it be preferable to amortize the cost of display houses on the basis of (a) the passage of time or (b) the number of shell houses sold? Explain. (AICPA adapted)

EXERCISES

exercise 4-1 (Calculation of net income)

Changes in account balances for the Flanigan Sales Co. during 1984 were as follows:

	Increase (Decrease)
Cash	$135,000
Accounts Receivable	15,000
Inventory	120,000
Buildings and Equipment (net)	360,000
Accounts Payable	(105,000)
Bonds Payable	300,000
Capital Stock	225,000
Additional Paid-In Capital	45,000

Dividends declared during 1984 were $75,000. Calculate the net income for the year assuming there were no transactions affecting retained earnings other than the dividends.

exercise 4-2 (Recognition of revenue or gain)

Indicate which of the following items involves the recognition of revenue or gain. Give the reasons for your answer.

(a) Land acquired in 1952 at $15,000 is now conservatively appraised at $100,000.
(b) Timberlands show a growth in timber valued at $40,000 for the year.
(c) An addition to a building was self-constructed at a cost of $3,600 after two offers from private contractors for the work at $4,650 and $5,000.
(d) Certain valuable franchise rights were received from a city for payment of annual licensing fees.
(e) A customer owing $4,600, which was delinquent for one year, gave securities valued at $5,000 in settlement of the obligation.
(f) Goods costing $1,000 are sold for $1,600 with a 50% down payment on a conditional sales contract, title to the goods being retained by the seller until the full contract price is collected.
(g) Cash is received on the sale of gift certificates redeemable in merchandise in the following period.

exercise 4-3 (Revenue and expense recognition)

State the amount of revenue and/or expense for 1984 in each of the following transactions of the Kryton Tractor Co. The accounting period ends December 31, 1984. Treat each item individually.

(a) On December 15, 1984, Kryton received $12,000 as rental revenue for a 6-month period ending June 15, 1985.
(b) Kryton, on July 1, 1984, sold one of its tractors and received $10,000 in cash and a note for $50,000 at 12% interest, payable in one year. The fair market value of the tractor is $60,000.
(c) One of Kryton's steady customers is presently in a weak cash flow position. To maintain its goodwill with this customer, Kryton sells them 2 tractors with a normal combined selling price of $112,000, but allows them a special discount of $8,000.
(d) During 1984, tractors sold for $400,000 are accompanied by a Kryton guarantee for one year. Past experience indicates that repairs equal to 1% of sales revenue will be required in year of sale, and an additional 3% of sales revenue will be needed for repairs in the subsequent year.
(e) On December 28, 1984, Kryton sold 5 tractors for a total of $435,000. As of December 31, 1984, 3 of the tractors were still in Kryton's warehouse.

exercise 4-4 (Classification of income statement items)

Where in a multiple-step income statement would each item be reported?

(a) Gain on sale of land.
(b) Purchase discounts.
(c) Charge for doubtful accounts in anticipation of failure to collect receivables.
(d) Loss from long-term investments written off as worthless.
(e) Loss from a strike.
(f) Loss from inventory price decline.
(g) Depletion expense.
(h) Sales discounts.
(i) Dividends received on long-term investments.
(j) Income tax for current period.
(k) Collection of life insurance policy upon death of officer.
(l) Vacation pay of office employee.

exercise 4-5 (Preparation of schedule of cost of goods manufactured)

Prepare a schedule of cost of goods manufactured in good form selecting the proper items from the following:

Purchases	$200,000	Indirect labor	$ 9,000
Purchase returns and allowances	20,000	Selling expenses	36,000
Beginning inventory—finished goods	40,000	Direct labor	52,000
Beginning inventory—goods in process	26,000	Other overhead	30,000
Beginning inventory—raw materials	30,000	Ending inventory—finished goods	32,000
Accounts receivable	170,000	Ending inventory—goods in process	24,000
Equipment	52,000	Ending inventory—raw materials	36,000
		Cash	22,000

exercise 4-6 (Analysis and preparation of income statement)

The selling expenses of Robinson, Inc., for 1984 are 10% of sales. General expenses, excluding doubtful accounts, are 25% of cost of goods sold but only 15% of sales. Doubtful accounts are 2% of sales. The beginning inventory was $124,000 and it decreased 25% during the year. Income for the year before income tax of 40% is $104,000. Prepare an income statement, including earnings per share data, giving supporting computations. Robinson, Inc., has 110,000 shares of common stock outstanding.

exercise 4-7 (Multiple-step income statement)

From the following list of accounts, prepare a multiple-step income statement in good form showing all appropriate items properly classified, including disclosure of earnings per share data. Assume a supporting schedule of cost of goods manufactured has been prepared. (No monetary amounts are to be recognized.)

Accounts Payable
Accumulated Depreciation—Office Building
Accumulated Depreciation—Delivery Equipment
Accumulated Depreciation—Office Furniture and Fixtures
Accumulated Depreciation—Tools
Advertising Expense
Allowance for Doubtful Accounts
Amortization of Patents
Cash
Common Stock, $20 par (10,000 shares outstanding)
Delivery Salaries
Depreciation Expense—Office Building
Depreciation Expense—Delivery Equipment
Depreciation Expense—Office Furniture and Fixtures
Depreciation Expense—Tools
Direct Labor
Dividend Revenue
Dividends Payable
Dividends Receivable
Doubtful Accounts Expense
Extraordinary Gain (net of income tax)
Factory Heat, Light, and Power
Factory Supervision
Factory Supplies
Factory Supplies Used
Finished Goods
Freight In
Federal Unemployment Tax Payable
Goods in Process
Goodwill
Income Tax
Income Tax Payable
Insurance Expense
Interest Expense—Bonds
Interest Expense—Other
Interest Payable
Interest Receivable
Interest Revenue
Miscellaneous Delivery Expense
Miscellaneous Factory Overhead
Miscellaneous General Expense
Miscellaneous Selling Expense
Office Salaries
Office Supplies
Office Supplies Used
Officers' Salaries
Patents
Property Tax
Purchase Discounts
Raw Materials
Raw Materials Purchases
Raw Materials Returns and Allowances
Retained Earnings
Royalties Received in Advance
Royalty Revenue
Salaries and Wages Payable
Sales
Sales Discounts
Sales Returns and Allowances
Sales Salaries and Commissions
Sales Tax Payable
Tools

exercise 4-8 (Single-step income statement and statement of retained earnings)

The Marville Steel Co. reports the following for 1984:

Retained earnings, January 1, 1984	$384,500
Selling expenses	212,200
Sales revenue	958,050
Interest expense	12,360
General and administrative expenses	237,800
Cost of goods sold	383,220
Dividends declared—1984	23,000

Common stock outstanding: average for 1984, 30,000 shares

Prepare a single-step income statement (including earnings per share data) and a statement of retained earnings for Marville. Assume a 40% tax rate for all items.

exercise 4-9 (Corrected income statement)

The following is the pre-audit income statement for the 10 months ended December 31, 1984, of Best Toy Company, a firm which started operations on March 1, 1984.

Best Toy Company
Income Statement
For Period Ended December 31, 1984

Sales			$497,000
Cost of goods sold:			
Completed units—5,000		$401,000	
Ending inventory—1,000		80,200	320,800
Gross profit on sales			$176,200
Selling expenses:			
Advertising	$13,200		
Miscellaneous selling expenses	60,000	$ 73,200	
General and administrative expenses:			
Officers' salaries	$32,100		
Depreciation expense	16,900		
Miscellaneous general and administrative expenses	3,300	52,300	125,500
Income before income tax			$50,700

During the course of the year-end audit, the auditors observed the following:

(a) Factory depreciation of $11,200 was included in general and administrative expenses.
(b) Sales returns and allowances of $2,750 were not recorded.
(c) Accrued sales commissions of $5,230 were not recorded as of December 31, 1984.
(d) Advertising expense of $13,200, paid on March 1, 1984, was for newspaper ads appearing each month for the next 12 months.
(e) Income tax was charged at a 40 percent rate.

Prepare a corrected income statement for the period ended December 31, 1984. (Round amounts to the nearest dollar.)

exercise 4-10 (Statement of retained earnings)

From the following data for Jenneson Carpet Sales, prepare a statement of retained earnings for 1984.

Net loss—1984	$ 97,775
Total assets at December 31, 1984	3,033,750
Common stock at December 31, 1984	750,000
Paid-in capital in excess of par at December 31, 1984	253,000
Dividends declared during 1984	35,600

The debt-to-equity ratio (liabilities ÷ owners' equity) is 50% at December 31, 1984.

exercise 4-11 (Correction of retained earnings statement)

B. Herman has been employed as the bookkeeper for the Staid Corporation for a number of years. With the assistance of a clerk, Herman handles all accounting duties, including the preparation of financial statements. The following is a "Statement of Earned Surplus" prepared by Herman for 1984.

Staid Corporation
Statement of Earned Surplus
For 1984

Balance at beginning of year		$ 76,949
Additions:		
Amortization overstatement	$ 2,800	
Gain on sale of land	8,350	
Dividend revenue	1,500	
Profit and loss for 1984	13,680	
Total additions		26,330
Total		$103,279
Deductions:		
Dividends declared and paid	$10,000	
Loss on sale of equipment	3,860	
Depreciation understatement	2,400	
Loss from major casualty (extraordinary)	17,730	
Total deductions		33,990
Balance at end of year		$69,289

(1) Prepare a schedule showing the correct net income for 1984. (Ignore income taxes.) (2) Prepare a retained earnings statement for 1984. (3) Explain why you have changed the retained earnings statement.

PROBLEMS

problem 4-1 (Single-step income statement)

The Thompson Co. on July 1, 1983, reported a retained earnings balance of $1,525,000. The books of the company showed the following account balances on June 30, 1984:

Sales	$2,500,000
Inventory: July 1, 1983	160,000
June 30, 1984	165,000
Sales Returns and Allowances	30,000
Purchases	1,536,000
Purchase Discounts	24,000
Dividends	260,000
Selling and General Expenses	250,000
Income Tax	285,200

Instructions: Prepare a single-step income statement and a retained earnings statement. The Thompson Co. has 400,000 shares of common stock outstanding.

problem 4-2 (Combined income and retained earnings statement)

Selected account balances of the Edwards Company along with additional information as of December 31, 1984, are as follows:

Contribution to Employees Pension Fund	$ 290,000
Delivery Expense	425,000
Depreciation Expense—Delivery Trucks	29,000
Depreciation Expense—Office Buildings and Equipment	35,000
Depreciation Expense—Store Equipment	25,000
Dividends	150,000
Dividend Revenue	5,000
Doubtful Accounts Expense	22,000
Federal Income Tax, 1984	515,600
Freight In	145,000
Gain on Sale of Office Equipment	10,000
Interest Revenue	1,500
Loss on Sale of Marketable Securities	50,000
Loss from Write-Down of Obsolete Inventory	$ 125,000
Inventory, Jan. 1, 1984	1,050,000
Miscellaneous General Expense	45,000
Miscellaneous Selling Expense	50,000
Officers' and Office Salaries	950,000
Purchase Discounts	47,700
Purchases	4,633,200
Retained Earnings, Jan. 1, 1984	550,000
Sales	9,125,000
Sales Discounts	55,000
Sales Returns and Allowances	95,000
Sales Salaries	601,000
State and Local Taxes	100,000
Store Supplies Expense	50,000

(a) Inventory at year-end was valued at $750,000—$875,000 cost less the $125,000 write-down of obsolete inventory.
(b) Edwards Company has 100,000 shares of common stock outstanding.

Instructions: Prepare a combined statement of income and retained earnings for the year ended December 31, 1984. (Use a multiple-step form.)

problem 4-3 (Multiple-step income statement with supporting schedules)

The London Supply Co. prepares a multiple-step income statement. The statement is supported by (1) a schedule of cost of goods manufactured, (2) a selling expense schedule, and (3) a general and administrative expense schedule. You are supplied the following data.

Income tax for the current year: Applicable to ordinary income	$30,404

Inventory balances at the end of the fiscal period as compared with balances at the beginning of the fiscal period were as follows:

Finished goods	$18,500 decrease
Goods in process	4,500 increase
Raw materials	10,000 decrease

Other account balances include the following:

Advertising Expense	$ 15,000
Delivery Expense	23,000
Depreciation Exp.—Machinery	5,600
Direct Labor	184,000
Dividend Revenue	300
Dividends	30,000
Doubtful Accounts Expense	1,600
Extraordinary gain (net of income tax of $2,400)	3,600
Factory Heat, Light, and Power	26,990
Factory Maintenance	15,000
Factory Supervision	60,000
Factory Supplies Expense	14,000
Factory Taxes	14,000
Freight In on Raw Materials	10,000
Gain on Sale of Land	$ 8,000
Indirect Labor	74,000
Interest Expense	10,200
Miscellaneous Factory Costs	10,500
Miscellaneous General Expense	3,200
Miscellaneous Selling Expense	2,150
Officers' Salaries	116,200
Office Salaries	70,000
Office Supplies Expense	3,200
Raw Materials Purchases	206,350
Raw Materials Returns	2,000
Royalty Revenue	2,700
Sales	1,031,500
Sales Discounts	8,000
Sales Returns and Allowances	6,500
Sales Salaries	65,000

London Supply Co. has 50,000 shares of common stock outstanding.

Instructions: Prepare an income statement with supporting schedules using the data for the year ended April 30, 1984.

problem 4-4 (Income statement and cash receipts and disbursements)

The Stinson Corporation was organized on March 21, 1984, 15,000 shares of no-par stock being issued in exchange for land, buildings, and equipment valued at $60,000 and cash of $15,000. The following data summarize activities for the initial fiscal period ending December 31, 1984:

(a) Net income for the period ending December 31, 1984, was $20,000.
(b) Raw materials on hand on December 31 were equal to 25% of raw materials purchased in 1984.
(c) Manufacturing costs in 1984 were distributed as follows:

Materials used 50%
Direct labor. 30%
Factory overhead . . 20% (includes depreciation of building, $2,500)

(d) Goods in process remaining in the factory on December 31 were equal to 33⅓% of the goods finished and transferred to stock.
(e) Finished goods remaining in stock were equal to 25% of the cost of goods sold.
(f) Operating expenses were 30% of sales.
(g) Cost of goods sold was 150% of the operating expenses total.
(h) Ninety percent of sales were collected in 1984; the balance was considered collectible in 1985.
(i) Seventy-five percent of the raw materials purchased were paid for; there were no expense accruals or prepayments at the end of the year.

Instructions:

(1) Prepare an income statement and a supporting schedule of cost of goods manufactured. (Disregard income tax.)
(2) Prepare a summary of cash receipts and disbursements to support the cash balance that would be reported on the balance sheet at December 31, 1984.

problem 4-5 (Analysis of income items—multiple-step income statement preparation)

On December 31, 1984, analysis of the Clancey Furniture Store's operations for 1984 revealed the following:

(a) Total cash collections from customers, $105,600.
(b) December 31, 1983 inventory balance, $10,020.
(c) Total cash payments, $87,364.
(d) Accounts receivable, December 31, 1983, $20,350.
(e) Accounts payable, December 31, 1983, $9,870.
(f) Accounts receivable, December 31, 1984, $10,780.
(g) Accounts payable, December 31, 1984, $4,130.
(h) General and administrative expenses total 20% of sales. This amount includes the depreciation on store and equipment.
(i) Selling expenses of $11,661 total 30% of gross profit on sales.
(j) No general and administrative or selling expense liabilities existed at December 31, 1984.
(k) Wages and salaries payable at December 31, 1983, $1,050.
(l) Depreciation expense on store and equipment total 13.5% of general and administrative expenses.
(m) Shares of stock issued and outstanding, 4,500.
(n) The income tax rate is 40%.

Instructions: Prepare a multiple-step income statement for the year ended December 31, 1984.

problem 4-6 (Corrected income and retained earnings statements)

Selected account balances and adjusting information of Cutler Appliance Co. for the year ended December 31, 1984, follow:

Retained Earnings, December 31, 1983	$245,730
Sales Salaries and Commissions	21,000
Advertising Expense	10,030
Legal Services	1,130
Insurance and Licenses	6,315
Travel Expense—Sales Representatives	3,170
Depreciation Expense—Sales and Delivery Equipment	4,200
Depreciation Expense—Office Equipment	3,740
Interest Revenue	1,100
Utilities	7,500
Telephone and Postage	1,380
Supplies Expense	2,180
Miscellaneous Selling Expense	2,740
Dividends	23,000
Dividend Revenue	3,115
Interest Expense	4,520
Allowance for Doubtful Accounts (credit balance)	5,260
Officers' Salaries	33,600
Sales	355,000
Sales Returns and Allowances	3,200
Sales Discounts	970
Gain on Sale of Assets	7,315
Inventory, January 1, 1984	92,645
Inventory, December 31, 1984	18,770
Purchases	132,500
Freight In	6,625
Accounts Receivable, December 31, 1984	250,000

Cutler has 35,000 shares of common stock outstanding.

(a) Cost of inventory in the possession of consignees as of December 31, 1984, totaled $15,300. This amount has not been included in the ending inventory balance.
(b) After preparing an analysis of aged accounts receivable, a decision was made to increase the allowance for doubtful accounts to 3% of the ending accounts receivable balance.
(c) Purchase returns and allowances totaling 7% of purchases were unrecorded.
(d) Sales commissions for the last day of the year had not been accrued. Sales for the day totaled $1,200 with sales commissions averaging 3% of sales.
(e) A freight bill for $575 was received on January 3, 1985, for goods received on December 29, 1984. No accrual had been made.
(f) An advertising campaign was initiated on November 1, 1984, at a cost of $1,212. This amount was recorded as "prepaid advertising" and should be amortized over a six-month period. No amortization had been recorded for 1984.
(g) Freight charges paid on sold merchandise are netted against sales. Freight charges on such sales totaled $4,100 during 1984.
(h) Interest earned but not accrued totaled $510.
(i) Depreciation expense on a new forklift purchased March 1, 1984, for $7,500 with an estimated life of 10 years had not been recognized. (Assume the equipment will have no salvage value and the straight-line method is to be used; depreciation is to be calculated to the nearest month.)
(j) Supplies on hand at year end total $1,150. A "real" account is debited upon receipt of supplies.
(k) The income tax rate is 40%.

Instructions: Prepare a corrected multiple-step income statement and a retained earnings statement for the year ended December 31, 1984. Assume all amounts are material.

problem 4-7 (Income statement and retained earnings statement)

The adjusted trial balance of the BINS Company included the following items at the end of 1984:

Sales	$575,680
Rent Received in Advance	5,000

Rent Revenue	$ 6,000
Gain on Sale of Machinery	1,800
Loss on Sale of Office Equipment	750
Extraordinary Casualty Loss (pretax)	23,400
Cost of Goods Sold	356,925
Dividend Revenue	4,200
Dividends	18,650
Interest Expense	3,600
Interest Revenue	1,500
Selling Expenses	54,600
General and Administrative Expenses	89,500
Common Stock (par $10 per share)	300,000
Retained Earnings, January 1, 1984	176,900

Instructions: Assuming a tax rate of 40% on all items, prepare the following for the year 1984:

(1) A multiple-step income statement.

(2) A combined single-step income statement and statement of retained earnings.

5 AN OVERVIEW OF THE BALANCE SHEET AND STATEMENT OF CHANGES IN FINANCIAL POSITION

CHAPTER OBJECTIVES

Describe the purposes and limitations of the balance sheet.

Identify and define the major elements on the balance sheet.

Discuss and illustrate the general reporting format for the balance sheet.

Present an overview of the nature and purposes of the statement of changes in financial position.

Chapter 4 discussed the income statement. The main subject of this chapter is the balance sheet. The statement of changes in financial position is also introduced but is explained in more detail in Chapter 23 when students are better able to understand its complexities.

PURPOSES AND LIMITATIONS OF THE BALANCE SHEET

The **balance sheet,** also known as the **statement of financial position,** reports as of a given point in time the resources of a business (**assets**), its obligations (**liabilities**), and the residual ownership claims against an entity's resources (**owners' equity**). By analyzing the relationships among these items, investors, creditors, and others can assess a firm's **liquidity**, i.e., its ability to meet short-term obligations, and **solvency**, i.e., its ability to pay all current and long-term debts as they come due. The balance sheet also shows the composition of assets and liabilities, the relative proportions of debt and equity financing, and how much of a firm's earnings have been retained in the business. Collectively, this information can be used by external parties to help assess the financial status of a firm at a particular date.

Following the traditional accounting model, the balance sheet is a historical report presenting the cumulative results of all past transactions of a business measured in terms of historical costs. It is an expression of the basic accounting equation—**Assets = Liabilities + Owners' Equity.** The balance sheet shows both the character and the amount of the assets, liabilities, and owners' equity.

For many years, the emphasis on earnings and profitability measures has resulted in the income statement receiving more attention than the balance sheet. While it does not appear that the prominence of reporting earnings is likely to decrease, the business community has shown a renewed interest in the balance sheet in recent years. Consider the following excerpts from an article entitled "Focus on Balance Sheet Reform."

> A quiet, but potentially explosive, revolution is sweeping the U.S. business world as lenders, investors, regulators, accountants, and corporate managers rediscover what should never have been lost: the balance sheet.
>
> ★ ★ ★
>
> Only by studying the balance sheet can a lender or an investor—or a regulator—measure a company's liquidity and its ability to generate profits and pay debts and dividends year after year. "The balance sheet is the anchor to windward," says John H. Kennedy, vice-president for finance at Alco Standard Corp. in Valley Forge, Pa. "It shows whether the company will survive, how profitable it can be, and whether it has a major obstacle to profits, like a pile of debt coming due."
>
> Because the balance sheet tells so much, it is astonishing that it could ever have gotten lost. Four decades ago, Benjamin Graham and David Dodd, the founding fathers of security analysis, stressed the balance sheet as they taught investors to look at a company's "intrinsic value" before they bought. Then came the go-go years of the late 1960s and early 1970s, when the only thing that seemed to matter was how fast a company could grow, a game that the biggest, most sophisticated institutional investors played as avidly as the rankest amateur in for a fast kill.
>
> But the go-go years ended in the inflation-recession agony of 1974–75, and people are focusing on the balance sheet as they have not in years...[1]

Balance sheets, especially when compared over time and with additional data, provide a great deal of useful information to those interested in analyzing the financial well-being of a company. Specific relationships, such as a company's current ratio, its debt to equity ratio, and its rate of return on investment can be highlighted.[2] Future commitments, favorable and unfavorable trends, problem areas in terms of collection patterns, and the relative equity positions of creditors and owners can also be analyzed, all of which assist in evaluating the financial position of a company.

---

[1] "Focus on Balance Sheet Reform," *Business Week,* June 7, 1976, p. 52.
[2] These ratios and relationships are discussed in detail in Chapter 25.

Notwithstanding its usefulness, the balance sheet has some serious limitations. External users often need to know a company's worth. The balance sheet, however, does not reflect the current values of a business. Instead, the entity's resources and obligations are shown at historical costs based on past transactions and events. The historical cost measurements represent market values existing at the dates the transactions or events occurred. However, when the prices of specific assets change significantly after the acquisition date, as has certainly been the case recently in the United States, then the balance sheet numbers are not relevant for evaluating a company's current worth.

A related problem with the balance sheet is the instability of the dollar, the standard accounting measuring unit in the United States. Because of general price changes in the economy, the dollar does not maintain a constant purchasing power. Yet the historical costs of resources and equities shown on the balance sheet are not adjusted for changes in the purchasing power of the measuring unit. The result is a balance sheet that reflects assets, liabilities, and equities in terms of unequal purchasing power units. Some elements, for example, may be stated in terms of 1960 dollars and some in terms of 1983 dollars. The variations in purchasing power of the amounts reported in the balance sheet make comparisons among companies and even within a single company less meaningful.

An additional limitation of the balance sheet, also related to the need for comparability, is that all companies do not classify and report all like items similarly. For example, titles and account classifications vary; some companies provide considerably more detail than others; and some companies with apparently similar transactions report them differently. Such differences make comparisons difficult and diminish the potential value of balance sheet analysis.

The balance sheet may be considered deficient in another respect. Due primarily to measurement problems, some entity resources and obligations are not reported on the balance sheet. For example, the employees of a company may be one of its most valuable resources; yet, they are not shown on the balance sheet because their future service potentials are not measurable in monetary terms. Similarly, a company's potential liability for polluting the air would not normally be shown on its balance sheet. The assumptions of the traditional accounting model identified in Chapter 3, specifically the requirements of arm's-length transactions or events measurable in monetary terms, add to the objectivity of balance sheet disclosures but at the same time cause some information to be omitted that is likely to be relevant to certain users' decisions.

The FASB has attempted to correct, at least partially, two of the above problems by requiring supplemental disclosures of both current values and constant dollar amounts for selected items. These reporting requirements are discussed in detail in Chapter 24. As indicated in Chapter 3, the Board is also working on other reporting problems through their conceptual framework project.

CONTENT OF THE BALANCE SHEET

For accounting purposes, **assets** are defined as "probable future economic benefits obtained or controlled by a particular entity as a result of past transactions or events."[3] They include those costs that have not been matched with revenues in the past and are expected to afford economic utility in the production of revenues in the future. Assets include both **monetary assets**, such as cash, certain marketable securities, and receivables, and **nonmonetary assets**—those costs recognized as recoverable and hence properly assignable to revenues of future periods, such as inventories, prepaid insurance, equipment, and patents.

Liabilities are defined as "probable future sacrifices of economic benefits arising from present obligations of a particular entity to transfer assets or provide services to other entities in the future as a result of past transactions or events."[4] They measure the claims of creditors against entity resources. The method for settlement of liabilities varies. Liabilities may call for settlement by cash payment or settlement through goods to be delivered or services to be performed.

Owners' equity is defined as "the residual interest in the assets of an entity that remains after deducting its liabilities."[5] It measures the interest of the ownership group in the total resources of the enterprise. This interest arises from investments by owners, and the equity increase or decrease from the change in net assets resulting from operations. An ownership equity does not call for settlement on a certain date; in the event of business dissolution, it represents a claim on assets only after creditors have been paid in full.

Balance sheet items are generally classified in a manner that facilitates analysis and interpretation of financial data. Information of primary concern to all parties is the business unit's liquidity and solvency—its ability to meet current and long-term obligations. Accordingly, assets and liabilities are classified as (1) **current** or **short-term** items and (2) **noncurrent** or **long-term** items. When assets and liabilities are so classified, the difference between current assets and current liabilities may be determined. This is referred to as the company's **working capital**—the liquid buffer available in meeting financial demands and contingencies of the future.

Current Assets and Current Liabilities

Current assets include cash and resources that are reasonably expected to be converted into cash during the normal operating cycle of a business or within one year, whichever period is longer. As depicted on the following page, the **normal operating cycle** is the time required for cash to be converted to inventories, inventories into receivables, and receivables ultimately into

---

[3]*Statement of Financial Accounting Concepts No. 3,* "Elements of Financial Statements of Business Enterprises" (Stamford: Financial Accounting Standards Board, December 1980), par. 19.

[4]*Ibid.*, par. 28.

[5]*Ibid.*, par. 43.

cash. When the operating cycle exceeds twelve months, for example, in the tobacco, distillery, and lumber industries, the longer period is used.

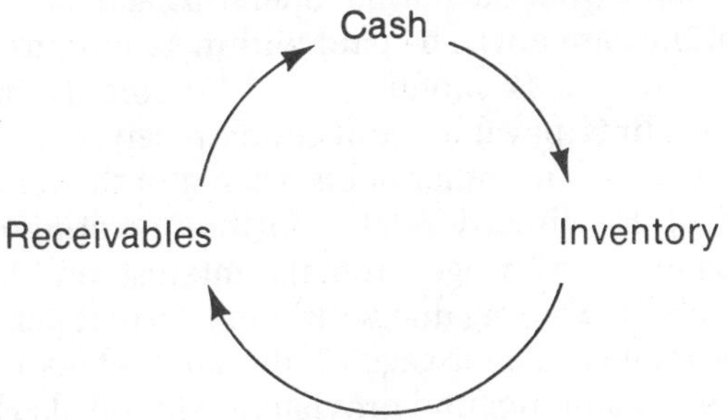

Normal Operating Cycle

Some exceptions to the general definition of current assets should be noted. Cash that is restricted as to use, e.g., designated for the acquisition of noncurrent assets or segregated for the liquidation of noncurrent debts, should not be included in current assets. Also, in classifying assets not related to the operating cycle, a one-year period is always used as the basis for current classification. For example, a note receivable due in 18 months that arose from the sale of land previously held for investment would be classified as noncurrent even if the normal operating cycle exceeds 18 months.

In addition to cash, receivables, and inventories, current assets typically include such resources as prepaid expenses and marketable securities. Prepayments of such items as insurance and interest are not current assets in the sense that they will be converted into cash but on the basis that, if they had not been prepaid, the use of cash or other current assets during the operating cycle period would have been required. Long-term prepayments should be reported as noncurrent assets and charged to the operations of several years. If securities of companies, whether marketable or not, are acquired for purposes of control rather than conversion back to cash during the normal operating cycle, they should not be designated as current assets. Other items that might be converted into cash, but are not expected to be converted and therefore should not be classified as current assets, include the cash surrender value of life insurance policies, land, and depreciable assets.

Current assets are normally listed on the balance sheet in the order of their liquidity. These assets, with the exception of marketable securities and inventories, are usually reported at their estimated realizable values. Thus, current receivable balances are reduced by allowances for estimated uncollectible accounts. Marketable equity securities should be reported at the lower of aggregate cost or market.[6] Inventories may be reported at cost or on the basis of "cost or market, whichever is lower."

Current liabilities are those obligations that are reasonably expected to be paid using existing resources properly classified as current assets or by

---

[6] *Statement of Financial Accounting Standards No. 12,* "Accounting for Certain Marketable Securities" (Stamford: Financial Accounting Standards Board, 1975), par. 8.

creating other current liabilities. Generally, if a liability will be paid within 12 months, it is properly classified as current. As with receivables, payables arising from the normal operating activities may be classified as current even if they are not to be paid within 12 months, but within the operating cycle if it exceeds 12 months. Items commonly included as current liabilities are accounts payable, collections received in advance of delivery of goods or services, and other debts arising in the normal operations of a business and that are directly related to the operating cycle. Examples are accruals for salaries and wages, rentals, interest, and taxes. The amount of a long-term liability coming due within the current period, such as the current portion of a long-term mortgage or the amount required to be paid within one year under sinking fund provisions, should also be classified as a current liability.

The current liability classification, however, generally does not include the following items, since these do not require the use of resources classified as current.

(1) Short-term obligations expected to be refinanced.[7]
(2) Debts to be liquidated from funds that have been accumulated and are reported as noncurrent assets.
(3) Loans on life insurance policies made with the intent that these will not be paid but will be liquidated by deduction from the proceeds of the policies upon their maturity or cancellation.
(4) Obligations for advance collections that involve long-term deferment of the delivery of goods or services.[8]

With respect to short-term obligations that normally would come due within the operating cycle but are expected to be refinanced, i.e., discharged by means of the issuance of new obligations in their place, the FASB has concluded that such obligations should be excluded from current liabilities if the following conditions are met: (1) the intent of the company is to refinance the obligations on a long-term basis, and (2) the company's intent is supported by an ability to consummate the refinancing as evidenced by a post-balance-sheet-date issuance of long-term obligations or equity securities or an explicit financing agreement.[9]

In effect, the FASB is recognizing that certain short-term obligations will not require the use of working capital during a period even though they are scheduled to mature during that period. Thus, they should not be classified as current liabilities.

Few problems occur in the valuation of current liabilities. Payables can usually be determined with reasonable accuracy, even though some items may require estimates as to the amounts ultimately to be paid. These claims, however determined, if payable currently, must be included under the current heading.

---

[7]*Statement of Financial Accounting Standards No. 6*, "Classification of Short-Term Obligations Expected to be Refinanced" (Stamford: Financial Accounting Standards Board, 1975).

[8]*Accounting Research and Terminology Bulletins—Final Edition, No. 43*, "Restatement and Revision of Accounting Research Bulletins" (New York: American Institute of Certified Public Accountants, 1961), par. 8 and footnotes 2 and 3.

[9]*Statement of Financial Accounting Standards No. 6, op. cit.*, par. 9–11.

The importance of an adequate working capital position cannot be minimized. A business may not be able to survive in the absence of a satisfactory relationship between current assets and current liabilities. Furthermore, its ability to prosper is largely determined by the composition of the current asset pool. There must be a proper balance between liquid assets in the form of cash and temporary investments, and receivables and inventories. Activities of the business center around these assets. Cash and temporary investments, representing immediate purchasing power, are used to meet current claims and purchasing, payroll, and expense requirements; receivables are the outgrowth of sales effort and provide cash in the course of operations; inventory is also a source of cash as well as the means of achieving a profit. Management, in setting policies with respect to selling, purchasing, financing, expanding, and the paying of dividends, must work within the limitations set by the company's working capital position.

Noncurrent Assets and Noncurrent Liabilities

Assets and liabilities not qualifying for presentation under the current headings are classified under a number of noncurrent headings. Noncurrent assets may be listed under separate headings, such as "Long-term investments," "Land, buildings, and equipment," "Intangible assets," and "Other long-term assets." Noncurrent liabilities are generally listed under separate headings, such as "Long-term debt," "Unearned revenues," and "Other long-term liabilities."

Long-Term Investments. Investments held for such long-term purposes as regular income, appreciation, or ownership control are reported under the heading "Long-term investments." Examples of items properly reported under this heading are long-term stocks, bonds, and mortgage holdings; securities of affiliated companies and advances to such companies; sinking fund assets consisting of cash and securities held for the redemption of bonds or stocks, the replacement of buildings, or the payment of pensions; land held for investment purposes; the cash surrender value of life insurance; and other miscellaneous investments not used directly in the operations of the business. Although many long-term investments are reported at cost, there are modifications to the valuation of some investments that will be discussed in later chapters.

Land, Buildings, and Equipment. Properties of a tangible and relatively permanent character that are used in the normal business operations are reported under "Land, buildings, and equipment" or other appropriate headings. Land, buildings, machinery, tools, furniture, fixtures, and vehicles are included under this heading. Most tangible properties except land are normally reported at cost less accumulated depreciation.

Intangible Assets. The long-term rights and privileges of a nonphysical nature acquired for use in business operations are often reported under the heading "Intangible assets." Included in this class are such items as goodwill, patents, trademarks, franchises, copyrights, formulas, leaseholds, and organization costs. Intangible assets are normally reported at cost less amounts previously amortized.

Other Long-Term Assets. Those noncurrent assets not suitably reported under any of the previous classifications may be listed under the general heading "Other long-term assets" or may be listed separately under special descriptive headings. Such assets include, for example, long-term advances to officers and deposits made with taxing authorities and utility companies.

Prepayments for services or benefits to be received over a number of periods are properly regarded as noncurrent. Among these are such items as plant rearrangement costs and developmental and improvement costs. These long-term prepayments are frequently reported under a "Deferred costs" or "Deferred charges" heading. However, objection can be raised to a deferred costs category since this designation could be applied to all costs assignable to future periods including inventories, buildings and equipment, and intangible assets. The deferred costs heading may be avoided by reporting long-term prepayments within the other long-term assets section or under separate descriptive headings.

A debit balance in the deferred income tax account may be shown under "Other long-term assets" or may be reported separately. Income tax is considered to be prepaid when paid on a computed taxable income that is more than the income reported on the financial statements. The difference between taxable income and income reported from operations may be a temporary timing difference that will be offset in the future. It may be caused by recognizing a taxable item of revenue or expense in one accounting period for tax purposes and in a different accounting period for purposes of reporting operating income. Under these circumstances, matching of income tax expense with revenue requires that the tax paid on taxable income in excess of the book income be deferred and recognized as an addition to tax expense in the period when the income is ultimately recognized on the books. Most of the time, the account Deferred Income Taxes has a credit balance and, as indicated on page 135, is properly shown as a long-term liability. Accounting for income tax is considered in detail in Chapter 20.

Contingent Assets. Circumstances at the balance sheet date may indicate the existence of certain rights or claims that could materialize as valuable assets depending on the favorable outcome of certain events. In the absence of a legal right to the properties at that time, these can be viewed only as **contingent assets**. Contingencies that might result in gains are not recorded in the accounts; they may be disclosed by a special note or by appropriate comment under a separate "Contingent assets" heading following the "Other asset" classifications. Care should be exercised not to present misleading implications with respect to possible realization.[10] Tax claims, insurance claims, and claims against suppliers may warrant such treatment, but usually do not. Reference to contingent assets on the balance sheet is rare in practice.

---

[10] *Statement of Financial Accounting Standards No. 5*, "Accounting for Contingencies" (Stamford: Financial Accounting Standards Board, 1975), par. 17.

Long-Term Debt. Long-term notes, bonds, mortgages, and similar obligations not requiring the use of current funds for their retirement are generally reported on the balance sheet under the heading "Long-term debt."

When an amount borrowed is not the same as the amount ultimately required in settlement of the debt, and the debt is stated in the accounts at its maturity amount, a debt discount or premium is reported. The discount or premium should be related to the debt item; a discount, then, should be subtracted from the amount reported for the debt, and a premium should be added to the amount reported for the debt. The debt is thus reported at its present value as measured by the proceeds from its issuance. Amortization of the discount or premium brings the obligation to the maturity amount by the end of its normal term. When a note, a bond issue, or a mortgage formerly classified as a long-term obligation becomes payable within a year, it should be reclassified and presented as a current liability, except when the obligation is to be refinanced, as discussed earlier, or is to be paid out of a sinking fund.

Unearned Revenues. Cash may be received or other assets recognized for goods and services to be supplied in future periods. Such transactions are recognized in the accounts by debits to assets and credits to liability accounts reporting the advance payments. The latter balance is properly carried forward until the company meets its responsibilities through the delivery of goods or the performance of services. Examples of transactions that call for revenue deferral and recognition as long-term obligations include fees received in advance on long-term service contracts, and long-term leasehold and rental prepayments. These prepayments are normally reported on the balance sheet under the heading of "Unearned revenues."

All revenues received in advance for goods and services are frequently reported under the "Unearned revenues" heading, including those calling for settlement in the near future. However, the noncurrent classification is appropriate only when an item represents no significant claim upon current assets. When significant costs are involved in satisfying a claim and these costs will be met from the company's current assets, the prepayment should be recognized as a current liability. The obligation arising from the receipt of cash in advance on magazine subscriptions, for example, is properly recognized as a current liability in view of the claim it makes upon current assets.

Other Long-Term Liabilities. Those noncurrent liabilities not suitably reported under the "Long-term debt" or "Unearned revenues" headings may be listed under the general heading "Other long-term liabilities" or may be listed separately under special descriptive headings. Such liabilities include long-term obligations to company officers or affiliated companies, matured but unclaimed bond principal and interest obligations, and long-term liabilities under pension plans.

A credit balance in the deferred income tax account may be shown under "Other long-term liabilities" or may be reported separately. Income tax is considered to have accrued when tax is paid on a computed taxable income that is less than the income reported on the financial statements. The difference, as previously mentioned in discussing other long-term assets, may be a temporary one caused by a timing difference. In this case, however, the timing difference has resulted in postponing income tax until a later period. Timing differences may occur, for example, in recognizing a different amount of depreciation on the tax return than on the books.

Contingent Liabilities. Past activities or circumstances may give rise to possible future liabilities, although legal obligations do not exist on the date of the balance sheet. These possible claims are known as **contingent liabilities**. They are potential obligations involving uncertainty as to possible losses. As future events occur or fail to occur, this uncertainty will be resolved. Thus, a contingent liability is distinguishable from an **estimated liability**. The latter is a definite obligation with only the amount of the obligation in question and subject to estimation at the balance sheet date. There may not be any doubt as to the amount of a contingent liability, for example, a pending lawsuit, but there is considerable uncertainty as to whether the obligation will actually materialize.

In the past, contingent liabilities were not recorded in the accounts nor presented on the balance sheet. When they were disclosed, it was in the notes to the financial statements. Since the issuance of FASB Statement No. 5, if a future payment is considered probable, the liability should be recorded by a debit to a loss account and a credit to a liability account.[11] Otherwise, the contingent nature of the loss is disclosed in a note to the financial statements or ignored depending on the degree of remoteness of the expected occurrence. Examples of contingent liabilities and further discussion of their treatment are presented in Chapter 13.

Owners' Equity

The method of reporting the owners' equity varies with the form of the business unit. Business units are typically divided into three categories: (1) **proprietorships**, (2) **partnerships**, and (3) **corporations**. In the case of a proprietorship, the owner's equity in assets is reported by means of a single capital account. The balance in this account is the cumulative result of the owner's investments and withdrawals as well as past earnings and losses. In a partnership, capital accounts are established for each partner. Capital account balances summarize the investments and withdrawals and shares of past earnings and losses of each partner, and thus measure the partners' individual equities in the partnership assets.

In a corporation, the difference between assets and liabilities is referred to as **stockholders' equity, shareholders' equity**, or simply, **capital**. In presenting the stockholders' equity on the balance sheet, a distinction is made between the equity originating from the stockholders' investments, referred to as **contributed capital** or **paid-in capital**, and the equity originating from earnings, referred to as **retained earnings**.

---

[11] *Ibid.*, par. 8-13.

The relationship and distinction between the amount of capital contributed or paid in by the owners of the corporation relative to the amount the company has earned and retained in the business is a significant one. Such disclosure helps creditors and investors assess the long-term ability of a company to internally finance its own operations. If the contributed capital of a corporation is large relative to the total owners' equity, it means the corporation has been financed primarily from external sources, usually from the sale of stock to investors. If the earned capital of a corporation is large relative to the total owners' equity, it means the company has been profitable in the past and has retained those earnings in the business to help finance its activities. This distinction between earned and contributed capital is not as important for a proprietorship or partnership because the owners of those types of businesses generally are also involved in their management and therefore are aware of how the company activities are being financed.

Contributed Capital. Contributed or paid-in capital is generally reported in two parts: (1) **capital stock** representing that portion of the contribution by stockholders assignable to the shares of stock issued; (2) **additional paid-in capital** representing investments by stockholders in excess of the amounts assignable to capital stock as well as invested capital from other sources.

Capital stock outstanding having a par value is shown on the balance sheet at par. Capital stock having no par value is stated at the amount received on its original sale or at some other value as stipulated by law or as assigned by action of the board of directors of the corporation. When more than a single class of stock has been issued and is outstanding, the stock of each class is reported separately. **Treasury stock**, which is stock issued but subsequently reacquired by the corporation and not retired or canceled, is subtracted from the total stock issued or from the sum of contributed capital and retained earnings balances. The capital stock balance is viewed as the **legal capital** or **permanent capital** of the corporation.

The amount received in excess of par value on the sale of par-value stock or the amount received in excess of the value assigned to no-par stock is recognized as additional paid-in capital. Additional paid-in capital may also arise from transactions other than the sale of stock, such as from the acquisition of property as a result of a donation or from the sale of treasury stock at more than cost. The additional paid-in capital balances are normally added to capital stock so the full amount of the contributed capital may be reported. Contributed capital is discussed in detail in Chapter 17.

Retained Earnings. The amount of undistributed earnings of past periods is reported as **retained earnings**. The total amount thus shown will probably not represent cash available for payment as dividends since past years' earnings will usually already have been reinvested in other assets. An excess of dividends and losses over earnings results in a negative retained earnings balance called a **deficit**. The balance of retained earnings is added to the contributed capital total in summarizing the stockholders' equity; a deficit is subtracted.

Portions of retained earnings are sometimes reported as restricted and unavailable as a basis for dividends. Restricted earnings may be designated as *appropriations*. Appropriations are sometimes made for such purposes as sinking funds, plant expansion, loss contingencies, and the reacquisition of capital stock. Often such appropriations are disclosed in a note rather than in the accounts. When appropriations have been made in the accounts, retained earnings on the balance sheet consists of an amount designated as *appropriated* and a balance designated as *unappropriated* or *free*. The term "reserve" should not generally be used to designate appropriations. Retained earnings is fully discussed in Chapter 18.

Offsets on the Balance Sheet

A number of balance sheet items are frequently reported at gross amounts calling for the recognition of offset balances in arriving at proper valuations. Such offset balances are found in asset, liability, and owners' equity categories. In the case of assets, for example, an allowance for doubtful accounts is subtracted from the sum of the customers' accounts in reporting the net amount estimated as collectible; accumulated depreciation is subtracted from the related buildings and equipment balances in reporting the costs of the assets still assignable to future revenues. In the case of liabilities, reacquired bonds or *treasury bonds*, are subtracted from bonds issued in reporting the amount of bonds outstanding; a bond discount is subtracted from the face value of bonds outstanding in reporting the net amount of the debt. In the stockholders' equity section of the balance sheet, treasury stock is deducted in reporting total stockholders' equity.

The types of offsets described above, utilizing contra accounts, are required for proper reporting of particular balance sheet items. Offsets are improper, however, if applied to different asset and liability balances or to asset and owners' equity balances even when there is some relationship between the items. For example, a company may accumulate cash in a special fund to discharge certain tax liabilities; but as long as control of the cash is retained and the liabilities are still outstanding, the company should continue to report both the asset and the liabilities separately. Or a company may accumulate cash in a special fund for the redemption of preferred stock outstanding; but until the cash is applied to the reacquisition of the stock, the company must continue to report the asset as well as the owners' equity item. A company may have made advances to certain salespersons while at the same time reporting accrued amounts payable to others; but a net figure cannot be justified here, just as a net figure cannot be justified for the offset of trade receivables against trade payables.

Form of the Balance Sheet

The form of the balance sheet presentation varies in practice. Its form may be influenced by the nature and size of the business, by the character of the business properties, by requirements set by regulatory bodies, or by display preferences in presenting key relationships. The balance sheet is prepared in one of two basic forms: (1) the **account form**, with assets being reported on the left-hand side and liabilities and owners' equity on the right-hand side, or (2) the **report form**, with assets, liabilities, and owners' equity sections appearing in vertical arrangement.

The order of asset and liability classifications may vary, but usually emphasis is placed on a company's working capital position and liquidity, with asset and liability groups, as well as the items within such groups, presented in the order of liquidity. However, within the land, buildings, and equipment section, assets are usually listed in the order of their permanence, that is, land, then buildings, equipment, and so on. A balance sheet in account form with financial data reported in the order of liquidity is illustrated on pages 140 and 141. The balance sheet of General Mills, reproduced in Appendix B, illustrates the report form.

When the report form is used, liability and owners' equity totals may be added together to constitute an amount equal to the asset total. In other instances, total liabilities are subtracted from total assets, and owners' equity is reported as the difference. A variation of the report form referred to as the **financial position form** has found some favor. This form emphasizes the current position and reports a working capital balance. The financial position form is illustrated below. (Individual assets and liabilities are omitted in the example.)

Balance sheets in published financial statements are frequently presented in **condensed form**, with many related items combined. For example,

Barnsby Corporation
Balance Sheet
December 31, 1984

Current assets		$310,000
Less current liabilities		67,000
Working capital		$243,000
Add:		
Long-term investments	$ 31,500	
Land, buildings, and equipment	250,000	
Intangible assets	88,500	
Other long-term assets	20,000	390,000
Total assets less current liabilities		$633,000
Deduct:		
Long-term liabilities less unamortized bond discount	$ 95,000	
Unearned revenues	20,000	
Deferred income tax	3,000	
Long-term advances to officers	65,000	183,000
Net assets		$450,000
Stockholders' equity:		
Contributed capital		$295,000
Retained earnings		155,000
Total stockholders' equity		$450,000

Financial Position Form of Balance Sheet

Barnsby
Balance
December

Assets				
Current assets:				
Cash in bank and on hand			$ 36,500	
Marketable securities (reported at cost; market value, $71,500)			70,000	
Notes receivable, trade debtors (Note 2)		$ 15,000		
Accounts receivable		50,000		
		$ 65,000		
Less allowance for doubtful notes and accounts receivable		5,000	60,000	
Claim for income tax refund			9,000	
Creditors accounts with debit balances			750	
Advances to employees			1,250	
Interest receivable			250	
Inventories (Note 1a)			125,000	
Prepaid expenses:				
Supply inventories		$ 3,000		
Insurance		4,250	7,250	$310,000
Long-term investments:				
Investment in land and unused facilities (Note 1d)			$ 22,500	
Cash surrender value of officers' life insurance policies			9,000	31,500
Land, buildings, and equipment (Note 1b):				
	Cost	Accumulated Depreciation	Book Value	
Land	$ 80,000		$ 80,000	
Buildings	150,000	$ 35,000	115,000	
Equipment	100,000	45,000	55,000	
	$330,000	$ 80,000		250,000
Intangible assets (Note 1c):				
Patents			$ 70,000	
Goodwill			18,500	88,500
Other long-term assets:				
Advances to officers			$ 15,000	
Utility deposits			5,000	20,000
Total assets				$700,000

See accompanying notes to financial statements.

Account Form

land, buildings, and equipment may be reported as a single item, and all long-term investments may be reported in total. Consolidation of similar items within reasonable limits may actually serve to clarify the business position and data relationships. Supporting detail for individual items, when considered of particular significance or when required by GAAP, may be supplied by means of special summaries referred to as **supplementary** or **supporting schedules**. For example, a listing of all long-term debt with appropriate interest rates and maturity dates might be shown as a useful supporting schedule to the notes payable account. Disclosure of segment or product line data is another example of information often shown as a supple-

Corporation
Sheet
31, 1984

Liabilities			
Current liabilities:			
Notes payable, trade creditors		$ 14,250	
Accounts payable		12,500	
Dividends payable		5,000	
Advances from customers		5,750	
Income tax payable		27,000	
Other liabilities:			
Salaries and wages payable	$ 1,000		
Taxes payable	1,500	2,500	$ 67,000
Long-term debt:			
8% First-mortgage bonds due December 31, 2000 (Note 3)		$100,000	
Less unamortized bond discount		5,000	95,000
Unearned revenues:			
Unearned lease revenue (Note 1d)			20,000
Other long-term liabilities:			
Deferred income tax		$ 3,000	
Long-term advances to officers		65,000	68,000
Total liabilities			$250,000
Stockholders' Equity			
Contributed capital:			
Common stock, $5 par value, 100,000 shares authorized, 50,000 shares issued and outstanding	$250,000		
Paid-in capital from sale of common stock at more than par value	45,000	$295,000	
Retained earnings		155,000	
Total stockholders' equity			450,000
Total liabilities and stockholders' equity			$700,000

Balance Sheet

mentary schedule. In Appendix B, Notes 7 and 16 for General Mills demonstrate the effective use of supporting schedules.

Parenthetical notation is another technique commonly used in balance sheet presentations. For example, in the current assets section of the balance sheet on page 140, the marketable securities are presented as follows:

Marketable securities (reported at cost; market value, $71,500)	70,000

Such disclosure shows the current market value of the securities as well as their cost. Thus, parenthetical disclosures can add significantly to the total understanding of the reader.

Balance sheet data are generally presented in comparative form. With comparative reports for two or more dates, information is made available concerning the nature and trend of financial changes taking place within the periods between balance sheet dates. Currently, a minimum of two years of balance sheets and three years of income statements and funds statements are required by the SEC to be included in the annual report to shareholders.

Notes to the Financial Statements

Notes to the financial statements are an integral part of any formal financial statement presentation. They are essential in explaining the basic financial data and should be prepared and read with care. Notes are commonly used to provide additional information about balance sheet and income statement items that cannot conveniently be shown, parenthetically or otherwise, directly on the statements. Frequently, notes deal with methods of valuation, the existence and amounts of dividends in arrears, the existence of contingencies, special financing arrangements, significant accounting policies and changes in policies, or unusual events or items that would be better understood with additional explanation.

The balance sheet for Barnsby Corporation, on pages 140 and 141, refers to Note 2 in connection with the trade notes receivable. In that note, shown below, the company discloses its contingent liability on $40,000 worth of guaranteed notes. Note 3, referenced under long-term debt, describes the nature of the bonds outstanding, especially with respect to the call option on the bonds.

Barnsby Corporation
Notes to Financial Statements—Year Ended December 31, 1984

1. Summary of significant accounting policies:
   (a) Inventories are valued at cost or market, whichever is lower. Cost is calculated by the first-in, first-out method.
   (b) Depreciation is computed by the straight-line method for the financial statements and by using the ACRS guidelines on the tax return.
   (c) Intangible assets are being amortized over the period of their estimated useful lives: patents, 10 years, and goodwill, 20 years.
   (d) The company leased Market Street properties for a 15-year period ending January 1, 1992. The lease does not meet criteria for capitalization and the leasehold payment received in advance is being recognized as revenue over the life of the lease.
2. The company is contingently liable on guaranteed notes and accounts totaling $40,000. Also, various suits are pending on which the ultimate payment cannot be determined. In the opinion of counsel and management, such liability, if any, will not be material.
3. Bonds may be called at the option of the board of directors at 105 plus accrued interest on or before December 31, 1986, and at gradually reduced amounts but at not less than 102½ plus accrued interest after January 1, 1992.

The overall objective of note disclosure is clarification of the information presented in the financial statements. It is a real challenge to present concisely and clearly the information needed by the various users of financial statements. The notes provided with General Mills' statements, presented as Appendix B, demonstrate how one company has attempted to meet that challenge. Disclosure requirements are so extensive that they cannot be completely discussed in a single chapter. Specific requirements will be noted as appropriate throughout the text. The notes to the financial statements illustrated in this chapter and in the end-of-chapter material do not necessarily provide complete disclosure, but are only illustrative of the general nature and content of notes included with financial statements.[12]

Summary of Significant Accounting Policies

In addition to the other notes, a summary of the significant accounting policies followed should be presented with the financial statements. In this regard, the Accounting Principles Board concluded in APB Opinion No. 22:

> ...When financial statements are issued purporting to present fairly financial position, changes in financial position, and results of operations in accordance with generally accepted accounting principles, a description of all significant accounting policies of the reporting entity should be included as an integral part of the financial statements.[13]

The Board further stated:

> ...In general, the disclosure should encompass important judgments as to appropriateness of principles related to recognition of revenue and allocation of asset costs to current and future periods; in particular it should encompass those accounting principles and methods that involve any of the following: (a) A selection from existing acceptable alternatives; (b) Principles and methods peculiar to the industry in which the reporting entity operates, even if such principles and methods are predominantly followed in that industry; (c) Unusual or innovative applications of generally accepted accounting principles (and, as applicable, of principles and methods peculiar to the industry in which the reporting entity operates).[14]

Examples of disclosures of accounting policies required by this opinion would include, among others, those relating to depreciation methods, amortization of intangible assets, inventory pricing methods, the recognition of profit on long-term construction-type contracts, and the recognition of revenue from leasing operations.[15]

The exact format for reporting the summary of accounting policies was not specified by the APB. However, the Board recommended such disclosure be included as the initial note or as a separate summary preceding the notes to the financial statements. The summary of significant accounting policies for the Barnsby Corporation is presented on the preceding page as the first note to the financial statements.

---

[12]Notes to financial statements in end-of-chapter material need only be prepared when specifically required by the exercise or problem.

[13]*Opinions of the Accounting Principles Board, No. 22*, "Disclosure of Accounting Policies" (New York: American Institute of Certified Public Accountants, 1972), par. 8.

[14]*Ibid.*, par. 12.

[15]*Ibid.*, par. 13.

Careful classification of items under descriptive headings, appropriate explanatory notes, and the presentation of data in comparative form provide more meaningful statements. Presentations in condensed forms and the rounding of numbers to the nearest dollar, hundred or thousands of dollars clarify relationships and facilitate analysis. A variety of different balance sheet disclosures are found in practice. As noted earlier, an illustrative set of financial statements, complete with applicable notes, is provided in Appendix B of this textbook. Included is a balance sheet illustrating one approach taken in the development of a statement summarizing financial status.

OVERVIEW OF THE STATEMENT OF CHANGES IN FINANCIAL POSITION

The **statement of changes in financial position,** also commonly referred to as the **funds statement,** is a condensed report of how the activities of a business have been financed and how the financial resources have been used. It is a flow statement, emphasizing the inflows and outflows of resources related to the significant financial events of an enterprise during a reporting period. The remainder of this chapter provides an overview of the statement of changes in financial position.

Nature and Purpose of the Funds Statement

The funds statement provides a summary of the sources from which funds became available during a period and the purposes to which funds were applied. An important part of the summary is the presentation of data concerning the extent to which funds were generated by income-oriented operations of the business. In addition to reporting funds provided by operations, funds inflow is also related to such sources as the sale of property items, the issuance of long-term obligations, and the issuance of capital stock. Funds outflow is related to such uses as the acquisition of property items, the retirement of long-term obligations, the reacquisition of outstanding stock, and the payment of dividends.

These primary inflows and outflows are illustrated diagrammatically on the following page.

Although based on the same data as the balance sheet and the income statement, the statement of changes in financial position helps to answer questions not readily apparent from examination of either or both of the other two statements. For example, the funds statement helps the reader answer questions such as: Where did the profits go? Why were dividends not larger in view of rising earnings? How can dividends be distributed in excess of current earnings or when there was a reported net loss? Why are current assets decreasing when the results of operations are positive? How was the plant expansion financed? What use was made of the proceeds from the sale of stock? How was bonded indebtedness paid off even though there was a substantial operating loss? These questions require answers if the various

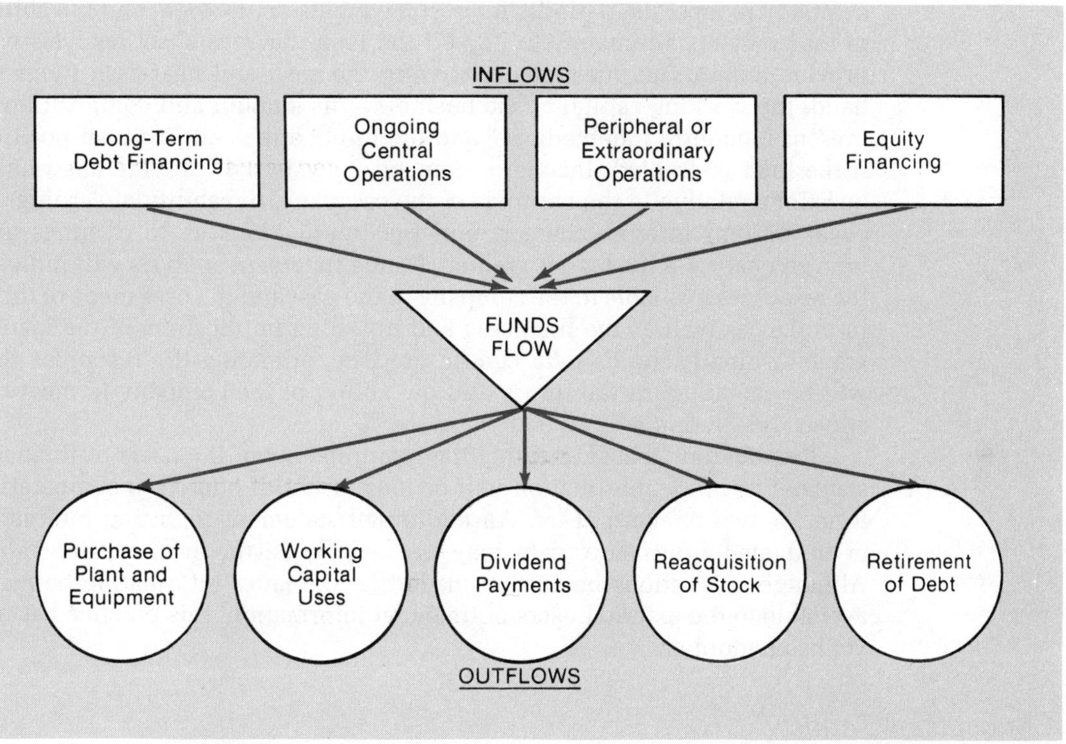

users of financial statements are to be provided the means of fully evaluating the operations of a business unit and the management of its resources.

Thus, although related to the balance sheet and the income statement, the funds statement cannot be considered in any sense a duplication of or substitution for the other financial statements. The Accounting Principles Board, in Opinion No. 19, points out:

> The funds statement is related to both the income statement and the balance sheet and provides information that can be obtained only partially, or at most in piecemeal form, by interpreting them. An income statement together with a statement of retained earnings reports results of operations but does not show other changes in financial position. Comparative balance sheets can significantly augment that information, but the objectives of the funds statement require that all such information be selected, classified, and summarized in meaningful form. The funds statement cannot supplant either the income statement or the balance sheet but is intended to provide information that the other statements either do not provide or provide only indirectly about the flow of funds and changes in financial position during the period.[16]

To illustrate the special contribution made by the funds statement, consider the needs of a prospective creditor and the means for meeting these needs. An individual or group asked to make a long-term loan to a company is concerned with the company's proposed use of the loan, the ability of the

[16] *Opinions of the Accounting Principles Board, No. 19,* "Reporting Changes in Financial Position" (New York: American Institute of Certified Public Accountants, 1971), par. 5.

company to meet the periodic interest payments on the loan, and the ability of the company ultimately to pay off the loan. Balance sheet analysis will provide answers to questions relative to the cash and near-cash items on hand, the working capital of the business—its amount and composition—present long-term indebtedness, and the implications on financial position if the loan is granted. Income statement analysis will provide answers to questions relative to the earnings of the company, the ability of earnings to cover current interest charges, and the implications as to earnings and interest charges if the loan is granted. Funds statement analysis will indicate the resources available to the company in the past and the uses made of those resources as well as the financing and investing implications if the loan is granted. Finally, funds data can be used in estimating the resources that will be generated in the future and the ability of the company to meet the added indebtedness.

It is obvious that in meeting the requirements of the users of financial statements, funds information will be most useful if offered in comparative form for two or more years. An additional statement reporting forecasted or budgeted funds-flow data may prove of equal or even greater value. Although suggestions have been made that the latter information be made available to the external users of financial information, this practice has not yet been adopted.

Concepts of Funds

The term **funds** has been defined in several different ways, and its definition will determine the character of the funds statement prepared. Traditionally, "funds" has most frequently been used to mean working capital, and when so defined, the funds statement reports financing and investing activities in terms of working capital. Defined in those terms, the funds statement provides a summary of the individual sources and uses of working capital for the period. More recently, several companies have begun to define funds as cash, and a funds statement applying this concept provides a presentation of the individual sources and uses of cash for the period and the resulting change in the cash balance.

As noted in Chapter 3, one of the primary objectives of financial reporting is to assist in the predicting of future cash flows. The recent trend toward preparing cash flow funds statements instead of working capital funds statements is consistent with this objective. A cash flow statement stresses liquidity and is intended to help companies with cash management. Thus, companies recognize the need, internally as well as for external reporting, to report the primary inflows and outflows of cash. The Financial Executives Institute and the Financial Accounting Standards Board have both expressed preferences for cash flow statements. A modification of the cash concept defines funds as net current monetary assets—current assets excluding inventory and prepaid items less current liabilities—or simply cash and temporary investments combined. In applying alternative definitions, the funds statement would report the sources and applications of such funds and reconcile their change in successive balance sheets. In practice, funds reporting generally employs the working capital or cash concepts, and subsequent discussions in this text will describe the preparation of funds statements using these concepts.

Illustration of a Funds Statement

By helping to answer questions such as those mentioned earlier, the funds statement serves an important function. The format of the statement, presented on a cash basis, is shown in the following statement for the Barnsby Corporation.

Barnsby Corporation
Statement of Changes in Financial Position—Cash Basis
For the Year Ended December 31, 1984

Cash was provided by:			
Operations:			
Net Income		$ 25,000	
Add items not requiring cash:			
Depreciation	$10,000		
Amortization of patents and goodwill	10,600	20,600	
Working capital from operations		$ 45,600	
Adjustments to cash basis:			
Increase in notes and accounts receivable	$(5,400)		
Decrease in inventory	4,600		
Decrease in notes and accounts payable	(2,500)	(3,300)	
Cash provided by operations		$ 42,300	
Issuance of bonds		95,000	
Issuance of common stock to acquire land		70,000	$207,300
Cash was applied to:			
Payment of dividends		$ 20,000	
Retirement of long-term debt		100,000	
Acquisition of land by issuance of common stock		70,000	190,000
Increase in cash			$ 17,300

Note: The above figures are illustrative only. They cannot be derived from the financial statements presented because comparative statements are not provided.

Another example of a statement of changes in financial position is included in Appendix B. In that example, General Mills uses the concept of cash and short-term investments. This is a change in 1982 for General Mills from previously using a working capital concept of funds. While working capital from operations is still disclosed, the company now highlights and emphasizes the amount of cash provided from operations, cash provided from financing activities, and the amount of cash used for investment activities.

Using the format illustrated, the funds statement has two main sections, showing the **sources** of funds and the **applications** or uses of funds. The difference between total sources and applications is the net increase or decrease in cash or working capital.

As highlighted in the funds statement for Barnsby Corporation, cash was provided by operations and from the issuance of bonds. Additional resources were obtained from the sale of stock and were used to acquire land. The cash generated was applied to dividends and to retire long-term debt, with the difference increasing the cash balance. Thus, the funds statement has accomplished its main purpose—that of identifying the primary sources and applications of funds and, therefore, the major financing activities of the business during a period of time. In Chapter 23 the techniques of preparing and analyzing funds statements are discussed in detail.

QUESTIONS

1. What are the purposes and limitations of the balance sheet?
2. What is the composition of the balance sheet? How is it related to the income statement and the statement of changes in financial position?
3. What is the balance sheet equation? Define each of the elements of that equation.
4. Why is the distinction between current and noncurrent assets and liabilities so important?
5. What criteria are generally used (a) in classifying assets as current or noncurrent? (b) in classifying liabilities as current or noncurrent?
6. Barker's Inc. reports the cash surrender value of life insurance on company officials as a current asset in view of its immediate convertibility into cash. Do you support this treatment? Explain.
7. Indicate under what circumstances each of the following can be considered noncurrent: (a) cash, (b) receivables.
8. Under what circumstances may bonds payable due in six months be reported as a long-term liability, even though they will not be liquidated from accumulated noncurrent funds?
9. What objections can be made to the use of the heading "Deferred costs"?
10. What justification is there for treating intangible items as assets on the balance sheet?
11. Distinguish between the following: (a) contingent liabilities and estimated liabilities, (b) appropriated retained earnings and free retained earnings.
12. What are the major classifications of (a) assets, (b) liabilities, and (c) owners' equity items? Indicate the nature of the items reported within each major classification.
13. Under what circumstances may offset balances be properly recognized on the balance sheet?
14. What is the nature and purpose of notes to financial statements?
15. What is the basic purpose of the statement of changes in financial position? What kind of information does this statement provide that is not readily available from the other general purpose statements?

16. What are the major categories of funds flow for a business entity?
17. What are the most common concepts of funds applied in preparing the statement of changes in financial position? Describe the statement under each of the different fund concepts. Which approach do you support?
18. Why are some companies beginning to report cash flow funds statements instead of working capital funds statements?

DISCUSSION CASES

case 5-1 (Net worth of a business) Consolidated Freight is actively seeking to purchase J. B. Publishing Co. J. B. is resisting such a "take over" primarily on the grounds that the offer is not high enough. Consolidated's offer is $1.5 million based on J. B.'s net worth as of the December 31, 1984, audited balance sheet. J. B. is a fairly diversified company with holdings in real estate in Arizona, Colorado, Wyoming, and Utah, and a fast food operation in California. You have been hired as an "expert witness" to testify as to the reasonableness of the $1.5 million net worth on J. B.'s books. Based on the facts given, for which side of the case would you prefer to testify—Consolidated Freight or J. B. Publishing Co.? Explain.

case 5-2 (Where does all the money go?) Price Brothers Auto Parts has hired you as a consultant to analyze the company's financial position. One of the owners, Dave Price, is in charge of the financial affairs of the company. He makes all the deposits and pays the bills, but has an accountant prepare a balance sheet and an income statement once a year. The business has been quite profitable over the years. In fact, two years ago Price Brothers opened a second store and is considering a third outlet. However, the economy has slowed and the cash position has become very tight. The company is having an increasingly difficult time paying its bills. Dave has not been able to satisfactorily explain to his brothers what is happening. What factors should you consider and what recommendations might you make to Price Brothers?

EXERCISES

exercise 5-1 (Balance sheet classification)

A balance sheet contains the following classifications:

(a) Current assets
(b) Long-term investments
(c) Land, buildings, and equipment
(d) Intangible assets

(e) Other long-term assets
(f) Current liabilities
(g) Long-term debt
(h) Unearned revenues
(i) Other long-term liabilities
(j) Capital stock
(k) Additional paid-in capital
(l) Retained earnings

Indicate by letter how each of the following accounts would be classified. Place a minus sign (−) after all accounts representing offset or contra balances.

___ (1) Discount on Bonds Payable
___ (2) Stock of Subsidiary Corporation
___ (3) 12% Bonds Payable (due in six months)
___ (4) U.S. Treasury Notes
___ (5) Income Tax Payable
___ (6) Sales Tax Payable
___ (7) Estimated Claims Under Guarantees for Service and Replacements
___ (8) Accounts Payable (debit balance)
___ (9) Unearned Rental Revenue (three years in advance)
___ (10) Long-term Advances to Officers
___ (11) Interest Receivable
___ (12) Preferred Stock Retirement Fund
___ (13) Trademarks
___ (14) Allowance for Doubtful Accounts
___ (15) Dividends Payable
___ (16) Accumulated Depreciation
___ (17) Petty Cash Fund
___ (18) Prepaid Rent
___ (19) Prepaid Interest
___ (20) Organization Costs

exercise 5-2 (Balance sheet classification)

State how each of the following accounts should be classified on the balance sheet.

(a) Accumulated Patent Amortization
(b) Retained Earnings
(c) Vacation Pay Payable
(d) Retained Earnings Appropriated for Loss Contingencies
(e) Allowance for Doubtful Accounts
(f) Liability for Pension Payments
(g) Marketable Securities
(h) Paid-In Capital from Sale of Stock at More Than Stated Value
(i) Unamortized Bond Issue Costs
(j) Goodwill
(k) Receivables—U.S. Government Contracts
(l) Advances to Salespersons
(m) Customers Accounts with Credit Balances
(n) Inventory
(o) Patents
(p) Unclaimed Payroll Checks
(q) Employees Income Tax Payable
(r) Subscription Revenue Received in Advance
(s) Interest Payable
(t) Deferred Income Tax (debit balance)
(u) Tools
(v) Deferred Income Tax (credit balance)
(w) Loans to Officers
(x) Leasehold Improvements

exercise 5-3 (Balance sheet classification)

Indicate how each of the following items should be classified on the balance sheet:

(a) Cash surrender value of life insurance.
(b) Sinking fund cash for retirement of bonds.
(c) Bonds payable in six months out of sinking fund cash.
(d) Note receivable that will be collected in 10 annual installments.
(e) Cash deposited with broker on option to buy real estate.
(f) Land held for investment purposes.
(g) Warehouse in process of construction.
(h) Cash fund representing sales tax collections.
(i) Goods in process that will require more than one year for completion.

exercise 5-4 (Determining balance sheet amounts and classifications)

For each of the following items, indicate the proper amount and account classification(s) for the December 31, 1984, balance sheet.

(a) A serial note payable of $80,000 carries an interest rate of 12%, payable semiannually September 1, and March 1. On March 1 of each year $20,000 of the principal is paid.
(b) $30,000 cash has been restricted for the purchase of a factory addition.
(c) Excess cash on hand of $12,000 has been used to purchase securities. As soon as the need for cash arises, these securities will be sold.
(d) A short-term note payable of $15,000 coming due on August 1, 1985; probably will be refinanced during 1985 with a long-term note.
(e) Company's twenty-year bonds payable with a face value of $100,000 were sold on December 28, 1984, for $103,000.

exercise 5-5 (Balance sheet preparation—financial position form)

Using the following data, prepare a balance sheet in financial position form for Frye Company at December 31, 1984.

Accounts payable	$20,000
Accounts receivable	22,000
Accumulated depreciation	18,000
Bonds payable	23,000
Cash	10,000
Land, buildings, and equipment	50,000
Inventory	10,000
Contributed capital	15,000
Rent revenue received in advance	5,000
Retained earnings	11,000

exercise 5-6 (Corrected balance sheet)

The bookkeeper for Fuja Inc. submitted the following balance sheet as of December 31, 1984.

Fuja Inc.
Balance Sheet
December 31, 1984

Assets		Liabilities and Stockholders' Equity	
Cash	$ 60,000	Accounts payable—trade	$100,000
Accounts receivable—trade	100,000	Salaries payable	40,000
Inventories	160,000	Stockholders' equity	280,000
Machinery	40,000		
Goodwill	60,000		
	$420,000		$420,000

Reference to the records of the company indicated the following:

(a) Cash included:

Petty cash	$ 2,000
Payroll account	20,000
Savings account for cash to be used for building remodeling	20,000
General account	18,000
	$60,000

(b) State and local taxes of $4,800 were accrued on December 31. However, $4,800 had been deposited in a special cash account to be used to pay these and neither cash nor the accrued taxes were reported on the balance sheet.
(c) Twenty-five percent of Fuja Inc.'s inventory is rapidly becoming obsolete. The obsolete portion of the inventory as of the balance sheet date was worth only one half of what Fuja Inc. paid for it.
(d) Goods costing $6,000 were shipped to customers on December 30 and 31, at a sales price of $8,800. Goods shipped were not included in the inventory as of December 31. However, receivables were not recognized for the shipment since invoices were not sent out until January 3.
(e) One of Fuja Inc.'s machines costing $16,000 is located on the Autonomous Island Republic, Tropicana. The dictator of Tropicana nationalized several foreign businesses during 1984 and is almost sure to expropriate Fuja Inc.'s machinery for personal use. All machinery was acquired in July of 1984 and will not be depreciated this year.
(f) The corporation had been organized on January 1, 1984, by exchanging 22,000 shares of stock with a par value of $10 per share for the net assets of the partnership Kazu and Komino.

Prepare a corrected balance sheet as of December 31, 1984.

exercise 5-7 (Balance sheet preparation—account form)

From the following chart of accounts, prepare a balance sheet in account form showing all balance sheet items properly classified. (No monetary amounts are to be recognized.)

Accounts Payable
Accounts Receivable
Accumulated Depreciation—Buildings
Accumulated Depreciation—Equipment
Advertising Expense
Allowance for Decline in Value of Marketable Securities
Allowance for Doubtful Accounts
Bonds Payable
Buildings
Cash
Common Stock
Cost of Goods Sold
Deferred Income Tax (debit balance)
Depreciation Expense—Buildings
Dividends
Doubtful Accounts Expense
Equipment
Estimated Warranty Expense Payable
Gain on Sale of Land
Gain on Sale of Marketable Securities
Goodwill
Income Summary
Income Tax Expense
Income Tax Payable
Interest Receivable
Interest Revenue
Inventory
Investment in Bonds
Land
Loss on Purchase Commitments
Marketable Securities
Miscellaneous General Expense
Notes Payable
Paid-In Capital from Sale of Common Stock at More Than Stated Value
Paid-In Capital from Sale of Treasury Stock
Patents
Pension Fund
Premium on Bonds Payable
Prepaid Insurance
Property Tax Expense
Purchases
Purchase Discounts
Retained Earnings
Salaries Payable
Sales
Sales Salaries
Travel Expense

exercise 5-8 (Balance sheet relationships)

For each of the items (a) through (o), indicate the amount that should appear on the balance sheet.

Cook and Company Inc.
Consolidated Balance Sheet
December 31, 1984

Assets			
Current assets:			
Cash			$ (a)
Marketable securities			22,153
Accounts and notes receivable		$ (b)	
Allowance for doubtful accounts and notes receivable		9,622	165,693
Inventories			235,813
Other current assets			10,419
Total current assets			$ (c)
Land, buildings, and equipment		$ (d)	
Accumulated depreciation		352,186	419,418
Other noncurrent assets			9,631
Total assets			$876,312
Liabilities and Stockholders' Equity			
Current liabilities:			
Accounts payable			$ 98,670
Payable to banks			22,858
Income taxes payable			8,328
Current installments of long-term debt			(e)
Accrued expenses			6,610
Total current liabilities			$139,186
Long-term debt		$ (f)	
Deferred income taxes		40,406	
Minority interest in subsidiaries		3,309	
Total noncurrent liabilities			(g)
Total liabilities			$308,655
Contributed Capital:			
Preferred stock, no par value (authorized 1,618 shares; issued 1,115 shares)		$ 16,596	
Common stock, $1 par value per share (authorized 60,000 shares, issued 25,939 shares)	$ (h)		
Additional paid-in capital	(i)	(j)	
Total contributed capital		$ (k)	
Retained earnings:			
Appropriated	$100,000		
Unappropriated	(l)	504,744	
Total contributed capital and retained earnings		$ (m)	
Less treasury stock, at cost (1,236 shares)		26,688	
Total stockholders' equity			(n)
Total liabilities and stockholders' equity			$ (o)

exercise 5-9 (Balance sheet schedules)

In its annual report to stockholders, Truax Inc. presents a condensed balance sheet with detailed data provided in supplementary schedules. From the trial balance of Truax, prepare the following schedules, properly classifying all accounts as to balance sheet categories:

(a) Current assets
(b) Land, buildings, and equipment
(c) Intangible assets
(d) Total assets
(e) Current liabilities
(f) Long-term liabilities
(g) Owners' equity
(h) Total liabilities and owners' equity

Truax Inc.
Trial Balance
December 31, 1984

Cash	18,500	
Marketable Securities—at cost (market, $23,400)	20,000	
Notes Receivable—trade debtors	30,000	
Accrued Interest on Notes Receivable	1,800	
Accounts Receivable—debit balances	79,000	
Accounts Receivable—credit balances		3,600
Allowance for Doubtful Accounts		4,300
Notes Receivable Discounted		10,000
Inventory	56,900	
Prepaid Expenses	3,100	
Accounts Payable—credit balances		26,500
Accounts Payable—debit balances	7,400	
Notes Payable—trade creditors		12,500
Accrued Interest on Notes Payable		800
Land	80,000	
Buildings	170,000	
Accumulated Depreciation—Buildings		34,000
Equipment	48,000	
Accumulated Depreciation—Equipment		5,600
Patents	20,000	
Accumulated Amortization—Patents		5,000
Franchises	10,000	
Bonds Payable, 8%—issue 1 (mature 12/31/87)		50,000
Bonds Payable, 12%—issue 2 (mature 12/31/97)		100,000
Accrued Interest on Bonds Payable		8,000
Premium on Bonds Payable—issue 1		1,500
Discount on Bonds Payable—issue 2	6,500	
Mortgage Payable		72,000
Accrued Interest on Mortgage Payable		2,160
Capital Stock, par value $25, 10,000 shares authorized, 4,000 shares issued		100,000
Additional Paid-In Capital		16,800
Retained Earnings Appropriated for Bond Redemption		35,000
Unappropriated Retained Earnings		73,440
Treasury Stock—at cost (500 shares)	10,000	
	561,200	561,200

exercise 5-10 (Format of funds statement)

From the following information for the MJB Corporation, prepare a statement of changes in financial position on a cash basis for the year ended December 31, 1984.

Amortization of patent	$ 2,200
Depreciation expense	7,000
Issuance of common stock	25,000
Issuance of new bonds payable	15,000
Net income	44,000
Payment of dividend	22,500
Purchase of equipment	33,200
Retirement of long-term debt	45,000
Sale of land (no gain or loss)	3,500
Decrease in accounts receivable	2,100
Increase in inventory	1,200
Increase in accounts payable	1,500

PROBLEMS

problem 5-1 (Computing balance sheet components)

Booth Tractors Inc. furnishes you with the following list of accounts.

Accounts Payable	$ 55,000	Investment in Kemp Oil Co. Stock (70% of outstanding Stock owned for control purposes)	$85,000
Accounts Receivable	40,000	Investment in Tooke Co. Stock (current marketable securities)	21,000
Accumulated Depreciation	44,000	Paid-In Capital in Excess of Par	45,000
Advances to Salespersons	5,000	Premium on Bonds Payable	6,000
Advertising Expense	72,000	Prepaid Interest Expense	3,000
Allowance for Doubtful Accounts	8,000	Rent Revenue	27,000
Bonds Payable	70,000	Rent Revenue Received in Advance	2,000
Cash	12,000	Retained Earnings	40,000
Certificates of Deposit	20,000	Retained Earnings Appropriated for Loss Contingencies	30,000
Common Stock (par)	120,000	Taxes Payable	10,000
Customer Accounts with Credit Balances	4,000	Tools	68,000
Deferred Income Tax (credit balance)	53,000		
Equipment	184,000		
Inventory	49,000		

Instructions: From the above list of accounts, determine working capital, total assets, total liabilities, and stockholders' equity per share of stock (50,000 shares outstanding).

problem 5-2 (Classified balance sheet)

Below is a list of account titles and balances for the Lott Company as of January 31, 1985.

Accounts Payable	$85,800	Inventory	$154,600
Accounts Receivable	106,000	Investment in Undeveloped Properties	212,000
Accumulated Depreciation—Buildings	140,000	Land	130,000
Accumulated Depreciation—Machinery and Equipment	40,000	Machinery and Equipment	144,000
Allowance for Doubtful Notes and Accounts	4,200	Miscellaneous Supplies Inventories	6,200
Buildings	300,000	Notes Payable (current)	69,260
Cash in Banks	107,300	Notes Payable (due 1990)	50,000
Cash on Hand	8,880	Notes Receivable	22,400
Cash Surrender Value of Life Insurance	17,000	Preferred Stock, $6 par	300,000
Claim for Income Tax Refund	5,000	Premium on Common Stock	60,000
Common Stock, $20 par	600,000	Prepaid Insurance	4,500
Employees Income Tax Payable	3,640	Retained Earnings (debit balance)	11,740
Income Tax Payable	24,600	Salaries and Wages Payable	7,400
Interest Payable	2,000	Temporary Investments in Marketable Securities	156,880
Interest Receivable	400		

Instructions: Prepare a properly classified balance sheet.

problem 5-3 (Classified balance sheet—account form including notes)

Account balances and supplemental information for Sunshine Research Corp. as of December 31, 1984, are as follows:

Accounts Payable	$ 32,160	Furniture, Fixtures, and Store Equipment	$769,000
Accounts Receivable—Trade	57,731	Inventory	201,620
Accumulated Depreciation—Leasehold Improvements and Equipment	579,472	Investment in Unconsolidated Subsidiary	80,000
Additional Paid-In Capital	100,000	Insurance Claims Receivable	120,000
Allowance for Doubtful Accounts	1,731	Land	6,000
Automotive Equipment	132,800	Leasehold Improvements	65,800
Cash	30,600	7½–12% Mortgage Notes	200,000
Cash Surrender Value of Life Insurance	3,600	Notes Payable—Banks	17,000
Common Stock	200,000	Notes Payable—Trade	63,540
Deferred Income Tax (credit balance)	45,000	Patent Licenses	57,402
Dividends Payable	37,500	Prepaid Insurance	5,500
Franchises	12,150	Profit Sharing, Payroll, and Vacation Payable	40,000
		Retained Earnings	225,800
		Tax Receivable—In Litigation	13,000

Supplemental information:

(a) Depreciation is provided by the straight-line method over the estimated useful lives of the assets.
(b) Common stock is $5 par, and 40,000 of the 100,000 authorized shares were issued and are outstanding.
(c) The cost of an exclusive franchise to import a foreign company's ball bearings and a related patent license are being amortized on the straight-line method over their remaining lives: franchise, 10 years; patents, 15 years.
(d) Inventories are stated at the lower of cost or market: cost was determined by the specific identification method.
(e) Insurance claims based upon the opinion of an independent insurance adjustor are for property damages at the central warehouse. These claims are estimated to be one-half collectible in the following year and one-half collectible thereafter.
(f) The company leases all of its buildings from various lessors. Estimated fixed lease obligations are $50,000 per year for the next ten years. The leases do not meet the criteria for capitalization.
(g) The company is currently in litigation over a claimed overpayment of income tax of $13,000. In the opinion of counsel, the claim is valid. The company is contingently liable on guaranteed notes worth $17,000.

Instructions: Prepare a properly classified balance sheet in account form. Include all notes and parenthetical notations necessary to properly disclose the essential financial data.

problem 5-4 (Corrected balance sheet)

The following balance sheet was prepared by the accountant for Pioneer Company.

Pioneer Company
Balance Sheet
June 30, 1985

Cash	$ 25,500
Marketable securities (includes 25% ownership in stock of Pine Mountain Developers, at cost of $250,000)	332,000
Inventories (net of amount still due suppliers of $75,980)	624,600
Prepaid expenses (includes a deposit of $10,000 made on inventories to be delivered in 18 months)	32,100
Plant assets (excluding $50,000 of equipment still in use, but fully depreciated)	220,000
Goodwill (based upon estimate of President of Pioneer Company)	50,000
Total assets	$1,284,200

Liabilities and Stockholders' Equity	
Notes payable ($75,000 due in 1987)	$ 135,000
Accounts payable (not including amount due to suppliers of inventory—see above)	142,000
Long-term liability under pension plan	80,000
Appropriation for building expansion	90,000
Accumulated depreciation—fixed assets	73,000
Taxes payable	44,500
Bonds payable (net of discount of $30,000)	270,000
Deferred income tax credit	83,000
Common stock (20,000 shares @ $10 par)	200,000
Premium on common stock	50,500
Unappropriated retained earnings	116,200
Total liabilities and stockholders' equity	$1,284,200

Instructions: Prepare a corrected statement in report form using appropriate account titles.

problem 5-5 (Classified balance sheet—report form)

The Oakley Ranch summarizes its financial position in the following letter to their accountant.

January 20, 1985

Dear Collin:

The following information should be of value to you in preparing the balance sheet for Oakley Ranch as of December 31, 1984. The balance of cash as of December 31 as reported on the bank statement was $43,825. There were still outstanding checks of $9,320 that had not cleared the bank and cash on hand of $3,640 was not deposited until January 4, 1985.

Customers owed the company $40,500 at December 31. We estimated 5% of this amount will never be collected. We owe suppliers $32,000 for poultry feed purchased in November and December. About 80% of this feed was used before December 31.

Because we think the price of grain will rise in 1985, we are holding 10,000 bushels of wheat and 5,000 bushels of oats until spring. The market value at December 31 was $3.50 per bushel of wheat and $1.50 per bushel of oats. We estimate that both prices will increase 10% by selling time. We are not able to estimate the cost of raising this product.

Oakley Ranch owns 1,850 acres of land. Two separate purchases of land were made as follows: 1,250 acres at $200 per acre in 1967, and 600 acres at $400 per acre in 1972. Similar land is currently selling for $800 per acre. The balance of the mortgage on the two parcels of land is $270,000 at December 31; 10% of this mortgage must be paid in 1985.

Our farm buildings and equipment cost us $176,400 and on the average are 50% depreciated. If we were to replace these buildings and equipment at today's prices, we believe we would be conservative in estimating a cost of $300,000.

We have not paid property tax of $5,500 for 1985 billed us in late November. Our estimated income tax for 1984 is $18,500. A refund claim for $2,800 has been filed relative to the 1982 income tax return. The claim arose because of an error made on the 1982 return.

The operator of the ranch will receive a bonus of $7,000 for 1984 operations. It will be paid when the entire grain crop has been sold.

As you will recall, we issued 14,000 shares of $10 par stock upon incorporation. The ranch received $255,000 as net proceeds from the stock issue. Dividends of $45,000 were declared last month and will be paid on February 1, 1985.

The new year appears to hold great promise. Thanks for your help in preparing this statement.

Sincerely,
Alice Mahle
President—Oakley Ranch

Instructions: Based upon this information, prepare a properly classified balance sheet in report form as of December 31, 1984.

problem 5-6 (Corrected balance sheet—report form)

The bookkeeper for the Streamline Furniture Company submits the following condensed balance sheet.

Streamline Furniture Company
Balance Sheet
June 30, 1985

Current assets	$252,150	Current liabilities	$136,550
Other assets	638,400	Other liabilities	90,000
		Capital	664,000
	$890,550		$890,550

A review of the account balances reveals the following data:

(a) An analysis of current assets discloses the following:

Cash	$ 49,250
Marketable securities held as temporary investment	60,000
Trade accounts receivable	57,400
Inventories, including advertising supplies of $2,500	85,500
	$252,150

(b) Other assets include:

Land, buildings, and equipment, cost $665,000, depreciated value	$549,000
Deposit with a supplier for merchandise ordered for August delivery	2,000
Goodwill recorded on the books to cancel losses incurred by the company in prior years	87,400
	$638,400

(c) Current liabilities include:

Payroll payable	$ 7,650
Taxes payable	4,000
Rent payable	12,000
Trade accounts payable, $90,400, less a $1,500 debit balance reported in the account of a vendor to whom merchandise had been returned after the account had been paid in full	88,900
Notes payable	24,000
	$136,550

(d) Other liabilities include:

9% mortgage on land, buildings and equipment, payable in semiannual installments of $9,000 through June 30, 1990	$ 90,000

(e) Capital includes:

20,000 shares of preferred stock, $20 par	$400,000
160,000 shares of common stock at stated value	264,000
	$664,000

(f) Common shares were originally issued for a total consideration of $400,000, but the losses of the company for past years were charged against the common stock balance.

Instructions: Using the balance sheet and the related data, prepare a corrected balance sheet in report form showing individual asset, liability, and capital balances properly classified.

problem 5-7 (Corrected balance sheet—report form)

The following balance sheet is submitted to you for inspection and review.

Aaron Freight Company
Balance Sheet
December 31, 1984

Assets		Liabilities and Stockholders' Equity	
Cash	$ 50,000	Miscellaneous liabilities	$ 2,500
Accounts receivable	180,000	Loan payable	56,250
Inventories	220,000	Accounts payable	146,250
Prepaid insurance	12,500	Capital stock	250,000
Land, buildings, and equipment	325,000	Paid-in capital	332,500
	$787,500		$787,500

In the course of the review you find the data listed below:

(a) The possibility of uncollectible accounts on accounts receivable has not been considered. It is estimated that uncollectible accounts will total $5,000.
(b) $50,000 representing the cost of a large-scale newspaper advertising campaign completed in 1984 has been added to the inventories, since it is believed that this campaign will benefit sales of 1985. It is also found that inventories include merchandise of $16,250 received on December 31 that has not yet been recorded as a purchase.
(c) Prepaid insurance consists of $1,000, the cost of fire insurance for 1985, and $11,500, the cash surrender value on officers' life insurance policies.
(d) The books show that land, buildings, and equipment have a cost of $525,000 with depreciation of $200,000 recognized in prior years. However, these balances include fully depreciated equipment of $75,000 that has been scrapped and is no longer on hand.
(e) Miscellaneous liabilities of $2,500 represent salaries payable of $7,500, less noncurrent advances of $5,000 made to company officials.
(f) Loan payable represents a loan from the bank that is payable in regular quarterly installments of $6,250.
(g) Tax liabilities not shown are estimated at $11,250.
(h) Deferred income tax (credit) arising from timing differences in recognizing income totals $23,750. This tax was not included in the balance sheet.
(i) Capital stock consists of 6,250 shares of preferred 6% stock, par $20, and 12,500 shares of common stock, stated value $10.
(j) Capital stock had been issued for a total consideration of $312,500, the amount received in excess of the par and stated values of the stock being reported as paid-in capital.

Instructions: Prepare a corrected balance sheet in report form with accounts properly classified.

problem 5-8 (Classified balance sheet—report form)

Billy Bailey incorporated his concrete manufacturing operations on January 1, 1984, by issuing 10,000 shares of $10 par common stock to himself. The following balance sheet for the new corporation was prepared.

Concrete Corporation
Balance Sheet
January 1, 1984

Cash	$ 10,000	Accounts payable—suppliers	$ 45,000
Accounts receivable	45,000	Capital stock, $10 par	100,000
Inventory	75,000	Premium on capital stock	100,000
Equipment	115,000		
	$245,000		$245,000

During 1984, Concrete Corporation engaged in the following transactions:

(a) Concrete Corporation produced concrete costing $270,000. Concrete costs consisted of $200,000, raw materials purchases; $25,000, labor; and $45,000, overhead. Concrete Corporation paid the $45,000 owed to suppliers as of January 1, and $130,000 of the $200,000 of raw materials purchased during the year. All labor, except for $1,500, and recorded overhead were paid for in cash during the year. Other operating expenses of $15,000 were incurred and paid in 1984.
(b) Concrete costing $300,000 was sold during 1984 for $425,000. All sales were made on credit, and collections on receivables were $365,000.
(c) Concrete Corporation purchased machinery (fair market value = $190,000) by trading in old equipment costing $50,000 and paying $140,000 in cash. There is no accumulated depreciation on the old equipment as it was revalued when the new corporation was formed.
(d) Concrete Corporation issued an additional 4,000 shares of common stock for $25 per share and declared a dividend of $4 per share to all stockholders of record as of December 31, 1984, payable on January 15, 1985.
(e) Depreciation expense for 1984 was $27,000. The allowance for doubtful accounts after year-end adjustments is $2,500.

Instructions: Prepare a properly classified balance sheet in report form for the Concrete Corporation as of December 31, 1984.

problem 5-9 (Analysis of financial position)

Fairbanks Realty Inc., a dealer in land, is searching for funds for a long-term expansion program. Fairbanks must maintain a working capital balance of $12,000,000 to be in a favorable position for borrowing. The post-closing trial balance as of December 31, 1984, is as follows:

Accounts Payable—Trade		3,678,000
Accounts Receivable	14,700,000	
Accumulated Depreciation—Office Buildings		24,000,000
Additional Paid-In Capital		22,500,000
Advances to Affiliates	1,650,000	
Allowance for Doubtful Accounts		189,000
Bonds (payable in installments of $1,500,000 on June 1 of each year)		22,500,000
Cash Surrender Value of Life Insurance	45,000	
Common Stock, $10 par		20,000,000
First National Bank Fund for Construction of Office Building	2,400,000	
First National Bank—General Account	1,866,000	
Income Tax Payable		1,455,000
Land	42,000,000	
Loans on Life Insurance Policies		30,000
Marketable Securities	9,000,000	
Notes Payable to Bank		6,000,000
Office Building	36,000,000	
Office Supplies Inventory	225,000	
Prepaid Insurance	75,000	
Retained Earnings		7,159,000
Salaries and Wages Payable		450,000

Additional investigation revealed:

(a) Accounts receivable consist of:

Employee advances—long-term	$ 1,500,000
Due in 1986 from sale of old office building	3,750,000
Installment notes receivable—trade	7,500,000
Accounts receivable—trade	1,950,000
	$14,700,000

(b) Land includes several parcels purchased for $15,000,000, which have become subject to severe flooding, thus lowering the value to $750,000. All the land is for sale except the $15,900,000 site for Fairbanks new office building.
(c) Fairbanks purchased 25% of the voting stock of a savings and loan company for $7,500,000 and included the acquisition in marketable securities.
(d) The loans on the life insurance policies come due in 18 months; the bank notes fall due in 8 months.

Instructions: Show whether Fairbanks Realty Inc. is in a favorable position for borrowing money by preparing the first portion of a balance sheet in financial position form: current assets less current liabilities equal working capital. Because of the nature of the business, land for sale is considered inventory.

problem 5-10 (Corrected balance sheet—financial position form)

The bookkeeper for the Sweet Tooth Bakery prepares the following condensed balance sheet.

Sweet Tooth Bakery
Condensed Balance Sheet
December 31, 1984

Current assets	$53,415
Less current liabilities	29,000
Working capital	$24,415
Add other assets	60,120
	$84,535
Deduct other liabilities	3,600
Investment in business	$80,935

A review of the account balances disclosed the following data:

(a) An analysis of the current asset grouping revealed the following:

Cash	$ 4,600
Trade accounts receivable (fully collectible)	12,500
Notes receivable (notes of customer who has been declared bankrupt and is unable to pay anything on the obligations)	1,000
Marketable securities, at cost (market value, $2,575)	4,250
Inventory	28,965
Cash surrender value of insurance on officers' lives	2,100
Total current assets	$53,415

The inventory account was found to include the cost of supplies of $425, a delivery truck acquired at the end of 1984 at a cost of $2,100, and fixtures at a depreciated value of $10,400. The fixtures had been acquired in 1981 at a cost of $12,500.

(b) The total for other assets was determined as follows:

Land and buildings, at cost of acquisition on July 1, 1982	$77,000
Less balance due on mortgage, $16,000, and accrued interest on mortgage, $880 (mortgage is payable in annual installments of $4,000 on July 1 of each year together with interest for the year at that time at 11%).	16,880
Total other assets	$60,120

It was estimated that the land, at the time of purchase, was worth $30,000. Buildings as of December 31, 1984, were estimated to have a remaining life of 17½ years.

(c) Current liabilities represented balances that were payable to trade creditors. Other liabilities consisted of withholding, payroll, real estate and other taxes payable to the federal, state, and local governments. However, no recognition was given the accrued salaries, utilities, and other miscellaneous items totaling $350.

(d) The company was originally organized in 1980 when 5,000 shares of no par stock with a stated value of $5 per share were issued in exchange for business assets that were recognized on the books at their fair market value of $55,000.

Instructions: Prepare a corrected balance sheet in financial position form with the items properly classified.

problem 5-11 (Format of funds statement)

The following data were taken from the records of Peabody Produce Company for the year ended June 30, 1984.

Borrowed on long-term notes	$20,000
Issued capital stock	50,000
Purchased equipment	27,000
Net income	37,000
Purchased treasury stock	2,000
Paid dividends	30,000
Depreciation expense	12,000
Retired bonds payable	70,000
Goodwill amortization	2,000
Sold long-term investment (at cost)	5,000
Decrease in working capital	3,000
Increase in cash	4,000

Instructions:

(1) From the information given, prepare in good form a statement of changes in financial position on (a) a working capital basis, (b) a cash basis.

(2) Briefly explain what an interested party would learn from studying Peabody Produce Company's funds statement.

Part 2 Assets

6 CASH AND TEMPORARY INVESTMENTS

CHAPTER OBJECTIVES

Identify criteria for classifying and disclosing the various components of cash.

Discuss potential problems in cash control and methods of reducing the probability of loss and misappropriation.

Describe and illustrate the imprest system of accounting for petty cash.

Describe and illustrate procedures for reconciling book cash balances and bank statement balances.

Discuss the nature of temporary investments.

Describe and illustrate accounting for purchases and sales of marketable securities.

Describe, illustrate, and evaluate alternative methods of accounting for changes in market values of marketable securities.

The first part of this book has established a perspective of accounting and its theoretical foundation. Part II explores items classified as **assets,** beginning with the most liquid assets, cash and temporary investments.

CASH

Cash is an important item on the financial statements. It is involved in most business transactions. This is due to the nature of business transactions, which include a price and conditions calling for settlement in terms of a medium of exchange. The standard medium of exchange is cash. Even if cash is not directly involved in a transaction, it provides the basis for measurement and accounting for all other items.

In striking contrast to the activity of cash is its unproductive nature. Since cash is the measure of value, it cannot expand or grow unless it is converted into other properties. Excessive balances of cash on hand are often referred to as **idle cash.** Efficient cash management requires available cash to be continuously working in one of several ways—e.g., as part of the operating cycle or as a short-term or long-term investment.

Composition of Cash

Cash is composed of commercial and savings deposits in banks and elsewhere and items on hand that can be used as a medium of exchange or that are acceptable for deposit at face value by a bank. **Cash on hand** would include petty cash funds, change funds, and other regularly used and unexpended funds, together with items such as personal checks, travelers' checks, cashiers' checks, bank drafts, and money orders.

"Acceptance at face value on deposit" is a satisfactory test in classifying as cash the items found in the cash drawer. It is assumed that deposits in a bank are made regularly and that deposits become the basis for disbursements by the depositor. Although postage stamps may in some instances pass for mail payments of small amounts, they are not accepted for deposit and should be classified as office supplies. Post-dated checks are in effect notes receivable and should not be recognized as cash until the time they can be deposited. Checks deposited but returned by the bank because of insufficient funds in the debtor's account are receivables. Cash-due memorandums for money advanced to officers and employees are receivable items, in some instances less satisfactory receivables than those of trade customers. A note or draft left at a bank for collection represents a receivable until collection is made and the amount is added to the depositor's account. Stocks, bonds, and other marketable securities, although immediately convertible into cash, generally are not used as a means for making payments, hence do not constitute cash but should be recognized as temporary or long-term investments.

Since the concept of cash embodies the standard of value, no valuation problems are encountered in reporting those items qualifying as cash. When cash is comprised solely of cash on hand and unrestricted demand deposits, the total generally appears on the balance sheet as a single item "Cash." Other components of cash, however, should be disclosed or reported as separate items.

Deposits that are not immediately available due to withdrawal restrictions require separate identification. Certificates of deposit (CDs), for example, generally may be withdrawn only at specified maturity dates. Thus, CDs are preferably reported parenthetically or separately as short-term or long-term investments.

Deposits in foreign banks subject to immediate and unrestricted withdrawal qualify as cash. Such balances should be converted into their U.S. dollar equivalents as of the date of the balance sheet. However, cash in foreign banks that is restricted as to use or withdrawal and cash in closed banks should be designated as claims or receivables of a current or noncurrent character and should be reported subject to allowances for losses on their realization.

Cash balances specifically designated by management for special purposes may be separately reported. Those cash balances to be applied to some current purpose or current obligation are properly reported in the current section on the balance sheet. For example, cash funds for employees' travel, payment of current interest and dividends, or payment of taxes or other obligations included in the current liabilities may be separately reported but are still classified as current.

Cash restricted as to use by agreement should be separately designated and reported. Restricted cash should be reported as a current item only if it is to be applied to some current purpose or obligation. Classification of the cash balance as current or noncurrent should parallel the classification applied to the liability.

Cash balances not available for current purposes require separate designation and classification under a noncurrent heading on the balance sheet. The noncurrent classification applies to items such as the following: time deposits not currently available as a result of withdrawal restrictions; cash deposits on bids or options that may be applied to the acquisition of noncurrent assets; and cash funds held by trustees for plant acquisitions, bond retirement, and pension payments.

A credit balance in the cash account resulting from the issuance of checks in excess of the amount on deposit is known as a **cash overdraft** and should be reported as a current liability. An overdraft does not necessarily embarrass a company if a number of checks are outstanding and deposits are made to cover the checks before clearance. When a company has two balances with a single bank, there can be no objection to the offsetting of the overdraft against an account with a positive balance; failure by the depositor to meet the overdraft will actually result in bank action to effect such an offset. However, when a company has accounts with two different banks and there is a positive balance in one account and an overdraft in the other, both an asset balance and a liability balance should be recognized in view of the claim against one bank and an obligation to the other; if recognition of an overdraft is to be avoided, cash should actually be transferred to cover the deficiency.

In summary, cash is a current asset comprised of coin, currency, and other items which (1) serve as a medium of exchange and (2) provide the basis for measurement in accounting. Most negotiable instruments (e.g., checks, bank drafts, and money orders) qualify as cash because they can be converted to coin or currency on demand or are acceptable for deposit at face value by a bank. Components of cash restricted as to use or withdrawal should be disclosed or separately reported and classified as an investment, a receivable, or other asset. The objective of disclosure is to provide the user of financial statements with information to assist in evaluating the entity's ability to meet obligations (its liquidity and solvency) and in assessing the effectiveness of cash management.

Compensating Balances. In connection with financing arrangements, it is common practice for a company to agree to maintain a minimum or average balance on deposit with a bank or other lending institution. These **compensating balances** are defined by the SEC as "...that portion of any demand deposit (or any time deposit or certificate of deposit) maintained by a corporation...which constitutes support for existing borrowing arrangements of the corporation...with a lending institution. Such arrangements would include both outstanding borrowings and the assurance of future credit availability."[1]

Compensating balances provide a source of funds to the lender as partial compensation for credit extended. In effect, such arrangements raise the interest rate of the borrower because a portion of the amount on deposit with the lending institution cannot be used. These balances present an accounting problem from the standpoint of disclosure. Readers of financial statements are likely to assume the entire cash balance is available to meet current obligations, when, in fact, part of the balance is restricted.

The solution to this problem is to disclose the extent of compensating balances. The SEC recommends any "legally restricted" deposits held as compensating balances be segregated and reported separately. If the balances are the result of short-term financing arrangements, they should be shown separately among the "cash items" in the current asset section; if the compensating balances are in connection with long-term agreements, they should be classified as noncurrent, either as investments or "other assets." Where deposits are not legally restricted, but where compensating balance agreements still exist, the amounts and nature of the arrangements should be disclosed in the notes to the financial statements.

Electronic Funds Transfer. During the past several years, some companies have experimented with a new method of transferring funds called **Electronic Funds Transfer (EFT).** This is a method of transferring funds to and from a bank electronically with no paper (e.g., currency or checks) involved in the transaction. EFT also makes cash information available upon request at any time through the use of a computer hook-up between the bank and its client.

Current uses of EFT systems include:

(1) *Balance reporting systems,* which provide the user with the bank balance through terminal-based computers.

---

[1]Securities and Exchange Commission, *Accounting Series Release No. 148*, "Disclosure of Compensating Balances and Short-Term Borrowing Arrangements" (Washington: U. S. Government Printing Office, 1973).

(2) *Zero-balance receipt and disbursement accounts,* where the bank has instructions from its customer to maintain the customer's demand account (non-interest-bearing) at zero and to transfer funds to these accounts from interest-bearing accounts only as needed. The purpose of these accounts is obviously to keep idle funds to a minimum.
(3) *Direct payroll deposit,* which involves a corporation transferring electronically the amount due an employee to the employee's bank through an automated clearing house rather than issuing paychecks to its employees. Some corporations are not supportive of this use of EFT because the widely used "float period" is eliminated. The float period is the time required for the company's check to actually clear the bank. Usually it takes 2-5 days from the time the company issues a check to the time the check is deposited and eventually charged to the company's account.
(4) *Individual-to-business bill payment,* an arrangement where the individual authorizes the business to electronically bill the individual's demand account for the amount due. The bank transfers the funds to the business and notifies the individual of the charge to the individual's account.

The future possibilities of EFT are limitless. While EFT will not alter the general nature of cash, if EFT is widely accepted, it will certainly impact on the manner of handling cash, especially where computer accounting systems are concerned. As one individual has stated, "With the development of electronic funds transfer systems (EFTS), electronic data processing in business is about to undergo a revolution as profound as that caused by the introduction of computers to accounting in the early 1960s."[2]

Control of Cash

The term **internal control** encompasses the systems, procedures, and policies employed by an enterprise to help assure that its transactions are properly authorized and are appropriately executed and recorded. It is a term that embraces both administrative controls and accounting controls. **Administrative controls** relate to the plan of organization and procedures required for management's authorization of transactions. This is the first step in establishing **accounting controls,** which include the plans, procedures, and records necessary for safeguarding assets and producing reliable financial records. Accounting controls are specifically designed to provide reasonable assurance that:

(a) Transactions are executed in accordance with management's general or specific authorization.
(b) Transactions are recorded as necessary (1) to permit preparation of financial statements in conformity with generally accepted accounting principles or any other criteria applicable to such statements and (2) to maintain accountability for assets.
(c) Access to assets is permitted only in accordance with management's authorization.

---

[2]Norman R. Lyons, "Segregation of Functions in EFTS," *Journal of Accountancy,* October 1978, p. 89. See also Sanford Rose, "Checkless Banking is Bound to Come," *Fortune,* June 1977.

(d) The recorded accountability for assets is compared with the existing assets at reasonable intervals and appropriate action is taken with respect to any differences.[3]

Managers and auditors have long recognized the need for effective internal controls. However, with the passage of the Foreign Corrupt Practices Act of 1977, the emphasis on internal controls is significantly increased. This is due to a provision in the Act that requires all public companies, not just those with foreign operations, to keep good accounting records and to maintain a sufficient system of internal accounting controls. The Act amends portions of the Securities and Exchange Act of 1934 and incorporates the definitions of internal control quoted previously. Thus, by law, all companies falling under the jurisdiction of the SEC are now required to devise and maintain a "sufficient" system of internal control. The exact meaning of sufficient is not clear; to date specific guidelines have not been established. It is apparent, however, that managers, accountants, and others involved with public companies should consider carefully the increased responsibilities being imposed in the internal control area.

Obviously, the system of internal control must be developed with appropriate regard to the size and nature of the particular unit to be served. Its design should provide the maximum contributions practicable considering the special risks faced as well as the costs of providing controls. The increased use of data processing equipment for processing accounting transactions has not eliminated the need for carefully designed control systems; on the contrary, it may have increased the need. As new equipment is acquired and introduced into a system, the establishment or modification of controls should be considered.

In any system of internal accounting control, special emphasis must be placed on the procedures for handling and accounting for cash.

Problems in Cash Control. Because of the characteristics of cash—its small bulk, its lack of owner identification, and its immediate transferability—it is the asset most subject to misappropriation, intentional or otherwise. Losses can be avoided only by careful control of cash from the time it is received until the time it is spent.

Control over business cash normally requires as a minimum the separation of cash custodial functions and cash recording functions. When the same persons have access to cash and also to cash records, the business becomes vulnerable to the misappropriation of cash and to the manipulation or falsification of cash records. The following are representative of practices that may develop under these circumstances: (1) cash receipts from sales, from recoveries of accounts previously written off, from refunds on invoice overpayments, and from other sources are understated, the unrecorded cash being pocketed; (2) receivables are not entered on the books and cash col-

---

[3]*Statement on Auditing Standards No. 1*, "Codification of Auditing Standards and Procedures" (New York: American Institute of Certified Public Accountants, 1973), par. 320.28.

lected on these receivables is withheld; (3) customers' accounts are credited for remittances but Sales Returns or Doubtful Accounts Expense is debited and the cash is withheld; (4) checks for personal purposes are debited to business expense; (5) invoices, vouchers, receipts, payroll records, or vouchers once approved and paid are used in support of fictitious charges, and endorsements on checks issued in payment of these charges are subsequently forged; (6) the cash balance is misstated by erroneous footings in the cash receipts and disbursement records, cash equivalent to the misstatement being withheld.

Two additional practices, check kiting and lapping, may be found when those who handle cash also maintain the cash records of the business.

Check kiting occurs when at the end of a month a transfer of funds is made by check from one bank to another to cover a cash shortage, and the entry to record the issue of the check is held over until the beginning of the new period. A cash increase in the customer's balance is recognized by the second bank in the current month as a result of the receipt of the check, but a corresponding decrease in the customer's balance is not recognized by the first bank because the check has not yet been presented for payment. When the bank statements are received, the balance in the bank in which the check was deposited shows an increase. At the same time, the balance shown in the bank on which the check was drawn remains unchanged. A cash shortage is thus temporarily concealed.

Lapping occurs when a customer's remittance is misappropriated, the customer's account being credited when cash is collected from another customer at a later date. This process may be continued with further misappropriations and increasing delays in postings. To illustrate lapping, assume that on successive days cash is received from customers A, B, and C in amounts of $75, $125, and $120. A's payment is misappropriated. A is subsequently credited with $75 out of B's payment and the difference, $50, is misappropriated. B is credited for $125 upon C's $120 payment and $5 is returned on the amounts originally *borrowed*. The shortage at this point is $120, the unrecorded credit to C's account. This procedure can be continued with but slight delay in recording any customer's payment. The embezzler frequently invests the money, intending to return it after a profit has been made on the investment. Unable to make restitution, the embezzler may resort to a fictitious entry debiting Doubtful Accounts Expense or some other expense account and crediting the customers' balances to bring these up to date.

Cash Shortage and Overage. When cash records and summaries report a cash total differing from the amount available for deposit, and it is assumed that cash has been lost or errors have been made in making change, an adjustment is made to a **cash short and over** account. The offsetting part of the entry is to the regular cash account. Unless theft is involved, the cash short and over account will usually "net" to a nominal amount during the year. Any balance in this account may be reported as miscellaneous expense or revenue in summarizing net income. However, a cash shortage resulting from employee defalcation should be charged to an employee account or the bonding company liable for such losses. Failure to recover the shortage requires the recognition of a loss from this source.

Attributes of Cash Control Systems. The system for controlling cash must be adapted to a particular business. It is not feasible to describe all the features and techniques employed in businesses of various kinds and sizes. In general, however, systems of cash control deny access to the accounting records to those who handle cash. This reduces the possibility of improper entries to conceal the misuse of cash receipts and cash payments. The probability of misappropriation of cash is greatly reduced if two or more employees must conspire in an embezzlement. Further, systems normally provide for separation of the receiving and paying functions. The basic characteristics of a system of cash control are:

(1) Specifically assigned responsibility for handling cash receipts.
(2) Separation of handling and recording cash receipts.
(3) Daily deposit of all cash received.
(4) Voucher system to control cash payments.
(5) Internal audits at irregular intervals.

Specifically Assigned Responsibility for Handling Cash Receipts. A fundamental principle in controlling any asset is that the responsibility be specifically assigned to one person. This principle is especially vital in the area of cash. If more than one person must have access to the same cash fund at different times, a reconciliation of the cash on hand should be made each time the responsibility is shifted. Any shortage or questionable transaction can then be identified with a particular person.

Separation of Handling and Recording Cash Receipts. An adequate control system normally requires cash from sales and cash remittances from customers be made available directly to the treasurer or the cashier for deposit, while records related to these transactions, as well as records related to bank deposits, be made available directly to the accounting department. It is also desirable that comparisons of bank deposits with the book records of cash be made regularly by a third party who is engaged neither in the cash handling nor in the cash recording functions. Frequently, for example, a clerk opens the mail, prepares lists of remittances in duplicate, and then sends the cash and one copy of the list of remittances to the cashier and the second copy of the list to the accounting department. Readings of cash registers are made by some responsible individual other than the cashier at the end of the day. The cash, together with a summary of the receipts, is sent to the cashier; a summary of the receipts is also sent to the accounting department. Although deposits in the bank are made by the cashier or treasurer, entries on the books are made from lists of remittances and register readings prepared by individuals not otherwise involved in handling or recording cash. Members of the accounting or auditing staff compare periodic bank statements with related data on the books to determine whether the data are in agreement. If customers' remittances are not listed and the cash is misused, statements to customers will report excessive amounts and protests will lead to sources of the discrepancies; if cash receipts listed are not deposited properly, the bank record will not agree with the cash records.

Daily Deposit of All Cash Received. The daily deposit of all cash received prevents sums of cash from lying around the office and being used for other than business purposes. Officers and employees have less opportunity to borrow on IOUs. Both the temptation for misappropriation of cash and the risk of theft of cash are avoided. The bank protects company funds and releases these only upon proper company authorization. When the full receipts are deposited daily, the bank's record of deposits must agree with the depositor's record of cash receipts. This double record provides an automatic check over cash receipts.

Voucher System to Control Cash Payments. The use of a voucher system to control cash payments is a desirable feature of cash control. Vouchers authorizing disbursements of cash by check are made at the time goods or services are received and found acceptable. Entries in the voucher register recording the expenditures and the authorizations for payment are made by the accounting department. Checks are also prepared and are sent, together with documents supporting the disbursements, to the person specifically authorized to make payment, normally the official designated as treasurer. This person signs and issues checks only after careful inspection of the vouchers supporting and authorizing payments. The accounting department, upon notification of the issuance of checks, makes appropriate records of payments. Receiving and paying functions of the business are maintained as two separate systems. In each instance, custodial and recording activities are exercised by different parties.

Internal Audits at Irregular Intervals. Internal audits at irregular and unannounced intervals may be made a part of the system of cash control. A member of the internal auditing staff verifies the records and checks on the activities of those employees handling cash to make sure the provisions of the system are being carried out. Such control is particularly desirable over petty cash and other cash funds where cash handling and bookkeeping are generally combined.

Double Record of Cash. A preceding section listed the daily deposit of all cash received as an important factor in the control of cash. If all cash receipts are deposited daily, then the bank record of deposits will agree with the depositor's record of cash receipts. As a complementary device, all cash payments should be made by check; the bank's record for checks should agree with the depositor's record of cash payments. Two complete cash summaries are thus available, one in the cash account and the other on the monthly bank statement. In addition to the advantages resulting from organized and consistent routines applied to cash receipts and disbursements, a duplicate record of cash maintained by an outside agency is made available as a check on the accuracy of the records kept by the company.

Petty Cash

Immediate cash payments and payments too small to be made by check may be made from a **petty cash fund.** Under an **imprest system,** the petty cash fund is created by cashing a check for the amount of the fund. In recording the establishment of the fund, Petty Cash is debited and Cash is credited. The cash is then turned over to a cashier or some person who is solely responsible for payments made out of the fund. The cashier should require a signed receipt for all payments made. These receipts may be printed in prenumbered form. Frequently, a bill or other memorandum is submitted when a payment is requested. A record of petty cash payments may be kept in a *petty cash journal.*

Whenever the amount of cash in the fund runs low and also at the end of each fiscal period, the fund is replenished by writing a check equal to the payments made. In recording replenishment, expenses and other appropriate accounts are debited for petty cash disbursements and Cash is credited. The cash short and over account, mentioned earlier, may be used when the fund fails to balance. Replenishment is necessary whenever statements are to be prepared since petty cash disbursements are recognized on the books only when the fund is replenished. Typical journal entries to establish and then to replenish a petty cash fund, based on assumed amounts, are illustrated below.

Petty Cash	1,000	
Cash		1,000
To establish a $1,000 petty cash fund.		
Office Supplies Expense	280	
Postage	150	
Advances to Employees	200	
Miscellaneous Expenses	40	
Cash Short or Over	10	
Cash		680
To replenish the petty cash fund.		

The request for cash to replenish the fund is supported by a summary and analysis of the signed receipts required at the time of disbursement from the fund. This analysis is the basis for the debits recognized on the books when the replenishing check is issued. The signed receipts, together with appropriate documents, are filed as evidence supporting petty cash disbursements.

The cashier of the petty cash fund is held accountable for the total amount of the fund. The person responsible must have on hand at all times cash and signed receipts equal in amount to the original balance of the fund. The cashier should be discouraged from cashing employees' checks from petty cash or otherwise engaging in a banking function. If a banking function is to be undertaken, it should represent a separate activity with a fund established for this purpose.

The petty cash operation should be maintained apart from other cash funds employed for particular business purposes. For example, a retail store may require funds for making change. Certain sums of coins and currency are withheld from deposit at the end of each day to be carried forward as the change funds for the beginning of business on the next day. A separate account should be established to report a cash supply always on hand. Also, special funds or bank accounts may be established for payrolls, dividend distributions, and bond interest payments. Each fund requires a separate accounting.

Reconciliation of Bank Balances

When daily receipts are deposited and payments other than those from petty cash are made by check, the bank's statement of its transactions with the depositor can be compared with the record of cash as reported on the depositor's books. A comparison of the bank balance with the balance reported on the books is usually made monthly by means of a summary known as a **bank reconciliation statement.** The bank reconciliation statement is prepared to disclose any errors or irregularities in either the records of the bank or those of the business unit. It is developed in a form that points out the reasons for discrepancies in the two balances. It should be prepared by an individual who neither handles nor records cash. Any discrepancies should be brought to the immediate attention of appropriate company officials.

When the bank statement and the depositor's records are compared, certain items may appear on one and not the other, resulting in a difference in the two balances. Most of these differences result from temporary timing lags, and are thus normal. Four common types of differences arise in the following situations:

(1) A deposit made near the end of the month and recorded on the depositor's books is not received by the bank in time to be reflected on the bank statement. This amount, referred to as a **deposit in transit,** has to be added to the bank statement balance to make it agree with the balance on the depositor's books.

(2) Checks written near the end of the month have reduced the depositor's cash balance, but have not cleared the bank as of the bank statement date. These **outstanding checks** must be subtracted from the bank statement balance to make it agree with the depositor's records.

(3) The bank normally charges a monthly fee for servicing an account. The bank automatically reduces the depositor's account balance for this **bank service charge** and notes the amount on the bank statement. The depositor must deduct this amount from the recorded cash balance to make it agree with the bank statement balance. The return of a customer's check for which insufficient funds are available, known as a **not-sufficient-funds (NSF) check,** is handled in a similar manner.

(4) An amount owed to the depositor is paid directly to the bank by a third party and added to the depositor's account. Upon receipt of the bank statement (assuming prior notification has not been received from the bank), this amount must be added to the cash balance on the depositor's books. Examples include, in the case of an individual, a direct payroll deposit by the individual's employer; or, in the case of a business, collection by the bank of a note receivable from a customer of the depositor. Banks often charge a fee for providing the latter type of collection service.

If, after considering the items mentioned, the bank statement and the book balances cannot be reconciled, a detailed analysis of both the bank's records and the depositor's books may be necessary to determine whether errors or irregularities exist on the records of either party.

There are two common forms of bank reconciliations: (1) reconciliation of bank and book balances to a corrected balance and (2) reconciliation of the bank balance to the book balance. The first form is prepared in two sections, the bank statement balance being adjusted to the corrected cash balance in the first section, and the book balance being adjusted to the same corrected cash balance in the second section. The first section, then, contains items the bank has not recognized as well as any corrections for errors made by the bank; the second section contains items the depositor has not yet recognized and any corrections for errors made on the depositor's books.

The other form begins with the bank statement balance and reports the adjustments that must be applied to this balance to obtain the cash balance on the depositor's books. The second form, then, simply reports the items accounting for the discrepancy between the bank and book balances. Both forms are illustrated below and on the next page.

The reconciliation of bank and book balances to a corrected balance may be considered preferable because it develops a corrected cash figure and shows separately all items requiring adjustment on the depositor's books.

Graham Inc.
Bank Reconciliation Statement
November 30, 1984

Balance per bank statement, November 30, 1984		$2,979.72
Add: Deposits in transit	$658.50	
Charge for interest made to depositor's account by bank in error	12.50	671.00
		$3,650.72
Deduct outstanding checks:		
No. 1125	$ 58.16	
No. 1138	100.00	
No. 1152	98.60	
No. 1154	255.00	
No. 1155	192.07	703.83
Corrected bank balance		$2,946.89
Balance per books, November 30, 1984		$2,552.49
Add: Proceeds of draft collected by bank November 30 ($500 face less $1.50 bank charges)	$498.50	
Check No. 1116 to Ace Advertising for $46 recorded by depositor as $64 in error	18.00	516.50
		$3,068.99
Deduct: Bank service charges	$ 3.16	
Customer's check deposited November 25 and returned marked NSF	118.94	122.10
Corrected book balance		$2,946.89

Reconciliation of Bank and Book Balances to Corrected Balance

Graham Inc. Bank Reconciliation Statement November 30, 1984			
Balance per bank statement, November 30, 1984			$2,979.72
Add: Deposits in transit		$658.50	
Charge for interest made to depositor's account by bank in error		12.50	
Bank service charges		3.16	
Customer's check deposited November 25 and returned marked NSF		118.94	793.10
			$3,772.82
Deduct: Outstanding checks:			
No. 1125	$ 58.16		
No. 1138	100.00		
No. 1152	98.60		
No. 1154	255.00		
No. 1155	192.07	$703.83	
Check No. 1116 to Ace Advertising for $46 recorded by depositor as $64 in error		18.00	
Proceeds of draft collected by bank on November 30		498.50	1,220.33
Balance per books, November 30, 1984			$2,552.49

Reconciliation of Bank Balance to Book Balance

However, some accountants prefer to use the second form, which is consistent with the nature of the reconciliation required for many other accounts.

After preparing the reconciliation, the depositor should record any items appearing on the bank statement and requiring recognition on the company's books as well as any corrections for errors discovered on its own books. The bank should be notified immediately of any bank errors. The following entries are required on the books of Graham Inc. as a result of the reconciliation just made:

Cash	498.50	
Miscellaneous General Expense	1.50	
Notes Receivable		500.00
To record collection of a $500 time draft by the bank on which bank charges were $1.50.		
Cash	18.00	
Advertising Expense		18.00
To record correction for check in payment of advertising recorded as $64 instead of the actual amount, $46.		
Accounts Receivable	118.94	
Miscellaneous General Expense	3.16	
Cash		122.10
To record customer's uncollectible check and bank charges for November.		

After these entries are posted, the cash account will show a balance of $2,946.89. This is the amount to be reported on the balance sheet. As noted, these adjustments are clearly distinguishable when using the first form of bank reconciliation. They are shown separately as adjustments on the books.

If the second form is used, adjustments can be determined only after careful analysis of all reconciling items.

The bank reconciliation is frequently expanded to incorporate a proof of both receipts and disbursements as separate steps in the reconciliation process. This is often referred to as a **four-column reconciliation** or a **proof of cash.** Two reconciliation forms may be employed here as in the previous examples. The form preferred by the authors develops corrected balances for both receipts and disbursements of the bank and the depositor, as illustrated below.

Graham Inc.
Reconciliation of Receipts, Disbursements, and Bank Balance
November 30, 1984

	Beginning Reconciliation October 31	Receipts	Disbursements	Ending Reconciliation November 30
Balance per bank statement	$5,895.42	$21,212.40	$24,128.10	$2,979.72
Deposits in transit:				
October 31	515.40	(515.40)		
November 30		658.50		658.50
Outstanding checks:				
October 31	(810.50)		(810.50)	
November 30			703.83	(703.83)
Charge for interest made by bank in error			(12.50)	12.50
Corrected bank balance	$5,600.32	$21,355.50	$24,008.93	$2,946.89
Balance per books	$5,406.22	$21,057.00	$23,910.73	$2,552.49
Bank service charges:				
October	(5.90)		(5.90)	
November			3.16	(3.16)
Customer's check deposited November 25 found to be uncollectible			118.94	(118.94)
Drafts collected by bank:				
October	200.00	(200.00)		
November		498.50		498.50
Check No. 116 for $46 recorded by depositor as $64 in error			(18.00)	18.00
Corrected book balance	$5,600.32	$21,355.50	$24,008.93	$2,946.89

Reconciliation of Bank and Book Balances to Corrected Balance

In preparing a four-column reconciliation, columns are provided for the beginning reconciliation, receipts, disbursements, and the ending reconciliation. The first column contains a reconciliation as of the end of the preceding period. The receipts of the period are added to the beginning balances and the disbursements are subtracted to arrive at the ending balances. Receipts are reconciled in the second column and disbursements in the third column. The amounts must reconcile both vertically and horizontally for the ending bank and book balances to agree.

In order to complete this type of reconciliation, each adjustment must be carefully analyzed. Note that two columns are always affected for each adjustment. For example, deposits of $515.40 on October 31, 1984, were received by the bank in November and are included in the total bank receipts of $21,212.40 for November. However, the deposit was properly recorded on the books as a receipt in October; thus, the $515.40 is not included in the book receipts of $21,057 for November, but is included in the beginning book balance. The reconciliation accounts for this by deducting the in-transit receipt from the total bank receipts and by adding the receipt to the beginning October 31 bank statement balance.

The illustrations for Graham Inc. assume adjustments of the book amounts are made in the month subsequent to their discovery. If the adjustments were made in the same month, as might be true at year-end, there would be no adjustments in the first column for adjusting the book amounts.

The expanded reconciliation procedure normally reduces the time and effort required to find errors made by either the bank or the depositor. In developing comparisons of both receipts and disbursements, the areas in which errors have been made, as well as the amounts of the discrepancies within each area, are immediately identified and checking procedures can be directed and narrowed accordingly. This procedure is frequently used by auditors when there is any question of possible discrepancies in the handling of cash.

Proper Disclosure of Cash and Current Condition

Although a system of internal control may provide for the effective safeguarding of cash, careful examination of the records is still necessary at the end of an accounting period to determine whether transactions have been satisfactorily recorded and cash and the current position of the business are properly presented. Certain practices designed to present a more favorable financial condition than is actually the case may be encountered. Such practices are sometimes referred to as *window dressing*. For example, cash records may be held open for a few days after the close of a fiscal period and cash received from customers during this period reported as receipts of the preceding period. An improved cash position is thus reported. If this balance is then used as a basis for drawing predated checks in payment of accounts payable, the ratio of current assets to current liabilities may be improved. For example, if current assets are $30,000 and current liabilities are $20,000 providing a current ratio of 1.5 to 1, recording payments to creditors of $10,000 will produce balances of $20,000 and $10,000, a current ratio of 2 to 1. The current ratio may also be improved by writing checks in payment of obligations and entering these on the books even though checks are not to be mailed until the following period. Or the current position, as well as earnings and owners' equity, may be overstated by predating sales made at the beginning of a new period. A careful review of the records will disclose whether improper practices have been employed. If such practices are discovered, the accounts should be corrected.

A companion function to cash control is cash planning. This is an important responsibility within a company and does not take place without management effort. Many companies that are basically sound in organization and product control frequently have financial problems because management does not understand the basic importance of cash planning. A knowledge of the techniques of budgeting and forecasting is essential to sound financial control. These topics are important but are outside the scope of this book. They are considered in detail in managerial accounting texts.

TEMPORARY INVESTMENTS

Temporarily available excess cash may be invested in time deposits, various money market funds, and similar instruments, or it may be used to purchase securities. As a result, revenue will be produced that would not be available if cash were left idle. Investments made during seasonal periods of low activity can be converted into cash in periods of expanding operations. Asset items arising from temporary conversions of cash are reported in the "Current assets" section of the balance sheet as "Temporary investments." Accounting and reporting considerations applicable to investments of a long-term nature are discussed in Chapters 12 and 14.

Criteria for Reporting Securities as Temporary Investments

Investments in securities qualify for reporting as **temporary investments** provided (1) there is a ready market for converting such securities into cash, and (2) it is management's intention to sell them if the need for cash arises.

Securities are considered marketable when a day-to-day market exists and when they can be sold on short notice. The volume of trading in the securities should be sufficient to absorb a company's holdings without materially affecting the market price. Generally, marketable securities include such items as listed stocks, high-grade bonds, and first-mortgage notes. United States government securities, despite their relatively low yield, are also a highly favored form of marketable security because of their stable prices and wide market. Securities having a limited market and fluctuating widely in price are not suitable for temporary investments.

Marketable securities may be converted into cash shortly after being acquired or they may be held for some time. In either case, however, they are properly classified as temporary investments as long as management intends to sell them if the need for cash arises. The deciding factor is management's intent, not the length of time the securities are held. Therefore, the following types of investments do not qualify as temporary investments even though the securities may be marketable: (1) reacquired shares of a corporation's own stock; (2) securities acquired to gain control of a company; (3) securities held for maintenance of business relations; and (4) any other securities that cannot be used or are not intended to be used as a ready source of cash.

Recording Purchase and Sale of Marketable Securities

Stocks and bonds acquired as temporary investments are recorded at cost, which includes brokers' fees, taxes, and other charges incurred in their acquisition. Stocks are normally quoted at a price per single share; bonds are quoted at a price per $100 face value although they are normally issued in $1,000 denominations. The purchase of 100 shares of stock at 5⅛, then, would indicate a purchase price of $512.50; the purchase of a $1,000 bond at 104¼ would indicate a purchase price of $1,042.50.

When interest-bearing securities are acquired between interest payment dates, the amount paid for the security is increased by a charge for accrued interest to the date of purchase. This charge should not be reported as part of the investment cost. Two assets have been acquired—the security and the accrued interest receivable—and should be reported in two separate asset accounts. Upon the receipt of interest, the accrued interest account is closed and Interest Revenue is credited for the amount of interest earned since the purchase date. Instead of recording the interest as a receivable (asset approach), Interest Revenue may be debited for the accrued interest paid. The subsequent collection of interest would then be credited in full to Interest Revenue. The latter procedure (revenue approach) is usually more convenient.

To illustrate the entries for the acquisition of securities, assume that $100,000 in U.S. Treasury notes are purchased at 104¼, including brokerage fees, on April 1. Interest is 9% payable semiannually on January 1 and July 1. Accrued interest of $2,250 would thus be added to the purchase price. The entries to record the purchase of the securities and the subsequent collection of interest under the alternate procedures would be as follows:

Asset Approach:

Apr. 1	Marketable Securities—9% U.S. Treasury Notes	104,250	
	Interest Receivable	2,250	
	Cash		106,500
July 1	Cash	4,500	
	Interest Receivable		2,250
	Interest Revenue		2,250

Revenue Approach:

Apr. 1	Marketable Securities—9% U.S. Treasury Notes	104,250	
	Interest Revenue	2,250	
	Cash		106,500
July 1	Cash	4,500	
	Interest Revenue		4,500

When such securities are acquired at a higher or lower price than their maturity value and it is expected that they will be held until maturity, periodic amortization of the premium or accumulation of the discount with corresponding adjustments to interest revenue is required. However, when securities are acquired as a temporary investment and it is not likely they will be held until maturity, such procedures are normally not necessary. When a temporary investment is sold, the difference between the sales proceeds and the cost is reported as a gain or loss on the sale. For example, if the U.S. Treasury notes in the preceding illustration were sold on July 1 for $105,000, and the brokerage fees were $500, the sale would be recorded as follows:

July 1	Cash	104,500	
	Marketable Securities—9% U.S. Treasury Notes		104,250
	Gain on Sale of Marketable Securities		250

The gain would be reported on the income statement as "Other revenue." Note that the brokerage fees reduce the cash proceeds and the recognized gain on the sale.

Valuation of Marketable Securities

Three different methods for the valuation of marketable securities have been advanced: (1) cost, (2) cost or market, whichever is lower, and (3) market.

Cost. Valuation of marketable securities at cost refers to the original acquisition price of a marketable security including all related fees, unless a new cost basis has been assigned to recognize a permanent decline in the value of the security. Cost is to be used unless circumstances require another method as is the case with marketable equity securities, to be explained in the next section. The recognition of gain or loss is deferred until the asset is sold, at which time investment cost is matched against investment proceeds. The cost basis is consistent with income tax procedures, recognizing neither gain nor loss until there is a sale or exchange.

Cost or Market, Whichever is Lower. When using the lower of cost or market method, if market is lower than cost, security values are written down to the lower value; if market is higher than cost, securities are maintained at cost, gains awaiting confirmation through sale.

Traditionally, the lower of cost or market method has been used only under special conditions when market was considered substantially lower than cost, and the decline was considered permanent. Because of the difficulty in defining substantial and nontemporary declines, the lower of cost or market method was not widely used in practice prior to 1976.[4]

Significant fluctuations in the stock market in recent years have created many more situations where market values are lower than cost. After due consideration of the issues involved, the FASB issued Statement No. 12 requiring that **marketable equity securities** be carried at the lower of aggregate cost or market value.[5] An equity security is defined by the FASB in Statement No. 12 as

---

[4]In the AICPA trends and technique survey, only 25 out of 291 companies reported marketable securities at the lower of cost or market. *Accounting Trends & Techniques*, 30th ed. (New York: American Institute of Certified Public Accountants, 1976), p. 80.

[5]*Statement of Financial Accounting Standards No. 12*, "Accounting for Certain Marketable Securities" (Stamford: Financial Accounting Standards Board, 1975), par. 8.

"...any instrument representing ownership shares (e.g., common, preferred, and other capital stock), or the right to acquire (e.g., warrants, rights, and call options) or dispose of (e.g., put options) ownership shares in an enterprise at fixed or determinable prices. The term does not encompass preferred stock that by its terms either must be redeemed by the issuing enterprise or is redeemable at the option of the investor, nor does it include treasury stock or convertible bonds."[6]

FASB Statement No. 12 deals only with marketable equity securities. Other marketable securities, primarily marketable debt securities (corporate and government bonds), still may be carried at cost unless there is a substantial decline that is not due to temporary conditions. It seems logical, however, to treat all short-term marketable securities similarly. All temporary investments are acquired for the same reason—utilization of idle cash to generate a short-term return. Both equity securities and debt securities must meet the same criteria to qualify as temporary investments, and their valuation should reflect a similar concept, i.e., the amount of cash that could be realized upon liquidation at the balance sheet date. Therefore, in the illustrations and end-of-chapter material in this text, the lower of cost or market method is used for all short-term marketable securities. It should be recognized, however, that actual practice varies. Some companies interpret FASB No. 12 strictly and account for only marketable equity securities on the lower of cost or market basis.

The lower of cost or market method may be employed in two ways: (1) it may be applied to securities in the aggregate; or (2) it may be applied to individual items. To illustrate, assume marketable securities with cost and market values on December 31, 1984, as follows:

	Cost	Market	Lower of Cost or Market on Individual Basis
1,000 shares of Carter Co. common	$20,000	$16,000	$16,000
$25,000 10% U.S. Treasury Notes	25,000	26,500	25,000
$10,000 U.S. Government 8% bonds	10,000	7,500	7,500
	$55,000	$50,000	$48,500

The lower of cost or market value on an aggregate basis is $50,000; on an individual basis, $48,500.

In accounting for marketable equity securities, it should be noted that FASB Statement No. 12 requires the use of the **aggregate method.** An important factor in choosing the aggregate basis is that many companies consider their marketable securities portfolios as collective assets. Further, the Board felt that applying the lower of cost or market procedure on an individual security basis would be unduly conservative.

However, the FASB did recognize that many companies classify separately their current and noncurrent securities portfolios. Therefore, when a classified balance sheet is presented, the lower of aggregate cost or market is to be applied to the separate current and noncurrent portfolios. When an

[6] *Ibid*, par. 7a.

unclassified balance sheet is presented, the entire marketable equity securities portfolio is to be considered a noncurrent asset. The application of FASB Statement No. 12 to long-term marketable equity securities is discussed in detail in Chapter 12.

In adopting the lower of aggregate cost or market method for marketable equity securities, the FASB chose to recognize declines in the realizable value of short-term marketable equity securities portfolios as a charge against income of the current period. The possibility of a future recovery in the market value was not considered sufficient reason to maintain the carrying value at cost.

Recognition of a decline in value on the books calls for a reduction of the asset and a debit to a loss account. Various titles are used for the loss account: Unrealized Loss on Marketable Securities; Loss on Valuation of Marketable Equity Securities; Recognized Decline in Value of Current Marketable Securities. The authors prefer the last title to avoid confusion with the entry required upon the final sale of the securities or with the title used in accounting for long-term marketable equity securities. It should also be noted that the valuation loss is not recognized for income tax purposes, and the basis of the securities for measurement of the ultimate gain or loss on final disposition continues to be cost. Cost can be preserved on the books by the use of a valuation account to reduce the securities to market. The following entry may be made to illustrate this procedure.

Recognized Decline in Value of Current Marketable Securities	5,000	
Allowance for Decline in Value of Current Marketable Securities		5,000

The balance sheet would show:

Current assets:		
Marketable securities (at cost)	$55,000	
Less allowance for decline in value of current marketable securities	5,000	
Marketable securities (at market, December 31, 1984)..........		$50,000

In practice a shorter form is often used, such as the following:

Current assets:	
Marketable securities (reported at market; cost, $55,000)	$50,000

The $5,000 loss must be reported on the current income statement, probably as a charge related to financial management. If in the future there is an increase in the market value of the short-term marketable securities portfolio, the write-down should be reversed to the extent that the resulting carrying value does not exceed original cost. The original write-down is to be viewed as a valuation allowance, representing an estimated decrease in the realizable value of the portfolio. Any subsequent market increase reduces or eliminates this valuation allowance. The reversal of a write-down is considered a change in accounting estimate of an unrealized loss.[7] Changes in estimates and other accounting changes are discussed in Chapter 21.

---

[7]See *FASB Statement No. 5*, par. 2 and *APB Opinion No. 20*, par. 10.

In subsequent periods, the portfolio of temporary investments will change through purchases and sales of individual securities. Because cost remains the accepted basis for recognition of gain or loss on final disposition and for income tax purposes, it is preferable to record the sale of marketable securities as though no valuation account existed; i.e., on a cost basis. At the end of each accounting period, an analysis can then be made of cost and aggregated market values for the securities held and the allowance account adjusted to reflect the new difference between cost and market. If market exceeds cost at a subsequent valuation date, the allowance account would be eliminated, and the securities would be valued at cost, the lower of the two values. The offsetting revenue account for the adjustment may be titled Recovery of Recognized Decline in Value of Current Marketable Securities.

To illustrate accounting for subsequent years' transactions, assume in the preceding example that in 1985 the Carter Co. stock is sold for $17,000 and $25,000 of 9% U. S. Treasury notes are purchased for $24,500. The following entries are made:

Cash	17,000	
Loss on Sale of Marketable Securities	3,000	
Marketable Securities—Carter Co. Common		20,000
Marketable Securities—9% U. S. Treasury Notes	24,500	
Cash		24,500

Assuming the market value of the remaining securities in the portfolio is unchanged and the market value of the U. S. Treasury notes remains at cost, the aggregate market value of the temporary investments is $58,500 ($26,500 + $7,500 + $24,500). When comparing the aggregate market value to the aggregate cost value of $59,500 ($25,000 + $10,000 + $24,500), the following adjusting entry would be made at the end of 1985:

Allowance for Decline in Value of Current Marketable Securities	4,000	
Recovery of Recognized Decline in Value of Current Marketable Securities		4,000

This entry leaves the valuation account with a balance of $1,000 which, when subtracted from cost of $59,500, will report the marketable securities at their aggregate market value of $58,500.

If the aggregate market value of the securities portfolio had fallen during 1985 to $53,000 (compared to cost of $59,500), the adjusting entry would be:

Recognized Decline in Value of Current Marketable Securities	1,500	
Allowance for Decline in Value of Current Marketable Securities		1,500

This entry increases the allowance account to $6,500 which, when subtracted from cost of $59,500, will report marketable securities at their aggregate market value of $53,000.

On the other hand, if the aggregate market value of the securities portfolio had risen to $60,000 (compared to cost of $59,500), the adjusting entry at year end would be:

Allowance for Decline in Value of Current Marketable Securities	5,000	
Recovery of Recognized Decline in Value of Current Marketable Securities		5,000

This entry cancels the allowance account since the $59,500 original cost of securities is lower than their current $60,000 aggregate market value.

If the classification of a marketable equity security changes from current to noncurrent or vice versa, the security must be transferred to the applicable portfolio at the lower of cost or market value at date of transfer. If the market value is lower than cost, the market value becomes the new cost basis and a realized loss is to be included in determining net income.[8] In essence, this procedure recognizes the loss upon transfer as though it had been realized. This should reduce the likelihood of income being manipulated through the transfer of securities between current and long-term portfolios.

To summarize the accounting for short-term marketable equity securities under FASB Statement No. 12, securities are originally recorded at cost. Subsequent valuation is at lower of cost or market on an aggregate basis. The adjustment is made at year-end through a valuation allowance account. Any reduction in value is recognized as a current period loss in the income statement; any recovery of the write-down, up to the original cost but no higher, is recognized as a current period recovery in the income statement. These gains or losses would be shown after operating income as "other revenues" or "other expenses." The amount of gain or loss on the ultimate sale of a marketable security is still the difference between the sales price and the original cost of the security without consideration for any previous year-end allowance adjustments. Then, at year-end, the allowance will be adjusted once again to reflect the proper lower of cost or market amount for the remaining securities portfolio.

Any permanent declines in securities values are to be recognized as losses currently, just like any other asset, with the new value being considered cost from thence forward. No subsequent partial recovery would be allowed.

FASB Statement No. 12 requires extensive disclosure of information with respect to marketable equity securities, including aggregate cost and market values, gross unrealized gains and losses, and the amount of net realized gain or loss included in net income.[9]

Market. Market value refers to the current market price of a marketable security. In applying the market value method, permanent declines in market prices of securities are recognized as losses in the current period. Temporary declines in market values are treated the same as under the lower of cost or market method. That is, security values are written down to market through a valuation adjustment at the end of the accounting period. Where the market method differs is in the valuation of securities whose prices have increased above cost. With the market method, current market prices are recognized as affording an objective basis for the valuation of marketable securities; therefore, such securities would be reported on the balance sheet at their current values, whether higher or lower than cost.

---

[8] *Statement of Financial Accounting Standards No. 12, op..cit.*, par. 10.

[9] *Ibid.*, par. 12.

If under the market method marketable securities are to be reported at current values that exceed cost, it is necessary to recognize the increase in the value of the securities. This may be done by debiting the securities and crediting a gain from the appreciation in market values. The gain would be reported in the gains and losses section of the income statement. However, if it is felt that recognition of gains resulting from market value increases should await the sale of securities, a separate capital account, such as Unrealized Appreciation in Value of Marketable Securities, may be credited. When the securities are sold, the unrealized appreciation account is eliminated, and any realized gain or loss is recognized in the income statement. In the interim, the balance in the unrealized appreciation account would be reported in the equity section of the balance sheet.

To illustrate the procedures that may be followed when using a market value approach, assume that at the end of 1984, securities costing $50,000 have quoted market values of $60,000. At the end of 1985, the market values have declined to $58,000. The securities are then sold on March 5, 1986, for $62,000. Assuming that unrealized gains from market value increases are not to be reported as income, the following entries would be made. Note that when the securities are sold in 1986, the sale would be reported as realized in the income statement. Up to that point, the changes in market values would be reflected in the unrealized appreciation account.

1984			
Dec. 31	Marketable Securities	10,000	
	Unrealized Appreciation in Value of Marketable Securities		10,000
1985			
Dec. 31	Unrealized Appreciation in Value of Marketable Securities	2,000	
	Marketable Securities		2,000
1986			
Mar. 5	Cash	62,000	
	Unrealized Appreciation in Value of Marketable Securities	8,000	
	Marketable Securities		58,000
	Gain on Sale of Marketable Securities		12,000

In the preceding illustration, the valuation changes are reflected only in the balance sheet through the net amount in the unrealized appreciation account. Alternatively, the changes could be recognized in the income statement by crediting a revenue account such as Unrealized Gain on Marketable Securities for 1984 and by debiting Unrealized Loss on Marketable Securities for 1985 instead of the special capital account.

Market value has been and continues to be an acceptable method for valuing marketable securities within certain industries that follow specialized accounting practices with respect to marketable securities. Enterprises within these industries, such as securities brokers and dealers, that carry marketable equity securities at market value are not required by FASB Statement No. 12 to change to lower of cost or market. For most companies, however, the market value method is not presently considered generally accepted accounting practice, and the lower of cost or market method should be used.

Evaluation of Methods

Valuation at cost finds support on the grounds that it is an extension of the cost principle; the asset is carried at cost until a sale or exchange provides an alternative asset and confirms a gain or loss. The cost method offers valuation on a consistent basis from period to period. It is the simplest method to apply and adheres to income tax requirements. However, certain objections to cost can be raised. The use of cost means investments may be carried at amounts differing from values objectively determinable at the balance sheet date, and the integrity of both balance sheet and income statement measurements can be challenged. The use of cost also means identical securities may be reported at different values because of purchases at different prices. A further objection is that management, in controlling the sale of securities, can determine the periods in which gains or losses are to be recognized even though the changes in values may have accrued over a number of periods.

The use of market value is advocated on the basis that there is evidence of the net realizable value of the marketable securities held at the balance sheet date and any changes from previous carrying values should be recognized as gains or losses in the current period. Assuming marketable securities are defined as having a readily available sales price or bid and ask price from one of the national securities exchanges or over-the-counter markets, this method is objective and relatively simple to apply. The major drawback of this method is that gains or losses may be recognized prior to realization, i.e., prior to the actual sale of the securities. In addition, market values fluctuate, often significantly, which would require continual changing of the carrying value of marketable securities on the balance sheet. Market is also challenged as a departure from the cost principle and as lacking in conservatism. Furthermore, market is not acceptable for general accounting or income tax purposes.

The lower of cost or market procedure provides for recognizing market declines and serves to prevent potential mistakes arising in analyzing statements when these declines are not reported. The lower of cost or market is supported as a conservative procedure. This approach may be challenged on the basis that it may be the most complicated method to follow, and it fails to apply a single valuation concept consistently. Securities carried at cost at the end of one period may be reported at market value in the subsequent period. Critics argue that if net realizable value is a desirable measurement concept, its use should not depend on whether portfolio values are greater or less than original cost.

CASH AND TEMPORARY INVESTMENTS ON THE BALANCE SHEET

For statement purposes, cash may be reported as a single item or it may be summarized under several descriptive headings, such as cash on hand, commercial deposits, and savings deposits. Since current assets are normally reported in the order of their liquidity, cash is listed first, followed by temporary investments, receivables, and inventories. When temporary investments are pledged for some particular purpose, the nature and the purpose of the pledge should be disclosed parenthetically or by note.

Cash and temporary investments may be reported on the balance sheet in the following manner:

Current assets:			
Cash on hand and demand deposits in banks			$ 46,000
Special cash deposits (to pay interest and dividends). .			24,000
Temporary investments:			
Certificates of deposit		$100,000	
Marketable securities:			
U. S. Government obligations (reported at cost; market, $158,500; $50,000 in bonds has been pledged as security on short-term bank loan) ...	$150,000		
Other stocks and bonds (reported at cost; market, $44,200)...........................	35,000	185,000	285,000

Using lower of cost or mkt

QUESTIONS

1. Why is cash on hand both necessary and yet potentially unproductive?
2. State how each of the following items should be reported on the balance sheet: (a) demand deposits with bank, (b) restricted cash deposits in foreign banks, (c) payroll fund to pay accrued salaries, (d) change funds on hand, (e) cash in a special cash account to be used currently for the construction of a new building.
3. The following items were included as cash on the balance sheet for the Lawrence Co. How should each of the items have been reported?
   - (a) Customers' checks returned by the bank marked "Not Sufficient Funds."
   - (b) Customers' postdated checks.
   - (c) Cashier's note with no due date.
   - (d) Postage stamps received in the mail for merchandise.
   - (e) Postal money orders from customers awaiting deposit.
   - (f) Receipts for advances to buyers.
   - (g) Notes receivable in the hands of the bank for collection.
   - (h) Special bank account in which sales tax collections are deposited.
   - (i) Customers' checks not yet deposited.
4. On reconciling the cash account with the bank statement, it is found that the general cash fund is overdrawn $436 but the bond redemption account has a balance of $5,400. The treasurer wishes to show cash as a current asset at $4,964. Discuss.
5. The Lehi Fence Company shows in its accounts a cash balance of $66,500 with Bank A, and an overdraft of $1,500 with Bank B on December 31. Bank B regards the

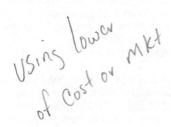

overdraft as in effect a loan to the Lehi Fence Company and charges interest on the overdraft balance. How would you report the balances with Banks A and B? Would your answer be any different if the overdraft arose as a result of certain checks deposited and proved to be uncollectible and the overdraft was cleared promptly by the Lehi Fence Company at the beginning of January?

6. Under certain conditions it is proper to offset either assets against liabilities or liabilities against assets. Comment upon the following practices of the Pioneer Kitchens Company.

(a) An overdraft of $300 in the payroll fund kept with Farmers and Mechanics Bank is offset against a restricted savings account balance kept with the same bank.
(b) A mortgage of $130,000 is offset against the buildings account of $180,000 to reflect a net equity in the buildings of $50,000.
(c) Advances to employees of $500 are offset against Salaries Payable of $1,100.

7. Bartholomew Manufacturing is required to maintain a compensating balance of $15,000 with its bank to maintain a line of open credit. The compensating balance is legally restricted as to its use. How should the compensating balance be reported on the balance sheet and why?

8. What are some current and possible future uses of EFT?

9. (a) Explain check kiting and lapping. (b) Mention at least six other practices resulting in misappropriations of cash in the absence of an adequate system of internal control. (c) What is the basic principle of cash control making fraudulent practices extremely difficult?

10. As an auditor, what basic features would you hope to find in your client's system of cash control?

11. (a) What are the major advantages in using imprest petty cash funds? (b) What dangers must be guarded against when petty cash funds are used?

12. (a) Give at least four common sources of differences between depositor and bank balances. (b) Which of the differences in (a) require an adjusting entry on the books of the depositor?

13. (a) What two methods may be employed in reconciling the bank and the cash balances? (b) Which would you recommend? Why?

14. (a) What purposes are served by preparing a four-column reconciliation of receipts and disbursements? (b) Why might this form be used by auditors?

15. International Cosmetics Corporation engaged in the following practices at the end of a fiscal year:

(a) Sales on account from January 1–January 5 were predated as of the month of December.
(b) Checks in payment of accounts were prepared on December 31 and were entered on the books, but they were placed in the safe awaiting instructions for mailing.
(c) Customers' checks returned by the bank and marked "Not Sufficient Funds" were ignored for statement purposes.
(d) Amounts owed company officers were paid off on December 31 and re-borrowed on January 2.

Explain what is wrong with each of the practices mentioned and give the entries that are required to correct the accounts.

16. Define *temporary investments*. What criteria must be met for a security to be considered a temporary investment?

17. What two methods may be used to record the payment for accrued interest on interest-bearing securities? Which method is preferable?

18. (a) What positions are held with respect to the valuation of marketable securities? (b) What arguments can be advanced in support of each and which position do you feel has greatest merit?

19. Resorts International reports marketable securities on the balance sheet at the lower of cost or market. What adjustments are required on the books at the end of the year in each situation below:

(a) Securities are purchased early in 1983 and at the end of 1983 their market value is more than cost.
(b) At the end of 1984 the market value of the securities is less than cost.
(c) At the end of 1985 the market value of the securities is greater than at the end of 1984 but is still less than cost.
(d) At the end of 1986 the market value of the securities is more than the amount originally paid.

20. One of the arguments advanced for using market as the valuation procedure for temporary investments is that it assists in a "proper evaluation of managerial decisions and activities relative to purchases, sales, and holdings of marketable securities." How might you support this statement using the following example? Marketable securities purchased for $500 rose in value to $900 as of the end of the fiscal year, and were sold in the subsequent year for $650.

DISCUSSION CASES

case 6-1. (Where has the cash gone?) As the auditor of Riverside Country Club, you make an unannounced visit to your client's office to count the $2,500 change fund. The office manager, Carl Steele, appears nervous, and as he shows you to the vault where the fund is kept, indicates that the cash "isn't all there." Following a count of the fund which totals only $1,000, Steele takes you to his office where he reveals a stack of daily reports indicating how each day the cash count has shown either an overage or a shortage. But the shortages have exceeded the overages, and the deficit has steadily grown. "It's been like this for two months, and I don't have time to do any of my office work. I keep looking for the missing cash!" His untidy office is ample evidence of his time problems.

You decide to review the system for handling cash to identify the cause of the shortage. Your investigation reveals that the fund has been used to cash members' checks and to pay miscellaneous bills under $50. Four different people in the office (including the bookkeeper) have access to the fund depending on which one is free when a need for cash arises. At the close of each day, the money collected from the cash registers in the club is merged with the change fund and with collections on members' accounts. All checks and sufficient cash to equal daily receipts are deposited, and the remainder is returned to the fund. You know you must do something immediately because a shortage occurs the very day you are studying the system. Your superior instructs you to prepare a memorandum outlining your recommendations and reasons for them.

case 6-2. (Valuation of securities) The TenCo Corporation has a current securities portfolio consisting of the following stocks and bonds:

	Cost	Market
Air Lite Corp. common stock	$100,000	$200,000
FCR Inc. preferred stock	200,000	140,000
1st National 8½% mortgage bonds	150,000	130,000
Midwest Co. 9% bonds	140,000	160,000
Madison Municipal 10% bonds	200,000	100,000

In a meeting between John Price, CPA, and the audit committee of TenCo, a question is raised as to the valuation method to be used for the current securities portfolio. Price explains that under the present guidelines of the FASB, marketable equity securities are to be recorded on an aggregate lower of cost or market basis. Other securities classified as current, such as bonds, may be recorded at cost unless a permanent decline has taken place. Joan Simmons of the audit committee doesn't understand why the entire portfolio can't be considered together for valuation purposes. Changes in the market values of bonds are as relevant for decision-making purposes as are market values for stocks. Another member of the committee, Mark Tracy, doesn't understand why the aggregate market value must be used. Tracy recalls a method learned in an accounting class in which each security is valued at the lower of its cost or market. He believes this would give a more accurate figure for purposes of valuation. After listening to the interchange, Barb Murphy, the chairman of the audit committee asks the CPA, "John, what are we talking about as far as impact on net income is concerned? How would the charge against income differ between the methods described? Do we have some flexibility in this matter, or are we locked into the FASB recommendation?" Forgetting the FASB for a moment, what do you recommend?

EXERCISES

exercise 6-1 (Reporting cash on the balance sheet)

R. Walton, proprietor of the Bennett Fabricating Co., would like to know how much cash may be reported on Bennett's balance sheet. Bennett has the following bank accounts and balances:

Overdrawn checking account	$(20)
United States savings bonds	400
Payroll account	100
Sales tax account	150

In addition to the bank accounts, Bennett has the following items in the office:

Postage stamps	$ 20
Employee's postdated check	30
IOU from Walton's brother	100
A wristwatch (reported at market value; surrendered as security by a customer who forgot his wallet)	30
Credit memo from a vendor for a purchase return	64
Traveler's check	40
Insufficient funds check	18
Ten cases of empty soft drink bottles (returnable value)	24
Petty cash fund ($16 in currency and expense receipts for $84)	100
Money order	36

How much may be reported as cash on Bennett's balance sheet?

exercise 6-2 (Accounting for petty cash)

An examination on the morning of January 2 by the auditor for the Pearson Lumber Company discloses the following items in the petty cash drawer:

Currency and coin		$ 105.66
IOUs from members of the office staff		135.00
An envelope containing collections for a football pool, with office staff names attached		45.00
Petty cash vouchers for:		
Typewriter repairs	$24.00	
Stamps	45.00	
Telegram charges	28.50	97.50
Employee's check postdated January 15		150.00
Employee's check marked "NSF"		210.00
Check drawn by Pearson Lumber Company to Petty Cash		345.00
		$1,088.16

The ledger account discloses a $1,050 balance for Petty Cash. (1) What adjustments should be made on the auditor's working papers so petty cash may be correctly stated on the balance sheet? (2) What is the correct amount of petty cash for the balance sheet? (3) How could the practice of borrowing by employees from the fund be discouraged?

exercise 6-3 (Compensating balances)

Kendall Home Repair borrowed $50,000 at 12%, but was required to maintain a compensating balance of $10,000. (1) In this case, what is Kendall's actual rate of interest? (2) How should this information be disclosed?

exercise 6-4 (Bank to book reconciliation)

The following data are assembled in the course of reconciling the bank balance as of December 31, 1984, for Fuente Inc. What cash balance will be found on the company books, assuming no errors on the part of the bank and the depositor?

Balance per bank statement	$607.80
Checks outstanding	880.00
December 31 receipts recorded but not deposited	175.00
Bank charges for December not recognized on books	3.75
Draft collected by bank but not recognized on books	275.00

exercise 6-5 (Adjusting the cash account)

The accounting department supplied the following data in reconciling the bank statement for Broberg Jewelers:

Cash balance per books	$14,692.71
Deposits in transit	2,615.23
Bank service charge	21.00
Outstanding checks	3,079.51
Note collected by bank including $45 interest (Broberg not yet notified)	1,045.00
Error by bank—check drawn by Brobert was charged to Broberg's account	617.08
Sale and deposit of $1,729.00 was entered in the sales journal and cash receipts journal as $1,792.00	

Give the journal entry required on the books to adjust the cash account.

exercise 6-6 (Bank reconciliation—correct balances)

The Mirro Lake Manufacturing Co. receives its bank statement for the month ending June 30 on July 2. The bank statement indicates a balance of $2,550. The cash account as of the close of business on June 30 has a balance of $270. In reconciling the balances, the auditor discovers the following:

(a) Receipts on June 30, $10,500, were not deposited until July 1.
(b) Checks outstanding on June 30 were $13,290.

(c) The bank has charged the depositor for overdrafts, $60.
(d) A canceled check to H. M. Ship for $9,618 was entered in cash payments in error as $9,168.

Prepare a bank reconciliation statement. (Use the form reconciling bank and depositor figures to corrected cash balance.)

exercise 6-7 (Bank reconciliation—analysis of outstanding checks)

The following information was included in the bank reconciliation for Ashman Plastics Inc. for June. What was the total of the outstanding checks at the beginning of June? Assume all other reconciling items are listed below.

Checks and charges returned by bank in June, including a June service charge of $10	$16,435
Service charge made by bank in May and recorded on books in June	5
Total of credits to Cash in all journals during June	19,292
Customer's NSF check returned as a bank charge in June (no entry made on books)	100
Customer's NSF check returned in May and redeposited in June (no entry made on books in either May or June)	250
Outstanding checks at June 30	8,060
Deposit in transit at June 30	600

exercise 6-8 (Four-column bank reconciliation—correct balances)

Tetzlaff Corporation began doing business with Fidelity Bank on October 1. On that date the correct cash balance was $4,000. All cash transactions are cleared through the bank account. Subsequent transactions during October and November relating to the records of Tetzlaff and Fidelity are summarized below:

	Tetzlaff Company Books	Fidelity Bank Books
October deposits	$7,360	$7,110
October checks	6,290	6,130
October service charge	—	10
October 31 balance	5,070	4,970
November deposits (regular)	8,220	8,280
November checks	9,410	9,220
November service charge	—	15
Note collected by bank (includes $15 interest)	—	1,015
October service charge	10	
November 30 balance	3,870	5,030

On the basis of the foregoing data: (1) prepare a reconciliation of receipts and disbursements and bank balance for November, and (2) assuming November 30 is the end of Tetzlaff's fiscal year, give entries that would be required by the bank reconciliation.

exercise 6-9 (Journalizing marketable securities transactions)

Give the entries necessary to record these transactions of Frampton Inc. during 1984.

(a) Purchased $100,000 U.S. Treasury 8% bonds, paying 102½ plus accrued interest of $3,000. Broker's fees were $740. Frampton Inc. uses the revenue approach to record accrued interest on purchased bonds.
(b) Purchased 1,000 shares of Byland Co. common stock at 256 plus brokerage fees of $1,200.
(c) Received semiannual interest on the U.S. Treasury bonds.
(d) Sold 300 shares of Byland Co. common at 261.
(e) Sold $60,000 of U.S. Treasury 8% bonds at 103 plus accrued interest of $800.
(f) Purchased a $20,000 six-month certificate of deposit.

exercise 6-10 (Accounting for marketable securities)

During 1984, Diann's Novelty Shop purchased the following marketable securities:

	Cost	Year-End Market
Astpo Co. common	$12,000	$14,000
10% U.S. Treasury Notes	18,000	11,000

Marketable securities are to be reported on the balance sheet at the lower of aggregate cost or market. (1) What entry would be made at year-end assuming the above values? (2) What entry would be made during 1985 assuming one half of the Astpo Co. common stock is sold for $7,000? (3) What entry would be made at the end of 1985 assuming: (a) the market value of remaining securities is $18,000? (b) The market value of remaining securities is $21,000? (c) The market value of remaining securities is $28,000?

exercise 6-11 (Valuation of marketable securities)

Midwestern Steel Corp. acquires marketable securities in 1983 at a cost of $225,000. Market values of the securities at the end of each year are as follows: 1983, $210,000; 1984, $219,000; 1985, $240,000. Give the entries at the end of 1983, 1984, and 1985 indicating how the securities would be reported on the balance sheet at the end of each year under each of the following assumptions:

(a) Securities are reported at cost.
(b) Securities are reported at the lower of cost or market on an aggregate basis.
(c) Securities are reported at market, using an unrealized appreciation valuation account.

exercise 6-12 (Multiple choice review)

For each of the following select the *one best* answer.

1. If a marketable equity security that was classified as noncurrent in a prior period were to be reclassified as current in the current period, what would be the effect upon the valuation allowance attendant to that security assuming no change in its market value?

   (a) The valuation allowance should be reclassified to current also.
   (b) The valuation allowance should be recognized as a loss in the current period.
   (c) The valuation allowance should be adjusted to zero and the security reclassified at cost.
   (d) The valuation allowance should be recognized as a gain in the subsequent period.

2. The Carson Company's marketable equity securities portfolio which is appropriately included in current assets is as follows:

	December 31, 1984		
	Cost	Market	Unrealized Gain (Loss)
Archer Inc.	$100,000	$100,000	—
Kelly Corp.	200,000	150,000	$(50,000)
Pelt Company	250,000	260,000	10,000
	$550,000	$510,000	$(40,000)

	December 31, 1983		
	Cost	Market	Unrealized Gain (Loss)
Archer Inc.	$100,000	$120,000	$ 20,000
Kelly Corp.	300,000	260,000	(40,000)
Pelt Company	200,000	240,000	40,000
	$600,000	$620,000	$ 20,000

Ignoring income taxes, what amount should be reported as a charge against income in Carson's 1984 income statement? (a) $0. (b) $10,000. (c) $40,000. (d) $60,000.

3. Which of the following conditions generally exists before market value can be used as the basis for valuation of a company's marketable equity securities?

(a) Market value must approximate historical cost.
(b) Management's intention must be to dispose of the security within one year.
(c) Market value must be less than cost for each security held in the company's marketable equity security portfolio.
(d) The aggregate valuation of a company's marketable equity security portfolio must be less than the aggregate cost of the portfolio.

4. On January 10, 1984, Conroy Corporation acquired 1,000 shares of Alva Corporation common stock at $70 per share as a short-term investment. On that date Alva had 100,000 shares issued and outstanding. On November 1, 1984, Alva declared and paid cash dividends of $2 per share on its outstanding common stock. On December 31, 1984, the market value of Alva's common stock was $62 per share. At what value should Conroy report the investment in common stock of Alva on its December 31, 1984, balance sheet? (a) $60,000. (b) $62,000. (c) $68.000. (d) $70,000.

5. A marketable equity security must have a ready market in order to be classified as current, and

(a) Be available to management for use in short run operations.
(b) Be traded on a recognized national exchange.
(c) Have a current market value in excess of original cost.
(d) Have been owned less than one year. (AICPA adapted)

PROBLEMS

problem 6-1 (Composition of cash and marketable securities)

The balance of $147,000 in the cash account of Lisonbee Inc. consists of these items:

Petty cash fund	$ 600
Receivable from an employee	300
Cash in bond sinking fund	13,500
Cash in a foreign bank unavailable for withdrawal	30,000
Cash in Central Bank	90,000
Currency on hand	12,600

The balance in the marketable securities account consists of:

U.S. Treasury bonds	31,260
Voting stock of a subsidiary company (70% interest)	366,000
Advances to a subsidiary company (no maturity date specified)	90,000
A note receivable from a customer	30,000
The company's own shares held as treasury stock	15,000
Stock of Western Telephone Co.	42,000

Instructions: Calculate the correct Cash and Marketable Securities balances and state in what accounts and in what sections of the balance sheet the other items would be properly reported.

problem 6-2 (Accounting for petty cash)

On December 1, 1983, TSS Corporation established an imprest petty cash fund. The operations of the fund for the last month of 1983 and the first month of 1984 are summarized below:

Dec. 1 The petty cash fund was established by cashing a company check for $1,250 and delivering the proceeds to the petty cash cashier.

21 A request for replenishment of the petty cash fund was received by the accounts payable department, supported by appropriate signed vouchers summarized as follows:

Selling expenses	$ 234
Administrative expenses	531
Special equipment	96
Telephone, telegraph, and postage	24
Miscellaneous expenses	154
Total	$1,039

22 A check for $1,039 was drawn payable to the petty cash cashier.

31 The company's independent certified public accountant counted the fund in connection with the year-end audit work and found the following:

Cash in petty cash fund		$ 505
Employees' checks with January dates (postdated checks)		90
Expense vouchers properly approved as follows:		
Selling expenses	$125	
Administrative expenses	238	
Office supplies	48	
Telephone, telegraph, and postage	28	
Miscellaneous expenses	214	653
Total		$1,248

The petty cash fund was not replenished at December 31, 1983.

Jan. 15 The employees' checks held in the petty cash fund at December 31 were cashed and the proceeds retained in the petty cash fund.

31 A request for replenishment of the petty cash fund was received by the accounts payable department and a check was drawn to restore the fund to its original balance of $1,250. The support vouchers for January expenditures are summarized below.

Selling expenses	$ 75
Administrative expenses	256
Telephone, telegraph, and postage	18
Miscellaneous expenses	169
Total	$518

Instructions: Record the transactions in general journal form.

problem 6-3 (Bank reconciliation—corrected balance)

The cash account of Stanford Glass Service Inc. disclosed a balance of $17,056.48 on October 31, 1984. The bank statement as of October 31 showed a balance of $21,209.45. Upon comparing the statement with the cash records, the following facts were developed:

(a) Stanford's account had been charged for a customer's uncollectible check amounting to $1,143 on October 26.

(b) A two-month, 9%, $3,000 customer's note dated August 25, discounted on October 12, had been protested October 26, and the bank had charged Stanford for $3,050.83, which included a protest fee of $5.83.

(c) A customer's check for $725 had been entered as $625 both by the depositor and the bank but was later corrected by the bank.

(d) Check No. 661 for $1,242.50 had been entered in the cashbook as $1,224.50, and check No. 652 for $32.90 had been entered as $329. The company uses the voucher system.
(e) There were bank service charges for October of $39.43 not yet recorded on the books.
(f) A bank memo stated that M. Stum's note for $2,500 and interest of $62.50 had been collected on October 29, and the bank had made a charge of $12.50. (No entry had been made on the books when the note was sent to the bank for collection.)
(g) Receipts of October 29 for $6,850 were deposited November 1.

The following checks were outstanding on October 31:

No. 620	$1,250.00	No. 671	$ 732.50
621	3,448.23	673	187.90
632	2,405.25	675	275.72
670	1,775.38	676	2,233.15

Instructions:

(1) Construct a bank reconciliation statement, using the form where both bank and book balances are brought to a corrected cash balance.
(2) Give the journal entries required as a result of the preceding information. (Assume the company makes use of the voucher system.)

problem 6-4 (Bank to book reconciliation)

Analysis of the December bank statement for Cutlery Corp. discloses the following information:

(a) Statement balance at December 31, 1984, was $33,350.
(b) Check issued by Cutco Inc. for $630 was charged to Cutlery Corp. in error.
(c) December bank charges were $60.
(d) Deposit of $1,400 was erroneously credited to Cutlery Corp., account by the bank.
(e) Outstanding checks at December 31, 1984, were $10,560. They included a $600 check outstanding for 8 months to Amco Products which was canceled in December and a new check issued. No entry was made for the cancellation.
(f) Receipts on December 31 were $9,000. Receipts were deposited on January 2.
(g) An error in addition was made on the December 23 deposit slip. This slip showed a total of $2,220. The correct balance as credited to the account by the bank was $2,020. A count of cash on hand showed an overage of $200 as of December 31.
(h) The Cash in Bank balance in the general ledger as of December 31, 1984, was $31,280.

Instructions:

(1) Prepare a bank reconciliation statement which reconciles the bank balance with the balance per books.
(2) Give all entries required on the books at December 31, 1984.

problem 6-5 (Four-column bank reconciliation—corrected balance)

The following data are applicable to the Rogers Building Co.

(a) The July 31 bank statement balance of $74,875 included a bank service charge of $235 not previously reported to the company but recorded on the company's books in August.
(b) The cash account balance in the general ledger on July 31 was $66,715.
(c) Outstanding checks at July 31 were $13,475. Undeposited receipts on July 31 were $5,080.
(d) The bank statement on August 31 had a balance of $78,265, recognizing receipts of $105,360, and disbursements of $101,970. The disbursements included a service charge for August of $270 not yet reported to Rogers Building Co.
(e) The cash account balance in the general ledger on August 31 was $80,435, recognizing receipts of $104,405 for August and checks written during August of $90,450. Receipts of $4,125 are in transit to the bank, and checks of $2,225 have not yet cleared the bank.

Instructions:

(1) Prepare a four-column bank reconciliation as of August 31. Use the form that reconciles both bank and book balances to a correct balance.
(2) Give any entries at August 31 that may be required on the company's books.

problem 6-6 **(Four-column bank reconciliation — corrected balance)**

The following information is related to Tiny Tot Toy Supplies.

	1984 August	1984 September
Bank statement balance — at month end	$ 2,412	$ 2,782
Cash account balance — at month end	1,955	2,276
Bank charges for NSF check returned (normally written off in month following return)	38	80
Outstanding checks — at month end	600	965
Deposits in transit — at month end	300	470
Bank service charges (normally recorded in month following bank charge)	5	9
Drafts collected by bank (not recorded by company until month following collection)	200	150
Total credits to cash account	14,853	17,979
Total deposits on bank statement		18,080

Check #411 was erroneously recorded in the company checkbook and journal as $286; the correct amount is $236. (This check was not outstanding on September 30.)

The outstanding checks on September 30 include a company check for $100 certified by the bank on September 18.

All disbursements were made by check.

Instructions: Prepare a four-column bank reconciliation for the month of September, 1984. Use the form where both bank and book balances are brought to a corrected cash balance.

problem 6-7 **(Comprehensive four-column bank reconciliation)**

The following information concerning the cash accounts of Adams Group Insurance is available:

(a) Balance per bank:
- November 30, 1984 .... $37,140
- December 31, 1984 38,724

(b) Balance per books:
- November 30, 1984 .... $24,736
- December 31, 1984 37,616

(c) Outstanding checks:
- November 30, 1984 .... $12,704
- December 31, 1984 15,008

(d) December deposits, per bank statement, $270,080.
(e) December cash receipts, per cash receipts journal, $341,020.
(f) NSF checks returned by the bank are recorded as a reduction in the cash receipts journal. Those redeposited are recorded as regular cash receipts. Data regarding NSF checks are as follows:
  (1) Returned by the bank in November and recorded by company as a reduction in cash receipts in December, $300.
  (2) Returned by the bank in December and recorded by company as a reduction in cash receipts in December, $2,700.
  (3) Returned by the bank in December and recorded by company as a reduction in cash receipts in January, $460.
  (4) Redeposited by company during December, $1,600.

(g) According to the repayment terms of a large loan with the bank, the bank credits the company's checking account with 80% of the amount presented for deposit. The remaining 20% is applied to reduce the unpaid balance of the loan. The following summary entries, recorded in the cash receipts and cash disbursements journals, for December indicate the company's treatment of the deposits and resulting loan reductions:

Cash in Bank	344,020	
Cash on Hand		344,020
Bank Loan	68,804	
Cash in Bank		68,804

(h) The above summary entries include one deposit in transit on December 31, in the amount of $6,420. There were no deposits in transit on November 30, 1984. There was no undeposited cash on hand on December 31, 1984.
(i) Interest on the bank loan for the month of December was charged by the bank against the checking account, $3,658.
(j) On December 31, 1984, a $4,646 check of Adams Garage was charged to the company's account in error.

Instructions:
(1) Prepare a four-column reconciliation of receipts, disbursements, and bank balance for December 31, 1984. Use the form where both bank and book balances are brought to a corrected cash balance.
(2) Give the December 31, 1984, adjusting entries relating to the cash accounts of Adams Group Insurance.

problem 6-8 (Bank reconciliation and correcting entries)

A bank statement for Elkins Products shows a balance as of December 31, 1984, of $11,772.56. The cash account for the company as of this date shows an overdraft of $542.24. In reconciling the statement with the books, the following items are discovered:

(a) The cash balance includes $600 representing change cash on hand. When the cash on hand is counted, only $517 is found.
(b) The cash balance includes $800 representing a petty cash fund. Inspection of the petty cash fund reveals cash of $640 on hand and a replenishing check drawn on December 31 for $160.
(c) Proceeds from cash sales of $1,180 for December 27 were stolen. The company expects to recover this amount from the insurance company and has made no entry for the loss.
(d) The bank statement shows the depositor charged with a customer's NSF check for $94, bank service charges of $31.20, and a check for $260 drawn by Elkars Produce and incorrectly cleared through this account.
(e) The bank statement does not show receipts of December 31 of $3,330, which were deposited on January 3.
(f) Checks outstanding were found to be $18,610. This includes the check transferred to the petty cash fund and also two checks for $228 each payable to J. Miner. Miner had notified the company she had lost the original check and had been sent a second one, the company stopping payment on the first check.

Instructions:
(1) Prepare a bank reconciliation statement, using the form in which both bank and book balances are brought to a corrected cash balance.
(2) Give the correcting entries for Elkins Products required by the foregoing.
(3) List the cash items as they should appear on the balance sheet on December 31.

problem 6-9 (Journalizing securities transactions)

The following data are furnished by Laser Products Inc. Laser uses the lower of cost or market method of reporting all current marketable securities, and has a fiscal year end of December 31.

1984

June 1 Purchased 30, $1,000 Landoth Inc. 10% bonds at 103 plus brokerage fees of $200. Interest is paid January 1 and July 1. Laser uses the revenue approach to record accrued interest on purchased bonds.

July 1 Received semiannual interest from the Landoth Inc. bonds.

Sept. 1 Purchased $50,000 of 9% U.S. Treasury notes for $52,000 plus accrued interest. Brokerage fees were $350. Interest is paid semiannually on January 1 and July 1.

Oct. 31 Sold $20,000 of U.S. Treasury notes for $22,000 plus accrued interest. Brokerage fees were $200.

Dec. 31 Accrual of interest on the marketable securities.

31 Market prices of securities were: Landoth Inc. bonds, 105; U.S. Treasury notes, 101.

1985

Feb. 1 Sold all Landoth Inc. bonds for $30,300 plus accrued interest. Brokerage fees were $200.

Instructions: Give the journal entries for the above data.

CASH ↑ 30,300
+ 250 INT Rev
− 200 BF
30,350

problem 6-10 (Recording and valuing temporary investments)

Freeman & Associates reports the following on their December 31, 1983 balance sheet:

Marketable securities (at cost)	$225,850	
Less allowance for decline in value of marketable securities	2,260	$223,590

Supporting records of Freeman's temporary holdings show marketable securities as follows:

	Cost	Market
200 shares of Jarvis Co. common	$ 25,450	$ 24,300
$80,000 U.S. Treasury 7% bonds	79,650	77,400
$120,000 U.S. Treasury 7½% bonds	120,750	121,890
	$225,850	$223,590

Interest dates on the treasury bonds are January 1 and July 1. Freeman & Associates makes reversing entries and uses the revenue approach to recording the purchase of bonds with accrued interest.

During 1984 and 1985 Freeman & Associates completed the following transactions related to their temporary investments:

1984

Jan. 1 Received semiannual interest on U.S. Treasury bonds. (The entry to reverse the interest accrual at the end of the last year has already been made.)

Apr. 1 Sold $60,000 of the 7½% U.S. Treasury bonds at 102 plus accrued interest. Brokerage fees were $200.

May 21 Received dividends of 25 cents per share on the Jarvis Co. common stock. The dividend had not been recorded on the declaration date.

July 1 Received semiannual interest on U.S. Treasury bonds, then sold the 7% treasury bonds at 97½. Brokerage fees were $250.

Aug. 15 Purchased 100 shares of Ottley Inc. common stock at 116 plus brokerage fees of $50.

Nov. 1 Purchased $50,000 of 8% U.S. Treasury bonds at 101 plus accrued interest. Brokerage fees were $125. Interest dates are January 1 and July 1.

Dec. 31 Market prices of securities were: Jarvis Co. common, 110; 7½% U.S. Treasury bonds, 101¾; 8% U.S. Treasury bonds, 101; Ottley Inc. common, 116¾. Freeman & Associates reports all marketable securities at the lower of aggregate cost or market.

1985

Jan. 2 Recorded the receipt of semiannual interest on the U.S. Treasury bonds.

Feb. 1 Sold the 7½% U.S. Treasury bonds at 101 plus accrued interest. Brokerage fees were $300.

Instructions:

(1) Prepare journal entries for the foregoing transactions and accrue required interest on December 31. Give computations in support of your entries.

(2) Show how marketable securities would be presented on the December 31, 1984 balance sheet.

problem 6-11 (Lower of cost or market valuation of marketable securities)

Seletos Inc. purchased marketable securities during 1984 with the following costs and year-end market values:

	Cost	Market
600 shares of Toko Machinery common	$ 33,600	$ 39,375
200 shares of Kit Inc. common	51,960	46,770
$20,000 Goodplace Municipal 7% bonds	27,540	20,130
	$113,100	$106,275

Seletos Inc. values marketable securities at the lower of cost or market on an aggregate basis. On August 10, 1985, Seletos Inc. sold 150 shares of Kit Inc. common for $35,325. Market prices of the remaining securities on December 31, 1985, were: Toko common, 63; Kit Inc. common, 235½; and Goodplace Municipal 7% bonds, 106⅞.

Instructions: Give all required entries for the valuation and sale of securities in 1984 and 1985. Ignore entries for interest revenue on the bonds.

problem 6-12 (Alternative methods of valuing marketable securities)

Easy Grow Seed Co. made the following investments in marketable securities in 1983:

Ferrell Inc., 1,400 shares @ 45¾	$ 64,050
Brogan Corp., 1,750 shares @ 22½	39,375
Turner Bros. first-mortgage 8% bonds, 105 $1,000 bonds at par	105,000
	$208,425

Brogan Corp. shares were sold at the end of 1985 for $29,750. The market values of the securities at the end of 1983, 1984, and 1985 were as follows:

	1983	1984	1985
Ferrell Inc.	$ 68,250	$ 55,650	$ 60,375
Brogan Corp.	35,700	30,100	—
Turner Bros. first-mortgage 8% bonds	108,500	110,250	105,350

Instructions: Give whatever entries are required in 1983, 1984, and 1985 for the valuation and for the sale of securities, and show how the securities would be reported on the balance sheet prepared at the end of 1983, 1984, and 1985 under each of the following assumptions:

(1) Securities are valued at cost.

(2) Securities are valued at the lower of cost or market (aggregate basis).

(3) Securities are valued at market, using an unrealized appreciation valuation account.

problem 6-13 (Correcting entries for temporary investments)

During 1983 and 1984, the Domingues Co. made the following journal entries to account for transactions involving temporary investments.

1983				
(a)	Nov. 1	Marketable Securities—10% U.S. Treasury Bonds	106,883	
		Cash		106,883
		To record the purchase of $100,000 of U.S. Treasury bonds at 103¼. Brokerage fees were $300.00. Interest is payable semiannually on January 1 and July 1.		
(b)	Dec. 31	Recognized Decline in Value of Current Marketable Securities	4,283	
		Allowance for Decline in Value of Current Marketable Securities		4,283
		To record the decrease in market value of the current marketable securities based on the following data:		

	Cost	Market
Peabody Co. stock	$ 25,250	$ 23,350
Willard Co. stock	32,450	33,950
10% U.S. Treasury bonds	106,883	103,000
	$164,583	$160,300

The beginning allowance account balance was $500. There were no other entries.

1984				
(c)	Jan. 1	Cash	5,000	
		Interest Revenue		5,000
		To record interest revenue for six months.		
(d)	July 1	Cash	5,000	
		Interest Revenue		5,000
		To record interest revenue for six months.		
(e)	Dec. 6	Marketable Securities—Thomas Co. Stock (10,000 shares)	50,000	
		Long-Term Investment in Equity Securities		50,000
		To record the reclassification of Thomas Co. stock, which was selected by management for sale in 1985. Market price was $4.80 per share.		
(f)	Dec. 31	Recognized Decline in Value of Current Marketable Securities	5,483	
		Allowance for Decline in Value of Current Marketable Securities		5,483
		To record the decrease in the market value of the current marketable securities based on the following data:		

	Cost	Market
Peabody Co. stock	$ 25,250	$ 24,950
Willard Co. stock	32,450	32,650
10% U.S. Treasury bonds	106,883	103,500
Thomas Co. stock	50,000	48,000
	$214,583	$209,100

There were no other entries.

Instructions: For each incorrect entry, give the entry that should have been made. Assume the revenue approach and the lower of cost or market method.

problem 6-14 (Reporting cash and temporary investments)

The balance sheet of Bailey Home Furnishings shows the following balances for cash and temporary investments within its current assets section as of December 31, 1984:

Current assets:		
Cash	$ 76,429	
Temporary Investments	173,291	$249,720

In examining the books, it is found that Cash consists of the following:

(a) A demand deposit of $16,337 at the First Security Bank.
(b) A time deposit of $5,500 that cannot be withdrawn until after April 1, 1986.
(c) Customers' checks not yet deposited, $500.
(d) Customers' returned NSF checks, $200.
(e) A demand deposit of $9,184, which is unavailable, being in a bank in a foreign country at war.
(f) An overdraft of $192 in the Merchants Bank.
(g) A time deposit of $4,500 in a closed building and loan savings association.
(h) Advances of $1,675 to officers.
(i) Sinking fund cash of $16,525.
(j) A pension fund of $22,000 for employees.
(k) A petty cash fund of $200, of which $65 is cash, $45 is in the form of employees' IOUs, and $90 is supported by the receipts for expenses paid out of the fund.

The following securities are included under the temporary investments heading:

	Cost	Market (Including Accrued Interest)
Bailey Home Furnishings treasury stock	$ 5,876	$ 7,358
All-Star Product Co. common stock (temporary holding)	3,490	3,250
Bohn Co., 8% bonds (interest payable March 1 and September 1). Face value, $9,000. Acquired on September 1, 1984 (temporary holding)	9,190	9,140
7% United States Treasury bonds (interest payable on March 1 and September 1). Face value, $30,000. Purchased with pension sinking fund cash. Acquired September 1, 1984	30,600	30,750
Jensen Bros. common stock (temporary holding)	7,235	5,500
Parkland Inc. common stock (stock of subsidiary company)	112,000	106,300
Timp Utilities preferred stock (temporary holding)	4,900	6,300

Instructions: Show cash and temporary investments as these items should properly appear in the current assets section of the balance sheet. Provide schedules to indicate how foregoing balances are determined and what disposition is to be made of items not appropriately shown under the cash and temporary investments headings. Assume that marketable securities are reported at cost or aggregate market, whichever is lower, by means of a valuation account.

7 RECEIVABLES

CHAPTER OBJECTIVES

Identify the various types of receivables and the appropriate classifications for reporting purposes.

Explain the concept of net realizable value as it relates to accounts receivable.

Describe and illustrate methods of estimating collectibility of receivables.

Describe and illustrate the use of accounts receivable as a source of immediate cash.

Explain the concept of present value in accounting for notes receivable.

Describe and illustrate the discounting of notes receivable.

For many businesses, receivables are a significant item, often representing a major portion of the liquid assets of a company. Therefore, it is important to establish effective credit policies and collection procedures to ensure timely collection of receivables and to minimize losses from uncollectible accounts. Sound internal controls and proper accounting for receivables can be important influences on the profitability of company operations.

NATURE AND COMPOSITION OF RECEIVABLES

In its broadest sense, the term **receivables** is applicable to all claims against others for money, goods, or services. For accounting purposes, however, the term is generally employed in a narrower sense to designate claims expected to be settled by the receipt of cash.

Classification of Receivables

Usually, the chief source of receivables is the normal operating activities of a business, i.e., credit sales of goods and services to customers. These **trade receivables** may be evidenced by a formal written promise to pay and classified as **notes receivable.** In most cases, however, trade receivables are unsecured "open accounts," often referred to simply as **accounts receivable.**

Trade accounts receivable represent an extension of short-term credit to customers. Payments are generally due within thirty to ninety days. The credit arrangements are typically informal agreements between seller and buyer supported by such business documents as invoices, sales orders, and delivery contracts. Normally trade receivables do not involve interest, although an interest or service charge may be added if payments are not made within a specified period. Trade receivables are the most common type of receivable and are generally the most significant in total dollar amount.

Nontrade receivables include all other types of receivables. They arise from a variety of transactions such as: (1) sale of securities or property other than goods or services; (2) advances to stockholders, directors, officers, employees, and affiliated companies; (3) deposits with creditors, utilities, and other agencies; (4) purchase prepayments; (5) deposits to guarantee contract performance or expense payment; (6) claims for losses or damages; (7) claims for rebates and tax refunds; (8) subscriptions for capital stock; and (9) dividends and interest receivable. Nontrade receivables are generally supported by formal, often written, agreements. Nontrade receivables should be summarized in appropriately titled accounts and reported separately in the financial statements.

Another classification relates to the **current** or short-term vs **noncurrent** or long-term nature of receivables. As indicated in Chapter 5, the "Current assets" classification as broadly conceived includes all receivables identified with the normal operating cycle. Receivables arising outside the inventory-to-cash cycle qualify as current only if they are expected to be collected within one year. Thus, for classification purposes, all trade receivables are considered current; each nontrade item requires separate analysis to determine whether it is reasonable to assume that it will be collected within one year. Noncurrent receivables are reported under the "Long-term investments" or "Other long-term assets" caption, whichever is appropriate.

Amounts due from officers, directors, and major stockholders arising out of sales and subject to the usual credit terms are normally considered current; however, when claims have arisen from transactions other than sales and current recovery is not assured, such items are properly classified as noncurrent. Sales to affiliated companies give rise to current claims, but advances are generally regarded as long-term in nature. Deposits on materials and merchandise ordered will soon represent inventories and are reported as current, but deposits on utility contracts are reported as long-term. Deposits for machinery and equipment ordered are noncurrent in view of the ultimate application of the deposit. Claims from the sale of assets other than merchandise and calling for periodic collections over a period exceeding one year require special analysis to determine the portion of the claim to be reported as current and the portion to be reported as noncurrent.

Subscriptions to capital stock are classified as current only if currently collectible. When current collection is not probable, such balances are reported as noncurrent assets or as subtractions from capital balances so that only the amount actually paid by stockholders and subscribers is reported as contributed capital.

When income tax refund claims or other claims have been granted and collection is expected within one year, they qualify for current presentation. When claims are still being processed and recovery is assured although the period required for such processing is uncertain, they are shown under a noncurrent heading.

Receivables are established in the accounts only when supportable claims exist, and when it can be reasonably assumed that the claims will be realized. When a claim does not involve a material amount and there is little likelihood of recovery, no reference need be made to it on the balance sheet. On the other hand, if a material amount is involved and there is prospect of a favorable settlement, the claim is properly viewed as a contingent receivable and should be disclosed by a special note or by appropriate comment under a separate contingent asset heading.

In summary, receivables may be classified in various ways, e.g., as accounts or notes receivable, as trade or nontrade receivables, and as current or long-term receivables. These categories are not mutually exclusive. For example, accounts receivable are trade receivables and are current; notes receivable may also be trade receivables and may be current in some circumstances, but are nontrade, long-term receivables in other situations. The classifications used most often in practice and throughout this book will be simply accounts receivable, notes receivable, and other receivables.

Accounting Considerations

The basic problems in accounting for receivables include appropriate valuation, proper classification, and accurate reporting of receivables. The collection of receivables and their proper use in cash planning are also important considerations. These accounting issues are addressed in the remaining sections of this chapter.

ACCOUNTS RECEIVABLE

Accounts receivable broadly include all trade receivables not supported by some form of commercial paper. Although it would be appropriate to refer to open accounts with customers arising from the sale of goods and services as Trade Accounts Receivable to distinguish these from other receivables, it has become established practice to use Accounts Receivable to designate these claims. For reporting purposes, accounts receivable should be limited to trade accounts expected to be converted into cash in the regular course of business.

Recognition and Reporting Considerations

A receivable arising from the sale of goods is generally recognized when the title to goods passes to the buyer. Because the point at which title passes may vary with the terms of the sale, it is general practice to recognize the receivable when goods are shipped to the customer. Receivables should not be recognized for goods shipped on approval where the shipper retains title to the goods until there is a formal acceptance, or for goods shipped on consignment where the shipper retains title to the goods until they are sold by the consignee.

Receivables for services to customers are properly recognized when the services are performed. When work under a contract has not been completed at the end of the period, the amount due as of the balance sheet date will have to be calculated. Receivables should be recognized for the portion of work completed under construction contracts and for reimbursable costs and accrued fees on cost-plus-fixed-fee contracts.

Ordinarily, detailed records of customer transactions and customers' balances are carried in subsidiary records. Entries to subsidiary records may be made from original business documents evidencing the transactions. With machine methods, subsidiary records are frequently maintained simultaneously with the preparation of invoices and remittance records.

Certain revenues accrue with the passage of time and are most conveniently recognized when collections are made. At the end of the period, it is necessary to calculate the amounts accrued since the last collections and to establish appropriate accrued receivables. Accrued interest is recognized on assets such as bank deposits, notes, bonds, and annuities. Rentals may accrue on real estate holdings. Royalties and patent fees may accrue on certain rights and properties. For some business units, accrued receivables may be small in total; for others, they may involve large amounts.

Creditor Account Debit Balances. Creditor accounts with debit balances require special attention. These balances are found by an analysis of subsidiary ledger detail. For example, assume that the accounts payable control account reports a balance of $10,000. Inspection of subsidiary account detail reveals accounts with credit balances of $10,500 and accounts with debit balances of $500. The nature of the debit balances should be investigated. If the debit balances have arisen as a result of overpayments or returns and allowances after payment, they are reportable as current assets in view of the claims they represent for cash or merchandise from vendors. Such balances are properly reported under a title, such as "Creditors' accounts with debit balances." If debit balances represent advance payments on the purchase of raw materials or merchandise, these too are current assets reportable under some descriptive title, such as "Advances on purchase contracts." In either case, Accounts Payable is reported at $10,500. Although both an asset and a liability are reported, no adjustment to the control account or the subsidiary ledger detail is required. Debit balances in the subsidiary ledger are carried forward and are ultimately canceled by purchases or cash settlement.

Customer ledger detail requires similar analysis. Customers' accounts with credit balances may result from overpayments, from customer returns after full payment, or from advance payments by customers. Such credits should be recognized as current liabilities, and accounts receivable should be reported at the sum of the debit balances in the subsidiary ledger.

When contra balances in customer and creditor accounts are not material in amount, they are frequently disregarded and only the net receivable or payable balance is reported on the balance sheet.

Credit Card Sales. An increasing amount of business is being transacted with credit cards. Credit cards issued by department stores, such as Sears or J. C. Penney, are essentially open accounts and are treated like other accounts receivable. Periodic bills are sent to cardholders for merchandise purchased, cash is collected, and any uncollectible amounts are recognized as bad debts. An interest or service charge is usually assessed for credit extended.

The major oil and gas companies follow similar procedures in accounting for their credit cards. The station owner periodically submits the credit card receipts to the company headquarters, using the receipts as though they were cash to pay for gas and other supplies received from the company. The company then bills the individual customers for their purchases, and follows procedures similar to those of a department store for accounts receivable.

Bank cards, such as VISA and MasterCard, are handled somewhat differently. When a retailer receives a bank credit card from a customer in payment for merchandise, the sale is treated like a cash sale. Periodically the credit card receipts are summarized, and the total is recorded on a regular, but separate, bank deposit slip. The receipts are then deposited as though they were cash.

When the bank receives the deposit slip and the credit card receipts, the retailer's bank account is credited for the amount of the deposit. Monthly, the bank debits the retailer's bank account for a credit card service fee which is usually a percentage (generally 3–5 percent) of net credit card sales. The customer pays the bank directly. In effect, it is the bank which holds the receivables.

As an example, assume that Hall & Nielsen, a small clothing retailer, had VISA credit card sales of $650 on June 9, 1984. The journal entry for these sales would be:

Cash	650	
Sales		650

Upon deposit, $650 would be added to Hall & Nielsen's bank account. Eventually, the customers purchasing the $650 worth of merchandise would pay their credit card balances to the bank. At the end of the month, assuming that Hall & Nielsen had monthly credit card sales of $14,300 and the bank charges a fee of 4 percent of net credit card sales, the journal entry to record the expenses charged by the bank would be:

Credit Card Service Fee	572	
Cash		572
Credit card service fee, $14,300 × .04 = $572.		

Valuation of Accounts Receivable

Theoretically, receivables arising from the sale of goods or services should be reported at their **net realizable or expected cash value.** This would indicate that accounts receivable should be recorded net of any discounts expected to be taken and any anticipated sales returns or allowances. Further, it would suggest that the receivables should be reduced by any unearned finance or interest charges included in their face amounts, and any anticipated uncollectible items. The objective is to report as receivables the amount of claims from customers actually expected to be collected in cash.

Trade Discounts. Many companies bill their customers at a gross sales price less an amount designated as a **trade discount.** The discount may vary by customer depending on the volume of business or size of order from the customer. In effect, the trade discount reduces the gross or list sales price to the net price actually charged the customer. This net price is the amount at which the receivable and corresponding revenue should be recorded.

Cash Discounts. It is common business practice to offer **cash discounts** to customers to encourage prompt payment of bills. Cash discounts may be taken only if payment is received within a specified period of time, generally thirty days or less. It is almost always beneficial for customers to take all cash discounts, even if a short-term loan is required to raise sufficient cash to make the payment. Therefore, receivables may be recorded net of cash discounts on the assumption that all such discounts will be taken. If a discount is not taken and the gross amount is collected, the extra cash is considered additional revenue from discounts not taken. While this procedure is logical, the more common method followed in practice is to record the receivable at its gross amount. If payment is received within the discount period, Sales Discounts is debited for the difference between the recorded amount of the receivable and the total cash collected. This method is simple and widely used. Cash discounts are explained more fully in Chapter 8.

Sales Returns and Allowances. In the normal course of business, it is likely that some goods will be returned and some allowances will have to be made for such factors as goods damaged during shipment, spoiled or otherwise defective goods, or shipment of an incorrect quantity or type of goods. When goods are returned or an allowance is necessary, net sales and accounts receivable are reduced. To illustrate, assume merchandise costing $1,000 is sold and later returned. The return would be recorded in the following manner:

Sales Returns and Allowances	1,000	
Accounts Receivable		1,000

While the charge could be made directly to Sales, the use of a separate account preserves information that may be useful to management.

Some industries, such as the publishing industry, experience a relatively high rate of sales returns. When expected future returns are likely to have a material impact on the financial statements, an end-of-period adjustment should be made to recognize estimated returns.[1]

To illustrate, assume that the Byland Co. began operating in January 1984, and estimated that 3% of its $2 million accounts receivable outstanding at December 31, 1984, would not be collected due to returns and allowances. For illustrative purposes the amount is considered to have a material effect on the company's income. Therefore, the following year-end adjusting entry is made:

Sales Returns and Allowances	60,000	
Allowance for Sales Returns and Allowances		60,000

Computation:
3% × $2,000,000 = $60,000

During the following year, Byland would record various sales returns and allowances. Allowance for Sales Returns and Allowances, if not adjusted during the year, would still have a $60,000 credit balance at the end of 1985. If the year-end Accounts Receivable balance is $1.5 million and 3% is still deemed an appropriate rate, the allowance account should be adjusted to a credit balance of $45,000 ($1,500,000 × 3% = $45,000) with the following entry:

Allowance for Sales Returns and Allowances	15,000	
Sales Returns and Allowances		15,000

The allowance account is a contra asset valuation account to be deducted from accounts receivable on the balance sheet, thus reporting accounts receivable at their estimated net realizable value. The sales returns and allowances account is subtracted from sales on the income statement. This procedure is consistent with the fundamental matching principle. It is an attempt to recognize the proper amount of sales revenue for a particular period. The realized revenues can then be properly matched with appropriate expenses to produce a realistic income measurement for the period. Failure to anticipate sales returns and allowances or other charges affecting the

---

[1]*Statement of Financial Accounting Standards No. 48,* "Revenue Recognition When Right of Return Exists" (Stamford: Financial Accounting Standards Board, 1981).

realizable value of receivables will have little effect on periodic net income when sales volume and the rate of occurrence of such charges do not vary significantly from period to period. The anticipation of sales returns and allowances is not allowed for income tax purposes.

Unearned Finance Charges Included in Receivables. Amounts charged to customers on sales contracts often include finance, interest, and other charges related to the extension of credit. These charges are actually earned with the passage of time and should be recognized as unearned at the time of the sale. The Accounting Principles Board in Opinion No. 6 makes the following observation:

> Unearned discounts (other than cash or quantity discounts and the like), finance charges and interest included in the face amount of receivables should be shown as a deduction from the related receivables.[2]

The entry at the time of sale should establish the unearned customer charges, and periodic adjustments should be made to recognize the amounts earned. To illustrate, assume that installment sales contracts of $27,600 for one year include finance charges of 2% a month, or a total of approximately $3,277. Payments are to be made in 12 equal monthly installments. Installment sales would be reported as follows:

Installment Accounts Receivable	27,600	
Sales		24,323
Unearned Customer Finance Charges		3,277
To record installment sales.		

Computation:
$PV_n = R(PVAF_{\overline{n}|i})$
$PV_n = (\$27{,}600 \div 12)(PVAF_{\overline{12}|2\%})$; $PV_n = \$2{,}300(10.5753) = \$24{,}323$.
See Appendix A, Table IV.

As collections are made on installment accounts, the finance charges on the net receivable balance would be recognized as earned. Assuming that the monthly finance charge is 2%, the entry for the first month is shown below.

Cash	2,300	
Unearned Customer Finance Charges	486	
Installment Accounts Receivable		2,300
Revenue from Customer Finance Charges		486

Computation:
Finance charge: 2% × ($27,600 − $3,277) = $486 (rounded).

The revenue from customer finance charges is reported under "Other revenues and expenses" in the income statement. Any unearned finance charges would be reported on the balance sheet as a deduction from the related receivable account as follows:

Installment accounts receivable	$25,300	
Less unearned customer finance charges	2,791	$22,509

[2] *Opinions of the Accounting Principles Board, No. 6,* "Status of Accounting Research Bulletins" (New York: American Institute of Certified Public Accountants, 1965), par. 14.

Estimating Collectibility of Accounts Receivable

Almost invariably some receivables will prove uncollectible. Uncollectible amounts must be anticipated if the charge for them is to be related to the period of the sale and if receivables are to be stated at their estimated realizable amounts.

The amount of receivables estimated to be uncollectible is recorded by a debit to expense and a credit to an allowance account. The terminology for these account titles has changed somewhat over time. The term Allowance for Doubtful Accounts has largely replaced the earlier term of Reserve for Bad Debts following the recommendation of the AICPA terminology bulletin regarding restrictive use of the term "reserve." Other possible terms besides Doubtful Accounts are Uncollectible Accounts or Bad Debts. The expense account title usually is consistent with that of the allowance account, and thus becomes Doubtful Accounts Expense, Uncollectible Accounts Expense, or Bad Debts Expense.

The charge for doubtful accounts may be reported as a deduction from sales on the theory that it is net sales—sales after uncollectibles—that must cover current charges and yield a profit. However, instead of being treated as a contra-sales balance, the bad debt item is usually regarded as a failure of management, and, hence, is reported as a selling, general and administrative, or financial charge, depending upon the division held responsible for approving sales on account. The allowance account is reported as a subtraction from accounts receivable. Use of the allowance account avoids premature adjustments to individual receivable accounts.

When positive evidence is available concerning the partial or complete worthlessness of an account, the account is written off by a debit to the allowance account and a credit to the receivable. Positive evidence of a reduction in value is found in the bankruptcy, death, or disappearance of a debtor, failure to enforce collection legally, or a barring of collection by the statute of limitations. Write-offs should be supported by evidence of the uncollectibility of the accounts from appropriate parties, such as courts, lawyers, or credit agencies, and should be authorized in writing by appropriate company officers.

Bases for Estimating Charge for Doubtful Accounts. The estimate for doubtful accounts may be based on (1) the amount of sales for the period or (2) the amount of receivables outstanding at the end of the period. When sales are used as the basis for calculation, the problem of estimating the charge for doubtful accounts is viewed as one involving primarily the proper measurement of income. When receivables are used as the basis for calculation, the problem is viewed as one involving primarily the proper valuation of receivables.

If the sales basis is used in computing the periodic charge for doubtful accounts, any existing balance in the allowance account resulting from past period charges is disregarded. For example, if 2 percent of sales are considered doubtful in terms of collection and sales for the period are $100,000, the charge for doubtful accounts expense would be 2 percent of the current period's sales, or $2,000, regardless of the carryover balance in the allowance account. On the other hand, if the amount of receivables is used as a basis for estimating the charge for doubtful accounts, a corrected allowance figure is established each period by adjusting the existing balance. For example, if it is determined that the allowance for doubtful accounts should be $1,500 and the current credit balance in the allowance account is $600, the debit to Doubtful Accounts Expense and corresponding credit to the allowance account would be $900. These two methods, described in the paragraphs that follow, are applicable to notes receivable as well as accounts receivable.

Adjustment for Doubtful Accounts Based on Sales. The charges for doubtful accounts of recent periods are related to the sales of those periods in developing a percentage of the charge for doubtful accounts to sales. This percentage may be modified by expectations based on current experience. Since doubtful accounts occur only with credit sales, it would seem logical to develop a percentage of doubtful accounts to credit sales of past periods. This percentage would be applied to credit sales of the current period. However, since extra work may be required in maintaining separate records of cash and credit sales or in analyzing sales data, the percentage is frequently developed in terms of total sales. Unless there is considerable periodic fluctuation in the proportion of cash and credit sales, the total sales method will give satisfactory results.

The **sales percentage method** for anticipating doubtful accounts is widely used in practice because it is sound in theory and simple to apply. Although normally offering a satisfactory approach to income measurement by providing equitable charges to periodic revenue, the method may not offer a "cash realizable" valuation for receivables. This shortcoming can be overcome by analyzing receivables at different intervals and correcting the allowance for any significant excess or deficiency.

Adjustment for Doubtful Accounts Based on Receivables. There are two methods of establishing and maintaining an allowance for doubtful accounts when receivables are used as the basis for the adjustment:

(1) The allowance is adjusted to a certain percentage of receivables.
(2) The allowance is adjusted to an amount determined by aging the accounts.

In adjusting the allowance account to a certain **percentage of receivables,** the uncollectible accounts experiences of recent periods are related to accounts outstanding for those periods, and the data are considered in terms of special current conditions. An estimate of the probable uncollectibles is developed and Doubtful Accounts Expense is debited and Allowance for Doubtful Accounts credited for an amount bringing the allowance to the desired balance. To illustrate, assume that receivables are $60,000 and the allowance account has a credit balance of $200 at the end of the period. Doubtful accounts are estimated at 2% of accounts receivable, or $1,200. The following entry brings the allowance to the desired amount:

Doubtful Accounts Expense	1,000	
Allowance for Doubtful Accounts		1,000

Although this method provides a satisfactory approach to the valuation of receivables, it may fail to provide equitable period charges to revenue. This is particularly true in view of the irregular determinations of actual uncollectibles as well as the lag in their recognition. After the first year, periodic provisions are directly affected by the current reductions in the allowance resulting from a recognition of uncollectible accounts originating in prior periods.

The most commonly used method for establishing an allowance based on outstanding receivables involves **aging receivables.** Individual accounts are analyzed to determine those not yet due and those past due. Past-due accounts are classified in terms of the length of the period past due. An analysis sheet used in aging accounts receivable is shown below:

Cash and Carry Inc.
Analysis of Receivables—December 31, 1984

Customer	Amount	Not Yet Due	Not More Than 30 Days Past Due	31–60 Days Past Due	61–90 Days Past Due	91–180 Days Past Due	181–365 Days Past Due	More Than One Year Past Due
A. B. Andrews........	$ 450			$ 450				
B. T. Brooks..........	300				$ 100	$ 200		
B. Bryant............	200		$ 200					
L. B. Devine..........	2,100	$ 2,100						
K. Martinez..........	200							$ 200
M. A. Young..........	1,400	1,000		100	300			
Total................	$47,550	$40,000	$3,000	$1,200	$ 650	$ 500	$ 800	$1,400

It is desirable to review each overdue balance with an appropriate company official and to arrive at estimates concerning the degree of collectibility of each item listed. An alternative procedure is to develop a series of estimated loss percentages and apply these to the different receivable classifications. The calculation of the allowance on the latter basis is illustrated below.

Cash and Carry Inc.
Estimated Amount of Uncollectible Accounts—December 31, 1984

Classification	Balances	Uncollectible Accounts Experience Percentage	Estimated Amount of Uncollectible Accounts
Not yet due....................................	$40,000	2%	$ 800
Not more than 30 days past due....................	3,000	5%	150
31–60 days past due..............................	1,200	10%	120
61–90 days past due..............................	650	20%	130
91–180 days past due.............................	500	30%	150
181–365 days past due............................	800	50%	400
More than one year past due.......................	1,400	80%	1,120
	$47,550		$2,870

Doubtful Accounts Expense is debited and Allowance for Doubtful Accounts is credited for an amount bringing the allowance account to the required balance. Assuming uncollectibles estimated at $2,870 as shown in the preceding tabulation and a credit balance of $620 in the allowance before adjustment, the following entry would be made:

Doubtful Accounts Expense	2,250	
Allowance for Doubtful Accounts		2,250

The aging method provides the most satisfactory approach to the valuation of receivables at their cash realizable amounts. Furthermore, data developed through aging receivables may be quite useful to management for purposes of credit analysis and control. On the other hand, application of this method may require considerable time and may prove expensive. The method still involves estimates, and the added refinement achieved by the aging process may not warrant the additional cost. As with the preceding method, charges based upon the recognizable impairment of asset values rather than upon sales may fail to provide equitable periodic charges against revenue.

Corrections in Allowance for Doubtful Accounts. As previously indicated, the allowance for doubtful accounts balance is established and maintained by means of adjusting entries at the close of each accounting period. If the allowance provisions are too large, the allowance account balance will be unnecessarily inflated and earnings will be understated; if the allowance provisions are too small, the allowance account balance will be inadequate and earnings will be overstated.

Care must be taken to see that the allowance balance follows the credit experience of the particular business. The process of aging receivables at different intervals may be employed as a means of checking the allowance balance to be certain that it is being maintained satisfactorily. Such periodic reviews may indicate the need for a correction in the allowance as well as a change in the rate or in the method employed.

When the uncollectible accounts experience approximates the anticipation of the losses, the allowance procedure may be considered satisfactory and no adjustment is required. When it appears that there has been a failure to estimate uncollectible accounts satisfactorily, resulting in an allowance balance clearly inadequate or excessive, an adjustment is in order. Such an adjustment would be considered a change in accounting estimate under APB Opinion No. 20, and the effect would be reported in the current and future periods as an ordinary item on the income statement, usually as an addition to or subtraction from Doubtful Accounts Expense.

The recognition of current period receivables as uncollectible by debits to the allowance and credits to the receivable accounts may result in a debit balance in the allowance account. A debit balance arising in this manner does not indicate the allowance is inadequate; debits to the allowance simply predate the current provision for uncollectible accounts, and the adjustment at the end of the period should cover uncollectibles already determined as well as those yet to be recognized.

Occasionally, accounts that have been charged off as uncollectible are unexpectedly collected. Entries are required to reverse the original entry and record the collection. Assuming an account of $1,500 was determined to be uncollectible but was subsequently collected, the entries would be as follows:

Allowance for Doubtful Accounts	1,500	
Accounts Receivable		1,500
To write off a customer's account as uncollectible.		
Accounts Receivable..	1,500	
Allowance for Doubtful Accounts		1,500
To reverse the original entry made in writing off the account.		
Cash...	1,500	
Accounts Receivable..		1,500
To record collection of account.		

Direct Write-Off Method

Many businesses may feel that the accounting refinement to be gained by anticipating uncollectibles hardly warrants the additional work required. Instead of anticipating uncollectible accounts, these businesses may prefer simply to recognize them in the periods in which accounts are determined to be uncollectible. This is referred to as the **direct write-off method.** When the loss is not anticipated by the establishment of an allowance, uncollectible accounts are written off by a debit to Uncollectible Accounts Expense or Bad Debt Expense and a credit to the customer's account. Because the loss is now certain, and the write-off is made directly to the customer's account rather than to an allowance, the term Doubtful Accounts Expense is not appropriate.

The recognition of uncollectibles in the period of their discovery is simple and convenient. However, accounting theory supports the anticipation of uncollectibles so that current revenues may carry the full burden of related expenses. Failure to use the allowance method is a departure from generally accepted accounting principles.

Accounts Receivable as a Source of Cash

Accounts receivable are a part of the normal operating cycle of a business. Cash is used to purchase inventory which in turn is often sold on account. The receivables are then collected, providing the cash to start the cycle over. Generally the operating cycle takes several months to complete. Sometimes companies find themselves in need of immediate cash and cannot wait for completion of the normal cycle. At other times companies are not in financial stress but want to accelerate the receivable collection process or shift the risk of credit and the effort of collection to someone else. In these circumstances, receivables from customers can be used as a source of financing.

Three types of financing arrangements using accounts receivable to obtain cash from a bank or finance company are: (1) pledge of accounts receivable, (2) transfer of accounts receivable with recourse, and (3) sale of accounts receivable without recourse.

Pledge of Accounts Receivable. Advances are frequently obtained from banks or other lending institutions by **pledging accounts receivable** as security on a loan. Ordinarily, the receivable collections are made by the borrower who is required to use this cash in meeting the obligation to the lender. The lender may be given access to the borrower's records to determine whether remittances are being properly made on pledged accounts.

No special accounting problems are encountered in the pledge of receivables. When receivables are pledged, the books simply report the loan (a debit to Cash and a credit to a liability account) and subsequently the settlement (a debit to the liability account and a credit to Cash). However, disclosure should be made on the balance sheet, by parenthetical comment or note, of the amount of receivables pledged to secure the obligation to the lender.

Transfer of Accounts Receivable with Recourse. Finance companies may agree to advance cash over a period of time as accounts receivable are transferred to them. These transfers may be made on a nonnotification basis, i.e., customers are not informed of the transfer and make their payments to the transferor who is then required to turn the collections over to the transferee (finance company). When transfers are made on a notification basis, customers are instructed to make their payments directly to the finance company.

In some cases, the transferee retains the right to collect from the transferor when debtors (customers) fail to make payments when due. This type of transfer is accounted for and reported as a **sale of accounts receivable with recourse** if all of the following conditions are met:[3]

(1) The transferor surrenders control of the future economic benefits relating to the receivables.
(2) The transferor can reasonably estimate its obligation under the recourse provisions.
(3) The transferee cannot require the transferor to repurchase the receivables except to the extent provided by the recourse provisions for failure of the debtor to pay when due.

If these conditions are not met, the transfer is reported as a secured loan, i.e., in the same manner as a pledge of receivables discussed previously. When a transfer of receivables with recourse meets the conditions specified and is recorded as a sale, the difference between the amount received from the finance company (the transfer price) and the net amount of the receivables transferred (the gross amount of the receivable adjusted for allowance for doubtful accounts and any finance and service charges) is to be recognized as a gain or loss on the sale. In effect, the accounting procedures are the same

---

[3] *Exposure Draft (Revised),* "Reporting by Transferors for Transfers of Receivables with Recourse" (Stamford: Financial Accounting Standards Board, August 31, 1982), par. 7.

as those discussed in the following section for the sale of receivables without recourse. The major difference is that a contingent liability exists if the receivables are sold with recourse. The specific disclosure requirements for contingent liabilities are discussed in Chapter 13.

Sale of Accounts Receivable Without Recourse. Certain banks, dealers, and finance companies purchase accounts receivable outright on a non-recourse basis. A **sale of accounts receivable without recourse** is commonly referred to as accounts receivable **factoring,** and the buyer is referred to as a **factor.** Customers are usually notified that their bills are payable to the factor, and this party assumes the burden of billing and collecting accounts. The flow of activities involved in factoring is presented below.

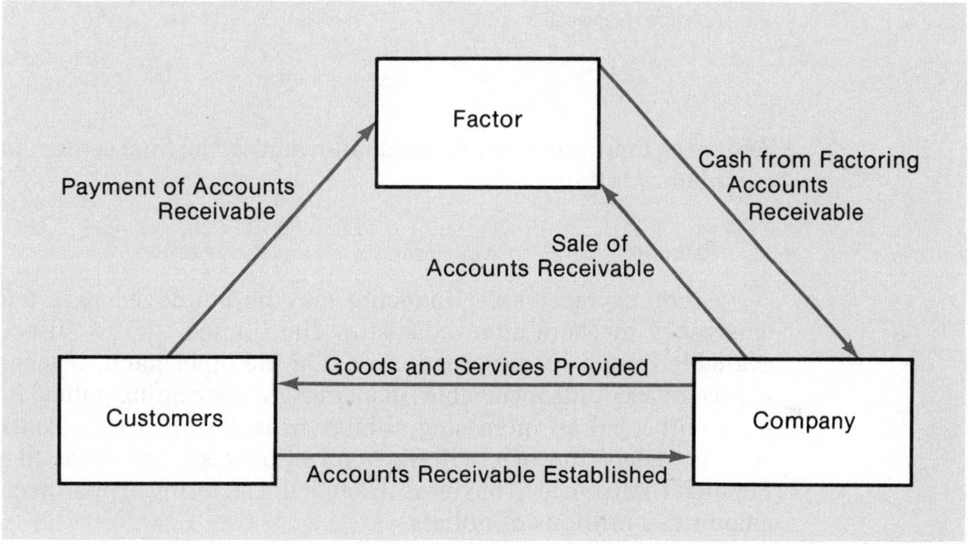

In many cases, factoring involves more than the purchase and collection of accounts receivable. Factoring frequently involves a continuing agreement whereby a financing institution assumes the credit function as well as the collection function. Under such an arrangement, the factor grants or denies credit, handles the accounts receivable records, bills customers, and makes collections. The business unit is relieved of all these activities. The sale of goods provides immediate cash for business use. Because the factor absorbs the losses from bad accounts and frequently assumes credit and collection responsibilities, the charges associated with factoring generally exceed the interest charges on a loan or the charges involved in a transfer of receivables with recourse. The factor may withhold a portion of the purchase price for possible future charges for customer returns and allowances or other special adjustments. Final settlement is made after receivables have been collected.

When receivables are sold outright, without recourse, Cash is debited, receivables and related allowance balances are closed, and an expense account is debited for factoring charges. When part of the purchase price is withheld by the factor, a receivable is established pending final settlement. Upon receipt of the total purchase price from the finance company, the receivable account is eliminated. To illustrate, assume that $10,000 of receivables are sold without recourse to a finance company for $8,500. An allowance for doubtful accounts equal to $300 was previously established. The finance company withheld 5% of the purchase price as protection against sales returns and allowances. The entry to record the sale of the accounts would be:

Cash	8,075	
Receivable from Finance Company	425	
Allowance for Doubtful Accounts	300	
Factoring Expense	1,200	
Accounts Receivable		10,000

Computations:
Cash = $8,500 − $425 = $8,075; receivable = $8,500 × 5% = $425; factoring expense = ($10,000 − $300) − $8,500 = $1,200.

Assuming there were no returns or allowances, the final settlement would be recorded as follows:

Cash	425	
Receivable from Finance Company		425

Accounts receivable financing may be employed as a temporary or emergency measure after exhausting the limited line of unsecured credit available from a lending institution. On the other hand, management may engage in accounts receivable financing as a continuing policy. Recent years have witnessed an increasing number of factoring arrangements involving the full delegation of credit and collection responsibilities to specialists. Financial assistance to business through the factoring of open accounts today amounts to millions of dollars.

NOTES RECEIVABLE

A **note** is an unconditional written promise by one party to another to pay a certain sum of money at a specified time. The note may be negotiable or nonnegotiable. It is **negotiable,** i.e., legally transferable by endorsement and delivery, only if it provides for payment to the order of the second party or bearer. Such notes are commonly accepted by commercial banks for discount; hence, they are more liquid than other classes of receivables.

For reporting purposes notes receivable should include only negotiable short-term instruments acquired from trade debtors and not yet due. Trade notes generally arise from sales involving relatively high dollar amounts where the buyer wants to extend payment beyond the usual trade credit period of thirty to ninety days. Also, sellers sometimes request notes from customers whose open accounts are past due.

Nontrade notes receivable should be separately designated on the balance sheet under an appropriate title. For example, notes arising from loans to customers, officers, employees, and affiliated companies should be reported separately.

Valuation of Notes Receivable

Notes receivable are initially recorded at their **present value** which may be defined as the sum of future receipts discounted to the present date at an appropriate rate of interest.[4] In a lending transaction, the present value is the amount of cash received by the borrower. When a note is exchanged for property, goods, or services, the present value equals the current cash selling price of the items exchanged. The difference between the present value and the amount to be collected at the due date or **maturity date** is a charge for interest.

All notes arising in arm's-length transactions between unrelated parties involve an element of interest. However, a distinction as to form is made between interest-bearing and non-interest-bearing notes. **Interest-bearing notes** are written as a promise to pay a **face amount** plus interest at a specified rate. In the absence of special valuation problems discussed in the next section, the face amount of an interest-bearing note is the present value upon issuance of the note.

Non-interest-bearing notes do not specify an interest rate, but the face amount includes the interest charge. Thus, present value is the difference between the face amount and the interest included in that amount.

In recording receipt of a note, Notes Receivable is debited for the face amount of the note. When the face amount differs from the present value, as is the case with non-interest-bearing notes, the difference is recorded as a premium or discount and amortized over the life of the note.

To illustrate, assume the Alpha Corporation sells goods on January 1, 1984, with a price of $1,000. The buyer gives Alpha a promissory note due December 31, 1985. The maturity value of the note includes interest at 10%. Thus, Alpha will receive $1,210 ($1,000 × 1.21)[5] when the note is paid. The following entries show the accounting procedures for an interest-bearing note and one written in a non-interest-bearing form.

Disc. →

	Interest-Bearing Note Face Amount = Present Value = $1,000 Stated Interest Rate = 10%			Non-Interest-Bearing Note Face Amount = Maturity = $1,210 No Stated Interest Rate		
1984						
Jan. 1	Notes Receivable	1,000		Notes Receivable	1,210	
	Sales		1,000	Sales		1,000
				Discount on Notes Receivable		210
	To record note received in exchange for goods selling for $1,000.					
Dec. 31	Interest Receivable	100		Discount on Notes Receivable	100	
	Interest Revenue		100	Interest Revenue		100
	To recognize interest earned for one year; $1,000 × .10.					

[4]See Appendix A for a discussion of present value concepts and applications.

[5]The future value of $1 due in two years at an annual rate of 10% is $1.21. See Table I of Appendix A.

	Interest-Bearing Note Face Amount = Present Value = $1,000 Stated Interest Rate = 10%			Non-Interest-Bearing Note Face Amount = Maturity = $1,210 No Stated Interest Rate		
1985						
Dec. 31	Cash	1,210		Cash	1,210	
	Notes Receivable		1,000	Discount on Notes Receivable	110	
	Interest Receivable		100	Notes Receivable		1,210
	Interest Revenue		110	Interest Revenue		110

To record settlement of note at maturity and recognize interest earned for one year: ($1,000 + $100) × .10.

If the non-interest-bearing note were recorded at face value with no recognition of the interest included therein, the sales price and profit to the seller would be overstated. In subsequent periods interest revenue would be understated. Failure to record the discount would also result in an overstatement of assets. At December 31, 1984, the unamortized discount of $110 would be deducted from notes receivable on the balance sheet.

Although the proper valuation of receivables calls for the amortization procedure just described, exceptions may be appropriate in some situations due to special limitations or practical considerations. The Accounting Principles Board in Opinion No. 21 provided guidelines for the recognition of interest on receivables and payables and the accounting subsequently to be employed. However, the Board indicated that this process is not to be regarded as applicable under all circumstances. Among the exceptions are the following:

> ...receivables and payables arising from transactions with customers or suppliers in the normal course of business which are due in customary trade terms not exceeding approximately one year.[6]

Accordingly, short-term notes and accounts receivable arising from trade sales may be properly recorded at the amounts collectible in the customary sales terms.

Notes, like accounts receivable, are not always collectible. If notes receivable comprise a significant portion of regular trade receivables, a provision should be made for uncollectible amounts and an allowance account established using procedures similar to those for accounts receivable already discussed.

Special Valuation Problems

APB Opinion No. 21 was issued to clarify and refine existing accounting practice with respect to receivables and payables.[7] The opinion is especially applicable to nontrade, long-term notes such as secured and unsecured notes, debentures, equipment obligations, and mortgage notes.

---

[6] *Opinions of the Accounting Principles Board, No. 21,* "Interest on Receivables and Payables" (New York: American Institute of Certified Public Accountants, 1971), par. 3(a). It may be noted that the primary objective of the Opinion was not to suggest new principles but simply to clarify and refine the manner of applying existing principles.

[7] *Ibid.,* par. 1.

Notes Exchanged for Cash. When a note is exchanged for cash, and there are no other rights or privileges involved, the present value of the note is presumed to be the amount of the cash proceeds. The note should be recorded at its face amount and any difference between the face amount and the cash proceeds should be recorded as a premium or discount on the note. The premium or discount should be amortized over the life of the note as illustrated previously for the Alpha Corporation. The total interest is measured by the difference in actual cash received by the borrower and the total amount to be received in the future by the lender. Any unamortized premium or discount on notes is reported on the balance sheet as a direct addition to or deduction from the face amount of the receivables, thus showing their net present value.

Notes Exchanged for Property, Goods, or Services. When a note is issued in exchange for property, goods, or services in an arm's-length transaction, the present value of the note is usually evidenced by the terms of the note or supporting documents. There is a general presumption that the interest specified by the parties to a transaction represents fair and adequate compensation for the use of borrowed funds.[8] Valuation problems arise, however, when one of the following conditions exists:[9]

(1) No interest rate is stated.
(2) The stated rate does not seem reasonable, given the nature of the transaction and surrounding circumstances.
(3) The stated face amount of the note is significantly different from the current cash equivalent sales price of similar property, goods, or services or from the current market value of similar notes at the date of the transaction.

Under any of the above conditions, APB No. 21 requires accounting recognition of the economic substance of the transaction rather than the form of the note. The note should be recorded at (1) the fair market value of the property, goods, or services exchanged or (2) the current market value of the note, whichever is more clearly determinable. The difference between the face amount of the note and the present value is recognized as a discount or premium and amortized over the life of the note.

To illustrate, assume that Delta Corporation on July 1 sells a tract of land purchased two years ago at a cost of $250,000. The buyer gives Delta a one-year note with a face amount of $280,000 bearing interest at a stated rate of 18%. An appraisal of the land prior to sale indicated a market value of $300,000, which in this example is considered to be the more appropriate basis for recording the sale as follows:

1984				
July	1	Notes Receivable	280,000	
		Premium on Notes Receivable	20,000	
		Land		250,000
		Gain on Sale of Land		50,000

[8] *Opinions of the Accounting Principles Board, No. 21, op. cit.*, par. 12.
[9] *Ibid.*

When the note is paid at maturity, Delta will receive the face value ($280,000) plus stated interest of $50,400 ($280,000 × .18) or a total of $330,400. The interest to be recognized, however, is $30,400—the difference between the maturity value of the note and the market value of the land at the date of the exchange. Thus, the **effective rate of interest** on the note is 10.13% ($30,400 ÷ $300,000).

Assuming that Delta's year-end is December 31, the following entries would be made to recognize interest revenue and record payment of the note at maturity.

1984			
Dec. 31	Interest Receivable	25,200	
	Premium on Notes Receivable		10,000
	Interest Revenue		15,200
1985			
June 30	Cash	330,400	
	Notes Receivable		280,000
	Premium on Notes Receivable		10,000
	Interest Receivable		25,200
	Interest Revenue		15,200

The unamortized premium balance of $10,000 would be added to notes receivable on the December 31, 1984 balance sheet.

Imputing an Interest Rate. If there is no current market price for either the property, goods, or services or the note, then the present value of the note must be determined by selecting an appropriate interest rate and using that rate to discount future receipts to the present. The **imputed interest rate** is determined at the date of the exchange and is not altered thereafter.

The selection of an appropriate rate is influenced by many factors including the credit standing of the issuer of the note and prevailing interest rates for debt instruments of similar quality and length of time to maturity. APB Opinion No. 21 states:

> In any event, the rate used for valuation purposes will normally be at least equal to the rate at which the debtor can obtain financing of a similar nature from other sources at the date of the transaction. The objective is to approximate the rate which would have resulted if an independent borrower and an independent lender had negotiated a similar transaction under comparable terms and conditions with the option to pay the cash price upon purchase or to give a note for the amount of the purchase which bears the prevailing rate of interest to maturity.[10]

To illustrate the process of imputing interest rates, assume that Sabin & Associates surveyed 800,000 acres of mountain property for the Bar X Ranch. On December 31, 1984, Sabin accepted a $45,000 note as payment for services. The note is non-interest-bearing and comes due in three yearly installments of $15,000 each beginning December 31, 1985. There is no market for the note, nor can an objective estimate be made of the fair

[10] *Ibid.*, par. 13.

market value of the services rendered. After considering the current prime interest rate, the credit standing of Bar X, the collateral available, the terms for repayment, and the prevailing rates of interest for the issuer's other debt, a 10% imputed interest rate is considered appropriate. The note should be recorded at its present value and a discount recognized. The computation is based on Present Value Table IV in Appendix A as follows:

Face amount of note	$45,000
Less present value of note:	
$PV_n = R(PVAF_{\overline{3}|10\%})$	
$PV_n = \$15,000(2.4869)$	37,303*
Discount on note	$ 7,697

*Rounded to nearest dollar.

The entry to record the receipt of the note would be:

1984			
Dec. 31	Notes Receivable	45,000	
	Discount on Notes Receivable		7,697
	Service Revenue		37,303
	To record a non-interest-bearing note receivable at its present value based on an imputed interest rate of 10% per year.		

A schedule showing the amortization of the discount on the note is presented below.

	(1) Face Amount Before Current Installment	(2) Unamortized Discount	(3) Net Amount (1) − (2)	(4) Discount Amortization 10% × (3)	(5) Payment Received
December 31, 1985	$45,000	$7,697	$37,303	$3,730	$15,000
December 31, 1986	30,000	3,967	26,033	2,603	15,000
December 31, 1987	15,000	1,364	13,636	1,364	15,000
				$7,697	$45,000

At the end of each year, an entry similar to the following would be made.

1985			
Dec. 31	Cash	15,000	
	Discount on Notes Receivable	3,730	
	Interest Revenue		3,730
	Notes Receivable		15,000
	To record the first year's installment on notes receivable and recognize interest earned during period.		

By using these procedures, at the end of the three years the discount will be completely amortized to interest revenue, the face amount of the note receivable will have been collected, and the appropriate amount of service revenue will have been recognized in the year it was earned. At the end of each year, the balance sheet will reflect the net present value of the receivable by subtracting the unamortized discount balance from the face amount of the note.

It is necessary to impute an interest rate only when the present value of the receivable cannot be determined through evaluation of existing market values of the elements in the transaction. The valuation and income measurement objectives remain the same regardless of the specific circumstances—to report receivables at their net present values and to record appropriate amounts of interest revenue during the collection period of the receivable.

Discounting Notes Receivable

As discussed earlier in the chapter, accounts receivable can be a source of immediate cash. Notes receivable can also provide a source of cash for a company through the process of **bank discounting.** This common business practice is not to be confused with the discounting of future cash receipts to arrive at asset values as discussed previously. Bank discounting is the sale of notes receivable for cash to a bank or to some other agency willing to accept such instruments. If a note is non-interest-bearing, cash is received for the face value of the note less a charge for interest, known as a **discount,** for the period from the date the note is discounted to the date of its maturity. If the note is interest-bearing, the maturity value of the note is first determined. The amount received from the bank (**proceeds**) is the maturity value of the note less a discount calculated on this maturity value from the date the note is discounted to its maturity.

To illustrate entries for a non-interest-bearing note, assume a 90-day, $1,000 note dated December 1 is received; the note is discounted on December 16 at 18%. The following entries are made:

Dec. 1	Notes Receivable	1,000.00	
	Accounts Receivable		1,000.00
16	Cash	962.50	
	Interest Expense	37.50	
	Notes Receivable		1,000.00

Computation:
Discount: $1,000 × .18 × 75/360 = $37.50

To illustrate the accounting for an interest-bearing note, assume that the note received in the previous example provides for the payment of interest at 10% at its maturity and it is discounted at the bank at 18%. Under these circumstances, the following entries would be appropriate:

Dec. 1	Notes Receivable	1,000.00	
	Accounts Receivable		1,000.00
16	Cash	986.56	
	Interest Expense	13.44	
	Notes Receivable		1,000.00

Computation:

Maturity value of note:
$1,000 + interest ($1,000 × .10 × 90/360) = $1,025
Discount:
$1,025 × .18 × 75/360 = $38.44

Proceeds:
$1,025 − $38.44 = $986.56
Net interest expense:
$1,000 − $986.56 = $13.44

A note endorsed "without recourse" relieves the endorser of any liability for the inability of the maker of the note or any prior endorser to pay the note upon its maturity. When a note is endorsed without making any qualification, the endorser becomes liable to subsequent holders of the note if it is not paid at maturity. However, if the endorser is held liable on the note, that person has the right to recover amounts paid from the maker of the note or prior endorsers who failed to comply with its terms.

Normally, endorsement without qualification is required in discounting a note, and the endorser becomes contingently liable on the note. Under these circumstances Notes Receivable Discounted instead of Notes Receivable may be credited when the note is discounted. Pending final settlement on the note, the discounted portion of notes receivable would be regarded as a contingent asset. Notes Receivable Discounted, in turn, would be an accompanying contingent liability. When the person who holds the note at maturity receives payment from the maker, both payment and recovery contingencies are ended, and Notes Receivable Discounted can be applied against Notes Receivable.

The use of the notes receivable discounted account gives the same final result as that obtained when Notes Receivable is credited for notes discounted. Since data concerning the contingent liability are of concern only on the balance sheet date and these can be determined readily at the end of the period from an examination of the detailed record of notes discounted, the extra work involved in maintaining a notes receivable discounted account may not be warranted. When a notes receivable discounted balance is carried in the accounts, this balance is subtracted from Notes Receivable in reporting the notes receivable balance. When a notes receivable discounted account is not used, information concerning the contingent liability is provided on the balance sheet by means of a parenthetical remark or note or by special reference under a separate contingent liabilities heading.

If a note is not paid when it is due, the holder of the note must give the endorser prompt notice of such dishonor. The endorser is then required to make payment to the holder. Payment consists of the face value of the note plus interest and any fees and costs relating to collection. The full amount paid is recoverable from the maker of the note, and Accounts Receivable, Notes Receivable Dishonored, or Notes Receivable Past Due may be debited. If Notes Receivable Discounted was credited at the time the note was discounted, this balance, together with the original notes receivable balance, should be canceled. Subsequent recovery on the note is recorded by a debit to Cash and a credit to the account with the debtor. It should be noted that this subsequent payment by the debtor would generally include additional interest from date of dishonor to date of payment as well as the protest fee which the endorser has had to pay. Failure to recover any portion of the balance due would call for writing off the unpaid balance.

To illustrate, assume that in the preceding example Notes Receivable Discounted instead of Notes Receivable was credited when the note was discounted. The following entry would be made when the note is paid at maturity.

Notes Receivable Discounted	1,000	
Notes Receivable		1,000

If the note was not paid at maturity and the bank charged the endorser with a $10 protest fee, an entry would be made as follows:

Accounts Receivable	1,035	
Notes Receivable Discounted	1,000	
Cash		1,035
Notes Receivable		1,000

Computation:
Maturity value of note, $1,025 + $10 protest fee = $1,035

Subsequent payment from the customer, assuming 30 days of additional interest, is recorded as follows:

Cash	1,043.63	
Accounts Receivable		1,035.00
Interest Revenue		8.63

Computation:
Value of receivable at dishonor date: $1,035 × .10 × 30/360 = $8.63 interest + $1,035 = $1,043.63

PRESENTATION OF RECEIVABLES ON THE BALANCE SHEET

Normally, the receivables qualifying as current items are grouped for presentation in the following classes: (1) notes—trade debtors, (2) accounts—trade debtors, (3) other receivables, and (4) accrued receivables. Reporting should disclose nonnegotiable notes. The detail reported for other and accrued receivables depends upon the relative significance of the various items included. When trade accounts or installment contracts are properly reported as current but involve collections beyond one year, particulars of such deferred collections should be provided. Valuation accounts are deducted from the individual receivable balances or combined balances to which they relate. Notes receivable may be reported gross with notes receivable discounted shown as a deduction from this balance, or notes may be reported net with appropriate reference to the contingent liability arising from notes discounted. If notes or accounts receivable have been pledged to secure a loan, the amount should be disclosed.

Current receivable items as they might appear on the balance sheet are shown below. An alternative to parenthetical disclosure would be to present the supplemental information in a note to the financial statements.

Receivables:		
Trade notes receivable (notes of $20,000 have been pledged to secure bank borrowing)	$39,500	
Less notes receivable discounted	1,500	$ 38,000
Accounts receivable (including installment contracts of approximately $30,000 not due for 12-18 months)	$154,000	
Less allowance for doubtful accounts	11,000	143,000
Miscellaneous notes and accounts, including short-term loans to employees of $6,500		12,000
Accrued receivables		4,500
Total receivables		$197,500

QUESTIONS

1. Explain how each of the following factors affects the classification of a receivable: (a) the form of the receivable, (b) the source of the receivable, and (c) the expected length of time to maturity or collection.

2. The Summer Corporation shows on its balance sheet one receivable balance including the following items: (a) advances to officers, (b) deposits on machinery and equipment being produced by various companies for the Summer Corporation, (c) advances for traveling expenses, (d) damage claims against transportation companies approved by such companies, (e) estimated federal income tax refunds, (f) accrued interest on notes receivable, (g) overdue notes, (h) receivables from a foreign subsidiary company, (i) subscriptions receivable on a new bond issue, and (j) creditor overpayments. Suggest the proper treatment of each item.

3. The Collins Co. includes in its current receivable total an investment in a joint venture with the Lars Corporation. Officials of the Collins Co. justify this practice on the grounds the assets of the joint venture are all in current form. Comment on this practice.

4. The Clarke Manufacturing Co. has filed a lawsuit against a competitor for alleged patent infringement. Clarke is seeking a very large sum in damages. The president of Clarke feels that the potential proceeds should "show up somewhere on the balance sheet." How would you respond to this comment?

5. (a) Give three methods for the establishment and the maintenance of an allowance for doubtful accounts. (b) What are the advantages and disadvantages of each method?

6. How would the percentages used in estimating uncollectible accounts be determined under any of the methods of maintaining an allowance for doubtful accounts?

7. What entries are necessary when an account previously written off is collected?

8. An analysis of the accounts receivable balance of $8,702 on the records of Bookkeepers, Inc. on December 31 reveals the following:

Accounts from sales of last three months (appear to be fully collectible)	$7,460
Accounts from sales prior to October 1 (of doubtful value)	1,312
Accounts known to be worthless	320
Dishonored notes charged back to customers' accounts	800
Credit balances in customers' accounts	1,190

(a) What adjustments are required?
(b) How should the various balances be shown on the balance sheet?

9. How do the accounting procedures for recognizing uncollectible accounts in the period of discovery (direct write-off) differ from those of anticipating uncollectible accounts?

10. List and explain three items that may be deducted under certain circumstances in reducing accounts receivable to a net realizable value.

11. If unearned customer finance charges for installment receivables are carried as a separate valuation account balance, what difficulties do you foresee in calculating a proper allowance for doubtful accounts?

12. In what section of the income statement would you report (a) doubtful accounts expense, (b) sales discounts?

13. (a) Distinguish between the practices of (1) pledging, (2) selling accounts receivable with recourse, and (3) selling accounts receivable without recourse. (b) Describe the accounting procedures to be followed in each case.

14. The Dunn Co. enters into a continuing agreement with H & S Finance Inc., whereby the latter company buys without recourse all of the trade receivables as they arise and assumes all credit and collection functions. (a) Describe the advantages that may accrue to the Dunn Co. as a result of the factoring agreement. (b) Are there any disadvantages? Explain.

15. Comment on the statement, "There is no such thing as a non-interest-bearing note."

16. (a) When should a note receivable be recorded at an amount different from its face value? (b) Describe the procedures employed in accounting for the difference between a note's face value and its recorded value.

17. (a) What is meant by imputing a rate of interest? (b) How is such a rate determined?

18. The Lambert Optical Co. discounts at 20% the following three notes at the Security First Bank on July 1 of the current year. Compute the proceeds on each note using 360 days to a year.

(a) A 90-day, 11% note receivable for $10,000 dated June 1.
(b) A 6-month, 12% note receivable for $14,000 dated May 13.
(c) Its own 4-month note payable dated July 1 with face value of $5,000 and no stated interest rate.

19. Indicate several methods for presenting information on the balance sheet relating to (a) notes receivable discounted, and (b) pledged accounts receivable.

DISCUSSION CASES

case 7-1 (Deferred payment receivables) The Sandee Corporation sells home air-conditioning units. The cash price of these units is $800; the price on a deferred payment plan is $900. Those acquiring the units on the deferred payment plan sign a note providing for payments of $50 per month for eighteen months. What accounting issues are involved? How would you recommend the deferred payment sales and subsequent collections be reported in the accounts?

case 7-2 (Accounts receivable as a source of cash) Assume you are the treasurer for Fullmer Products Inc. and one of your responsibilities is to ensure that the company always takes available cash discounts on purchases. The corporation needs $100,000 within one week in order to take advantage of current cash discounts. The lending officer at the bank insists on adequate collateral for a $100,000 loan. For various reasons, your plant assets are not available as collateral, but your accounts receivable balance is $130,000. What might you do?

case 7-3 (Selling receivables instead of merchandise) The following excerpts are from an article printed in the Wall Street Journal. What aspects appear to be unique to this actual example of the sale of receivables?

> Sears, Roebuck & Co. said it arranged to sell $550 million of customer accounts receivable to a group of 16 institutional investors headed by Continental Illinois National Bank & Trust Co.
>
> Under the plan, the investors will assume ownership of the receivables, representing about 8% of Sears' total receivables outstanding as well as additions resulting from new purchases. The receivables will be sold to the institutional investors without recourse. And they will receive subsequent finance charge income on the accounts.
>
> Edward R. Telling, Sears chairman, said the agreement calls for the sale by Sears of additional receivables each month with the total to be sold expected to reach $625 million by February 1, 1979. Subject to further negotiations, the total could reach $1 billion by 1983, he added.
>
> The initial $550 million will be sold at 99.015% of face value with Sears receiving an administrative fee from the institutional buyers for handling the accounts. Initially, the fee will equal 5.62% of the unpaid balance.

EXERCISES

exercise 7-1 (Balance sheet presentation of receivables)

The accounts receivable control account for the Brix Corporation shows a debit balance of $113,900; Allowance for Doubtful Accounts shows a credit balance of $7,600. Subsidiary ledger detail reveals the following:

Trade accounts receivable (accounts pledged to secure bank loan, $16,000)	$24,000
Subscriptions receivable for common stock due in 60 days	45,000
Interest receivable on bonds	3,750
Installment receivables due 1-18 months hence (including unearned finance charge of $1,000)	6,000
Trade receivables from officers, due currently	800
Customers' accounts reporting credit balances arising from sales returns	250
Advance payments to creditors on purchase orders	7,500
Advance payments to creditors on orders for machinery	12,000
Customers' accounts reporting credit balances arising from advance payments	1,500
Accounts known to be worthless	900
Trade accounts on which post-dated checks are held (no entries were made on receipt of checks)	700
Advances to affiliated companies	15,000

Show how this information would be reported on the balance sheet.

exercise 7-2 (Computing the accounts receivable balance)

The information below, pertaining to the Selker Company's first year of operations, is to be used in testing the accuracy of Accounts Receivable, which has a balance of $33,000 at December 31, 1984.

(a) Collections from customers, $50,000
(b) Merchandise purchased, $80,000
(c) Ending merchandise inventory, $20,000
(d) Goods sell at 50% above cost
(e) All sales are on account

Compute the balance that Accounts Receivable should show and determine the amount of any shortage or overage.

exercise 7-3 (Recording credit card sales)

José Rubio's Mexican Restaurant accepts only cash or VISA and MasterCard credit cards. During June, total sales amounted to $16,800, including $10,000 worth of net bank card sales. The bank charges a 3.5% fee on net credit card sales. Record the monthly summary entry to reflect the above transactions.

exercise 7-4 (Estimating doubtful accounts)

Accounts Receivable of the Fakler Manufacturing Co. on December 31, 1984, had a balance of $150,000. The Allowance for Doubtful Accounts had a $4,500 debit balance. Sales in 1984 were $1,125,000 less sales discounts taken of $9,000.

Give the adjusting entry for estimated doubtful accounts expense, assuming:

(1) One half of 1% of 1984 net sales will probably never be collected.
(2) Two percent of outstanding accounts receivable are doubtful.
(3) An aging schedule shows that $7,500 of the outstanding accounts receivable are doubtful.

exercise 7-5 (Journal entries for doubtful accounts)

Willie's Gas Station had sales of $605,000 during 1984, 30% of which were on credit. Accounts receivable outstanding at December 31, 1984, totaled $30,000, and the allowance for doubtful accounts had a $500 credit balance. Willie had cash discounts (for credit customers who paid within the discount period) of $10,000. He also had $5,000 of merchandise returned by dissatisfied customers, 30% of which were by credit customers.

Give the adjusting entry for estimated doubtful accounts expense, assuming:

(1) One percent of net credit sales will be uncollectible.
(2) Two and one-half percent of current accounts receivable are doubtful.

exercise 7-6 (Estimating doubtful accounts—percentage of sales method)

Prior to 1985, Jeske Inc. followed the percentage-of-sales method of estimating doubtful accounts. The following data are gathered by the accounting department:

	1981	1982	1983	1984
Total sales	$1,050,000	$2,100,000	$3,600,000	$6,300,000
Credit sales	600,000	960,000	1,950,000	3,600,000
Accounts receivable (end-of-year balance)	186,000	234,000	360,000	750,000
Allowance for doubtful accounts (end-of-year credit balance)	3,000	18,000	12,000	66,000
Accounts written off	27,000	6,000	42,000	9,000

(1) What amount was debited to expense for 1982, 1983, and 1984?
(2) Compute the balance in the valuation account at the beginning of 1981 assuming there has been no change in the percentage of sales used over the four-year period.
(3) What explanation can be given for the fluctuating amount of write-off?
(4) Why do the actual write-offs fail to give the correct charge to expense?

exercise 7-7 (Aging accounts receivable)

The Ivar Company's accounts receivable subsidiary ledger reveals the following information.

Buyer	Account Balance December 31, 1984	Invoice Amounts	and Dates
Alford Inc.	$ 8,795	$3,500	12/6/84
		5,295	11/29/84
Banks Bros. Inc.	5,230	3,000	9/27/84
		2,230	8/20/84
Krop & Co.	7,650	5,000	12/8/84
		2,650	10/25/84
Marr Inc.	11,285	5,785	11/17/84
		5,500	10/09/84
Sage Inc.	7,900	4,800	12/12/84
		3,100	12/2/84
Westring Co.	4,350	4,350	9/12/84

Ivar Company's receivable collection experience indicates that losses have occurred as follows:

Age of Accounts	Uncollectible Percentage
0-30 days	.7%
31-60 days	1.4%
61-90 days	3.5%
91-120 days	10.2%
121 days and over	60.0%

The Allowance for Doubtful Accounts balance on December 31, 1984, was $2,245 before adjustment.

(1) Prepare an accounts receivable aging schedule.
(2) Using the aging schedule from part (1), compute the Allowance for Doubtful Accounts balance as of December 31, 1984.
(3) Prepare the end-of-year adjusting entry.
(4) (a) Where accounts receivable are few in number, such as in this exercise, what are some possible weaknesses in estimating doubtful accounts by the aging method? (b) Would the other methods of estimating doubtful accounts be subject to these same weaknesses? Explain.

exercise 7-8 (Analysis of allowance for doubtful accounts)

The Technical Publishing Company follows the procedure of debiting Doubtful Accounts Expense for 2% of all new sales. Sales for four consecutive years and year-end allowance account balances were as follows:

Year	Sales	Allowance for Doubtful Accounts (end-of-year credit balance)
1981	$2,100,000	$21,500
1982	1,975,000	35,500
1983	2,500,000	50,000
1984	2,350,000	66,000

(1) Compute the amount of accounts written off for the years 1982, 1983, and 1984.
(2) The external auditors are concerned with the growing amount in the allowance account. What action do you recommend the auditors take?
(3) What arguments might Technical use to justify the balance in the valuation account? Allowance for Doubtful Accounts is the only accounts receivable valuation account used by Technical Publishing.

exercise 7-9 (Accounts receivable as a source of cash)

The Beta Corporation decides to use accounts receivable as a basis for financing. Its current position is as follows:

Accounts receivable....	$80,000	Cash overdraft.........	$ 400
Inventories	81,000	Accounts payable......	57,500

Prepare a statement of its current position, assuming cash is obtained as indicated in each case below:

(1) Cash of $60,000 is borrowed on short-term notes and $35,000 is applied to the payment of creditors; accounts of $70,000 are pledged to secure the loan.
(2) Cash of $60,000 is advanced to the company by Eakins Finance Co., the advance representing 80% of accounts transferred on a recourse basis. (Assume the transfer meets the FASB conditions to be accounted for as a sale.)
(3) Cash of $60,000 is received on the sale of accounts receivable of $78,000 on a nonrecourse basis.

exercise 7-10 (Accounting for a non-interest-bearing note)

Johnson Corporation sells equipment with a book value of $6,000, receiving a non-interest-bearing note due in three years with a face amount of $8,000. There is no established market value for the equipment. The interest rate on similar obligations is estimated at 12%. Compute the gain or loss on the sale and the discount on notes receivable, and make the necessary entry to record the sale.

exercise 7-11 (Accounting for an interest-bearing note)

Brady Inc. sold a piece of machinery with an original cost of $40,000 and accumulated depreciation of $15,000. The buyer, lacking sufficient cash to pay for the machine, issued a 6-month, 10% note for $28,000. Make the entries for Brady to record (1) the sale and (2) settlement of the note at maturity.

exercise 7-12 (Discounting notes—computations)

On December 21, the following notes are discounted by the bank at 16%. Determine the cash proceeds from each note.

(1) 30-day, $3,500, non-interest-bearing note dated December 15.
(2) 60-day, $2,379, 9% note dated December 1.
(3) 60-day, $10,000, 13% note dated November 6.
(4) 90-day, $6,775, 19% note dated November 24.

exercise 7-13 (Accounting for notes receivable discounted)

G. C. Larsen sold Andersen Farm Machinery a used tractor and received a 90-day, 10% note for $5,000 on May 13, 1984. On May 29, Larsen discounted the note at 11%. On August 11, the bank notified Larsen that the note was not paid and charged Larsen a $10 protest fee. On September 1, Larsen collected the note plus 12% interest from the maturity date on the account receivable balance. Record the entries for the above events on Larsen's books.

exercise 7-14 (Accounting for notes receivable discounted)

B. Richmond received from J. Harman, a customer, a 90-day, 12% note for $4,000, dated June 6, 1984. On July 6, Richmond had Harman's note discounted at 10% and recorded the contingent liability. The bank protested nonpayment of the note and charged the endorser with protest fees of $10 in addition to the amount of the note. On September 28, 1984, the note was collected with interest at 14% from the maturity date on the account receivable balance. What entries would appear on Richmond's books as a result of the foregoing?

exercise 7-15 (Discounting a note receivable)

On June 1, 1984, J. Sparks received a $4,107 note from a customer on an overdue account. The note matures on August 30 and bears interest at 10%. On July 1, Sparks discounted the note at 11% and applied the proceeds to the payment of creditors. On August 30, the customer is unable to make payment to the bank and the bank charges Sparks' account for the maturity value of the note plus a $6 protest fee. On September 29, Sparks accepted the customer's offer to cancel the liability in exchange for marketable securities valued at $4,290. Give all entries on Sparks' books to record the foregoing.

exercise 7-16 (AICPA adapted multiple choice)

For each of the following, select the *one* best answer.

(1) At the beginning of 1982, Garmar Company received a three-year non-interest-bearing $1,000 trade note. The market rate for equivalent notes was 12% at that time. Garmar reported this note as $1,000 trade notes receivable on its 1982 year-end statement of financial position and $1,000 as sales revenue for 1982. What effect did this accounting for the note have on Garmar's net earnings for 1982, 1983, and 1984, and its retained earnings at the end of 1984, respectively?

(a) Overstate, understate, understate, zero.
(b) Overstate, understate, understate, understate.
(c) Overstate, overstate, understate, zero.
(d) No effect on any of these.

(2) At the close of its first year of operations December 31, 1984, the Walker Company had accounts receivable of $250,000, which were net of the related allowance for doubtful accounts. During 1984, the company had charges to bad debt expense of $40,000 and wrote off, as uncollectible, accounts receivable of $10,000. What should the company report on its balance sheet at December 31, 1984, as accounts receivable before the allowance for doubtful accounts?

(a) $250,000.
(b) $260,000.
(c) $280,000.
(d) $300,000.

(3) For the month of December 1984, the records of Ranger Corporation show the following information:

Cash received on accounts receivable	$35,000
Cash sales	30,000
Accounts receivable, December 1, 1984	80,000
Accounts receivable, December 31, 1984	74,000
Accounts receivable written off as uncollectible	1,000

The corporation uses the direct write-off method in accounting for uncollectible accounts receivable. What are the gross sales for the month of December 1984?

(a) $59,000.
(b) $60,000.
(c) $65,000.
(d) $72,000.

(4) The Mitchell Company received a seven-year non-interest-bearing note on February 22, 1983, in exchange for property it sold to the Grispin Company. There was no established exchange price for this property and the note has no ready market. The prevailing rate of interest for a note of this type was 10% on February 22, 1983, 10.2% on December 31, 1983, 10.3% on February 22, 1984, and 10.4% on December 31, 1984. What interest rate should be used to calculate the interest revenue from this transaction for the year ended December 31, 1984 and 1983, respectively?

(a) 0% and 0%.
(b) 10% and 10%.
(c) 10% and 10.3%.
(d) 10.2% and 10.4%.

(5) The following accounts were abstracted from the trial balance of Marion Company at December 31, 1984:

	Debit	Credit
Gross Sales		$500,000
Sales Discount	$10,000	

On January 1, 1984, Allowance for Doubtful Accounts had a credit balance of $12,000. During 1984, $20,000 of accounts receivable deemed uncollectible were written off.

Historical experience indicates that 3% of gross sales proved uncollectible. What should be the balance in Allowance for Doubtful Accounts after the current provision is made?

(a) $6,700.
(b) $7,000.
(c) $14,700.
(d) $23,000.

(AICPA adapted)

PROBLEMS

problem 7-1 (Journal entries and balance sheet presentation)

The balance sheet for the Ashley Cosmetic Corporation on December 31, 1983, includes the following receivable balances:

Interest receivable		$ 325
Notes receivable	$47,500	
Less notes receivable discounted	15,500	32,000
Accounts receivable	$90,000	
Less allowance for doubtful accounts	3,950	86,050

Transactions during 1984 included the following:

(a) Sales on account were $767,800.
(b) Cash collected on accounts totaled $571,000, which included accounts of $97,000 on which cash discounts of 2% were allowed.
(c) Notes received in payment of accounts totaled $84,000.
(d) Notes receivable discounted as of December 31, 1983, were paid at maturity with the exception of one $8,000 note on which the company had to pay $8,090, which included interest and protest fees. It is expected that recovery will be made on this note in 1985.
(e) Customers' notes of $50,000 were discounted during the year, proceeds from their sale being $48,500. Of this total, $34,500 matured during the year without notice of protest.
(f) Customers' accounts of $8,420 were written off during the year as worthless.
(g) Recoveries of doubtful accounts written off in prior years were $1,020.
(h) Notes receivable collected during the year totaled $26,000 and interest collected was $2,150.
(i) On December 31, accrued interest on notes receivable was $635.
(j) Uncollectible accounts are estimated to be 5% of the December 31, 1984, Accounts Receivable balance.
(k) Cash of $35,000 was borrowed from the bank, accounts receivable of $42,000 being pledged on the loan. Collections of $19,500 had been made on these receivables (included in the total given in transaction [b]) and this amount was applied on December 31, 1984, to payment of accrued interest on the loan of $500, and the balance to partial payment of the loan.

Instructions:
(1) Prepare journal entries summarizing the transactions and information given above.
(2) Prepare a summary of current receivables for balance sheet presentation.

problem 7-2 (Analysis of accounts receivable)

The Tammarack Co., which began business on January 1, 1984, decided to establish an allowance for doubtful accounts. It was estimated that uncollectibles would amount to 1% of credit sales. At the end of each month, an entry was made to record doubtful accounts expense equal to 1% of credit sales for the month. On December 31, 1984, outstanding receivables are $23,000; Allowance for Doubtful Accounts has a credit balance of $500 after recording estimated doubtful accounts expense for December and after $250 of uncollectible accounts had been written off. Following is additional data for 1984.

(a) Collections from customers (excluding cash purchases), $60,000.
(b) Merchandise purchased, $90,000.
(c) Ending merchandise inventory, $15,000.
(d) Goods were sold at 40% above cost.
(e) 80% of sales were on account.

Instructions: Determine if accounts receivable and the allowance for doubtful accounts are correctly stated at December 31, 1984.

problem 7-3 (Accounting for receivables—journal entries)

The following transactions affecting the accounts receivable of Southern States Manufacturing Corporation took place during the year ended January 31, 1984.

Sales (cash and credit)	$591,050
Cash received from credit customers (customers who paid $298,900 took advantage of the discount feature of the corporation's credit terms, 2/10, n/30)	302,755
Cash received from cash customers	205,175
Accounts receivable written off as worthless	4,955
Credit memoranda issued to credit customers for sales returns and allowances	56,275
Cash refunds given to cash customers for sales returns and allowances	16,972
Recoveries on accounts receivable written off as uncollectible in prior periods (not included in cash amount stated above)	10,615

The following two balances were taken from the January 31, 1983 balance sheet:

Accounts receivable	$95,842
Allowance for doubtful accounts	9,740

The corporation provides for its net uncollectible account losses by crediting Allowance for Doubtful Accounts for 1½% of net credit sales for the fiscal period.

Instructions:

(1) Prepare the journal entries to record the transactions for the year ended January 31, 1984.
(2) Prepare the adjusting journal entry for estimated uncollectible accounts on January 31, 1984.

problem 7-4 (Estimating uncollectible accounts by aging receivables)

Starr Company, a wholesaler, uses the aging method to estimate bad debt losses. The following schedule of aged accounts receivable was prepared at December 31, 1985.

Age of Accounts	Amount
0-30 days	$461,200
31-60 days	196,100
61-90 days	83,600
91-120 days	18,500
More than 120 days	8,400
	$767,800

The following schedule shows the year-end receivable balance and uncollectible account experience for the previous five years.

		Loss Experience—Percent of Uncollectible Accounts				
Year	Year-End Receivables	0-30 days	31-60 days	61-90 days	91-120 days	Over 120 days
1984	$785,700	.5%	1.0%	10.2%	49.1%	77.6%
1983	750,400	.4	1.1	9.8	51.2	77.3
1982	680,900	.7	1.2	11.0	51.7	79.0
1981	698,200	.5	.8	10.1	48.8	78.5
1980	719,500	.4	.9	8.9	49.2	77.6

The unadjusted Allowance for Doubtful Accounts balance on December 31, 1985, is $30,697.

Instructions: Compute the correct balance for the allowance account based on the average loss experience for the last five years and prepare the appropriate end-of-year adjusting entry.

problem 7-5 (Pledging and factoring accounts receivable)

Live-Wire Electric Supply Company has run into financial difficulties. It decides to improve its cash position by factoring one third of its accounts receivable and pledging one half of the remaining receivables on a loan from the local bank. Details of these arrangements were as follows:

Accounts receivable, December 31, 1983	$420,000	(before financing)
Allowance for doubtful accounts, December 31, 1983	3,000	(credit)
Estimated uncollectibles, December 31, 1983....		3% of accounts receivable balance
Factoring expense.......		20% of gross receivables financed
Note payable to bank	100,000	@ 15% interest

Instructions:

(1) Prepare the journal entries to record the receipt of cash from (a) factoring, and (b) pledging the accounts receivable.
(2) Prepare the journal entry to record the necessary adjustment to Allowance for Doubtful Accounts.
(3) Prepare the accounts receivable section of the balance sheet as it would appear after these transactions.
(4) What entry would be made on the company books of the Live-Wire Electric Supply Company when factored accounts have been collected?

problem 7-6 (Discounting notes)

Parco Marketing Corporation completed the following transactions, among others:

May 5 Received a $5,000, 60-day, 10% note dated May 5 from C. I. Parker, a customer.
24 Received a $1,800, 90-day, non-interest-bearing note dated May 23 from E. Silva as settlement for unpaid balance of $1,752.
25 Had Parker's note discounted at the bank at 13%.
June 7 Had Silva's note discounted at the bank at 15%.
25 Received from B. Avery, a customer, a $7,000, 90-day, 12% note dated June 5, payable to B. Avery and signed by the Barlow Corp. Upon endorsement, gave the customer credit for the maturity value of the note less discount at 13%.
29 Received a $3,500, 60-day, 9% note dated June 29 from P. L. Edwards, a customer.
July 5 Received notice from the bank that Parker's note was not paid at maturity. Protest fees of $15 were charged by the bank.
21 Received payment from Parker on the dishonored note, including interest at 16% on the account receivable balance from maturity date.

Instructions:

(1) Give the journal entries to record the above transactions, showing contingent liabilities in the accounts. (Show data used in calculations with each entry.)
(2) Give the adjusting entries required on July 31.

problem 7-7 (Accounting for discounted notes)

The following transactions were completed by M. D. Forsyth over a three-month period:

Nov. 10 Received from G. R. Jackman, a customer, a $4,000, 60-day, 9% note dated Nov. 9.
11 Received from M. C. Leshner on account, a $1,800, 60-day, 12% note dated Nov. 10.
20 Discounted Leshner's note at the bank at 10%.
24 Discounted Jackman's note at the bank at 10%.
Dec. 3 Received a $2,950, 30-day, non-interest-bearing note dated Dec. 1 from D. H. Prado, crediting Prado's account at face value.
7 Discounted Prado's note at the bank at 9%.
29 Received from W. E. Averett, a $500, 90-day, 12% note dated Dec. 14 and made by Bellaire Realty Inc. Gave the customer credit for the maturity value of the note less discount at 10%.

Dec. 29 Received a $3,500, 10-day, 7% note dated Dec. 29 from S. Sullivan, a customer.
Jan. 10 Received notice from the bank that Jackman's note was not paid at maturity. A protest fee of $15 was charged by the bank.
22 Received a $15,000, 120-day, 9% note dated Jan. 22 from C. B. Thorgood, a customer.
28 Received payment on Sullivan's note, including interest at 10%, the legal rate, on the face value from the maturity date.

Instructions:

(1) Give the entries to record the preceding transactions showing the contingent liabilities in the accounts. (Show data used in calculations with each entry; round amounts to nearest dollar.)
(2) Give the necessary adjusting entries on January 31. Assume all notes discounted are paid when due unless otherwise indicated.

problem 7-8 (Accounting for a non-interest-bearing note)

On January 1, 1984, Austin Manufacturing sold a tract of land to three doctors as an investment. The land, purchased ten years ago, was carried on Austin's books at a value of $55,000. Austin received a non-interest-bearing note for $110,000 from the doctors. The note is due December 31, 1985. There is no market value readily available for the land, but the current market rate of interest for comparable notes is 12%.

Instructions:

(1) Give the journal entry to record the sale of land on Austin's books.
(2) Prepare a schedule of discount amortization for the note with amounts rounded to the nearest dollar.
(3) Give the adjusting entries to be made at the end of 1984 and 1985 to record the effective interest earned.

problem 7-9 (Imputing interest)

Jimco Cement purchased a patent for a quick drying cement from C. F. Schaefer, an independent inventor. On December 31, 1983, Shaefer accepted a note for $20,000 as payment for the patent. The note is non-interest-bearing and comes due in four equal annual installments beginning December 31, 1984. A 10% imputed interest rate is considered appropriate.

Instructions: Give the entries required on Schaefer's books for the life of the note.

problem 7-10 (Factoring receivables)

Barrett Factors Inc. was incorporated December 31, 1983. The capital stock of the company consists of 100,000 shares of $10 par value each, all of which were paid in at par. The company was organized for the purpose of factoring the accounts receivable of various businesses requiring this service.

Barrett Factors Inc. charges a commission to its clients of 2% of all receivables factored and assumes all credit risks. Besides the commission, an additional 10% of gross receivables is withheld on all purchases and is credited to Client Retainer. This retainer is used for merchandise returns, etc., made by customers of the clients for which a credit memo would be due. Payments are made to the clients by Barrett Factors Inc. at the end of each month to adjust the retainer so that it equals 10% of the unpaid receivables at the month's end.

Based on the collection experience of other factoring companies in this area, officials of Barrett Factors Inc. have decided to make monthly provisions to Allowance for Doubtful Accounts based on ¼% of all receivables purchased during the month.

The company also decided to recognize commission revenue on only the factored receivables which have been collected; however, for bookkeeping simplicity all commissions are originally credited to Commission Revenue and an adjustment is made to Unearned Commissions at the end of each quarter based on 2% of receivables then outstanding.

Operations of the company during the first quarter of 1984 resulted in the following:

Accounts receivable factored:

January	$200,000
February	400,000
March	300,000

Collections on the above receivables totaled $700,000.

General and administrative expenses paid during the period:

Salaries	$5,000
Office rent	900
Advertising	500
Equipment rent	1,600
Miscellaneous	1,000

On February 1, 1984, a three-month 10% bank loan was obtained for $500,000 with interest payable at maturity.

For the first three months of the year, the company rented all of its office furniture and equipment; however, on March 31, 1984, it purchased various equipment at a cost of $5,000, the liability for which had not been recorded as of March 31.

Instructions:

(1) Give all entries necessary to record the above transactions and to close the books as of March 31, 1984. (Disregard all taxes.)
(2) Prepare a balance sheet and an income statement as of March 31, 1984. (AICPA adapted)

problem 7-11 (Balance sheet presentation of receivables)

On December 31, 1984, the notes receivable account of the Imbler Company consisted of the following notes:

Trade notes receivable, considered 100% collectible:	
Due in 12 months or less	$ 27,000
Due in more than 12 months	46,000
Trade notes receivable, considered 80% collectible:	
Due in 12 months or less	22,000
Trade notes receivable, considered worthless	4,500
Trade notes receivable, considered 100% collectible, and discounted with the First National Bank (with offsetting credits to Notes Receivable Discounted). Of these notes, $44,000 have been paid	98,000
Notes receivable accepted on sale of diesel equipment (plant asset), $72,000. This amount was payable $2,000 plus interest monthly, and the purchaser was considered a good credit risk	72,000
Note receivable of Ivan Imbler, president, payable on demand. This note was received in payment of his subscription to 1,000 shares of common stock of Imbler Company at par. Upon receipt of this note, the corporation issued a certificate of capital stock for 1,000 shares	120,000
	$389,500

Instructions: Indicate how each of the company's notes receivable would be classified on the balance sheet of December 31, 1984.

8 INVENTORIES—COST PROCEDURES

CHAPTER OBJECTIVES

Describe the nature, classification, and cost of items included in inventory.

Explain the basic accounting problem of allocating inventory costs between the balance sheet and income statement.

Describe the impact of changing price levels on inventory cost allocation.

Describe and illustrate the traditional methods for allocating inventory costs.

Compare and evaluate inventory cost allocation methods.

Describe and illustrate the effects of inventory errors on financial statements.

The primary source of revenue for a business entity is the sale of goods or services. The selling price of the goods or services must exceed all directly and indirectly related expenses in order for a company to realize a profit on its operations. For a nonservice enterprise, the cost of goods sold and the cost of those held for future sale are significant items in the measurement of income and the determination of financial position.

NATURE OF INVENTORIES

The term **inventories** designates goods held for sale in the normal course of business and, in the case of a manufacturer, goods in production or to be placed in production. The nature of goods classified as inventory varies widely with the nature of business activities, and in some cases includes assets not normally thought of as inventories. For example, land and buildings held for resale by a real estate firm, partially completed buildings to be sold in the future by a construction firm, and marketable securities held for resale by a stockbroker are all properly classified as inventories by the respective firms.

Inventories represent one of the most active elements in business operations, being continuously acquired or produced and resold. A large part of a company's resources is frequently invested in goods purchased or manufactured. The cost of these goods must be recorded, grouped, and summarized during the accounting period. At the end of the period, costs must be allocated between current and future activities, i.e., between goods sold during the current period and those on hand to be sold in future periods. This allocation is a major element in financial reporting. Failure to allocate costs properly can result in serious distortions of financial progress and position.

IMPACT OF INFLATION ON INVENTORIES

Of the many accounting problems that complicate the allocation procedure, one of the most perplexing is the effect of changing prices. In recent decades, economies throughout most of the world have experienced moderate to extensive inflation. When prices increase while inventory is being held or produced, a higher than normal profit is recognized when the inventory is sold. Increases in the value of inventories due to rising prices have been labeled **holding gains** in the accounting literature. These are distinguished from **operating gross profit,** which reflects the normal markup between cost and selling price. The holding gain share of profits must be used to replace the sold inventory. Thus, a portion of the reported profit is really illusory and is not available for return to stockholders as dividends.

For example, assume that a company purchased 100 units of inventory for $10 each or a total of $1,000. At the time of purchase, it was anticipated that the inventory would be sold for $12.50 per unit, a markup on cost of 25%. Assume further that, prior to resale, the cost to acquire identical goods increased to $12 per unit, and the resale price was increased to $15 to maintain the 25% markup. If the 100 units were sold, historical cost accounting would recognize sales revenue of $1,500 and cost of $1,000, or a gross profit of $500. However, replacement of the 100 units now requires $1,200 of the proceeds. Thus, $200 of the reported profit is really a holding gain, and $300 is the true gross profit from operations.

As discussed in Chapter 4, historical cost reporting fails to reflect the fact that a company's real position is improved only to the extent of the true operating profit. In addition to the impact on cost of sales, the increased cost of inventory replacement is not reflected in the balance sheet under the historical cost system. Failure to recognize the holding gains as a separate revenue item occurring at the time of the price increase produces a balance sheet with asset values lower than their current replacement cost. To continue the preceding example, assume that the inventory was not sold in the current period. Historical cost accounting would require the asset to be reported at its cost of $1,000. However, if the unrealized holding gain were recognized, the inventory would be reported at $1,200. The $200 unrealized holding gain could be reported either as a revenue item on the income statement or as a direct increase to owners' equity. The choice between these alternatives would depend upon the income recognition rule being applied.

As discussed in Chapter 3, the accounting standards currently accepted in the United States are still based upon historical costs. However, because of the increasingly significant influence of inflation on our economy, the Securities and Exchange Commission ruled in 1976 that certain large companies must report the replacement cost of inventories as supplemental information.[1] The SEC stopped short of requiring adjustment of the actual income statement and balance sheet accounts. In 1979 the FASB extended this supplementary information requirement for certain large entities to include computation of a supplemental net income figure that includes a cost of sales computation based upon current replacement costs.[2] In response to the FASB's action, the SEC agreed to phase out its own replacement cost disclosure requirements.

Pending a more complete acceptance of accounting for inflation, accountants in the United States have developed some unique methods of inventory valuation in their attempt to cope with the deteriorating value of the dollar. These methods, only partially successful, are explored in both this and the subsequent chapter. If prices remained constant, inventory valuation would prove to be rather simple. But when prices continually change, which is the current situation, the allocation of a constant cost to present and future periods' revenue challenges the most experienced accountant.[3]

CLASSES OF INVENTORIES

The term **inventory** or **merchandise inventory** is generally applied to goods held by a merchandising firm, either wholesale or retail, when such goods have been acquired in a condition for resale. The terms **raw materials, goods in process,** and **finished goods** refer to the inventories of a manufacturing enterprise. The latter items require description.

---

[1] Securities and Exchange Commission, *Accounting Series Release No. 190,* "Disclosure of Certain Replacement Cost Data" (Washington: U. S. Government Printing Office, 1976).

[2] *Statement of Financial Accounting Standards, No. 33,* "Financial Reporting and Changing Prices" (Stamford: Financial Accounting Standards Board, 1979), par. 29–30.

[3] See Chapter 24 for in-depth discussion of accounting for inflation.

Raw Materials

Raw materials are goods acquired for use in the production process. Some raw materials are obtained directly from natural sources. More often, however, raw materials are acquired from other companies and represent the finished products of the suppliers. For example, newsprint is the finished product of the paper mill but represents raw material to the printer who acquires it.

Although the term raw materials can be used broadly to cover all materials used in manufacturing, this designation is frequently restricted to materials that will be physically incorporated in the products being manufactured. The term **factory supplies,** or **manufacturing supplies,** is then used to refer to auxiliary materials, i.e., materials that are necessary in the production process but are not directly incorporated in the products. Oils and fuels for factory equipment, cleaning supplies, and similar items fall into this grouping since these items are not incorporated in a product but simply facilitate production as a whole. Raw materials directly used in the production of certain goods are frequently referred to as **direct materials;** factory supplies are referred to as **indirect materials.**

Although factory supplies may be summarized separately, they should be reported as a part of a company's inventories since they will ultimately be consumed in the production process. Supplies purchased for use in the delivery, sales, and general administrative functions of the enterprise should not be reported as part of the inventories, but as prepaid expenses.

Goods in Process

Goods in process, alternately referred to as **work in process,** consists of materials partly processed and requiring further work before they can be sold. This inventory includes three cost elements: (1) **direct materials,** (2) **direct labor,** and (3) **factory overhead** or **manufacturing overhead.** The cost of materials directly identified with the goods in production is included under (1). The cost of labor directly identified with goods in production is included under (2). The portion of factory overhead assignable to goods still in production forms the third element of cost.

Factory overhead consists of all manufacturing costs other than direct materials and direct labor. It includes factory supplies used and labor not directly identified with the production of specific products. It also includes general manufacturing costs such as depreciation, maintenance, repairs, property taxes, insurance, and light, heat, and power, as well as a reasonable share of the managerial costs other than those relating solely to the selling and administrative functions of the business. Overhead may be designated as **fixed, variable,** or **semivariable.** Overhead charges that remain constant in amount regardless of the volume of production are referred to as **fixed.** Depreciation, insurance, rent, and property taxes normally fall into this category. Overhead charges that fluctuate in proportion to the volume of production are called **variable.** Some indirect materials and labor vary directly with production. Some charges vary, but the variations are not in direct proportion to the volume. These charges have both fixed and variable components and are designated as **semivariable** or **mixed** costs. Factory supervision is an example of a semivariable item when it is fixed within a certain range of production but changes when production is not within this range.

Finished Goods

Finished goods are the manufactured products awaiting sale. As products are completed, the costs accumulated in the production process are transferred from Goods in Process to the finished goods inventory account. The diagram below illustrates the basic flow of product costs through the inventory accounts of a manufacturer.

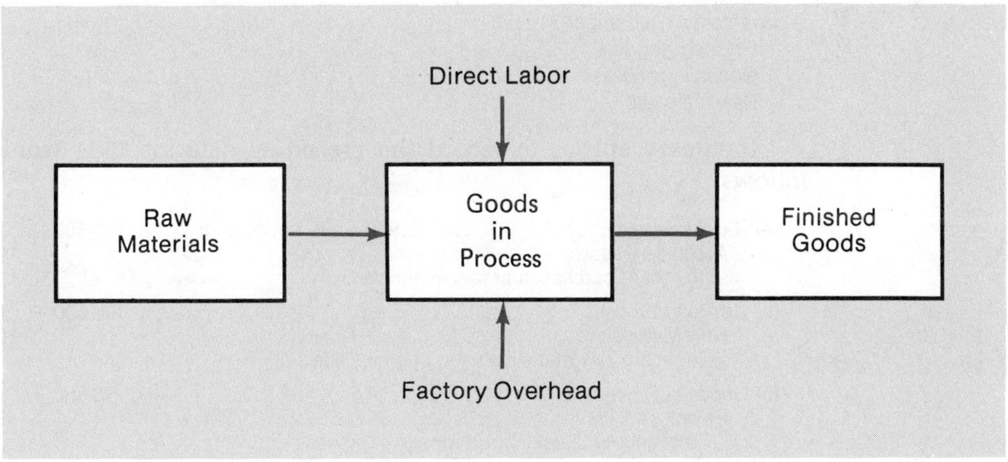

INVENTORY SYSTEMS

Inventory records may be maintained on either a **periodic** or **perpetual** basis. A **periodic inventory system** requires a **physical inventory,** i.e., a counting, measuring, or weighing of goods, at the end of the accounting period to determine the quantities on hand. Values are then assigned to the quantities to determine the portion of the recorded costs to be carried forward.

The **perpetual inventory system** requires the maintenance of records that provide a continuous summary of inventory items on hand. Individual accounts are kept for each class of goods. Inventory increases and decreases are recorded in the individual accounts, the resulting balances representing the amounts on hand. Perpetual records may be kept in terms of quantities only or in terms of both quantities and costs. In a manufacturing organization, a perpetual system applied to inventories requires recording the full movement of goods through individual accounts for raw materials, goods in process, and finished goods. To illustrate, assume the following data for the Dover Corporation, a manufacturing company that uses a perpetual inventory system:

Inventories, January 1, 1984:	
Finished goods	$ 45,000
Goods in process	29,400
Raw materials	21,350
Charges incurred during 1984:	
Raw materials purchased	107,500
Raw materials used	106,500
Direct labor	96,850
Factory overhead	134,055
Cost of goods completed in 1984	340,305
Cost of goods sold in 1984	334,305
Inventories, December 31, 1984:	
Finished goods	51,000
Goods in process	26,500
Raw materials	22,350

Summary entries to record the preceding data for 1984 would be as follows:

(a) Raw Materials	107,500	
Accounts Payable		107,500
To record purchases of raw materials.		
(b) Goods in Process	106,500	
Raw Materials		106,500
To record raw materials used in production.		
(c) Goods in Process	96,850	
Payroll		96,850
To distribute direct labor to goods in process.		
(d) Factory Overhead	134,055	
Various accounts (e.g., liabilities, accumulated depreciation, and prepaid expenses)		134,055
To record factory overhead charges.		
(e) Goods in Process	134,055	
Factory Overhead		134,055
To apply factory overhead to goods in process.		
(f) Finished Goods	340,305	
Goods in Process		340,305
To transfer completed goods.		
(g) Cost of Sales	334,305	
Finished Goods		334,305
To record the cost of goods sold.		

After posting, the inventory and cost of sales accounts would appear in the ledger as follows:

Raw Materials

Jan. 1	21,350	(b)	106,500
(a)	107,500		
Dec. 31	22,350		

Finished Goods

Jan. 1	45,000	(g)	334,305
(f)	340,305		
Dec. 31	51,000		

Goods in Process				Cost of Goods Sold	
Jan. 1	29,400	(f)	340,305	(g) 334,305	
(b)	106,500				
(c)	96,850				
(e)	134,055				
Dec. 31	26,500				

When preparing the income statement for a manufacturing company, it is useful to prepare a separate manufacturing schedule that shows the detail supporting the cost of goods completed and transferred to Finished Goods. An illustration of this schedule, based on the preceding data and additional factory overhead detail, follows:

Dover Corporation
Schedule of Cost of Goods Manufactured
For Year Ended December 31, 1984

Direct materials:		
Raw materials inventory, January 1, 1984	$ 21,350	
Purchases	107,500	
Cost of raw materials available for use	$128,850	
Less raw materials inventory, December 31, 1984	22,350	
Raw materials used in production		$106,500
Direct labor		96,850
Factory overhead:		
Indirect labor	$ 40,000	
Factory supervision	29,000	
Depreciation expense—factory buildings and equipment	20,000	
Light, heat, and power	18,000	
Factory supplies expense	15,000	
Miscellaneous factory overhead	12,055	134,055
Total manufacturing costs		$337,405
Add goods in process inventory, January 1, 1984		29,400
		$366,805
Less goods in process inventory, December 31, 1984		26,500
Cost of goods manufactured		$340,305

When the perpetual system is employed, physical counts of the units on hand should be made at least once a year to confirm the balances on the books. The frequency of physical inventories will vary depending upon the nature of the goods, their rate of turnover, and the degree of internal control. A plan for continuous counting of inventory items on a rotation basis is frequently employed. Variations may be found between the recorded amounts and the amounts actually on hand as a result of recording errors, shrinkage, breakage, theft, and other causes. The inventory accounts should be adjusted to agree with the physical count when a discrepancy exists. To illustrate, assume that a physical inventory of raw materials resulted in a value which is $2,500 less than the recorded inventory. The entry to adjust the inventory account would be as follows:

Inventory Adjustment	2,500	
Raw Materials Inventory		2,500

Normal adjustments for shrinkage and breakage are reported as adjustments to cost of goods sold. Abnormal shortages or thefts may be reported separately as operating expenses.

Practically all large trading and manufacturing enterprises and many relatively small organizations have adopted the perpetual inventory system as an integral part of their record keeping and internal control. This system offers a continuous check and control over inventories. Purchasing and production planning are facilitated, adequate inventories on hand are assured, and losses incurred through damage and theft are fully disclosed. The additional costs of maintaining such a system are usually well repaid by the benefits provided to management.

ITEMS TO BE INCLUDED IN INVENTORY

As a general rule, goods should be included in the inventory of the party holding title. The passing of title is a legal term designating the point at which ownership changes. In some situations, the legal rule may be waived for practical reasons or because of certain limitations in its application. When the rule of passing of title is not observed, there should be appropriate disclosure on the statements of the special practice followed and the factors supporting such practice. Application of the legal test under a number of special circumstances is described in the following paragraphs.

Goods in Transit

When terms of sale are **FOB (free on board) shipping point,** title passes to the buyer with the loading of goods at the point of shipment. Under these terms, application of the legal rule to a year-end shipment calls for recognition of a sale and an accompanying decrease in goods on hand on the books of the seller. Since title passes at the shipping point, **goods in transit** at year-end should be included in the inventory of the buyer despite the lack of physical possession. A determination of the goods in transit at year-end is made by a review of the incoming orders during the early part of the new period. The purchase records may be kept open beyond the fiscal period to permit the recognition of goods in transit as of the end of the period, or goods in transit may be recorded by means of an adjusting entry.

When terms of a sale are **FOB destination,** application of the legal test calls for no recognition of the transaction until goods are received by the buyer. In this case, because of the difficulties involved in ascertaining whether goods have reached their destination at year-end, the seller may prefer to ignore the legal rule and employ shipment as a basis for recognizing a sale and the accompanying inventory decrease. In some cases, title to goods may pass before shipment takes place. For example, if the parties agree that the buyer will pick up the goods at the seller's place of business, and if the goods are **segregated** awaiting pick-up, title has passed and the goods should be recognized as in transit to the buyer. If the sale is recognized upon segregation by the seller, care must be taken to exclude such goods from the seller's inventory. The buyer, on the other hand, could recognize the in-transit goods as a purchase and thus part of its inventory.

Goods on Consignment

Goods are frequently transferred to a dealer (**consignee**) on a consignment basis. The shipper (**consignor**) retains title and includes the goods in inventory until their sale by the consignee. **Consigned goods** are properly reported at the sum of their cost and the handling and shipping costs incurred in their transfer to the consignee. The goods may be separately designated on the balance sheet as merchandise on consignment. The consignee does not own the consigned goods; hence neither consigned goods nor obligations for such goods are reported on the consignee's financial statements. Accounting for consignments is discussed in Chapter 19. Other merchandise owned by a business but in the possession of others, such as goods in the hands of salespersons and agents, goods held by customers on approval, and goods held by others for storage, processing, or shipment, should also be shown as a part of the owner's ending inventory.

Conditional and Installment Sales

Conditional sales and installment sales contracts may provide for a retention of title by the seller until the sales price is fully recovered. Under these circumstances, the seller, who retains title, may continue to show the goods, reduced by the buyer's equity in such goods as established by collections; the buyer, in turn, can report an equity in the goods accruing through payments made. However, in the usual case when the possibilities of returns and defaults are very low, the test of passing of title should be relinquished and the transaction recorded in terms of the expected outcome: the seller, anticipating completion of the contract and the ultimate passing of title, recognizes the transaction as a regular sale involving deferred collections; the buyer, intending to comply with the contract and acquire title, recognizes the transaction as a regular purchase. Installment sales are discussed in detail in Chapter 19.

DETERMINATION OF INVENTORY COST

After the goods to be included as inventory have been identified, the accountant must assign a dollar value to the physical units. As indicated earlier, the profession has historically favored retention of some measure of **incurred cost** for this purpose. Attention is directed in this chapter to identifying the elements that comprise cost, and to a consideration of how to determine the portion of historical costs to be retained as the inventory amount reported on the balance sheet and the amount to be charged against current revenues.

Items Included in Cost

Inventory cost consists of all expenditures, both direct and indirect, relating to inventory acquisition, preparation, and placement for sale. In the case of raw materials or goods acquired for resale, cost includes the purchase price, freight, receiving, storage, and all other costs incurred to the time goods are ready for sale. Certain expenditures can be traced to specific acquisitions or can be allocated to inventory items in some equitable manner. Other expenditures may be relatively small and difficult to allocate. Such items are normally excluded in the calculation of inventory cost and are thus charged in full against current revenue as **period costs.**

The charges to be included in the cost of manufactured products have already been mentioned. Proper accounting for materials, labor, and factory overhead items and their identification with goods in process and finished goods inventories is best achieved through adoption of a cost accounting system designed to meet the needs of a particular business unit. Certain costs relating to the acquisition or the manufacture of goods may be considered abnormal and may be excluded in arriving at inventory cost. For example, costs arising from idle capacity, excessive spoilage, and reprocessing are normally considered abnormal items chargeable to current revenue. Only those portions of general and administrative costs that are clearly related to procurement or production should be included in inventory cost.

In practice, companies take different positions in classifying certain costs. For example, costs of the purchasing department, costs of accounting for manufacturing activities, and costs of pensions for production personnel may be treated as inventoriable costs by some companies and period costs by others.

Discounts as Reductions in Cost

Discounts treated as a reduction of cost in recording the acquisition of goods should similarly be treated as a reduction in the cost assigned to the inventory. **Trade discounts** are discounts converting a catalog price list to the prices actually charged to a buyer. The discount available may vary with such factors as the quantity purchased. Thus, trade discounts are frequently stated in a series. For example, given trade discount terms based on the quantity ordered of 30/20/10, a customer would be entitled to a discount of either 30%, 30% and 20%, or 30% and 20% and 10%, depending on the size of the order. Each successive discount is applied to the net invoice cost after deducting any earlier discounts. To illustrate, assume that an inventory item is listed in a catalog for $5,000 and a buyer is given terms of 20/10/5. The net invoice price is calculated as follows:

	Discount	Net Invoice Amount
$5,000 × 20%	$1,000	$5,000 − $1,000 = $4,000
$4,000 × 10%	$ 400	$4,000 − $ 400 = $3,600
$3,600 × 5%	$ 180	$3,600 − $ 180 = $3,420

An alternative approach to the preceding computation is to compute a composite discount rate which can be applied to the initial gross amount. The following computation could be made for the above invoice:

Discount Rate	×	Percentage of Original Invoice Cost	=	Composite Discount Rate
20%		100%		20.00%
10%		80% (100% − 20%)		8.00
5%		72% (80% − 8%)		3.60
		Composite rate		31.60%

Computation of discount: $5,000 × 31.6% = $1,580 discount
Net price = $5,000 − $1,580 = $3,420

The advantage of the composite approach is that once a composite rate is computed, it can be used directly for all purchases that have the same trade discount terms.

Cost is defined as the list price less the trade discount. No record needs to be made of the discount, and the purchases should be recorded at the net price.

Cash discounts are discounts granted for payment of invoices within a limited time period. Business use of such discounts has declined in popularity over the past years, although they are still found in some industries. Cash discounts are usually stated as a certain percentage rate to be allowed if the invoice is paid within a certain number of days, with the full amount due within another time period. For example, 2/10, n/30 (two ten, net thirty) means that 2% is allowed as a cash discount if the invoice is paid within 10 days after the invoice date, but that the full or "net" amount is due within 30 days. Terms of 3/10 eom mean a 3% discount is allowed if the invoice is paid within 10 days after the end of the month in which the invoice is written.

Theoretically, inventory should be recorded at the discounted amount, i.e., the gross invoice price less the allowable discount. This **net method** reflects the fact that discounts not taken are in effect credit-related expenditures incurred for failure to pay within the discount period. They are recorded in the discounts lost account and reported as a separate item on the income statement. Discounts lost usually represent a relatively high rate of interest and indicate a failure on the part of financial management due to either carelessness in considering payment alternatives or financial inability to avoid the extra charge.

This inefficiency is not reflected when inventory records are maintained at the gross unit price for convenience, as is often the case. Under the **gross method** cash discounts taken are reflected through a contra purchases account, Purchase Discounts, when a periodic inventory system is used. With a perpetual inventory system, discounts are credited directly to Inventory.

Because of its control features, the net method of accounting for purchases is strongly preferred; however, many companies still follow the historical practice of recognizing cash discounts only as payments are made. If the payment is made in the same period the inventory is sold, use of either method will result in the same net income. However, if inventory is sold in one period and payment is made in a subsequent period, net income is affected and a proper matching of costs against revenue will not take place. If the net method is used, an adjusting entry should be made at the end of each period to record the discounts lost on unpaid invoices for which the discount period has passed.

The entries required for both the gross and net methods are illustrated below. A perpetual inventory method is assumed.

Transaction	Purchases Reported Net			Purchases Reported Gross		
Purchase of merchandise priced at $2,500 less trade discount of 30/20 and a cash discount of 2%: $2,500 less 30% = $1,750 $1,750 less 20% = $1,400 $1,400 less 2% = $1,372	Inventory .... Accounts Payable	1,372	 1,372	Inventory .... Accounts Payable	1,400	 1,400
(a) Assuming payment of the invoice within discount period.	Accounts Payable ..... Cash	1,372	 1,372	Accounts Payable ..... Inventory .... Cash	1,400	 28 1,372
(b) Assuming payment of the invoice after discount period.	Accounts Payable ..... Discounts Lost .... Cash	1,372 28	 1,400	Accounts Payable ..... Cash	1,400	 1,400
(c) Required adjustment at the end of the period assuming that the invoice was not paid and the discount period has lapsed.	Discounts Lost .... Accounts Payable	28	 28	No entry required		

Purchase Returns and Allowances

Adjustments to invoice cost are also made when merchandise either is damaged or is of a lesser quality than ordered. Sometimes the merchandise is physically returned to the supplier. In other instances, a credit is allowed to the buyer by the supplier to compensate for the damage or the inferior quality of the merchandise. In either case, the liability is reduced and a credit is made either directly to the inventory account under a perpetual inventory system, or to a contra purchases account, Purchase Returns and Allowances, under a periodic inventory system.

TRADITIONAL COST ALLOCATION METHODS

Four commonly applied allocation methods are discussed in this section: (1) **specific identification,** (2) **first-in, first-out (fifo),** (3) **weighted average,** and (4) **last-in, first-out (lifo).** Each has certain characteristics that make it preferable under certain conditions. One of them, the last-in, first-out method, was specifically developed as an attempt to reduce the impact of inventory inflation on net income. All four methods have in common the fact that inventory cost, as defined in this chapter, is allocated between the income statement and the balance sheet. No adjustment for price changes is made to the total amount to be allocated.

Specific Identification

Costs may be allocated between goods sold during the period and goods on hand at the end of the period according to the actual cost of specific units. This **specific identification** procedure requires a means of identifying the historical cost of each unit of inventory up to the time of sale. When perpetual inventory records are maintained, Cost of Goods Sold is debited and Inventory is credited for the actual cost of each item sold. In a periodic system, cost allocation is based on the identified cost of items on hand at the end of the period. Thus, under either system the flow of recorded costs matches the physical flow of goods.

The specific identification procedure is a highly objective approach to matching historical costs with revenues. As stated in Accounting Research Study No. 13, "There appears to be little theoretical argument against the use of specific identification of cost with units of product if that method of determining inventory costs is practicable."[4] Application of this method, however, is often difficult or impossible. When inventory is composed of a great many items or identical items acquired at different times and at different prices, cost identification procedures are likely to be slow, burdensome, and costly. Furthermore, when units are identical and interchangeable, this method opens the doors to possible profit manipulation through the selection of particular units for delivery. Finally, significant changes in costs during a period may warrant charges to revenue on a basis other than past identifiable costs.

First-In, First-Out Method

The **first-in, first-out (fifo) method** is based on the assumption that costs should be charged to revenue in the order in which incurred. Inventories are thus stated in terms of most recent costs. To illustrate the application of this method, assume the following data:

Jan. 1	Inventory	200	units at $10	$ 2,000
12	Purchase	400	units at 12	4,800
26	Purchase	300	units at 11	3,300
30	Purchase	100	units at 12	1,200
	Total	1,000		$11,300

A physical inventory on January 31 shows 300 units on hand. The most recent costs would be assigned to the units as follows:

Most recent purchase, Jan. 30	100	units at $12	$1,200
Next most recent purchase, Jan. 26	200	units at 11	2,200
Total	300		$3,400

[4]Horace G. Barden, *Accounting Research Study No. 13,* "The Accounting Basis of Inventories" (New York: American Institute of Certified Public Accountants, 1973) p. 83.

If the ending inventory is recorded at $3,400, cost of goods sold is $7,900 ($11,300 − $3,400). Thus, revenue is charged with the earliest costs incurred.

When perpetual inventory accounts are maintained, a form similar to that illustrated below is used to record the cost assigned to units issued and the cost relating to the goods on hand. The columns show the quantities and values of goods acquired, goods issued, and balances on hand. It should be observed that identical values for physical and perpetual inventories are obtained when fifo is applied.

COMMODITY: X **(fifo)**

	RECEIVED			ISSUED			BALANCE		
DATE	QUANTITY	UNIT COST	TOTAL COST	QUANTITY	UNIT COST	TOTAL COST	QUANTITY	UNIT COST	TOTAL COST
Jan. 1							200	$10	$2,000
12	400	$12	$4,800				200 400	10 12	2,000 4,800
16				200 300	$10 12	$2,000 3,600	100	12	1,200
26	300	11	3,300				100 300	12 11	1,200 3,300
29				100 100	12 11	1,200 1,100	200	11	2,200
30	100	12	1,200				200 100	11 12	2,200 1,200

Fifo can be supported as a logical and realistic approach to the flow of costs when it is impractical or impossible to achieve specific cost identification. Fifo assumes a cost flow closely paralleling the usual physical flow of goods sold. Revenue is charged with costs considered applicable to the goods actually sold; ending inventories are reported in terms of most recent costs—costs closely approximating the current value of inventories at the balance sheet date. Fifo affords little opportunity for profit manipulation because the assignment of costs is determined by the order in which costs are incurred.

Average Cost Methods

The **weighted average method** is based on the assumption that goods sold should be charged at an average cost, such average being influenced or *weighted* by the number of units acquired at each price. Inventories are stated at the same weighted average cost per unit. Using the cost data in the preceding section, the weighted average cost of a physical inventory of 300 units on January 31 would be as follows:

Jan. 1 Inventory	200	units at $10	$ 2,000
12 Purchase	400	units at 12	4,800
26 Purchase	300	units at 11	3,300
30 Purchase	100	units at 12	1,200
Total	1,000		$11,300

Weighted average cost .... $11,300 ÷ 1,000 = $11.30.
Ending inventory .... 300 units at $11.30 = $3,390.

The ending inventory is recorded at a cost of $3,390, cost of goods sold is $7,910 ($11,300 − $3,390), thus charging revenue with a weighted average cost. The calculations above were made for costs of one month. Similar calculations could be developed in terms of data for a quarter or for a year.

When perpetual records of quantities issued are maintained but the costs of units issued are not recorded until the end of a period, a weighted average cost for the period, such as that discussed above, is calculated at that time and the accounts are credited for the cost of total units issued. Frequently, however, costs relating to issues are recorded currently, and it is necessary to calculate costs on the basis of the weighted average on the date of issue. This requires calculating a new weighted average cost immediately after the receipt of each additional purchase. This method of successive average recalculations is referred to as the **moving average method.** The use of this method is illustrated below.

COMMODITY: X **(moving average)**

	RECEIVED			ISSUED			BALANCE		
DATE	QUANTITY	UNIT COST	TOTAL COST	QUANTITY	UNIT COST	TOTAL COST	QUANTITY	UNIT COST	TOTAL COST
Jan. 1							200	$10.00	$2,000
12	400	$12	$4,800				600	11.33	6,800
16				500	$11.33	$5,665	100	*11.35	1,135
26	300	11	3,300				400	11.09	4,435
29				200	11.09	2,218	200	11.09	2,217
30	100	12	1,200				300	11.39	3,417

*Increase in unit cost due to rounding.

On January 12 the new unit cost of $11.33 was found by dividing $6,800, the total cost, by 600, the number of units on hand. Then on January 16, the balance of $1,135 represented the previous balance of $6,800, less $5,665, the cost assigned to the 500 units issued on this date. New unit costs were calculated on January 26 and 30 when additional units were acquired.

With successive recalculations of cost and the use of such different costs during the period, the cost identified with the ending inventory will differ from that determined when cost is assigned to the ending inventory in terms of average cost for all goods available during the period. A physical inventory and use of the weighted average method resulted in a value for the ending inventory of $3,390; a perpetual inventory and use of the moving average method resulted in a value for the ending inventory of $3,417.

The average cost approach can be supported as realistic and as paralleling the physical flow of goods, particularly where there is an intermingling of identical inventory units. Unlike the other inventory methods, the average approach provides the same cost for similar items of equal utility. The method does not permit profit manipulation. Limitations of the average method are inventory values that perpetually contain some degree of influence of earliest costs and inventory values that may lag significantly behind current prices in periods of rapidly rising or falling prices.

Last-In, First-Out Method

The **last-in, first-out (lifo) method** is based on the assumption that the latest costs of a specific item should be charged to cost of goods sold. Inventories are thus stated at earliest costs. Using the cost data in the preceding section, a physical inventory of 300 units on January 31 would have a cost as follows:

Earliest costs relating to goods, Jan. 1	200 units at $10	$2,000
Next earliest cost, Jan. 12	100 units at 12	1,200
Total	300	$3,200

The ending inventory is recorded at a cost of $3,200 and cost of goods sold is $8,100 ($11,300 − $3,200). Thus, revenue is charged with the most recently incurred costs.

When perpetual inventories are maintained, it is necessary to calculate costs on a last-in, first-out basis using the cost data on the date of each issue as illustrated at the top of the next page.

It should be noted that lifo values obtained under a periodic system will usually differ from those determined on a perpetual basis. In the example, a cost of $3,200 was obtained for the periodic inventory, whereas $3,300 was obtained when costs were calculated as goods were issued. This difference results because it was necessary to "dip into" the beginning inventory layer and charge 100 units of the beginning inventory at $10 to the issue of January 16. The ending inventory thus reflects only 100 units at the beginning unit cost.

These temporary liquidations of inventory frequently occur during the year, especially for companies with seasonal business. These liquidations cause monthly reports prepared on the lifo basis to be unrealistic and meaningless. Because of this, most companies using lifo maintain their internal records using other inventory methods, such as fifo or weighted average, and adjust the statements to lifo at the end of the year with a **lifo allowance**

COMMODITY: X **(lifo)**

DATE	RECEIVED			ISSUED			BALANCE		
	QUANTITY	UNIT COST	TOTAL COST	QUANTITY	UNIT COST	TOTAL COST	QUANTITY	UNIT COST	TOTAL COST
Jan. 1							200	$10	$2,000
12	400	$12	$4,800				200 400	10 12	2,000 4,800
16				400 100	$12 10	$4,800 1,000	100	10	1,000
26	300	11	3,300				100 300	10 11	1,000 3,300
29				200	11	2,200	100 100	10 11	1,000 1,100
30	100	12	1,200				100 100 100	10 11 12	1,000 1,100 1,200

account. Companies frequently refer to this account as the *lifo reserve* account. Because the profession has recommended that the word *reserve* not be used for asset valuation accounts, the term allowance is used in this text.

The lifo inventory method was developed in the United States during the late 1930's as a method to permit deferral of illusory inventory profits during periods of rising prices. Petition was made to Congress by companies desiring to use this method, and in 1939 Congress agreed to allow the use of lifo for income tax purposes *if* companies also used the method for financial reporting. This represents one of the few accounting areas in which tax and book accounting must agree.

Because lifo developed primarily as a tax shelter, the Internal Revenue Service controls the method of computing and applying this inventory method. As the IRS changes its rules, book accounting for inventories must also change. This has proven to be a serious disadvantage to the use of lifo.

Specific-Goods Lifo Pools. With large and diversified inventories, application of the lifo procedures to specific goods proved to be extremely burdensome. Because of the complexity and cost involved, companies frequently selected only a few very important inventory items, usually raw materials, for application of the lifo method. As a means of simplifying the valuation process and extending its applicability to more items, an adaptation of lifo applied to specific goods was developed and approved by the IRS. This adaptation permitted the establishment of **inventory pools** of substantially identical goods. At the end of a period, the quantity of items in the pool is determined, and costs are assigned to those items. Units equal to the beginning quantity in the pool are assigned the beginning unit costs. If the number of units in ending inventory exceeds the number of beginning units, the additional units are regarded as an incremental **layer** within the pool. The unit cost assigned to the items in the new layer may be based on (1) actual costs of earliest acquisitions within the period (lifo), (2) the weighted average cost of acquisitions within the period, or (3) actual costs of the latest acquisitions within the period (fifo). Increments in subsequent periods form successive inventory layers. A decrease in the number of units in an inventory pool during a period is regarded as a reduction in the most recently added layer, then in successively lower layers, and finally in the original or base quantity. Once a specific layer is reduced or eliminated, it is not restored.

To illustrate the above lifo valuation process, assume that there are three inventory pools, and the changes in the pools are as listed below. The inventory calculations that follow the listing are based on the assumption that weighted average costs are used in valuing annual incremental layers.

Inventory pool increments and liquidations:

	Class A Goods	Class B Goods	Class C Goods
Inv., Dec. 31, 1983	3,000 @ $6	3,000 @ $5	2,000 @ $10
Purchases—1984	3,000 @ $7	2,000 @ $6	3,000 @ $11
	1,000 @ $9		
Total available for sale	7,000	5,000	5,000
Sales—1984	3,000	1,000	3,500
Inv., Dec. 31, 1984	4,000	4,000	1,500
Purchases—1985	1,000 @ $8	2,000 @ $6	3,000 @ $11
	3,000 @ $10		
Total available for sale	8,000	6,000	4,500
Sales—1985	3,500	2,500	2,000
Inv., Dec. 31, 1985	4,500	3,500	2,500

Inventory valuations using specific-goods lifo pools:

	Class A Goods		Class B Goods		Class C Goods	
Inv., Dec. 31, 1983	3,000 @ 6	$18,000	3,000 @ $5	$15,000	2,000 @ $10	$20,000
Inv., Dec. 31, 1984	3,000 @ $6	$18,000	3,000 @ $5	$15,000	1,500 @ $10	$15,000
	1,000 @ $7.50[1]	7,500	1,000 @ $6	6,000		
	4,000	$25,500	4,000	$21,000	1,500	$15,000
Inv., Dec. 31, 1985	3,000 @ $6	$18,000	3,000 @ $5	$15,000	1,500 @ $10	$15,000
	1,000 @ $7.50	7,500	500 @ $6	3,000	1,000 @ $11	11,000
	500 @ $9.50[2]	4,750				
	4,500	$30,250	3,500	$18,000	2,500	$26,000

[1]Cost of units acquired in 1984, $30,000, divided by number of units acquired, 4,000, or $7.50.
[2]Cost of units acquired in 1985, $38,000, divided by number of units acquired, 4,000, or $9.50.

The layer process for lifo inventories may be further illustrated as shown on page 257.

A new layer was added to the inventory of Class A goods each year. Previously established layers were reduced in 1985 for Class B goods and in 1984 for Class C goods.

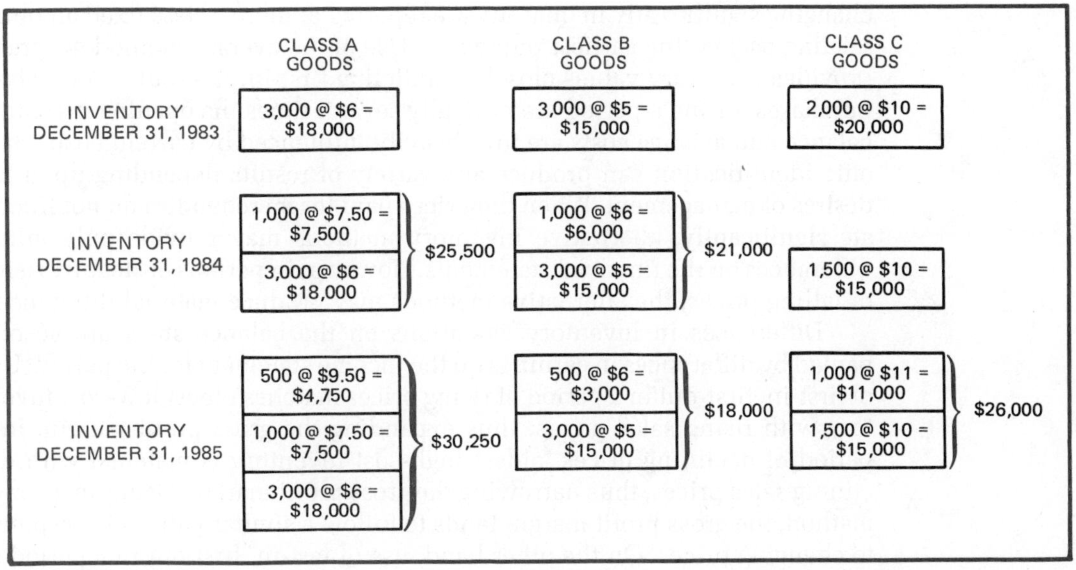

Dollar-Value Lifo Pools. Even the grouping of substantially identical items into quantity pools does not produce all the benefits desired from the use of the lifo method. Technological changes sometimes introduce new products thus requiring the elimination of inventory in old pools, and requiring the establishment of new pools for the new product that no longer qualifies as being substantially identical. For example, the introduction of synthetic fabrics to replace cotton meant that "cotton" pools were eliminated and new "synthetic fabric" pools established. This change resulted in the loss of lower lifo bases by companies changing the type of fabrics they used. To overcome this type of problem and to further simplify the clerical work involved, the **dollar-value lifo inventory method** was developed. Under this method, the unit of measurement is the dollar rather than the quantity of goods. All similar items, such as all raw materials for a given line of business, are grouped into a pool and layers are determined based upon total dollar changes. The dollar-value method is currently the most widely used adaptation of the lifo concept and is now acceptable for tax purposes.[5] The procedures to apply this adaptation of lifo are discussed in Chapter 9.

COMPARISON OF COST ALLOCATION PROCEDURES

In using the first-in, first-out procedure, inventories are reported on the balance sheet at or near current costs. With last-in, first-out, inventories not

[5] Maurice E. Stark, "A Survey of LIFO Inventory Application Techniques," *The Accounting Review* (January, 1978), pp. 182–185.

changing significantly in quantity are reported at more or less fixed amounts relating back to the earliest purchases. Use of the average method generally provides inventory values closely paralleling first-in, first-out values, since purchases during a period are normally several times the opening inventory balance and average costs are thus heavily influenced by current costs. Specific identification can produce any variety of results depending upon the desires of management. When the prices paid for merchandise do not fluctuate significantly, alternative inventory methods may provide only minor differences on the financial statements. However, in periods of steadily rising or falling prices, the alternative methods may produce material differences.

Differences in inventory valuations on the balance sheet are accompanied by differences in earnings on the income statement for the period. Use of first-in, first-out in a period of rising prices matches oldest low-cost inventory with rising sales prices, thus expanding the gross profit margin. In a period of declining prices, oldest high-cost inventory is matched with declining sales prices, thus narrowing the gross profit margin. Using an average method, the gross profit margin tends to follow a similar pattern in response to changing prices. On the other hand, use of last-in, first-out in a period of rising prices relates current high costs of acquiring goods with rising sales prices. Thus lifo tends to have a stabilizing effect on gross profit margins.

The application of the different methods, excluding specific identification, in periods of rising and falling prices is illustrated in the following example. Assume that the Welch Sales Co. sells its goods at 50% over prevailing costs from 1982 to 1985. The company sells its inventories and terminates activities at the end of 1985. Sales, costs, and gross profits using each of the three methods are shown in the following tabulation.

	Fifo			Weighted Average[1]			Lifo		
1982:									
Sales, 500 units @ $9			$4,500			$4,500			$4,500
Inventory, 200 units	@ $5	$1,000		200 @ $5	$1,000		200 @ $5	$1,000	
Purchases, 500 units	@ $6	3,000		500 @ $6	3,000		500 @ $6	3,000	
Goods available for sale		$4,000			$4,000			$4,000	
Ending Inv., 200 units	@ $6	1,200		200 @ $5.71 ($4,000 ÷ 700)	1,142		200 @ $5	1,000	
Cost of goods sold			2,800			2,858			3,000
Gross profit on sales			$1,700			$1,642			$1,500
1983:									
Sales, 450 units @ $12			$5,400			$5,400			$5,400
Inventory, 200 units	@ $6	$1,200		200 @ $5.71	$1,142		200 @ $5	$1,000	
Purchases, 500 units	@ $8	4,000		500 @ $8	4,000		500 @ $8	4,000	
Goods available for sale		$5,200			$5,142			$5,000	
Ending Inv., 250 units	@ $8	2,000		250 @ $7.35 ($5,142 ÷ 700)	1,838		200 @ $5		
							50 @ $8	1,400	
Cost of goods sold			3,200			3,304			3,600
Gross Profit on Sales			$2,200			$2,096			$1,800

[1]Totals in the illustration are calculated to the nearest dollar.

	Fifo		Weighted Average		Lifo	
1984:						
Sales, 475 units @ $10.50		$4,988		$4,988		$4,988
Inventory, 250 units	@ $8 $2,000		250 @ $7.35 $1,838		200 @ $5 50 @ $8 } $1,400	
Purchases, 450 units	@ $7 3,150		450 @ $7 3,150		450 @ $7 3,150	
Goods available for sale	$5,150		$4,988		$4,550	
Ending Inv., 225 units	@ $7 1,575		225 @ $7.13 ($4,988 ÷ 700) 1,604		200 @ $5 25 @ $8 } 1,200	
Cost of goods sold		3,575		3,384		3,350
Gross profit on sales		$1,413		$1,604		$1,638
1985:						
Sales, 625 units @ $7.50		$4,688		$4,688		$4,688
Inventory, 225 units	@ $7 $1,575		225 @ $7.13 $1,604		200 @ $5 25 @ $8 } $1,200	
Purchases, 400 units	@ $5 2,000		400 @ $5 2,000		400 @ $5 2,000	
Cost of goods sold		3,575		3,604		3,200
Gross profit on sales		$1,113		$1,084		$1,488

The foregoing transactions are summarized below:

		Fifo			Weighted Average			Lifo		
Year	Sales	*Cost of Goods Sold*	*Gross Profit on Sales*	*Gross Profit % to Sales*	*Cost of Goods Sold*	*Gross Profit on Sales*	*Gross Profit % to Sales*	*Cost of Goods Sold*	*Gross Profit on Sales*	*Gross Profit % to Sales*
1982	$ 4,500	$ 2,800	$1,700	37.8%	$ 2,858	$1,642	36.5%	$ 3,000	$1,500	33.3%
1983	5,400	3,200	2,200	40.7	3,304	2,096	38.8	3,600	1,800	33.3
1984	4,988	3,575	1,413	28.3	3,384	1,604	32.2	3,350	1,638	32.8
1985	4,688	3,575	1,113	23.7	3,604	1,084	23.1	3,200	1,488	31.7
	$19,576	$13,150	$6,426	32.8%	$13,150	$6,426	32.8%	$13,150	$6,426	32.8%

Although the different methods give the same total gross profit on sales for the four-year period, use of first-in, first-out resulted in increased gross profit percentages in periods of rising prices and a contraction of gross profit percentages in periods of falling prices, while last-in, first-out resulted in relatively steady gross profit percentages in spite of fluctuating prices. The weighted average method offered results closely comparable to those obtained by first-in, first-out. Assuming operating expenses at 30% of sales, use of last-in, first-out would result in a net income for each of the four years; first-in, first-out would result in larger net incomes in 1982 and 1983, but net losses in 1984 and 1985. Inventory valuation on the last-in, first-out basis tends to smooth the peaks and fill the troughs of business fluctuations.

Income Tax Consequences of Lifo

The above comparison was made without considering the income tax impact of the method used. As indicated earlier, if a company elects to use lifo for tax purposes, it must also use lifo in its financial reporting. In a period of inflation, the lower reported profit using lifo results in lower income taxes. Thus, the tax liability on gross profit, assuming a 45% tax rate, for the three illustrated methods over the four-year period would be as follows:

	Fifo	Weighted Average	Lifo
1982	$ 765	$ 739	$ 675
1983	990	943	810
1984	636	722	737
1985	501	488	670
Total	$2,892	$2,892	$2,892

In this example, a complete cycle of price increases and decreases occurred over the four-year period; thus the total income tax liability for the four years was the same under each method. However, by using lifo to defer part of the tax during 1982 and 1983, more cash was available to the company for operating purposes. In periods of constantly increasing inflation, the deferral tends to become permanent and is a condition sought by many companies. When inflation started to accelerate in the United States in the mid 1970's, many companies began to report larger net incomes primarily caused by the illusory influence of holding gains. To protect their cash flows, a significant number of companies changed to lifo inventory to reduce their present and future tax liabilities. These changes had to be approved by the Internal Revenue Service, and were subject to specific rules governing adoption of the lifo method. The complexity of some of these rules deterred other companies from making the change even though the tax consequences promised to be favorable. Some of the rules were relaxed, especially for small businesses, by the Economic Recovery Act of 1981.

Evaluation of Lifo as a Cost Allocation Method

Because so many companies have resorted to lifo as a means of reducing income and, consequently, their income tax liability, it is important to identify the advantages and disadvantages of this unique inventory method. Because it allocates only the incurred cost between the balance sheet and the income statement, it can only partially account for the effects of inflation.

Major Advantages of Lifo. The advantages of lifo may be summarized as follows:

Tax Benefits. As mentioned earlier, temporary or permanent deferrals of income taxes can be achieved with lifo, resulting in current cash savings. These deferrals continue as long as the price level is increasing and inventory quantities do not decline. The improved cash flow enables a company to either decrease its borrowing and reduce interest cost, or invest the savings to produce revenue.

Better Measurement of Income. Because lifo allocates the most recently incurred costs to cost of sales, this method produces an income figure that tends to report only the operating income and defers recognition of the holding gain until prices or quantities decline. The illusory inflation profits discussed earlier tend not to appear as part of net income when lifo inventory is used.

Major Disadvantages of Lifo. The disadvantages of lifo are more subtle than the advantages. Companies adopting lifo sometimes realize too late that lifo can produce some severe side effects.

Reduced Income. The application of the most recent prices against current revenue produces a decrease in net income in an inflationary period. If management's goal is to maximize reported income, the adoption of lifo will produce results that are in opposition to that goal.

Investors and other users of financial statements frequently base their evaluations of a company's performance on the "bottom line" or net income. Failure on the part of users to recognize that a lower net income is due to the use of lifo rather than a decline in operating proficiency may have a depressing effect on the market price of a company's stock. The reduced income may be perceived as a failure on the part of management. Further, the use of lifo will reduce bonus payments to employees that are based on net income and could reduce the amount of dividends distributed to shareholders.

Unrealistic Inventory Balances on the Balance Sheet. The allocation of older inventory costs to the balance sheet can cause a serious understatement of inventory values. Depending upon the length of time the lifo layers have been developing, and the severity of the price increase, the reported inventory values can be substantially lower than current replacement values. For example, Note 4 to the General Mills statements reproduced in Appendix B states that if the fifo method had been used, inventories would be $75.5 million higher in 1982 than the reported lifo inventory. This is approximately 34% of the lifo valued inventory. Because inventory costs enter into the determination of working capital, the current ratio can be seriously distorted under a lifo inventory system. Although this discussion of lifo assumes an inflationary economy, if prices were to decrease, lifo would produce inventory values higher than current replacement costs. It is fair to assume that should this occur, there would be strong pressure for special action to permit the write-down of inventory balances to replacement cost.

Unanticipated Profits Created by Failing to Maintain Inventory Quantities. The income advantages summarized previously will be realized only if inventory quantity levels are maintained. If the ending inventory quantities decline, the layers of cost eliminated are charged against current revenue. If the inventory costs of these layers are significantly less than the current replacement costs, the reported profit will be artificially increased by the failure to maintain inventory levels.

Two specific examples may clarify this weakness.

(1) Many companies who rely upon steel as a basic raw material for their production processes use the lifo inventory method. Assume that during an

extended steel strike many manufacturing companies find their steel stock dwindling as their fiscal year-end approaches. Unless they can restock their inventories, they will be forced to match lower inventory costs against current revenue, thus reporting a substantial holding gain in current profit. Assume, for instance, that company sales for the year are $6,000,000 and that the cost of goods sold using current year prices is $5,000,000, but using a mixture of current year and earlier years' lower priced lifo layers, the cost of goods sold is $4,000,000. The resulting increase in profit of $1,000,000 is caused solely by the inability of the company to replace its normal stocks.

(2) The failure to protect lifo layers may be caused by a timing error in requesting shipments of purchases. Assume that a lumber company normally received its lumber by ship, but that at year-end, orders were mishandled and a boat load was not received as planned. The company, in failing to record the boat load of lumber as a current year purchase, would have to apply older lifo costs against sales. The resulting profit could lead to conclusions that would not be justified by the facts.

To avoid the distortion caused by a temporary reduction of lifo layers at the end of a year, some accountants advocate establishing a replacement allowance that charges the current period for the extra replacement cost expected to be incurred in the subsequent period when the inventory is replenished. However, the use of an allowance for temporary liquidation of lifo layers, sometimes referred to as the **base-stock method,** is not currently acceptable for financial reporting or tax purposes. The use of this type of allowance on the books could disqualify a company from filing its tax returns on the lifo basis, and therefore, it is seldom used in practice.

Unrealistic Flow Assumptions. The cost assignment resulting from the application of lifo does not normally approximate the physical movement of goods through the business. One would seldom encounter in practice the actual use or transfer of goods on a last-in, first-out basis.

Artificial Adjustments for Inflation. Although lifo comes the closest of the four cost allocation methods discussed to recognizing the impact of inflation on inventories, it fails to recognize the full impact. As discussed earlier, a full recognition of the effects of inflation on inventory would require a balance sheet valuation at current cost, as well as the use of current replacement cost as the cost of each sale. If the last purchase of inventory was made before a significant price rise, lifo would still fail to properly match current cost and current income. Only a replacement cost or a "next-in, first-out" system would fully reflect the effects of inflation on the income statement.

OTHER COST PROCEDURES

The methods previously described for arriving at inventory cost are the ones most widely used. Several other procedures are sometimes encountered and deserve mention.

Cost of Latest Purchases

Sometimes goods are valued at cost of the latest purchase regardless of quantities on hand. When the inventory consists largely of recent purchases, this method may give results closely approximating those obtained through specific cost identification or first-in, first-out procedures with considerably less work. However, when the quantities of goods on hand are significantly in excess of the latest quantities purchased and major price changes have taken place, use of latest costs may result in significant cost misstatement.

Standard Costs

Manufacturing inventories are frequently reported at **standard costs**—predetermined costs based upon representative or normal conditions of efficiency and volume of operations. Differences between actual costs and standard costs for materials, labor, and factory overhead result in **standard cost variances** indicating favorable and unfavorable operational or cost experiences. Excessive materials usage, inefficient labor application, excessive spoilage, and idle time, for example, produce unfavorable variances, and these would be separately summarized in variance accounts.

Standard costs are developed from a variety of sources. Past manufacturing experiences may be carefully analyzed; time and motion studies, as well as job and process studies, may be undertaken; data from industry and economy-wide sources may be consulted. Standards should be reviewed at frequent intervals to determine whether they continue to offer reliable cost criteria. Changing conditions require adjustment in the standards, so that at the balance sheet date, standard costs will reasonably approximate costs computed under one of the recognized costing methods.

Direct Costing

A practice widely debated for many years is referred to as **direct costing, marginal costing,** or **variable costing.** Inventories under direct costing are assigned only the variable costs incurred in production—direct materials, direct labor, and the variable components of factory overhead. Fixed costs are treated as period charges and assigned to current revenue. Only costs directly related to output are assigned to goods and charged to the period in which the goods are sold; costs that are a function of time and that are continuing regardless of the volume of output—for example, supervisory salaries, depreciation, and property tax—are charged against revenue of the period in which they are incurred.

The difference between direct costing and conventional **full costing** is illustrated at the top of the next page.

With conventional full costing applied to inventories, a high gross profit may emerge in a period of high production even though sales are declining. With direct costing, cost of goods sold varies directly with sales and a high gross profit emerges in a period of high sales; changes in the volume of production have no effect upon gross profit. For example, assume in the

	Full Costing		Direct Costing	
Sales		$200,000		$200,000
Variable cost of goods sold	$110,000		$110,000	
Fixed cost of goods sold	55,000		62,500	
Total cost of goods sold		165,000		172,500
Gross profit		$ 35,000		$ 27,500
Inventory value:				
Variable costs		$ 15,000		$ 15,000
Fixed costs		7,500		—
Total cost of inventory		$ 22,500		$ 15,000

illustration above that, although sales remained the same, production had been greater and as a result the ending inventory was double the amount shown. Variable costs identified with the inventory would amount to $30,000. Under full costing, a different allocation of fixed costs would be appropriate. Assuming that $12,500 in fixed costs is allocated to the inventory reducing the fixed costs assigned to operations by $5,000, the gross profit would increase to $40,000. Under direct costing, the gross profit would remain unchanged at $27,500.

Support for direct costing is made on the grounds that it provides more meaningful and useful data to management than full costing. Direct costing enables management to appraise the effects of sales fluctuations on net income. Sales, current and potential, can be evaluated in terms of out-of-pocket costs to achieve such sales. The direct costing approach becomes a valuable tool for planning and control and is used by management to analyze cost, price, and volume relationships.

Although no objection can be raised to the use of direct costing when it is used for internal reporting and as a means for assisting management in decision-making, objection can be raised to the extension of direct costing procedures to the annual financial statements. In measuring financial position and the results of operations, inventories must carry their full costs including a satisfactory allocation of the fixed overhead costs. Fixed costs, no less than variable costs, are incurred in contemplation of future benefits and should be matched against the revenues ultimately produced through such efforts. When inventories are valued by direct costing procedures for internal reporting, they should be restated in terms of full costing whenever financial statements are to be prepared.

SELECTION OF AN INVENTORY METHOD

As indicated in this chapter, companies have many alternative ways to value inventories. Guidelines for the selection of a proper method are very broad, and a company may justify almost any accepted method. After a lengthy study of inventory practices, Horace Barden, retired partner of Ernst and Whinney, concluded his Research Study by stating:

> ...one must recognize that no neat package of principles or other criteria exists to substitute for the professional judgment of the responsible accountant. The

> need for the exercise of judgment in accounting for inventories is so great that I recommend to authoritative bodies that they refrain from establishing rules that, in isolation from the conditions and circumstances that may exist in practice, attempt to determine the accounting treatment to be applied under any and all circumstances.[6]

Many companies use more than one method. For example, General Mills values some domestic inventories at the lower of lifo cost or market and other inventories at the lower of fifo cost or market.[7] The decision as to which method to use depends upon not only the tax consequences but also the nature of the inventories themselves. Except for lifo, a company may use a different inventory method for tax purposes than it uses for reporting purposes.

As indicated earlier in this chapter, companies sometimes change their inventory methods, especially as economic conditions change. When inventories are a material item, a change in the inventory method by a company may impair comparability of that company's financial statements with prior years' statements and with the financial statements of other entities. Such changes require careful consideration and should be made only when management can clearly demonstrate the preferability of the alternative method. This position was emphasized by the Accounting Principles Board in Opinion No. 20 with the statement, "The burden of justifying other changes rests with the entity proposing the change."[8] If a change is made, complete disclosure of the impact of the change is encouraged by the FASB.

EFFECTS OF ERRORS IN RECORDING INVENTORY POSITION

Failures to report the inventory position accurately result in misstatements on both the balance sheet and the income statement. The effect on the income statement is sometimes difficult to evaluate because of the different amounts which can be affected by an error. Analysis of the impact is aided by recalling the structure of the cost of goods sold section of the income statement:

Beginning Inventory
+
Purchases
=
Goods Available for Sale
−
Ending Inventory
=
Cost of Goods Sold

An overstatement of the beginning inventory will thus result in an overstatement of goods available for sale and cost of goods sold. Because the cost

[6] Barden, *op. cit.*, p. 141.

[7] See Appendix B, Note 1D and Note 4.

[8] *Opinions of the Accounting Principles Board, No. 20,* "Accounting Changes" (New York: American Institute of Certified Public Accountants, 1971), par. 16.

of goods sold is deducted from sales to determine the gross profit, the overstated cost of goods sold results in an understated gross profit and finally an understated net income. Sometimes an error may affect two of the amounts in such a way that they offset each other. For example, if a purchase in transit under the fifo method is neither recorded as a purchase nor included in the ending inventory, the understatement of purchases results in an understatement of goods available for sale; however, the understatement of ending inventory subtracted from goods available for sale offsets the error and creates a correct cost of goods sold, gross profit, and net income. Inventory and accounts payable, however, will be understated on the balance sheet.

Because the ending inventory of one period becomes the beginning inventory of the next period, undetected accounting errors affect two accounting periods. If left undetected, the errors will offset each other under a fifo or average method. Errors in lifo layers may, however, perpetuate themselves until the layer is eliminated.

This type of analysis is required for all inventory errors. It is unwise to try to memorize the impact an error has on the income statement. It is preferable to analyze each situation as illustrated. The following analyses of four typical inventory errors, with their impact on both the current and succeeding years, provide additional opportunity for students to practice the above type of analysis.

(1) Overstatement of the ending inventory through errors in the count of goods on hand, pricing, or the inclusion in inventory of goods not owned or goods already sold:

Current year:

Income statement—overstatement of the ending inventory will cause the cost of goods sold to be understated and the net income to be overstated.

Balance sheet—the inventory will be overstated and the owners' equity will be overstated.

Succeeding year:

Income statement—overstatement of the beginning inventory will cause the cost of goods sold to be overstated and the net income to be understated.

Balance sheet—the error of the previous year will have been counterbalanced on the succeeding income statement and the balance sheet will be correctly stated.

(2) Understatement of ending inventory through errors in the count of goods on hand, pricing, or the failure to include in inventory goods purchased or goods transferred but not yet sold:

Misstatements indicated in (1) above are reversed.

(3) Overstatement of ending inventory accompanied by failure to recognize sales and corresponding receivables at end of period:

Current year:

Income statement—sales are understated by the sales price of the goods and cost of goods sold is understated by the cost of the goods relating to the sales; gross profit and net income are thus understated by the gross profit on the sales.

Balance sheet—receivables are understated by the sales price of the goods and the inventory is overstated by the cost of the goods that were sold; current assets and owners' equity are thus understated by the gross profit on the sales.

Succeeding year:

Income statement—sales of the preceeding year are recognized in this year in sales and cost of sales; gross profit and net income, therefore, are overstated by the gross profit on such sales.

Balance sheet—the error of the previous year is counterbalanced on the succeeding income statement and the balance sheet will be correctly stated.

(4) Understatement of ending inventory accompanied by failure to recognize purchases and corresponding payables at end of period:

Current year:

Income statement—purchases are understated, but this is counterbalanced by the understatement of the ending inventory; gross profit and net income are correctly stated as a result of the counterbalancing effect of the error.

Balance sheet—although owners' equity is reported correctly, both current assets and current liabilities are understated.

Succeeding year:

Income statement—the beginning inventory is understated, but this is counterbalanced by an overstatement of purchases, as purchases at the end of the prior year are recognized currently; gross profit and net income are correctly stated as a result of the counterbalancing effect of the error.

Balance sheet—the error of the previous year no longer affects balance sheet data.

This analysis can be summarized in tabular form as follows; (+) indicates overstatement, (−) indicates understatement, and (0) indicates no effect.

	Current year						Subsequent year					
	Assets	*Liabilities*	*Equity*	*Sales*	*Cost of goods sold*	*Net income*	*Assets*	*Liabilities*	*Equity*	*Sales*	*Cost of goods sold*	*Net income*
(1) Overstatement of ending inventory	+	0	+	0	−	+	0	0	0	0	+	−
(2) Understatement of ending inventory	−	0	−	0	+	−	0	0	0	0	−	+
(3) Overstatement of ending inventory and understatement of sales	−	0	−	−	−	−	0	0	0	+	+	+
(4) Understatement of ending intory and understatement of purchases	−	−	0	0	0	0	0	0	0	0	0	0

Summary of Impact of Inventory Errors on Financial Statements

The correcting entry for each of these errors depends upon when the error is discovered. If it is discovered in the current year, adjustments can be made to current accounts, and the reported net income and balance sheet amounts will be correct. If the error is not discovered until the subsequent period, the correcting entry qualifies as a prior period adjustment if the net income of the prior period was misstated. The error to the prior years' income is corrected through retained earnings. To illustrate these entries, assume that error number three has occurred. The correcting entries required, depending upon when the error is discovered, would be as follows. Assume the use of a perpetual inventory system.

Error discovered in current year (Cost of inventory $1,000; sales price of inventory, $1,500).

Accounts Receivable	1,500	
Cost of Goods Sold	1,000	
Inventory		1,000
Sales		1,500

Error discovered in subsequent year (sale has been recorded in subsequent year).

Sales	1,500	
Cost of Goods Sold		1,000
Retained Earnings		500

If trend statistics are included in the annual reports, prior years' balances should be adjusted to reflect the correction of the error. Present-day audit techniques can substantially reduce the probability of material inventory errors.

QUESTIONS

1. (a) Distinguish between holding gains and operating profit. (b) Are holding gains really "gains"? Explain.

2. (a) What are the three cost elements entering into goods in process and finished goods? (b) What items enter into factory overhead? (c) Define fixed overhead, variable overhead, and semivariable or mixed overhead and give an example of each.

3. Distinguish between raw materials and factory supplies. Why are the terms direct materials and indirect materials often used to refer to raw materials and factory supplies, respectively?

4. What are the advantages of using the perpetual inventory system as compared with the periodic system?

5. Does the adoption of a perpetual inventory system eliminate the need for a physical count or measurement of inventories? Explain.
6. Under what conditions is merchandise in transit legally reported as inventory by the (a) seller? (b) buyer?
7. Under what conditions would an accounting failure to recognize incoming merchandise in transit that was shipped FOB shipping point have no effect on income?
8. The Miller Company has followed the practice of recording all goods shipped on consignment as current period sales and has not carried consigned goods as inventory. Under what conditions would this practice have no effect on income?
9. How should the following items be treated in computing year-end inventory costs: (a) segregated goods? (b) conditional sales?
10. State how you would report each of the following items on the financial statements:

(a) Manufacturing supplies.
(b) Goods on hand received on a consignment basis.
(c) Materials of a customer held for processing.
(d) Goods received without an accompanying invoice.
(e) Goods in stock to be delivered to customers in subsequent periods.
(f) Goods in hands of agents and consignees.
(g) Deposits with vendors for merchandise to be delivered next period.
(h) Goods in hands of customers on approval.
(i) Defective goods requiring reprocessing.

11. (a) What types of expenditures are included in inventory costs? (b) What distinguishes a cost that is treated as a period cost from one included in inventory?
12. (a) What are the two methods of accounting for cash discounts? (b) Which method is generally preferred? Why?
13. Describe and explain the year-end adjustments necessary under the net method of accounting for cash discounts assuming: (a) The discount period has not elapsed and it is assumed that the invoice will be paid before the period expires. (b) The discount period has elapsed.
14. Theoretically, there is little wrong with inventory costing by the specific cost identification method. What objections can be raised to the use of this method?
15. What is meant by inventory layers? Why are they significant with respect to the fifo and lifo methods?
16. In recent years, some companies have changed from fifo to lifo for computing their inventory values. What effect does a change from fifo to lifo during an inflationary period have on net earnings and working capital? Explain.
17. Discuss the advantages and disadvantages of lifo as a cost allocation method.
18. As stated in the text, lifo can only partially account for the effects of inventory inflation. Explain this statement. (Include in your explanation the concept of incurred costs.)
19. The Wallace Co. decides to adopt specific goods lifo as of the beginning of 1984, and determines the cost of the different lines of merchandise carried as of this date. (a) What three different methods may be employed at the end of each period in assigning costs to quantity increases in specific lines? (b) What procedure is employed at the end of each period for quantity decreases in specific lines?
20. (a) What type of company is likely to use standard costs? (b) What precautions are necessary in the use of standard costs?
21. What effect would each of the following situations have upon the current year's net income for a company manufacturing a single product if it used direct costing to value its ending inventory rather than full costing? Assume fixed costs are the same for each year.

(a) Quantity of items produced and sold are the same for the year.
(b) Quantity of items produced exceeds the quantity sold.
(c) Quantity of items sold exceeds the quantity produced.

22. State the effect of each of the following errors made by Cole Inc. upon the balance sheet and the income statement (1) of the current period and (2) of the succeeding period:

(a) The company fails to record a sale of merchandise on account; goods sold are excluded in recording the ending inventory.
(b) The company fails to record a sale of merchandise on account; the goods sold are included, however, in recording the ending inventory.
(c) The company fails to record a purchase of merchandise on account; goods purchased are included in recording the ending inventory.
(d) The company fails to record a purchase of merchandise on account; goods purchased are not recognized in recording the ending inventory.
(e) The ending inventory is understated as the result of a miscount of goods on hand.

DISCUSSION CASES

case 8-1 (Should we adopt lifo?) You are the controller of the Mirage Steel Co. The economy has entered a period of rapidly increasing inflation. The turnover of inventory in your company occurs about once every nine months. The inflation is causing revenue to rise more rapidly than the historical cost of the goods sold. Although profits are higher this year than last, you realize that the cost to replace the sold inventory is also higher. You are aware that many companies are changing to the lifo inventory method. But you are concerned that what goes up will eventually come down, and when prices decline, the lifo method will result in high profits and taxes. Since declining prices are usually equated with economic recession, it is likely that the higher taxes will have to be paid at a time when revenues are declining.

What factors should you consider before making a change to lifo? Based on the above considerations, what would you recommend?

case 8-2 (What is an inventoriable cost?) You have been hired by Western Products Co. to work in their accounting department. As part of your assignment, you have been asked to review the inventory costing procedures. In the past, the company has attempted to keep its inventory as low as possible to hedge against future declines in demand. One way of doing this has been to charge off as many costs as can be justified as expenses of the current period. Sales have declined, however, and the controller wants to include as high an ending inventory valuation as possible to show the stockholders a better income figure for the current year. Your study shows the following costs have been consistently treated as period costs:

Depreciation of plant
Fringe payroll benefits for factory personnel
Repairs of equipment
Salaries of foremen
Warehouse rental for storage of finished products
Pension costs for factory personnel
Training program—all employees
Cafeteria costs—all employees
Interest expense
Depreciation and maintenance of fleet of delivery trucks

Which of the items do you suggest could be deferred by including them as inventoriable costs? Evaluate the wisdom and propriety of making the suggested changes.

case 8-3 (Lifo—a major contributor to illiquidity?) In 1982, many companies were finding their lifo inventories declining due to the economic recession. In a letter to the Wall Street Journal on August 12, 1982, a CPA wrote as follows:

> The last-in, first-out inventory method is a major contributor to the illiquidity of firms. In this period of inventory contraction, the Journal almost daily informs us of companies that report millions of dollars in "lifo profits." These companies pay a cash-draining income tax on their spurious inventory earnings. Or, alternatively, they are denied a refund of prior years' taxes, because the false lifo income offsets real operating losses.
>
> It is accounting ritual, not accounting reason that causes enterprises to report that a profit—which will never be confirmed by the receipt of cash—has been realized by theoretically dipping into old, low-historic-cost levels of inventory, inventory which in fact was disposed of long ago, but through accounting pretense is still carried on the books.

What risks does this article identify with the adoption of lifo? Are they sufficient to suggest lifo use should be avoided?

EXERCISES

exercise 8-1 (Holding gains and operating profit)

J & D Lawn Products purchased a large piece of machinery for $15,000. The machine was placed in inventory awaiting sale. Prior to resale, the cost of similar equipment had increased by 10%. J & D sells all inventory at 50% over the cost necessary to replace the inventory.

(1) Determine the gross profit on the sale of the machine.
(2) Break the gross profit from part (1) into (a) the holding gain and (b) the operating profit.
(3) What argument might be made for presenting the two components of gross profit separately in the financial statements?

exercise 8-2 (Passage of title)

The management of Ledbetter Company has engaged you to assist in the preparation of year-end (December 31) financial statements. You are told that on November 30, the correct inventory level was 120,000 units. During the month of December sales totaled 50,000 units including 25,000 units shipped on consignment to Farnsworth Company. A letter received from Farnsworth indicates that as of December 31, they had sold 10,000 units and were still trying to sell the remainder. A review of the December purchase orders, to various suppliers, shows the following:

Date of Purchase Order	Invoice Date	Quantity in Units	Date Shipped	Date Received	Terms
12-2-84	1-3-85	10,000	1-2-85	1-3-85	FOB shipping point
12-11-84	1-3-85	8,000	12-22-84	12-24-84	FOB destination
12-13-84	1-2-85	13,000	12-28-84	1-2-85	FOB destination
12-23-84	12-26-84	12,000	1-2-85	1-3-85	FOB shipping point
12-28-84	1-10-85	10,000	12-31-84	1-5-85	FOB shipping point
12-31-84	1-10-85	15,000	1-3-85	1-6-85	FOB destination

Ledbetter Company uses the "passing of legal title" for inventory recognition. Compute the number of units which should be included in the year-end inventory.

exercise 8-3 (Passage of title)

The Carol Manufacturing Company reviewed its in-transit inventory and found the following items. Indicate which items should be included in the inventory balance at December 31, 1984. Give your reasons for the treatment you suggest.

(a) Merchandise costing $2,350 was received on January 3, 1985, and the related purchase invoice was recorded January 5. The invoice showed the shipment was made on December 29, 1984, FOB shipping point.
(b) Merchandise costing $625 was received on December 28, 1984, and the invoice was not recorded. The invoice was in the hands of the purchasing agent; it was marked "on consignment."
(c) A packing case containing a product costing $816 was standing in the shipping room when the physical inventory was taken. It was not included in the inventory because it was marked "Hold for shipping instructions." The customer's order was dated December 18, but the case was shipped and the customer billed on January 10, 1985.
(d) Merchandise received on January 6, 1985, costing $720 was entered in the purchase register on January 7. The invoice showed shipment was made FOB destination on December 31, 1984. Since it was not on hand during the inventory count, it was not included.
(e) A special machine, fabricated to order for a particular customer, was finished and in the shipping room on December 30. The customer was billed on that date and the machine was excluded from inventory although it was shipped January 4, 1985. (AICPA adapted)

exercise 8-4 (Trade and cash discounts)

Taylor Carpet Service regularly buys merchandise from Mountain Suppliers and is allowed a trade discount of 10/20/5 from the list price. Taylor uses the net method to record purchases and discounts. On August 15, Taylor Carpet purchased material from Mountain Suppliers. The invoice, received by Taylor, showed a list price of $2,500, and terms of 2/10, n/30. Payment was sent to Mountain Suppliers on August 28. Prepare the journal entries to record the purchase and subsequent payment. (Round to nearest dollar.)

exercise 8-5 (Net and gross method—entries)

On December 3, Thomas Photo purchased inventory listed at $8,550 from Ewing Photo. Terms of the purchase were 2/10, n/20. Thomas Photo also purchased inventory from Terry Wholesale on December 10, for a list price of $7,450. Terms of this purchase were 2/10 eom. On December 16, Thomas paid both suppliers for these purchases. Thomas does not use a perpetual inventory system.

(1) Give the entries to record the purchases and invoice payments assuming that (a) the net method is used, (b) the gross method is used.
(2) Assume that Thomas had not paid either of the invoices at December 31. Give the year-end adjusting entries, if the net method is being used. Also assume that Thomas plans to pay Terry Wholesale within the discount period.

exercise 8-6 (Inventory computation using different cost flows)

The Hansen Store shows the following information relating to Product A:

Inventory, January 1	300 units @ $17.50
Purchases, January 10	900 units @ $18.00
Purchases, January 20	1200 units @ $18.25
Sales, January 8	150 units
Sales, January 18	600 units
Sales, January 25	1000 units

What are the values of ending inventory under (1) perpetual and (2) periodic methods assuming the cost flows below? (Carry your unit costs to four places and round to three.)

(a) Fifo
(b) Lifo
(c) Average

exercise 8-7 (Inventory computation using different cost flows)

Flex Corporation had the following transactions relating to Product 500 during September.

Date		Units	Unit Cost
September 1	Balance on hand.....	500 units	$5.00
September 6	Purchase............	100 units	4.50
September 12	Sale	300 units	
September 13	Sale	200 units	
September 18	Purchase............	200 units	6.00
September 20	Purchase............	300 units	4.00
September 25	Sale	200 units	

Determine the ending inventory value under each of the following costing methods:

(1) Fifo (perpetual)
(2) Fifo (periodic)
(3) Lifo (perpetual)
(4) Lifo (periodic)

exercise 8-8 (Computing lifo inventory from fifo inventory)

Rushforth Farm Supply's records for the first three months of its existence show purchases of Commodity A as follows:

	Number of units	Cost
August..............	5,500	$29,975
September	8,000	41,600
October.............	4,370	24,035

The inventory at the end of October of Commodity A using fifo is valued at $33,811. Assuming that none of Commodity A was sold during August and September, what value would be shown at the end of October if a lifo cost flow was assumed?

exercise 8-9 (Inventory computation—average methods)

The following data are for Product 102, stocked by the Merrill Company.

Date		Units	Unit Cost	Unit Sales Price
July 1	Balance......	150	$6.50	
July 3	Purchase.....	250	6.20	
July 11	Sale	120		$10.00
July 12	Sale	100		10.20
July 15	Purchase.....	110	6.70	
July 21	Purchase.....	70	6.80	
July 22	Sale	95		10.15
July 28	Sale	105		10.25
July 30	Purchase.....	100	6.67	

Using the appropriate average costing method compute (1) cost of goods sold and (2) ending inventory value for the month of July under the following assumptions. (Carry unit costs to four places and round to three. Round totals to nearest dollar.)

(a) Periodic inventory method is used by the Merrill Company.
(b) Perpetual inventory method is used by the Merrill Company.

exercise 8-10 (Inventory computation from incomplete records)

A flood recently destroyed many of the financial records of Hymas Manufacturing Company. Management has hired you to re-create as much financial information as possible for the month of October. You are able to find out that the company uses a weighted average inventory costing system. You also learn that Hymas makes a physical count at the end of each month in order to determine monthly ending inventory values. By examining various documents you are able to gather the following information:

Ending inventory at October 31	50,000 units
Total cost of units available for sale in October	$118,800
Cost of goods sold during October	$ 99,000
Cost of beginning inventory, October 1	35¢ per unit
Gross margin on sales for October	$101,000

October Purchases

Date	Units	Unit Cost
October 4	60,000	$0.40
October 11	50,000	0.41
October 15	40,000	0.42
October 16	50,000	0.45

You are asked to provide the following information:

(1) Number of units on hand, October 1.
(2) Units sold during October.
(3) Unit cost of inventory at October 31.
(4) Value of inventory at October 31.

exercise 8-11 (Computation of beginning inventory from ending inventory)

The Lopez Company sells Product A. During a move to a new location, the inventory records for Product A were misplaced. The bookkeeper has been able to gather some information from the sales records, and gives you the data shown below:

July sales: 53,500 units at $10.00

July purchases:

Date	Quantity	Unit Price
July 5	10,000	$6.50
July 9	12,500	6.25
July 12	15,000	6.00
July 25	14,000	6.20

On July 31, 18,000 units were on hand with a total value of $110,800. Lopez has always used a periodic fifo inventory costing system. Gross profit on sales for July was $205,875. Reconstruct the beginning inventory (quantity and dollar value) for the month of July.

exercise 8-12 (Impact on profit of failure to replace lifo layers)

Calder Lumber Company uses a periodic lifo method for inventory costing. The following information relates to the plywood inventory carried by Calder Lumber.

Plywood Inventory

	Quantity	Lifo Costing Layers
May 1	500 Sheets	300 Sheets at $ 8.00
		125 Sheets at 11.00
		75 Sheets at 13.00

Plywood Purchases

May 8	115 Sheets at $14.00
May 17	95 Sheets at $15.00
May 29	200 Sheets at $13.00

All sales of plywood during May were at $20 per sheet. On May 31, there were 310 sheets of plywood in the storeroom.

(1) Compute the gross profit on sales for May, as a dollar value and as a percent of sales.
(2) Assume that because of a lumber strike, Calder Lumber is not able to purchase the May 29 order of lumber until June 10. If sales remained the same, recompute the gross profit on sales for May, as a dollar value and as a percent of sales.
(3) Compare the results of part (1) and part (2) and explain the difference.

exercise 8-13 (Income differences—fifo vs. lifo)

First-in, first-out has been used for inventory valuation by the Harper Co. since it was organized in 1981. Using the data that follow, redetermine the net incomes for each year on the assumption of inventory valuation on the last-in, first-out basis:

	1981	1982	1983	1984
Reported net income (fifo basis)	$15,500	$ 30,000	$ 34,250	$ 44,000
Reported ending inventories—fifo basis	61,500	102,000	126,000	130,000
Inventories—lifo basis	59,000	75,100	95,000	105,000

exercise 8-14 (Income differences—fifo vs. lifo)

The following data relate to the Pratt Company's first three years of operations.

	1982	1983	1984
Net income under fifo	$20,000	$30,000	$12,000
Net income under lifo	15,000	17,000	13,000
Ending inventory under fifo	70,000	76,000	70,000

Compute the ending inventory under lifo for each year.

exercise 8-15 (Impact on profit of direct costing)

Parson Battery Company began operations of January 1, 1984. Sales for 1984 amounted to $500,000 (50,000 batteries). Because of an expected increase in demand during the coming year, production was increased and 80,000 units were manufactured during 1984. Variable costs for 1984 were $6.00 per battery. Depreciation, salaries, and other fixed factory overhead costs totaled $87,488 for the year.

Determine (1) the gross profit on sales, and (2) the value of remaining inventory (as of December 31) under:

(a) the full costing method,
(b) the direct costing method.

exercise 8-16 (Correction of inventory errors)

Annual income for the Robinson Co. for the period 1980–1984 appears on the next page. However, a review of the records for the company reveals inventory misstatements as listed. Calculate corrected net income for each year.

	1980	1981	1982	1983	1984
Reported net income (loss)	$18,000	$20,000	$2,000	$(7,500)	$16,000
Inventory overstatement, end of year	2,500		2,800		1,600
Inventory understatement, end of year				4,000	

exercise 8-17 (Effect on net income of inventory errors)

The Evans Company reported income before taxes of $105,000 for 1982, and $120,000 for 1983. A later audit produced the following information:

(a) The ending inventory for 1982 included 200 units erroneously priced at $5.90 per unit. The correct cost was $9.50 per unit.
(b) Merchandise costing $1,800 was shipped to the Evans Company, FOB shipping point, on December 26, 1982. The purchase was recorded in 1982, but the merchandise was excluded from the ending inventory since it was not received until January 4, 1983.
(c) On December 28, 1982, merchandise costing $1,200 was sold to Cole Paint Shop. Cole had asked Evans to keep the merchandise for him until January 2, when he would come and pick it up. Because the merchandise was still in the store at year-end, the merchandise was included in the inventory count. The sale was correctly recorded in December 1982.
(d) Holt Company sold merchandise costing $1,500 to Evans Company. The purchase was made on December 29, 1982, and the merchandise was shipped on December 30. Terms were FOB shipping point. Because the Evans Co. bookkeeper was on vacation, neither the purchase nor the receipt of goods was recorded on the books until January 1983.

Assuming all amounts are material and a physical count is taken every December 31,

(1) Compute the corrected income before taxes for each year.
(2) By what amount did the total net income change for the two years combined?
(3) Assume all errors were found in January 1984, before the books were closed for 1983; what journal entry would be made?

PROBLEMS

problem 8-1 (Inventory computation using different cost flows)

The Ashbury Corporation uses Part 100 in a manufacturing process. Information as to balances on hand, purchases, and requisitions of Part 100 are given in the following table:

	Quantities			
Date	Received	Issued	Balance	Unit Price of Purchase
January 8	—	—	200	$1.55
January 29	200	—	400	1.70
February 8	—	80	320	—
March 20	—	160	160	—
July 10	150	—	310	1.75
August 18	—	110	200	—
September 6	—	110	90	—
November 14	200	—	290	2.00
December 29	—	110	180	—

Instructions: What is the closing inventory under each of the following pricing methods? (Carry unit costs to four places and round.)

(1) Perpetual fifo
(2) Periodic fifo
(3) Perpetual lifo
(4) Periodic lifo
(5) Moving average
(6) Weighted average

problem 8-2 (Inventory computation using different cost flows)

Records of the Murray Sales Co. show the following data relative to Product A:

March 2 Inventory.......	325 units at $25.50		March 3 Sales.........	300 units at $37.50
6 Purchase.......	300 units at 26.00		20 Sales.........	200 units at 35.70
13 Purchase.......	350 units at 27.00		28 Sales.........	125 units at 36.00
25 Purchase.......	50 units at 27.50			

Instructions: Calculate the inventory balance and the gross profit on sales for the month on each of the following bases:

(1) First-in, first-out. Perpetual inventories are maintained and costs are charged out currently.
(2) First-in, first-out. No book inventory is maintained.
(3) Last-in, first-out. Perpetual inventories are maintained and costs are charged out currently.
(4) Last-in, first-out. No book inventory is maintained.
(5) Moving average. Perpetual inventories are maintained and costs are charged out currently. (Carry calculations to four places and round to three.)
(6) Weighted average. No book inventory is maintained.

problem 8-3 (Inventory calculation—lifo and fifo)

The Lay Manufacturing Co. was organized in 1982 to produce a single product. The company's production and sales records for the period 1982–1984 are summarized below:

	Units Produced		Sales	
	No. of Units	Production Costs	No. of Units	Sales Revenue
1982	320,000	$144,000	200,000	$160,500
1983	310,000	161,200	290,000	230,000
1984	270,000	156,600	260,000	210,300

Instructions: Calculate the gross profit for each of the three years assuming that inventory values are calculated in terms of:

(1) Last-in, first-out. (Average cost used for incremental layers.)
(2) First-in, first-out.

problem 8-4 (Impact on income of using different cost flows)

The Brush Corporation began operations in 1984. A summary of the first quarter appears below:

	Purchases	
	Units	Total Cost
January 2	250	$23,250
February 11	100	9,500
February 20	400	38,400
March 21	200	19,600
March 27	225	22,275

Other Data

	Sales in Units	Sales Price per Unit	Operating Expenses
January	200	$140	$9,575
February	225	142	7,820
March	350	145	7,905

The Brush Corporation used the lifo perpetual inventory method and computed an inventory value of $38,300, at the end of the first quarter. Management is considering changing to a fifo costing method. They have also considered using a periodic system instead of the perpetual system presently being used. You have been hired to assist management in making the decision.

Instructions:

(1) Prepare a condensed comparative income statement for the first quarter of 1984, with columns for each of the four methods under consideration (periodic fifo, periodic lifo, perpetual fifo, perpetual lifo). Ignore taxes.
(2) Compute net income as a percent of sales for each of the four methods used in part (1).
(3) Prepare a list of factors management should consider in selecting an inventory costing method.

problem 8-5 (Computation of lifo inventory with lifo pools)

The Durrant Company sells three different products. Five years ago management adopted the lifo inventory method and established three specific pools of goods. Durrant values all incremental layers of inventory at the average cost of purchases within the period. Information relating to the three products for the first quarter of 1984 is given below.

	Product 201	Product 202	Product 203
Purchases:			
January	1,000 @ $12.00	500 @ $25	5,000 @ $5.30
February	1,500 @ $12.50	250 @ $26	4,850 @ $5.38
March	1,200 @ $12.25	—	3,500 @ $5.42
First quarter sales (units)	2,850	825	10,750
January 1, 1984 inventory	950 @ $11.50	155 @ $24	3,760 @ $5.00

Instructions: Compute the ending inventory value for the first quarter of 1984. (Round unit inventory values to the nearest cent and final inventory values to the nearest dollar.)

problem 8-6 (Computation of lifo inventory)

The Bramble Products Company's inventory record appears below:

	Purchases		Sales
	Quantity	Unit Cost	Quantity
1982	9,000	$5.60	6,500
1983	9,500	5.75	10,000
1984	7,200	5.78	5,000

The company uses a lifo cost flow assumption. It reported ending inventories as follows:

1982	$14,000
1983	11,600
1984	24,410

Instructions: Determine if the Bramble Products Company has reported their inventory correctly. Assuming that 1984 accounts are not yet closed, make any necessary correcting entries.

problem 8-7 (Computation of inventory from balance sheet and transaction data)

A portion of the Mower Company's balance sheet appears below:

	December 31, 1984	December 31, 1983
Assets:		
Cash	$353,300	$ 50,000
Notes receivable	–0–	25,000
Inventory	To be determined	199,875
Liabilities:		
Accounts payable	To be determined	$ 50,000

Mower Company pays for all operating expenses with cash, and purchases all inventory on credit. During 1984, cash totaling $471,000 was paid on accounts payable. Operating expenses for 1984 totaled $200,000. All sales are cash sales. The inventory was restocked by purchasing 1,500 units per month, and valued by using periodic fifo. The unit cost of inventory was $32.60 during January 1984 and increased $.10 per month during the year. All sales are made for $50 per unit. The ending inventory for 1983 was valued at $32.50 per unit.

Instructions:

(1) Compute the number of units sold during 1984.
(2) Compute the December 31, 1984 accounts payable balance.
(3) Compute the beginning inventory quantity.
(4) Compute the ending inventory quantity and value.
(5) Prepare an income statement for 1984 (including a detailed cost of goods sold section). Ignore income tax.

problem 8-8 (Impact of lifo inventory system)

The Weimer Corporation sells household appliances and uses lifo for inventory costing. The inventory contains ten different products, and historical lifo layers are maintained for each of them. The lifo layers for one of their products, Wonder Blender, were as follows at December 31, 1984:

1983 layer	4,000 @ $100
1978 layer	3,500 @ $ 85
1974 layer	1,000 @ $ 75
1972 layer	3,000 @ $ 52

Instructions:

(1) What was the value of the ending inventory of Wonder Blenders at December 31, 1984?
(2) How did the December 31, 1984 quantity of blenders compare with the December 31, 1983 quantity of blenders?
(3) What was the value of the ending inventory of Wonder Blenders at December 31, 1985, assuming that there were 10,500 blenders on hand?
(4) How would income in part (3) be affected if, in addition to the quantity on hand, 1,250 blenders were in transit to Weimer Corporation at December 31, 1985? The shipment was made on December 26, 1985, terms FOB shipping point. Total invoice cost was $131,250.

problem 8-9 (Inventory error correction)

The Wallace Corporation has adjusted and closed its books at the end of 1984. The company arrives at its inventory position by a physical count taken on December 31 of each year. In March of 1985, the following errors were discovered.

(a) Merchandise which cost $2,500 was sold for $3,200 on December 29, 1984. The order was shipped December 31, 1984, with terms of FOB shipping point. The merchandise was not included in the ending inventory. The sale was recorded on January 12, 1985, when the customer made payment on the sale.
(b) On January 3, 1985, Wallace Corporation received merchandise which had been shipped to them on December 30, 1984. The terms of the purchase were FOB shipping point. Cost of the merchandise was $1,750. The purchase was recorded and the goods included in the inventory when payment was made in January of 1985.
(c) On January 8, 1985, merchandise which had been included in the ending inventory was returned to Wallace because the consignee had not been able to sell it. The cost of this merchandise was $1,200 with a selling price of $1,800.
(d) Merchandise costing $950, located in a separate warehouse, was overlooked and excluded from the 1984 inventory count.
(e) On December 26, 1984, Wallace Corporation purchased merchandise from a supplier costing $1,175. The order was shipped December 28 (terms FOB destination) and was still "in-transit" on December 31. Since the invoice was received on December 31, the purchase was recorded in 1984. The merchandise was not included in the inventory count.
(f) The corporation failed to make an entry for a purchase on account of $835 at the end of 1984, although it included this merchandise in the inventory count. The purchase was recorded when payment was made to the supplier in 1985.
(g) The corporation included in its 1984 ending inventory, merchandise with a cost of $1,290. This merchandise had been custom-built and was being held until the customer could come and pick up the merchandise. The sale, for $1,425, was recorded in 1985.

Instructions: Give the entry in 1985 (1984 books are closed) to correct each error. Assume that the errors were made during 1984 and all amounts are material.

problem 8-10 (Inventory error correction)

The Jennings Corporation adjusted and closed its books on December 31, 1984. Net income of $52,000 was reported for the year. Several months later, the independent auditors discovered the following material errors. Jennings used a periodic inventory method.

(a) 3,000 units of Product A, costing $8.95, were recorded at a unit cost of $8.59 in summarizing the ending inventory.
(b) A sale of merchandise shipped on January 3, 1985, was included in the ending inventory count. The cost of this merchandise was $4,750, and the sale was properly recorded at $5,950 on December 31, 1984.
(c) Merchandise costing $5,550 was included in the inventory although it was shipped to a customer on December 31, 1984, with terms of FOB shipping point. The corporation recorded the sale ($7,400) on January 3, 1985.
(d) Merchandise in the storeroom on December 31 (costing $1,500) was included in the 1984 ending inventory although the purchase invoice was not received or recorded until January 5, 1985.
(e) Merchandise in the hands of a consignee, costing $4,000, was included in the inventory; however, $2,400 of the merchandise had been sold as of December 31. The sale was not recorded until January 31, 1985, when the consignee made a full remittance of $3,200 on the merchandise sold.
(f) On December 31, 1984, a purchase of merchandise costing $2,500 was still in a delivery truck parked in the corporation's receiving dock. Because of the rush at year-end, the truck had not been unloaded. The terms of the purchase were FOB destination. The merchandise was not included in the ending inventory, but the purchase was recorded in the books in 1984.

Instructions:
(1) Compute the corrected net income for 1984.
(2) Give the entries that are required in 1985 to correct the accounts.

problem 8-11 (Inventory error corrections—cut-off)

The Oakland Company is a wholesale distributor of automotive replacement parts. Initial amounts taken from Oakland's accounting records are as follows:

Inventory at December 31, 1984 (based on physical count of goods in Oakland's warehouse on December 31, 1984)			$1,250,000
Accounts payable at December 31, 1984:			
Vendor	Terms	Amount	
Holly Company	2% 10 days, net 30	$ 265,000	
Marie Inc.	Net 30	210,000	
Becca Corporation	Net 30	300,000	
Steve Company	Net 30	225,000	
Bob Bottle Company	Net 30	—	
		$1,000,000	
Sales in 1984			$9,000,000

Additional information is as follows:

(a) Parts held on consignment from Marie to Oakland, the consignee, amounting to $155,000, were included in the physical count of goods in Oakland's warehouse on December 31, 1984, and in accounts payable at December 31, 1984.

(b) $22,000 of parts which were purchased from Bob Bottle and paid for in December 1984 were sold in the last week of 1984 and appropriately recorded as sales of $28,000. The parts were included in the physical count of goods in Oakland's warehouse on December 31, 1984, because the parts were on the loading dock waiting to be picked up by customers.

(c) Parts in transit on December 31, 1984, to customers, shipped FOB shipping point on December 28, 1984, amounted to a cost of $34,000. The customers received the parts on January 6, 1985. Sales of $40,000 to the customers for the parts were recorded by Oakland on January 2, 1985.

(d) Retailers were holding $210,000 at cost ($250,000 at retail) of goods on consignment from Oakland, the consignor, at their stores on December 31, 1984.

(e) Goods were in transit from Marie to Oakland on December 31, 1984. The cost of the goods was $25,000, and they were shipped FOB shipping point on December 29, 1984. The transaction was recorded when the goods were received.

(f) A freight bill in the amount of $2,000 specifically relating to merchandise purchases in December 1984, all of which were still in the inventory at December 31, 1984, was received on January 3, 1985. The freight bill was not included in either the inventory or in accounts payable at December 31, 1984.

(g) All of the purchases from Holly occurred during the last seven days of the year. These items have been recorded in accounts payable and accounted for in the physical inventory at cost before discount. Oakland's policy is to pay invoices in time to take advantage of all cash discounts, adjust inventory accordingly, and record accounts payable, net of cash discounts.

Instructions: Prepare a schedule of adjustments to the initial amounts using the format shown below. Show the effect, if any, of each of the transactions separately and if the transactions would have no effect on the amount shown, state NONE.

	Inventory	Accounts Payable	Sales
Initial amounts	$1,250,000	$1,000,000	$9,000,000
Adjustments			
Total adjustments			
Adjusted amounts	$	$	$

(AICPA adapted)

problem 8-12 (Change from fifo to lifo inventory)

The Topanga Manufacturing Company manufactures two products: Mult and Tran. At December 31, 1984, Topanga used the first-in, first-out (fifo) inventory method. Effective

January 1, 1985, Topanga changed to the last-in, first-out (lifo) inventory method. The cumulative effect of this change is not determinable and, as a result, the ending inventory of 1984 for which the fifo method was used, is also the beginning inventory for 1985 for the lifo method. Any layers added during 1985 should be costed by reference to the first acquisitions of 1985 and any layers liquidated during 1985 should be considered a permanent liquidation.

The following information was available from Topanga's inventory records for the two most recent years:

	Mult		Tran	
	Units	Unit Cost	Units	Unit Cost
1984 purchases:				
January 7	5,000	$4.00	22,000	$2.00
April 16	12,000	4.50		
November 8	17,000	5.00	18,500	2.50
December 13	10,000	6.00		
1985 purchases:				
February 11	3,000	7.00	23,000	3.00
May 20	8,000	7.50		
October 15	20,000	8.00		
December 23			15,500	3.50
Units on hand:				
December 31, 1984	15,000		14,500	
December 31, 1985	16,000		13,000	

Instructions: Compute the effect on income before income taxes for the year ended December 31, 1985, resulting from the change from the fifo to the lifo inventory method.

(AICPA adapted)

problem 8-13 (Lifo inventory pools—unit lifo)

On January 1, 1980, Grover Company changed its inventory cost flow method from fifo to lifo for its raw material inventory. The change was made for both financial statement and income tax reporting purposes. Grover uses the multiple-pools approach under which substantially identical raw materials are grouped into lifo inventory pools; weighted average costs are used in valuing annual incremental layers. The composition of the December 31, 1982, inventory for the Class F inventory pool is as follows:

	Units	Weighted Average Unit Cost	Total Cost
Base year inventory—1980	9,000	$10.00	$ 90,000
Incremental layer—1981	3,000	11.00	33,000
Incremental layer—1982	2,000	12.50	25,000
Inventory, December 31, 1982	14,000		$148,000

Inventory transactions for the Class F inventory pool during 1983 and 1984 were as follows:

1983

Mar. 1 4,800 units were purchased at a unit cost of $13.50 for $64,800.
Sept. 1 7,200 units were purchased at a unit cost of $14.00 for $100,800.
A total of 15,000 units were used for production during 1983.

1984

Jan. 10 7,500 units were purchased at a unit cost of $14.50 for $108,750.
May 15 5,500 units were purchased at a unit cost of $15.50 for $85,250.
Dec. 29 7,000 units were purchased at a unit cost of $16.00 for $112,000.
A total of 16,000 units were used for production during 1984.

Instructions:

(1) Prepare a schedule to compute the inventory (unit and dollar amounts) of the Class F inventory pool at December 31, 1983. Show supporting computations in good form.
(2) Prepare a schedule to compute the cost of Class F raw materials used in production for the year ended December 31, 1983.
(3) Prepare a schedule to compute the inventory (unit and dollar amounts) of the Class F inventory pool at December 31, 1984. Show supporting computations in good form.

(AICPA adapted)

9 INVENTORIES — ESTIMATION AND VALUATION PROCEDURES

CHAPTER OBJECTIVES

Explain and illustrate the use of the gross profit and retail methods in estimating inventory quantities and costs.

Explain and illustrate general procedures for using dollar-value lifo and application of the procedures to the retail inventory method.

Identify and describe alternatives to cost as a basis for valuing inventories.

Describe and illustrate currently accepted accounting procedures for recognizing declines in the market value of goods on hand.

Describe and illustrate the presentation of inventories on the balance sheet and the required disclosure of supplemental information.

The basic concepts and methods of inventory cost allocation were presented in Chapter 8. Some specialized cost methods and required departures from valuation at cost are discussed in this chapter.

GROSS PROFIT METHOD

Estimates are frequently employed in developing inventory quantities and costs. The **gross profit method** of estimation is based on an assumed relationship between gross profit and sales. A gross profit percentage is applied to sales to determine cost of goods sold; then cost of goods sold is subtracted from the cost of goods available for sale to arrive at an estimated inventory balance.

The gross profit method is useful when:

(1) A periodic system is in use and inventories are required for interim statements or for the determination of the week-to-week or month-to-month inventory position, and the cost of taking physical inventories would be excessive for such purposes.
(2) Inventories have been destroyed or lost by fire, theft, or other casualty, and the specific data required for inventory valuation are not available.
(3) It is desired to test or check the validity of inventory figures determined by other means. Such application is referred to as the **gross profit test.**

The gross profit percentage used must be a reliable measure of current experience. In developing a reliable rate, reference is made to past rates and these are adjusted for variations considered to exist currently. Past gross profit rates, for example, may require adjustment when inventories are valued at last-in, first-out, and significant fluctuations in inventory position and/or prices have occurred. Current changes in cost-price relationships or in the sales mix of specific products also create a need for modifying past rates.

The calculation of cost of goods sold depends on whether the gross profit percentage is developed and stated in terms of sales or in terms of cost. The procedures to be followed in each case are illustrated below.

Example 1—Gross profit as a percentage of sales. Assume sales are $100,000 and goods are sold at a gross profit of 40% of sales.

If gross profit is 40% of sales, then cost of goods sold must be 60% of sales.

Sales	100%		Sales	100%
Cost of goods sold	?	=	Cost of goods sold	60%
Gross profit	40%		Gross profit	40%

Cost of goods sold, then, is 60% of $100,000, or $60,000. Goods available for sale less the estimated cost of goods sold gives the estimated cost of the remaining inventory. Assuming the cost of goods available for sale is $85,000, this balance less the estimated cost of goods sold, $60,000, gives an estimated inventory of $25,000.

Example 2—Gross profit as a percentage of cost. Assume sales are $100,000 and goods are sold at a gross profit that is 60% of their cost.

If sales are made at a gross profit of 60% of cost, then sales must be equal to the sum of cost, considered 100%, and the gross profit on cost, 60%. Sales, then, are 160% of cost:

Sales	?		Sales	160%
Cost of goods sold	100%	=	Cost of goods sold	100%
Gross profit	60%		Gross profit	60%

To find cost, or 100%, sales may be divided by 160 and multiplied by 100, or sales may simply be divided by 1.60. Cost of goods sold, then, is $100,000 ÷ 1.60 = $62,500. This amount is subtracted from the cost of goods available for sale to determine the estimated inventory.

When various lines of merchandise are sold at different gross profit rates, it may be possible to develop a reliable inventory value only by making separate calculations for each line. Under such circumstances, it is necessary to develop summaries of sales, goods available for sale, and gross profit data for the different merchandise lines.

Use of Gross Profit Method for Interim Inventory Calculations

When a periodic inventory system is used and inventory quantities are determined only at year-end, the gross profit method can be employed to provide management with information not otherwise available. For example, assume that data are needed to compute the inventory turnover for a business. If only year-end inventories are available, the turnover would be computed using the average of the beginning and ending inventories. A more representative average inventory can be obtained by analyzing sales and purchases and computing estimated monthly inventories by the gross profit method. To illustrate the impact of this difference, assume that a company had the following annual income information:

Sales		$500,000
Cost of goods sold:		
Inventory, January 1	$ 20,000	
Purchases	310,000	
Goods available for sale	$330,000	
Inventory, December 31	30,000	
Cost of goods sold		300,000
Gross profit on sales		$200,000

If only these data are available, the average inventory is $25,000, the sum of the beginning and ending balances divided by 2. Using this average, the inventory turnover, the number of times the average inventory has been replenished during the year, is 12 times, calculated as follows:

$$\frac{\text{Cost of goods sold}}{\text{Average inventory (using year-end balances)}} = \frac{\$300{,}000}{\$25{,}000} = 12$$

A more representative average inventory to use for computing turnover can be obtained by analyzing sales and purchases and computing estimated monthly inventories by the gross profit method. These computations are given at the top of the next page.

The average inventory can now be calculated from the monthly inventory balances, including the beginning inventory, and the turnover determined as follows:

$$\frac{\text{Total of inventories}}{\text{Number of inventories}} = \frac{\$476{,}000}{13} = \$36{,}615$$

$$\frac{\text{Cost of goods sold}}{\text{Average inventory (using monthly balances)}} = \frac{\$300{,}000}{\$36{,}615} = 8.2$$

This figure is more accurate than the one developed on the basis of the year-end inventories which were not representative of the inventory activity during the year.

	A	B	C	D	E	F
		Cost of Goods Sold				
	Purchases	*Sales*	*Cost as a Percentage of Sales*	*Cost of Goods Sold (B × C)*	*Inventory Increase or (Decrease) (A − D)*	*Inventory (F + E)*
January 1						$ 20,000
January	$ 20,000	$ 30,000	60%	$ 18,000	$ 2,000	22,000
February	20,000	30,000	60	18,000	2,000	24,000
March	20,000	30,000	60	18,000	2,000	26,000
April	20,000	30,000	60	18,000	2,000	28,000
May	30,000	40,000	60	24,000	6,000	34,000
June	30,000	40,000	60	24,000	6,000	40,000
July	30,000	60,000	60	36,000	(6,000)	34,000
August	30,000	40,000	60	24,000	6,000	40,000
September	40,000	40,000	60	24,000	16,000	56,000
October	40,000	50,000	60	30,000	10,000	66,000
November	20,000	50,000	60	30,000	(10,000)	56,000
December	10,000	60,000	60	36,000	(26,000)	30,000
	$310,000	$500,000	60%	$300,000	$ 10,000	$476,000

Use of the gross profit method to estimate inventories on a monthly, weekly, or other basis can also (1) serve as a control measure to avoid overstocking or shortages of goods and (2) provide information for the preparation of interim financial statements.

Use of Gross Profit Method for Computation of Casualty Loss

A common application of the gross profit method is the estimation of inventory when a physical count is impossible due to the loss or destruction of goods. For example, assume that on October 31, 1984, a fire in the warehouse of a wholesale distributing company totally destroyed the contents, including many accounting records. Remaining records indicated that the last physical inventory was taken on December 31, 1983, and that the inventory at that date was $329,500. Microfilm bank records of canceled checks disclosed that during 1984 payments to suppliers for inventory items were $1,015,000. Unpaid invoices at the beginning of 1984 amounted to $260,000, and communication with suppliers indicated a balance due at the time of the fire of $315,000. Bank deposits for the ten months amounted to $1,605,000. All deposits came from customers for goods purchased except for a loan of $100,000 obtained from the bank during the year. Accounts receivable at the beginning of the year were $328,000, and an analysis of the available records indicated that accounts receivable on October 31 totaled $275,000. Gross profit percentages on sales for the preceding four years were:

1980.........	28%	1982........	23%
1981.........	25%	1983........	24%

From these facts, the inventory in the warehouse at the time of the fire could be estimated as follows:

Estimate of sales January 1 to October 31, 1984		
Collection of accounts receivable ($1,605,000 − $100,000)		$1,505,000
Add accounts receivable at October 31, 1984		275,000
		$1,780,000
Deduct accounts receivable at January 1, 1984		328,000
Estimate of sales January 1 to October 31, 1984		$1,452,000
Average gross profit percentage on sales for past 4 years		25%
Average cost percentage on sales for past 4 years		75%
Estimate of cost of goods sold to October 31, 1984 ($1,452,000 × 75%)		$1,089,000
Estimate of inventory on October 31, 1984		
Inventory January 1, 1984		$ 329,500
Add: Payments to suppliers—1984	$1,015,000	
Amounts payable to suppliers, October 31, 1984	315,000	
	$1,330,000	
Deduct accounts payable to suppliers, January 1, 1984	260,000	
Estimate of purchases January 1 to October 31, 1984		1,070,000
Goods available for sale		$1,399,500
Estimate of cost of goods sold for 1984 (from above)		1,089,000
Estimated inventory, October 31, 1984		$ 310,500

RETAIL INVENTORY METHOD

The **retail inventory method** is widely employed by retail concerns, particularly department stores, to arrive at reliable estimates of inventory position whenever desired. This method, like the gross profit method, permits the calculation of an inventory amount without the time and expense of taking a physical inventory or maintaining a detailed perpetual inventory record for each of the thousands of items normally included in a retail inventory. When this method is used, records of goods purchased are maintained at two amounts—cost and retail. **A cost percentage** is computed by dividing the goods available for sale at cost by the goods available for sale at retail. This cost percentage can then be applied to the ending inventory at retail, an amount that can be readily calculated by subtracting sales for the period from the total goods available for sale at retail.

The computation of a retail inventory at the end of a month is illustrated by the following example:

	Cost	Retail
Inventory, January 1	$30,000	$45,000
Purchases in January	20,000	35,000
Goods available for sale	$50,000	$80,000
Cost percentage ($50,000 ÷ $80,000) = 62.5%		
Deduct sales for January		25,000
Inventory, January 31, at retail		$55,000
Inventory, January 31, at estimated cost ($55,000 × 62.5%)	$34,375	

The effect of the above procedure is to provide an inventory valuation in terms of average cost. No cost sequence, such as lifo or fifo, is recognized; the percentage of cost to retail for the ending inventory is the same as the percentage of cost to retail for goods sold.

Use of the retail inventory method offers the following advantages:

(1) Estimated interim inventories can be obtained without a physical count.
(2) When a physical inventory is actually taken for periodic statement purposes, it can be taken at retail and then converted to cost without reference to individual costs and invoices, thus saving time and expense.
(3) Shoplifting losses can be determined and monitored. Since physical counts of inventory should agree with the calculated retail inventory, any difference not accounted for by clerical errors in the company records must be attributable to actual physical loss by shoplifting or employee theft.

Although this method permits the estimation of a value for inventory, errors can occur in accounting for the dual prices and in applying the retail method. Thus, a physical count of the inventory to be reported on the annual financial statements is generally required at least once a year. Retail inventory records should be adjusted for variations shown by the physical count so that records reflect the actual status of the inventory for purposes of future estimates and control.

The accounting entries for the retail inventory method are similar to those made using a periodic inventory system. The retail figures are part of the analysis necessary to compute the cost of the inventory; however, they do not actually appear in the accounts. Thus, the following entries would be made to record the inventory data included in the preceding example.

Purchases	20,000	
Accounts Payable		20,000
Accounts Receivable	25,000	
Sales		25,000
Income Summary	30,000	
Inventory		30,000
To close the beginning inventory.		
Inventory	34,375	
Income Summary		34,375
To record the ending inventory.		

After closing Purchases and Sales to Income Summary, the income summary account has a balance of $9,375. This is the gross profit on sales that would be reported on the income statement.

Markups and Markdowns

In the earlier inventory calculations, it was assumed that there were no changes in retail prices after the goods were originally recorded. Frequently, however, retail prices do change because of changes in the price level, shifts in consumer demand, or other factors. The following terms are used in discussing the retail method:

(1) **Original retail**—the initial sales price, including the original increase over cost referred to as the **markon** or **initial markup.**
(2) **Additional markups**—increases that raise sales prices above original retail.
(3) **Markup cancellations**—decreases in additional markups that do not reduce sales prices below original retail.
(4) **Net markups**—Additional markups less markup cancellations.
(5) **Markdowns**—decreases that reduce sales prices below original retail.
(6) **Markdown cancellations**—decreases in the markdowns that do not raise the sales prices above original retail.
(7) **Net markdowns**—markdowns less markdown cancellations.

The difference between cost and actual selling price as adjusted for the described changes is referred to as the **maintained markup.**

To illustrate the use of these terms, assume that goods originally placed for sale are marked at 50% above cost. Merchandise costing $4 a unit, then, is marked at $6, which is the **original retail.** The **initial markup** of $2 is referred to as a "50% markup on cost" or a "33⅓% markup on sales price." In anticipation of a heavy demand for the article, the retail price is subsequently increased to $7.50. This represents an **additional markup** of $1.50. At a later date the price is reduced to $7. This is a **markup cancellation** of 50 cents and not a markdown since the retail price has not been reduced below the original sales price. But assume that goods originally marked to sell at $6 are subsequently marked down to $5. This represents a **markdown** of $1. At a later date the goods are marked to sell at $5.25. This is a **markdown cancellation** of 25 cents and not a markup, since sales price does not exceed the original retail.

Retail inventory results will vary depending on whether net markdowns are used in computing the cost percentage. When applying the most commonly used retail method, net markups are added to goods available for sale at retail before calculating the cost percentage; net markdowns, however, are not deducted in arriving at the percentage. This method is sometimes referred to as the **conventional retail inventory method.** It results in a lower cost percentage and correspondingly a lower inventory amount and a higher cost of goods sold than would be obtained if net markdowns were deducted before calculating the cost percentage. This can be illustrated as follows:

Net markdowns not deducted to calculate cost percentage (Conventional retail):

	Cost	Retail
Beginning inventory	$ 8,600	$ 14,000
Purchases	72,100	110,000
Additional markups		13,000
Markup cancellations		(2,500)
Goods available for sale	$80,700	$134,500
Cost percentage ($80,700 ÷ $134,500) = 60%		
Deduct: Sales		$108,000
Markdowns		4,800
Markdown cancellations		(800)
		$112,000
Ending inventory at retail		$ 22,500
Ending inventory at estimated cost ($22,500 × 60%)	$13,500	

Net markdowns deducted to calculate cost percentage:

	Cost	Retail
Beginning inventory	$ 8,600	$ 14,000
Purchases	72,100	110,000
Net markups		10,500
Net markdowns		(4,000)
Goods available for sale	$80,700	$130,500
Cost percentage ($80,700 ÷ $130,500) = 61.84%		
Deduct sales		108,000
Ending inventory at retail		$ 22,500
Ending inventory at estimated cost ($22,500 × 61.84%)	$13,914	

The lower inventory obtained with the conventional method approximates a **lower of average cost or market** valuation. The lower of cost or market concept, discussed in detail later in this chapter, requires recognition of declines in the value of inventory in the period such declines occur. Under the conventional retail method, markdowns are viewed as indicating a decline in the value of inventory and are deducted as a current cost of sales. When markdowns are included in the cost percentage computation, the result is an average cost allocated proportionately between cost of sales and ending inventory. Thus, only a portion of the decline in value is charged in the current period. The remainder is carried forward in ending inventory to be charged against future sales.

Markdowns may be made for special sales or clearance purposes, or they may be made as a result of market fluctuations and a decline in the replacement cost of goods. In either case their omission in calculating the cost percentage is necessary in order to value the inventory at the lower of cost or market. This is illustrated in the two examples that follow:

Example 1—Markdowns for special sales purposes. Assume that merchandise costing $50,000 is marked to sell for $100,000. To dispose of part of the goods immediately, one fourth of the stock is marked down $5,000 and is sold. The cost of the ending inventory is calculated as follows:

	Cost	Retail
Purchases	$50,000	$100,000
Cost percentage ($50,000 ÷ $100,000) = 50%		
Deduct: Sales		$ 20,000
Markdowns		5,000
		$ 25,000
Ending inventory at retail		$ 75,000
Ending inventory at estimated cost ($75,000 × 50%)	$37,500	

If cost, $50,000, had been related to sales price after markdowns, $95,000, a cost percentage of 52.6% would have been obtained, and the inventory, which is three fourths of the merchandise originally acquired, would have been reported at 52.6% of $75,000, or $39,450. The inventory would thus be stated above the $37,500 cost of the remaining inventory and cost of goods sold would be understated by $1,950. A markdown relating to goods no longer on hand would have been recognized in the development of a cost percentage to be applied to the inventory. Reductions in the goods available at sales prices resulting from shortages or damaged goods should likewise be disregarded in calculating the cost percentage.

Example 2—Markdowns as a result of market declines. Assume that merchandise costing $50,000 is marked to sell for $100,000. With a drop in replacement cost of merchandise to $40,000, sales prices are marked down to $80,000. Three fourths of the merchandise is sold. The cost of the ending inventory is calculated as follows:

	Cost	Retail
Purchases	$50,000	$100,000
Cost percentage ($50,000 ÷ $100,000) = 50%		
Deduct: Sales		$ 60,000
Markdowns		20,000
		$ 80,000
Ending inventory at retail		$ 20,000
Ending inventory at estimated cost ($20,000 × 50%)	$10,000	

If cost, $50,000, had been related to sales price after markdowns, $80,000, a cost percentage of 62.5% would have been obtained and the inventory would have been reported at 62.5% of $20,000, or $12,500. The use of the 50% cost percentage in the example reduces the inventory to $10,000, a balance providing the usual gross profit in subsequent periods if current prices and relationships between cost and retail prices prevail.

Freight, Discounts, Returns, and Allowances

In calculating the cost percentage, freight in should be added to the cost of the purchase; purchase discounts and returns and allowances should be deducted. A purchase return affects both the cost and the retail computations, while a purchase allowance affects only the cost total unless a change in retail price is made as a result of the allowance. Sales returns are proper adjustments to gross sales since the inventory is returned; however, sales discounts and sales allowances are not deducted to determine the estimated ending retail inventory. The deduction is not made because the sales price of an item is added into the computation of the retail inventory when it is purchased and deducted when it is sold, all at the gross sales price. Subsequent price adjustments included in the computation would leave a balance in the inventory account with no inventory on hand to represent it. For example, assume the sales price for 100 units of Product A is $5,000. When these units are sold for $5,000, the retail inventory balance would be zero. Subsequently, if an allowance of $100 is granted to the customer, the allowance would not be included in the computation of the month-end retail inventory balance. It would be recorded on the books, however, in the usual manner: debit Sales Allowances and credit Accounts Receivable.

Limitations of Retail Method

The calculation of a cost percentage for all goods carried is valid only when goods on hand can be regarded as representative of the total goods handled. Varying markon percentages and sales of high- and low-margin items in proportions that differ from purchases will require separate records and the development of separate cost percentages for different classes of goods. For example, assume that a store operates three departments and that for July the following information pertains to these departments:

	Department A		Department B		Department C		Total	
	Cost	Retail	Cost	Retail	Cost	Retail	Cost	Retail
Beginning inventory.........	$20,000	$ 28,000	$10,000	$15,000	$16,000	$ 40,000	$ 46,000	$ 83,000
Net purchases	57,000	82,000	20,000	35,000	20,000	60,000	97,000	177,000
Goods available for sale.....	$77,000	$110,000	$30,000	$50,000	$36,000	$100,000	$143,000	$260,000
Cost percentage		70%		60%		36%		55%
Sales........................		80,000		30,000		40,000		150,000
Inventory at retail		$ 30,000		$20,000		$ 60,000		$110,000
Inventory at cost............		$ 21,000		$12,000		$ 21,600		$ 60,500
				$54,600				

Because of the range in cost percentages from 36% to 70% and the difference in mix of the purchases and ending inventory, the ending inventory balance, using an overall cost percentage, is $5,900 higher ($60,500 – $54,600) than when the departmental rates are used. When material variations exist in the cost percentages by departments, separate departmental rates should be computed and applied.

The retail method is acceptable for income tax purposes, provided the taxpayer maintains adequate and satisfactory records supporting inventory calculations and applies the method consistently on successive tax returns.

An adaptation of the conventional retail method using lifo concepts has been developed. Before discussing this method, commonly called the retail-lifo method, a further discussion of the dollar-value lifo method introduced in Chapter 8 will aid in understanding the adaptation of lifo to retail inventories.

DOLLAR-VALUE LIFO METHOD

The concept of dollar-value lifo pools was introduced in Chapter 8. The **dollar-value lifo method** has become the most popular of the lifo methods. The greatest flexibility in using lifo is available under this method, and it can apply to almost any kind of inventory.

The income tax regulations specify that a taxpayer should ordinarily use the **double extension technique** for computing the base-year and the current-year cost of a dollar-value inventory pool. This method requires extending all items in the ending inventory at *both* the base-year prices *and* the end-of-year prices. The beginning inventory at base-year prices is then compared with the ending inventory at base-year prices to determine whether inventory quantities have increased or decreased. If a decrease has occurred, a corresponding reduction is required in the most recently created layers. If an increase has occurred, a new layer is added.

In many cases it is impractical to double-extend all items because of the large number of items involved or because of changing products due to technological or other changes. In these situations, the taxpayer may use an **index technique** for computing all or a part of the base-year values of the inventories. One method of arriving at an index is to double-extend a representative sample of the ending inventory and compute from this an index between the base-year and current-year prices. A modification of the **double-extension index,** known as the **link-chain index,** is also accepted. In some limited situations, the regulations permit the use of published price indexes that show price movements for a specific type of business. In this chapter, the index technique is used for both dollar-value lifo and retail-lifo examples.

General Procedures—Dollar-Value Lifo

All goods in the inventory or in the separate pools to which dollar-value lifo is to be applied are viewed as though they were identical items. Ending inventories are valued in terms of current prices. Beginning and ending inventory values are then converted by means of appropriate price deflator indexes to base-year prices, i.e., price levels existing at the time the lifo method was adopted. The difference between the converted beginning and ending dollar balances is a measure of the inventory **quantity change** for the year. An inventory increase is recognized as an inventory layer to be added to the beginning inventory, and such increase is converted by an inflator index to current prices and added to the dollars identified with the beginning balance.

An inventory decrease is recognized as a shrinkage to be applied to the most recent or top layer and to successively lower layers of the beginning inventory. This decrease is converted at the price indexes applying to such layers and subtracted from the dollars identified with the beginning inventory. The following example illustrates dollar-value lifo calculations over a five-year period. The index numbers and inventories at end-of-year prices are as follows:

Date	Year-End Price Index[1]	Inventory at End-of-Year Prices
December 31, 1980	1.00	$38,000
December 31, 1981	1.20	54,000
December 31, 1982	1.32	66,000
December 31, 1983	1.40	56,000
December 31, 1984	1.25	55,000

[1]Many published indexes appear as percentages without decimals, e.g., 100, 120, 132, 140, 125.

Date	Inventory at End-of-Year Prices		Deflator Index		Inventory at Base-Year Prices	Layers in Base-Year Prices		Incremental Layer Inflator Index		Dollar-Value Lifo Cost
December 31, 1980	$38,000	÷	1.00	=	$38,000	$38,000	×	1.00	=	$38,000
December 31, 1981	$54,000	÷	1.20	=	$45,000	$38,000	×	1.00	=	$38,000
						7,000	×	1.20	=	8,400
						$45,000				$46,400
December 31, 1982	$66,000	÷	1.32	=	$50,000	$38,000	×	1.00	=	$38,000
						7,000	×	1.20	=	8,400
						5,000	×	1.32	=	6,600
						$50,000				$53,000
December 31, 1983	$56,000	÷	1.40	=	$40,000	$38,000	×	1.00	=	$38,000
						2,000	×	1.20	=	2,400
						$40,000				$40,400
December 31, 1984	$55,000	÷	1.25	=	$44,000	$38,000	×	1.00	=	$38,000
						2,000	×	1.20	=	2,400
						4,000	×	1.25	=	5,000
						$44,000				$45,400

The following items should be observed in the example:

December 31, 1981—With an ending inventory of $45,000 in terms of base prices, the inventory has increased in 1981 by $7,000; however, the $7,000 increase is stated in terms of the pricing when lifo was adopted and needs to be restated in terms of 1981 year-end prices which are 120% of the base level.

December 31, 1982—With an ending inventory of $50,000 in terms of base prices, the inventory has increased in 1982 by another $5,000; however, the $5,000 increase is stated in terms of the pricing when lifo was adopted and needs to be restated in terms of 1982 year-end costs which are 132% of the base level.

December 31, 1983—When the ending inventory of $40,000 (expressed in base-year dollars) is compared to the beginning inventory of $50,000 (also expressed in base-year dollars), it is apparent that the inventory has been decreased by $10,000, in base-year terms. Under lifo procedures, the decrease is assumed to take place in the most recently added layers, reducing or eliminating them. As a result, the 1982 layer, priced at $5,000 in base-year terms, is completely eliminated, and $5,000 of the $7,000 layer from 1981 is eliminated. This leaves only $2,000 of the 1981 layer, plus the base-year amount. The remaining $2,000 of the 1981 layer is multiplied by 1.20 to restate it to 1981 dollars, and is added to the base-year amount to arrive at the ending inventory amount of $40,400.

December 31, 1984—The ending inventory of $44,000 in terms of the base prices indicates an inventory increase for 1984 of $4,000; this increase requires restatement in terms of 1984 year-end prices which are 125% of the base level.

As discussed in Chapter 8, the Internal Revenue Service allows the incremental lifo layer to be valued using fifo, average, or lifo costing. Thus the inflator index used to compute the new layer may be (1) a year-end index, as previously illustrated, based on costs of the most recent purchases (fifo costing); (2) an average index, based on average purchases during the year (average costing); or (3) a beginning-of-year index, representing costs of the earliest purchases during the year (lifo costing).

When fifo costing is used to value the incremental layer, as in the previous example, the inflator index is the same as the deflator index used to determine if a new layer exists. However, if average or lifo costing is used to compute the new layer, the inflator index will differ from the deflator index. To illustrate, using data from the preceding example, assume that lifo costing is used to value incremental inventory layers. The beginning-of-year indexes, representing the earliest purchases in each year, are as follows:

Date	Price Index Beginning-of-Year Purchases
December 31, 1981	1.02
December 31, 1982	1.21
December 31, 1983	1.35
December 31, 1984	1.38

The computation of year-end inventories would then be made as follows:

Date	Inventory at End-of-Year Prices		Deflator Index		Inventory at Base-Year Prices	Layers in Base-Year Prices		Incremental Layer Inflator Index		Dollar-Value Lifo Cost
December 31, 1980	$38,000	÷	1.00	=	$38,000	$38,000	×	1.00	=	$38,000
December 31, 1981	$54,000	÷	1.20	=	$45,000	$38,000	×	1.00	=	$38,000
						7,000	×	1.02	=	7,140
						$45,000				$45,140
December 31, 1982	$66,000	÷	1.32	=	$50,000	$38,000	×	1.00	=	$38,000
						7,000	×	1.02	=	7,140
						5,000	×	1.21	=	6,050
						$50,000				$51,190
December 31, 1983	$56,000	÷	1.40	=	$40,000	$38,000	×	1.00	=	$38,000
						2,000	×	1.02	=	2,040
						$40,000				$40,040
December 31, 1984	$55,000	÷	1.25	=	$44,000	$38,000	×	1.00	=	$38,000
						2,000	×	1.02	=	2,040
						4,000	×	1.38	=	5,520
						$44,000				$45,560

In some cases, the index for the first year of the lifo layers is not 1.00. This is especially true when an externally generated index is used. When this occurs, it is simpler to convert all inventories to a base of 1.00 rather than to use the index for the initial year of the lifo layers. The computations are done in the same manner as in the previous example except the inventory is stated in terms of the base year of the index, not the first year of the inventory layers. To illustrate, assume the same facts as stated for the example on page 294 except that the base year of the external index is 1977; in 1980, the index is 1.20; and, in 1981, it is 1.44. The schedule showing the lifo inventory computations would be modified as follows for the first two years. Note that the inventory cost is the same under either situation.

Date	Inventory at End-of-Year Prices		Deflator Index		Inventory at Base = 1.00 (1977 Prices)	Layers in Base = 1.00 (1977 Prices)		Incremental Layer Inflator Index		Dollar-Value Lifo Cost
December 31, 1980	$38,000	÷	1.20	=	$31,667	$31,667	×	1.20	=	$38,000
December 31, 1981	$54,000	÷	1.44	=	$37,500	$31,667	×	1.20	=	$38,000
						5,833	×	1.44	=	8,400
						$37,500				$46,400

Retail-Lifo Method

The dollar-value lifo procedures just described can be applied to the retail inventory method in developing inventory values reflecting a last-in, first-out valuation approach. The **retail-lifo method** requires that index numbers be applied to inventories stated at retail in arriving at the quantitative changes in inventories. When the quantitative changes have been determined, ending inventories are restated in terms of the retail base amounts, and the indexes for the layers involved in their composition and related cost percentages are applied to such values.

The retail-lifo procedures require two modifications to the conventional retail procedures to determine a cost percentage.

(1) Beginning inventory values are disregarded. The lifo inventory is composed of a base cost and subsequent cost layers that have not been assigned to revenues. Because costs for prior periods remain unchanged, only the cost of a current incremental layer requires calculation.

(2) Markdowns, as well as markups, are recognized in calculating the cost percentage applicable to goods stated at retail. Markdowns were not recognized in arriving at the cost percentage when the objective was to arrive at a lower of cost or market valuation. However, because lifo measurements require inventory valuation in terms of cost, the recognition of both markups and markdowns is appropriate.

These modifications in calculating cost percentages are illustrated in the following example:

	Cost	Retail
Purchases	$63,000	$ 98,000
Purchase returns	(2,000)	(3,000)
Purchase discounts	(1,000)	
Freight in	2,220	
Markups, net of cancellations		8,000
Markdowns, net of cancellations		(1,000)
Total current period purchases adjusted for markups and markdowns	$62,220	$102,000

Retail-lifo cost percentage ($62,220 ÷ $102,000) = 61%

It is important to note that this cost percentage will be used only if an incremental layer is added to the inventory in the current period. If the inventory level has declined, previous inventory layers will be reduced.

Retail-lifo computations are illustrated in the example that follows. Incremental layers are costed at end-of-year prices. The cost and index data relating to each year are as follows:

Date	Year-End Price Index	Cost Percentage	Inventory at End-of-Year Retail Prices
December 31, 1980	1.00	.60	$60,000
December 31, 1981	1.05	.62	69,300
December 31, 1982	1.10	.64	77,000
December 31, 1983	1.12	.65	77,280
December 31, 1984	1.08	.60	78,300

Date	Inventory at End-of-Year Retail Prices		Deflator Index		Inventory at Base-Year Retail Prices	Layers		Incremental Layer Inflator Index		Cost Percentage		Retail-Lifo Cost
December 31, 1980	$60,000	÷	1.00	=	$60,000	$60,000	×	1.00	×	.60	=	$36,000
December 31, 1981	$69,300	÷	1.05	=	$66,000	$60,000	×	1.00	×	.60	=	$36,000
						6,000	×	1.05	×	.62	=	3,906
						$66,000						$39,906
December 31, 1982	$77,000	÷	1.10	=	$70,000	$60,000	×	1.00	×	.60	=	$36,000
						6,000	×	1.05	×	.62	=	3,906
						4,000	×	1.10	×	.64	=	2,816
						$70,000						$42,722
December 31, 1983	$77,280	÷	1.12	=	$69,000	$60,000	×	1.00	×	.60	=	$36,000
						6,000	×	1.05	×	.62	=	3,906
						3,000	×	1.10	×	.64	=	2,112
						$69,000						$42,018
December 31, 1984	$78,300	÷	1.08	=	$72,500	$60,000	×	1.00	×	.60	=	$36,000
						6,000	×	1.05	×	.62	=	3,906
						3,000	×	1.10	×	.64	=	2,112
						3,500	×	1.08	×	.60	=	2,268
						$72,500						$44,286

Change to Retail-Lifo Method

In the preceding example, it was assumed that retail-lifo was used from the beginning of the company's existence. However, if a company has been using the conventional retail method and decides to change to retail-lifo, the beginning inventory in the year of change must be adjusted from a lower of average cost or market valuation to a strict cost situation for the period involved. This can be done by including markdowns and excluding the beginning inventory when computing the cost percentage. To illustrate, assume the company whose conventional retail inventory of $13,500 was computed on page 290 decided to change its inventory method to retail-lifo. The cost percentage, rather than being 60%, would be 61.89% as a result of deducting the net markdowns of $4,000 from the retail value and excluding the beginning inventories at both cost and retail: ($80,700 − $8,600 = $72,100; $134,500 − $4,000 − $14,000 = $116,500; $72,100 ÷ $116,500 = 61.89%). The ending inventory would be $13,925 ($22,500 × 61.89%), an increase of $425 ($13,925 − $13,500). This inventory would become the first layer for the new year. The $425 increase in inventory would be reported as a special income item relating to the effect of changing an accounting method. (See Chapter 21 for a discussion of reporting changes in accounting methods). The entry to record the change would be:

Inventory	425	
Inventory Adjustment Due to Change in Accounting Methods		425

Determination of Price Indexes

As indicated earlier, there are two common approaches for determining price indexes for a particular inventory: (1) using a published external index relating to the inventory; or (2) developing a specific internal index from the company's inventory records.

External Indexes. Although many price-level indexes are published by governmental and private agencies, only the Bureau of Labor Statistics' (BLS) department store indexes were automatically acceptable for income tax purposes until the Economic Recovery Tax Act of 1981 was passed. This Act directed the IRS to prescribe regulations providing for an expansion of external indexes for use by lifo companies. As a result, regulations were issued in 1982 permitting small businesses with annual sales of $2 million or less to use either monthly consumer price indexes (CPI) or monthly producer price indexes (PPI).[1] Companies that do not qualify as small businesses may use these same indexes, but they may only incorporate in their inventory calculations 80 percent of the reported change in the index being used. A separate index must be used for each inventory item that comprises more than 10 percent of the total inventory value. However, aggregation is permitted of each item comprising less than 10 percent of the total inventory value.

The BLS department store indexes that are still acceptable for retail department stores are divided into twenty groups, and each group becomes a separate dollar-value pool.

The increased number of external indexes available should increase the popularity of the lifo method and reduce the cost of implementation required if an internal index must be developed. For this reason, the use of these new external indexes is being referred to as "simplified lifo." The IRS has decided that adoption of these external indexes in place of internal indexes is a change in accounting method. Except for limited situations, companies making the change must obtain prior approval from the Commissioner of Internal

[1] *IRS Income Tax Regulations,* Section 1.472-8(e)(3)

Revenue. The acceptability of the simplified lifo method for financial reporting purposes is still under consideration by the accounting profession. In the opinion of the authors, if the method is acceptable for income tax purposes, it should be acceptable for financial reporting purposes. The lifo method is a creation of the income tax regulations, and it seems unwise to accept some parts of the regulations and reject others.

Internal Indexes. When published indexes are not available, specific indexes must be developed from the company's inventory records. A widely used technique for developing indexes for dollar-value lifo is double extension. As indicated earlier, a **double extension index** is computed by extending a representative portion of a specific inventory at both base-year prices and at current prices. Thus, if the sample ending inventory was $126,500 valued at current prices and $105,400 when the individual items in the sample inventory were valued at base-year prices, the index relationship between these values would be 1.20 ($126,500 ÷ $105,400). The Internal Revenue Service has stated that a nonstatistical sample must include at least 50% of the items and represent 70% or more of the dollar value. Fewer items are necessary if a carefully constructed random sample is used.

The double extension index has two principal disadvantages: (1) it is time consuming and costly for companies having a large number of different inventory items; and (2) if the inventory items are changing, it may be difficult to determine base year prices for newly added items. This latter disadvantage is overcome with the **link-chain index.** This modification of the double extension index requires extending a statistically representative portion of the ending inventory at end-of-year prices and beginning-of-year, rather than base-year prices. The index computed from this valuation is then multiplied by a cumulative index carried forward from previous years to determine the current index. The BLS department store indexes are established using this approach.

The computation of a link-chain index is illustrated as follows:

Valuation at year-end prices of representative portion of inventory	$215,040
Valuation at beginning-of-year prices of above portion of inventory	$204,800
Yearly index ($215,040 ÷ $204,800)	1.05
Cumulative index from previous years	1.40
Cumulative index as of end of current year (1.40 × 1.05 = 1.47)	1.47

This approach has the advantage of simplicity because historical records of base-year costs are not necessary. It permits changing inventory items without causing difficulty in computing base-year prices for the new items. A company may change from the double extension index method to the link-chain index if it has had at least a 90% turnover of inventory items in the preceding five-year period.

Selection of Pools

The selection of inventory pools is critical in dollar-value lifo. A company should have a minimum number of pools to benefit most by the use of the lifo method. For manufacturers and processors, **natural business unit pools** are recommended. If it can be shown that a business has only one natural business unit, one pool may be used for all of its inventory, including raw materials, goods in process, and finished goods. If, however, a business enterprise is composed of more than one natural business unit, more than one pool will be required. If the company maintains separate divisions for internal management purposes, has distinct production facilities and processes, or maintains separate income records for different units, more than one business unit pool is inferred. The Income Tax Regulations give the following example of a company with more than one natural business unit pool:

> A corporation manufactures, in one division, automatic clothes washers and driers of both commercial and domestic grade as well as electric ranges, mangles, and dishwashers. The corporation manufactures, in another division, radios and television sets. The manufacturing facilities and processes used in manufacturing the radios and television sets are distinct from those used in manufacturing the automatic clothes washers, etc. Under these circumstances, the enterprise would consist of two business units and two pools would be appropriate, one consisting of all of the LIFO inventories entering into the manufacture of clothes washers and driers, electric ranges, mangles, and dishwashers and the other consisting of all of the LIFO inventories entering into the production of radio and television sets.[2]

A manufacturer or processor may choose to use **multiple pools** rather than include all inventory in natural business units. Each pool should consist of inventory items that are substantially similar, including raw materials.

Pools for wholesalers, retailers, etc., are usually defined by major lines, types, or classes of goods. The departments of a retail store are examples of separate pools for these entities. The number and propriety of inventory pools is reviewed periodically by the IRS, and continued use of established pools is subject to the results of the evaluation.

The Economic Recovery Tax Act of 1981 simplified the selection of pools for smaller businesses. Any business with average gross receipts not in excess of $2 million for the three most recent taxable years may elect to use a single inventory pool rather than identifying natural product pools.

Adopting Lifo—IRS Requirement

An application to use the lifo method of inventory valuation for tax purposes must be filed with the Internal Revenue Service. The application form is reproduced on the following page. Note the choices the taxpayer must specifically make in defining the lifo techniques to be used. While no permission from the IRS is required to adopt lifo, the IRS may question the techniques being used based on the application. Changing from lifo to another inventory valuation method requires prior IRS approval.

---

[2] *Ibid.*, Section 1.472-8(b)(2)(ii)

Form **970** (Rev. November 1981) Department of the Treasury Internal Revenue Service

Application to Use LIFO Inventory Method

▶ Attach to your tax return.
▶ For Paperwork Reduction Act Notice, see instructions on back.

OMB No. 1545-0042
Expires 11-30-84

Name | Identifying number *(See instructions)*

Address *(Number, street, city, State and ZIP code)*

CHECK ONE:
☐ Initial Election
☐ Subsequent Election

Statement of Election and Other Information:

A. I apply to adopt and use the LIFO inventory method provided by section 472. I will use this method for the first time (or modify this method) as of (date tax year ends) ...., for the following goods (give details as explained in instructions; use more sheets if necessary):

B. I agree to make any adjustments that the District Director of Internal Revenue may require, on examination of my return, to reflect income clearly for the years involved in changing to or from the LIFO method or in using it.

1. Nature of business

2. **(a)** Inventory method used until now

(b) Will inventory be taken at actual cost regardless of market value? If "No," attach explanation. . . . . ☐ Yes ☐ No

3. **(a)** Was the closing inventory of the specified goods valued at cost as of the end of the immediately preceding tax year, as required by section 472(d)? If "No," attach explanation . . . . ☐ Yes ☐ No

(b) Did you file an amended return to include in the prior year's income any adjustments that resulted from changing to LIFO? See Rev. Proc. 76-6, 1976-1, C.B. 545. If "No," attach explanation. ☐ Yes ☐ No

4. **(a)** List goods subject to inventory that are not to be inventoried under the LIFO method

(b) Were the goods of the specified type included in opening inventory counted as acquired at the same time and at a unit cost equal to the actual cost of the total divided by the number of units on hand? If "No," attach explanation . . . . . ☐ Yes ☐ No

5. **(a)** Did you issue credit statements, or reports to shareholders, partners, other proprietors, or beneficiaries, covering the first tax year to which this application refers? . . . . ☐ Yes ☐ No

(b) If "Yes," state to whom, and on what dates

(c) Show the inventory method used in determining income, profit, or loss in those statements

6. Method used to determine the cost of the goods in the closing inventory over those in the opening inventory. *(See Regulations section 1.472-2.)*
☐ Most recent purchases ☐ Earliest acquisitions during the year ☐ Average cost of purchases during the year ☐ Other—Attach explanation

7. Method used in valuing LIFO inventories
☐ Unit method ☐ Dollar-value method

8. **(a)** If you use pools, list and describe contents of each pool

(b) Describe briefly the cost system used

(c) Method used in computing LIFO value of dollar-value pools
☐ Double extension method ☐ Other method *(If other, describe and justify—see instructions.)*

9. Did you change your method of valuing inventories for this tax year with the Commissioner's permission? If "Yes," attach a copy of the National Office's "grant letter" to this Form 970 . . . . ☐ Yes ☐ No

10. Were you ever on LIFO before? If "Yes," attach a statement to list the tax years you used LIFO and to explain why you discontinued it . . . . ☐ Yes ☐ No

Under penalties of perjury, I declare that I have examined this application, including any accompanying schedules and statements, and to the best of my knowledge and belief it is true, correct, and complete.

.... Date .... Signature of taxpayer

.... Date .... Signature of officer .... Title

INVENTORY VALUATIONS AT OTHER THAN COST

The basic cost procedures for determining inventory values have been discussed in this and the previous chapter. In some cases, generally accepted accounting principles permit deviations from cost, especially if a write-down of inventory values is warranted. The remainder of this chapter discusses some of these departures from historical cost and the circumstances under which they are appropriate.

Inventory Valuation at Lower of Cost or Market

As discussed in the preceding chapter, the accounting profession has not permitted the recognition of unrealized holding gains on inventories, i.e., goods on hand cannot be "written up" to reflect price-level increases prior to sale. Conversely, however, the recognition of unrealized losses is required under generally accepted accounting principles. This is a reflection of the long-standing and often debated tradition of conservatism in asset valuation and income recognition.

Recognition of a decline in the value of inventory as a loss in the period in which the decline occurs is referred to as **valuation at cost or market, whichever is lower,** or simply **valuation at the lower of cost or market.** The AICPA sanctioned this departure from cost in the following statement:

> A departure from the cost basis of pricing the inventory is required when the utility of the goods is no longer as great as its cost. Where there is evidence that the utility of goods, in their disposal in the ordinary course of business, will be less than cost, whether due to physical deterioration, obsolescence, changes in price levels, or other causes, the difference should be recognized as a loss of the current period. This is generally accomplished by stating such goods at a lower level commonly designated as market.[3]

In applying the lower of cost or market method, the cost of the ending inventory, as determined under an appropriate cost allocation method, is compared with market value at the end of the period. If market is less than cost, an adjusting entry is made to record the loss and restate ending inventory at the lower value. It should be noted that no adjustment to lifo cost is permitted for tax purposes; however, for financial reporting purposes, the lower of cost or market method applies to all inventories. This does not violate the "lifo conformity" rules.

Definition of Market. **Market** in "lower of cost or market" is interpreted as replacement cost with upper and lower limits which reflect estimated realizable values. This concept of market was stated by the American Institute of Certified Public Accountants as follows:

> As used in the phrase *lower of cost or market,* the term *market* means current replacement cost (by purchase or by reproduction, as the case may be) except that:

---

[3]*Accounting Research and Terminology Bulletins—Final Edition,* No. 43, "Restatement and Revision of Accounting Research Bulletins" (New York: American Institute of Certified Public Accountants, 1961), Ch. 4, statement 5.

(1) Market should not exceed the net realizable value (i.e., estimated selling price in the ordinary course of business less reasonably predictable costs of completion and disposal); and
(2) Market should not be less than net realizable value reduced by an allowance for an approximately normal profit margin.[4]

Replacement cost, sometimes referred to as **entry cost,** includes the purchase price of the product or raw materials plus all other costs incurred in the acquisition or manufacture of goods. Because wholesale and retail prices are generally related, declines in entry costs usually indicate declines in selling prices or **exit values.** However, exit values do not always respond immediately and in proportion to changes in entry costs. If selling price does not decline, there is no loss in utility and a write-down of inventory values would not be warranted. On the other hand, selling prices may decline in response to factors unrelated to replacement costs. Perhaps an inventory item has been used as a demonstrator which reduces its marketability as a new product. Or perhaps an item is damaged in storage or becomes shopworn from excessive handling.

The AICPA definition considers exit values as well as entry costs by establishing a ceiling for the market value at sales price less costs of completion and disposal and a floor for market at sales price less both the costs of completion and disposal and the normal profit margin. The ceiling limitation is applied so the inventory is not valued at more than its net realizable value. Failure to observe this limitation would result in charges to future revenue that exceed the utility carried forward and an ultimate loss on the sale of the inventory. The floor limitation is applied so the inventory is not valued at less than its net realizable value minus a normal profit. The concept of normal profit is a difficult one to measure objectively. Profits vary by item and over time. Records are seldom accurate enough to determine a normal profit by individual inventory item. Despite these difficulties, however, the use of a floor prevents a definition of market that would result in a write-down of inventory values in one period to create an abnormally high profit in future periods.

To illustrate, assume that a certain commodity sells for one dollar; selling expenses are twenty cents; the normal profit is 25% or twenty-five cents. The lower of cost or market as modified by the AICPA is developed in each case as shown in the illustration below.

		Market				
Case	Cost	*Replacement Cost*	*Floor (Estimated sales price less selling expenses and normal profit)*	*Ceiling (Estimated sales price less selling expenses)*	*Market (Limited by floor and ceiling values)*	Lower of Cost or Market
A	$.65	$ .70	$.55	$.80	$.70	$.65
B	.65	.60	.55	.80	.60	.60
C	.65	.50	.55	.80	.55	.55
D	.50	.45	.55	.80	.55	.50
E	.75	.85	.55	.80	.80	.75
F	.90	1.00	.55	.80	.80	.80

[4] *Ibid.*, statement 6.

A: Market is not limited by floor or ceiling; cost is less than market.
B: Market is not limited by floor or ceiling; market is less than cost.
C: Market is limited to floor; market is less than cost.
D: Market is limited to floor; cost is less than market.
E: Market is limited to ceiling; cost is less than market.
F: Market is limited to ceiling; market is less than cost.

The following dollar line graphically illustrates the floor and ceiling range. B and A replacement costs clearly are within bounds and therefore are defined as market. D and C are below the floor and thus the market is the floor; E and F are above the ceiling and market therefore is the ceiling.

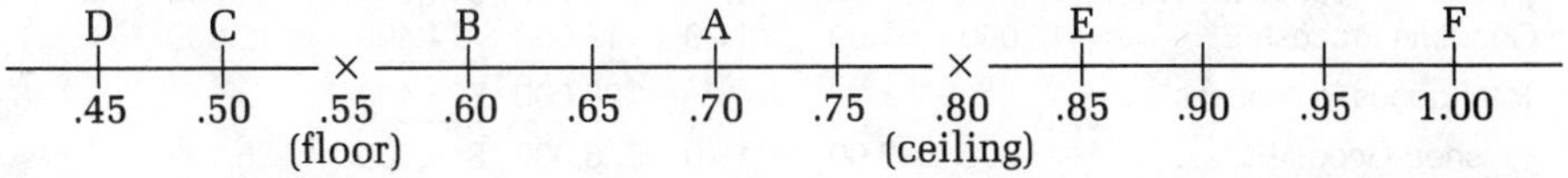

The market value is always the middle value of three amounts; replacement cost, floor, and ceiling.

Applying Lower of Cost or Market Method. The lower of cost or market method may be applied to each inventory item, to the major classes or categories of inventory items, or to the inventory as a whole. Application of this procedure to the individual inventory items will result in the lowest inventory value. However, application to inventory groups or to the inventory as a whole may provide a more representative valuation with considerably less effort. For example, assume that balanced stocks of raw materials are on hand, some have declined in value and others have gone up. When raw materials are used as components of a single finished product, a loss in the value of certain materials may be considered to be counterbalanced by the gains that are found in other materials, and the lower of cost or market applied to this category as a whole may provide an adequate measure of the utility of the goods.

The illustration at the top of the next page shows the valuation procedure applied to (1) individual inventory items, (2) independent classes of the inventory, and (3) inventory as a whole.

In valuing manufacturing inventories, raw materials declines are applicable to the raw materials inventory and also to raw materials costs in goods in process and finished goods inventories. Declines in direct labor and factory overhead costs also affect the values of goods in process and finished goods, but these are usually ignored when they are relatively minor.

The method that is chosen for reducing an inventory to a lower value should be applied consistently in successive valuations. When valuing inventories by individual items, a lower market value assigned to goods at the end of a period is considered to be its cost for purposes of inventory valuation in subsequent periods; cost reductions once made, then, are not restored in subsequent inventory determinations. This restriction cannot be applied to inventories valued by major classes or as a whole when a record of the individual price changes is not maintained.

	Quan-tities	Unit Cost	Market	Total Cost	Total Market	Cost or Market, Whichever is Lower (1) If Applied to Individual Inventory Items	(2) If Applied to Inventory Classes	(3) If Applied to Inventory as a Whole
Material A	4,000	$1.20	$1.10	$ 4,800	$ 4,400	$ 4,400		
Material B	5,000	.50	.40	2,500	2,000	2,000		
Material C	2,000	1.00	1.10	2,000	2,200	2,000		
Total raw materials				$ 9,300	$ 8,600		$ 8,600	
Goods in Process D	10,000	1.60	1.40	$16,000	$14,000	14,000		
Goods in Process E	12,000	1.00	1.20	12,000	14,400	12,000		
Total goods in process				$28,000	$28,400		28,000	
Finished Goods F	3,000	2.00	1.70	$ 6,000	$ 5,100	5,100		
Finished Goods G	2,000	1.50	1.60	3,000	3,200	3,000		
Total finished goods				$ 9,000	$ 8,300		8,300	
				$46,300	$45,300			$45,300
Inventory valuation						$42,500	$44,900	$45,300

Accounting for Declines in Inventory Value. In valuing inventories at the lower of cost or market, a decline in asset value may be reflected directly in the inventory account or in a separate inventory valuation account. The loss on the decline in market value may be shown as a separate item in the income statement after cost of goods sold. Alternatively, the loss may be reflected directly in the cost of goods sold section by valuing the ending inventory at market rather than cost. Separate reporting of these changes has the advantage of providing readers with increased information to forecast operations and cash flows.

Conflict Between Tax Laws and Lower of Cost or Market Rule. A decline in inventory value may be deducted for federal income tax purposes as a loss in the taxable year in which such decline occurs. However, the deductible loss must be computed on an individual item basis. Thus, a company which applies lower of cost or market to classes of inventory or to inventory as a whole for financial reporting purposes must make a separate item-by-item computation to obtain a tax deduction.

Disputes between taxpayers and IRS as to what constitutes a recognizable decline in inventory value have led to a number of court decisions. An important tax case in this area was settled by the U. S. Supreme Court in 1979.[5] The taxpayer, Thor Power Tool Co., had followed the practice of writing down the value of spare parts inventories that were being held to cover future warranty requirements. Although the sales price did not decline, the probability of the parts being sold, and thus the net realizable value, decreased as time passed. The write-down to reflect the current decline in value is consistent with the accounting principle of matching current costs

[5]Thor Power Tool Company vs. Commissioner of Internal Revenue, *United States Supreme Court Reports*, Vol. 439, p. 532 (1979).

and revenues. The Supreme Court, however, upheld the IRS position that recognition of declines in inventory values for tax purposes must await actual decline in the sales price for the parts in question.

This case is another illustration of a situation in which tax and financial accounting practices differ. Because the objective of levying taxes is not always compatible with an attempt to measure results of operations, differences will probably always exist. As explained in Chapter 20, this creates a constant need for interperiod tax allocation under the assumption that taxes are accruable as an expense. The U. S. Supreme Court recognized this difference in objectives in their conclusion to the Thor case as follows:

> Given this diversity, even contrariety, of objectives, any presumptive equivalency between tax and financial accounting would be unacceptable.[6]

Evaluation of Lower of Cost or Market Method. As mentioned earlier, the lower of cost or market method is evidence of the concept of accounting conservatism. Its strict application has been applied to avoid valuing inventory on the balance sheet at more than replacement cost. As discussed earlier, the AICPA replaced this strict entry valuation with a utility measure that relies partially upon the exit prices. If selling prices for the inventory have declined and the decline is expected to hold until the inventory is sold, the adjustment of income in the period of the decline seems justified. The value of the inventory has been impaired which requires current adjustment. However, care must be taken in using this method not to manipulate income by allowing excessive charges against income in one period to be offset by excessive income in the next period.

Some accountants have argued against the use of cost or market because it violates the cost concept. Market valuations are often subjective and based upon expectations. To the extent these expectations are not realized, misleading financial statements will be produced. To illustrate, assume that activities summarized in terms of cost provide the following results over a three year period:

	1983		1984		1985	
Sales		$200,000		$225,000		$250,000
Cost of goods sold:						
Beginning inventory	$ 60,000		$ 80,000		$127,500	
Purchases	120,000		160,000		90,000	
Goods available for sale	$180,000		$240,000		$217,500	
Less ending inventory	80,000	100,000	127,500	112,500	92,500	125,000
Gross profit on sales		$100,000		$112,500		$125,000
Operating expenses		80,000		90,000		100,000
Net income		$ 20,000		$ 22,500		$ 25,000
Rate of income to sales		10%		10%		10%

Assume estimates as to the future utility of ending inventories indicated market values as follows:

[6] *Ibid.*, pp. 542–3.

1983	1984	1985
$75,000	$110,000	$92,500

If the expected decline in selling prices did not occur, inventory valuation at the lower of cost or market would provide the following results.

	1983		1984		1985	
Sales		$200,000		$225,000		$250,000
Cost of goods sold:						
Beginning inventory	$ 60,000		$ 75,000		$110,000	
Purchases	120,000		160,000		90,000	
Goods available for sale	$180,000		$235,000		$200,000	
Less ending inventory	75,000	105,000	110,000	125,000	92,500	107,500
Gross profit on sales		$ 95,000		$100,000		$142,500
Operating expenses		80,000		90,000		100,000
Net income		$ 15,000		$ 10,000		$ 42,500
Rate of income to sales		7.5%		4.4%		17.0%

Reduction of an inventory below cost reduces the net income of the period in which the reduction is made and increases the net income of a subsequent period over what it would have been. In the example just given, total net income for the three-year period is the same under either set of calculations. But the reduction of inventories to lower market values reduced the net income for 1983 and for 1984 and increased the net income for 1985. The fact that inventory reductions were not followed by decreases in the sales prices resulted in net income determinations that varied considerably from those that might reasonably have been expected from increasing sales and costs that normally vary with sales volume.

Objection to valuation at the lower of cost or market is also raised on the grounds it produces inconsistencies in the measurements of both the financial position and the operations of the enterprise. Market decreases are recognized but increases are not. Although this system does produce some inconsistent application to the upward and downward movement of market, the authors feel that the lower of cost or market concept is preferable to a strict cost measurement. A loss in the utility of any asset should be reflected in the period the impairment is first recognized and a reasonable estimate of its significance can be determined. However, the lower of cost or market method fails to meet the needs of an inflationary economy as emphasized in Chapter 8. Most prices are increasing in our present economy; therefore, there is a reduced probability that, in any situation, the inventory market values will be lower than incurred cost.

Valuation at Market

As discussed in Chapter 8, due to inflationary conditions, there has been increasing pressure on accountants to move from the cost method of valuing inventories toward replacement cost or some other form of market valuation.

Advocates of a market approach to inventory valuation argue that if market is a relevant measure of value when it is less than cost, it is equally valid when greater than cost.

Although the market method has not become *generally* accepted for statement presentation, it has been adopted for valuing certain types of inventories. Market valuation has become an accepted practice within the mining industry for products such as gold and silver for which market is readily defined and tends to fluctuate dramatically, often in response to speculative trading activity. Similar conditions have led to the wide-spread use of market in valuing inventories of agricultural commodities. As discussed in Chapter 6, market is an acceptable method for valuing inventories of securities held by financial institutions and brokers and dealers in securities. These have been recognized by the accounting profession as special cases, acceptable within the framework of GAAP.

In applying the market method, the market price replaces cost regardless of whether market is greater or less than cost. Increases and decreases are normally reflected in the income statement. Some companies, however, credit a special equity account for unrealized holding gains and charge only losses against income. Thus, net income would be the same as that reported using a lower of cost or market valuation.

Although the current recommendations of the FASB require supplemental disclosure of market values, the authors believe that financial information would be more realistic and relevant if a market-based accounting system were adopted for use on the books and in the general statements. Only when market valuation is uniformly adopted for all purposes can users of financial statements clearly evaluate the impact of inflation on a specific company. Such a procedure would eliminate the various alternative cost allocation methods currently acceptable. Because market can be defined in different ways, the use of market valuation will not totally eliminate differences among companies, nor will it eliminate completely opportunities for manipulation of net income. However, issuance of specific guidelines by the FASB for applying market valuation should reduce the severity of these problems.

Losses on Purchase Commitments

Commitments are frequently made for the future purchase of goods at fixed prices. No entry is required to record the purchase prior to delivery of the goods. However, when price declines take place subsequent to such commitments, it is considered appropriate to measure and recognize these losses on the books just as losses on goods on hand are recognized. A decline is recorded by a debit to a special loss account and a credit to either a contra asset account or an accrued liability account, such as Estimated Losses on Purchase Commitments. Acquisition of the goods in a subsequent period is recorded by a credit to Accounts Payable, a debit canceling the credit balance in the contra asset or accrued liability account, and a debit to Purchases for the difference.

For example, assume that Monroe Manufacturing Company entered into a purchase contract for $120,000 of materials to be delivered in March of the following year. At the end of the current year, the market price for this order had fallen to $100,000. The entries to record this decline and subsequent delivery of the materials would be as follows:

Dec. 31	Loss on Purchase Commitments	20,000	
	Estimated Loss on Purchase Commitments		20,000
Mar. 1	Estimated Loss on Purchase Commitments	20,000	
	Purchases	100,000	
	Accounts Payable		120,000

The loss is thus assigned to the period in which the decline took place, and a subsequent period is charged for no more than the economic utility of the goods it receives. Current loss recognition would not be appropriate when commitments can be canceled, when commitments provide for price adjustment, when hedging transactions[7] prevent losses, or when declines do not suggest reductions in sale prices. No adjustments are customarily made if a recovery occurs prior to delivery.

Valuation of Trade-Ins and Repossessions

When goods are acquired in secondhand condition as a result of repossessions and trade-ins, they should be recorded at their estimated cash purchase price. In some industries, these prices are defined and made available to dealers. One of the more organized used markets is that for automobiles. A "blue book" is published frequently in the various geographical markets of the country. This book lists low, medium, and high market values for the different models and makes of cars. It also distinguishes between retail and wholesale values. Similar lists are provided for machinery and equipment in some lines. When these publications exist, the prices listed may be used to value repossessed or trade-in inventory.

However, in the absence of published prices, it is more difficult to measure the equivalent cash purchase price of the inventory. Under these conditions, the consistent use of **floor values**—amounts which, after adding reconditioning charges and selling expenses, will permit the recognition of normal profits—would be appropriate.

The accounting for trade-ins is illustrated by the following example: Daynes Department Store sells a new washing machine to a customer for $350 cash and a trade-in of an old washer. It is estimated that a realistic floor value for the trade-in is $50. Reconditioning costs of $30 are incurred after which the trade-in washer is sold for $120, an amount that provides a normal profit. Perpetual inventory records are maintained for trade-ins but not for the regular inventory. The entries shown below reflect these transactions:

Cash	350	
Trade-In Inventory	50	
Sales		400

[7]Purchases or sales entered into for the purpose of balancing, respectively, sales or purchases already made or under contract, in order to offset the effects of price fluctuations.

Trade-In Inventory	30	
Cash		30
Cash	120	
Sales—Trade-Ins		120
Cost of Trade-Ins Sold	80	
Trade-In Inventory		80

Another approach to valuing trade-in inventories is to establish clearly the sales price of the new inventory being sold, and charge the trade-in inventory for the difference between a cash sales price and the cash required with the trade-in. Assume in the case of the washing machine that the regular cash sales price without a trade-in could be established at $390. The value assigned to the trade-in would thus be $40, the difference between $390 and $350.

Accounting for repossessions requires a slightly different approach. Assume Daynes Department Store sold another washing machine on account for $350 plus interest on the unpaid balance. The customer made principal payments of $200 on the machine and then defaulted on the contract. The machine was repossessed and overhauled at a cost of $40. It was then sold for $150, a price that provided a normal profit of 50% on cost.

The following entries reflect the repossession and subsequent resale.

Loss on Repossession	90	
Repossessed Inventory	60	
Accounts Receivable		150

Computation:
Value of repossession established to permit 50% normal profit on cost. (33⅓% on selling price.)

Selling price	$150
Less profit at 33⅓%	50
Cost of repossessed goods sold	$100
Less cost of overhaul	40
Value of repossessed inventory	$ 60

Repossessed Inventory	40	
Cash		40
Cost to overhaul repossessed washing machine.		
Cash	150	
Sales—Repossessed Inventory		150
Sale of repossessed washing machine.		
Cost of Repossessed Goods Sold	100	
Repossessed Inventory		100
Cost of repossessed washing machine.		

INVENTORIES ON THE BALANCE SHEET

It is customary to report both trading and manufacturing inventories as current assets even though in some situations, considerable time will elapse before portions of such inventories are realized in cash. Among the items that are generally reported separately under the inventories heading are merchandise inventory or finished goods, goods in process, raw materials, factory supplies, goods and materials in transit, goods on consignment, and goods in the hands of agents and salespersons. Inventories are normally listed in the order of their liquidity. Any advance payments on purchase commitments should be reported separately and should not be included with inventories. Such advances are preferably listed after inventories in the current asset section since they have not entered the inventory phase of the operating cycle.

The valuation procedures employed must be disclosed in a note to the financial statements outlining all significant accounting policies followed.[8] The basis of valuation (such as cost or lower of cost or market), together with the method of arriving at cost (lifo, fifo, average, or other method), should be indicated. The reader of a statement may assume that the valuation procedures indicated have been consistently applied and financial statements are comparable with those of past periods. If this is not the case, a special note should be provided stating the change in the method and the effects of the change upon the financial statements. Further discussion of reporting changes in accounting methods is found in Chapter 21.

If significant inventory price declines take place between the balance sheet date and the date the statement is prepared, such declines should be disclosed by parenthetical remark or note. When relatively large orders for merchandise have been placed by the reporting company in a period of widely fluctuating prices, but the title to such goods has not yet passed, such commitments should be described by special note. Information should also be provided concerning possible losses on purchase commitments. Similar information may be appropriate for possible losses on sales commitments.

Replacement cost of inventories is now required to be included as a footnote to balance sheets of the larger corporations.[9] Until such time as market valuation of inventories becomes generally acceptable for reporting purposes, only supplemental disclosure of such values is required.

When inventories or sections of an inventory have been pledged as security on loans from banks, finance companies, or factors, the amounts pledged should be disclosed parenthetically in the inventory section of the balance sheet.

Inventory items may be reported as follows:

Inventories:		
Finished goods:		
On hand (goods of $100,000 have been pledged as security on loans of $75,000 from First State Bank)	$300,000	
On consignment	15,000	$315,000
Goods in process		300,000
Raw materials		240,000
Factory supplies		12,000
Total inventories		$867,000

[8] *Opinions of the Accounting Principles Board, No. 22,* "Disclosure of Accounting Policies" (New York: American Institute of Certified Public Accountants, 1972), par. 12.

[9] *Statement of Financial Accounting Standards, No. 33,* "Financial Reporting and Changing Prices" (Stamford: Financial Accounting Standards Board, 1979).

QUESTIONS

1. What is your understanding of the meaning of the "gross profit test"?
2. Distinguish between: (a) gross profit as a percentage of cost and gross profit as a percentage of sales; (b) the gross profit method of calculating estimated inventory cost and the retail inventory method of calculating estimated inventory cost.
3. What effect would the use of the lifo inventory method have upon the applicability of the gross profit method of valuing inventory?
4. Define (a) initial markup, (b) additional markup, (c) markup cancellation, (d) markdown, (e) markdown cancellation, and (f) maintained markup.
5. How are purchase discounts and sales discounts treated in using the retail inventory method?
6. A merchant taking inventory by the retail method maintains no separate record of markup cancellations and markdown cancellations. Instead the former is included in markdowns and the latter in markups, as "these represent price decreases and increases respectively." How will this procedure affect the inventory at (a) retail? (b) cost?
7. What are the major advantages of dollar-value lifo?
8. (a) Describe retail lifo. (b) What modifications in the conventional retail procedures are required in adopting and applying retail lifo?
9. How would a company determine appropriate indexes for the dollar-value lifo method?
10. Under what circumstances would a decline in replacement cost of an item not justify a departure from the cost basis of valuing inventory?
11. The use of cost or market, whichever is lower, is an archaic continuation of conservative accounting. Comment on this view.
12. Why is a ceiling and floor limitation on replacement cost considered necessary by the AICPA?
13. The inventory of the Prince Co. on December 31, 1984, had a cost of $85,000. However, prices had been declining and the replacement cost of the inventory on this date was $70,000. Prices continued to decline and in early March, 1985, when the statements were being drawn up, the replacement cost for the inventory was only $55,000. How would you recommend that the inventory be reported on the statements for 1984?
14. The Berg Corporation began business on January 1, 1983. Information about inventories, as of December 31 for three consecutive years, under different valuation methods is shown below. Using this information and assuming that the same method is used each year, you are to choose the phrase which best answers each of the following questions:

	Lifo Cost	Fifo Cost	Market	Lower of Cost or Market*
1983	$10,200	$10,000	$ 9,600	$ 8,900
1984	9,100	9,000	8,800	8,500
1985	10,300	11,000	12,000	10,900

*Fifo cost, item by item valuation.

(a) The inventory basis that would result in the highest net income for 1983 is: (1) Lifo cost, (2) Fifo cost, (3) Market, (4) Lower of cost or market.
(b) The inventory basis that would result in the highest net income for 1984 is: (1) Lifo cost, (2) Fifo cost, (3) Market, (4) Lower of cost or market.
(c) The inventory basis that would result in the lowest net income for the three years combined is: (1) Lifo cost, (2) Fifo cost, (3) Market, (4) Lower of cost or market.
(d) For the year 1984, how much higher or lower would net income be on the fifo cost basis than on the lower of cost or market basis? (1) $400 higher, (2) $400 lower, (3) $600 higher, (4) $600 lower, (5) $1,000 higher, (6) $1,000 lower, (7) $1,400 higher, (8) $1,400 lower.

15. There has been increasing support for the use of market values in reporting inventories on the financial statements. What are the major arguments that are raised in supporting such use?

16. How does the accounting treatment for losses on purchase commitments differ between actual losses which have already occurred and losses which may occur in the future?
17. What is the justification for valuing trade-ins or repossessions so that a normal profit can be realized upon their sale?
18. How should repossessed goods be valued for inventory purposes? Give reasons for your answers.
19. How would you recommend that the following items be reported on the balance sheet?

(a) Unsold goods in the hands of consignees.
(b) Purchase orders outstanding.
(c) Advance payments on purchase commitments.
(d) Raw materials pledged by means of warehouse receipts on notes payable to bank.
(e) Raw materials in transit from suppliers
(f) Goods produced by special order and set aside to be picked up by customer.
(g) Finished parts to be used in the assembly of final products.
(h) Office supplies.

DISCUSSION CASES

case 9-1 (Must we lose lifo layers?) The Energy Production Co. has used the lifo method of valuing its inventories for several years. Layers for some of the inventory items are valued at amounts ⅓ to ½ of the current market price. The products manufactured and marketed by the company are subject to rapid technological obsolescence, and the company is continually developing new products and phasing out old ones. As items are discontinued, the company finds its income and taxes increasing as old costs are matched against current revenues. However, since new products must be produced at higher costs, it has been difficult to maintain a positive cash flow for the company. The president of Energy Production, having heard a competitor mention dollar-value lifo, approaches you, the chief accountant, with the following questions. "Would this help us? What differences are there between our lifo system and dollar-value lifo?"

case 9-2 (Where has the inventory gone?) Happy Service Department Store uses the retail inventory method. Periodically, a physical count is made of the inventory and compared with the book figure computed from the company sales and purchase records. This year the extended valuation of the physical count resulted in a total inventory value 10% lower than the book figure. Jane Alexander, the controller, is concerned by the variance. A 2 to 3% loss from shoplifting has been tolerated through the years. But 10% is too much. The branch manager, Harvey Colfax, who is summoned to account for the discrepancy, insists that the book figures must be wrong. He is confident that the shortage could not be that high, but that bookkeeping errors must be at fault. Alexander, however, is not satisified with the explanation, and asks Colfax to outline specifically what types of errors could have caused such a variance.

case 9-3 (Inventory valuation without records) The Corner Grocery Store has never kept many records. The proceeds from sales are used to pay suppliers for goods delivered. When the owner, Martin Krebs, needs some cash, he withdraws it from the till without any record being made of it. Krebs realizes that eventually tax returns must be filed, but for three years "he just doesn't get around to it." Finally, the Internal Revenue Service catches up with Krebs, and an audit of the company records is conducted. The auditor requests the general ledger, special journals, inventory counts, and supporting documentation—very little of which is available. Records of expenditures are extremely sketchy because most expenses are paid in cash. If you were the IRS auditor, what might you do to make a reasonable estimate of income for the company.

case 9-4 (But those repair parts aren't worth that much!) Thor Power Tool Company maintains a large inventory of spare parts for the various machines it produces. The average life of these machines is 10-15 years, and Thor tries to maintain sufficient parts to meet repair demands throughout the entire life of the machines. Because of the difficulty in predicting demand, Thor often accumulates excess inventory items. In the past, rather than waiting until the parts are either sold or discarded, Thor's accountant prepared estimates of the remaining parts required and, if a loss was indicated, recognized the loss as the usage period expired. The Internal Revenue Service objected to this procedure and disallowed the losses because no reduction in sales price of the repair parts was made. Thus, in their view, no loss had occurred. Thor's management argued that past experience can provide fairly reliable estimates based upon actual usage to date. Evaluate the positions of the Internal Revenue Service and Thor Power Tool Company. What theoretical support exists for each position?

EXERCISES

exercise 9-1 (Inventory loss—gross profit method)

On August 15, 1984, a hurricane damaged a warehouse of RP & JS Merchandise Company. The entire inventory and many accounting records stored in the warehouse were completely destroyed. Although the inventory was not insured, a portion could be sold for scrap. Through the use of microfilmed records, the following data are assembled:

Inventory, January 1	$ 250,000
Purchases, January 1–August 15	1,150,000
Cash sales, January 1–August 15	225,000
Collection of accounts receivable, January 1–August 15	1,562,500
Accounts receivable, January 1	187,500
Accounts receivable, August 15	250,000
Salvage value of inventory	5,000
Gross profit percentage on sales	30%

Compute the inventory loss as a result of the hurricane.

exercise 9-2 (Inventory loss—gross profit method)

On June 30, 1984, a flash flood damaged the warehouse and factory of Padway Corporation, completely destroying the work-in-process inventory. There was no damage to either the raw materials or finished goods inventories. A physical inventory taken after the flood revealed the following valuations:

Finished goods	$119,000
Work in process	–0–
Raw materials	62,000

The inventory on January 1, 1984, consisted of the following:

Finished goods	$140,000
Work in process	100,000
Raw materials	30,000
	$270,000

A review of the books and records disclosed that the gross profit margin historically approximated 25% of sales. The sales for the first six months of 1984 were $340,000.

Raw material purchases were $115,000. Direct labor costs for this period were $80,000, and factory overhead has historically been applied at 50% of direct labor.

Compute the value of the work-in-process inventory lost at June 30, 1984. Show supporting computations in good form. (AICPA adapted)

exercise 9-3 (Retail inventory method)

"Big D" Department Store uses the retail inventory method. On December 31, 1984, the following information relating to the inventory was gathered:

	Cost	Retail
Inventory, January 1, 1984	$ 21,625	$ 40,500
Sales		350,000
Purchases	280,000	400,000
Purchase Discounts	4,705	
Freight in	4,200	
Net markups		30,000
Net markdowns		10,000
Sales discounts		5,000

Compute the ending inventory value at December 31, 1984, using the conventional retail inventory method.

exercise 9-4 (Retail inventory method)

The Supreme Clothing Store values its inventory under the retail inventory method at the lower of cost or market. The following data are available for the month of November 1984:

	Cost	Selling Price
Inventory, November 1	$ 53,800	$ 80,000
Markdowns		21,000
Markups		29,000
Markdown cancellations		13,000
Markup cancellations		9,000
Purchases	173,200	223,600
Sales		244,000
Purchase returns	3,000	3,600
Sales returns		12,000

Based upon the data presented above, prepare a schedule in good form to compute the estimated inventory at November 30, 1984, at the lower of cost or market under the retail inventory method. (AICPA adapted)

exercise 9-5 (Dollar-value lifo inventory method)

The Rumsey Manufacturing Company manufactures a single product. The management of Rumsey decided on December 31, 1981, to adopt the dollar-value lifo inventory method. The inventory value on that date using the newly adopted dollar-value lifo method was determined to be $500,000. Additional information follows:

	Inventory at Respective Year-End Prices	Relevant Price Index
December 31, 1982	$583,000	1.10
December 31, 1983	598,000	1.15
December 31, 1984	664,900	1.22

Compute the inventory value at December 31 of each year using the dollar-value lifo method, assuming incremental layers are costed at year-end prices.

exercise 9-6 (Dollar-value lifo inventory method)

Rawlins Inc. adopted dollar-value lifo in 1981. Information for 1981-1984 follows:

	Inventory at End-of-Year Prices	Year-End Index	Beginning-of-Year Index
December 31, 1981.........	$250,000	1.00	1.00
December 31, 1982.........	299,750	1.10	1.02
December 31, 1983.........	330,960	1.20	1.12
December 31, 1984.........	346,240	1.28	1.20

(1) Compute the inventory value for each year under the dollar-value lifo method, assuming incremental layers are costed at beginning-of-year prices.
(2) Compute the inventory value for 1984 assuming that dollar-value lifo procedures were adopted at the beginning of 1983 rather than in 1981.

exercise 9-7 (Dollar-value lifo; link-chain index)

The Valdez Department Store has hired you to assist with some year-end financial data preparation. The company's accountant quit three weeks ago and left many items incomplete. Information for computation of yearly price indexes and the inventory summary is in the table below. Valdez uses the link-chain index for lifo inventory valuation.

	1982	1983	1984
Ending inventory at beginning-of-year prices (December 31)...............................	$150,000	?	?
Ending inventory at end-of-year prices (December 31)........	?	$174,900	?
Beginning cumulative index at January 1....................	?	?	1.749
Yearly price index ...	1.100	1.060	?
Cumulative index at end of current year...................	?	1.749	1.924

Determine the inventory data that are missing from the table. Carry each index to three decimal places.

exercise 9-8 (Double extension and link-chain indexes)

On December 31, 1984, the controller of Squeeze-Em Baby Toys selected five items to use as a representative sample of the company's inventory. Information relative to these products was compiled and summarized in the following schedule. 1979 is used as a base year. Cumulative index at January 1, 1984, was 1.15.

	Products in Sample Inventory				
	1	2	3	4	5
Historical cost.........................	$20	$45	$10	$60	$100
January 1, 1979 price.................	20	50	8	50	92 = 220
January 1, 1984 price.................	24	51	13	60,	102 = 250
December 31, 1984 price	26	55	17	66	111 = 275

Compute a price index for use in deflating the December 31, 1984 inventory, assuming the use of:

(1) double extension.
(2) link-chain.

(1) 275/220 = 1.25
(2) 275/250 = 1.1 1.1×1.5 = 1.265

exercise 9-9 (Cumulative link-chain index)

The Dixie Newspaper Corporation took a statistical sample of its inventory at December 31, 1984. The inventory revealed the following information:

	Quantity	Cost 1983	Cost 1984
Printing Ink	75	$ 5.00	$ 5.60
Art Pencils	250	1.80	2.10
Drawing Pads	140	10.00	10.60

The link-chain cumulative price index at December 31, 1983 was 1.51. Compute the cumulative index at December 31, 1984.

exercise 9-10 (Retail-lifo inventory method)

The Neve Variety Store began using the retail-lifo method in 1983 for determining inventory values. In 1983, the cost percentage was computed at 65%. Information relating to the inventory for 1984 is given below:

	Cost	Retail
Inventory, January 1	$ 29,510	$ 45,400
Purchases	120,000	172,000
Freight in	20,000	
Purchases returns	3,500	5,000
Sales		190,000
Net markups		40,000
Net markdowns		12,000

Price index:

1983—All year	1.00
1984—December 31	1.05

(1) Compute the cost percentage for 1984.
(2) Compute the inventory value to be reported at December 31, 1984, assuming incremental layers are costed at end-of-year prices.

exercise 9-11 (Retail-lifo inventory method)

Gardner Inc. has compiled the following information concerning inventory for five years. They have been using the retail-lifo inventory method.

Date	Deflator Price Index	Inflator Price Index	Cost Percentage	Inventory at Retail
December 31, 1981	1.00	1.00	.70	$150,000
December 31, 1982	1.05	1.02	.72	190,953
December 31, 1983	1.12	1.08	.65	192,500
December 31, 1984	1.10	1.11	.62	193,200
December 31, 1985	1.15	1.12	.68	195,200

Compute the inventory cost at the end of each year under the retail-lifo method. (Round all dollar amounts to the nearest dollar.)

exercise 9-12 (Lower of cost or market valuation)

Determine the proper carrying value of the following inventory items if priced in accordance with the recommendations of the AICPA.

Item	Cost	Replacement Cost	Sales Price	Cost of Completion	Normal Profit
Product 501	$1.65	$1.82	$2.30	$.35	$.20
Product 502	.69	.65	1.00	.30	.04
Product 503	.31	.24	.59	.15	.07
Product 504	.92	.84	1.05	.27	.05
Product 505	.79	.82	1.00	.19	.09
Product 506	1.19	1.15	1.25	.13	.11

exercise 9-13 (Loss on purchase commitments)

On October 1, 1984, River City Distributors Inc. entered into a six-month $500,000 purchase commitment for a supply of Product A. On December 31, 1984, the market value of this material has fallen so that current acquisition of the ordered quantity would cost $425,550. It is anticipated that a further decline will occur during the next three months and that market at date of delivery will be approximately $340,000. What entries would you make on December 31, 1984, and on March 31, 1985, assuming the expected decline in prices did occur?

exercise 9-14 (Valuation of trade-in)

Reliance Inc. sells new equipment for a $9,000 cash price. Assume that Reliance sells one unit of equipment and accepts a trade-in plus $8,400 in cash. The expected sales price of the reconditioned equipment is $900, the reconditioning expenses are estimated to be $150, and normal profit is 30% of the sales price.

(1) What value should be placed on the trade-in assuming that floor values are used?
(2) What value should be placed on the trade-in assuming that the sale of new equipment is recorded at its normal cash price?

exercise 9-15 (Repossessed inventory)

Big Wheel Inc. sells its equipment on a time basis. In about 5% of the sales, the customer defaults in the payments and the equipment must be repossessed. Assume that equipment was sold for $14,000 which included interest of $1,500 (company uses an allowance for unearned finance charges account). The customer defaulted after making payments of $6,900 which included $900 interest. The equipment was repossessed and overhauled at a cost of $1,800. It was then sold on a thirty day account for $11,000, a price that provided a normal profit of 25% on cost. What journal entries would be required to record the repossession and subsequent resale of the equipment?

PROBLEMS

problem 9-1 (Inventory fire loss)

Norris Manufacturing began operations five years ago. On August 13, 1984, a fire broke out in the warehouse destroying all inventory and many accounting records relating to the inventory. The information available is presented below. All sales and all purchases are on account.

	January 1, 1984	August 13, 1984
Inventory	$128,590	
Accounts receivable	130,590	$107,320
Accounts payable	88,140	122,850

Collection on accounts receivable, January 1–August 13	$697,250
Payments to suppliers, January 1–August 13	487,500
Goods out on consignment at August 13, at cost	45,000

Summary of previous years sales:

	1981	1982	1983
Sales	$626,000	$675,000	$680,000
Gross profit on sales	200,320	175,500	217,600

Instructions: Determine the inventory loss suffered as a result of the fire.

problem 9-2 (Interim inventory computation–gross profit method)

The following information was taken from the records of the Card Company.

	1/1/83–12/31/83	1/1/84–9/30/84
Sales (net of returns)	$2,500,000	$1,500,000
Beginning inventory	420,000	730,000
Purchases	2,152,000	1,061,000
Freight in	116,000	72,000
Purchase discounts	30,000	15,000
Purchase returns	40,000	13,000
Purchase allowances	8,000	5,000
Ending inventory	730,000	
Selling and general expenses	450,000	320,000

Instructions: Compute by the gross-profit method the value to be assigned to the inventory as of September 30, 1984, and prepare an interim statement summarizing operations for the nine-month period ending on this date.

problem 9-3 (Inventory theft loss)

In December, 1984, Bullseye Merchandise Inc. had a significant portion of its inventory stolen. The company determined the cost of inventory not stolen to be $38,046. The following information was taken from the records of the company.

	January 1, 1984 to Date of Theft	1983
Purchases	$154,854	$161,320
Purchase returns and allowances	7,225	8,420
Sales	236,012	243,980
Sales returns and allowances	2,882	2,600
Salaries	9,600	10,800
Rent	6,480	6,480
Insurance	1,160	1,178
Light, heat, and water	1,361	1,525
Advertising	5,100	3,216
Depreciation expense	1,506	1,536
Beginning inventory	57,456	59,040

Instructions: Estimate the cost of the stolen inventory.

problem 9-4 (Retail inventory method)

The following information was taken from the records of Locust Inc. for the years 1983 and 1984.

	1984	1983
Sales	$138,600	$135,600
Sales discounts	1,840	1,200
Sales returns	2,040	1,600
Freight in	4,000	3,640
Purchases (at cost)	78,000	68,560
Purchases (at retail)	100,560	92,480
Purchase discounts	1,178	1,000
Beginning inventory (at cost)		65,600
Beginning inventory (at retail)		87,520

Instructions: Compute the value of the inventory at the end of 1983 and 1984 using the conventional retail inventory method.

problem 9-5 (Retail inventory method)

The Reed Clothing Store values its inventory under the retail inventory method. The following data are available for 1984:

	Cost	Selling Price
Inventory, January 1	$ 50,673	$ 79,100
Additional markdowns		21,000
Additional markups		40,600
Markdown cancellations		13,000
Markup cancellations		9,000
Purchases	170,000	221,600
Sales		246,500
Purchases returns	3,600	6,000
Sales allowances		12,000
Freight in	14,600	

Instructions:

(1) Prepare a schedule to compute the estimated inventory at December 31, 1984, at the lower of average cost or market under the retail method.

(2) Prepare the summary accounting journal entries to record the above inventory data (include entries to record the purchases, sales, and closing of inventory to income summary).

(3) What gross profit on sales would be reported on the income statement for 1984?

problem 9-6 (Dollar-value lifo inventory method)

Do-It-Yourself Repair Shop began operations on January 1, 1979. Management concluded that dollar-value lifo should be used for inventory costing. Information concerning the inventory of Do-It-Yourself is shown below:

	Year-End Index	Inventory at Year-End Prices
December 31, 1979	1.00	$15,000
December 31, 1980	1.20	31,200
December 31, 1981	1.35	54,000
December 31, 1982	1.15	34,500
December 31, 1983	1.70	72,250
December 31, 1984	2.00	39,400

Instructions: Compute the December 31 inventory value for each year (1979–1984) under the dollar-value lifo method, assuming incremental layers are costed at end-of-year prices.

problem 9-7 (Dollar-value lifo inventory method)

The Acute Company manufactures a single product. On December 31, 1979, Acute adopted the dollar-value inventory method. The inventory on that date using the dollar-value lifo inventory method was determined to be $300,000; the price index at the end of 1979 (the base year) was 1.20. Inventory data for succeeding years are as follows:

	Inventory at End-of-Year Prices	Deflator Price Index	Inflator Price Index
December 31, 1980	$363,000	1.320	1.240
December 31, 1981	420,000	1.440	1.362
December 31, 1982	430,000	1.500	1.450
December 31, 1983	416,640	1.536	1.510
December 31, 1984	452,232	1.584	1.548

Instructions: Compute the inventory amounts at December 31 of each year using the dollar-value lifo inventory method. (AICPA Adapted)

problem 9-8 (Retail-lifo inventory method)

In 1982, Crossley Inc. adopted the retail-lifo inventory method. The January 1, 1982 price index was 1.00. The following data are available for a four-year period ending December 31, 1985.

		Cost	Retail
1982	Inventory, January 1	$141,750	$225,000
	Purchases	387,500	625,000
	Sales		575,000
	Year-end price index		1.10
1983	Purchases	363,000	550,000
	Sales		593,125
	Year-end price index		1.06
1984	Purchases	390,000	650,000
	Sales		625,375
	Year-end price index		1.08
1985	Purchases	504,000	800,000
	Sales		762,500
	Year-end price index		1.12

Instructions: Calculate the inventories to be reported at the end of 1982, 1983, 1984, and 1985. Incremental layers are costed at end-of-year prices.

problem 9-9 (Retail-lifo inventory method)

The Mountain View Sports Shop values its inventory on the retail-lifo basis. Incremental inventory layers are costed at end-of-year prices. At December 31, 1983, the inventory was valued as follows:

Lifo Layer Year	Cost	Actual Retail	Year-End Price Index	Retail at Base of 1.00
1977	$14,760	$24,600	1.00	$24,600
1979	9,482	13,545	1.05	12,900
1981	13,442	26,884	1.03	26,100
1982	4,500	6,000	1.10	5,454
	$42,184	$71,029		$69,054

The following data were also compiled:

December 31, 1983 inventory at 1983 retail prices	$ 77,340
Purchases—cost	435,600
Purchases—selling price	673,845
Freight in	9,900
Sales returns	11,220
Sales discounts	1,950
Markups	4,740
Markup cancellations	1,080
Markdowns	2,505
Gross sales	702,000
Year-end price index for 1984	1.08

Instructions: Based upon the above information, compute:
(1) The 1984 cost ratio.
(2) The inventory amount that would be reported on the balance sheet at December 31, 1984.

problem 9-10 (Lower of cost or market valuation)

Austin Inc. carries four items in inventory. The following data are relative to such goods at the end of 1984:

			Per Unit			
	Units	Cost	Replacement Cost	Estimated Sales Price	Selling Cost	Normal Profit
Commodity A	2,000	$5.50	$5.00	$ 8.00	$ .90	$2.00
Commodity B	1,650	6.00	6.00	10.00	.80	1.25
Commodity C	5,000	2.50	2.00	4.75	.95	.50
Commodity D	3,250	7.00	7.50	7.50	1.20	1.75

Instructions: Calculate the value of the inventory under each of the following methods:

(1) Cost.
(2) The lower of cost or market without regard to market floor and ceiling limitations, applied to the individual inventory items.
(3) The lower of cost or market without regard to market floor and ceiling limitations applied to the inventory as a whole.
(4) The lower of cost or net realizable value applied to the individual inventory items.
(5) The lower of cost or market recognizing floor and ceiling limitations applied to the individual inventory items.

problem 9-11 (Lower of cost or market valuation)

Red Robin Lawn Supplies Co. uses the first-in, first-out method in calculating cost of goods sold for three of the products that Red Robin handles. Inventories and purchase information concerning these three products are given for the month of August.

		Shovels	Fertilizer	Lawn Seed
Aug. 1	Inventory	5,000 units at $6.00	3,000 units at $10.00	6,500 units at $ .90
Aug. 1–15	Purchases	7,000 units at $6.50	4,500 units at $10.50	3,000 units at $1.25
Aug. 16–31	Purchases	3,000 units at $7.50		
Aug.	Sales	10,000 units	5,000 units	4,500 units
Aug. 31	Sale Price	$8.00 per unit	$11.00 per unit	$2.00 per unit

On August 31, Red Robin's suppliers reduced their price from the last purchase price by the following percentages: Shovels, 20%; Fertilizer, 10%; Lawn Seed 8%. Accordingly Red Robin decided to reduce their sales prices on all items by 10% effective September 1. Red Robin's selling cost is 10% of sales price. Shovels and fertilizer have a normal profit (after selling costs) of 30% on sales prices, while the normal profit on lawn seed (after selling costs) is 15% of sales price.

Instructions:

(1) Calculate the value of the inventory at August 31, using the lower of cost or market method (applied to individual items).
(2) Calculate the fifo cost of goods sold for August and the amount of inventory write-off due to the market decline.

problem 9-12 (Trade-ins and repossessed inventory)

The Watson Appliance Company began business on January 1, 1983. The company decided from the beginning to grant allowances on merchandise traded in as part payment on new sales. During 1984 the company granted trade-in allowances of $64,035. The wholesale value of merchandise traded in was $40,875. Trade-ins recorded at $39,000 were sold for their wholesale value of $27,000 during the year.

The following summary entries were made to record annual sales and trade-in sales for 1984:

Accounts Receivable	439,890	
Trade-In Inventory	64,035	
Sales		503,925
Cash	27,000	
Loss on Trade-In Inventory	12,000	
Trade-In Inventory		39,000

When a customer defaults on the accounts receivable contract, the appliance is repossessed. During 1984 the following repossessions occurred:

	Original Sales Price	Unpaid Contract Balance
On 1983 contracts	$37,500	$20,250
On 1984 contracts	24,000	18,750

The wholesale value of these goods is estimated by the trade as follows:

(a) Goods repossessed during year of sale are valued at 50% of original sales price.
(b) Goods repossessed in later years are valued at 25% of original sales price.

Instructions:

(1) At what values should Watson Appliance report the trade-in and repossessed inventory at December 31, 1984?
(2) Give the entry that should have been made to record the repossessions of 1984.
(3) Give the entry that is required to correct the trade-in summary entries.

problem 9-13 (Inventory transactions–journal entries)

The Ainge Company values its perpetual inventory at the lower of fifo cost or market. The inventory accounts at December 31, 1983, had the following balances:

Raw Materials	$ 81,000
Allowance to Reduce Raw Material Inventory from Cost to Market	5,700
Work in Process	131,520
Finished Goods	205,200

The following are some of the transactions that affected the inventory of the Ainge Company during 1984:

Feb. 10 Purchased raw materials at an invoice price of $30,000; terms 3/15, n/30. Ainge Company uses the net method of valuing inventories.

Mar. 15 Ainge Company repossessed an inventory item from a customer who was overdue in making payment. The unpaid balance on the sale was $175. The repossessed merchandise is to be refinished and placed on sale. It is expected that the item can be sold for $250 after estimated refinishing cost of $50. The normal profit for this item is considered to be $40.

Apr. 1 Refinishing costs of $55 are incurred on the repossessed item.

Apr. 10 The repossessed item is resold for $250 on account; 20% down.

May 30 A sale on account is made of finished goods that have a list price of $740 and a cost of $480. A reduction from the list price of $100 is granted as a trade-in allowance. The trade-in item is to be priced to sell at $80 as is. The normal profit on this type of inventory is 25% of the sales price.

Nov. 30 Ordered materials to be delivered January 31, 1985, at a cost of $21,600. No discount terms were included.

Dec. 31 The following information was available to adjust the accounts for the annual statements:

(a) The market value of the items ordered on November 30 had declined to $18,000.
(b) The raw material inventory account had a cost balance of $110,400. Current market value was $101,400.
(c) The finished goods inventory account had a cost balance of $177,600. Current market value was $189,000.

Instructions: Record this information in journal entry form, including any required adjusting entries at December 31, 1984.

problem 9-14 (Gross profit method)

The Borow Corporation is an importer and wholesaler. Its merchandise is purchased from a number of suppliers and is warehoused by Borow Corporation until sold to consumers.

In conducting the audit for the year ended June 30, 1985, the company's CPA determined that the system of internal control was good. Accordingly, the physical inventory was observed at an interim date, May 31, 1985, instead of at year end.

The following information was obtained from the general ledger:

Inventory, July 1, 1984	$ 87,500
Physical inventory, May 31, 1985	95,000
Sales for 11 months ended May 31, 1985	840,000
Sales for year ended June 30, 1985	960,000
Purchases for 11 months ended May 31, 1985 (before audit adjustments)	675,000
Purchases for year ended June 30, 1985 (before audit adjustments)	800,000

The CPA's audit-disclosed the following information:

Shipments received in May and included in physical inventory but recorded as June purchases	$ 7,500
Shipments received in unsalable condition and excluded from physical inventory. Credit memos had not been received nor had chargebacks to vendors been recorded.	
Total at May 31, 1985	1,000
Total at June 30, 1985 (including the May unrecorded chargebacks)	1,500
Deposit made with vendor and charged to purchases in April, 1985. Product was shipped in July, 1985	2,000
Deposit made with vendor and charged to purchases in May 1985. Product was shipped, FOB destination, on May 29, 1985, and was included in May 31, 1985, physical inventory as goods in transit	5,500
Through the carelessness of the receiving department a June shipment was damaged by rain. This shipment was later sold in June at its cost of $10,000.	

In audit engagements in which interim physical inventories are observed, a frequently used auditing procedure is to test the reasonableness of the year-end inventory by the application of gross profit ratios.

Instructions: Prepare the following schedules:

(1) Computation of the gross profit ratio for 11 months ended May 31, 1985.
(2) Computation by the gross profit method of cost of goods sold during June 1985.
(3) Computation by the gross profit method of the inventory at June 30, 1985.

(AICPA adapted)

problem 9-15 (Retail and retail-lifo inventory methods)

Russo Department Store converted from the conventional retail method to the retail-lifo method on January 1, 1984. Management requested during your examination of the financial statements for the year ended December 31, 1985, that you furnish a summary showing certain computations of inventory costs for the past three years.

Available information follows:

(a) The inventory at January 1, 1983, had a retail value of $45,000 and a cost of $27,500 based on the conventional retail method. (There were no markdowns in 1982.)
(b) Transactions during 1983 were as follows:

	Cost	Retail
Gross purchases	$282,000	$490,000
Purchase returns	6,500	10,000
Purchase discounts	5,000	
Gross sales (exclusive of employee discounts)		492,000
Sales returns		5,000
Employee discounts		3,000
Freight in	26,500	
Net markups		25,000
Net markdowns		10,000

(c) The retail value of the December 31, 1984 inventory was $56,100, the cost percentage for 1984 under the retail-lifo method was 62%, and the regional price index was 102% of the January 1, 1984 price level.
(d) The retail value of the December 31, 1985 inventory was $48,300, the cost percentage for 1985 under the retail-lifo method was 61%, and the regional price index was 105% of the January 1, 1984 price level.

Instructions:

(1) Prepare a schedule showing the computation of the cost of inventory on hand at December 31, 1983, based on the conventional retail method.
(2) Prepare a schedule showing the computation of the cost of inventory on hand at the store on December 31, 1983, based on the retail-lifo method. Russo Department Store does not consider beginning inventories in computing its retail-lifo cost ratio. Assume that the retail value of the inventory on December 31, 1983, was $50,000.
(3) Without prejudice to your solution to part (2), assume that you computed the inventory on December 31, 1983, (retail value $50,000) under the retail-lifo method at a cost of $28,000. Prepare a schedule showing the computations of the cost of the 1984 and 1985 year-end inventories under the retail-lifo method. (AICPA adapted)

10 PLANT AND INTANGIBLE ASSETS—ACQUISITION

CHAPTER OBJECTIVES

Distinguish between capital and revenue expenditures.

Describe the nature and classification of plant assets and intangible assets.

Describe and illustrate the recording of asset acquisitions under various acquisition methods—purchase, exchange, issuance of securities, construction, and donation or discovery.

Discuss by asset category special accounting problems in determining the cost of plant assets and intangible assets.

Describe the treatment of expenditures made subsequent to asset acquisition.

Many expenditures made by an entity are for the acquisition of resources that will contribute to the production of revenue for more than one fiscal period. The basic accounting concept of **matching costs with revenues** requires that this type of expenditure be charged against all the periods benefited rather than allocated entirely to the period in which the expenditure is made. Such an expenditure is properly "capitalized," i.e., recognized as an asset on the balance sheet, and is commonly referred to as a **capital**

expenditure or a **deferred cost.** The expenditure is then allocated against future revenue in some pattern which attempts to reflect the value received from the use of the asset acquired.

The first critical accounting question is what degree of assurance is there that a future direct benefit will actually be realized from the expenditure. If the future benefit is highly uncertain, the expenditure is not capitalized but is written off as an expense of the period. The expenditure is then commonly referred to as a **revenue expenditure** because it is matched against revenue of the current period. Once an expenditure is identified as a capital expenditure, the next accounting question is what portion of the total expenditure should be considered part of the asset cost and thus capitalized. This chapter considers these questions for both tangible and intangible assets. The allocation of acquisition cost over time and the accounting for the eventual retirement or abandonment of assets are considered in the next chapter.

CLASSIFICATION OF PLANT AND INTANGIBLE ASSETS

Assets may be tangible or intangible. **Tangible assets** can be observed by one or more of the physical senses. They may be seen and touched and, in some environments, heard and smelled. **Plant assets,** sometimes referred to as fixed assets, are tangible assets of a durable nature employed in the operating activities of an enterprise. The term **plant** includes land, buildings, fixtures, machinery, and other equipment used to produce or facilitate the sale of goods and services. Plant assets may be reported on the balance sheet under the heading "Land, buildings, and equipment." Other common classifications include "Property, plant, and equipment" and "Plant and equipment," with the term *plant* used in a restricted sense to designate buildings only or land and buildings.

Intangible assets cannot be directly observed. Evidence of the asset in the form of agreements, contracts, or patents sometimes exists, but the asset itself has no physical existence. Intangible assets include such items as copyrights, patents, goodwill, and franchise agreements. The "most intangible" asset is goodwill. Unlike other intangible assets, goodwill does not represent any specific contractual future rights or privileges. Goodwill is recorded on the accounting records only when one business entity acquires another business entity, and then only if the purchase price exceeds the total fair market value of the net assets of the company acquired. Because of the relatively greater uncertainty concerning the ultimate benefit of most intangible assets, they are generally classified near the end of the asset section of the balance sheet.

CAPITAL AND REVENUE EXPENDITURES

The decision as to whether a given expenditure is a capital or revenue expenditure is one of many areas in which an accountant must exercise judgment. Generally, expenditures must be individually analyzed. In some companies, however, a lower limit to the definition of capital expenditure is established to avoid excessive costs of accounting for relatively small deferred costs. Thus, any expenditure under the established limit is always expensed currently even though future benefits are expected from that expenditure. This practice is justified on the grounds of expediency. The amount of the limit varies with the size of the company. Limits of $100, $500, and $1,000 are not unusual. This treatment is acceptable as long as it is consistently applied and no material misstatements arise due to unusual expenditure patterns or other causes.

Income cannot be fairly measured unless expenditures are properly identified and recorded as revenue or capital expenditures. For example, an incorrect debit to an equipment account instead of an expense account results in the overstatement of current earnings on the income statement and the overstatement of assets and owners' equity on the balance sheet. As the charge is assigned to operations in subsequent periods, earnings of such periods will be understated; assets and equity on the successive balance sheets will continue to be overstated, although by lesser amounts each year, until the asset is written off and the original error is fully counterbalanced. On the other hand, an incorrect debit to an expense instead of an equipment account results in the understatement of current earnings and the understatement of assets and equity. Earnings of subsequent periods will be overstated in the absence of debits for depreciation or amortization; assets and equity will continue to be understated, although by lesser amounts each year, until the original error is completely offset.

Because of the need to exercise judgment in determining the revenue or capital nature of expenditures, there is considerable diversity in practice as to which expenditures are capitalized. Two areas in which the FASB has attempted to reduce or eliminate such diversity are accounting for development stage expenditures and accounting for research and development expenditures.

Accounting for Development Stage Expenditures

In the past, some development stage companies deferred many costs without regard to recoverability or matching on the basis that they were not yet fully operating enterprises. Advocates of this approach maintain that all charges for interest, taxes, and general and administrative services during the development stage of a new company should be capitalized. Support for this procedure is based on the theory that future periods are benefited by necessary initial costs and it is unreasonable to assume losses have been incurred before sales activities begin. The Financial Accounting Standards Board reviewed this practice and concluded that accounting principles for companies in the organizational or developmental stage should be the same as for more mature companies. No special rules or principles should apply. Therefore, capitalization policies would not be different for these companies, and the above expenditures should be expensed in the period incurred, unless their deferral can be justified by identifiable future benefits.[1]

Accounting for Research and Development Expenditures

Historically, expenditures for research and development purposes were reported sometimes as capital expenditures and sometimes as revenue expenditures. The FASB inherited this problem from the Accounting Principles Board, and made this area the subject of their first definitive standard.[2] The Board defined **research** activities as those undertaken to discover new knowledge that will be useful in developing new products, services, or processes or that will result in significant improvements of existing products or processes. **Development** activities involve the application of research findings to develop a plan or design for new or improved products and processes. Development activities include the formulation, design, and testing of products, construction of prototypes, and operation of pilot plants.

In general, the FASB concluded that research and development expenditures should be treated as revenue expenditures and expensed in the period incurred.[3] This decision was reached after much analysis and after many attempts to establish criteria for selectively capitalizing some research and development expenditures and expensing others. Among the arguments for expensing these costs was the frequent inability to find a definite causal relationship between the expenditures and future revenues. Sometimes very large expenditures do not generate any future revenue, while relatively small expenditures lead to significant discoveries that generate large revenues. The Board found it difficult to establish criteria that would distinguish between those research and development expenditures that would most likely benefit future periods and those that would not.

As defined by the FASB in Statement No. 2, research and development costs include those costs of materials, equipment, facilities, personnel, purchased intangibles, contract services, and a reasonable allocation of indirect costs that are specifically related to research and development activities and that have no alternative future uses.[4] Such activities include:

(1) Laboratory research aimed at discovery of new knowledge.
(2) Searching for applications of new research findings or other knowledge.
(3) Conceptual formulation and design of possible product or process alternatives.
(4) Testing in search for or evaluation of product or process alternatives.
(5) Modification of the formulation or design of a product or process.
(6) Design, construction, and testing of pre-production prototypes and models.
(7) Design of tools, jigs, molds, and dies involving new technology.

---

[1] *Statement of Financial Accounting Standards No. 7,* "Accounting and Reporting by Development Stage Enterprises" (Stamford: Financial Accounting Standards Board, 1975), par. 10.

[2] *Statement of Financial Accounting Standards No. 2,* "Accounting for Research and Development Costs" (Stamford: Financial Accounting Standards Board, 1974).

[3] *Ibid.,* par. 12.

[4] *Ibid.,* par. 11.

(8) Design, construction, and operation of a pilot plant that is not of a scale economically feasible to the enterprise for commercial production.
(9) Engineering activity required to advance the design of a product to the point that it meets specific functional and economic requirements and is ready for manufacture.[5]

The Board stipulated, however, that expenditures for certain items having alternative future uses, either in additional research projects or for productive purposes, can be capitalized and allocated against future projects or periods. This exception permits the deferral of costs incurred for materials, equipment, facilities, and purchased intangibles, but only if an alternative use can be identified.

Research and development costs vary widely among companies. Many expenditures do have future worth, while others are so highly uncertain as to future worth that capitalization is clearly improper. For the FASB to ignore these differences and issue a blanket rule that all research and development expenditures should be handled the same seems arbitrary and without theoretical support. The International Accounting Group studying this area disagreed with the FASB and identified general situations in which they felt capitalization and deferral of development costs would be justified:

> Development costs of a project may be deferred to future periods if all the following criteria are satisfied:
>
> (a) the product or process is clearly defined and the costs attributable to the product or process can be separately identified;
> (b) the technical feasibility of the product or process has been demonstrated;
> (c) the management of the enterprise has indicated its intention to produce and market, or use, the product or process;
> (d) there is a clear indication of a future market for the product or process or, if it is to be used internally rather than sold, its usefulness to the enterprise can be demonstrated; and
> (e) adequate resources exist, or are reasonably expected to be available, to complete the project and market the product or process.[6]

While guidelines to help distinguish between capital and revenue expenditures are desirable, specific rules, such as those issued for research and development expenditures, that mandate by definition the treatment of all expenditures ignore the reality of the great diversity of conditions existing in practice.

RECORDING ACQUISITION OF PLANT AND INTANGIBLE ASSETS

Plant assets and intangible assets are recorded initially at cost—the initial bargained or cash sales price. The **cost** of property includes not only the original purchase price or equivalent value, but also any other ex-

[5] *Ibid.*, par. 9.
[6] *International Accounting Standard, No. 9,* "Accounting for Research and Development Activities" (London, England: International Accounting Standards Committee, 1978), par. 17.

penditures required in obtaining and preparing it for its intended use. Any taxes and duties, freight, installation, and other expenditures related to the acquisition should be included in the asset cost.

In a competitive economy, the cost should be representative of the market value of the asset as of the acquisition date. While "bargain purchases" can occur in our less-than-perfect competitive economy, they are generally ignored and the cash or equivalent price is used to record the acquisition. There are a number of different arrangements that can be used to acquire assets, some of which present special problems relating to asset cost. The acquisition of assets is discussed under the following headings: (1) purchase for cash, (2) purchase on long-term contract, (3) exchange, (4) issuance of securities, (5) self-construction, and (6) donation or discovery.

Purchase for Cash

An asset acquired for cash is recorded at the amount of cash paid, including all incidental outlays relating to its purchase or preparation for use.

As suggested in Chapter 8, sound accounting theory requires discounts on purchases to be regarded as reductions in costs: earnings arise from sales, not from purchases. In applying this theory, any available discounts on property acquisitions should be treated as reductions to asset cost. Failure to take such discounts should be reported as Discounts Lost or Interest Expense.

A number of assets may be acquired for one lump sum. Some of the assets may be depreciable, others nondepreciable. Depreciable assets may have different useful lives. If there is to be accountability for the assets on an individual basis, the total purchase price must be allocated among the individual assets. When part of a purchase price can be clearly identified with specific assets, such a cost assignment should be made and the balance of the purchase price allocated among the remaining assets. When no part of the purchase price can be related to specific assets, the entire amount must be allocated among the different assets acquired. Appraisal values or similar evidence provided by a competent independent authority should be sought to support such allocation.

To illustrate the allocation of a joint asset cost, assume that land, buildings, and equipment are acquired for $80,000. Assume further that assessed values for the individual assets as reported on the property tax bill are considered to provide an equitable basis for cost allocation. The allocation is made as shown below.

	Assessed Values	*Cost Allocation According to Relative Assessed Values*	*Cost Assigned to Individual Assets*
Real properties:			
Land	$14,000	14,000/50,000 × $80,000	$22,400
Improvements (building)	30,000	30,000/50,000 × $80,000	48,000
Personal property (equipment)	6,000	6,000/50,000 × $80,000	9,600
	$50,000		$80,000

An asset acquired in secondhand or used condition should be recorded at its cost without reference to the balance on the seller's books. Expenditures to repair, recondition, or improve the asset before it is placed in use should be capitalized as part of the cost. It must be assumed that the buyer knew additional expenditures would be required when the purchase was made.

Purchase on Long-Term Contract

The acquisition of real estate or other property frequently involves deferred payment of all or part of the purchase price. The indebtedness of the buyer is usually evidenced by a note, debenture, mortgage, or other contract that specifies the terms of settlement of the obligation. The debt instrument may call for one payment at a given future date or a series of payments at specified intervals. Interest charged on the unpaid balance of the contract should be recognized as an expense. To illustrate the accounting for a long-term purchase contract, assume that land is acquired for $100,000; $35,000 is paid at the time of purchase and the balance is to be paid in semiannual installments of $5,000, plus interest on the unpaid principal at an annual rate of 10%. Entries for the purchase and for the first payment on the contract are shown below.

Transaction	Entry		
January 2, 1984 Purchased land for $100,000 paying $35,000 down, the balance to be paid in semiannual payments of $5,000 plus interest at 10%.	Land .... Cash .... Contract Payable............	100,000	 35,000 65,000
June 30, 1984 Made first payment. Amount of payment: $5,000 + $3,250 (5% of $65,000) = $8,250	 Interest Expense.............. Contract Payable.............. Cash	 3,250 5,000	 8,250

In the preceding example, the contract specified both a purchase price and interest at a stated rate on the unpaid balance. Sometimes, however, a contract may simply provide for a payment or series of payments without reference to interest or may provide for a stated interest rate that is unreasonable in relation to the market. As indicated in Chapter 7, APB No. 21, "Interest on Receivables and Payables," requires that in these circumstances, the note, sales price, and cost of the property, goods, or services exchanged for the note should be recorded at the fair market value of the property, goods, or services or at the current market value of the note, whichever value is more clearly determinable.[7] Application of Opinion No. 21 with respect to the seller was illustrated in Chapter 7. The following example illustrates the accounting by the purchaser.

Assume that certain equipment, which has a cash price of $50,000, is acquired under a long-term contract. The contract specifies a down payment of $15,000 plus seven annual payments of $7,189.22 each, or a total price,

[7]The term *notes* is used by the Board in Opinion No. 21 as a general term for contractual rights to receive money or contractual obligations to pay money at specified or determinable dates.

including interest, of $65,324.54. Although not stated, the effective interest rate implicit in this contract is 10%, the rate that discounts the annual payments of $7,189.22 to a present value of $35,000, the cash price less the down payment.[8] As specified in APB Opinion No. 21, if the cash equivalent price, that is, the fair market value of the asset varies from the contract price because of delayed payments, the difference should be recorded as a discount and amortized over the life of the contract using the implicit or effective interest rate. The entries to record the purchase, the amortization of the discount for the first two years, and the first two payments would be as follows:

Transaction	Entry		
January 2, 1984 Purchased equipment with a cash price of $50,000 for $15,000 down plus seven annual payments of $7,189.22 each, or a total contract price of $65,324.54.	Equipment.................... Discount on Equipment Contract Payable............ Equipment Contract Payable Cash....................	50,000.00 15,324.54	 50,324.54 15,000.00
December 31, 1984 Made first payment of $7,189.22. Amortization of debt discount: 10% × $35,000 = $3,500 ($50,324.54 − $15,324.54 = $35,000)	Equipment Contract Payable .... Cash .... Interest Expense.............. Discount on Equipment Contract Payable..........	7,189.22 3,500.00	 7,189.22 3,500.00
December 31, 1985 Made second payment of $7,189.22. Amortization of debt discount: 10% × $31,310.78* = $3,131.08	Equipment Contract Payable .... Cash .... Interest Expense.............. Discount on Equipment Payable..................	7,189.22 3,131.08	 7,189.22 3,131.08

*$50,324.54 − $7,189.22 = $43,135.32 Equipment contract payable
$15,324.54 − $3,500.00 = 11,824.54 Discount on equipment contract payable
$31,310.78 Present value of equipment contract payable end of first year

When there is no established cash price for the property, goods, or services, and there is no stated rate of interest on the contract, or the stated rate is unreasonable under the circumstances, an imputed interest rate must be used. A discussion of the determination and application of imputed interest rates is included in Chapter 7.

Property may be acquired under a conditional sales contract whereby legal title to the asset is retained by the seller until payments are completed. The failure to acquire legal title may be disregarded by the buyer and the transaction recognized in terms of its substance—the acquisition of an asset and assumption of a liability. The buyer has the possession and use of the asset and must absorb any decline in its value; title to the asset is retained by the seller simply as a means of assuring payment on the purchase contract.

[8] The effective or implicit interest rate is computed as follows:

$$PV_n = R(PVAF_{\overline{n}|i})$$

$$\$50,000 - \$15,000 = \$7,189.22\ (PVAF_{\overline{7}|i})$$

$$PVAF_{\overline{7}|i} = \frac{\$35,000.00}{\$\ 7,189.22}$$

$$PVAF_{\overline{7}|i} = 4.8684$$

From Table IV, Appendix A, the interest rate for the present value of 4.8684 when $n = 7$ is 10%. Additional examples of computing an implicit rate of interest are presented in Appendix A.

Acquisition by Exchange—General Case

When one **nonmonetary asset**[9] is traded for another, the new asset should generally be recorded at the fair market value of the asset given up, or the fair market value of the asset received if its fair market value is more clearly evident.[10] If a used asset is surrendered for a new asset, the fair market value of the new asset is often more clearly evident than the market value of the old asset, and thus would be used to value the exchange. Care must be taken to determine the true market value of the new asset. Frequently, the quoted price is not a good indicator of market and is higher than the actual cash price for the new asset. A higher list price permits the seller to increase the trade-in allowance for the used asset. The price for which the asset could be acquired in a strictly cash transaction is the fair market value that should be used.

Any difference between the fair market value assigned to the asset received and the book value (carrying value) of the old asset should be recognized as a gain or loss on the exchange. If the exchange involves a monetary consideration, or **boot**, the new asset should be recorded at the fair market value of the surrendered asset plus boot paid or minus boot received. Any trade-in allowance should be carefully examined to determine whether it measures fairly the value of the asset exchanged. The use of an inflated trade-in allowance as representative of the market value of the surrendered asset will result in the overstatement of the newly acquired asset and also in the subsequent overstatment of depreciation charges.

To illustrate an exchange involving nonmonetary assets under the general case, assume that a new truck with a fair market value of $8,200 is acquired in exchange for $600 cash and used equipment which originally cost $10,000 and has a book value of $8,000. The following entry would be made to record the exchange:

Trucks	8,200	
Accumulated Depreciation—Equipment	2,000	
Loss on Exchange of Equipment	400	
Equipment		10,000
Cash		600

Computations:
Trade-in allowance: $8,200 − $600 = $7,600
Accumulated depreciation: $10,000 cost − $8,000 book value = $2,000 accumulated depreciation
Loss:
$8,000 book value − $7,600 trade-in allowance = $400 loss

In the example, the asset was assumed to have been exchanged at the beginning of a fiscal period. When a depreciable asset is exchanged within a fiscal period, depreciation should be recognized to the time of the ex-

[9] *Monetary assets* are those whose amounts are fixed in terms of units of currency by contract or otherwise. Examples include cash and short or long-term accounts receivable. *Nonmonetary assets* include all other assets, such as inventories, land, buildings, and equipment.

[10] *Opinions of the Accounting Principles Board, No. 29,* "Accounting for Nonmonetary Transactions" (New York: American Institute of Certified Public Accountants, 1973), par. 18.

change, and the entry to record the exchange should recognize the book value of the asset at that date.

Acquisition by Exchange—Special Cases

The Accounting Principles Board recognized three exceptions to the general rule of using market values to determine the gain or loss on exchange of nonmonetary assets.[11] They are:

(1) If market values are not determinable within reasonable limits.
(2) If the exchange indicates a gain, but does not culminate the earnings process:
  (a) Exchange of inventory between dealers to facilitate sales to customers other than the parties involved in the exchange.
  (b) Exchange of *similar productive assets* not held for sale.
(3) If nonmonetary assets are transferred to owners in a spin-off, or other form of reorganization.[12]

In the first case, since there are no market values available, the new asset is recorded at the book value of the old asset and no gain or loss is recognized. In the second case, market values are available and indicated gains or losses can be computed. However, the Board concluded that both the exchanges identified above are interim transactions, and do not culminate the earnings process. Inventories are often swapped between dealers or other firms to obtain a different model, style, or color for a specific sale. The Board felt that no income should be recognized until a sale actually was made to an external customer. Likewise, they felt that income from an exchange of **similar productive assets**[13] occurs from the sale of items produced by the productive assets, not from their exchange. Thus, any **gain** indicated by comparing market values with book values is deferred unless boot is received. The asset acquired is valued at the book value of the asset relinquished. However, if a **loss** is indicated because the fair market value of the asset given up is less than its book value, the general case would apply and the entire loss should be recognized. If boot is *received* in the exchange, the Board felt that a partial culmination of the earnings process has occurred and part of the gain represented by the boot should be recognized immediately.

APB Opinion No. 29, "Accounting for Nonmonetary Transactions," is not specific as to whether the special case applies to exchanges in which one of the two contract parties does in fact culminate the earnings process. This type of exchange, the most common type, occurs when a company acquires a productive asset from a dealer and turns in an old productive asset as a trade-in on the new asset. In this case the earnings process has culminated for the dealer, but not for the purchaser of the new asset.

---

[11] *Ibid.*, par. 20–23.

[12] Further discussion of Exception 3 is beyond the scope of this textbook.

[13] *Similar productive assets* are assets of the same general type, that perform the same function, or that are employed in the same line of business.

An investigation of APB Opinion No. 29 by James B. Hobbs and D.R. Bainbridge led them to conclude that the Board did not intend to include these dealer-nondealer exchanges as part of the special case.[14] Thus an exchange between a dealer and a nondealer would be viewed as the general case, with any gain or loss recognized by both parties. The dealer treats the transaction as a sale of inventory and, as discussed in Chapter 9, recognizes a profit or loss on the transaction after assigning a value to the trade-in. The purchaser recognizes any indicated gain or loss on the exchange and records the new asset at its fair market value.

The authors agree with the conclusions of Hobbs and Bainbridge, and thus the discussion of the special case will be limited to exchanges of similar productive assets between two nondealers or two dealers. Because of the complexities of accounting for exchanges not culminating the earnings process, the following examples will illustrate journal entries for exchanges with and without monetary asset transfers or boot.

Exchanges Not Culminating the Earnings Process—No Boot Involved. To illustrate the exchange of similar assets when no boot is involved, assume that Company A exchanged equipment costing $9,000, with accumulated depreciation of $6,000 and a fair market value of $5,000, for similar equipment from Company B costing $12,000, with accumulated depreciation on Company B's books of $7,500, and a fair market value of $5,000. The entries on the books of Company A and Company B would be:

Company A

Equipment	3,000	
Accumulated Depreciation—Equipment	6,000	
Equipment		9,000

Computation:
$9,000 cost of old equipment—$6,000 accumulated depreciation = $3,000 carrying value of the old equipment.

Company B

Equipment	4,500	
Accumulated Depreciation—Equipment	7,500	
Equipment		12,000

Computation:
$12,000 cost of old equipment − $7,500 accumulated depreciation = $4,500 carrying value of the old equipment.

Since the fair market value ($5,000) exceeded the book value of each asset involved in the exchange, each company had an indicated gain ($2,000 for Company A and $500 for Company B), but it is deferred and not recognized.

If the fair market values of the assets exchanged had been $4,000 at the time of the exchange, Company A would still have an indicated gain ($1,000) and would record the exchange as above with the gain deferred. However, Company B would have an indicated loss of $500 on the exchange, $4,500 − $4,000, and would value the new equipment at $4,000 after

[14] James B. Hobbs and D.R. Bainbridge, "Nonmonetary Exchange Transactions: Clarification of APB Opinion No. 29," *Accounting Review* (January, 1982), pp. 171-175.

recognizing the loss of $500. This latter treatment differs from the income tax treatment for exchanges with an indicated loss. Under income tax regulations, no gain or loss is recognized on exchange of productive, like-kind assets.[15]

Exchange Not Culminating the Earnings Process—Boot Involved. When a small amount of monetary consideration (boot) is *given* in an exchange, the same procedures apply as when no boot is involved.[16] No indicated gain is recognized, and the new asset is recorded at the carrying value of the old asset plus the cash given. However, if boot is *received* in the exchange, and there is an indicated gain on the transaction, a portion of the gain is recognized. The formula for the amount of gain recognized is as follows:[17]

$$\text{Recognized Gain} = \frac{\text{Boot}}{\text{Boot} + \text{Fair Market Value of Acquired Asset}} \times \text{Total Indicated Gain}$$

The total indicated gain is the difference between the fair market value of the asset given up and its book value. The recognized gain is determined by computing the percentage the boot received is of the total consideration received and applying this percentage to the indicated gain. This is a somewhat arbitrary rule, and difficult to justify in theory. It also differs from the income tax rule which requires recognition of the gain to the extent boot is received.

To illustrate this situation, assume that Company A exchanged equipment costing $15,000 with accumulated depreciation of $9,000 and a fair market value of $8,000 plus cash of $500 for similar equipment from Company B costing $12,000 with accumulated depreciation on Company B's books of $5,000 and a fair market value of $8,500. Company A would have an indicated gain of $2,000 ($8,000 fair market value of the asset given up less its carrying value of $6,000). The gain can also be computed as the difference between the fair market value of the asset received ($8,500), and the book value of the equipment exchanged ($6,000) plus boot paid ($500). The exchange is not viewed as culminating the earnings process, and since the boot was given by Company A, that company's entire gain is deferred. The entry on the books of Company A would be as follows:

Company A (boot given in exchange)

Equipment	6,500	
Accumulated Depreciation—Equipment	9,000	
Cash		500
Equipment		15,000

Computation:
$15,000 cost of old equipment − $9,000 accumulated depreciation + $500 cash = $6,500 carrying value of the old equipment plus cash paid.

---

[15]Internal Revenue Code, Sec. 1031.

[16]Opinion No. 29 does not define a "small amount of monetary consideration." Presumably, if the monetary amount exceeds the concept of being small, the transaction no longer qualifies as a nonmonetary exchange and the exchange would be accounted for as a monetary exchange with any gain or loss recognized.

[17]*Opinions of the Accounting Principles Board, No. 29, op. cit.,* par. 22.

Company B would have an indicated gain of $1,500 ($8,500 fair market value of asset given up less its carrying value of $7,000). However, since Company B received the boot, a portion of the gain will be recognized and the balance deferred. The recognized gain is computed from the formula as follows:

$$\text{Recognized Gain} = \frac{\$500}{\$500 + \$8{,}000} \times \$1{,}500$$

$$= 1/17 \times \$1{,}500 = \underline{\underline{\$88}}$$

The entry on the books of Company B would be as follows:

Company B (boot received in exchange)

Equipment	6,588	
Accumulated Depreciation—Equipment	5,000	
Cash	500	
Equipment		12,000
Gain on Exchange of Equipment		88

Computation:
$12,000 cost of old equipment − $5,000 accumulated depreciation − $500 cash = $6,500 carrying value of the old equipment minus cash paid. $6,500 + $88 gain = $6,588.

Acquisition by Issuance of Securities

A company may acquire certain property by issuing its own bonds or stock. When a market value for the securities can be determined, such value is assigned to the asset; in the absence of a market value for the securities, the fair market value of the asset acquired would be sought. If bonds or stock are selling at more or less than par value, Bonds Payable or Capital Stock should be credited at par and the difference recorded as a premium or discount. To illustrate, assume that a company issues 1,000 shares of $25 par stock in acquiring land; the stock is currently selling on the market at $45. An entry should be made as follows:

Land	45,000	
Common Stock		25,000
Premium on Common Stock		20,000

When securities do not have an established market value, appraisal of the assets by an independent authority may be required to arrive at an objective determination of their fair market value. If satisfactory market values cannot be obtained for either securities issued or the assets acquired, values as established by the board of directors may have to be accepted for accounting purposes. Disclosure should be provided on the balance sheet of the source of the valuation. The assignment of values by the board of directors is normally not subject to challenge unless it can be shown that the board has acted fraudulently. Nevertheless, evidence should be sought to validate the fairness of original valuations, and if within a short time after an acquisition, the sale of stock or other information indicates that original valuations were erroneous, appropriate action should be taken to restate asset and owners' equity accounts.

Property is frequently acquired in exchange for securities pursuant to a corporate merger or consolidation. When such combination represents the transfer of properties to a new owner, the combination is designated a *purchase* and the acquired assets are reported at their cost to the new owner. But when such combination represents essentially no more than a continuation of the original ownership in the enlarged entity, the combination is designated a *pooling of interests* and accounting authorities have approved the practice of recording properties at the original book values as shown on the books of the acquired company. Specific guidelines for distinguishing between a purchase and a pooling of interests are included in APB Opinion No. 16 and are discussed in detail in advanced accounting texts.[18]

Acquisition by Self-Construction

Sometimes buildings or equipment items are constructed by a company for its own use. This may be done to save on construction costs, to utilize idle facilities, or to achieve a higher quality of construction. A number of special problems arise in arriving at the cost of self-constructed assets.

Overhead Chargeable to Self-Construction. All costs that can be related to construction should be charged to the assets under construction. There is no question about the inclusion of charges directly attributable to the new construction. However, there is a difference of opinion regarding the amount of overhead properly assignable to the construction activity. Some accountants take the position that assets under construction should be charged with no more than the incremental overhead—the increase in a company's total overhead resulting from the special construction activity. Others maintain that overhead should be assigned to construction just as it is assigned to normal operations. This would call for the inclusion of not only the increase in overhead resulting from construction activities but also a pro rata share of the company's fixed overhead.

The argument for limiting overhead charges to incremental amounts is that the cost of construction is actually no more than the extra costs incurred. Charges should not be shifted from normal operations to construction activities. Management is aware of the cost of normal operations and decides to undertake a project on the basis of the anticipated added costs. The position that construction should carry a fair share of the fixed overhead if the full cost of the asset is to be reported is based on the premise that overhead has served a dual purpose during the construction period and this is properly reflected in reduced operating costs. The latter argument may be particularly persuasive if construction takes place during a period of subnormal operations and utilizes what would otherwise represent idle capacity cost, or if construction restricts production or other regular business activites.

---

[18]See Paul M. Fischer, William James Taylor, and J. Arthur Leer, *Advanced Accounting* (Cincinnati: South-Western Publishing Co., 1982).

The assignment to construction of normal overhead otherwise chargeable to current operations will increase net income during the construction period. The recognition of a portion of overhead is postponed and related to subsequent periods through charges in the form of depreciation.

The accounting profession has not been successful in coming to an agreement on the issue. Authors of a research study for the AICPA have suggested the following criteria to help resolve the issue.

> ...in the absence of compelling evidence to the contrary, overhead costs considered to have "discernible future benefits" for the purpose of determining the cost of inventory should be presumed to have "discernible future benefits" for the purpose of determining the cost of a self-constructed depreciable asset.[19]

This criterion would charge both normal and incremental overhead costs to self-constructed fixed assets and has the advantage of providing consistency within a company in the treatment of overhead costs.

Saving or Loss on Self-Construction. When the cost of self-construction of an asset is less than the cost to acquire it through purchase or construction by outsiders, the difference for accounting purposes is not a profit but a savings. The construction is properly reported at its actual cost. The savings will emerge as income over the life of the asset as lower depreciation is charged against periodic revenue. Assume, on the other hand, the cost of self-construction is greater than bids originally received for the construction. There is generally no assurance that the asset under alternative arrangements might have been equal in quality to that which was self-constructed. In recording this transaction, just as in recording others, accounts should reflect those courses of action taken, not the alternatives that might have been selected. However, if there is evidence indicating cost has been materially excessive because of certain construction inefficiencies or failures, the excess is properly recognized as a loss; subsequent periods should not be burdened with charges for depreciation arising from costs that could have been avoided.

Interest During Period of Construction. In public utility accounting, interest during a period of building construction is recognized as a part of asset cost. This practice applies both to interest actually paid and to an implicit interest charge if the public utility uses its own funds. Interest, then, emerges as a charge for depreciation in the periods in which the properties are income-producing. Service rates established by regulatory bodies are based upon current charges and may provide for a recovery of past interest in this manner.

The practice of capitalizing interest has sometimes been carried into accounting for industrial companies. Support for this practice is based on the grounds that interest is a cost of construction, and the proper matching of revenues and expenses suggests it be deferred and charged over the life of the

---

[19]Charles Lamden, Dale L. Gerboth, and Thomas McRae, "Accounting for Depreciable Assets," *Accounting Research Monograph No. 1* (New York: American Institute of Certified Public Accountants, 1975), pp. 57.

constructed asset. It can also be argued that if buildings or equipment were acquired by purchase rather than by self-construction, a charge for interest during the construction period would be implicit in the purchase price.

Arguments advanced against this practice are:

(1) It is difficult to follow cash once it is invested in a firm. Is the interest charge really related to the constructed asset, or is it a payment made to meet general financial needs? Even when a loan is made for specific purposes, it frees cash raised by other means to be used for other projects.
(2) To be consistent, implicit interest on all funds used, not just borrowed funds, should be charged to the asset cost. This practice is followed in utility accounting and requires determining a cost of capital for internal funds used, a very difficult task.

Traditionally, nonutility companies have not capitalized interest. However, in the mid 1970's an increasing number of companies changed their accounting method to a policy of capitalizing interest, an action that tended to increase net income. In reaction to these changes, the Securities and Exchange Commission, in 1974, declared a moratorium on companies changing their methods of accounting for interest costs pending study of the issue by the Financial Accounting Standards Board.[20]

Such a study was conducted, and in October 1979, FASB Statement No. 34 was issued recommending limited capitalization of interest cost.[21] If the development of an asset for use or in limited cases, for sale or lease, requires a significant period of time between the initial expenditure related to its development and its readiness for intended use, interest cost on borrowed funds should be capitalized as part of the asset cost.

The amount of interest to be capitalized is

> ...that portion of the interest cost incurred during the assets' acquisition periods that theoretically could have been avoided (for example, by avoiding additional borrowings or by using the funds expended for the assets to repay existing borrowings) if expenditures for the assets had not been made.[22]

The amount to be capitalized for a given accounting period is determined by applying an appropriate interest or **capitalization rate** to the **average accumulated expenditures** for the asset during the period. The rate to be applied to the expenditures is based on the interest rates applicable to borrowings outstanding during the period. If an enterprise's financing plan associates a specific new borrowing with a qualifying asset, the enterprise may use the rate on the borrowing for the portion of the average accumulated expenditures that does not exceed that borrowing. The capitalization rate to be applied to any excess average expenditures is a weighted average of the rates applicable to other borrowings. In no instance should the capitalized interest exceed the total interest cost incurred by the enterprise in a given period. Thus, no imputed interest on the company's own funds is to be capitalized.

---

[20]Securities and Exchange Commission, *Accounting Series Release No. 163*, "Capitalization of Interest by Companies Other than Public Utilities" (Washington: U.S. Government Printing Office 1974).

[21]*Statement of Financial Accounting Standards No. 34*, "Capitalization of Interest Cost" (Stamford: Financial Accounting Standards Board, 1979).

[22]*Ibid.*, par. 12.

The period of capitalization begins with the first expenditure and ends with completion or suspension of active development. FASB Statement No. 34 specifies that interest capitalization shall continue as long as three conditions are present:[23]

(1) Expenditures for the asset have been made.
(2) Activities that are necessary to get ready for its intended use are in progress (including administrative and technical activities in the preconstruction stage, such as development of plans and obtaining special permits).
(3) Interest costs are being incurred.

To illustrate the required capitalization of interest cost, assume that a company has decided to construct its own building. For the current year, expenditures for the building totaled $3,000,000. Assuming that the expenditures were incurred evenly throughout the year, average accumulated construction expenditures on the partially completed building would be $1,500,000 ($3,000,000 ÷ 2). Debt related directly to the project consists of a $1,000,000, 10% mortgage. Debt not directly related includes $200,000 of long-term notes issued at 12% interest and additional debt of $1,000,000 on the books at an average rate of 9%. The interest cost that would be capitalized in the current period would be $147,500 computed as follows:

Interest cost related directly to the project:	
10% × $1,000,000	$100,000
Interest cost on remaining $500,000 of average accumulated expenditures at 9.5%* weighted average rate:	
9.5% × $500,000	47,500
Total capitalized interest cost	$147,500

*$200,000 × 12%	=	$ 24,000
$1,000,000 × 9%	=	90,000
Total interest	=	$114,000
Weight average rate	=	$114,000 ÷ $1,200,000 = 9.5%

Acquisition by Donation or Discovery

When property is received through donation by a governmental unit or other source, there is no cost that can be used as a basis for its valuation. It is classified as a **nonreciprocal transfer of a nonmonetary asset.**[24] Even though certain expenditures may have to be made incident to the gift, these expenditures are generally considerably less than the value of the property. Here cost obviously fails to provide a satisfactory basis for asset accountability as well as for future income measurement.

Property acquired through donation should be appraised and recorded at its fair market value.[25] A donation increases owners' equity, therefore Donated Capital is credited. To illustrate, if the Beverly Hills Chamber of Commerce donates land and buildings appraised at $50,000 and $150,000 respectively, the entry on the books of the donee would be:

---

[23] *Ibid.*, par. 17.
[24] *Opinions of the Accounting Principles Board, No. 29, op. cit.*, par. 3(d).
[25] *Ibid.*, par. 18.

Land	50,000	
Buildings	150,000	
Donated Capital		200,000

Depreciation of an asset acquired by gift should be recorded in the usual manner; the value assigned to the asset providing the basis for the depreciation charge.

If a gift is contingent upon some act to be performed by the donee, the contingent nature of the asset and the capital item should be indicated in the account titles. Account balances should be reported "short" or a special note should be made on the balance sheet. When conditions of the gift have been met, both the increase in assets and in owners' equity should be recognized in the accounts and on the financial statements.

Occasionally, valuable resources are discovered on already owned land. The discovery greatly increases the value of the property. However, because the cost of the land is not affected by the discovery, it is common practice to ignore this increase in value. Similarly, the increase in value for assets that change over time, such as growing timber or aging wine, is ignored in common practice. Failure to recognize these discovery or accretion values ignores the economic reality of the situation and tends to materially understate the assets of the entity. More meaningful decisions could probably be made if the user of the statements was aware of these changes in value.

Recently, special attention has been focused on the discovery value of oil and gas reserves. Most of the increased attention has been caused by the energy shortages experienced in the United States, and the volatile changes in oil and gas prices charged by oil-producing companies in the Near East and Mexico. Exploration and drilling costs in the oil industry have historically been recorded in one of two ways; either as an asset to be written off against revenue from producing wells (**full cost**), or as an immediate write-off unless successful discoveries of oil are made (**successful efforts**). Both the FASB and the SEC have attempted to establish guidelines for a uniform method of accounting by oil and gas producing companies. The FASB advocated a form of successful efforts accounting, while the SEC favored development of a new method, referred to as **revenue recognition accounting (RRA)**, a form of discovery value accounting. The FASB accounting requirements were suspended before they could be put into effect, and the SEC withdrew its support for RRA after a few years of experimenting with the new method as supplemental information.

In November, 1982, the FASB issued Statement No. 69, "Disclosures about Oil and Gas Producing Activities." The statement does not specify a single method of accounting, but requires disclosure of the method used. Statement No. 69 also establishes a comprehensive set of supplemental disclosure requirements for publicly traded companies.

RECORDING ACQUISITION OF SPECIFIC ASSETS

Special accounting problems arise in recording the acquisition of certain property items. Attention is directed in the following sections to specific properties and their special problems.

Real Property

All property is divided into two basic categories—real property and personal property. **Real property**, alternatively referred to as realty or real estate, includes land and most things affixed to it. The latter element includes buildings, building fixtures such as plumbing that cannot be removed without damage to the structure, and most land improvements such as trees, shrubs, and sidewalks. All other property is **personal property**.

Land. Rights to land arising from purchase should be distinguished from rights under leaseholds and under easements. With a **purchase**, the buyer acquires title and ownership **in fee simple**, and the property is properly recognized as an asset. A **leasehold** provides rights to the possession and profits of land for a certain period. An **easement** provides rights for the use of land as in the case of rights-of-way or other special privileges. Recognition of asset balances for leaseholds and easements is limited to prepayments of rents and fees to the owners of land for the acquired rights unless the leasehold or easement is in substance a purchase. In this case, the present value of future rental payments is capitalized.[26]

When land is purchased, its cost includes not only the negotiated purchase price but also all other costs related to the acquisition including brokers' commissions, legal fees, title, recording, and escrow fees, and surveying fees. Any existing unpaid tax, interest, or other liens on the property assumed by the buyer are added to cost.

Costs of clearing, grading, subdividing, or otherwise permanently improving the land after its acquisition should also be treated as increases in the cost of land. When a site secured for a new plant is already occupied by a building that must be torn down, the cost of removing the old structure less any recovery from salvage is added to land cost. If salvage exceeds the cost of razing buildings, the excess may be considered a reduction of land cost. Special assessments by local governments for certain local benefits, such as streets and sidewalks, lighting, and sewers and drainage systems that will be maintained by the government, may be regarded as permanently improving land and thus chargeable to the asset. When expenditures are incurred for land improvements having a limited life and requiring ultimate replacement as, for example, paving, fencing, water and sewage systems, and landscaping, such costs should be summarized separately in an account entitled Land Improvements and depreciated over the estimated useful life of the improvements. The useful life of some improvements may be limited to the life of the buildings on the land; other improvements may have an independent service life.

Land qualifies for presentation in the land, buildings, and equipment category only when it is being used in the normal activities of the business. Land held for future use or for speculation should be reported under the long-term investments heading; land held for current sale should be reported

---

[26]See Chapter 15 for discussion of capitalization of leases.

as a current asset. A descriptive account title should be used to distinguish land not used in normal operations from the land in use.

Buildings. A purchase involving the acquisition of both land and buildings requires the cost to be allocated between the two assets. Allocable cost consists of the purchase price plus all charges incident to the purchase. The cost allocated to buildings is increased by expenditures for reconditioning and repairs in preparing the asset for use as well as by expenditures for improvements and additions.

When buildings are constructed, their costs consist of materials, labor, and overhead related to construction. Costs of excavation or grading and filling required for purposes of the specific project, rather than for making land usable, are charged to buildings. Charges for architects' fees, building permits and fees, workers' compensation and accident insurance, fire insurance for the period of construction, and temporary buildings used for construction activities, form part of the total building cost. Tax on property improvements, as well as financing costs during a period of construction, are generally capitalized as a cost of buildings.

It was suggested earlier that when land and buildings are acquired and buildings are immediately demolished, the cost of demolishing buildings is added to land as a cost of preparing land for its intended use. However, the cost of demolishing buildings that have been previously occupied by the company requires different treatment. This is a cost that should be identified with the original buildings. The recovery of salvage upon asset retirement serves to reduce the cost arising from the use of an asset and is frequently anticipated in calculating periodic charges for depreciation; a cost arising from asset retirement serves to increase the cost of asset use but is seldom anticipated in developing periodic charges.

In many instances, careful analysis is required in determining whether an expenditure should be recognized as buildings or whether it should be identified with the land or equipment categories. For example, expenditures for sidewalks and roads that are part of a building program are normally reported as buildings, but these would be properly reported as land improvements when they improve land regardless of its use; expenditures for items such as shelving, cabinets, or partitions in the course of building construction are normally reported as buildings, but these would be properly reported as equipment items when they are movable, can be used in different centers, and are considered to have independent lives. Particular care should be directed to charges against revenues under different classification and recording alternatives. Frequently alternative classifications can be supported and the ultimate choice will be a matter of judgment.

If depreciation on buildings is to be recognized satisfactorily, separate accounts should be maintained for each building with a different life as well as for those structural elements of a building requiring modification or replacement before the building is fully depreciated, such as loading and shipping quarters, storage facilities, and garages. Separate recording should also be extended to building equipment and appurtenances requiring replacement before the building is fully depreciated, such as boilers, heating and ventilating systems, plumbing and lighting systems, elevators, and wiring and piping installations. The latter items are frequently summarized in an account titled Building Equipment or Building Improvements, but detailed records will be required in support of this balance of the different service lives of the individual items.

Third-Party Financing of Land and Buildings. Real property is usually purchased through a real estate broker in conjunction with a bank or other financial institution. Frequently the financial institution holds the down payment "in escrow" prior to transfer of the property and prepares the necessary documents to complete the transfer. At the time of settlement, the financial institution acts as a third-party intermediary for the collection of funds from the buyer and disbursement of funds to the seller, the real estate broker, and other payees such as attorneys and taxing authorities.

Generally, both buyer and seller must pay certain costs in connection with the transaction. These costs and the settlement between the buyer and seller are summarized in an **escrow statement** prepared by the financial institution. An example of such a document showing both the seller's and the buyer's interest in the transaction is presented below. Usually, however, each party to the transaction receives a separate statement.

Mountain West Escrow Company
Escrow Statements

	Statement of Seller		Statement of Buyer	
	Charges	*Credits*	*Charges*	*Credits*
Selling price		$739,600	$739,600	
Mortgage assumed by buyer	$276,200			$276,200
Property taxes—pro rata (to be paid by buyer)	7,000			7,000
Commission	30,000			
Title insurance (cost split)	4,000		4,000	
Fire insurance—pro rata (paid by seller)		1,200	1,200	
Title insurance (cost split)	2,000		2,000	
Escrow fee (buyer pays all)			4,000	
Interest—pro rata (to be paid by buyer)	700			700
Recording fee			100	
Deposit placed in escrow				200,000
Cash to balance accounts	420,900			267,000
	$740,800	$740,800	$750,900	$750,900

The escrow statement is somewhat confusing at first glance, but it is not difficult to interpret after becoming familiar with the terminology. Two columns are provided for each party—one representing the charges and the other the credits. The mortgage balance owed by the seller and closing costs allocated to the seller are charged against the selling price, unexpired fire insurance as of the settlement date is credited to the seller, and the balance of $420,900 is paid to the seller by the financial institution. The seller's cost include property taxes of $7,000 and mortgage interest of $700 accrued as of the transfer date, both of which will be paid by the buyer when due. The balance to be paid by the buyer to the financial institution is $267,000—the selling price plus the buyer's closing costs less the credits for the mortgage assumed, the deposit, and the accrued taxes and interest.

The entry to record the acquisition would be as follows, assuming the land portion of the purchase is $100,000 with the remainder assigned to the building.

Land	100,000	
Unexpired Insurance	1,200	
Building	649,700	
Escrow Deposit		200,000
Mortgage Payable		276,200
Taxes Payable		7,000
Interest Payable		700
Cash		267,000

Equipment

Equipment covers a wide range of items that vary with the particular enterprise and its activities. The discussion in the following paragraphs is limited to machinery, tools, patterns and dies, furniture and fixtures, motor vehicles, and returnable containers.

Machinery of a manufacturing concern includes such items as lathes, stamping machines, ovens, and conveyor systems. The machinery account is debited for all expenditures identified with the acquisition and the preparation for use of factory machines. Machinery cost includes the purchase price, tax and duties on purchase, freight charges, insurance charges while in transit, installation charges, expenditures for testing and final preparation for use, and costs for reconditioning used equipment when purchased.

Two classes of **tools** are employed in productive activities: (1) **machine tools**, representing detachable parts of a machine, such as dies, drills, and punches; and (2) **hand tools**, such as hammers, wrenches, and saws. Both classes of tools are normally of small individual cost and are relatively short-lived as a result of wear, breakage, and loss. These factors frequently suggest that these items be accounted for as a single asset. Replacement of these small tools may then either be charged directly to expense or added to the single asset account and written off by reasonable annual depreciation charges.

Patterns and dies are acquired for designing, stamping, cutting, or forging out a particular object. The cost of patterns and dies is either a purchase cost or a developmental cost composed of labor, materials, and overhead. When patterns and dies are used in normal productive activities, their cost is reported as an asset and the asset values are written off over the period of their usefulness. When the use of such items is limited to the manufacture of a single job, their cost is recognized as a part of the cost of that job.

Furniture and fixtures include such items as desks, chairs, carpets, showcases, and display fixtures. Acquisitions should be identified with production, selling, or general and administrative functions. Such classification makes it possible to assign depreciation accurately to the different business activities. Furniture and fixtures are recorded at cost, which includes purchase price, tax, freight, and installation charges.

Automobile and truck acquisitions should also be identified with production, selling, or general and administrative functions. Depreciation can then be accurately related to the different activities. Automotive equipment is recorded at its purchase price increased by any sales and excise tax and delivery charges paid. When payment for equipment includes charges for items, such as current license fees, personal property tax, and insurance, these should be recognized separately as expenses relating to both the current and the future use of the equipment.

Goods are frequently delivered in **containers** to be returned and reused. Returnable containers consist of such items as tanks, drums, and barrels. Containers are depreciable assets used in the business and are included in the equipment group. Adjustments must be made periodically to reduce the asset account and its related accumulated depreciation for containers not expected to be returned. The reduction is reported as a current loss.

Leaseholds

A **leasehold** is a contractual agreement whereby a **lessee** is granted a right to use property owned by the **lessor** for a specified period of time for a specified periodic cost. Many leases are in effect purchases of property. In such cases, the property should be recorded on the lessee's books as an asset at the present value of the future lease payments. Because lease accounting is a complex area, an entire chapter (Chapter 15) is devoted to accounting for lease contracts. Even when a lease is not considered to be the same as a purchase and the periodic payments are written off as rental expense, certain lease prepayments or improvements to the property by the lessee may be treated as capital expenditures. Since leasehold improvements, such as partitions in a building, additions, and attached equipment, revert to the owner at the expiration of the lease, they are properly capitalized on the books of the lessee and amortized over the remaining life of the lease. Some lease costs are really expenses of the period and should not be capitalized. This includes improvements that are made in lieu of rent; e.g., a lessee builds partitions in a leased warehouse for storage of its product. The lessor allows the lessee to offset the cost against rental expense for the period. These costs should be expensed by the lessee.

Patents

A **patent** is an exclusive right granted by the government to an inventor enabling the inventor to control the manufacture, sale, or other use of the invention for a specified period of time. The United States Patent Office issues patents that are valid for **seventeen years** from the date of issuance. Patents are not renewable although effective control of an invention is frequently maintained beyond the expiration of the original patent through new patents covering improvements or changes. The owner of a patent may grant its use to others under royalty agreements or the patent may be sold.

The issuance of a patent does not necessarily indicate the existence of a valuable right. The value of a patent stems from whatever advantage it might afford its owner in excluding competitors from utilizing a process resulting in lower costs or superior products. Many patents cover inventions that cannot be exploited commercially and may actually be worthless.

Patents are recorded at their **acquisition costs.** When a patent is purchased, it is recorded at the new owner's purchase price. When a patent is developed through company-sponsored research, the accounting treatment falls under FASB Statement No. 2, "Accounting for Research and Development Costs," described previously. Only patent licensing and related legal fees are included as its costs. All related experimental and developmental expenditures, along with the cost of models and drawings not required by the patent application, are considered research and development costs and are to be debited to expense when incurred.[27]

The validity of a patent may be challenged in the courts. The cost of successfully prosecuting or defending infringement suits is regarded as a cost of establishing the legal rights of the holder and may be added to the other costs of the patent. In the event of unsuccessful litigation, the litigation cost, as well as other patent costs, should be written off as a loss.

Copyrights

A **copyright** is an exclusive right granted by the federal government permitting an author, composer, or artist to publish, sell, license, or otherwise control a literary, musical, or artistic work. In 1978, a new copyright law became effective in the United States. Under the new law, a copyright expires fifty years after the death of the creator of the work. Formerly, copyrights expired after a maximum of 56 years from the time they were granted. The new law permits the United States to be part of the Bern Union, the most widely recognized international copyright agreement.

The cost assigned to a copyright consists of those charges required to establish the right. When a copyright is purchased, it is recorded at its purchase price. The cost of any subsequent litigation to protect the copyright, if successful, should be capitalized as an additional cost of the copyright.

Trademarks and Trade Names

Trademarks and **trade names,** together with distinctive symbols, labels, and designs, are important to all companies that depend on a public demand for their products. It is by means of these distinctive markings that particular products are differentiated from competing brands. In building the reputa-

---

[27] *Statement of Financial Accounting Standards No. 2,* "Accounting for Research and Development Costs" (Stamford, Conn.: Financial Accounting Standards Board, 1974), par. 10(i).

tion of a product, relatively large costs may be incurred. The federal government offers legal protection for trademarks through their registry with the United States Patent Office. Prior and continuous use is the important factor in determining the ownership of a particular trademark. The right to a trademark is retained as long as continuous use is made of it. Protection of trade names and brands that cannot be registered must be sought in the common law. Distinctive trademarks, trade names, and brands can be assigned or sold.

The cost of a trademark consists of those expenditures required to establish it, including filing and registry fees, and expenditures for successful litigation in defense of the trademark. When a trademark is purchased, it is recorded at its purchase price.

Organization Costs

In forming a corporation, certain expenditures are incurred including legal fees, promotional costs, stock certificate costs, underwriting costs, and state incorporation fees. The benefits to be derived from these expenditures normally extend beyond the first fiscal period. Further, the recognition of these expenditures as expenses at the time of organization would commit the corporation to a deficit before it actually begins operations. These factors support the practice of recognizing the initial costs of organization as an intangible asset.

Expenditures relating to organization may be considered to benefit the corporation during its entire life. Thus, there is theoretical support for carrying organization costs as an intangible asset until the corporation is dissolved or becomes inactive. On the other hand, it may be argued that the organizational and start-up costs of a business are of primary benefit during the first few years of operation. Beyond that point, these costs generally become insignificant in terms of impact on the success or failure of the enterprise.

It is sometimes suggested that operating losses of the first few years should be capitalized as organization costs or as goodwill. It is argued that the losses cannot be avoided in the early years when the business is being developed, and hence it is reasonable that these losses should be absorbed in later years. Although losses may be inevitable, they do not necessarily carry any future service potential. To report these losses as intangible assets would result in the overstatement of assets, net income, and owners' equity. This practice cannot be condoned.

Franchises

A **franchise** is an exclusive right or privilege received by a business or individual (**franchisee**) to perform certain business functions or use certain products or services, usually in a specified geographical area. The **grantor** of the franchise (**franchisor**) usually specifies a period of time over which the right may be exercised and the conditions under which the franchise can be revoked. Some grantors are governmental units such as municipalities, that frequently grant business concerns the right to use public property to provide services such as utilities, refuse collection, and public transportation. Other grantors are private companies who grant exclusive rights to market their products or to use their name.

The cost of a franchise includes any sum paid specifically for a franchise as well as legal fees and other costs incurred in obtaining it. Although the value of a franchise at the time of its acquisition may be substantially in excess of its cost, the amount recorded should be limited to actual outlays. When a franchise is purchased from another company, the amount paid is recorded as the franchise cost.

A franchise agreement may require that periodic payments be made to the grantor. Payments may be fixed amounts or they may be variable amounts depending on revenue, utilization, or other factors. These payments should be recognized by the franchisee as charges to periodic revenue. When certain property improvements are required under terms of the franchise, the costs of the improvements should be capitalized and charged to revenue over the life of the franchise. The revenue recognition problems related to the franchisor are discussed in Chapter 19.

Goodwill

Goodwill is generally regarded as the summation of all the special advantages, not otherwise identifiable, related to a going concern. It includes such items as a good name, capable staff and personnel, high credit standing, reputation for superior products and services, and favorable location. Unlike most other assets, tangible or intangible, goodwill cannot be transferred without transferring the entire business.

From an accounting point of view, goodwill is recognized as the ability of a business to earn above-normal earnings with the identifiable assets employed in the business. Above-normal earnings mean a rate of return greater than that normally required to attract investors into a particular type of business.

The recording of goodwill has been the subject of many discussions and publications. Under currently accepted accounting principles, goodwill is recorded on the books only when it is **acquired by purchase** or otherwise established through a business transaction. The latter condition includes its recognition in connection with a merger or a reorganization of a corporation or a change of partners in a partnership.

Although goodwill is recognized on the company books only when it is acquired in an arm's-length transaction, this procedure makes it more difficult to compare a company that has recorded goodwill and one that doesn't. Just because a company has not purchased another company does not mean it does not have goodwill as defined above. Thus, current accounting principles may result in misleading users as far as goodwill is concerned. On the other hand, to allow companies to place a value on their own goodwill would undoubtedly lead to abuse. These difficulties have led some accountants to suggest that all purchased goodwill should be written off to expense as soon as it is acquired. Advocates of this position include the authors of Accounting Research Study No. 10, "Accounting for Goodwill," whose justification for immediate write-off was given as follows:

(1) Goodwill is not a resource or property right that is consumed or utilized in the production of earnings. It is the result of expectations of future earnings by investors and thus is not subject to normal amortization procedures.
(2) Goodwill is subject to sudden and wide fluctuations. That value has no reliable or continuing relation to costs incurred in its creation.
(3) Under existing practices of accounting, neither the cost nor the value of nonpurchased goodwill is reported in the balance sheet. Purchased goodwill has no continuing, separately measurable existence after the combination and is merged with the total goodwill value of the continuing business entity. As such, its write-off cannot be measured with any validity.
(4) Goodwill as an asset account is not relevant to an investor. Most analysts ignore any reported goodwill when analyzing a company's status and operations.[28]

This position has been consistently rejected by the accounting principles-setting bodies, and the immediate write-off of purchased goodwill is strongly discouraged. They maintain that a price has been paid for the excess earnings power, and it should be recognized as an asset. Because of the poor connotative image the term *goodwill* has acquired, some companies use more descriptive titles for reporting purposes, such as "Excess of Cost over Net Assets of Acquired Companies."

In the purchase of a going business, the actual price paid for goodwill usually results from bargaining and compromises between the parties concerned. A basis for negotiation in arriving at a price for goodwill could involve many variables:

(1) The level of projected future earnings.
(2) An appropriate rate of return.
(3) Current valuation of the net business assets other than goodwill.

Several ways in which these variables may be used to aid in the negotiations are presented in the Appendix to this chapter. These are not really accounting methods, but financial models that utilize accounting data.

When a lump-sum amount is paid for an established business and no explicit evaluation is made of goodwill, goodwill may still be recognized. In this case the identifiable net assets require appraisal, and the difference between the full purchase price and the value of identifiable net assets can be attributed to the purchase of goodwill. In appraising properties for this purpose, current market values should be sought rather than the values reported in the accounts. Receivables should be stated at amounts estimated to be realized. Inventories and securities should be restated in terms of current market values. Land, buildings, and equipment may require special

[28]George R. Catlett and Norman O. Olson, "Accounting for Goodwill," *Accounting Research Study No. 10* (New York: American Institute of Certified Public Accountants, 1968).

appraisals in arriving at their present replacement or reproduction values. Intangible assets, such as patents and franchises, should be included at their current values even though, originally, expenditures were reported as expenses or were reported as assets and amortized against revenue. Care should be taken to determine that liabilities are fully recognized. Assets at their current fair market values less the liabilities to be assumed provide the net assets total that, together with estimated future earnings, is used in arriving at a purchase price.

To the extent possible, the amount paid for any existing company should be related to identifiable assets. If an excess does exist, the use of a term other than goodwill can avoid the implication that only companies that purchase other companies have goodwill.

EXPENDITURES SUBSEQUENT TO ACQUISITION

During the lives of property items, regular as well as special expenditures are incurred. Certain expenditures are required to maintain and repair assets; others are incurred to increase their capacity or efficiency or to extend their useful lives. Each expenditure requires careful analysis to determine whether it should be assigned to revenue of the current period, hence charged to an expense account, or whether it should be assigned to revenue of more than one period, which calls for a debit to an asset account or to an accumulated depreciation account. In many cases the answer may not be clear, and the procedure chosen may be a matter of judgment.

The terms maintenance, repairs, betterments, improvements, additions, and rearrangements are used in describing expenditures made in the course of asset use. These are described in the following sections.

Maintenance

Expenditures to maintain plant assets in fit condition are referred to as **maintenance.** Among these are expenditures for painting, lubricating, and adjusting equipment. Maintenance items are ordinary and recurring and do not improve the asset or add to its life; therefore, they are recorded as expenses.

Repairs

Expenditures to restore assets to a fit condition upon their breakdown or to restore and replace broken parts are referred to as **repairs.** When these expenditures are ordinary and benefit only current operations, they are debited to expense. When they are extraordinary and **extend the life of the asset,** they may be debited to the accumulated depreciation account. The depreciation rate is then redetermined in view of changes in the asset book value and estimated life. Debits for repairs extending the useful life of the asset are made against the accumulated depreciation account to avoid a build-up of gross asset values. The book value of the asset will be the same whether the debit is made to the asset account directly or to the accumulated depreciation account.

Repairs involving the overhauling of certain assets are frequently referred to as **renewals.** Substitutions of parts or entire units are referred to as **replacements.** The cost of the replacement may be expensed or capitalized depending on how the property unit is defined. For example, components of a major piece of equipment, such as the motor, the frame, and the attachments, may be considered separate property units, or the entire machine may be considered the property unit. If the component parts are the property units, replacement of a component requires entries cancelling the book value related to the old component and capitalizing the cost of new equipment. If the property unit is the entire machine, the replacement of the component would be debited to an expense if it is considered to be a normal replacement, or debited to accumulated depreciation if it is considered to be an extraordinary replacement. General criteria as to what constitutes a property unit have not been developed by the profession. Companies have had to establish their own guidelines and consistently apply them. Research indicates that companies do not feel that this lack of guidelines has led to serious abuses in practice.[29]

Repairs arising from flood, fire, or other casualty require special analysis. An expenditure to restore an asset to its previous condition should be reported as a loss from casualties.

Betterments or Improvements

Changes in assets designed to provide increased or improved services are referred to as **betterments** or **improvements.** Installation of improved lighting systems, heating systems, or sanitary systems represent betterments. Minor expenditures for betterments may be recorded as ordinary repairs. Major expenditures call for entries to cancel the book value related to the old asset and to establish a value for the improved asset, or entries to reduce the accumulated depreciation related to the original asset. The latter method is sometimes required when the cost of the item replaced is not readily separable from the whole unit.

Additions

Enlargements and extensions of existing facilities are referred to as **additions.** A new plant wing, additional loading docks, or the expansion of a paved parking lot represent additions. These expenditures are capitalized, and the cost is written off over the service life of the addition.

Another type of addition occurs with intangible assets such as patents, copyrights, trademarks, and franchises. Sometimes legal costs are incurred to protect a patent or a copyright. If the legal action is successful, the legal cost

---

[29]Lamden, Gerboth, and McRae, *op. cit.,* pp. 48–49.

could be deferred over the remaining life of the asset. This would be proper because the successful conclusion of the suit means the asset will still be a valuable piece of property to the company. On the other hand, if the suit is lost, the costs should be expensed and the remaining value of the asset should be written off against revenue.

Rearrangements

Movement of machinery and equipment items and reinstallations to secure economies or greater efficiencies are referred to as **rearrangements.** Costs related to rearrangements should be assigned to those periods benefiting from such changes. When more than one period is benefited, an asset account—appropriately designated to indicate the nature of the cost deferral—should be established and this balance allocated systematically to revenue. When rearrangements involve reinstallation costs, the portion of asset book value related to an original installation should be written off; the cost of the new installation should be added to the asset and written off over its remaining life.

SUMMARY

The most challenging issue facing accountants in the area of asset acquisitions is which costs should be deferred and matched against future revenue, and which should be expensed immediately. Costs to acquire new property items with lives in excess of one fiscal period should clearly be capitalized and charged against future periods. Accounting for repairs, additions, and similar costs incurred subsequent to the initial acquisition is less clear, and such expenditures must be individually evaluated in light of existing conditions. The historical acquisition cost of the asset is widely accepted as the basis for the gross investment, whether for tangible or intangible assets. Methods for matching these costs against future revenues will be discussed in the next chapter, as well as accounting for the retirement of assets.

APPENDIX

As indicated previously, there are many factors that can be considered in determining the purchase price for a business. In deciding whether more than the current value of identifiable net assets should be paid, management may utilize one or more of the following goodwill valuation methods:

(1) Capitalization of average net earnings
(2) Capitalization of average excess net earnings

(3) Number of years' excess earnings
(4) Present value of future excess net earnings

VARIABLES USED IN GOODWILL VALUATION

Before discussing these methods, two variables that are used in all methods are discussed: (1) an estimate of future earnings and (2) the appropriate rate of return.

Estimating the Level of Future Earnings

Past earnings ordinarily offer the best basis on which to develop an estimate of the level of future earnings. In considering past earnings as a basis for projection into the future, reference should be made to earnings most recently experienced. A sufficient number of periods should be included in the analysis so a representative measurement of business performance is available and significant trends are observable. In certain instances, it may be considered necessary to restate revenue and expense balances to give effect to alternative depreciation or amortization methods, inventory methods, or other measurement processes considered desirable in summarizing past operations. Irregular or extraordinary gains and losses that cannot be considered a part of regular activities would be excluded from past operating results. Depending on the circumstances, these items may include gains and losses from the sale of investments and land, buildings, and equipment, gains and losses from the retirement of debt, and losses from casualties.

The regular earnings from operations should be analyzed to determine their trend and stability. If earnings over a period of years show a tendency to decline, careful analysis is necessary to determine whether this decline may be expected to continue. There may be greater confidence in possible future earnings when past earnings have been relatively stable rather than widely fluctuating.

Any changes in the operations of the business that may be anticipated after the transfer of ownership should also be considered. The elimination of a division, the disposal of substantial property items, or the retirement of long-term debt, for example, could materially affect future earnings.

The regular earnings of the past are used as a basis for estimating earnings of the future. Business conditions, the business cycle, sources of supply, demand for the company's products or services, price structure, competition, and other significant factors must be studied in developing data making it possible to convert past earnings into estimated future earnings.

Determining the Appropriate Rate of Return

The existence of above-normal earnings, if any, can be determined only by reference to a normal rate of return. The **normal earnings rate** is that which would ordinarily be required to attract investors in the particular type of business being acquired. In judging this rate, consideration must be given to such factors as money market rates, business conditions at the time of the purchase, competitive factors, risks involved, entrepreneurial abilities required, and alternative investment opportunities.

In general, the greater the risk entailed in an investment, the higher the rate of return required. Because most business enterprises are subject to a considerable amount of risk, investors generally expect a relatively high rate of return to justify their investment. A long history of stable earnings or the existence of certain tangible assets that can be easily sold reduce the degree of risk in acquiring a business and thus reduce the rate of return required by a potential investor.

If goodwill is to be purchased, it should be looked upon as an investment and must offer the prospect of sufficient return to justify the commitment. Special risks are associated with goodwill. The value of goodwill is uncertain and fluctuating. It cannot be separated from the business as a whole and sold, as can most other business properties. Furthermore, it is subject to rapid deterioration and may be totally lost in the event of business sale or liquidation. As a result of the greater risk, a higher rate of return would normally be required on the purchase of goodwill than on the purchase of other business properties.

METHODS OF VALUING GOODWILL

Assume that the following information is available for Company A:

Net earnings after adjustment and elimination of unusual and extraordinary items:

1980	$120,000
1981	80,000
1982	110,000
1983	75,000
1984	115,000
Total	$500,000

Average net earnings 1980-1984: $500,000 ÷ 5 = $100,000. Net assets as appraised on January 2, 1985, before recognizing goodwill, $1,000,000. (Land, buildings, equipment, inventories, and receivables, $1,200,000; liabilities to be assumed by purchaser, $200,000.)

The average net earnings figure of $100,000 for the five-year period 1980-1984 was used in arriving at an estimate of the probable future net earnings.

Different goodwill amounts may be computed using these data depending on which of the four valuation methods enumerated on page 356 and 357 is used. Each of these will be described and illustrated with examples.

Capitalization of Average Net Earnings

The amount to be paid for a business may be determined by capitalizing expected future earnings at a rate representing the required return on the investment. Capitalization of earnings, as used in this sense, means calculation of the principal value that will yield the stated earnings at the specified rate indefinitely or in perpetuity. This is accomplished by dividing the earnings by the specified rate.[30] The difference between the amount to be paid for the business as thus obtained and the appraised values of the individual property items may be considered the price paid for goodwill.

If, in the example, a return of 8% were required on the investment and earnings were estimated at $100,000 per year, the business would be valued at $1,250,000 ($100,000 ÷ .08). Since net assets, with the exception of goodwill, were appraised at $1,000,000, goodwill would be valued at $250,000. If a 10% return were required on the investment, the business would be worth only $1,000,000. In acquiring the business for $1,000,000, there would be no payment for goodwill.

Capitalization of Average Excess Net Earnings

In the above method, a single rate of return was applied to the estimated annual earnings in arriving at the value of the business. No consideration was given to the extent the earnings were attributable to net identifiable assets and the extent the earnings were attributable to goodwill. It would seem reasonable, however, to expect a higher return on an investment in goodwill than on the other assets acquired. To illustrate, assume the following facts:

	Company A	*Company B*
Net assets as appraised	$1,000,000	$500,000
Estimated future net earnings	100,000	100,000

If the estimated earnings are capitalized at a uniform rate of 8%, the value of each company is found to be $1,250,000. The goodwill for Company A is then $250,000, and for Company B, $750,000 as shown:

	Company A	*Company B*
Total net asset valuation (earnings capitalized at 8%)	$1,250,000	$1,250,000
Deduct net assets as appraised	1,000,000	500,000
Goodwill	$ 250,000	$ 750,000

These calculations ignore the fact that the appraised value of the net assets identified with Company A exceed those of Company B. Company A, whose earnings of $100,000 are accompanied by net assets valued at $1,000,000, would certainly command a higher price than Company B, whose earnings of $100,000 are accompanied by net assets valued at only $500,000.

Satisfactory recognition of both earnings and asset contributions is generally effected by (1) requiring a fair return on identifiable net assets, and (2) viewing any excess earnings as attributable to goodwill and capitalizing

[30]This may be shown as follows: P = principal amount or the capitalized earnings to be computed; r = the specified rate of return; E = expected annual earnings. Then, $E = P \times r$, and $P = E \div r$.

the excess at a higher rate in recognition of the degree of risk that characterizes goodwill. To illustrate, assume in the previous cases that 8% is considered a normal return on identifiable net assets and that excess earnings are capitalized at 20% in determining the amount to be paid for goodwill. Amounts to be paid for Companies A and B would be calculated as follows:

	Company A	*Company B*
Estimated net earnings	$ 100,000	$ 100,000
Normal return on net assets:		
Company A—8% of $1,000,000	80,000	
Company B—8% of $ 500,000		40,000
Excess net earnings	$ 20,000	$ 60,000
Excess net earnings capitalized at 20%	÷ .20	÷ .20
Value of goodwill	$ 100,000	$ 300,000

	Company A	*Company B*
Value of net assets offering normal return of 8%	$1,000,000	$ 500,000
Value of goodwill, excess net earnings capitalized at 20%	100,000	300,000
Total net asset valuation	$1,100,000	$ 800,000

Number of Years' Excess Earnings

Behind each of the capitalization methods just described, there is an implicit assumption that the superior earning power attributed to the existence of goodwill will continue indefinitely. The very nature of goodwill, however, makes it subject to rapid decline. A business with unusually high earnings may expect the competition from other companies to reduce earnings over a period of years. Furthermore, the high levels of earnings may frequently be maintained only by special efforts on the part of the new owners, and they cannot be expected to pay for something they themselves must achieve.

As the goodwill being purchased cannot be expected to last beyond a specific number of years, one frequently finds payment for excess earnings stated in terms of *years* of excess earnings rather than capitalization in perpetuity.[31] For example, if excess annual earnings of $20,000 are expected and payment is to be made for excess earnings for a five-year period, the purchase price for goodwill would be $100,000. If the excess annual earnings are expected to be $60,000 and the payment is to be made for four years' excess earnings, the price for goodwill would be $240,000.

The years of excess earnings method has the advantage of conceptual simplicity. It is related to the common business practice of evaluating investment opportunities in terms of their *payback period*—the number of years expected for recovery of the initial investment.

[31]Calculation of goodwill in terms of number of years of excess earnings will yield results identical to the capitalization method when the number of years used is equal to the reciprocal of the capitalization rate. Payment for the five years' earnings, for example, is equivalent to capitalizing earnings at a 20% rate (1 ÷ .20 = 5). Payment of four years' earnings is equivalent to capitalization at a 25% rate (1 ÷ .25 = 4).

Present Value Method

The concept of number of years' purchase can be combined with the concept of a rate of return on investment. Excess earnings can be expected to continue for only a limited number of years, but an investment in these earnings should provide an adequate return, considering the risks involved. The amount to be paid for goodwill, then, is the discounted or present value of the excess earnings amounts expected to become available in future periods.

To illustrate the calculation of goodwill by the present value method, assume the earnings of Company A exceed a normal return on the net identifiable assets used in the business by $20,000 per year. These excess earnings are expected to continue for a period of five years, and a return of 12% is considered necessary to attract investors in this industry. The amount to be paid for goodwill, then, may be regarded as the discounted value at 12% of five installments of $20,000 to be received at annual intervals. Present value tables may be used in determining the present value of the series of payments. The present value of 5 annual payments of $1 each, to provide a return of 12%, is found to be 3.6048.[32] The present value of five payments of $20,000 each would then be calculated as $20,000 × 3.6048 = $72,096.

The principal advantage of the present value method is the explicit recognition of the anticipated duration of excess earnings together with the use of a realistic rate of return. Thus, it focuses on the factors most relevant to the goodwill evaluation.

QUESTIONS

1. What are the characteristics that distinguish intangible assets from tangible assets?
2. (a) Distinguish between capital expenditures and revenue expenditures. (b) Give five examples of each.
3. Which of the following items would be recorded as a revenue expenditure and which would be recorded as a capital expenditure?

(a) Cost of installing machinery.
(b) Cost of moving and reinstalling machinery.
(c) Extensive repairs as a result of fire.
(d) Cost of grading land.
(e) Insurance on machinery in transit.
(f) Bond discount amortization during construction period.
(g) Cost of major overhaul on machinery.
(h) New safety guards on machinery.
(i) Commission on purchase of real estate.
(j) Special tax assessment for street improvements.
(k) Cost of repainting offices.

---

[32]See Appendix A, Table IV.

4. Indicate the effects of the following errors on the balance sheet and the income statement in the current year and in succeeding years:

(a) The cost of a depreciable asset is incorrectly recorded as a revenue expenditure.
(b) A revenue expenditure is incorrectly recorded as an addition to the cost of a depreciable asset.

5. What types of activities are considered research and development activities?
6. How are identifiable intangible assets more similar to tangible assets than to the intangible asset, goodwill?
7. What additional accounting problems are introduced when a company purchases equipment on a long-term contract rather than with cash?
8. Under what circumstances is a gain or loss recognized when a productive asset is exchanged for a similar productive asset?
9. Christie Inc. decides to construct a building for itself and plans to use whatever plant facilities it has to further such construction. (a) What costs will enter into the cost of construction? (b) What two positions can the company take with respect to general overhead allocation during the period of construction? Evaluate each position and indicate your preference.
10. When the Boatman Corporation finds that the lowest bid it can get on the construction of an addition to its building is $40,000, it proceeds to erect the building with its own workers and equipment. (a) Assuming that the cost of construction is $35,000, how would you treat the savings? (b) Assuming the cost of construction is $50,000, how would you treat the excess cost?
11. Evaluate the practice of including interest paid on borrowed funds and the imputed interest on equity capital as a cost of construction for (a) public utilities, (b) commercial entities.
12. How should development stage enterprises report (a) their organization costs and (b) any net operating losses?
13. The Parkhurst Corporation acquires land and buildings valued at $250,000 as a gift from Industrial City. The president of the company maintains that since there was no cost for the acquisition, neither cost of the facilities nor depreciation needs to be recognized for financial statement purposes. Evaluate the president's position assuming (a) the donation is unconditional; (b) the donation is contingent upon the employment by the company of a certain number of employees for a ten-year period.
14. In the balance sheets of many companies, the largest classification of assets in amount is plant assets. Name the items, in addition to the amount paid to the former owner or contractor, that may be properly included as part of the acquisition cost of the following property items: (a) land, (b) buildings, and (c) equipment.
15. How would a trademark worth $5,000,000 be reported on the balance sheet if (a) the trademark were purchased for $5,000,000 or (b) the trademark gradually became identified over the years as a company symbol?
16. (a) What items are normally considered to comprise the organization costs of a company? (b) Would you approve the inclusion of the following items: (1) first-year advertising costs; (2) first-year loss from operations?
17. What costs are capitalized as (a) copyrights, (b) franchises, (c) trademarks?
18. (a) Under what conditions may goodwill be reported as an asset? (b) The Radcliff Company engages in a widespread advertising campaign on behalf of new products, charging above-normal expenditures to goodwill. Do you approve of this practice? Why or why not?
19. Distinguish between (a) maintenance and repairs, (b) ordinary repairs and extraordinary repairs, (c) betterments and additions.
* **20.** What factors should be considered in estimating the future earnings of a business in order to develop a fair valuation of goodwill?
* **21.** Give four methods for arriving at a goodwill valuation, using estimated future earn-

*Questions to Appendix material.

ings as a basis for these calculations. Which method do you think would give the most relevant valuation of goodwill?

DISCUSSION CASES

case 10-1 (Where should we charge it?) Biltmore Energy Corp. has recently purchased the assets of a small local company, Banks Inc., for $553,500 cash. The chief accountant of Biltmore has been given the assignment of preparing the journal entry to record the purchase. An investigation disclosed the following information about the assets of Banks Inc.:

(a) Banks owned land and a small manufacturing building. The book value of the property on Banks' records was $115,000. An appraisal for fire insurance purposes had been made during the year. The building was appraised by the insurance company at $150,000. Property tax assessment notices showed that the building's worth was five times the worth of the land.
(b) Banks' equipment had a book value of $75,000. It is estimated by Banks that it would take six times the amount of book value to replace the equipment new. The old equipment is, on the average, 50% depreciated.
(c) Banks had a franchise to produce and sell solar energy units from another company in a set geographic area. The franchise was transferred to Biltmore as part of the purchase. Banks carried the asset on its books at $40,000, the amortized balance of the original cost of $90,000. The franchise is for an unlimited time. Similar franchises are now being sold by the company for $120,000 per geographic area.
(d) Banks had two excellent research scientists who were responsible for much of the company's innovation in product development. They are each paid $50,000 per year by Banks. They have agreed to work for Biltmore Energy at the same salary.
(e) Banks held two patents on its products. Both had been fully amortized and were not carried as assets on Banks' books. Banks feels they could have been sold separately for $75,000 each.

Evaluate each of the above items and prepare the journal entry that should be made to record the purchase on Biltmore's books.

case 10-2 (How much does it cost?) The Waters Co. decides to construct a piece of specialized machinery using personnel from the maintenance department. This is the first time the maintenance personnel have been used for this purpose, and the cost accountant for the factory is concerned as to the accounting for costs of the machine. Some of the issues raised by the maintenance department management are highlighted below:

(a) The supervisor of the maintenance department has instructed the workers to schedule work so all the overtime hours are charged to the machinery. Overtime is paid at 150% of the regular rate, or at a 50% premium.
(b) Material used in the production of the machine is charged out from the materials storeroom at 125% of cost, the same markup used when material is furnished to subsidiary companies.
(c) The maintenance department overhead rate is applied on maintenance hours. No extra overhead is anticipated as a result of constructing the machine.
(d) The maintenance department personnel is not qualified to test the machine on the production line. This will be done by production employees.
(e) Although the machine will take about one year to build, no extra borrowing of funds will be necessary to finance its construction. The company does, however, have outstanding bonds from earlier financing.
(f) It is expected that the self-construction of the machinery will save the company at least $20,000.

What advice can you give the cost accountant to help in the determination of a proper cost for the machine?

EXERCISES

exercise 10-1 (Research and development costs)

In 1984 the MSA Corporation incurred research and development costs as follows:

Materials and equipment	$100,000
Personnel	100,000
Indirect costs	50,000
	$250,000

These costs relate to a product that will be marketed in 1985. It is estimated that these costs will be recouped by December 31, 1988.

(1) What is the amount of research and development costs which should be charged to income in 1984?

(2) Assume that of the above costs, equipment of $60,000 can be used on other research projects. Estimated useful life of the equipment is five years, and it was acquired at the beginning of 1984. What is the amount of research and development costs that should be charged to income in 1984 under these conditions. Assume depreciation on all equipment is computed on a straight-line basis. (AICPA adapted)

exercise 10-2 (Determining cost of machinery)

Spencer Inc. acquires a machine priced at $82,000. Payment of this amount may be made within 60 days; a 5% discount is allowed if cash is paid at time of purchase. Give the entry to record the acquisition, assuming:

(a) Cash is paid at time of purchase.
(b) Payment is to be made at the end of 60 days.
(c) A long-term contract is signed whereby a down payment of $25,000 is made with 12 payments of $6,000 to be made at monthly intervals thereafter.

exercise 10-3 (Lump-sum acquisition)

The Red Sky Shipping Co. acquired land, buildings, and equipment at a lump-sum price of $380,000. An appraisal of the assets at the time of acquisition disclosed the following values:

Land	$150,000
Buildings	225,000
Equipment	125,000

What cost should be assigned to each asset?

exercise 10-4 (Lump-sum acquisition)

The Dixon Corporation purchased land, a building, a patent, and a franchise for the lump sum of $950,000. A real estate appraiser estimated the building to have a resale value of $400,000 (⅔ of the total worth of land and building). The franchise had no established resale value. The patent was valued by management at $300,000. Give the journal entry to record the acquisition of the assets.

exercise 10-5 (Equipment purchase on contract)

Braithwaite Co. purchases equipment costing $120,000 with a down payment of $30,000 and sufficient semiannual installments of $7,000 (including interest on the unpaid principal at 10% per year) to pay the balance.

(1) Give the entries to record the purchase and the first two semiannual payments.
(2) Assume that there was no known cash price and twenty semiannual installments were to be made in addition to the $30,000 down payment. Give the entries to record the purchase and the first two semiannual payments.

exercise 10-6 (Exchange of productive assets)

Moore Math Analysis Inc. purchased a new computer from a dealer. The following data relate to the purchase:

(a) List price of new computer with trade-in—$60,000.
(b) Cash price of new computer with no trade-in—$53,700.
(c) Moore Math Analysis Inc. received a trade-in allowance (based on list price) of $15,000 on a machine costing $25,000 new and having a present book value of $12,000. The balance was paid in cash.
(d) The Express Delivery Service charged Moore $1,200 to deliver the computer.

Give the entry to record the acquisition of the new computer.

exercise 10-7 (Exchange of machinery)

Assume that Alpine Corporation has a machine that cost $22,000, has a book value of $16,000, and has a market value of $20,000. For each of the following situations, indicate the value at which Alpine should record the new asset and why it should be recorded at that value.

(a) Alpine exchanged the machine for a truck with a list price of $25,000.
(b) Alpine exchanged the machine with another company for another machine qualifying as a similar productive asset with a list price of $20,500.
(c) Alpine exchanged the machine for a newer model machine from a dealer with a list price of $24,000. Alpine paid $1,000 in the transaction.
(d) Alpine exchanged the machine plus $750 cash for a similar machine from Payson Inc. (a nondealer). The newly acquired machine is carried on Payson's books at $25,000 with accumulated depreciation of $15,000; its fair market value is $20,750. In addition to determining the value, give the journal entries for both companies to record the exchange.

exercise 10-8 (Exchange of truck)

On January 2, 1984, Wilbur Delivery Company traded with a dealer an old delivery truck for a newer model. Data relative to the old and new trucks follow:

Old truck:	
Original cost	$8,000
Accumulated depreciation as of January 2, 1984	6,000
Average published retail value	1,700
New truck:	
List price	$10,000
Cash price without trade-in	9,000
Cash paid with trade-in	7,800

(1) Give the journal entries on Wilbur's books to record the purchase of the new truck.
(2) Give the journal entries on Wilbur's books if the cash paid was $6,800.

(AICPA adapted)

exercise 10-9 (Lump-sum acquisition with stock)

On January 31, 1984, Cherrytown Corp. exchanged 10,000 shares of its $25 par common stock for the following assets:

(a) A trademark valued at $150,000.
(b) A building, including land, valued at $650,000 (20% of the value is for the land).
(c) A franchise right. No estimate of value at time of exchange.

Cherrytown Corp. stock is selling at $95 per share on the date of the exchange. Give the entries to record the exchange on Cherrytown's books.

exercise 10-10 (Purchase of building with bonds and stock)

The Rabbit Co. enters into a contract with the Taulbee Construction Co. for construction of an office building at a cost of $720,000. Upon completion of construction the Taulbee Construction Co. agrees to accept in full payment of the contract price Rabbit Co. 10% bonds with a face value of $400,000 and common stock with a par value of $300,000 and no established fair market value. Rabbit Co. bonds are selling on the market at this time at 98. How would you recommend the building acquisition be recorded?

exercise 10-11 (Acquisition of land and building)

Chester's Music Store acquired land and an old building in exchange for 50,000 shares of its common stock, par $10, and cash of $25,000. The auditor ascertains that the company's stock was selling on the market at $14 when the purchase was made. The following additional costs were incurred to complete the transaction.

Escrow cost to complete transaction	$10,000
Property tax for previous year	30,000
Cost of building demolition	18,000
Salvage value of demolished building	4,000

What entry should be made to record the acquisition of the property?

exercise 10-12 (Cost of self-constructed asset including interest capitalization)

The Mid-Town Manufacturing Company decided to construct its own special equipment for a new product it has developed. A bid to construct the equipment by an outside company was received for $540,000. The actual cost to construct the equipment was as follows:

Direct material	$220,000
Direct labor	80,000

It is estimated that variable overhead costs amount to 125% of direct labor costs. In addition, nonvariable costs (exclusive of interest) of $700,000 are incurred and allocated to production on the basis of total prime costs (direct labor plus direct material). The prime costs required to build the new equipment amount to 15% of the total prime cost incurred for the period. The company follows the policy of capitalizing all possible costs on self-construction projects.

In order to finance the construction of the equipment, a $400,000 10% loan was acquired. Construction on the equipment required six months. Assume expenditures are incurred evenly over the six-month period, and interest charges are to be capitalized in accordance with FASB Statement No. 34. Compute the cost to be assigned to the new equipment upon its completion.

exercise 10-13 (Capitalization of interest)

Home Department Stores Inc. constructs its own stores. In the past, no cost has been added to the asset value for interest on monies borrowed for construction. Management has decided to change its policy, and desires to include interest as part of the cost for a new store just being completed. Based on the following information, how much interest would be added to the cost of the store?

Total construction costs:	
Costs spread evenly over one-year period	$3,500,000
Outstanding company debt:	
Mortgage related directly to new store:	
Interest rate 12%; term, five years from beginning of construction	1,000,000
General bond liability:	
Bonds issued just prior to construction of store; interest rate 10% for ten years	500,000
Bonds issued previously—8%; mature in five years	1,500,000
Estimated cost of equity capital	14%

exercise 10-14 (Cost of specific plant items)

The following expenditures were incurred by the Merrill Food Co. in 1985: purchase of land, $300,000; land survey, $1,500; fees for search of title for land, $350; building permit, $500; temporary quarters for construction crews, $10,750; payment to tenants of old building for vacating premises, $2,000; razing of old building, $25,000; excavation of basement, $10,000; special assessment tax for street project, $2,000; dividends, $5,000; damages awarded for injuries sustained in construction, $4,200 (no insurance was carried; the cost of insurance would have been $200); costs of construction, $750,000; cost of paving parking lot adjoining building, $25,000; cost of shrubs, trees, and other landscaping, $5,000. What is the cost of the land, land improvements, and building?

exercise 10-15 (Determining cost of patent)

Wong and Fong Enterprises Inc. developed a new machine that reduces the time required to insert the fortunes into their fortune cookies. Because the process is considered very valuable to the fortune cookie industry, Fong had the machine patented. The following expenses were incurred in developing and patenting the machine.

Research and development laboratory expenses	$15,000
Metal used in the construction of machine	5,000
Blueprints used to design the machine	500
Legal expenses to obtain patent	10,000
Wages paid for Fong's work on the research, development, and building of the machine (60% of the time was spent in actually building the machine)	30,000
Expense of drawings required by the patent office to be submitted with the patent application	150
Fees paid to government patent office to process patent application	500

One year later, Wong and Fong Enterprises Inc. paid $12,000 in legal fees to successfully defend the patent against an infringement suit by the Golden Dragon Cookie Co.

Give the entries on Wong and Fong's books indicated by the above events. Ignore any amortization of the patent or depreciation of the machine.

exercise 10-16 (Recording acquisition of intangibles)

Brookstone Corporation acquired the following assets at the beginning of 1984. Give the entries to record the acquisition of the assets.

(a) Paperback copyright to a best seller novel in exchange for 120 shares of Brookstone Corporation stock; $50 par, common stock selling for $224 per share.
(b) A fast food franchise in exchange for one acre of prime real estate. Franchises of this type are selling for $50,000 cash. The land was purchased 15 years ago for $2,500. The franchise has an unlimited life as long as Brookstone Corporation maintains the quality standards of the grantor.
(c) Enoc Enterprises for $212,500 cash. Net identifiable assets of Enoc enterprises are fairly valued at $187,500. The purchased goodwill is expected to grow every year as Brookstone Corporation plans to expend substantial resources for advertising and other promotional activities.

exercise 10-17 (Correcting organization costs account)

The Mustang Manufacturing Co. was incorporated on January 1, 1984. In reviewing the accounts in 1985, you find the organization costs account appears as follows:

Account **Organization Costs**

Item	Debit	Credit	Balance Debit	Balance Credit
Incorporation fees	3,750		3,750	
Legal fees relative to organization	21,150		24,900	
Stock certificate cost	6,000		30,900	
Cost of rehabilitating building acquired at end of 1984	165,600		196,500	
Advertising expenditures to promote company products	18,000		214,500	
Amortization of organization costs for 1984, 20% of balance of organization cost (per board of directors' resolution)		42,900	171,600	
Net loss for 1984	54,000		225,600	

Give the entry or entries required to correct the account.

exercise 10-18 (Capital vs. revenue expenditures)

One of the most difficult problems facing an accountant is the determination of which expenditures should be deferred as assets and which should be immediately charged off as expenses. What position would you take in each of the following instances?

(a) Painting of partitions in a large room recently divided into four sections.
(b) Labor cost of tearing down a wall to permit extension of assembly line.
(c) Replacement of motor on a machine. Life used to depreciate the machine is 8 years. The machine is 4 years old. Replacement of the motor was anticipated when the machine was purchased.
(d) Cost of grading land prior to construction.
(e) Assessment for street paving.
(f) Cost of moving and reinstalling equipment.
(g) Cost of tearing down a previously occupied old building in preparation for new construction; old building is fully depreciated.

* exercise 10-19 (Calculation of normal pretax earnings)

In analyzing the accounts of Alexander's Inc. in an attempt to measure goodwill, you find pretax earnings of $500,000 for 1984 after debits and credits for the items listed below. Land, buildings, and equipment are appraised at 50% above cost for purposes of the sale.

Depreciation of land, buildings, and equipment (at cost)	$ 75,000
Special year-end bonus to president of company	25,000
Gain on sale of securities	45,000
Gain on revaluation of securities	15,000
Write-off of goodwill	150,000
Amortization of patents and leaseholds	62,500
Income tax refund for 1982	20,000

What is the normal pretax earnings balance for purposes of your calculations?

* exercise 10-20 (Calculation of goodwill—various methods)

The appraised value of net assets of the Cherrington Co. on December 31, 1984, was $500,000. Average net earnings for the past 5 years after elimination of unusual or extraordinary gains and losses were $82,500. Calculate the amount to be paid for goodwill under each of the following assumptions:

(a) Earnings are capitalized at 15% in arriving at the business worth.
(b) A return of 9% is considered normal on net assets at their appraised value; excess earnings are to be capitalized at 15% in arriving at the value of goodwill.
(c) A return of 12% is considered normal on net assets at their appraised value; goodwill is to be valued at 5 years' excess earnings.
(d) A return of 10% is considered normal on net identifiable assets at their appraised value. Excess earnings are expected to continue for six years. Goodwill is to be valued by the present value method using a rate of 12%. (Use present value table in Appendix A.)

* exercise 10-21 (Computation of goodwill—decision)

Because of superior earning power, Patterson Inc. is considering paying $603,830 for the Predmore Proprietorship with the following assets and liabilities:

	Cost	Fair Market Value
Accounts receivable	$240,000	$220,000
Inventory	140,000	150,000
Prepaid insurance	10,000	10,000
Buildings and equipment (net)	170,000	300,000
Accounts payable	(160,000)	(160,000)
Net assets	$400,000	$520,000

Estimated future earnings are expected to exceed normal earnings by $27,600 for four years. Patterson Inc. uses the present value method of valuing goodwill. Patterson is willing to purchase Predmore if the normal rate of return for Predmore exceeds 10%. Should Patterson purchase Predmore Proprietorship? (Use present value table in Appendix A.)

* exercise 10-22 (Computation of goodwill)

The owners of the Zoot Suit Clothing Store are contemplating selling the business to new interests. The cumulative earnings for the past 5 years amounted to $450,000 including extraordinary gains of $10,000. The annual earnings based on an average rate of return on investment for this industry would have been $76,000. Excess earnings are to be capitalized at 10%. What is the amount of implied goodwill?

(AICPA adapted)

*Exercises to Appendix material.

PROBLEMS

problem 10-1 (Lump-sum acquisition of plant)

The Parowan Wholesale Company incurred the following expenses in 1984 for their office building acquired on July 1, 1984, the beginning of its fiscal year:

Cost of land	$ 75,000
Cost of building	425,000
Remodeling and repairs prior to occupancy	67,500
Escrow fee	6,000
Landscaping	25,000
Unpaid property tax for period prior to acquisition	20,000
Real estate commission	30,000

The company signed a non-interest-bearing note for $500,000 on the acquisition. The implicit interest rate is 12%. Payments of $25,000 are to be made semiannually beginning January 1, 1985, for 10 years.

Instructions: Give the required journal entries to record (1) the acquisition of the land and building (assume that cash is paid to equalize the cost of the assets and the present value of the note), and (2) the first two semiannual payments, including amortization of note discount.

problem 10-2 (Transactions involving plant)

The following transactions were completed by the Terry Toy Co. during 1984:

Mar. 1 Purchased real property for $536,775 which included a charge of $11,775 representing property tax for March 1–June 30 that had been prepaid by the vendor; 20% of the purchase price is deemed applicable to land and the balance to buildings. A mortgage of $375,000 was assumed by the Terry Toy Co. on the purchase.

2–30 Previous owners had failed to take care of normal maintenance and repair requirements on the building, necessitating current reconditioning at a cost of $24,900.

May 15 Garages in the rear of the building were demolished, $4,500 being recovered on the lumber salvage. The company proceeded to construct a warehouse. The cost of such construction was $37,500 which was almost exactly the same as bids made on the construction by independent contractors. Upon completion of construction, city inspectors ordered extensive modifications in the buildings as a result of failure on the part of the company to comply with the Building Safety Code. Such modifications, which could have been avoided, cost $8,400.

June 1 The company exchanged its own stock with a fair market value of $35,000 (par $30,000) for a patent and a new plastic doll-making machine. The machine has a market value of $25,000.

July 1 The new machinery for the new building arrived. In addition to the machinery a new franchise was acquired from the manufacturer of the machinery to produce Double Duck dolls. Payment was made by issuing bonds with a face value of $50,000 and by paying cash of $15,000. The value of the franchise is set at $20,000 while the fair market value of the machine is $40,000.

Nov. 20 The company contracted for parking lots and landscaping at a cost of $45,000 and $9,600 respectively. The work was completed and billed on November 20.

Dec. 31 The business was closed to permit taking the year-end inventory. During the taking of the inventory, required redecorating and repairs were completed at a cost of $4,500.

Instructions: Give the journal entries to record each of the preceding transactions. (Disregard depreciation.)

problem 10-3 (Correcting plant capitalization)

On December 31, 1984, the Bushman Co. shows the following account for machinery it had assembled for its own use during 1984:

Account **Machinery (Job Order #90)**

Item	Debit	Credit	Balance Debit	Balance Credit
Cost of dismantling old machine..........	12,480		12,480	
Cash proceeds from sale of old machine...		10,000	2,480	
Raw materials used in construction of new machine..............................	63,000		65,480	
Labor in construction of new machine.....	49,000		114,480	
Cost of installation.......................	11,200		125,680	
Materials spoiled in machine trial runs....	2,400		128,080	
Profit on construction.....................	27,600		155,680	
Purchase of machine tools................	14,400		170,080	

An analysis of the detail in the account disclosed the following:

(a) The old machine, which was removed in the installation of the new one, had been fully depreciated.
(b) Cash discounts received on the payments for materials used in construction totaled $1,600 and these were reported in the purchases discount account.
(c) The factory overhead account shows a balance of $292,000 for the year ended December 31, 1984; this balance exceeds normal overhead on regular plant activities by approximately $14,800 and is attributable to machine construction.
(d) A profit was recognized on construction for the difference between costs incurred and the price at which the machine could have been purchased.

Instructions:

(1) Determine the machinery and machine tools balances as of December 31, 1984.
(2) Give individual journal entries necessary to correct the accounts as of December 31, 1984, assuming that the nominal accounts are still open.

problem 10-4 (Acquisition of plant)

The Carter Co. planned to open a new store. The company narrowed the possible sites to two lots and decided to take purchase options on both lots while they studied traffic densities in both areas. They paid $7,200 for the option on Lot A and $14,400 for the option on Lot B. After studying traffic densities, they decided to purchase Lot B. The company opened a single real estate account that shows the following:

Debits:	Option on Lot A..	$ 7,200
	Option on Lot B..	14,400
	Payment of balance on Lot B................................	120,000
	Title insurance..	2,100
	Assessment for street improvements.........................	5,100
	Recording fee for deed......................................	300
	Cost of razing old building on Lot B........................	9,000
	Payment for erection of new building.......................	300,000
Credit:	Sale of salvaged materials from old building................	9,000

The salvage value of material obtained from the old building and used in the erection of the new building was $7,500. The depreciated value of the old building, as shown by the books of the company from which the purchase was made, was $54,000. The old building was razed immediately after the purchase.

Instructions:

(1) Determine the cost of the land, listing the items included in the total.
(2) Determine the cost of the new building, listing the items included in the total.

problem 10-5 (Analysis of an escrow statement)

The following escrow statement summarizes the purchase of land and buildings by Sun Products Inc. from Abbot Medical Center.

Foster Escrow Company
Escrow Statement

	Abbot Medical Center Statement of Seller		Sun Products Inc. Statement of Buyer	
	Charge	Credit	Charge	Credit
Selling price (10% land)		$1,296,000	$1,296,000	
Mortgage assumed by buyer	$ 629,000			$ 629,000
Property taxes—seller's share (to be paid by buyer)	25,000			25,000
Title policy	10,000			
Fire insurance—buyer's share (to be paid by seller)		4,000	4,000	
Appraisal fees	2,000		2,000	
Commission	60,000			
Escrow fee			6,000	
Interest—seller's share (to be paid by buyer)	2,500			2,500
Cash deposit placed in escrow				400,000
Cash to balance accounts	571,500			251,500
Totals	$1,300,000	$1,300,000	$1,308,000	$1,308,000

Instructions: Based on the statement of escrow, prepare the journal entries to be made by Sun Products Inc. and by Abbot Medical Center. Assume the land is carried on Abbot's books at $20,000 and the building has a carrying value of $1,100,000 (cost $1,900,000) on Abbot's books.

problem 10-6 (Acquisition of land and construction of plant)

The Halverson Corporation was organized in June, 1984. In auditing the books of the company, you find a land, buildings, and equipment account with the following details:

Account **Land, Buildings, and Equipment**

Date		Item	Debit	Credit	Balance Debit	Balance Credit
1984						
June	8	Organization fees paid to the state	10,000		10,000	
	16	Land site and old building	325,000		335,000	
	30	Corporate organization costs	10,000		345,000	
July	2	Title clearance fees	8,400		353,400	
Aug.	28	Cost of razing old building	16,000		369,400	
Sept.	1	Salaries of Halverson Corporation executives	60,000		429,400	
	1	Cost to acquire patent for special equipment	70,000		499,400	
Dec.	12	Stock bonus to corporate promoters, 2,000 shares of common stock, $40 par	80,000		579,400	
	15	County real estate tax	14,400		593,800	
	15	Cost of new building completed and occupied on this date	1,600,000		2,193,800	

An analysis of the foregoing account and of other accounts disclosed the following additional information:

(a) The building acquired on June 16, 1984, was valued at $35,000.
(b) The company paid $16,000 for the demolition of the old building, then sold the scrap for $1,000 and credited the proceeds to Miscellaneous Revenue.
(c) The company executives did not participate in the construction of the new building.
(d) The county real estate tax was for the six-month period ended December 31, 1984, and was assessed by the county on the land.

Instructions: Prepare journal entries to correct the books of the Halverson Corporation. Each entry should include an explanation.

problem 10-7 (Exchange of assets)

The Union Development Co. acquired the following assets in exchange for various nonmonetary assets.

1984
Mar. 15 Acquired from another company a computerized lathe in exchange for 3 old lathes. The old lathes had a total cost of $35,000 and had a remaining book value of $13,000. The new lathe had a market value of $20,000, approximately the same value as the three old lathes.

June 1 Acquired 200 acres of land by issuing 2,000 shares of common stock with par value of $10 and market value of $90. Market analysis reveals that the market value of the stock was a reasonable value for the land.

July 15 Acquired a used piece of heavy earth-moving equipment, market value $25,000, by exchanging a used molding machine with a market value of $5,000 (book value $2,000; cost $10,000) and land with a market value of $25,000 (cost $10,000). Cash of $5,000 was received by Union Development Co. as part of the transaction.

Aug. 15 Acquired a patent, franchise, and copyright for 2 used milling machines. The book value of each milling machine was $1,500 and each had originally cost $10,000. The market value of each machine is $12,500. It is estimated that the patent and franchise have about the same market values, and the market value of the copyright is 50% of the market value of the patent.

Nov. 1 Acquired from a dealer a new packaging machine for 4 old packaging machines. The old machines had a total cost of $50,000 and a total remaining book value of $20,000. The new packaging machine has an indicated market value of $25,000, approximately the same value of the four old machines.

Instructions: Prepare the journal entries required on Union Development Co. books to record the exchanges.

problem 10-8 (Exchange of assets)

A review of the books of Busbee Electric Co. disclosed that there were five transactions involving gains and losses on the exchange of fixed assets. The transactions were recorded as indicated in the following ledger accounts.

Cash				Plant Assets				Accum. Depr. — Plant Assets		
(2)	5,000	(5)	1,000	(1)	10,000	(3)	118,000	(3)	110,000	
(3)	6,000			(2)	25,000	(4)	300,000	(4)	390,000	

Intangible Assets		Gain on Exchange — Plant Assets			Loss on Exchange — Plant Assets		
(5)	1,000		(1)	10,000	(3)	2,000	
			(2)	30,000			
			(4)	90,000

Investigation disclosed the following facts concerning these dealer-dealer transactions:

(1) Exchanged a piece of equipment with a $50,000 original cost, $20,000 book value, and $30,000 current market value for a piece of similar equipment owned by Creer Electric that had a $60,000 original cost, $10,000 book value, and a $30,000 current market value.
(2) Exchanged a machine, cost $70,000, book value $10,000, current market value $40,000, for a similar machine, market value $35,000, and $5,000 in cash.
(3) Exchanged a building, cost $150,000, book value $40,000, current market value $30,000, for a building with market value of $24,000 plus cash of $6,000.
(4) Exchanged a factory building, cost $850,000, book value $460,000, current market value $550,000, for equipment owned by Crestwood Inc. that had an original cost of $900,000, accumulated depreciation of $325,000, and current market value of $550,000.
(5) Exchanged a patent, cost $12,000, book value $6,000, current market value $3,000 and cash of $1,000 for another patent with market value of $4,000.

Instructions: Analyze each recorded transaction as to its compliance with generally accepted accounting principles. Prepare adjusting journal entries where required.

problem 10-9 (Acquisition of intangible assets)

In your audit of the books of Quist Corporation for the year ending September 30, 1984, you found the following items in connection with the company's patents account:

(a) The company had spent $102,000 during its fiscal year ended September 30, 1983, for research and development costs and debited this amount to its patent account. Your review of the company's cost records indicated the company had spent a total of $123,500 for the research and development of its patents, of which only $21,500 spent in its fiscal year ended September 30, 1982, had been debited to Research and Development Expense.
(b) The patents were issued on April 1, 1983. Legal expenses in connection with the issuance of the patents of $14,280 were debited to Legal and Professional Fees.
(c) The company paid a retainer of $7,500 on October 5, 1983, for legal services in connection with an infringement suit brought against it. This amount was debited to Deferred Costs.
(d) A letter dated October 15, 1984, from the company's attorneys in reply to your inquiry as to liabilities of the company existing at September 30, 1984, indicated that a settlement of the infringement suit had been arranged. The other party had agreed to drop the suit and to release the company from all future liabilities for $16,000. Additional fees due to the attorneys amounted to $590.

Instructions: From the information given, prepare correcting journal entries as of September 30, 1984.

problem 10-10 (Acquisition of intangible assets)

Transactions during 1984 of the newly organized Barstow Corporation included the following:

Jan. 2 Paid legal fees of $10,000 and stock certificate costs of $3,200 to complete organization of the corporation.

15 Hired a clown to stand in front of the corporate office for two weeks and hand out pamphlets and candy to create goodwill for the new enterprise. Clown cost $800; candy and pamphlets, $500.

Apr. 1 Patented a newly developed process with the following costs:

Legal fees to obtain patent	$22,400
Patent application and licensing fees	3,200
Total	$25,600

It is estimated that in five years other companies will have developed improved processes making the Barstow Corporation process obsolete.

May 1 Acquired both a license to use a special type of container and a distinctive trademark to be printed on the container in exchange for 600 shares of Barstow Corporation no par common stock selling for $80 per share. The license is worth twice as much as the trademark, both of which may be used for 6 years.

July 1 Constructed a shed for $50,000 to house prototypes of experimental models to be developed in future research projects.

Dec. 31 Salaries for an engineer and a chemist involved in product development totaled $100,000 in 1984.

Instructions:

(1) Give journal entries to record the foregoing transactions. (Give explanations in support of your entries.)

(2) Present in good form the "Intangible assets" section of the Barstow Corporation balance sheet at December 31, 1984.

problem 10-11 (Capital vs. revenue expenditures)

The Romney Company completed a program of expansion and improvement of its plant during 1984. You are provided with the following information concerning its buildings account:

(a) On October 31, 1984, a 30-foot extension to the present factory building was completed at a contract cost of $108,000.

(b) During the course of construction, the following costs were incurred for the removal of the end wall of the building where the extension was to be constructed:

(1) Payroll costs during the month of April arising from employees' time spent in removing of the wall, $6,940.

(2) Payments to a salvage company for removing unusual debris, $780.

(c) The cost of the original structure allocable to the end wall was estimated to be $26,400, with accumulated depreciation thereon of $11,100; $7,080 was received by Romney Company from the construction company for windows and other assorted materials salvaged from the old wall.

(d) The old flooring was covered with a new type long-lasting floor covering at a cost of $5,290.

(e) The interior of the plant was repainted in new bright colors for a contract price of $4,875.

(f) New and improved shelving was installed at a cost of $858.

(g) Old electrical wiring was replaced at a cost of $10,218. Cost of the old wiring was determined to be $4,650 with accumulated depreciation to date of $2,055.

(h) New electrical fixtures using fluorescent bulbs were installed. The new fixtures were purchased on the installment plan; the schedule of monthly payments showed total payments of $9,300, which included interest and carrying charges of $720. The old fixtures were carried at a cost of $2,790 with accumulated depreciation to date of $1,200. The old fixtures had no scrap value.

Instructions: Prepare journal entries including explanations for the above information. Briefly justify the capitalization vs. revenue decision for each item.

problem 10-12 (Self-construction of equipment)

Ellford Corporation received a $400,000 low bid from a reputable manufacturer for the construction of special production equipment needed by Ellford in an expansion program. Because the company's own plant was not operating at capacity, Ellford decided to construct the equipment there and recorded the following production costs related to the construction:

Services of consulting engineer	$ 10,000
Work subcontracted	20,000
Materials	200,000
Plant labor normally assigned to production	65,000
Plant labor normally assigned to maintenance	100,000
Total	$395,000

Management prefers to record the cost of the equipment under the incremental cost method. Approximately 40% of the corporation's production is devoted to government supply contracts which are all based in some way on cost. The contracts require that any self-constructed equipment be allocated its full share of all costs related to the construction.

The following information is also available:

(a) The above production labor was for partial fabrication of the equipment in the plant. Skilled personnel were required and were assigned from other projects. The maintenance labor would have been idle time of nonproduction plant employees who would have been retained on the payroll whether or not their services were utilized.
(b) Payroll taxes and employee fringe benefits are approximately 30% of labor cost and are included in manufacturing overhead cost. Total manufacturing overhead for the year was $5,630,000 including the $100,000 maintenance labor used to construct the equipment.
(c) Manufacturing overhead is approximately 50% variable and is applied on the basis of production labor cost. Production labor cost for the year for the corporation's normal products totaled $6,810,000.
(d) General and administrative expenses include $22,500 of executive salary cost and $10,500 of postage, telephone, supplies, and miscellaneous expenses identifiable with this equipment construction.

Instructions:

(1) Prepare a schedule computing the amount that should be reported as the full cost of the constructed equipment to meet the requirements of the government contracts. Any supporting computations should be in good form.
(2) Prepare a schedule computing the incremental cost of the constructed equipment.
(3) What is the greatest amount that should be capitalized as the cost of the equipment? Why? (AICPA adapted)

problem 10-13 (Valuation of plant assets)

At December 31, 1983, certain accounts included in the property, plant, and equipment section of the Townsand Company's balance sheet had the following balances:

Land	$100,000
Buildings	800,000
Leasehold Improvements	500,000
Machinery and Equipment	700,000

During 1984 the following transactions occurred:

(a) Land site number 621 was acquired for $1,000,000. Additionally, to acquire the land Townsand paid a $60,000 commission to a real estate agent. Costs of $15,000 were incurred to clear the land. During the course of clearing the land, timber and gravel were recovered and sold for $5,000.
(b) A second tract of land (site number 622) with a building was acquired for $300,000. The closing statement indicated that the land value was $200,000 and the building value was $100,000. Shortly after acquisition, the building was demolished at a cost of $30,000. A new building was constructed for $150,000 plus the following costs:

Excavation fees	$11,000
Architectural design fees	8,000
Building permit fee	1,000
Imputed interest on funds used during construction	6,000

The building was completed and occupied on September 30, 1984.
(c) A third tract of land (site number 623) was acquired for $600,000 and was put on the market for resale.
(d) Extensive work was done to a building occupied by Townsand under a lease agreement that expires on December 31, 1993. The total cost of the work was $125,000, which consisted of the following:

Painting of ceilings	$ 10,000	(estimated useful life is one year)
Electrical work	35,000	(estimated useful life is ten years)
Construction of extension to current working area	80,000	(estimated useful life is thirty years)
	$125,000	

The lessor paid ½ of the costs incurred in connection with the extension to the current working area.

(e) During December 1984 costs of $65,000 were incurred to improve leased office space. The related lease will terminate on December 31, 1986, and is not expected to be renewed.

(f) A group of new machines was purchased under a royalty agreement which provides for payment of royalties based on units of production for the machines. The invoice price of the machines was $75,000, freight costs were $2,000, unloading charges were $1,500, and royalty payments for 1984 were $13,000.

Instructions:

(1) Prepare a detailed analysis of the changes in each of the following balance sheet accounts for 1984: Land, Buildings, Leasehold Improvements, and Machinery and Equipment. (Disregard the related accumulated depreciation accounts.)

(2) List the items in the fact situation which were not used to determine the answer to (1), and indicate where, or if, these items should be included in Townsand's financial statements.

(AICPA adapted)

*problem 10-14 (Computation of goodwill)

The Escondido Corp. in considering acquisition of the Mapleton Company assembles the following information relative to the company.

Mapleton Company
Balance Sheet
December 31, 1984

	Per Company's Books	As Adjusted by Appraisal and Audit
Assets		
Current assets	$ 96,000	$ 92,000
Investments	32,000	28,000
Land, buildings, and equipment (net)	279,200	260,000
Goodwill	64,000	64,000
	$471,200	$444,000
Liabilities and Stockholders' Equity		
Current liabilities	$ 15,000	$ 15,000
Long-term liabilities	160,000	160,000
Capital stock	160,000	160,000
Retained earnings	136,200	109,000
	$471,200	$444,000

An analysis of retained earnings discloses the following information:

	Per Company's Books	As Adjusted by Appraisal and Audit
Retained earnings, January 1, 1982	$115,560	$ 94,600
Add net income, 1982–1984*	49,440	43,200
Deduct dividends 1982–1984	(28,800)	(28,800)
Retained earnings, December 31, 1984	$136,200	$109,000
*After loss on sale of assets in 1984	$ 48,960	$ 52,800

*Problem to Appendix material

Instructions:

(1) Calculate the amount to be paid for goodwill, assuming that earnings of the future are expected to be the same as average normal earnings of the past three years, 10% is accepted as a reasonable return on net assets other than goodwill as of December 31, 1984, and average earnings in excess of 10% are capitalized at 16% in determining goodwill.

(2) Give the entry on the books of the Escondido Corp., assuming purchase of the assets of the Mapleton Company and assumption of its liabilities on the basis as indicated in (1). Cash is paid for net assets acquired.

*problem 10-15 (Computation of goodwill)

West Coast Industries Inc. assembles the following data relative to the Tacoma Corp. in determining the amount to be paid for the net assets and goodwill of the latter company:

Assets at appraised value (before goodwill)	$1,700,000
Liabilities	640,000
Stockholders' equity	$1,060,000

Net earnings (after elimination of extraordinary items):

1980	$180,000
1981	144,000
1982	194,000
1983	190,000
1984	202,000

Instructions: Calculate the amount to be paid for goodwill under each of the following assumptions:

(1) Average earnings are capitalized at 16% in arriving at the business worth.

(2) A return of 12% is considered normal on net assets at appraised values; goodwill is valued at 5 years' excess earnings.

(3) A return of 14% is considered normal on net assets at appraised values; excess earnings are to be capitalized at 20%.

(4) Goodwill is valued at the sum of the earnings of the last 3 years in excess of a 10% annual yield on net assets at appraised values. (Assume that net assets are the same for the 3-year period.)

(5) A return of 10% is considered normal on net identifiable assets at their appraised values. Excess earnings are expected to continue for 10 years. Goodwill is to be valued by the present value method using a 20% rate. (Use Appendix A present value table.)

*Problem to Appendix material

11 PLANT AND INTANGIBLE ASSETS —UTILIZATION AND RETIREMENT

CHAPTER OBJECTIVES

Explain the concept of periodic charges to represent the utilization of assets in producing revenue.

Discuss the allocation of historical asset cost versus periodic charges based on current cost.

Identify and describe the factors determining the periodic depreciation charge.

Describe, illustrate, and evaluate alternative methods of depreciation.

Discuss the amortization of intangible assets and the depletion of wasting assets.

Describe and illustrate the accounting for asset retirements.

A fundamental characteristic of most plant and intangible assets is that as they are used to produce revenue, their utility for future services declines. A notable exception to this generalization is land—even farm land can be kept productive indefinitely with proper fertilization and care. Other plant assets, however, have limited lives and are literally "used up" in producing revenue. Intangible assets, although not physically used up or exhausted, tend to decline in utility with the passage of time.

As an asset is used to produce revenue, a charge against revenue to represent the usage is required if proper matching is to occur and a meaningful income figure is to be reported. In practice, three different terms have evolved to describe this charge depending on the type of asset involved. For plant assets, generally the charge is referred to as **depreciation.** For mineral and other natural resources, sometimes referred to as *wasting assets*, the charge that describes the depleting of the source of the revenue is appropriately called **depletion.** For intangible assets, such as patents, copyrights and goodwill, the charge is referred to as **amortization.** Sometimes the latter term is used generically to encompass all of the other terms. Because the principles underlying each of these terms are similar, they are discussed together in this chapter.

HISTORICAL COST VERSUS CURRENT COST ALLOCATION

A difficult problem in accounting for plant and intangible asset utilization arises in determining the periodic charges to revenues, especially in periods of changing prices. In accounting practice, depreciation, depletion, and amortization have traditionally been viewed as an allocation of the acquisition cost over the life of the asset. This meaning can be observed in the definition of depreciation accounting adopted by the Committee on Terminology in the 1940's and still accepted today:

> *Depreciation accounting* is a system of accounting which aims to distribute the cost or other basic value of tangible capital assets, less salvage (if any), over the estimated useful life of the unit (which may be a group of assets) in a systematic and rational manner. It is a process of allocation, not of valuation. *Depreciation for the year* is the portion of the total charge under such a system that is allocated to the year. Although the allocation may properly take into account occurrences during the year, it is not intended to be a measurement of the effect of all such occurrences.[1]

Under this view, the total amount charged against revenue is fixed by the acquisition cost less any estimated recoverable salvage or residual value. While the pattern of charges may vary with the allocation method used, the total amount charged against revenue cannot exceed the historical cost of the asset. For any group of assets at any given time, the cumulative amount charged against past revenue plus the remaining asset carrying or book value will equal the original acquisition cost adjusted by any additions or betterments.

There are many who advocate a charge against revenue based on a current asset value referred to as **replacement cost** or **current cost.** This allocation approach matches current rather than past costs against current revenues, resulting in a net income figure that better reflects income available for dividends and that is more useful for estimating future cash flows of the business entity. The concept of replacement cost was discussed in

[1] *Accounting Research and Terminology Bulletins—Final Edition*, "Accounting Terminology Bulletins, No. 1, Review and Résumé" (New York: American Institute of Certified Public Accountants, 1961), par. 56.

conjunction with inventories in Chapter 8. Plant assets, like inventories, must be replaced, and that portion of current and future earnings needed for replacement will not be available for distribution to owners or for payments to creditors.

Replacement costs reflect changes in the prices of specific assets. Another approach to accounting for the impact of price changes is **constant-dollar adjustment** of historical costs. This approach restates historical costs to reflect general price-level changes, i.e., changes in the value of the monetary unit measured by a general index.

As discussed in previous chapters, increasing inflationary pressures prompted the SEC, and later the FASB, to require supplemental disclosure of the effects of changing prices. Currently, under FASB Statement No. 33, companies with inventories and tangible fixed assets totaling more than $125 million or total assets exceeding $1 billion are required to report, as supplemental information, both constant-dollar and current-cost information. For plant assets, disclosure requirements apply to both the remaining asset cost and the charge against current revenue.

Historical cost is still the basis for financial statement reporting. However, various attempts have been made to modify the application of historical cost allocation to partially soften the impact of changing price levels. Emphasis in this chapter is on the methods used to allocate the historical acquisition cost against revenue and the modifications made to consider price changes. Supplemental disclosures for price changes are discussed and illustrated in Chapter 24.

DEPRECIATION OF PLANT ASSETS

Depreciation is the allocation of asset cost over the periods benefited by the use of the asset. There has been a tendency, however, on the part of many readers of financial statements to interpret depreciation accounting as somehow related to the accumulation of a fund for asset replacement. The use of such terms as "provision for depreciation" and "reserve for depreciation" has contributed toward this misinterpretation.

The charge for depreciation is the recognition of the declining service value of an asset. The nature of this charge is no different from those made to recognize the expiration of insurance premiums or patent rights. It is true that revenues equal to or in excess of expenses for a period result in a recovery of these expenses; salary expense is thus recovered by revenues, as is insurance expense, patent amortization, and charges for depreciation. But this does not mean that cash equal to the recorded depreciation will be segregated for property replacement. Revenues may be applied to many uses: to the increase in receivables, inventories, or other working capital items; to the acquisition of new property or other noncurrent items; to the retirement of debt or the redemption of stock; or to the payment of dividends. If a special fund is to be available for the replacement of property, special authorization by management would be required. Such a fund is seldom found, however, because fund earnings would usually be less than the return from alternative uses of the resources.

Factors Determining the Periodic Depreciation Charge

Four factors must be recognized in arriving at the periodic charge for the use of a depreciable asset: (1) **asset cost,** (2) **residual or salvage value,** (3) **useful life,** and (4) **pattern of use.**

Asset Cost. The **cost** of an asset includes all the expenditures relating to its acquisition and preparation for use as described in Chapter 10. The cost of an asset less the expected residual value, if any, is the depreciable cost or depreciation base, i.e., the portion of asset cost to be charged against future revenue.

Residual or Salvage Value. The **residual** or **salvage value** of a plant asset is the amount that can reasonably be expected to be realized upon retirement of the asset. This may depend on the retirement policy of the company as well as market conditions and other factors. If, for example, the company normally uses equipment until it is physically exhausted and no longer serviceable, the residual value, represented by the scrap or junk that may be salvaged, may be nominal. But if the company normally trades its equipment after a relatively short period of use, the residual value, represented by the value in trade, may be relatively high. In some cases there may be a cost to dismantle and remove an asset. The residual value should be adjusted to a lower amount to reflect these anticipated costs. From a theoretical point of view, any net estimated residual value should be subtracted from cost in arriving at the cost of the asset to be allocated. Therefore, if dismantling and removal costs are expected to exceed the ultimate salvage value, the excess or "negative salvage value" should be added to the cost in arriving at the total cost to be allocated.

In practice, both salvage values and dismantling and removal costs are frequently ignored in determining periodic depreciation charges. Disregard of these items is not objectionable when they are relatively small or not subject to reasonable estimation and when it is doubtful whether greater accuracy will be gained through such refinement.

A theoretical question related to residual or salvage values is whether the effects of changing prices should be anticipated in its estimation. The general approach to this question by the accounting principles-setting bodies has been that if price changes are ignored in the allocation process, they should be ignored in the estimation of residual or salvage values. Thus, the salvage value used to determine the depreciable cost is based on the conditions existing at the date of asset acquisition.

Useful Life. Plant assets other than land have a limited **useful life** as a result of certain physical and functional factors. The **physical factors** that limit the service life of an asset are (1) *wear and tear,* (2) *deterioration and decay,* and (3) *damage or destruction.* Everyone is familiar with the processes of wear and tear that render an automobile, a typewriter, or furniture no longer usable. A tangible asset, whether used or not, is also subject to deterioration and decay through aging. Finally, fire, flood, earthquake, or accident may reduce or terminate the useful life of an asset.

The **functional factors** limiting the lives of these assets are (1) *inadequacy* and (2) *obsolescence.* An asset may lose its usefulness when, as a result of altered business requirements or technical progress, it no longer can produce sufficient revenue to justify its continued use. Although the asset is still usable, its inability to produce revenue has cut short its service life. An example of rapid obsolescence can be observed in the computer industry. The rapid technological changes in this field have rendered perfectly good electronic equipment obsolete for efficient continued use long before the physical asset itself wore out.

Both physical and functional factors must be recognized in estimating the useful life of a depreciable plant asset. This recognition requires estimating what events will take place in the future and requires careful judgment on the part of the accountant.[2] Physical factors are more readily apparent than functional factors in predicting asset life. But when functional factors are expected to hasten the retirement of an asset, these must also be recognized.

Both physical and functional factors may operate gradually or may emerge suddenly. Recognition of depreciation is usually limited to the conditions that operate gradually and are reasonably foreseeable. For example, a sudden change in demand for a certain product may make an asset worthless, or an accident may destroy an asset, but these are unforeseeable events requiring recognition when they occur.

Since the service life of a depreciable plant asset is affected by maintenance and repairs, the policy with respect to these matters must be considered in estimating useful life. Low standards of maintenance and repair keep these charges at a minimum but may hasten the physical deterioration of the asset, thus requiring higher-than-normal allocations for depreciation. On the other hand, high standards of maintenance and repairs will mean higher charges for these items; but with a policy prolonging the usefulness of assets, periodic allocations for depreciation may be reduced.

The useful life of a depreciable plant asset may be expressed in terms of either an estimated time factor or an estimated use factor. The time factor may be a period of months or years; the use factor may be a number of hours of service or a number of units of output. The cost of the asset is allocated in accordance with the lapse of time or degrees of use. The rate of cost allocation may be modified by other factors, but basically depreciation must be recognized on a time or use basis.

The useful life of assets has often been used by Congress and the Treasury Department to offset the effects of inflation on the tax return and to

---

[2]Although the concept of useful life is generally recognized to be difficult to apply, there has been relatively little written on it in accounting literature. For a thorough discussion of the topic, see Charles Lamden, Dale L. Gerboth, and Thomas McRae, "Accounting for Depreciable Assets," *Accounting Research Monograph No. 1* (New York: American Institute of Certified Public Accountants, 1975), Ch. 5.

stimulate investment and economic growth. For example, during World War II, a tax provision was passed by Congress permitting companies that had provided facilities and equipment to produce emergency war products to depreciate these assets over a very short period of time. This enabled a company to write off its cost against revenue rapidly, thus reducing taxable income and deferring payment of income tax on current revenues until after the short life had expired. In 1971 the Treasury Department introduced the Asset Depreciation Range (ADR) system which allowed companies to vary the lives of their depreciable assets over a range 20% above or below the guideline lives provided in the regulations for different types of depreciable assets. This permitted greater flexibility on the part of users to adjust their depreciation charge by altering useful lives.

More recently, Congress passed the Economic Recovery Tax Act (ERTA) of 1981 that introduced a new approach to depreciation for tax purposes. The traditional depreciation methods were replaced with an approach referred to as the **accelerated cost recovery system (ACRS).** In general, this method permits companies to write off the cost of assets over a shorter period than the actual economic life. The purpose of the legislation was to encourage businesses to invest in new assets and thus stimulate the economy that had been suffering from a recession. The accelerated cost recovery system is discussed in detail later in the chapter.

Pattern of Use. In order to match service cost against revenue, it is necessary to consider how an asset's services are actually expected to be used over the life of the asset. Periodic depreciation charges should reflect as closely as possible the **pattern of use.** If the asset produces a varying revenue pattern, then the depreciation charges should vary in a corresponding manner. When depreciation is measured in terms of a time factor, the pattern of use must be estimated. Several somewhat arbitrary methods have come into common use. Each method represents a different pattern and is designed to make the time basis approximate the use basis. The time factor is employed in two general classes of methods, *straight-line depreciation* and *decreasing-charge depreciation.* When depreciation is measured in terms of a use factor, the units of use must be estimated. The depreciation charge varies periodically in accordance with the services provided by the asset. The use factor is employed in *service-hours depreciation* and in *productive-output depreciation.*

Recording Periodic Depreciation

The periodic allocation of plant asset costs is made by debiting either a production overhead cost account or a selling or administrative expense account, and crediting an allowance or contra asset account. If the charge is made to a production overhead account, it becomes part of the cost of the finished and unfinished goods inventories and is deferred to the extent inventory has not been sold or completed. If the charge is made to selling or administrative expenses, it is considered to be a period cost and is written off against revenue as an operating expense of the current period.

The valuation or allowance account that is credited in recording periodic depreciation is commonly titled Accumulated Depreciation. The accumulation of expired cost in a separate account rather than crediting the asset account directly permits identification of the original cost of the asset and the accumulated depreciation. The FASB requires disclosure of both cost and accumulated depreciation for plant assets on the balance sheet or notes to the financial statements. This enables the user to estimate the relative age of all assets and provides some basis for evaluating the effects of price-level changes on the company's plant assets.

A separate valuation account is maintained for each asset or class of assets requiring the use of a separate depreciation rate. When a subsidiary property ledger is maintained for land, buildings, and equipment, it normally provides for the accumulation of depreciation allocations on the individual assets. Such records are variously termed Unit Property Records, Property Ledger, or Plant Asset Control Records. They usually involve the control account principle, assets being summarized in the general ledger, and detail being recorded in subsidiary ledgers.

The use of a property record consisting of cards or separate sheets provides a flexible record since assets can be arranged in any desired order. One card or one sheet is provided for each asset on which all information with respect to the item is listed. For buildings and equipment, this information usually includes a description of the asset, location, name of the vendor, guarantee period, insurance carried, date acquired, original cost, transportation charge, installation cost, estimated life, estimated residual value, depreciation rate, depreciation to date, major expenditures for repairs and improvements, and proceeds from final disposal. Property files are frequently maintained on tabulating cards, magnetic tapes, or in the memory of an electronic computer. When the information is maintained and stored in this form, it may be easily sorted and used to make depreciation computations and accounting entries.

Separate debits relating to individual property items in the subsidiary ledger support the land, buildings, and equipment balance in the general ledger; separate credits representing individual property item cost allocations in the subsidiary ledger support the accumulated depreciation balance in the general ledger. When a property item consists of a number of units or structural elements with varying lives and these units are recorded separately, depreciation is recognized in terms of the respective lives of the different units.

Methods of Depreciation

As mentioned earlier, there are a number of different methods for allocating the costs of depreciable assets. The method used in any specific instance is a matter of judgment and should be selected to most closely approximate the actual pattern of use expected from the asset. The following methods are described in this chapter:

Time-Factor Methods
- (1) Straight-line depreciation
- (2) Decreasing-charge depreciation
  - (a) Sum-of-the-years-digits method
  - (b) Declining-balance method
  - (c) Double-declining-balance method
- (3) Accelerated cost recovery system

Use-Factor Methods
- (1) Service-hours method
- (2) Productive-output method

Group-Rate and Composite-Rate Methods
- (1) Group depreciation
- (2) Composite depreciation

Two other time-factor methods each providing for increasing charges, the *annuity method* and the *sinking fund method*, require the use of compound interest calculations. These methods are rarely encountered in practice.

The examples that follow assume the acquisition of a machine at a cost of $10,000 with a salvage value at the end of its useful life of $500. The following symbols are employed in the formulas for the development of depreciation rates and charges:

C = Asset cost
S = Estimated salvage value
n = Estimated life in years, hours of service, or units of output
r = Depreciation rate per period, per hour of service, or per unit of output
D = Periodic depreciation charge

Time-Factor Methods. The most common methods of cost allocation are related to the passage of time. In general, a productive asset is used up over time. Possible obsolescence due to technological changes is also a function of time. Of the time-factor methods, straight-line depreciation has been the most popular. Decreasing-charge methods and the accelerated cost recovery system are widely used for tax purposes, however, because they provide for higher charges than other methods in the early years of asset use. The result is a deferral of income tax due to the higher deductions for depreciation in the earlier years. These "accelerated depreciation" methods are based largely on the assumption that there will be rapid reductions in asset efficiency, output, or other benefits in the early years of an asset's life. Such reductions may be accompanied by increased charges for maintenance and repairs. Charges for depreciation decline, then, as the economic advantages afforded through ownership of the asset decline. The most commonly used decreasing-charge methods are sum-of-the-years-digits and some variation of a declining-balance method.

Both decreasing-charge methods and asset lives have been used by Congress and the Treasury Department to provide investment incentives and relief for companies when price levels change and replacement costs of existing facilities greatly increase. As a result, many companies use accelerated depreciation methods for tax purposes, but compute depreciation on a straight-line basis for financial reporting purposes. This is the policy followed by General Mills as disclosed in Note 1B in the financial statements reproduced in Appendix B. The difference between taxable income and income reported in the financial statements requires interperiod tax allocation as discussed in Chapter 20.

Straight-line Depreciation. **Straight-line depreciation** relates cost allocation to the passage of time and recognizes equal periodic charges over the life of the asset. The allocation assumes equal usefulness per time period, and in applying this assumption, the charge is not affected by asset productivity or efficiency variations. In developing the periodic charge, an estimate is made of the useful life of the asset in terms of months or years. The difference between the asset cost and residual value is divided by the useful life of the asset in arriving at the cost assigned to each time unit.

Using data for the machine referred to earlier and assuming a 10-year life, annual depreciation is determined as follows:

$$D = \frac{C - S}{n}, \quad \text{or} \quad \frac{\$10{,}000 - \$500}{10} = \$950$$

The depreciation rate is commonly expressed as a percentage to be applied periodically to asset cost. The depreciation rate in the example is calculated as follows: (100% − 5%) ÷ 10 = 9.5%. This percentage applied to cost provides a periodic charge of $950. The rate may also be expressed as a percentage to be applied to depreciable cost—cost less residual value. Expressed in this way the rate is simply the reciprocal value of the useful life expressed in periods, or r (per period) = 1 ÷ n. In the example, then, the annual rate would be 1 ÷ 10 = 10%, and this rate applied to depreciable cost, $9,500, gives an annual charge of $950. A table to summarize the process of cost allocation follows:

Asset Cost Allocation—Straight-Line Method

End of Year	Debit to Depreciation Expense and Credit to Accumulated Depreciation	Balance of Accumulated Depreciation	Asset Book Value
			$10,000
1	$ 950	$ 950	9,050
2	950	1,900	8,100
3	950	2,850	7,150
4	950	3,800	6,200
5	950	4,750	5,250
6	950	5,700	4,300
7	950	6,650	3,350
8	950	7,600	2,400
9	950	8,550	1,450
10	950	9,500	500
	$9,500		

It was indicated earlier that residual value is frequently ignored when this is a relatively minor amount. If this were done in the example, depreciation would be recognized at $1,000 per year instead of $950.

Sum-of-the-Years-Digits Method. The **sum-of-the-years-digits method** provides decreasing charges by applying a series of fractions, each of a smaller value, to depreciable asset cost. Fractions are developed in terms of the sum of the asset life periods. Weights for purposes of developing reducing fractions are the years-digits listed in reverse order. The denominator for the fraction is obtained by adding these weights; the numerator is the weight assigned to the specific year. The denominator for the fraction can be obtained by an alternate calculation: the sum of the digits for the first and last years can be divided by 2 and multiplied by the number of years of asset life. In the example, the denominator can be determined as follows: $([10 + 1] \div 2) \times 10 = 55$. Periodic charges for depreciation using the sum-of-the-years-digits method for the asset previously described are developed as follows:

	Reducing Weights	Reducing Fractions
First year	10	10/55
Second year	9	9/55
Third year	8	8/55
Fourth year	7	7/55
Fifth year	6	6/55
Sixth year	5	5/55
Seventh year	4	4/55
Eighth year	3	3/55
Ninth year	2	2/55
Tenth year	1	1/55
	55	55/55

Depreciation computed by the application of reducing fractions to depreciable cost is summarized in the table below:

Asset Cost Allocation—Sum-of-the-Years-Digits Method

End of Year		Debit to Depreciation Expense and Credit to Accumulated Depreciation	Balance of Accumulated Depreciation	Asset Book Value
				$10,000.00
1	(10/55 × $9,500)	$1,727.27	$1,727.27	8,272.73
2	(9/55 × 9,500)	1,554.55	3,281.82	6,718.18
3	(8/55 × 9,500)	1,381.82	4,663.64	5,336.36
4	(7/55 × 9,500)	1,209.09	5,872.73	4,127.27
5	(6/55 × 9,500)	1,036.36	6,909.09	3,090.91
6	(5/55 × 9,500)	863.64	7,772.73	2,227.27
7	(4/55 × 9,500)	690.91	8,463.64	1,536.36
8	(3/55 × 9,500)	518.18	8,981.82	1,018.18
9	(2/55 × 9,500)	345.45	9,327.27	672.73
10	(1/55 × 9,500)	172.73	9,500.00	500.00
		$9,500.00		

Declining-Balance Method. The **declining-balance method** provides decreasing charges by applying a constant percentage rate to a declining asset book value. The rate to be applied to the declining book value in producing the estimated salvage value at the end of the useful life of the asset is calculated by the following formula:

$$r \text{ (rate per period applicable to declining book value)} = 1 - \sqrt[n]{S \div C}$$

Using the previous asset data and assuming a 10-year asset life, the depreciation rate is determined as follows:

$$1 - \sqrt[10]{\$500 \div \$10{,}000} = 1 - \sqrt[10]{.05} = 1 - .74113 = .25887, \quad \text{or} \quad 25.887\%$$

Dividing the estimated salvage value by cost in the formula above gives .05, the proportion that salvage value at the end of 10 years should be to cost. The tenth root of this value is .74113. Multiplying cost and the successive declining book values by .74113 ten times will reduce the asset to .05 of its cost. The difference between 1 and .74113, or .25887, then, is the rate of decrease to be applied successively in bringing the asset down to .05 of its original balance. Since it is impossible to bring a value down to zero by a constant multiplier, a residual value must be assigned to the asset in using the formula. In the absence of an expected residual value, a nominal value of $1 can be assumed for this purpose.

Depreciation calculated by application of the 25.887% rate to the declining book value is summarized in the following table:

Asset Cost Allocation—Declining-Balance Method

End of Year	Debit to Depreciation Expense and Credit to Accumulated Depreciation		Balance of Accumulated Depreciation	Asset Book Value
				$10,000.00
1	(25.887% × $10,000.00)	$2,588.70	$2,588.70	7,411.30
2	(25.887% × 7,411.30)	1,918.56	4,507.26	5,492.74
3	(25.887% × 5,492.74)	1,421.91	5,929.17	4,070.83
4	(25.887% × 4,070.83)	1,053.82	6,982.99	3,017.01
5	(25.887% × 3,017.01)	781.01	7,764.00	2,236.00
6	(25.887% × 2,236.00)	578.83	8,342.83	1,657.17
7	(25.887% × 1,657.17)	428.99	8,771.82	1,228.18
8	(25.887% × 1,228.18)	317.94	9,089.76	910.24
9	(25.887% × 910.24)	235.63	9,325.39	674.61
10	(25.887% × 674.61)	174.61*	9,500.00	500.00
		$9,500.00		

*Discrepancy due to rounding.

Instead of developing an exact rate that will produce a salvage value of $500, it is usually more convenient to approximate a rate that will provide satisfactory cost allocation; since depreciation involves an estimate, there is little assurance that rate refinement will produce more accurate results. In the previous illustration, the use of a rate of 25% is more convenient than 25.887%; differences are not material.

Double-Declining-Balance Method. Federal income tax regulations provide that for certain assets acquired before 1981, depreciation is allowed at a fixed percentage equal to double the straight-line rate. This is referred to as the **double-declining-balance method.** Although a residual value is not taken into account in employing this method, depreciation charges should not be made after reaching the residual balance. The percentage is readily calculated as follows:

Estimated Life in Years	Straight-Line Rate	Double-Declining-Balance Rate
3	33⅓%	66⅔%
5	20	40
6	16⅔	33⅓
8	12½	25
10	10	20
20	5	10

Depreciation using the double-declining-balance method for the asset described earlier is summarized in the table that follows:

Asset Cost Allocation—Double-Declining-Balance Method

End of Year	Debit to Depreciation Expense and Credit to Accumulated Depreciation		Balance of Accumulated Depreciation	Asset Book Value
				$10,000.00
1	(20% × $10,000.00)	$2,000.00	$2,000.00	8,000.00
2	(20% × 8,000.00)	1,600.00	3,600.00	6,400.00
3	(20% × 6,400.00)	1,280.00	4,880.00	5,120.00
4	(20% × 5,120.00)	1,024.00	5,904.00	4,096.00
5	(20% × 4,096.00)	819.20	6,723.20	3,276.80
6	(20% × 3,276.80)	655.36	7,378.56	2,621.44
7	(20% × 2,621.44)	524.29	7,902.85	2,097.15
8	(20% × 2,097.15)	419.43	8,322.28	1,677.72
9	(20% × 1,677.72)	335.54	8,657.82	1,342.18
10	(20% × 1,342.18)	268.44	8,926.26	1,073.74
		$8,926.26		

It should be noted that the rate of 20% is applied to the book value of the asset each year. In applying this rate, the book value after ten years exceeds the residual value by $573.74 ($1,073.74 − $500.00). This condition arises wherever residual values are relatively low in amount. One way to make the book value equal the residual value is to change from the double-declining-balance method to another acceptable method prior to the end of the asset's useful life.

Accelerated Cost Recovery System (ACRS). As mentioned previously, the Economic Recovery Tax Act (ERTA) of 1981 introduced a new time-factor method of computing depreciation for tax purposes called the **accelerated cost recovery system (ACRS).** The new method was intended to both simplify the computation of depreciation and provide for a more rapid recovery of asset cost to offset inflation and stimulate investment.

In general, the new system requires that property acquired after December 31, 1980, be depreciated over three, five, ten, or fifteen years, depending on the type of property. The appropriate recovery period for a specific asset is determined by reference to the asset depreciation range (ADR) midpoint lives previously used for tax depreciation. Examples of three-year recovery property include automobiles, light-duty trucks, and machinery and equipment used in connection with research and experimentation. The five-year property class includes most machinery, equipment, and furniture. The ten-year class includes certain real property with an ADR midpoint life of twelve and one-half years or less and certain types of specialized equipment. The fifteen-year class includes all real property except for the limited types of real property included in the ten-year class.

Cost recovery tables for each class of property specify the percentage of cost recovery for each year. The tables developed for this purpose provide for a declining pattern of recovery (depreciation) with built-in switches to straight-line depreciation to assure 100 percent recovery in the time specified. The tables provide for one-half year's depreciation in the year of acquisition for three, five, and ten-year property. For fifteen-year property, the percentage depends on the month in which the property was acquired. Salvage values are ignored under ACRS, and the recovery percentage is applied to asset cost.

The following table shows the cost percentages for three, five, and ten-year property:

Year	Three-Year Property	Five-Year Property	Ten-Year Property
1	25%	15%	8%
2	38	22	14
3	37	21	12
4		21	10
5		21	10
6			10
7			9
8			9
9			9
10			9
	100%	100%	100%

To illustrate application of ACRS, assume that the machine used in previous examples was purchased in 1982. Although the machine has an estimated useful life of ten years, it is classified as five-year recovery property under the ACRS guidelines. Depreciation charges on the machine for tax purposes are as follows:

Year	Cost	Recovery Percentage	ACRS Depreciation
1982	$10,000	15%	$ 1,500
1983	10,000	22	2,200
1984	10,000	21	2,100
1985	10,000	21	2,100
1986	10,000	21	2,100
		100%	$10,000

The depreciation charge for the first year is 15 percent regardless of when the machine was purchased during 1982. At the end of the fifth year, the entire cost of the machine has been written off without regard to salvage value.

For tax purposes, ACRS is mandatory for most assets acquired after December 31, 1980. In lieu of the cost recovery table percentages, however, a taxpayer may elect to use straight-line depreciation over specified recovery periods. A taxpayer may also elect to apply one of the use-factor methods, discussed later in the chapter, instead of ACRS. For assets acquired before 1981, depreciation is computed using the method elected in the year of acquisition.

Evaluation of Time-Factor Methods. Using the straight-line method, depreciation is a constant or fixed charge each period. When the life of an asset is affected primarily by the lapse of time rather than by the degree of use, recognition of depreciation as a constant charge is generally appropriate. However, net income measurements become particularly sensitive to changes in the volume of business activity. With above-normal activity, there is no increase in the depreciation charge; with below-normal activity, revenue is still charged with the costs of assets standing ready to serve.

Straight-line depreciation is a widely used procedure. It is readily understood and frequently parallels observable asset deterioration. It has the advantage of simplicity and under normal conditions offers a satisfactory means of cost allocation. Normal asset conditions exist when (1) assets have been accumulated over a period of years so that the total of depreciation plus maintenance is comparatively even from period to period, and (2) service potentials of assets are being steadily reduced by functional as well as physical factors. The absence of either of these conditions may suggest the use of some depreciation method other than straight line.

Decreasing-charge methods can be supported as reasonable approaches to asset cost allocation when the annual benefits provided by a property item decline as it grows older. These methods, too, are suggested when an asset requires increasing maintenance and repairs over its useful life.[3] When straight-line depreciation is employed, the combined charges for depreciation, maintenance, and repairs will increase over the life of the asset; when the decreasing-charge methods are used, the combined charges will tend to be equalized.

Other factors suggesting the use of a decreasing-charge method include: (1) the anticipation of a significant contribution in early periods with the extent of the contribution to be realized in later periods less definite; (2) the possibility that inadequacy or obsolescence may result in premature retire-

---

[3]The AICPA Committee on Accounting Procedure has stated, "The declining-balance method is one of those which meets the requirements of being 'systematic and rational.' In those cases where the expected productivity or revenue-earning power of the asset is relatively greater during the earlier years of its life, or where maintenance charges tend to increase during the later years, the declining-balance method may well provide the most satisfactory allocation of cost." The Committee would apply these conclusions to other decreasing-charge methods, including the sum-of-the-years-digits method, that produce substantially similar results. See *Accounting Research and Terminology Bulletins—Final Edition,* "No. 44 (Revised), Declining-Balance Depreciation" (New York: American Institute of Certified Public Accountants, 1961), par. 2.

ment of the asset. In the event of premature retirement, depreciation charges will have absorbed what would otherwise require recognition as a loss.

In passing the Economic Recovery Tax Act of 1981, members of Congress were concerned with economic recovery rather than accounting principles. Asset life and pattern of use were not considered important in the establishment of recovery periods and percentages. Both the AICPA and FASB have expressed concern over this new tax incentive and have stated that ACRS should be used for financial reporting only if the lives and patterns inherent in the ACRS tables coincide closely with actual asset lives and patterns of use. In general, most accountants feel that this will seldom occur. Thus, the periodic depreciation charge on the income tax return will differ from the one reported in the financial statements even more frequently than in the past.

Depreciation for Partial Periods. The discussion thus far has assumed that assets were purchased on the first day of a company's fiscal period. In reality, of course, asset transactions occur throughout the year. When a time-factor method is used, depreciation on assets acquired or disposed of during the year may be based on the number of days the asset was held during the period. When the level of acquisitions and retirements is significant, however, companies often adopt a less burdensome policy for recognizing depreciation for partial periods. Some alternatives found in practice include the following:

(1) Depreciation is recognized to the nearest whole month. Assets acquired on or before the 15th of the month are considered owned for the entire month; assets acquired after the 15th are not considered owned for any part of the month. Conversely, assets sold on or before the 15th of the month are not considered owned for any part of the month; assets sold after the 15th are considered owned for the entire month.

(2) Depreciation is recognized to the nearest whole year. Assets acquired during the first six months are considered held for the entire year; assets acquired during the last six months are not considered in the depreciation computation. Conversely, no depreciation is recorded on assets sold during the first six months and a full year's depreciation is recorded on assets sold during the last six months.

(3) One-half year's depreciation is recognized on all assets purchased or sold during the year. A full year's depreciation is taken on all other assets.

(4) No depreciation is recognized on acquisitions during the year but depreciation for a full year is recognized on retirements.

(5) Depreciation is recognized for a full year on acquisitions during the year but no depreciation is recognized on retirements.

Methods 2 through 5 are attractive because of their simplicity. However, Method 1 provides greater accuracy and its use is assumed in the examples and problems in the text unless otherwise specified. For tax purposes, Method 1 is generally used for assets acquired prior to 1981 and for fifteen-year recovery property under ACRS. For other classes of ACRS property, one-half year's depreciation is recognized in the year of acquisition, but no depreciation is recognized in the year an asset is sold.

If a company uses the sum-of-the-years-digits method of depreciation and recognizes partial year's depreciation on assets purchased or sold, each year's computation after the first year must be divided into two parts. The depreciation expense for each full year must be computed and then prorated over the partial periods. For example, assume that the asset discussed on page 386 was acquired midway through a fiscal period. The computation of depreciation for the first two years recognizing partial period depreciation would be as follows:

First Year:		
Depreciation for first full year (see page 388)	$1,727.27	
One-half year's depreciation		$ 863.64
Second Year:		
Depreciation for balance of first year		$ 863.63
Depreciation for second full year (see page 388)	$1,554.55	
One-half year's depreciation		777.28
Total depreciation—second year		$1,640.91

Use-Factor Methods. Use-factor methods view asset exhaustion as related primarily to asset use or output and provide periodic charges varying with the degree of such service. Service life for certain assets can best be expressed in terms of hours of service: for others in terms of units of production.

Service-Hours Method. Service-hours depreciation is based on the theory that purchase of an asset represents the purchase of a number of hours of direct service. This method requires an estimate of the life of the asset in terms of service hours. Depreciable cost is divided by total service hours in arriving at the depreciation rate to be assigned for each hour of asset use. The use of the asset during the period is measured, and the number of service hours is multiplied by the depreciation rate in arriving at the periodic depreciation charge. Depreciation charges against revenue fluctuate periodically according to the contribution the asset makes in service hours.

Using asset data previously given and an estimated service life of 20,000 hours, the rate to be applied for each service hour is determined as follows:

$$r \text{ (per hour)} = \frac{C - S}{n}, \quad \text{or} \quad \frac{\$10{,}000 - \$500}{20{,}000} = \$.475$$

Allocation of asset cost in terms of service hours is summarized in the table at the top of the next page.

It is assumed that the original estimate of service hours is confirmed and the asset is retired after 20,000 hours are reached in the tenth year. Such precise confirmation would seldom be found in practice.

It should be observed that straight-line depreciation resulted in an annual charge of $950 regardless of fluctuations in productive activity. When asset life is affected directly by the degree of use, and when there are significant fluctuations in such use in successive periods, the service-hours method, which recognizes hours used instead of hours available for use, normally provides the more equitable charges to operations.

Asset Cost Allocation—Service-Hours Method

End of Year	Service Hours	Debit to Depreciation Expense and Credit to Accumulated Depreciation		Balance of Accumulated Depreciation	Asset Book Value
					$10,000.00
1	1,500	(1,500 × $.475)	$ 712.50	$ 712.50	9,287.50
2	2,500	(2,500 × .475)	1,187.50	1,900.00	8,100.00
3	2,500	(2,500 × .475)	1,187.50	3,087.50	6,912.50
4	2,000	(2,000 × .475)	950.00	4,037.50	5,962.50
5	1,500	(1,500 × .475)	712.50	4,750.00	5,250.00
6	1,500	(1,500 × .475)	712.50	5,462.50	4,537.50
7	3,000	(3,000 × .475)	1,425.00	6,887.50	3,112.50
8	2,500	(2,500 × .475)	1,187.50	8,075.00	1,925.00
9	2,000	(2,000 × .475)	950.00	9,025.00	975.00
10	1,000	(1,000 × .475)	475.00	9,500.00	500.00
	20,000		$9,500.00		

Productive-Output Method. Productive-output depreciation is based on the theory that an asset is acquired for the service it can provide in the form of production output. This method requires an estimate of the total unit output of the asset. Depreciable cost divided by the total estimated output gives the equal charge to be assigned for each unit of output. The measured production for a period multiplied by the charge per unit gives the charge to be made against revenue. Depreciation charges fluctuate periodically according to the contribution the asset makes in unit output.

Using the previous asset data and an estimated productive life of 2,500,000 units, the rate to be applied for each thousand units produced is determined as follows:

$$r \text{ (per thousand units)} = \frac{C - S}{n}, \quad \text{or} \quad \frac{\$10{,}000 - \$500}{2{,}500} = \$3.80$$

Asset cost allocation in terms of productive output is summarized in the following table:

Asset Cost Allocation—Productive-Output Method

End of Year	Unit Output	Debit to Depreciation Expense and Credit to Accumulated Depreciation		Balance Accumulated Depreciation	Asset Book Value
					$10,000
1	80,000	(80 × $3.80)	$ 304	$ 304	9,696
2	250,000	(250 × 3.80)	950	1,254	8,746
3	400,000	(400 × 3.80)	1,520	2,774	7,226
4	320,000	(320 × 3.80)	1,216	3,990	6,010
5	440,000	(440 × 3.80)	1,672	5,662	4,338
6	360,000	(360 × 3.80)	1,368	7,030	2,970
7	280,000	(280 × 3.80)	1,064	8,094	1,906
8	210,000	(210 × 3.80)	798	8,892	1,108
9	120,000	(120 × 3.80)	456	9,348	652
10	40,000	(40 × 3.80)	152	9,500	500
	2,500,000		$9,500		

Evaluation of Use-Factor Methods. When quantitative uses of plant assets can be reasonably estimated and readily measured, the use-factor methods provide highly satisfactory approaches to asset cost allocation. Depreciation as a fluctuating charge tends to follow the revenue curve: high depreciation charges are assigned to periods of high activity; low charges are assigned to periods of low activity. When the useful life of an asset is affected primarily by the degree of its use, recognition of depreciation as a variable charge is particularly appropriate.

However, certain limitations in using the use-factor methods need to be pointed out. Asset performance in terms of service hours or productive output is often difficult to estimate. Measurement solely in terms of these factors could fail to recognize special conditions, such as increasing maintenance and repair costs as well as possible inadequacy and obsolescence. Furthermore, when service life expires even in the absence of use, a use-factor method may conceal actual fluctuations in earnings; by relating periodic depreciation charges to the volume of operations, periodic operating results may be smoothed out, thus creating a false appearance of stability.

Group-Rate and Composite-Rate Methods. It was assumed in preceding discussions that depreciation expense is associated with individual assets and is applied to each separate unit. This practice is commonly referred to as **unit depreciation.** However, there may be certain advantages in associating depreciation with a group of assets and applying a single rate to the collective cost of the group at any given time. Group cost allocation procedures are referred to as **group depreciation** and **composite depreciation.**

Group Depreciation. When useful life is affected primarily by physical factors, a group of similar items purchased at one time should have the same expected life, but in fact some will probably remain useful longer than others. In recording depreciation on a unit basis, the sale or retirement of an asset before or after its anticipated lifetime requires recognition of a gain or loss. Such gains and losses, however, can usually be attributed to normal variations in useful life rather than to unforeseen disasters and windfalls.

The **group-depreciation** procedure treats a collection of similar assets as a single group. Depreciation is accumulated in a single valuation account, and the depreciation rate is based on the average life of assets in the group. Because the accumulated depreciation account under the group procedure applies to the entire group of assets, it is not related to any specific asset. Thus, no book value can be calculated for any specific asset and there are no fully depreciated assets. To arrive at the periodic depreciation charge, the depreciation rate is applied to the recorded cost of all assets remaining in service, regardless of age.

When an item in the group is retired, no gain or loss is recognized; the asset account is credited with the cost of the item and the valuation account is debited for the difference between cost and any salvage. With normal variations in asset lives, the losses not recognized on early retirements are offset by the continued depreciation charges on those assets still in service after the average life has elapsed. Group depreciation is generally computed as an adaptation of the straight-line method, and the illustrations in this chapter assume this approach.

To illustrate, assume that 100 similar machines having an average expected useful life of 5 years are purchased at a total cost of $2,000,000. Of this group, 30 machines are retired at the end of four years, 40 at the end of five years, and the remaining 30 at the end of the sixth year. Based on the average expected useful life of 5 years, a depreciation charge of 20% is reported on those assets in service each year. The charges for depreciation and the changes in the group asset and accumulated depreciation accounts are summarized below.

Asset Cost Allocation—Group Depreciation

End of Year	Debit to Depreciation Expense (20% of Cost)	Asset			Accumulated Depreciation			Asset Book Value
		Debit	Credit	Balance	Debit	Credit	Balance	
		$2,000,000		$2,000,000				$2,000,000
1	$ 400,000			2,000,000		$ 400,000	$ 400,000	1,600,000
2	400,000			2,000,000		400,000	800,000	1,200,000
3	400,000			2,000,000		400,000	1,200,000	800,000
4	400,000		$ 600,000	1,400,000	$ 600,000	400,000	1,000,000	400,000
5	280,000		800,000	600,000	800,000	280,000	480,000	120,000
6	120,000		600,000	—	600,000	120,000	—	—
	$2,000,000	$2,000,000	$2,000,000		$2,000,000	$2,000,000		

It should be noted that the depreciation charge is exactly $4,000 per machine-year. In each of the first four years, 100 machine-years of service[4] are utilized, and the annual depreciation charge is $400,000. In the fifth year, when only 70 machines are in operation, the charge is $280,000 (20% of $1,400,000). In the sixth year, when 30 units are still in service, a proportionate charge for such use of $120,000 (20% of $600,000) is made.

If the 30 machines retired after four years had been sold for $50,000, the entry to record the sale using the group depreciation method would have been as follows:

Cash	50,000	
Accumulated Depreciation—Equipment	550,000	
Equipment		600,000

If unit depreciation had been used for these 100 machines, the retirement entry would have reflected four years depreciation expense charged for the machines sold, and a loss of $70,000 would be charged against revenue as follows:

[4]It should be observed that in the example the original estimates of an average useful life of 5 years is confirmed in the use of the assets. Such precise confirmation would seldom be the case. In instances where assets in a group are continued in use after their cost has been assigned to operations, no further depreciation charges would be recognized. On the other hand, where all of the assets in a group are retired before their cost has been assigned to operations, a special charge related to such retirement would have to be recognized.

Cash	50,000	
Accumulated Depreciation—Equipment	480,000	
Loss on Sale of Equipment	70,000	
Equipment		600,000

If additional assets are purchased and added to the group, the depreciation rate is applied to the larger gross cost of all assets in the group. Application of the group depreciation procedure under circumstances such as the foregoing provides an annual charge that is more closely related to the quantity of productive facilities being used. Gains and losses due solely to normal variations in asset lives are not recognized, and operating results are more meaningfully stated. The convenience of applying a uniform depreciation rate to a number of similar items may also represent a substantial advantage.

Composite Depreciation. The basic procedures employed under the group method for allocating the cost of substantially identical assets may be extended to include dissimilar assets. This special application of the group procedure is known as **composite depreciation.** The composite method retains the convenience of the group method, but because assets with varying service-lives are aggregated to determine an average life, it is unlikely to provide all the reporting advantages of the group method.

A composite rate is established by analyzing the various assets or classes of assets in use and computing the depreciation as an average of the straight-line annual depreciation as follows:

Asset	Cost	Residual Value	Depreciable Cost	Estimated Life in Years	Annual Depreciation Expense (Straight-line)
A	$ 2,000	$ 120	$ 1,880	4	$ 470
B	6,000	300	5,700	6	950
C	12,000	1,200	10,800	10	1,080
	$20,000	$1,620	$18,380		$2,500

Composite depreciation rate to be applied to cost: $2,500 ÷ $20,000 = 12.5%
Composite or average life of assets: $18,380 ÷ $2,500 = 7.35 years.

It will be observed that a rate of 12.5 percent applied to the cost of the assets, $20,000, results in annual depreciation of $2,500. Annual depreciation of $2,500 will accumulate to a total of $18,380 in 7.35 years; hence 7.35 years may be considered the composite or average life of the assets. Composite depreciation would be reported in a single accumulated depreciation account. Upon the retirement of an individual asset, the asset account is credited and Accumulated Depreciation is debited with the difference between cost and residual value. As with the group procedure, no gains or losses are recognized at the time individual assets are retired.

After a composite rate has been set, it is ordinarily continued in the absence of significant changes in the lives of assets or asset additions and retirements having a material effect upon the rate. It is assumed in the preceding example that the assets are replaced with similar assets when retired. If they are not replaced, continuation of the 12.5 percent rate will misstate depreciation charges.

AMORTIZATION OF INTANGIBLE ASSETS

The life of an intangible asset is usually limited by the effects of obsolescence, shifts in demand, competition, and other economic factors. Because of the difficulty in estimating such highly uncertain future events, companies sometimes did not amortize the cost of intangible assets, but assumed their value was never used up. This practice was frequently followed for trademarks, goodwill, and some franchises. The Accounting Principles Board, however, felt that eventually all intangible assets became of insignificant worth to the company. The Board, therefore, issued Opinion No. 17, requiring that the recorded costs of all intangible assets acquired after October 31, 1970—the effective date of the Opinion—be amortized over the estimated useful life.[5] Many companies do not amortize certain intangibles, notably goodwill, acquired prior to November 1, 1970, although amortization of these assets was encouraged by the Board.[6]

The useful life of an intangible asset may be affected by a variety of factors, all of which should be considered in determining the amortization period. Useful life may be limited by legal, regulatory, or contractual provisions. These factors, including options for renewal or extension, should be evaluated in conjunction with the economic factors noted above and other pertinent information. A patent, for example, has a legal life of 17 years; but if the competitive advantages afforded by the patent are expected to terminate after 5 years, then the patent cost should be amortized over the shorter period.

Although the life of an intangible asset is to be estimated by careful analysis of the surrounding circumstances, a maximum life of 40 years was established for amortization purposes. APB Opinion No. 17 included this limitation as follows:

> The cost of each type of intangible asset should be amortized on the basis of the estimated life of that specific asset and should not be written off in the period of acquisition....
>
> The period of amortization should not, however, exceed forty years. Analysis at the time of acquisition may indicate that the indeterminate lives of some intangible assets are likely to exceed forty years and the cost of those assets should be amortized over the maximum period of forty years, not an arbitrary shorter period.[7]

The requirement that the recorded cost of all intangible assets be amortized and the arbitrary selection of a 40-year life are of questionable theoretical merit. An analysis of the expected future benefits to be derived from a particular asset should be the basis for capitalizing and amortizing the cost of any asset, whether tangible or intangible.

---

[5] *Opinions of the Accounting Principles Board, No. 17*, "Intangible Assets" (New York: American Institute of Certified Public Accountants, 1970).

[6] See, for example, the notes to financial statements at the end of this chapter for The Bendix Corporation and Note 1E in the financial statements for General Mills Inc., reproduced in Appendix B.

[7] *Opinions of the Accounting Principles Board, No. 17, op. cit.*, par. 28–29.

Recording Periodic Amortization

Amortization, like depreciation, may be charged as an operating expense of the period or allocated to production overhead if the asset is directly related to the manufacture of goods. In practice the credit entry is often made directly to the asset account rather than to a separate allowance account. This practice is arbitrary, and there is no reason why charges for amortization cannot be accumulated in a separate account in the same manner as depreciation. The FASB requires disclosure of both cost and accumulated depreciation for plant assets, but does not require similar disclosure for intangible assets. When amortization is recorded in a separate account, such account is typically called Accumulated Amortization.

Method of Amortization

Amortization of intangible assets is made evenly in most instances, or on a straight-line allocation basis. APB Opinion No. 17 states:

> The Board concludes that the straight-line method of amortization—equal annual amounts—should be applied unless a company demonstrates that another systematic method is more appropriate.[8]

Although practice favors straight-line amortization, analysis of many intangibles such as patents, franchises, and even goodwill suggests that greater benefit is often realized in the early years of the asset's life than in the later years. In those instances, a decreasing-charge amortization seems justified.

DEPLETION OF NATURAL RESOURCES

Natural resources, also called **wasting assets,** move toward exhaustion as the physical units representing these resources are removed and sold. The withdrawal of oil or gas, the cutting of timber, and the mining of coal, sulphur, iron, copper, or silver ore are examples of processes leading to the exhaustion of natural resources. Depletion expense is a charge for the using up of the resources.

Recording Periodic Depletion

Because depletion expense is recognized as the cost of the material that becomes directly embodied in the product of the company, it is always charged to inventory. If the inventory is sold, depletion expense becomes part of the cost of goods sold. If it is unsold at the end of an accounting period, it is deferred in the cost of inventory. The credit is made to either Accumulated Depletion or directly to the natural resource asset account.

---

[8] *Ibid.*, par. 30.

Computing Periodic Depletion

The computation of depletion expense is an adaptation of the productive-output method of depreciation. Perhaps the most difficult problem in computing depletion expense is estimating the amount of resources available for economical removal from the land. Generally, a geologist, mining engineer, or other expert is called upon to make the estimate, and it is subject to continual revision as the resource is extracted or removed.

Developmental costs, such as costs of drilling, sinking mine shafts, and constructing roads should be capitalized and added to the original cost of the property in arriving at the total cost subject to depletion. These costs are often incurred before normal activities begin.

To illustrate the computation of depletion expense, assume the following facts: Land containing natural resources is purchased at a cost of $5,500,000. The land has an estimated value after removal of the resources of $250,000; the natural resource supply is estimated at 1,000,000 tons. The unit depletion charge and the total depletion charge for the first year, assuming the withdrawal of 80,000 tons are calculated as follows:

Depletion charge per ton: ($5,500,000 − $250,000) ÷ 1,000,000 = $5.25

Depletion charge for the first year: 80,000 tons × $5.25 = $420,000

If the 80,000 tons are sold, the entire $420,000 becomes a part of the cost of goods sold. If only 60,000 tons are sold in the current period, $105,000 becomes part of the inventory shown on the ending balance sheet.

When buildings and improvements are constructed in connection with the removal of natural resources and their usefulness is limited to the duration of the project, it is reasonable to recognize depreciation on such properties on an output basis consistent with the charges to be recognized for the natural resources themselves. For example, assume buildings are constructed at a cost of $250,000; the useful lives of the buildings are expected to terminate upon exhaustion of the natural resource consisting of 1,000,000 units. Under these circumstances, a depreciation charge of $.25 ($250,000 ÷ 1,000,000) should accompany the depletion charge recognized for each unit. When improvements provide benefits expected to terminate prior to the exhaustion of the natural resource, the cost of such improvements may be allocated on the basis of the units to be removed during the life of the improvements or on a time basis, whichever is considered more appropriate.

CHANGES IN ESTIMATES OF VARIABLES

The allocation of asset costs benefiting more than one period cannot be precisely determined at acquisition because so many of the variables cannot be known with certainty until a future time. Only one factor in determining the periodic charge for depreciation, amortization or depletion is based on historical information—asset cost. Other factors—residual value, useful life or output, and the pattern of use or benefit—must be estimated. The question frequently facing accountants is how adjustments to these estimates, which arise as time passes, should be reflected in the accounts. As indicated in Chapter 4, a change in estimate is normally reported in the current and future periods rather than as an adjustment of prior periods. This type of adjustment would be made for residual value and useful life changes. However, a change in the cost allocation method based on a revised expected pattern of use, is a change in accounting principle and is accounted for in a different manner. Changes in accounting principles are discussed in Chapter 21.

To illustrate the procedure for a change in estimate affecting allocation of asset cost, assume that a company purchased $50,000 of equipment and estimated a ten-year life for depreciation purposes. Using the straight-line method with no residual value, the annual depreciation would be $5,000. After four years, accumulated depreciation would amount to $20,000, and the remaining undepreciated book value would be $30,000. Assume in the fifth year, a re-evaluation of the life indicates only four more years of service can be expected from the asset. An adjustment must therefore be made for the fifth and subsequent years to reflect the change. A new annual depreciation charge is calculated by dividing the remaining book value by the remaining life of four years. In the illustration above, this would result in an annual charge of $7,500 for the fifth through eighth years ($30,000 ÷ 4 = $7,500).

A change in the estimated life of an intangible asset is accounted for in the same manner, i.e., the unamortized cost is allocated over the remaining life based on the revised estimate. Because of the uncertainties surrounding the estimation of the life of an intangible asset, frequent evaluation of the amortization period should be made to determine if a change in estimated life is warranted.

Another change in estimate occurs in accounting for wasting assets when the estimate of the recoverable units changes as a result of further discoveries, improved extraction processes, or changes in sales prices that indicate changes in the number of units that can be extracted profitably. A revised depletion rate is established by dividing the remaining resource cost balance by the estimated remaining recoverable units.

To illustrate, assume the facts used in the example on page 401. Land is purchased at a cost of $5,500,000 with estimated residual value of $250,000. The original estimated supply of natural resources in the land is 1,000,000 tons. As indicated previously, the depletion rate under these conditions would be $5.25 per ton, and the depletion charge for the first year when 80,000 tons were mined would be $420,000. Assume that in the second year of operation, 100,000 tons of ore are withdrawn, but before the books are closed at the end of the second year, appraisal of the expected recoverable tons indicates a remaining tonnage of 950,000. The new depletion rate and the depletion charge for the second year would be computed as follows:

Cost assignable to recoverable tons at the beginning of the second year:	
Original costs applicable to depletable resources	$5,250,000
Deduct depletion charge for the first year	420,000
Balance of cost subject to depletion	$4,830,000

Estimated recoverable tons as of the beginning of the second year:	
Number of tons withdrawn in the second year	100,000
Estimated recoverable tons as of the end of the second year	950,000
Total recoverable tons at the beginning of the second year	1,050,000

Depletion charge per ton for the second year: $4,830,000 ÷ 1,050,000 = $4.60
Depletion charge for the second year: 100,000 × $4.60 = $460,000.

Sometimes an increase in estimated recoverable units arises from additional expenditures for capital developments. When this occurs, the additional costs should be added to the remaining recoverable cost and divided by the number of tons remaining to be extracted. To illustrate this situation, assume in the preceding example that $525,000 additional costs had been incurred at the beginning of the second year. The preceding computation of depletion rate and depletion expense would be changed as follows:

Cost assignable to recoverable tons as of the beginning of the second year:	
Original costs applicable to depletable resources	$5,250,000
Add additional costs incurred in the second year	525,000
	$5,775,000
Deduct depletion charge for the first year	420,000
Balance of cost subject to depletion	$5,355,000
Estimated recoverable tons as of the beginning of the second year; as above:	1,050,000

Depletion charge per ton for the second year: $5,355,000 ÷ 1,050,000 = $5.10
Depletion charge for the second year: 100,000 × $5.10 = $510,000

Accounting is made up of many estimates. The procedures outlined in this section are designed to prevent the continual restating of reported income from prior years. Adjustments to prior period income figures are made only if actual errors have occurred, not when reasonable estimates have been made that later prove inaccurate.

PERIODIC COST ALLOCATION ON THE INCOME STATEMENT

Because depreciation, depletion, and amortization expenses are different from other expenses since they do not require current cash disbursements, and because of their significance monetarily for most companies, practice has favored reporting all of these charges as a separate item on a single-step income statement. This approach can be observed in the General Mills income statement in Appendix B.

ASSET RETIREMENTS

Assets may be retired by sale, trade, or abandonment. Generally, when an asset is disposed of, the asset account and allowance account balance if applicable are canceled, and a gain or loss is recognized for the difference between the amount recovered on the asset and its book value. The gain or loss would be reported as "other income" in the year of asset disposition. As noted earlier, however, no gain or loss is recognized on the retirement of plant assets depreciated using the group or composite method.

Recording Asset Retirements

In recording a disposal, any unrecorded depreciation, amortization, or depletion should be recognized to the date of disposition. To illustrate the accounting for an asset retirement, assume that certain machinery is sold on April 10, 1984, for $1,250. The machinery was originally acquired on November 20, 1975, for $10,000 and had been depreciated at 10% per year. The company's policy is to recognize depreciation to the nearest month in the period of acquisition and disposal. The entries to record depreciation for 1984 and sale of the machinery are as follows:

Depreciation Expense—Machinery	250	
Accumulated Depreciation—Machinery		250
To record depreciation for three months in 1984.		

Computation:
$10,000 × 10% × 3/12 = $250.

Cash	1,250	
Accumulated Depreciation—Machinery	8,333	
Loss on Sale of Machinery	417	
Machinery		10,000
To record sale of machinery.		

Computation:

Cost	$10,000
Depreciation to date of sale:	
November 20, 1975—April 10, 1984 (10% per year for 8 4/12 years)	8,333
Asset book value	$ 1,667
Proceeds from sale	1,250
Loss on sale	$ 417

The preceding entries can be combined in the form of a single compound entry as follows:

Cash	1,250	
Depreciation Expense—Machinery	250	
Accumulated Depreciation—Machinery	8,083	
Loss on Sale of Machinery	417	
Machinery		10,000

If an asset is scrapped or abandoned without cash recovery, a loss would be recognized equal to the asset book value; if the full cost of the asset has been written off, the asset and its offset balance would simply be canceled. When an asset is retired from active or standby service but is not immediately disposed of, the asset and accumulated depreciation balances should be closed and the lesser of book value or salvage value of the asset established as a separate asset account. If the estimated salvage value is less than book value, the difference should be recognized as a loss on the retirement. Prior to ultimate disposition of the asset, the salvage value should be reported as an asset but separately from the land, buildings, and equipment section of the balance sheet.

Property Damage or Destruction

Special accounting problems arise when property is damaged or destroyed as a result of fire, flood, storm, or other casualty. When a company owns many properties and these are widely distributed, the company itself may assume the risk of loss. However, companies ordinarily carry insurance for casualties that may involve large sums.

When uninsured properties are partly or wholly destroyed, asset book values should be reduced or canceled and a loss recorded for such reductions. When property items are insured and these are damaged or destroyed, entries on the books must be made to report asset losses and also the insurance claims arising from such losses.

The most common casualty loss incurred by a business is that from fire. Of all of the various types of protection offered by insurance, fire is the risk most widely covered. Because of the importance of fire insurance in business and because of special accounting problems that arise in the event of fire, a discussion of this matter is included in this chapter.

Fire Insurance. Fire insurance policies are usually written in $100 or $1,000 units for a period of three years. Insurance premiums are normally paid annually in advance. The amount of the premium is determined by the conditions prevailing in each case.

The insurance contract may be canceled by either the insurer or the insured. When the insurance company cancels the policy, a refund is made on a pro rata basis. When the policyholder cancels the policy, a refund may be made on what is known as a short-rate basis that provides for a higher insurance rate for the shorter period of coverage.

A **coinsurance clause** is frequently written into a policy by the insurance companies to offset the tendency by the buyer to purchase only a minimum insurance coverage. A business with assets worth $100,000 at fair market value, for example, may estimate that any single loss could not destroy more than one half of these assets and might consider itself adequately protected by insurance of $50,000. With an 80% coinsurance clause, however, the business would have to carry insurance equal to 80% of the fair market value of the property, or $80,000, to recover the full amount on claims up to the face of the policy. When less than this percentage is carried, the insured shares in the risk with the insurer.

To illustrate the calculation of the amount recoverable on a policy failing to meet coinsurance requirements, assume the following: assets are insured for $70,000 under a policy containing an 80% coinsurance clause; on the date of a fire, assets have a fair market value of $100,000. Because insurance of only $70,000 is carried when coinsurance requirements are $80,000, any loss will be borne 7/8 by the insurance company and 1/8 by the policyholder;

furthermore, whatever the loss, the maximum to be borne by the insurance company is $70,000, the face of the policy. The amount recoverable from the insurance company if a fire loss is $50,000, for example, is calculated as follows:

$$\frac{\$70{,}000 \text{ (policy)}}{\$80{,}000 \text{ (coinsurance requirement)}} \times \$50{,}000 \text{ (loss)} = \$43{,}750$$

The same calculations are made when the loss is greater than the face of the policy. Assume the same facts given above, but assume a fire loss of $75,000. The amount recoverable from insurance is calculated as follows:

$$\frac{\$70{,}000 \text{ (policy)}}{\$80{,}000 \text{ (coinsurance requirement)}} \times \$75{,}000 \text{ (loss)} = \$65{,}625$$

In the preceding example, application of the formula gives an amount still less than the face of the policy and hence fully recoverable. But if application of the formula results in an amount exceeding the face value of the policy, the claim is limited to the latter amount. If, for example, the loss is $90,000, the following calculation is made:

$$\frac{\$70{,}000 \text{ (policy)}}{\$80{,}000 \text{ (coinsurance requirement)}} \times \$90{,}000 \text{ (loss)} = \$78{,}750$$

Recovery from the insurance company, however, is limited to $70,000, the ceiling set by the policy.

When the insurance coverage is equal to or greater than the percentage required by the coinsurance clause, the formula need not be applied since any loss is paid in full up to the face value of the policy. It is important to note that coinsurance requirements are based not on the cost or book value of the insured property but upon the actual market value of the property on the date of a fire. If coinsurance requirements are to be met, a rise in the value of insured assets requires that insurance coverage be increased.

The following general rules may be formulated:

(1) In the absence of a coinsurance clause the amount recoverable is the lower of the loss or the face of the policy.
(2) When a policy includes a coinsurance clause, the amount recoverable is the lower of the loss as adjusted by the coinsurance formula or the face of the policy.

Insurance policies normally include a **contribution clause** that provides that if other policies are carried on the same property, recovery of a loss on a policy shall be limited to the ratio which the face of the policy bears to the total insurance carried. Such a limitation on the amount to be paid eliminates the possibility of recovery by the insured of amounts in excess of the actual loss. When coinsurance clauses are found on the different policies, the recoverable amount on each is limited to the ratio of the face of the policy to the higher of (a) the total insurance carried, or (b) the total insurance required to be carried by the policy. To illustrate the limitations set by contribution clauses, assume a fire loss of $30,000 on property with a value of $100,000 on which policies are carried as follows: Co. A, $50,000; Co. B, $15,000; Co. C, $10,000.

(1) Assuming policies have no coinsurance clauses, amounts that may be recovered from each company are as follows:

Co. A:	$\frac{\$50,000 \text{ (policy)}}{\$75,000 \text{ (total policies)}} \times \$30,000 \text{ (loss)}$	$20,000
Co. B:	$\frac{\$15,000 \text{ (policy)}}{\$75,000 \text{ (total policies)}} \times \$30,000 \text{ (loss)}$	6,000
Co. C:	$\frac{\$10,000 \text{ (policy)}}{\$75,000 \text{ (total policies)}} \times \$30,000 \text{ (loss)}$	4,000
Total amount recoverable		$30,000

(2) Assuming each policy includes an 80% coinsurance clause, coinsurance requirements on each policy would exceed the total insurance carried and amounts recoverable from each company are as follows:

Co. A:	$\frac{\$50,000 \text{ (policy)}}{\$80,000 \text{ (coinsurance requirement)}} \times \$30,000 \text{ (loss)}$	$18,750
Co. B:	$\frac{\$15,000 \text{ (policy)}}{\$80,000 \text{ (coinsurance requirement)}} \times \$30,000 \text{ (loss)}$	5,625
Co. C:	$\frac{\$10,000 \text{ (policy)}}{\$80,000 \text{ (coinsurance requirement)}} \times \$30,000 \text{ (loss)}$	3,750
Total amount recoverable		$28,125

(3) Assuming each policy includes a 70% coinsurance clause, total insurance carried exceeds coinsurance requirements on each policy and amounts recoverable from each company are the same as in (1).

(4) Assuming that coinsurance requirements are Co. A—none, Co. B—70%, and Co. C—80%, recovery on each policy is based on its relationship to the total insurance carried or the coinsurance requirement where this is higher, as follows:

Co. A:	$\frac{\$50,000 \text{ (policy)}}{\$75,000 \text{ (total policies)}} \times \$30,000 \text{ (loss)}$	$20,000
Co. B:	$\frac{\$15,000 \text{ (policy)}}{\$75,000 \text{ (total policies)}} \times \$30,000 \text{ (loss)}$	6,000
Co. C:	$\frac{\$10,000 \text{ (policy)}}{\$80,000 \text{ (coinsurance requirement)}} \times \$30,000 \text{ (loss)}$	3,750
Total amount recoverable		$29,750

Accounting for Fire Losses. When a fire occurs and books of account are destroyed, account balances to the date of the fire will have to be reconstructed from the best available evidence. As the first step in summarizing the fire loss, books as maintained or as reconstructed are adjusted as of the date of the fire. With accounts brought up to date, the loss may be summarized in a fire loss account. The fire loss account is debited for the book value of properties destroyed, and it is credited for amounts recoverable from insurance companies and amounts recoverable from salvage. A debit balance in the account is normally recognized as an ordinary loss and is closed into the income summary account.

A number of special problems are encountered in arriving at the charges to be made to the fire loss account. When depreciable assets are destroyed, the book values of the properties must be brought up to date and these balances in total or in part transferred to the fire loss account. When merchandise is destroyed, the estimated cost of the merchandise on hand at the time of the fire must be determined. If perpetual inventory records are available, the goods on hand may be obtained from this source. In the absence of such records, the inventory is generally calculated by the gross profit method. The inventory may be set up by a debit to the inventory account and a credit to the income summary account. The inventory total or portion destroyed may now be transferred to the fire loss account.

Insurance expired to the date of the fire is recorded as an expense. The balance in the unexpired insurance account is carried forward when policies continue in force and offer original protection on rehabilitated properties or newly acquired replacements. If a business does not plan to repair or replace the assets, it may cancel a part or all of a policy and recover cash on a short-rate basis. The difference between the unexpired insurance balance and the amount received on the short-rate basis is a loss from insurance cancellation brought about by the fire and is recorded as an addition to the fire loss balance.

Because the insurance proceeds are based upon appraised values, insurance proceeds may exceed the book value of assets destroyed, resulting in a credit balance in the fire loss account. If the assets destroyed must be replaced at current market prices, the credit balance can hardly be viewed as indicating an economic gain. The credit balance may be designated for reporting purposes as "Excess of Insurance and Salvage over Book Value of Assets Lost by Fire."

BALANCE SHEET PRESENTATION AND DISCLOSURE

Plant assets, natural resources, and intangible assets are usually shown separately on the balance sheet. As indicated earlier in this chapter, both the gross cost and accumulated depreciation must be disclosed for plant assets. Such disclosure is not required for intangible and wasting assets, and many companies report only net values for these assets. Because of the alternative methods available to compute the asset cost allocation charge, the method used must be disclosed in the financial statements. Without this information, a user of the statements might be misled in trying to compare the financial results of one company with another. Cost allocation methods are normally reported in the first note to the financial statements, "Summary of Significant Accounting Policies."

Selected portions of the financial statements published in the 1982 Annual Report of The Bendix Corporation are reproduced on the following page. In the Consolidated Balance Sheet, plant assets and intangible assets are reported at their net values. Plant asset cost and accumulated depreciation are disclosed in notes to the financial statements. Though not required, similar information is provided for intangible assets. Appendix B provides another illustration of reporting and disclosure practices for plant and intangible assets.

QUESTIONS

1. Distinguish between depreciation, depletion, and amortization.

2. What has been the historical definition of depreciation, depletion, and amortization commonly used by accountants?

3. (a) What arguments can be made for charging more than an asset's cost against revenue? (b) What methods have been suggested to adjust cost allocation for inflation?

4. The president of the Vega Co. recommends that no depreciation be recorded for 1984 since the depreciation rate is 5% per year and price indexes show that prices during the year have risen by more than this figure. Evaluate this recommendation.

5. The policy of the Lyons Co. is to recondition its building and equipment each year so they may be maintained in perfect repair. In view of the extensive periodic costs involved in keeping the property in such condition, officials of the company feel the need for recognizing depreciation is eliminated. Evaluate this argument.

6. Distinguish between functional depreciation and physical depreciation of assets.

7. What factors must be considered to determine the periodic depreciation charges that should be made for a company's depreciable plant assets?

8. The computer has greatly simplified accounting for buildings and equipment. In what ways has this simplification taken place?

9. In what ways, if any, do accelerated methods of depreciation increase the flow of cash into a company?

10. There are several different methods that may be used to allocate the cost of assets against revenue. Wouldn't it be better to require all companies to use the same method? Discuss briefly.

11. The Egnew Manufacturing Company purchased a new machine especially built to perform one particular function on their assembly line. A difference of opinion has arisen as to the method of depreciation to be used in connection with this machine. Three methods are now being considered:

(a) The straight-line method.
(b) The productive-output method.
(c) The sum-of-the-years-digits method.

List separately the arguments for and against each of the proposed methods from both the theoretical and the practical viewpoints. In your answer, you need not express your preference and you are to disregard income tax consequences.

12. The accelerated cost recovery system of depreciation is used for tax purposes but is usually not acceptable for financial reporting. Why is this true?

The Bendix Corporation and Consolidated Subsidiaries

CONSOLIDATED BALANCE SHEET

September 30	1982	1981
Assets		
Current Assets		
Cash and marketable securities	$ 148.1	$ 572.2
Trade receivables (less allowance for doubtful receivables)	575.6	622.0
Inventories and contracts in progress (less progress payments)	764.8	901.6
Prepaid expenses	39.1	43.3
Total Current Assets	1,527.6	2,139.1
Investments	1,347.6	98.3
Land, Buildings, Equipment, and Tooling—Net	776.3	780.0
Goodwill and Other Intangibles (Less Amortization)	92.7	88.7
Miscellaneous Assets	126.6	114.5
Total	$3,870.8	$3,220.6

Details to Consolidated Balance Sheet

	1982	1981
Land, Buildings, Equipment, and Tooling		
Land and improvements	$ 61.2	$ 56.5
Buildings	301.0	304.3
Machinery and equipment	721.1	728.2
Construction in progress	78.8	65.8
Total	1,162.1	1,154.8
Less—Accumulated depreciation	422.2	417.5
Land, Buildings, and Equipment—Net	739.9	737.3
Unamortized special tools	36.4	42.7
Land, Buildings, Equipment, and Tooling—Net	$ 776.3	$ 780.0
Goodwill and Other Intangibles		
Goodwill and other intangibles	$ 104.2	$ 101.1
Patents	6.8	3.1
Total	111.0	104.2
Less—Accumulated amortization	18.3	15.5
Remainder	$ 92.7	$ 88.7

NOTES TO CONSOLIDATED FINANCIAL STATEMENTS

Summary of Significant Accounting Policies

LAND, BUILDINGS, EQUIPMENT, and TOOLING   Land, buildings, and equipment are stated at cost. Interest costs incurred during the construction period for certain plant and equipment are capitalized as part of the acquisition cost. Depreciation is provided generally on a straight-line basis over the estimated service lives of the respective classes of property. Because of the numerous classifications of property and equipment, it is impracticable to enumerate depreciation rates. Fully depreciated assets still in service are not included in the property accounts. Amortization of leasehold improvements is credited directly to the asset accounts and is based upon the shorter of the life of the asset or the term of the respective lease. The amortization of special tools generally is provided over a three-year period and is credited directly to the asset account.

For physical properties not fully depreciated, the cost of the assets retired or sold is credited to the asset accounts and the related accumulated depreciation is charged to the accumulated depreciation accounts. The gain or loss from sale or retirement of property is taken into income.

GOODWILL AND OTHER INTANGIBLES   Goodwill arising prior to November 1970 represents the excess of cost over the amount ascribed to the net assets of going businesses purchased and is not amortized; goodwill and other intangibles arising from acquisitions entered into after October 1970 are amortized on a straight-line basis over periods up to forty years.

Purchased patents are stated at cost, less amortization, and are amortized over their estimated economic lives. The cost of internally developed patents is charged to income as incurred.

13. The certified public accountant is frequently called upon by management for advice regarding methods of computing depreciation. Although the question arises less frequently, of comparable importance is whether the depreciation method should be based on the consideration of the property items as units, as groups, or as having a composite life.

(a) Briefly describe the depreciation methods based on recognizing property items as (1) units, (2) groups, or (3) as having a composite life.
(b) Present the arguments for and against the use of each of these methods.
(c) Describe how retirements are recorded under each of these methods.

14. Wells, Inc. has valuable patent rights that are being amortized over their legal lives. The president of the company believes these patents are contributing substantially to company goodwill and recommends patent amortization be capitalized as company goodwill. What is your opinion of this proposal?

15. What factors should be considered in estimating the useful lives of intangible assets?

16. (a) What method is commonly used to amortize the cost of intangible assets? (b) Under what circumstances might an alternative method be appropriate?

17. What procedures must be followed when the estimate of recoverable wasting assets is changed due to subsequent development work?

18. Machinery in the finishing department of the Gerhardt Co., although less than 50% depreciated, has been replaced by new machinery. The company expects to find a buyer for the old machinery, and on December 31 the machinery is in the yards and available for inspection. How should it be reported on the balance sheet?

19. (a) What is a coinsurance clause and why is it found in fire insurance policies? (b) What is a contribution clause? How does it affect recovery of a loss?

20. How should plant assets, wasting assets, and intangibles be reported on the balance sheet? What footnote disclosure should be made for these assets?

DISCUSSION CASES

case 11-1 (How long will it last?) Below is an excerpt from an article in the Wall Street Journal (February 13, 1979) concerning life to be used in depreciating certain assets by the Xerox Corporation.

IRS Seeks $88 Million from Xerox Corp. in a Dispute over Depreciation Claimed

By a "Wall Street Journal" *Staff Reporter*

STAMFORD, Conn.—A tax battle involving $88 million is shaping up between Xerox Corp. and the Internal Revenue Service.

The IRS is seeking that sum from the office-equipment company, which said the claim will be "vigorously contested."

Xerox disclosed that the IRS is disputing the amount of depreciation claimed on the company's tax returns for 1972 and 1973. For tax purposes, depreciation is an expense that lowers pretax earnings and thus reduces the tax bill.

The company said the IRS wants Xerox to depreciate its copying and duplicating equipment over a longer period. The longer the period, the smaller the deduction for any single year—and the greater the tax bill. Xerox is allowed to depreciate machines that it leases or rents, as opposed to sells, to customers.

According to its annual report, Xerox, in preparing its public financial statement, depreciates rental equipment over an estimated useful life of five to seven years. A company spokesman said that the same practice is followed in filing federal tax returns. Xerox declined to give the number of years over which the IRS wants the equipment written off.

(1) Assume that you are representing Xerox Corp. in the dispute with IRS. What factors would you consider in developing an argument in support of the company's depreciation policies? (2) The Economic Recovery Tax Act of 1981 should significantly reduce the number of tax disputes involving useful lives of depreciable assets. Why is this true?

case 11-2 (Do shorter lives overcome the impact of inflation?) After several years of proposed legislation to accelerate depreciation for productive assets, the Economic Recovery Tax Act of 1981 adopted a 3-5-10-15 year accelerated cost recovery system. One of the arguments given in support of its adoption is that it will help overcome the impact of inflation in depreciation. Evaluate the reasonableness of this argument.

case 11-3 (Why write off goodwill?) The Reno Corporation purchased the Stardust Club for $500,000, which included $100,000 for goodwill. Reno Corporation incurs large promotional and advertising expenses to maintain Stardust Club's popularity. As the annual financial statements are being prepared, the CPA of the Reno Corporation, Alice Boggs, insists that some of the goodwill be amortized against revenue. Boggs cites APB Opinion No. 17 that requires all intangible assets to be written off over a maximum life of 40 years. Phil Brooks, the Reno Corporation controller, feels that amortization of the purchased goodwill in the same periods as heavy expenses are incurred to maintain the goodwill in effect creates a double charge against income of the period. Brooks argues that no write-off of goodwill is necessary. Indeed, goodwill has increased in value and should even be increased on the books to reflect this improvement. Evaluate the logic of these two positions.

EXERCISES

exercise 11-1 (Computation of asset cost and depreciation expense)

A machine is purchased at the beginning of 1984 for $31,000. Its estimated life is 6 years. Freight in on the machine is $1,400. Installation costs are $800. The machine is estimated to have a residual value of $2,000 and a useful life of 40,000 hours. It was used 6,000 hours in 1984.

(1) What is the cost of the machine for accounting purposes?
(2) Compare the depreciation charge for 1984 using (a) the straight-line method, and (b) the service-hours method.

exercise 11-2 (Computation of depreciation expense)

The Table Company purchased a machine for $90,000 on June 15, 1984. It is estimated that the machine will have a 10-year life and will have a salvage value of $9,000. Its working hours and production in units are estimated at 36,000 and 600,000 respectively. It is the company's policy to take a half-year's depreciation on all assets for which they use the straight-line or double-declining-balance depreciation method in the year of purchase. During 1984, the machine was operated 4,000 hours and produced 67,000 units. Which of the following methods will give the greatest depreciation expense for 1984? (1) double-declining balance; (2) productive-output; or (3) service-hours. (Show computations for all three methods.)

exercise 11-3 (Computation of book and tax depreciation)

On July 1, 1983, Benjamin Corporation purchased factory equipment for $25,000. Salvage value was estimated to be $3,000. The equipment will be depreciated for financial reporting purposes over its estimated useful life of 10 years, counting the year of acquisition as one-half year.

(1) What amount should Benjamin Corporation record for depreciation expense for 1984 using the (a) double-declining-balance method? (b) sum-of-the-years-digits method?
(2) Assuming the factory equipment is classified as 5-year property under the accelerated cost recovery system (ACRS), what amount should Benjamin Corporation deduct for depreciation on its 1984 tax return?

exercise 11–4 (Productive-output depreciation and asset retirement)

Equipment was purchased at the beginning of 1982 for $50,000 with an estimated product life of 300,000 units. The estimated salvage value was $5,000. During 1982, 1983, and 1984, the equipment produced 80,000 units, 120,000 units, and 40,000 units respectively. The machine was damaged at the beginning of 1985, and the equipment was scrapped with no salvage value.

(1) Determine depreciation using the productive-output method for 1982, 1983, and 1984.
(2) Give the entry to write off the equipment at the beginning of 1985.

exercise 11-5 (Composite depreciation)

The Medallion Co. records show the following assets:

	Acquired	Cost	Salvage	Estimated Useful Life
Machinery	7/1/84	$105,000	$7,500	10 years
Equipment	1/1/85	33,000	1,500	7 years
Fixtures	1/1/85	45,000	4,500	4 years

For 1985, what is (a) the composite depreciation rate to be applied to cost and (b) the composite life of the assets?

exercise 11-6 (Composite depreciation)

A schedule of machinery owned by Lester Manufacturing Company is presented below:

	Total Cost	Estimated Salvage Value	Estimated Life in Years
Machine A	$550,000	$50,000	20
Machine B	200,000	20,000	15
Machine C	40,000	—	5

Lester computes depreciation on the straight-line method. Based on the information presented, calculate the composite depreciation rate and the composite life of these assets. (AICPA adapted)

exercise 11-7 (Depreciation of special component)

The Box Manufacturing Co. acquired a machine at a cost of $19,080 on March 1, 1978. The machine is estimated to have a life of 10 years except for a special component that will require replacement at the end of 6 years. The asset is recorded in two accounts, $14,400 being assigned to the main unit, and $4,680 to the special component. Depreciation is recorded by the straight-line method to the nearest month, salvage values being disregarded. On March 1, 1984, the special component is scrapped and is replaced with a similar component; the cost of the replacement at this time is $11,200, and it is estimated that the component will have a residual value of approximately 25% of cost at the end of the useful life of the main unit. What are the depreciation charges to be recognized for the years 1978, 1984, and 1985?

exercise 11-8 (Accounting for patents)

The Qualis Co. applied for and received numerous patents at a total cost of $30,345 at the beginning of 1979. It is assumed the patents will be useful evenly during their full legal life. At the beginning of 1981, the company paid $7,875 in successfully prosecuting an attempted infringement of these patent rights. At the beginning of 1984, $25,200 was paid to acquire patents that could make its own patents worthless: the patents acquired have a remaining life of 15 years but will not be used.

(1) Give the entries to record the expenditures relative to patents.
(2) Give the entries to record patent amortization for the years, 1979, 1981, and 1984.

exercise 11-9 (Depletion and depreciation expense)

On July 1, 1984, Stubs Mining, a calendar-year corporation, purchased the rights to a copper mine. Of the total purchase price, $1,400,000 was appropriately allocable to the copper. Estimated reserves were 400,000 tons of copper. Stubs expects to extract and sell 5,000 tons of copper per month. Production began immediately. The selling price is $25 per ton.

To aid production, Stubs also purchased some new equipment on July 1, 1984. The equipment cost $152,000 and had an estimated useful life of 8 years. However, after all the copper is removed from this mine, the equipment will be of no use to Stubs and will be sold for an estimated $8,000.

If sales and production conform to expectations, what is Stubs' depletion expense on this mine and depreciation expense on the new equipment for financial accounting purposes for the calendar year 1984?

exercise 11-10 (Change in estimated useful life)

Eastside Corporation purchased a machine on July 1, 1981, for $75,000. The machine was estimated to have a useful life of 10 years with an estimated salvage value of $5,000. During 1984 it became apparent that the machine would become uneconomical after December 31, 1988, and that the machine would have no scrap value. Accumulated depreciation on this machine as of December 31, 1983, was $17,500. What should be the charge for depreciation in 1984 under a new annual depreciation charge for the remaining life? (AICPA adapted)

exercise 11-11 (Change in estimated useful life)

Indec Corporation purchased a machine on January 1, 1979, for $150,000. At the date of acquisition, the machine had an estimated useful life of 15 years with no salvage value. The machine is being depreciated on a straight-line basis. On January 1, 1984, as a result of Indec's experience with the machine, it was decided that the machine had an estimated useful life of 10 years from the date of acquisition. What is the amount of depreciation expense on this machine in 1984 using a new annual depreciation charge for the remaining 5 years?

exercise 11-12 (Computation and recording of depletion expense)

The Manning Mining Company in 1981 paid $3,200,000 for property with a supply of natural resources estimated at 2,000,000 tons. The property was estimated to be worth $400,000 after removal of the natural resource. Developmental costs of $600,000 were incurred in 1982 before withdrawals of the resources could be made. In 1983 resources removed totaled 400,000 tons. In 1984 resources removed totaled 600,000 tons. During 1984 discoveries were made indicating that available resources subsequent to 1984 will total 3,000,000 tons. Additional developmental costs of $880,000 were incurred in 1984. What entries should be made to recognize depletion for 1983 and 1984?

exercise 11-13 (Recording the sale of equipment)

Star Inc. purchased equipment costing $100,000 on June 30, 1983, having an estimated life of 5 years and a residual value of $10,000. The company uses the sum-of-the-years-digits method of depreciation, and takes one-half year's depreciation on assets in the year of purchase. The asset was sold on December 31, 1985, for $31,000. Give the entry to record the sale of the equipment.

exercise 11-14 (Recording the sale of equipment with note)

On December 31, 1984, Majestic Corporation sold for $15,000 an old machine having an original cost of $50,000 and a book value of $6,000. The terms of the sale were as follows: $5,000 down payment, $5,000 payable on December 31 of the next two years. The agreement of sale made no mention of interest, however, 10% would be a fair rate for this type transaction. Give the journal entries on Majestic's books to record the sale of the machine and receipt of the two subsequent payments. (AICPA adapted)

exercise 11-15 (Computation of fire loss and insurance proceeds)

M. R. Sabin Inc. purchased a building for $500,000 on August 1, 1974. Depreciation was recorded at 3% a year. On October 31, 1984, 50% of the building was destroyed. On this date the building had a fair market value of $1,200,000. A policy for $500,000 was carried on the building, the policy containing a 80% coinsurance clause. What entries would be made to record (a) the loss from destruction of the building and (b) the amount due from the insurance company? (Assume the company's fiscal period is the calendar year.)

exercise 11-16 (Coinsurance computations)

Beck Corporation had a fire which destroyed their warehouse No. 12 to the extent that it will have to be torn down. The fair market value of the building was $150,000. The contents were valued at $50,000; however, $20,000 was salvaged in a fire-goods sale. The corporation had two insurance policies on the building: one with Fire Prevention Company for $100,000, and one with Safety Company for $90,000. What amount will each company pay to Beck Corporation assuming: (a) Both companies require 80% coinsurance? (b) Fire Prevention Company requires 90% coinsurance and Safety Company requires 100% coinsurance?

PROBLEMS

problem 11-1 (Time-factor methods of depreciation)

A delivery truck was acquired by Sports Inc. for $10,000 on January 1, 1984. The truck was estimated to have a 3-year life and a trade-in value at the end of that time of $1,000. The following depreciation methods are being considered.

(a) Depreciation is to be calculated by the straight-line method.
(b) Depreciation is to be calculated by the sum-of-the-years-digits method.

(c) Depreciation is to be calculated by applying a fixed percentage to the declining book value of the asset that will reduce the asset book value to its residual value at the end of the third year. (The third root of .10 = .464.)
(d) Depreciation is to be calculated using the accelerated cost recovery system for 3-year recovery property.

Instructions: Prepare tables reporting periodic depreciation and asset book value over the 3-year period for each assumption listed.

problem 11-2 (Maintenance charges and depreciation of components)

A company buys a machine for $9,600. The maintenance costs for the years 1982–1985 are as follows: 1982, $100; 1983, $110; 1984, $2,548 (includes $2,496 for cost of a new motor installed in December 1984); 1985, $140.

Instructions:

(1) Assume the machine is recorded in a single account at a cost of $9,600. No record is kept of the cost of the component parts. Straight-line depreciation is used and the asset is estimated to have a useful life of 8 years. It is assumed there will be no residual value at the end of the useful life. What is the sum of the depreciation and maintenance charges for each of the first four years?
(2) Assume the cost of the frame of the machine was recorded in one account at a cost of $7,200 and the motor was recorded in a second account at a cost of $2,400. Straight-line depreciation is used with a useful life of 10 years for the frame and 4 years for the motor. Neither item is assumed to have any residual value at the end of its useful life. What is the sum of depreciation and maintenance charges for each of the first four years?
(3) Evaluate the two methods.

problem 11-3 (Group depreciation and asset retirement)

The Omrat Manufacturing Co. acquired 25 similar machines at the beginning of 1979 for $50,000. Machines have an average life of 5 years and no residual value. The group-depreciation method is employed in writing off the cost of the machines. Machines were retired as follows:

2 machines at the end of 1981	11 machines at the end of 1983
6 machines at the end of 1982	6 machines at the end of 1984

Instructions: Give the entries to record the retirement of machines and the periodic depreciation for the years 1979–1984 inclusive.

problem 11-4 (Composite depreciation)

Machines are acquired by McArthur Inc. on March 1, 1984, as follows:

	Cost	Estimated Salvage Value	Estimated Life in Years
Machine 101	$54,000	$12,000	6
102	20,000	2,000	8
103	2,000	800	8
104	18,000	1,700	10
105	7,500	None	10

Instructions:

(1) Calculate the composite depreciation rate for this group.
(2) Calculate the composite or average life in years for the group.
(3) Give the entry to record the depreciation for the year ending December 31, 1984.

problem 11-5 (Computation of asset cost and depreciation)

Thompson Corporation, a manufacturer of steel products, began operations on October 1, 1984. The accounting department of Thompson has started the plant asset and depreciation schedule presented below. You have been asked to assist in completing this schedule. In addition to ascertaining that the data already on the schedule are correct, you have obtained from the company's records and personnel the information shown below the schedule.

Thompson Corporation
Plant Asset and Depreciation Schedule
For Years Ended September 30, 1985, and September 30, 1986

Assets	Acquisition Date	Cost	Salvage	Depreciation Method	Estimated Life in Years	Depreciation Expense Year Ended September 30, 1985	1986
Land A..................	October 1, 1984	$ (1)	N/A*	N/A	N/A	N/A	N/A
Building A..............	October 1, 1984	(2)	$47,500	Straight line	(3)	$14,000	(4)
Land B..................	October 2, 1984	(5)	N/A	N/A	N/A	N/A	N/A
Building B..............	Under Construction	210,000 to date	—	Straight line	30	—	(6)
Donated Equipment......	October 2, 1984	(7)	2,000	Double-declining balance	10	(8)	(9)
Machinery A............	October 2, 1984	(10)	5,500	Sum-of-the years-digits	10	(11)	(12)
Machinery B............	October 1, 1985	(13)	—	Straight line	15	—	(14)

*N/A—Not Applicable

(a) Depreciation is computed from the first of the month of acquisition to the first of the month of disposition.

(b) Land A and Building A were acquired from a predecessor corporation. Thompson paid $812,500 for the land and building together. At the time of acquisition, the land had an appraised value of $72,000 and the building had an appraised value of $828,000.

(c) Land B was acquired on October 2, 1984, in exchange for 3,000 newly issued shares of Thompson's common stock. At the date of acquisition, the stock had a par value of $5 per share and a fair value of $25 per share. During October, 1984, Thompson paid $10,400 to demolish an existing building on this land so it could construct a new building.

(d) Construction of Building B on the newly acquired land began on October 1, 1985. By September 30, 1986, Thompson had paid $210,000 of the estimated total construction costs of $300,000. Estimated completion and occupancy are July, 1987.

(e) Certain equipment was donated to the corporation by a local university. An independent appraisal of the equipment when donated placed the fair value at $16,000 and the salvage value at $2,000.

(f) Machinery A's total cost of $110,000 includes installation expense of $550 and normal repairs and maintenance of $11,000. Salvage value is estimated at $5,500. Machinery A was sold on February 1, 1986.

(g) On October 1, 1985, Machinery B was acquired with a down payment of $4,000 and the remaining payments to be made in ten annual installments of $4,000 each beginning October 1, 1986. The prevailing interest rate was 8%.

Instructions: For each numbered item on the preceding schedule determine the correct amount. Round each answer to the nearest dollar. (AICPA adapted)

problem 11–6 (Adjusting entries—plant assets)

You are engaged in the examination of the financial statements of the Smoky Mountain Mfg. Company and are auditing the machinery and equipment account and the related depreciation accounts for the year ended December 31, 1984.

Your permanent file contains the following schedules:

Machinery and Equipment

Year	Balance 12/31/82	1983 Retirements	1983 Additions	Balance 12/31/83
1970-73	$ 8,000	$2,100	—	$ 5,900
1974	400	—	—	400
1975	—	—	—	—
1976	—	—	—	—
1977	3,900	—	—	3,900
1978	—	—	—	—
1979	5,300	—	—	5,300
1980	—	—	—	—
1981	4,200	—	—	4,200
1982	—	—	—	—
1983	—	—	$5,700	5,700
	$21,800	$2,100	$5,700	$25,400

Accumulated Depreciation

Year	Balance 12/31/82	1983 Retirements	1983 Provision	Balance 12/31/83
1970-73	$ 7,840	$2,100	$ 160	$ 5,900
1974	340	—	40	380
1975	—	—	—	—
1976	—	—	—	—
1977	2,145	—	390	2,535
1978	—	—	—	—
1979	1,855	—	530	2,385
1980	—	—	—	—
1981	630	—	420	1,050
1982	—	—	—	—
1983	—	—	285	285
	$12,810	$2,100	$1,825	$12,535

A transcript of the machinery and equipment account for 1984 follows:

Machinery and Equipment

Date	Item	Debit	Credit
1984			
Jan. 1	Balance forward	$25,400	
Mar. 1	Burnham grinder	1,200	
May 1	Air compressor	7,500	
June 1	Power lawnmower	600	
June 1	Lift truck battery	320	
Aug. 1	Rockwood saw		$ 150
Nov. 1	Electric spot welder	4,500	
Nov. 1	Baking oven	2,800	
Dec. 1	Baking oven	325	
		$42,645	$ 150
Dec. 31	Balance		42,495
		$42,645	$42,645

Your examination reveals the following information:

(a) The company uses a ten-year life for all machinery and equipment for depreciation purposes. Depreciation is computed by the straight-line method. Six months' depreciation is recorded in the year of acquisition or retirement. For 1984 the company recorded depreciation of $2,800 on machinery and equipment.

(b) The Burnham grinder was purchased for cash from a firm in financial distress. The chief engineer and a used machinery dealer agreed that the practically new machine was worth $2,100 in the open market.

(c) For production reasons the new air compressor was installed in a small building that was erected in 1984 to house the machine and will also be used for general storage. The cost of the building, which has a 25-year life, was $5,000 and is included in the $7,500 voucher for the air compressor.

(d) The power lawnmower was delivered to the home of the company president for personal use.

(e) On June 1 the battery in a battery-powered lift truck was accidentally damaged beyond repair. The damaged battery was included at a price of $600 in the $4,200 cost of the lift truck purchased on July 1, 1981. The company decided to rent a replacement battery rather than buy a new battery. The $320 expenditure is the annual rental for the battery paid in advance, net of a $40 allowance for the scrap value of the damaged battery that was returned to the battery company.

(f) The Rockwood saw sold on August 1 had been purchased on August 1, 1971, for $1,500. The saw was in use until it was sold.

(g) On September 1 the company determined that a production casting machine was no longer needed and advertised it for sale for $1,800 after determining from a used machinery dealer that this was its market value. The casting machine had been purchased for $5,000 on September 1, 1979.

(h) The company elected to exercise an option under a lease-purchase agreement to buy the electric spot welder. The welder had been installed on February 1, 1984, at a monthly rental of $100.

(i) On November 1 a baking oven was purchased for $10,000. A $2,800 down-payment was made and the balance will be paid in monthly installments over a three-year period. The December 1 payment includes interest charges of $125. Legal title to the oven will not pass to the company until the payments are completed.

Instructions: Prepare the auditor's adjusting journal entries required at December 31, 1984, for equipment and the related depreciation. (AICPA adapted)

problem 11-7 (Accounting for patents)

On January 10, 1976, the Briggs Company spent $24,000 to apply for and obtain a patent on a newly developed product. The patent had an estimated useful life of 10 years. At the beginning of 1980, the company spent $18,000 in successfully prosecuting an attempted infringement of the patent. At the beginning of 1981, the company purchased for $50,000 a patent that was expected to prolong the life of its original patent by 5 years. On July 1, 1984, a competitor obtained rights to a patent which made the company's patent obsolete.

Instructions: Give all the entries that would be made relative to the patent for the period 1976-1984, including entries to record the purchase of the patent, annual patent amortization, and ultimate patent obsolescence. (Assume the company's accounting period is the calendar year.)

problem 11-8 (Financial statements for mining company)

The Dutch Corp. was organized on January 2, 1984. It was authorized to issue 80,000 shares of common stock, par $50. On the date of organization it sold 20,000 shares at par and gave the remaining shares in exchange for certain land bearing recoverable ore deposits estimated by geologists at 800,000 tons. The property is deemed to have a value of $3,000,000 with no residual value.

During 1984 mine improvements totaled $144,000. During the year 50,000 tons were mined; 4,000 tons of this amount were on hand unsold on December 31, the balance of the tonnage being sold for cash at $17 per ton. Expenses incurred and paid for during the year, exclusive of depletion and depreciation, were as follows:

Mining	$151,750
Delivery	15,000
General and administrative	12,800

Cash dividends of $2 per share were declared on December 31, payable January 15, 1985.

It is believed that buildings and sheds will be useful only over the life of the mine; hence depreciation is to be recognized in terms of mine output.

Instructions: Prepare an income statement and a balance sheet for 1984. Submit working papers showing the development of statement data.

problem 11-9 (Computation of depletion expense)

The Silver Mining Company paid $2,700,000 in 1983 for property with a supply of natural resources estimated at 2,000,000 tons. The estimated cost of restoring the land for use after the resources are exhausted is $225,000. After the land is restored, it will have an estimated value of $325,000. Development costs, such as drilling and road construction, were $825,000. Buildings, such as bunk houses and mess hall, were constructed on the site for $175,000. The useful lives of the buildings are expected to terminate upon exhaustion of the natural resources. Operations were not begun until January 1, 1984. In 1984, resources removed totaled 600,000 tons. During 1985, an additional discovery was made indicating that available resources subsequent to 1985 will total 1,875,000 tons. Because of a strike, only 400,000 tons of resources were removed during 1985.

Instructions: Compute the debits to Depletion Expense for 1983, 1984, and 1985. (Include development costs and buildings together in account entitled Mine Improvements.)

problem 11-10 (Purchase and sale of plant and intangible assets)

The Lakeview Company entered into the following transactions involving its plant and intangible assets in 1984. Lakeview uses the calendar year as its fiscal year.

Jan. 1 The Lakeview Company sold land to the Falls Company which originally cost Lakeview $600,000. There was *no* established exchange price for this property. Falls gave Lakeview a $1,000,000 noninterest-bearing note payable in five equal annual installments of $200,000 with the first payment due December 31, 1984. The note has *no* ready market. The prevailing interest rate for a note of this type is 10%.

Mar. 1 Lakeview sold a machine for $800. The machine had been purchased on May 1, 1975, for $25,000. At the time of acquisition, the machine was estimated to have a useful life of ten years and a salvage value of $1,000. The company has recorded monthly depreciation using the straight-line method.

July 1 Lakeview sold a machine for $27,000. It was acquired for $74,000 on November 1, 1978. At the time of acquisition, the machine was estimated to have a useful life of 8 years and a salvage value of $2,000.

Dec. 31 Lakeview had purchased patents on January 1, 1981, at a cost of $56,000. The patents had been estimated to have a 10-year life. It is now estimated that the remaining benefit from the patents will be negligible after 1987.

Instructions: Prepare journal entries to record each of the above transactions or adjustments required by the information provided.

problem 11-11 (Computation of depreciation and depletion)

The following independent situations describe facts concerning the ownership of various assets.

(a) The Apex Company purchased a tooling machine in 1974 for $30,000. The machine was being depreciated on the straight-line method over an estimated useful life of 20 years, with no salvage value. At the beginning of 1984, when the machine had been in use for 10 years, Apex paid $5,000 to overhaul the machine. As a result of this improvement, Apex estimated that the useful life of the machine would be extended an additional 5 years.

(b) Samson Manufacturing Co., a calendar-year company, purchased a machine for $65,000 on January 1, 1982. At the date of purchase, Samson incurred the following additional costs:

Loss on sale of old machinery	$1,000
Freight in	500
Installation cost	2,000
Testing costs prior to regular operation	300

The estimated salvage value of the machine was $5,000 and Samson estimated that the machine would have a useful life of 20 years, with depreciation being computed on the straight-line method. In January 1984, accessories costing $3,600 were added to the machine in order to reduce its operating costs. These accessories neither prolonged the machine's life nor did they provide any additional salvage value.

(c) On July 1, 1984, Gusto Corporation purchased equipment at a cost of $22,000. The equipment has an estimated salvage value of $3,000 and is being depreciated over an estimated life of eight years under the double-declining-balance method of depreciation. For the six months ended December 31, 1984, Gusto recorded one-half year's depreciation.

(d) The Gunther Company acquired a tract of land containing an extractable natural resource. Gunther is required by its purchase contract to restore the land to a condition suitable for recreational use after it has extracted the natural resource. Geological surveys estimate that the recoverable reserves will be 4,000,000 tons, and that the land will have a value of $1,000,000 after restoration. Relevant cost information follows:

Land	$9,000,000
Estimated restoration costs	$1,200,000
Tons mined and sold in 1984	800,000

(e) In January 1984, Action corporation entered into a contract to acquire a new machine for its factory. The machine, which had a cash price of $150,000, was paid for as follows:

Down payment	$ 15,000
Notes payable in 10 equal monthly installments, interest 10%	120,000
500 shares of Action common stock with an agreed value of $50 per share	25,000
Total	$160,000

Prior to the machine's use, installation costs of $4,000 were incurred. The machine has an estimated useful life of 10 years and an estimated salvage value of $5,000.

Instructions: In each case, compute the amount of cost allocation for the current year, 1984. (AICPA adapted)

problem 11-12 (Computation and recording of fire loss)

On March 1, 1982, the Blue Co. took out a $1,000,000, 4-year fire insurance policy on a building that was completed at a cost of $1,760,000 at the end of June, 1966. The insurance policy contains an 80% coinsurance clause. Depreciation is calculated at 2½% annually. On July 5, 1984, the building was 50% destroyed by fire. The insurance company accepted a value for the property of $1,375,000 and agreed to make settlement on this basis. The fiscal period for the Blue Co. is the calendar year.

Instructions: Prepare the journal entries necessary as of July 5, 1984, to summarize the foregoing information in the fire loss account and to close the account to Income Summary.

problem 11-13 (Computation of fire loss)

The ABC Corporation is a small manufacturing company producing a highly flammable cleaning fluid. On May 31, 1984, the company had a fire which completely destroyed the processing building and the in-process inventory; some of the equipment was saved.

The cost of the fixed assets destroyed and their related accumulated depreciation accounts at May 31, 1984, were as follows:

	Cost	Accumulated Depreciation
Buildings	$40,000	$24,667
Equipment	15,000	4,375

At present prices, the cost to replace the destroyed property would be: building, $80,000; equipment, $37,500. At the time of the fire, it was determined that the destroyed building was 62½% depreciated, and the destroyed equipment was 33⅓% depreciated.

After the fire a physical inventory was taken. The raw materials were valued at $30,000, the finished goods at $50,000 and supplies at $5,000.

The inventories on January 1, 1984 consisted of:

Finished goods	$ 70,000
Goods in process	50,000
Raw materials	15,000
Supplies	2,000
Total	$137,000

A review of the accounts showed that the sales and gross profit for the last five years were:

	Sales	Gross Profit
1979	$300,000	$ 86,200
1980	320,000	102,400
1981	330,000	108,900
1982	250,000	62,500
1983	280,000	84,000

The sales for the first five months of 1984 were $150,000. Raw materials purchases were $50,000. Freight on purchases was $5,000. Direct labor for five months was $40,000; for the past five years manufacturing overhead was 50% of direct labor.

Insurance on the property and inventory was carried with three companies. Each policy included an 80% coinsurance clause. The amount of insurance carried with the various companies was:

	Buildings and Equipment	Inventories
Company A	$30,000	$38,000
Company B	20,000	35,000
Company C	15,000	35,000

The cost of cleaning up the debris was $7,000. The value of the scrap salvaged from the fire was $600.

Instructions:

(1) Compute the value of inventory lost.
(2) Compute the expected recovery from each insurance company. (AICPA adapted)

problem 11-14 (Balance sheet presentation of plant and intangible assets)

The following account balances pertain to the North Ice Company.

Account Title	Dr.	Cr.
Equipment	675,000	
Goodwill	435,000	
Inventory	90,000	
Land	200,000	
Franchises	575,000	

	Dr.	Cr.
Cash	65,000	
Accounts Receivable	137,000	
Buildings	1,400,000	
Patents	15,000	
Notes Receivable	456,000	
Accumulated Depreciation—Equipment		235,000
Accounts Payable		147,000
Notes Payable		1,500,000
Accumulated Depreciation—Buildings		385,000

Additional information:

(a) $600,000 of the notes payable are secured by a direct lien on the building.
(b) The company uses the sum-of-the-years-digits method of cost allocation for buildings and equipment and uses straight-line for patents, franchises, and goodwill.
(c) Inventory valuation was made using the retail method.

Instructions: Prepare the land, buildings, and equipment section and the intangible asset section of the balance sheet.

12 LONG-TERM INVESTMENTS IN EQUITY SECURITIES, FUNDS, AND MISCELLANEOUS ASSETS

CHAPTER OBJECTIVES

Explain the nature and classification of long-term investments.

Describe and illustrate the accounting for acquisitions of equity securities under various acquisition methods.

Explain the concepts underlying the recognition of revenue from long-term investments in common stock, and illustrate the application of the cost and equity methods of revenue recognition.

Discuss the accounting treatment of corporate distributions in the form of stock dividends, stock splits, and stock rights.

Describe and illustrate the valuation of equity securities subsequent to acquisition.

Describe and illustrate the accounting for dispositions of stock by sale, redemption, and exchange.

Discuss the accounting for long-term investments in funds and miscellaneous assets.

A company invests funds in inventories, receivables, land, buildings, equipment, and other assets in order to engage in the sale of goods and services. Some available funds, however, may be applied to the acquisition of assets not directly identified with a company's primary activities. These assets, referred to as **investments,** are expected to contribute to the success of the business either by exercising a favorable influence on sales and operations generally, or by making an independent contribution to business earnings over the long term.

CLASSIFICATION OF INVESTMENTS

From the standpoint of the owner, investments are either temporary or long-term. As discussed in Chapter 6, investments are classified as current only where they are (1) readily marketable and (2) it is management's intent to use them in meeting current cash requirements. Investments not meeting both of these tests are considered **long-term** or **permanent investments** and are usually reported on the balance sheet under a separate noncurrent heading.

Long-term or permanent investments include a variety of items. For discussion purposes, long-term investments will be classified in four groups: (1) investments in equity securities, both preferred and common stock; (2) investments in bonds, mortgages, and similar debt instruments; (3) funds for bond retirement, stock redemption, and other special purposes; and (4) miscellaneous investments including real estate held for appreciation, advances to affiliates, interests in life insurance contracts, ownership equities in partnerships or joint ventures, and interests in trusts and estates. The accounting problems relating to all long-term investments except bonds are considered in this chapter; those relating to bonds are considered in Chapter 14.

LONG-TERM INVESTMENTS IN EQUITY SECURITIES

One of the characteristics of our free enterprise financial community is the considerable level of intercorporate investment. A corporation may acquire securities of another established corporation to obtain instant growth in assets and earning power and/or a diversification in the products or services sold. In other cases, the investment insures the acquiring company a source for its raw materials or a distribution outlet for its finished product. Whatever the objective, an investment in equity securities of another corporate entity is expected to enhance the economic well-being of the acquiring company.

Acquisition of Equity Securities

Shares of stock are usually acquired through brokers on the New York Stock Exchange, the American Stock Exchange, regional exchanges, or over the counter. Stock may also be acquired directly from an issuing company or from a private investor.

Cash Purchase. Stock purchase for cash is recorded at the amount paid, including brokers' commissions, taxes, and other fees incidental to the purchase. When payment of all or part of the purchase price is deferred, the full cost of the stock should be recorded as an asset. An agreement or **subscription** entered into with a corporation for the purchase of its stock is recognized by a debit to an asset account for the securities to be received and a credit to a liability account for the amount to be paid. A purchase of stock that is partially financed by a broker is referred to as a purchase **on margin.** Stock acquired on margin should be recorded at its purchase price and a liability recognized for the unpaid balance.

To illustrate, assume a company purchases 2,000 shares of common stock in another company at a price of $30 per share. Existing margin requirements call for an initial payment of two thirds of the purchase price or $20 per share. The purchase would be recorded as follows:

Investment in Common Stock	60,000	
Cash		40,000
Payable to Broker		20,000

To report only the initial cash invested would be, in effect, to offset the obligation to the broker against the investment account. A charge for interest on any obligation arising from a stock purchase should be reported as an expense.

Noncash Acquisition. When stock is acquired in exchange for properties or services, the fair market value of such considerations or the value at which the stock is currently selling, whichever is more clearly determinable, should be used as a basis for recording the investment. In the absence of clearly defined values for assets or services exchanged or a market price for the security acquired, appraisals and estimates are required in arriving at cost. Any gain or loss is recognized as an element of income in the period of the exchange. To illustrate, assume that a company purchases common stock with inventory; cost is $20,000, normal selling price, $30,000. The market value of the securities is not well established. If the company uses the perpetual inventory system the exchange would be recorded as follows:

Cost of Sales	20,000	
Investment in Common Stock	30,000	
Inventory		20,000
Sales		30,000

The $10,000 gross profit on the exchange would be included in total gross profit reported for the period of the exchange.

Lump-Sum Purchase. When two or more securities are acquired for a lump-sum price, this cost should be allocated in some equitable manner to the different acquisitions. When market prices are available for each security, cost can be apportioned on the basis of the relative market prices. When there is a market price for one security but not for the other, it may be reasonable to assign the market price to one and the cost excess to the other. When market prices are not available for either security, cost apportionment may have to be postponed until support for an equitable division becomes available. In some cases, it will be necessary to carry the two securities in a single account until disposition, and to treat the proceeds from the sale of one security as a subtraction from total cost. The residual cost can then be identified with the other security.

To illustrate these procedures, assume the purchase of 100 units of preferred and common stock at $75 per unit; each unit consists of one share of preferred and two shares of common. Market prices at the time the stock is acquired are $60 per share for preferred and $10 per share for common. The investment cost is recorded in terms of the relative market values of the securities, as follows:

Investment in Preferred Stock	5,625	
Investment in Common Stock	1,875	
Cash		7,500

Computation:
Value of preferred: 100 × $60 = $6,000
Value of common: 200 × $10 = 2,000
$8,000

Cost assigned to preferred: 6,000/8,000 × $7,500 = $5,625.
Cost assigned to common: 2,000/8,000 × $7,500 = $1,875.

If there is no market value for common stock, the investment may be recorded as follows:

Investment in Preferred Stock	6,000	
Investment in Common Stock	1,500	
Cash		7,500

Computation:

Cost of preferred and common stock	$7,500
Cost identified with preferred stock (market)	6,000
Remaining cost identified with common stock	$1,500

If the division of cost must be deferred, the following entry is made:

Investment in Preferred and Common Stock	7,500	
Cash		7,500

The joint investment balance may be eliminated when a basis for apportionment is established and costs can be assigned to individual classes.

In some limited situations, stock is subject to special calls or assessments requiring additional capital contributions from stockholders. Such payments to the corporation are recorded as additions to the costs of the holdings. Pro rata contributions by the stockholders to the corporation to eliminate a deficit, to retire bonds, or to effect a reorganization, are also treated as additions to investment cost.

Revenue from Long-Term Investments in Common Stocks

The accounting profession has developed a variety of methods to account for investments in common stock. The key concept in accounting for and reporting equity investments subsequent to purchase is the **degree of influence** exercised by the acquiring company (**investor**) over the acquired company (**investee**).

When a company acquires a majority voting interest in another company through acquisition of **more than 50 percent** of its voting common stock, the investor and investee are referred to respectively as the **parent** company and **subsidiary** company. Financial statement balances of the parent and subsidiary are added together or **consolidated** after necessary adjustments are made. This treatment reflects the fact that majority ownership of common stock assures control by the parent over the decision-making processes of the subsidiary. In certain limited situations, the financial statements of a subsidiary are not consolidated with those of the parent. Generally, however, the reporting entity is the economic unit consisting of the parent and all its subsidiaries. Accounting for consolidated entities is covered in advanced accounting texts.[1]

The Cost and Equity Methods of Revenue Recognition. Consolidated financial statements are appropriate only when the investor holds a majority voting interest in the investee. A considerable degree of control, however, may be exercised by an investor owning **50 percent or less** of the common stock of the investee. If conditions indicate that the acquiring company exercises **significant influence** over the financial and operational decisions of the other company, the basic accounting principle of substance over form suggests that accounting procedures should be designed to parallel as closely as possible those followed when voting control exists and consolidated statements are prepared. The **equity method** of accounting is used to produce these results. Because adjustments are made directly to a single investment account, this method is often referred to as a "one-line consolidation."

When the acquiring company does not exercise significant influence over the acquired company, accounting for the investment should recognize the separate identities of the companies. At present, this is accomplished by the **cost method** of accounting; subsequent to acquisition, adjustments are made to the carrying value of the investment only to recognize a decline in market value below cost. Since preferred stock does not provide for significant influence, the cost method is used for these investments.

The ability to exercise significant influence over such decisions as dividend distribution and operational and financial administration may be indicated in several ways: e.g., representation on the investee's board of directors, participation in policy-making processes, material intercompany transactions, interchange of managerial personnel, or technological dependency. Another important consideration is the extent of ownership by an investor in relation to the concentration of other shareholdings. While it is clear that ownership of over 50 percent of common stock assures control by the acquiring company, ownership of a lesser percentage may give effective control if the balance of the stock is widely held and no significant blocks of stockholders are consistently united in their ownership.

The Accounting Principles Board in Opinion No. 18 recognized that the degree of influence and control will not always be clear and that judgment will be required in assessing the status of each investment. To achieve a reasonable degree of uniformity in the application of its position, the Board set 20 percent as an ownership standard; the ownership of 20 percent or more of the voting stock of the company carries the presumption, in the absence of evidence to the contrary, that an investor has the ability to exercise

[1]See Paul M. Fischer, William James Taylor, and J. Arthur Leer, *Advanced Accounting* (Cincinnati: South-Western Publishing Co., 1982.)

significant influence over that company. Conversely, ownership of less than 20 percent leads to the presumption that the investor does not have the ability to exercise significant influence unless such ability can be demonstrated.[2]

Because other control factors are usually very subjective, the percentage-of-ownership criterion set forth in APB Opinion No. 18 has been widely accepted as the basis for determining the appropriate method of revenue recognition for investments in equity securities when the investor does not possess absolute voting control. Thus, in the absence of persuasive evidence to the contrary, the **cost method** is used when ownership is **less than 20 percent;** the **equity method,** when ownership is **20 percent to 50 percent.**

In May 1981, the FASB issued Interpretation No. 35 that emphasized the guideline nature of the 20-50 percent criterion. To illustrate this point, the FASB listed five illustrative examples of indications that an investor is not able to exercise significant influence.[3]

(1) Opposition by the investee, such as litigation or complaints to governmental regulatory authorities.
(2) An agreement between the investor and investee under which the investor surrenders significant rights as a shareholder.
(3) Majority ownership of the investee is concentrated among a small group of shareholders who operate the investee without regard to the views of the investor.
(4) The investor needs or wants more financial information to apply the equity method than is available to the investee's other shareholders (for example, the investor wants quarterly financial information from an investee who publicly reports only annually), tries to obtain the information, and fails.
(5) The investor tries and fails to obtain representation on the investee's board of directors.

Applying the Equity Method. The equity method of recognizing revenue reflects the economic substance of the relationship between the investor and investee rather than the legal distinction of the separate entities. Although the earnings of the investee are not legally available to stockholders until their distribution as dividends has been authorized by the board of directors, the timing of the distribution can be affected by a stockholder with significant influence over the dividend decision. Failure to recognize income as earned by the investee would permit such a stockholder to affect its own income by the distribution policy followed.

Under the equity method of accounting for controlled investments, a proportionate share of the earnings or losses of an investee is recognized by the investor in the year earned or incurred. The earnings are generally reflected in a single account unless the investee has special items such as extraordinary gains or losses or cumulative adjustments from changing accounting methods. Separate revenue accounts should be used for ordinary

[2] *Opinions of the Accounting Principles Board, No. 18,* "The Equity Method of Accounting for Investments in Common Stock" (New York: American Institute of Certified Public Accountants, 1971).

[3] *FASB Interpretation No. 35,* "Criteria for Applying the Equity Method of Accounting for Investments in Common Stock" (Stamford: Financial Accounting Standards Board, 1981), par. 4.

income and for these special items. The investment account is increased by the proportionate share of the earnings and decreased by the proportionate share of the losses and the proportionate distribution of dividends.

For example, assume that Probert Manufacturing Co. held a 40 percent interest in the common stock of Stewart Inc. In 1984, Stewart Inc. reported net income of $150,000, which included an extraordinary gain of $30,000. Dividends of $70,000 were distributed to stockholders. The following entries would be made on the books of Probert Manufacturing Co. to record its share of the 1984 earnings of Stewart Inc.

Investment in Stewart Inc. Common Stock	60,000	
Share of Ordinary Income—Stewart Inc. Common Stock		48,000
Share of Extraordinary Income—Stewart Inc. Common Stock		12,000
To recognize 40% of the income earned by Stewart Inc. common stock.		
Cash	28,000	
Investment in Stewart Inc. Common Stock		28,000
To record receipt of cash dividend.		

If an investee company has preferred stock outstanding, dividends on this stock must be deducted from income before the investor computes the proportionate share of income earned.

One of the objectives of the equity method is that the recorded investment reflect as closely as possible a proportionate share of the underlying value of an investee company as if 100 percent of the company had been purchased and consolidated with the parent company. When a company is purchased, the purchase price often differs from the recorded book values of the company. If the purchase price exceeds the recorded value, the acquiring company must allocate this purchase price among the assets acquired using their current market values as opposed to the amounts carried on the books of the acquired company. If part of the purchase price is still unallocated after this division, the difference is identified as goodwill. If the recorded value exceeds the purchase price, asset values must be reduced to equal the purchase price. Future income determination for the acquired company will use the new recorded values to determine the depreciation and amortization charges.

When only a portion of a company is purchased and the equity method is used to reflect the income of the partially owned company, a similar adjustment may be required to the reported income. In order to determine whether such an adjustment is necessary, an acquiring company must compare the implied value of the company based on the purchase price of the common stock with the recorded book value of the company at the date of purchase. If the implied value exceeds the reported value, the computed excess must be analyzed in the same way as described above for a 100% purchase, although no entries are made to the books for the new values. To the extent assets have limited lives, the proportionate share of additional depreciation or amortization implied in the purchase price must be deducted from the income reported by the acquired company. This adjustment serves to meet the objective of computing the income reported using the equity method in the same manner as would be done if the company were 100% purchased and consolidated financial statements prepared.

For example, assume that the total common stockholders' equity of Stewart Inc. was $500,000 at the time Probert Manufacturing Co. purchased 40 percent of its common shares for $250,000. The implied value of the total common stockholders' equity of Stewart Inc. would be $625,000 ($250,000 ÷ .40), or $125,000 in excess of common stockholders' equity. Assume that review of the asset values discloses that the market value of depreciable properties with an average remaining life of ten years exceeds the carrying value of these assets by $50,000. The remaining $75,000 difference ($125,000 − $50,000) is attributed to goodwill. The adjustment to Stewart Inc.'s revenue to be recognized by Probert Manufacturing Co. would be a deduction of $2,000 for the proportionate depreciation of the excess market value on depreciable property, ($50,000 × .40) ÷ 10, and a deduction of $750 for the proportionate amortization of goodwill over a 40 year period, ($75,000 × .40) ÷ 40. The entry for this adjustment would be as follows:

Share of Ordinary Income—Stewart Inc. Common Stock........	2,750	
Investment in Stewart Inc. Common Stock....................		2,750
To adjust share of ordinary income on Stewart Inc. common stock for proportionate depreciation on excess market value of depreciable property, $2,000, and for amortization of implied goodwill from acquisition, $750.		

This illustration assumes that the fiscal years of the two companies coincide and that the purchase of the stock is made at the first of that year. If a purchase is made at other times, the income earned up to the date of the purchase is assumed to be included in the cost of purchase. Only income earned subsequent to acquisition should be recognized as revenue on the books of the investor.

If the purchase cost is less than the underlying book value at the time of acquisition, it is assumed that specific assets of the investee are overvalued and an adjustment is necessary to reduce the depreciation or amortization taken by the investee. The journal entry to reflect this adjustment is the reverse of the one just illustrated.

If the investor and the investee are engaged in intercompany revenue producing activities, adjustments must also be made to eliminate intercompany profits. These adjustments are similar to those made when consolidated statements are prepared for parents and 50 percent or more owned subsidiaries. A more complete description of these intercompany problems is found in advanced accounting texts.

Applying the Cost Method. When investment in another company's stock does not involve either a controlling interest or significant influence, the revenue recognized is limited to the distribution of the dividends declared by the investee. The receipt of cash dividends by a stockholder is recorded by a debit to Cash and a credit to Dividend Revenue. Three dates are generally included in the formal dividend announcement: (1) date of declaration, (2) record date, and (3) date of payment. The formal dividend announcement may read somewhat as follows: "The Board of Directors at their meeting on November 5, 1984, declared a regular quarterly dividend on outstanding common stock of 50 cents per share payable on January 15, 1985, to stockholders of record at the close of business, December 29, 1984." The stockholder becomes aware of the dividend action upon its announcement. If stock is sold and a new owner is recognized by the corporation prior to the record date, the dividend is paid to the new owner. If a stock transfer is not recognized by the corporation until after the record date, the dividend will be paid to the former owner, i.e., the shareholder of record. After the record date, stock no longer carries a right to dividends and sells **ex-dividend.**[4] Accordingly, a stockholder is justified in recognizing the corporate dividend action on the record date. At this time a receivable account may be debited and Dividend Revenue credited. Upon receipt of the dividend, Cash is debited and the receivable credited. Practice frequently omits accrual and recognizes revenue as the cash is received.

If dividends paid by the investee exceed the income earned by the investee since the stock was acquired, the excess represents a return of the investment price. This portion should be credited to the investment account rather than to Dividend Revenue. For example, assume that a 15 percent interest in Security Manufacturing Co. is acquired by Midwest Manufacturing Co. for $100,000. At the end of the first full year of ownership, Security Manufacturing reports an income of $50,000 and pays a dividend to its shareholders of $80,000. The $12,000 dividend received by Midwest Manufacturing Co. should be recorded as follows:

Cash ($80,000 × 15%)	12,000	
Dividend Revenue ($50,000 × 15%)		7,500
Investment in Security Manufacturing Co. Common Stock		4,500

A similar allocation of dividends between revenue and investment is required when an investee makes distributions in excess of current and prior years' accumulated earnings. Although these **liquidating dividends** can occur in any company, they are most common in a company consuming natural resources in its operations. When natural resources are limited and irreplaceable, the company may choose to distribute full proceeds becoming available from operations. Dividends paid, then, represent in part a distribution of earnings and in part a distribution of invested capital. Distributions involving both earnings and invested capital may also be found when a company makes full distribution of the proceeds from the sale of certain properties, such as land or securities, or when a distribution represents the proceeds from business liquidation.

Information regarding the portion of dividends representing earnings and the portion representing invested capital should be reported to the stockholder by the corporation making the distribution. This is necessary because return *of* capital is not taxable income; however, return *on* capital is recognized as taxable income. This report may not accompany each dividend

[4]Stock on the New York Stock Exchange is normally quoted ex-dividend or ex-rights four full trading days prior to the record date because of the time required to deliver the stock and to record the stock transfer.

check but instead may be provided annually and may cover the total dividends paid during the year. If dividends have been recorded as revenue during the year, the revenue account is debited and the investment account is credited when notification is received of the amount to be recognized as a distribution of invested capital.

When liquidating dividends exceed investment cost, excess distributions are reported as a gain from the investment. If liquidation is completed and the investment cost is not fully recovered, the balance of the investment account should be written off as a loss.

Change Between Cost and Equity Methods. Variations in percentage of ownership caused by additional purchases or sales of stock by the investor or by the additional sale or retirement of stock by the investee may require a change in accounting method. If the equity method has been used but subsequent events reduce the investment ownership below 20 percent, a change should be made to the cost method effective for the year when the reduced ownership occurs. No adjustment to the investment account is necessary at the time of the change. The values determined by the equity method for prior years are left in the investment account.

If the cost method has been used but subsequent acquisitions increase the investment ownership to 20 percent or more, a change should be made to the equity method with a retroactive adjustment to prior years to reflect the income that would have been reported using the equity method. To illustrate this latter condition, assume that Basic Foods Corporation acquired stock of Dehydrated Foods Inc. over the three year period 1982-1984. Purchase, dividend, and income information for these years are as follows (the purchases were made on the first day of each year):

			Dehydrated Foods Inc.	
Year	*Percentage Ownership Acquired*	*Purchase Price**	*Dividends Paid Dec. 31*	*Income Earned*
1982	10%	$ 50,000	$100,000	$200,000
1983	5	30,000	120,000	300,000
1984	15	117,000	180,000	400,000

*Purchase price equal to underlying book value at date of purchase

The following entries would be made on the books of Basic Foods Corporation to reflect the cost method for the years 1982 and 1983:

1982			
Jan. 1	Investment in Dehydrated Foods Inc. Common Stock . . .	50,000	
	Cash		50,000
	To record purchase of 10% interest.		
Dec. 31	Cash	10,000	
	Dividend Revenue		10,000
	To record receipt of dividends from Dehydrated Foods Inc. (10% × $100,000).		
1983			
Jan. 1	Investment in Dehydrated Foods Inc. Common Stock . . .	30,000	
	Cash		30,000
	To record purchase of 5% interest. Total interest now 15%.		

Dec. 31	Cash	18,000	
	Dividend Revenue		18,000
	To record receipt of dividends from Dehydrated Foods Inc. (15% × $120,000).		

The additional acquisition of stock at the beginning of 1984 increases ownership to 30%, and a retroactive adjustment to the equity method must be made at the time of acquisition. The adjustment is for the difference between the revenue reported using the cost method and that which would have been reported if the equity method had been used. The adjustment would be computed as follows:

Year	Percentage Ownership	Revenue Recognized— Cost Method	Revenue Recognized— Equity Method	Required Retroactive Adjustment
1982	10%	$10,000	$20,000[1]	$10,000
1983	15%	18,000	45,000[2]	27,000
			Total adjustment	$37,000

[1]$200,000 × 10%
[2]$300,000 × 15%

The following entries on the books of Basic Foods Corporation would be made to reflect the equity method for 1984:

1984			
Jan. 1	Investment in Dehydrated Foods Inc. Common Stock ...	117,000	
	Cash		117,000
	To record purchase of 15% interest. Total interest now 30%.		
1	Investment in Dehydrated Foods Inc. Common Stock ...	37,000	
	Retained Earnings		37,000
	To retroactively reflect revenue for 1982 and 1983 for investment in Dehydrated Foods Inc. as if the equity method had been used.		
Dec. 31	Investment in Dehydrated Foods Inc. Common Stock ...	120,000	
	Share of Income—Dehydrated Foods Inc. Common Stock..		120,000
	To record 30% of income earned by Dehydrated Foods Inc. using equity method.		
31	Cash	54,000	
	Investment in Dehydrated Foods Inc. Common Stock..		54,000
	To record receipt of dividend from Dehydrated Foods Inc. using equity method.		

Property Dividends. Dividend distributions under either the cost or equity method may involve assets other than cash. Such dividends are referred to as **property dividends.** In distributing earnings by means of a property dividend, the corporation credits the asset account for the cost of the asset distributed, debits Retained Earnings for the market value of the asset distributed, if determinable, and accounts for the difference as a gain or a loss. APB Opinion No. 29 defines this type of transaction as a nonreciprocal transfer to an owner and recommends that it be treated as a dividend.[5] The stockholder

[5]*Opinions of the Accounting Principles Board, No. 29,* "Accounting for Nonmonetary Transactions" (New York: American Institute of Certified Public Accountants, 1973), par. 3.

debits an asset account and credits Dividend Revenue or the investment account depending on whether the cost or equity method is being used. The stockholder also recognizes the dividend in terms of the market value of the property item at the date of its distribution.

To illustrate these situations, assume that the Wells Corporation with 1,000,000 shares of common stock outstanding distributes as a dividend its holdings of 50,000 shares of Barnes Co. stock acquired at a cost of $11 per share. The distribution of one share of Barnes Co. stock for every 20 shares of Wells Corporation held is made when Barnes Co. shares are selling at $16. Wells Corporation would record the dividend as follows:

Retained Earnings	800,000	
Investment in Barnes Co. Common Stock		550,000
Gain from Distribution of Barnes Co. Common Stock		250,000
To record distribution of 50,000 shares of Barnes Co. stock as a property dividend.		

A stockholder owning 100 shares of Wells Corporation stock would make the following entry in recording the receipt of the dividend:

Investment in Barnes Co. Common Stock	80	
Dividend Revenue		80
Received 5 shares of Barnes Co. common stock, market price $16 per share, as a dividend on 100 shares of Wells Corporation.		

Nonrevenue Distributions from Investee

Certain types of distributions or stock adjustments do not produce immediate revenue for investors, but may enhance the value of their investment over time. The most common of these are stock dividends, stock splits, and stock rights. Although differing in nature, each requires a recomputation of cost per share of the investment. In some cases, an allocation of the investment cost is necessary to reflect the additional investment securities held.

Stock Dividends. A company may distribute a dividend in the form of additional shares that are the same as those held by its stockholders. Such a dividend does not affect company assets but simply results in the transfer of retained earnings to invested capital. The increase in total shares outstanding is distributed pro rata to individual stockholders. The receipt of additional shares by stockholders leaves their respective equities exactly as they were. Although the number of shares held by individual stockholders has gone up, there are now a greater number of shares outstanding and proportionate interests remain unchanged. The division of equities into a greater number of parts cannot be regarded as giving rise to revenue. To illustrate, assume that Eagle Corporation has 10,000 shares of common stock outstanding. Total stockholders' equity is $330,000; the book value per share is $33. If a 10 percent stock dividend is declared, an additional 1,000 shares of stock will be issued and the book value per share will decline to $30. A stockholder who held 10 shares with a book value of $330 (10 × $33) will hold 11 shares after the stock dividend, with the book value remaining at $330 (11 × $30).

The market value of the stock may or may not react in a similar manner. Theoretically, the same relative decrease should occur in the market value as occurred in the book value; however, there are many variables influencing the market price of securities. If the percentage of the stock dividend issued is comparatively low, under 20–25 percent, there is generally less than a pro rata immediate effect on the stock market price. This means that while a stockholder after receiving a stock dividend will have no greater interest in the company, the investment may have a greater market value.

Because no assets are distributed, there is no effect on the underlying book value of the investment; only a memorandum entry needs to be made by the stockholder in recognizing the receipt of additional shares. Original investment cost applies to a greater number of shares, and this cost is divided by the total shares now held in arriving at the cost per share to be used upon subsequent disposition of holdings. The new per-share cost basis is indicated in the memorandum entry.

When stock has been acquired at different dates and at different costs, the stock dividend will have to be related to each different acquisition. Adjusted costs for shares comprising each lot held can then be developed. To illustrate, assume that H. C. De Soto owns stock of the Banner Corporation acquired as follows:

	Shares	Cost per Share	Total Cost
Lot 1	50	$120	$6,000
Lot 2	30	90	2,700

A stock dividend of 1 share for every 2 held is distributed by the Banner Corporation. A memorandum entry on De Soto's books to report the number of shares now held and the cost per share within each lot would be made as follows:

Received 40 shares of Banner Corporation stock, representing a 50% stock dividend on 80 shares held. Number of shares held and costs assigned to shares are now as follows:

	Shares	Total Cost	Revised Cost per Share
Lot 1	75 (50 + 25)	$6,000	$80 ($6,000 ÷ 75)
Lot 2	45 (30 + 15)	2,700	60 ($2,700 ÷ 45)

The number of shares to be issued as a stock dividend may include fractional shares. Usually a cash payment is made to the stockholder by the issuing company in lieu of issuing fractional shares.

Receipt of a dividend in the form of stock of a class different from that held should not be regarded as revenue. As in the case of a like dividend, a portion of the retained earnings relating to the original holdings is formally labeled invested capital. All owners of the stock on which the dividend is declared participate pro rata in the distribution and now own two classes of stock instead of a single class. A book value can now be identified with the new stock, but this is accompanied by a corresponding decrease in the book value identified with the original holdings. A similar position can be taken when an investor receives dividends in the form of bonds or other contractual obligations of the corporation.

One difference between the receipt of stock of the same class and securities of a different class should be noted. When common stock is received on common, all shares are alike and original cost may be equitably assigned in terms of the total number of units held after the dividend. When different securities are received whose value is not the same as that of the shares originally held, it would not be proper to assign an equal amount of original cost to both old and new units. Instead, equitable apportionment of cost would require use of the relative market values of the two classes of securities.

To illustrate, assume the ownership of 100 shares of Bell Co. common stock acquired at $100 per share. A stock dividend of 50 shares of $25 par preferred stock is received on the common stock held. On the date of distribution, the common stock is selling for $65 and the preferred stock for $20. The receipt of the dividend and the apportionment of the $10,000 investment cost is recorded as follows:

Investment in Bell Co. Preferred Stock	1,333.33	
Investment in Bell Co. Common Stock		1,333.33
To record receipt of 50 shares of preferred stock as a dividend on 100 shares of common.		

Computation:
Cost of common apportioned to common and preferred shares on the basis of relative market values of the two securities on the date of distribution:

Value of preferred: 50 × $20 = $1,000
Value of common: 100 × $65 = 6,500
$7,500

Cost assigned to preferred: 1,000/7,500 × $10,000 = $1,333.33.
(Cost per share: $1,333.33 ÷ 50 = $26.67.)
Cost assigned to common: 6,500/7,500 × $10,000 = $8,666.67.
(Cost per share: $8,666.67 ÷ 100 = $86.67.)

Stock dividends may be reported as revenue if they are regarded as having been made in lieu of cash. The distribution is regarded as having been made in lieu of cash if (1) it is made in discharge of dividends on preferred stock for the current year or for the preceding taxable year, or (2) the stockholder is given the option of receiving cash or other property instead of stock.

Stock Splits. A corporation may effect a **stock split** by reducing the par or stated value of capital stock and increasing the number of shares outstanding accordingly. For example, a corporation with 1,000,000 shares outstanding may decide to split its stock on a 3-for-1 basis. After the split the corporation will have 3,000,000 shares outstanding; each stockholder will have three shares for every share originally held. However, each share will now represent only one third of the interest previously represented; furthermore, each share of stock can be expected to sell for approximately one third of its previous value.

The stockholders ledger is revised to show the increased number of shares identified with each stockholder and the reduced par value, if any. Accounting for a stock split on the books of the investor is the same as that for a stock dividend. With an increase in the number of shares, each share now carries only a portion of the original cost. When shares have been acquired at different dates and at different prices, the shares received in a split will have to be associated with the original acquisitions and per-share costs for each lot revised. A memorandum entry is made to report the increase in the number of shares and the allocation of cost to the shares held after the split.

Stock Rights. A corporation that wishes to raise cash by the sale of additional stock may be required to offer existing stockholders the right to subscribe to the new stock. This privilege attaching to stock is called the **preemptive right** and is designed to enable stockholders to retain their respective interest in the corporation. For example, assume that a stockholder owns 50 percent of a company's outstanding stock. If the stock is doubled and the additional shares are offered and sold to other parties, that stockholder's interest in the company would drop to 25 percent. With the right to subscribe to the pro rata share of any new offering, the stockholder can maintain the same proportionate interest in the corporation. Although the preemptive right is a general requirement in most state corporation laws, the right may be nullified in the articles of incorporation of a company. There is an increasing movement by corporations to eliminate the preemptive right because of the extra time and expense of granting stockholders this right.

In order to make subscription privileges attractive and to insure sale of the stock, it is customary for corporations to offer the additional issues to its stockholders at less than the market price of the stock. Certificates known as **rights** or **warrants** are issued to stockholders enabling them to subscribe for stock in proportion to the holdings on which they are issued. One right is offered for each share held. But more than one right is generally required in subscribing for each new share. Rights may be sold by stockholders who do not care to exercise them.

As in the case of cash and other dividends, the directors of the corporation in declaring rights to subscribe for additional shares designate a record date that follows the declaration date. All stockholders on the record date are entitled to the rights. Up to the record date, stock sells **rights-on**, since parties acquiring the stock will receive the rights when they are issued; after the record date, the stock sells **ex-rights**, and the rights may be sold separately by those owning the rights as of the record date. A date on which the rights expire is also designated when the rights are declared. Rights not exercised are worthless beyond the expiration date. Generally, rights have a limited life of only a few weeks.

The receipt of stock rights is comparable to the receipt of a stock dividend in that the corporation has made no asset distribution and stockholders' equities remain unchanged. However, the stockholders' investment is now evidenced by shares originally acquired and by rights that have a value of their own since they permit the purchase of shares at less than market price. These circumstances call for an **allocation of cost** between the original shares and the rights. Since the shares and the rights have different values, an apportionment should be made in terms of the relative market values as of the date the stock sells ex-rights. A separate accounting for each class of security is subsequently followed. The accounting for stock rights is illustrated in the following example.

Assume that in 1981 Interior Design Co. acquired 100 shares of Superior Products no-par common at $180 per share. In 1985 the corporation issues rights to purchase 1 share of common at $100 for every 5 shares owned. Interior Design Co. thus receives 100 rights — one right for each share owned. However, since 5 rights are required for the acquisition of a single share, the 100 rights enable Interior to subscribe for only 20 new shares. Interior's original investment of $18,000 now applies to two assets, the shares and the rights. This cost is apportioned on the basis of the relative market values of each security as of the date that the rights are distributed to the stockholders. The cost allocation may be expressed as follows:

$$\text{Cost assigned to rights: } \frac{\text{Market Value of Rights}}{\text{Market Value of Stock Ex-rights} + \text{Market Value of Rights}} \times \begin{array}{c}\text{Original}\\ \text{Cost of}\\ \text{Stock}\end{array}$$

$$\text{Cost assigned to stock: } \frac{\text{Market Value of Stock Ex-rights}}{\text{Market Value of Stock Ex-rights} + \text{Market Value of Rights}} \times \begin{array}{c}\text{Original}\\ \text{Cost of}\\ \text{Stock}\end{array}$$

Assume that Superior Products common is selling ex-rights at $121 per share and rights are selling at $4 each. The cost allocation would be made as follows:

$$\text{To rights: } \frac{4}{121 + 4} \times \$18{,}000 = \$576 \text{ } (\$576 \div 100 = \$5.76\text{, cost per right})$$

To stock (balance): $18,000 − $576 = $17,424 ($17,424 ÷ 100 = $174.24, cost per share)

The following entry may be made at this time:

Investment in Superior Products Stock Rights....................	576	
Investment in Superior Products Common Stock		576
Received 100 rights permitting the purchase of 20 shares at $100. Cost of stock was apportioned on the basis of the relative market values of stock and rights on the date rights were distributed.		

The cost apportioned to the rights is used in determining the gain or the loss arising from the sale of rights. Assume that the rights in the preceding example are sold at 4½. The following entry would be made:

Cash..	450	
Loss on Sale of Superior Products Stock Rights.................	126	
Investment in Superior Products Stock Rights.................		576
Sold 100 rights at 4½.		

If the rights are exercised, the cost of the new shares acquired consists of the cost assigned to the rights plus the cash that is paid in the exercise of rights. Assume that, instead of selling the rights, Interior Design Co. exercises its privilege to purchase 20 additional shares at $100. The following entry is made.

Investment in Superior Products Common Stock	2,576	
Investment in Superior Products Stock Rights..............		576
Cash..		2,000
Exercised rights acquiring 20 shares at $100.		

Upon exercising the rights, Interior Design's records show an investment balance of $20,000 consisting of two lots of stock as follows:

Lot 1 (1981 acquisition) 100 shares:	
($17,424 ÷ 100 = $174.24, cost per share as adjusted)	$17,424
Lot 2 (1985 acquisition) 20 shares:	
($2,576 ÷ 20 = $128.80, cost per share acquired through rights).........	2,576
Total	$20,000

These costs provide the basis for calculating gains or losses upon subsequent sales of the stock.

Frequently the receipt of rights includes one or more rights that cannot be used in the purchase of a whole share. For example, assume that the owner of 100 shares receives 100 rights; 6 rights are required for the purchase of 1 share. Here the holder uses 96 rights in purchasing 16 shares. Several options are available to the holder: allow the remaining 4 rights to lapse; sell the rights and report a gain or a loss on such sale; or supplement the rights held by the purchase of 2 or more rights making possible the purchase of an additional share of stock.

If the owner of valuable rights allows them to lapse, it would appear that the cost assigned to such rights should be written off as a loss. This can be supported on the theory that the issuance of stock by the corporation at less than current market price results in some dilution in the equities identified with original holdings. However, when changes in the market price of the stock make the exercise of rights unattractive to all investors and none of the rights can be sold, no dilution has occurred and any cost of rights reported separately should be returned to the investment account.

Valuation of Marketable Equity Securities

The valuation of marketable equity securities held as a temporary investment and included with current assets was discussed in Chapter 6. In general, current marketable equity securities are valued at the lower of aggregate cost or market, and an allowance is used to reduce the cost to market. Any change in the allowance account is recognized in the income statement in the period of change.

When marketable equity securities are classified as long-term investments because management's intent is not to use the securities as a current source of cash, the advantages of market valuations are less certain. Stock market prices can fluctuate greatly while the stock is being held, and if the investment is to be retained for long-range purposes, the impact of gains or losses on the net income could be misleading. The Financial Accounting Standards Board in its Statement No. 12 considered this classification difference to be significant, and recommended a slightly different treatment for valuation of noncurrent equity investments than for current equity investments.[6]

Temporary Changes in Market Value. If the investor can exercise significant influence over the decisions of the investee, the equity method described earlier in this chapter is used and no recognition is given for temporary fluctuations in the market price. If the cost method is appropriate because significant influence does not exist, the lower of aggregate cost or market is to be used for valuation thus following the recommended procedures for marketable equity securities classified as current assets. Temporary declines in value are reflected in an allowance account, which is deducted from the investment account on the balance sheet.

Adjustments for temporary changes in value of noncurrent marketable equity securities do not affect current income as do adjustments for current marketable equity securities. Instead, a **contra stockholders' equity** account is created. This account, which in FASB Statement No. 12 is entitled Net Unrealized Loss on Noncurrent Marketable Equity Securities, is to be deducted from the total stockholders' equity balance in the balance sheet. Both the allowance account that reduces the cost to market and the contra stockholders' equity account should have the same balance at all times. As the market price of the noncurrent equity security portfolio varies, these accounts will be adjusted to bring the valuation to the lower of aggregate cost or market. When equity securities are sold, the transaction is recorded on the historical cost basis and a gain or loss recognized. These procedures are illustrated in the following example.

A company carries a long-term investment marketable equity portfolio that has a cost of $125,000. At December 31, 1984, the market value of the securities held has fallen to $110,000. The decline is judged to be temporary. The following entries would be required to reduce the securities valuation from cost to market.

Net Unrealized Loss on Noncurrent Marketable Equity Securities..	15,000	
Allowance for Decline in Value of Noncurrent Marketable Equity Securities..........		15,000

Assume that at the end of 1985, the portfolio has increased through additional purchases to an original cost of $155,000. The market value of the portfolio is $148,000. The amount in the allowance account and in the contra equity account can now be reduced to $7,000 as follows:

Allowance for Decline in Value of Noncurrent Marketable Equity Securities..........	8,000	
Net Unrealized Loss on Noncurrent Marketable Equity Securities..........		8,000

Permanent Declines in Market Value. If a decline in the market value of an individual security in the portfolio is judged to be other than temporary,

---

[6]*Statement of Financial Accounting Standards No. 12,* "Accounting for Certain Marketable Securities" (Stamford: Financial Accounting Standards Board, 1975), par. 9.

the cost basis of that security should be reduced by crediting the investment rather than the allowance account. The write-down should be recognized as a loss and charged against income.[7] The new cost basis for the security may not be adjusted upward to its original cost for any subsequent increases in market value.

To illustrate the accounting for a permanent decline, assume the long-term marketable equity securities portfolio of a company at the end of its first year of operations contains the following securities:

	Cost	Market
Company A	$ 50,000	$ 40,000
Company B	30,000	35,000
Company C	100,000	60,000
Total	$180,000	$135,000

On an aggregate basis, the allowance adjustment would be for the difference between cost and market, or $45,000. However, if evaluation of market conditions for the securities of Company C indicates the decline in value is other than temporary, the security should be written down to market, and a reevaluation made of the portfolio to determine the need for an allowance. The write-down entry would be as follows:

Recognized Loss from Permanent Decline in Market Value of Noncurrent Marketable Equity Securities	40,000	
Long-Term Investment in Marketable Securities		40,000

The recognized loss account would be closed to Income Summary at the end of the year. The portfolio of long-term securities would now appear as follows:

	Cost	Market
Company A	$ 50,000	$ 40,000
Company B	30,000	35,000
Company C	60,000	60,000
Total	$140,000	$135,000

The $5,000 difference would be recognized as a charge against the unrealized loss account and as a credit to the allowance for decline.

The valuation of marketable equity securities as discussed on the preceding pages is summarized in the flowchart on the following page. By studying the flowchart carefully in conjunction with the discussion and examples, the decision points and accounting treatment can be more clearly understood.

If there is a change in the classification of a marketable equity security between current and noncurrent assets, the transfer should be made at the lower of cost or market at the date of the transfer, and the lower figure is defined as the new cost basis with a realized loss being recorded in the current period as was done for permanent declines in value.

The above action of the Financial Accounting Standards Board places a high premium on the classification of marketable equity securities. Because

[7] *Ibid.*, par. 21.

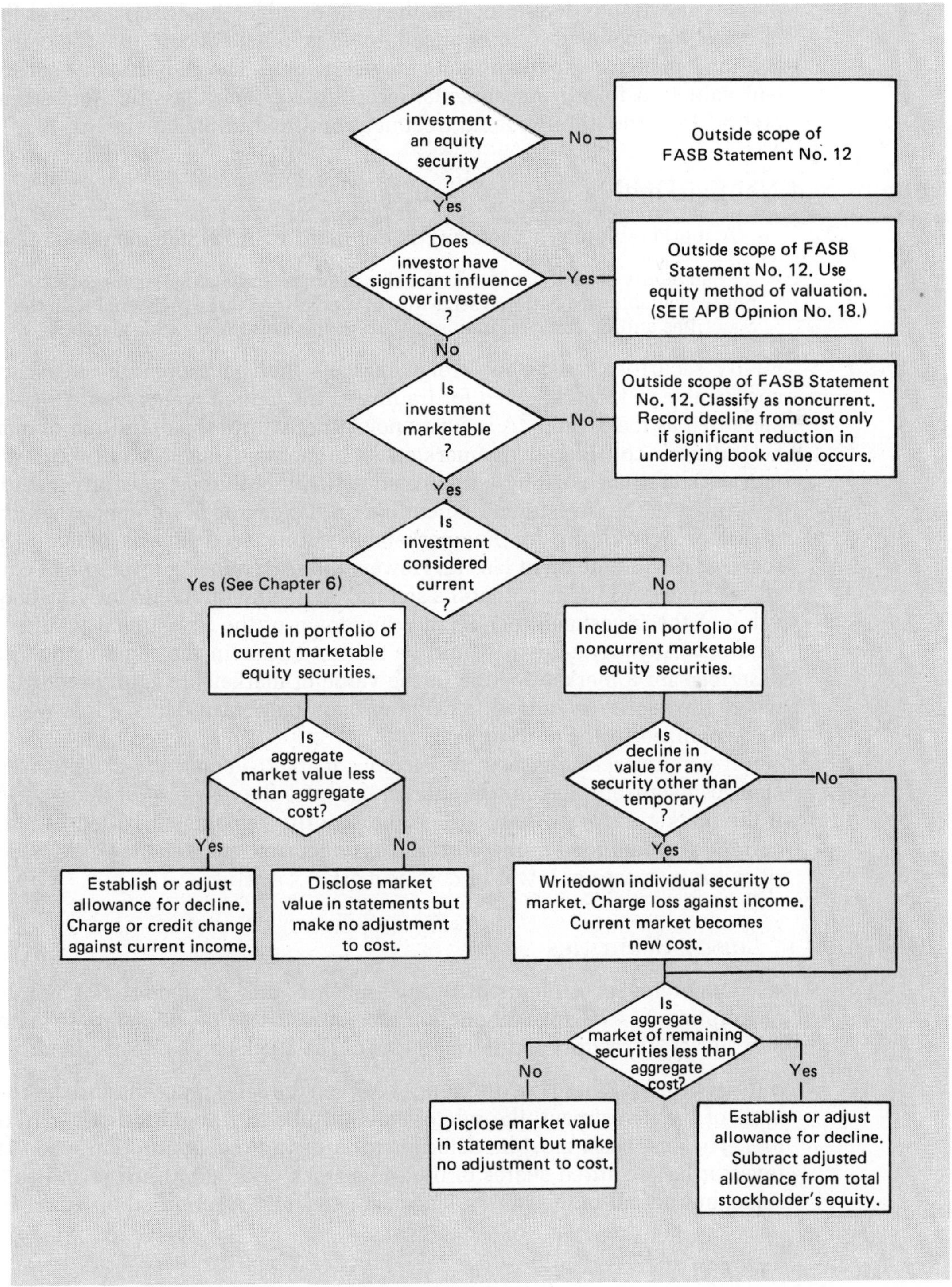

Flowchart of Valuation for Marketable Equity Securities as Prescribed by FASB Statement No. 12

the classification is determined on the basis of subjective criteria, such as the intent of management to hold or sell, there is much concern that the classification can be used to manipulate the net income. The adoption of a consistent valuation for all investments, regardless of their classification, seems preferable to the differentiated treatment outlined in Statement No. 12.

Valuation of Nonmarketable Equity Securities

A marketable equity security is defined in FASB Statement No. 12 as

> . . . an equity security as to which sales prices or bid and ask prices are currently available on a national securities exchange (i.e., those registered with the Securities and Exchange Commission) or in the over-the-counter market.[8]

Equity securities traded in foreign markets that have breadth and scope comparable to that indicated for trading in the United States would also be classified as marketable. A security not fitting within the definition of marketability is considered nonmarketable. A nonmarketable equity security must be classified as a long-term investment. Either the cost or equity method is applied to the investment depending on the degree of influence over the investee. Accounting for nonmarketable equity securities is outside the scope of FASB Statement No. 12. However, the accounting principle of conservatism would indicate that if a significant decline in the underlying book value of the investment occurs, a write-down of the investment would be required. Any write-down would be accounted for in the same manner as described for a market decline in the value of marketable equity securities where the decline is judged to be other than temporary. Thus, a loss would be recognized in the current year.

If a nonmarketable security becomes marketable and the classification changes to current, the current market becomes the new cost of the security if the market is lower than cost. If the security remains classified as noncurrent, it is included in the portfolio of noncurrent marketable equity securities for purposes of lower of cost or market valuation.

Disposition of Equity Securities

Long-term investments in equity securities may be disposed of by sale, redemption, or exchange for another type of security. It is necessary to maintain sufficient records so the cost basis of the stock can be determined.

Sale of Stock. If there is a difference between the sales proceeds and the cost basis of the investment, the sale of stock results in recognition of a gain or loss. The cost basis must be determined under a flow assumption when an investor has acquired shares of the same stock at different prices and sells some, but not all of the shares. The cost is usually determined on a first-in,

---

[8] *Ibid.*, par. 7.

first-out (fifo) basis or by specific identification. A weighted average cost may be used for book purposes, although it is not acceptable for tax purposes.

A gain or loss on the sale of stock is considered to be realized when the sale occurs. Any prior adjustments for unrealized valuation losses for the investment portfolio are disregarded when recording the sale unless a new cost basis had been assigned to reflect a permanent decline in value. Valuation adjustments are made at each statement date and are reflections of existing portfolio values at that date. Since only realized gains and losses are recognized for tax purposes, this method of accounting produces amounts needed on the tax return.

To illustrate the accounting for realized and unrealized gains and losses, assume that a company had the following portfolio of noncurrent marketable equity securities as of December 31, 1984:

	Cost	Market
A Company	$ 50,000	$ 40,000
B Company	30,000	35,000
C Company	100,000	60,000
Total	$180,000	$135,000

If none of the decline were considered permanent, an adjusting entry would be made as follows:

Net Unrealized Loss on Noncurrent Marketable Equity Securities	45,000	
Allowance for Decline in Value of Noncurrent Marketable Equity Securities		45,000

Assume that Company A stock is sold in 1985 for $35,000. The entry to record the sale would be:

Cash	35,000	
Loss on Sale of Noncurrent Marketable Equity Securities	15,000	
Long-Term Investments in Marketable Securities		50,000

At the end of 1985, the long-term portfolio would again be evaluated and adjustments made to the contra asset and contra equity accounts to reflect the new cost and market value amounts. Assume that the cost of the portfolio at December 31, 1985, was $110,000 and the market value was $90,000. The new balance in the valuation account should be $20,000, and the valuation entry at that date would be as follows:

Allowance for Decline in Value of Noncurrent Marketable Equity Securities	25,000	
Net Unrealized Loss on Noncurrent Marketable Equity Securities		25,000

As indicated earlier, if a decline in market value of the noncurrent marketable equity securities is considered permanent, market becomes the new cost or carrying value. Gains and losses upon sale of the security are measured from the new carrying value. If, for example, the decline in value of A Company securities at the end of 1984 had been considered permanent, the loss on the sale in 1985 would have been $5,000 instead of $15,000. For income tax purposes, the 1985 loss would still be $15,000.

Redemption of Stock. Stock, particularly preferred issues, may be called in for redemption and cancellation by the corporation under conditions set by the issue. The call price is ordinarily set at a figure higher than the price at which the stock was originally issued, but this call price may be more or less than the cost to the holder who acquired the stock after its original issue. When stock is surrendered to the corporation, an entry is made debiting Cash and crediting the investment account. Any difference between the cash proceeds and the investment cost is recorded as a gain or a loss. For example, assume that an investor acquires 100 shares of Y Co. 6 percent, $100 par preferred stock at 97. These shares are subsequently called in at 105. The redemption is recorded on the stockholder's books by the following entry.

Cash	10,500	
Investment in Y Co. 6% Preferred Stock		9,700
Gain on Redemption of Y Co. Preferred Stock		800
Received $10,500 on call of Y Co. preferred stock, cost $9,700.		

Exchange of Stock. When shares of stock are exchanged for other securities, the investor opens an account for the newly acquired security and closes the account of the security originally held. The new securities should be recorded at their fair market value or at the fair market value of the shares given up, whichever is more clearly determinable. A gain or loss is recognized on the exchange for the difference between the value assigned to the securities acquired and the carrying value of the shares given up. To illustrate, assume that the Z Co. offers its preferred stockholders two shares of no-par common stock in exchange for each share of $100 par preferred. An investor exchanges 100 shares of preferred stock carried at a cost of $10,000 for 200 shares of common stock. Common shares are quoted on the market at the time of exchange at $65. The exchange is recorded on the books of the stockholder by the following entry:

Investment in Z Co. Common Stock	13,000	
Investment in Z Co. Preferred Stock		10,000
Gain on Exchange of Z Co. Preferred Stock		3,000
Acquired 200 shares of common stock valued at $65 in exchange for 100 shares of preferred stock costing $100.		

If market values cannot be determined for the old or the new securities, the carrying value of the shares given up will have to be recognized as the cost of the new securities.

LONG-TERM INVESTMENTS IN FUNDS

Cash and other assets set apart for certain common purposes are called **funds, sinking funds**, or **redemption funds**. Some funds are to be used for specific current purposes, such as the payment of expenses or the discharge of current obligations, and are appropriately reported as current assets.

Examples of these are petty cash funds, payroll funds, interest funds, dividend funds, and withholding, social security, and other tax funds. Other funds are accumulated over a long term for such purposes as the acquisition or replacement of properties, retirement of long-term debt, the redemption of capital stock, operation of a pension plan, or possible future contingencies. These funds are properly considered noncurrent and are reported under the long-term investment heading.

Establishment of Funds

A fund may be established through the voluntary action of management or it may be established as a result of contractual requirements. It may arise from a single deposit or from a series of deposits, or it may be composed of the sum of the deposits plus the earnings identified with such deposits. The fund may be used for a single purpose, such as the redemption of preferred stock, or it may be used for several related purposes, such as the periodic payment of interest on bonds, the retirement of bonds at various intervals, and the ultimate retirement of the remaining bond indebtedness.

When a fund is voluntarily created by management, control of the fund and its disposition are arbitrary matters depending on the wishes of management. When a fund is created through some legal requirement, it must be administered and applied in accordance therewith. Such a fund may be administered by one or more independent trustees under an agreement known as a **trust indenture**. If the trustee assumes responsibility for fulfillment of the requirement, as may be true for a bond retirement or pension program, neither the fund nor the related liability is carried on the company's books. However, if the indenture does not free the company from further obligation, the fund must be accounted for as if there were no trustee.

Fund Accumulation

When a corporation is required by agreement to establish a fund for a certain purpose, such as the retirement of bonds or the redemption of stock, the agreement generally provides that fund deposits (1) shall be fixed amounts, (2) shall vary according to gross revenue, net income, or units of product sold, or (3) shall be equal periodic sums that, together with earnings, will produce a certain amount at some future date. The latter arrangement is based on compound-interest factors, and compound-interest or annuity tables are used to determine the equal periodic deposits. In order to accumulate a fund of $100,000 by a series of 5 equal annual deposits at 8 percent compounded annually, a periodic deposit of $17,045.65 is required.[9] A schedule

---

[9]This amount can be determined from Table III, Appendix A. The rent or annual payment for an annuity of $100,000 at 8% for 5 periods is computed as follows:

$$R = \frac{FV_n}{FVAF_{\overline{n}|i}} = \frac{FV_n}{\text{Table III}_{\overline{5}|8\%}} = \frac{\$100{,}000}{5.8666} = \$17{,}045.65$$

can be developed to show the planned fund accumulation through deposits and earnings. Such a schedule is illustrated below:

Fund Accumulation Schedule

Year	Earnings on Fund Balance for Year	Amount Deposited in Fund	Total Increase in Fund for Year	Accumulated Fund Total
1		$17,045.65	$17,045.65	$ 17,045.65
2	$1,363.65	17,045.65	18,409.30	35,454.95
3	2,836.40	17,045.65	19,882.05	55,337.00
4	4,426.96	17,045.65	21,472.61	76,809.61
5	6,144.74	17,045.65	23,190.39	100,000.00

Assuming deposits at the end of each year, the table shows a fund balance at the end of the first year of $17,045.65 resulting from the first deposit. At the end of the second year the fund is increased by (1) earnings at 8 percent on the investment in the fund during the year, $1,363.65, and (2) the second deposit to the fund, $17,045.65. The total in the fund at this time is $35,454.95. Fund earnings in the following year are based on a total investment of $35,454.95 as of the beginning of the year.

The schedule is developed on the assumption of annual earnings of 8%. However, various factors, such as fluctuations in the earnings rate and gains and losses on investments, may provide earnings that differ from the assumed amounts. If the fund is to be maintained in accordance with the accumulation schedule, deposits must be adjusted for earnings that differ from estimated amounts. Smaller deposits, then, can be made in periods when earnings exceed the assumed rate; larger deposits are necessary when earnings fail to meet the assumed rate.

Accounting for Funds

A fund is usually composed of cash and securities. The accounting for stock held in a fund is the same as that described earlier in this chapter except the securities are reported as part of the fund balance. The accounting for investments in bonds will be discussed in Chapter 14.

To illustrate the accounting for a fund held by a company, assume that a preferred stock redemption fund is established with annual payments to the fund of $20,000. The fund administrator invests 90 percent of its assets in stock and places the remainder in bank certificates of deposit paying 10 percent interest. Journal entries for the first year's transactions are as follows:

Stock Redemption Fund Cash	20,000	
Cash		20,000
Annual fund contribution		
Stock Redemption Fund Securities	18,000	
Stock Redemption Fund Cash		18,000
Investment of fund cash in securities.		
Stock Redemption Fund Certificates of Deposit	2,000	
Stock Redemption Fund Cash		2,000
Investment of fund cash in certificates of deposit.		

Stock Redemption Fund Cash	1,400	
Stock Redemption Fund Revenue		1,400
Dividends on fund securities.		
Stock Redemption Fund Cash	200	
Stock Redemption Fund Revenue		200
Interest on certificates of deposit.		
Stock Redemption Fund Expenses	200	
Stock Redemption Fund Cash		200
Expenses to operate fund.		

At the end of the year, the stock redemption fund assets are as follows:

Stock redemption fund cash	$ 1,400
Stock redemption fund certificates of deposit	2,000
Stock redemption fund securities	18,000
Total	$21,400

This total amount would be reported under the "Long-term investments" heading on the balance sheet.

Stock redemption fund revenue for the year is $1,600 and stock redemption fund expense is $200, resulting in a net income from the fund operation of $1,400. This amount is reported on the income statement as other revenue. When stock is redeemed, the payment is made from Stock Redemption Fund Cash after the securities are converted to cash.

LONG-TERM INVESTMENTS IN MISCELLANEOUS ASSETS

In addition to securities and funds, many other assets of an auxiliary character in relation to primary business activities are properly reported under the "Long-term investments" heading.

Cash Surrender Value of Life Insurance

Many business enterprises carry life insurance policies on the lives of their executives because the business has a definite stake in the continuing services of its officers. In some cases the insurance plan affords a financial cushion in the event of loss of such personnel. In other instances the insurance offers a means of purchasing a deceased owner's interest in the business, thus avoiding a transfer of such interest to some outside party or the need to liquidate the business in effecting settlement with the estate of the deceased. In these cases, the company is the beneficiary.

Insurance premiums normally consist of an amount for insurance protection and the balance for a form of investment. The investment portion is manifest in a growing **cash surrender value** available to the policyholder in the event of policy surrender and cancellation. If this cash surrender value belongs to the business, it should be reported as a long-term investment. Insurance expense for a fiscal period is the difference between the insurance premium paid and the increase in the cash surrender value of the policy. The increase in the cash surrender value is relatively uniform after the first year of the policy. At the end of the first year there may be no cash surrender value, or, if there is such a value, it may be quite low because the insurance company must recover certain costs connected with selling and initiating the policy. The cost of life insurance to the business, then, may be considered higher during the first year of the policy than in later years because of the starting costs involved. Cash surrender value tables are included in the life insurance contract.

An insurance policy with a cash surrender value also has a **loan value**. The amount an insurance company will loan on a policy is normally limited to the cash surrender value at the end of the policy year less discount from the loan date to the cash surrender value date. For example, assume a cash surrender value of $3,000 at the end of the fifth policy year. The maximum loan value on the policy at the beginning of the fifth policy year, assuming the insurance premium for the fifth year is paid, is $3,000 discounted for one year. If the discount rate applied by the insurance company is 5 percent, the policy loan value is calculated as follows: $3,000 ÷ 1.05 = $2,857.14.

When the policyholder uses the policy as a basis for a loan, the amount borrowed should be recorded as a liability and not as a reduction in the cash value. Such a loan may be liquidated by payments of principal and interest, or the loan may be continuing, to be applied against the insurance proceeds upon policy cancellation or ultimate settlement. Although it is possible for the policyholder to recognize policy loan values instead of cash surrender values, the latter values are generally used.

The policyholder may authorize the insurance company to apply any dividends declared upon insurance policies to the reduction of the annual premium payment or to the increase in cash surrender value, or the dividends may be collected in cash. Dividends should be viewed as a reduction in the cost of carrying insurance rather than as a source of supplementary revenue. Hence, if dividends are applied to the reduction of the annual premium, Insurance Expense is simply debited for the net amount paid. If the dividend is applied to the increase in the policy cash surrender value or if it is collected in cash, it should still be treated as an offset to the periodic expense of carrying the policy; the policy cash surrender value or Cash is debited and Insurance Expense is credited. After a number of years, the periodic dividends plus increases in the cash surrender value may exceed the premium payments, thus resulting in revenue rather than expense on policy holdings.

Collection of a policy upon death of the insured requires cancellation of any cash surrender balance. The difference between the insurance proceeds and the balances relating to the insurance policy is recognized as a gain in the period of death. The nature of the insurance policies carried and their coverage should be disclosed by appropriate comment on the balance sheet.

For income tax purposes, no deduction may be taken by an employer for the payment of life insurance premiums on officers or employees when the employer is directly or indirectly the policy beneficiary. The amount recovered on the surrender of an insurance contract represents taxable income to the extent this exceeds total premium payments; the policy here is viewed as an investment that has realized an amount exceeding its cost. However, amounts collected on a policy by reason of the death of the insured are not subject to income tax.

The entries to be made for an insurance contract are illustrated in the following example. The Andrews Manufacturing Company insured the life of its president, W. E. Andrews, on October 1, 1982. The amount of the policy was $50,000; the annual premiums were $2,100.

Policy Year	Gross Premium	Dividend	Net Premium	Increase in Cash Value	Insurance Expense
1	$2,100	—	$2,100	—	$2,100
2	2,100	—	2,100	$1,150	950
3	2,100	$272	1,828	1,300	528

The fiscal period for the company is the calendar year. Andrews died on July 1, 1985. The premium rebate for the period July 1—October 1, 1985, is $525, and the dividend accrued as of July 1, 1985 is $210. The entries made in recording transactions relating to the insurance contract are shown on the next page.

Cash surrender value increases are recognized on the books whenever a premium is paid. The periodic insurance premium includes a charge for the increase in the policy cash surrender value but the increase actually becomes effective as of the end of the policy year. Hence, anticipation of the cash surrender value on the date of the premium payment needs to be accompanied by a notation as to its effective date. Anticipation of the cash surrender value should also be disclosed in presenting this asset on the balance sheet. Dividends in the example reduce the insurance charge of the period in which they are applied against a premium. Actually the dividend applied against the premium for the third year accrues at the end of the second year and could be considered as a correction in the expense of the second year. Dividends received in the period of policy termination are recognized as a part of policy proceeds in final settlement rather than as a correction of insurance expense. The procedures illustrated involve certain concessions in theoretical accuracy but are normally preferred because of their practicality.

Interests in Real Estate

Improved property purchased for supplementary income and possible price appreciation may also be shown under the long-term investment heading. The expenses relating to such holdings should be deducted from any revenue produced by the property. Unimproved property is frequently acquired for possible future use or for sale. Land while unused makes no contribution to periodic revenue. Costs incident to holding the land should be added to the investment balance. When the land is used for construction purposes or is sold, its cost will include all expenditures related to its acquisition and holding. Market or appraised values, when available, may be reported parenthetically.

Transaction		Entry		
October 1, 1982 Paid first annual premium, $2,100.		Prepaid Insurance........... Cash	2,100.00	 2,100.00
December 31, 1982 To record insurance expense for Oct. 1–Dec. 31: ¼ × $2,100 = $525.		Life Insurance Expense...... Prepaid Insurance.........	525.00	 525.00
October 1, 1983 Paid second annual premium, $2,100. Premium................................ Less cash surrender value................ Net insurance charge	 $2,100 1,150 $ 950	Cash Surrender Value of Life Insurance (as of 9/30/84) .. Prepaid Insurance........... Cash	 1,150.00 950.00	 2,100.00
December 31, 1983 To record insurance expense for the year: ¾ × $2,100 (Jan. 1–Sept. 30) .... ¼ × $950 (Oct. 1–Dec. 31)...............	 $1,575.00 237.50 $1,812.50	Life Insurance Expense...... Prepaid Insurance.........	1,812.50	 1,812.50
October 1, 1984 Paid third annual premium, $2,100. Premium.......................... Less: Cash surrender value.........$1,300 Dividend .... 272 Net insurance charge	 $2,100 1,572 $ 528	Cash Surrender Value of Life Insurance (as of 9/30/85) .. Prepaid Insurance........... Cash	 1,300.00 528.00	 1,828.00
December 31, 1984 To record insurance expense for the year: ¾ × $950 (Jan. 1–Sept. 30).............. ¼ × $528 (Oct. 1–Dec. 31)..............	 $712.50 132.00 $844.50	Life Insurance Expense...... Prepaid Insurance.........	844.50	 844.50
July 1, 1985 To record insurance expense for Jan. 1–July 1: ½ × $528 = $264.		Life Insurance Expense...... Prepaid Insurance.........	264.00	 264.00
July 1, 1985 To record cancellation of policy upon death of insured: Amount recoverable on policy: Face of policy.......................... Premium rebate for period July 1–Oct. 1 and current year dividend............ Cancellation of asset values: Cash surrender value .... Prepaid insurance .... Gain on policy settlement..................	 $50,000 735 $50,735 $ 2,450 132 $ 2,582 $48,153	Receivable from Insurance Company .... Cash Surrender Value of Life Insurance .... Prepaid Insurance....... Gain on Settlement of Life Insurance	 50,735.00	 2,450.00 132.00 48,153.00

To illustrate, assume that in 1984, land is acquired as a speculative investment for $40,000. The land is ultimately sold in 1994 for $75,000; taxes and other carrying charges over the 10-year period totaled $20,000. The investment in land may be regarded as $60,000 and the gain as $15,000. The land represented, in effect, goods in process during the holding period; $75,000 is ultimately realized on an investment totaling $60,000. If carrying charges had been assigned to the periodic revenues, net income during the ten-year holding period would have been reduced by $20,000 and a gain of

$35,000 would be reported on the sale of the property. The latter treatment fails to offer a satisfactory accounting for period earnings and for the gain emerging from the investment.

It is difficult to support capitalizing expenditures for carrying assets when market values fail to confirm increasing property values; here conservatism requires the treatment of such expenditures as charges to periodic revenues. The capitalization procedure is likewise inappropriate when land is used for such purposes as rental or farming and produces current revenue; expenditures under these circumstances should be treated as charges against such revenue.

Other Long-Term Investments

Long-term investments include such items as: advances to subsidiaries that are of a permanent nature; deposits made to guarantee contract performance; and equity interests in partnerships, trusts, and estates. Most of these assets produce either current revenue or have a favorable business effect in some other way. Although cost is the underlying basis for these miscellaneous investments, the accounting procedure varies according to the type of investment involved.

LONG-TERM INVESTMENTS ON THE BALANCE SHEET

Long-term investments are generally reported on the balance sheet following the current assets classification. The long-term investment section should not include temporary investments held as a ready source of cash. Headings should be provided for the different long-term investment categories and individual long-term investments reported within such groupings. Detailed information relative to individual long-term investments may be provided in separate supporting schedules. Long-term investment costs should be supplemented by market quotations in parenthetical or note form if market exceeds cost. Information concerning the pledge of long-term investments as collateral on loans should be provided. When long-term investments are carried at amounts other than cost, the valuation that is employed should be described.

In reporting funds to be applied to specific purposes or paid to specific parties, disclosure should be made by special note of the conditions relative to their establishment and ultimate application. A fund arrearage or other failure to meet contractual requirements should be pointed out; deposit requirements in the succeeding fiscal period should also be disclosed when material. Offset of a fund balance against a liability item is proper only when an asset transfer to a trustee is irrevocable and actually serves to discharge the obligation.

The "Long-term investments" section of a balance sheet might appear as follows:

Long-term investments:			
Affiliated companies:			
Investment in Wilson Co. common stock, reported by the equity method (Investment consists of 90,000 shares representing a 40% interest acquired on July 1, 1980, for $1,500,000. Retained earnings of the subsidiary since date of acquisition have increased by $120,000; 40% of this amount, or $48,000, is identified with the parent company equity and has been recognized in the accounts.)	$1,548,000		
Advances to Wilson Co.	115,000	$1,663,000	
Miscellaneous stock investments, at cost (stock has an aggregate quoted market value of $112,000; stock has been deposited as security on bank loan—refer to notes payable, contra).		100,000	
Stock redemption fund, composed of:			
Cash	$ 15,000		
Stocks and bonds, at cost (aggregate quoted market value, $420,000)	410,500		
Dividends and interest receivable.............	4,500	430,000	
Investment in land and unused facilities		125,000	
Cash surrender value of life insurance carried on officers' lives		12,500	
Total long-term investments			$2,330,500

QUESTIONS

1. Why would a manufacturing company invest funds in stocks, bonds, and other securities?

2. How should each of the following be classified on the balance sheet?

(a) Stock held for purposes of controlling the activities of a subsidiary.
(b) Listed stock rights to be sold.
(c) Stock intended to be transferred to a supplier in cancellation of an amount owed.

3. David Giles purchases 1,000 shares of Bart Motors at $90 a share in November, paying his broker $65,000. The market value of the stock on December 31 is $125 a share; Giles has made no further payment to his broker. On this date he shows on his balance sheet Bart Motors stock, $100,000, the difference between market value and the unpaid balance to the broker. Do you approve of this report? Explain.

4. How would you record the purchase of stock and bond units acquired for a lump sum when (a) only one of the securities is quoted on the market? (b) both securities are quoted? (c) neither security is quoted?

5. Define: (a) parent company, (b) subsidiary company.

6. (a) What factors may indicate the ability of an investor owning less than a majority voting interest to exercise significant influence over the investee's operating and financial policies? (b) What percentage of stock ownership is required to exercise significant influence?

7. A corporation is a legal entity, separate and distinct from its owners and any other business unit. In view of this legal entity concept, how can use of the equity method by an investor be justified?

8. What is the difference between consolidated financial statements and a oneline consolidation achieved by using the equity method?

9. Current generally accepted accounting principles require that a retroactive adjustment be made when additional stock acquisitions cause a change from the cost method to the equity method. However, no retroactive adjustment is made when a declining ownership percentage causes a switch from the equity method to the cost method. Why are the treatments different?

10. How is the retroactive adjustment made for a switch from the cost to the equity method?

11. Distinguish between the following types of dividends: (a) cash, (b) liquidating, (c) stock, (d) property.

12. What reasons may be offered for the infrequent use of property dividends by a corporation?

13. J. M. Child receives $400 representing a dividend of $4 per share on Marimount, Inc., common stock, accompanied by a statement that $1.56 represents a distribution of income and $2.44 represents a dividend in partial liquidation. (a) What is the meaning of this statement? (b) What entry should Child make in recording the dividend?

14. Some accounting writers have suggested that certain stock dividends should constitute revenue to the recipients. What is the basis for this view?

15. Distinguish between the valuation method recommended for current marketable equity securities and that recommended for noncurrent marketable equity securities.

16. How are nonmarketable equity securities classified and valued on the balance sheet?

17. Name and describe five funds that would be listed as current assets and five that would be listed as long-term investments.

18. (a) Distinguish between life insurance cash surrender value and loan value. (b) How is the loan value on a life insurance policy calculated?

19. Name ten items properly reported under the "Long-term investments" heading on the balance sheet.

DISCUSSION CASES

case 12-1 (What is significant influence?) The Wheeling Corporation's Board of Directors has been wrestling with a basic decision concerning its involvement with other business entities. Bill Bradford, President, wants to acquire major controlling interest in several companies which serve as suppliers of basic materials used by Wheeling and other companies which are distributors of its varied products. Jane Allan, Chairman of the Board, feels part of the capital required to obtain more than 50% ownership should be used to expand Wheeling's working capital. Allan argues that significant influence over vital operating decisions can be obtained with far less than 50% of the stock. By reducing the investment, more funds can be freed for other vital needs. Both Bradford and Allan are concerned about the impact acquisitions will have on the company profits, especially the accounting differences as more substantial investments in other companies are made. They have come to you as the controller of Wheeling to shed some light on this issue and to obtain your recommendation as to the path they should follow. What factors would you stress in your answer to them?

case 12-2 (Must we recognize market declines in investments?) Virginia Corporation is having some financial difficulties, and these difficulties are reflected in a declining profit pattern. Some of the decline in profits has resulted from falling market prices on marketable equity securities carried as a current asset. S. M. Davis, controller, has learned that under some circumstances, generally accepted accounting principles do not require market reductions to be written off against current revenues. Davis has called you, a CPA, to obtain additional information as to how he can avoid reflecting these losses on Virginia's income statement. How would you advise him?

case 12-3 (How does increased ownership in another company affect our books?) For the past five years Herbert Corp. has maintained an investment (properly accounted for and reported upon) in Broome Co. amounting to a 10% interest in the voting common stock of Broome. The purchase price was $700,000 and the underlying net equity in Broome at the date of purchase was $620,000. On January 2 of the current year, Herbert purchased an additional 15% of the voting common stock of Broome for $1,200,000; the underlying net equity of the additional investment at January 2 was $1,000,000. Broome has been profitable and has paid dividends annually since Herbert's initial acquisition.

Discuss how this increase in ownership affects the accounting for and reporting upon the investment in Broome. Include in your discussion adjustments, if any, to the amount shown prior to the increase in investment to bring the amount into conformity with generally accepted accounting principles. Also include how current and subsequent periods would be reported upon. (AICPA adapted)

EXERCISES

exercise 12-1 (Lump-sum purchase of stock on margin)

Metal Magic Inc. acquired on margin 2,500 shares of Ferrus Co. preferred stock and 25,000 shares of Ferrus Co. common stock for $500,000 plus broker's commission of 1%. Market prices at the time the stock was acquired were $40 per share for preferred and $16 per share for common. Terms of the margin agreement provided for payment at acquisition date of the broker's commission plus 25% of the stock purchase price. The balance due the broker, plus 10% interest, must be paid within six months.

(1) What entry should have been made to record the purchase?
(2) What entry would be made to pay the balance due the broker three months after purchase?

exercise 12-2 (Investment in common stock)

National Environment Technologies purchased 12,000 shares of common stock of Landreth Inc. on May 13, 1983, for $15 per share. At the time of the purchase, Landreth Inc. had outstanding 40,000 shares, and the total stockholders' equity was $600,000. Thereafter, the following took place:

(a) On July 5, 1984, National Environment Technologies received from Landreth Inc. a dividend of $2 per share.
(b) On December 31, 1984, Landreth Inc. reported net income of $250,000 for the calendar year 1984.

Give the entries that would be required to reflect the purchase and subsequent events on National Environment Technologies' books.

exercise 12-3 (Investment in common stock)

In 1983, Frost Corporation acquired 22,500 shares of Al-Artica Inc. for a cost of $360,000. Although this purchase represented only 15% of the 150,000 shares of Al-Artica Inc. common voting stock outstanding, it allowed Frost Corporation to elect its president, Harold Baca, chairman of Al-Artica Inc.'s board of directors. What entries would Frost make to record the following events?

1984
Dec. 31 Al-Artica announces net income of $275,000 for the year ended December 31, 1984 and pays a dividend of 80¢ per share.

1985
Jan. 2 Frost Corporation acquires an additional 37,500 shares of Al-Artica for $600,000.
Dec. 31 Al-Artica announces ordinary income of $325,000 for the year ended December 31, 1985, an extraordinary gain of $75,000, and pays a dividend of $1.00 per share.

exercise 12-4 (Investment in common stock)

Darl Co. purchased 100,000 shares of Washburn Manufacturing Co. common stock on July 1, 1984, at book value as of that date. Washburn Manufacturing Co. had 400,000 common shares outstanding at the time of the purchase. Prior to this purchase, Darl Co. had no interest in Washburn Manufacturing Co. In its second quarterly statement, Washburn Manufacturing Co. reported net income of $56,000 for the six months ended June 30, 1984. Darl Co. received a dividend of $7,000 from Washburn Manufacturing Co. on August 1, 1984. Washburn Manufacturing Co. reported net income of $120,000 for the year ended December 31, 1984. Give the entries Darl Co. would make to reflect its share of Washburn Manufacturing Co.'s earnings for the year and the receipt of the dividends.

exercise 12-5 (Investment in common stock)

On January 1, 1984, Western Co. purchased 8,000 shares of Colvin Corporation common stock for $40,000. At that date there were 40,000 shares of Colvin common stock authorized and outstanding. The net assets of Colvin at January 1 were valued at $150,000. You determine that plant assets with a remaining life of 10 years have a fair market value of $20,000 above their net book value, and that the remainder of the excess is attributed to goodwill and amortized over 40 years.

Give the entries required in 1984 and 1998 on Western's books if the investment in Colvin permits Western to exercise significant influence and if (a) net income in 1984 of Colvin is $60,000; and (b) net loss in 1998 is $10,000.

exercise 12-6 (Investment in common stock—cost to equity method)

Garza Manufacturing Co. purchased 5% of the 100,000 outstanding common shares of Kit Inc. on January 1, 1983, for a total purchase price of $7,500. Net assets of Kit Inc. at the time had a book value of $150,000. Net income for Kit Inc. for the year ended December 31, 1983, was $50,000. Garza received dividends during the year of $1,500. There was no change of Garza ownership of Kit Inc. during the year 1984; Kit Inc. had net income of $70,000 for the year ended December 31, 1984. Garza received dividends of $2,000 for that year. On January 1, 1985, Garza Manufacturing Co. purchased an additional 20% of Kit Inc.'s common stock or 20,000 shares for a total price of $40,000. Kit Inc.'s net asset value at the time of the purchase was $200,000. For the year ended December 31, 1985, Kit Inc. had net income of $100,000; Garza received dividends from Kit Inc. totaling $10,000 for the year ended December 31, 1985. Prepare journal entries for Garza Manufacturing Co. to reflect the above transactions, including adjusting entries necessary to reflect the change from the cost method to the equity method of accounting for Garza Manufacturing Co.'s investment in Kit Inc.

exercise 12-7 (Receipt of stock dividend and sale of stock)

H. Gividen owns stock of Hjorth Inc. acquired in two lots as follows:

	Shares	Cost per Share	Total Cost
January 29, 1982	75	$24	$1,800
June 22, 1983	100	30	3,000

In 1984, a stock dividend of 35 shares was received. Gividen needed cash and sold the 35 shares at $15 per share, crediting the proceeds to a revenue account, Gain on Sale of Hjorth Inc. Stock. If the first-in, first-out method is used to record stock sales, what correction in the accounts is necessary assuming (a) the books are still open for 1984; (b) the error is not detected until 1985 after the 1984 financial reports were prepared?

exercise 12-8 (Cost per share after stock dividends and splits)

L. Brock owns 240 shares of Carp Co. common acquired at $20 per share. Give the cost basis per share for Brock's investment holdings if:

(a) A common stock dividend of 1 for 3 is received.
(b) Common stock is exchanged in a 4-for-1 split.
(c) A preferred stock dividend of 1 share for every 5 shares of common held is received; common is selling ex-dividend at $25; preferred is selling at $125.
(d) A property dividend of 1 share of Merritt Co. common, market price $10, for every 6 shares held is received.

exercise 12-9 (Dividends and stock rights)

On April 1, 1984, Bartholomew Co. purchased 1500 shares of Thompson Co. common stock, par $5, at $24. On June 1, Bartholomew received a stock dividend of 1 share for every 5 owned. On October 26, Bartholomew received a cash dividend of 50¢ on the stock and was granted the right to purchase 1 share at $15 for every 6 shares held. On this date stock had a market value ex-rights of $23.50, and each right had a value of $1.50; stock cost was allocated on this basis. On November 15, Bartholomew sold 600 rights at $1 each and exercised the remaining rights. What entries will appear on Bartholomew's books as a results of the foregoing?

exercise 12-10 (Stock rights)

P. Falcon bought 2,000 shares of the Maltese Mining Co. for $15 per share, on April 3, 1983. On June 22, 1984, Maltese Mining Co. issued stock rights to its holders of common stock, one right for each share owned. The terms of the exercise required 4 rights plus $15 for each share purchased. Maltese stock is selling ex-rights for $19 per share, and the rights have a market value of $1 each. On September 1, 1984, Falcon exercises 1,000 rights, but before the remaining rights can be exercised or sold, the stock price declines to $10 per share. On December 31, 1984, Falcon receives a $1 per share dividend, of which 20% represents a return of capital. What entries would be required to reflect the foregoing in Falcon's accounting records?

exercise 12-11 (Stock rights)

The Murray Co. holds stock of Hales Inc. acquired as follows:

	Shares	Total Cost
Lot A, 1982	75	$ 6,000
Lot B, 1983	125	11,000

In 1984, Murray Co. receives 200 rights to purchase Hales Inc. stock at $80 per share. Five rights are required to purchase one share. At issue date, rights had a market value of $4 each and stock was selling ex-rights at $96. Murray Co. used rights to purchase 30 additional shares of Hales Inc. and allowed the unexercised rights to lapse. Assume use of the first-in, first-out method of identifying stock rights exercised. What entries are required to record the preceding events?

exercise 12-12 (Valuation of long-term marketable equity securities)

The long-term marketable equity securities portfolio for Valley Industries Inc. contained the following securities at December 31, 1984. No previous market declines had been recorded.

	Cost	Market Value
Salt Valley common	$32,000	$39,000
Pinkerton Co. common	20,000	14,000
Layton Oil Co. common	40,000	33,000

(1) Give the December 31, 1984 valuation entry required under FASB Statement No. 12 if none of the declines in market value are considered permanent.
(2) Assume the Pinkerton Co. common was sold for $17,000 in 1985 and that the market value of the remaining securities in the portfolio was the same at December 31, 1985, as it was at December 31, 1984. Give the journal entries to record the sale of the stock and the valuation entries necessary at December 31, 1985.
(3) Give the December 31, 1984 valuation entries required under FASB Statement No. 12 if the decline in value of the Layton Oil Co. stock is considered permanent.

exercise 12-13 (Valuation of marketable equity securities)

Bridgeman Paper Co. reported the following selected balances on its financial statements for each of the four years 1982-1985.

	1982	1983	1984	1985
Allowance for Decline in Value of Noncurrent Marketable Equity Securities	0	$25,000	$18,000	$30,000
Recognized Loss from Permanent Decline in Market Value of Noncurrent Marketable Equity Securities	0	0	$ 4,000	0
Allowance for Decline in Value of Current Marketable Equity Securities	0	$ 5,000	$ 8,000	$ 3,000

Based on these balances, reconstruct the valuation journal entries that must have been made each year.

exercise 12-14 (Sale of stock under various flow assumptions)

The Clapson Co. holds stock of Waico Inc. acquired as follows:

	Shares	Total Cost
1983	200	$6,200
1984	100	2,800
1985	100	2,900

Give the entries that would be made upon the sale of 100 shares in 1986 at $29 per share assuming that cost is determined by (a) the first-in, first-out method, (b) the weighted average cost method, (c) identification of lot sold as the 1984 purchase.

exercise 12-15 (Fund investments)

On December 31, 1983, Casper Corporation set up a stock redemption fund, with an initial deposit of $100,000.

On February 1, 1984, Casper Corporation invested $85,000 stock redemption fund cash in 10% preferred stock of Rader Inc., par value of $50,000. Rader normally declares and pays dividends on the preferred stock semiannually: March 1 and September 1. On April 1, 1985, Casper exchanged the stock with another investor for 3,000 shares of Wright Corporation common stock. The market value of the common at the date of exchange was $35 per share.

Give all the entries necessary to record the preceding transactions assuming semi-annual dividends were paid.

exercise 12-16 (Sinking fund accumulation schedule)

Sinking fund tables show that 5 annual deposits of $16,379.75 accruing interest at 10% compounded annually will result in a total accumulation of $100,000 immediately after the fifth payment. (a) Prepare a fund accumulation schedule showing the theoretical growth of a property acquisition fund over the 5-year period. (b) Give all of the entries that would appear on the books for the increases in the property acquisition fund balance for the first 3 years.

exercise 12-17 (Cash surrender value)

The Dove Company insured the life of its president for $200,000. Annual premiums of $8,200 are paid beginning October 1, 1983. A dividend of $1,000 is to be paid on the policy annually beginning October 1, 1984. Cash surrender value at September 30, 1985, is $4,200 (recognized on October 1, 1984). At September 30, 1986, cash surrender value is $8,460 (recognized on October 1, 1985). The president died on January 1, 1986. A premium refund of $6,150 and accrued dividend of $250 are received in addition to the face value of the policy. If Dove Company closes its books on December 31, give the required entries on its books for the years 1983-1986.

exercise 12-18 (Investment in real estate)

In 1974, the Lockland Manufacturing Co. purchased for $108,000 ten acres adjoining its manufacturing plant to provide for possible future expansion. From 1974-1984 the company paid a total of $25,000 in taxes and $20,000 in special assessments. In 1984 it sold one half of the land for $120,000 and erected a building at a cost of $450,000 on the other half. All of these transactions were recorded in a "plant" account. The company books on December 31, 1984, show a "plant" account balance of $483,000. Give the journal entries to correct the accounts.

PROBLEMS

problem 12-1 (Investments in common stock)

Galland Inc. and the Noble Corp. each have 200,000 shares of no-par common stock outstanding. Rollins Inc. acquired 20,000 shares of Galland stock and 50,000 shares of Noble stock in 1980. Changes in retained earnings for Galland and Noble for 1983 and 1984 are as follows:

	Galland Inc.		Noble Corp.	
Retained earnings (deficit), January 1, 1983		$200,000		$(35,000)
Cash dividends, 1983		(25,000)		—
		$175,000		$(35,000)
Income before extraordinary items	$40,000		$20,000	
Extraordinary gain	—		45,000	
Net income, 1983		40,000		65,000
Retained earnings, December 31, 1983		$215,000		$30,000
Cash dividends, 1984		(30,000)		(10,000)
Market value of stock dividends issued—10,000 shares (transferred to paid-in capital section)		(30,000)		
Net income, 1984 (no extraordinary items)		60,000		25,000
Retained earnings, December 31, 1984		$215,000		$45,000

Instructions: Give the entries required on the books of Rollins Inc. for 1983 and 1984 to account for its investments.

problem 12-2 (Investment in common stock)

Prado Inc. purchases 10,000 shares of Darron Inc. which represents 25% of its outstanding common voting stock. The purchase price was $35,000. The carrying value of the net assets of Darron at the time of purchase was $120,000. Assets with an average remaining life of 5 years have a current market value which is $35,000 in excess of their carrying values. The remaining difference between the purchase price and the value of the underlying stockholder's equity cannot be attributable to any tangible asset; however, the company is carrying goodwill on its books valued at $40,000, which is being amortized at the rate of $1,250 per year for 32 more years. At the end of the year of purchase, Darron reports net income of $30,000. Give the entries necessary to reflect Prado Inc.'s share of the income, and any necessary adjusting entries. (Carry computations to nearest dollar.)

problem 12-3 (Investment in common stock—cost to equity method)

On January 2, 1983, Jenkins Co. purchased 15% of Walt Enterprises common voting stock for $75,000 when the net carrying value of Walt Enterprises assets was $400,000. The excess of the implied fair market value over the net carrying value is attributable to goodwill. On December 31, 1983, Walt Enterprises reported net income of $50,000 for the year then ended; Jenkins Co. received $1,500 in dividends in 1983. On January 2, 1984, Jenkins Co. purchased an additional 5% of Walt Enterprises stock for $27,000 when the net carrying value of Walt Enterprises assets was $440,000. The excess of implied fair market value over carrying value is attributable to goodwill. The 20 percent ownership interest enabled Jenkins Co. to exercise significant influence over Walt Enterprises. Dividends received from Walt Enterprises for 1984 totaled $5,000; net income reported by Walt Enterprises for the year ended December 31, 1984, was $85,000. Jenkins Co. amortizes goodwill on a straight-line basis over 40 years.

Instructions: Give the entries necessary to record the above transactions on the books of Jenkins Co.

problem 12-4 (Dividends and stock rights)

H. Rodriquez owns 500 shares of Varco. Inc. acquired on August 1, 1980, for $9,000. During 1983 and 1984, the following transactions took place with respect to this investment:

1983
Mar. 1 Received cash dividend of 75¢ per share and stock dividend of 20%.
Sept. 20 Received stock rights offering the purchase of 1 share at $25 for every 4 shares held. At this time stock was quoted ex-rights at $29 and rights were quoted at $1; stock cost was apportioned on this basis. Rights were exercised.

1984
Mar. 1 Received a cash dividend of 80¢ per share and a stock dividend of 10%.
Aug. 15 Received stock rights offering the purchase of 1 share at $20 for every 4 shares held. At this time stock was quoted ex-rights at $24 and rights were quoted at $1; stock cost was apportioned on this basis. Rights were sold at $1.50, less brokerage charges of $50.

Instructions:

(1) Give journal entries to record the foregoing transactions.
(2) Give the investment account balance as of December 31, 1984, including shares and costs in support of this balance.

problem 12-5 (Stock rights and stock dividends)

Transactions in the Manning Corp. investment account during 1984 included the following (assume the specific identification method is used in accounting for stock transactions):

Jan. 7 Purchased 750 units of Gomez Co. preferred and common stock at $90 per unit. Each unit consisted of one share of preferred and three shares of common. No market costs were available.
Feb. 1 Common stock market value became established at $14 per share. No market price is yet available for preferred stock.

Mar. 15 Received stock rights permitting the purchase of one share of common at $10 for every 4 shares held. On this day, rights were being traded at $1 each and stock was being traded ex-rights at $14 per share.

26 Exercised 1,800 rights and sold the remainder at $1 each less $25 brokerage costs.

May 10 Sold the Gomez Co. preferred stocks at $50 per share.

July 22 Received a 10% stock dividend on Gomez Co. common and one share of Gomez Co. 8% preferred stock for every 50 shares of Gomez Co. common held before the 10% stock dividend. On this date, preferred stock was selling for $60 per share, and common stock was selling for $15 per share. Costs were allocated first to preferred stock dividend, then to the common stock dividend.

Oct. 13 Sold 500 shares of Gomez Co. common; 495 shares of Lot 2 and 5 shares from Lot 1. The sales price was $14 per share.

Dec. 10 Gomez Co. redeemed 25 shares of the preferred stock at a call price of $65 per share. These came from the preferred identified with Lot 1.

Instructions:

(1) Give the journal entries to record the foregoing transactions. (Give computations in support of your entries.)
(2) Give the investment account balance on December 31, 1984, and the shares and costs making up this balance.

problem 12-6 (Stock rights and stock dividends)

The following balances appeared in the ledger of the Dalton Company on December 31, 1981.

Investment in Quist Corp. Common Stock, par $10, 500 shares	$10,000
Investment in Quist Corp. 8% Preferred Stock, par $50, 20 shares	$ 1,500

The Dalton Company uses the first-in, first-out method in accounting for stock transactions. In 1982, 1983, and 1984 the following transactions took place relative to the above investments:

1982

Feb. 15 Holders of Quist Corp. 8% preferred were given the right to exchange their holdings at the rate of 5 shares of Quist Corp. common for each share of preferred, and the Dalton Co. made such exchange. Common shares on the date of exchange were quoted on the market at $30 per share.

Nov. 21 Received cash dividends of $1 per share on Quist Corp. common.

1983

June 15 Received additional shares of Quist common in a 2-for-1 stock split. (Par value of common was reduced to $5.)

Nov. 21 Exercised option to receive 1 share of Quist Corp. common for each 15 shares held in lieu of a cash dividend of $1 per share held. The market value of Quist Corp. common on the date of distribution was $20 per share. Dividend revenue was recognized at the value of the shares received.

1984

May 14 Received a stock dividend of 20% on Quist common.

Sept. 16 Received warrants representing right to purchase 1 share of Quist Corp. common for every 6 shares held. On date of warrants issue, the market value of shares ex-rights was $28.50, and the market value of rights was $1.50. Cost of the stock was allocated on this basis. The exercise price was $20 per share.

Sept. 30 Exercised 900 rights identified with the first lot of stock acquired and sold remaining rights at $1.25 per right less brokerage charges of $75.

Dec. 31 Sold 1400 shares of Quist Corp. common at $32 per share less brokerage charges of $225.

Instructions:

(1) Prepare journal entries to record the transactions in Quist Corp. holdings.
(2) Prepare a schedule showing the balance of Quist Corp. common stock held by Dalton Company on December 31, 1984.

problem 12-7 (Stock rights, stock splits, and stock dividends)

The Clawson Co. has the following securities on hand on January 1, 1984.

Hicken Inc. 8% preferred stock, par $100, 50 shares	$5,500
Mangum Inc. common stock, 200 shares	$6,600

During 1984, the following transactions were completed relative to investments.

Jan. 29	Purchased 75 shares of Randall Inc. common for $2,700.
Feb. 14	Received a cash dividend of 60¢ and stock dividend of 20% on Mangum Inc. common.
Apr. 25	Purchased 125 shares of Randall Inc. common for $5,000.
June 30	Received the semiannual dividend on Hicken Inc. 8% preferred.
July 1	Randall Inc. common was split on a 4-for-1 basis.
Aug. 14	Received a dividend of 50¢ on Randall Inc. common.
Aug. 21	Received a cash dividend of 60¢ and a stock dividend of 10% on Mangum Inc. common.
Sept. 13	Sold 100 shares of Randall Inc. common for $2,000 and also sold 25 shares of Hicken Inc. 8% preferred for $3,000.
Oct. 26	Received rights on Randall Inc. common to subscribe for additional shares as follows: 1 share could be acquired at $15 for every 4 shares held. On this date stock was selling for 23 and rights were selling at 2; stock cost was apportioned on this basis.
Nov. 16	Exercised the Randall Inc. rights
Dec. 1	Received a special year-end dividend on Mangum Inc. common of $2.

Instructions:

(1) Assuming the use of first-in, first-out in assigning costs to sales, give journal entries to record the foregoing transactions. (Give calculations in support of your entries.)
(2) Give the investment account balance as of December 31, 1984, including the number of shares and costs comprising such balances.

problem 12-8 (Correction of investment account)

During your December 31, 1984 audit of Monroe Enterprises, you find the following items in the account summarizing the investment in Rubio Manufacturing Co. common stock:

Account **Investment in Rubio Manufacturing Co. Common Stock**

Date		Item	Debit	Credit	Balance Debit	Balance Credit
1984						
Jan.	2	Purchased 6,000 shares at $35	210,000		210,000	
Feb.	15	Cash dividend		6,000	204,000	
June	30	Share of net income for first half of 1984	10,000		214,000	
Oct.	15	Received stock rights		21,400	192,600	
	30	Cash dividend		12,000	180,600	
Nov.	11	Exercised stock rights to purchase 1,500 shares at $35	63,200		243,800	
Dec.	31	Share of net income for second half of 1984	11,250		255,050	

After inquiry, the following additional data were obtained:

(a) Rubio Manufacturing Co. net income for the first and second halves of 1984 was $500,000 and $600,000 respectively.
(b) Broker's fees of $3,000 on the original purchase were recorded as an expense.

(c) The dividend of February 15 represented a distribution of earnings from the second half of 1983.
(d) The dividend of October 30 was $2 per share; $1.50 per share represents earnings and the balance represents a liquidating dividend.
(e) Rubio Manufacturing Co. offered its stockholders the opportunity to subscribe to new stock at $35 per share up to 50% of their holdings. At distribution date, stock rights were selling for $5. Stock was quoted ex-rights at 45.

Instructions:

(1) Give the individual entries for each correction required in the Rubio Manufacturing Co. investment account on December 31, 1984, to bring this account in conformity with generally accepted accounting principles.
(2) Give the corrected balance for the investment account on December 31, 1984, and the shares and costs making up this balance.

problem 12-9 (Investment in common stock—cost to equity to cost method)

Chenowith Inc. wants to gain a controlling interest in Williams Chemical Co. in order to assure a steady source of a raw material manufactured by Williams. The following transactions occurred with respect to Chenowith and Williams. Both companies keep their books on a calendar year basis.

1981

Jan. 2 Chenowith purchased 5,000 shares (5%) of Williams common stock for $10 per share. The assets of Williams had a net carrying value of $800,000. At that date, certain depreciable equipment owned by Williams had a fair market value $30,000 in excess of its carrying value, with an estimated remaining useful life of 10 years. Chenowith also carried land on its books that had a fair market value $70,000 in excess of its book value. The balance of the excess of the cost of the stock over the underlying equity in net assets was attributable to goodwill which is amortized over 40 years. (Unless circumstances indicate otherwise, Chenowith's policy is to amortize any recognized goodwill evenly over a 40-year period from date of recognition.)

Feb. 15 Chenowith received a dividend of $3,000 representing a distribution from income earned in 1980.

July 1 Chenowith purchased 10,000 additional shares of Williams stock for $11 per share. Williams' net income for the first six months of 1981 was $150,000. The net carrying value of Williams stockholders' equity at July 1, 1981, was $890,000. The difference between the fair market value of Williams' depreciable assets and their carrying value at this date was $30,000, and the equipment had an estimated remaining useful life of 9.5 years from the date of the purchase. The market value of the land remained $70,000 over book value. Williams had not issued any new stock during the past six months.

Dec 31 Williams reported net income for the year of $260,000.

1982

Feb. 15 Chenowith received a dividend from Williams of $18,000.

Dec. 31 Williams reported net income for the year of $320,000.

1983

Jan. 2 Chenowith purchased 20,000 additional shares of Williams stock for $13 per share which permitted Chenowith to exercise significant influence over Williams. At this time Williams was experiencing a boycott of its products which was expected to last indefinitely. Although the difference between the fair market values of its assets and their carrying values remained the same, Williams' boycott problems detracted from the long-term attractiveness of its shares, and no implied goodwill was included in the purchase price. (There has been no change in the estimated useful lives of depreciable assets from the date of the original purchase on January 2, 1981).

Feb. 15 Chenowith received a dividend of $49,000 from Williams Co.

Dec. 31 Williams reported net income of $280,000. In view of Williams' boycott situation, Chenowith decided to write off remaining goodwill over a period of 10 years, beginning this year.

1984
Feb. 15 Chenowith received a dividend of $39,200 from Williams Co.
Apr. 1 Chenowith, after experiencing a series of reversals in the marketplace, ceased manufacturing the product containing the raw material from Williams Co. On this date, Chenowith sold 20,000 shares of Williams Co. stock for $12 per share. Chenowith used the average cost of its investment in Williams Co. in calculating its basis in the investment. Assume Williams Co. had no income for the first quarter of 1984.
Dec. 31 Williams reported net income of $295,000 for the year ended December 31, 1984.

1985
Feb. 15 Chenowith received a dividend of $17,700 from Williams Co.
Mar. 20 Chenowith sold its remaining 15,000 shares of Williams Co. stock for $11.50 per share.

Instructions: Give all the entries necessary to record these transactions on the books of Chenowith Inc. (Round computations to the nearest dollar.)

problem 12-10 (Valuation of marketable equity securities)

Transactions of Valley Corp. in securities during 1984 were as follows:

Jan. 29 Purchased 1,500 shares of Colton Inc. common stock for $45,000.
June 22 Purchased 10,000 shares of Riggs Co. preferred stock for $140,000.
Aug. 5 Sold 750 shares of Colton Inc. common stock for $18,750.

The fair market value of Riggs Co. preferred and Colton Inc. common stock on December 31, 1984, the date of the annual audit, was $12 and $20 per share respectively. The president of the company recommends that the cost balance in the investments account be retained because the investments are in reality long-term and the declines in market values seem to be temporary. The auditor counters that since one half of the Colton Inc. common stock has been sold during the year and since the investment in Riggs Co. is in preferred stock, the investments appear to be current assets rather than long-term investments.

Instructions:

(1) Give journal entries to record any valuation adjustments that would be made if the auditor's recommendations are followed.
(2) Give journal entries to record any valuation adjustments that would be made if the president's recommendations are followed.
(3) Give journal entries to record any valuation adjustments that would be made if the Colton Inc. common is identified as long-term, but the decline is felt to be permanent. The Riggs Co. stock is still classified as a current asset.

problem 12-11 (Valuation of long-term marketable equity securities)

The long-term investment portfolio of Roylance Inc. at December 31, 1984, contains the following securities:

Arnold Company common, 1% ownership, 2,000 shares; cost, $45,000; market value $35,000.
Graves Inc. preferred, 1,000 shares; cost $80,000; market value $85,000.
Wilson Inc. 10% bonds, $10,000 face value; cost $12,000; market value $12,400.
Affiliated Inc. common, 30% ownership; carrying value $120,000; market value $115,000.
Parry Company common, 10% ownership, 10,000 shares; cost $67,500; market value $50,000.
Jones Company common, 5% ownership, 6,000 shares; cost $35,000; no market value.

Instructions:

(1) Give the valuation adjustment required at December 31, 1984, assuming market values in the past for the long-term investment portfolio have always exceeded cost and none of the indicated declines in market value are considered permanent.
(2) Assume the Parry Company common stock market decline is considered permanent. Give the valuation entries required at December 31, 1984, under this change in assumption.

(continued)

(3) Assume the market values for the long-term investment portfolio at December 31, 1985, were as follows:

Arnold Co. common	$ 48,000
Graves Inc. preferred	82,000
Wilson Inc. bonds	12,500
Affiliated Inc. common	125,000
Parry Company common	45,000
Jones Company common	no market

Give the valuation entries at December 31, 1985, assuming the conditions at December 31, 1984, were as described in (2).

problem 12-12 (Fund accumulation)

On December 31, 1983, a four-payment fund is set up to redeem $50,000 of preferred stock. The fund is guaranteed to earn 8% compounded annually and must generate enough income to enable the company to retire the stock after the fourth payment. The annual installments paid to the fund trustee are $11,096.07. The first deposit is made immediately.

Instructions:

(1) Give the journal entries in connection with the fund for the years 1983 and 1984. (Assume the company keeps its books on the calendar year basis.)
(2) Suppose that on December 31, 1987, the fund balance of $50,000 consisted of $12,000 cash and $38,000 in securities. The securities are sold for $44,000. Give all of the journal entries that would be made to sell the securities, retire the $50,000 of preferred stock, and liquidate any balance in the fund account.

problem 12-13 (Cash surrender value)

During the course of the audit of Huff Inc., which closes its accounts on December 31, you examine the life insurance policies, premium receipts, and confirmations returned by the insurance companies in response to your request for information. You find that in 1984 the company had paid premiums on the life of the president, Bill Huff, as shown below:

Sole Owner and Beneficiary	Face of Policy	Billed Premium 1984	Dividend Used to Reduce Premium	Annual Premium Date	Cash Surrender Value December 31 1984	Cash Surrender Value December 31 1983
(1) Huff Inc.	$100,000	$2,200	$900	Aug. 30	$32,000	$30,500
(2) Sue Huff, wife of Bill Huff	50,000	2,600	700	Sept. 30	15,000	13,000
(3) Huff Inc.	100,000	3,700	500	Mar. 1	22,000	20,000

Instructions:

(1) Prepare all of the journal entries required for the year 1984.
(2) What balances relating to these insurance policies would appear on the balance sheet prepared on December 31, 1984?

problem 12-14 (Investment in long-term securities—cost to equity method)

On January 1, 1983, Jeffries Inc. paid $700,000 for 10,000 shares of Wolf Company's voting stock, which was a 10% interest in Wolf. At that date, the net assets of Wolf totaled $6,000,000. The fair market values of all of Wolf's identifiable assets and liabilities were equal to their book values. Jeffries does not have the ability to exercise significant influence over the operating and financial policies of Wolf. Jeffries received dividends of $.90 per share from Wolf on October 1, 1983. Wolf reported net income of $400,000 for the year ended December 31, 1983.

On July 1, 1984, Jeffries paid $2,300,000 for 30,000 additional shares of Wolf Company's voting common stock, which represents a 30% investment in Wolf. The fair market values of all of Wolf's identifiable assets net of liabilities were equal to their book values of $6,500,000. As a result of this transaction, Jeffries has the ability to exercise significant influence over the operating and financial policies of Wolf. Jeffries received dividends of $1.10 per share from Wolf on April 1, 1984 and $1.35 per share on October 1, 1984. Wolf reported net income of $500,000 for the year ended December 31, 1984 and $200,000 for the six months ended December 31, 1984. Jeffries amortizes goodwill over a forty-year period.

Instructions:

(1) Compute the income or loss before income taxes for the year ended December 31, 1983 that Jeffries should report from its investment in Wolf in its income statement issued in March 1984.

(2) During March 1985, Jeffries issues comparative financial statements for 1983 and 1984. Compute the income or loss before income taxes for the years ended December 31, 1983 and 1984, that Jeffries should report from its investment in Wolf. Show supporting computations. (AICPA adapted)

problem 12-15 (Investments)

The Putnam Company owned marketable securities at December 31, 1983, which were appropriately recorded as current assets as follows:

	Cost	Market Value
Bart Corporation, 500 shares of $200 par value 6% cumulative preferred stock	$110,000	$240,000
Behrend Corporation, 1,000 shares of $3 no-par convertible preferred stock	225,000	230,000
Bella Company, 10,000 shares of common stock	200,000	250,000
Chockey Inc., 3,000 shares of common stock	90,000	92,000
Dempsey Co., 4,000 shares of common stock	24,000	25,000
Total marketable securities	$649,000	$837,000

Putnam appropriately recorded cash surrender value of life insurance carried on the president of Putnam's life of $42,000 at December 31, 1983. During 1984, the following transactions occurred:

(a) Bart Corporation could not pay dividends on preferred stock in 1984 due to adverse business conditions. The market value of the stock was $120,000 at December 31, 1984.

(b) Behrend Corp., issued cash dividends once a year to stockholders of record on May 31. The cash was received on June 10, 1984. On June 15, 1984, Putnam converted 500 shares of Behrend Corp., $3 no-par convertible preferred stock into 1,000 shares of Behrend Corp., common stock, which had a market value of $114,000 at the date of conversion and $116,000 at December 31, 1984. The market value of the remaining $3 no-par convertible preferred stock was $117,000 at December 31, 1984.

(c) Bella Company issues a 10% stock dividend in 1984. The market value of the common stock at December 31, 1984, was $24 per share.

(d) Chockey, Inc. effected a 2 for 1 split in 1984. The market value of the common stock at December 31, 1984, was $91,000.

(e) Dempsey Co., issued cash dividends to stockholders of record on March 31, 1984, and June 30, 1984, of 30¢ per share at each date. The cash was received on April 15, 1984, and July 15, 1984, respectively. On July 4, 1984, Putnam sold all of its shares of Dempsey for $7 per share.

(f) In January 1984, premiums for the six months ended June 30, 1984, of $2,500 were paid on the president of Putnam's $100,000 life insurance policy. During the six-month period, the cash surrender value of the policy increased $1,300. The president of Putnam died on July 1, 1984, and Putnam received the proceeds from the insurance policy shortly thereafter.

(g) On October 1, 1984, Putnam purchased 100,000 shares representing 40% of the outstanding stock of Neville Company for cash of $1,600,000 when the underlying equity in net assets of 40% of Neville was $1,200,000. Putnam amortizes goodwill over a forty-year period with a full year's amortization taken in the year of the purchase. As a result of this transaction, Putnam has the ability to exercise significant influence over the operating and financial policies of Neville. The net income for Neville for the three months ended December 31, 1984, was $90,000 and for the year ended December 31, 1984, was $170,000. On December 1, 1984, Putnam made a long-term loan to Neville of $500,000. The market value of the stock was $1,605,000 at December 31, 1984. On January 20, 1985, cash dividends of 20¢ per share were paid to stockholders of record on December 31, 1984.

Instructions:

(1) Prepare a schedule of the balance in marketable securities at December 31, 1984, for Putnam. Show supporting computations in good form.

(2) Prepare a schedule of the balance in long-term investments at December 31, 1984, for Putnam. Show supporting computations in good form.

(3) List, and compute the amounts of the above transactions that affect the income statement of Putnam. Ignore income tax and deferred tax considerations in your answer. Show supporting computations in good form. (AICPA adapted)

Part 3 Liabilities and Equity

13 LIABILITIES—CURRENT AND CONTINGENT

CHAPTER OBJECTIVES

Define liabilities and explain how the definition is applied in practice.

Describe how liabilities are reported in the financial statements.

Identify liabilities that are definite in amount and describe how they are recorded and reported.

Identify liabilities that are estimated in amount, and describe how they are estimated, recorded, and reported.

Identify contingent liabilities and describe how they are reported.

Part II focused on the accounts comprising the assets of a company, or the debit side of the balance sheet. Liabilities and owners' equity, the credit side of the balance sheet, are considered in Part III. In this chapter, liabilities in general and some specific current and contingent liabilities are discussed. Subsequent chapters focus on noncurrent liabilities that are relatively complex in nature and, in some cases, directly related to asset accounts. These include bonds and long-term notes, leases, and pensions.

DEFINITION OF LIABILITIES

Liabilities have been defined by the FASB as "probable future sacrifices of economic benefits arising from present obligations of a particular entity to transfer assets or provide services to other entities in the future as a result of past transactions or events."[1] This definition contains significant elements that need to be explored before individual liability accounts are discussed.

A liability is a result of **past transactions or events.** Thus, a liability is not recognized until incurred. This part of the definition excludes contractual obligations from an exchange of promises if performance by both parties is still in the future. Such contracts are referred to as *executory contracts.* This aspect of the liability definition has been subject to much discussion in accounting. The signing of a labor contract that obligates both the employer and the employee does not give rise to a liability in current accounting practice, nor does the placing of an order for the purchase of merchandise. However, under some conditions, the signing of a lease is recognized as an event that requires the current recognition of a liability even though a lease is essentially an executory contract. Clarification of this area is needed.

A liability must involve a **probable future transfer of assets or services.** Although liabilities result from past transactions or events, an obligation may be contingent upon the occurrence of another event sometime in the future. When occurrence of the future event seems probable, the obligation is defined as a liability. Although the majority of liabilities are satisfied by payment of cash, some obligations are satisfied by transferring other types of assets or by providing services. For example, revenue received in advance requires recognition of an obligation to provide goods or services in the future. Usually, the time of payment is specified by a debt instrument, e.g., a note requiring payment of interest and principal on a given date or series of dates. Some obligations, however, require the transfer of assets or services over a period of time, but the exact dates cannot be determined when the liability is incurred, e.g., obligations to provide parts or service under a warranty agreement.

A liability is the **obligation of a particular entity,** i.e., the entity that has the responsibility to transfer assets or provide services. As long as the payment or transfer is probable, it is not necessary that the entity to whom the obligation is owed be identified. Thus, a warranty to make any repairs necessary to an item sold by an entity is an obligation of that entity even though it is not certain which customers will receive benefits. Generally, the obligation rests on a foundation of legal rights and duties. However, obligations created, inferred, or construed from the facts of a particular situation may also be recognized as liabilities. For example, if a company regularly pays vacation pay or year-end bonuses, accrual of these items as a liability is warranted even though no legal agreement exists to make these payments.

---

[1]*Statement of Financial Accounting Concepts No. 3,* "Elements of Financial Statements of Business Enterprises" (Stamford: Financial Accounting Standards Board, December 1980), par. 28.

CLASSIFICATION OF LIABILITIES

Liabilities may be classified as **current** or **noncurrent**. Generally, the distinction between current and noncurrent liabilities is an important one. Such distinction is necessary for the computation of working capital, a measure of the liquidity of an enterprise. However, for some types of entities, such as banks and other financial institutions, the distinction between current and noncurrent assets and liabilities has little or no significance. All assets and liabilities must be considered together to evaluate the liquidity and solvency of these entities.

Generally, the same rules apply for the classification of liabilities as for assets. If a liability arises in the course of an entity's normal operating cycle, it is considered current if it must be satisfied with current assets before the operating cycle is completed or within one year, whichever period is longer. On the other hand, bank borrowings, notes, mortgages and similar obligations are related to the general financial condition of the entity rather than directly to the operating cycle, and are classified as current only if they are to be paid with current assets within one year.

When debt that has been classified as noncurrent will mature within the next year, the liability should be reported as a current liability in order to reflect the expected drain on current assets. However, if the liability is to be paid by transfer of noncurrent assets that have been accumulated for the purpose of liquidating the liability, the obligation continues to be classified as noncurrent.

Short-term obligations that will be refinanced on a long-term basis should not be included in current liabilities. This applies to the currently maturing portion of long-term debt and to all other short-term obligations except those arising in the normal course of operations that are due in customary terms. The refinancing must be more than a mere possibility. The FASB has ruled that noncurrent classification is appropriate only if one of the following conditions is met: (1) the refinancing must actually take place in the period between the balance sheet date and the date the balance sheet is issued or (2) a definite agreement for the refinancing must have been reached prior to issuance of the balance sheet.[2]

Timing is an important factor. If the obligation is paid prior to the actual refinancing, the obligation should be included in current liabilities on the balance sheet.[3] To illustrate, assume that the liabilities of Donnelly Inc. at December 31, 1984, include a note payable for $200,000 due January 15, 1985. The management of Donnelly intends to refinance the note by issuing 10-year bonds. The bonds are actually issued before the issuance of the December 31, 1984, balance sheet on February 15, 1985. If the bonds were issued prior to payment of the note, the note should be classified as noncurrent on the

[2]*Statement of Financial Accounting Standards No. 6*, "Classification of Short-Term Obligations Expected to be Refinanced" (Stamford: Financial Accounting Standards Board, 1975), par. 11.

[3]*FASB Interpretation No. 8*, "Classification of a Short-Term Obligation Repaid Prior to Being Replaced by a Long-Term Security" (Stamford: Financial Accounting Standards Board, 1976).

December 31, 1984, balance sheet. If payment of the note preceded the sale of the bonds, however, the note should be included in current liabilities.

MEASUREMENT OF LIABILITIES

The definition of liabilities established by the FASB does not include measurement considerations. As outlined in Chapter 3, the measurement of the defined elements is a separate part of the conceptual framework project yet to be completed. Before liabilities can be included in the traditional balance sheet, they must be measured in financial terms. They should normally be reported at the amount necessary to liquidate the claim if it were being paid today. Thus, if the claim isn't to be paid until sometime in the future, the claim should either provide for interest to be paid on the debt, or the obligation should be reported at the discounted value of its maturity amount. Only in recent years have discounted values been used in accounting practice. Obligations arising in the course of normal business operations involving the buying and selling of merchandise or raw materials, and due within a one-year period, normally are not discounted.[4] Thus, regular accounts payable are not discounted even though they carry no interest provision. However, nonoperating business transactions such as the borrowing of money, purchase of assets over time, and long-term leases, do involve the discounting process. The obligation in these instances is the present value of the future resource outflows.

Some liabilities, such as the principal payments on notes, are definite in amount. Other liabilities, such as warranty obligations, are estimated. Liabilities in both categories are normally reported on a balance sheet as claims against recorded assets. Some items that resemble liabilities are contingent upon the occurrence of some future event, and are not recorded until it is probable that the event will occur. If no reasonable basis exists for estimating the amount of liability or a probable contingent liability, no recording of the obligation can take place. However, disclosure of the obligation should be made in a note to the financial statements.

The remaining sections of this chapter are divided into liabilities that are definite in amount, liabilities that are estimated in amount, and contingent liabilities. Several examples of liabilities in each area are presented to clarify the accounting issues involved.

LIABILITIES THAT ARE DEFINITE IN AMOUNT

Representative of liabilities that are definite in amount and are frequently found on the balance sheet are notes payable, accounts payable, and miscellaneous operating payables including salaries, payroll taxes, property and sales taxes, and income taxes. Some liabilities accrue as time passes.

---

[4] *Opinions of the Accounting Principles Board No. 21*, "Interest on Receivables and Payables" (New York: American Institute of Certified Public Accountants, 1971), par. 3.

Most notable in this category are interest and rent, although the latter is frequently paid in advance. Some of the problems arising in determining the balances to be reported for liabilities that are definite in amount are described in the following sections.

Short-Term Notes Payable

Notes payable may include notes issued to trade creditors for the purchase of goods and services, to banks for loans, to officers and stockholders for advances, and to others for the purchase of plant assets. It is normally desirable to classify current notes payable on the balance sheet in terms of their origin. Such presentation provides information concerning the sources of business indebtedness and the extent to which the business has relied on each source in financing its activities.

The problems encountered in the valuation of notes payable are similar to those discussed in Chapter 7 with respect to notes receivable. In reporting notes receivable, it was recognized that theoretical accuracy would require reporting at present values. It was further observed that valuation accounts should be established for amounts estimated to be uncollectible to arrive at the net realizable value of the asset. In reporting notes payable, similar considerations apply. When property, goods, or services are acquired at an amount payable at some future date, this amount may be regarded as composed of a purchase price and a charge for interest for the period of payment deferral. If determinable, an established exchange or purchase price may be used to arrive at the present value of the note payable. In the absence of such a price, the present value of the note payable should be determined by discounting the amount payable at an appropriate interest rate for the period payment is deferred. The acquisition, then, is recorded by a debit to the account reporting the purchase at the amount computed, a debit to the discount on the note payable, and a credit to the note payable at its face amount. The discount is amortized over the life of the note payable as a debit to interest expense; in preparing a balance sheet, any unamortized discount is reported as a direct subtraction from the note payable.

Individual notes are frequently secured by the pledge of certain assets. Assets pledged may consist of marketable securities, notes receivable, accounts receivable, inventories, or plant assets. The pledge of an asset limits the use or the disposition of the asset or its proceeds until the related obligation is liquidated. In the event of bankruptcy, the cash realized on a pledged asset must first be applied to the satisfaction of the related obligation. A liability is **partly secured** or **fully secured** depending on whether the value of the pledged property is less than the amount of the obligation or whether such value is equal to or in excess of the obligation. As stated earlier, reference is made to a lien on an asset by a parenthetical remark in the "Assets" section of the balance sheet. It is also desirable to provide a parenthetical remark in connection with the secured liability identifying the asset pledged and its present market value.

There are many kinds of notes. However, two types frequently create difficulty in recording: (1) a note payable with no stated interest rate or an unreasonable rate, and (2) a note payable that is discounted at a financial institution. An example of each type is included in the following paragraphs:

(1) Assume that equipment is purchased in exchange for a $10,000 non-interest-bearing note for one year. If the equipment and the related obligation are recorded at $10,000, this would fail to recognize the charge for interest implicit in the deferred payment arrangement, and both asset and liability balances would be overstated. If the prevailing interest rate on similar obligations is 10%, the asset, as well as the liability, must be recognized at a cash-equivalent value of $9,090.91 ($10,000 ÷ 1.10). The following entry should be made:

Equipment	9,090.91	
Discount on Notes Payable........................	909.09	
Notes Payable................................		10,000.00

In reporting the note on the balance sheet prior to its payment, an adjustment should be made to recognize the accrual of interest at 10% on the amount of the debt of $9,090.91 to the date of the balance sheet. The accrual of interest is recorded by a debit to Interest Expense and a credit to Discount on Notes Payable. The balance of the discount on the notes payable is subtracted from notes payable in reporting the liability on the balance sheet. A similar procedure would be required if a note provided for a nominal interest rate that was substantially lower than the current market rate.

(2) Assume that a company borrows $10,000 by discounting its own $10,000 one-year note at the bank, receiving $10,000 less a discount of 10% or $9,000. If the amount of the discount is recognized as prepaid interest and the note is recorded at $10,000, both asset and liability balances would be overstated: interest has not been paid in advance but is still to be paid; the obligation at the time of borrowing is no greater than the amount borrowed. The following entry should be made:

Cash	9,000	
Discount on Notes Payable........................	1,000	
Notes Payable................................		10,000

In reporting the note on the balance sheet prior to its payment, an adjustment should be made to recognize the accrual of interest just as in the first example. However, a discount of 10% is, in effect, a charge for interest at the rate of 11.1% ($1,000 ÷ $9,000). The accrual of interest, then, is computed at 11.1% on the amount of the debt of $9,000 to the date of the balance sheet.

Accounts Payable

Most goods and services in today's economic environment are purchased on credit. The term **accounts payable** usually refers to the amount due for the purchase of materials by a manufacturing company or merchandise by a wholesaler or retailer. Other obligations, such as salaries and wages, rent, interest, and utilities are reported as separate liabilities in accounts descriptive of the nature of the obligation. Accounts payable are not recorded when purchase orders are placed, but only when legal title to the goods passes to the buyer. The rules for the customary recognition of legal passage of title were presented in Chapter 8. If goods are in transit at year-end, the purchase should be recorded if the shipment terms indicate that title has passed. This means that care must be exercised to review the purchase of goods and services near the end of an accounting period to assure a proper cut-off and reporting of liabilities and inventory.

It is customary to report accounts payable at the expected amount of the payment. Because the payment period is normally short, no recognition of interest by reporting the present value of the liability is required. As indicated in Chapter 8, if cash discounts are available, the liability should be reported net of the expected cash discount. Failure to use the net method in recording purchases reports liabilities in excess of the payment finally made.

Miscellaneous Operating Payables

Many miscellaneous payables arise in the course of a company's operating activities. Three of these are specifically discussed in this section. They are indicative of other specific liabilities that could be reported by a given entity. In general, the points made in discussing the definition of liabilities in the opening section of this chapter apply to these miscellaneous operating liabilities.

Salaries and Bonuses Payable. In an ongoing entity, salaries and wages of officers and other employees accrue daily. Normally, no entry is made for these expenses until payment is made. A liability for unpaid salaries and wages is recorded, however, at the end of an accounting period when a more precise matching of revenues and expenses is desired. An estimate of the amount of unpaid wages and salaries is made, and an adjusting entry is prepared to recognize the amount due. Usually the entire accrued amount is identified as salaries payable with no attempt to identify the withholdings associated with the accrual. When payment is made in the subsequent period, the amount is allocated between the employee and other entities such as government taxing units, unions, and insurance companies.

For example, assume that a company has 15 employees who are paid every two weeks. At December 31, four days of unpaid wages have accrued. Analysis reveals that the 15 employees earn a total of $1,000 a day. Thus the adjusting entry at December 31 would be:

Salaries and Wages Expense	4,000	
Salaries and Wages Payable		4,000

This entry may be reversed at the beginning of the next period, or, when payment is made, Salaries and Wages Payable may be debited for $4,000.

Additional compensation in the form of accrued bonuses or commissions should also be recognized. Bonuses are often based on some measure of the employer's income. Employee bonuses, even those viewed as a sharing of profits with employees, are deductible expenses for the purposes of income tax.

An agreement may provide for a bonus computed on the basis of gross revenue or sales, or on the basis of income. When income is used, the computation will depend on whether the bonus is based on: (1) income before deductions for bonus or income tax, (2) income after deduction for bonus but before deduction for income tax, (3) income after deduction for income tax but before deduction for bonus, or (4) net income after deductions for both bonus and income tax. The degree of difficulty in computing a bonus based on income varies with the measure of income used. To illustrate the computations required in each case, assume the following: Barker Sales Inc. gives the sales managers of its individual stores a bonus of 10 percent of store earnings. Income for 1984 for store No. 1 before any charges for bonus or income tax was $100,000. The income tax rate is 40 percent.

Let B=Bonus
T=Income Tax

(1) *Assuming the bonus is based on income before deductions for bonus or income tax:*

$$B = .10 \times \$100{,}000$$
$$B = \$10{,}000$$

(2) *Assuming the bonus is based on income after deduction for bonus but before deduction for income tax:*

$$B = .10\,(\$100{,}000 - B)$$
$$B = \$10{,}000 - .10B$$
$$B + .10B = \$10{,}000$$
$$1.10B = \$10{,}000$$
$$B = \$9{,}090.91$$

Calculation of the bonus may be proved as follows:

Income before bonus and income tax	$100,000.00
Deduct bonus	9,090.91
Income after bonus but before income tax	$ 90,909.09
Bonus rate	10%
Bonus	$ 9,090.91

(3) *Assuming the bonus is based on income after deduction for income tax but before deduction for bonus:*

$$B = .10\,(\$100{,}000 - T)$$
$$T = .40\,(\$100{,}000 - B)$$

Substituting for T in the first equation and solving for B:

$$B = .10\,[\$100{,}000 - .40\,(\$100{,}000 - B)]$$
$$B = .10\,(\$100{,}000 - \$40{,}000 + .40B)$$
$$B = \$10{,}000 - \$4{,}000 + .04B$$
$$B - .04B = \$6{,}000$$
$$.96B = \$6{,}000$$
$$B = \$6{,}250$$

Substituting for B in the second equation and solving for T:

$$T = .40\ (\$100{,}000 - \$6{,}250)$$
$$T = .40 \times \$93{,}750$$
$$T = \$37{,}500$$

Calculation of the bonus may be proved as follows:

Income before bonus and income tax	$100,000
Deduct income tax	37,500
Income after income tax but before bonus	$ 62,500
Bonus rate	10%
Bonus	$ 6,250

(4) *Assuming the bonus is based on net income after deductions for bonus and income tax:*

$$B = .10\ (\$100{,}000 - B - T)$$
$$T = .40\ (\$100{,}000 - B)$$

Substituting for T in the first equation and solving for B:

$$B = .10\ [\$100{,}000 - B - .40\ (\$100{,}000 - B)]$$
$$B = .10\ (\$100{,}000 - B - \$40{,}000 + .40B)$$
$$B = \$10{,}000 - .1B - \$4{,}000 + .04B$$
$$B + .1B - .04B = \$10{,}000 - \$4{,}000$$
$$1.06B = \$6{,}000$$
$$B = \$5{,}660.38$$

Substituting for B in the second equation and solving for T:

$$T = .40\ (\$100{,}000 - \$5{,}660.38)$$
$$T = .40 \times \$94{,}339.62$$
$$T = \$37{,}735.85$$

Calculation of the bonus is proved in the following summary:

Income before bonus and income tax		$100,000.00
Deduct: Bonus	$ 5,660.38	
Income tax	37,735.85	43,396.23
Net income after bonus and income tax		$ 56,603.77
Bonus rate		10%
Bonus		$ 5,660.38

The bonus should be reported on the income statement as an expense before arriving at net income regardless of the method employed in its computation.

Payroll Taxes and Income Tax Withheld. Social security and income tax legislation impose four taxes based on payrolls:

(1) Federal old-age, survivors, disability and hospital insurance
(2) Federal unemployment insurance
(3) State unemployment insurance
(4) Income tax withheld

Federal Old-Age, Survivors, Disability, and Hospital Insurance. The Federal Insurance Contributions Act (FICA), generally referred to as social security legislation, provides for taxes on employers and employees to provide funds for federal old-age, survivors, disability, and hospital insurance benefits for certain individuals and members of their families. At one time, only employees were covered by this legislation; however, coverage now includes most individuals who are self-employed.

Provisions of the legislation require equal contributions by the employee and the employer. The contribution is based on a tax rate applied to annual gross wages up to a designated maximum. Both the tax rate and the wage base have greatly increased since the inception of the social security legislation to provide for increasing benefits. In the mid-thirties, an employer and employee each contributed one percent of the employee's annual earnings up to $3,000. In 1983, the rate was 6.7 percent on earnings up to $35,700, with additional increases projected for subsequent years.

Employers of one or more persons, with certain exceptions, come under the law. The amount of the employee's tax is withheld from the wage payment by the employer. The employer remits this amount together with a matched amount. The employer is required to maintain complete records and submit detailed support for the tax remittance. The employer also is responsible for the full amount of the tax even when the employee contributions are not withheld. Self-employed persons who carry on a trade or business are assessed a tax rate somewhat higher than the employee's rate but less than the sum of the employee and employer contributions.

Federal Unemployment Insurance. The Federal Social Security Act and the Federal Unemployment Tax Act provide for the establishment of unemployment insurance plans. Employers with covered workers employed in each of 20 weeks during a calendar year or who pay $1,500 or more in wages during any calendar quarter are affected.

Under present provisions of the law, the federal government taxes eligible employers on the first $7,000 paid to every employee during the calendar year. The rate of tax in effect for 1983 and 1984 is 3.5 percent, but the employer is allowed a tax credit limited to 2.7 percent for taxes paid under state unemployment compensation laws. No tax is levied on the employee. When an employer is subject to a tax of 2.7 percent or more as a result of state unemployment legislation, the federal unemployment tax, then, is 0.8 percent of the wages. A significant increase in the federal unemployment tax rate is projected for 1985 and subsequent years.

Payment to the federal government is required quarterly. Unemployment benefits are paid by the individual states. Revenues collected by the federal government under the acts are used to meet the cost of administering state and federal unemployment plans as well as to provide supplemental unemployment benefits.

State Unemployment Insurance. State unemployment compensation laws are not the same in all states. In most states, laws provide for tax only on employers; but in a few states, taxes are applicable to both employers and employees. Each state law specifies the classes of exempt employees, the number of employees required or the amount of wages paid before the tax is applicable, and the contributions that are to be made by employers and employees. Exemptions are frequently similar to those under the federal act. Tax payment is generally required on or before the last day of the month following each calendar quarter.

Although the normal tax on employers may be 2.7 percent, states have merit rating or experience plans providing for lower rates based on employers' individual employment experiences. Employers with stable employment records are taxed at a rate in keeping with the limited amount of benefits required for their former employees; employers with less satisfactory employment records contribute at a rate more nearly approaching 2.7 percent in view of the greater amount of benefits paid to their former employees. Savings under state merit systems are allowed as credits in the calculation of the federal contribution, so the federal tax does not exceed 0.8 percent even though payment of less than 2.7 percent is made by an employer entitled to a lower rate under the merit rating system.

Income Tax Withheld. Federal income tax on the wages of an individual are collected in the period in which the wages are paid. The "pay-as-you-go" plan requires employers to withhold income tax from wages paid to their employees. Most states and many local governments also impose income taxes on the earnings of employees that must be withheld and remitted by the employer. Withholding is required not only of employers engaged in a trade or business, but also of religious and charitable organizations, educational institutions, social organizations, and governments of the United States, the states, the territories, and their agencies, instrumentalities, and political subdivisions. Certain classes of wage payments are exempt from withholding although these are still subject to income tax.

An employer must meet withholding requirements under the law even if wages of only one employee are subject to such withholdings. The amounts to be withheld by the employer are developed from formulas provided by the law or from tax withholding tables made available by the government. Withholding is based on the length of the payroll period, the amount earned, and the number of withholding exemptions claimed by the employee. Taxes required under the Federal Insurance Contributions Act (both employees' and employer's portions) and income tax that has been withheld by the employer are paid to the federal government at the same time. These combined taxes are deposited in an authorized bank quarterly, monthly, or several times each month depending on the amount of the liability. Quarterly and annual statements must also be filed providing a summary of all wages paid by the employer.

Accounting for Payroll Taxes and Income Tax Withheld. To illustrate the accounting procedures for payroll taxes and income tax withheld, assume that in January, 1984, salaries for a retail store with 15 employees are $15,000. The state unemployment compensation law provides for a tax on employers of 2.7 percent. Income tax withholdings for the month are $1,600. Assume FICA rates are 7 percent for employer and employee. Entries for the payroll and the employer's payroll taxes follow:

Salaries Expense	15,000	
FICA Tax Payable		1,050
Employees Income Tax Payable		1,600
Cash		12,350
To record payment of payroll.		
Payroll Taxes Expense	1,575	
FICA Tax Payable		1,050
State Unemployment Tax Payable		405
Federal Unemployment Tax Payable		120
To record the payroll tax liability of the employer.		

Computation:

Tax under Federal Insurance Contributions Act: 7% × $15,000	$1,050
Tax under state unemployment insurance legislation: 2.7% × $15,000	405
Tax under Federal Unemployment Tax Act: 0.8% (3.5% − credit of 2.7%) × $15,000	120
Total payroll taxes expense	$1,575

When tax payments are made to the proper agencies, the tax liability accounts are debited and Cash is credited.

The employer's payroll taxes, as well as the taxes withheld from employees, are based on amounts paid to employees during the period regardless of the basis employed for reporting income. When financial reports are prepared on the accrual basis, the employer will have to recognize both accrued payroll and the employer's payroll taxes relating thereto by adjustments at the end of the accounting period.

For example, assume that the salaries and wages accrued at December 31 were $4,000. Of this amount, $1,000 was subject to unemployment tax and $2,500 to FICA tax. The accrual entry for the employer's payroll taxes would be as follows:

Payroll Taxes Expense	210	
FICA Tax Payable		175
State Unemployment Tax Payable		27
Federal Unemployment Tax Payable		8
To accrue the payroll tax liability of the employer.		

Computation:

Tax under Federal Insurance Contributions Act: 7% × $2,500	$175
Tax under state unemployment insurance legislation: 2.7% × $1,000	27
Tax under Federal Unemployment Tax Act: 0.8% × $1,000	8
	$210

As was true with the accrual entry for the salaries and wages discussed on page 475, the preceding entry may be reversed at the beginning of the new period, or the accrued liabilities may be debited when the payments are made to the taxing authorities.

Agreements with employees may provide for payroll deductions and employer contributions for other items, such as group insurance plans, pension plans, savings bonds purchases, or union dues. Such agreements call for accounting procedures similar to those described for payroll taxes and income tax withholdings.

Other Tax Liabilities. There are many different types of taxes imposed on business entities. In addition to the several payroll taxes discussed in the previous section, a company usually must pay property taxes, federal and state income taxes on their earnings, and serve as an agent for the collection of sales taxes. Each of these liabilities has some unusual features that can complicate accounting for them.

Property Taxes. Real and personal property taxes are based on the assessed valuation of properties as of a particular date. This has given rise to the view held by courts and others that taxes accrue as of a particular date. Generally, the date of accrual has been held to be the date of property assessment, or lien date, and a liability for the full year's property tax can be established at that date. The offset to the liability is a deferred expense and is generally recognized as a charge against revenue over the fiscal year of the taxing authority for which the taxes are levied. This procedure relates the tax charge to the period in which the taxes provide benefits through government service. The date for payment of the liability is determined by the taxing authority and is accounted for independently from the monthly recognition of property tax expense.

To illustrate accounting for property taxes, assume that the taxing authority is on a July 1 to June 30 fiscal year, but the entity paying the tax is on a calendar year basis. Property taxes assessed for the period July 1, 1984, to June 30, 1985, are $60,000, and the full year's tax is to be paid on or before November 15, 1984. The following entry is made by the taxpaying entity at July 1, 1984, to accrue property taxes for the year:

Deferred Property Taxes	60,000	
Property Taxes Payable		60,000

Each month, the following entry would be made to recognize the expense:

Property Tax Expense	5,000	
Deferred Property Taxes		5,000

The entry to record payment of the property taxes on November 15, 1984, would be:

Property Taxes Payable	60,000	
Cash		60,000

At December 31, 1984, the deferred property tax account would have a debit balance of $30,000, representing the property taxes to be recognized as expenses in 1985. If the tax were due in January, 1985, and no payment had been made as of December 31, 1984, Property Taxes Payable would have a $60,000 credit balance, that would be reported as a current liability on the balance sheet.

Although the preceding approach seems to reflect the current definition of liabilities as established by the FASB, some companies recognize the liability ratably over the year rather than on the assessment or lien date. Under this latter approach, a prepaid property tax account is created when the full year's tax is paid before the end of the taxing authority's fiscal year. In the authors' opinion, this practice is not as informative and useful as that illustrated.

Income Taxes. Both federal and state governments raise a large portion of their revenue from income taxes assessed against both individuals and businesses. The taxable income of a business entity is determined by applying the tax rules and regulations to the operations of the business. As indicated in Chapter 3, the income tax rules do not always follow generally accepted accounting principles. Thus, the income reported for tax purposes may differ from that reported on the income statement. This difference can give rise to deferred income taxes, a special liability item discussed more fully in Chapter 20. The actual amount payable for the current year must be determined after all adjusting entries are made at the close of a fiscal period. Federal and some state income tax regulations require companies to estimate their tax liability, and make periodic payments during the year in advance of the final computation and submission of the tax returns. Thus, the amount of income tax liability at year-end is usually much lower than the total tax computed for the year. Because income tax returns are always subject to government audit, a contingent liability exists for any year within the statute of limitations not yet reviewed by the Internal Revenue Service. If an additional liability arises as a result of an audit, the additional assessment should be reported as a liability until the payment is made.

Sales and Use Taxes. With the passage of sales and use tax laws by state and local governments, additional duties are required of a business unit. Laws generally provide that the business unit must act as an agent for the governmental authority in the collection from customers of sales tax on the transfers of tangible personal properties. The buyer is responsible for the payment of sales tax to the seller when both buyer and seller are in the same tax jurisdiction; however, the buyer is responsible for the payment of use tax directly to the tax authority when the seller is outside the jurisdiction of such authority. Provision must be made in the accounts for the liability to the government for the tax collected from customers and the additional tax that the business must absorb.

The sales tax payable is generally a stated percentage of sales. The actual sales total and the sales tax collections are usually recorded separately at the time of sale. Cash or Accounts Receivable is debited; Sales and Sales Tax Payable are credited. The amount of sales tax to be paid to the taxing authority is computed on the recorded sales. If sales tax collections are not exactly equal to the sales tax liability because either more or less sales tax was collected than was required by law, the payable account will require adjustment to bring it to the balance due. In making this adjustment, a gain or a loss on sales tax collection is recognized. In some cases, sales tax collections as well as sales are recorded in total in the sales account. Under these conditions it becomes necessary to divide this amount into its component parts, sales and sales tax payable. For example, if the sales tax is 5 percent of sales, then the amount recorded in the sales account is equal to sales + .05 of sales, or 1.05 times the sales total. The amount of sales is obtained by dividing the sales account balance by 1.05, and 5 percent of the sales amount as thus derived is the tax liability. To illustrate, assume that the sales account balance is $100,000, which includes sales tax of 5 percent. Sales, then, are

$100,000 ÷ 1.05 = $95,238.10. The sales tax liability is then 5 percent of $95,238.10 = $4,761.90. The liability can also be determined by subtracting the sales figure, $95,238.10 from $100,000.00. To record the liability, Sales would be debited and Sales Tax Payable would be credited for $4,761.90.

Unearned Revenues

A significant class of liabilities is represented by **unearned revenues.** Frequently, these liabilities represent an obligation to provide services rather than tangible resources. Common types of unearned revenue include advances from customers, unearned rent, unearned subscription revenue for publishing companies, unearned interest, and unearned commissions. Unearned revenue accounts are classified as current or noncurrent liabilities depending on when the revenue will be earned. When the revenue is earned, e.g., when services are performed, the unearned revenue account is debited and an appropriate revenue account is credited. If advances are refunded without providing goods or services, the liability is reduced by the payment, and no revenue is recognized. A full discussion of revenue recognition is presented in Chapter 19.

LIABILITIES ESTIMATED IN AMOUNT

The amount of an obligation is generally established by contract or accrues at a specified rate. There are instances, however, when an obligation clearly exists on a balance sheet date but the amount ultimately to be paid cannot be definitely determined. Because the amount to be paid is not definite does not mean the liability can be ignored or given a contingent status. The claim must be estimated from whatever data are available. Obligations arising from current operations, for example, the cost of meeting warranties for service and repairs on goods sold, must be estimated when prior experience indicates there is a definite liability. Here, uncertainty as to the amount and timing of expenditures is accompanied by an inability to identify the payees; but the fact that there are charges yet to be absorbed is certain.

Representative of liabilities that are estimated in amount and frequently found on financial statements are the following:

(1) Refundable deposits, reporting the estimated amount to be refunded to depositors.
(2) Warranties for service and replacements, reporting the estimated future claims by customers as a result of past guarantees of services or products or product part replacements.
(3) Customer premium offers, reporting the estimated value of premiums or prizes to be distributed as a result of past sales or sales promotion activities.
(4) Tickets, tokens, and gift certificates, reporting the estimated obligations in the form of services or merchandise arising from the receipt of cash in past periods.
(5) Compensated absences, reporting the estimated future payments attributable to past services of employees.

Refundable Deposits

Liabilities of a company may include an obligation to refund amounts previously collected from customers as deposits. **Refundable deposits** may be classified as current or noncurrent liabilities depending on the purpose of the deposit. If deposits are made to protect the company against nonpayment for future services to be rendered, and the services are expected to be provided over a long period, the deposit should be reported as a noncurrent liability. Utility companies characteristically charge certain customers, such as those renting their homes, a deposit that is held until a customer discontinues the service, usually because of a move.

Another type of customer deposit is one made for reusable containers, such as bottles or drums, that hold the product being purchased. When a sale is recorded, a liability is recognized for the deposit. When a container is returned, a refund or credit is given for the deposit made. Periodically, an adjustment is recorded for containers not expected to be returned. The asset "containers" and the related accumulated depreciation account should be reduced to eliminate the book value of containers not expected to be returned, and any gain or loss is recognized on the "sale" of the containers.

Warranties for Service and Replacements

Many companies agree to provide free service on units failing to perform satisfactorily or to replace defective goods. When these agreements, or **warranties**, involve only minor costs, such costs may be recognized in the periods incurred. When these agreements involve significant future costs and when experience indicates a definite future obligation exists, estimates of such costs should be made and matched against current revenues. Such estimates are usually recorded by a debit to an expense account and a credit to a liability account. Subsequent costs of fulfilling warranties are debited to the liability account and credited to an appropriate account, e.g., Cash or Inventory.

To illustrate accounting for warranties, consider the following example. Supersonic Sound Inc. sells compact stereo systems with a two-year warranty. Past experience indicates that 10 percent of all sets sold will need repairs in the first year, and 20 percent will need repairs in the second year. The average repair cost is \$50 per system. The number of systems sold in 1984 and 1985 was 5,000 and 6,000, respectively. Actual repair costs were \$12,500 in 1984 and \$55,000 in 1985; it is assumed that all repair costs involved cash expenditures.

1984	Warranty Expense	75,000	
	Estimated Liability Under Warranties		75,000
	Estimated warranty expense based on systems sold: 5,000 × .30 × \$50 = \$75,000.		
	Estimated Liability Under Warranties	12,500	
	Cash		12,500
	Repairs actually made in 1984.		

1985	Warranty Expense	90,000	
	Estimated Liability Under Warranties		90,000
	Estimated warranty expense based on systems sold: 6,000 × .30 × $50 = $90,000.		
	Estimated Liability Under Warranties	55,000	
	Cash		55,000
	Repairs actually made in 1985.		

Periodically, the warranty liability account should be analyzed to see if the actual repairs approximate the estimate. Adjustment to the liability account will be required if experience differs appreciably from the estimates. These adjustments are changes in estimates and are reported in the period of change. If sales and repairs in the preceding example are assumed to occur evenly through the year, analysis of the liability account at the end of 1985 shows the ending balance of $97,500 ($75,000 + $90,000 − $12,500 − $55,000) is reasonably close to the predicted amount of $100,000 based upon the 10 percent and 20 percent estimates.

Computation:	
1984 sales still under warranty for 6 months: $50 × [5,000 (½ × .20)]	$ 25,000
1985 sales still under warranty for 18 months: $50 × [6,000 (½ × .10) + 6,000 (.20)]	75,000
Total	$100,000

Assume, however, that warranty costs incurred in 1985 were only $35,000. Then the ending balance of $117,500 would be much higher than the $100,000 estimate. If the $17,500 difference were considered to be material, an adjustment to warranty expense would be made in 1985 as follows:

Estimated Liability Under Warranties	17,500	
Warranty Expense		17,500
Adjustment of estimate for warranty repairs.		

In certain cases, customers are charged special fees for a service or replacement warranty covering a specific period. When fees are collected, an unearned revenue account is credited. The unearned revenue is then recognized as revenue over the warranty period. Costs incurred in meeting the contract requirements are debited to expense; Cash, Inventory, or other appropriate account is credited. The **service contract** is in reality an insurance contract, and the amount charged for the contract is based on the past repair experience of the company for the item sold. The fee usually is set at a rate that will produce a profit margin on the contract if expectations are realized.

To illustrate accounting for service contracts, assume a company sells three-year service contracts covering its product. During the first year, $50,000 was received on contracts, and expenses incurred in connection with these contracts totaled $5,000 all of which was for replacement parts. It is estimated from past experience that the pattern of repairs, based on the total dollars spent for repairs, is 25 percent in the first year of the contract, 30 percent in the second year, and 45 percent in the third year. In addition, it is assumed that sales of the contracts are made evenly during the year. The following entries would be made in the first year.

Cash	50,000	
Unearned Revenue from Service Contracts		50,000
Sale of service contracts.		
Unearned Revenue from Service Contracts	6,250	
Revenue from Service Contracts		6,250
Estimated revenue earned from contracts. 12½% (½ of 25%) of $50,000, or $6,250.		
Service Contract Expense	5,000	
Inventory		5,000
Repairs actually made during the year.		

Based on the above entries, a profit of $1,250 on service contracts would be recognized in the first year. If future expectations change, adjustments will be necessary to the unearned revenue account to reflect the change in estimate.

The accounts Estimated Liability Under Warranties and Unearned Revenue from Service Contracts are classified as current or noncurrent liabilities depending on the period remaining on the warranty. Those warranty costs expected to be incurred within one year or unearned revenues expected to be earned within one year are classified as current; the balance as long-term. In the above illustration, the expected revenue percentage for the second year would be 27½ percent of the contract price, i.e., 12½ percent for balance of first year expectations and 15 percent (½ of 30 percent) for one-half of the second year expectations, or $13,750. This amount would be classified as current. The remaining 60 percent, or $30,000, of unearned revenue would be classified as noncurrent.

The method of accounting illustrated above does not recognize any income on the initial sale of the contract, but only as the period of the service contract passes and the actual costs are matched against an estimate of the earned revenue. Alternatively, a company could estimate in advance the cost of the repairs and recognize the difference between the amount of the service contract and the expected repair cost in the period of the contract sale. The choice of which method to use depends on the degree of confidence in the estimated repair cost. As discussed more fully in Chapter 19, revenue recognition varies with the facts involved. When collection is reasonably assured and future costs are known with a high degree of certainty, immediate income recognition is recommended. In the case of service contracts, the uncertainty of future expenses usually dictates use of the illustrated method.

Customer Premium Offers

Many companies offer special premiums to customers to stimulate the regular purchase of certain products. These offers may be open for a limited time or may be of a continuing nature. The premium is normally made available when the customer submits the required number of product labels or other evidence of purchase. In certain instances the premium offer may provide for an optional cash payment.

If a premium offer expires on or before the end of the company's fiscal period, adjustments in the accounts are not required. Premium obligations are fully met and the premium expense account summarizes the full charge for the period. However, when a premium offer is continuing, an adjustment must be made at the end of the period to recognize the liability for future redemptions—Premium Expense is debited and an appropriate liability account is credited. The expense is thus charged to the period benefiting from the premium plan and current liabilities reflect the claim for premiums outstanding. If premium distributions are debited to an expense account, the liability balance may be reversed at the beginning of the new period.

To illustrate the accounting for a premium offer, assume the following: Smart Foods offers a set of breakfast bowls upon the receipt of 20 certificates, one certificate being included in each package of the cereal distributed by this company. The cost of each set of bowls to the company is $2. It is estimated that only 40 percent of the certificates will be redeemed. In 1984, the company purchased 10,000 sets of bowls at $2 per set; 400,000 packages of cereal containing certificates were sold at a price of $1.20 per package. By the end of 1984, 30 percent of the certificates had been redeemed. Entries for 1984 are as follows:

Transaction		Entry		
1984:				
Premium purchases:		Premiums—Bowl Sets	20,000	
10,000 sets × $2 = $20,000		Cash		20,000
Sales:		Cash	480,000	
400,000 packages × $1.20 = $480,000		Sales		480,000
Premium claim redemptions:		Premium Expense	12,000	
120,000 certificates, or 6,000 sets × $2 = $12,000.		Premiums—Bowl Sets		12,000
December 31, 1984:				
Coupons estimated redeemable in future periods:		Premium Expense	4,000	
Total estimated redemptions—		Estimated Premium Claims Outstanding		4,000
40% of 400,000	160,000			
Redemptions in 1984	120,000			
Estimated future redemptions	40,000			
Estimated claims outstanding:				
40,000 certificates, or 2,000 sets @ $2	$ 4,000			
January 1, 1985 (optional):		Estimated Premium Claims Outstanding	4,000	
Reversal of accrued liability balance.		Premium Expense		4,000

The balance sheet at the end of 1984 will show premiums of $8,000 as a current asset and estimated premium claims outstanding of $4,000 as a current liability; the income statement for 1984 will show premium expense of $16,000 as a selling expense.

Experience indicating a redemption percentage that differs from the assumed rate will call for an appropriate adjustment in the subsequent period and the revision of future redemption estimates.

The estimated cost of the premiums may be shown as a direct reduction of sales by recording the premium claim at the time of the sale. This requires an estimate of the premium cost at the time of the sale. For example, in the previous illustration, the summary entry for sales recorded during the year, employing the sales reduction approach, would be as follows:

Cash	480,000	
Sales		464,000
Estimated Premium Claims Outstanding		16,000

The redemption of premium claims would call for debits to the liability account. Either the expense method or the sales reduction method is acceptable and both are found in practice.

Some organizations have adopted plans for the issuance to customers of trading stamps, cash register tapes, or other media redeemable in merchandise, premiums, or cash. The accounting procedure followed will depend on the nature of the plan. A business may establish its own plan, prepare its own stamps or other trading media, and assume redemption responsibilities. Under these circumstances, the accounting procedure would parallel that just illustrated for specific premium offers. On the other hand, a business unit may enter into an agreement for a stamp plan with a trading-stamp company. The latter normally assumes full responsibility for the redemption of stamps and sells the trading stamps for a set unit price whether they are redeemed or not. The business would report stamps purchased as an asset and stamps issued as a selling expense; the trading-stamp company would recognize on its books the sale of stamps, purchase of premiums, distributions of premiums, and the estimated liability for the costs of merchandise and related services identified with stamps expected to be redeemed.

To illustrate accounting for trading stamps, assume that on January 3, 1984, Quik Mart Grocery Store purchased trading stamps from Silver Streak Stamp Company for $10,000. During the month of January, $2,000 worth of the stamps were issued to customers. The purchase and distribution of stamps would be recorded on Quik Mart's books as follows:

Trading Stamp Inventory	10,000	
Cash		10,000
Trading Stamp Expense	2,000	
Trading Stamp Inventory		2,000

Continuing the example, assume that Silver Streak's total stamp sales during January, 1984, amounted to $100,000. Past experience indicates that approximately 95% of the stamps are eventually redeemed for merchandise. The cost of the merchandise is on the average 90% of the price charged to merchants for the stamps. Assume also that during January, 1984, $30,000 worth of the stamps sold in January are redeemed for merchandise. The summary entries for Silver Streak Stamp Company relating to stamp activity in January would be:

Cash	100,000	
Revenue from Sale of Stamps		100,000
Cost of Sales—Trading Stamps	85,500	
Estimated Liability for Stamp Sales		85,500
Recognition of estimated cost to redeem trading stamps; 95% redemption rate, 90% cost: ($100,000 × .95 × .90 = $85,500).		
Estimated Liability for Stamp Sales	27,000	
Inventory		27,000
Issuance of merchandise: ($30,000 × .90 = $27,000).		

In the preceding example, it is assumed that the cost of the merchandise to be issued is known with sufficient certainty to enable the company to recognize the income of $14,500 ($100,000 − $85,500) immediately. As discussed on page 486 dealing with service contracts, when this certainty does not exist, income should be deferred and recognized as the merchandise is redeemed. Again, the particular practice followed depends on the specific circumstances.

One of the more difficult questions in accounting for the liability for unredeemed trading stamps is the expected redemption rate. Past experience provides the best basis for making this determination.[5]

Tickets, Tokens, and Gift Certificates Outstanding

Many companies sell tickets, tokens, and gift certificates that entitle the owner to services or merchandise: for example, airlines issue tickets used for travel; local transit companies issue tokens good for fares; department stores sell gift certificates redeemable in merchandise.

When instruments redeemable in services or merchandise are outstanding at the end of the period, accounts should be adjusted to reflect the obligations under such arrangements. The nature of the adjustment will depend on the entries originally made in recording the sale of the instruments.

Ordinarily, the sale of instruments redeemable in services or merchandise is recorded by a debit to Cash and a credit to a liability account. As instruments are redeemed, the liability balance is debited and Sales or an appropriate revenue account is credited. Certain claims may be rendered void by lapse of time or for some other reason as defined by the sales agreement. In addition, experience may indicate a certain percentage of outstanding claims will never be presented for redemption. These factors must be considered at the end of the period, when the liability balance is reduced to the balance of the claim estimated to be outstanding and a revenue account is credited for the gain indicated from forfeitures. If Sales or a special revenue account is originally credited on the sale of the redemption instrument, the adjustment at the end of the period calls for a debit to the revenue account and a credit to a liability account for the claim still outstanding.

Compensated Absences

Compensated absences include payments by employers for vacation, holiday, illness, or other personal activities. Employees often earn paid absences based on the time employed. Generally, the longer an employee works for a company, the longer the vacation allowed, or the more liberal the time allowed for illnesses. At the end of any given accounting period, a company has a liability for earned but unused compensated absences. The matching principle requires that the estimated amounts earned be charged against

[5]For an illustration of models used to estimate the liability, see Davidson, Neter, and Petran, "Estimating the Liability for Unredeemed Stamps," *Journal of Accounting Research,* Autumn 1967, pages 186–207.

current revenue, and a liability established for that amount.[6] The difficult part of this accounting is estimating how much should be accrued. In Statement No. 43, the FASB requires a liability to be recognized for compensated absences that (1) have been earned through services already rendered, (2) vest or can be carried forward to subsequent years, and (3) are estimable and probable.

For example, assume that a company has a vacation pay policy for all employees. If all employees had the same anniversary date for computing time in service, the computations would not be too difficult. However, most plans provide for a flexible employee starting date. In order to compute the liability, a careful inventory of all employees must be made that includes the number of years of service, rate of pay, carryover of unused vacation from prior periods, turnover, and the probability of taking the vacation.

The FASB decided that sick pay needs to be accrued only if it vests with the employee, i.e., the employee is entitled to compensation for a certain number of "sick days" regardless of whether the employee is actually absent for that period. Upon leaving the firm, an employee would be compensated for any unused sick time. If the sick pay does not vest, it is recorded as an expense only when actually paid.[7]

Although compensated absences are not deductible for income tax purposes until the vacation, holiday, or illness occurs and the payment is made, they are required to be recognized as liabilities on the financial statements if the FASB requirements are met.

CONTINGENT LIABILITIES

Contingencies are defined in FASB Statement No. 5 as:

> ...an existing condition, situation, or set of circumstances involving uncertainty as to possible gain...or loss...to an enterprise that will ultimately be resolved when one or more future events occur or fail to occur.[8]

As defined, contingencies may apply broadly to either assets or liabilities, and to either a gain or a loss. In this chapter, attention is focused on contingent losses that might give rise to a liability. Historically, liabilities classified as contingent were not recorded on the books, but were disclosed in notes to financial statements. The distinction between a recorded liability and a contingent liability was not always clear. If a legal liability existed and the amount of the obligation was either definite or could be estimated with reasonable certainty, the liability was recorded on the books. If the existence of the obligation depended on the happening of a future event, recording of the liability was deferred until the event occurred. In an attempt to make the distinction more precise, the FASB used three terms in FASB Statement

---

[6] *Statement of Financial Accounting Standards No. 43,* "Accounting for Compensated Absences" (Stamford: Financial Accounting Standards Board, 1980), par. 6.

[7] *Ibid.,* par. 7.

[8] *Statement of Financial Accounting Standards No. 5,* "Accounting for Contingencies" (Stamford: Financial Accounting Standards Board, 1975), par. 1.

No. 5 to identify the range of likelihood possibilities of the event occurring. Different accounting action was recommended for each term. The terms, their definition, and the accounting action recommended are as follows:[9]

Term	*Definition*	*Accounting Action*
Probable	The future event or events are likely to occur	Record the probable event in the accounts if the amount can be reasonably estimated. If not estimable, disclose facts in note.
Reasonably possible	The chance of the future event or events occurring is more than remote but less than likely	Report the contingency in a note.
Remote	The chance of the future event or events occurring is slight	No recording or reporting unless contingency represents a guarantee. Then note disclosure is required.

If the happening of the event that would create a liability is probable, and if the amount of the obligation can be reasonably estimated, the contingency should be recognized as a liability. Some of the liabilities already presented as estimated liabilities may be considered probable contingent liabilities because the existence of the obligation is dependent on some event occurring, e.g., warranties are dependent on the need for repair or service to be given, gift certificates are dependent on the certificate being turned in for redemption, and vacation pay is dependent on a person taking a vacation. These liabilities are not included in this section, however, because historically they have been recognized as recorded liabilities. Other liabilities, such as unsettled litigation claims, self insurance, and loan guarantees have more traditionally been considered as unrecorded contingent liabilities, and these will be explored separately in the following pages.

Inasmuch as all liabilities have some element of contingency associated with them, the authors feel that the classification "contingent liability" should be reserved for those items that fit into one of the latter two terms, i.e., reasonably possible or remote. If the happening of the event is probable and the amount of the obligation can be estimated, the liability is no longer a contingent liability, but a recorded estimated liability. Such liabilities meet the definition for liabilities established by the FASB. This approach avoids having to say that some contingent liabilities are recorded and others are not. By this definition, a contingent liability is never recorded but is either disclosed in a footnote or ignored depending on the degree of remoteness of its expected occurrence.

The FASB statement provided no specific guidelines as to how these three terms should be interpreted in probability percentages. Surveys made of statement preparers and users disclosed a great diversity in the probability interpretation of the terms. It is unlikely, therefore, that FASB Statement No. 5 has greatly reduced the diversity in practice in recording some of these contingent items.

[9] *Ibid.*, par. 3.

Litigation

An increasing number of lawsuits are being filed against companies and individuals. Lawsuits may result in substantial liabilities to successful plaintiffs. Typically, litigation takes a long time to conclude. Even after a decision has been rendered by a lower court, there are many appeal opportunities available. Thus, both the amount and timing of a loss arising from litigation are generally highly uncertain. Some companies carry insurance to protect them against these losses, so the impact of the losses on the financial statements is minimized. For uninsured risks, however, a decision must be made as to when the liability for litigation becomes probable, and thus a recorded loss.

FASB Statement No. 5 identifies several key factors to consider in making the decision. These include:[10]

(1) The nature of the litigation.
(2) The period when the cause of action occurred. (Liability is not recognized in any period before the cause of action occurred.)
(3) Progress of the case in court, including progress between date of the financial statements and their issuance date.
(4) Views of legal counsel as to the probability of loss.
(5) Prior experience with similar cases.
(6) Management's intended response to the litigation.

If analysis of these and similar factors results in the judgment that a loss is probable, and the amount of the loss can be reasonably estimated, the liability should be recorded. A settlement after the balance sheet date but before the statements are issued would be evidence that the loss was probable at the year-end, and would result in a reporting of loss in the current financial statements.

Another area of potential liability involves unasserted claims, i.e., a cause of action has occurred but no claim has yet been asserted. For example, a person may be injured on the property of the company, but as of the date the financial statements are issued, no legal action has been taken; or a violation of a government regulation may occur, but no federal action has yet been taken. If it is probable that a claim will be filed, and the amount of the claim can be reasonably estimated, accrual of the liability should be made. If the amount cannot be reasonably estimated, note disclosure is required. If assertion of the claim is not judged to be probable, no accrual or disclosure is necessary.

The following example illustrates accounting for litigation that is judged to be probable of adverse settlement. Assume a claim for $10 million is filed in 1984 against Sky-Ways Limited for injuries suffered in an airplane crash. The case is in court, and an out-of-court settlement is in the process of being negotiated. Even though the nature of the accident made the loss uninsured, Sky-Ways has agreed to a payment of $2 million. Attorneys for Sky-Ways believe an eventual settlement will be reached for about that amount. Based

[10] *Ibid.*, par. 36.

on these facts, management decides the $2 million loss is probable, and the estimated loss is recorded as follows:

1984	Loss from Damage Suit	2,000,000	
	Estimated Liability Arising from Damage Suit		2,000,000

Assume further that in 1985 a settlement is finally made for $2,500,000. Since the entry in the preceding year was based on an estimate, the additional $500,000 is recorded as a loss in 1985.

1985	Loss from Damage Suit	500,000	
	Estimated Liability Arising from Damage Suit	2,000,000	
	Cash		2,500,000

If the actual loss is less than the amount recorded, the adjustment is made to the current year's income statement as would be true for revision of any estimates. Reference to Note Fifteen of General Mills' financial statements in Appendix B reveals no identified recorded liability for litigation. The note does, however, describe the dismissal of a contingent loss from litigation with the Federal Trade Commission.

Self Insurance

Some large companies with widely distributed risks may decide not to purchase insurance for protection against the normal business risks of fire, explosion, flood, or damage to other persons or their property. These companies in effect insure themselves against these risks. The accounting question that arises is whether a liability should be accrued and a loss recognized for the possible occurrence of the uninsured risk. Sometimes companies have recorded as an expense an amount equal to the insurance premium that would have been paid had commercial insurance been carried. The FASB considered this specific subject in Statement No. 5, and concluded that no loss or liability should be recorded until the loss has occurred. Fires, explosions, or other casualties are random in occurrence, and as such, are not accruable. Further, they stated that

> ...unlike an insurance company, which has a contractual obligation under policies in force to reimburse insureds for losses, an enterprise can have no such obligation to itself and, hence, no liability.[11]

Thus, although an exposed condition does exist, it is a future period that must bear any loss that occurs, not a current period.

Loan Guarantees

Enterprises sometimes enter into a contract guaranteeing a loan for another enterprise, frequently a subsidiary company, a supplier, or even a favored customer. These guarantees obligate the entity to make the loan

[11] *Ibid.*, par. 28.

payment if the principal borrower fails to make the payment. A similar contingent obligation exists when the payee of a note receivable discounts it at a bank, but is held contingently liable in the event the maker of the note defaults. Discussion of discounted notes receivable was included in Chapter 7. If the default on the loan or the note is judged to be probable based on the events that have occurred prior to the issuance date of the financial statements, the loss and liability should be accrued in accordance with the general guidelines discussed in this section. Otherwise, note disclosure is required even if the likelihood of making the payment is remote. This exception to not disclosing remote contingencies arose because companies have traditionally disclosed guarantees in notes to the financial statements, and the FASB did not want to reduce this disclosure practice.

Future Commitments

Various types of contracts or agreements may be entered into that could result in losses to the entity making them. For example, a contract for a future sale of a product may be made with the selling price fixed. If a rapid rise in prices occurs before the date of the sale, a loss rather than a profit may be incurred by the seller on the contract. When a loss arising from such a commitment is probable, it should be accrued in the current period rather than waiting for it to be recognized when the commitment is fulfilled.

For example, assume a $10,000 sale of a product is made with the item to be purchased and delivered in six months. The present cost of the product is $9,000. The financial statements are prepared after four months, and the cost of the product has risen rapidly and is now $11,000. Since the inventory must still be purchased, the $1,000 loss is probable and should be recognized as follows:

Loss from Future Sales Commitment	1,000	
Estimated Loss Arising from Sales Commitment		1,000

Assume further that the sale is made in the next year, and the purchase cost of the inventory was $11,000. The entry to record the sale and its cost under a perpetual inventory system would be as follows:

Inventory	11,000	
Cash		11,000
Accounts Receivable	10,000	
Sales		10,000
Cost of Sales	10,000	
Estimated Loss Arising from Sales Commitment	1,000	
Inventory		11,000

Other commitments, such as purchase commitments discussed in Chapter 9 would be recorded similarly.

Companies sometimes **hedge** their future commitments to avoid a loss. This means that at the same time a sales contract is entered into for six months in the future, a purchase contract for the item or its major component parts is entered into for delivery also in the future. A hedge enables a company to avoid the risk of loss. Of course, future commitments can result in profits, and a hedge prevents this from occurring as well. Probable gains arising from future commitments are not recognized in current practice until the event occurs. Thus, in the preceding example, if the cost fell to $8,000, the extra $1,000 profit would be recognized in the year the sale was made.

BALANCE SHEET PRESENTATION

The liability section of the balance sheet is usually divided between current and noncurrent liabilities as previously discussed. The nature of the detail to be presented for current liabilities depends on the use to be made of the financial statement. A balance sheet prepared for stockholders might report little detail; on the other hand, creditors may insist on full detail concerning current debts.

Assets are normally recorded in the order of their liquidity, and consistency would suggest that liabilities be reported in the order of their maturity. The latter practice may be followed only to the extent it is practical; observance of this procedure would require an analysis of the different classes of obligations and separate reporting for classes with varying maturity dates. A bank overdraft should be listed first in view of the immediate demand it makes on cash.

Liabilities should not be offset by assets to be applied to their liquidation. Disclosure as to future debt liquidation, however, may be provided by an appropriate parenthetical remark or note. Disclosure of liabilities secured by specific assets should also be made by a parenthetical remark or note.

The current liabilities section of a balance sheet prepared on December 31, 1984, might appear as shown below:

Current liabilities:			
Notes payable:			
Trade creditors	$12,000		
Banks (secured by pledge of monies to become due under certain contracts)	20,000		
Officers	10,000		
Miscellaneous	2,500	$44,500	
Accounts payable:			
Trade creditors	$30,500		
Credit balances in customers' accounts	1,250		
Miscellaneous	3,500	35,250	
Long-term liability installments due in 1985		10,000	
Cash dividends payable		4,500	
Income tax payable		6,000	
Other liabilities:			
Salaries and wages payable	$ 1,250		
Real and personal property taxes	1,550		
Miscellaneous liabilities	1,400		
Customer advances	7,500		
Estimated repair costs on goods sold with service warranties	2,500	14,200	$114,450

Because most of the noncurrent liabilities are discussed in separate chapters that follow, illustration of the details of the noncurrent liabilities section is deferred until Chapter 18 and illustrated with owners' equity. For a further illustration of a liabilities section of a balance sheet with related notes, see the General Mills' financial statements reproduced in Appendix B.

QUESTIONS

1. Identify the major elements included in the definition of liabilities established by the FASB.
2. (a) What is meant by an executory contract? (b) Do these contracts fit the definition of liabilities included in this chapter?
3. (a) Distinguish between the definition of liabilities and their measurement. (b) Why is present value used so extensively in liability accounting?
4. Distinguish between current and noncurrent liabilities.
5. Under what conditions would debt that will mature within the next year be reported as a noncurrent liability?
6. The Cable Co. issues a non-interest-bearing note due in one year in payment for equipment. Describe the accounting procedures that should be employed for the purchase.
7. The sales manager for Bonneville Sales Co. is entitled to a bonus of 12% of profits. What difficulties may arise in the interpretation of this profit-sharing agreement?
8. Gross payroll is taxed by both federal and state governments. Identify these taxes and indicate who bears the cost of the tax, the employer or the employee?
9. How should a company account for revenue received in advance for a service contract?
10. What uncertainties are present when accounting for trading stamps?
11. What information must a firm accumulate in order to adequately account for estimated liabilities on tickets, tokens and gift certificates?
12. How should contingent liabilities that are reasonably possible of becoming liabilities be reported on the financial statements?
13. What factors are important in deciding whether a lawsuit in process should be reported as a liability on the balance sheet?
14. Why does accounting for self-insurance differ from accounting for insurance premiums with outside carriers?
15. Under what circumstances can a future sales commitment give rise to a loss? How can the possibility of loss be eliminated?

DISCUSSION CASES

case 13-1 (Is it really self-insurance?) The auditors of Information Retrieval Systems are concerned with how to account for the insurance liability on a policy carried with a large insurance company. Premiums on the policy are based on the average loss experience of the past five years. In some years, no liability loss occurs; however, the company follows the practice of recognizing expenses for the premiums paid to the insurance company regardless of actual loss. The senior auditor, Gary Wells, has read FASB Statement No. 5, and argues that the premiums paid are really deposits with the insurance company. Since the premiums are based on the losses actually incurred, income should be charged only when the losses occur, not when the premiums are paid. By charging the premiums to expense, an artificial smoothing of income results, something FASB Statement No. 5 was designed to prevent. Barbara Orton, controller, argues that the premiums are arm's-length payments, that FASB Statement No. 5 applies only to self-insurance reserves, and that the policy carried by Information Retrieval Systems is obviously with an outside carrier. Thus, Orton believes the premiums should be recognized as a valid period expense. As audit manager, you are asked to render your opinion on the matter.

case 13-2 (When is a loss a loss?) The following three **independent** sets of facts relate to (a) the possible accrual or (b) the possible disclosure by other means of a loss contingency.

Situation I

A company offers a one-year warranty for the product that it manufactures. A history of warranty claims has been compiled and the probable amount of claims related to sales for a given period can be determined.

Situation II

Subsequent to the date of a set of financial statements, but prior to the issuance of the financial statements, a company enters into a contract which, because of a sudden shift in the economy, will probably result in a significant loss to the company. The amount of the loss can be reasonably estimated.

Situation III

A company has adopted a policy of recording self-insurance for any possible losses resulting from injury to others by the company's vehicles. The premium for an insurance policy for the same risk from an independent insurance company would have an annual cost of $20,000. During the period covered by the financial statements, there were no accidents involving the company's vehicles which resulted in injury to others.

Discuss the accrual and/or type of disclosure necessary (if any) and the reason(s) why such disclosure is appropriate for each of the three independent sets of facts above.
(AICPA adapted)

case 13-3 (Leave my current ratio alone) Snell Inc. a closely held corporation, has never been audited and is seeking a large bank loan for plant expansion. The bank has requested audited statements. In conference with the president and majority stockholder of Snell, the auditor is informed that the bank looks very closely at the current ratio. The auditor's proposed reclassifications and adjustments include the following:

(a) A note payable issued 4½ years ago matures in six months from the balance sheet date. The auditor wants to reclassify it as a current liability. The controller says no because "we are probably going to refinance this note with other long-term debt."

(b) An accrual for compensated absences. Again the controller objects because the amount of the pay for these absences cannot be estimated. "Some employees quit in the first year and don't get vacation, and it is impossible to predict which employees will be absent for illness or other causes. Without being able to identify the employees, we can't determine the rate of compensation."

How would you as auditor respond to the controller?

EXERCISES

exercise 13-1 (Accounting for notes payable)

The following notes were issued by the Yale Marble Company:

(a) Note issued to purchase office equipment. Face amount $25,000; no stated interest rate; market rate of interest, 12%; term of note, one year; date of note, November 1, 1984.
(b) Note issued to bank for a cash loan. Maturity value of note, $25,000; bank discount rate, 12%; term of note, one year; date of note, October 1, 1984.

(1) Give the entries required at the time the notes were issued. Round to nearest dollar.
(2) Give the adjusting entries required on December 31, 1984, to recognize the accrual of the interest on each note.

exercise 13-2 (Purchase with non-interest-bearing note)

On September 1, 1984, Bart Manufacturing Co. purchased two new company automobiles from Easy-Terms Auto Sales. The purchase was made on September 1, 1984. The terms of the sale called for Bart to pay $19,992 to Easy-Terms on September 1, 1985. Bart gave the seller a non-interest-bearing note for that amount. At the date of purchase, the interest rate for short-term loans was 12%. Prepare the journal entries necessary on September 1, 1984, December 31, 1984 (year-end adjusting), and September 1, 1985.

exercise 13-3 (Calculation of bonus)

Riggs Wholesale Company, has an agreement with its sales manager whereby the latter is entitled to 6% of company earnings as a bonus. Company income for a calendar year before bonus and income tax is $150,000. Income tax is 45% of income after bonus. Compute the amount of the bonus under each of the conditions below.

(a) The bonus is calculated on income before deductions for bonus and income tax.
(b) The bonus is calculated on income after deduction for bonus but before deduction for income tax.
(c) The bonus is calculated on income after deduction for income tax but before deduction for bonus.
(d) The bonus is calculated on net income after deductions for both bonus and income tax.

exercise 13-4 (Calculation of bonus)

Martin Distributors is considering two different proposals for computing a bonus for the company president. The first proposal states that the president's bonus is equal to 10% of the company's income (before income tax, but after deducting the bonus) in excess of $200,000. The alternative plan states that the bonus is equal to 15% of the company's income after deducting income tax, but before deducting the bonus. Assuming income before income tax and bonus of $794,000, compute the bonus under each alternative plan. Assume the company's tax rate is 40%. (Round all numbers to the nearest dollar.)

exercise 13-5 (Calculation of bonus rate)

The Rodriguez Furniture Company provides a special bonus for its executive officers based upon income before bonus or income tax. Income before bonus and income tax for 1985 was $1,250,000. The combined state and federal income tax rate is 55%, and the total income tax liability for 1985 is $632,500. What was the bonus rate?

exercise 13-6 (Recording payroll and payroll taxes)

Quickie Cleaners paid one week's wages of $10,600 in cash (net pay after all withholdings and deductions) to its 40 employees. Income tax withholdings were equal to 17% of the gross payroll, and the only other deductions were 6.7% for FICA tax and

$160 for union dues. Give the entries that should be made on the books of the store to record the payroll and the tax accruals to be recognized by the employer, assuming that the company is subject to unemployment taxes of 2.7% (state) and .8% (federal).

exercise 13-7 (Accounting for property taxes)

On November 20, 1984, Red Rose Floral Shop received a property tax assessment of $144,000 for the fiscal year ending June 30, 1985. No entry was made to record the assessment. Several months later, Red Rose's accountant was preparing the yearly financial statements (based on a February 1 to January 31 fiscal year) and came across the property tax assessment. Give the journal entries to record the tax payment (if any) and any adjusting entries necessary on January 31, assuming:

(a) The full tax of $144,000 had been paid on January 5, 1985.
(b) The full tax of $144,000 had not been paid.
(c) A portion of the tax ($90,500) had been paid on January 20, 1985.

exercise 13-8 (Accounting for sales tax)

Total sales plus sales tax for the Universal Power Company in 1984 was $122,850; 70% of the sales are normally made on account. Prepare an entry summarizing these data for 1984 if the sales tax rate is 5%.

exercise 13-9 (Warranty liability)

In 1984 Daynes Office Supply began selling a new calculator that carried a two-year warranty against defects. Based on the manufacturer's recommendations, Daynes projects the estimated warranty costs (as a percent of dollar sales) as follows:

First year of warranty	4%
Second year of warranty	10%

Sales and actual warranty repairs for 1984 and 1985 are presented below:

	1984	1985
Sales	$250,000	$475,000
Actual warranty repairs	4,750	26,175

(1) Give the necessary journal entries to record the liability at the end of 1984 and 1985.
(2) Analyze the warranty liability account as of the year ending December 31, 1985, to see if the actual repairs approximate the estimate. Should Daynes revise the manufacturer's warranty estimate? (Assume sales and repairs occur evenly throughout the year).

exercise 13-10 (Warranty liability)

Quick Service Appliance Company's accountant has been reviewing the firm's past television sales. For the past two years, Quick Service has been offering a special service warranty on all televisions sold. With the purchase of a television, the customer has the right to purchase a three-year service contract for an extra $50. Information concerning past television and warranty contract sales is given below:

Color-All Model II Television

	1984	1985
Television sales in units	450	525
Sales price per unit	$ 400	$ 500
Number of service contracts sold	300	350
Expenses relating to television warranties	$2,950	$7,360

Quick Service's accountant has estimated from past records that the pattern of repairs has been 40% in the first year after sale, 36% in the second year, and 24% in the third year. Give the necessary journal entries related to the service contracts for 1984 and

1985. In addition, indicate how much profit on service contracts would be recognized in 1985. Assume sales of the contracts are made evenly during the year.

exercise 13-11 (Premium liability)

In an effort to increase sales, Nick Razor Blade Company began a sales promotion campaign on June 30, 1984. Part of this new promotion included placing a special coupon in each package of razor blades sold. Customers were able to redeem 5 coupons for a bottle of shaving lotion. Each premium costs Nick $.50. Nick estimated that 60% of the coupons issued will be redeemed. For the six months ended December 31, 1984, the following information is available:

Packages of razor blades sold	800,000
Premiums purchased	60,000
Coupons redeemed	200,000

What is the estimated liability for premium claims outstanding at December 31, 1984?
(AICPA adapted)

exercise 13-12 (Premium liability)

On January 2, 1984, the Russell Beverage Company began marketing a new soft drink called "TINGLE." To help promote TINGLE, the management of Russell is offering a special TINGLE T-shirt to each customer who returns 24 bottle caps. Russell estimates that out of the 450,000 bottles of TINGLE sold during 1984, only 60% of the bottle caps will be redeemed. On December 31, 1984, the following information was collected.

	Units	Amount
T-Shirts purchased by Russell	14,250	$18,525
T-Shirts distributed to customers	5,000	

(1) What is the amount of the liability that Russell should record on their 1984 financial statements?
(2) Give the journal entries to record the purchase, distribution, and year-end liability relating to the T-shirts.

exercise 13-13 (Trading stamp liability)

Reliance Food Stores purchases trading stamps from Checkerboard Stamp Company. Checkerboard has agreed to handle full responsibility for the redemption of the stamps. During 1984, Reliance issued $7,025 worth of stamps to their customers. Reliance's records show the following information relating to their trading stamp inventory:

Trading Stamp Inventory—Reliance	
January 1, 1984	$12,750
December 31, 1984	9,225

Besides selling to Reliance, Checkerboard also sells to other grocery outlets. During 1984, Checkerboard sold $175,000 worth of stamps to other grocery stores. Checkerboard estimates that 94% of the stamps will be eventually redeemed for merchandise. Checkerboard uses various household items as gifts to customers returning a predetermined number of stamps. The cost of the gifts averages 80% of the price paid by the merchants for the redeemed stamps. During 1984, $65,000 worth of stamps were redeemed by Checkerboard. Give the journal entries to record the sale and redemption of trading stamps during 1984 for Checkerboard and the purchase and distribution of stamps in 1984 for Reliance Foods.

exercise 13-14 (Compensated absences—vacation pay)

Rosenbaum Builders Inc. employs five people. Each employee is entitled to two weeks' paid vacation every year the employee works for the company. The conditions of the paid vacation are: (a) for each full year of work, an employee will receive two weeks of paid vacation (no vacation accrues for a portion of a year), (b) each employee will receive the same pay for vacation time as the regular pay in the year taken, and (c) unused vacation pay can be carried forward. The following data were taken from the firm's personnel records:

Employee	Starting Date	Cumulative Vacation Taken as of December 31, 1985	Weekly Salary
John Palermo	December 21, 1978	11 weeks	$375
Robert Gorman	March 6, 1983	2 weeks	500
Mary Ann Tyler	August 13, 1984	none	350
Frank Huang	December 17, 1983	3 weeks	300
Rebecca Lewis	March 29, 1985	none	400

Compute the liability for vacation pay as of December 31, 1985.

exercise 13-15 (Contingent losses)

Conrad Corporation sells motorcycle helmets. In 1984, Conrad sold 4 million helmets before discovering a significant defect in the helmet's construction. By December 31, 1984, two lawsuits had been filed against Conrad. The first lawsuit, which Conrad has little chance of winning, is expected to be settled out of court for $900,000 in January of 1985. In the second lawsuit, which is for $400,000, Conrad's attorneys think the company has a fifty-fifty chance of winning. What accounting treatment should Conrad give the pending lawsuits in the year-end financial statements? (Include any necessary journal entries.)

exercise 13-16 (Loss from sales commitment)

Whipple Corporation is a wholesale distributor of lumber products. On September 4, an agreement was reached to deliver a large shipment of plywood to Gaffin Inc. on February 4 of the following year. The sales price was firmly established at $16,500. The cost to Whipple at September 4 would have been $13,750, but they decided not to purchase at this price because they hoped prices would fall. A severe shortage of plywood during December drastically increased prices. By December 31, the date of Whipple's financial statements, the purchase price of the plywood had risen to $17,000. On February 3, the plywood was purchased for $18,000. Give the journal entries required to record the above transactions. (Assume a perpetual inventory system.)

exercise 13-17 (Balance sheet classification of liabilities)

Prepare the current liabilities section of the balance sheet for the McQueen Mattress Company on December 31, 1984, from the information appearing below:

(a) Notes payable: arising from purchases of goods, $58,680; arising from loans from banks, $18,000, on which marketable securities valued at $26,100 have been pledged as security; arising from short-term advances by officers, $21,600.
(b) Accounts payable arising from purchase of goods, $55,800.
(c) Cash balance with Farmers Bank, $9,900; cash overdraft with Merchants Bank, $5,976.
(d) Dividends in arrears on preferred stock, $32,400.
(e) Employees income tax payable, $1,584.
(f) First-mortgage serial bonds, $125,000, payable in semiannual installments of $5,000 due on March 1 and September 1 of each year.
(g) Advances received from customers on purchase orders, $4,140.
(h) Customers' accounts with credit balances arising from purchase returns, $1,500.
(i) Estimated expense of meeting warranty for service requirements on merchandise sold, $4,860.

PROBLEMS

problem 13-1 (Recording various liabilities)

The information below comes from the books of the D. E. Calder Supply Co. at December 31, 1984.

Sales on account (including sales tax of 5%)	$262,500
Net income	30,500
Cash dividends (declared December 30, 1984)	20,000
Machinery purchased, October 1, 1984 (a one-year non-interest-bearing note was issued in payment)	60,000
Notes payable (a one-year note for $10,000 was discounted at the bank at 13% on September 1, 1984)	10,000
Marketable securities	8,000
Common stock, $100 par	50,000

Instructions: Prepare necessary journal entries to record the following transactions: Round to nearest dollar.

(1) Discounting the note payable.
(2) Purchase of machinery (money is worth 12% per year).
(3) Declaration of cash dividend.
(4) Sales and sales tax.
(5) Record the interest to be charged to this year at year end as a result of the issuance of the notes.

problem 13-2 (Calculation of bonus)

Miller Manufacturing Corporation pays bonuses to its sales manager and two sales agents. The company had income for 1984 of $1,500,000 before bonuses and income tax. Income taxes average 45%.

Instructions: Compute the bonuses assuming:

(1) Sales manager gets 6% and each sales agent gets 5% of income before tax and bonuses.
(2) Each bonus is 9% of income after income tax but before bonuses.
(3) Each bonus is 12% of net income after income tax and bonuses.
(4) Sales manager gets 12% and each sales agent gets 10% of income after bonuses but before income tax.

problem 13-3 (Accrued payroll and payroll taxes)

Kingston Clothiers' employees are paid on the 10th and 25th of each month for the period ending the previous 5th and 20th respectively. An analysis of the payroll on Thursday, November 5, 1984, revealed the following data:

	Gross Pay	FICA	Federal Income Tax	State Income Tax	Insurance	Net Pay
Office salaries	$10,500	$ 504	$1,200	$ 200	270	$ 8,326
Officers' salaries	27,000	324	5,100	1,500	510	19,566
Sales salaries	18,000	648	3,000	750	390	13,212
Total	$55,500	$1,476	$9,300	$2,450	$1,170	$41,104

It is determined that for the November 5 pay period, no additional employees exceeded the wage base for FICA purposes than had done so in prior periods. All of the officers' salaries, 70% of the office salaries, and 60% of the sales salaries for the payroll period ending November 5 were paid to employees that had exceeded the wage base for unemployment taxes. Assume the rates in force are as follows: FICA, 7%; federal unemployment tax, .8% and state unemployment tax, 2.7%.

Instructions: Prepare the adjusting entries that would be required at October 31, the end of Kingston's fiscal year, to reflect the accrual of the payroll and any related payroll taxes. Separate salary and payroll taxes expense accounts are used for each of the three employee categories; office, officers', and sales salaries.

problem 13-4 (Miscellaneous operating payables)

The Marston Corporation closes its books and prepares financial statements on an annual basis. The following information is gathered by the chief accountant to assist in preparing the liability section of the balance sheet:

(a) Property taxes of $45,000 were assessed on the property in May 1984, for the subsequent period of July 1 to June 30. The payment of the taxes is divided into three equal installments, November 1, February 1, and May 1. The November 1 payment was made and charged to Property Tax Expense. No other entries have been made for property taxes relative to the 1984–85 assessment.

(b) The estimated 1984 pretax income for Marston is $629,000. The effective state income tax rate is 10% (applied to pretax income). The effective rate for federal income taxes is estimated at 40% (applied to income after deducting state income taxes). Income tax payments of $280,000 were made by Marston during 1984, including $50,000 as the final payment on 1983 federal income taxes, $20,000 for 1984 state estimated taxes, the balance for 1984 federal estimated taxes.

(c) Taxable sales for 1984 were $7,500,000. The state sales tax rate is 4.5%. Quarterly statements have been filed, and the following tax payments were made with the return.

1st Quarter	$76,000
2d Quarter	80,000
3d Quarter	70,000

The balance in the account Sales Tax Payable is $110,800 at December 31, 1984.

Instructions:

(1) Based on the above data, what amounts should be reported on the balance sheet as liabilities at December 31, 1984?

(2) Prepare the necessary adjusting entries to record the liabilities.

problem 13-5 (Premium liability)

The Cascade Corp. manufactures a special type of low-suds laundry soap. A dish towel is offered as a premium to customers who send in two proof-of-purchase seals from these soap boxes and a remittance of $2. Data for the premium offer are summarized below:

	1984	1985
Soap sales ($2.50 per package)	$2,500,000	$3,125,000
Dish towel purchases ($2.50 per towel)	$ 130,000	$ 156,250
Number of dish towels distributed as premiums	40,000	60,000
Number of dish towels expected to be distributed in subsequent periods	7,500	2,000

Mailing costs are 26¢ per package.

Instructions:

(1) Give the entries for 1984 and 1985 to record product sales, premium purchases and redemptions, and year-end adjustments.

(2) Present "T" accounts with appropriate amounts as of the end of 1984 and 1985.

problem 13-6 (Compensated absences)

Card Electronics Inc. has a plan to compensate its employees for certain absences. Each employee can receive five days' sick leave each year plus 10 days' vacation. The benefits carry over for two additional years, after which the provision lapses on a fifo flow basis. Thus the maximum accumulation is 45 days. In some cases, the company permits vacations to be taken before they are earned. Payments are made based upon current compensation levels, not on the level in effect when the absence time was earned.

Employee	Days Accrued Jan. 1, 1984	Daily Rate Jan. 1, 1984	Days Earned 1984	Days Taken 1984	Days Accrued Dec. 31, 1984	Daily Rate Dec. 31
A	10	$36	15	10	15	$40
B	—	$46	15	10	5	$50
C	30	$40	7	37	—	Terminated June 15— Rate = $45
D	−5	$34	15	20	−10	$40
E	40	$60	15	5	50	$70
F	Hired July 1— Rate = $40	—	8	0	8	$40

Instructions:

(1) How much is the liability for compensated absences at December 31, 1984?
(2) Prepare a summary journal entry to record compensation absence payments during the year and the accrual at the end of the year. Assume the payroll liability account is charged for all payments made during the year for both sickness and vacation leaves. The average rate of compensation for the year may be used to value the hours taken except for Employee C who took leaves at the date of termination. The end-of-year rate should be used to establish the ending liability.

problem 13-7 (Contingent liabilities)

The Western Supply Co. has several contingent liabilities at December 31, 1984. The following brief description of each liability is obtained by the auditor.

(a) In May 1983, Western Supply became involved in litigation. In December 1984, a judgment for $800,000 was assessed against Western by the court. Western is appealing the amount of the judgment. Attorneys for Western feel it is probable that they can reduce the assessment on appeal by 50%. No entries have been made by Western pending completion of the appeal process, which is expected to take at least a year.
(b) In July 1984, Morgan County brought action against Western for polluting the Jordan River with its waste products. It is reasonably possible that Morgan County will be successful, but the amount of damages Western might have to pay should not exceed $200,000. No entry has been made by Western to reflect the possible loss.
(c) Western Supply has elected to self-insure its fire and casualty risks. At the beginning of the year, the account Reserve for Insurance, had a balance of $2,500,000. During 1984, $750,000 was debited to insurance expense and credited to the reserve account. After payment for losses actually sustained in 1984, the reserve account had a balance of $2,800,000 at December 31, 1984. The opening balance was a result of several years activity similar to 1984.
(d) Western Supply has signed as guarantor for a $50,000 loan by Guaranty Bank to Midwest Parts Inc. a principal supplier to Western. Because of financial problems at Midwest, it is probable that Western Supply will have to pay the $50,000 with only a 40% recovery anticipated from Midwest. No entries have been made to reflect the contingent liability.

Instructions:

(1) What amount should be reported as a liability on the December 31, 1984 balance sheet?
(2) What note disclosure should be included as part of the balance sheet for each of the above items?
(3) Prepare the journal entries necessary to adjust Western's books to reflect your answers in (1) and (2).

problem 13-8 (Balance sheet classification of liabilities)

The following data are made available for purposes of stating the financial position of Imperial Cabinets Inc. on December 31, 1984.

Cash in bank.		$29,000
Petty cash, which includes IOU's of employees totaling $350 that are to be repaid to the petty cash fund		1,000
Marketable securities, valued at $75,000, securities valued at $25,000 having been pledged on a note payable to the bank for $20,000, reported on the books at cost		55,000
Notes receivable, which have been reduced by notes discounted of $10,000 that are not yet due and on which the company is contingently liable.		25,000
Accounts receivable, which include accounts with credit balances of $560 and past-due accounts of $2,650 on which a loss of 80% is anticipated.		34,700
Merchandise inventory, which includes goods held on a consignment basis, $1,800. After the inventory count goods were received on December 31, in the amount of $2,600; this item has not been recorded as a purchase.		156,000
Prepaid insurance, which includes cash surrender value of life insurance policies, $8,400		18,200
Rents paid in advance		1,560
Furniture and fixtures, which include fixtures that were fully depreciated and that have just been scrapped, $4,500:		
Cost	$56,000	
Accumulated depreciation.	11,750	44,250
Notes payable, which are trade notes with the exception of a 6-month, $20,000 note payable to Commerce First National Bank on June 15, 1985.		37,830
Accounts payable, which include accounts with debit balances of $675.		18,100
Miscellaneous accrued expenses		3,650
Long-term notes, which are payable in annual installments of $2,500 on February 1 of each year (ignore interest).		10,000
Preferred 10% stock, $15 par, cumulative, on which dividends for 3 years are in arrears		45,000
No-par common stock, 40,000 shares authorized and outstanding		250,000
Retained earnings		130

The following data are not included in the above account balances:

(a) A special sales offer made in December will result in redemption of premiums estimated at a cost of $4,000 during the next year.

(b) Product replacement warranties outstanding are estimated to result in costs to the company of $6,000.

Instructions: Prepare a classified balance sheet, including whatever notes are appropriate in support of balance sheet data.

problem 13-9 (Warranty liability)

The Rapid Communications Corporation, a client, requests that you compute the appropriate balance for its estimated liability for product warranty account for a statement as of June 30, 1985.

The Rapid Communications Corporation manufactures television tubes and sells them with a six-month warranty under which defective tubes will be replaced without a charge. On December 31, 1984, Estimated Liability for Product Warranty had a balance of $510,000. By June 30, 1985, this balance had been reduced to $80,250 by debits for estimated net cost of tubes returned that had been sold in 1984.

The company started out in 1985 expecting 8% of the dollar volume of sales to be returned. However, due to the introduction of new models during the year, this estimated percentage of returns was increased to 10% on May 1. It is assumed that no tubes sold during a given month are returned in that month. Each tube is stamped with a date at time of sale so that the warranty may be properly administered. The following table of percentages indicates the likely pattern of sales returns during the six-month period of the warranty, starting with the month following the sale of tubes.

Month Following Sale	Percentage of Total Returns Expected
First	20%
Second	30
Third	20
Fourth through sixth—10% each month	30
Total	100%

Gross sales of tubes were as follows for the first six months of 1985:

Month	Amount	Month	Amount
January	$3,600,000	April	$2,850,000
February	3,300,000	May	2,000,000
March	4,100,000	June	1,800,000

The company's warranty also covers the payment of freight cost on defective tubes returned and on the new tubes sent out as replacements. This freight cost runs approximately 10% of the sales price of the tubes returned. The manufacturing cost of the tubes is roughly 80% of the sales price, and the salvage value of returned tubes averages 15% of their sales price. Returned tubes on hand at December 31, 1984, were thus valued in inventory at 15% of their original sales price.

Instructions: Using the data given, draw up a suitable working-paper schedule for arriving at the balance of the estimated liability for product warranty account and give the proposed adjusting entry. (AICPA adapted)

14 ACCOUNTING FOR BONDS AND LONG-TERM NOTES

CHAPTER OBJECTIVES

Describe the various types of long-term debt used to finance an entity's operations.

Explain and illustrate currently accepted accounting procedures followed by both investors and issuers for the issuance and servicing of long-term debt, including bonds and notes.

Describe and illustrate currently accepted accounting procedures for the conversion and termination of long-term debt including troubled debt restructuring.

Illustrate the presentation of long-term debt on the balance sheets of both investors and issuers.

Long-term financing of a corporation is accomplished either through the issuance of long-term debt instruments, usually bonds or notes, or through the sale of additional stock. The issuance of bonds or notes instead of stock may be preferred by stockholders for the following reasons: (1) the charge against earnings for interest is normally less than the share of earnings that would be payable as dividends on a new issue of preferred stock or on the sale of additional common stock; (2) present owners continue in control of the corporation; and, (3) interest is a deductible expense in arriving at taxable income while dividends are not.

But there are certain limitations and disadvantages of financing through bonds and long-term notes. Debt financing is possible only when a company is in a satisfactory financial condition and can offer adequate security to a new creditor group. Furthermore, interest must be paid regardless of the company's earnings and financial position. With operating losses and the inability of a company to raise sufficient cash to meet periodic interest payments, bondholders may take legal action to assume control of company properties.

Most bonds and long-term notes differ only in terms of the time to maturity. Generally speaking, bonds carry a maturity date five years or more after issue. Some bonds may not mature for twenty-five years or more. Long-term notes, however, generally mature in a period of one to seven years from issuance date. Other characteristics of bonds and long-term notes are usually identical. Therefore, in the discussion that follows, references to bonds can also be applied to long-term notes.

Bonds and notes are purchased for both short-term and long-term purposes by corporations, principally insurance companies, banks, trust companies, and educational and charitable institutions. Because of the similarity in accounting for bonds and notes by issuers and investors, both sides of bond and long-term note transactions will be presented in this chapter.

NATURE OF BONDS

The power of a corporation to create bonded indebtedness is found in the corporation laws of a state and may be specifically granted by charter. In some cases formal authorization by a majority of stockholders is required before a board of directors can approve a bond issue.

Borrowing by means of bonds involves the issuance of certificates of indebtedness. Bond certificates may represent equal parts of the bond issue or they may be of varying denominations. Bonds of a business unit are commonly issued in $1,000 denominations, referred to as the **bond face, par,** or **maturity value.**

The group contract between the corporation and the bondholders is known as the **bond** or **trust indenture.** The indenture details the rights and obligations of the contracting parties, indicates the property pledged as well as the protection offered on the loan, and names the bank or trust company that is to represent the bondholders.

Bonds may be sold by the company directly to investors, or they may be underwritten by investment bankers or a syndicate. The underwriters may agree to purchase the entire bond issue or that part of the issue which is not sold by the company, or they may agree simply to manage the sale of the security on a commission basis.

Most companies attempt to sell their bonds to underwriters to avoid a loss occurring after the bonds are placed on the market. An interesting example of this occurred in 1979 when IBM Corporation went to the bond market for the first time and issued a record one billion dollars worth of bonds and long-term notes. After the issue was released by IBM to the underwriters, interest rates soared as the Federal Reserve Bank sharply increased its rediscount rate. The market price of the IBM securities fell, and the brokerage houses and investment bankers participating in the underwriting incurred a loss in excess of 50 million dollars on the sale of the securities to investors.

Issuers of Bonds

Bonds and similar debt instruments are issued by private corporations, the United States Government, state, county and local governments, school districts, and government sponsored organizations such as the Federal Home Loan Bank and the Federal National Mortgage Association. The total amount of debt issued by these organizations is now well in excess of one trillion dollars.

The U.S. debt includes not only Treasury bonds, but also Treasury bills, which are notes with less than one year to maturity date, and Treasury notes, which mature in one to seven years. Both Treasury bills and Treasury notes are more in demand in the marketplace than Treasury bonds.

Debt securities issued by state, county, and local governments and their agencies are collectively referred to as **municipal debt.** A unique feature of municipal debt is that the interest received by investors from such securities is exempt from federal income tax. Because of this tax advantage, "municipals" generally carry lower interest rates than debt securities of other issuers, enabling these governmental units to borrow at favorable interest rates. The tax exemption is in reality a subsidy granted by the federal government to encourage capital investment in state and local governments.

Types of Bonds

Bonds may be classified in many different ways. When all the bonds mature on a single date, they are called **term bonds**; when bonds mature in installments, they are known as **serial bonds**. Bonds issued by private corporations may be **secured** or **unsecured**. Secured bonds provide protection to the investor in the form of a mortgage covering the company's real estate and perhaps other property, or a pledge in the form of certain collateral. A **first-mortgage bond** represents a first claim against the property of a corporation in the event of the company's inability to meet bond interest and principal payments. A **second-mortgage bond** is a secondary claim ranking only after the claim of the first-mortgage bonds or senior issue has been completely satisfied. A **collateral trust bond** is usually secured by stocks and bonds of other corporations owned by the issuing company. Such securities are generally transferred to a trustee who holds them as collateral on behalf of the bondholders and, if necessary, will sell them to satisfy the bondholders' claim.

Unsecured bonds are not protected by the pledge of certain property and are frequently termed **debenture bonds**. Holders of debenture bonds simply rank as general creditors with other unsecured parties. The risk involved in these securities varies with the financial strength of the debtor. Debentures issued by a strong company may involve little risk; debentures issued by a weak company whose properties are already heavily mortgaged may involve considerable risk. Quality ratings for bonds are made by both Moody's and Standard and Poor's investment publication companies. For example, Moody's bond ratings range from Aaa, or highest quality, to C for a high-risk bond.

Bonds may provide for their conversion into some other security at the option of the bondholder. Such bonds are known as **convertible bonds**. The conversion feature generally permits the owner of bonds to exchange them for common stock. The bondholder is thus able to convert the claim into an ownership interest if corporate operations prove successful and conversion becomes attractive; in the meantime the special rights of a creditor are maintained.

Other bond features may serve the issuer's interests. For example, bond indentures frequently give the issuing company the right to call and retire the bonds prior to their maturity. Such bonds are termed **callable bonds**. When a corporation wishes to reduce its outstanding indebtedness, bondholders are notified of the portion of the issue to be surrendered, and they are paid in accordance with call provisions. Interest does not accrue after the call date.

Bonds may be classified as (1) **registered bonds** or (2) **bearer** or **coupon bonds**. Registered bonds call for the registry of the owner's name on the corporation books. Transfer of bond ownership is similar to that for stock. When a bond is sold, the corporate transfer agent cancels the bond certificate surrendered by the seller and issues a new certificate to the buyer. Interest checks are mailed periodically to the bondholders of record. Bearer or coupon bonds are not recorded in the name of the owner, title to such bonds passing with delivery. Each bond is accompanied by coupons for individual interest payments covering the life of the issue. Coupons are clipped by the owner of the bond and presented to a bank for deposit or collection. The issue of bearer bonds eliminates the need for recording bond ownership changes and preparing and mailing periodic interest checks. But coupon bonds fail to offer the bondholder the protection found in registered bonds in the event bonds are lost or stolen. In some cases, bonds provide interest coupons but require registry as to principal. Here, ownership safeguards are afforded while the time-consuming routines involved in making interest payments are avoided. Most bonds of recent issue are registered.

In recent years, some bonds and long-term notes have been issued with **floating interest rates**. Because of the wide fluctuations in interest rates that have occurred in the past few years, the floating interest rate security reduces the risk to the investor when interest rates are rising and to the issuer when interest rates are falling.

Bond Market Price

The market price of bonds varies with the safety of the investment. When the financial condition and earnings of a corporation are such that payment of interest and principal on bonded indebtedness is virtually assured, the interest rate a company must offer to dispose of a bond issue is relatively low. As the risk factor increases, a higher interest return is necessary to attract investors. The amount of interest paid on bonds is a specified percentage of the face value. This percentage is termed the **stated** or **contract rate**. This rate, however, may not be the same as the prevailing or **market rate** for bonds of similar quality and length of time to maturity at the time the issue is sold. Furthermore, the market rate constantly fluctuates. These factors often result in a difference between bond face values and the prices at which the bonds sell on the market.

The purchase of bonds at face value implies agreement between the bond rate of interest and the prevailing market rate of interest. If the bond rate exceeds the market rate, the bonds will sell at a **premium**; if the bond rate is less than the market rate, the bonds will sell at a **discount**. The premium or the discount is the discounted value of the difference between the stated rate and the market rate of the series of interest payments. A declining market rate of interest subsequent to issuance of the bonds results in an increase in the market value of the bonds; a rising market rate of interest results in a decrease in their market value. The stated rate adjusted for the premium or the discount on the purchase gives the actual rate of return on the bonds, known as the **effective interest rate**. Bonds are quoted on the market as a percentage of face value. Thus, a bond quotation of 96.5 means the market price is 96.5% of face value, or at a discount; a bond quotation of 104 means the market price is 104% of face value, or at a premium. U.S. Government note and bond quotations are made in 32's rather than 100's. Thus a Government bond selling at 98.16 is selling at $98\frac{16}{32}$, or in terms of decimal equivalents, 98.5%.

The market price of a bond at any date can be determined by discounting the maturity value of the bond and each remaining interest payment at the effective rate of interest for similar debt on that date. Present value tables that can be used for discounting are included in Appendix A.

To illustrate the computation of a bond market price from the tables, assume 10-year, 8% bonds of $100,000 are to be sold on the bond issue date. The effective interest rate for these bonds is 10%, compounded semiannually. The computation may be divided into two parts:

(1) *Present Value of Maturity Value:*

Maturity value of bonds after ten years or twenty semiannual periods = $100,000

Effective interest rate—10% per year, or 5% per semiannual period:

$PV_n = A(PVF_{\overline{n}|i}) = \$100{,}000(\text{Table II}_{\overline{20}|5\%}) = \$100{,}000(.3769) = \$37{,}690.$

(2) *Present Value of Twenty Interest Payments:*

Semiannual payment, 4% of $100,000 = $4,000

Effective interest rate—10% per year, or 5% per semiannual period:

$PV_n = R(PVAF_{\overline{n}|i}) = \$4{,}000(\text{Table IV}_{\overline{20}|5\%}) = \$4{,}000(12.4622) = \$49{,}849$

The market price for the bonds would thus be $87,539, the sum of the two parts. Because the effective interest rate is higher than the stated interest rate, the bonds would sell at a $12,461 discount at the issuance date.

Special adaptation of present value tables is available to determine the price to be paid for the bonds if they are to provide a certain return. A portion of such a bond table is illustrated below.

Values to the Nearest Dollar of 8% Bond for $100,000
Interest Payable Semiannually

Yield	8 years	8½ years	9 years	9½ years	10 years
7.00	$106,046	$106,325	$106,595	$106,855	$107,107
7.25	104,495	104,699	104,896	105,090	105,272
7.50	102,971	103,100	103,232	103,360	103,476
7.75	101,472	101,537	101,595	101,658	101,718
8.00	100,000	100,000	100,000	100,000	100,000
8.25	98,552	98,494	98,437	98,372	98,325
8.50	97,141	97,012	96,893	96,787	96,678
8.75	95,746	95,568	95,398	95,232	95,070
9.00	94,383	94,147	93,920	93,703	93,496
9.25	93,042	92,757	92,480	92,214	91,953
9.50	91,723	91,380	91,055	90,751	90,452
9.75	90,350	89,960	89,588	89,238	88,902
10.00	89,162	88,726	88,310	87,914	87,539

Note that the present value from the table of 8% bonds to return 10% in 10 years is $87,539, the same amount computed on page 511. If the effective rate were 7.5%, the present value would be $103,476.

The table can also be used to determine the effective rate on a bond acquired at a certain price. To illustrate, assume that a $1,000, 8% bond due in 10 years is selling at $951. Reference to the column "10 years" for $95,070 shows a return of 8.75% is provided on an investment of $950.70.

BOND ISSUANCE

Bonds may be sold directly to investors by the issuer or they may be sold on the open market through securities exchanges or through investment bankers. Over 50% of bond issues are privately placed with large investors.

An issuer normally records bonds at their face value—the amount that the company must pay at maturity. Hence, when bonds are issued at an amount other than face value, a bond discount or premium account is established for the difference between the cash received and the bond face value. The premium is added to or the discount is subtracted from the bond face value in the liability section of the balance sheet. This results in bonds being reported at their present value.

The issuance of bonds normally involves costs to the issuer for legal services, printing and engraving, taxes and underwriting. Traditionally, these costs have been either (1) summarized separately as bond issuance costs, classified as deferred charges and charged to revenue over the life of the bond issue, or (2) offset against any premium or added to any discount arising on the issuance and thus netted against the face value of the bonds. The Accounting Principles Board in Opinion No. 21 recommended that these costs be reported on the balance sheet as deferred charges.[1] However, in Statement of Concepts No. 3, the FASB stated that such costs fail to meet the definition of assets adopted by the Board.[2] The authors agree with the position of the FASB, and favor netting the issuance costs against the bonds payable as part of the premium or discount on the bonds. Concepts Statements do not establish GAAP, however, and until such time as the FASB addresses the issue, the APB Opinion governs generally accepted practice.

Although an investor could record the investment in bonds at their face value with a premium or discount account as described for the issuer, traditionally investors record their investment at cost, or net of any premium or discount. Cost includes brokerage fees and any other costs incident to the purchase. Bonds acquired in exchange for noncash assets or services are recorded at the fair market value of the bonds, unless the value of the exchanged assets or services is more clearly determinable. When bonds and other securities are acquired for a lump sum, an apportionment of such cost among the securities is required. Purchase of bonds on a deferred payment basis calls for recognition of both the asset and the liability balances.

When bonds are issued or sold between interest dates, an adjustment is made for the interest accrued between the last interest payment date and the date of the transaction. A buyer of the bonds adds the amount of accrued interest to the purchase price and then receives this payment back plus interest earned subsequent to the purchase date when the next interest payment is made. This practice avoids the problem an issuer of bonds would have in trying to split interest payments for a given period between two or more owners of the securities. For example, if the interest dates of 10% bonds are March 1 and September 1, and $600,000 of bonds are sold at par on May 1, the two months' interest from March 1 to May 1 of $10,000 would be added to the amount paid by the investor to the issuer. When the September 1 payment of $30,000 is made to the investor, the $10,000 is offset against the $30,000 received, and the net difference of $20,000 is reported as interest earned for the period from May 1 to September 1. Similarly, $20,000 is reported as interest expense by the issuer. The $10,000 interest payment may be debited to Interest Receivable on the investor's books and credited to Interest Payable on the issuer's books as shown below:

Issuer's Books

May 1	Cash	610,000	
	Bonds Payable		600,000
	Interest Payable		10,000
Sept. 1	Interest Payable	10,000	
	Interest Expense	20,000	
	Cash		30,000

[1] *Opinions of the Accounting Principles Board, No. 21,* "Interest on Receivables and Payables" (New York: American Institute of Certified Public Accountants, 1971), par. 16.

[2] *Statement of Financial Accounting Concepts No. 3,* "Elements of Financial Statements of Business Enterprises" (Stamford: Financial Accounting Standards Board, December 1980), par. 161.

Investor's Books

May 1	Interest Receivable	10,000	
	Investment in Bonds	600,000	
	Cash		610,000
Sept. 1	Cash	30,000	
	Interest Receivable		10,000
	Interest Revenue		20,000

Alternatively, as illustrated in the example below, the accrued interest could be initially credited to Interest Expense by the issuer and debited to Interest Revenue by the investor.

To further illustrate the accounting for bond issuance, assume a 10-year, \$200,000, 8% bond issue is sold at 103, on May 1. Interest payment dates are February 1 and August 1. The entries on the books of the issuer and the investor would be as follows:

Issuer's Books

May 1	Cash	210,000	
	Bonds Payable		200,000
	Premium on Bonds		6,000
	Interest Expense		4,000
	To record issuance of bonds.		

Computation:
\$200,000 × 1.03 = \$206,000 purchase price.
Interest: \$200,000 × .08 × 3/12 = \$4,000

Investor's Books

May 1	Investment in Bonds	206,000	
	Interest Revenue	4,000	
	Cash		210,000
	To record investment in bonds.		

A 360-day year (12 months, 30 days per month) was assumed in the illustration for convenience. With the aid of computers, a 365-day year is increasingly being used for bond accounting.

When bonds are issued in exchange for property, the transaction should be recorded at the cash price at which the bonds could be issued. When difficulties are encountered in arriving at a cash price, the market or appraised value of the property acquired would be used. A difference between the face value of the bonds and the cash value of the bonds or the value of the property acquired is recognized as bond discount or bond premium.

Issuance of Convertible Bonds

The issuance of **convertible debt securities**, most frequently bonds, has become popular. These securities are convertible into the common stock of the issuing company or an affiliate at a specified exchange value and at the option of the holder. These securities usually have the following characteristics:[3]

[3]*Opinions of the Accounting Principles Board, No. 14,* "Accounting for Convertible Debt and Debt Issued with Stock Purchase Warrants" (New York: American Institute of Certified Public Accountants, 1969), par. 3.

(1) An interest rate lower than the issuer could establish for nonconvertible debt.
(2) An initial conversion price higher than the market value of the common stock at time of issuance.
(3) A call option retained by the issuer.

The popularity of these securities may be attributed to the advantages to both an issuer and a holder. An issuer is able to obtain financing at a lower interest rate because of the value of the conversion feature to the holder. Because of the call provision, an issuer is in a position to exert influence upon the holders to exchange the debt for equity securities if stock values increase; the issuer has had the use of relatively low interest rate financing if stock values do not increase. On the other hand, the holder has a debt instrument that, barring default, assures the return of investment plus a fixed return, and at the same time offers an option to transfer his or her interest to equity capital should such transfer become attractive.

Many convertible bond issues place no restriction on when an issuer can call in bonds, and interest accrued on such bonds is sometimes absorbed in a conversion and not paid to the investor. Thus, a company can have the use of interest-free money as a result of calling in bonds prior to the first interest payment. Widespread use of early call provisions in the early 1980s led some investors to demand a provision restricting exercise of the call provision for a specified time period.[4]

Differences of opinion exist as to whether convertible debt securities should be treated by an issuer solely as debt, or whether part of the proceeds received from the issuance of debt should be recognized as equity capital. One view holds that the debt and the conversion privilege are inseparably connected, and therefore the debt and equity portions of a security should not be separately valued. A holder cannot sell part of the instrument and retain the other. An alternate view holds that there are two distinct elements in these securities and that each should be recognized in the accounts: that portion of the issuance price attributable to the conversion privilege should be recorded as a credit to Paid-In Capital; the balance of the issuance price should be assigned to the debt. This would decrease the premium otherwise recognized in the debt or perhaps result in a discount.

These views are compared in the illustration that follows. Assume that 500 ten-year bonds, face value $1,000, are sold at 105. The bonds contain a conversion privilege that provides for exchange of a $1,000 bond for 20 shares of stock, par value $40. The interest rate on the bonds is 8%. It is estimated that without the conversion privilege, the bonds would sell at 96. The journal entries to record the issuance on the issuer's books under the two approaches follow.

Debt and Equity Not Separated

Cash	525,000	
Bonds Payable		500,000
Premium on Bonds Payable		25,000

[4] Ben Weberman, "The Convertible Bond Scam," *Forbes* (January 19, 1981), p. 92.

Debt and Equity Separated

Cash	525,000	
Discount on Bonds Payable	20,000	
Bonds Payable		500,000
Paid-In Capital Arising from Bond Conversion Privilege		45,000

The periodic charge for interest will differ depending on which method is employed. To illustrate the computation of interest charges, assume that the straight-line method is used to amortize bond premium or discount. Under the first approach, the annual interest charge would be $37,500 ($40,000 paid less $2,500 premium amortization). Under the second approach, the annual interest charge would be $42,000 ($40,000 paid plus $2,000 discount amortization).

The Accounting Principles Board stated that when convertible debt is sold at a price or with a value at issuance not significantly in excess of the face amount, "... no portion of the proceeds from the issuance... should be accounted for as attributable to the conversion feature."[5]

The APB stated that greater weight for this decision was placed on the inseparability of the debt and the conversion option than upon the practical problems of valuing the separate parts. However, the practical problems are considerable. Separate valuation requires asking the question: How much would the security sell for without the conversion feature? In many instances this question would appear to be unanswerable. Investment banks responsible for selling these issues are frequently unable to separate the two features for valuation purposes; they contend that the cash required simply could not be raised without the conversion privilege.

There would seem to be strong theoretical support for separating the debt and equity portions of the proceeds from the issuance of convertible debt on the issuer's books. Despite these theoretical arguments, current practice follows APB Opinion No. 14, and no separation is usually made between debt and equity. This is true even when separate values are determinable.

Issuance of Bonds with Stock Purchase Warrants Attached

Another type of potential equity interest arises when bonds are issued with detachable stock purchase warrants. Because the debt instrument and the warrants are separate, they can and do trade on the market separately. The decision to exercise the warrants depends on the movement of the stock market.

Because the warrants are separable from the debt instrument, a value can be assigned to the warrants based on the relative fair value of the debt security without the warrants and the value of the warrants themselves at the time of issuance. Assume the same example used in the discussion of convertible bonds except that stock warrants are substituted for the conversion feature: 500 ten-year bonds, face value $1,000, are sold at 105. Each bond is accompanied by one warrant that permits the holder to purchase 20 shares

[5]*Ibid.*, par. 12.

of stock, par value $40. Each bond without the warrant has a market value of $960, and each warrant has a market value of $90. The proceeds of $525,000 would be allocated $480,000 to the debt and $45,000 to the owners' equity on the issuer's books as follows:

Cash	525,000	
Discount on Bonds Payable	20,000	
Bonds Payable		500,000
Common Stock Purchase Warrants		45,000

In the preceding example, the sum of the market values for bonds and stock warrants equaled the issue price of the joint offering. Due to market imperfections, however, such relationships are rare. Usually, sales proceeds must be allocated between the two securities on the basis of their relative market values at the time of their issuance. When purchase warrants are used to acquire stock, the amount allocated to equity is transferred to the account Premium on Common Stock.

BOND INTEREST—TERM BONDS

When coupon bonds are issued, cash is paid by the company in exchange for interest coupons on the interest dates. Payments on coupons may be made by the company directly to bondholders, or payments may be cleared through a bank or other disbursing agent. Subsidiary records with bondholders are not maintained since coupons are redeemable by bearers. In the case of registered bonds, interest checks are mailed either by the company or its agent. When bonds are registered, the bonds account requires subsidiary ledger support. The subsidiary ledger shows holdings by individuals and changes in such holdings. Checks are sent to bondholders of record as of the interest payment dates.

When an agent is to make interest payments, the company normally transfers cash to the agent in advance of the interest payment date. Since the company is not freed from its obligation to bondholders until payment has been made by its agent, it records the cash transfer by a debit to Cash Deposited with Agent for Bond Interest and a credit to Cash. On the date the interest is due, the company debits Interest Expense and credits Interest Payable. Upon receipt from the agent of paid interest coupons, a certificate of coupon receipt and appropriate disposal, or other evidence that the interest was paid, the company debits Interest Payable and credits Cash Deposited with Agent for Bond Interest.

Amortization of Premium or Discount

When bonds are issued at a premium or discount, the market acts to adjust the stated interest rate to a market or effective interest rate. Because of the initial premium or discount, the periodic interest payments made over the bond life by the issuer to the investors do not represent the complete revenue and expense for the periods involved. An adjustment to the cash transfer for the periodic write-off of the premium or discount is necessary to reflect the effective interest rate being incurred or earned on the bonds. This adjustment is referred to as **bond premium** or **discount amortization**. The periodic adjustment of bonds results in a gradual adjustment of the carrying value toward the bond's face value.

A premium on issued bonds recognizes that the stated interest rate is higher than the market interest rate. Amortization of the premium reduces the interest revenue or expense below the amount of cash transferred. A discount on issued bonds recognizes that the stated interest rate is lower than the market interest rate. Amortization of the discount increases the amount of interest revenue or expense above the amount of cash transferred.

Two principal methods are used to amortize the premium or discount: (1) the straight-line method and (2) the interest method.

Straight-Line Method. The straight-line method provides for the recognition of an equal amount of premium or discount amortization each period. The amount of monthly amortization is determined by dividing the premium or discount at purchase or issuance by the number of months remaining to the bond maturity date. For example, if a 10-year, 10% bond issue with a maturity value of $200,000 was sold on the issuance date at 103, the $6,000 premium would be amortized evenly over the 120 months until maturity, or at a rate of $50 per month, ($6,000 ÷ 120). If the bonds were sold three months after the issuance date, the $6,000 premium would be amortized evenly over 117 months, or a rate of $51.28 per month, ($6,000 ÷ 117). The amortization period is always the time from original sale to maturity. The premium amortization would reduce both interest expense on the issuer's books and interest revenue on the investor's books. A discount amortization would have the opposite results: both accounts would be increased.

It is necessary to set some arbitrary minimum time unit in the straight-line amortization of bond premium or bond discount. The month is used in this text as the minimum unit. Transactions occurring during the first half of the month are treated as though they were made at the beginning of the month; transactions occurring during the second half are treated as though made at the start of the following month. Use of a longer term, such as the quarter or half year, is possible, although this offers less accuracy than the use of a shorter time unit.

Interest Method. The interest method of amortization uses a uniform interest rate based on a changing investment balance and provides for an increasing premium or discount amortization each period. In order to use this method, the effective interest rate for the bonds must first be determined. This is the rate of interest at bond issuance that discounts the maturity value of the bonds and the periodic interest payments to the market price of the bonds. This rate is used to determine the effective revenue or expense to be recorded on the books.

For example, as shown on page 512, $100,000, 10-year, 8% bonds sold to return 10% would sell for $87,539, or at a discount of $12,461. If the bonds were sold on the issuance date, the straight-line discount amortization for each six month period would be $623.05 [($100,000 − $87,539) ÷ 20]. The discount amortization for the first six months using the interest method would be computed as follows:

Investment balance at beginning of first period	$87,539
Effective rate per semiannual period	5%
Stated rate per semiannual period	4%
Interest amount based on effective rate ($87,539 × .05)	$ 4,377
Interest payment based on stated rate ($100,000 × .04)	4,000
Difference between interest amount based on effective rate and stated rate	$ 377

This difference is the discount amortization for the first period using the interest method. For the second semiannual period, the bond carrying value increases by the discount amortization. The amortization for the second semiannual period would be computed as follows:

Investment balance at beginning of second period ($87,539 + $377)	$87,916
Interest amount based on effective rate ($87,916 × .05)	$ 4,396
Interest payment based on stated rate ($100,000 × .04)	4,000
Difference between interest amount based on effective rate and stated rate	$ 396

The amount of interest for each period is computed at a uniform rate on an increasing balance. This results in an increasing discount amortization over the life of the bonds that is graphically demonstrated and compared with straight-line amortization below.

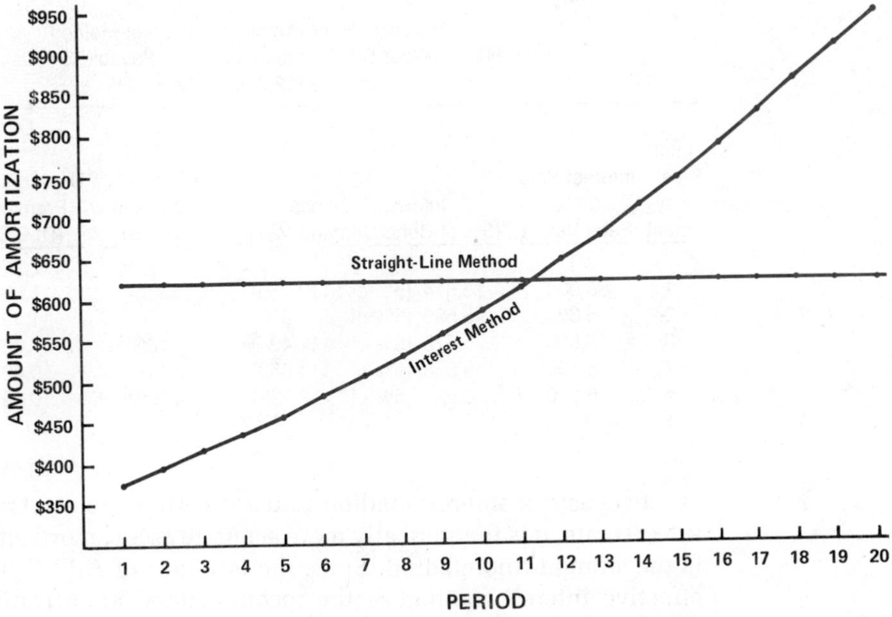

Premium amortization would be computed in a similar way except that the interest amount based on the stated interest rate would be higher than the amount based on the effective rate. For example, $100,000, 10-year, 12% bonds sold to return 10% would sell for $112,285, or at a premium of $12,285. If the bonds were sold on the issuance date, the premium amortization for the first and second six-month periods would be computed as follows:

Investment balance at beginning of first period	$112,285
Effective rate per semiannual period	5%
Stated rate per semiannual period	6%
Interest payment based on stated rate ($100,000 × .06)	$ 6,000
Interest amount based on effective rate ($112,285 × .05)	5,614
Difference between interest amount based on stated rate and effective rate, or premium amortization	$ 386
Investment balance at beginning of second period ($112,285 − $386)	$111,899
Interest payment based on stated rate ($100,000 × .06)	$ 6,000
Interest amount based on effective rate ($111,899 × .05)	5,595
Difference between interest amount based on stated rate and effective rate	$ 405

As illustrated, as the investment or liability balance is reduced by the premium amortization, the interest based on the effective rate also decreases. The difference between the interest payment and the interest based upon the effective rate increases in a manner similar to discount amortization. Special bond amortization tables, such as the partial one illustrated below, may be prepared to determine the periodic adjustments to the bond carrying value.

Amortization of Premium—Interest Method
$100,000, 10-Year Bonds, Interest at 12% Payable Semiannually,
Sold at $112,285 to Yield 10%

	A	B	C	D	E
Interest Payment	Interest Paid (6% of Face Value)	Interest Expense (5% of Bond Carrying Value)	Premium Amortization (A − B)	Unamortized Premium (D − C)	Bond Carrying Value ($100,000 + D)
				$12,285	$112,285
1	$6,000	$5,614 (5% of $112,285)	$386	11,899	111,899
2	6,000	5,595 (5% of 111,899)	405	11,494	111,494
3	6,000	5,575 (5% of 111,494)	425	11,069	111,069
4	6,000	5,553 (5% of 111,069)	447	10,622	110,622
5	6,000	5,531 (5% of 110,622)	469	10,153	110,153
⋮	⋮	⋮	⋮	⋮	⋮

Because the interest method adjusts the stated interest rate to an effective interest rate, it is theoretically more accurate as an amortization method than is the straight-line method. Since the issuance of APB Opinion No. 21, the effective interest method is the recommended amortization method. The more popular straight-line method may be used by a company if the results of using it do not differ materially from the amortization using the interest method.[6]

Accounting for Bond Interest

Entries for premium or discount amortization may be made as adjusting entries at the end of a company's fiscal year or interim period, or as each interest payment is made. The accounting entries for bond interest and first year discount amortization on both the issuer's and investor's books would be as follows. Assume the bonds are issued at a discount as described at the bottom of page 518, and the discount is amortized by the interest method when each payment is made or received.

Issuer's Books

First payment:	Interest Expense	4,377	
	Cash		4,000
	Discount on Bonds Payable		377
Second payment:	Interest Expense	4,396	
	Cash		4,000
	Discount on Bonds Payable		396

Investor's Books

First payment:	Cash	4,000	
	Investment in Bonds	377	
	Interest Revenue		4,377
Second payment:	Cash	4,000	
	Investment in Bonds	396	
	Interest Revenue		4,396

If the bonds were sold at a premium, the investment or liability balance would be reduced over the life of the bonds to maturity value. Assume a 10-year, $200,000, 8% bond issue is sold at 103 on May 1 and is recorded as shown on page 514. Interest payment dates are February 1 and August 1, and the straight-line method of amortization is used. The following entries on both the issuer's and investor's books for the first year would be required. (Adjusting entries at the end of fiscal year are not included.)

Issuer's Books

Aug. 1	Interest Expense	7,846	
	Premium on Bonds Payable	154	
	Cash		8,000

Computation:
Premium amortization for 3 months:
$6,000/117 months = $51.28 per month
$51.28 × 3 = $153.84, or $154

Feb. 1	Interest Expense	7,692	
	Premium on Bonds Payable	308	
	Cash		8,000

Computation:
Premium amortization for 6 months:
$51.28 × 6 = $307.68, or $308

---

[6]*Opinions of the Accounting Principles Board, No. 21*, "Interest on Receivables and Payables" (New York: American Institute of Certified Public Accountants, 1972), par. 15.

Investor's Books

Aug. 1	Cash	8,000	
	Investment in Bonds		154
	Interest Revenue		7,846
Feb. 1	Cash	8,000	
	Investment in Bonds		308
	Interest Revenue		7,692

When bonds are acquired as a temporary investment, investment cost is maintained in the accounts without adjustment for premium or discount amortization. Any difference between the purchase and sales price is recognized as a gain or loss at the time of the sale.

BOND INTEREST—SERIAL BONDS

Serial bonds mature at various dates. Usually, each bond indicates when it will mature. Because of the difference in time to maturity, the interest rate often varies depending on the due date. For example, the following schedule for Iowa Housing Finance Authority Bonds shows bonds maturing each year for 19 years. The stated interest rate for bonds maturing each year differs, reflecting the added risk of accepting a fixed rate for periods in the future.

$108,215,000 Serial Bonds—Price 100%

Principal Amount	Due August 1	Interest Rate	Principal Amount	Due August 1	Interest Rate	Principal Amount	Due August 1	Interest Rate
$5,270,000	1981	5.50%	$6,825,000	1987	6.05%	$4,915,000	1994	6.40%
5,270,000	1982	5.60	6,735,000	1988	6.10	4,790,000	1995	6.45
6,235,000	1983	5.70	6,515,000	1989	6.15	4,715,000	1996	6.50
6,785,000	1984	5.80	6,255,000	1990	6.20	4,640,000	1997	6.60
7,200,000	1985	5.90	5,640,000	1991	6.25	4,445,000	1998	6.70
7,315,000	1986	6.00	5,350,000	1992	6.30	4,195,000	1999	6.80
			5,120,000	1993	6.35			

In some instances, the stated interest rate remains constant for all maturity dates, but the effective interest rate differs as the selling prices for the different maturity dates vary to reflect the added risk. When serial bonds are issued at other than 100%, the premium or discount could be related to the bonds maturing on each specific date, and the amortization of the premium or discount could be made as though each maturity date was a separate bond issue. No new problems related to accounting for interest arise under this approach.

However, an entire serial bond issue is sometimes sold directly to underwriters at a lump-sum price that differs from the total face value of the issue. When this occurs, the issue price usually cannot be identified with each maturity date. Under these circumstances, the premium or discount on the entire serial bond issue must be amortized as a unit. This requires that either an average effective rate be determined for the entire issue, and the interest method used to determine the amortization; or that a variation of the straight-line method known as the **bonds outstanding** method be applied. Both methods provide for decreases in the amortization schedule as the principal amounts of the serial bonds mature.

Bonds-Outstanding Method

Amortization by the bonds-outstanding method is illustrated in the example that follows. Assume that bonds with a face value of $100,000, dated January 1, 1984, are issued on this date for a lump-sum price of $101,260. Bonds of $20,000 mature at the end of each year starting on December 31, 1984. The bonds pay interest of 8% annually. The company's accounting period ends on December 31; the accounting period and the bond year thus coincide. A table showing the premium to be amortized each year is developed as shown in the schedule below.

Amortization Schedule—Bonds-Outstanding Method

Year	Bonds Outstanding	Fraction of Premium to be Amortized	Annual Premium Amortization (Fraction × $1,260)
1984	$100,000	100,000/300,000 (or 10/30)	$ 420
1985	80,000	80,000/300,000 (or 8/30)	336
1986	60,000	60,000/300,000 (or 6/30)	252
1987	40,000	40,000/300,000 (or 4/30)	168
1988	20,000	20,000/300,000 (or 2/30)	84
	$300,000	300,000/300,000 (or 30/30)	$1,260

The annual premium amortization is found by multiplying the premium by a fraction whose numerator is the number of bond dollars outstanding in that year and whose denominator is the total number of bond dollars outstanding for the life of the bond issue. As bonds are retired, the amounts of premium amortization decline accordingly.

An alternative computation can be made by computing the amount of amortization related to each $1,000 of outstanding bonds. In the above example, this would be $4.20 per 1,000 bond ($1,260 ÷ 300). Applying this amount to the number of $1,000 bonds outstanding each year would result in the same amortization computed above; e.g., for 1985, 80 × $4.20, or $336. The use of this alternative method of computing the amortization is especially useful when computing the unamortized premium or discount on serial bonds retired early.

Periodic amortization may be incorporated in a table summarizing the interest charges and changes in bond carrying values as shown below.

Amortization of Premium—Serial Bonds
Bonds-Outstanding Method

Date	A Interest Payment (8% of Face Value	B Premium Amortization	C Interest Expense (A − B)	D Principal Payment	E Bond Carrying Value Decrease (B + D)	F Bond Carrying Value (F − E)
Jan. 1, 1984						$101,260
Dec. 31, 1984	$8,000	$420	$7,580	$20,000	$20,420	80,840
Dec. 31, 1985	6,400	336	6,064	20,000	20,336	60,504
Dec. 31, 1986	4,800	252	4,548	20,000	20,252	40,252
Dec. 31, 1987	3,200	168	3,032	20,000	20,168	20,084
Dec. 31, 1988	1,600	84	1,516	20,000	20,084	—

Interest Method

Tables show that the bonds discussed on the preceding page were sold to return approximately 7½%. Use of this rate results in the following interest charges and premium amortization using the interest method:

Amortization of Premium—Serial Bonds
Interest Method

	A	B	C	D	E	F
Date	Interest Payment (8% of Face Value)	Interest Expense (7½% of Bond Carrying Value)	Premium Amortization (A – B)	Principal Payment	Bond Carrying Value Decrease (C + D)	Bond Carrying Value (F – E)
Jan. 1, 1984						$101,260
Dec. 31, 1984	$8,000	$7,595	$405	$20,000	$20,405	80,855
Dec. 31, 1985	6,400	6,064	336	20,000	20,336	60,519
Dec. 31, 1986	4,800	4,539	261	20,000	20,261	40,258
Dec. 31, 1987	3,200	3,019	181	20,000	20,181	20,077
Dec. 31, 1988	1,600	1,523*	77*	20,000	20,077	—

*The last payment is adjusted because the effective rate was not exactly 7½%. On the final payment the premium balance is closed and interest expense is reduced by this amount.

The bonds-outstanding method of amortization provides for the recognition of uniform amounts of amortization in terms of the par value of bonds outstanding. The interest method provides for the recognition of interest at a uniform rate on the declining debt balance.

BOND TRANSFERS BETWEEN INVESTORS

Bonds are negotiable, and thus may be sold on the market after purchase. As explained earlier, any accrued interest is paid for by the purchaser, thus giving the seller interest revenue for the period the investment was held. For example, assume Alco Inc. owns Jessup Co. bonds with a maturity value of $100,000 and a carrying value of $98,000. Accrued interest of $2,500 is due on the bonds at the date of sale to Majestic Inc. The bonds are sold at 99 plus accrued interest. The following entries on the seller's and buyer's books would be made.

Alco Inc. (Seller)

Cash	101,500	
Investment in Jessup Co. Bonds		98,000
Interest Revenue		2,500
Gain on Sale of Bond Investment		1,000

Majestic Inc. (Buyer)

Investment in Jessup Co. Bonds	99,000	
Interest Revenue	2,500	
Cash		101,500

CONVERSION OF BONDS

Convertible bonds grant to an investor the right to convert debt to equity under certain conditions. The conversion privilege is granted when the bonds are sold, but as discussed earlier, the value of the conversion privilege is normally combined with the cost of the debt instrument. When conversion takes place, a special valuation question must be answered. Should the market value of the securities be used to compute a gain or loss on the transaction? If the security is viewed as debt, then the conversion to equity would seem to be a significant economic transaction and a gain or loss would be recognized. If, however, the security is viewed as equity, the conversion is really an exchange of one type of equity capital for another, and the historical cost principle would seem to indicate that no gain or loss would be recognized. In practice, the latter approach seems to be most commonly followed by both the issuer and investor of the bonds. No gain or loss is recognized either for book or tax purposes. The book value of the bonds is transferred to become the book value of the stock issued. However, this treatment seems inconsistent with APB Opinion No. 14 as discussed earlier in this chapter.[7] In that opinion, convertible debt was considered to be debt rather than equity.

If an investor viewed the security as debt, conversion of the debt could be viewed as an exchange of one asset for another. The general rule for the exchange of nonmonetary assets is that the market value of the asset exchanged should be used to measure any gain or loss on the transaction.[8] If there is no market value of the asset surrendered or if its value is undeterminable, the market value of the asset received should be used. The market value of convertible bonds should reflect the market value of the stock to be issued on the conversion, and thus the market value of the two securities should be similar.

To illustrate bond conversion for the investor recognizing a gain or loss on conversion, assume Carl Co. offers bondholders 40 shares of Carl Co. common stock, $25 par, in exchange for each $1,000, 8% bond held. An investor exchanges bonds of $10,000 (book value as brought up to date, $9,850) for 400 shares of common stock having a market price at the time of the exchange of $26 per share. The exchange is completed at the interest payment date. The exchange is recorded as follows:

Investment in Carl Co. Common Stock	10,400	
Investment in Carl Co. Bonds		9,850
Gain on Conversion of Carl Co. Bonds		550

If the investor chose not to recognize a gain or loss, the journal entry would be as follows:

Investment in Carl Co. Common Stock	9,850	
Investment in Carl Co. Bonds		9,850

[7]See page 515.
[8]*Opinions of the Accounting Principles Board, No. 29,* "Accounting for Nonmonetary Transactions" (New York: American Institute of Certified Public Accountants, 1973), par. 18.

Similar differences would occur on the issuer's books depending on the viewpoint assumed. If the issuer desired to recognize the conversion of the convertible debt as a significant transaction, the market value of the securities would be used to record the conversion. To illustrate the journal entries for the issuer using this reasoning, assume 100 bonds, face value $1,000, are exchanged for 2,000 shares of common stock, $40 par value, $55 market value. At the time of the conversion, there is an unamortized premium on the bond issue of $3,000. The conversion would be recorded as follows:

Bonds Payable	100,000	
Premium on Bonds Payable	3,000	
Loss on Conversion of Bonds	7,000	
Common Stock		80,000
Premium on Common Stock		30,000

Computation:		
Market value of stock issued (2,000 shares at $55)		$110,000
Face value of bonds payable	$100,000	
Plus unamortized premium	3,000	103,000
Loss to company on conversion of bonds		$ 7,000

If the issuer did not consider the conversion as a culminating transaction, no gain or loss would be recognized. The bond carrying value would be transferred to the capital stock account on the theory that the company upon issuing the bonds is aware of the fact that bond proceeds may ultimately represent the consideration identified with stock. Thus, when bondholders exercise their conversion privileges, the value identified with the obligation is transferred to the security that replaces it. Under this assumption, the conversion would be recorded as follows:

Bonds Payable	100,000	
Premium on Bonds Payable	3,000	
Common Stock, $40 par		80,000
Premium on Common Stock		23,000

The profession has not resolved the accounting issues surrounding convertible debt. Although the practice of not recognizing gain or loss on either the issuer's or the investor's books is widespread, it seems inconsistent with the treatment of other items that are transferred by an entity. The economic reality of the transaction would seem to require a recognition of the change in value at least at the time conversion takes place. The movement toward the use of current values in the accounts would require recognition of gains or losses on these securities at even earlier dates if the market reflected a change in value.

RETIREMENT OF BONDS AT MATURITY

Bonds always include a specified termination or maturity date. At that time, the issuer must pay the current investors the maturity or face value of the bonds. When bond discount or premium and issue cost balances have been properly amortized over the life of the bonds, bond retirement simply calls for elimination of the liability or the investment by a cash transaction. Any bonds not presented for payment at their maturity date should be removed from the bonds payable balance on the issuer's books and reported separately as Matured Bonds Payable; these are reported as a current liability except when they are to be paid out of a sinking fund. Interest does not accrue on matured bonds not presented for payment.

If a bond fund is used to pay off a bond issue, any cash remaining in the fund may be returned to the cash account. Appropriations of retained earnings established during the life of the issue may be returned to retained earnings.

TERMINATION OF BONDS PRIOR TO MATURITY

Bonds (and other long-term debt instruments) may be terminated prior to the maturity date through either a purchase or a redemption. In a **purchase**, the issuer buys individual bonds on the market. In a **redemption**, the issuer utilizes the call provision frequently included in bond indentures and redeems all or part of the bond issue prior to maturity. Bonds purchased or redeemed prior to maturity may be retired or held as treasury bonds for possible future reissuance.

Acquisition of bonds prior to their maturity calls for recognition by the issuer of a gain or a loss for the difference between the bond carrying value and the amount paid.[9] This gain or loss is classified as an **early extinguishment of debt,** and according to FASB Statement No. 4 is reported as an extraordinary item on the income statement.[10] An exception to this extraordinary classification is made if the early termination is necessary to satisfy bond sinking fund requirements within a one-year period.[11] Payment of accrued interest on bond termination is separately reported as a debit to Interest Expense.

In 1983, the FASB issued an exposure draft clarifying the nature of transactions that are properly recognized as early extinguishment of debt. The exposure draft was issued to establish guidelines for a procedure used by some companies in recent years to reduce the amount of long-term indebtedness reported on their balance sheets. The practice involved transferring assets to a trust that was to be used solely for satisfying certain long-term debt obligations. The transfer of assets was treated as an extinguishment of debt, and a gain was recognized even though the debt had not actually been paid. These transactions were referred to as "in-substance defeasance" arrangements. In the exposure draft, the Board stated that these transactions could be treated as extinguishment of debt only if the debtor is virtually assured

---

[9] *Opinions of the Accounting Principles Board, No. 26,* "Early Extinguishment of Debt" (New York: American Institute of Certified Public Accountants, 1972), par. 20.

[10] *Statement of Financial Accounting Standards No. 4,* "Reporting Gains and Losses from Extinguishment of Debt" (Stamford: Financial Accounting Standards Board, 1975), par. 8.

[11] *Statement of Financial Accounting Standards No. 64,* "Extinguishment of Debt Made to Satisfy Sinking-Fund Requirements" (Stamford: Financial Accounting Standards Board, 1982), par. 3.

that no further payment will be required with respect to that debt. The exposure draft defines criteria for "virtual assurance."[12]

The following sections discuss the accounting procedures applicable to the early termination of bonds through purchase and redemption.

Purchase of Bonds by Issuer Prior to Maturity

Corporations frequently purchase their own bonds on the market when prices or other factors make such actions desirable. When bonds are purchased, amortization of bond premium or discount and issue costs should be brought up to date. Purchase by the issuer calls for the cancellation of the bond face value together with any related premium, discount, or issue costs as of the purchase date.

When bonds are purchased and canceled, Bonds Payable is debited. When bonds are purchased but are held for possible future reissue, Treasury Bonds instead of Bonds Payable may be debited. Treasury bonds are evidence of a liquidated liability. Although treasury bonds may represent a ready source of cash, their sale creates new creditors, a situation that is no different from the debt created by any other type of borrowing. Treasury bonds, then, should be recorded at their face value and subtracted from the bonds payable balance in reporting bonds issued and outstanding. If treasury bonds are sold at a price other than face value, Cash is debited, Treasury Bonds is credited, thus reinstating the bond liability, and a premium or a discount on the sale is recorded, the latter balance to be amortized over the remaining life of this specific bond group. While held, treasury bonds occupy the same legal status as unissued bonds. At the maturity of the bond issue, any balance in a treasury bonds account is applied against Bonds Payable.

To illustrate bond purchase prior to maturity, assume that $100,000, 8% bonds of Atlas Inc. are not held until maturity, but are sold back to the issuer on February 1, 1985, at 97 plus accrued interest. The book value of the bonds on both the issuer's and investor's books is $97,700 as of January 1. Discount amortization has been recorded at $50 a month using the straight-line method. Interest payment dates on the bonds are November 1 and May 1; accrued interest adjustments are reversed. Entries on both the issuer's and investor's books at the time of purchase would be as follows:

Issuer's Books

Feb. 1	Interest Expense	50	
	Discount on Bonds Payable		50
	To record discount amortization for January, 1985.		
1	Bonds Payable (*or* Treasury Bonds)	100,000	
	Interest Expense	2,000	
	Discount on Bonds Payable		2,250
	Cash		99,000
	Gain on Bond Reacquisition		750
	To record purchase of bonds and payment of three months' interest.		

[12]Exposure Draft, "Extinguishment of Debt" (Stamford: Financial Accounting Standards Board, 1983).

Computation:

Book value of bonds, January 1, 1985	$97,700
Discount amortization for January	50
Book value of bonds, February 1, 1985	$97,750
Purchase price	97,000
Gain on purchase	$ 750

Interest expense for 3 months:
$100,000 × .08 × 1/4 = $2,000

Investor's Books

Feb. 1	Investment in Atlas Inc. Bonds	50	
	Interest Revenue		50
	To record discount amortization for January, 1985.		
1	Cash	99,000	
	Loss on Sale of Bonds	750	
	Investment in Atlas Inc. Bonds		97,750
	Interest Revenue		2,000
	To record sale of bonds and receipt of three month's interest.		

Bond Redemption Prior to Maturity—Term Bonds

Provisions of a bond indenture frequently give the issuer the option of calling bonds for payment prior to maturity. Frequently the call must be made on an interest payment date, and no further interest accrues on the bonds not presented at this time. When only a part of an issue is to be redeemed, the bonds called may be determined by lot.

The inclusion of call provisions in a bond agreement is a feature favoring the issuer. The company is in a position to terminate the bond agreement and eliminate future interest charges whenever its financial position makes such action feasible. Furthermore, the company is protected in the event of a fall in the market interest rate by being able to retire the old issue from proceeds of a new issue paying a lower rate of interest. A bond contract normally requires payment of a premium if bonds are called. A bondholder is thus offered special compensation if the investment is terminated.

When bonds are called, the difference between the amount paid and the bond carrying value is reported as a gain or a loss on both the issuer's and investor's books. Any interest paid at the time of the call is recorded as a debit to Interest Expense on the issuer's books and a credit to Interest Revenue on the investor's books. The entries to be made are the same as illustrated previously for the purchase of the bonds by the issuer.

When an investor acquires callable bonds at a premium, conservatism calls for an amortization policy that prevents the bonds from being reported at more than their redemption values at the various call dates. To illustrate, assume bonds of $10,000 are acquired for $10,800 on January 1, 1985. The bonds were originally issued on January 1, 1983, and have a maturity date of January 1, 2003. The following table of redemption values is included in the indenture.

Redeemable January 1, 1988, to December 31, 1992, at 105
Redeemable January 1, 1993, to December 31, 1997, at 102½
Redeemable January 1, 1998, to December 31, 2002, at 101

Regular premium amortization and accelerated amortization based upon bond redemption values of $10,500, $10,250 and $10,100, are compared below:

Regular Amortization	Accelerated Amortization
$800 ÷ 18 years = $44.44 per year (1985-2003)	($10,800 − $10,500) ÷ 3 years (1985-1987) = $100 per year
	($10,500 − $10,250) ÷ 5 years (1988-1992) = $ 50 per year
	($10,250 − $10,100) ÷ 5 years (1993-1997) = $ 30 per year
	($10,100 − $10,000) ÷ 5 years (1998-2002) = $ 20 per year

If regular amortization procedures are followed on the books of the investor, bond redemption prior to maturity will result in a recovery of cash that is less than bond carrying value and will require recognition of a loss that nullifies in part the earnings recognized in the past. Accelerated amortization reduces the investment to its redemption value at the beginning of each redemption period. Obviously, bonds reported at a discount, or bonds reported at a premium reduced by normal amortization to an amount that is not greater than redemption value, require no special treatment.

Bond Redemption Prior to Maturity—Serial Bonds

When serial bonds are redeemed prior to their maturities, it is necessary to cancel the unamortized premium or discount relating to that part of the bond issue that is liquidated. For example, assume the issuance of serial bonds previously described on page 523 and amortization of the premium by the bonds-outstanding method as given on that page. On April 1, 1985, $10,000 of bonds due December 31, 1986, and $10,000 of bonds due December 31, 1987, are redeemed at 100½ plus accrued interest. The premium for the period January 1—April 1, 1985, relating to redeemed bonds affects bond interest for the current period and will be written off as an adjustment to expense. The balance of the premium from the redemption date to the respective maturity dates of the series redeemed must be canceled. The premium balance relating to redeemed bonds is calculated as follows:

Premium identified with 1985: 20,000/80,000 × $336 × 9/12	= $ 63
Premium identified with 1986: 20,000/60,000 × 252	= 84
Premium identified with 1987: 10,000/40,000 × 168	= 42
Premium identified with redeemed bonds	$189

Instead of the above procedure, the premium amortization per year on each $1,000 bond may be applied to bonds of each period that are redeemed. As shown on page 523, the annual amortization per $1,000 bond is $4.20.

The premium to be canceled may now be determined as follows:

Year	Number of $1,000 Bonds	Annual Premium Amortization per $1,000 Bond	Fractional Part of Year	Total Premium Cancellation
1985	20	$4.20	9/12	$ 63
1986	20	4.20		84
1987	10	4.20		42
Premium identified with redeemed bonds				$189

Bonds, carrying value $20,189, are redeemed at a cost of $20,100 resulting in a gain of $89. Payment is also made for interest on bonds of $20,000 for three months at 8%, or $400. The entry to record the redemption of bonds and the payment of interest on the series retired follows:

Bonds Payable	20,000	
Premium on Bonds Payable	189	
Interest Expense	400	
Cash		20,500
Gain on Bond Redemption		89

The following is a revised schedule for the amortization of bond premium.

Amortization Schedule—Bonds-Outstanding Method
Revised for Bond Retirement

Year	Annual Premium Amortization per Original Schedule	Premium Cancellation on Bond Retirement	Annual Premium Amortization Adjusted for Bond Retirement
1984	$ 420		$ 420
1985	336	$ 63	273
1986	252	84	168
1987	168	42	126
1988	84		84
	$1,260	$189	$1,071

If serial bonds are amortized using the interest method, the present value of the early payments must be computed using the effective interest rate, and the carrying value of the bond issue reduced by this value. Subsequent years' amortization can then be computed using the reduced carrying value as the basis for applying the effective interest rate.

BOND REFUNDING

Cash for the retirement of a bond issue is frequently raised through the sale of a new issue and is referred to as **bond refunding;** the original issue is said to be refunded. Bond refunding may take place when an issue matures. Bonds may also be refunded prior to their maturity when the interest rate has dropped and the interest savings on a new issue will more than offset the cost of retiring the old issue. To illustrate, assume that a corporation has outstanding 12% bonds of $1,000,000 callable at 102 and with a remaining 10-year term, and similar 10-year bonds can be marketed currently at an interest rate of only 10%. Under these circumstances it would be advantageous to retire the old issue with the proceeds from a new 10% issue since the future savings in interest will exceed by a considerable amount the premium to be paid on the call of the old issue.

The desirability of refunding may not be so obvious as in the preceding example. In determining whether refunding is warranted in marginal cases, careful consideration must be given to such factors as the different maturity dates of the two issues, possible future changes in interest rates, changed loan requirements, different indenture provisions, income tax effects of refunding, and legal fees, printing costs, and marketing costs involved in refunding.

When refunding takes place before the maturity date of the old issue, the problem arises as to how to dispose of the call premium and unamortized discount and issue costs of the original bonds. Three positions have been taken with respect to disposition of these items:

(1) Such charges are considered a loss on bond retirement.
(2) Such charges are considered deferrable and to be amortized systematically over the remaining life of the original issue.
(3) Such charges are considered deferrable and to be amortized systematically over the life of the new issue.

Although arguments can be presented supporting each of these alternatives, the Accounting Principles Board concluded that "all extinguishments of debt before schedule maturities are fundamentally alike. The accounting for such transactions should be the same regardless of the means used to achieve the extinguishment."[13] The first position, immediate recognition of the gain or loss, was selected by the Board for all early extinguishment of debt. The Financial Accounting Standards Board considered the nature of this gain or loss and defined it as being an extraordinary item requiring separate income statement disclosure.[14]

BOND FUNDS

Bond indentures for term bonds frequently require the issuing company to establish a **sinking fund** to be used to retire the bonds at maturity. The annual amount to be paid into the fund is computed using compound interest tables as illustrated in Chapter 12. Bond funds may be administered directly by a company or by an independent trustee.

When funds are administered by the issuing company, separate accounts are usually maintained for the different assets comprising the fund. If desired, separate revenue and expense accounts may also be maintained, Account titles should be descriptive of their special nature, e.g., Bond Cash Fund, Bond Fund Securities, and Bond Fund Revenue. If the issuing company does not want fund detail in the general ledger, a separate ledger consisting of the bond accounts may be employed.

When separate books are maintained by a trustee, an asset account is created on the issuing company's books equal to the amount transferred to the trustee plus any net earnings reported by the trustee less any retirement of bonds. A liability account is created on the trustee's books, increasing as assets are received and decreasing as disbursements are made. These two accounts are reciprocal accounts since the credit balance in the liability

---

[13] *Opinions of the Accounting Principles Board, No. 26, op. cit.*, par. 19.
[14] *Statement of Financial Accounting Standards No. 4, op. cit.*

account on the trustee's books should be equal to the debit balance in the asset account on the issuing company's books.

When a company retires its own bonds through bond fund cash, the liability is canceled, the bond fund cash account is credited, and a loss or gain on the retirement is recorded. For example, assume that the books of a company show bonds of $100,000 outstanding with an unamortized bond discount balance relating to this issue of $3,500. The company acquires and formally retires bonds with a face value of $20,000 at a cost of $19,500. The entry to record the bond retirement follows:

Bonds Payable	20,000	
Loss on Bond Retirement	200	
Bond Fund Cash		19,500
Unamortized Bond Discount		700
To record bond retirement.		

Computation:	
Amount paid on retirement	$19,500
Book value of bonds retired: face value of bonds, $20,000, less unamortized discount applicable to bonds, $700	19,300
Loss on retirement	$ 200

The treatment of bond reacquisition as a retirement by an entry similar to that above may call for an increase in the deposit schedule to compensate for the loss of interest in the fund accumulation. The larger transfers to the fund, however, are accompanied by reduced interest payments in the absence of interest accruals on bonds reacquired. If bonds are resold, the sale is treated just as an original issue, any premium or discount on the reissue being identified with the remaining life of the bond lot resold. The treatment of bond reacquisitions as bond retirement should be followed even though this calls for adjustments in a plan for systematic fund accumulation.

Generally, bond sinking fund assets are reported in the Investments section of the issuing company's balance sheet. In some cases, however, a trustee may assume the liability for payment of the bonds. In these circumstances, the bond liability is reduced as payments are made to the trustee, and no fund assets are reported on the issuer's balance sheet.

The issuance of serial bonds eliminates the need for a bond sinking fund. When a sinking fund cannot produce earnings at a rate equivalent to that paid on the bond issue, serial bonds are advantageous to the issuing company. In this case, cash otherwise deposited in the fund is applied directly to the retirement of debt, and the payment of interest relating to that portion of the debt is terminated.

VALUATION OF BONDS AND LONG-TERM NOTES

Thus far, no reference has been made in this chapter to adjusting investments and liabilities when the debt or investment valuation differs from cost. In Chapter 12, accounting for declines in value of long-term equity securities was presented. There it was noted that temporary declines in the market value of equity securities are recognized on the books of the investor by a debit to an equity offset account and by a credit to an allowance account. Permanent declines are recognized by a debit to a recognized loss account on the income statement and a credit to the Investment account. Debt instruments were not explicitly included in FASB Statement No. 12. However, if a market decline in debt securities is deemed to be permanent, and it is probable that the maturity value will not be paid when due, entries similar to those made for permanent declines in equity securities are normally made on the investor's books. If the market declines are considered temporary, no accounting entries are usually made, but the decline in value is recognized in a note to the financial statements. Entries likewise are not made to reflect increases in the market values of bond investments. Changes in the market value of the liability are ignored by the issuer unless a troubled debt restructuring takes place.

TROUBLED DEBT RESTRUCTURING

Economic conditions sometimes arise making it difficult for the issuer of long-term debt to make the cash payments required by the indenture. These payments include interest payments, principal payments to retire serial bonds, or notes, periodic payments into sinking funds, or even payments at the maturity of the debt. To avoid bankruptcy proceedings or foreclosure on the debt, investors in such situations may agree to make concessions and revise the original terms of the debt to permit the issuer to recover from financial problems. The restructuring may take many different forms. For example, there may be a suspension of interest payments for a period of time, a reduction in the interest rate, an extension of the maturity date of the debt, or even an exchange of assets or equity securities for the debt. The principal accounting question in these cases, on both the books of the issuer and the investor, is whether a gain or loss should be recognized upon the restructuring of the debt.

The issue became critical in the mid 1970's when several issues of municipal bonds, notably New York City bonds, were restructured due to the financial difficulties of the issuing organizations. Investors in the bonds were faced with interest and fund payments in arrears, and a near bankrupt situation for New York City. Most investors felt the decline was only temporary, and so did not recognize any loss on the books. After considerable negotiation, the terms of the bonds were restructured. Changes included a moratorium on interest and fund payments and extended maturity dates. Other municipalities and private companies experienced similar restructuring needs.

The Financial Accounting Standards Board considered this area carefully, and issued Statement No. 15 in 1977. In this statement the Board defined **troubled debt restructuring** as a situation where "the creditor for economic or legal reasons related to the debtor's financial difficulties grants a concession to the debtor that it would not otherwise consider. That concession either stems from an agreement between the creditor and the debtor or is imposed by law or a court."[15] The key word in this definition is *concession*. If a concession is not made by creditors, accounting for the restructuring follows the procedures discussed under the heading Termination of Bonds.

The major issue addressed by the FASB in Statement No. 15 is whether a troubled debt restructuring agreement should be viewed as a significant economic transaction. It was decided that if it is considered to be a significant economic transaction, entries should be made on both the issuer's and the investor's books to reflect the gain or loss. If the restructuring is not considered to be a significant economic transaction, no entries are required. The accounting treatment thus depends upon the nature of the restructuring. The FASB conclusions are summarized in the following table.

Accounting for Different Types of Troubled Debt Restructuring

Type	Restructuring Considered Significant Economic Transaction: Gain or Loss Recognized	Restructuring Not Considered Significant Economic Transaction: No Gain or Loss Recognized
Transfer of assets in full settlement (asset swap)	X	
Grant of equity interest in full settlement (equity swap)	X	
Modification of terms: total payment under new structure exceeds debt carrying value		X
Modification of terms: total payment under new structure is less than debt carrying value	X	

Each of the above types of restructuring is discussed and illustrated in the following sections.

Transfer of Assets in Full Settlement (Asset Swap)

A debtor that transfers assets, such as real estate, inventories, receivables, or investments, to a creditor to fully settle a payable usually will recognize two types of gains or losses: (1) **a gain or loss on disposal of the asset,** and (2) **a gain arising from the concession** granted in the restructuring of the debt. The computation of these gains and/or losses is made as follows:

Carrying value of assets being transferred	
	Difference represents gain or loss on disposal
Market value of asset being transferred	
	Difference represents gain on restructuring
Carrying value of debt being liquidated	

[15] *Statement of Financial Accounting Standards No. 15,* "Accounting by Debtors and Creditors for Troubled Debt Restructuring" (Stamford: Financial Accounting Standards Board, 1977), par. 2.

The gain or loss on disposal of an asset is usually reported as an ordinary income item unless it meets criteria for reporting it is an unusual or irregular item. However, the gain on restructuring is considered to arise from an early extinguishment of debt and must be reported as an extraordinary item.[16] An investor always recognizes **a loss on the restructuring** due to the concession granted unless the investment has already been written down in anticipation of the loss. The computation of the loss is made as follows:

Carrying value of investment liquidated	Difference represents loss on restructuring
Market value of asset being transferred	

The classification of this loss depends on the criteria being used to recognize irregular or extraordinary items. However, usually the loss is anticipated as market values of the investment decline, and it is recognized as an ordinary loss, either prior to the restructuring or as part of the restructuring.

To illustrate these points, assume that McElroy Industries is behind in its interest payments on outstanding bonds of $500,000, and is threatened with bankruptcy proceedings. The carrying value of the bonds on McElroy's books is $545,000 after deducting the unamortized discount of $5,000 and adding unpaid interest of $50,000. To settle the debt, McElroy transfers long-term investments it holds in Boswell common stock with a carrying value of $350,000 and a current market value of $400,000, to all investors on a pro-rata basis. Assume Reliance Inc. holds $40,000 face value of bonds. Because of the troubled financial condition of McElroy Industries, Reliance Inc. has previously recognized as a loss a $5,000 decline in the value of the debt, and is carrying the investment at $35,000 on its books plus interest receivable of $4,000. The entries to record the asset transfer would be as follows:

McElroy Industries (Issuer)

Interest Payable	50,000	
Bonds Payable	500,000	
Discount on Bonds		5,000
Long-Term Investments—Boswell Common		350,000
Gain on Disposal of Boswell Common		50,000
Gain on Restructuring of Debt		145,000

Computation:

Carrying value of Boswell Common	$350,000	$50,000 gain on disposal
Market value of Boswell Common	400,000	$145,000 gain from restructuring
Carrying value of debt liquidated	545,000	

Reliance Inc. (Investor)

Long-Term Investments—Boswell Common	32,000	
Loss on Restructuring of Debt	7,000	
Long-Term Investments—McElroy Bonds		35,000
Interest Receivable		4,000

Computation:
Percentage of debt held by Reliance Inc.: $40,000/$500,000 = 8%
Market value of long-term investment received in settlement of debt: 8% × $400,000 = $32,000

[16] *Ibid.*, par. 21.

If an active market does not exist for the assets being transferred, estimates of the value should be made based upon transfer of similar assets or by analyzing future cash flows from the assets.[17]

Grant of Equity Interest (Equity Swap)

A debtor that grants an equity interest to the investor as a substitute for a liability must recognize an extraordinary gain equal to the difference between the fair market value of the equity interest and the carrying value of the liquidated liability. A creditor (investor) must recognize a loss equal to the difference between the same fair market value of the equity interest and the carrying value of the debt as an investment. For example, assume that McElroy Industries transferred 20,000 shares of common stock to satisfy the $500,000 face value of bonds. The par value of the common stock per share is $15 and the market value at the date of the restructuring is $20 per share. Assume the other facts described in the illustration of an asset swap on page 536 are unchanged. The entries to record the grant of the equity interest on both sets of books would be as follows:

McElroy Industries (Issuer)

Interest Payable	50,000	
Bonds Payable	500,000	
Discount on Bonds		5,000
Common Stock		300,000
Premium on Common Stock		100,000
Gain on Restructuring of Debt		145,000

Computation:

Market value of common stock	$400,000	$145,000 gain from restructuring
Carrying value of debt liquidated	$545,000	

Reliance Inc. (Investor)

Long-Term Investments- McElroy Common	32,000	
Loss on Restructuring of Debt	7,000	
Long-Term Investment-McElroy Bonds		35,000
Interest Receivable		4,000

The entry on McElroy's books for an equity swap differs from that made for the asset swap because there can be no gain or loss on disposal of a company's own stock. However, the entry on Reliance's books for an equity swap is identical with that for an asset swap except that the investment is in McElroy common stock.

Modification of Debt Terms

There are many ways debt terms may be modified to aid a troubled debtor. Modification may involve either the interest, the maturity value, or both. Interest concessions may involve a reduction of the interest rate, forgiveness of unpaid interest, or a moratorium on interest payments for a

[17] *Ibid.*, par. 13.

period of time. Maturity value concessions may involve an extension of the maturity date or a reduction in the amount to be repaid at maturity. Basically, the FASB decided that most modifications of debt did not result in a significant economic transaction, and thus did not give rise to a gain or loss at the date of restructuring. They argued that the new terms were merely an extension of an existing debt and that the modifications should be reflected in future periods through modified interest charges based on computed implicit interest rates. The only exception to this general rule occurs if the total payments to be made under the new structure, including all future interest payments, are less than the carrying value of the debt or the investment at the time of restructuring. Under this exception, the difference between the total future cash payments required and the carrying value of the debt or investment is recognized as a gain on the debtor's books and a loss on the creditor's books.

To illustrate the accounting for this type of restructuring, assume the interest rate on the McElroy Industries bonds (see page 536) is reduced from 10% to 7%, the maturity date is extended from 3 to 5 years from the restructuring date, and the past interest due of $50,000 is forgiven. The total future payments to be made after this restructuring are as follows:

Maturity value of bonds	$500,000
Interest—7% × $500,000 × 5 years	175,000
Total payments to be made after restructuring	$675,000

Since the $675,000 exceeds the carrying value of $545,000, no gain is recognized on the books of McElroy Industries at the time of restructuring. A similar computation for Reliance Inc. results in total future payments of $54,000 [$40,000 + ($2,800 × 5)] as compared with a carrying value of $39,000. Thus, no further loss is recognized on Reliance Inc. books at the time of restructure.

However, if in addition to the above changes, $200,000 of maturity value is forgiven, the future payments would be reduced as follows:

Maturity value of bonds	$300,000
Interest—7% × $300,000 × 5 years	105,000
Total payments to be made after restructuring	$405,000

Now the carrying value exceeds the future payments by $140,000, and this gain would be recognized by McElroy as follows:

Interest Payable	50,000	
Bonds Payable	500,000	
Discount on Bonds		5,000
Restructured Debt		405,000
Gain on Restructured Debt		140,000
To reclassify restructured debt and recognize a gain of $140,000 on restructuring.		

Similar computations could be made on Reliance's books assuming 40% of the debt is cancelled ($200,000/$500,000 = 40%).

Maturity value—($40,000 × 60%)	$24,000
Interest—7% × $24,000 × 5 years	8,400
Total receipts after restructuring	$32,400
Carrying value of investment	39,000
Loss on restructuring	$ 6,600

The entry to record the loss on Reliance's books would be as follows:

Loss on Restructuring	6,600	
Investment in McElroy Bonds		2,600
Interest Receivable		4,000
To recognize a loss of $6,600 on restructuring.		

When terms are modified, the amount recognized as interest expense or interest revenue in the remaining periods of the debt instrument's life is based on a computed implicit interest rate. The implicit interest rate is the rate that equates the present value of all future debt payments to the present carrying value of the debt or investment. The interest expense or interest revenue for each period is equal to the carrying value of the debt for the period involved times the implicit interest rate. The computation of the implicit interest rate can be complex, and usually requires the use of a computer program. However, approximations can be made by using a trial and error approach from the present value tables in Appendix A.

To illustrate the computation of an implicit interest rate, the restructuring of McElroy Industries described on page 538 will be used. The question to be answered is what rate of interest will equate the total payments of $675,000 to the present carrying value of $545,000. Trial and error use of Tables II and IV in Appendix A shows that the rate is between 4% and 6% per year. The computations are as follows:

	Interest Rate 6% (3% per Semiannual Period)	*Interest Rate 4% (2% per Semiannual Period)*
Present value of maturity value due in five years (ten semiannual periods)	.7441 × $500,000 = $372,050	.8203 × $500,000 = $410,150
Present value of $17,500 interest payments for ten semiannual payments	8.5302 × $17,500 = 149,279	8.9826 × $17,500 = 157,196
Total present value	$521,329	$567,346

Interpolation of the above results indicates that the present value of $545,000 lies almost exactly midway between the above values; therefore, the approximate interest rate is 5%. For purposes of the illustration, the 5% rate will be used, or 2½% per semiannual payment period.

Using this rate, the recorded interest expense for the first six months would be $13,625, or 2½% of $545,000. Since the actual cash payment for interest is $17,500, the carrying value of the debt will decline by $3,875 ($17,500 − $13,625). The interest expense for the second semiannual period will be less than for the first period because of the decrease in the carrying value of the debt. [($545,000 − $3,875) × 2.5%] = $13,528 interest expense). These computations are identical with those used in using the interest method of amortization described on pages 518–520. If the exact implicit interest rate were used, continuation of the procedure for the ten periods would leave a balance of $500,000, the maturity value, in the liability account of McElroy Industries. The entries to record the restructuring on McElroy's books and the first two interest payments would be as follows:

Bonds Payable	500,000	
Interest Payable	50,000	
Discount on Bonds		5,000
Restructured Debt		545,000
To reclassify debt into one account.		
Interest Expense	13,625	
Restructured Debt	3,875	
Cash		17,500
Payment of first semiannual interest after restructuring.		
Interest Expense	13,528	
Restructured Debt	3,972	
Cash		17,500
Payment of second semiannual interest after restructuring.		

A similar computation of an implicit interest rate could be made for Reliance based on future receipts of $54,000 [$40,000 + ($2,800 × 5)], and the present carrying value of the investment of $39,000. Use of this rate would increase the investment account to $40,000 at the end of the ten periods, or the maturity value of the investment held.

The above discussion covers all situations when bond restructuring reflects a modification of terms except when the cash to be received after the restructuring is less than the carrying value of the debt or investment. Under these conditions the implicit interest rate is negative. In order to raise the rate to zero, the carrying value must be reduced to the cash to be realized and a gain or loss recognized for the difference. All interest payments or receipts in the future are offset directly to the debt or investment account. No interest expense or revenue will be earned or incurred in the future because of the extreme concessions made in the restructuring. By charging or crediting all interest payments to the debt or investment account, the balance remaining at the maturity date will be the maturity value of the debt.

Any combination of these methods of bond restructuring may be employed. Accounting for these multiple restructurings can become very complex, and must be carefully evaluated.

REPORTING OF LONG-TERM DEBT ON THE BALANCE SHEET

Bond and long-term note accounts are frequently very significant items on the balance sheet of both the investor and the issuer. Generally, they are reported in the noncurrent section; however, under some circumstances they may be reported as current items. The valuation and reporting problems for the investor and issuer will be considered separately.

Reporting Bonds and Long-Term Notes as Investments

The market value of long-term debt varies with changes in the financial strength of the issuing company, changes in the level of interest rates, and shrinkage in the remaining life of the issue. In the absence of material price declines, bonds held as long-term investments are reported on the balance sheet at book value. This book value approaches maturity value as the bonds move closer to maturity. To this extent, then, the accounting can be considered to follow a similar change that is taking place on the market as the bond life is reduced and a correspondingly lower valuation is attached to the difference between the actual rate and the market rate of remaining interest payments. Although investments are usually reported at book value, parenthetical disclosure of the aggregate market value of the securities makes the financial statements more informative.

When bonds are purchased *flat*, that is, when interest on bonds is in arrears and one price is paid for the bonds together with all accrued and unpaid interest, this price is recorded as the bond investment cost. Any amounts subsequently received on the bonds, whether designated as payments of principal or defaulted interest, should be treated as a recovery of investment cost as long as there is uncertainty of ultimate recovery of more than the amount invested. No interest should be accrued on the bonds until solvency of the debtor is restored and the regular receipt of interest is assured. Such bonds are reported at their unrecovered cost with full information as to the nature of the investment.

Bond funds are also normally classified as long-term investments. Even when the maturity date of term bonds will occur during the next fiscal period, the fund and the liability usually continue to be reported as noncurrent items.

Data relative to long-term note and bond investments and bond sinking fund assets might be reported as follows:

Long-term investments:		
Investment in Golden Corp. Long-Term Note, 14%, $50,000 face value, due July 1, 1988. (Market value, $48,500 at December 31, 1984)		$ 50,000
Investment in Wilkins Co. Bonds; 12%, $1,000,000 face value, due July 1, 1992 (reported at cost as adjusted for amortized discount)		982,500
Bond retirement fund in hands of trustee, composed of:		
Cash	$ 15,000	
Stocks and bonds (reported at cost; aggregate quoted market value, $540,000)	510,500	
Dividends and interest receivable	4,500	530,000

Reporting Bonds and Long-Term Notes as Liabilities

In reporting long-term debt on the balance sheet, the nature of the liabilities, maturity dates, interest rates, methods of liquidation, conversion privileges, sinking fund requirements, borrowing restrictions, and other significant matters should be indicated. For an example of a note describing long-term debt, see Note Seven to General Mills Financial Statements, Appendix B. When assets have been pledged to secure a liability, full particulars of the pledge should be indicated in the description of the obligation. This may be accompanied by identification on the asset side of the balance sheet of the specific assets pledged. When an agreement with a creditor limits the ability of a company to pay dividends, such limitation should be disclosed.

The portion of serial bonds payable within one year and other long-term debt maturing within one year should be reported as a current liability only if retirement will claim current assets. If the debt is to be paid from a bond retirement fund or is to be retired through some form of refinancing, it would continue to be reported as noncurrent with an explanation of the method to be used in its liquidation.[18]

Bond liabilities may be reported on a balance sheet as of December 31, 1984, as follows:

Current liabilities:		
Serial 10% debenture bonds, installment due May 1, 1985		$ 10,000
Long-term liabilities:		
5-year, 12% notes outstanding, due January 1, 1987............		100,000
20-year, 9% first-mortgage bonds outstanding, due January 1, 1996	$210,000	
Less unamortized bond discount	4,500	205,500
Serial 10% debenture bonds, due May 1, 1986 to May 1, 1995, inclusive		100,000

QUESTIONS

1. What factors should be considered in determining whether cash should be raised by the issue of bonds or by the sale of additional stock?

2. Distinguish between (a) secured and unsecured bonds, (b) collateral trust and debenture bonds, (c) convertible bonds and callable bonds, (d) coupon bonds and registered bonds and (e) municipal bonds and corporate bonds.

3. What is meant by bond market rate, stated or contract rate, and effective rate? Which of these rates changes during the lifetime of the bond issue?

4. How should bond issuance costs be accounted for on the issuer's books?

5. An investor purchases bonds with a face value of $100,000. Payment for the bonds includes (a) a premium, (b) accrued interest, and (c) brokerage fees. How would each of these charges be recorded and what disposition would ultimately be made of each of these charges?

6. (a) Why do companies find the issuance of convertible bonds a desirable method of financing? (b) What are the normal characteristics of convertible bonds?

---

[18] *Statement of Financial Accounting Standards No. 6*, "Classification of Short-Term Obligations Expected to be Refinanced" (Stamford: Financial Accounting Standards Board, 1975).

7. Convertible bonds provide something extra over a regular bond. That "extra" is really part of the owners' equity of the company, and part of the bond proceeds should be allocated to the stockholders' equity. What are the chief arguments against this proposal?
8. (a) What is the difference in the accounting treatment between convertible bonds and bonds issued with detachable stock warrants? (b) Do you think this difference is justified? Give your reasons.
9. Distinguish between straight-line and interest methods of bond premium amortization. What arguments can be offered in support of each method?
10. The interest method of bond premium or discount amortization is not desirable for the issuer because it results in higher net income than would be found with straight-line amortization. Under what conditions would this be true?
11. (a) Describe the bonds-outstanding method for premium or discount amortization. (b) How does this method differ from the interest method of amortization?
12. The conversion of convertible bonds to common stock by an investor may be viewed as an exchange involving no gain or loss, or as a transaction for which market values should be recognized and a gain or loss reported. What arguments support each of these views for the investor and for the issuer?
13. What is an early extinguishment of debt?
14. What purpose is served by using callable bonds? What effect does a call feature have upon the amortization of a bond premium?
15. What is meant by refunding a bond issue? Why may refunding be advisable?
16. What are the major differences in accounting for a bond fund when transactions are recorded directly on the issuer's books and when they are recorded directly by the trustee on its books?
17. How should bonds recorded as long-term investments be adjusted for price changes in periods subsequent to their purchase so that their valuation will be in accordance with GAAP?
18. What distinguishes a troubled debt restructuring from other debt restructurings?
19. What is the recommended accounting treatment for bond restructurings effected as:

(a) An asset swap?
(b) An equity swap?
(c) A modification of terms?

20. Under what circumstances would bonds maturing within the current year not be reported as long-term liabilities?

DISCUSSION CASES

case 14-1 (Do we really have income?) The Madison Corporation has $40,000,000 of 10% bonds outstanding. Because of cash flow problems, the company is behind in interest payments and in contributions to its sinking fund. The market value of the bonds has declined until it is currently only 50% of the face value of the bonds. After lengthy negotiations, the principal bondholders have agreed to exchange their bonds for preferred stock that has a current market value of $20,000,000. The accountant for Madison Corporation recorded the transaction by charging the bond liability for the entire $40,000,000, and crediting Preferred Stock for the same amount. This entry thus transfers the amount received by the company from debt to equity.

The CPA firm performing the annual audit, however, does not agree with this treatment. The auditors argue that this transfer represents a troubled debt restructuring due to the significant concessions made by the bondholders, and under these conditions, the FASB requires Madison to use the market value of the preferred stock as its recorded value. The difference between the $40,000,000 face value of the bonds and the $20,000,000 market value of the preferred stock is a reportable gain.

The controller of Madison, G. L. Rutgers, is flabbergasted. "Here we are, almost bankrupt, and you tell us we must report the $20,000,000 as a gain. I don't care what the PASB or whatever it is says, that's a ridiculous situation. You can't be serious." But the auditor in charge of the engagements is adamant. "We really have no choice. You have had a forgiveness of debt for $20,000,000. You had use of the money, and based on current conditions, you won't have to pay it back. That situation looks like a gain to me."

What position do you think should be taken? Consider the external users of the statement and their needs in your discussion.

case 14-2 (Can we take a loss today for a gain in the future?) Jubilee Investment Group follows the policy of borrowing money for relatively long periods of time and loaning the money to newly formed companies on a medium term basis. At December 31, 1984, Jubilee has several loans outstanding, and all but one are current in their interest payments and are living up to the covenant agreements made in conjunction with the loan. However, one loan to Direct Contact Corporation for $10,000,000 made at 14% interest is of much concern to Jubilee. The company has not been successful in generating a steady cash flow, and thus has fallen behind in its interest payments. The current position of the company is also far below the amount specified in the loan agreement. The president of Direct Contact has asked Jubilee for help and suggests a two-year suspension of interest payments followed by a new rate of 4% on the debt. The owners of Jubilee initially refuse, saying that for the risk now involved, the going interest rate would really be more like 20%. After a somewhat bitter discussion, the president of Direct Contact says that Jubilee leaves them no alternative; they must declare bankruptcy. After renewed discussion, the new terms requested are agreed upon and the past accrued interest is removed from the books by crediting accrued interest expense.

After reviewing the situation, Jubilee's auditor argues that present value accounting for debt requires Jubilee to restate the loan so that it would reflect the present value of the future payments at the 20% effective interest rate. This means that the present value of the $10,000,000 investment would be significantly reduced and the loss recognized in the current year. Future income would then reflect interest revenue at the 20% rate rather than the greatly reduced 4% rate. Now Jubilee's partners are really upset. "Must we take a loss now just to report an increased profit in the future? That is ridiculous accounting!"

Before agreement is reached, the Financial Accounting Standards Board issues its Statement No. 15 that supports Jubilee's position. But their auditors are still concerned. How can we argue for present value accounting and ignore the impact of the changed terms on the indebtedness? The FASB has abandoned the conceptual basis for expediency.

How would you evaluate the above situation?

case 14-3 (Is there a loss on conversion?) Zakin Co. recently issued $1,000,000 face value, 8%, 30-year subordinated debentures at 97. The debentures are redeemable at 103 upon demand by the issuer at any date upon 30 days notice ten years after issue. The debentures are convertible into $10 par value common stock of the company at the conversion price of $12.50 per share for each $500 or multiple thereof of the principal amount of the debentures. ($500 ÷ $12.50 = 40 shares for each $500 of face value.)

Assume that no value is assigned to the conversion feature upon issue of the debentures. Assume further that five years after issue, debentures with a face value of $100,000 and book value of $97,500 are tendered for conversion on an interest payment date when the market price of the debentures is 104 and the common stock is selling at $14 per share and that S. R. Lee, the company accountant, records the conversion as follows:

Bonds Payable	100,000	
Discount on Bonds Payable		2,500
Common Stock		80,000
Premium on Common Stock		17,500

J. F. Rich, staff auditor for the CPA firm, reviews the transaction and feels the conversion entry should reflect the market value of the stock. According to Rich's analysis, a loss on the bond conversion of $14,500 should be recognized. Lee objects to recognizing a loss, so Rich discusses the problem with the audit manager, K. Edmonds. Edmonds has a different view and recommends using the market value of the debentures as a basis for recording the conversion and recognizing a loss of only $6,500.

Evaluate the various positions. Include in your evaluation the substitute entries that would be made under both Rich's and Edmonds' proposals.

case 14-4 (Stabilizing the Mexican peso) The following article appeared in the Wall Street Journal, August 23, 1982:

> International bankers have heard Mexico's plea for assistance and tentatively pledged some help.
>
> Foreign bankers who hold a large slice of Mexico's estimated $60 billion of public foreign debt tentatively agreed Friday in New York to postpone the repayment of about $10 billion of principal that will fall due in the next 90 days. The bankers also formed a 14-member committee to work out a restructuring plan for longer-term debt, and try to raise $500 million to $1 billion in new money for Mexico.
>
> Bankers, economists and government officials agreed over the weekend, however, that this was just a start. The bankers believe they have little choice but to accept postponement of principal payments, as Mexico simply doesn't have the cash to pay its debt. But now the banks must restructure Mexico's huge debt—the largest in the Third World—so that the country has a chance of eventually paying back the money.

What methods of restructuring the Mexican debt are possible? How would each of these methods be accounted for according to the FASB?

EXERCISES

exercise 14-1 (Computation of market values of bond issues)

What is the market value of each of the following bond issues? Round to the nearest dollar.

(a) 10% bond of $50,000 sold on the bond issue date; 10-year life, interest payable semiannually, effective rate 12%.
(b) 9% bond of $200,000 sold on bond issue date; 20-year life, interest payable semiannually, effective rate 8%.
(c) 6% bond of $100,000 sold 30 months after bond issue date; 15-year life, interest payable semiannually, effective rate 10%.

exercise 14-2 (Evaluation of bonds and stock for raising capital)

The Aspen Co. has issued 10,000 shares of $50 par common stock. The company requires additional working capital and finds it can sell 6,000 additional shares of common at $70, or it can issue $420,000 of 9% bonds at par. Earnings of the company before income tax have been $100,000 annually, and it is expected that these will increase 20% (before additional interest charges) as a result of additional funds. Assuming that the income tax rate is estimated at 45%, which method of financing would you recommend as a common stockholder? Why? (Show calculations.)

exercise 14-3 (Issuance of convertible bonds)

Wright Insurance decides to finance expansion of its physical facilities by issuing convertible debenture bonds. The terms of the bonds are: maturity date 20 years after May 1, 1983, the date of issuance; conversion at option of holder after 2 years, 40 shares of $30 par value stock for each $1,000 bond held; interest rate of 10% and call provision on the bonds of 103. The bonds were sold at 101.

(1) Give the entry on Wright's books to record the sale of 1,000 bonds on July 1, 1984; interest payment dates are May 1 and November 1.
(2) Assume the same condition as in (1) above, except that the sale of the bonds is to be recorded in a manner that will recognize a value related to the conversion privilege. The estimated sales price of the bonds without the conversion privilege is 98.

exercise 14-4 (Issuance of serial bonds)

On January 1, 1984, JVJ Corporation issued and sold $1,000,000 in five-year, 10% serial bonds to be repaid in the amount of $200,000 on January 1 of 1985, 1986, 1987, 1988, and 1989. Interest is payable at the end of each year. The bonds were sold to yield a rate of 12%. Prepare the entry to record the issuance of the serial bonds on the books of JVJ Corporation.

exercise 14-5 (Detachable warrants)

On April 7, 1984, the Micro-Sense Corporation sold a $1,000,000 20-year, 10% bond issue for $1,030,000. Each $1,000 bond has a detachable warrant that permits the purchase of one share of the corporation's common stock for $30. The stock has a par value of $25 per share. Bond issue costs were $5,000, assignable entirely to the debt provision. Immediately after the sale of the bonds, the corporation's securities had the following market values:

10% bonds without warrants.......	$1,020
Warrants..........................	10
Common stock.....................	28

On September 30, 1984, all warrants are exercised. The market value of the stock at the exercise date has risen to $40. Prepare the journal entries to record the issuance of the bonds with detachable warrants and the exercise of the detachable warrants on both the issuer's and the investor's books.

exercise 14-6 (Retirement of debt before maturity)

The long-term debt section of Viking Company's balance sheet as of December 31, 1984, included 8% bonds payable of $100,000 less unamortized discount of $5,000. Further examination revealed that these bonds were issued to yield 10%. The amortization of the bond discount was recorded using the interest method. Interest was paid on January 1 and July 1 of each year. On July 1, 1985, Viking retired the bonds at 102 before maturity. Prepare the journal entries to record the July 1, 1985 payment of interest, the amortization of the discount since December 31, 1984, and the early retirement on the books of Viking Company.

exercise 14-7 (Interest and discount amortization)

Assume that $100,000 City School District 6% bonds are purchased on the bond issue date for $92,894. Interest is payable semiannually and the bonds mature in 10 years. The purchase price provides a return of 7% on the investment.

(1) What entries would be made on the investor's books for the receipt of the first two interest payments, assuming discount amortization on each interest date by (a) the straight-line method and (b) the interest method? Round to nearest dollar.
(2) What entries would be made on City School District's books to record the first two interest payments, assuming discount amortization on each interest date by (a) the straight-line method and (b) the interest method? Round to nearest dollar.

exercise 14-8 (Discount and premium amortization)

The ASA Corporation issued $100,000 of 8% debenture bonds on a basis to return 10%, receiving $92,278. Interest is payable semiannually and the bonds mature in 5 years.

(1) What entries would be made for the first two interest payments, assuming discount amortization on interest dates by (a) the straight-line method and (b) the interest method? Round to nearest dollar.
(2) If the sale is made on a 7% return, $104,158 being received, what entries would be made for the first two interest payments, assuming premium amortization on interest dates by (a) the straight-line method and (b) the interest method? Round to nearest dollar.
(3) What entries would be made on the books of the investor for the first two interest receipts assuming one party obtained all the bonds and the straight-line method of amortization was used? Round to nearest dollar.

exercise 14-9 (Bonds-outstanding table)

Robin Corporation purchased 8% serial bonds on April 1, 1983, face value $2,000,000. The bonds mature in $400,000 lots on April 1 of each of the following years. Interest is payable semiannually; the issue has an overall discount of $50,000. Assuming that Robin operates on a calendar year, prepare a table summarizing interest charges and bond carrying values by the bonds-outstanding method.

exercise 14-10 (Sale of bond investment)

L. Durfee acquired $80,000 of Bedrock Corp. 9% bonds on July 1, 1982. The bonds were acquired at 92; interest is paid semiannually on March 1 and September 1. The bonds mature September 1, 1989. Durfee's books are kept on a calendar year basis. On February 1, 1985, Durfee sold the bonds for 97 plus accrued interest. Assuming a straight-line discount amortization, give the entry to record the sale of the bonds on February 1. Round to the nearest dollar.

exercise 14-11 (Conversion of bonds)

On June 30, 1984, the original issue date, T. Taylor purchases $300,000 of 20-year, 7% convertible bonds of Jones Corporation at 104. Jones bonds are convertible to 50 shares of $10 par common stock for each $1,000 bond. The bond interest is payable semiannually, June 30 and December 31. On March 31, 1989, Taylor converts $200,000 of the bonds. Both Taylor and Jones Corporation use the calendar year as their fiscal year and amortize the bond premium on the straight-line basis.

(1) Give entries on both Taylor's and Jones Corporation's books to record the conversion in the absence of a market value for the stock.
(2) Give the entries on both Taylor's and Jones Corporation's books if the market value of the stock is $25 at the conversion date and a gain or a loss is to be recognized on the conversion.

exercise 14-12 (Convertible bonds)

On January 1, 1984, when its $30 par value common stock was selling for $80 per share, a corporation issued $10,000,000 of 8% convertible debentures due in ten years. The conversion option allowed the holder of each $1,000 bond to convert the bond into five shares of the corporation's $30 par value common stock. The debentures were issued for $11,000,000. The present value of the bond payments at the time of issuance was $9,750,000 and the corporation believes the difference between the present value and the amount paid is attributable to the conversion feature. On January 1, 1985, the corporation's $30 par value common stock was split 3 to 1. On January 1, 1986, when the corporation's $10 par value common stock was selling for $90 per share, holders of 40% of the convertible debentures exercised their conversion options. The corporation uses the straight-line method for amortizing any bond discounts or premiums.

(1) Prepare in general journal format the entry to record the original issuance of the convertible debentures in accordance with GAAP.
(2) Prepare in general journal format the entry to record the exercise of the conversion option, using the book value method. Show supporting computations in good form.

(AICPA adapted)

exercise 14-13 (Issuance and reacquisition of bonds)

On December 1, 1982, the Taylor Company issues 10-year bonds of $200,000 at 104. Interest is payable on December 1 and June 1 at 10%. On April 1, 1984, the Taylor Company reacquires and retires 40 of its own $1,000 bonds at 98 plus accrued interest. The fiscal period for the Taylor Company is the calendar year. Prepare entries to record (a) the issuance of the bonds, (b) the interest payments and adjustments relating to the debt in 1983, (c) the reacquisition and retirement of bonds in 1984, and (d) the interest payments and adjustments relating to the debt in 1984. Round to the nearest dollar. Assume the premium is amortized on a straight-line basis.

exercise 14-14 (Amortization of bond premium)

On January 1, 1983, Tony Bell purchased $40,000 of Midwest Company 10% bonds at 108. Bonds are due on January 1, 1998, but can be redeemed by the company at earlier dates at premium values as follows:

January 1, 1991, to December 31, 1994, at 103
January 1, 1995, to December 31, 1997, at 101

(1) What alternatives does Bell have as to the method of recognizing the amortization of premium? Which is preferable? Why?
(2) What amortization amounts should Bell recognize over the life of the bond issue?

exercise 14-15 (Retirement of bonds)

The December 31, 1984, balance sheet of Baylor Company includes the following items:

9% bonds payable due December 31, 1993	$400,000
Premium on bonds payable	10,000

The bonds were issued on December 31, 1983, at 103, with interest payable on June 30 and December 31 of each year. The straight-line method is used for premium amortization.

On March 1, 1985, Baylor retired $200,000 of these bonds at 98, plus accrued interest. Prepare the journal entries to record retirement of the bonds, including accrual of interest since the last payment and amortization of the premium.

exercise 14-16 (Serial bonds—early retirement)

The Beckham Manufacturing Co. issued $1,500,000 of 7-year, 12% serial bonds on January 1, 1982, at a lump-sum price of $1,452,000. The following bonds outstanding schedule was prepared to amortize the $48,000 discount on the issue. The last $300,000 payment is to be made on January 1, 1989.

Year End	Bonds Outstanding	Fraction of Discount to be Amortized	Annual Discount Amortization (Fraction × $48,000)
1982	$1,500,000	15/72 = 5/24	$10,000
1983	1,500,000	5/24	10,000
1984	1,200,000	4/24	8,000
1985	1,200,000	4/24	8,000
1986	900,000	3/24	6,000
1987	600,000	2/24	4,000
1988	300,000	1/24	2,000
	$7,200,000	24/24	$48,000

(1) Compute the amount of extra discount amortization required in 1984 if the January 1, 1987 retirement of $300,000 is made on January 1, 1984, using the bonds outstanding method.
(2) Prepare the journal entry to retire the bonds early on January 1, 1984, using the bonds outstanding method of amortization. Assume the bonds are retired at 101 and that all interest payments are current.
(3) Recompute the discount amortization for the years 1984–1988 after the early retirement has taken place.

exercise 14-17 (Retirement and reissuance of bonds)

Joplin Corporation has $500,000 of 12% bonds callable at 103, with a remaining 10-year term, and interest payable semiannually. The bonds are currently valued on the books at $480,000 and the company has just made the interest payment and adjustments for amortization of the discount. Similar bonds can be marketed currently at 10% and would sell at par.

(1) Give the journal entries to retire the old debt and issue $500,000 of new 10% bonds at par.
(2) In what year will the reduction in interest offset the cost of refunding the bond issue?

exercise 14-18 (Valuation of bonds used as investment)

Several years ago, Buffalo Life Insurance Company bought $1,000,000 of New York City 6% bonds at par. The bonds are currently selling at 78. Because of the recent troubles the bond issuer has been in meeting bond payments, the bondholder has decided to write down the market decline as a permanent decline. It is felt that only 80% of the original bond value will be recovered. Buffalo Life Insurance Company also holds $500,000 of Picto City 8% bonds that were bought at par but are selling at 96. They perceive this to be a temporary decline.

(1) What journal entries would you make to record the above decisions?
(2) What disclosure would you make in the financial statements?

exercise 14-19 (Troubled-debt restructuring—asset swap)

The Sanchez Machine Company has outstanding a $100,000 note payable to the Ontario Investment Corporation. Because of financial difficulties, Sanchez negotiates with Ontario to exchange inventory of machine parts to satisfy the debt. The cost of the inventory transferred is carried on Sanchez's books at $60,000. The estimated retail value of the inventory is $75,000. Sanchez uses a perpetual inventory system. Prepare journal entries for the exchange on the books of both Sanchez Machine Company and Ontario Investment Corporation according to the requirement of FASB Statement No. 15.

exercise 14-20 (Troubled-debt restructuring—equity swap)

Lucky Enterprises is threatened with bankruptcy due to its inability to meet interest payments and sinking fund requirements on $10,000,000 of long-term notes. The notes are all held by Fidelity Insurance Company. In order to prevent bankruptcy, Lucky has entered into an agreement with Fidelity to exchange equity securities for the debt. The terms of the exchange are as follows: 500,000 shares of $5 par common stock, current market value $8 per share, and 40,000 shares of $100 par preferred stock, current market value $70 per share. Prepare journal entries for the exchange on the books of both Fidelity Insurance Company and Lucky Enterprises according to the requirements of FASB Statement No. 15.

exercise 14-21 (Troubled-debt restructuring—modification of terms)

The Metashbi Corporation is about to enter voluntary bankruptcy procedures. In a last minute effort to avoid such action, holders of $10,000,000 worth of 10% corporate bonds maturing in eight years agree to the following change of principal and interest terms: (a) reduction in bond principal by 40%; (b) moratorium on interest payments for two years; (c) reduction of interest rate on the new principal amount from 10% to 6% for the remaining six years. Prepare any journal entries required on the books of Metashbi as a result of the restructuring. An unamortized discount of $500,000 is associated with the bonds.

exercise 14-22 (Disclosure of bond investments)

For the Bectel Corporation, arrange the following information as you would present it on the balance sheet dated December 31, 1986.

(a) Items in the possession of a sinking fund trustee for the first-mortgage bonds include: cash of $8,000 and stocks of $84,000 (market value $94,500).
(b) Investment in Holder Company 10% bonds, $100,000 face value, due July 1, 1990, (cost as adjusted for unamortized premium $103,000) currently selling at 99.
(c) 20-year, 9% Bectel Corp., first-mortgage bonds, $500,000 face value, due January 1, 2003 (cost as adjusted for unamortized discount $493,000).
(d) Investment in Stahman Corporation long-term notes, 12%, $60,000 face value, due September 1, 1992 (market value $63,000).
(e) Bectel Corporation, serial debenture bonds, 8%, last installment due July 1, 1987, $100,000 face value, carried on the books at par.

PROBLEMS

problem 14-1 (Computation of bond market price and amortization of discount)

Martin Products decided to issue $2,000,000 in 10-year bonds. The interest rate on the bonds is stated at 7%, payable semiannually. At the time the bonds were sold, the market rate had increased to 8%.

Instructions:

(1) Determine the maximum amount an investor should pay for these bonds. Round to the nearest dollar.
(2) Assuming that the amount in (1) is paid, compute the amount at which the bonds would be reported after being held for one year. Use two recognized methods of handling amortization of the difference in cost and maturity value of the bonds, and give support to the method you prefer. Round to the nearest dollar.

problem 14-2 (Convertible bonds and detachable warrants)

The Escalante Mining Company needs to raise additional capital, and on July 1, 1984, sold two types of debt securities as follows:

(a) $1,000,000 of 10%, 12-year convertible debentures, each $1,000 bond convertible into 25 shares of $15 par common stock. The bond issue date was April 1, 1984. The bonds sold on July 1, 1984, at 102 plus accrued interest. It is estimated that without the conversion feature, the bonds would have sold at about 97.

(b) $500,000 of 10%, 7-year notes with one detachable warrant attached for each $1,000 note were issued and sold on July 1, 1984. Each warrant provides for the right to purchase 20 shares of $15 par common stock for $20 each. The market value of the common stock was $23.50 per share at July 1, 1984. The detachable warrant market price was $70 per warrant at the time the warrants were issued, and the market value of the notes without the warrants attached is 97. The notes sold at 104.

Instructions:

(1) Prepare the journal entries at July 1, 1984, to record the sale for both of the above debt securities. Use current GAAP.

(2) Prepare the journal entry to record the exercise of the warrants on December 31, 1984. The market value of the stock was $30 at the date the warrants were exercised.

problem 14-3 (Bond issuance and interest entries)

Salter Inc. was authorized to issue 8-year, 9% bonds of $500,000. The bonds are dated January 1, 1983, and interest is payable semiannually on January 1 and July 1. Checks for interest are mailed on June 30 and December 31. Bond sales were as follows:

April 1, 1983	$250,000 at 96 plus accrued interest.
July 1, 1984	$150,000 at 102.

On September 1, 1984, remaining unissued bonds were pledged as collateral on the issue of $84,000 of short-term notes.

Instructions:

(1) Give the journal entries relating to bonds that would appear on the corporation's books in 1983 and 1984. (Straight-line amortization is used. Adjustments are made annually.) Round to nearest dollar.

(2) Show how information relative to the bond issue will appear on the balance sheet prepared on December 31, 1984. (Give balance sheet section headings and accounts and account balances appearing within such sections.)

problem 14-4 (Premium amortization table)

The Young Co. acquired $20,000 of Mexico Sales Co. 7% bonds, interest payable semiannually, bonds maturing in 5 years. The bonds were acquired at $20,850, a price to return approximately 6%.

Instructions:

(1) Prepare tables to show the periodic adjustments to the investment account and the annual bond earnings, assuming adjustment by each of the following methods: (a) the straight-line method, and (b) the interest method. Round to nearest dollar.

(2) Assuming use of the interest method, give entries for the first year on the books of both companies.

problem 14-5 (Bonds-outstanding tables)

The Macy Manufacturing Company issued $2,000,000 of 8% serial bonds on January 1, 1977, at 98. The bonds mature in units of $250,000 beginning January 1, 1982, with interest payable semiannually on January 1 and July 1. On June 1, 1985, Macy reacquired at 101 plus accrued interest, $200,000 of bonds due January 1, 1987, and $100,000 due January 1, 1988.

Instructions:

(1) Assuming discount amortization by the bonds-outstanding method and bond retirements as scheduled, prepare a table summarizing interest charges and bond carrying values for the bond life, supported by a schedule showing the calculation of amortization amounts. Round to nearest dollar.
(2) Prepare a similar table summarizing interest charges and bond carrying values for the bond life taking into consideration bond redemptions in advance of maturity dates as indicated (round to nearest dollar).
(3) Record in general journal form the retirement of bonds on June 1, 1985.

problem 14-6 (Bond entries—investor and issuer)

Bobco Inc. issued $500,000 of 8-year, 12% notes payable dated April 1, 1984. Interest on the notes is payable semiannually on April 1 and October 1. The notes were sold on April 1, 1984, to an underwriter for $480,000 net of issuance costs. The notes were then offered for sale by the underwriter, and on July 1, 1984, J. Farmer purchased the entire issue as a long-term investment. Farmer paid 101 plus accrued interest for the notes. On June 1, 1987, Farmer sold the investment in Bobco notes to M. Barney as a short-term investment. Barney paid 96 plus accrued interest for the notes as well as $1,500 for brokerage fees. Farmer paid $1,000 broker's fees to sell the notes. Barney held the investment until April 1, 1988, when the notes were called at 102 by Bobco.

Instructions:

Prepare all journal entries required on the books of Bobco Inc. for 1984 and 1988; on the books of Farmer for 1984 and 1987; and on the books of Barney for 1987 and 1988. Assume each entity uses the calendar year for reporting purposes and that issue costs are netted against the note proceeds by Bobco. Any required amortization is made using the straight-line procedure at the end of each calendar year or when the bonds are transferred.

problem 14-7 (Bond entries—issuer)

The Pine Company issued $10 million of 7% convertible bonds with interest payment dates of April 1 and October 1. The bonds were sold on July 1, 1974, and mature on April 1, 1994. The bond discount totaled $533,250. The bond contract entitles the bondholders to receive 25 shares of $15 par value common stock in exchange for each $1,000 bond. On April 1, 1984, the holders of bonds, face value $1,000,000, exercised their conversion privilege. On July 1, 1984, the Pine Company reacquired bonds, face value $500,000 on the open market. The balances in the capital accounts as of December 31, 1983 were:

Common Stock, $15 par, authorized 3 million shares, issued and outstanding, 250,000 shares	$3,750,000
Premium on Common Stock	2,500,000

Market values of the common stock and bonds were as follows:

Date	Bonds (per $1,000)	Common Stock (per share)
April 1, 1984	$1,220	$47
July 1, 1984	1,250	51

Instructions:

Prepare journal entries on the issuer's books for each of the following transactions. (Use straight-line amortization for the bond discount.)

(1) Sale of the bonds on July 1, 1974.
(2) Interest payment on October 1, 1974.
(3) Interest accrual on December 31, 1974, including bond discount amortization.

(continued)

(4) Conversion of bonds on April 1, 1984. (Assume that interest and discount amortization are correctly shown as of April 1, 1984. No gain or loss on conversion is recognized.)
(5) Reacquisition and retirement of bonds on July 1, 1984. (Interest and discount amortization are correctly reported as of July 1, 1984.)

problem 14-8 (Adjustment of bond investment account)

In auditing the books for the Chemical Corporation as of December 31, 1984, before the accounts are closed, you find the following long-term investment account balance:

Account **Investment in Big Oil 9% Bonds (Maturity date, June 1, 1988)**

Date		Item	Debit	Credit	Balance	
					Debit	Credit
1984						
Jan.	21	Bonds, $200,000 par, acquired at 102 plus accrued interest	206,550		206,550	
Mar.	1	Proceeds from sale of bonds, $100,000 par and accrued interest		106,000	100,550	
June	1	Interest received		4,500	96,050	
Nov.	1	Amount received on call of bonds, $40,000 par, at 101 and accrued interest		41,900	54,150	
Dec.	1	Interest received		2,700	51,450	

Instructions:

(1) Give the entries that should have been made relative to the investment in bonds, including any adjusting entries that would be made on December 31, the end of the fiscal year. (Assume bond premium amortization by the straight-line method.)
(2) Give the journal entries required at the end of 1984 to correct and bring the accounts up to date in view of the entries actually made.

problem 14-9 (Reacquisition of bonds)

Johnson Company issued $1,000,000 of 10%, 10-year debentures on January 1, 1979. Interest is payable on January 1 and July 1. The entire issue was sold on April 1, 1979, at 102 plus accrued interest. On April 1, 1984, $500,000 of the bond issue was reacquired and retired at 99 plus accrued interest. On June 30, 1984, the remaining bonds were reacquired at 96 plus accrued interest and refunded with $400,000, 8% bonds issue sold at 100.

Instructions:

Give the journal entries for 1979 and 1984 (through June 30) on the Johnson Company books. The company's books are kept on a calendar year basis. Round to nearest dollar. Assume straight-line amortization of premium.

problem 14-10 (Bond entries—investor)

On May 1, 1981, the Timp Co. acquired $40,000 of XYZ Corp. 9% bonds at 97 plus accrued interest. Interest on bonds is payable semiannually on March 1 and September 1, and bonds mature on September 1, 1984.

On May 1, 1982, the Timp Co. sold bonds of $12,000 for 103 plus accrued interest.

On July 1, 1983, bonds of $16,000 were exchanged for 2,250 shares of XYZ Corp. no-par common, quoted on the market on this date at $8. Interest was received on bonds to date of exchange.

On September 1, 1984, remaining bonds were redeemed.

Instructions:

Give journal entries for 1981–1984 to record the foregoing transactions on the books of the Timp Co., including any adjustments that are required at the end of each fiscal year ending on December 31. Assume bond discount amortization by the straight-line method. (Show all calculations.)

problem 14-11 (Troubled-debt restructuring—modification of terms)

On June 30, 1981, the Hargrove Company issued at par $100,000 of 8% bonds with interest payable semiannually. The bonds were due 5 years later on June 30, 1986, and were bought by Daniels Inc. As the due date approached, it became obvious that Daniels had made a poor investment. By May 1986, Hargrove Company was $16,000 in arrears on the interest payments. During negotiations in May the following terms were agreed to by the two companies:

(a) Daniels would forgive all interest payments in arrears.
(b) Daniels would forgive $20,000 of the principal.
(c) Hargrove would pay one half of the remaining principal on December 1, 1986, and the other one half on June 1, 1987, with interest from June 1, 1986, at a 12% annual rate.

The agreement was signed by both parties on June 1, 1986. Both companies are on a calendar year.

Instructions:

(1) Give all entries during 1986 and 1987 for Hargrove Company. (Show computations)
(2) Give all entries during 1986 and 1987 for Daniels Inc.

problem 14-12 (Troubled-debt restructuring—modification of terms)

In the latter part of 1985, Whitney Air Company experienced severe financial pressure and is in default in meeting interest payments on long-term debt of $5,000,000 due on December 31, 1990. The interest rate on the debt is 10% payable semiannually. In an agreement with Iowa Investment Corporation, Whitney obtained acceptance of a change in principal and interest terms for the remaining five-year life of the note. The changes in terms are as follows:

(a) A reduction of principal of $600,000.
(b) A reduction in the interest rate to 8%.
(c) Whitney agreed to pay on December 31, 1985, both the $500,000 of interest in arrears and the normal interest payment under the old terms.

Instructions:

(1) What is the total dollar difference in cash payments by Whitney over the five-year period as a result of the restatement of terms?
(2) What journal entries for the restructuring of the debt, payment of interest under the old terms, and the first two interest payments under the new terms would Whitney make? (Assume an implicit interest rate of 6%)
(3) What journal entries would Iowa Investment make in 1985 and 1986?

problem 14-13 (Convertible bonds)

The Beck Co. issued $1,000,000 of convertible 10-year debentures on July 1, 1983. The debentures provide for 9% interest payable semiannually on January 1 and July 1. The discount in connection with the issue was $19,500 which is being amortized monthly on a straight-line basis.

The debentures are convertible after one year into 7 shares of the Beck Co.'s $100 par value common stock for each $1,000 of debentures.

On August 1, 1984, $100,000 of debentures were turned in for conversion into common. Interest has been accrued monthly and paid as due. Accrued interest on debentures is paid in cash upon conversion.

Instructions:

Prepare the journal entries to record the conversion, amortization, and interest in connection with the debentures as of: August 1, 1984; August 31, 1984; and December 31, 1984—including closing entries for end of year. No gain or loss is to be recognized on the conversion. Round to nearest cent. (AICPA adapted)

problem 14-14 (Bond entries—issuer)

The McDouglas Company issued $3,000,000 of 8% first-mortgage bonds on October 1, 1976, at $2,873,640 plus accrued interest. The bonds were dated July 1, 1981; interest payable semiannually on January 1 and July 1; redeemable after June 30, 1981, and to June 30, 1983, at 101, and thereafter until maturity at 100; and convertible into $100 par value common stock as follows:

Until June 30, 1981, at the rate of 6 shares for each $1,000 of bonds.
From July 1, 1981, to June 30, 1984, at the rate of 5 shares for each $1,000 of bonds.
After June 30, 1984, at the rate of 4 shares for each $1,000 of bonds.

The bonds mature in 10 years from their date. The company adjusts its books monthly and closes its books as of December 31 each year. It follows the practice of writing off all unamortized bond discount in the period of bond retirement.

The following transactions occur in connection with the bonds:

1982
July 1 $500,000 of bonds were converted into stock.
1983
Dec. 31 $500,000 face amount of bonds were reacquired at 99¼ and accrued interest. These were immediately retired.
1984
July 1 The remaining bonds were called for redemption. For purpose of obtaining funds for redemption and business expansion, a $4,000,000 issue of 7% bonds was sold at 97. These bonds were dated July 1, 1984, and were due in 20 years.

Instructions:

Prepare in journal form the entries necessary for the company in connection with the preceding transactions, including monthly adjustments where appropriate, as of the following dates. Round to nearest dollar.

(1) October 1, 1976
(2) December 31, 1976
(3) July 1, 1982
(4) December 31, 1983
(5) July 1, 1984

(AICPA adapted)

problem 14-15 (Bond entries—investor)

On June 1, 1984, Warner Inc. purchased as a long-term investment 800 of the $1,000 face value, 8% bonds of Universal Corporation for $738,300. The bonds were purchased to yield 10% interest. Interest is payable semiannually on December 1 and June 1. The bonds mature on June 1, 1989. Warner uses the interest method of amortization. On November 1, 1985, Warner sold the bonds for $785,000. This amount includes the appropriate accrued interest.

Instructions:

Prepare a schedule showing the income or loss before income taxes from the bond investment that Warner should record for the year ended December 31, 1984, and 1985. Show supporting computations.

(AICPA adapted)

15 ACCOUNTING FOR LEASES

CHAPTER OBJECTIVES

Discuss the nature of leasing transactions and the historical development of accounting for leases.

Identify the four general classification criteria in FASB Statement No. 13 for distinguishing ordinary rental agreements from capital transactions.

Describe and illustrate accounting and disclosure by the lessee for operating leases and capital leases.

Describe and illustrate accounting and disclosure by the lessor for operating leases, sales-type leases, and direct financing leases.

Identify and describe some complexities of lease agreements, including leases of real estate and sale-leaseback transactions.

The use of leases as a means of transferring the right to use property to others has experienced a great growth in the decades since World War II. Indeed, much of the growth that has occurred in American businesses can be attributed to the added flexibility lease financing offers both to the one transferring the property (**lessor**) and the one receiving and using the property (**lessee**). The Financial Accounting Standards Board recognized this growth and commented as follows:

> Leasing as a means of acquiring the right to use property has proliferated markedly throughout the post-war period. But it was the decade of the 1960s that saw the greatest expansion, not only in the volume of leasing transactions, but also in the variety of application and degree of sophistication of the techniques employed. During that period, according to some estimates, leasing grew at an average annual rate of between 15 percent and 20 percent. It was

estimated that over $11 billion in new equipment was leased in 1974 and that by the end of 1975 equipment on lease would total $100 billion.[1]

Simple lease rental contracts have, of course, existed for many decades. Lessees frequently rent equipment or real property for relatively short periods of time with no intent of using the property throughout its economic life. Such contracts generally do not present any accounting problems–periodic payments are recognized as rent expense by the lessee and as rent revenue by the lessor. Some lease agreements, however, are in reality long-term financing arrangements that effectively transfer ownership of the "leased" asset. Such transactions should be accounted for as a sale by the lessor and a purchase by the lessee. Criteria for determining whether a lease is a rental agreement or a sale/purchase and problems in accounting for the latter are discussed in this chapter.

HISTORICAL DEVELOPMENT OF LEASE ACCOUNTING

Historically, leases were accounted for as rental contracts regardless of the terms of a specific agreement. But as lease arrangements became more sophisticated, it became increasingly difficult to distinguish between a rental contract and a sale/purchase of an asset. Leases were frequently noncancelable or cancelable only with severe penalty. They contained terms that extended over the life of the asset, required the lessee to pay the costs of ownership, including taxes and maintenance, and even included options to purchase or renew the lease at bargain amounts. Since there was no recording of the implied liability arising from the lease agreement, there was increasing concern among accountants that accounting for these types of leases as simple rentals no longer described the true nature of the transaction. The legal form of the transaction was different from a sale/purchase transaction, but the substance of the transaction was frequently the same.

Perhaps the earliest accounting recognition of the importance of leasing as a financing device occurred in 1949 when the Committee on Accounting Procedures issued *Accounting Research Bulletin No. 38,* "Disclosure of Long-Term Leases in Financial Statements of Lessees." When the Accounting Principles Board and Accounting Research Division were formed in 1959, the topic of leases was one of the initial ones to be considered by the Accounting Research Division. This resulted in the publication of *Accounting Research Study No. 4,* "Reporting of Leases in Financial Statements."[2] The Accounting Principles Board responded to this research and continued need with four opinions on the subject spread over its brief fourteen-year history. Two of the opinions, Number 5 and Number 31, dealt with accounting for leases by lessees. The other two, Number 7 and Number 27, dealt with accounting for

---

[1] *Financial Accounting Standards Board Exposure Draft (Revised): Proposed Statement of Financial Accounting Standards,* "Accounting for Leases" (Stamford: Financial Accounting Standards Board, 1976), par. 51.

[2] John H. Myers, *Accounting Research Study No. 4,* "Reporting of Leases in Financial Statements" (New York: American Institute of Certified Public Accountants, 1962).

leases by lessors. But the profession was not satisfied with the results of these opinions. Inconsistencies developed between accounting for lessees and lessors, and much of the opinions dealt with footnote disclosure rather than the accounting procedures themselves. Rules for requiring capitalization of leases on the balance sheet were vague, and few companies actually reported leases as assets with the accompanying liabilities.

The Financial Accounting Standards Board put the topic of leases on its original agenda, and in 1976 issued Statement No. 13, "Accounting for Leases." The apparent objective of the FASB in issuing Statement No. 13 was to reflect the economic reality of leasing by requiring that the majority of long-term leases be accounted for as capital acquisitions by the lessee and as sales by the lessor. However, comparatively few leases have been capitalized as a result of the statement because of the liberal interpretations applied to the criteria used to define a capital lease.[3] An example of the broad interpretation of Statement No. 13 can be observed in the financial statements of General Mills, Inc. reproduced in Appendix B. Note thirteen refers to the company's existing leases, all of which are apparently reported as rental agreements rather than capitalized, even though they are labeled noncancelable, and require future rental payments totaling $234 million.

The failure of Statement No. 13 to achieve the desired objective forced the FASB to issue additional pronouncements in the area of leasing. By 1980, several Interpretations of Statement No. 13 and seven new statements had been issued in an attempt to achieve the original goal of increased lease capitalization. In May 1980, the FASB issued an integrated revision of Statement No. 13 and its amendments and interpretations.[4] Since 1980, there have not been any further statements issued involving leases as the FASB has turned its attention to the conceptual framework project and more specialized industry pronouncements. Leases are in concept executory contracts and, as indicated in Chapter 13, such contracts are inconsistently treated in accounting today. Thus, additional analysis of leases may be necessary as the conceptual framework is completed.

NATURE OF LEASES

All types of assets are subject to lease, including manufacturing equipment, data processing equipment, transportation equipment, and land and buildings. Leases vary widely in their contractual terms. Variables include length of the lease term, renewal and purchase options, cancelation provisions and penalties, guarantees by lessees of residual values, amount and timing of lease payments, interest rates implicit in the lease agreement, and the degree of risk assumed by lessee, including payment of certain costs such as maintenance, insurance, and taxes. These and any other relevant facts

[3]For an interesting analysis of these problems, see Richard Dieter, "Is Lessee Accounting Working?" *CPA Journal*, August 1979, pp. 13–19.

[4]*FASB Statement No. 13* as amended and interpreted through May 1980 incorporating Statements 13, 17, 22, 23, 26, 27, 28, & 29, and Interpretations 19, 21, 23, 24, 26, & 27.

must be considered in determining the appropriate accounting treatment of a lease.

The **inception of the lease** is also an important accounting consideration. It is defined as the date of the lease agreement or earlier written commitment if all the principal provisions have been negotiated. This is true even if the leased asset must yet be constructed or acquired by the lessor.[5] The inception of the lease should be distinguished from the beginning of the lease term or period. The **lease term** begins when the lease agreement takes effect, i.e., when the leased property is transferred to the lessee. A considerable amount of time may elapse between the inception date and the beginning of the lease term.

LEASE CLASSIFICATION CRITERIA

A critical question that has generated much controversy and discussion is what criteria should be used to classify a lease as a capital transaction. In Statement No. 13, the FASB identified the following four criteria:[6]

(1) The lease transfers ownership of the property to the lessee by the end of the lease term.
(2) The lease contains a bargain purchase option.
(3) The lease term is equal to 75% or more of the estimated economic life of the leased property.
(4) The present value at the beginning of the lease term of the minimum lease payments excluding that portion representing executory costs equals or exceeds 90% of the fair market value of the property.

In general, if a lease meets any one of the above criteria, it should be accounted for as a purchase by the lessee and a sale by the lessor[7] (additional conditions applicable to the lessor are discussed later in the chapter). An exception should be noted with regard to used assets and the third and fourth criteria, i.e., neither criterion is applicable if the beginning of the lease term falls within the last 25 percent of the total estimated economic life of the asset.

Application of the above classification criteria is discussed in the following sections. Although the terms of a lease apply to both lessee and lessor, there are different accounting problems associated with each side of the lease transaction. Because of these differences, accounting for leases by lessees will be presented first, followed by a discussion of accounting for leases by lessors. Leases involving real estate and sale-leaseback transactions are discussed separately later in the chapter.

---

[5] *Statement of Financial Accounting Standards No. 23,* "Inception of the Lease" (Stamford: Financial Accounting Standards Board, 1978), par. 6 and 7.

[6] *Statement of Financial Accounting Standards No. 13,* "Accounting for Leases" (Stamford: Financial Accounting Standards Board, 1976), par.7.

[7] For an interesting analysis that demonstrates that the first three criteria are in reality redundant and are incorporated in the fourth criteria for the lessor and, in most cases, for the lessees see John W. Coughlan, "Regulation, Rents, and Residuals," *Journal of Accountancy,* February 1980, pp. 58–66.

ACCOUNTING FOR LEASES—LESSEE

A lessee has access to designated leased property during the term of the lease, perhaps with some specific renewal or purchase privileges. Title to the property remains with the lessor; however, many of the normal ownership responsibilities may be transferred to the lessee by contract. These could include payment of such **executory costs** as maintenance, insurance, and taxes. Basically, all leases as viewed by the lessee may be divided into two types: **operating leases** and **capital leases**. If a lease meets any one of the four classification criteria mentioned previously, it is treated as a capital lease. Otherwise, it is accounted for as an operating lease.

Accounting for operating leases involves the recognition of rent expense over the term of the lease. The leased property is not reported as an asset on the lessee's balance sheet nor is a liability recognized for the obligation to make future payments for use of the property. Information concerning the lease is limited to disclosure in notes to the financial statements. Accounting for a capital lease essentially requires the lessee to report on the balance sheet the present value of the future lease payments, both as an asset and a liability. The asset is amortized as though it had been purchased by the lessee. The liability is accounted for in the same manner as would be a mortgage on the property. The difference in the impact of these two methods on the financial statements is frequently significant.

Accounting for Operating Leases–Lessee

Operating leases are considered to be simple rental agreements with debits being made to an expense account as the payments are made. For example, assume the lease terms for manufacturing equipment were $40,000 a year on a year-to-year basis. The entry to record the payment for a year's rent would be as follows:

Rent Expense	40,000	
Cash		40,000

Rent payments are frequently made in advance. In this event, if the lease period does not coincide with the lessee's fiscal year, or if the lessee prepares interim reports, a prepaid rent account would be required to record the unexpired portion of rent at the end of the accounting period involved. Amortization of the prepayment should be made on a straight-line basis. In some cases, the terms of an operating lease provide for a large initial payment, and smaller annual charges in the future. Other patterns that vary from straight-line may also be encountered, including small payments in the early years and larger payments in the later years. In these instances, recording of rent expense should approximate a straight-line pattern, and differences between the actual payments and the debit to expense would be reported either as Prepaid Rent or Rent Payable. For example, assume the terms of the lease were $70,000 rent each year for the first two years of a five-year lease, with annual payments for the last three years reduced to $20,000 a year. The total lease payments for the five years would be $200,000, or $40,000 a year on a straight-line basis. The required entries in the first two years would be as follows:

Prepaid Rent	30,000	
Rent Expense	40,000	
Cash		70,000

The entries for each of the last three years would be as follows:

Rent Expense	40,000	
Prepaid Rent		20,000
Cash		20,000

Even though a lease is accounted for by the lessee as an operating lease, users of financial statements need to be informed as to the nature of the agreement if the amounts involved are significant. The Financial Accounting Standards Board recommended the following disclosures for operating leases:

> For operating leases having initial or remaining noncancelable lease terms in excess of one year:
> (i) Future minimum rental payments required as of the date of the latest balance sheet presented, in the aggregate and for each of the five succeeding fiscal years.
> (ii) The total minimum rentals to be received in the future under noncancelable subleases as of the date of the latest balance sheet presented.
> For all operating leases, rental expense for each period for which an income statement is presented, with separate amounts for minimum rentals, contingent rentals, and sublease rentals. Rental payments under leases with terms of a month or less that were not renewed need not be included.[8]

In addition, disclosure of restrictions on such items as dividends, additional debt, and further leasing should be included for all leases.

Accounting for Capital Leases—Lessee

Capital leases are considered to be more like a purchase of property than a rental. Consequently, the accounting for capital leases requires entries similar to those required for the purchase of an asset with long-term credit terms. The amount to be recorded as an asset and a liability should represent the present value of future **minimum lease payments,** which include: (1) minimum rental payments required over the lease term and (2) any payment called for by a bargain purchase option or other guarantee by the lessee of the residual value of the property.

Minimum Rental Payments. The **minimum rental payments** to be capitalized by the lessee do not include executory costs such as insurance, maintenance, and taxes or any profit charged the lessee on these costs. Executory costs may be paid directly by the lessee apart from rental payments to the lessor, or they may be included in the rental payments and paid by the lessor. These costs are period costs and are recognized as expenses when paid or accrued. If executory costs are included in the rental payment and the

[8] *Ibid.*, par. 16b, c.

amount is not determinable from the lease provisions, the lessee must estimate the portion of the rental payment representing executory costs.[9]

The **lease term** to be used to establish the minimum rental payments is the fixed noncancelable term of the lease plus all periods for which renewal is reasonably assured, including periods covered by bargain renewal options. A **bargain renewal** provision gives the lessee the option to renew the lease for a rental that is significantly less than the expected fair rental of the property at the date the option becomes exercisable. The renewal rental must be sufficiently low in relation to the expected fair rental value that exercise of the option appears, at the inception of the lease, to be reasonably assured. The lease term also includes any periods for which a penalty is imposed on the lessee for failure to renew the lease if the amount of the penalty is such that, at the inception of the lease, renewal appears to be reasonably assured. The lease term includes all periods covered by ordinary renewal options preceding the date at which a bargain purchase option becomes exercisable. Regardless of other provisions, the lease term for purposes of computing minimum lease payments shall not extend beyond the date at which a bargain purchase option becomes exercisable.[10]

Bargain Purchase or Guarantee of Residual Value. A **bargain purchase option** gives the lessee the right to purchase the leased property at a price that is sufficiently lower than the expected fair value of the property at the date the option becomes exercisable that exercise of the option appears, at the inception of the lease, to be reasonably assured.[11] If a lease contains a bargain purchase option, the minimum lease payments include the minimum rental payments required up to the date the option becomes exercisable and the price to be paid by the lessee to exercise the purchase option.

Any **guarantee of the estimated residual value** of the leased property by the lessee is included in determining the minimum lease payments, whether or not payment of the guarantee constitutes a purchase of the property. The **estimated residual value** is the expected fair market value of the property at the end of the lease term.[12] The lessor, for example, may have the right to require the lessee to purchase the property at the end of the lease term at a specified or determinable price, or the lessee may have to make up any deficiency below a stated amount upon disposition of the property by the lessor. In the latter case, the amount to be included in minimum lease payments is the stated amount of the guarantee rather than an estimate of the deficiency.[13]

Present Value of Minimum Lease Payments. Once the minimum lease payments have been determined from an evaluation of the lease provisions, they must be discounted to their present value. The discount rate to be used by the lessee is the lessee's **incremental borrowing rate**, the rate that, at the inception of the lease, the lessee would have incurred to borrow over a

[9]*Ibid.*, par. 10.
[10]*Ibid.*, par. 5(f).
[11]*Ibid.*, par. 5d.
[12]*Ibid.*, par. 5h.
[13]*Ibid.*, par. 5j.

similar period of time the funds necessary to purchase the leased asset. An exception applies, however, if the lessee knows the **implicit rate of interest in the lease** as computed by the lessor. Then, the lessee should use the lower of the implicit rate or the incremental borrowing rate.[14] The implicit interest rate in a lease is the discount rate that, when applied to the minimum lease payments causes the aggregate present value at the beginning of the lease term to be equal to the fair value of the leased property to the lessor at the inception of the lease. The FASB had proposed requiring the lessee to estimate the lessor's implicit rate if it is not known; however, no change to Statement No. 13 was finalized. Since the implicit rate is often less than the incremental borrowing rate, such a requirement would increase the computed present value of the minimum lease payments and thus make the fourth criterion more effective.

An important exception to the use of the present value of future minimum lease payments as a basis for recording a capital lease was included by the FASB in Statement No. 13 as follows:

> However, if the amount so determined exceeds the fair value of the leased property at the inception of the lease, the amount recorded as the asset and obligation shall be the fair value.[15]

This means that if the leased asset has a determinable sales price, the present value of the future minimum lease payments should be compared with that price. If the sales price is lower, it should be used as the capitalized value of the lease, and an implicit interest rate would have to be computed using the sales price as the capitalized value of the asset.

Illustrative Entries for Capital Leases. Assume that Buehner Corporation leases equipment from Universal Leasing Company with the following terms:

Lease period: Five years, beginning January 1, 1984. Noncancelable.
Rental amount: $43,000 per year payable annually in advance; includes $3,000 to cover executory costs to be paid by lessor.
Estimated economic life of equipment: Five years.
Expected residual value of equipment at end of lease period: None.

Because the rental payments are payable in advance, the formula to find the present value of the lease is the annuity-due formula described in Appendix A. Assuming the Buehner Corporation's incremental borrowing rate is 8 percent and that rate is equal to or less than the implicit rate, the present value for the lease would be $172,484 computed as follows:

$$PV_n = R(PVAF_{\overline{n-1}|i} + 1)$$
$$PV_n = \$40{,}000(\text{Table IV}_{\overline{4}|8\%} + 1)$$
$$PV_n = \$40{,}000(3.3121 + 1)$$
$$PV_n = \$172{,}484^{16}$$

The journal entry to record the lease at the beginning of the lease term would be as follows:

---

[14] *Ibid.*, par. 7(d).
[15] *Ibid.*, par. 10.
[16] All computations of present value in this chapter will be rounded to the nearest dollar. This will require some adjustment at times to the final figures in the tables to balance the amounts.

1984			
Jan. 1	Leased Equipment Under Capital Leases	172,484	
	Obligations Under Capital Leases		172,484[17]
1	Lease Expense	3,000	
	Obligations Under Capital Leases	40,000	
	Cash		43,000

Although the asset and liability balances are the same at the inception of the lease, they seldom remain the same during the lease period. The asset value should be amortized in accordance with the lessee's normal depreciation policy over the asset's life. The life to be used depends upon which of the criteria was used to qualify the lease as a capital lease. If the lease qualified under either of the first two criteria as listed previously, the asset life should be used for amortizing the capitalized value of the leased asset. If the lease qualified under either of the last two criteria and the lease term is shorter than the estimated life of the asset, the lease term should be used for amortization purposes. In the preceding example, the lease qualifies under the third criterion and presumably the fourth since the lessor would not lease the asset over its entire economic life if the present value of the lease payments were less than the fair market value of the asset at the inception of the lease. The liability should be reduced each period so as to produce a constant rate of interest expense on the remaining balance of the obligation. The lessee's incremental borrowing rate, or the lessor's implicit rate if lower, is the constant interest rate for the lessee under the provisions of FASB Statement No. 13. Table 1 below shows how the $40,000 payments (excluding executory costs) would be separated between payment on the obligation and interest expense. To simplify the schedule, it is assumed that the lease payments after the first payment are made on December 31 of each year. If the payments were made in January, an accrual of interest at December 31 would be required. Because of this assumption, the portion of the lease payment that represents executory costs must be recorded as a prepayment and charged to lease expense in the following year.

TABLE 1
Schedule of Lease Payments
[Five-Year Lease, $40,000 Annual Payments (Net of Executory Costs) 8% Interest]

		Lease Payment			
Date	Description	*Amount*	*Interest Expense**	*Principal*	Lease Obligation
1– 1–84	Initial balance				$172,484
1– 1–84	Payment	$40,000		$40,000	132,484
12–31–84	Payment	40,000	$10,599	29,401	103,083
12–31–85	Payment	40,000	8,247	31,753	71,330
12–31–86	Payment	40,000	5,706	34,294	37,036
12–31–87	Payment	40,000	2,964	37,036	0

*Preceding lease obligation × 8%.

[17]It is also possible to record the liability at the gross amount of the payments ($200,000) and offset it with a discount account–Discount on Lease Contract. The net method is more common in accounting for leases by the lessee and will be used in this chapter.

If the normal company depreciation policy for this type of equipment is straight-line, the required entry at December 31, 1984, for amortization of the asset would be as follows:

1984			
Dec. 31	Amortization Expense on Leased Equipment	34,497	
	Accumulated Amortization of Leased Equipment Under Capital Leases		34,497

Computation:
$172,484 ÷ 5 = $34,497

Similar entries would be made for each of the remaining four years. Although the credit could be made directly against the asset account, the use of a contra asset account provides the necessary disclosure information about the original lease value and accumulated amortization to date.

Another entry is required at December 31, 1984, to record the second lease payment. As indicated in Table 1, the interest expense for 1984 would be computed by applying the incremental borrowing rate of 8% against the initial present value of the obligation less the immediate $40,000 first payment, or $10,599 [($172,484 − $40,000) × .08].

1984			
Dec. 31	Prepaid Executory Costs	3,000	
	Obligations Under Capital Leases	29,401	
	Interest Expense	10,599	
	Cash		43,000

The December 31, 1984, balance sheet of Buehner Corporation would include information concerning the leased equipment and related obligation as illustrated below:

Buehner Corporation
Balance Sheet
December 31, 1984

Assets		Liabilities	
Land, buildings, and equipment:		Current liabilities:	
Leased equipment under capital leases	$172,484	Obligations under capital leases, current portion	$31,753
Less accumulated amortization of leased equipment under capital leases	34,497	Long-term liabilities:	
Net value	$137,987	Obligations under capital leases, exclusive of $31,753 included in current liabilities	71,330

Note that the principal portion of the December 31, 1985, payment is reported as a current liability.

The income statement would include the amortization on leased property of $34,497, interest expense of $10,599, and executory costs of $3,000 as expenses for the period. The total expense of $48,096 exceeds the $43,000 rental payment made in the first year. As the amount of interest expense declines each period, the total expense will be reduced and, for the last two years, will be less than the $43,000 payments (Table 2 below). The total amount debited to expense over the life of the lease will, of course, be the same regardless of whether the lease is accounted for as an operating lease or as a capital lease. If a declining-balance method of amortization is used, the difference in the early years between the expense and the payment would be even larger. In addition to this statement disclosure, a note to the financial statements would be necessary to explain the terms of the lease and future rental payments in more detail.

TABLE 2
Schedule of Amounts Charged to Operations—
Capital and Operating Leases Compared

	Charge to Operations—Capital Lease				Charge to Operations—Operating Lease	
Year	*Interest*	*Executory Costs*	*Amortization*	*Total*	Lease	Difference
1984	$10,599	$ 3,000	$ 34,497	$ 48,096	$ 43,000	$ 5,096
1985	8,247	3,000	34,497	45,744	43,000	2,744
1986	5,706	3,000	34,497	43,203	43,000	203
1987	2,964	3,000	34,497	40,461	43,000	(2,539)
1988	—	3,000	34,496	37,496	43,000	(5,504)
	$27,516	$15,000	$172,484	$215,000	$215,000	$ 0

If in this example, the fair market value of the leased asset had been less than $172,484, the exception discussed previously would be applied, and the lower fair market value would be used for the capitalized value of the lease. For example, assume the fair market value, or sales price, of the leased asset is $166,796. By using the present value tables and the method illustrated in Appendix A, the implicit interest rate of the lease can be computed as being 10%. A table similar to Table 1 may now be constructed using $166,796 as the initial balance and 10% as the interest rate. For complex lease situations involving something other than equal annual lease payments, computation of the implicit rate of interest must be done from the present value formulas themselves. This computation is facilitated by use of a computer.

Accounting for Lease with Bargain Purchase Option. Frequently, the lessee is given the option of purchasing the property at some future date at a bargain price. As discussed previously, the present value of the purchase option should be included in the capitalized value of the lease. Assume in the above example that there was a bargain purchase option of $60,000 exercisable after five years, and the economic life of the equipment was expected to be ten years. The other lease terms remain the same. The present value of the revised lease would be increased by the present value of the bargain purchase amount of $60,000, or $40,836 computed as follows:

$$PV = A(PVF_{\overline{n|}i})$$
$$PV = \$60{,}000(\text{Table II}_{\overline{5|}8\%})$$
$$PV = \$60{,}000(.6806)$$
$$PV = \$40{,}836$$

The total present value of the lease is $213,320 ($172,484 + $40,836). This amount will be used to record the initial asset and liability. The asset balance of $213,320 will be amortized over the asset life of ten years because of the existence of the bargain purchase option, which makes the transaction in reality a sale. The liability balance will be reduced as shown in Table 3.

TABLE 3
Schedule of Lease Payments
[Five-Year Lease with Bargain Purchase Option of $60,000 after Five Years, $40,000 Annual Payments (Net of Executory Costs) 8% Interest]

		Lease Payment			
Date	Description	*Amount*	*Interest Expense*	*Principal*	Lease Obligation
1– 1–84	Initial balance				$213,320
1– 1–84	Payment	$40,000		$40,000	173,320
12–31–84	Payment	40,000	$13,866	26,134	147,186
12–31–85	Payment	40,000	11,775	28,225	118,961
12–31–86	Payment	40,000	9,517	30,483	88,478
12–31–87	Payment	40,000	7,078	32,922	55,556
12–31–88	Purchase	60,000	4,444	55,556	0

At the date of exercising the option, the net balance in the asset account, Leased Equipment Under Capital Leases, and its related accumulated amortization account would be transferred to the regular equipment account. The entries at the exercise of the option would be as follows:

Obligations Under Capital Leases	55,556	
Interest Expense	4,444	
Cash		60,000
To record exercise of bargain purchase option.		
Equipment	106,660	
Accumulated Amortization of Leased Equipment Under Capital Leases	106,660	
Leased Equipment Under Capital Leases		213,320
To transfer remaining balance in leased asset account to equipment account.		

Computation:
Accumulated amortization:
One half amortized after five years of a ten-year life: $213,320 ÷ 2 = $106,660

If the equipment is not purchased and the lease is permitted to lapse, a loss in the amount of the net remaining balance in the asset account, less any remaining liabilities, would have to be recognized by the following entry:

Loss from Failure to Exercise Bargain Purchase Option on Capital Lease	46,660	
Obligations Under Capital Leases	55,556	
Interest Expense	4,444	
Accumulated Amortization of Leased Equipment Under Capital Leases	106,660	
Leased Equipment Under Capital Leases		213,320

Purchase of Asset During Lease Term. When a bargain purchase option does not exist, it is still possible that a lessee may purchase leased property during the term of the lease. Usually the purchase price will differ from the recorded lease obligation at the purchase date. The FASB issued Interpretation No. 26 to cover this situation. The Board decided that no gain or loss should be recorded on the purchase, but the difference between the payment made and the obligation still on the books should be charged or credited to the acquired asset's carrying value.[18]

To illustrate, assume that on December 31, 1986, rather than making the lease payment due on that date the lessee purchased the leased property described on page 563 for $85,000. At that date, the remaining liability recorded on the lessee's books is $77,036 ($71,330 + $5,706), and the net book value of the recorded leased asset is $68,993, the original capitalized value of $172,484 less $103,491 amortization ($34,497 × 3). The entry to record the purchase on the lessee's books would be as follows:

Interest Expense	5,706	
Obligations Under Capital Leases	71,330	
Equipment	76,957	
Accumulated Amortization of Leased Equipment	103,491	
Leased Equipment Under Capital Leases		172,484
Cash		85,000

The purchased equipment is capitalized at $76,957, which is the book value of the leased asset, $68,993, plus $7,964, the excess of the purchase price over the carrying value of the lease obligation ($85,000 − $77,036).

Disclosure Requirements for Capital Leases. The FASB has prescribed the following specific disclosure requirements for capital leases by the lessee.[19]

(1) The gross amount of assets recorded under capital leases as of the date of each balance sheet presented by major classes according to nature of function. This information may be combined with comparable information for owned assets.

(2) Future minimum lease payments as of the date of the latest balance sheet presented, in the aggregate and for each of the five succeeding fiscal years, with separate deductions from the total for the amount representing executory costs included in the minimum lease payments and for the amount of the imputed interest necessary to reduce the net minimum lease payments to present value.

In addition , disclosure of information concerning subrentals and contingent rentals is required. A note, adapted from Statement No. 13, that meets these requirements is illustrated on page 569.[20]

ACCOUNTING FOR LEASES—LESSOR

The lessor in a lease transaction gives up the physical possession of the property to the lessee. If the transfer of the property is considered temporary

[18] *FASB Interpretation No. 26,* "Accounting for Purchase of a Leased Asset by the Lessee during the Term of the Lease" (Stamford: Financial Accounting Standards Board, 1978), par 5.

[19] *Statement of Financial Accounting Standards No. 13, op. cit.,* par. 16a.

[20] *Ibid.,* Appendix D.

Note 2—Capital Leases

The following is an analysis of the leased property under capital leases by major classes:

Classes of Property	Asset Balances at December 31, 1984	1983
Manufacturing plant	$XXX	$XXX
Store facilities	XXX	XXX
Other	XXX	XXX
	$XXX	$XXX
Less accumulated amortization	(XXX)	(XXX)
	$XXX	$XXX

The following is a schedule by years of future minimum lease payments under capital leases together with the present value of the net minimum lease payments as of December 31, 1984:

Year ending December 31:	
1985	$XXX
1986	XXX
1987	XXX
1988	XXX
1989	XXX
Later years	XXX
Total minimum lease payments	$XXX
Less amount representing estimated executory costs (such as taxes, maintenance, and insurance), including profit thereon, included in total minimum lease payments	(XXX)
Net minimum lease payments	$XXX
Less amount representing interest	(XXX)
Present value of net minimum lease payments	$XXX

in nature, the lessor will continue to carry the leased asset as an owned asset on the balance sheet, and the revenue from the lease will be reported as it is earned. Depreciation of the leased asset will be matched against the revenue. This type of lease is described as an **operating lease** and is similar to the operating lease described for the lessee. However, if a lease has terms that make the transaction similar in substance to a sale or a permanent transfer of the asset to the lessee, the lessor should no longer report the asset as though it were owned, but should reflect the transfer to the lessee.

From the standpoint of the lessor, a lease is accounted for as an operating lease unless it meets one of the classification criteria on page 559 and also meets both of the following conditions at the inception of the lease:[21]

(1) Collectibility of the minimum lease payments is reasonably predictable.

(2) No important uncertainties surround the amount of unreimbursable costs yet to be incurred by the lessor. This test is to be applied at the date construction of the leased asset is completed or when the property is acquired if these dates are after the inception of the lease.[22]

[21] *Ibid.*, par. 8.

[22] *Statement of Financial Accounting Standards No. 23,* "Inception of the Lease" (Stamford: Financial Accounting Standards Board, 1978), par. 7.

Leases that meet these two conditions and one or more of the previously discussed criteria are classified by the lessor as either a **sales-type lease** or a **direct financing lease**. Thus, a lease that qualifies as a capital lease for the lessee is either a sales-type or direct financing lease for the lessor assuming the additional conditions applicable to the lessor are met. However, if one or both of the additional conditions are not met, the lessor would account for the lease as an operating lease and the lessee would account for the lease as a capital lease.

Sales-type lease transactions involve a profit or loss to the lessor on the transfer of the asset to the lessee. The lessors in such transactions are normally manufacturers or dealers who use leases as a means of facilitating the marketing of their products. The profit or loss recognized by the lessor is the difference between the fair value of the leased asset at the inception of the lease and its cost or carrying value. Direct financing leases do not involve any manufacturer's or dealer's profit or loss. The lessor in such transactions typically is primarily engaged in financing operations. Thus, direct financing leases are essentially financial arrangements between a financial institution and the lessee.

The three types of leases from the lessor's standpoint—operating leases, sales-type leases, and direct financing leases—are discussed in the following sections.

Accounting for Operating Leases—Lessor

Accounting for operating leases for the lessor is very similar to that described for the lessee. The lessor recognizes the payments as they are received as revenue. If there are significant variations in the payment terms, entries will be necessary to reflect a straight-line pattern of revenue recognition.

A lessor may incur certain costs in connection with a lease transaction. These costs, referred to as **initial direct costs**, were defined by the FASB as follows:

> Those costs incurred by the lessor that are directly associated with negotiating and consummating completed leasing transactions. Those costs include, but are not necessarily limited to, commissions, legal fees, costs of credit investigations, and costs of preparing and processing documents for new leases acquired.... No portion of supervisory and administrative expenses or other indirect expenses, such as rent and facilities costs, shall be included in initial direct costs.[23]

Initial direct costs incurred in connection with an operating lease are deferred and amortized over the term of the lease.

To illustrate accounting for an operating lease on the lessor's books, assume that the equipment leased for five years by Buehner Corporation for

---

[23] *Statement of Financial Accounting Standards No. 13, op. cit.*, par. 5m as amended by *Statement of Financial Accounting Standards No. 17*, "Accounting for Leases—Initial Direct Costs" (Stamford: Financial Accounting Standards Board, 1977), par. 8.

$43,000 a year including executory costs of $3,000 per year had a cost of $300,000 to the lessor. Initial direct costs of $5,000 were incurred to obtain the lease. It is expected that the equipment has a ten-year life, with no salvage value at the end of ten years. Assuming no purchase or renewal options or guarantees by the lessee, the lease does not meet any of the four general classification criteria and would be treated as an operating lease. The entries to record the payment of the initial direct costs and the receipt of rent would be as follows:

1984			
Jan. 1	Deferred Initial Direct Costs	5,000	
	Cash		5,000
1	Cash	43,000	
	Rent Revenue		43,000

Assuming the lessor depreciates the equipment on a straight-line basis over its expected life of 10 years and amortizes the initial direct costs on a straight-line basis over the five-year lease term, the depreciation and amortization entries at the end of the first year would be:

1984			
Dec. 31	Amortization of Initial Direct Costs	1,000	
	Deferred Initial Direct Costs		1,000
31	Depreciation Expense on Leased Equipment	30,000	
	Accumulated Depreciation on Leased Equipment		30,000

Executory costs would be recognized as expense when paid or accrued. If the rental period and the lessor's fiscal year do not coincide, or if the lessor prepares interim reports, a rent received in advance account would be required to record the unearned rent revenue at the end of the accounting period.

There are no special reporting problems for this type of lease; however, a note disclosure of the lease terms similar to those included by the lessee (page 561) is recommended. The leased property with its accumulated depreciation should be disclosed separately in the "Land, buildings, and equipment" section of the balance sheet. Deferred initial direct costs should be reported as a long-term deferred charge on the balance sheet.

Specific disclosures required for operating leases by the lessor are as follows.[24]

(1) The cost and carrying amount, if different, of property on lease or held for leasing by major classes of property according to nature or function, and the amount of accumulated depreciation in total as of the date of the latest balance sheet presented.
(2) Minimum future rentals on noncancelable leases as of the date of the latest balance sheet presented, in the aggregate and for each of the five succeeding years.

In addition, information concerning any contingent rentals included in the income statements should be included in the disclosure.

[24] *Statement of Financial Accounting Standards No. 13, op. cit.,* par. 23b.

Accounting for Sales-Type Leases

As discussed previously, under the provisions of a lease, the lessee may acquire the asset at the end of the lease term, e.g., through exercise of a bargain purchase option. If ownership does not revert to the lessee, the residual value, if any, accrues to the benefit of the lessor. The lease may require the lessee to guarantee the estimated residual value or some portion thereof. Any residual value not covered by a guarantee is referred to as the **unguaranteed residual value**. Because the existence of an unguaranteed residual value complicates the accounting for sales-type leases, leases without such residual values will be considered first.

Sales-Type Leases with No Unguaranteed Residual Value. Leases used to market products normally have two income components—financial revenue or interest and manufacturer's or dealer's profit (or loss). Three values must be identified to determine these income elements:

(1) The minimum lease payments as defined previously for the lessee, i.e., rental payments over the lease term net of any executory costs included therein plus the amount to be paid under a bargain purchase option or guarantee of residual value by the lessee.
(2) The fair market value of the asset, which equals the present value of the minimum lease payments.
(3) The cost or carrying value of the asset to the lessor increased by any initial direct costs.

The manufacturer's or dealer's profit is the difference between the fair market value of the asset [(2) above] and the cost or carrying value of the asset to the lessor [(3) above]. If cost exceeds the fair market value, a loss will be reported. The difference between the gross rentals [(1) above] and the fair market value of the asset [(2) above] is interest revenue and arises because of the time delay in paying for the asset as described by the lease terms. The relationship between these three values can be demonstrated as follows:

(1) Minimum lease payments	
	Financial Revenue (Interest)
(2) Fair market value of leased asset	
	Manufacturer's or Dealer's Profit (Loss)
(3) Cost or carrying value of leased asset to lessor	

To illustrate this type of lease, assume the equipment described on page 563 had a fair market value equal to its present value at 8% interest or $172,484 and a cost of $125,000 including initial direct costs of $5,000. The three values and their related revenue amounts would be as follows:

(1) Minimum lease payments: ($43,000 – $3,000) × 5	$200,000	
		$27,516 (Interest Revenue)
(2) Fair market value of equipment	$172,484	
		$47,484 (Manufacturer's Profit)
(3) Cost of leased equipment to lessor	$125,000	

The interest revenue is recognized as revenue over the life of the lease so as to produce a constant periodic rate of return on the net investment of the lease in a manner similar to the recognition of interest expense on the lessee's books (see Table 1, page 564). The manufacturer's profit is recognized as revenue in the current period by including the fair market value of the asset as a sale and debiting the cost of the equipment carried in the finished goods inventory to Cost of Sales. The reimbursement of executory costs to the lessor is either credited to Miscellaneous Revenue or to the executory expense accounts involved. The entries to record this information on the lessor's books at the beginning of the lease term would be as follows:

1984			
Jan. 1	Minimum Lease Payments Receivable	200,000[25]	
	Cost of Leased Equipment Recorded as a Sale	125,000	
	Finished Goods Inventory		120,000
	Unearned Interest Revenue		27,516
	Sales		172,484
	Deferred Initial Direct Costs		5,000
1	Cash	43,000	
	Miscellaneous Revenue (or Executory Expenses)		3,000
	Minimum Lease Payments Receivable		40,000
	First year lease receipts.		

At the end of the first year, interest revenue would be recognized when the payment is received as indicated in Table 4.

1984			
Dec. 31	Cash	43,000	
	Minimum Lease Payments Receivable		40,000
	Miscellaneous Revenue		3,000
31	Unearned Interest Revenue	10,599	
	Interest Revenue		10,599

TABLE 4
Schedule of Lease Receipts and Interest Revenue
[Five-Year Lease, $40,000 Annual Payments
(Exclusive of Executory Costs) 8% Interest]

Date	Description	Interest Revenue*	Lease Receipt	Lease Payments Receivable	Unearned Interest Revenue
1– 1–84	Initial balance			$200,000	$27,516
1– 1–84	Receipt		$40,000	160,000	27,516
12–31–84	Receipt	$10,599	40,000	120,000	16,917
12–31–85	Receipt	8,247	40,000	80,000	8,670
12–31–86	Receipt	5,706	40,000	40,000	2,964
12–31–87	Receipt	2,964	40,000	0	0

*Preceding lease payment receivable less unearned interest revenue × 8%.

The balance sheet of the lessor at December 31, 1984, will report the lease receivable less the unearned interest revenue as follows:

[25]It is also possible to record the receivable at the net difference between the gross receivable and the unearned interest revenue. The gross method is more common in accounting for the lessor and is used in this chapter.

Universal Leasing Company Balance Sheet December 31, 1984		
Assets		
Current assets:		
Minimum lease payment receivable	$40,000	
Less unearned interest revenue	8,247	$31,753
Long-term assets:		
Minimum lease payments receivable (exclusive of $40,000 included in current assets)	$80,000	
Less unearned interest revenue	8,670	71,330

The 1984 income statement would include the sales and cost of sales amounts yielding the manufacturer's profit of $47,484, and interest revenue of $10,599. A note to the statements would describe in more detail the nature of the lease and its terms.

In the preceding example, it was implied that the fair market value of the leased equipment was determined by discounting the minimum lease payments at a rate of 8 percent. Normally, however, the fair market value is known, and the minimum lease payments are set at an amount that will yield the desired rate of return to the lessor.

Sales-Type Leases with Unguaranteed Residual Value. Frequently, the economic life of a leased asset exceeds the initial lease term, and thus a significant economic value may still exist at the end of the initial lease term. In many leases, no bargain purchase or guarantee of the residual value exists, and the lessor receives the benefit of the residual value at the expiration of the lease. Thus, in recording the lease, the lessor recognizes not only the minimum lease payments receivable, but also the estimated residual value that reverts to the lessor at the end of the lease term. The combined amount of the minimum lease payments and the unguaranteed residual value is referred to as the **gross investment** in the lease. The fair market value of the leased asset is viewed as the **net investment**, i.e., the present value of the two components of the gross investment. In determining manufacturer's or dealer's profit or loss, the present value of the unguaranteed residual value is deducted from cost.

To illustrate the accounting for unguaranteed residual values, assume that in the example of the Universal Leasing Company lease on page 563 there was an expected unguaranteed residual value of $60,000 at the end of the five-year period with no bargain purchase option. The residual value would be added to the minimum lease payments to determine the gross investment by the lessor in the leased asset ($200,000 + $60,000 = $260,000). Assume the fair market value of the property with residual value was $213,320. Because the terms of the lease now include both an annuity and a future lump-sum value, the computation of the implicit interest rate is more complex and would require use of the formulas rather than the normally established tables. In this example, the implicit rate is 8%. The present value of the residual value using this rate is $40,836 ($60,000 × .6806), and the entry to record the lease initially on the lessor's books would be as follows:

1984			
Jan. 1	Gross Investment in Leased Assets	260,000	
	Cost of Leased Equipment Recorded as a Sale	84,164	
	Finished Goods Inventory		120,000
	Unearned Interest Revenue		46,680
	Sales		172,484
	Deferred Initial Direct Costs		5,000

Computations:

Cost of leased equipment recorded as a sale:	
Cost from finished goods and initial direct costs	$125,000
Less present value of residual value	40,836
	$ 84,164
Unearned interest revenue:	
Gross investment in lease	$260,000
Less fair market value of lease	213,320
	$ 46,680

Sales:
Same as computation on page 563. Also equals fair market value of property less present value of residual value ($213,320 − $40,836 = $172,484).

The manufacturer's profit in this case would be $88,320 ($172,484 − $84,164), or $40,836 (present value of unguaranteed residual value) more than the example on page 572. The annual recognition of interest revenue would also differ from the earlier example because of the higher net investment base that includes the present value of the residual amount. For example, the interest revenue for the first year would be $13,866 (Table 3, page 567) rather than $10,599 (Table 4, page 573) computed without the residual value.

Because of the significance of the residual value in lease accounting, the estimate of its amount should be reviewed at least annually. If it is felt to be excessive and the decline is other than temporary, the accounting should be revised to reflect the changed estimate. The resulting reduction in the net investment is recognized as a loss in the period when the estimate is changed. If the residual value is felt to be too low, adjustment would result in a gain. The Financial Accounting Standards Board, however, has recommended that no upward adjustment be made in the estimate, again demonstrating the conservative bias of accounting principles setting bodies.[26]

Accounting for Direct Financing Leases

If the cost of the leased property and its fair market value are the same, no manufacturer's or dealer's profit exists, and the entire difference between the total amount of the minimum lease payments plus unguaranteed residual

[26]*Statement of Financial Accounting Standards No. 13, op. cit.*, par 17d.

value and the cost is considered to be interest revenue to be recognized over the life of the lease. Usually, the lessors of direct financing leases are primarily engaged in financing operations rather than in manufacturing or dealerships. Renewals of sales-type leases are frequently considered to be direct financing leases inasmuch as no manufacturer's or dealer's profits could exist at the time of the renewal.

Illustrative Entries for Direct Financing Leases. Referring to the example on page 563, assume that the cost of the equipment to the lessor was the same as its fair market value, $172,484, and the purchase by the lessor had been entered into the account Equipment Purchased for Lease. The entry to record the initial lease would be as follows:

Minimum Lease Payments Receivable	200,000	
Equipment Purchased for Lease............................		172,484
Unearned Interest Revenue................................		27,516

No sales or cost of sales figures would be reported. The entries for recognition of interest revenue would be the same as in the example for a sales-type lease.

Unguaranteed residual value is added to the minimum lease payments to determine the lessor's gross investment in a direct financing lease. The difference between the gross investment and the cost of the asset to the lessor is the amount of unearned revenue to be recognized over the term of the lease. If, in the preceding example, the leased asset had an unguaranteed residual value of $60,000 and a cost to the lessor of $213,320 equal to the fair market value, the lessor would record the lease as follows:

Gross Investment in Leased Assets..........................	260,000	
Equipment Purchased for Lease............................		213,320
Unearned Interest Revenue................................		46,680

Interest revenue would be recognized in accordance with Table 3, page 567. At the end of the first year, for example, the lessor would make the following entries:

Cash..	43,000	
Gross Investment in Leased Assets........................		40,000
Miscellaneous Revenue		3,000
Unearned Interest Revenue..................................	13,866	
Interest Revenue		13,866

At the end of the lease term, the lessor would make the following entry to record the recovery of the leased asset assuming the residual value was the same as originally estimated:

Equipment...	60,000	
Unearned Interest Revenue..................................	4,444	
Gross Investment in Leased Assets........................		60,000
Interest Revenue		4,444

As mentioned earlier, the unguaranteed residual value should be reviewed at least annually by the lessor and adjusted for any decline that is considered other than temporary. Such adjustment is accounted for as a change in estimate.

Initial Direct Costs Related to Direct Financing Lease. If the lessor incurs any initial direct costs in connection with a direct financing lease, those costs are to be charged against income when incurred, and a portion of unearned income equal to the initial direct costs is recognized as income in the same period.[27]

To illustrate, assume that the lessor in the preceding example incurred initial direct costs of $5,000. The entries relating to these costs would be as follows:

Lease Expense	5,000	
Cash		5,000
To record payment of initial direct costs.		
Unearned Interest Revenue	5,000	
Interest Revenue		5,000
To recognize portion of unearned revenue equal to initial direct costs.		

The remaining unearned revenue of $41,680 ($46,680 − $5,000) would be recognized over the lease term. The present value formulas would be used to calculate a new implicit rate of interest for recognizing the reduced amount of unearned revenue. In the example, the new rate is approximately 7 percent.

Sale of Asset During Lease Term

If the lessor sells an asset being leased, a gain or loss is recognized on the difference between the receivable balance, after deducting any unearned finance charges, and the selling price of the asset. Thus, if the leased asset described in Table 4, page 573, is sold on December 31, 1986, for $90,000 before the $40,000 rental payment is made, a gain of $12,964 would be reported. ($90,000 − $80,000 + $8,670 − $5,706). The following journal entry would be made to record the sale.

Unearned Interest Revenue	8,670	
Cash	90,000	
Interest Revenue		5,706
Minimum Lease Payments Receivable		80,000
Gain on Sale of Leased Asset		12,964

It should be remembered that although the lessor does recognize a gain or loss on the sale, the lessee defers any gain or loss in the value placed on the purchased asset.

Disclosure Requirements for Sales-Type and Direct Financing Leases

The FASB has prescribed the following disclosure requirements for sales-type and direct financing leases by the lessor.[28]

(1) The components of the net investment in sales-type and direct financing leases as of the date of each balance sheet presented:

[27] *Ibid.*, par. 18b.
[28] *Ibid.*, par. 23a.

(a) Future minimum lease payments to be received, with separate deductions for (i) amounts representing executory costs, including any profit thereon, included in the minimum lease payments and (ii) the accumulated allowance for uncollectible minimum lease payments receivable.
(b) The unguaranteed residual values accruing to the benefit of the lessor.
(c) Unearned income.

(2) Future minimum lease payments to be received for each of the five succeeding fiscal years as of the date of the latest balance sheet presented.

In addition, information concerning contingent rentals is required to be included. The following note, adapted from Statement No. 13, illustrates the preceding disclosure requirements.[29]

Note 2—Net Investment in Direct Financing and Sales-Type Leases

The following lists the components of the net investment in direct financing and sales-type leases as of December 31:

	1984	1983
Total minimum lease payments to be received	$XXX	$XXX
Less amounts representing estimated executory costs (such as taxes, maintenance, and insurance), including profit thereon, included in total minimum lease payments	(XXX)	(XXX)
Minimum lease payments receivable	$XXX	$XXX
Less allowance for uncollectibles	(XXX)	(XXX)
Net minimum lease payments receivable	$XXX	$XXX
Estimated residual values of leased property (unguaranteed)	XXX	XXX
Less unearned income	(XXX)	(XXX)
Net investment in direct financing and sales-type leases	$XXX	$XXX

RENEWALS AND EXTENSIONS OF EXISTING LEASES

If the renewal or extension of a lease was not contemplated at the inception of the lease because no bargain renewal option existed, it is treated as a new lease arrangement for purpose of applying the criteria to determine if the lease is a capital lease or an operating lease. No new accounting issues are involved if the lease renewal comes at the end of the initial lease term. However, if the renewal of a sales-type or direct financing lease occurs in the middle of the initial lease term, the lessor has a restriction on considering the renewal a sales-type lease. To avoid a duplication of the manufacturer's profit, if the renewal of such a lease would qualify as a sales-type lease, it is treated as a direct financing lease on the renewal and no manufacturer's or dealer's profit is recognized.[30]

---

[29] *Ibid.*, Appendix D.

[30] *Statement of Financial Accounting Standards No. 27*, "Classification of Renewal or Extensions of Existing Sales-Type or Direct Financing Leases" (Stamford: Financial Accounting Standards Board, 1979), par. 14 and 15.

CRITERIA FOR CAPITALIZATION OF REAL ESTATE LEASES

A significant percentage of leases involve real estate. If the real estate includes both nondepreciable land and depreciable buildings and equipment, special problems arise in determining how the lease should be treated. Some of the criteria used to evaluate a lease do not apply to leases of land. The FASB treated leases of real estate separately in Statement No. 13. This treatment is summarized in the following flowchart and in subsequent sections.

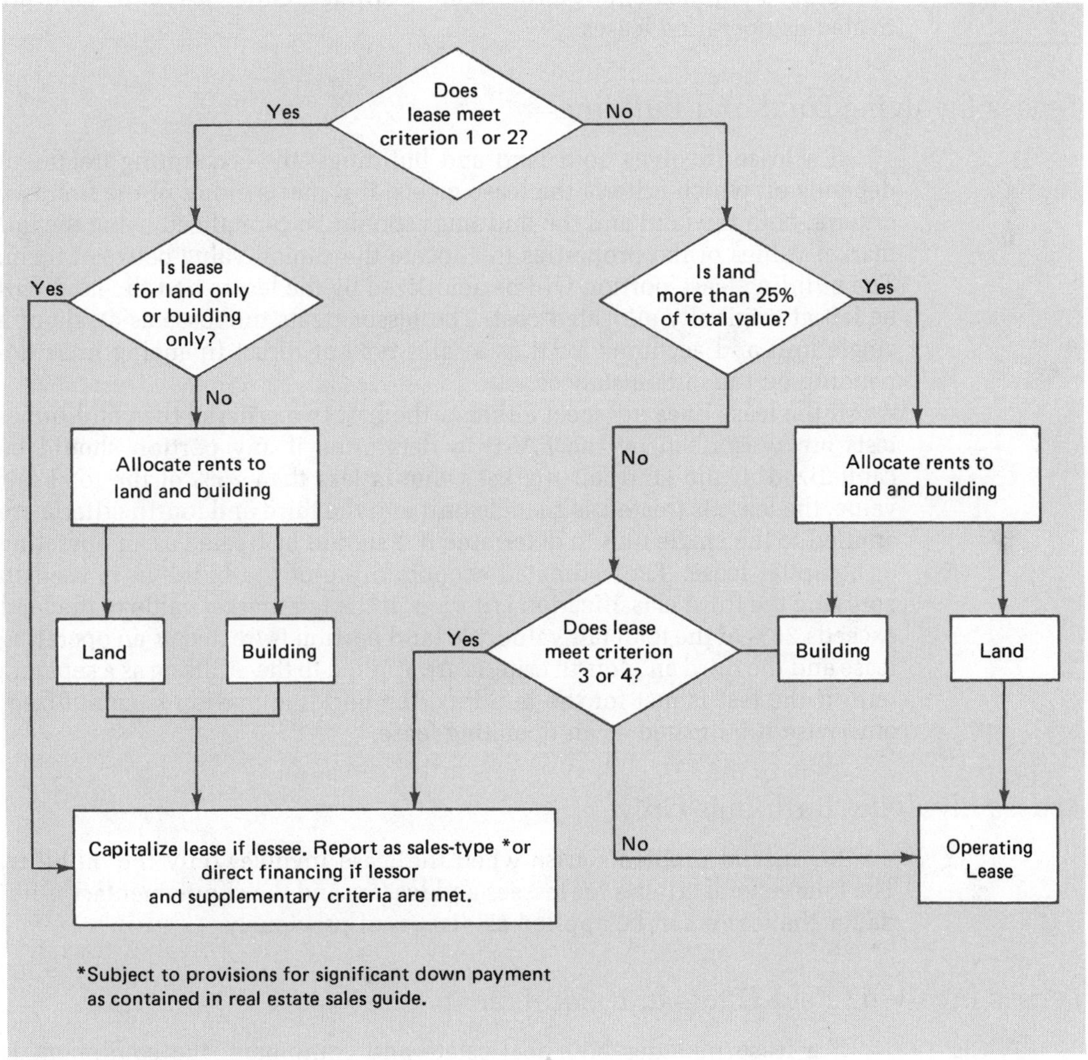

Leases Involving Land Only

The Board felt that leases of land should be capitalized only if title to the land is certain to be transferred in the future or if transfer is reasonably assured based on the existence of a bargain purchase option. Thus, only the first two general criteria listed on page 559 apply to the leasing of land. The third criterion cannot apply because land has an unlimited life. The fourth criterion was not felt to be applicable, because under this criterion no actual ownership transfer is contemplated. Ownership transfer is an important consideration, because the residual value of the land to the lessor would be material since there is no depreciation on land. Leases of land that meet either of the first two general criteria are capitalized on the lessee's books and treated as sales-type or direct financing leases on the lessor's books if both of the lessor's supplementary criteria are also met. Other leases of land are treated as operating leases.

Leases Involving Land and Buildings

If a lease involves both land and buildings, the accounting treatment depends on which criteria the lease meets. If it meets either of the first two criteria, both the land and the buildings should be capitalized using the fair market values of the properties to allocate the capital value between them. The building lease portion will be amortized by the lessee and the land will be left at originally allocated cost. The lessor treats the lease as a sale of a single unit and accounts for it as a sales-type or direct financing lease depending on the circumstances.

If the lease does not meet either of the first two criteria, then additional tests are prescribed by the FASB to determine if any portion should be capitalized. If the land fair market value is less than 25% of the total fair value, the lease is treated as a single unit and the third and fourth criteria are applied to the single unit to determine if it should be treated as an operating or a capital lease. The estimated economic life of the building is used in applying the third classification criterion. If the fair market value of the land exceeds 25% of the total fair value, the land portion is treated as an operating lease and the third and fourth criteria are applied to the building as a separate unit. If the test is met for the building, the building portion is capitalized, otherwise it is treated as an operating lease.

Leases Involving Buildings Only

No special problems arise when the lease involves only the building. The four general criteria for lessees and lessors and the supplementary criteria for the lessor can be applied as discussed previously.

Leases Involving Real Estate and Equipment

If a lease includes both real estate and equipment, the equipment is considered separately in determining the appropriate classification by the lessee and lessor and is accounted for separately over the term of the lease. The real estate portion of the lease is then classified and accounted for in accordance with the criteria applicable to leases of real estate.

Profit Recognition on Sales-Type Real Estate Leases

The provisions of profit recognition on sales of real estate (see Chapter 19) have an impact on the lessor's classification of real estate leases. Under the guidelines for sales of real estate, a substantial down payment (approximately 25%) must be made before the profit on the sale can be recognized in full. The FASB amended Statement No. 13 to specify that leases that fail to meet the criteria for full and immediate profit recognition if the real estate had been sold should be classified as operating leases, and no immediate profit recognized. This amendment does not apply to direct financing leases, or sales-type leases where a loss is indicated.[31]

ACCOUNTING FOR SALE-LEASEBACK TRANSACTIONS

A common type of lease arrangement is referred to as a **sale-leaseback** transaction. Typical of this type of lease is an arrangement whereby one party sells the property to a second party, and then the first party leases the property back. Thus, the seller becomes a seller-lessee and the purchaser a purchaser-lessor. The accounting problem raised by this transaction is whether the seller-lessee should recognize the profit from the original sale immediately, or defer it over the lease term. The Financial Accounting Standards Board has recommended that if the initial sale produces a profit, it should be deferred and amortized in proportion to the amortization of the leased asset if it is a capital lease or in proportion to the rental payments if it is an operating lease. If the transaction produces a loss because the fair market value of the asset is less than the undepreciated cost, an immediate loss should be recognized.[32]

To illustrate the accounting treatment for a sale at a gain, assume that on January 1, 1984, Morgan Inc. sells a warehouse having a carrying value of $5,500,000 on its books to Scowcroft Co. for $7,500,000 and immediately leases the warehouse back. The following conditions are established to govern the transaction.

(1) The land value is less than 25% of the total fair market value.
(2) The term of the lease is ten years, noncancelable. Equal rental payments of $1,071,082 are paid at the beginning of each year.
(3) The warehouse has a fair value of $7,500,000 on January 1, 1984, and an estimated economic life of twenty years. Straight line depreciation is used on all owned assets.
(4) The lessee has an option to renew the lease for $100,000 per year for ten years, the rest of its economic life.

Analysis of this lease shows that it qualifies as a capital lease under both the third and fourth criteria. Since the land value is less than 25% of the total

---

[31] *Statement of Financial Accounting Standards No. 26,* "Profit Recognition on Sales-Type Leases of Real Estate" (Stamford: Financial Accounting Standards Board, 1978).

[32] *Statement of Financial Accounting Standards No. 13, op. cit.,* par. 32–33.

fair value, the lease is treated as a single depreciable unit. It meets the third "75% of economic life" criterion because of the bargain renewal option which makes both the lease term and the economic life of the warehouse 20 years. It meets the fourth "90% of fair market value" criterion, because the present value of the rental payments is equal to the fair market value of the warehouse ($7,500,000).[33] The entries for recording the sale and the lease-back on both the seller-lessee's books and the purchaser-lessor's books for the first year of the lease are as follows:

Morgan Inc. (Seller-Lessee)

1984			
Jan. 1	Cash	7,500,000	
	Warehouse		5,500,000
	Unearned Profit on Sale-Leaseback		2,000,000
	Original sale of warehouse.		
1	Leased Warehouse Under Capital Lease	7,500,000	
	Obligations Under Capital Lease		7,500,000
	Lease of warehouse.		
1	Obligations Under Capital Lease	1,071,082	
	Cash		1,071,082
	First lease payment. Payable in advance.		
Dec. 31	Amortization Expense on Leased Warehouse	375,000	
	Accumulated Amortization of Leased Warehouse		375,000
	Amortization of warehouse over 20 year period: ($7,500,000 ÷ 20).		
31	Interest Expense	642,892	
	Obligations Under Capital Lease	428,190	
	Cash		1,071,082
	Second lease payment. Interest expense: ($7,500,000 − $1,071,082) = $6,428,918; $6,428,918 × 10% = $642,892.		
31	Unearned Profit on Sale-Leaseback	100,000	
	Revenue Earned on Sale-Leaseback		100,000
	Recognition of revenue over 20 year life in proportion to the amortization of the leased asset.		

Scowcroft Co. (Purchaser-Lessor)

1984			
Jan. 1	Warehouse	7,500,000	
	Cash		7,500,000
	Purchase of warehouse.		
1	Minimum Lease Payments Receivable	11,710,820	
	Warehouse		7,500,000
	Unearned Interest Revenue		4,210,820
	Direct financing leaseback to Morgan Inc. Total receivable = (10 × $1,071,082) + (10 × $100,000) = $11,710,820.		

---

[33] *Computation of present value of lease:*
(a) Present value of 10 years' rentals:
$R(PVAF_{\overline{10-1}|\,10\%} + 1) = \$1,071,082 \times 6.7590 = \$7,239,443$
(b) Present value of second 10 years' rentals:
$R(PVAF_{\overline{10-1}|\,10\%} + 1) = \$100,000 \times 6.7590 = \$675,900$, present value at beginning of second ten years' lease period.
Present value at beginning of lease, 10 years earlier:
$A(PVF_{\overline{10}|\,10\%}) = \$675,900 \times .3855 = \$260,559$.
(c) Total present value, $7,239,443 + $260,559 = $7,500,000 (rounded).

Jan. 1	Cash	1,071,082	
	Minimum Lease Payments Receivable		1,071,082
	Receipt of first lease payment.		
Dec. 31	Cash	1,071,082	
	Unearned Interest Revenue	642,892	
	Lease Payments Receivable		1,071,082
	Interest Revenue		642,892
	Receipt of second lease payment. See computations under Morgan Inc.		

The amortization entries and recognition of the deferred gain on the sale for Morgan Inc. would be the same each year for the twenty year lease term. The interest expense and interest revenue amounts would decline each year using the interest method of computation.

If the lease had not met criteria three or four, it would have been recorded as an operating lease. The gain on the sale would have been deferred and recognized in proportion to the lease payments. If the initial sale had been at a loss, an immediate recognition of the loss would have been recorded.

CONCLUDING COMMENT

This chapter has discussed the basics of accounting for leases. Many lease arrangements are very complex and often involve third parties who assist in financing the transactions. These three party leases, referred to as **leveraged leases,** are considered to be beyond the scope of Intermediate Accounting, and thus are not discussed in this chapter. Adjustments to some of the lease amounts discussed in this chapter would be required if investment tax credits were involved for the leased property.

As indicated at the beginning of this chapter, the Board is convinced that more leases should be reported as capital items. Until such time as companies respond, more statements and interpretations from the Board on leases can be expected. In the meantime, full disclosure of lease arrangements seems to be a minimum requirement to meet the spirit of Statement No. 13.

QUESTIONS

1. Accounting for leases has changed markedly since World War II. Describe the changes in lease terms that have taken place and why these changes caused modifications in lease reporting.

2. What criteria must be met before a lease can be properly accounted for as a capital lease on the books of the lessee?

3. The third and fourth criteria for classifying a lease as a capital transaction are not as restrictive as originally intended. Explain how each of these criteria can be circumvented.

4. What is the basic difference between an operating lease and a capital lease from the viewpoint of the lessee?
5. If an operating lease requires the payment of uneven rental amounts over its life, how should the lessee recognize rental expense?
6. Rental expense for operating leases should be disclosed for each period for which an income statement is presented, with separate amounts for minimum rentals, contingent rentals, and sublease rentals. What further disclosure is required for operating leases with terms greater than one year?
7. What amount should be recorded as an asset and a liability for capital leases on the books of the lessee?
8. The FASB has identified a situation in which the present value of future minimum payments would not be used as the amount for the initial recording of an asset and liability for lessees under capital leases. Describe this situation and how an interest rate would be calculated for determining interest expense.
9. Why do asset and liability balances for capital leases usually differ after the first year?
10. A capitalized lease should be amortized in accordance with the lessee's normal depreciation policy. What life should be used for lease amortization?
11. The use of the capital lease method for a given lease will always result in a lower net income than the operating lease method. Do you agree? Explain fully.
12. If a lease contains a bargain purchase option, what entries are required on the books of the lessee under each of the following conditions?
(a) The bargain purchase option is exercised.
(b) The bargain purchase option is not exercised and no renewal of the lease is made.
(c) The bargain purchase option is not exercised, but a renewal of the lease is obtained.
13. Describe the specific disclosure requirements for lessees under capital leases.
14. How does classification of leases by the lessor differ from the classification by the lessee?
15. Contrast a sales-type lease from a direct financing lease.
16. In determining the classification of a lease, a lessor uses the criteria of the lessee plus two other criteria. What are these other criteria and why are they included in the determination of the classification of lessors' leases?
17. Under what circumstances would a lessor recognize as interest revenue over the lease term an amount greater than the difference between the gross amount of lease receivables and the cost of the asset to the lessor?
18. What disclosure is required by the FASB for sales-type and direct financing leases?
19. Unguaranteed residual values may accrue to the lessor at the expiration of the lease. How are these values treated in a sales-type lease?
20. Real estate leases can include land and/or buildings. Explain how the four criteria for determining lease capitalization are applied to the following:
(a) Leases involving land only.
(b) Leases involving land and buildings.
(c) Leases involving buildings only.
21. When should the profit or loss be recognized by the seller-lessee in a sale-leaseback arrangement?

DISCUSSION CASES

case 15-1 (More leases mean lower profits) In 1979, International Business Machines Inc. experienced a 55% or $4.2 billion increase in its computers out on lease.

The increase was partially caused by IBM's introducing a new series of medium sized computers, the 4300, at greatly reduced prices for the computing capacity. Potential purchasers of large-scale IBM computers jumped to the conclusion that maybe IBM would offer the same bargain prices for the new "H" series of large-scale computers under development, and switched from purchasing existing systems to leasing them to gain greater flexibility should their assumptions prove correct.

The following excerpt concerning these leases is taken from a *Fortune* article, "I.B.M.'s Battle to Look Superhuman Again," May 19, 1980, page 110.

> Equipment leased in 1979 probably had an if-sold value of some $15 billion. If leases had grown at a more normal rate of, say, 15 percent, and if I.B.M. had shipped the same number of machines, the company would have sold roughly $4 billion more equipment than it did. At I.B.M.'s usual after-tax margin of 13 or 14 percent, those extra sales should have added some $540 million to the company's 1979 profit, enough to lift it by 14 percent above the 1978 level.

IBM's overall profits for 1979 declined by 3.2%, the first year-to-year drop in two decades.

Based upon this excerpt, what method of accounting do you think IBM is using to record its leases of computers? How would alternative methods have altered the impact on income of this sudden switch by IBM's customers to leasing?

case 15-2 (How should the leases be recorded?) Milton Corporation entered into a lease arrangement with James Leasing Corporation for a certain machine. James's primary business is leasing and it is not a manufacturer or dealer. Milton will lease the machine for a period of three years, which is 50% of the machine's economic life. James will take possession of the machine at the end of the initial three-year lease and lease it to another smaller company that does not need the most current version of the machine. Milton does not guarantee any residual value for the machine and will not purchase the machine at the end of the lease term.

Milton's incremental borrowing rate is 10% and the implicit rate in the lease is $8\frac{1}{2}$%. Milton has no way of knowing the implicit rate used by James. Using either rate, the present value of the minimum lease payments is between 90% and 100% of the fair value of the machine at the date of the lease agreement.

Milton has agreed to pay all executory costs directly and no allowance for these costs is included in the lease payments.

James is reasonably certain that Milton will pay all lease payments, and, because Milton has agreed to pay all executory costs, there are no important uncertainties regarding costs to be incurred by James.

(a) With respect to Milton (the lessee) answer the following:
  (1) What type of lease has been entered into? Explain the reason for your answer.
  (2) How should Milton compute the appropriate amount to be recorded for the lease or asset acquired?
  (3) What accounts will be created or affected by this transaction and how will the lease or asset and other costs related to the transaction be matched with earnings?
  (4) What disclosures must Milton make regarding this lease or asset?

(b) With respect to James (the lessor) answer the following:
  (1) What type of leasing arrangement has been entered into? Explain the reason for your answer.
  (2) How should this lease be recorded by James and how are the appropriate amounts determined?
  (3) How should James determine the appropriate amount of earnings to be recognized from each lease payment?
  (4) What disclosures must James make regarding this lease?

(AICPA adapted)

EXERCISES

exercise 15-1 (Criteria for capitalizing leases)

Missile Supply Co. leases its equipment from Lloyd's Leasing Company. In each of the following cases, assuming none of the other criteria for capitalizing leases is met, determine whether the lease would be a capital lease or an operating lease under FASB Statement No. 13 on leases. Your decision is to be based only on the terms presented, considering each case independently of the others.

(a) At the end of the lease term, the market value of the equipment is expected to be $20,000. Missile has the option of purchasing it for $5,000.
(b) The fair market value of the equipment is $75,000. The present value of the lease payments is $60,000 (excluding any executory costs).
(c) Ownership of the property automatically reverts to Missile at the end of the lease term.
(d) The economic life of the equipment is 15 years. The lease term is for 12 years.
(e) The lease requires payments of $9,500 per year in advance, plus executory costs of $500 per year. The lease period is for three years, and Missile's incremental borrowing rate is 12%. The fair market value of the equipment is $28,000.
(f) The lease requires payments of $6,000 per year in advance which includes executory costs of $500 per year. The lease period is for three years, and Missile's incremental borrowing rate is 10%. The fair market value of the equipment is $17,000.

exercise 15-2 (Entries for operating lease—lessor and lessee)

The Marne Company purchased a machine on January 1, 1984, for $1,250,000 for the express purpose of leasing it. The machine was expected to have a six-year life from January 1, 1984, no salvage value, and be depreciated on a straight-line basis. On March 1, 1984, Marne leased the machine to Dal Company for $300,000 a year for a four-year period ending February 28, 1988. Marne incurred total maintenance and other related costs under the provisions of the lease of $15,000 relating to the year ended December 31, 1984. Dal paid $300,000 to Marne on March 1, 1984. Give all the 1984 entries relating to the lease on (a) Marne Company's books, (b) Dal Company's books. Assume both sets of books are maintained on the calendar-year basis.

(AICPA adapted)

exercise 15-3 (Entries for operating lease—lessee)

Mitchell Inc. leases equipment on a five-year lease. The lease payments are to be made in advance as shown below.

January 1, 1984	$125,000
January 1, 1985	80,000
January 1, 1986	75,000
January 1, 1987	60,000
January 1, 1988	50,000
Total	$390,000

The equipment is to be used evenly over the five-year period. For each of the five years, give the entry that should be made at the time the lease payment is made to allocate the proper share of rent expense to each period. The lease is classified as an operating lease by Mitchell Inc.

exercise 15-4 (Entries for capital lease—lessee)

Beckham Smelting Company entered into a fifteen-year old noncancelable lease beginning January 1, 1984, for equipment to use in its smelting operations. The term of the lease is essentially the expected economic life of the equipment. Beckham uses straight-line depreciation on all its owned assets. The operating terms of the lease call for annual payments of $125,000 in advance plus $5,000 per year as payment for executory costs, such as taxes and insurance, for the fifteen-year period of the lease. At the end of the fifteen years, the equipment is expected to be junked. The incremental borrowing rate of Beckham is 10%. The lessor's computed implicit interest rate is unknown to Beckham.

Record the lease on the books of Beckham and give all the entries necessary to record the lease for its first year plus the entry to record the second lease payment on December 31, 1984. Round to nearest dollar.

exercise 15-5 (Entries for capital lease—lessee)

On January 2, 1984, the Northeast Company entered into a noncancelable lease for a new warehouse. The warehouse was built to the Northeast Company's specifications and is in an area where rental to another lessee would be difficult. Rental payments are $250,000 a year for ten years, payable in advance. The warehouse has an estimated economic life of twenty years. The taxes and maintenance are to be paid by the Northeast Company, and the title to the warehouse is to be transferred to Northeast at the end of the lease term. Assume the cost of borrowing funds for this type of an asset by Northeast Company is 12%.

(1) Give the entry on Northeast's books that should be made at the inception of the lease.
(2) Give the entries for 1984 and 1985 assuming the second payment and subsequent payments are made on December 31 and assuming straight-line amortization.

exercise 15-6 (Schedule of lease payments)

Juab Construction Co. is leasing equipment from Chavez Inc. The lease calls for payments of $60,000 a year plus $5,000 a year executory costs for five years. The first payment is due on January 1 when the lease is signed with the other four payments due on December 31 of each year. Juab has also been given the option of purchasing the equipment at the end of the lease at a bargain price of $100,000. Juab has an incremental borrowing rate of 10%, the same as the implicit interest rate of Chavez. Juab has hired you as an accountant and asks for a schedule of its obligations under the lease contract. Prepare a schedule that shows all of the lessee's obligations.

exercise 15-7 (Entry for purchase by lessee)

The Gunn Enterprise Company leases many of its assets and capitalizes most of the leased assets. At December 31, 1984, the company had the following balances on its books in relation to a piece of specialized equipment.

Leased Equipment Under Capital Lease	$62,000
Accumulated Amortization—Leased Equipment	49,300
Remaining Obligation Due on Capital Leases	19,500

Amortization has been recorded up to the end of the year, and no accrued interest is involved. At that date, Gunn decided to purchase the equipment for $27,500, and paid cash to complete the purchase. Give the entry required on Gunn's books to record the purchase.

exercise 15-8 (Lease disclosures—lessee)

The following lease information was obtained by a staff auditor for a client, Natures Way Inc. at December 31, 1984. Indicate how this information should be presented in Natures Way's two-year comparative financial statements. Include any notes to the statements required to meet generally accepted accounting principles. Lease payments are made on January 1 of each year.

Leased building; minimum lease payments per year; ten years remaining life	$36,200
Executory costs per year (included in above minimum lease payments)	1,200

(continued)

Capitalized lease value, 12% interest	$266,987
Accumulated amortization of leased building at December 31, 1984	88,995
Amortization expense for 1984	17,799
Obligations under capital leases; balance at December 31, 1984	221,487
Obligations under capital leases; balance at December 31, 1983	232,757

exercise 15-9 (Computation of implicit interest rate)

Johnson Leasing leases equipment to Melville Manufacturing. The fair market value of the equipment is $442,974. Lease payments, excluding executory costs, are $70,000 per year, payable in advance, for ten years. What is the implicit rate of interest Johnson Leasing should use to record this capital lease on its books?

exercise 15-10 (Sales-type lease—lessor)

Barnes Co. leased equipment to Wills Inc. on April 1, 1984. The lease is appropriately recorded as a sale by Barnes. The lease is for an eight-year period ending March 31, 1992. The first of 8 equal annual payments of $250,000 (excluding executory costs) was made on April 1, 1984. The cost of the equipment to Barnes is $1,400,000. The equipment has an estimated useful life of eight years with no residual value expected. Barnes uses straight-line depreciation and takes a full year's depreciation in the year of purchase. The cash selling price of the equipment is $1,467,000.

(1) Give the entry required to record the lease on Barnes' books.
(2) How much interest revenue will Barnes recognize in 1984?

exercise 15-11 (Sales-type lease—lessor)

The Moss Leasing and Manufacturing Company uses leases as a means of financing sales of its equipment. Moss leased a machine to Eastman Awning for $15,000 per year, payable in advance, for a ten-year period. The cost of the machine to Moss was $90,000. The fair market value at the date of the lease was $97,500. Assume a residual value of zero at the end of the lease.

(1) Give the entry required to record the lease on Moss's books.
(2) How much profit will Moss recognize initially on the lease, excluding any interest revenue?
(3) How much interest revenue would be recognized in the first year?

exercise 15-12 (Direct financing lease—lessor)

The Armstrong Finance Company purchased a printing press to lease to the Walton Printing Company. The lease was structured so that at the end of the lease period of fifteen years Walton would own the printing press. Lease payments required in this lease were $75,000 (excluding executory costs) per year, the annual payment being payable in advance. The cost of the press to Armstrong was $627,503, which is also considered to be its fair market value at the time of the lease.

(1) Why is this a direct financing lease?
(2) Give the entry to record the lease transaction on the books of Armstrong Finance Company.
(3) Give the entry at the end of the first year on Armstrong Finance Company's books to recognize interest revenue.

exercise 15-13 (Direct financing lease with residual value)

The Flemming Insurance Company has decided to enter the leasing business. It acquires a specialized packaging machine for $300,000, and leases it for a period of six years after which the machine is returned to the insurance company for disposition. The expected unguaranteed residual value of the machine is $20,000. The lease terms are arranged so that a return of 12% is earned by the insurance company.

(1) Calculate the annual rent, payable in advance, required to yield the desired return.
(2) Prepare entries for the lessor for the first year of the lease assuming the machine is acquired and the lease is entered into on January 1, 1984. The first lease payment is made on January 1, 1984, and subsequent payments are made each December 31.
(3) Assuming the packaging machine is sold by Flemming at the end of the six years for $25,000, give the required entry to record the sale.

exercise 15-14 (Table for direct financing lease—lessor)

The Western Savings and Loan Company acquires a piece of specialized hospital equipment for $1,500,000 that it leases on January 1, 1984, to a local hospital for $391,006 per year, payable in advance. Because of rapid technological developments, the equipment is expected to be replaced after four years. It is expected that the machine will have a residual value of $200,000 to Western Savings at the end of the lease term. The implicit rate of interest in the lease is 10%.

Prepare a four-year table for Western Savings and Loan similar to Table 4 on page 573, but with a Gross Investment column replacing Lease Payments Receivable.

exercise 15-15 (Direct financing lease with residual value)

The Petty Automobile Company leases automobiles under the following terms: A three-year lease agreement is signed in which the lessor receives annual rental of $2,500 (in advance). At the end of the three years, the lessee agrees to make up any deficiency in residual value below $2,400 (guaranteed residual value to lessor); any excess over this amount accrues to the benefit of the lessee. The cash price of the automobile is $8,433. The implicit interest rate is 12%, which is known to the lessee and is less than the lessee's incremental borrowing rate. The lessee estimates the residual value at the end of three years to be $2,700, and depreciates its automobiles on a straight-line basis.

(1) Give the entries on the lessee's books required in the first year of the lease. Assume the lease begins May 1, 1984, the beginning of the lessee's fiscal year.
(2) What balances relative to the lease would appear on the lessee's balance sheet at the end of year 3?
(3) Assume the automobile is sold by the lessee for $2,900. Prepare the entries to record the sale and settlement with Petty Automobile Company.

exercise 15-16 (Entries for real estate lease with residual value—lessee)

Family Enterprises Inc. leases its land and building from an investment company. The terms of the lease are as follows:

(a) Lease term is twenty years, after which title to the property can be acquired for 25% of the market value at that date. The estimated remaining life of the building is thirty years.
(b) Annual lease payments payable in advance are $250,000 (excluding executory costs). Expected residual value of the property in twenty years is $800,000.
(c) Assume the current market value of the combined land and buildings is $2,370,945, of which the market value of the land is $350,000. The implicit interest rate of the lease is 10%.

What entries would be required on Family Enterprise's books for the first year of the lease? Assume the second lease payment is made on the last day of the first year.

exercise 15-17 (Lease of real estate—lessee)

Murdock Entertainment Company leased its land and buildings on a 10-year lease from M. L. Tenneysen. The property includes ten acres of land that is used for parking and an amusement area. The market value of the leased land is $500,000, and the market value of the leased buildings is $1,000,000. The annual rent for the property payable in advance is $221,926. There is no provision in the lease for Murdock to purchase the property at the conclusion of the lease. The buildings are estimated to have a twelve year remaining life, and are depreciated on a straight-line basis.

(1) Does the lease of Murdock Entertainment Company qualify as a capital lease? If yes, what criteria apply?
(2) Record the lease on Murdock's books and give the entries for the first full year of the lease assuming the first payment is made on January 1, 1984, and the second payment is made on December 31, 1984.

exercise 15-18 (Sale-leaseback accounting)

On July 1, 1984, Groberg Corporation sold equipment it had recently purchased to an unaffiliated company for $550,000. The equipment had a book value on Groberg's books of $450,000 and a remaining life of six years. On that same day, Groberg leased back the equipment at $100,000 per year, payable in advance, for a five-year period. Groberg's incremental borrowing rate is 10%, and it does not know the lessor's implicit interest rate. What entries are required for Groberg to record the transactions involving the equipment during the first full year assuming the second lease payment is made on June 30, 1985? Ignore consideration of the lessee's fiscal year. The lessee uses the double-declining balance method of depreciation for similar assets it owns outright.

PROBLEMS

problem 15-1 (Disclosure requirements — operating leases)

Aztec Mining and Manufacturing Company leases from Granite Leasing Company three machines under the following terms:

Machine #1	Lease Period — ten years, beginning April 1, 1978.
	Lease Payment — $18,000 per year, payable in advance.
Machine #2	Lease Period — ten years, beginning July 1, 1982.
	Lease Payment — $30,000 per year, payable in advance.
Machine #3	Lease Period — fifteen years, beginning January 1, 1983
	Lease Payment — $12,500 per year, payable in advance.

All of the above leases are classified as operating leases.

Instructions: Prepare the note to the 1984 financial statements that would be required to disclose the lease commitments of Aztec Mining and Manufacturing Company. Aztec uses the calendar year as its accounting period.

problem 15-2 (Entries for capital lease — lessee; lease criteria)

The Friel Company leased a machine on July 1, 1984, under a ten-year lease. The economic life of the machine is estimated to be 15 years. Title to the machine passes to Friel Company at the expiration of the lease and thus the lease is a capital lease. The lease payments are $40,500 per year, including executory costs of $3,000 per year, all payable in advance annually. The incremental borrowing rate of the company is 10% and the lessor's implicit interest rate is unknown. The Friel Company uses the straight-line method of depreciation and uses the calendar year as its fiscal year.

Instructions:

(1) Give all entries on the books of the lessee relating to the lease for 1984.
(2) Assume the lessor retains title to the machine at the expiration of the lease, there is no bargain renewal or purchase option, and that the fair market value of the equipment was $270,000 as of the lease date. Using the criteria for distinguishing between operating and capital leases according to FASB Statement No. 13, what would be the amortization or depreciation expense for 1984?

problem 15-3 (Entries for capital lease — lessee)

Ellis Electric Company has a policy of acquiring its equipment by leasing. On January 2, 1984, the company signed a lease for a coiling machine. The lease stipulates that payments of $45,000 (excluding executory costs) will be made annually for five years. The payments are to be made in advance on December 31 of each year. At the end of the five-year period, the company may purchase the machine for $20,000. Its estimated fair market value at that date is $75,000. The company's incremental borrowing rate is 12%, which is less than the implicit interest rate. The estimated economic life of the equipment is eight years. Ellis uses straight-line depreciation for all equipment and uses the calendar year for reporting purposes.

Instructions:

(1) Compute the amount to be capitalized as an asset for the lease of the coiling machine.
(2) Prepare a table similar to Table 3, page 567, that shows the computation of the interest expense for each period.
(3) Give the journal entries that would be made on Ellis Electric Company's books for the first two years of the lease.
(4) Assume on December 31, 1988, the purchase option is exercised. Give the journal entry to record the exercise of the option on Ellis Electric Company's books.

problem 15-4 (Sales-type lease — lessor)

The Royal Shipbuilding Company uses leases as a method of selling its products. In 1983, the company constructed a ferry to ply the waters of the Puget Sound between Seattle and Bremerton. The ferry was leased to Sea Brem Ferry Line on April 1, 1984, for $150,000 (excluding executory costs) per year for twenty years, paid annually in advance. The fair market value of the ferry on the lease date was $1,404,735. The cost of the ferry was $1,294,855. At the end of the lease period, the title to the property passes to Sea Brem.

Instructions:

(1) From the information given above, compute the amount of financial revenue that will be earned over the lease term and the manufacturer's profit that will be earned immediately by Royal.
(2) Give the entries to record the lease on Royal's books. What is the implicit rate of interest on the lease?
(3) Give all the entries necessary to record the operating of the lease for the first three years, exclusive of initial entry. Royal's accounting period is the calendar year.
(4) What would be the balance in each of the following accounts at December 31, 1986: Unearned Interest Revenue and Minimum Lease Payments Receivable?

problem 15-5 (Entries for capital lease — lessee and lessor)

The Truman Company leased equipment from the Roosevelt Company on October 1, 1981. The lease is appropriately recorded as a purchase by Truman and as a sale by Roosevelt. The lease is for an eight-year period expiring September 30, 1989. Equal annual payments under the lease are $600,000 (excluding executory costs) and are due on October 1 of each year. The first payment was made on October 1, 1981. The cost of the equipment reported as inventory on Roosevelt's accounting records was $3,000,000. The equipment has an estimated useful life of eight years with no residual value expected. Truman uses straight-line depreciation and computes depreciation to the nearest month. The rate of interest agreed to in the lease is 10%. On October 1, 1984, Truman Company purchased the leased equipment for $2,700,000.

Instructions: Prepare journal entries on the books of both the lessee and the lessor as follows:

(1) Entries in 1981 to record the lease, including adjustments necessary at December 31, 1981, the end of each company's fiscal year.
(2) All entries required in 1982. The companies do not make reversing entries.
(3) Entry at October 1, 1984, to record the sale and purchase assuming no previous entries had been made in connection with the lease during the year.

problem 15-6 (Accounting for capital lease—lessee and lessor)

The Jorgensen Equipment Company both leases and sells its equipment to its customers. The most popular line of equipment includes a machine that costs $140,000 to manufacture. The standard lease terms provide for five annual payments of $55,000 each (excluding executory costs), with the first payment due when the lease is signed and subsequent payments due on December 31 of each year. The implicit rate of interest in the contract is 10% per year. Madison Powder Co. leases one of these machines on January 2, 1984. Initial direct costs of $10,000 are incurred by Jorgensen on January 2, 1984, to obtain the lease. Madison's incremental borrowing rate is determined to be 12%. The equipment is very specialized, and it is assumed it will have no salvage value after five years. Assume the lease qualifies as a capital lease and a sales-type lease for lessee and lessor respectively. Also assume that both the lessee and the lessor are on a calendar-year basis and that the lessee is aware of the lessor's implicit interest rate.

Instructions:

(1) Give all entries required on the books of Madison Powder Co. to record the lease of equipment from Jorgensen Equipment Company for the year 1984. The depreciation on owned equipment is computed once a year on the straight-line basis.
(2) Give entries required on the books of Jorgensen Equipment Company to record the lease of equipment to Madison Powder Co. for the year 1984.
(3) Prepare the balance sheet section involving lease balances for both the lessee's and lessor's financial statements at December 31, 1984.
(4) Determine the amount of expense Madison Powder Co. will report relative to the lease for 1984 and the amount of revenue Jorgensen Equipment Company will report for the same period.

problem 15-7 (Accounting for direct financing lease—lessee and lessor)

The Fuller Leasing Company buys equipment for leasing to various manufacturing companies. On October 1, 1983, Fuller leases a strap press to the Cordon Shoe Company. The cost of the machine to Fuller, which approximated its fair market value on the lease date, was $163,590. The lease payments stipulated in the lease are $27,500 per year in advance for the ten-year period of the lease. The payments include executory costs of $2,500 per year. The expected economic life of the equipment is also ten years. The title to the equipment remains in the hands of Fuller Leasing Company at the end of the lease term, although only nominal scrap value is expected at that time. Cordon's incremental borrowing rate is 10% and it uses the straight-line method of depreciation on all owned equipment. Both Cordon and Fuller have a fiscal year end of September 30 and lease payments are made on September 30.

Instructions:

(1) Prepare the entries to record the lease on the books of the lessor and lessee assuming the lease meets the criteria of a direct-financing lease for the lessor and a capital lease for the lessee.
(2) Compute the implicit rate of interest of the lessor.
(3) Give all entries required to account for the lease on both the lessee's and lessor's books for the fiscal years 1984, 1985, and 1986 [exclusive of the initial entry required in (1)].

problem 15-8 (Accounting for sales-type lease—lessee and lessor)

Lewis Manufacturing Company manufactures and leases a variety of items. On January 2, 1984, Lewis leased a hydraulic left-handed skyhook to Tew Industries Co. The lease is for six years with an annual amount of $38,000 payable annually in advance. The skyhook has an estimated useful life of eight years, and was manufactured by Lewis at a cost of $130,000. The lease payment includes executory costs of $1,500 per year. It is estimated that the skyhook will have a residual value of $50,000 at the end of the six-year lease term. There is no guarantee by the lessee of this amount, nor is there any provision for purchase or renewal of the skyhook by Tew at the end of the lease term. The skyhook has a fair market value at the lease inception of $203,089. The implicit rate of interest in the contract is 10%, the same rate at which Tew Industries Co. can borrow money at their bank. Tew depreciates assets on a straight-line basis. All lease payments after the first one are made on December 31 of each year.

Instructions:

(1) Give the entries required on the books of the lessor and lessee to record the incurrence of the lease and its operation for the first year, assuming the lease meets the qualifications for a capital lease for the lessee and a sales-type lease for the lessor.
(2) Show how the lease would appear on the balance sheet of Lewis Manufacturing Company and Tew Industries Co. (if applicable) as of December 31, 1984.
(3) Assume Lewis Manufacturing Co. sold the skyhook at the end of the six-year lease for $60,000. Give the entry to record the sale assuming all lease entries have been properly made.

problem 15-9 (Capital lease computations—lessee and lessor)

Dumont Corporation, a lessor of office machines, purchased a new machine for $450,000 on December 31, 1984. The machine was delivered the same day (by prior arrangement) to Finley Company, the lessee. The following information relating to the lease transaction is available:

(a) The leased asset had an estimated useful life of seven years which coincides with the lease term.
(b) At the end of the lease term, the machine will revert to Dumont, at which time it is expected to have a residual value of $60,000 (none of which is guaranteed by Finley).
(c) Dumont's implicit interest rate (on its net investment) is 12%, which is known by Finley.
(d) Finley's incremental borrowing rate is 14% at December 31, 1984.
(e) Lease rentals consist of seven equal annual payments, the first of which was paid on December 31, 1984.
(f) The lease is appropriately accounted for as a direct financing lease by Dumont and as a capital lease by Finley. Both the lessor and lessee are calendar-year corporations and depreciate all plant assets on the straight-line basis.

Instructions:

(1) Compute the annual rental under the lease. Round to nearest dollar.
(2) Compute the amounts of the minimum lease payments receivable and the unearned interest revenue that Dumont should disclose at the inception of the lease on December 31, 1984.
(3) What expense should Finley record for the year ended December 31, 1985?

(AICPA adapted)

16 ACCOUNTING FOR PENSIONS

CHAPTER OBJECTIVES

Describe the characteristics of corporate pension plans, and define the terminology commonly employed in these plans.

Trace the development of accounting standards for pensions.

Identify and describe the accounting issues related to pension accounting for employers.

Illustrate methods of accounting for employers' pension costs, including financial statement disclosure requirements.

Identify and describe the accounting issues related to financial statement disclosure for pension plans.

Pension accounting is another specialized area that has become prominent on the agenda of the Financial Accounting Standards Board. Like leases discussed in the previous chapter, pension agreements can often be very complex and can have a material effect on the financial statements of employers who typically pay for a major part of the plan. Also like leases, there has been much controversy over how much of a pension contract should be recognized in the formal financial statements at its inception. Another set of problems revolves around financial reporting of pension plans as separate entities. Before looking at the many accounting issues dealing with pensions, it is necessary that a general discussion of pension plans and their unique terminology be presented.

CHARACTERISTICS OF PENSION PLANS

The general objective of all pension plans is to set aside funds during an employee's productive years so that at retirement the funds and earnings from investment of the funds may be returned to the employee in lieu of earned wages. The primary responsibility for setting funds aside has varied over time and with the economic environment. In some societies and times, the emphasis has been placed upon individuals assuming the responsibility for setting funds aside for future use, usually through prudent investment of a portion of current earnings. In other societies and times, the individual responsibility has been shared with the employer and/or government. This latter condition has become prominent in the United States, especially in the mid and late twentieth century. The depression of the 1930s led to the involvement of the United States Government in providing retirement benefits through the social security system. As described in Chapter 13, the costs of this program are shared between the employee and the employer. However, this program has always been a minimal one in terms of benefits and has been supplemented extensively by private pension plans, frequently negotiated between labor unions and employers. In more recent years, the United States Government has emphasized shared responsibility for retirement benefits by providing tax incentives for individuals to establish their own tax-sheltered retirement programs. Illustrative of this is the widely advertised encouragement for individuals to establish Individual Retirement Accounts (IRAs), contributions to which can be deducted directly from taxable income.

Growth of Private Pension Plans

The number of pension plans and the size of their investment portfolios have grown sharply in the period since World War II. In a report issued in 1979 by Johnson & Higgins, a professional consulting firm, it was stated that:

> Pension assets of corporations and other non-governmental entities comprise the largest part of private capital in America—in excess of $300 billion at the end of 1978 and estimated to exceed one trillion dollars by the late 1980's.[1]

With assets of this magnitude, these plans greatly influence economic institutions, such as the stock market and employer corporations that continually contribute to these plans.

The rapid growth of pension plans, not surprisingly, has been accompanied by many abuses. Until recently, little control was exercised over the pension plans themselves. Some employers tried initially to carry their own plans, and employees often found money for retirement payments to be lacking when retirement time arrived. Some employees were reportedly terminated a short time before retirement, with no benefits accruing to them. Employees of companies that entered into bankruptcy found the obligation

[1] *Funding Costs and Liabilities of Large Corporate Pension Plans* (New York: Johnson & Higgins, 1979), p. 1.

of the company to them for retirement benefits dissolved with the company. Pension plans themselves were sometimes subject to dilution of their resources through mismanagement or even fraud. Reporting standards for pension plans were inadequate and sometimes totally lacking. To overcome these problems, often associated with company-operated plans, institutions such as insurance companies, banks, and unions assumed a trustee role and began to administer the plans. With outside trustees, more order was introduced to the pension plans through actuarial refinement and more careful management of the burgeoning assets. Yet, very few plans were subject to independent financial audit. As a result of pension plan irregularities and abuses, Congress enacted a massive piece of legislation in 1974 officially known as the **Employee Retirement Income Security Act of 1974 (ERISA)**, commonly called the Pension Reform Act of 1974. The act effected a wide spectrum of reforms and many regulations covering all pensions. Included in the act were provisions requiring minimum funding of plans, minimum rights to employees upon termination of their employment, and minimum disclosure and audit requirements for trustees of pension plans. In addition to these provisions, the Act called for creation of a special federal agency, the **Pension Benefit Guaranty Corporation (PBGC)**, to help protect employee pension benefits when pension plans are terminated as a result of bankruptcy or other causes. When a plan is terminated, ERISA requires the employer to contribute up to 30 percent of its net assets to provide benefits for the employees covered by the plan. In effect, PBGC actually becomes the trustee for pension plans that terminate. The PBGC also administers a fund supported by premiums charged to participating companies.

The economic recession of the early 1980s and the resultant business failures of many large U.S. companies led to a heavy drain on the PBGC fund. When the PBGC was formed, the premium charged to employers was $1 per employee per year. In January 1981, the premium was increased to $2.60. Even with the increase, in 1981 the PBGC paid $57 million to 39,000 participants and finished the year with a deficit of $147 million. This led to a request for a $6 premium per employee per year. With companies such as financially troubled International Harvester Inc. having an unfunded pension liability of over $1 billion, the ability of the PBGC to truly stand behind the pension is highly questionable.[2]

As discussed later in this chapter, under currently accepted accounting principles, employers are not required to recognize certain unfunded pension liabilities. This is the major area of controversy surrounding pension accounting. Past failures and threatened failures of U.S. companies demonstrate forcefully the magnitude of the unrecorded pension liability for many companies.

The provisions of ERISA are complex, but they are playing a dominant role in establishing a framework for identifying the accounting issues that

---

[2] "Some Fear Harvester Could Dump Big Pension Debt on U.S. Agency," *Wall Street Journal*, December 7, 1982, p. 27.

must be resolved to properly report pension plans on the statements of the involved parties.

Types of Pension Plans

Many different types of pension plans have evolved through the years. Some plans are individualized and cover a **single employer**. Others cover many companies, and are referred to as **multiemployer** plans. Federal regulations vary depending on which type of plan is involved. Pension plans may be **contributory** or **noncontributory**, depending on whether the employee contributes to the cost of the plan. Under noncontributory plans, the employer pays the entire cost of the plan. If a pension plan meets certain requirements of the Internal Revenue Code, it is referred to as a **qualified plan**. Most plans are designed to meet the qualifying criteria because of the substantial tax advantages of a qualified plan. An employer's contributions to a qualified plan are deductible when paid, within certain limitations. Earnings from plan investments are exempt from income tax, and the benefits are taxable to employees only when received.

Most pension plans can be classified as defined benefit plans or defined contribution plans. **Defined benefit plans** specify the benefits employees will receive upon retirement. Contributions to these plans are based on the specified benefits and are usually determined through formulas that consider the current level of employee compensation, years of service, and other variables that directly affect estimated future benefits. These include future compensation levels, life expectancies, employee turnover, rates of investment returns, and rates of inflation. The quantitative determination of the contribution is made by actuaries based on estimates of these variables referred to as **actuarial assumptions**.

In contrast, **defined contribution plans** specify the amount to be contributed annually by the employer rather than the benefits to be paid. Typically, the contribution is related to the employer's earnings (profit sharing), employees' salaries, or possibly employee productivity. Benefits eventually paid are based on the amount contributed. Although the amount of future benefits can be estimated, no promise is made as to the actual amount to be paid to the employee.

More accounting problems are associated with defined benefit plans than with defined contribution plans. A majority of single employer pension plans are defined benefit plans, and most of the accounting literature dealing with pensions concentrates on this type.

In addition to accounting for formal pension plans, companies must determine how to account for other **postemployment benefits**. Such benefits include postemployment health care and life insurance benefits. Because these benefits are also related to the productive service years of an employee, the accounting treatment for these costs is directly related to the accounting treatment for pensions. The remainder of this chapter will emphasize accounting and reporting for defined benefit pension plans and postemployment benefits.

Vesting Provisions

Vested benefits are those benefits that are not contingent upon any future services by employees. These benefits are those available to the employee at retirement should he or she leave the company's employment before retirement. To the extent these vested benefits exceed the amount of assets in the pension plan, the vested benefits are unfunded. ERISA established some definite guidelines for vesting, generally requiring pension plans to grant vesting rights faster than had been true in existing pension plans. Three alternative minimum vesting schedules were described:

(1) A graduated schedule under which 25 percent of accrued benefits becomes vested after five years of service, an additional 5 percent becomes vested in each of the following five years, and an additional 10 percent becomes vested in each of the succeeding five years.
(2) Vesting of accrued benefits is 100 percent by the end of ten years of service.
(3) The "rule of 45" under which accrued benefits of an employee with at least five years of service becomes 50 percent vested when the sum of his or her age and years of service equals forty-five (or ten years of service without regard to age), and an additional 10 percent of accrued benefits vests in each of the following five years.

With more rapid vesting requirements, the number of plans with unfunded vested benefits has significantly increased.

PENSION COSTS

There are three major issues related to pension costs: measurement, recognition, and disclosure. Measurement is essentially an actuarial problem; however, the cost of providing future benefits as determined by the actuary normally provides the basis for recognition and disclosure by accountants. An understanding of these issues requires an understanding of the elements of pension costs.

Elements of Pension Costs

Because retirement benefits under defined benefit plans are affected by the years of employee service, new pension plans must provide funds for benefits earned prior to the inception of the plan. The costs relating to these benefits are referred to as **past service costs**, and are defined as the present value of the future benefits arising from services performed by employees before the pension plan was initiated. After a plan is adopted, additional future benefits accrue to employees for current services. The costs of these benefits are referred to as **normal costs** and are defined as the present value of the increase in future benefits arising from the current year of service to the company. At any given date (valuation date) after the plan is in effect, all past service costs and normal costs preceding the valuation date are referred to as **prior service costs**. Because these various costs are accounted for somewhat differently, the relationship between them is important. The following illustration helps to distinguish these cost elements:

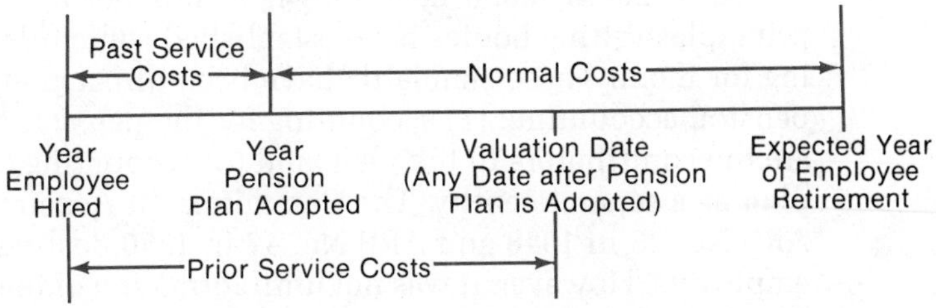

Frequently, pension plans are amended to provide additional benefits to offset the impact of inflation on retirement benefits. Usually these amendments increase benefits related to services rendered prior to the amendment, thus increasing prior service costs. Prior service costs attributable to a plan amendment are accounted for in the same manner as past service costs.

Methods of Determining Pension Costs

As mentioned previously, the costs of providing retirement benefits under a defined benefit plan are determined by actuaries based on a set of actuarial assumptions. There are several different types of **actuarial cost methods,** sometimes referred to as **funding methods.** However, most of these can be divided into two categories: (1) the accrued benefit cost method and (2) the projected benefit cost methods.

The **accrued benefit cost method,** also referred to as the **unit credit method,** identifies a distinct unit of retirement benefit with each year of credited service, and the present value of the unit can be computed at any date. The computation of past service costs under this method is easily made. The **projected benefit cost methods** relate the cost to the prospective benefits of a closed group of employees. Costs are computed so as to remain constant over the life of the employee. Projected benefit methods include the following popular methods:

(1) Entry age normal
(2) Attained age normal
(3) Aggregate
(4) Individual level premium

The latter two methods spread past service costs over the entire pension period rather than over just a predetermined number of years, and thus do not provide for a separate computation of past service costs. Consistent use of any plan provides for an orderly accrual of funds for the plan.

The type of funding used determines the timing of employer contributions to the trustee. In many cases, the amount of periodic cost charged as an expense by the employer is equal to the contribution for the period.

DEVELOPMENT OF ACCOUNTING STANDARDS FOR PENSION COSTS AND PENSION PLANS

As pension plans have grown in number and popularity, accounting principles-setting bodies have established standards to govern the accounting for them. These standards have been directed at two different levels of pension accounting: (1) accounting for the **pension costs of employers** who are the contributors to the plan, and (2) accounting for the **trusteed pension plan** as a separate entity. The Committee on Accounting Procedures issued ARB No. 36 in 1948 and ARB No. 47 in 1956 dealing with pension costs for employers. However, it was not until formation of the Accounting Principles Board that a comprehensive approach was taken to pension accounting. In 1965, the Accounting Research Division of the AICPA issued Accounting Research Study No. 8, "Accounting for the Cost of Pension Plans." This was followed in 1966 by APB Opinion No. 8 that established some significant guidelines to reduce the amount of income manipulation in employers' statements made possible through the lack of comprehensive standards to govern accounting for pension costs.[3]

This standard became widely adopted, and was considered an adequate document by the majority of accountants until ERISA was enacted. Because ERISA required pension plans to be audited, it became more important to have standards governing accounting for the trusteed *pension plans* themselves. The Financial Accounting Standards Board placed this on its early agenda and, in 1975, issued a discussion memorandum on pension plans. After extensive public hearings, two exposure drafts, and over 1,000 letters of comment from accountants and interested parties, FASB Statement No. 35, "Accounting and Reporting by Defined Benefit Pension Plans," was issued in March 1980.

As soon as the pension plan project was completed, the FASB authorized a reexamination of certain parts of APB Opinion No. 8 dealing with accounting for pension costs for employers. The Board had earlier issued an interpretation to Opinion No. 8 stating that there was no obvious conflict between ERISA and the requirements of APB Opinion No. 8.[4] However, the research and discussions leading to FASB Statement No. 35 raised issues that could have an impact on Opinion No. 8. Thus, the FASB began an intensive study of employers' accounting for pensions and other postemployment benefits in light of ERISA and Statement No. 35.

As a preliminary guide, the Board issued a background paper, "Accounting for Pensions by Employers," in early 1980. The study led to the issuance of a discussion memorandum in February 1981.[5] In November 1982, the Board issued a document setting forth its preliminary views, including some significant recommendations for changing the accounting and report-

---

[3]*Opinions of the Accounting Principles Board, No. 8,* "Accounting for the Cost of Pension Plans" (New York: American Institute of Certified Public Accountants, 1966).

[4]*FASB Interpretation No. 3,* "Accounting for the Cost of Pension Plans Subject to the Employee Retirement Income Security Act of 1974" (Stamford: Financial Accounting Standards Board, 1974).

[5]*FASB Discussion Memorandum,* "Employers' Accounting for Pensions and Other Postemployment Benefits" (Stamford: Financial Accounting Standards Board, February 1981).

ing by employers.[6] Because of the importance of the pension area, a long period of time for discussion was provided by the Board. No final action on pension accounting for employers is anticipated before 1985.

As an interim measure pending the results of the current study, in May 1980, the FASB issued Statement No. 36, "Disclosure of Pension Information." This statement, an amendment to APB Opinion No. 8, was directed to employers and specified additional disclosure considered necessary to make reporting requirements for employers more like those for the pension plans.

Because accounting for pensions by employers is still governed by APB Opinion No. 8 and the disclosure guidelines in FASB Statement No. 36, the requirements of these two documents are outlined in this chapter. However, the authors believe that the recommendations and preliminary views of the Board also should be presented as an appendix to the chapter. The recommendations are significantly different from present practice and are controversial. The final FASB statement may be quite different from the preliminary position of the Board and will require careful study when issued.

ISSUES RELATED TO PENSION ACCOUNTING FOR EMPLOYERS

Recognition was identified earlier as a major issue in accounting for pension costs of employers. The principal problems include: (1) accounting for unfunded prior service costs, (2) determining the amount of periodic pension expense, and (3) accounting for actuarial gains and losses on the pension investment portfolio. Each of these areas will be explored in depth in the following pages.

Accounting for Unfunded Prior Service Costs

Unfunded prior service costs are those prior pension costs, including past service costs, past normal costs, and prior service costs arising from a plan amendment, not yet funded to the trustee. APB Opinion No. 8 does not require reporting this amount as a liability unless the company clearly "has a legal obligation for pension cost in excess of amounts paid or accrued."[7] This sometimes occurs when vesting rights must be legally funded, and failure to do so constitutes a legal liability. For example, if the amount funded fails to meet the minimum funding standards specified by ERISA, and a waiver of the requirement has not been secured from the Secretary of the Treasury, a liability must be created. In addition, a liability should be recognized when a plan is terminated, and there is a company liability for the benefits in excess of the plan assets as defined by ERISA. Other than these exceptions, the only liability for pension costs currently required to be recognized by GAAP is that arising when the amount funded in a given year

---

[6] *Preliminary Views of the Financial Accounting Standards Board,* "Employers' Accounting for Pensions and Other Postemployment Benefits" (Stamford: Financial Accounting Standards Board, November 1982).

[7] *Opinions of the Accounting Principles Board, No. 8, op cit.,* par. 18.

is less than the amount charged to expense in that year. This limited liability requirement is discussed more fully in the next section, accounting for the amount of periodic pension cost.

Prior to ERISA, an employer often had only limited liability for unfunded prior service costs. In the event bankruptcy occurred, claims against the plan by the employee were usually limited to the amount of funds in the plan. ERISA extends significantly the liability of employers to their employees, including the previously mentioned requirement that up to 30% of an employer's net assets be allocated to the employees' benefit in the event the pension plan is terminated. In light of this extended liability, the failure to record unfunded prior service costs has become a central issue in the reexamination of employer pension costs being made by the FASB.

If a liability for unfunded prior service costs were to be recorded, the offsetting debit to the liability should be to a deferred charge. This deferred charge would be written off over future periods and the liability would be reduced as payments were made. In form, this accounting would be much like that for a capitalized lease on the books of the lessee. For example, assume the prior service costs of a new plan were computed at $300,000. The following entry would be made at the inception of the plan:

Deferred Pension Costs	300,000	
Unfunded Prior Service Costs		300,000

If the funding is to take place with equal payments over ten years at 10 percent interest, payments being made at the end of each year, the annual funding contribution would be $48,823.[8] Assuming the deferred charge is written off on a straight-line basis over ten years, the following entries would be made at the end of the first year to record the amortization of the deferred charge and the first prior service cost payment:

Amortization of Prior Service Costs	30,000	
Deferred Pension Costs		30,000
Interest Expense	30,000	
Unfunded Prior Service Costs	18,823	
Cash		48,823

$300,000 × 10% = $30,000 interest expense.
$48,823 − $30,000 = $18,823.

This example is a very simplified illustration of what would happen if a liability for unfunded prior service costs were to be recorded. Complicating factors, such as amendments to the plan and changes in actuarial variables that alter the benefits to be paid or the value of the plan's investment portfolio, would affect the accounting entries required and must be studied as part of any decision to change current practice. The accrual of unfunded prior service costs is one of the preliminary recommendations discussed in the appendix to this chapter.

---

[8] $PV_n = R(PVAF_{\overline{n}|i})$
$\$300{,}000 = R(PVAF_{\overline{10}|10\%})$
$R = \$300{,}000 \div 6.1446$
$R = \$48{,}823$

Determining the Amount of Periodic Pension Cost

Since no entries generally have been made on the employer's books at the inception of a pension plan, charges to pension expense have traditionally been related to the amount of funds contributed to the plan. Contributions to the trustee usually consist of both normal costs and a portion of past service costs. Although normal cost contributions are usually made each year because they relate to current service, past service contributions may be more flexible depending on the actuarial cost method used for funding. Because of this flexibility, contributions may not represent a proper charge to expense under the accrual concept required by APB Opinion No. 8. The Opinion requires that past service costs be allocated in a rational and systematic manner to current and future periods. No part of past service cost is considered a charge against periods preceding the adoption of a plan. Similarly, prior service costs arising from a plan amendment are allocated to periods subsequent to the amendment date. The Committee on Accounting Procedures made this decision in 1948, and it has been supported by succeeding standard-setting bodies.

Different Funding Methods. If an employer decides to recognize pension costs on a basis different from the funding, the difference is either debited to an asset account or credited to a liability account. Because the computation of pension plan contributions includes an assumed rate of return on plan investments (interest rate), **interest equivalents** must be considered when the pattern of expense recognition differs from the funding pattern. Three different conditions can arise in any given year: Condition A—the contribution and the expense recognized are the same; Condition B—the contribution exceeds the expense recognized thus creating a deferred charge; Condition C—the expense recognized exceeds the contribution thus creating a liability. Assuming both the funding and expense recognition are computed as level amounts using annuity formulas, the accounting entries for each of these three conditions are given in the following sections. It is assumed in these illustrations that normal costs are funded each year.

Condition A—Contribution and Expense Recognition the Same. To illustrate this condition, assume that the past service costs for the Andrus Co. at the adoption of a pension plan are \$310,500. The interest rate used in the plan is 5%. If contributions are made at the end of each year for twenty years, the amount of each contribution (rent) and the expense recognized each year would be computed as follows:

$$PV_n = R(PVAF_{\overline{n}|i})$$

$$R = \frac{PV_n}{PVAF_{\overline{n}|i}}$$

$$R = \frac{\$310{,}500}{\text{Table IV}_{\overline{20}|5\%}}$$

$$R = \frac{\$310{,}500}{12.4622}$$

$$R = \$24{,}915$$

Thus, payments of $24,915 for twenty years would liquidate the past service cost liability. Because the company is charging the past service cost over the same twenty-year period that the contributions are being made, no asset or liability will arise. If normal costs for the first year are $26,500, the entry to record pension cost for the year would be as follows:

Pension Expense	51,415	
Cash		51,415
$24,915 + $26,500 = $51,415.		

Because normal costs will usually vary each year as conditions change, the amount charged to expense and contributed to the trustee will vary. However, the past service cost charge will be the same each year.

Condition B—Contribution Faster Than Expense Accrual. If the employer decides to amortize the past service costs over a longer period, say twenty-five years, the trustee has funds in advance of the accrual period, and pension expense is reduced by the interest equivalent revenue. This is illustrated in Table 1. The annual annuity amortization for twenty-five years is $22,031 ($310,500 ÷ 14.0939).

TABLE 1
Andrus Company
Past Service Cost Accounting Accrual of
Deferred Pension Expense Amortization Period—25 Years

Year	(A) Funding Contribution 20 Years	(B) Annuity Amortization	(C) Less Interest (5%) of Previous Deferred Balance	(D) Pension Expense (B − C)	(E) Deferred Charge Increase (Decrease) (A − D)	(F) Deferred Pension Expense Balance
1	$24,915	$22,031	$ 0	$22,031	$ 2,884	$ 2,884
2	24,915	22,031	144	21,887	3,028	5,912
3	24,915	22,031	296	21,735	3,180	9,092
4	24,915	22,031	455	21,576	3,339	12,431
5	24,915	22,031	622	21,409	3,506	15,937
6	24,915	22,031	797	21,234	3,681	19,618
7	24,915	22,031	981	21,050	3,865	23,483
8	24,915	22,031	1,174	20,857	4,058	27,541
9	24,915	22,031	1,377	20,654	4,261	31,802
10	24,915	22,031	1,590	20,441	4,474	36,276
11	24,915	22,031	1,814	20,217	4,698	40,974
12	24,915	22,031	2,049	19,982	4,933	45,907
13	24,915	22,031	2,295	19,736	5,179	51,086
14	24,915	22,031	2,554	19,477	5,438	56,524
15	24,915	22,031	2,826	19,205	5,710	62,234
16	24,915	22,031	3,112	18,919	5,996	68,230
17	24,915	22,031	3,412	18,619	6,296	74,526
18	24,915	22,031	3,726	18,305	6,610	81,136
19	24,915	22,031	4,057	17,974	6,941	88,077
20	24,915	22,031	4,404	17,627	7,288	95,365
21	0	22,031	4,768	17,263	(17,263)	78,102
22	0	22,031	3,905	18,126	(18,126)	59,976
23	0	22,031	2,999	19,032	(19,032)	40,944
24	0	22,031	2,047	19,984	(19,984)	20,960
25	0	22,031	1,071*	20,960	(20,960)	–0–

*Adjusted for rounding differences

Assuming the same normal costs of $26,500 included in the preceding illustration, the entry for the first year to record pension costs would be as follows:

Pension Expense.	48,531	
Deferred Pension Expense	2,884	
Cash.		51,415
$22,031 + $26,500 = $48,531.		

The deferred pension expense would increase each year by the difference between the amount contributed and the amount expensed, including an interest equivalent adjustment, until the twenty-year funding period has expired. During the remaining five years of the accrual period, the balance in the deferred account would be charged to expense.

Condition C—Expense Accrual Faster Than Contribution. If the employer decides to amortize past service costs over a shorter period, say fifteen years, the trustee has deferred receiving funds as compared with the period of accrual, and an addition to pension expense for the interest equivalent must be made as illustrated in Table 2 below. The annual annuity amortization for fifteen years is $29,914 ($310,500 ÷ 10.3797).

TABLE 2
Andrus Company
Past Service Cost Accounting Accrual of
Pension Liability Amortization Period—15 Years

Year	(A) *Funding Contribution 20 Years*	(B) *Annuity Amortization*	(C) *Add Interest (5%) on Previous Liability Balance*	(D) *Pension Expense (B + C)*	(E) *Liability Increase (Decrease) (D − A)*	(F) *Liability Balance*
1	$24,915	$29,914	$ 0	$29,914	$ 4,999	$ 4,999
2	24,915	29,914	250	30,164	5,249	10,248
3	24,915	29,914	512	30,426	5,511	15,759
4	24,915	29,914	788	30,702	5,787	21,546
5	24,915	29,914	1,077	30,991	6,076	27,622
6	24,915	29,914	1,381	31,295	6,380	34,002
7	24,915	29,914	1,700	31,614	6,699	40,701
8	24,915	29,914	2,035	31,949	7,034	47,735
9	24,915	29,914	2,387	32,301	7,386	55,121
10	24,915	29,914	2,756	32,670	7,755	62,876
11	24,915	29,914	3,144	33,058	8,143	71,019
12	24,915	29,914	3,551	33,465	8,550	79,569
13	24,915	29,914	3,978	33,892	8,977	88,546
14	24,915	29,914	4,427	34,341	9,426	97,972
15	24,915	29,914	4,899	34,813	9,898	107,870
16	24,915	0	5,394	5,394	(19,521)	88,349
17	24,915	0	4,417	4,417	(20,498)	67,851
18	24,915	0	3,393	3,393	(21,522)	46,329
19	24,915	0	2,316	2,316	(22,599)	23,730
20	24,915	0	1,185*	1,185	(23,730)	0

*Adjusted for rounding differences

Again assuming the same normal costs of $26,500 in the first year, the entry for the first year to record pension costs under this condition would be as follows:

Pension Expense	56,414	
Liability Under Pension Plan		4,999
Cash		51,415
$29,914 + $26,500 = $56,414.		

The liability for pension costs would increase each year by the difference between the amount contributed and the amount expensed, including an interest equivalent adjustment, until the fifteen-year expense recognition period expired. During the remaining five years of funding, the pension expense would be limited to the interest equivalent on the remaining liability.

These three conditions are only examples of how funding and expense recognition patterns might vary. Only if the funding period is clearly not representative of service benefits will an employer select an expense recognition period that differs from the funding period.

Limitations Placed on Pension Expense by GAAP. APB Opinion No. 8 did not specify exactly how past service costs should be recognized over current and future years. In order to avoid some of the extreme fluctuations prevalent in practice at that time, the Accounting Principles Board established a range within which the charge to pension expense could vary. The extremes of this range were labeled the **minimum** and the **maximum**. The Opinion requires that normal cost always be charged to expense each year, whether or not the normal costs are funded. In addition, the Board established limitations concerning the portion of past service costs that could be charged against revenue in any given year.

Accountants generally rely upon actuaries to evaluate the expense accrual to determine if it meets the limitations imposed by APB Opinion No. 8. Most plans provide for funding of past service costs over a period of ten to forty years. In the past, if the expense recognition followed the same pattern as the contributions, the maximum and minimum provisions were usually met. However, with inflation and variable interest rates, companies may find their contributions not falling within the limits placed on pension expense by the Accounting Principles Board. This problem is discussed further after the variables entering into the computation of the minimum and maximum are defined.

Minimum Charge. The annual pension expense recognized should not be less than the total of:

(1) The normal cost.
(2) An amount equivalent to interest on any unfunded prior service cost.
(3) If indicated, a provision for vested benefits.[9]

The interest rate to be used in the second provision is the rate that actuaries estimate to be the rate of return on the plan's investments. If none

[9]*Opinions of the Accounting Principles Board, No. 8, op. cit.,* par. 17a.

of the past service costs are initially funded, the amount of the second provision would be the interest rate applied to the present value of past service costs at the beginning of the pension plan.

The third provision for vested benefits arises only when the unfunded vested benefits are not being reduced by at least 5 percent each year, and if the interest equivalent on unfunded prior service costs results in an allocation of past service costs over a period longer than forty years. The provision for vested benefits is complex, and with the more restrictive funding and vesting requirements of ERISA, is rarely encountered. For these reasons, it will not be discussed further in this chapter.

Maximum Charge. The annual pension expense recognized should not be more than the total of:

(1) The normal cost.
(2) Ten percent of the past service cost (until fully amortized).
(3) Ten percent of the amounts of any increases or decreases in prior service cost arising on amendments of the plan (until fully amortized).
(4) Interest equivalents on the difference between provisions and the amount funded.[10]

The maximum charge is similar to the maximum charge for past service costs permitted for income tax purposes, and the APB was influenced by the tax regulations in establishing this limit.

Application of Minimum and Maximum. When a pension plan is initiated, only the first two provisions apply for either the minimum or the maximum computations. For example, the minimum and maximum for the first year of the pension plan described on page 603 would be computed as follows:

Minimum		Maximum	
Normal cost	$26,500	Normal cost	$26,500
Interest on unfunded prior service cost ($310,500 × 5%)	15,525	10% of past service cost ($310,500 × 10%)	31,050
	$42,025		$57,550

The payment of $51,415 falls within this range, and could therefore be used for expense recognition purposes. After the first year, the minimum provision declines as the prior service costs are funded. The maximum provision does not change unless there are amendments to the plan, or unless the accrual amount differs from the amount funded. When the latter occurs, the fourth provision of the maximum must be applied. Thus, when funding is faster than the expense recognition as illustrated in Table 1, the maximum is decreased each period by the interest equivalent adjustment in column C. When funding is slower than the expense recognition as illustrated in Table 2, the maximum is increased each period by the interest equivalent adjustment, also in column C. To illustrate this further, in the fifth year the maxi-

[10] *Ibid.*, par. 17b.

mum under Table 1 conditions is reduced by $622 or to $56,928, and under Table 2 conditions, it is increased by $1,077 to $58,627. With the interest rate of 5% used in the tables, the recognized expense always falls in the defined range.

A contradiction exists, however, in the definition of the maximum as interest rates rise. The definitions are applicable only if the interest rate used in the minimum does not exceed 10 percent, the maximum amount of amortization permitted. If the earnings rate on pension investment were to exceed 10 percent, the minimum apparently could exceed the maximum, and a "no solution" situation would exist. This problem arises at lower interest rates if the annuity method of amortization illustrated on pages 603 to 606 is followed. Pension expense will exceed the maximum in the first year of a pension plan any time a combination of the amortization period and the interest rate results in an annuity factor from Appendix A, Table IV, less than 10. As can be seen by examining the table, this occurs at relatively low interest rates, e.g., 12 years, 3%; 15 years, 6%; 20 years, 8%. This contradiction is one of the areas that is being studied by the FASB as outlined in the chapter appendix.

Accounting for Gains and Losses

The amount of required contributions to a pension plan is based on many actuarial assumptions including mortality tables for employees, expected employee turnover rates, anticipated investment revenue from dividends, interest and sales of securities, amount of future compensation to be paid to employees, and vesting benefits. When these variables differ from the estimates, more or less funds are provided than planned. These differences are referred to as **actuarial gains and losses**. Alternative ways of accounting for these gains and losses are *immediate recognition*; spreading in a consistent manner over a reasonable number of years, defined as between ten and twenty years; or *averaging*, the average being determined from past experience.

The Accounting Principles Board rejected the immediate recognition method except under certain limited circumstances because of its fluctuating impact upon the amount of pension expense. Accordingly, it recommended that actuarial gains and losses should be spread over the current and future years by either the **spreading** or **averaging** technique. Some of the actuarial cost methods used to determine periodic pension costs automatically provide for spreading. If the method used does not accomplish this, special amortization adjustments to normal costs may be required, as illustrated in Tables 3 and 4 adapted from the interpretations of APB Opinion No. 8.[11] The methods used in this illustration are only examples of those that are acceptable. More complex methods of spreading and averaging are permitted. The major objective of these methods is to avoid significant year-to-year fluctuations due to actuarial gains and losses. The journal entries required to record

---

[11] *Accounting Interpretations of APB Opinion No. 8*, "Accounting for the Cost of Pension Plans" (New York: American Institute of Certified Public Accountants, 1966), par. 15, Exhibit D.

actuarial gains and losses when they are considered a separate component of pension expense are illustrated on page 610 for Year 3 from the spreading table below. Assume normal costs without actuarial gain are $20,000.

TABLE 3
Actuarial Gains and Losses
Spreading Technique
10-Year Straight-Line

Year	*(A)* *Actual Gain (Loss)*	*(B)* *Cumulative Actual (B + A)*	*(C)* *Applied to Reduce Pension Expense (B ÷ 10)*	*(D)* *Increase (Decrease) in Deferred Amount (A − C)*	*(E)* *Deferred to Future Years (E + D)*
1	$ 5,000	$ 5,000	$ 500	$4,500	$ 4,500
2	2,000	7,000	700	1,300	5,800
3	6,000	13,000	1,300	4,700	10,500
4	(1,000)	12,000	1,200	(2,200)	8,300
5	7,000	19,000	1,900	5,100	13,400
6	3,000	22,000	2,200	800	14,200
7	(8,000)	14,000	1,400	(9,400)	4,800
8	1,000	15,000	1,500	(500)	4,300
9	10,000	25,000	2,500	7,500	11,800
10	1,000	26,000	2,600	(1,600)	10,200

TABLE 4
Actuarial Gains and Losses
Averaging Technique
5-Year Moving-Average

Year	*(A)* *Actual Gain (Loss)*	*(B)* *5-Year Total*	*(C)* *Applied to Reduce Pension Expense (B ÷ 5)*	*(D)* *Increases in Deferred Amount (A − C)*	*(E)* *Deferred to Future Years (E + D)*
−4	$ 1,000*				
−3	4,000*				
−2	(2,000)*				
−1	3,000*				
1	5,000	$11,000	$2,200	$2,800	$2,800
2	2,000	12,000**	2,400	(400)	2,400
3	6,000	14,000	2,800	3,200	5,600
4	(1,000)	15,000	3,000	(4,000)	1,600
5	7,000	19,000	3,800	3,200	4,800
6	3,000	17,000	3,400	(400)	4,400
7	(8,000)	7,000	1,400	(9,400)	(5,000)
8	1,000	2,000	400	600	(4,400)
9	10,000	13,000	2,600	7,400	3,000
10	1,000	7,000	1,400	(400)	2,600

*Before Year 1, the gains and losses were recognized in the year of determination; they are used here, however, to develop a starting point in the averaging computation.
**$4,000 − $2,000 + $3,000 + $5,000 + $2,000 = $12,000. Each year the previous earliest year is dropped from the average and the new year is added.

Pension Expense	20,000	
Liability Under Pension Plan		20,000
Normal costs for year.		
Liability Under Pension Plan	6,000	
Pension Expense		1,300
Deferred Actuarial Gain		4,700
Actuarial gains and losses using spreading technique.		

Assume normal costs are again $20,000 and the spreading technique is used, the entries for Year 4 would be as follows:

Pension Expense	20,000	
Liability Under Pension Plan		20,000
Normal costs for year.		
Deferred Actuarial Gain	2,200	
Pension Expense		1,200
Liability Under Pension Plan		1,000
Actuarial gains and losses using spreading technique.		

Postemployment Benefits

Employers frequently continue to provide employees with certain benefits subsequent to their retirement. Some of these benefits arise from union pressures during contract negotiations. Most commonly, these benefits are related to life insurance and medical insurance. However, they may also include additional benefits such as employee merchandise discounts and use of company vehicles or office space. Sometimes employers voluntarily increase pension benefits to their retired employees because of the impact of inflation. For example, in 1979 General Electric Co. increased its benefits by 7 percent for 70,000 retired employees.

The accounting question arising from these and similar plans and actions is whether the cost of these benefits can be estimated in advance and thus charged to the service-producing periods. The standards for determining when to record a liability seem to apply to this area. If it is *probable* that postemployment benefits will be paid, and the amount can be reasonably measured in advance, then an accrual of these benefits seems appropriate. Otherwise, the pay-as-you-go basis that is most commonly followed would be acceptable. The accrual of these costs is complicated by the fact that many employers do not record separately the cost of those benefits related to retired employees. For example, some insurance premiums are computed on an aggregate basis that considers the average of employee ages, and does not distinguish cost by age category. Also, some employers essentially self-insure their employees thus not accruing charges in advance of the loss.

Early Retirement Incentives

Special benefits are sometimes offered to a limited group of employees for a short period of time in connection with termination of employment. Frequently, these benefits relate to employees who have reached early retirement age and receive bonus settlements either as a lump-sum or spread over a specified period of years. The FASB considered these plans and in 1983 issued Statement No. 74 that requires companies to recognize a liability and an expense on the books when it is probable that those termination benefits will be paid and the amount can be reasonably estimated.[12]

This requirement applies regardless of how the payments are made. The amount to be recognized is the total of the lump-sum cash payment, the actuarially determined present value of future payments, and any actuarial loss (or less any actuarial gain) under an existing pension plan that results from termination of the employees.

Disclosure Requirements

Pension plans are of great importance to the proper understanding of both financial position and the results of operations. There is a need for the adequate disclosure of such plans. Since the issuance of APB Opinion No. 8, employers have been required to make the following disclosures relative to pension plans:

(1) A statement that such plans exist, identifying or describing the employee groups covered.
(2) A statement of the company's accounting and funding policies.
(3) The provision for pension cost for the period.
(4) The excess, if any, of the actuarially computed value of vested benefits over the total of the pension fund and any balance-sheet pension accruals, less any pension prepayments or deferred charges.
(5) Nature and effect of significant matters affecting comparability for all-periods presented, such as changes in accounting methods (actuarial cost method, amortization of past and prior service cost, treatment of actuarial gains and losses, etc.), changes in circumstances (actuarial assumptions, etc.), or adoption or amendment of a plan.[13]

FASB Statement No. 36 amended Opinion No. 8 and replaced the fourth item in the list with the following requirements:

> For its defined benefit pension plans, an employer shall disclose for each complete set of financial statements the following data determined in accordance with Statement 35 as of the most recent benefit information date for which the data are available:
> (a) The actuarial present value of vested accumulated plan benefits.
> (b) The actuarial present value of nonvested accumulated plan benefits.
> (c) The plan's net assets available for benefits.
> (d) The assumed rates of return used in determining the actuarial present values of vested and nonvested accumulated plan benefits.
> (e) The date as of which the benefit information was determined.[14]

---

[12]*Statement of Financial Accounting Standards No. 74,* "Accounting for Special Termination Benefits Paid to Employees" (Stamford: Financial Accounting Standards Board, 1983).

[13]*Opinions of the Accounting Principles Board, No. 8, op. cit.,* par. 46.

[14]*Statement of Financial Accounting Standards No. 36,* "Disclosure of Pension Information" (Stamford: Financial Accounting Standards Board, 1980), par. 8.

If the required data are not available, the fourth disclosure requirement contained in APB Opinion No. 8 should be followed. The reason for the failure to report the data required by Statement No. 36 should be disclosed.

These disclosure requirements may be altered by the FASB after the reexamination of APB Opinion No. 8 is concluded, and any new standards issued. For the present, the requirement provides data that could be used by an astute reader to make different adjustments for pension costs.

For an example of disclosure of pension information, see Note 10 of General Mills Financial Statements, Appendix B. Note that the disclosure includes both the fair value of the plan assets and the present value of future benefits, both now required under FASB No. 36.

ISSUES RELATED TO ACCOUNTING FOR DEFINED BENEFIT PENSION PLANS

Before 1974, financial reporting by defined benefit pension plans was quite limited. ERISA required, among other things, submission of summarized information about the pension plan to plan participants. In many cases, this meant full financial statement presentation. However, no authoritative accounting pronouncement regarding these plans had ever been issued by the FASB or any earlier standard setting body. The FASB put this item on its technical agenda in 1974, and in 1980 Statement No. 35 was finally passed by a 4–3 decision of FASB members. Several significant accounting issues were addressed in this standard. Although not necessarily related to employer's reporting of pension plans, Statement No. 35 may have long range implications for these related areas of pension reporting.

Before discussing these accounting issues, it is necessary that the objective of financial statements for pension plans be clearly defined. The FASB states:

> The primary objective of a pension plan's financial statements is to provide financial information that is useful in assessing the plan's present and future ability to pay benefits when due.[15]

Although the statement does not identify any one group as the primary user, Appendix B of the statement, "Basis for Conclusions," indicates that the needs of plan participants should be the primary focus since pension plans exist for their benefit.[16] The Board then proceeds to identify information considered important to meet this objective. Three types of information were identified that would provide plan participants and others with information necessary in their analysis: (1) fair value of plan investments, (2) present value of estimated future pension benefits, and (3) changes in asset values and the present value of future benefits during the year. A full development

[15] *Statement of Financial Accounting Standards No. 35,* "Accounting and Reporting by Defined Benefit Pension Plans" (Stamford: Financial Accounting Standards Board, March 1980), par. 5.

[16] *Ibid,* par. 49.

of the material in Statement No. 35 is considered to be beyond the scope of Intermediate Accounting. However, because Statement No. 35 may signal significant changes in employer liabilities for pension plans, these required disclosures will be briefly explored.

Valuation of Assets

Plan investments, whether equity or debt securities, real estate, or others (excluding contracts with insurance companies) shall be presented at their fair value at the reporting date. Fair value is defined as the amount the plan could reasonably expect to receive for the asset in a current sale between a willing buyer and seller; that is, in other than a forced liquidation.[17] The Board believes that the current or fair value of the investment assets is the most significant information to help participants evaluate the plan's ability to pay present and future benefits to them. While it is true that such values can fluctuate significantly, and may be quite different by the time benefits must be actually paid, it still is considered to be the best estimate of the plan's ability to pay at any given date. Contracts with insurance companies are exempted from this valuation requirement because of their complex nature, and because valuation of these contracts is specifically defined by ERISA.

The Board recommended that the valuation be made at the end of the reporting year. However, because most benefit computations historically have been made as of the beginning of the year, the Board concluded that the net assets should also be valued at this same date. They did urge, however, that pension plans move toward reporting both assets *and* benefits as of the end of the reporting year. While investment assets are reported at fair values, operating assets, such as buildings and equipment, furniture and fixtures, and leasehold improvements shall continue to be reported at cost less accumulated depreciation or amortization.[18]

Present Value of Estimated Future Benefits

Other needed information relates to the liability incurred by the plan for future payment of accumulated plan benefits. Accumulated plan benefits are those future benefit payments attributed under the plan's provisions to employees' service rendered to the benefit information date. The actuarial assumptions that must be made in order to report this information include (1) a reasonable rate of return to determine present value, (2) reasonable estimates of retirement, death, disability, automatic benefit increases, or termination of plan participants, and (3) expected dates of benefit payments. The computation should assume the plan will continue to operate indefinitely. Accountants will probably enlist the services of actuaries to provide these data.

---

[17] *Ibid*, par. 11.
[18] *Ibid*, par. 14.

Changes in Asset Values and Benefit Data

In addition to a "snapshot" of the plan's status at a given date, Statement No. 35 also requires information about changes in the value of the assets and in the present value of benefits due between the prior and the current year. These changes may include such factors as changing market values of the assets, changing interest rates, and changes in environmental conditions or actuarial assumptions that affect the future benefits to be paid.

It is not required that this information be audited, at least for the present. It is also recognized that trend data and summary financial information for several years will be more useful than information for a single year. The following exhibits reproduced from Statement No. 35 illustrate how this information may be presented. The detailed notes that would accompany the statements are not reproduced.[19]

EXHIBIT D-1

C & H COMPANY PENSION PLAN

STATEMENT OF NET ASSETS AVAILABLE FOR BENEFITS

	December 31
Assets	
Investments, at fair value (Notes B(1) and E) United States Government securities	$ 350,000
Corporate bonds and debentures	3,500,000
Common stock:	
C & H Company	690,000
Other	2,250,000
Mortgages	480,000
Real estate	270,000
	$7,540,000
Deposit administration contract, at contract value (Notes B(1) and F)	1,000,000
Total investments	$8,540,000
Receivables:	
Employees' contributions	$ 40,000
Securities sold	310,000
Accrued interest and dividends	77,000
	$ 427,000
Cash	$ 200,000
Total assets	$9,167,000
Liabilities	
Accounts payable	$ 70,000
Accrued expenses	85,000
Total liabilities	$ 155,000
Net assets available for benefits	$9,012,000

[19]For complete statements, including notes, see *Statement of Financial Accounting Standards No. 35, op. cit.*, Appendix D, pages 121–141.

EXHIBIT D-2

C & H COMPANY PENSION PLAN

STATEMENT OF CHANGES IN NET ASSETS AVAILABLE FOR BENEFITS

	Year Ended December 31
Investment income:	
Net appreciation in fair value of investments (Note E)	$ 207,000
Interest	345,000
Dividends	130,000
Rents	55,000
	$ 737,000
Less investment expenses	39,000
	$ 698,000
Contributions (Note C):	
Employer	$ 780,000
Employees	450,000
	$1,230,000
Total additions	$1,928,000
Benefits paid directly to participants	$ 740,000
Purchases of annuity contracts (Note F)	257,000
	$ 997,000
Administrative expenses	65,000
Total deductions	$1,062,000
Net increase	$ 866,000
Net assets available for benefits:	
Beginning of year	8,146,000
End of year	$9,012,000

EXHIBIT D-3

C & H COMPANY PENSION PLAN

STATEMENT OF ACCUMULATED PLAN BENEFITS

	Year Ended December 31
Actuarial present value of accumulated plan benefits (Notes B(2) and C):	
Vested benefits:	
Participants currently receiving payments	$ 3,040,000
Other participants	8,120,000
	$11,160,000
Nonvested benefits	2,720,000
Total actuarial present value of accumulated plan benefits	$13,880,000

EXHIBIT D-4

C & H COMPANY PENSION PLAN

STATEMENT OF CHANGES IN ACCUMULATED PLAN BENEFITS

	Year Ended December 31
Actuarial present value of accumulated plan benefits at beginning of year	$11,880,000
Increase (decrease) during the year attributable to:	
Plan amendment (Note G)	$ 2,410,000
Change in actuarial assumptions (Note B(2))	(1,050,500)
Benefits accumulated	895,000
Increase for interest due to the decrease in the discount period (Note B(2))	742,500
Benefits paid	(997,000)
Net increase	$ 2,000,000
Actuarial present value of accumulated plan benefits at end of year	$13,880,000

As indicated in the discussion of disclosure requirements for employers, much of the information required for reporting the pension plan is now required for employer disclosure. This results in more consistent reporting, especially for single employer plans.

APPENDIX

MAJOR ISSUES RELATED TO EMPLOYERS' ACCOUNTING FOR PENSIONS AND OTHER POSTEMPLOYMENT BENEFITS

After almost two years of intensive study since issuing a discussion memorandum on employers' accounting for pensions, the FASB issued in November 1982, a document containing its preliminary views. This publication is intended to precede an exposure draft addressing this area and makes recommendations that would lead to some dramatic changes in accounting for pensions. The proposed requirements apply only to an employer that sponsors a noncontributory defined benefit pension plan for its U.S. employees. Issues relating to multi-employer plans, foreign plans, and plans funded by contracts with insurance companies were addressed in a separate discussion memorandum issued in April 1983.[20] Final resolution of these related matters will probably be made after the basic pension issues are resolved.

[20]FASB *Discussion Memorandum,* "Employers' Accounting for Pensions and Other Postemployment Benefits" (Stamford: Financial Accounting Standards Board, April 19, 1983).

Many accountants feel that the pension area is one of the most complex and difficult areas that the FASB has studied. The impact of the Board's conclusions will be felt by almost all business entities because of the widespread use of retirement plans.

Preliminary Views of the FASB

The major changes recommended in the preliminary views publication are as follows:

(1) Liability for vested and nonvested unfunded prior service costs should be recorded and a charge made to an intangible asset. Because the Board views a defined benefit pension plan as an employer's promise to pay retirement benefits in exchange for employee service, it feels that an obligation has been incurred for unfunded benefits earned. The Board also felt that these unfunded amounts met the definition of liabilities included in Concepts Statement No. 3. When the liability is recorded, a charge is made to an intangible asset. The asset represents benefits that are realizable in the future through improved productivity, reduced demand for wage increases, reduced employee turnover, and other factors.

(2) Investment assets in the pension trust should be valued at fair value and deducted from the pension fund liability in arriving at net pension liability or asset on the balance sheet. Because plan assets will be used to pay pension liabilities, the right of offset exists. If plan assets exceed benefit obligations, a net pension asset would be reported.

(3) Actuarial (experience) gains and losses and price changes in the value of plan assets will not be included in income immediately, but will be recorded in a measurement valuation allowance (MVA) account and amortized over the average remaining service period of plan participants. The use of a valuation allowance will remove the wide fluctuations in pension expense and pension liability that could occur because of temporary and unusual fluctuations in financial markets.

(4) The intangible asset and liability will be measured at the present value of future benefits to be paid. If the plan defines benefits in terms of future salary, these future salaries should be considered in the accounting measurement. Otherwise, a flat benefit assumption may be made. The Board felt that the difference in plan provisions concerning measuring the future service benefits should be reflected in the accounting entries.

(5) Rather than allowing a range for measuring the amount of pension expense as is currently done, all employers would recognize a charge equivalent to the sum of the increase in the present value of future benefit obligations attributable to employee service, accrual of interest on the obligation, the amortization of the intangible asset, the amortization of the measurement valuation allowance, and less the interest earned on the plan assets. The Board felt that a single measurement method for expense is desirable to increase comparability among different companies.

(6) The cost of postemployment health care and life insurance benefits should be accrued over the periods in which employees render service

provided the amounts involved are material. The Board recognized that the accrual of these benefits must be based on estimates, and they do not anticipate specifying a single approach to making these estimates. The pay-as-you-go, or cash, basis and terminal funding, or accrual at retirement, do not adequately recognize the liability being accrued over the employees' service life.

(7) Two different transition methods are proposed as being permissible. Under the first method, a retroactive application of all provisions would be required. Under the second method, the intangible asset and liability would be set equal at the date of the change and future amortization would be based on these initial amounts. Many loan covenants, contracts, and individual expectations will be affected by the proposed pension accounting. To ease the economic impact of the change, the FASB is recommending a flexible transition policy.

Opposing Views

The preliminary views of the FASB on pensions have not received full support from the accounting profession. Arguments against making such dramatic changes in pension accounting include the following:

(1) Because of the many variables affecting the final payment of pension benefits, no liability amount can be reliably measured. Disclosure of such "soft data" is best left to financial statement notes where readers can attach their own probability estimates to the numbers.

(2) Pension contracts that have unfunded prior service costs are in reality executory contracts, i.e., neither side has yet performed. Future service will "earn" the pension benefits, and therefore the liability should be recorded only as the services are performed. Executory contracts are typically not recognized in the financial statements. To do so with pensions would result in a piecemeal approach to accounting principles.

(3) A single method of measuring pension expense is not desirable when the actual funding methods differ among companies. Since one of the objectives of financial reporting contained in Concepts Statement No. 1 is to assist in predicting future cash flows, the present method of allowing recognition of pension expense based on pension funding better meets the cash flow objective.

(4) The intangible asset for deferred pension expense would be misunderstood by readers of the statements. There would be a tendency for analysts to reduce stockholders' equity by this charge (as they often do for goodwill), with no corresponding reduction in pension liability. This could lead to an overly conservative statement of financial position.

(5) Comparability among companies would be made more difficult if two transition methods were permitted. This approach could be very confusing to statement readers.

Concluding Comment

The preceding arguments against the preliminary views can be contrasted with the Board's rationale as summarized earlier in this appendix.

Undoubtedly there will be an attempt at compromise among Board members on this issue. Rather than making the change in one step, there may be a more gradual movement to greater statement disclosure of pension obligations. One possible compromise would be the offsetting of the deferred pension charge (intangible asset) against the pension liability, thus reporting only the difference as an asset or a liability. This would reduce the impact on financial statement ratios and prevent analysts from subtracting deferred pension charges from stockholders' equity. This compromise, however, is not consistent with the elements definition included in Concepts Statement No. 3 and could lead to an increase in offsetting assets against liabilities even when only a remote relationship exists. Leases and mortgages on real estate are examples of situations where the rule of offset could be logically extended.

Another compromise might be to have the liability computed on present salaries rather the projected future salary amounts. While this might provide more verifiable results, it would fail to reflect the reality of a pension contract that is based on future salary amounts.

The preliminary views of the Board appear to be based on a sound application of the concepts statements developed as part of the conceptual framework project. If the conceptual framework is to have a significant impact on the development of accounting standards, the Board's final conclusions in the area of pensions must not compromise the framework. However, care must be exercised so that widespread disruptive economic results do not occur because of the issuance of a pension standard. The careful study and long discussion period attached to this complex area should assist the profession and the Board in attaining a clearer understanding of the basic issues.[21]

QUESTIONS

1. The rapid growth of pension plans has been accompanied by many abuses. What are some of the major problems employees have had with pension plans, and how has ERISA helped to reduce the magnitude of these problems?
2. What is the PBGC, and how does it assist the employees of terminated pension plans?
3. Distinguish between each of the following types of pension plans:
(a) Single employer and multiemployer plans
(b) Contributory and noncontributory plans
(c) Qualified and nonqualified plans
(d) Defined benefit and defined contribution plans
4. Define (a) normal costs, (b) past service costs, (c) prior service costs.
5. (a) What are vested benefits? (b) What vesting requirements for pension plans are included in ERISA?
6. Why did the passage of ERISA focus increased attention on the financial statements of the pension plan as opposed to earlier concern only with the impact of pension plans on employer's financial statements?
7. What are the principal accounting problems relating to pension costs?

---

[21]For a further discussion of the issues relating to the board's preliminary views, see Timothy S. Lucas and Betsy Ann Hollowell, "Pension Accounting: The Liability Question," *Journal of Accountancy* (October 1981), pp. 57–66.

8. What alternative ways might unfunded prior service costs be recorded in the employer's accounting records? Which of these is currently required by GAAP?
9. Why are past service costs considered a charge against future earnings rather than an adjustment of past earnings?
10. What are interest equivalents and why must they be included in computing pension expense when the expense accrual and the contribution differ?
11. What are the variables in computing (a) minimum limits on pension expense, and (b) maximum limits on pension expense?
12. (a) Define actuarial gains and losses. (b) What are the three alternative ways of accounting for the gains and losses? Which do you recommend?
13. What are postemployment benefits? What alternative ways are there for reporting the cost of these benefits during an employee's productive years?
14. What pension information should be disclosed in employers' annual reports?
15. What special information must be disclosed by defined benefit pension plans in their financial statements to meet the requirements of FASB Statement No. 35?

DISCUSSION CASES

case 16-1 (Are unfunded prior service costs really liabilities?) As a partner for a regional CPA firm, you have been asked to serve on a state society committee that is studying the issue of pension costs for employers. You have been asked to come to your first committee meeting to present arguments for and against recording unfunded prior service costs as a liability, regardless of the amount of vested benefits. Outline the presentation you will make.

case 16-2 (What does our pension funding method do to net income?) The Royal Aviation Company decides to begin a pension plan for its employees. The trustees of the plan outline three alternative ways for funding the past service costs: (1) An immediate payment of $600,000; (2) 15 annual payments of $57,805, payable at the end of each year; (3) 20 annual payments of $48,146 payable at the end of each year. R. M. Gray, president of Royal, is concerned about how these alternatives would affect the company's net income assuming that past service pension costs are to be written off over a 15-year period. You have been hired as the chief accountant of Royal Aviation Company, and have been asked to prepare a comparative report for the president. You may assume the company earns 8% before taxes on its new investments. Your report should include computations showing the net pension cost (pension expense less revenue that could be earned on the $600,000 past service cost if not funded initially) for the first two years.

case 16-3 (Are pensions over or underfunded?) Much disagreement exists between economic observers as to whether or not American pension funds are underfunded. Some sources, for example, suggest that many plans are overfunded. Other sources, however, warn of dangerous underfunding and talk of possible pension collapses. Analysts explaining the contradictory dialogue point to two or three factors that are being considered differently by these sources thus causing the different results. What do you think these factors are, and how do such widely different conclusions occur?

case 16-4 (When is the insurance expense a proper charge against revenue?) After lengthy union negotiations, the employees of Mesa Alliance received a new package of fringe benefits that included company payment of major medical insurance premiums for the life of the employees, plus continuation of employee discount privileges for the purchase of company products up to ten years after retirement. These postemployment benefits are going to be charged to expense as paid. What alternative methods of accruing the expense for the benefits are possible? Evaluate them in light of the concepts of income determination and measurability.

case 16-5 (Is the disclosure adequate?) The following notes were included in the 1982 financial statements of Digital Equipment Corporation, BankAmerica Corporation, and The Houghton Mifflin Company.

Digital Equipment Corporation, Notes, page 43:

The Company and its subsidiaries have pension plans covering substantially all of their employees. Total pension expense was $61,801,000 in fiscal 1982, $46,896,000 in fiscal 1981, and $34,784,000 in fiscal 1980. Annual contributions are made to the plans equal to the amounts accrued for pension expense. There was no unfunded past service liability as of July 3, 1982.

A comparision of accumulated plan benefits and plan net assets for the Company's domestic defined benefit plans and for those foreign subsidiaries with defined benefit plans, determined as of the beginning of each respective fiscal year is presented in the accompanying table. Foreign subsidiaries with insured plans, rather than defined benefit plans, have been excluded from this information.

(In Thousands)	July 3, 1982	June 27, 1981
Actuarial present value of accumulated plan benefits:		
Vested	$ 45,889	$ 34,063
Nonvested	32,888	23,375
	$ 78,777	$ 57,438
Net assets available for benefits	$172,853	$117,323

The weighted average assumed rate of return used in determining the actuarial present value of accumulated plan benefits was 6 percent for both 1982 and 1981.

BankAmerica Corporation, Note 17, page 44:

Substantially all permanent, salaried, domestic employees of the corporation are covered by non-contributory defined benefit pension plans. Total pension expense, which includes amortization of past service costs over not more than 40 years, aggregated $62,512,000 in 1982, $52,469,000 in 1981, and $47,103,000 in 1980. The corporation makes annual contributions to the plan equal to the amounts accrued for pension expense.

The following is a summary of accumulated benefits and net plan assets:

(In Thousands)	Dec. 31, 1982	Dec. 31, 1981
Actuarial present value of accumulated plan benefits of participants:		
Vested	$395,158	$272,639
Nonvested	50,130	33,965
	$445,288	$306,604
Current value of net plan assets available for benefits	$491,773	$375,856

In determining the actuarial present value of accumulated plan benefits for 1982, the rate of return assumptions established by the Pension Benefit Guaranty Corporation (PBGC) for calculating such benefits were used and approximated 9.5%. For 1981 the rate of return assumed was 14.2%; however, if the PBGC rate of return assumptions, approximating 10.2%, had been used in 1981, the actuarial present value of accumulated plan benefits would have been $78,335,000 more than reported.

The corporation also has plans for employees in certain non-U.S. operations. Each plan generally covers the employees in a specific country. The actuarial value of accumulated benefits and the net assets available for benefits are not determined annually for these plans.

The Houghton Mifflin Company, Note 6, page 24:

The Company has a noncontributory trusteed defined benefit pension plan that covers substantially all of its employees. The total pension expense for 1982, 1981 and 1980 was $2,200,000, $2,400,000 and $1,800,000 respectively. A comparison of plan benefits and plan net assets at the end of the most recent plan year is shown opposite.

(In Thousands)	July 1, 1982	July 1, 1983
Actuarial present value of accumulated benefits:		
Vested	$15,971	$14,471
Nonvested	951	710
	$16,922	$15,181
Net assets available for benefits	$19,918	$19,725

The weighted average assumed rate of return used in determining the actuarial present value of plan benefits was 8% for both years.

The information contained in these notes is required by FASB Statement No. 36. A member of your staff comes to you, a partner in an international CPA firm, with the following questions about these disclosures:

(a) Why is disclosure of interest rates important? In these three companies, the 1982 rates vary from 6% for Digital Equipment Corporation to 14.2% for BankAmerica Corporation. What guidelines are there for selecting the interest rate? How does the interest rate affect the amounts in the note?
(b) Why is it important to distinguish between vested and nonvested accumulated plan benefits? Shouldn't they be combined and disclosed as one sum?
(c) Of what significance, for accounting entries, is the statement that annual contributions are made to the plan equal to the amount accrued for pension expense.
(d) Do the accumulated plan benefits involved in these notes use current salary amounts or projected ones?

Respond to these questions.

EXERCISES

exercise 16-1 (Pension accrual entries)

The Montoya Company accrued pension costs of $25,000 for 1984 and 1985. Give the entries to record pension costs for 1984 and 1985 if the company funds (a) $25,000; (b) $19,000; and (c) $28,000. The interest rate related to the pensions is 6%.

exercise 16-2 (Pension liability table)

The Marlon Corporation funds its past service pension costs over 20 years and amortizes them over 15 years. Past service pension costs at the adoption of the pension plan are

$360,000 and the interest rate is 5%. The corporation accountant has prepared the following four-year table accounting for past service costs.

Marlon Corporation
Past-Service Cost Accounting
Accrual of Pension Liability
Amortization Period—15 Years

Year	Funding Contribution 20 Years	Annuity Amortization	Add Interest (5%) on Previous Liability Balance	Pension Expense	Liability Increase (Decrease)	Liability Balance
1983	$28,887	$36,000	-0-	$36,000	$7,113	$ 7,113
1984	28,887	36,000	$ 356	36,356	7,469	14,582
1985	28,887	36,000	729	36,729	7,842	22,424
1986	28,887	36,000	1,121	37,121	8,234	30,658

(1) Prepare a correct table for 1983–1986.
(2) Give the entry to record past service pension cost for 1985.

exercise 16-3 (Minimum and maximum limits—pensions)

The following pension plan information is provided by the actuary for Piston Builders Inc. at December 31, 1984:

Normal cost	$ 210,000
Unfunded prior service cost	$1,300,000
Interest rate used for actuarial purposes	8%
Unfunded vested benefits—December 31, 1983	$ 430,000
Unfunded vested benefits—December 31, 1984	$ 400,000
10% of past service costs	$ 200,000
(There have been no plan amendments)	
Balance in pension liability account on company's books	$ 60,000

Based on this information, compute the minimum and maximum pension expense allowed under APB Opinion No. 8.

exercise 16-4 (Actuarial gains and losses)

Actuarial gains and losses for 1978–1984 are shown below:

1978	$(4,000)
1979	5,000
1980	2,000
1981	(500)
1982	2,000
1983	4,000
1984	(2,000)

(1) Using the five-year averaging technique, compute the amount applied to reduce pension expense in 1983 and 1984 if the actuarial gains and losses are computed separately each year.
(2) Prepare the journal entries in 1984 if normal costs are $15,000.

exercise 16-5 (Postemployment benefits)

The Crossley Manufacturing Company decides to continue paying medical and life insurance premiums for its retired employees beginning with employees retiring after 4 more years. No funds are going to be accumulated for these premiums. The company has only 5 employees. It is anticipated that, on the average, $8,000 in insurance premiums must be spent for each retired employee. The remaining years to retirement for the 5 employees are as follows:

Employee	Remaining Years Until Retirement
A	10
B	5
C	16
D	2
E	8

The company decides to accrue the liability for postemployment benefits based on the remaining years of service. Give the entry required to accrue postemployment benefits as of the end of the first year. (Ignore present value considerations.)

exercise 16-6 (Financial statement pension disclosure—employer)

Based on the following information, indicate how Pixton Enterprises would report information required by FASB No. 36 relative to its defined benefit pension plan in its own financial statements at December 31, 1984. The company is funding past service costs to an independent trustee over 20 years and accruing these costs on its books over 15 years. Actuarial gains and losses are being spread on a straight-line basis over 10 years.

Excess of accumulated accruals of pension expense over amount funded	$ 165,000
Actuarial present value of vested accumulated plan benefits	4,200,000
Market value of plan assets	2,600,000
Cost of plan assets	2,200,000
Actuarial present value of nonvested accumulated plan benefits	1,300,000
Pension expense for year	420,000
Contributions for year	350,000
Unfunded past service costs—December 31, 1984	4,300,000
Rate of return used in determining values	6%

Plan statements are prepared as of June 30, 1984.

exercise 16-7 (Financial statement disclosure—pension plan)

The Morgan Inc. pension plan had the following activity during 1984.

Administrative expenses	$ 110,000
Employee contributions to plan	362,000
Appreciation in fair value of investments	295,000
Cost of investments at December 31, 1984	4,926,000
Market value of investments at December 31, 1984	6,950,000
Interest revenue	312,000
Employer contributions to plan	719,000
Benefits accumulated during year	1,196,000
Benefits paid during the year	1,200,000
Actuarial present value of accumulated plan benefits	9,260,000
Investment expenses	38,000
Dividend revenue	320,000

Based upon this data, prepare the statement of changes in net assets available for benefits for the year ended December 31, 1984.

PROBLEMS

problem 16-1 (Deferred pension expense table)

The Glencoe Corporation institutes a pension plan on January 2, 1984. Normal costs for 1984 are $20,000. Other information is as follows:

(a) Unfunded past service costs are $175,000.
(b) The Glencoe Corporation accrues past-service costs over a 25-year period, and funds them over 15 years.
(c) Minimum pension cost for 1984 is computed to be $34,000.
(d) Interest on unfunded prior service costs is 8%.
(e) Maximum pension cost for 1984 is computed to be $60,000.

Instructions:

(1) Construct a table for the first four years of the pension showing the computation of accrual of deferred pension expense.
(2) Prepare journal entries for the first and fourth years.

problem 16-2 (Deferred pension expense table and minimum—maximum limits)

The Clampett Corporation adopted a pension plan on January 6, 1983. Past service costs are estimated by the firm's actuary to be $427,975. The plan will be funded over 10 years and is expected to earn an average rate of 6%. Past service costs will be amortized over 16 years.

Normal costs are $35,000 each year.

Instructions:

(1) Construct a table for the first four years showing the computation of annual past service pension expense and accrued pension liability.
(2) Compute the minimum and maximum limits for 1983, the first year of the plan. Does the pension expense computed for 1983 in the table fall between these limits?
(3) Prepare journal entries to record pension related transactions for 1985.

problem 16-3 (Pension accrual entries)

Liberty Inc., a calendar-year corporation, adopted a company pension plan at the beginning of 1984. This plan is to be funded and noncontributory. Liberty used an appropriate actuarial cost method to determine its normal annual pension cost for 1984 and 1985 as $15,000 and $16,000 respectively, which was paid in the same year.

Liberty's actuarially determined past service costs were funded on December 31, 1984, at an amount properly computed as $106,000. These past service costs are to be amortized at the maximum amount permitted by generally accepted accounting principles. The interest factor assumed by the actuary is 6%.

Instructions: Prepare journal entries to record the funding of past service costs on December 31, 1984, and the pension expenses for the years 1984 and 1985. Under each journal entry give the reasoning to support your entry. Round to the nearest dollar.

(AICPA adapted)

problem 16-4 (Financial statement pension disclosure—employer)

The CMA Corporation, which has been in operation for the past 23 years, decided late in 1983 to adopt a funded pension plan for its employees, beginning on January 1, 1984. The pension plan is to be noncontributory, and will provide for vesting after 5 years of service by each eligible employee. A trust agreement has been entered into whereby a large national insurance company will receive the yearly pension fund contributions and administer the fund.

Management, through extended consultation with the fund trustee, internal accountants, and independent actuaries, arrived at the following conclusions:

(a) The normal pension cost for 1984 will be $30,000.
(b) The present value of the past service cost at date of inception of the pension plan (January 1, 1984) is $200,000.

(c) Because of the large sum of money involved, the past service costs will be funded at a rate of $23,365 per year for the next 15 years. The first payment will not be due until January 1, 1985.
(d) In accordance with APB Opinion No. 8, the "unit credit method" of accounting for the pension costs will be followed. Pension costs will be amortized over a 10-year period. The 10-year accrual factor is $29,805 per year. Neither the maximum nor minimum amortization amounts as prescribed by APB Opinion No. 8 will be violated.

Instructions:

(1) What amounts (use xxx if amount cannot be calculated) will be reported in the company's (a) income statement for 1984, (b) balance sheet as of December 31, 1984, and (c) notes to the statements? Give account titles with the amounts.
(2) What amounts (use xxx if amount cannot be calculated) will be reported in the company's (a) income statement for 1985 (assume normal cost of $30,000), (b) balance sheet as of December 31, and (c) notes to the statements? Give account titles with the amounts.

(CMA adapted)

problem 16-5 (Actuarial gains and losses)

The Ruff Company experienced actuarial gains and losses in relation to its pension plan as follows:

Year	
1	$7,000
2	2,000
3	(3,000)
4	(1,500)
5	4,000

Actuarial gains and losses are spread over 10 years using a straight-line basis.

Instructions:

(1) Construct a table showing the spreading of Ruff Company's actuarial gains and losses for 5 years.
(2) Assuming past service costs are being amortized according to Table 2 on page 605, record pension expense for Year 4. Normal costs are $125,000.

problem 16-6 (Financial statement disclosure—pension plan)

The following information for the year ending December 31, 1984, is obtained in the course of an auditor's examination of the Signal Peak Corporation Pension Plan.

Investments	Cost	Market
Stocks	$2,820,000	$3,460,000
Bonds	1,300,000	1,200,000
Real estate	350,000	600,000
	$4,470,000	$5,260,000

Cash and receivables	$ 620,000
Accounts payable	120,000
Actuarial present value of vested accumulated plan benefits: 1984	8,250,000
1983	7,500,000
Actuarial present value of nonvested accumulated plan benefits: 1984	2,625,000
1983	2,100,000
Benefits paid during year	950,000
Benefits accumulated during year	1,025,000
Additions to accumulated plan benefits because of plan amendment	1,200,000
Investment revenue	450,000
Investment expense	42,000
Contributions by employer	1,300,000
Administration expense	72,000
Net assets available for benefits—1983	5,074,000

Instructions: From this data, prepare pension plan financial statements as required by FASB Statement No. 35 for the year ended December 31, 1984.

problem 16-7 (Minimum and maximum limits—pensions)

Dane Enterprises, which started operations in 1978, instituted a pension plan on January 1, 1983. The insurance company which is administering the pension plan has computed the present value of past service costs at $100,000 for the five years of operations through December 31, 1982.

The insurance company proposed that Dane Enterprises fund the past service cost in equal installments over 15 years calculated by the present value method. Using an interest rate of 5%, the annual payment for past service cost would be $9,634 for 15 years.

The normal cost for the pension fund is estimated to be $30,000 each year for the next 4 years. The annual payment to the insurance company covering the current year's normal cost and the annual installment on the past service cost is payable on December 31 each year, the end of Dane Enterprises' fiscal year. The insurance company was paid $39,634 ($30,000 + $9,634) on December 31, 1983, to cover the company's pension obligation for 1983.

Instructions:

(1) Calculate and label the components that comprise the maximum and minimum 1983 financial statement pension expense limits in accordance with generally accepted accounting principles for Dane Enterprises (ignore vesting).

(2) Assume that Dane Enterprises will be unable to remit the full pension payment ($39,634) in 1984 and will only submit $30,000 (the normal cost) to the insurance company. If Dane Enterprises can recognize $39,634 as pension expense in 1984, show the entry required. If the company cannot recognize the $39,634 as pension expense in 1984, explain why not. (CMA adapted)

17 OWNERS' EQUITY—CONTRIBUTED CAPITAL

CHAPTER OBJECTIVES

Describe the nature and classifications of capital stock.

Explain and illustrate proper accounting for the issuance of capital stock.

Explain and illustrate proper accounting for the reacquisition and resale or retirement of capital stock.

Describe and illustrate the accounting and reporting for stock rights and options, stock conversions, and stock splits.

Describe balance sheet disclosure of contributed capital.

The difference between assets and liabilities is owners' equity or capital. Assets represent entity resources while liabilities reflect the creditor claims against those resources. The owners' equity of an entity represents the residual interest of the owners in the net assets (total assets less total liabilities) of the business.

The capital of a business originates from two primary sources—investments by owners and business earnings. Reductions in capital result primarily from distributions to owners and business losses. In a proprietorship, the owner's entire equity resulting from investments, withdrawals, and earnings or losses is reflected in a single capital account. Similarly, in a partnership, a single capital account for each partner reports the partner's equity resulting from investments, withdrawals, and earnings or losses. In reporting corporate capital, however, a distinction is made between (1) investments by owners, called **contributed capital** or **paid-in capital** and (2) retention of net assets arising from earnings, designated as **retained earnings.** The issues surrounding contributed capital are discussed in this chapter, while those relating to retained earnings are considered in Chapter 18. Accounting for corporations is emphasized because they are the dominant form of organization in today's economy. Not only are corporations the major source of our national output, but they also provide the majority of employment opportunities. Millions of people hold equity securities (capital stock) in corporations throughout the world.

NATURE AND CLASSIFICATIONS OF CAPITAL STOCK

A corporation is an artificial entity created by law that has an existence separate from its owners and may engage in business within prescribed limits just as a natural person. Unless the life of a corporation is limited by law, it has perpetual existence. The modern corporation makes it possible for large amounts of resources to be assembled under one management. These resources are transferred to the corporation by individual owners because they believe they can earn a greater rate of return through the corporation's efficient use of the resources than would be possible from alternative investments. In exchange for these resources, the corporation issues **stock certificates** evidencing ownership interests. Directors elected by stockholders delegate to management responsibility for supervising the use, operation, and disposition of corporate resources.

Business corporations may be created under the incorporating laws of any one of the fifty states or of the federal government. Since the states do not follow a uniform incorporating act, the conditions under which corporations may be created and under which they may operate are somewhat varied.

In most states at least three individuals must join in applying for a corporate charter. Application is made by submitting **articles of incorporation** to the secretary of state or other appropriate official. The articles must set forth the name of the corporation, its purpose and nature, the stock to be issued, those persons who are to act as first directors, and other data required by law. If the articles conform to the state's laws governing corporate formation, they are approved and are recognized as the **charter** for the new corporate entity. When stock of a corporation is to be offered or distributed outside the state in which it is incorporated, registration with the Securities and Exchange Commission may be required. The objective of such registration is to assure that all facts relative to the business and its securities will be adequately and honestly disclosed. A stockholders' meeting is called at which a code of rules or **bylaws** governing meetings, voting procedures, and other internal operations are adopted; a **board of directors** is elected; and the board appoints company administrative officers. Corporate activities may now proceed in conformance with laws of the state of incorporation and charter authorization. A complete record of the proceedings of both the stockholders' and the directors' meetings should be maintained in a minutes book.

When a corporation is formed, a single class of stock, known as **common stock,** is usually issued. Corporations may later find that there are advantages to issuing one or more additional classes of stock with varying rights and priorities. Stock with certain preferences (rights) over the common stock is called **preferred stock.** All shares within a particular class of stock are identical in terms of ownership rights represented.

Unless restricted or withheld by terms of the stock contract, certain basic rights are held by each stockholder. These rights are as follows:

(1) To share in distributions of corporate earnings.
(2) To vote in the election of directors and in the determination of certain corporate policies.
(3) To maintain one's proportional interest in the corporation through purchase of additional capital stock if issued, known as the *preemptive right*. (In recent years, some states have eliminated this right.)
(4) To share in distributions of cash or other properties upon liquidation of the corporation.

If both preferred and common stocks are issued, the special features of each class of stock are stated in the articles of incorporation or in the corporation bylaws and become a part of the stock contract between the corporation and its stockholders. One must be familiar with the overall capital structure to understand fully the nature of the equity found in any single class of stock. Frequently, the stock certificate describes the rights and restrictions relative to the ownership interest it represents together with those pertaining to other securities issued. Shares of stock represent personal property and may be freely transferred by their owners in the absence of special restrictions.

Legal or Stated Value of Stock

As indicated, the capital of a corporation is divided between contributed capital and earned capital. This is an important distinction because readers of financial statements need to know the portion of equity derived from investments by owners as contrasted with the portion of equity that has been earned and retained by the business. The invested or contributed capital may be further classified into (a) an amount forming the corporate **legal or stated capital,** and (b) the balance, if any, in excess of legal capital. The amount of the investment representing the legal or stated capital is reported as **capital stock.** The remaining balance is recognized as **additional paid-in capital** or **premium.** Contributions of properties by outsiders may also be included in the additional paid-in capital grouping, although it would be possible to recognize these in a separate **donated capital** category.

The major components of owners' equity are shown on the following page. It should be recognized, however, that the definitions and classifications of legal and other capital categories may vary according to state statutes.

The significance of legal capital is that most state incorporation laws provide that dividends cannot reduce corporate capital below an amount designated as legal capital. Modern corporation laws normally go beyond

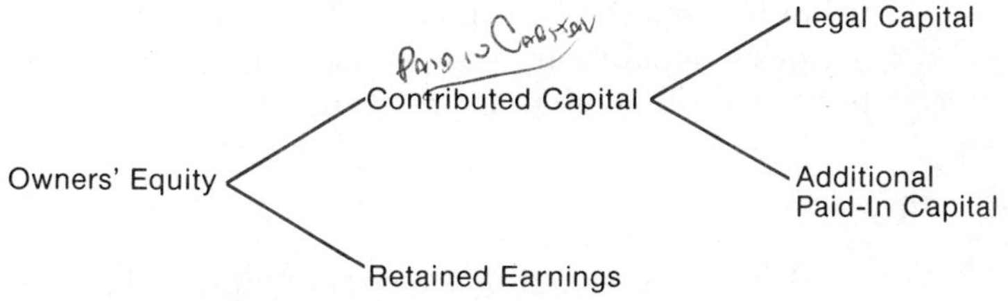

Elements of Owners' Equity

these limitations and add that legal capital cannot be impaired by the reacquisition of capital stock. Creditors of a corporation cannot hold individual stockholders liable for claims against the company. But with a portion of the corporate capital restricted as to distribution, creditors can rely on the absorption by the ownership group of losses equal to the legal capital before losses are applied to the creditors' equity. As a practical matter, the legal capital of a corporation is generally small in comparison to total capital and does not strongly influence dividend policy nor provide significant creditor protection.

When a value is assigned to each share of stock, whether common or preferred, and is reported on the stock certificate, the stock is said to have a **par value;** stock without such an assigned value is called **no-par** stock. When shares have a par value, the legal or stated capital is normally the aggregate par value of all shares issued and subscribed. When a corporation is authorized to issue capital stock with a par value, the incorporation laws of most states permit such issue only for an amount equal to or in excess of par. Par value may be any amount, for example, $100, $5, or 25 cents. An amount received on the sale of capital stock in excess of its par value is recorded as a premium; the premium is added to capital stock at par in reporting total contributed capital.

When shares are no-par, laws of certain states require that the total consideration received for the shares, even when they are sold at different prices, be recognized as legal capital. Laws of a number of states, however, permit the corporate directors to establish legal capital by assigning an arbitrary value to each share regardless of issue price, although in some instances the value cannot be less than a certain minimum amount. The value fixed by the board of directors or the minimum value required by law is known as the share's **stated value**, and an amount received in excess of stated value is reported as a premium. Descriptive account titles such as Additional Paid-In Capital or Paid-In Capital in Excess of Par (or Stated) Value, are often used to record premiums paid on par or stated value stock.

Prior to 1912, corporations were permitted to issue only stock with a par value. In 1912, however, New York state changed its corporation laws to permit the issuance of stock without a par value, and since that time all other states have followed with similar statutory provisions. Today many of the common stocks, as well as some of the preferred stocks, listed on the large securities exchanges are no-par. Usually, no-par stock must have a stated value for reporting purposes. This makes it very similar to par stock and defines a separation of the stock proceeds between stated value and additional paid-in capital or premium.

Preferred Stock

When a corporation issues both preferred and common stock, the preference rights attaching to preferred stock normally consist of prior claims to dividends. A dividend preference does not assure stockholders of dividends on the preferred issue but simply means that dividend requirements must be met on preferred stock before anything may be paid on common stock. Dividends do not legally accrue; a dividend on preferred stock, as on common stock, requires the ability on the part of the company to make such a distribution as well as appropriate action by the board of directors. When the board of directors fails to declare a dividend on preferred stock at the time such action would be called for, the dividend is said to be "passed." Although preferred stockholders have a prior claim on dividends, such preference is usually accompanied by limitations on the amount of dividends they may receive.

Preferred stock is generally issued with a par value. When preferred stock has a par value, the dividend is stated in terms of a percentage of par value. When preferred stock is no-par, the dividend must be stated in terms of dollars and cents. Thus, holders of 5% preferred stock with a $50 par value are entitled to an annual dividend of $2.50 per share before any distribution is made to common stockholders; holders of $5 no-par preferred stock are entitled to an annual dividend of $5 per share before dividends are paid to common stockholders.

A corporation may issue more than one class of preferred stock. For example, preferred issues may be designated first preferred or second preferred with the first preferred issue having a first claim on earnings and the second preferred having a second claim on earnings. In other instances the claim to earnings on the part of several preferred issues may have equal priority, but dividend rates or other preferences may vary. Holders of the common stock may receive dividends only after the satisfaction of all preferred dividend requirements.

Other characteristics and conditions are frequently added to preferred stock in the extension of certain advantages or in the limitation of certain rights. Such factors may be expressed in adjectives modifying preferred stock, as *cumulative* preferred stock, *convertible* preferred stock, and *callable* preferred stock. More than one of these characteristics may be applicable to a specific issue of preferred stock.

Cumulative and Noncumulative Preferred Stock. Cumulative preferred stock provides that whenever the corporation fails to declare dividends on this class, such dividends accumulate and require payment in the future before any dividends may be paid to common stockholders. For example, assume a corporation has outstanding 100,000 shares of 9% cumulative preferred stock, $10 par. Dividends were last paid through December 31, 1981, and the company wishes to resume payments at the end of 1984. The company will have to declare dividends on preferred for three years, or $270,000 before it may declare any dividends on common stock. Dividends on cumulative preferred stock that are passed are referred to as **dividends in arrears.** Although these dividends are not a liability until declared by the board of directors, this information is of importance to stockholders and other users of the financial statements. Disclosure of the amount of the dividends in arrears is made by special note on the balance sheet.

If preferred stock is **noncumulative,** it is not necessary to provide for passed dividends. A dividend omission on preferred stock in any one year means it is irretrievably lost. Dividends may be declared on common stock as long as the preferred stock receives the preferred rate for the current period. Preferred stock contracts, however, normally provide for cumulative dividends. Also, courts have generally held that dividend rights on preferred stock are cumulative in the absence of specific conditions to the contrary.

Convertible Preferred Stock. Preferred stock is **convertible** when terms of the issue provide that it can be exchanged by its owner for some other security of the issuing corporation. Conversion rights generally provide for the exchange of preferred stock into common stock. Since preferred stock normally has a prior but limited right to earnings, large earnings resulting from successful operations accrue to the common stockholders. The conversion privilege gives the preferred stockholders the opportunity to exchange their holdings for stock in which the rights to earnings are not limited. In some instances, preferred stock may be convertible into bonds, thus the investors have the option of changing their positions from stockholders to creditors. Convertible preferred issues have become increasingly popular in recent years.

The decision by a stockholder to convert preferred holdings into common stock is a difficult one. It involves many factors, including the time limitation, if any, on the conversion privilege and the relative dividend returns on common stock as compared with preferred stock.

Callable Preferred Stock. Preferred stock is **callable** when it can be called or redeemed at the option of the corporation. Many preferred issues are callable. The **call price** is usually specified in the original agreement and provides for payment of dividends in arrears as part of the repurchase price. When convertible stock has a call provision, the holders of the stock, at the time of the call, are frequently given the option of converting their holdings into common stock rather than accepting the call price. The decision made by the investor will be based on the market price of the common stock.

Redeemable Preferred Stock. Preferred stock is sometimes subject to mandatory redemption requirements or other redemption provisions that give the security overlapping debt and equity characteristics. This type of stock is referred to as **redeemable preferred stock** and is defined as preferred stock that is redeemable at the option of the holder, or at a fixed or determinable price on a specific date, or upon other conditions not solely within the control of the issuer (e.g., redemption upon reaching a certain level of earnings). The FASB currently requires disclosure of long-term obligations, including the extent of redemption requirements for all issues of capital stock that are redeemable at fixed or determinable prices on fixed or determinable dates. Redemption requirements may be disclosed separately for each issue or for all issues combined.[1]

Asset and Dividend Preferences upon Corporation Liquidation. Preferred stock is generally preferred as to assets distributed upon corporate liquidation. Such a preference, however, cannot be assumed but must be specifically stated in the preferred stock contract. The asset preference for stock with a par value is an amount equal to par, or par plus a premium; in the absence of a par value it is a stated amount. Terms of the preferred contract may also provide for the full payment of any dividends in arrears upon liquidation, regardless of the retained earnings balance reported by the company. When this is the case and there are insufficient retained earnings, i.e., a deficit, such dividend priorities must be met from paid-in capital of the common issue; common stockholders receive whatever assets remain after settlement with the preferred group.

Common Stock

Strictly speaking, there should be but one kind of common stock. Common stock represents the residual ownership equity and carries the greatest risk. In return for this risk, common stock ordinarily shares in earnings to the greatest extent if the corporation is successful. There is no inherent distinction in voting rights between preferred and common stocks; however, voting rights are frequently given exclusively to common stockholders as long as dividends are paid regularly on preferred stock. Upon failure to meet preferred dividend requirements, special voting rights may be granted to preferred stockholders, thus affording this group a more prominent role in the management. In some states, voting rights cannot be withheld on any class of stock.

ISSUANCE OF CAPITAL STOCK

The capital stock of a corporation may be authorized but unissued; it may be subscribed for and held for issuance pending receipt of cash on stock subscriptions; it may be outstanding in the hands of stockholders; it may be reacquired and held by the corporation for subsequent reissuance or bonus distribution; it may be canceled by appropriate corporate action. An accurate record of all transactions involving capital stock must be maintained by the corporation. Individual accounts should be maintained in the general ledger for each source of capital including each class of stock.

---

[1]*Statement of Financial Accounting Standards No. 47,* "Disclosure of Long-Term Obligations" (Stamford: Financial Accounting Standards Board, 1981), par. 10c.

A **stockholders ledger,** in which accounts are maintained for each stockholder, is controlled by the capital stock account. The issuance of stock by a corporation calls for a credit to a stockholder's account for the shares issued. A transfer of stock ownership is recorded by a debit to the account of the person making the transfer and a credit to the account of the person acquiring the stock; since the capital stock outstanding remains the same after transfer of individual holdings, general ledger accounts are not affected.

A **stock certificate book** also reports shares outstanding. Certificates in the book are usually serially numbered. As certificates are issued, the number of shares issued is reported on the certificate stubs. When ownership transfers, the original certificates submitted by the sellers are canceled and attached to the original stubs and new certificates are issued to the buyers. Frequently, a corporation will appoint banks or trust companies to serve as **registrars** and **transfer agents.** These parties are assigned various responsibilities, such as transferring stock certificates, maintaining the stockholders ledger, preparing lists of stockholders for meetings, and making dividend distributions.

Capital Stock Issued for Cash

The issuance of stock for cash is recorded by a debit to Cash and a credit to Capital Stock for the par or stated value.[2] When the amount of cash received from the sale of stock is greater than the par or stated value, the excess is recorded separately as a credit to a premium or special paid-in capital account.[3] This account is carried on the books as long as the stock to which it relates is outstanding. When stock is retired, the capital stock balance as well as any related premium balance is generally canceled.

To illustrate, assume the Whitni Corporation is authorized to issue 10,000 shares of $10 par common stock. On April 1, 1984, 4,000 shares are sold for $45,000 cash. The entry to record the transaction is:

1984			
April 1	Cash	45,000	
	Common Stock, $10 par		40,000
	Premium on Common Stock		5,000
	To record the issuance of 4,000 shares of $10 par common stock for $45,000.		

If, in the above example, the common stock were no-par stock but with a $10 stated value, the entry would be the same except the description of the stock would be Common Stock, $10 stated value and the $5,000 excess designated Paid-In Capital from Sale of Common Stock at More Than Stated Value. Generally, stock is assigned a par or a stated value. However, if there is no such value assigned, the entire amount of cash received on the sale of stock is credited to the capital stock account and there is no premium account involved. Assuming Whitni Corporation's stock were no-par com-

[2]The term *Capital Stock* is used in account titles in the text when the class of stock is not specifically designated. When preferred and common designations are given, these are used in the account titles.

[3]For conciseness, "premium" accounts are used in the text examples, even though account titles such as "Paid-In Capital in Excess of Par Value" are more descriptive.

mon without a stated value, the entry to record the sale of 4,000 shares for $45,000 would be:

1984			
April 1	Cash	45,000	
	Common Stock		45,000
	To record the issuance of 4,000 shares of no-par, no stated-value common stock for $45,000.		

Capital stock is seldom sold at less than par or stated value, often because state laws preclude such a sale. If it were, however, a *discount* would be recorded. A discount on the sale of stock indicates a potential claim by creditors against stockholders in the event the company becomes insolvent; from a going-concern point of view, however, the discount should be recognized as a deduction in presenting the company's contributed capital rather than as a liability.

Capital Stock Sold on Subscription

Capital stock may be issued on a subscription basis. A **subscription** is a legally binding contract between the subscriber (purchaser of stock) and the corporation (issuer of stock). The document states the number of shares subscribed, the subscription price, the terms of payment, and other conditions of the transaction. By express provisions, the contract may be binding only if the corporation receives subscriptions for a stated number of shares. A subscription, while giving the corporation a legal claim for the contract price, also gives the subscriber the legal status of a stockholder unless certain rights as a stockholder are specifically withheld by law or by terms of the contract. Ordinarily stock certificates evidencing share ownership are not issued until the full subscription price has been received by the corporation.

Upon receiving subscriptions, Capital Stock Subscriptions Receivable is debited for the subscription price, Capital Stock Subscribed is credited for the amount to be recognized as capital stock when subscriptions have been collected, and a paid-in capital account is credited for the amount of the subscription price in excess of par or stated value. A special *subscribers journal* may be used in recording capital stock subscriptions.

Capital Stock Subscriptions Receivable is a control account, individual subscriptions being reported in the subsidiary *subscribers ledger.* Subscriptions Receivable is regarded as a current asset when the corporation expects to collect the balance currently, which is the usual situation; remaining balances are regarded as noncurrent.

Subscriptions may be collected in cash or in other properties accepted by the corporation. When collections are made, the appropriate asset account is debited and the receivable account is credited. Credits are also made to subscribers' accounts in the subsidiary ledger.

The actual issuance of stock is recorded by a debit to Capital Stock Subscribed and a credit to Capital Stock. The following entries illustrate the recording and issuance of capital stock sold on subscription. It is assumed that the Bushman Corporation is authorized to issue 10,000 shares of $10 par value common stock.

Recording and Issuance of Capital Stock Sold on Subscription

November 1–30 Received subscriptions for 5,000 shares at 12½ with 50% down payment, balance payable in 60 days.	Common Stock Subscriptions Receivable	62,500	
	Common Stock Subscribed		50,000
	Premium on Common Stock		12,500
	Cash	31,250	
	Common Stock Subscriptions Receivable		31,250
December 1–31 Received balance due on one half of subscriptions and issued stock to the fully paid subscribers, 2,500 shares.	Cash	15,625	
	Common Stock Subscriptions Receivable		15,625
	Common Stock Subscribed	25,000	
	Common Stock		25,000
Stockholders' equity after the above transactions:	Stockholders' Equity		
	Contributed capital:		
	Common stock, $10 par, 10,000 shares authorized, 2,500 shares issued and outstanding		$25,000
	Common stock subscribed, 2,500 shares		25,000
	Premium on common stock		12,500
	Total stockholders' equity		$62,500

Subscription Defaults

If a subscriber defaults on a subscription by failing to make a payment when it is due, a corporation may (1) return to the subscriber the amount paid, (2) return to the subscriber the amount paid less any reduction in price or expense incurred upon the resale of the stock, (3) declare the full amount paid as forfeited, or (4) issue to the subscriber shares equal to the number paid for in full. The practice followed will depend on the policy adopted by the corporation within the legal limitations set by the state in which it is incorporated.

To illustrate the entries under these different circumstances, assume in the Bushman Corporation example described earlier (with subscriptions at 12½) that one subscriber for 100 shares defaults after making the 50% down payment. Defaulted shares are subsequently resold at 11. The entries to record the default by the subscriber and the subsequent resale of the defaulted shares would be as follows:

(1) *Assuming the amount paid in is returned:*

Common Stock Subscribed	1,000	
Premium on Common Stock	250	
Common Stock Subscriptions Receivable		625
Cash		625
Cash	1,100	
Common Stock		1,000
Premium on Common Stock		100

(2) *Assuming the amount paid in less the price reduction on the resale is returned:*

Common Stock Subscribed	1,000	
Premium on Common Stock	250	
Common Stock Subscriptions Receivable		625
Payable to Defaulting Subscriber (*payment withheld pending stock resale*)		625
Cash	1,100	
Payable to Defaulting Subscriber	150	
Common Stock		1,000
Premium on Common Stock		250
Payable to Defaulting Subscriber	475	
Cash		475

(3) *Assuming the full amount paid in is declared to be forfeited:*

Common Stock Subscribed	1,000	
Premium on Common Stock	250	
Common Stock Subscriptions Receivable		625
Paid-In Capital from Forfeited Stock Subscriptions		625
Cash	1,100	
Common Stock		1,000
Premium on Common Stock		100

(4) *Assuming shares equal to the number paid for in full are issued:*

Common Stock Subscribed	1,000	
Premium on Common Stock	125	
Common Stock		500
Common Stock Subscriptions Receivable		625
Cash	550	
Common Stock		500
Premium on Common Stock		50

Capital Stock Issued for Consideration Other Than Cash

When capital stock is issued for consideration in the form of property other than cash or for services, particular care is required in recording the transaction. When, at the time of the exchange, stock is sold by the company for cash or is quoted on the open market at a certain price, this price can be used in recording the consideration received and the capital increase. When means for arriving at the cash value of the securities are not available, it will be necessary to arrive at a value for the acquired consideration.

It may be possible to arrive at a satisfactory valuation of property received in exchange for stock through an appraisal by a competent outside authority. But this solution may not be available in arriving at a valuation for consideration in the form of certain services as, for example, promotional services in organizing the corporation.

Normally the board of directors is given the right by law to establish valuations for consideration other than cash received for stock. Such values will stand for all legal purposes in the absence of proof that fraud was involved in the action. The assignment of values by the board of directors should be subject to particularly careful scrutiny. There have been cases where directors have assigned excessive values to the consideration received for stock to improve the company's reported financial position. When the value of the consideration cannot be clearly established and the directors' valuations are used in reporting assets and invested capital, the source of the valuations should be disclosed on the balance sheet. When there is evidence that improper values have been assigned to the consideration received for stock, such values should be restated.

Stock is said to be **watered** when assets are overstated and capital items are correspondingly overstated. On the other hand, the balance sheet is said to contain **secret reserves** when there is an understatement of assets or an overstatement of liabilities accompanied by a corresponding understatement of capital. These misstatements may be intentional or unintentional. The accountant cannot condone either overstatement or understatement of net assets and capital. It should be observed once more that any failures in accounting for assets are not limited to the balance sheet: the overstatement of assets will result in understatements of net income as asset cost is assigned to revenue; the understatement of assets will result in overstatements of net income as asset cost is assigned to revenue.

Issuance of Capital Stock in Exchange for a Business

A corporation, upon its formation or at some later date, may be combined with another ongoing business, issuing capital stock in exchange for the net assets acquired. This is referred to as a **business combination.** In determining the amount of stock to be issued, the fair market value of the stock, as well as the values of the net assets acquired, must be considered.

Frequently the value of the stock transferred by a corporation will exceed the value of the identifiable assets acquired because of a favorable earnings record of the business acquired. If the exchange is accounted for as a *purchase,* the value of the stock in excess of the values assigned to identifiable assets is recognized as goodwill. Under this approach, the retained earnings of the company acquired *do not* become part of the combined retained earnings. On the other hand, if the exchange is treated as a *pooling of interests,* neither the revaluation of assets nor the recognition of goodwill is recorded. Assets are stated at the amounts previously reported; the retained earnings accounts of the two companies are added together and become the amount of retained earnings for the combined entity. The purchase method assumes that one of the companies is dominant and is acquiring the other company. The pooling of interests method assumes equal status and continuity of common ownership. The accounting for business combinations is dealt with in APB Opinion No. 16, and is discussed in detail in advanced accounting texts.

CAPITAL STOCK REACQUISITION AND RETIREMENT

A corporation may have the right to call certain classes of stock for redemption and may choose to exercise this right. In other cases, it may purchase stock on the open market and formally retire shares. Whether obtained through call for redemption or through purchase on the market, retirement of stock at a cost differing from the original issuance price presents special accounting problems.

The reacquisition and retirement of stock cannot be considered to give rise to income or loss. A company in issuing stock raises capital which it hopes to employ profitably; in reacquiring and retiring shares it reduces the capital to be employed in subsequent operations. Income or loss arises from the utilization of resources placed in the hands of a corporation, not from capital transactions between a company and its stockholders. Although there is general agreement on this matter, there are still certain problems in recording stock retirement.

If a class of stock is retired at the same amount originally recognized as capital stock, the capital stock account is debited and Cash is credited. All reference to the investment by the stockholders, then, is canceled. However, when the purchase price of the stock retired exceeds the par or stated value of the stock, the excess must be assigned in some satisfactory manner to paid-in capital and retained earnings.

The Accounting Principles Board in Opinion No. 6 commented upon the procedure to be followed when stock of a corporation is retired:

> (i) *an excess of purchase price over par or stated value* may be allocated between capital surplus [paid-in capital] and retained earnings. The portion of the excess allocated to capital surplus should be limited to the sum of (a) all capital surplus arising from previous retirements and net "gains" on sales of treasury stock of the same issue and (b) the pro rata portion of capital surplus paid in, voluntary transfers of retained earnings, capitalization of stock dividends, etc., on the same issue. For this purpose, any remaining capital surplus applicable to issues fully retired (formal or constructive) is deemed to be applicable pro rata to shares of common stock. Alternatively, the excess may be charged entirely to retained earnings in recognition of the fact that a corporation can always capitalize or allocate retained earnings for such purposes.
>
> (ii) *an excess of par or stated value over purchase price* should be credited to capital surplus.[4]

The effects of these provisions are illustrated in the following examples. Assume that a corporation reports the following balances related to an issue of preferred stock:

Preferred stock outstanding, par $10, 10,000 shares	$100,000
Premium on preferred stock	10,000

(1) Assume the corporation redeems and retires 2,000 shares, or 20%, of the preferred stock at $12.50 per share. Reductions are made in the preferred stock account for 2,000 shares, par $10, or $20,000, and in the premium on preferred stock for a pro rata share of the premium, 20% of $10,000, or $2,000, and the difference between the sum of these amounts and the amount paid is debited to Retained Earnings. The entry, then, is as follows:

[4] *Opinions of the Accounting Principles Board, No. 6,* "Status of Accounting Research Bulletins" (New York: American Institute of Certified Public Accountants, 1965), par. 12a.

Preferred Stock	20,000	
Premium on Preferred Stock	2,000	
Retained Earnings	3,000	
Cash		25,000

If the alternate method indicated by the Accounting Principles Board is followed, the entire amount paid over par or stated value of the retired shares would be debited to Retained Earnings. In the example, then, the entry would be:

Preferred Stock	20,000	
Retained Earnings	5,000	
Cash		25,000

(2) Assume the corporation redeems and retires the 2,000 shares of preferred stock at only $9 per share. The preferred stock account is reduced by the par value of the shares, $20,000, and the difference between the debit to Preferred Stock and the amount paid is credited to a paid-in capital account. The following entry is made:

Preferred Stock	20,000	
Cash		18,000
Paid-In Capital from Preferred Stock Reacquisition		2,000

It would also be possible to reduce Premium on Preferred Stock for a pro rata share of the premium, $2,000, and report the Paid-In Capital from Preferred Stock Reacquisition at the difference between the amount at which the preferred shares were originally issued and the amount paid on their retirement. The following entry can be made:

Preferred Stock	20,000	
Premium on Preferred Stock	2,000	
Cash		18,000
Paid-In Capital from Preferred Stock Reacquisition		4,000

If additional shares of preferred stock are subsequently retired at amounts in excess of par, the differences between the amounts paid and the par value of the preferred stock retired can be debited to the paid-in capital from the earlier preferred stock acquisition.

When stock is formally retired, there is a reduction in the corporate legal or stated capital. State laws normally do not bar the reduction of legal or stated capital when stock is issued subject to redemption and redemption is made at the price provided by terms of the stock issue.

Treasury Stock

When a company's own stock, previously paid for and issued, is reacquired and held in the name of the company rather than formally retired, it is known as **treasury stock.** A company may acquire its own stock by purchase, by acceptance in satisfaction of a claim, or by donation from stockholders. Treasury shares may subsequently be sold or formally retired.

There are many reasons a company finds it desirable to repurchase its own stock. A survey by the Conference Board cited seven major reasons for repurchasing shares.[5]

[5]Francis J. Walsh, Jr., *Repurchasing Common Stock* (New York: The Conference Board Inc., 1975), p. 5.

(1) To obtain shares for executive stock options and other compensation programs.
(2) To obtain stock to be used in acquisitions.
(3) To improve per-share earnings by reducing the number of shares outstanding.
(4) To obtain shares for conversion of other securities.
(5) To invest surplus cash temporarily.
(6) To support the market price of the stock.
(7) To increase the ratio of debt to equity.

State laws vary widely in their regulations concerning treasury stock. In some states, accounting for treasury stock is governed largely by statute. In other states, only general restrictions are applied. The accounting for treasury stock requires careful review of the state laws. State laws normally provide that the reacquisition of stock must serve some legitimate corporate purpose and must be made without injury or prejudice to the creditors or to the remaining stockholders. In almost every state, it is provided that the legal or stated capital of the corporation may not be reduced by reacquisition.

Despite the fact that the legal capital remains the same after a company has reacquired shares of its own stock, treasury stock cannot normally be viewed as an asset but should be regarded as a reduction in corporate capital. A company cannot have an ownership interest in itself; treasury stock generally does not confer upon the corporation dividend, voting, or subscription rights.

Although treasury stock has a number of similarities to unissued stock, there are some significant differences. Among these differences are the following: (1) stockholders' preemptive rights do not apply to treasury stock; (2) treasury stock may be reissued without authorization by stockholders; (3) having already been issued in accordance with legal requirements governing legal or stated capital, treasury stock may be reissued without the conditions imposed upon its original issue, for example, the discount liability on the original issue; and (4) treasury stock remains a part of legal capital in most states.

The sale of treasury stock increases the number of shares outstanding. However, the legal capital, remaining unchanged upon its purchase, is not increased through its sale. If treasury stock is to be retired, such retirement is formalized by the preparation of a certificate or notice of reduction filed with appropriate state officials. Upon the formal retirement of shares, these revert to the status of unissued shares and there is a reduction in the corporate legal or stated capital. For federal income tax purposes, treasury stock transactions provide no taxable gain or loss; stock reacquisition, as well as stock reissue or retirement, is regarded as a transaction related to a company's invested capital.

Purchase and Sale or Retirement of Treasury Stock. Two primary methods for recording treasury stock transactions have been suggested: (1) the **cost method,** where the purchase of treasury stock is viewed as giving rise to a capital element whose ultimate disposition remains to be resolved; and (2) the **par or stated value method,** where the purchase of treasury stock is viewed as effective retirement of outstanding stock.

Cost Method. Under the cost method, the purchase of treasury stock is recorded by debiting a treasury stock account for the cost of the purchase and crediting Cash. The cost is determined by the current market price of the stock and is not necessarily tied to the original stock issue price. The balance in the treasury stock account is reported as a deduction from total stockholders' equity on the balance sheet. If treasury stock is subsequently retired, the debit balance in the treasury stock account is eliminated by allocating proportionate amounts of the appropriate capital stock, paid-in capital, and retained earnings accounts, as noted previously according to APB Opinion No. 6. If treasury stock is subsequently sold, the difference between the acquisition cost and the selling price is reported as an increase or decrease in stockholders' equity. If stockholders' equity is increased, the account credited is Paid-In Capital from Treasury Stock Transactions. If stockholders' equity is decreased, paid-in capital accounts previously established may be debited or the entire amount may be debited to Retained Earnings.

To illustrate the entries required for treasury stock transactions using the cost method, consider the following:

Cost Method of Accounting for Treasury Stock

1983 Issue of stock, 10,000 shares, $10 par, at $15	Cash	150,000	
	Capital Stock		100,000
	Premium on Capital Stock		50,000
Net income for year, $30,000.	Income Summary	30,000	
	Retained Earnings		30,000
1984 Reacquisition of 1,000 shares at $16.	Treasury Stock	16,000	
	Cash		16,000
(1) Sale of treasury stock at $20.	Cash	20,000	
	Treasury Stock		16,000
	Paid-In Capital from Sale of Treasury Stock at More Than Cost		4,000
(2) Sale of treasury stock at $14.	Cash	14,000	
	Retained Earnings	2,000	
	Treasury Stock		16,000
(3) Retirement of treasury stock (10% of original issue).	Capital Stock	10,000	
	Premium on Capital Stock	5,000*	
	Retained Earnings	1,000	
	Treasury Stock		16,000
	*As indicated earlier, the entire $6,000 difference between the debit to Capital Stock and the cost to acquire the treasury stock may be debited to Retained Earnings.		
Illustration of stockholders' equity section of balance sheet prior to sale or retirement of treasury stock.	Stockholders' Equity		
	Contributed capital:		
	Capital stock		$100,000
	Premium on capital stock		50,000
	Retained earnings		30,000
	Total		$180,000
	Less treasury stock at cost		16,000
	Total stockholders' equity		$164,000

Par or Stated Value Method. If the par or stated value method (also known as the retirement method) is used, the purchase of treasury stock is regarded as a withdrawal of a group of stockholders. This calls for the cancellation of capital balances identified with this group. It follows that the sale of treasury stock, under this approach, represents the admission of a new group of stockholders calling for entries giving effect to the investment by this group. Thus, there are two separate transactions that must be recorded—the purchase and the sale.

Using the par or stated value method and the same basic data for 1983 as illustrated for the cost method, the following entries would be made in 1984:

Par Value Method of Accounting for Treasury Stock

1984 Reacquisition of 1,000 shares at $16 (assumed retirement of 10% of original issue).	Capital Stock..................	10,000	
	Premium on Capital Stock	5,000*	
	Retained Earnings	1,000	
	Cash.......................		16,000
	*Alternatively, the entire $6,000 may be debited to Retained Earnings.		
Sale of treasury stock at $20.	Cash.........................	20,000	
	Capital Stock................		10,000
	Paid-In Capital from Sale of Treasury Stock at More Than Par...		10,000**
	**Alternatively, this amount may be appropriately credited to Premium on Capital Stock.		
Illustration of stockholders' equity section of balance sheet prior to sale of treasury stock.	Stockholders' Equity		
	Contributed capital:		
	Capital stock		$ 90,000
	Premium on capital stock.................		45,000
	Retained earnings		29,000
	Total stockholders' equity..................		$164,000

Evaluating the Two Primary Methods of Accounting for Treasury Stock Transactions. Neither the AICPA, through the Accounting Principles Board, nor the Financial Accounting Standards Board has expressed a preference between the two approaches of accounting for treasury stock transactions. Although there is theoretical support for each approach, in practice the cost method is generally followed.

In comparing the results of the two approaches, it should be noticed that the total stockholders' equity will be the same regardless of which method is used. There may be differences, however, in the amounts of contributed and earned capital reported. It also should be noted that Retained Earnings may be decreased with treasury stock transactions, but can never be increased by buying and selling treasury stock.

Retained earnings may be restricted for dividend purposes while treasury stock is held. There are several ways these restrictions may be shown on the balance sheet. The most common are (1) as an appropriation of retained earnings discussed in the next chapter, (2) as a parenthetical remark in the body of the statement, and (3) as a note to the financial statements. The restriction would be reported regardless of the method used to record the purchase of the stock.

The procedures illustrated in this chapter may be modified to meet existing legal requirements relative to the status of treasury stock and to the effects upon capital balances when treasury stock is sold or retired.

Conclusions Relative to Treasury Stock Transactions. From the discussion of treasury stock, several important conclusions may be summarized as follows:

(1) Treasury stock is rarely includable as an asset on corporation books and does not qualify for dividends.
(2) Neither gain nor loss can be recognized on the income statement relative to transactions in a company's own stock.
(3) Retained earnings can be decreased as a result of treasury stock transactions; however, retained earnings cannot be increased through such transactions.
(4) In most states, retained earnings equal to the cost of treasury stock is legally unavailable for dividends. This restriction on retained earnings is reported on the balance sheet by an appropriation of retained earnings, by parenthetical remark, or by a note to the financial statements.
(5) The total stockholders' equity is not affected by the method used; however, the amounts reported for contributed capital and retained earnings can be affected by the accounting procedure followed.

Donated Treasury Stock

Treasury stock is occasionally acquired by donation from the stockholders. Shares may be donated to enable the company to raise capital by reselling the shares. In other cases, shares may be donated to eliminate a deficit. Ordinarily, all of the stockholders participate in the donation, each party donating a certain percentage of holdings so that relative interests in the corporation remain unchanged.

In the absence of an objective basis for valuation, the acquisition of treasury stock by donation may be reported on the corporation books by a memorandum entry. Assuming the assets of the company have been fairly valued, the sale of donated stock is then recorded by a debit to Cash and a credit to Donated Capital. If assets of the company have been overvalued, however, it would be improper to recognize an increase in capital arising from the sale of donated shares. Under these circumstances, the sale price for the stock should be employed as a basis for restating the company assets and contributed capital.

To illustrate this concept, assume the Bonanza Mining Co. is formed to take over the mining properties of partners Clark and Davis, and the corporation issues 10,000 shares of no-par stock to the partners in exchange for the properties. A value of $250,000 is assigned to the properties and an entry is made for the acquisition as follows:

Mining Properties	250,000	
Capital Stock		250,000

Shortly after corporate formation, Clark and Davis donate 4,000 shares to the corporation, and the corporation sells these for $15 per share. If $15 can be regarded as a measure of the fair value of the stock exchanged for the properties, the properties should be restated at $90,000, or $15 × 6,000, the number of shares actually exchanged. Upon the sale of the donated shares, then, entries should be made (1) to correct the property account and capital stock for both the stock overissue and the property overvaluation, and (2) to record the sale of the donated shares. These entries are:

Capital Stock	160,000	
Mining Properties		160,000
Cash	60,000	
Capital Stock		60,000

The balance sheet for the corporation would now show the following balances:

Cash	$60,000	Capital stock, no-par, 10,000 shares outstanding	$150,000
Mining properties	90,000		

When stock is donated so that a company may cancel a deficit, the company should take formal action to retire donated shares. Upon retirement, Capital Stock is debited for the decrease in legal capital and Additional Paid-In Capital is credited. The deficit can then be applied against the additional paid-in capital balance.

STOCK RIGHTS AND OPTIONS

As discussed in Chapter 12, a company may grant rights and options to buy its stock. These grants generally arise under the following circumstances:

(1) A company requiring additional capital may offer stockholders rights to make the purchase of additional shares attractive.
(2) A company may provide rights with the issue of various classes of securities to promote the sale of these securities.
(3) A company may offer promoters, officers, or employees special rights or options as compensation for services or other contributions.

Rights to purchase stock are evidenced by certificates called **stock purchase warrants.** The rights enable their owners to purchase shares at a specified price or a variable price dependent upon future events. The period for exercise is usually limited. Because the rights are represented by separate purchase warrants, they also have a market value and are traded on the exchange. The rights have a value because of the difference between the exercise price of the right as compared with a higher market value for the security, either present or potential.

The accounting problems faced by the issuing company under each of the circumstances listed above are described in the following paragraphs.

Rights Issued to Existing Stockholders

When rights are issued to stockholders, only a memorandum entry is made on the issuing company's books stating the number of shares that may be claimed under the outstanding rights. This information is required so the corporation may retain sufficient unissued or reacquired stock to meet the exercise of the rights. Upon surrender of the rights and the receipt of payments as specified by the rights, the stock is issued. At this time a memorandum entry is made to record the decrease in the number of rights outstanding accompanied by an entry to record the stock sale. The entry for the sale depends on the amount paid for the shares:

(1) When the cash received in the exercise of rights is less than the par or stated value of the stock, the difference is generally debited to Retained Earnings; retained earnings are permanently capitalized under these conditions.
(2) When the cash received is equal to the par or stated value of the stock, Cash is debited and Capital Stock is credited.
(3) When the cash received is more than the par or the stated value of the stock, the excess is recorded as a credit to Premium on Capital Stock or Paid-In Capital from Sale of Capital Stock at More Than Stated Value.

Usually the time period to exercise this type of right is very limited. As indicated earlier, some state laws require corporations to give existing stockholders first right to purchase new issues of stock to protect their percentage ownership in the business, the **preemptive right.** Because this process is often cumbersome and time consuming, corporate articles of incorporation are frequently written to limit this right.

Information concerning outstanding rights should be reported on the balance sheet so that the effects of the future exercise of remaining rights may be ascertained.

Rights Issued with Various Classes of Securities

When rights are issued with various classes of securities, such as debt or preferred stock, separate stock purchase warrants are issued to accompany the basic security. As described in Chapter 14, the Accounting Principles Board in Opinion No. 14 recommended assigning part of the issuance price of debt to any detachable stock purchase warrants and classifying it as part of owners' equity.[6] The value assigned to the warrant is determined by multiplying the total issue price by a fraction, the numerator of which is the fair market value of the warrant; the denominator is the fair market value of the security without the warrant plus the fair market value of the warrant. This valuation procedure is expressed in the following equation:

$$\text{Value assigned to purchase warrants} = \text{Total issue price} \times \frac{\text{Fair market value of warrant}}{\text{Fair market value of security without warrant} + \text{Fair market value of warrant}}$$

[6] *Opinions of the Accounting Principles Board, No. 14,* "Accounting for Convertible Debt and Debt Issued with Stock Purchase Warrants" (New York: American Institute of Certified Public Accountants, 1969), par. 16.

Although Opinion No. 14 is directed only to warrants attached to debt, it appears logical to extend the conclusions of that Opinion to warrants attached to preferred stock. Thus, if a market value does exist for the purchase warrants at the issuance date, a separate equity account is credited with that portion of the issuance price assigned to the warrants. If the rights are exercised, the value assigned to the common stock is the value allocated to the warrants plus the cash proceeds from the issuance of the common stock. If the rights are allowed to lapse, the value assigned to the warrants may be transferred to a permanent paid-in capital account.

Accounting for rights attached to a preferred stock issue is illustrated as follows: assume the Streuling Co. sells 1,000 shares of $50 par preferred stock for $60 per share. As an incentive for the sale, Streuling Co. gives the purchaser separate warrants enabling holders to subscribe to 1,000 shares of $20 par common stock for $25 per share. The rights expire after one year. Immediately following the issuance of the stock, the stock purchase warrants are selling at $5 per warrant. Assume the fair market value of the preferred stock without the warrant attached is $55. The proceeds of $60,000 should be allocated as follows:

$$\text{Value assigned to the purchase warrants} = \frac{\$5}{\$55 + \$5} \times \$60{,}000 = \$5{,}000$$

The entry to record the sale of the preferred stock with detachable warrants is as follows:

Cash	60,000	
Preferred Stock, $50 par		50,000
Premium on Preferred Stock		5,000
Common Stock Purchase Warrants		5,000

If the rights are exercised, the entry to record the issuance of common stock would be as follows:

Common Stock Purchase Warrants	5,000	
Cash	25,000	
Common Stock		20,000
Premium on Common Stock		10,000

This entry would be the same regardless of the market price of the common stock at the issuance date.

If the rights in the above example were allowed to lapse, the following entry would be made.

Common Stock Purchase Warrants	5,000	
Paid-In Capital from Lapsed Warrants		5,000

Rights or Options Issued to Employees

Many corporations have adopted various plans, contracts, and other agreements giving employees the opportunity to purchase stock in the employer corporation. These plans may be part of a corporate program to secure equity capital and to spread the ownership to the employee group.

Depending on the principal objectives of the corporation, plans may be classified as **noncompensatory** or **compensatory.** No special accounting problems arise if the plan is classified as noncompensatory; no compensation is recognized by the employer corporation when the stock is issued—the cash price is the issue price. If the plan is compensatory, compensation may or may not be recorded depending on the provisions of the issue.

Noncompensatory Plans. Because of the difference in accounting between compensatory and noncompensatory plans, the Accounting Principles Board in Opinion No. 25 identified four characteristics essential in a noncompensatory program.

(1) Substantially all full-time employees who meet limited employment qualifications may participate.
(2) Stock is offered to eligible employees equally or based on a uniform percentage of salary or wages.
(3) The time permitted for exercise of an option or purchase right is limited to a reasonable period.
(4) The discount from the market price of the stock is no greater than would be reasonable in an offer of stock to stockholders or others.[7]

Compensatory Plans. Stock purchase plans not meeting the four characteristics of noncompensatory plans are classified as compensatory plans. The compensation arises when an employee can purchase stock in the future at a price substantially lower than the market price. The major accounting questions associated with compensatory plans are: (1) what amount, if any, should be recognized as compensation, and (2) what period should be charged with the cost?

APB Opinion No. 25 specifies that "Compensation for services that a corporation receives as consideration for stock issued through employee stock option, purchase, and award plans should be measured by the quoted market price of the stock at the measurement date less the amount, if any, that the employee is required to pay."[8] However, some accountants argue that the appropriate amount of **compensation** is the fair market value of the services of employees. This presents both a measurement problem and a theoretical question as to whether the amount should be the opportunity cost of an employee's salary or the present value of ultimate receipts of payments, perhaps including a speculative gain or loss on the difference. In any event, stockholders should be aware of the significant opportunity costs of stock options that are paid to key employees.

Most of the accounting controversy relating to compensatory plans has focused on the appropriate **measurement date.** Several possibilities exist: (1) the date of adoption of a plan; (2) the date an option is granted to a specific individual; (3) the date on which the grantee may first exercise an option (exercisable date); (4) the date the grantee actually exercises an option (exercise date); (5) the date the grantee disposes of the stock acquired; or (6) when

[7]*Opinions of the Accounting Principles Board, No. 25,* "Accounting for Stock Issued to Employees" (New York: American Institute of Certified Public Accountants, 1972), par. 7.
[8]*Ibid.*, par. 10.

variable factors are involved, the date at which both the number of shares and the option prices are first known. These dates are not necessarily mutually exclusive. Depending on the plan, the exercisable date may coincide with the exercise date.

The Accounting Principles Board defined the measurement date as the first date on which the following are both known: (1) the number of shares that an individual employee is entitled to receive, and (2) the option or purchase price, if any.[9] For many plans, that date is the date of the option agreement. However, plans with variable terms would generally use a later measurement date, often the exercise date.

It is felt that a measurement date requiring both a definite number of shares and an option price is the date on which the company acknowledges the claim and takes action precluding any alternative use of the shares covered by the option. Dates prior to this time are not appropriate: plans calling for services are no more than proposed courses of action until services are formally recognized and the liability becomes effective. Dates after this time are not appropriate: changes in the values of the compensation award after its accrual are beyond the scope of the plan and represent matters of concern only to the grantee. Thus, a corporation will recognize compensation expense for compensatory plans only if the employee pays an amount less than the quoted market price at the measurement date.

If compensation expense is to be recognized, the remaining accounting problem is the determination of what period should be charged for the cost. Generally, the compensation should be charged to the current and future periods in which the employees perform the services for which the stock is issued. Past periods should not be adjusted. The grant may specify the period or periods during which the service is to be performed, or it may be inferred from the past patterns of grants or awards. When several periods of employment are involved before the stock is issued, the employer corporation should accrue compensation expense in each period involved. If the measurement date is later than the award date, the compensation expense each period must be estimated based on the quoted market price of the stock at the end of each period.[10] If stock is issued before some or all of the services are performed, part of the consideration received should be recorded in an unearned compensation account. Because it is related to issued stock, this account should be classified as a separate reduction of stockholders' equity rather than as a deferred charge in the asset section.

Options are sometimes issued as a payment for services that should be capitalized. For example, the employee receiving the option may be involved in producing specialized equipment for the company's own use, or in producing specialized inventory. In these cases, the appropriate asset account should be debited for the implicit value of the services included in the option. Upon exercise of the options, the sum of the cash received and the value previously assigned to options represents the consideration related to the issue of the stock.

---

[9] *Ibid.*, par. 10b.
[10] *Ibid.*, par. 13.

Illustrative Entries for Recording Compensatory Stock Options. Accounting for compensatory plans can be illustrated by the following examples: Assume that on December 31, 1982, the board of directors of the Lister Co. authorizes the grant of nontransferable stock options to supplement the salaries of certain executives. Options permit the purchase of 10,000 shares of $10 par common stock at a price of $47.50. Stock is currently selling at $50. Options can be exercised beginning January 1, 1985, but only if executives are still in the employ of the company; options expire at the end of 1986. All the options are exercised on December 31, 1985, when the $10 par stock is quoted on the market at $60.

The value of the stock options at the date of the grant (compensation expense) is determined as follows:

Market value of common stock on December 31, 1982, 10,000 shares at $50	$500,000
Option price, 10,000 shares at $47.50	475,000
Value of stock options (compensation expense)	$ 25,000

The terms of the grant indicate that the services are being performed for the period from the grant date to the exercisable date, or for 1983 and 1984.

The following entries are made by the corporation to record the grant of the options, the annual accrual of option rights, and the exercise of the options.

Transaction	Entry		
December 31, 1982 Grant of nontransferable stock options.	(Memorandum entry) Granted nontransferable options to executives for the purchase of 10,000 shares of common stock at $47.50. Options are exercisable beginning January 1, 1985, providing officers are in the employ of the company on that date. Options expire on December 31, 1986. Value of options on December 31, 1982, is $25,000 (market value of stock, $500,000; option price, $475,000).		
December 31, 1983 To record compensation and option credit accrual for 1983: value of stock options, $25,000; period of service covered by plan, 1983 and 1984; cost assigned to 1983: ½ × $25,000 = $12,500.	Executive Compensation Expense. Credit Under Stock Option Plan ..	12,500	 12,500
December 31, 1984 To record compensation and option credit accrual for 1984: ½ × $25,000 = $12,500.	Executive Compensation Expense. Credit Under Stock Option Plan ..	12,500	 12,500
December 31, 1985 To record exercise of stock options: cash received for stock, 10,000 shares at $47.50, or $475,000; par value of stock issued, 10,000 shares at $10, or $100,000.	Cash Credit Under Stock Option Plan Common Stock Premium on Common Stock	475,000 25,000	 100,000 400,000

The accrued compensation reported in Credit Under Stock Option Plan is properly reported as a part of paid-in capital because it represents investments of services made by employees that are expected to be paid for by the issuance of capital stock at a reduced price. If options expire through a failure of employees to meet the conditions of the option or through changes in the price of the stock making exercise of options unattractive, the balance of the account should be eliminated by decreasing compensation expense in the period of forfeiture.[11]

Special Treatment for Variable Stock Option Plans. In FASB Interpretation No. 28, plans involving stock appreciation rights and other variable plan awards, for example, plans that award a variable number of shares of stock as an option or with a variable option price, or both, are specifically included under the provisions of APB No. 25.[12] Special treatment is needed for these types of plans. The compensation expense is accrued and charged to the service period(s) as with other stock option plans. However, changes in the market values of variable stock option plans in periods subsequent to the grant date require an adjustment for the compensation accrual. The Interpretation indicates that changes in the market value, either up or down, between the grant date and the measurement date result in a change in the measurement of compensation associated with these rights or awards. If a quoted market price is not available, the best estimate of the market value should be used. A catch-up adjustment for the changes in values is to be reflected in the period when the change occurs and the new balance spread over current and future periods.

To illustrate, if the grant provisions offered by Lister Co. were variable and the measurement date occurred after the grant date, different entries would be required than those shown on page 651. Assume that on December 31, 1982, the executives of Lister Co. are given the right to purchase 10,000 shares of $10 par stock at 80% of the market price on December 31, 1984, two years after the grant date. In order to be eligible for the stock, the executives must remain with the company until the exercisable date, December 31, 1985. The market price for the stock is as follows: December 31, 1982, date of grant, $50; December 31, 1983, end of first year of service period, $60; December 31, 1984, end of second year of service period, $65; and December 31, 1985, exercisable date, $80.

The entries and computations on page 653 would be made to record the annual accruals of option rights and the exercise of the options for the variable stock option plans.

It should be noted in the example that the compensation expense accrual of $46,667 recognizes the "catch-up" adjustment for changes in market value in 1984, which is in accordance with Interpretation No. 28. Recall that Opinion No. 20 allows changes in estimates to be corrected in the current period or "spread" over current and future periods. If the $10,000 change in estimate in the example had been spread only over the current and future periods, the compensation expense entry for 1984 and 1985 would have been $45,000 in each year ($130,000 − $40,000 = $90,000 ÷ 2 = $45,000). Because the example deals with a variable stock option plan and falls specifically under

[11]*Ibid.*, par. 15.

[12]*FASB Interpretation No. 28*, "Accounting for Stock Appreciation Rights and Other Variable Stock Option or Award Plans" (Stamford: Financial Accounting Standards Board, 1978).

Transaction	Entry		
December 31, 1983 To record estimate of compensation expense accrual for 1983; market price of stock, December 31, 1983, $60; estimated option price, 80% of $60, or $48; estimated value of option per share, $12 ($60 − $48); total compensation, $120,000 ($12 × 10,000). Period of services rendered, three years or $40,000 each year.	Executive Compensation Expense. Credit Under Stock Option Plan . .	40,000	 40,000
December 31, 1984 To record estimate of compensation expense accrual for 1984; market price of stock, December 31, 1984, $65; estimated option price, 80% of $65, or $52; estimated value of option per share, $13 ($65 − $52); total compensation, $130,000 ($13 × 10,000). Compensation recognized 1983, $40,000. Compensation as adjusted for changes in market values, to be recognized in 1984, $46,667 = ($130,000 ÷ 3 = $43,333) plus $3,334 catch-up from 1983.	Executive Compensation Expense. Credit Under Stock Option Plan . .	46,667	 46,667
December 31, 1985 To record compensation expense for 1985, as adjusted, and issuance of stock.	Executive Compensation Expense. Credit Under Stock Option Plan . . Cash . . . . Credit Under Stock Option Plan . . . . Common Stock . . . . Premium on Common Stock	43,333 520,000 130,000	 43,333 100,000 550,000

Computations:

		Compensation				Accrual of Expense by Year		
Date	*Market Price*	*Per Share*	*Aggregate*	*Percentage Accrued*	*Accrued to Date*	*1983*	*1984*	*1985*
12/31/83	$60	$12	$120,000	33⅓%	$ 40,000	$40,000		
					46,667		$46,667	
12/31/84	$65	$13	$130,000	66⅔%	$ 86,667			
					43,333			$43,333
12/31/85	$65*	$13	$130,000	100%	$130,000			

*Measurement data value

Interpretation No. 28, a catch-up adjustment must be made to the current period, that is, in the period when the change was first determined.

Income Tax Treatment of Compensatory Stock Plans. Compensatory plans have frequently been awarded to key executives whose cash salaries place them in high tax rate brackets. Therefore, the detailed nature of stock option plans offered by employers is greatly affected by the provisions of the Internal Revenue Code in effect at the time the options are granted.

For example, the Economic Recovery Tax Act of 1981 provided for a new type of stock option called an **incentive stock option** which is similar in many respects to the former qualified and restricted stock options which were repealed in 1976. Under the incentive stock option plan, no tax consequences result from the grant of the option or from the exercise of the option by the employee. Gains on subsequent sales of stock purchased through the incentive stock option plan are taxed at lower capital gain rates if the stock is held for at least two years from the date of the option grant and one year after the stock was transferred. Because of these tax advantages, many companies began offering incentive stock options to their key executives.

Disclosure of Stock Options

When stock option plans are in existence, disclosure should be made as to the status of the option or plan at the end of the reporting period, including the number of shares under option, the option price, and the number of shares that were exercisable. Information on options exercised should also be provided, including the number of options exercised and the option price. Note Nine to the financial statements of General Mills, Inc., reproduced in Appendix B, provides a good illustration of disclosure for stock options.

STOCK CONVERSIONS

Stockholders may be permitted by the terms of their stock agreement or by special action by the corporation to exchange their holdings for stock of other classes. No gain or loss is recognized on these conversions because it is an exchange of one equity for another. In certain instances, the exchanges may affect only corporate contributed capital accounts; in other instances, the exchanges may affect both capital and retained earnings accounts.

To illustrate the different conditions, assume that the capital of the Oakey Corporation on December 31, 1984 is as follows:

Preferred stock, $100 par, 10,000 shares	$1,000,000
Premium on preferred stock	100,000
Common stock, $25 stated value, 100,000 shares	2,500,000
Paid-in capital from sale of common stock at more than stated value	500,000
Retained earnings	1,000,000

Preferred shares are convertible into common shares at any time at the option of the shareholder.

Case 1—Assume conditions of conversion permit the exchange of each share of preferred for 4 shares of common. On December 31, 1984, 1,000 shares of preferred stock are exchanged on the above basis. The amount originally paid for the preferred, $110,000, is now the consideration identified with 4,000 shares of common stock with a total stated value of $100,000. The conversion is recorded as follows:

Preferred Stock, $100 par	100,000	
Premium on Preferred Stock	10,000	
Common Stock, $25 stated value		100,000
Paid-In Capital from Conversion of Preferred Stock into Common Stock		10,000

Case 2 —Assume conditions of conversion permit the exchange of each share of preferred for 5 shares of common. In converting 1,000 shares of preferred for common, an increase in common stock of $125,000 must be recognized although it is accompanied by a decrease in the preferred equity of only $110,000; the increase in the legal capital related to the new issue is generally accomplished by a debit to Retained Earnings. The conversion, then, is recorded as follows:

Preferred Stock, $100 par	100,000	
Premium on Preferrred Stock	10,000	
Retained Earnings	15,000	
Common Stock, $25 stated value		125,000

The problems relating to the conversion of bonds for capital stock were described in Chapter 14. When either stocks or bonds have conversion rights, the company must be in a position to issue securities of the required class. Unissued or reacquired securities may be maintained by the company for this purpose. Detailed information should be given on the balance sheet relative to security conversion features as well as the means for meeting conversion requirements.

STOCK SPLITS AND REVERSE STOCK SPLITS

When the market price of shares is high and it is felt that a lower price will result in a better market and a wider distribution of ownership, a corporation may authorize the shares outstanding to be replaced by a larger number of shares. For example, 100,000 shares of stock, par value $100, are exchanged for 500,000 shares of stock, par value $20. Each stockholder receives 5 new shares for each share owned. The increase in shares outstanding in this manner is known as a **stock split** or **stock split-up.** The reverse procedure, replacement of shares outstanding by a smaller number of shares, may be desirable when the price of shares is low and it is felt there may be certain advantages in having a higher price for shares. The reduction of shares outstanding by combining shares is referred to as a **reverse stock split** or a **stock split-down.**

After a stock split or reverse stock split, the capital stock balance remains the same; however, the change in the number of shares of stock outstanding is accompanied by a change in the par or stated value of the stock. The change in the number of shares outstanding, as well as the change in the par or stated value, may be recorded by means of a memorandum entry. However, it may be desirable to establish a new account reporting the nature and the amount of the new issue. In any event, notations will be required in the subsidiary stockholders ledger to report the exchange of stock and the change in the number of shares held by each stockholder.

Stock splits are sometimes effected by issuing a large stock dividend. In this case, the par value of the stock is not changed and an amount equal to the par value of the newly issued shares is transferred to the capital account from either additional paid-in capital or from retained earnings. A further discussion on this type of stock split is included in Chapter 18.

BALANCE SHEET DISCLOSURE OF CONTRIBUTED CAPITAL

Contributed capital and its components should be disclosed separately from Retained Earnings in the balance sheet. Within the contributed capital section, it is important to identify the major classes of stock with their related additional paid-in capital accounts. Although it is common practice to report a single value for additional paid-in capital for each class of stock, separate accounts should be provided in the ledger to identify the individual sources of additional paid-in capital, e.g., premium on capital stock or paid-in capital in excess of stated value, paid-in capital from conversion of capital stock, from forfeited stock subscriptions, or from donations by stockholders.

A description of the major features should be disclosed for each class of stock such as par or stated value, dividend preference, or conversion option. The number of shares authorized, issued, and outstanding should also be disclosed. The balance sheet for General Mills Inc. in Appendix B illustrates many of these points.

QUESTIONS

1. M. Sears has owned and operated a small machine shop for several months. The business has grown, and Sears has given some thought to incorporating. What advantages and disadvantages would there be to such a change?

2. What are the four basic rights of stockholders?

3. (a) Define legal capital. (b) What limitations are placed on the corporation by law to safeguard legal capital?

4. (a) What preferences are usually granted preferred stockholders? (b) What is callable preferred stock? Redeemable preferred stock? Convertible preferred stock? (c) Distinguish between cumulative and noncumulative preferred stock. (d) What limitations on stockholders' rights may be placed on preferred stock?

5. The controller for the Forsey Co. contends that the redemption of preferred stock at less than its issuance price should be reported as an increase in retained earnings since redemption at more than issuance price calls for a decrease in retained earnings. How would you answer this argument?

6. A new company decides to issue both preferred and common stock. The par value for both types is $100. An investor decides to purchase the preferred stock. Under what conditions would this be a wise decision?

7. The Carver Co. treats proceeds from capital stock subscription defaults as miscellaneous revenue. Would you approve of this practice? Explain.
8. (a) What alternatives may a company have when a subscriber defaults on a subscription? (b) What limits the choice between these alternatives?
9. The Jeffs Company acquires the assets of the Marino Company in exchange for 10,000 shares of its common stock, par value $10. (a) Assuming the appraised value of the property acquired exceeds the par value of the stock issued, how would you record the acquisition? (b) Assuming the par value of the stock issued exceeds the appraised value of the property acquired, suggest different methods for recording the acquisition. What factors will determine the method to be used?
10. Why might a company purchase its own stock?
11. Energy Resources Inc. reports treasury stock as a current asset, explaining that it intends to sell the stock soon to acquire working capital. Do you approve of this reporting?
12. (a) Describe two approaches that may be taken in recording the reacquisition of treasury stock. (b) What are the entries in each case assuming: (1) the stock is purchased at more than its original issue price; (2) the stock is purchased at less than its original issue price?
13. There is frequently a difference between the purchase price and the sales price of treasury stock. Why isn't this difference properly shown as an income statement item, especially in view of accounting pronouncements that restrict entries to Retained Earnings?
14. The South West Co. issues 10,000,000 shares of no-par common stock in exchange for certain mineral lands. Property is established on the books at $5,000,000. Shortly thereafter, stockholders donate to the corporation 20% of their shares. The stock is resold by the company at 10¢ per share. What accounting problems arise as a result of the stock donation and resale?
15. (a) What entries should be made on the issuer's books when stock rights are issued to stockholders? (b) What entries should be made when stock is issued on rights? (c) What information, if any, should appear on the balance sheet relative to outstanding rights?
16. What characteristics are essential for a stock-option plan to be classified as noncompensatory?
17. What determines the measurement date for purposes of a stock option valuation?
18. Preferred stockholders of the Beacon Corporation exchange their holdings for no-par common stock in accordance with terms of the preferred issue. How should this conversion be reported on the corporation books?
19. Define a stock split and identify the major objectives of this corporate action.

DISCUSSION CASES

case 17-1 (Should par value be used to determine the amount of contributed capital?) The P & H Company, in payment for services, issues 5,000 shares of common stock to persons organizing and promoting the company, and another 20,000 shares in exchange for properties believed to have valuable mineral rights. The par value of the stock, $10 per share, is used in recording the consideration for the shares. Shortly after organization, the company decides to sell the properties and use the proceeds for another venture. The properties are sold for $265,000. What accounting issues are involved? How would you record the sale of properties and why?

case 17-2 (Giving something for nothing?) Excerpts from an article appearing in the May 1, 1979, *Wall Street Journal* are presented as follows:

Dividend News

IBM Holders Vote 4-for-1 Stock Split, Effective May 10

By a "Wall Street Journal" Staff Reporter

SAN DIEGO—International Business Machines Corp. shareholders as expected, authorized a four-for-one split of the company's stock, effective May 10.

At a quiet annual meeting attended by an estimated 1,400 of the computer giant's more than 600,000 shareholders, the split was opposed by less than 1% of the votes cast.

The split which is expected to make IBM's shares more attractive to small investors, will increase the number of authorized shares to 650 million from 162.5 million. About 583 million shares are expected to be outstanding after the split.

IBM has made numerous stock distributions in recent years so that 100 shares from 1958 ballooned to 1,135 shares at the annual meeting, but the forthcoming split is the first distribution since 1958 that will result in a change in the par value of IBM's shares. The par value will be reduced to $1.25 a share, from $5.00.

Regarding the mechanics of the split, IBM said that current stock certificates will remain in effect. Each shareholder of record May 10 will receive new certificates representing three shares for each held. The new certificates will be mailed around May 31.

Why did IBM propose the 4-for-1 stock split and why were the stockholders not opposed to the split? What will the impact be on the owners' equity section of IBM's balance sheet?

EXERCISES

exercise 17-1 (Common stock transactions)

The Spisak Corporation is authorized to issue 50,000 shares of $30 par value common stock. Record the following transactions in journal entry form.

(a) Issued 5,000 shares at par value; received cash.
(b) Issued 250 shares to attorneys for services in securing the corporate charter and for preliminary legal costs of organizing the corporation. The value of the services was $9,000.
(c) Issued 300 shares, valued objectively at $10,000, to the corporate promoters.
(d) Issued 8,500 shares of stock in exchange for buildings valued at $175,000 and land valued at $80,000.
(e) Received cash for 6,500 shares of stock sold at $38 per share.
(f) Issued 8,000 shares at $45 per share; received cash.

exercise 17-2 (Par and stated values)

At the time of formation, the Pruett Corporation was authorized to issue 25,000 shares of common stock. Pruett later received cash from the issuance of 20,000 shares at $12.50 per share. Record the entries for the authorization and issuance of the common stock under each of the following assumptions. (Consider each assumption separately.)

(a) Stock has a par value of $10 per share.
(b) Stock has a stated value of $7.50 per share with no par value.
(c) Stock has no par or stated value.

exercise 17-3 (Dividends per share: cumulative; noncumulative features)

The Samuelson Company paid dividends at the end of each year as follows: 1982, $150,000; 1983, $240,000; 1984, $560,000. Give the amount of dividends that was paid per share on common and preferred stock for each year, assuming capital structures as follows:

(a) 250,000 shares of no-par common; 20,000 shares of $100 par, 7%, noncumulative preferred.
(b) 250,000 shares of no-par common; 20,000 shares of $100 par, 7%, cumulative preferred, dividends three years in arrears at the beginning of 1982.
(c) 250,000 shares of $10 par common; 30,000 shares of $100 par, 7%, cumulative preferred, no dividends in arrears at the beginning of 1982.

exercise 17-4 (Computing liquidation amounts)

The stockholders' equity for the Brandon Company on July 1, 1984, is given below.

Contributed capital:	
Preferred stock, cumulative, $10 stated value, 37,000 shares outstanding, entitled upon involuntary liquidation to $12 per share plus dividends in arrears amounting to $4 per share on July 1, 1984	$370,000
Common stock, $2 stated value, 90,000 shares outstanding	180,000
Paid-in capital from sale of common stock at more than stated value	200,000
Retained earnings	56,000
Total stockholders' equity	$806,000

Determine the amounts that would be paid to each class of stockholders if the company is liquidated on this date, assuming cash available for stockholders after meeting all of the creditors' claims is (a) $300,000; (b) $500,000; (c) $640,000.

exercise 17-5 (Issuance of capital stock)

The Blackburn Corporation is organized with authorized capital as follows: 15,000 shares of no-par common and 2,000 shares of 8% preferred, par $200. Give the entries required for each of the following transactions:

(a) Assets formerly owned by G. Culligan are accepted as payment for 5,000 shares of common stock. Assets are recorded at values as follows: land, $20,000; buildings, $40,000; inventories, $80,000.
(b) Remaining common stock is sold at $15.
(c) Subscriptions are received for 1,250 shares of preferred stock at $206. A 50% down payment is made on preferred.
(d) One subscriber for 125 shares of preferred defaults and the down payment is retained pending sale of this lot. Remaining subscribers pay the balances due and the stock is issued.
(e) Lot of 125 shares of preferred is sold at $204. Loss on resale is charged against the account of the defaulting subscriber, and the down payment less the loss is returned to the subscriber.

exercise 17-6 (Accounting for defaulted subscriptions)

On January 1, 1984, RSK Corporation received authorization to issue 100,000 shares of no-par common stock with a stated value of $10 per share. The stock was offered to subscribers at a subscription price of $40 per share. Subscriptions were recorded by a debit to Subscriptions Receivable and credits to Common Stock Subscribed and to a paid-in capital account. Subsequently, a subscriber who had contracted to purchase 500 shares defaulted after paying 20% of the subscription price. Give four methods of accounting for the default, and give the journal entry to record the default under each method.

exercise 17-7 (Exchanging stock for properties)

The Giles Co. issues 10,000 shares of preferred stock and 45,000 shares of common stock, each with a par value of $10, in exchange for properties appraised at $600,000. Give the entry to record the exchange on the books of the corporation assuming:

(a) No price can be assigned at date of issuance to the preferred stock or common stock issues.
(b) Common stock is selling on the market at $10.50 per share; there was no preferred stock issued prior to this issue.
(c) Common stock is selling on the market at $10 per share, preferred stock is selling on the market at $15 per share.

exercise 17-8 (Acquisition and retirement of stock)

The Cowart Company reported the following balances related to an issuance of common stock:

Common Stock, $10 par, 50,000 shares issued and outstanding	$500,000
Premium on Common Stock	50,000

The company purchased and retired 5,000 shares at $13 on June 1, 1984, and 12,000 shares at $8 on December 31, 1984. Give the entries to record the acquisition and retirement of the common stock.

exercise 17-9 (Treasury stock: par value and cost methods)

The capital accounts for the Crawford Co. were as follows on June 1, 1984:

Common Stock, $15 par, 240,000 shares	$3,600,000
Premium on Common Stock	480,000
Retained Earnings	900,000

On this date the company purchased 15,000 shares of stock at $16; and in December of the same year it reissued this stock at $19.

(1) What entries should be made for the stock purchase and the reissuance if the par value method of recording treasury stock transactions is used? (If alternate treatments are possible, justify your selection).
(2) What entries should be made for the stock purchase and reissuance if the cost method is used?
(3) After the reissuance of the treasury stock, how does the stockholders' equity differ under the two methods?

exercise 17-10 (Acquisition of treasury stock)

The Rojo Company issued 10,000 shares of no-par stock at $30 and 20,000 shares at $45. The state in which Rojo is incorporated does not require any stated capital. During 1984, 2,000 shares were reacquired at $42. Assume the treasury stock is to be carried at the weighted average price per share. Prepare the journal entry to record the reacquisition.

exercise 17-11 (Valuation of donated capital)

In your first audit of a mining company, you note the following facts with respect to its capital stock transactions:

Authorized capital consists of 2,500,000 shares of $1 par value common stock.

All of the shares were issued initially in exchange for certain mineral properties. The properties were recorded on the company books at $5,000,000.

One million shares were received by the company as a donation shortly after incorporation and were sold immediately for cash of $1,500,000. This amount was recorded as a credit to Donated Capital.

(1) What values should be assigned to the mineral properties and the stockholders' equity? Discuss.
(2) Prepare any required correcting entry.

exercise 17-12 (Accounting for stock purchase warrants)

The Short Company needs to raise additional equity capital. After analysis of the available options, the company decides to issue 1,000 shares of $100 par preferred stock with detachable warrants attached. The package of the stock and warrants sells for 112. The warrants enable the holder to purchase 1,000 shares of $25 par common stock at $30 per share. Immediately following the issuance of the stock, the stock purchase warrants are selling at $9 per share. The market value of the preferred stock without the warrants is 104. What journal entries would be required to record the issuance of the stock and subsequent use of the warrants to purchase common stock? Round answers to the nearest dollar.

exercise 17-13 (Accounting for compensatory stock options)

The stockholders of the Wagner Co. on December 24, 1978, approved a plan granting certain officers of the company nontransferable options to buy 50,000 shares of no-par common stock at $16 per share. Stock was selling at this time at $20 per share. The option plan provides that the officers must be employed by the company for the next five years, that options can be exercised after January 1, 1984, and that options will expire at the end of 1985. One of the officers who had been granted options for 10,000 shares left the company at the beginning of 1982; remaining officers exercised their rights under the option plan at the end of 1985. Give the entries that should be made on the books of the corporation at the end of each year for 1978–1985 inclusive. The market price of the stock at January 1, 1984, was $30 per share.

exercise 17-14 (Accounting for variable stock option plans)

On March 31, 1981, the Board of Directors of Allen Industries approved a stock option plan for its twenty executives to purchase 500 shares of $25 par common stock each. The plan further indicated that the twenty executives must remain with the company until March 31, 1984, at which time they could exercise their options. The exercise price is 90% of the market price of the stock on December 31, 1983. All outstanding options expire on December 31, 1985. Assuming the following stock prices and that all options are exercised on June 27, 1984, give the journal entries for the company for its calendar years 1981, 1982, 1983, and 1984.

Date	Stock Price
March 31, 1981	$30
December 31, 1981	35
December 31, 1982	45
December 31, 1983	42
March 31, 1984	45
June 27, 1984	46

exercise 17-15 (Convertible preferred stock)

Capital accounts for the Dome Co. on December 31 are as follows:

Preferred Stock, $25 par, 30,000 shares issued and outstanding	$ 750,000
Premium on Preferred Stock	60,000
Common Stock, $5 par, 300,000 shares issued and outstanding	1,500,000
Premium on Common Stock	450,000
Retained Earnings	1,450,000

Preferred stock is convertible into common stock. Give the entry made on the corporation books assuming 1,800 shares of preferred are converted under each assumption listed:

(a) Preferred shares are convertible into common on a share-for-share basis.
(b) Each preferred share is convertible into 8 shares of common.
(c) Each preferred share is convertible into 4 shares of common.

exercise 17-16 (Analysis of owners' equity)

From the following information, reconstruct the journal entries that were made by the Starlight Corporation during 1984.

	December 31, 1984		December 31, 1983	
	Amount	Shares	Amount	Shares
Common stock	$175,000	7,000	$150,000	6,000
Premium on common stock	54,250		36,000	
Paid-in capital from sale of treasury stock at more than cost	1,000	200	—	—
Retained earnings	76,500*	—	49,000	—
Treasury stock	15,000	300	—	—

*Includes net income for 1984 of $40,000. There were no dividends.

Twenty-five hundred shares of common stock issued when the company was formed were purchased and retired during 1984. The cost method is used to record treasury stock transactions.

PROBLEMS

problem 17-1 (Stockholders' equity transactions and balance sheet preparation)

Pulsipher Co. was organized on May 25, 1984, and was authorized to issue 250,000 shares of no-par common stock, stated value $20, and 10,000 shares of 9% preferred stock, par value $50.

The following were the company's capital stock transactions through September 15, 1984:

June 1 Issued 55,000 shares of common stock to an investment group at $25.

June 15 Assets were obtained from Lawler Co. in exchange for 75,000 shares of common stock. The assets were appraised as follows:

Merchandise inventory	$400,000
Furniture and fixtures	150,000
Machinery and equipment	575,000
Land	475,000

July 1 Subscriptions were received for 120,000 shares of common stock at $30 and for 5,000 shares of preferred 9% stock at $55; each class of stock is to be paid for in two installments, 25% on the date of subscription and 75% within 90 days.

Sept. 15 The second installments on the common stock and preferred stock were paid in full and the stock was issued.

Instructions:

(1) Give the journal entries to record the preceding transactions.
(2) Prepare a balance sheet based on the results of the preceding transactions.

problem 17-2 (Accounting and reporting for capital stock subscriptions)

The Romero Company, organized on April 10, 1984, was authorized to issue stock as follows:

250,000 shares of $10 par common stock
10,250 shares of 8% preferred stock with a par value of $100

Capital stock transactions through September 15, 1984, were as follows:

May 15 Subscriptions were received for 100,000 shares of common stock at $16 on the following terms: 10% was paid in cash at the time of subscription, the balance being payable in three equal installments due on the fifteenth day of each succeeding month.

June 1 All of the preferred stock was issued to an investment company for cash at $102 and stock was issued.

June 15 The first installment on subscriptions to 95,000 shares was collected. Terms of the subscription contract provided that defaulting subscribers have 30 days in which to make payment and obtain reinstatement; failure to make payment within the specified period will result in the forfeiture of amounts already paid in.

July 15 The second installment on common subscriptions was collected. Collections included receipt of the first and second installment on 3,000 shares from subscribers who defaulted on their first installment; however, subscribers to 1,000 shares defaulted in addition to subscribers already in default.

Aug. 15 The third installment on common subscriptions was collected. Collections included receipt of the second and third installment from subscribers to 500 shares who defaulted on their second installment. Stock certificates were issued to fully paid subscribers.

Sept. 1 Stock in default was issued to an investment company at 14.

Instructions:

(1) Give the journal entries to record these transactions.
(2) Prepare the stockholders' equity section of the balance sheet on September 15, 1984.

problem 17-3 (Stockholders' equity transactions and balance sheet presentation)

The Seaman Corporation was organized on September 1, 1984, with authorized capital stock of 200,000 shares of 9% cumulative preferred with a $40 par value and 1,000,000 shares of no-par common stock with a $30 stated value. During the balance of the year, the following transactions relating to capital stock were completed:

Oct. 1 Subscriptions were received for 300,000 shares of common stock at $42, payable $22 down and the balance in two equal installments due November 1 and December 1. On the same date 16,500 shares of common stock were issued to Jim Williams in exchange for his business. Assets transferred to the corporation were valued as follows: land, $210,000; buildings, $250,000; equipment, $50,000; merchandise, $110,000. Liabilities of the business assumed by the corporation were: mortgage payable, $41,000; accounts payable, $11,000; accrued interest on mortgage, $550. No goodwill is recognized in recording the issuance of the stock for net assets.

Oct. 3 Subscriptions were received for 120,000 shares of preferred stock at $45, payable $15 down and the balance in two equal installments due November 1, and December 1.

Nov. 1 Amounts due on this date were collected from all common and preferred stock subscribers.

Nov. 12 Subscriptions were received for 480,000 shares of common stock at $44, payable $22 down and the balance in two equal installments due December 1, and January 1.

Dec. 1 Amounts due on this date were collected from all common stock subscribers and stock fully paid for was issued. The final installment on preferred stock subscriptions was received from all subscribers except one whose installment due on this date was $9,000. State corporation laws provide that the company is liable for the return to the subscriber of the amount received less the loss on the subsequent resale of the stock. Preferred stock fully paid for was issued.

Dec. 6 Preferred stock defaulted on December 1 was issued for cash at $36. Stock was issued, and settlement was made with the defaulting subscriber.

Instructions:

(1) Prepare journal entries to record the foregoing transactions.
(2) Prepare the stockholders' equity section for the corporation as of December 31.

problem 17-4 (Reconstruction of equity transactions)

The Hunter Company had the following account balances in its balance sheet at December 31, 1984, the end of its first year of operations. All stock was issued on a subscription basis, and the state laws permit the company to retain all partial subscriptions paid by defaulting subscribers.

Common Stock Subscriptions Receivable	$100,000
Common Stock, $25 par	50,000
Common Stock Subscribed	150,000
Premium on Common Stock	40,000
Preferred 8% Stock, $100 par	100,000
Premium on Preferred 8% Stock	50,000
Paid-In Capital from Default on Preferred 8% Stock (200 shares)	10,000
Preferred 10% Stock, $50 par	20,000
Retained Earnings	20,000

The reported net income for 1984 was $40,000.

Instructions: From the above data, reconstruct in summary form the journal entries to record all transactions involving the company's stockholders. Indicate the amount of dividends distributed to each class of stockholders.

problem 17-5 (Capital stock subscriptions)

The Jorgensen Machine Co. was incorporated on January 31, 1984, with authorized common stock of $1,200,000 and 9% cumulative preferred stock of $240,000, each class with a par value of $60.

Subscriptions were received for 6,000 shares of common stock at $65 a share, to be paid in four equal installments on March 1, April 1, May 1, and June 1. The first installment was paid in full.

Subscribers for 400 shares defaulted on the second installment, and the amounts already received from these subscribers were returned. The second, third, and fourth installments were paid in full on their due dates by the remaining subscribers, and the stock was issued.

During March, preferred stock was offered for sale at $80, 1 share of common stock being offered with each subscription for 10 shares of preferred. During March, the market price for the common stock was $65 per share. On this basis subscriptions were received for all of the preferred stock. Subscriptions were payable in two equal installments: the first was payable by the end of March and the second was payable at any time prior to June 15. The first installment was paid in full. By June 1, $136,000 had been received on the second installment, and stock was issued to the fully paid subscribers.

Instructions:

(1) Journalize the above transactions.
(2) Prepare the stockholders' equity section of the balance sheet as of June 1 reflecting the foregoing.

problem 17-6 (Reacquisition, retirement, and resale of capital stock)

The capital accounts of the Malmrose Company were as follows on June 1, 1984.

Preferred 9% Stock, $100 par, 7,000 shares issued and outstanding	$ 700,000
Premium on Preferred Stock	21,000
Common Stock, $20 par, 70,000 shares issued and outstanding	1,400,000

Premium on Common Stock	$ 350,000
Retained Earnings	190,000

During the remainder of 1984, the Malmrose Company called the preferred stock at $112 per share and then retired the stock. Also, the company reacquired 28,000 shares of common stock at $17, and 22,000 of the reacquired common shares were reissued at $24 per share.

Instructions:

(1) Give the entries to record the reacquisition and retirement of the preferred stock and the acquisition and reissue of the common stock assuming the par value method of recording treasury stock transactions is used.

(2) Give the entry to record the acquisition and resale of the common stock assuming the cost method of recording treasury stock transactions is used.

problem 17-7 (Comprehensive analysis and reporting of stockholders' equity)

The Monson Company has two classes of capital stock outstanding: 9%, $20 par preferred and $70 par common. During the fiscal year ending November 30, 1984, the company was active in transactions affecting the stockholders' equity. The following summarizes these transactions:

Type of Transaction	Number of Shares	Price per Share
(a) Issue of preferred stock	10,000	$28
(b) Issue of common stock	35,000	70
(c) Retirement of preferred stock	2,000	30
(d) Purchase of treasury stock—common (reported at cost)	5,000	80
(e) Stock split—common (par value reduced to $35)	2 for 1	
(f) Reissue of treasury stock—common	5,000	52

Balances of the accounts in the stockholders' equity section of the November 30, 1983, balance sheet were:

Preferred Stock, 50,000 shares	$1,000,000
Common Stock, 100,000 shares	7,000,000
Premium on Preferred Stock	400,000
Premium on Common Stock	1,200,000
Retained Earnings	550,000

Dividends were paid at the end of the fiscal year on the common stock at $1.20 per share, and on the preferred stock at the preferred rate. Net income for the year was $850,000.

Instructions: Based on the preceding data, prepare the stockholders' equity section of the balance sheet as of November 30, 1984. (Note: A work sheet beginning with November 30, 1983 balances and providing for transactions for the current year will facilitate the preparation of this section of the balance sheet.)

problem 17-8 (Treasury stock transactions)

Transactions of the Tinker Company during 1984, the first year of operations, that affected its stockholders' equity are given below.

(a) Issued 30,000 shares of 9% preferred stock, $20 par, at $26.
(b) Issued 50,000 shares of $30 par common stock at $33.
(c) Purchased and retired 4,000 shares of preferred stock at $28.
(d) Purchased 6,000 shares of its own common stock at $35.
(e) Reissued 1,000 shares of treasury stock at $37.
(f) Stockholders donated to the company 4,000 shares of common when shares had a market price of $36. One half of these shares were issued for $38.

No dividends were declared in 1984 and net income for 1984 was $185,000.

Instructions:

(1) Record each of the transactions. Assume treasury stock acquisitions are recorded at cost.
(2) Give the entries for (d) and (e) assuming treasury stock acquisitions are reported as capital stock retirement.
(3) Prepare the stockholders' equity section of the balance sheet, assuming treasury stock is recorded at cost and assuming retained earnings restrictions are shown by parenthetical remarks.

problem 17-9 (Accounting for stock options)

The board of directors of the Prince Production Co. adopted a stock option plan to supplement the salaries of certain executives of the company. Options to buy common stock were granted as follows:

		Number of Shares	Option Price	Price of Shares at Date of Grant
Jan. 10, 1981	Q. L. Peck	75,000	20	21
June 30, 1981	A. G. Byrd	50,000	25	26
	K. C. Nelson	20,000		

Options are nontransferable and can be exercised three years after date of grant providing the executive is still in the employ of the company. Options expire two years after the date they can first be exercised.

Nelson left the employ of the company at the beginning of 1983.

Stock options were exercised as follows:

		Number of Shares	Price of Shares at Date of Exercise
Jan. 15, 1984	Q. L. Peck	60,000	45
Dec. 20, 1984	Q. L. Peck	15,000	36
Dec. 22, 1984	A. G. Byrd	50,000	32

Stock of the company has a $14 par value. The accounting period for the company is the calendar year.

Instructions: Give all the entries that would be made on the books of the corporation relative to the stock option agreement for the period 1981 to 1984 inclusive.

problem 17-10 (Variable stock options)

On December 31, 1986, the executive stock option plan expired for Martin Distributing. The plan was adopted on January 1, 1983. Executives remaining with the company could exercise their options beginning January 1, 1986. The option price was to be at a percentage of the market price of the company's stock on December 31, 1984. The following information is given for the year 1986:

Change in common stock (par $5) from options exercised	$125,000
Change in premium on common stock from options exercised	325,000
Cash received on options exercised	382,500
Balance remaining in Credit Under Stock Option Plan	27,000
Stock price on December 31, 1983	15
Stock price on December 31, 1985	20

Instructions:

(1) Compute the following:
   (a) The December 31, 1984 stock price.
   (b) The option percentage.

(continued)

(c) The total shares optioned to the executives.
(d) The executive compensation expense for 1983, 1984, and 1985.

(2) Give the journal entries for 1986.

problem 17-11 (Accounting for various capital stock transactions)

The stockholders' equity section of Levy Inc. showed the following data on December 31, 1983: common stock, $30 par, 300,000 shares authorized, 150,000 shares issued and outstanding, $4,500,000; premium on common stock, $300,000; credit under stock option plan, $150,000; retained earnings, $480,000. The stock options were granted to key executives and provided them the right to acquire 30,000 shares of common stock at $35 per share. The stock was selling at $40 at the time the options were granted.

The following transactions occurred during 1984:

Mar. 31	4,500 options outstanding at December 31, 1983 were exercised. The market price per share was $42 at this time.
Apr. 1	The company issued bonds of $2,000,000 at par, giving each $1,000 bond a warrant enabling the holder to purchase two shares of stock at $40 for a one-year period. The stock was selling for $42 per share at that date.
June 30	The company issued rights to stockholders (one right on each share) permitting holders to acquire for a thirty-day period one share at $40 with every ten rights submitted. Shares were selling for $43 at this time. All but 7,000 rights were exercised on July 31, and the additional stock was issued.
Sept. 30	All shares were issued in connection with rights issued on the sale of bonds.
Nov. 30	The market price per share dropped to $32 and options came due. Since the market price was below the option price, no remaining options were exercised.

Instructions:

(1) Give entries to record the foregoing transactions.
(2) Prepare the stockholders' equity section of the balance sheet as of December 31, 1984, (assume net income of $160,000 for 1984).

problem 17-12 (Accounting for various capital stock transactions)

The Garfield Co., organized on June 1, 1983, was authorized to issue stock as follows:

60,000 shares of preferred 9% stock, convertible, $100 par
220,000 shares of common stock, $20 par

During the remainder of the Garfield Co.'s fiscal year, the following transactions were completed in the order given.

(a) 30,000 shares of preferred stock were subscribed for at $102 and 80,000 shares of the common stock were subscribed for at $23. Both subscriptions were payable 30% upon subscription, the balance in one payment.
(b) The second subscription payment was made, except one subscriber for 5,000 shares of common stock defaulted on payment. The full amount paid by this subscriber was returned and all of the fully paid stock was issued.
(c) 12,000 shares of common stock were reacquired by purchase at $17. (Treasury stock is recorded at cost.)
(d) Each share of preferred stock is converted into four shares of common stock.
(e) The treasury stock was exchanged for machinery with a fair market value of $230,000.
(f) There is a 2:1 stock split and the par value of the new common stock is $10.
(g) A major stockholder donated 100,000 shares of common stock to the company.
(h) Net income was $123,000.

Instructions:

(1) Give the journal entries to record the transactions described above. (For net income, give the entry to close the income summary account to Retained Earnings.)
(2) Prepare the stockholders' equity section as of May 31, 1984.

problem 17-13 (Auditing stockholders' equity)

You have been assigned to the audit of Naylor Inc., a manufacturing company. You have been asked to summarize the transactions for the year ended December 31, 1984, affecting stockholders' equity and other related accounts. The stockholders' equity section of Naylor's December 31, 1984, balance sheet follows:

Stockholders' Equity

Paid-in capital:		
Common stock, $20 par value, 500,000 shares authorized, 90,000 shares issued	$1,800,000	
Paid-in capital from treasury stock transactions	22,500	
Premium on common stock	200,000	$2,022,500
Retained earnings	$ 324,689	
Less cost of 1,210 shares of common stock in treasury	72,600	252,089
Total stockholders' equity		$2,274,589

You have extracted the following information from the accounting records and audit working papers.

1985

Jan. 15 Six hundred fifty shares of treasury stock were reissued for $40 per share. The 1,210 shares of treasury stock on hand at December 31, 1984, were purchased in one block in 1984. Naylor used the cost method for recording the treasury shares purchased.

Feb. 2 Ninety, $1,000, 9% bonds due February 1, 1988, were sold at 103 with one detachable stock purchase warrant attached to each bond. Interest is payable annually on February 1. The fair value of the bonds without the stock warrants is 97. The detached warrants have a fair value of $60 each and expire on February 1, 1986. Each warrant entitles the holder to purchase ten shares of common stock at $40 per share.

Mar. 6 Subscriptions for 1,400 shares of common stock were issued at $44 per share, payable 40% down and the balance by March 20.

Mar. 20 The balance due on 1,200 shares was received and those shares were issued. The subscriber who defaulted on the 200 remaining shares forfeited the down payment in accordance with the subscription agreement.

Nov. 1 Fifty-five stock warrants detached from the bonds were exercised.

Instructions: Give journal entries required to summarize the above transactions. (AICPA adapted)

18 OWNERS' EQUITY — RETAINED EARNINGS

CHAPTER OBJECTIVES

Describe the factors affecting retained earnings: prior period adjustments, earnings, dividends, recapitalization, and quasi-reorganizations.

Identify other possible additions to or deductions from owners' equity.

Explain the measurement of book value per share.

Describe and illustrate the equity section in balance sheets of corporations, and the statement of changes in stockholders' equity.

The nature of retained earnings is frequently misunderstood, and this misunderstanding may lead to seriously misleading inferences in reading and interpreting financial statements. Retained earnings is essentially the meeting place of the balance sheet accounts and the income statement accounts. In successive periods retained earnings are increased by income and decreased by losses and dividends. As a result, the retained earnings balance represents the net accumulated earnings of the corporation. If the retained earnings account were affected only by income (losses) and dividends, there would be little confusion in its interpretation. A number of other factors, however, can affect retained earnings. The purpose of this chapter is to identify and explain the different types of transactions and events that impact directly on retained earnings.

FACTORS AFFECTING RETAINED EARNINGS

In addition to earnings or losses and dividends, factors that affect Retained Earnings include: prior period adjustments for corrections of errors, certain types of recapitalizations, quasi-reorganizations, and treasury stock transactions (discussed in Chapter 17). The transactions and events that increase or decrease Retained Earnings may be summarized as follows:

Retained Earnings

Decreases	*Increases*
Prior period adjustments for overstatements of past earnings	Prior period adjustments for understatements of past earnings
Current net loss	Current net income
Dividends	Quasi-reorganizations
Recapitalizations	
Treasury stock transactions	

Prior Period Adjustments

In some situations, errors made in past years are discovered and corrected in the current year by an adjustment to Retained Earnings, referred to as a **prior period adjustment**. There are several types of errors that may occur in measuring the results of operations and the financial status of an enterprise. Accounting errors can result from mathematical mistakes, a failure to apply appropriate accounting procedures, or a misstatement or omission of certain information. In addition, a change from an accounting principle that is not generally accepted to one that is accepted is considered a correction of an error.[1]

Fortunately, most errors are discovered during the accounting period, prior to closing the books. When this is the case, corrections can be made by adjusting entries directly to the accounts. The proper balances are then shown on the balance sheet and an appropriate income measurement reported.

Sometimes errors go undetected during the current period, but they are affected by an equal misstatement in the subsequent period; that is, they are *counterbalanced*. When this happens, the under or overstatement of income in one period is counterbalanced by an equal over- or understatement of income in the next period, and after the closing process is completed for the second year, Retained Earnings is correctly stated. If a counterbalancing error is discovered during the second year, however, it should be corrected at that time.

When errors of past periods are not counterbalancing, Retained Earnings will be misstated until a correction is made in the accounting records. If the error is material, the Accounting Principles Board has specified it should be considered a prior period adjustment and the adjustment should be made

---

[1] *Opinions of the Accounting Principles Board, No. 20*, "Accounting Changes" (New York: American Institute of Certified Public Accountants, 1971) par. 13.

directly to the retained earnings account.[2] If an error resulted in an understatement of income in previous periods, a correcting entry would be needed to increase retained earnings; if an error overstated income in prior periods, then retained earnings would have to be decreased. These adjustments for corrections in net income of prior periods would typically be shown as a part of the total change in retained earnings as follows:

Retained Earnings, unadjusted beginning balance	$xxx
Add or deduct prior period adjustments	xx
Retained Earnings, adjusted beginning balance	$xxx
Add current year's net income or deduct current year's net loss	xx
	$xxx
Deduct dividends	xx
Retained Earnings, ending balance	$xxx

When errors are discovered, the accountant must be able to analyze the situation and determine what action is appropriate under the circumstances. This calls for an understanding of accounting standards as well as good judgment and skill in dealing with situations indicating a failure to meet such standards. The appendix to this chapter covers in detail the techniques for analyzing and correcting errors.

Earnings

The primary source of retained earnings is the net income generated by a business. The retained earnings account is increased by net income and is reduced by net losses from business activities. When operating losses or other debits to Retained Earnings produce a debit balance in this account, the debit balance is referred to as a **deficit**.

Corporate earnings originate from transactions with individuals or businesses outside the company. No earnings are recognized for the construction of machinery or other plant assets for a company's own use, even though the cost of such construction is below the market price for similar assets; self-construction at less than the asset purchase price is regarded simply as a savings in cost. No increases in retained earnings are recognized on transactions with stockholders involving treasury stock; however, as indicated in Chapter 17, decreases may be recognized. The receipt of properties through donation is not recognized as earnings, but as paid-in capital. The earnings of a corporation may be distributed to the stockholders or retained to provide for expanding operations.

Dividends

Dividends are distributions to stockholders of a corporation in proportion to the number of shares held by the respective owners. Distributions may

[2] *Ibid.*, par. 36.

take the form of (1) cash, (2) other assets, (3) notes or other evidence of corporate indebtedness, in effect, deferred cash dividends, and (4) shares of a company's own stock. Most dividends involve reductions in retained earnings. Exceptions include (1) some stock dividends issued in the form of stock splits, which involve a transfer from additional paid-in capital to legal capital, and (2) dividends in corporate liquidation, which represent a return to stockholders of a portion or all of the corporate legal capital and call for reductions in invested capital.

Use of the term *dividend* without qualification normally implies the distribution of cash. Dividends in a form other than cash should be designated by their special form, and distributions from a capital source other than retained earnings should carry a description of their special origin. The terms *property dividend* and *stock dividend* suggest distributions of a special form; designations such as *liquidating dividend* and *dividend distribution of paid-in capital* identify the special origin of the distribution.

"Dividends paid out of retained earnings" is an expression frequently encountered. Accuracy, however, requires recognition that dividends are paid out of cash, which serves to reduce retained earnings. Earnings of the corporation increase net assets or stockholders' equity. Dividend distributions represent no more than asset withdrawals that reduce net assets.

Dividend Policy. Among the powers delegated by the stockholders to the board of directors is the power to control the dividend policy. Whether dividends shall or shall not be paid, as well as the nature and the amount of dividends, are matters that the board determines. In setting dividend policy, the board of directors must answer two questions: Do we have the legal right to declare a dividend? Is such a distribution financially advisable?

In declaring dividends, the board of directors must observe the legal requirements governing the maintenance of legal or stated capital. The laws of different states range from those making any part of capital other than legal capital available for dividends to those permitting dividends only to the extent of retained earnings and under specified conditions. In most states dividends cannot be declared in the event of a deficit; in a few states, however, dividends equal to current earnings may be distributed despite a previously accumulated deficit. The availability of capital as a basis for dividends is a determination to be made by the legal counsel and not by the accountant. The accountant must report accurately the sources of each capital increase; the legal counsel investigates the availability of such sources as bases for dividend distributions.

The board of directors must also consider the financial aspect of dividend distributions—the company's asset position relative to present and future asset requirements. When a dividend is legally declared and announced, its revocation is not possible. In the event of corporate insolvency prior to payment of the dividend, stockholders have claims as a creditor group to the dividend, and as an ownership group to any assets remaining after all corporate liabilities have been paid. A dividend that was illegally declared, however, is revocable; in the event of insolvency at the time of declaration, such action is nullified and stockholders participate in asset distributions only after creditors have been paid in full.

Restrictions on Retained Earnings. Although state laws generally permit the distribution of dividends to the extent of retained earnings, other factors may limit the amount of dividends that can be declared. For example, a portion of retained earnings may be restricted as a result of contractual requirements, such as agreements with creditors that provide for the retention of earnings to ensure repayment of debt at maturity. Retained earnings may also be restricted at the discretion of the board of directors. For example, the board may designate a portion of retained earnings as restricted for a particular purpose, such as expansion of plant facilities.

If restrictions on retained earnings are material, they are generally disclosed in a note to the financial statements. Sometimes, however, the restricted portion of retained earnings is reported on the balance sheet separately from the unrestricted amount that is available for dividends. The restricted portion may be designated as **appropriated retained earnings** and the unrestricted portion as **unappropriated** or **free retained earnings**. Occasionally, the restrictions are recognized in the accounts by a debit to the regular retained earnings account and a credit to a special appropriated retained earnings account. Once the purpose of the appropriation has been served, the original entry creating the appropriated retained earnings balance is reversed. There is no segregation of funds, and no gain or loss is involved in the restriction of retained earnings.

Whatever the form of disclosure, the main idea behind restrictions on retained earnings is to alert stockholders that some of the assets that might otherwise be available for dividend distribution are being retained within the business for specific purposes. Because the amount of dividends actually paid is usually much less than the retained earnings balance, this is generally not a significant issue.

The Formal Dividend Announcement. Three dates are essential in the formal dividend statement: (1) date of declaration, (2) date of stockholders of record, (3) date of payment. Dividends are made payable to stockholders of record as of a date following the date of declaration and preceding the date of payment. The liability for dividends payable is recorded on the declaration date and is canceled on the payment date. No entry is required on the record date, but a list of the stockholders is made as of the close of business on this date. These are the persons who receive dividends on the payment date. In practice, stock is said to sell *ex-dividend* three or four trading days prior to the date of record. A full record of the dividend action must be provided in the minutes book.

Cash Dividends. The most common type of dividend is a **cash dividend**. For a corporation, these dividends involve a reduction in retained earnings and in cash. A current liability for dividends payable is recognized on the declaration date; this is canceled when dividend checks are sent to stockholders. Entries to record the declaration and the payment of a cash dividend follow:

Retained Earnings	100,000	
Dividends Payable		100,000
Dividends Payable	100,000	
Cash		100,000

In declaring a dividend, the board of directors must consider the limitations set by the current financial position and the cash balance of the company. For example, a corporation may have retained earnings of $500,000. If it has cash of only $150,000, however, cash dividends must be limited to this amount unless it converts certain assets into cash or borrows cash. If the cash required for regular operations is $100,000, the cash available for dividends is then only $50,000. Although legally able to declare dividends of $500,000, the company would be able to distribute no more than one tenth of that amount at this time. Generally, companies pay dividends that are significantly less than the legal amount allowed or the amount of cash on hand.

Property Dividends. A distribution to stockholders that is payable in some asset other than cash is generally referred to as a **property dividend**. Frequently the assets to be distributed are securities of other companies owned by the corporation. The corporation thus transfers to its stockholders its ownership interest in such securities. Property dividends usually occur only in closely held corporations.

This type of transfer is sometimes referred to as a *nonreciprocal transfer to owners* inasmuch as nothing is received by the company in return for its distribution to the stockholders. These transfers should be recorded using the fair market value (as of the day of declaration) of the assets distributed, and a gain or loss recognized for the difference between the carrying value on the books of the issuing company and the fair market value of the assets.[3] Property dividends are valued at carrying value if the fair market value is not determinable.

To illustrate the entries for a property dividend, assume that the State Oil Corporation owns 100,000 shares in the Valley Oil Co., cost $2,000,000, fair market value $3,000,000, which it wishes to distribute to its stockholders. There are 1,000,000 shares of State Oil Corporation stock outstanding. Accordingly, a dividend of 1/10 of a share of Valley Oil Co. stock is declared on each share of State Oil Corporation stock outstanding. The entries for the dividend declaration and payment are:

Retained Earnings	3,000,000	
Property Dividends Payable		3,000,000
Property Dividends Payable	3,000,000	
Investment in Valley Oil Co. Stock		2,000,000
Gain on Distribution of Property Dividends		1,000,000

Stock Dividends. A corporation may distribute to stockholders additional shares of the company's own stock as a **stock dividend**. A stock dividend

[3] *Opinions of the Accounting Principles Board, No. 29,* "Accounting for Nonmonetary Transactions" (New York: American Institute of Certified Public Accountants, 1973), par. 18.

permits the corporation to retain within the business net assets produced by earnings while at the same time offering stockholders tangible evidence of the growth of their equity.

A stock dividend usually involves (1) the capitalization of retained earnings, and (2) a distribution of common stock to common stockholders. These distributions are sometimes referred to as *ordinary stock dividends*. In some states, stock dividends may be effected by the capitalization of certain paid-in capital balances. In other instances, common stock is issued to holders of preferred stock or preferred stock is issued to holders of common stock. These distributions are sometimes referred to as *special stock dividends*.

A stock dividend makes a portion of retained earnings no longer available for distribution while raising the legal capital of the corporation. In recording the dividend, a debit is made to Retained Earnings and credits are made to appropriate paid-in capital balances. A stock dividend has the same effect as the payment by the corporation of a cash dividend and a subsequent return of the cash to the corporation in exchange for capital stock.

In distributing stock as a dividend, the issuing corporation must meet legal requirements relative to the amounts to be capitalized. If stock has a par or a stated value, an amount equal to the par or stated value of the shares issued will have to be transferred to capital stock; if stock has no par value and no stated value, the laws of the state of incorporation may provide specific requirements as to the amounts to be transferred, or they may leave such determinations to the corporate directors.

Although the minimum amounts to be transferred to legal or stated capital balances upon the issuance of additional stock are set by law, the board of directors is not prevented from going beyond legal requirements and authorizing increases in both capital stock and paid-in capital balances. For example, assume that $100 par stock was originally issued at $120. Legal requirements may call for the capitalization of no more than the par value of the additional shares issued. The board of directors, however, in order to preserve the paid-in capital relationship, may authorize a transfer from Retained Earnings of $120 per share; for every share issued, Capital Stock would be increased $100 and a paid-in capital account would be increased $20; or the board of directors may decide that the retained earnings transfer shall be made in terms of the fair value of shares that exceeds the legal value. Here, too, the credit to Capital Stock is accompanied by a credit to a paid-in capital account.

Small vs. Large Stock Dividends. The Committee on Accounting Procedure of the AICPA, in commenting on the issuance by a corporation of its own common stock to its common stockholders, has indicated that proper corporate policy in certain situations would call for the capitalization of an amount equal to the fair value of shares issued. The Committee pointed out:

> . . . a stock dividend does not, in fact, give rise to any change whatsoever in either the corporation's assets or its respective shareholders' proportionate interests therein. However, it cannot fail to be recognized that, merely as a consequence of the expressed purpose of the transaction and its characterization as

> a *dividend* in related notices to shareholders and the public at large, many recipients of stock dividends look upon them as distributions of corporate earnings and usually in an amount equivalent to the fair value of the additional shares received. Furthermore, it is to be presumed that such views of recipients are materially strengthened in those instances, which are by far the most numerous, where the issuances are so small in comparison with the shares previously outstanding that they do not have any apparent effect upon the share market price and, consequently, the market value of the shares previously held remains substantially unchanged. The committee therefore believes that where these circumstances exist the corporation should in the public interest account for the transaction by transferring from earned surplus to the category of permanent capitalization (represented by the capital stock and capital surplus accounts) an amount equal to the fair value of the additional shares issued. Unless this is done, the amount of earnings which the shareholder may believe to have been distributed to him will be left, except to the extent otherwise dictated by legal requirements, in earned surplus subject to possible further similar stock issuances or cash distributions.[4]

However, the Committee indicated that certain circumstances would suggest that retained earnings be debited for no more than the stock's par, stated, or other value as required by law. The Committee stated:

> Where the number of additional shares issued as a stock dividend is so great that it has, or may reasonably be expected to have, the effect of materially reducing the share market value, the committee believes that the implications and possible constructions discussed . . . are not likely to exist and that the transaction clearly partakes of the nature of a stock split-up . . . . Consequently, the committee considers that under such circumstances there is no need to capitalize earned surplus, other than to the extent occasioned by legal requirements. It recommends, however, that in such instances every effort be made to avoid the use of the word *dividend* in related corporate resolutions, notices, and announcements and that, in those cases where because of legal requirements this cannot be done, the transaction be described, for example, as a *split up effected in the form of a dividend.*[5]

The Committee indicated that the majority of stock dividends would probably fall within the first category stated above, suggesting debits to Retained Earnings of amounts exceeding legal requirements. Although reluctant to name a dividend percentage that would require adherence to this practice, the Committee did suggest that in stock distributions involving the issuance of less than 20–25 percent of the number of shares previously outstanding, referred to as a **small stock dividend**, the debits to Retained Earnings should normally be at the fair value of additional shares issued.

The following examples illustrate the entries for the declaration and the issue of a small stock dividend. Assume that the capital for the Hernandez Co. on July 1 is as follows:

Capital stock, $10 par, 100,000 shares outstanding	$1,000,000
Premium on capital stock	1,100,000
Retained earnings	750,000

[4] *Accounting Research and Terminology Bulletins—Final Edition,* "No. 43, Restatement and Revision of Accounting Research Bulletins" (New York: American Institute of Certified Public Accountants, 1961), Ch. 7, sec. B, par. 10.

[5] *Ibid.,* par. 11.

The company declares a 10 percent stock dividend, or a dividend of one share for every ten held. Shares are selling on the market on this date at $16 per share. The stock dividend is to be recorded at the market value of the shares issued, or $160,000 (10,000 shares at $16). The entries to record the declaration of the dividend and the issue of stock follow:

Retained Earnings	160,000	
Stock Dividends Distributable		100,000
Paid-In Capital from Stock Dividends		60,000
Stock Dividends Distributable	100,000	
Capital Stock, $10 par		100,000

Assume, however, that the company declares a **large stock dividend** of 50 percent, or a dividend of one share for every two held. Legal requirements call for the transfer to capital stock of an amount equal to the par value of the shares issued. This transfer may be made from retained earnings or paid-in capital. When the transfer is made from paid-in capital, it is preferable to refer to the transaction as a stock split effected in the form of a dividend rather than as a stock dividend. Entries for the declaration of the dividend and the issue of stock follow:

Retained Earnings (*or* Premium on Capital Stock)	500,000	
Stock Dividends Distributable		500,000
Stock Dividends Distributable	500,000	
Capital Stock, $10 par		500,000

Fractional Share Warrants. When stock dividends are issued by a company, it may be necessary to issue **fractional share warrants** to certain stockholders. For example, when a 10 percent stock dividend is issued, a stockholder owning twenty-five shares can be given no more than two full shares; however, the holdings in excess of an even multiple of ten shares are recognized by the issue of a fractional share warrant for one-half share. The warrant for one-half share may be sold, or a warrant for an additional half share may be purchased so a full share may be claimed from the company. In some instances, the corporation may arrange for the payment of cash in lieu of fractional warrants or it may issue a full share of stock in exchange for warrants accompanied by cash for the fractional share deficiency.

Assume that the Hernandez Company in distributing a stock dividend issues fractional share warrants totaling 500 shares, par $10. The entry for the fractional share warrants issued would be as follows:

Stock Dividends Distributable	5,000	
Fractional Share Warrants Issued		5,000

Assuming 80 percent of the warrants are ultimately turned in for shares and the remaining warrants expire, the following entry would be made:

Fractional Share Warrants Issued	5,000	
Capital Stock, $10 par		4,000
Paid-In Capital from Forfeitures of Fractional Share Warrants		1,000

Stock Dividends vs. Stock Splits. Although a stock dividend can be compared to a stock split from the investors' point of view, its effects on corporate capital differ from those of a stock split. A **stock dividend** results in an increase in the number of shares outstanding and in an increase in the capital stock balance, no change being made in the value assigned to each share of stock on the company records; the increase in capital stock outstanding is effected by a transfer from the retained earnings balance, retained earnings available for dividends being permanently reduced by this transfer. A **stock split** merely divides the existing capital stock balance into more parts with a reduction in the stated or legal value related to each share; there is no change in the retained earnings available for dividends, both the capital stock and the retained earnings balances remaining unchanged.

A stock split effected in the form of a large stock dividend is sometimes referred to simply as a stock split. This can be misleading because additional shares of stock are issued in this situation and the par value of the stock is not changed. A careful distinction should be made between a pure stock split as described in Chapter 17 and the large stock dividends discussed in this chapter.

Stock Dividends on the Balance Sheet. Special disclosure should be provided on the balance sheet when retained earnings have been reclassified as paid-in capital as a result of stock dividends, recapitalizations, or other actions. Information concerning the amount of retained earnings transferred to paid-in capital will contribute to an understanding of the extent to which business growth has been financed through corporate earnings. For example, assume the information for the Hernandez Co. on pages 676-677 and the transfer to paid-in capital of $500,000 as a result of the 50 percent stock dividend. The stockholders' equity may be presented as illustrated below.

Contributed capital:		
Capital stock, $10 par, 150,000 shares	$1,500,000	
Premium on capital stock	1,100,000	$2,600,000
Retained earnings	$ 750,000	
Less amount transferred to paid-in capital by stock dividend	500,000	250,000
Total stockholders' equity		$2,850,000

If a balance sheet is prepared after the declaration of a stock dividend but before issue of the shares, stock dividends distributable is reported in the stockholders' equity section as an addition to capital stock outstanding. Through stock dividends, the corporation reduces its retained earnings balance and increases its capital stock. The stock the corporation may still sell is limited to the difference between capital stock authorized and the sum of (1) capital stock issued, (2) capital stock subscribed, (3) stock reserved for the exercise of stock rights and stock options, and (4) stock dividends distributable.

Liquidating Dividends. A corporation will declare a **liquidating dividend** when the dividend is to be considered a return to stockholders of a portion of their original investments. These distributions by the corporation represent reductions of invested capital balances. Instead of actually debiting Capital Stock and paid-in capital accounts, however, it is possible to debit a separate account for the reduction in invested capital. This balance is subtracted from the invested capital balances in presenting the stockholders' equity on the balance sheet.

Corporations owning wasting assets may regularly declare dividends that are in part a distribution of earnings and in part a distribution of the corporation's invested capital. Entries on the corporation books for such dividend declarations should reflect the decrease in the two capital elements. This information should be reported to stockholders so they may recognize dividends as representing in part income and in part a return of investment.

Dividends on Preferred Stock. When dividends on preferred stock are cumulative, the payment of a stipulated amount on these shares is necessary before any dividends may be paid on common. When the board of directors fails to declare dividends on cumulative preferred stock, information concerning the amount of dividends in arrears should be reported parenthetically or in note form on the balance sheet; or retained earnings may be divided on the balance sheet to show the amount required to meet dividends in arrears and the free balance for other purposes.

Recapitalization

Corporate **recapitalization** occurs when an entire issue of stock is changed by appropriate action of the corporation. In some states, recapitalizations, including changes in the legal capital, are possible by action of the board of directors and stockholders; in other states, recapitalizations also require the approval of state authorities.

A typical recapitalization is a change from par to no-par stock. If the common stock balance is to remain the same after the change, the original common stock account is closed and an account for the new issue is opened. Any premium relating to the original stock issue should be transferred to some other paid-in capital account appropriately labeled. If the common stock balance is to exceed the consideration received on the original sale of the stock, a new capital stock account is credited for the value assigned to the new issue, original paid-in capital balances are closed, and the retained earnings account is debited for the difference. If the capital stock balance is to be reduced, the original account, as well as any premium account, is closed, a new capital stock account is credited for the value assigned to the new stock, and an appropriately titled paid-in capital account is credited for the difference.

To illustrate, assume capital for the Signal Corporation as follows:

Common stock, $10 par, 100,000 shares	$1,000,000
Premium on common stock	100,000
Retained earnings	250,000

Entries for each of the three possibilities follow:

Case 1—Assume the original stock is exchanged for no-par stock with a stated value of $10:

Common Stock, $10 par	1,000,000	
Premium on Common Stock	100,000	
Common Stock, $10 stated value		1,000,000
Paid-In Capital from Exchange of Par for No-Par Stock		100,000

Case 2—Assume the original stock is exchanged for no-par stock with a stated value of $12.50:

Common Stock, $10 par	1,000,000	
Premium on Common Stock	100,000	
Retained Earnings	150,000	
Common Stock, $12.50 stated value		1,250,000

Case 3—Assume the original stock is exchanged for no-par stock with a stated value of $5:

Common Stock, $10 par	1,000,000	
Premium on Common Stock	100,000	
Common Stock, $5 stated value		500,000
Paid-in Capital from Reduction in Value Assigned to Common Stock		600,000

Recapitalizations involving changes in the stated values of no-par stock or changes from no-par stock to stock with a par value call for similar procedures.

Quasi-Reorganization

A situation may arise in which a company's properties were acquired at costs that do not permit earnings under current conditions. There may also be a deficit from previous operations or a retained earnings balance insufficient to absorb a reduction in the carrying value of the property items. Yet such a reduction may be warranted by current conditions and indeed may be necessary if the company is to be able to report profitable operations in future periods. The company erred in acquiring property that could not be employed profitably in the business, but it should be recognized that a mistake was made and that the future operations of the company should not be burdened with past mistakes.

Under such circumstances a company may elect to write down property items and to accompany such action with a restatement of the capital structure, eliminating the deficit found after the write-off. The elimination of a deficit through a restatement of invested capital balances providing, in effect, a fresh start accounting-wise on the part of the corporation is called a **quasi-reorganization**. The quasi-reorganization procedure does not require recourse to the courts as in formal reorganization procedures; there is no change in the legal corporate entity or interruption in business activity.

To illustrate the nature of a quasi-reorganization, assume the Bradley Corporation has suffered losses from operations for some time and both current and future revenues appear to be insufficient to cover the depreciation on properties acquired when prices were considerably higher than at present. The company decides to restate its assets and paid-in capital in order to remove the deficit and make possible the declaration of dividends upon a return to profitable operations. A balance sheet for the company just prior to this action is given below.

Bradley Corporation
Balance Sheet
June 30, 1984

Assets			Liabilities and Stockholders' Equity		
Current assets		$ 250,000	Liabilities		$ 300,000
Land, buildings, and equipment	$1,500,000		Capital stock, $10 par, 100,000 shares	$1,000,000	
Less accumulated depreciation	600,000	900,000	Less deficit	150,000	850,000
Total assets		$1,150,000	Total liabilities and stockholders' equity		$1,150,000

The quasi-reorganization is to be accomplished as follows:

(1) Land, buildings, and equipment are to be reduced to their present fair market value of $600,000 by reductions in the asset and accumulated depreciation balances of 33⅓%.

(2) Capital stock is to be reduced to a par of $5, $500,000 in capital stock thus being converted into "additional paid-in capital."

(3) The deficit of $450,000 ($150,000 as reported on the balance sheet increased by $300,000 arising from the write-down of land, buildings and equipment) is to be applied against the capital from the reduction of the par value of stock.

Entries to record the changes follow:

Transaction	Entry	Debit	Credit
(1) To write down land, buildings, and equipment and accumulated depreciation balances by 33⅓%.	Retained Earnings (Deficit)	300,000	
	Accumulated Depreciation	200,000	
	Land, Buildings, and Equipment		500,000
(2) To reduce the capital stock balance from $10 par to $5 par and to establish paid-in capital from reduction in stock par value.	Capital Stock, $10 par	1,000,000	
	Capital Stock, $5 par		500,000
	Paid-In Capital from Reduction in Stock Par Value		500,000
(3) To apply the deficit after asset devaluation against paid-in capital from reduction in stock par value.	Paid-In Capital from Reduction in Stock Par Value	450,000	
	Retained Earnings (Deficit)		450,000

The balance sheet after the quasi-reorganization is shown below:

Bradley Corporation
Balance Sheet
June 30, 1984

Assets			Liabilities and Stockholders' Equity	
Current assets		$250,000	Liabilities	$300,000
Land, buildings, and equipment	$1,000,000		Capital stock, $5 par, 100,000 shares......................	500,000
Less accumulated depreciation......	400,000	600,000	Paid-in capital from reduction in stock par value	50,000
Total assets		$850,000	Total liabilities and stockholders' equity	$850,000

Following the quasi-reorganization, the accounting for the company's operations is similar to that for a new company. Earnings subsequent to the quasi-reorganization, however, should be accumulated in a *dated retained earnings* account. On future balance sheets, retained earnings dated as of the time of account readjustment will inform readers of the date of such action and of the fresh start in earnings accumulation.

The AICPA Committee on Accounting Procedure has recommended that a company electing to bring about a legitimate restatement of its assets, capital stock, and retained earnings through a quasi-reorganization, relieving future income or retained earnings of charges that would otherwise be made against them, should meet the following conditions:

(1) It should make a clear report to stockholders of the proposed changes and should obtain their formal consent.
(2) It should present a fair balance sheet with a reasonably complete restatement of values so that there will be no continuation of the circumstances that justify charges to invested capital.
(3) Assets should be carried forward as of the date of the quasi-reorganization at fair and not unduly conservative amounts, determined with due regard for the accounting to be employed thereafter. Excessive writedowns that will result in the overstatement of earnings or retained earnings on the ultimate realization of assets should be avoided.[6]

The Committee recognized that in some cases the fair value of an asset or the amount of potential losses or charges cannot be measured satisfactorily as of the date of a quasi-reorganization and estimates of asset and liability values will be required. In such cases, material differences between book values and ultimate realization or liquidation amounts that cannot be attributed to events or circumstances originating after the date of the readjustment should not be recognized as losses but should be reported as corrections identified with the readjustment.

---

[6] *Ibid.*, Ch. 7, sec. A., par. 3 & 4.

OTHER ADDITIONS TO OR DEDUCTIONS FROM OWNERS' EQUITY

The previous sections have discussed the major items affecting retained earnings. The three most common items are prior period adjustments, earnings, and dividends. When retained earnings are combined with capital stock and other paid-in capital, the amount of total owners' equity is usually determined. Sometimes, however, there are other additions to or deductions from owners' equity.

As discussed in previous chapters, deductions from total stockholders' equity are made for the cost of treasury stock (Chapter 17) and the accumulated changes in the valuation allowance for a marketable equity securities portfolio included in noncurrent assets (Chapter 12). These may be referred to as **contra-equity accounts.**[7]

These deductions from total stockholders' equity are dissimilar in origin, but both have the result of reducing stockholders' equity. As an example, some loan agreements may require a company to maintain a certain amount of stockholders' equity in relation to its debt. The reduction of stockholders' equity due to the decline in value of long-term investments could cause a violation of these requirements. To illustrate, assume that a company was required to maintain a debt-to-equity ratio of .66 or less, and that a market decline of $75,000 was incurred on long-term investments held by the company. Before the entry recognizing the market decline in long-term securities, the company had debt of $1,000,000 and stockholders' equity of $1,550,000, or a debt-to-equity ratio of .645 ($1,000,000 ÷ $1,550,000). This ratio meets the requirements. After the entry for the market decline, stockholders' equity would be reduced to $1,475,000 and the debt-to-equity ratio increased to .678, a figure that would be in violation of the loan agreement.

BOOK VALUE PER SHARE

Readers of corporate financial statements are interested in certain special measurements that can be developed from the data concerning stockholders' equity. One measurement is **book value per share**. The book value per share measurement is the dollar equity in corporate capital of each share of stock. It is the amount that would be paid on each share assuming the company is liquidated, and the amount available to stockholders is exactly the amount reported as the stockholders' equity.[8] The book value measurement is sometimes used as a factor in evaluating stock worth. However, care must be exercised because improper use may be misleading. Both single

---

[7]Losses due to changes in foreign exchange rates are also reported as a contra-equity item as required by FASB Statement No. 52; gains due to changes in foreign exchange rates are reported as an addition to equity. This area is discussed in detail in most advanced accounting texts.

[8]Financial analysts frequently follow the practice of subtracting any amounts reported for intangible assets from the total reported for the stockholders' equity in calculating share book value.

values and comparative values may be required, the latter to afford data relative to trends and growth in the stockholders' equity.

One Class of Outstanding Stock

When only one class of stock is outstanding, the calculation of book value is relatively simple; the total stockholders' equity is divided by the number of shares of stock outstanding at the close of the reporting period. When stock has been reacquired and treasury stock is reported, its cost should be recognized as a deduction in arriving at the stockholders' equity, and the shares represented by the treasury stock should be subtracted from the shares issued in arriving at the shares outstanding. When shares of stock have been subscribed for but are unissued, capital stock subscribed should be included in the total for the stockholders' equity and the shares subscribed should be added to the shares outstanding. To illustrate, assume a stockholders' equity for the Moore Corporation as shown below:

Contributed capital:	
Capital stock, $10 par, 100,000 shares issued, 5,000 shares reacquired and held as treasury stock (see below)	$1,000,000
Capital stock subscribed, 20,000 shares	200,000
Additional paid-in capital	350,000
Retained earnings	650,000
	$2,200,000
Less stock reacquired and held as treasury stock, at cost (5,000 shares)	75,000
Total stockholders' equity	$2,125,000

The book value per share of stock is calculated as follows:

$2,125,000 (total capital) ÷ 115,000 (shares issued, 100,000, plus shares subscribed, 20,000, minus treasury shares, 5,000) = $18.48.

More Than One Class of Outstanding Stock

When more than one class of stock has been issued, it is necessary to consider the rights of the different classes of stockholders. With preferred and common issues, for example, the prior rights of preferred stockholders must first be determined and the portion of the stockholders' equity related to preferred stockholders calculated. The preferred stockholders' equity when subtracted from the total stockholders' equity gives the equity related to the common stockholders, or the *residual equity.* The preferred equity divided by the number of preferred shares gives the book value of a preferred share; the common equity divided by the number of common shares gives the book value of a common share.

The portion of the stockholders' equity related to preferred would be that amount distributable to preferred stockholders in the event of corporate liquidation. This calls for consideration of the liquidation value and also the special dividend rights of the preferred issue.

Liquidation Value. Preferred shares may have a liquidation value equal to par, to par plus a premium, or to a stated dollar amount. Capital equal to this value for the number of preferred shares outstanding should be assigned to preferred stock. A preferred call price differing from the amount to be paid to preferred stockholders upon liquidation would not be applicable for book value computations; the call of preferred stock is not obligatory, hence call prices are not relevant in the apportionment of values between preferred and common stockholders.

Dividend Rights. (1) Preferred stock may have certain rights in retained earnings as a result of special dividend privileges. For example, preferred shares may be entitled to dividends not yet declared for a portion of the current year, assuming liquidation; here a portion of retained earnings equal to the dividend requirements would be related to preferred shares. (2) Preferred stock may be cumulative with dividends in arrears. When terms of the preferred issue provide that dividends in arrears must be paid upon liquidation regardless of any retained earning or deficit balance reported on the books, capital equivalent to the dividends in arrears must be assigned to preferred shares even though this impairs or eliminates the equity relating to common stockholders. When preferred stockholders are entitled to dividends in arrears only in the event of accumulated earnings, as much retained earnings as are available, but not in excess of such dividend requirements, are related to preferred stock.

The computation of book values for preferred and common shares is illustrated in the following series of examples. The examples are based upon the stockholders' equity reported by the Maxwell Corporation on December 31, 1984, which follows:

Preferred 6% stock, $50 par, 10,000 shares	$ 500,000
Common stock, $10 par, 100,000 shares	1,000,000
Retained earnings	250,000
Total stockholders' equity	$1,750,000

Example 1—Assume preferred dividends have been paid to July 1, 1984. Preferred stock has a liquidation value of $52 and is entitled to current unpaid dividends. Book values on December 31, 1984, are developed as follows:

Total stockholders' equity		$1,750,000
Equity identified with preferred:		
Liquidation value, 10,000 shares @ $52	$520,000	
Current dividends, 3% of $500,000	15,000	535,000
Balance—equity identified with common		$1,215,000

Book values per share:	
Preferred: $ 535,000 ÷ 10,000	$53.50
Common: $1,215,000 ÷ 100,000	$12.15

Example 2—Assume preferred stock has a liquidation value of $52. Preferred stock is cumulative with dividends 5 years in arrears that must be paid in the event of liquidation. Book values for common and preferred shares would be developed as follows:

Total stockholders' equity		$1,750,000
Equity identified with preferred:		
Liquidation value, 10,000 shares @ $52	$520,000	
Dividends in arrears, 30% of $500,000	150,000	670,000
Balance—equity identified with common		$1,080,000
Book values per share:		
Preferred: $ 670,000 ÷ 10,000		$67.00
Common: $1,080,000 ÷ 100,000		$10.80

Example 3—Assume preferred stock has a liquidation value equal to its par value. Preferred is cumulative with dividends 10 years in arrears payable in the event of liquidation even though impairing the invested capital of the common shareholders. Book values for common and preferred shares are developed as follows:

Total stockholders'equity		$1,750,000
Equity identified with preferred:		
Liquidation value, 10,000 shares @ $50	$500,000	
Dividends in arrears, 60% of $500,000	300,000	800,000
Balance—equity identified with common		$ 950,000
Book values per share:		
Preferred: $800,000 ÷ 10,000		$80.00
Common: $950,000 ÷ 100,000		$ 9.50

The nature and the limitations of the share book value measurements must be appreciated in using these data. Share book values are developed from the net asset values as reported on the books. Furthermore, calculations require the assumption of liquidation in the allocation of amounts to the several classes of stock. Book values of assets may vary materially from present fair values or immediate realizable values. Moreover, book values of property items are stated in terms of the "going concern"; the full implications of a "quitting concern" approach would call for many significant changes in the values as reported on the books.

REPORTING STOCKHOLDERS' EQUITY

The following is the stockholders' equity section of the balance sheet of Oslo Corporation as of December 31, 1984. It should be noted that companies rarely present as much detail as provided in the following illustration. Students are again referred to the actual financial statements of General Mills in Appendix B.

The following points should be observed in examining the illustrative equity section of the balance sheet:

(1) The stockholders' equity is reported in terms of its sources: (a) the amount paid in by stockholders; and (b) the amount representing earnings retained in the business.

(2) The classes of capital stock are reported separately and are described in detail. Information is offered concerning the nature of the stock, the number

Stockholders' Equity

Contributed capital:			
Preferred 6% stock, $100 par, cumulative, callable, 5,000 shares authorized and issued	$500,000		
No-par common stock, $5 stated value, 100,000 shares authorized, 60,000 shares issued; treasury stock, 5,000 shares—deducted below	300,000	$ 800,000	
Paid-in capital from sale of common stock at more than stated value	$260,000		
Paid-in capital from sale of treasury stock at more than cost	16,000	276,000	
Total contributed capital		$1,076,000	
Retained earnings:			
Appropriated for contingencies (Note X)	$125,000		
Unappropriated	225,000		
Total retained earnings		350,000	
Total contributed capital and retained earnings		$1,426,000	
Deduct: Common treasury stock, at cost (5,000 shares acquired at $8)	$ 40,000		
Net unrealized loss on noncurrent marketable equity securities	24,000	64,000	
Total stockholders' equity			1,362,000

of shares authorized, the number of shares issued, and the number of shares reacquired and held as treasury stock.

(3) A portion of retained earnings has been designated as restricted for contingencies, the nature of which is described in a note to the financial statements.

(4) The cost of treasury stock and the unrealized loss on noncurrent marketable equity securities are reported as contra-equity items and deducted in determining total stockholders' equity.

Readers of financial statements should be provided with an explanation of the changes during the period in individual equity balances. Frequently, such explanation is provided in notes to the financial statements. When stockholders' equity is composed of numerous accounts, as in the preceding example, a **statement of changes in stockholders' equity** is sometimes presented. An illustrative statement for the Oslo Corporation is shown on the following page.

The net ownership equity of a business is an important element. Analyses of the amounts and sources of contributed capital compared to those generated and retained by the company provide useful information for assessing the long-term profitability and solvency of a business. The techniques for analyzing financial statements are discussed in Chapter 25.

APPENDIX

ANALYSIS OF CORRECTION OF ERRORS

A number of special practices are usually adopted by a business unit to ensure accuracy in recording and summarizing business transactions. A

Oslo Corporation
Statement of Changes in Stockholders' Equity
For the Year Ended December 31, 1984

	Preferred Stock	Common Stock	Paid-In Capital	Appropriated Retained Earnings for Contingencies	Unappropriated Retained Earnings	Contra-Equity Balances	Total
Balances, December 31, 1983	$300,000	$300,000	$260,000*	$ 90,000	$222,500	–0–	$1,172,500
Prior period adjustment—correction of 1982 error, net of tax					(25,000)		(25,000)
Adjusted balances, December 31, 1983	$300,000	$300,000	$260,000	$ 90,000	$197,500	–0–	$1,147,500
Increase from sale of 1,000 shares of preferred stock in January, 1984, at par value	200,000						200,000
Increase from sale of 25,000 shares of treasury stock, common, in January, 1984, cost $20,000, for $36,000			16,000				16,000
Net income for 1984					120,000		120,000
Cash dividends:							
Preferred stock, $6 on 5,000 shares, $30,000; Common stock 50¢ on 55,000 shares, $27,500					(57,500)		(57,500)
Retained earnings appropriated for contingencies				35,000	(35,000)		
Purchase of 5,000 shares of common treasury stock @ cost, $8						$(40,000)	(40,000)
Net unrealized loss on noncurrent marketable equity securities						(24,000)	(24,000)
Balances, December 31, 1984	$500,000	$300,000	$276,000	$125,000	$225,000	$(64,000)	$1,362,000

*From sale of common stock at more than stated value.

prime requisite in achieving accuracy, of course, is the establishment of an accounting system providing safeguards against both carelessness and dishonesty. Despite the accounting system established and the verification procedures employed, some misstatements will enter into the financial statements. Misstatements may be minor ones having little effect on the financial presentations; others may be of a major character, resulting in material misrepresentations of financial position and the results of operations. Misstatements may arise from intentional falsifications by employees or officers as well as from unintentional errors and omissions by employees.

Kinds of Errors

There are a number of different kinds of errors. Some errors are discovered in the period in which they are made, and these are easily corrected. Others may not be discovered currently and are reflected on the financial statements until discovered. Some errors are never discovered; however, the effects of these errors are counterbalanced in subsequent periods and after this takes place, account balances are again accurately stated. Errors may be classified as follows.

(1) *Errors discovered currently in the course of normal accounting procedures.* Examples of this type of error are clerical errors, such as an addition error, posting to the wrong account, or misstating or omitting an account from the trial balance. These types of errors usually are detected during the regular summarizing process of the accounting cycle and are readily corrected.

(2) *Errors limited to balance sheet accounts.* Examples include debiting Marketable Securities instead of Notes Receivable, crediting Interest Payable instead of Notes Payable, or crediting Interest Payable instead of Salaries Payable. Another example is not recording the exchange of convertible bonds for stock. Such errors are frequently discovered and corrected in the period in which they are made. When such errors are not found until a subsequent period, corrections must be made at that time and balance sheet data subsequently restated for comparative reporting purposes.

(3) *Errors limited to income statement accounts.* The examples and correcting procedures for this type of error are similar to those in (2) above. For example, Office Salaries may be debited instead of Sales Salaries. This type of error should be corrected as soon as it is discovered. Even though the error would not affect net income, the misstated accounts should be restated for analysis purposes and comparative reporting.

(4) *Errors affecting both income statement accounts and balance sheet accounts.* Certain errors, when not discovered currently, result in the misstatement of net income and thus affect both the income statement accounts and the balance sheet accounts. The balance sheet accounts are carried into the succeeding period; hence, an error made currently and not detected will affect earnings of the future. Such errors may be classified into two groups:

(a) *Errors in net income that, when not detected, are automatically counterbalanced in the following fiscal period.* Net income amounts on the income statements for two successive periods are inaccurately stated; certain account balances on the balance sheet at the end of the first period are inaccurately stated, but the account balances in the balance sheet at the end of the succeeding period are accurately stated. In this class are errors such as the misstatement of inventories and the omission of adjustments for prepaid and accrued items at the end of the period.

(b) *Errors in net income that, when not detected, are not automatically counterbalanced in the following fiscal period.* Account balances on successive balance sheets are inaccurately stated until such time as entries are made compensating for or correcting the errors. In this class are errors such as the recognition of capital expenditures as revenue expenditures and the omission of charges for depreciation and amortization.

When these types of errors are discovered, careful analysis is required to determine the required action to correct the account balances. As indicated, most of these errors will be caught and corrected prior to closing the books. Those that are not detected during the current period may be *counterbalancing,* i.e., affected by an equal misstatement in the subsequent period. The few material, noncounterbalancing errors not detected until subsequent periods must be treated as prior period adjustments according to APB Opinion No. 20.

The remaining sections of this appendix describe and illustrate the procedures to be applied when error corrections qualify as prior period adjustments. Accordingly, it is assumed each of the errors named is material and calls for correction directly to the retained earnings account summarizing past earnings. When errors are discovered, they usually affect the income tax liability for a prior period. Amended tax returns are usually prepared either to claim a refund or to pay any additional tax assessment. For simplicity, the extended example on the following pages and the exercises and problems ignore the income tax effect of errors.

Illustrative Example of Error Correction

The following example illustrates the analysis required upon the discovery of errors of prior periods and the entries to correct these errors.

Assume the R & G Wholesale Co. began operations at the beginning of 1983. An auditing firm is engaged for the first time in 1985. Before the accounts are adjusted and closed for 1985, the auditor reviews the books and accounts, and discovers the errors summarized on pages 692 and 693. Effects of these errors on the financial statements are listed before any correcting entries. A plus sign (+) indicates an overstatement; a minus sign (−) indicates an understatement. Each error correction is discussed in the following paragraphs.

(1) *Understatement of merchandise inventory.* It is discovered that the merchandise inventory as of December 31, 1983, was understated by $1,000. The effects of the misstatement were as shown below.

	Income Statement	Balance Sheet
For 1983:	Cost of goods sold overstated (ending inventory too low)	Assets understated (inventory too low)
	Net income understated	Retained earnings understated
For 1984:	Cost of goods sold understated (beginning inventory too low) Net income overstated	Balance sheet items not affected, retained earnings understatement for 1983 being corrected by net income overstatement for 1984

Since this type of error counterbalances after two years, no correcting entry is required in 1985.

If the error had been discovered in 1984 instead of 1985, an entry could have been made to correct the account balances so that operations for 1984 might be reported accurately. The beginning inventory would have to be increased by $1,000, the asset understatement, and Retained Earnings would have to be credited for this amount representing the income understatement in 1983. The correcting entry in 1984 would have been:

Merchandise Inventory	1,000	
Retained Earnings		1,000

(2) *Failure to record merchandise purchases.* It is discovered that purchase invoices as of December 28, 1983, for $850 were not recorded until 1984. The goods were included in the inventory at the end of 1983. The effects of failure to record the purchases were as follows:

	Income Statement	Balance Sheet
For 1983:	Cost of goods sold understated (purchases too low) Net income overstated	Liabilities understated (accounts payable too low) Retained earnings overstated
For 1984:	Cost of goods sold overstated (purchases too high) Net income understated	Balance sheet items not affected, retained earnings overstatement for 1983 being corrected by net income understatement for 1984

Since this is a counterbalancing error, no correcting entry is required in 1985.

If the error had been discovered in 1984 instead of 1985, a correcting entry would have been necessary. In 1984, Purchases was debited and Accounts Payable credited for $850 for merchandise acquired in 1983 and included in the ending inventory of 1983. Retained Earnings would have to be debited for $850, representing the net income overstatement for 1983, and Purchases would have to be credited for a similar amount to reduce the Purchases balance in 1984. The correcting entry in 1984 would have been:

Retained Earnings	850	
Purchases		850

(3) *Failure to record merchandise sales.* It is discovered that sales on account for the last week of December, 1984, for $1,800 were not recorded until 1985. The goods sold were not included in the inventory at the end of 1984. The effects of the failure to report the revenue in 1984 were:

	Income Statement	Balance Sheet
For 1984:	Revenue understated (sales too low)	Assets understated (accounts receivable too low)
	Net income understated	Retained earnings understated

Analysis Sheet to Show Effects

	At End of 1983			
	Income Statement		Balance Sheet	
	Section	*Net Income*	*Section*	*Retained Earnings*
(1) Understatement of merchandise inventory of $1,000 on December 31, 1983.	Cost of Goods Sold +	–	Current Assets –	–
(2) Failure to record merchandise purchases on account of $850 in 1983, purchases were recorded in 1984.	Cost of Goods Sold –	+	Current Liabilities –	+
(3) Failure to record merchandise sales on account of $1,800 in 1984. (It is assumed that the sales for 1984 were recognized as revenue in 1985.)				
(4) Failure to record accrued sales salaries; expense was recognized when payment was made. On December 31, 1983, $450.	Selling Expense –	+	Current Liabilities –	+
On December 31, 1984, $300.				
(5) Failure to record prepaid taxes of $275 on December 31, 1983, amount was included as miscellaneous general expense.	General Expense +	–	Current Assets –	–
(6) Failure to record reduction in prepaid insurance balance of $350 on December 31, 1983, insurance for 1983 was charged to 1984.	General Expense –	+	Current Assets +	+
(7) Failure to record accrued interest on notes receivable of $150 on December 31, 1983, revenue was recognized on collection in 1984.	Other Revenue –	–	Current Assets –	–
(8) Failure to record unearned service fees; amounts received were included in Miscellaneous Revenue. On December 31, 1983, $175.	Other Revenue +	+	Current Liabilities –	+
On December 31, 1984, $225.				
(9) Failure to record reduction in unearned rent revenue balance on December 31, 1984, $125. (It is assumed that the rent revenue for 1984 was recognized as revenue in 1985).				
(10) Failure to record depreciation of delivery equipment. On December 31, 1983, $1,200.	Selling Expense –	+	Noncurrent Assets +	+
On December 31, 1984, $1,200.				

of Errors on Financial Statements

At End of 1984				At End of 1985			
Income Statement		Balance Sheet		Income Statement		Balance Sheet	
Section	*Net Income*	*Section*	*Retained Earnings*	*Section*	*Net Income*	*Section*	*Retained Earnings*
Cost of Goods Sold −	+						
Cost of Goods Sold +	−						
Sales −	−	Accounts Receivable −	−	Sales +	+		
Selling Expense +	−						
Selling Expense −	+	Current Liabilities −	+	Selling Expense +	−		
General Expense −	+						
General Expense +	−						
Other Revenue +	+						
Other Revenue −	−						
Other Revenue +	+	Current Liabilities −	+	Other Revenue −	−		
Other Revenue −	−	Deferred Revenues +	−	Other Revenue +	+		
		Noncurrent Assets +	+			Noncurrent Assets +	+
Selling Expense −	+	Noncurrent Assets +	+			Noncurrent Assets +	+

When the error is discovered in 1985, Sales is debited for $1,800 and Retained Earnings is credited for this amount representing the net income understatement for 1984. The following entry is made:

Sales	1,800	
Retained Earnings		1,800

(4) *Failure to record accrued expense.* Accrued sales salaries of $450 as of December 31, 1983, and $300 as of December 31, 1984, were overlooked in adjusting the accounts on each of these dates. Sales Salaries is debited for salary payments. The effects of the failure to record the accrued expense of $450 as of December 31, 1983, were as follows:

	Income Statement	Balance Sheet
For 1983:	Expenses understated (sales salaries too low)	Liabilities understated (accrued sales salaries not reported)
	Net income overstated	Retained earnings overstated
For 1984:	Expenses overstated (sales salaries too high) Net income understated	Balance sheet items not affected, retained earnings overstatement for 1983 being corrected by net income understatement for 1984.

The effects of failure to recognize the accrued expense of $300 on December 31, 1984, were as follows:

	Income Statement	Balance Sheet
For 1984:	Expenses understated (sales salaries too low)	Liabilities understated (accrued sales salaries not reported)
	Net income overstated	Retained earnings overstated

No entry is required in 1985 to correct the accounts for the failure to record the accrued expense at the end of 1983, the misstatement in 1983 having been counterbalanced by the misstatement in 1984. An entry is required, however, to correct the accounts for the failure to record the accrued expense at the end of 1984 if the net income for 1985 is not to be misstated. If accrued expenses were properly recorded at the end of 1985, Retained Earnings would be debited for $300, representing the net income overstatement for 1984, and Sales Salaries would be credited for a similar amount, representing the amount to be subtracted from salary payments in 1985. The correcting entry is:

Retained Earnings	300	
Sales Salaries		300

If the failure to adjust the accounts for the accrued expense of 1983 had been recognized in 1984, an entry similar to the one above would have been required in 1984 to correct the account balances. The entry in 1984 would have been:

Retained Earnings	450	
Sales Salaries		450

The accrued salaries of $300 as of the end of 1984 would be recorded at the end of that year by an appropriate adjustment.

(5) *Failure to record prepaid expense.* It is discovered that Miscellaneous General Expense for 1983 included taxes of $275 that should have been deferred in adjusting the accounts on December 31, 1983. The effects of the failure to record the prepaid expense were as follows:

	Income Statement	Balance Sheet
For 1983:	Expenses overstated (miscellaneous general expense too high)	Assets understated (prepaid taxes not reported)
	Net income understated	Retained earnings understated
For 1984:	Expenses understated (miscellaneous general expense too low) Net income overstated	Balance sheet items not affected, retained earnings understatement for 1983 being corrected by net income overstatement for 1984.

Since this is a counterbalancing error, no entry to correct the accounts is required in 1985.

If the error had been discovered in 1984 instead of 1985, a correcting entry would have been necessary. If prepaid taxes were properly recorded at the end of 1984, Miscellaneous General Expense would have to be debited for $275, the expense relating to operations of 1984, and Retained Earnings would have to be credited for a similar amount representing the net income understatement for 1983. The correcting entry in 1984 would have been:

Miscellaneous General Expense	275	
Retained Earnings		275

(6) *Overstatement of prepaid expense.* On January 2, 1983, $1,050 representing insurance for a three-year period was paid. The charge was made to the asset account, Prepaid Insurance. No adjustment was made at the end of 1983. At the end of 1984, the prepaid insurance account was reduced to the prepaid balance on that date, $350, insurance for two years, or $700, being charged to operations of 1984. The effects of the misstatements were as follows:

	Income Statement	Balance Sheet
For 1983:	Expenses understated (insurance expense not reported)	Assets overstated (prepaid insurance too high)
	Net income overstated	Retained earnings overstated
For 1984:	Expenses overstated (insurance expense too high) Net income understated	Balance sheet items not affected, retained earnings overstatement for 1983 being corrected by net income understatement for 1984.

Since the balance sheet items at the end of 1984 were correctly stated, no entry to correct the accounts is required in 1985.

If the error had been discovered in 1984 instead of 1985, an entry would have been necessary to correct the account balances. Prepaid Insurance would have been decreased for the expired insurance of $350 and Retained Earnings would be debited for this amount representing the net income overstatement for 1983. The correcting entry in 1984 would have been:

Retained Earnings	350	
Prepaid Insurance		350

The expired insurance of $350 for 1984 would be recorded at the end of that year by an appropriate adjustment.

(7) *Failure to record accrued revenue.* Accrued interest on notes receivable of $150 was overlooked in adjusting the accounts on December 31, 1983. The revenue was recognized when the interest was collected in 1984. The effects of the failure to record the accrued revenue were:

	Income Statement	Balance Sheet
For 1983:	Revenue understated (interest revenue too low) Net income understated	Assets understated (interest receivable not reported) Retained earnings understated
For 1984:	Revenue overstated (interest revenue too high) Net income overstated	Balance sheet items not affected, retained earnings understatement for 1983 being corrected by net income overstatement for 1984.

Since the balance sheet items at the end of 1984 were correctly stated, no entry to correct the accounts is required in 1985.

If the error had been discovered in 1984 instead of 1985, an entry would have been necessary to correct the account balances. If accrued interest on notes receivable had been properly recorded at the end of 1984, Interest Revenue would have to be debited for $150, the amount to be subtracted from receipts of 1984, and Retained Earnings would have to be credited for a similar amount representing the net income understatement for 1983. The correcting entry in 1984 would have been:

Interest Revenue	150	
Retained Earnings		150

(8) *Failure to record unearned revenue.* Fees received in advance for miscellaneous services of $175 as of December 31, 1983, and $225 as of December 31, 1984, were overlooked in adjusting the accounts on each of these dates. Miscellaneous Revenue had been credited when fees were received. The effects of the failure to recognize the unearned revenue of $175 at the end of 1983 were as follows:

	Income Statement	Balance Sheet
For 1983:	Revenue overstated (miscellaneous revenue too high) Net income overstated	Liabilities understated (unearned service fees not reported) Retained earnings overstated
For 1984:	Revenue understated (miscellaneous revenue too low) Net income understated	Balance sheet items not affected, retained earnings overstatement for 1983 being corrected by net income understatement for 1984.

The effects of the failure to recognize the unearned revenue of $225 at the end of 1984 were as follows:

	Income Statement	Balance Sheet
For 1984:	Revenue overstated (miscellaneous revenue too high) Net income overstated	Liabilities understated (unearned service fees not reported) Retained earnings overstated

No entry is required in 1985 to correct the accounts for the failure to record the unearned revenue at the end of 1983, the misstatement in 1983 having been counterbalanced by the misstatement in 1984. An entry is required, however, to correct the accounts for the failure to record the unearned revenue at the end of 1984 if the net income for 1985 is not to be misstated. If the unearned revenue were properly recorded at the end of 1985, Retained Earnings would be debited for $225, representing the net income overstatement for 1984, and Miscellaneous Revenue would be credited for the same amount, representing the revenue that is to be identified with 1985. The correcting entry is:

Retained Earnings	225	
Miscellaneous Revenue		225

If the failure to adjust the accounts for the unearned revenue of 1983 had been recognized in 1984, instead of 1985, an entry similar to the one above would have been required in 1984 to correct the account balances. The entry at that time would have been:

Retained Earnings	175	
Miscellaneous Revenue		175

The unearned service fees of $225 as of the end of 1984 would be recorded at the end of that year by an appropriate adjustment.

(9) *Overstatement of unearned revenue.* Unearned Rent Revenue was credited for $375 representing revenue for December, 1984, and for January and February, 1985. No adjustment was made on December 31, 1984. The effects of the failure to adjust the accounts to show revenue of $125 for 1984 were as follows:

	Income Statement	Balance Sheet
For 1984:	Revenue understated (rent revenue too low)	Liabilities overstated (unearned rent revenue too high)
	Net income understated	Retained earnings understated

When the error is discovered in 1985, Unearned Rent Revenue is debited for $125 and Retained Earnings is credited for this amount representing the net income understatement in 1984. The following entry is made:

Unearned Rent Revenue	125	
Retained Earnings		125

(10) *Failure to record depreciation.* Delivery equipment was acquired at the beginning of 1983 at a cost of $6,000. The equipment has an estimated five-year life, and depreciation of $1,200 was overlooked at the end of 1983 and 1984. The effects of the failure to record depreciation for 1983 were as follows:

	Income Statement	Balance Sheet
For 1983:	Expenses understated (depreciation of delivery equipment too low)	Assets overstated (accumulated depreciation of delivery equipment too low)
	Net income overstated	Retained earnings overstated
For 1984:	Expenses not affected	Assets overstated (accumulated depreciation of delivery equipment too low)
	Net income not affected	Retained earnings overstated

It should be observed that the misstatements arising from the failure to record depreciation are not counterbalanced in the succeeding year.

Failure to record depreciation for 1984 affected the statements as shown below:

	Income Statement	Balance Sheet
For 1984:	Expenses understated (depreciation of delivery equipment too low)	Assets overstated (accumulated depreciation of delivery equipment too low)
	Net income overstated	Retained earnings overstated

When the omission is recognized, Retained Earnings must be decreased by the net income overstatements of prior years and accumulated depreciation must be increased by the depreciation that should have been recorded. The correcting entry in 1985 for depreciation that should have been recognized for 1983 and 1984 is as follows:

Retained Earnings	2,400	
Accumulated Depreciation—Delivery Equipment		2,400

Working Papers to Summarize Corrections

It is assumed in the following sections that the errors previously discussed are discovered in 1985 before the accounts for the year are adjusted and closed. Accounts are corrected so that revenue and expense accounts report the balances identified with the current period and asset, liability, and retained earnings accounts are accurately stated. Instead of preparing a separate entry for each correction, a single compound entry may be made for all of the errors discovered. The entry to correct earnings of prior years as well as to correct current earnings may be developed by the preparation of working papers. Assume the following retained earnings account for the R & G Wholesale Co.:

Account **Retained Earnings**

Date		Item	Debit	Credit	Balance	
					Debit	Credit
1983						
Dec.	31	Balance...........				12,000
1984						
Dec.	20	Dividends declared .	5,000			7,000
	31	Net income		15,000		22,000

The working papers to determine the corrected retained earnings balance on December 31, 1983, and the corrected net income for 1984 are shown on page 699. As indicated earlier, no adjustment is made for income tax effects in this example.

The working papers indicate that Retained Earnings is to be decreased by $1,000 as of January 1, 1985, as shown at the top of page 700.

R & G Wholesale Co.
Working Papers for Correction of Account Balances
December 31, 1985

Explanation	Retained Earnings Dec. 31, 1983		Net Income Year Ended Dec. 31, 1984		Accounts Requiring Correction in 1985		
	Debit	Credit	Debit	Credit	Debit	Credit	Account
Reported retained earnings balance, Dec. 31, 1983		12,000					
Reported net income for year ended Dec. 31, 1984				15,000			
Corrections:*							
(1) Understatement of inventory on Dec. 31, 1983, $1,000		1,000	1,000				
(2) Failure to record merchandise purchases in 1983, $850.	850			850			
(3) Failure to record merchandise sales in 1984, $1,800				1,800	1,800		Sales
(4) Failure to record accrued sales salaries:							
(a) On Dec. 31, 1983, $450	450			450			
(b) On Dec. 31, 1984, $300			300			300	Sales Salaries
(5) Failure to record prepaid taxes on Dec. 31, 1983, $275		275	275				
(6) Failure to record insurance expense on Dec. 31, 1983, $350, insurance of $700 for 1983 and 1984 being charged to 1984	350			350			
(7) Failure to record accrued interest on notes receivable on Dec. 31, 1983, $150		150	150				
(8) Failure to record unearned service fees:							
(a) On Dec. 31, 1983, $175.	175			175			
(b) On Dec. 31, 1984, $225			225			225	Misc. Revenue
(9) Failure to record rent revenue on Dec. 31, 1984, $125				125	125		Unearned Rent
(10) Failure to record depreciation of delivery equipment:							
(a) On Dec. 31, 1983, $1,200.	1,200					1,200	Accumulated Depr.—Delivery Equipment
(b) On Dec. 31, 1984, $1,200.			1,200			1,200	
Corrected retained earnings balance, Dec. 31, 1983.	10,400						
	13,425	13,425					
Corrected net income for 1984.			15,600				
			18,750	18,750			
Net correction to retained earnings as of Jan. 1, 1985					1,000		Retained Earnings
					2,925	2,925	

*For a more detailed description of the individual errors and their correction, refer to pages 690–698.

Retained earnings overstatement as of December 31, 1983:		
Retained earnings as originally reported	$12,000	
Retained earnings as corrected	10,400	$1,600
Retained earnings understatement in 1984:		
Net income as corrected	$15,600	
Net income as originally reported	15,000	600
Retained earnings overstatement as of January 1, 1985		$1,000

The following entry is prepared from the working papers to correct the account balances in 1985:

Retained Earnings	1,000	
Sales	1,800	
Unearned Rent Revenue	125	
Sales Salaries		300
Miscellaneous Revenue		225
Accumulated Depreciation—Delivery Equipment		2,400

The retained earnings account after correction will appear with a balance of $21,000, as follows:

Account **Retained Earnings**

Date		Item	Debit	Credit	Balance Debit	Balance Credit
1985						
Jan.	1	Balance				22,000
Dec.	31	Corrections in net incomes of prior periods discovered during the course of the audit	1,000			21,000

The balance in Retained Earnings can be proved by reconstructing the account from the detail shown on the working papers. If the net incomes for 1983 and 1984 had been reported properly, Retained Earnings would have appeared as follows:

Account **Retained Earnings**

Date		Item	Debit	Credit	Balance Debit	Balance Credit
1983						
Dec.	31	Corrected balance per working papers				10,400
1984						
Dec.	20	Dividends declared	5,000			5,400
	31	Corrected net income for 1984		15,600		21,000

In the foregoing example, a corrected net income figure for only 1984 was required; hence any corrections in earnings for years prior to this date were shown as affecting the retained earnings balance as of December 31, 1983. Working papers on page 699 were constructed to summarize this information by providing a pair of columns for retained earnings as of December 31, 1983, and a pair of columns for earnings data for 1984. It may be desirable to determine corrected earnings for a number of years. When this is to be done, a pair of columns must be provided for retained earnings as of the beginning of the period under review and a separate pair of columns for each year for which corrected earnings are to be determined. For example, assume that corrected earnings for the years 1982, 1983, and 1984 are to be determined. Working papers for the correction of account balances would be constructed with headings as shown below. Corrections for the omission of accrued sales salaries for a four-year period would appear as follows:

	Retained Earnings Dec. 31, 1981		Net Income Year Ended Dec. 31, 1982		Net Income Year Ended Dec. 31, 1983		Net Income Year Ended Dec. 31, 1984		Accounts Requiring Correction in 1985		
Explanation	Debit	Credit	Debit	Credit	Debit	Credit	Debit	Credit	Debit	Credit	Account
Failure to record accrued sales salaries at end of:											
1981, $750.	750			750							
1982, $800.			800			800					
1983, $900.					900			900			
1984, $625.							625			625	Sales Salaries

QUESTIONS

1. Accumulated retained earnings are in general supported by a cross section of all the assets. Directors are criticized by stockholders for failure to declare dividends when retained earnings are present. Are these two statements related? Explain.

2. Which of the following transactions are a source of stockholders' equity?

(a) Operating profits.
(b) Cancellation of a part of a liability upon prompt payment of the balance.
(c) Reduction of par value of stock outstanding.
(d) Discovery of an understatement of income in a previous period.
(e) Release of Retained Earnings Appropriated for Purchase of Treasury Stock upon the sale of treasury stock.
(f) Issue of bonds at a premium.
(g) Purchase of the corporation's own capital stock at a discount.
(h) Increase in the company's earning capacity, taken to be evidence of considerable goodwill.
(i) Construction of equipment for the company's own use at a cost less than the prevailing market price of identical equipment.
(j) Donation to the corporation of its own stock.
(k) Sale of land, buildings, and equipment at a gain.
(l) Gain on bond retirement.

(continued)

(m) Revaluation of land, buildings, and equipment due to an increase in asset replacement values, resulting in an increase in asset book values.
(n) Collection of stock assessments from stockholders.
(o) Discovery of valuable resources on company property.
(p) Conversion of bonds into common stock.
(q) Conversion of preferred stock into common stock.

3. The following announcement appeared on the financial page of a newspaper:

> The Board of Directors of the Benton Co., at their meeting on June 15, 1984, declared the regular quarterly dividend on outstanding common stock of 70 cents per share and an extra dividend of $1.40 per share, both payable on July 10, 1984, to the stockholders of record at the close of business June 30, 1984.

(a) What is the purpose of each of the three dates given in the declaration? (b) When would the stock become "ex-dividend"? (c) Why is the $1.40 designated as an "extra" dividend?

4. The directors of The Fern Shoppe are considering issuance of a stock dividend. They have asked you to discuss the proposed action by answering the following questions:
(a) What is a stock dividend? How is a stock dividend distinguished from a stock split: (1) from a legal standpoint? (2) from an accounting standpoint?
(b) For what reasons does a corporation usually declare (1) a stock dividend? (2) a stock split? (3) a stock split in the form of a stock dividend?

5. Eastern Supply Inc. has 1,000,000 shares of no-par common stock outstanding. Dividends have been limited to approximately 20% of annual earnings, remaining earnings being used to finance expansion. With pressure from stockholders for an increase in dividends, the board of directors takes action to issue to stockholders an additional 1,000,000 shares of stock, and the president of the company informs stockholders that the company will pay a 100% stock dividend in view of the conservative dividend policy in the past. What is your comment on this statement?

6. It has been recommended that the balance sheet maintain a permanent distinction between contributed capital and retained earnings. How can such a distinction be maintained when action is taken to convert retained earnings into capital stock?

7. (a) What is a liquidating dividend? (b) Under what circumstances are such distributions made? (c) How would you recommend that liquidating dividends be recorded in the accounts of the corporation?

8. At the regular meeting of the board of directors of the Lawton Corporation, a dividend payable in the stock of the Colter Corporation is to be declared. The stock of the Colter Corporation is recorded on the books of the Lawton Corporation at $190,000; the market value of the stock is $230,000. The question is raised whether the amount to be recorded for the dividend payable should be the book value or the market value. What is the proper accounting treatment?

9. Snow White Cleaners, acting within the law of the state of incorporation, paid a cash dividend to stockholders for which it debited Paid-In Capital from Sale of Stock at a Premium. A stockholder protested, saying that such a dividend was a partial liquidation of her holdings. Is this true?

10. Why should Retained Earnings not be credited for gains arising from a company dealing in its own stock if losses for similar transactions are debited to the account?

11. A stockholder of Barker Inc. does not understand the purpose of the Appropriation for Bond Redemption Fund that has been set up by periodic debits to Retained Earnings. He is told that this balance will not be used to redeem the bonds at their maturity. (a) What account will be reduced by the payment of the bonds? (b) What purpose is accomplished by the Appropriation for Bond Redemption Fund? (c) What dispositions may be made of the appropriation?

12. Management of the Judd Construction Co., considering the possibility of a strike by employees, authorized the establishment of an appropriation for contingencies at the end of 1983 by a charge to revenue. The strike was called in 1984, and company losses incurred to the date of the strike settlement were charged against the appropriation. The company management points out that it exercised good judgment in anticipating strike losses and in providing a cushion for such losses. What criticism, if any, can you offer of the accounting procedures followed by the company?

13. What items are defined as contra-equity accounts and deducted from the total stockholders' equity?

14. Which of the following transactions change total stockholders' equity? What is the nature of the change?

(a) Declaration of a cash dividend.
(b) Payment of a cash dividend.
(c) Retirement of bonds payable for which both a redemption fund and an appropriation had been established.
(d) Declaration of a stock dividend.
(e) Payment of a stock dividend.
(f) Conversion of bonds payable into preferred stock.
(g) The passing of a dividend on cumulative preferred stock.
(h) Donation by the officers of shares of stock.
(i) Operating loss for the period.

15. How would you report the following items on the balance sheet: (a) dividends in arrears on cumulative preferred stock, (b) unclaimed bond interest and unclaimed dividends, (c) stock purchase rights issued but not exercised as of the balance sheet date, (d) stock that is callable at a premium at the option of the corporation?

16. Why is book value per share often a poor indicator of stock worth?

17. What adjustments are applied to the total stockholders' equity in computing book value per common share when there is more than one class of stock outstanding?

18. The liquidation value of preferred stock is 100 and the call price is 105. Which value should be used in computing book value for preferred stock? Why?

DISCUSSION CASES

case 18-1 (How much should our dividend be?) Fullen Upholstery Corp. has paid quarterly dividends of $.80 per share for the last three years and is trying to continue this tradition. Fullen's balance sheet is as follows:

Fullen Upholstery Corp.
Balance Sheet
December 31, 1984

Assets		Liabilities	
Cash	$ 60,000	Accounts payable	$ 570,000
Accounts receivable	490,000	Taxes payable	100,000
Inventory	1,200,000	Accrued liabilities	90,000
Total current assets	$1,750,000	Total current liabilities	$ 760,000
		Bonds payable	1,500,000
Investments	500,000	Total liabilities	$2,260,000
Land, buildings, and equipment (net)	1,600,000		
		Equity	
		Common stock ($10 par, 69,000 shares outstanding	$ 690,000
		Retained earnings	900,000
		Total equity	$1,590,000
Total assets	$3,850,000	Total liabilities and equity	$3,850,000

Discuss Fullen's possibilities concerning the issuance of dividends.

case 18-2 (Cash or stock dividend?) Elkington Ski Manufacturer is considering offering a 10% stock dividend rather than its normal cash dividend of $1 per share in the first quarter of 1985. However, some of Elkington's stockholders have expressed displeasure at the idea and say they strongly prefer cash dividends.

Discuss the issue of a stock dividend as opposed to a cash dividend from the point of view of (a) a stockholder and (b) the board of directors.

case 18-3 (Stock splits and stock dividends) IBM has been one of the more popular growth stocks during the past several years. In 1979, its stock was selling in the range of $300–$330, with about 146,000 shares outstanding. On May 1, 1979, IBM announced that, effective May 10, 1979, their stock would be split four for one. This was the first time since 1958 that IBM stock had been split, although several stock dividends had been issued during the past twenty years. (a) What are the differences between a stock dividend and a stock split both from the standpoint of the investor and of the company? (b) What possible reasons do you see for IBM using stock dividends as a means of capitalizing retained earnings until 1979 when the stock split was announced?

case 18-4 (The "value" of book value) Elias Snell, president and sole owner of the Snell Corporation, is looking for someone to purchase his company. Snell cites failing health as a reason for his "throwing in the towel" at the age of 87. He claims that it is getting too hard for him to keep abreast of the day-to-day operations at his plant which manufactures wooden wagon wheels.

In talking to a prospective buyer, Snell emphasized that he isn't trying to make a profit from the sale of his stock, but that he did expect to recoup his investment in the company. Snell then presented the prospective buyer with a copy of the corporation's balance sheet for the year ending December 31, 1984. The balance sheet follows:

Snell Corporation
Balance Sheet
December 31, 1984

Assets		Liabilities and Equity	
Cash	$ 350	Accounts payable	$14,750
Accounts receivable	5,600	Estimated liabilities under	
Prepaid expenses	7,800	warranties	2,000
Land, buildings, and equipment (net)		Capital stock ($10 par)	60,000
	53,000	Deficit	(10,000)
Total assets	$66,750	Total liabilities and equity	$66,750

After presenting the balance sheet, Snell explained that the book value represented an extremely attractive selling price and that he was practically giving the company away for that price. However, an independent audit of Snell's financial statements revealed that 90% of accounts receivable were past due by at least three years; prepaid expenses represent advance payments to employees who have never returned to work after having received their advances; the fair market value of all land, buildings, and equipment is $20,000; and current litigation tends to indicate that liabilities for warranties are drastically underestimated. Also, sales have continually declined for the past several years.

The prospective buyer believes that the book value per share indicates an attractive price for the company's stock since Snell is not even trying to make a profit on his investment in the company. As an investment consultant, you have been asked to advise the prospective buyer on this investment opportunity. Explain your reasoning.

EXERCISES

exercise 18-1 (Cash and stock dividends)

The balance sheet of the Jenks Warehouse Supply Company shows the following on July 1:

Cash	$300,000
Capital stock, $10 par, 100,000 shares authorized, 75,000 shares issued and outstanding	750,000
Paid-in capital	150,000
Retained earnings	345,000

On July 1, Jenks declared a cash dividend of $2 per share payable on October 1. Then on November 1, the corporation declared a 15% stock dividend with the shares to be issued on December 31. Market value on November 1 was $15 per share. Give the necessary entries to record the declaration and payment or issuance of the dividends.

exercise 18-2 (Property dividends)

Lamoreaux Lumber Co. distributed the following dividends to its stockholders:

(a) Investment of 400,000 shares of Accord Corporation stock, carrying value $1,200,000, fair market value $2,300,000.

(b) Investment of 230,000 shares of Pfeffer Trailer Company stock, a closely held corporation. The shares were purchased three years ago at $5.60 per share, but no current market price is available.

Give the journal entries to account for the declaration and the payment of the above dividends.

exercise 18-3 (Dividend computation)

Thornton Excavating has been paying quarterly dividends of $.50 and wants to pay the same amount in the third quarter of 1984. Given the following information, what is the total amount in dollars that Thornton will have to pay in dividends in the third quarter in order to pay $.50 per share?

1984	
Jan. 1	Shares outstanding, 600,000; $10 par (1,000,000 shares authorized)
Feb. 15	Issued 150,000 new shares at $16.50
Mar. 31	Paid quarterly dividends of $.50 per share
May 12	$1,600,000 of $1,000 bonds were converted to common stock at the rate of 80 shares of stock per $1,000 bond.
June 30	Paid quarterly dividends of $.50 per share. Also issued a 5% stock dividend.

exercise 18-4 (Stock dividends)

The balance sheet of the Far Valley Motors Co. shows the following:

Capital stock, $5 stated value, 80,000 shares issued and outstanding	$400,000
Paid-in capital	800,000
Retained earnings	350,000

A 25% stock dividend is declared, the board of directors authorizing a transfer from Retained Earnings to Capital Stock at the stock stated value.

(a) Give entries to record the declaration and payment of the dividend.

(b) What was the effect of the issue of the stock dividend on the ownership equity of each stockholder in the corporation?

(c) Give entries to record the declaration and payment of the dividend if the board of directors had elected to transfer amounts from Retained Earnings to Capital Stock equal to the market value of the stock ($10 per share).

exercise 18-5 (Stock dividends and stock splits)

The capital accounts for Kiddie Korner Furniture Inc. on June 30, 1984, follow:

Capital Stock, $20 par, 60,000 shares	$1,200,000
Premium on Capital Stock	435,000
Retained Earnings	2,160,000

Shares of the company's stock are selling at this time at 36. What entries would you make in each case below?

(a) A stock dividend of 10% is declared and issued.
(b) A stock dividend of 100% is declared and issued.
(c) A 2-for-1 stock split is declared and issued.

exercise 18-6 (Stock dividend computation)

The directors of Fairly Dry Cleaning Inc., whose $80 par value common stock is currently selling at $100 per share, have decided to issue a stock dividend. Fairly Dry has an authorization for 400,000 shares of common, has issued 220,000 shares of which 20,000 shares are now held as treasury stock, and desires to capitalize $2,400,000 of the retained earnings account balance. What percent stock dividend should be issued to accomplish this desire?

exercise 18-7 (Accounting for dividends)

The dividend declarations and distributions by the Fenton Company over a three-year period are listed below. Give the entry required in each case.

1983
July 1 Declared a 30% stock dividend on 1,000,000 shares of stock, par value $15. The stock was originally sold at $18, and Retained Earnings is to be debited for the stock dividend for an amount equal to the original stock issuance price.
15 Distributed the stock dividend declared on July 1, which included fractional warrants for 1,800 shares.
Sept. 1 1,100 shares were issued for fractional warrants; remaining fractional warrants expired.

1985
July 1 Declared a dividend of 1 share of Eastern Co. common stock on every share of Fenton Company stock owned. Eastern Co. common stock is carried on the books of the Fenton Company at a cost of $1.60 per share, and the market price is $1.80 per share.
15 Distributed Eastern Co. common stock to shareholders.

exercise 18-8 (Restricting retained earnings)

On January 1, 1983, Pacific Manufacturing Corporation floated a $14,000,000 bond issue. The bond issue agreement with the underwriters required Pacific Manufacturing to appropriate earnings of $875,000 at the end of each year until the bonds are retired. During their 1985 board meeting, the directors decided to change the company's financing policy to just short-term debt and equity, and to drop their present insurance policy in favor of a self-insurance plan. On July 1, 1985, the company retired the bond issue and set up their first annual appropriation for self-insurance for $14,000.

(1) Give the entries to record the periodic appropriations under the bond issue agreement for 1983 and 1984 and their cancellation in 1985.
(2) How should the appropriation for self-insurance be recorded?

exercise 18-9 (Appropriation of retained earnings)

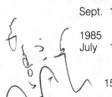

A physical inventory taken by the Eckles Storage Co. on December 31, 1984, discloses goods on hand with a cost of $2,580,000; the inventory is recorded at this figure less an allowance of $108,000 to reduce it to the lower of cost or market. At the same time, the company authorizes that an appropriation for possible future inventory decline of $900,000 be established.

(1) Give the entries made at the end of 1984 in recording the inventory and establishing the accounts as indicated.
(2) Give the entries in 1985 to close the beginning inventory and balances established at the end of 1984, assuming that the estimated inventory decline does not materialize and that the inventory at the end of 1985 is properly reported at cost, which is lower than market.
(3) Give the entries in 1985 to close the inventory and other account balances established at the end of 1984 if a decline in the value of the December 31, 1984 inventory of $480,000 is to be recognized; the inventory at the end of 1985 is properly reported at cost, which is lower than its market value at this date.

exercise 18-10 (Correcting the retained earnings account)

The retained earnings account for Brookside Corp. shows the following debits and credits. Give whatever entries may be required to correct the account.

Account **Related Earnings**

Date		Item	Debit	Credit	Balance Debit	Balance Credit
Jan.	1	Balance				263,200
(a)		Loss from fire	2,625			260,575
(b)		Write-off of goodwill	26,250			234,325
(c)		Stock dividend	70,000			164,325
(d)		Loss on sale of equipment	24,150			140,175
(e)		Officers compensation related to income of prior periods—accrual overlooked	162,750		22,575	
(f)		Loss on retirement of preferred shares at more than issuance price	35,000		57,575	
(g)		Premium on common stock		64,750		7,175
(h)		Stock subscription defaults		4,235		11,410
(i)		Gain on retirement of preferred stock at less than issuance price		12,950		24,360
(j)		Gain on early retirement of bonds at less than book value		7,525		31,885
(k)		Gain on life insurance policy settlement		5,250		37,135
(l)		Correction of prior period error		25,025		62,160

exercise 18-11 (Book value—one class of stock)

As of December 31, the equity section of the Intermountain Tile Corp. balance sheet contained the following information: capital stock, 120,000 shares issued, $1,200,000; capital stock subscribed, 20,000 shares, $200,000; additional paid-in capital, $400,000; retained earnings, $1,800,000; treasury stock at cost, 20,000 shares, $120,000. Compute the book value per share of common stock.

exercise 18-12 (Book value—two classes of stock)

The stockholders' equity of Greco Inc. on December 31, 1984, follows:

Common stock, $15 par, 100,000 shares	$1,500,000
Preferred 6% stock, $25 par, 10,000 shares	250,000
Additional paid-in capital	150,000
Retained earnings	100,000
Total stockholders' equity	$2,000,000

Compute the book values per share of preferred stock and common stock under each of the following assumptions:

(a) Preferred stock is noncumulative, callable at $30, and preferred as to assets at $27.50 upon corporate liquidation.
(b) Preferred stock is cumulative, with dividends in arrears for 6 years (including the current year). Upon corporate liquidation, shares are preferred as to assets up to par, and any dividends in arrears must be paid before distribution may be made to common shares.

exercise 18-13 (AICPA adapted multiple choice)

For each of the following, select the *one* best answer.

(1) The stockholders' equity section of the Larado Corporation as of December 31, 1984, was as follows:

Common stock, par value $4; authorized 20,000 shares; issued and outstanding 5,000 shares	$ 20,000
Capital contributed in excess of par	30,000
Retained earnings	60,000
Total stockholders' equity	$110,000

On March 1, 1985, the board of directors declared a 10% stock dividend, and accordingly 500 additional shares were issued. On March 1, 1985, the fair market value of the stock was $9 per share. For the two months ended February 28, 1985, Lorado sustained a net loss of $10,000.

What amount should Larado report as retained earnings as of March 1, 1985?

(a) $45,500.
(b) $47,500.
(c) $48,000.
(d) $50,000.

(2) On January 1, 1985, Wilson, Inc. declared a 5% stock dividend on its common stock when the market value of the common stock was $15 per share. Stockholders' equity before the stock dividend was declared consisted of:

Common stock, $10 par value. Authorized 200,000 shares; issued and outstanding 100,000 shares	$1,000,000
Additional paid-in capital on common stock	150,000
Retained earnings	700,000
Total stockholders' equity	$1,850,000

What was the effect on Wilson's retained earnings as a result of this dividend declaration?

(a) No effect.
(b) $50,000 decrease.
(c) $75,000 decrease.
(d) $150,000 decrease.

(3) Milner Company issued what is called a "100% stock dividend" on its common stock. Milner did not change the par value of the common stock. At what amount per share, if any, should either paid-in capital or retained earnings be reduced for this transaction?

(a) Zero because no entry is made.
(b) Par value.
(c) Market value at the declaration date.
(d) Market value at the date of issuance.

(4) The Shamus Company was organized on January 2, 1984, and issued the following stock:

200,000 shares of $5 par value common stock at $12 per share (authorized 200,000 shares).
50,000 shares of $10 par value 4% cumulative preferred stock at $25 per share (authorized 150,000 shares).

The net income for 1984 was $420,000 and cash dividends of $72,000 were declared and paid in 1984.

What were the dividends paid on the preferred and common stock, respectively?

(a) $20,000 and $52,000
(b) $24,000 and $48,000
(c) $46,000 and $26,000.
(d) $72,000 and $0.

exercise 18-14 (Recapitalization of equity)

McGregor Machinery Inc. reports its stockholders' equity as follows:

Common stock, $5 par, 500,000 shares	$2,500,000
Additional paid-in capital	200,000
Deficit	(350,000)
Total stockholders' equity	$2,350,000

The company wishes to cancel the deficit and is considering two possible alternatives. For each of the assumptions listed below, make the necessary entries that should appear on McGregor's books and prepare the stockholders' equity section of the balance sheet.

(a) One new share of no-par stock is to be exchanged for each share of common stock outstanding and the legal capital for the company is to be restated at $2,350,000.
(b) One new share of no-par stock with a stated value of $15 is to be exchanged for every four shares of common stock outstanding.

exercise 18-15 (Quasi-reorganization)

The Lincoln Lumber Company has a deficit in retained earnings of $100,000. Business appears to be turning around, so the president wants the company to go through a quasi-reorganization. The balance sheet of the company prior to the reorganization contains the following information: current assets, $50,000; land, $150,000; buildings, $500,000; accumulated depreciation, $100,000; liabilities $100,000; capital stock $20 par value, $600,000. As part of the reorganization, the building is to be written down to its fair value of $100,000 and the common stock is to be canceled and reissued at $5 par. Give the entries to record the quasi-reorganization.

*exercise 18-16 (Analysis of errors)

State the effect of each of the following errors made in 1983 upon the balance sheets and the income statements prepared in 1983 and 1984:

(a) The ending inventory is understated as a result of an error in the count of goods on hand.
(b) The ending inventory is overstated as a result of the inclusion of goods acquired and held on a consignment basis. No purchase was recorded on the books.
(c) A purchase of merchandise at the end of 1983 is not recorded until payment is made for the goods in 1984; the goods purchased were included in the inventory at the end of 1983.
(d) A sale of merchandise at the end of 1983 is not recorded until cash is received for the

(continued)

*Exercise to appendix material.

goods in 1984; the goods sold were excluded from the inventory at the end of 1983.

(e) Goods shipped to consignees in 1983 were reported as sales; good in the hands of consignees at the end of 1983 were not recognized for inventory purposes; sale of such goods in 1984 and collections on such sales were recorded as credits to the receivables established with consignees in 1983.

(f) One week's sales total during 1983 was credited to Gain on Sales—Machinery.

(g) No depreciation is taken in 1983 for machinery sold in April, 1983. The company is on a calendar year and computes depreciation to the nearest month.

(h) No depreciation is taken in 1983 for machinery purchased in October, 1983. The company is on a calendar year and computes depreciation to the nearest month.

(i) Customers' notes receivable are debited to Accounts Receivable.

*exercise 18-17 (Correction of errors—work papers)

The Nielson Co. reports net incomes for a three-year period as follows: 1982, $18,000; 1983, $10,500; 1984, $12,500.

In reviewing the accounts in 1985, after the books for the prior year have been closed, you find that the following errors have been made in summarizing activities:

	1982	1983	1984
Overstatement of ending inventories as a result of errors in count.	$1,600	$2,800	$1,800
Understatement of advertising expense payable.	300	600	450
Overstatement of interest receivable	250	—	200
Omission of depreciation on property items still in use	900	800	750

(a) Prepare working papers summarizing corrections and reporting corrected net incomes for 1982, 1983, and 1984.

(b) Give the entry to bring the books of the company up to date in 1985.

*exercise 18-18 (Journal entries to correct accounts)

The first audit of the books for the Warren Corporation was made for the year ended December 31, 1984. In reviewing the books, the auditor discovered that certain adjustments had been overlooked at the end of 1983 and 1984, and also that other items had been improperly recorded. Omissions and other failures for each year are summarized below:

	December 31	
	1983	1984
Sales salaries payable.	$1,300	$1,100
Interest receivable	325	215
Prepaid insurance.	450	300
Advances from customers . . . . (Collections from customers had been included in sales but should have been recognized as advances from customers since goods were not shipped until the following year.)	1,750	2,500
Equipment . . . . (Expenditures had been recognized as repairs but should have been recognized as cost of equipment; the depreciation rate on such equipment is 10% per year, but depreciation in the year of the expenditure is to be recognized at 5%).	1,400	1,200

Prepare journal entries to correct revenue and expense accounts for 1984 and record assets and liabilities that require recognition on the balance sheet as of December 31, 1984. Assume the nominal accounts for 1984 have not yet been closed into the income summary account.

*Exercises to appendix material.

PROBLEMS

problem 18-1 (Accounting for stock transactions)

Ernst Photography Equipment was organized on June 30, 1982. After two and one-half years of profitable operations, the equity section of Ernst's balance sheet was as follows:

Contributed capital:	
Common stock, $30 par, 500,000 shares authorized, 100,000 shares issued and outstanding	$3,000,000
Premium on common stock	500,000
Retained earnings	1,800,000
Total stockholders' equity	$5,300,000

During 1985, the following transactions affected the stockholders' equity:

Jan. 31 10,000 shares of common stock were reacquired at $33; treasury stock is reported at cost.
Apr. 1 The company declared a 35% stock dividend, (Applies to all issued stock.)
30 The company declared a $.50 cash dividend. (Applies only to outstanding stock.)
June 1 The stock dividend was issued and the cash dividend was paid.
Aug. 31 The treasury stock was sold at $36.

Instructions: Give journal entries to record the above stock transactions.

problem 18-2 (Accounting for stockholders' equity)

The stockholders' equity of the Ash Lumber Co. on June 30, 1984, was as follows:

Contributed capital:	
Preferred 8% stock, $50 par, cumulative, 20,000 shares issued, dividends 5 years in arrears	$1,000,000
Common stock, $20 par, 160,000 shares issued	3,200,000
	$4,200,000
Less deficit from operations	600,000
Total stockholders' equity	$3,600,000

On this date the following action was taken:

(a) Common stockholders turned in their stock and received in exchange new common stock, 1 share of the new stock being exchanged for every 4 shares of the old. New stock was given a stated value of $40 per share.
(b) One-half share of the new common stock was issued on each share of preferred stock outstanding in liquidation of dividends in arrears on preferred stock.
(c) The deficit from operations was applied against the paid-in capital arising from the common stock restatement.

Transactions for the remainder of 1984 affecting the stockholders' equity were as follows:

Oct. 1 10,000 shares of preferred stock were called in at $55 plus dividends for 3 months at 8%. Stock was formally retired.
Nov. 10 60,000 shares of new common stock were sold at 42.
Dec. 31 Net income for the six months ended on this date was $170,000. (Debit Income Summary.) The semiannual dividend was declared on preferred shares and a $.50 dividend on common shares, dividends being payable January 20, 1985.

Instructions:

(1) Record in journal form the transactions given above.
(2) Prepare the stockholders' equity section of the balance sheet as of December 31, 1984.

problem 18-3 (Stockholders' equity transactions)

Butler Inc. was organized on January 2, 1983, with authorized stock consisting of 40,000 shares of 16%, $200 par preferred, and 250,000 shares of no-par common. During the first two years of the company's existence, the following transactions took place:

1983

Jan.	2	Sold 10,600 shares of common stock at 16.
	2	Sold 2,600 shares of preferred stock at 216.
Mar.	2	Sold common stock as follows: 10,200 shares at 22; 2,400 shares at 24.
July	10	A nearby piece of land, appraised at $404,000 was acquired for 600 shares of preferred stock and 28,000 shares of common. (Preferred stock was recorded at 216, the balance being assigned to common.)
Dec.	16	The regular preferred and a $1.50 common dividend were declared.
	28	Dividends declared on December 16 were paid.
	31	The income summary account showed a credit balance of $408,000, which was transferred to retained earnings.

1984

Feb.	27	The corporation reacquired 12,000 shares of common stock at 18. The treasury stock is carried at cost. (State law requires that an appropriation of retained earnings be made for the purchase price of treasury stock. Appropriations are to be returned to retained earnings upon resale of the stock.)
June	17	Resold 10,000 shares of the treasury stock at 20.
July	31	Resold all of the remaining treasury stock at 19.
Sept.	30	The corporation sold 12,000 additional shares of common stock at 21.
Dec.	16	The regular preferred dividend and an $.80 common dividend were declared.
	28	Dividends declared on December 16 were paid.
	31	The income summary account showed a credit balance of $356,000, which was transferred to retained earnings.

Instructions:

(1) Give the journal entries to record the foregoing transactions.
(2) Prepare the stockholders' equity section of the balance sheet as of December 31, 1984.

problem 18-4 (Accounting for stockholders' equity)

A condensed balance sheet for Tax Trimmers Inc. as of December 31, 1981, appears below:

Tax Trimmers Inc.
Condensed Balance Sheet
December 31, 1981

Assets		Liabilities and Stockholders' Equity	
Assets	$525,000	Liabilities	$120,000
		Preferred 8% stock, $100 par	75,000
		Common stock, $50 par	150,000
		Premium on common stock	30,000
		Retained earnings	150,000
Total assets	$525,000	Total liabilities and stockholders' equity	$525,000

Capital stock authorized consists of: 750 shares of 8%, cumulative preferred stock with a prior claim on assets, and 15,000 shares of common stock.

Information relating to operations of the succeeding three years follows:

	1982	1983	1984
Dividends declared on Dec. 20, payable on Jan. 10 of the following year:			
Preferred stock	8% cash	8% cash	8% cash
Common stock	$1.00 cash 50% stock*	$1.25 cash	$1.00 cash
Net income for year	$67,500	$39,000	$51,000

*Retained earnings is reduced by the par value of the stock dividend.

1983

Feb. 12 Accumulated depreciation was reduced by $72,000 following an income tax investigation. (Assume that this was an error that qualifies as a prior period adjustment.) Additional income tax of $22,500 for prior years was paid.

Mar. 3 300 shares of common stock were purchased by the corporation at $54 per share; treasury stock is recorded at cost and retained earnings are appropriated equal to such cost.

1984

Aug. 10 All of the treasury stock was resold at $59 per share and the retained earnings appropriation was canceled.

Sept. 12 By vote of the stockholders, each share of the common stock was exchanged by the corporation for 4 shares of no-par common stock with a stated value of $15.

Instructions:

(1) Give the journal entries to record the foregoing transactions for the three-year period ended December 31, 1984.

(2) Prepare the stockholders' equity section of the balance sheet as it would appear at the end of 1982, 1983, and 1984.

problem 18-5 (Adjustments to Retained Earnings)

On March 31, 1984, the retained earnings account of State-Wide Wrecking Service showed a balance of $19,000,000. The board of directors of State-Wide made the following decisions during the remainder of 1984 that possibly affect the retained earnings account.

Apr. 1 State-Wide decided to assume the risk for workers' compensation insurance. The estimated liability for 1984 is $120,000. Also, a fund was set up to cover the estimated liability.

Apr. 30 State-Wide has not experienced even a small fire since 1946; therefore, the board of directors decided to start a self-insurance plan. They decided to start with a $400,000 appropriation.

May 15 A fire did considerable damage to the outside warehouse. It cost $360,000 to repair the warehouse.

Aug. 20 The board of directors received a report from the plant engineer which indicated that the company is possibly in violation of pollution control standards. The fine for such a violation is $800,000. As a result of the engineer's report, the board decided to set up a general contingency reserve for $800,000.

Sept. 1 The company reacquired 80,000 shares of their own stock at $29; treasury stock is recorded at cost. Due to legal restrictions, State-Wide has to set up an appropriation to cover the cost of the treasury stock.

Dec. 31 The company had to pay an $800,000 fine for pollution control violations and the treasury stock was sold at $31. No workers' compensation was paid during the year.

Instructions: Prepare all of the necessary entries to record the above transactions.

problem 18-6 (Reporting stockholders' equity)

Accounts of Alpine Ranch on December 31, 1984, show the following balances:

Accumulated Depreciation—Buildings		$ 272,000
Allowance for Purchase Discount	$ 2,400	
Bonds Payable		320,000
Bond Retirement Fund	128,000	
Buildings	1,200,000	
Capital Stock (80,000 shares authorized)		632,000
Capital Stock Subscribed (4,000 shares)		40,000
Current Assets	768,000	
Current Liabilities—Other		260,000
Customers' Deposits		20,000
Dividends Payable—Cash		16,000
Income Tax Payable		40,000
Paid-In Capital from Sale of Treasury Stock at More Than Cost		32,000
Premium on Capital Stock		24,000
Retained Earnings Appropriated for Contingencies		100,000
Retained Earnings Appropriated for Bond Retirement Fund		128,000
Retained Earnings Appropriated for Purchase of Treasury Stock		56,000
Stock Dividends Distributable		65,600
Treasury Stock, 4,800 shares at cost	56,000	
Unappropriated Retained Earnings		148,800
	$2,154,400	$2,154,400

Instructions: From these data prepare the stockholders' equity section as it would appear on the balance sheet.

problem 18-7 (Book value per share)

The stockholders' equity for the Kawakami Radio Corp. on December 31, 1984, follows:

Preferred 6% stock, $100 par, 20,000 shares	$2,000,000
Common stock, $25 par, 200,000 shares	5,000,000
Additional paid-in capital	500,000
Retained earnings	750,000
Total stockholders' equity	$8,250,000

Instructions: Calculate the book values of preferred shares and common shares as of December 31, 1984, under each of the following assumptions:

(1) Preferred dividends have been paid to October 1, 1984; preferred shares have a call value of $110, a liquidation value of $105, and are entitled to current unpaid quarterly dividends.
(2) Preferred shares have a liquidation value of $110; shares are cumulative, with dividends in arrears for 4 years including the current year and fully payable in the event of liquidation.
(3) Preferred shares have a liquidation value of par; shares are noncumulative, and no dividends have been paid for the past 5 years; however, the current year's dividend has been declared but not yet recorded on the books.

problem 18-8 (Quasi-reorganization)

Mathews Metal Works has experienced several poor earnings years and has several assets on its books that are overvalued. It desires to revalue its assets downward and eliminate the deficit. At December 31, 1984, the company owns the following net tangible assets:

	Cost	Accumulated Depreciation	Book Value	Current Value
Land	$ 500,000	—	$ 500,000	$300,000
Buildings	750,000	$350,000	400,000	200,000
Machinery and equipment	350,000	150,000	200,000	150,000
	$1,600,000	$500,000	$1,100,000	$650,000

The balance sheet on December 31, 1984, reported the following balances in the stockholders' equity section:

Common stock, $25 par, 80,000 shares	$2,000,000
Additional paid-in capital	200,000
Retained earnings (deficit)	(300,000)
Total	$1,900,000

As part of the reorganization, the common stock is to be canceled and reissued at $10 par.

Instructions:

(1) Prepare the journal entries to record the quasi-reorganization.
(2) Give the property section and stockholders' equity section of the company's balance sheet as they would appear after the entries are posted.

problem 18-9 (Balance sheet preparation)

The following trial balance was taken from the books of Eastern Plastics Inc. as of April 30, 1984:

Eastern Plastics Inc.
Trial Balance
April 30, 1984

Cash	310,000	
Accounts Receivable	800,000	
Finished Goods on Hand	500,000	
Finished Goods Out on Consignment	100,000	
Raw Materials on Hand	750,000	
Land, Buildings, and Equipment	1,460,000	
Prepaid Expenses	5,400	
Sales Returns and Allowances	25,000	
Administrative Salaries	65,000	
Cost of Goods Sold	2,350,000	
Travel Expense	30,030	
Interest Expense	10,570	
Accounts Payable		175,000
Notes Payable		100,000
Payroll Payable		6,000
Interest Payable on 6% Bonds		10,000
Capital Stock—6% Preferred		1,000,000
Capital Stock—Common		1,416,000
6% Bonds, due June 30, 1992		500,000
Sales		2,500,000
Retained Earnings, December 31, 1983		520
Paid-In Capital		698,480
	6,406,000	6,406,000

The following transactions had been completed by the company:

(a) The company has purchased various lots of its $100 par value common stock, aggregating 840 shares, at an average price of $65.50 per share, for $55,020. In recording these transactions the company has canceled the stock certificates and debited the common stock account with the par value of $84,000 and credited the paid-in capital account with the difference of $28,980 between par and the cash paid.
(b) Paid-in capital was previously credited with (1) a premium at $20 per share on 15,000 shares of common stock issued, and (2) adjustments arising from the appraisal of land, buildings, and equipment bought at a receivers' sale, $398,000.
(c) 6% bonds of the face amount of $250,000 falling due on December 31, 1990, were issued on January 1, 1966, at a 10% discount. To June 30, 1982, $16,500 of this discount had been

charged against revenues and as of this date the entire issue of these bonds was retired at par and the unamortized discount debited to Additional Paid-In Capital.

(d) A new issue of $500,000, 6% ten-year bonds was effected as of July 1, 1982, at par. Expenses incurred with respect to this issue in the amount of $20,000 were debited to Paid-In Capital.

Instructions: Prepare a balance sheet as of April 30, 1984, making any corrections necessary in view of the company's treatment of the preceding transactions. (AICPA adapted)

problem 18-10 (Computing cash dividends)

Tomasco Inc. began operations in January 1981 and had the following reported net income or loss for each of its five years of operations:

1981	$ 150,000 loss
1982	130,000 loss
1983	120,000 loss
1984	250,000 income
1985	1,000,000 income

At December 31, 1985, the Tomasco capital accounts were as follows:

Common stock, par value $10 per share; authorized 100,000 shares; issued and outstanding 50,000 shares	$ 500,000
4% noncumulative preferred stock, par value $100 per share; authorized, issued and outstanding 1,000 shares	100,000
8% cumulative preferred stock, par value $100 per share; authorized, issued and outstanding 10,000 shares	1,000,000

Tomasco has never paid a cash or stock dividend. There has been no change in the capital accounts since Tomasco began operations. The appropriate state law permits dividends only from retained earnings.

Instructions: Prepare a work sheet showing the maximum amount available for cash dividends on December 31, 1985, and how it would be distributable to the holders of the common shares and each of the preferred shares. Show supporting computations. (AICPA adapted)

problem 18-11 (Recapitalization)

Nick's Novelty Shops Inc. at December 31, 1984, is insolvent and must declare bankruptcy unless a large loan can be obtained immediately. A lender who is willing to advance $550,000 to the company has been located, but will only make the loan subject to the following conditions:

(a) A $700,000, 10% mortgage payable on the company's land and buildings held by a major stockholder will be canceled along with four months' accrued interest. The mortgage will be replaced by 6,000 shares of $100 par value, 10%, cumulative preferred stock.

(b) A $550,000, 12% mortgage payable over 15 years on the land and buildings will be given as security on the new loan.

(c) On May 1, 1983, the company's trade creditors accepted $360,000 in notes payable on demand at 10% interest in settlement of all past-due accounts. No payment has been made to date. The company will offer to settle these liabilities at $.75 per $1 owed or to replace the notes payable on demand with new notes payable for full indebtedness over five years at 10% interest. It is estimated that $200,000 of the demand notes will be exchanged for the longer-term notes and that the remainder will accept the offer of a reduced cash settlement.

(d) A new issue of 700 shares of $100 par value, 8%, noncumulative, preferred stock will replace 700 outstanding shares of $100 par value, 11%, cumulative, preferred stock. Preferred stockholders will relinquish all claims to $46,200 of dividends in arrears. The dividends have never been formally declared.

(e) A new issue of 1,000 shares of $40 par value, class A common stock will replace 1,000 outstanding shares of $80 par value, class A common stock.

(f) A new issue of 1,200 shares of $30 par value, class B common stock will replace 1,200 outstanding shares of $80 par value, class B common stock.

The following condensed account balances are on the books at December 31, 1984.

Bank overdraft	$ 24,000
Other current assets	380,000
Land, buildings, and equipment	940,000
Trade accounts payable	103,667
Other current liabilities	126,333
Paid-in capital at more than par value	200,000
Retained earnings deficit	440,000

Instructions:

(1) Prepare pro forma journal entries you would suggest to give effect to the foregoing transactions as of January 1, 1985. Entries should be keyed to lettered information in order.
(2) Prepare a pro forma balance sheet for Nick's Novelty Shops Inc. at January 1, 1985, as if the recapitalization had been consummated. (AICPA adapted)

*problem 18-12 (Correction of errors—work papers)

The auditors for the Hansen Co. in inspecting accounts on December 31, 1984, the end of the fiscal year, find that certain prepaid and accrued items had been overlooked in prior years and in the current year as follows:

	End of 1981	1982	1983	1984
Prepaid expenses	$700	$600	$750	$1,900
Expenses payable	500	800	950	1,000
Prepaid revenues	140			420
Revenues receivable		150	125	200

Retained earnings on December 31, 1981, had been reported at $25,600; and net income for 1982 and for 1983 were reported at $9,500 and $12,250 respectively. Revenue and expense balances for 1984 were transferred to the income summary account and the latter shows a credit balance of $12,500 prior to correction by the auditors. No dividends had been declared in the three-year period.

Instructions:

(1) Prepare working papers as illustrated on pages 699 and 701 to develop a corrected retained earnings balance as of December 31, 1981, and corrected earnings for 1982, 1983, and 1984. Disregard effects of corrections on income tax.
(2) Prepare a corrected statement of retained earnings for the three-year period ending December 31, 1984.
(3) Give the entry or entries required as of December 31, 1984, to correct the income summary account and retained earnings account and to establish the appropriate balance sheet accounts as of this date.

*problem 18-13 (Analysis and correction of errors)

An auditor is engaged by the Grayson Corp. in March, 1985, to examine the books and records and to make whatever corrections are necessary.

An examination of the accounts discloses the following:

(a) Dividends had been declared on December 15 in 1982 and 1983 but had not been entered in the books until paid.
(b) Improvements in buildings and equipment of $4,800 had been debited to expense at the end of April, 1981. Improvements are estimated to have an eight-year life. The company uses the straight-line method in recording depreciation.

*Problems to appendix material

(c) The physical inventory of merchandise had been understated by $1,500 at the end of 1982 and by $2,150 at the end of 1984.
(d) The merchandise inventories at the end of 1983 and 1984 did not include merchandise that was then in transit and to which the company had title. These shipments of $1,900 and $2,750 were recorded as purchases in January of 1984 and 1985 respectively.
(e) The company had failed to record sales commissions payable of $1,050 and $850 at the end of 1983 and 1984 respectively.
(f) The company had failed to recognize supplies on hand of $600 and $1,250 at the end of 1983 and 1984 respectively.

The retained earnings account on the date of the audit is as follows:

Account **Retained Earnings**

Date		Item	Debit	Credit	Balance Debit	Balance Credit
1982						
Jan.	1	Balance......................				40,500
Dec.	31	Net income for year		9,000		49,500
1983						
Jan.	10	Dividends paid...............	7,500			42,000
Mar.	6	Premium on capital stock		16,000		58,000
Dec.	31	Net loss for year.............	5,600			52,400
1984						
Jan.	10	Dividends paid...............	7,500			44,900
Dec.	31	Net loss for year.............	6,200			38,700

Instructions:

(1) Prepare working papers for the correction of account balances similar to those illustrated on pages 699 and 701, using the following columns (disregard effects of corrections on income tax):

	Retained Earnings Jan. 1, 1982		Net Income Year Ended Dec. 31, 1982		Net Income Year Ended Dec. 31, 1983		Net Income Year Ended Dec. 31, 1984		Accounts Requiring Correction in 1985		
Explanation	Debit	Credit	Debit	Credit	Debit	Credit	Debit	Credit	Debit	Credit	Account

(2) Journalize corrections required in March, 1985, in compound form.
(3) Prepare a statement of retained earnings covering the three-year period beginning January 1, 1982. The statement should report the corrected retained earnings balance on January 1, 1982, the annual changes in the account, and the corrected retained earnings balances as of December 31, 1982, 1983, and 1984.
(4) Set up an account for retained earnings before correction, and post correcting data to this account for part (2) above. Balance the account, showing the corrected retained earnings as of December 31, 1984.

Part 4 Special Problems in Income Determination and Reporting

19 REVENUE RECOGNITION

CHAPTER OBJECTIVES

Identify conditions under which revenue recognition can occur at other than point of sale or completion of a service contract.

Describe and illustrate the percentage-of-completion method for recognizing revenue prior to the delivery of goods.

Explain the proportional performance method for recognizing revenue prior to the completion of a service contract.

Distinguish among accounting procedures used in recognizing revenue after the delivery of goods or completion of a service contract including installment sales, cost recovery, and cash methods.

Identify and describe interim accounting methods used to account for receipt of monetary assets (deposit method) or disposition of inventory (consignment method) prior to revenue recognition.

As discussed in Chapter 4, accountants and users of financial statements have for many years focused attention on problems related to the income statement. In Chapters 5 through 18 of this text, the principles and procedures of accounting for balance sheet assets, liabilities, and equities have been presented. Because the balance sheet and income statement are interrelated, discussion of balance sheet accounts automatically relates to income measurement. Whenever possible, the discussion of balance sheet accounts has included a discussion of how accounting for them affects the reporting and measurement of income. There are, however, some special income items that are best considered separately rather than integrated throughout the text. These special items are presented in the four chapters comprising Part 4. In this chapter, attention is focused on special problems that arise when the time of revenue recognition is other than the date of delivery of goods or completion of a service contract. In subsequent chapters, the recording and reporting of income taxes, special disclosures required for nonoperating components of income, and the computation and presentation of earnings per share are discussed.

SPECIALIZED ACCOUNTING AND REPORTING PRINCIPLES AND PRACTICES

Many special revenue recognition problems have developed in specific industries such as construction, real estate, and franchising. In many areas, the AICPA has established committees to study industry-related accounting and auditing problems. Often these committees have issued either **Industry Accounting Guides** or **Industry Audit Guides** based on their work. In other cases, the Institute's Accounting Standards Executive Committee (AcSEC) has issued **Statements of Position (SOPs).** These publications are used by accountants to govern the accounting policies followed even though they do not qualify as FASB approved generally accepted accounting principles.

Because of the confusion arising in the minds of many users of financial statements with so many different sources of accounting principles, in 1979 the FASB agreed to bring all AICPA accounting pronouncements under the jurisdiction of the Board, and to eventually issue standards where they appear necessary. Beginning in the early 1980s, many specialized industry guides were adopted as FASB standards (see Appendix C for a list of such standards). Until standards were issued, the FASB identified the principles contained in the AICPA publications as **preferable accounting principles** for the purpose of justifying a change in accounting principle under APB Opinion No. 20. "Accounting Changes."[1]

REVENUE RECOGNITION IN THE CONCEPTUAL FRAMEWORK

The FASB identified revenue recognition as one of the basic elements of the conceptual framework. Because of the significant differences in practice among various types of business entities, this part of the framework is considered to be one of the most difficult to resolve. In an attempt to assist the FASB

---

[1] *Statement of Financial Accounting Standards No. 32,* "Specialized Accounting and Reporting Principles and Practices in AICPA Statements of Position and Guides on Accounting and Auditing Matters" (Stamford: Financial Accounting Standards Board, 1979).

in its deliberations, the following three research reports were issued in the early 1980s:

(1) *Recognition of Contractual Rights and Obligations,* Yuji Ijiri, 1980.
(2) *Survey of Present Practice in Recognizing Revenues, Expenses, Gains and Losses,* Henry R. Jaenicke, 1981.
(3) *Recognition in Financial Statements: Underlying Concepts and Practical Conventions,* L. Todd Johnson and Reed K. Storey, 1982.

The second report provides an excellent overview of the many variations in revenue recognition today, many of which are discussed in this chapter. Standards for making revenue recognition practices more comparable are definitely needed, and the FASB is continuing its efforts to provide these standards. The FASB statements currently being issued for specialized industries do not provide a well-defined, overall revenue recognition standard; therefore, some modification of these Statements may be required once the revenue recognition portion of the conceptual framework is completed.

REVENUE RECOGNITION CONCEPTS

Two basic approaches to defining income were discussed in Chapter 4: (1) the **economic approach** and (2) the **transaction approach.** Although theoretically there is a stronger argument for using the economic or asset valuation approach to income measurement, for practical reasons accountants have historically used the transaction approach. Reported revenue is the key element of the transaction approach. Once revenue is recognized, the matching of expenses with revenues is more easily accomplished.

The revenue recognition rules currently being applied (see page 102) generally lead to revenue recognition at the time goods are delivered or the service contract is completed. However, under some conditions, revenue recognition at other points in the production or service cycle may represent a better measure of the activity for a period. These exceptions to the general rule are discussed in the following sections of this chapter.

REVENUE RECOGNITION PRIOR TO DELIVERY OF GOODS OR PERFORMANCE OF SERVICES

Under some circumstances, revenue can be meaningfully reported prior to the delivery of the finished product or completion of a service contract. Usually this occurs when the construction period of the asset being sold or the period of service performance is relatively long; that is, more than one year. If a company waits until the production or service period is complete to recognize revenue, the income statement may not meaningfully report the periodic achievement of the company. All income from the contract will be related to the year of completion, even though only a small part of the earnings may be attributable to effort in that period. Previous periods receive no credit for their efforts; in fact, they may be penalized through the absorption of selling, general and administrative, and other overhead costs relating to the contract but not considered part of the inventory cost.

Percentage-of-completion accounting, an alternative to the **completed-contract** method, was developed to relate recognition of revenue on long-term construction-type contracts to the activities of a firm in fulfilling these contracts. Similarly, the **proportional performance method** has been developed to reflect revenue earned on service contracts under which many acts of service are to be performed before the contract is completed. Examples include contracts covering maintenance on electronic office equipment, correspondence schools, trustee services, health clubs, professional services such as those offered by attorneys and accountants, and servicing of mortgage loans by mortgage bankers. Percentage-of-completion accounting and proportional performance accounting are similar in their application. However, some special problems arise in accounting for service contracts. The discussion and examples in the following sections relate first to long-term construction contracts, then to the special problems encountered with service contracts.

General Concepts of Percentage-of-Completion Accounting

Under the percentage-of-completion method, a company recognizes revenues and costs on a contract as it progresses toward completion rather than deferring recognition of these items until the contract is completed. The amount of revenue to be recognized is based on some measure of progress toward completion. This requires an estimate of costs yet to be incurred. Changes in estimates of future costs arise normally, and the necessary adjustments are made in the year the estimates are revised. Thus, the revenues and costs to be recognized in a given year are affected by the revenues and costs already recognized. The actual costs incurred and the profit being recognized during the construction period are charged to inventory. If a company projects a loss on the contract prior to completion, the full amount of the loss is recognized immediately.

Necessary Conditions to Use Percentage-of-Completion Accounting

Most long-term construction-type contracts should be reported using the percentage-of-completion method. The guidelines presently in force, however, are not specific as to when a company must use percentage-of-completion and when it must use the alternative completed-contract method. The accounting standards that still govern this area were issued by the Committee on Accounting Procedure in 1955.[2] In January 1981, the Construction Contractor Guide Committee of the Accounting Standards Division of the AICPA issued Statement of Position 81-1, "Accounting for

---

[2]Committee on Accounting Procedure, *Accounting Research Bulletin No. 45,*"Long-Term Construction-Type Contracts" (New York: American Institute of Certified Public Accountants, 1955).

Performance of Construction-Type and Certain Production-Type Contracts." In this SOP, the committee strongly recommended which of the two common methods of accounting for these types of contracts should be required, depending on the specific circumstances involved. They further stated that the two methods should not be viewed as acceptable alternatives for the same circumstances. The committee identified several elements that should be present if percentage-of-completion accounting is to be used.[3]

(1) Dependable estimates can be made of the extent of progress towards completion, contract revenues, and contract costs.
(2) The contract clearly specifies the enforceable rights regarding goods or services to be provided and received by the parties, the consideration to be exchanged, and the manner and terms of settlement.
(3) The buyer can be expected to satisfy obligations under the contract.
(4) The contractor can be expected to perform the contractual obligation.

The completed-contract method should be used only when an entity has primarily short-term contracts, when the above conditions for using the percentage-of-completion accounting are not met, or when there are inherent uncertainties in the contract beyond the normal business risks.

In February 1982, the FASB issued Statement No. 56 designating the accounting and reporting principles and practices contained in SOP 81-1 and in the *AICPA Audit and Accounting Guide for Construction Contractors* as preferable accounting principles.[4] The Board indicated that they would consider adopting these principles as FASB standards after allowing sufficient time for the principles to be used in practice so that a basis can be provided for determining their usefulness. A critical issue involved in this area is the clear preference in the SOP for using the percentage-of-completion method of accounting.

Measuring the Percentage of Completion

Various methods are currently used in practice to measure progress on a contract. They can be conveniently grouped in two categories: input and output measures.

Input Measures. Input measures are made in relation to the efforts devoted to a contract. They are based on an established or assumed relationship between a unit of input and productivity. They include the popular cost-to-cost method and several variations of efforts-expended methods.

Cost-to-Cost Method. Perhaps the most popular of the input measures is the **cost-to-cost method.** Under this method, the degree of completion is determined by comparing costs already incurred with the most recent esti-

---

[3]Construction Contractor Guide Committee of the Accounting Standards Division, AICPA, *Statement of Position 81-1,* "Accounting for Performance of Construction-Type and Certain Production-Type Contracts" (New York: American Institute of Certified Public Accountants, 1981), par. 23.

[4]*Statement of Financial Accounting Standards No. 56,*"Designation of AICPA Guide and Statement of Position (SOP) 81-1 on Contractor Accounting and SOP 81-2 Concerning Hospital-Related Organizations as Preferable for Purposes of Applying APB Opinion 20" (Stamford: Financial Accounting Standards Board, 1982).

mates of total expected costs to complete the project. The percentage that costs incurred bear to total expected costs is applied to the expected net income on the project in arriving at earnings to date. Some of the costs incurred, particularly in the early stages of the contract, should be disregarded in applying this method because they do not directly relate to effort expended on the contract. These include such items as subcontract costs for work that has yet to be performed and standard fabricated materials that have not yet been installed. One of the most difficult problems in using this method is estimating the cost yet to be incurred. However, this estimation is required in reporting income regardless of how the percentage of completion is computed.

Efforts-Expended Methods. The **efforts-expended methods** are based on some measure of work performed. They include labor hours, labor dollars, machine hours, or material quantities. In each case, the degree of completion is measured in a way similar to that used in the cost-to-cost approach: the ratio of the efforts expended to date to the estimated total efforts to be expended on the entire contract. For example, if the measure of work performed is labor hours, the ratio of hours worked to date to the total estimated hours would produce the percentage for use in measuring income earned.

Output Measures. **Output measures** are made in terms of results achieved. Included in this category are methods based on units produced, contract milestones reached, and values added. For example, if the contract calls for units of output, such as miles of roadway, a measure of completion would be a ratio of the miles completed to the total miles in the contract. Architects or engineers are sometimes asked to evaluate jobs and estimate what percentage of a job is complete. These estimates are in reality output measures and are usually based on the physical progress made on a contract.

Accounting for Long-Term Construction-Type Contracts

There are relatively few differences in accounting for long-term construction-type contracts under either the percentage-of-completion or completed-contract methods. Only the timing of revenue recognition and the recognition of matching costs is different. All direct and allocable indirect costs of the contracts are charged to an inventory account, Construction in Progress, as they accrue. The inventory account is also increased by the profit recognized during the construction period. Usually, contracts require progress billings by the contractor and payments by the customer on these billings. The amount of these billings is usually specified by the contract terms, and may be related to the costs actually incurred. Generally, these contracts require inspection before final settlement is made. As a protection for the customer, the contract frequently provides for an amount to be held out from the progress payment. This retention is usually a percentage of the progress billings, 10–20 percent, and is paid upon final acceptance of the construction. The billings, including any amount to be retained, are debited to Accounts Receivable and credited to a deferred credit account, Progress Billings on Construction Contracts, that serves as an offset to the inventory account, Construction in Progress. The billing of the contract thus in reality transfers the asset value from inventory to receivables, but because of the long-term nature of the contract, the construction costs continue to be reflected in the accounts.

To illustrate accounting for a long-term construction contract, assume that a dam was constructed over a two-year period commencing in September 1983, at a contract price of $5,000,000. The direct and allocable indirect costs, billings, and collections for 1983, 1984, and 1985 were as follows:

Year	Direct and Allocable Indirect Costs	Billings Including 10% Retention	Collections
1983	$1,125,000	$1,000,000	$ 800,000
1984	2,250,000	2,300,000	1,900,000
1985	1,125,000	1,700,000	2,300,000

The following entries for the three years would be made on the contractor's books under either the percentage-of-completion or the completed-contract methods.

	1983		1984		1985	
Construction in Progress	1,125,000		2,250,000		1,125,000	
Materials, Cash etc.		1,125,000		2,250,000		1,125,000
Accounts Receivable	1,000,000		2,300,000		1,700,000	
Progress Billings on Construction Contracts		1,000,000		2,300,000		1,700,000
Cash	800,000		1,900,000		2,300,000	
Accounts Receivable		800,000		1,900,000		2,300,000

No other entries would be required in 1983 and 1984 under the completed-contract method. In both years, the balance of the construction in progress account exceeds the amount in Progress Billings on Construction Contracts, thus the latter account would be offset against the inventory account in the balance sheet. Because the operating cycle of a company that emphasizes long-term contracts is usually more than one year, all of the above balance sheet accounts would be classified as current. The balance sheet at the end of 1984 would disclose the following balances related to the dam construction contract.

Current assets:		
Accounts receivable, including 10% retention fee of $330,000		$600,000
Construction in progress	$3,375,000	
Less progress billings on construction contracts	3,300,000	75,000

If the billings exceeded the construction costs, the two accounts would be reported in the current liability section of the balance sheet.

At the completion of the contract, the following entries would be made under the completed-contract method to recognize revenue and costs and to close out the inventory and billings account.

Progress Billings on Construction Contracts	5,000,000	
Revenue from Long-Term Construction Contracts		5,000,000
Cost of Long-Term Construction Contracts	4,500,000	
Construction in Progress		4,500,000

The income statement for 1985 would report the gross revenues and the matched costs, thus recognizing the entire $500,000 profit in one year.

If the company used the percentage-of-completion method of accounting, the $500,000 profit would be spread over all three years of construction according to the estimated percentage of completion for each year. Assume that the estimated cost from the beginning of construction was $4,500,000, and that the estimate did not change over the three years. Also, assume that the cost-to-cost method of determining percentage of completion is used. The percentage for each year would be calculated as follows:

	1983	1984	1985
(1) Cost incurred to date	$1,125,000	$3,375,000	$4,500,000
(2) Estimated cost to complete	3,375,000	1,125,000	—0—
(3) Total estimated cost	$4,500,000	$4,500,000	$4,500,000
Percentage of completion to date [(1) ÷ (3)]	25%	75%	100%

These percentages may be used directly to determine the gross profit that should be recognized on the income statement. Preferably, however, they should be used to determine both revenues and cost. The income statement will then disclose the gross profit as the difference between these elements, a method more consistent with normal income statement reporting. The AICPA Audit and Accounting Guide for Construction Contractors recommended following this procedure, and the presentations in this chapter will follow their recommendations.[5]

Thus, for 1983, 25% of the fixed contract price of $5,000,000 would be recognized as revenue and 25% of the expected total cost of $4,500,000 would be reported as cost. Since the cost-to-cost method is being used, this will always result in the same amount as the costs actually incurred. The following revenue recognition entries would be made for each of the three years of the contract.

	1983		1984		1985	
Cost of Long-Term Construction Contracts	1,125,000		2,250,000		1,125,000	
Construction in Progress	125,000		250,000		125,000	
Revenue from Long-Term Construction Contracts		1,250,000		2,500,000		1,250,000

The gross profit recognized each year is added to the construction in progress account. This changes the valuation base for this account from cost to a measure of net realizable value. At the conclusion of the construction, the

[5] Construction Contractor Guide Committee of the Accounting Standards Division, AICPA, *Audit and Accounting Guide for Construction Contractors* (New York: American Institute of Certified Public Accountants, 1980), p. 44.

balance in Construction in Progress will be exactly equal to the amount in Progress Billings on Construction Contracts, and the following closing entry would complete the accounting process.

Progress Billings on Construction Contracts	5,000,000	
Construction in Progress		5,000,000

If the cost-to-cost method is not used to measure progress on the contract, the amount of costs recognized under this method may not be equal to the costs incurred. For example, assume in 1983 that an engineering estimate measure was used, and 20% of the contract was assumed to be completed. The gross profit recognized would therefore be computed and reported as follows:

Earned revenue (20% of $5,000,000)	$1,000,000
Cost of earned revenue (20% of $4,500,000)	900,000
Gross profit (20% of $500,000)	$ 100,000

This approach is labeled Alternative A in SOP 81-1.

Because some accountants felt that the amount of cost recognized should be equal to the costs actually incurred, an alternative to the preceding approach was included in the SOP.[6] Under this approach, labeled Alternative B in the SOP, revenue is defined as the costs incurred on the contract plus the gross profit earned for the period on the contract. Using the data from the previous example, the revenue and costs to be reported on the 1983 income statement would be as follows:

Costs incurred to date	$1,125,000
Gross profit (20% of $500,000)	100,000
Earned revenue	$1,225,000

This contrasts with the $1,000,000 revenue using Alternative A.

In a footnote to this discussion in the SOP, the Committee made it clear that Alternatives A and B are equally acceptable. However, because Alternative B results in a varying gross profit percentage from period to period whenever the measurement of completion differs from that which would occur if the cost-to-cost method were used, the authors feel that Alternative A is preferable. Unless a different method is explicitly stated, examples and end-of-chapter material will assume the use of Alternative A.

Revision of Estimates. In the example, it was assumed that the estimated cost did not vary from the beginning of the contract. This would rarely be true. As estimates change, cumulative catch-up adjustments are made in the year of the change. To illustrate the impact of changing estimates, assume that at the end of 1984 it was estimated that the remaining cost to complete the contract would be $1,225,000, making a total estimated cost of $4,600,000. Since costs of $3,375,000 had been incurred by the end of 1984, the estimated percentage of completion for 1984 using the cost-to-cost method would be 73.37% ($3,375,000 ÷ $4,600,000).

[6] *SOP 81-1, op. cit.*, par. 80 and 81.

The following analysis would be made to compute revenues and expenses for the three years of the contract under the change in estimate, assuming actual costs of $1,175,000 were incurred in 1985.

	(A) To Date	(B) Recognized in Prior Years	(C) Recognized in Current Year (A)—(B)
1983—(25% completed)			
Earned revenue ($5,000,000 × .25)	$1,250,000		$1,250,000
Cost of earned revenue ($4,500,000 × .25)	1,125,000		1,125,000
Gross profit	$ 125,000		$ 125,000
Gross profit rate	10%		10%
1984—(73.37% completed)			
Earned revenue ($5,000,000 × .7337)	$3,668,500	$1,250,000	$2,418,500
Cost of earned revenue ($4,600,000 × .7337)	3,375,000*	1,125,000	2,250,000
Gross profit	$ 293,500	$ 125,000	$ 168,500
Gross profit rate	8%	10%	6.97%
1985—(100% completed)			
Earned revenue	$5,000,000	$3,668,500	$1,331,500
Cost of earned revenue	4,550,000	3,375,000	1,175,000
Gross profit	$ 450,000	$ 293,500	$ 156,500
Gross profit rate	9%	8%	11.75%

*Made equal to cost incurred, difference due to rounding of completion percentage.

The entries to record revenue and expense for the three years under the above assumed estimate revision would be as follows:

	1983		1984		1985	
Cost of Long-Term Construction Contracts	1,125,000		2,250,000		1,175,000	
Construction in Progress	125,000		168,500		156,500	
Revenue from Long-Term Construction Contracts		1,250,000		2,418,500		1,331,500

The computation of gross profit rates shows how sensitive the reporting is to revisions in estimated costs, and why great care is required in making these estimates.

Reporting Anticipated Contract Losses. The examples thus far have assumed a profit is expected to be realized. If a loss on the total contract is anticipated, however, generally accepted accounting principles require reporting the loss *in its entirety* in the period when the loss is first anticipated. This is true under either the completed-contract or the percentage-of-completion methods. For example, assume that in the earlier dam construction example the estimated cost to complete the contract at the end of 1984 was $1,725,000. This would mean the total estimated cost of the contract would be $5,100,000 or $100,000 more than the contract price. If the completed-contract method were being used, the following entry would be required at the end of 1984.

Anticipated Loss on Long-Term Construction Contracts	100,000	
Construction in Progress		100,000

The inventory account, Construction in Progress, is thus reduced by the anticipated loss.

Accounting for such an anticipated loss is more complicated under the percentage-of-completion method because of the impact of prior years on the current year. Again referring to the dam construction example, the percentage of completion under the cost-to-cost method would be 66.18% under the changed assumptions ($3,375,000 ÷ $5,100,000). Cumulative earned revenue would be computed as before, 66.18% × $5,000,000, or $3,309,000. However, construction costs for the current period would be computed by adding the anticipated loss to the earned revenue, thus resulting in cumulative recognized costs of $3,409,000. The loss to be recognized in 1984 would thus be not only the $100,000 loss anticipated on the entire contract but also an additional loss of $125,000 to adjust for the 1983 recognized profit that is now not expected to be realized. These computations can be illustrated by reconstructing part of the earlier table as follows:

	(A) To Date	(B) Recognized in Prior Year	(C) Recognized in Current Year (A)—(B)
1984—(66.18% completed)			
Earned revenue $5,000,000 × .6618.......	$3,309,000	$1,250,000	$2,059,000
Cost of earned revenue $3,309,000 + $100,000	3,409,000	1,125,000	2,284,000
Gross profit (loss)	($ 100,000)	$ 125,000	($ 225,000)

The entry to record the revenue, costs, and adjustments to Construction In Progress for the loss would be as follows:

Cost of Long-Term Construction Contracts......................	2,284,000	
Revenue from Long-Term Construction Contracts		2,059,000
Construction in Progress		225,000

The construction in progress account under both methods would have a balance of $3,275,000 computed as follows:

Completed-contract method:

Construction in Progress

1983 cost	1,125,000	1984 loss	100,000
1984 cost	2,250,000		
Bal.	3,275,000		

Percentage-of-completion method:

Construction in Progress

1983 cost	1,125,000	1984 loss	225,000
1983 gross profit	125,000		
1984 cost	2,250,000		
Bal.	3,275,000		

Accounting for Contract Change Orders. Long-term construction contracts are seldom completed without change orders that affect both the contract price and the cost of performance. **Change orders** are modifications of an original contract that effectively change the provisions of the contract. They may be initiated by the contractor or the customer, and include changes in specifications or design, method or manner of performance, facilities, equipment, materials, location, site, etc. If the contract price is changed as a result of a change order, future computations are made with the revised expected revenue and any anticipated cost changes that will arise because of the change order. Change orders are often unpriced, that is, the work to be performed is defined, but the adjustment to the contract price is to be negotiated later. If it is probable that a contract price change will be negotiated to at least recover the increased costs, the increased costs may be included with the incurred costs of the period and the revenue may be increased by the same amount.

Income Tax Considerations

When a building, installation, or construction contract covers more than one year, federal income tax regulations permit the taxpayer to recognize income on a percentage-of-completion basis over the life of the project or in the year when the project is completed and accepted. General and administrative salaries, taxes, and other expenses that are not directly attributable to specific contracts have previously been expensed in the year incurred under either the completed contract or the percentage of completion method. The Tax Equity and Fiscal Responsibility Act of 1982 identified many of these costs as being more properly allocated to existing contracts, especially if the contracts have a construction period in excess of two years. The effect of this regulation is to make the completed contract method less favorable for tax deferral purposes.

Consistent application of the method of accounting chosen is required for tax purposes; a change from the percentage-of-completion method to the completed-contract method, or a change from the completed-contract method to the percentage-of-completion method, requires special permission. The use of different methods for financial statements and for income tax purposes will require the application of interperiod tax allocation procedures, which will be discussed in Chapter 20.

Accounting for Long-Term Service Contracts—the Proportional Performance Method

Thus far, the discussion in this chapter has focused on long-term construction contracts. As indicated earlier, another type of contract that frequently extends over a long period of time is a **service contract.** An increasing percentage of sales in our economy are classified as sales of services as opposed to sales of goods. When the service to be performed is completed as a single act or over a relatively short period of time, no revenue recognition problems arise. The revenue recognition criteria previously defined apply, and all direct and indirect costs related to the service are charged to expense in the period the revenue is recognized. However, when several acts over a period of time are involved, the same revenue recognition problems illustrated for long-term construction contracts arise. Although the FASB has not issued a standard dealing with these contracts, the Board did issue an Invitation to Comment on a proposed Statement of Position that had been issued by the AICPA's Accounting Standards Division.[7] The discussion in the following pages reflects the recommendations made by the Accounting Standards Division.

The Division recommends that unless the final act of service to be performed is so vital to the contract that earlier acts are relatively insignificant, e.g., the packaging, loading, and final delivery of goods in a delivery contract, revenue should be recognized under the **proportional performance method.**[8] Both input and output measures are identified as possible ways of measuring progress on a service contract. If a contract involves a specified number of identical or similar acts, e.g., the processing of monthly mortgage payments by a mortgage banker, an output measure derived by relating the number of acts performed to the total number of acts to be performed over the contract life is recommended. If a contract involves a specified number of defined but not identical acts, e.g., a correspondence school that provides evaluation, lessons, examinations, and grading, a cost-to-cost input measurement percentage would be applicable. If future costs are not objectively determinable, output measures such as relating sales value of the individual acts to the total sales value of the service contract may be used. If no pattern of performance can be determined, or if a service contract involves an unspecified number of similar or identical acts with a fixed period for performance, e.g., a maintenance contract for electronic office equipment, the Division recommends the use of the straight-line method, i.e., equally over the periods of performance.

These measures are used to determine what portion of the service contract fee should be recognized as revenue. Generally, the measures are only indirectly related to the pattern of cash collection; however, they are applicable only if cash collection is reasonably assured and if losses from nonpayment can be objectively determined.

The cost recognition problems of service contracts are somewhat different from long-term construction contracts. Most service contracts involve three different types of costs: (1) initial direct costs related to obtaining and performing initial services on the contract, such as commissions, legal fees, credit investigations, and paper processing; (2) direct costs related to performing the various acts of service; and (3) indirect costs related to maintaining the organization to service the contract, e.g., general and administrative expenses. Initial direct costs are generally charged against revenue using the same input or output measure used for revenue recognition. If the cost-to-cost method of input measurement is used, initial direct costs should be excluded from the cost incurred to date in computing the measure. Only direct costs related to the acts of service are relevant. Direct costs are usually

[7] *FASB Invitation to Comment*, "Accounting for Certain Service Transactions," (Stamford: Financial Accounting Standards Board, 1978).

[8] *Ibid*, pp. 12–13.

charged to expense as incurred because they are felt to relate directly to the acts for which revenue is recognized. Similarly, all indirect costs should be charged to expense as incurred. As is true for long-term construction contracts, any indicated loss on completion of the service contract is to be charged to the period in which the loss is first indicated. If collection of a service contract is highly uncertain, revenue recognition should not be related to performance but to the collection of the receivable using one of the methods described in the latter part of this chapter.

To illustrate accounting for a service contract using the proportional performance method, assume a correspondence school enters into one hundred contracts with students for an extended writing course. The fee for each contract is $500 payable in advance. This fee includes many different services such as providing the text material, evaluations of writing, examinations, and awarding of a certificate. The total initial direct costs related to the contracts are $5,000. Direct costs for the lessons actually completed during the period are $12,000. It is estimated that the total direct costs of these contracts will be $30,000. The facts of this case suggest that the cost-to-cost method is applicable, and the following entries would be made to record these transactions:

Cash	50,000	
Deferred Course Revenue		50,000
Deferred Initial Costs	5,000	
Cash		5,000
Contract Costs	12,000	
Cash		12,000
Deferred Course Revenue	20,000[1]	
Recognized Course Revenue		20,000
Contract Costs	2,000[2]	
Deferred Initial Costs		2,000

Computations:
[1]Cost-to-cost percentage: $12,000 ÷ $30,000 = 40%; $50,000 × .40 = $20,000
[2]$5,000 × .40 = $2,000

The gross profit reported on these contracts for the period would be $6,000 ($20,000 − $12,000 − $2,000). The deferred initial cost and deferred course revenues would normally be reported as current balance sheet deferrals because the operating cycle of a correspondence school would be equal to the average time to complete a contract or one year, whichever is longer.

Evaluation of Proportional Performance Method

The FASB has not issued a standard on service industries pending completion of the revenue recognition project in the conceptual framework. While the proportional performance method has theoretical support for its adoption, it tends to be extremely conservative, especially during a period of rapid growth in a company's revenues. This situation is often encountered with new companies, such as those in the rapidly expanding health-spa industry. Since no income is recognized until performance of the service is begun, the proportional performance method recognizes no income at the critical point of signing a service contract. Thus, in the growing years of a company, use of the proportional performance method will result in large losses being reported even though the operation might be very profitable over time. This can lead to the questionable conclusion that a company is no better off after service contracts are sold than it was before.

An alternative method of recognizing revenue for service contracts would be to recognize part of the income upon the signing of the contract, and then spread the balance of the income over the contract life using the proportional performance concept. The decision as to how much income should be recognized at the beginning of the contract would depend on the nature and terms of the contract, including any forfeiture or cancellation provisions.

REVENUE RECOGNITION AFTER DELIVERY OF GOODS OR PERFORMANCE OF SERVICES

The first revenue recognition principle enumerated in Chapter 4 states that revenue should not be recognized until the earnings process is complete or virtually so. Normally, the earnings process is virtually completed by the delivery of goods or performance of services. Collection of receivables is usually routine, and any future warranty costs can be reasonably estimated. In some cases, however, the circumstances surrounding a revenue transaction are such that considerable uncertainty exists as to whether payments will indeed be received. This can occur if the sales transaction is unusual in nature and involves a customer in such a way that default carries little cost or penalty. Under these circumstances, the uncertainty of cash collection suggests that revenue recognition should await the actual receipt of cash. There are at least three different approaches to revenue recognition that depend on the receipt of cash: **installment sales, cost recovery,** and **cash.** These methods differ as to the treatment of costs incurred and the timing of revenue recognition. They are summarized and contrasted with the full accrual method in the following table.

Method	Treatment of Product Costs or Initial Costs Under Service Contracts	Timing of Revenue and/or Income Recognition
Full accrual	Charge against revenue at time of sale or rendering of service.	At point of sale.
Installment sales	Defer to be matched against part of each cash collection. Usually done by deferring the estimated profit.	At collection of cash. Usually a portion of the cash payment is recognized as income.
Cost recovery	Defer to be matched against total cash collected.	At collection of cash, but only after all costs are recovered.
Cash	Charge to expense as incurred.	At collection of cash.

These methods are really not alternatives to each other; however, the guidelines for applying them are not well defined. As the uncertainty of the environment increases, generally accepted accounting principles would require moving from the full accrual method to installment sales, cost recovery and finally, a strict cash approach. The cash method is the most conservative approach because it would not permit the deferral of any costs, but would charge them to expense as incurred. In the following pages, each of these revenue recognition methods will be discussed and illustrated.

Installment Sales Method

Traditionally, the most commonly applied method for dealing with the uncertainty of cash collections has been the **installment sales method.** Under this method, income is recognized as cash is collected rather than at the time of sale. This method of accounting was developed after World War II in response to an increasing number of sales contracts that extended the time of payment over several years, with full title to the "sold" property being transferred only at the time of final collection. Consumer goods such as electrical appliances, jewelry, automobiles, and recreational equipment were commonly purchased and accounted for in this way. As this method of sales became more popular, and as credit rating evaluations became more sophisticated, the probability of collection on these contracts became more certain. The collection of cash was no longer the critical event, but the point of sale essentially completed the earnings process. Collection costs and the cost of uncollectible accounts could be estimated at the time of sale. Additional protection was afforded the seller because most contracts included a right of repossession. For these reasons, the Accounting Principles Board concluded in 1966 that, except for special circumstances, the installment method of recognizing revenue is not acceptable for reporting purposes.[9] The installment method continues to be widely used for income tax purposes because it permits the deferral of tax payments until cash is collected.

In more recent years, sales of other types of property, such as developed real estate and undeveloped land, have also been made with greatly extended terms. Commonly, these contracts involve little or no down payment, the payments are spread over ten to thirty or forty years, and the probability of default in the early years is high because of a small investment by the buyer in the contract and because the market prices of the property are often unstable. Application of the accrual method to these contracts frequently overstates income in the early years due to the failure to realistically provide for future costs related to the contract, including losses from contract defaults. The FASB considered these types of sales, and concluded that accrual accounting applied in these circumstances often results in "front-end loading," i.e., a recognition of all revenue at the time of the sales contract with

---

[9] *Opinions of the Accounting Principles Board, No. 10*, "Omnibus Opinion—1966" (New York: American Institute of Certified Public Accountants, 1967), par. 12.

improper matching of related costs. Thus, the Board has established criteria that must be met before real estate and retail land sales can be recorded using the full accrual method of revenue recognition. If the criteria are not fully met, then the use of the installment sales method, or in some cases the cost recovery or deposit methods, was recommended to reflect the conditions of the sale more accurately.[10] Because the installment sales method is often recommended in new sales environments, and because it is a popularly recognized income tax method, it is important for accountants to understand its application.

Accounting for installment sales using the deferred gross profit approach requires determining a gross profit rate for the sales of each year, and establishing an accounts receivable and a deferred revenue account identified by the year of the sale. As collections are made of a given year's receivables, a portion of the deferred revenue equal to the gross profit rate times the collections made is recognized as income. The most common application of this method has been for the sale of merchandise. However, any sale of property or services may be recorded using the concept. The following examples of transactions and journal entries will illustrate this method of recognizing revenue.

Installment Sales of Merchandise. Assume that the Riding Corporation sells merchandise on the installment basis, and that the uncertainties of cash collection make the use of the installment sales method acceptable. The following data relate to three years of operations. To simplify the presentation, interest charges are excluded from the example.

	1984	1985	1986
Installment sales	$150,000	$200,000	$300,000
Cost of installment sales	100,000	140,000	204,000
Gross profit	$ 50,000	$ 60,000	$ 96,000
Gross profit percentage	33.3%	30%	32%
Cash collections:			
1984 Sales	$ 30,000	$ 75,000	$ 30,000
1985 Sales		70,000	80,000
1986 Sales			100,000

The entries to record the transactions for 1984 would be as follows:

Installment Accounts Receivable—1984	150,000	
Installment Sales		150,000
Cost of Installment Sales	100,000	
Inventory		100,000
Cash	30,000	
Installment Accounts Receivable—1984		30,000
Installment Sales	150,000	
Cost of Installment Sales		100,000
Deferred Gross Profit—1984		50,000

[10] *Statement of Financial Accounting Standards No. 66*, "Accounting for Sales of Real Estate" (Stamford: Financial Accounting Standards Board, October, 1982).

Deferred Gross Profit—1984	10,000*	
Realized Gross Profit on Installment Sales		10,000

*$30,000 × 33.3%

The sales and costs related to sales are recorded in a manner identical with the accounting for sales discussed in Chapter 7. At the end of the year, however, the sales and cost of sales accounts are closed to a deferred gross profit account rather than to Income Summary. The realized gross profit is then recognized by applying the gross profit percentage to cash collections. All other general and administrative expenses are normally written off in the period incurred.

Entries for the next two years are summarized in the following schedule:

	1985		1986	
Installment Accounts Receivable—1985	200,000			
Installment Accounts Receivable—1986			300,000	
Installment Sales		200,000		300,000
Cost of Installment Sales	140,000		204,000	
Inventory		140,000		204,000
Cash	145,000		210,000	
Installment Accounts Receivable—1984		75,000		30,000
Installment Accounts Receivable—1985		70,000		80,000
Installment Accounts Receivable—1986				100,000
Installment Sales	200,000		300,000	
Cost of Installment Sales		140,000		204,000
Deferred Gross Profit—1985		60,000		
Deferred Gross Profit—1986				96,000
Deferred Gross Profit—1984	25,000[1]		10,000[3]	
Deferred Gross Profit—1985	21,000[2]		24,000[4]	
Deferred Gross Profit—1986			32,000[5]	
Realized Gross Profit on Installment Sales		46,000		66,000

Computations:
[1] $75,000 × .333 = $25,000
[2] $70,000 × .30 = $21,000
[3] $30,000 × .333 = $10,000
[4] $80,000 × .30 = $24,000
[5] $100,000 × .32 = $32,000

Although this method of recording installment sales is the one most commonly followed, it would also be possible to defer both the gross revenue and the gross costs rather than just the net difference. If this approach is followed, the resulting entries would be more similar to those illustrated for percentage-of-completion accounting. Each year a portion of the gross revenue and gross costs would be recognized with the difference being the realized gross profit. Both methods produce the same net income.

If a company is heavily involved in installment sales, the operating cycle of the business is normally the period of the average installment contract. Thus, the currently accepted definition of current assets and current liabilities requires the receivables and their related deferred gross profit accounts to be reported in the current asset section of classified balance sheets. The deferred gross profit accounts should be reported as an offset to the related accounts receivable. Thus, at the end of 1984 the current asset section would include the following accounts:

Installment accounts receivable	$120,000	
Less deferred gross profit	40,000	$80,000

Complexities of Installment Sales of Merchandise. In the previous example, no provision was made for interest. As discussed in Chapter 7, installment sales contracts always include interest, either expressed or implied. It is assumed that the interest portion of the payments is recognized as income in the period accrued, and the balance of the payment is treated as a collection on the installment sale. Thus, if in the example on page 735 the $75,000 collection of 1984 sales in 1985 included interest of $40,000, only $35,000 would be used to compute the realized gross profit from 1984 sales. A complete example involving interest is illustrated in the next section dealing with real estate installment sales.

Additional complexities can arise in installment sales accounting in providing for uncollectible accounts. Because of the right to repossess merchandise in the event of nonpayment, the provision for uncollectible accounts can be less than might be expected. Only the amount of the receivable in excess of the current value of the repossessed merchandise is a potential loss. Accounting for repossessions was discussed in Chapter 9. Theoretically, a proper matching of estimated losses against revenues would require allocating the expected losses over the years of collection. Practically, however, the provision is made and charged against income in the period of the sale. Thus, the accounting entries for handling estimated uncollectible accounts are the same as illustrated in Chapter 7.

Installment Sales of Real Estate. The installment sales method of accounting is often used for sales of real estate on a long-term contract basis. These sales are frequently characterized by small down payments with long payout periods on the balance. Usually the seller retains title to the real estate until the final payment is made, thus giving the seller the right of repossession. In an inflationary economy, this right is valuable and in most cases means that ultimate collection of the debt, either through payment or repossession, is virtually assured. However, if circumstances reduce the probability of collection or if the market value of the property is unstable, then the installment sales method may be applied, or in extreme cases, the cost recovery method may be required.

To illustrate the accounting for real estate sales using the installment method, assume that Carbon Industries Inc. sells land and buildings on January 1, 1984, for $4,000,000. Carbon receives a down payment of $300,000 and a promissory note for the remaining $3,700,000 plus interest at 12 percent to be paid in equal installments of $471,752 at the end of each of the next 25 years. The land has a carrying value on Carbon's books at the time of sale of $200,000, and the buildings have a carrying value of $2,000,000. The sale does not meet the FASB's criteria for the full accrual method of revenue recognition, and the installment method of accounting is assumed to be appropriate. The following entries would be made to record the initial transaction:

1984			
Jan. 1	Cash	300,000	
	Notes Receivable	11,793,800[1]	
	Discount on Notes Receivable		8,093,800[2]
	Real Estate Sales		4,000,000
	Cost of Real Estate Sales	2,200,000	
	Land		200,000
	Building (net of accumulated depreciation)		2,000,000
	Real Estate Sales	4,000,000	
	Cost of Real Estate Sales		2,200,000
	Deferred Gross Profit on Real Estate Sales		1,800,000

Computations:
[1]$471,752 × 25 = $11,793,800
[2]$11,793,800 − $3,700,000 = $8,093,800

The gross profit percentage for this sale is 45 percent ($1,800,000 ÷ $4,000,000). This percentage is applied to each cash collection reduced by the amount of interest included in the cash receipt. Thus, $135,000 would be recognized immediately upon receipt of the $300,000 down payment (.45 × $300,000) and the following entry would be made to recognize this profit.

1984			
Jan. 1	Deferred Gross Profit on Real Estate Sales	135,000	
	Realized Gross Profit on Real Estate Sales		135,000

At the end of the first year, cash of $471,752 will be collected in accordance with the contract terms. Included in this amount is interest earned of $444,000 (.12 × $3,700,000). The remainder of the cash collected, $27,752, is payment on the principal amount of the debt; 45% of this portion of the payment, or $12,488 (.45 × $27,752), would also be recognized as realized gross profit in the first year.

1984			
Dec. 31	Cash	471,752	
	Discount on Notes Receivable	444,000	
	Notes Receivable		471,752
	Interest Revenue		444,000
	Deferred Gross Profit on Real Estate Sales	12,488	
	Realized Gross Profit on Real Estate Sales		12,488

The following T-accounts summarize these transactions for the first year before closing entries.

Notes Receivable

Debit		Credit	
	11,793,800		471,752
Bal.	11,322,048		

Land

Debit	Credit
200,000	200,000

Discount on Notes Receivable

Debit		Credit	
	444,000		8,093,800
		Bal.	7,649,800

Buildings (net of accumulated depreciation)

Debit	Credit
2,000,000	2,000,000

Real Estate Sales

4,000,000	4,000,000

Cost of Real Estate Sales

2,200,000	2,200,000

Interest Revenue

	444,000

Deferred Gross Profit on Real Estate Sales

135,000	1,800,000
12,488	
	Bal. 1,652,512

Realized Gross Profit on Real Estate Sales

	135,000
	12,488
	Bal. 147,488

Cash collections in subsequent years would be divided between interest and principal in the same manner, and a portion of the deferred profit would be recognized each year. Because the collections are constant, and the interest revenue is declining as the carrying value of the receivable declines, the gross profit recognized would increase each year.

Care must be taken in evaluating a sale of real estate. In some cases, the contract may be in reality a financial arrangement or an operating lease, or it may be a deposit on a possible future sale. Revenue should be recognized only after careful evaluation of the contractual arrangements and application of the criteria in FASB Statement No. 66.

Cost Recovery Method

Under the cost recovery method, no income is recognized on a sale until the cost of the item sold is recovered through cash receipts. Then, all subsequent receipts are reported as revenue. Because all costs have been recovered, the recognized revenue after cost recovery represents income. This method is used only when the circumstances surrounding a sale are so uncertain that earlier recognition is impossible.

To illustrate the accounting entries required under this method, assume that collection on the real estate sales contract for Carbon Industries Inc. is felt to be so uncertain that the cost recovery method should be used. Under this method, the $2,200,000 carrying value of the real estate must be collected before any revenue or income is recognized, including any recognition of interest revenue on the contract. The same entries would be made to record the sale, the cost of the sale, and the deferred gross profit as was done under the installment sales method. The difference between the book value of the property and the down payment received equals the unrecovered cost of $1,900,000 ($2,200,000 – $300,000). Unrecovered cost may also be computed as follows:

Notes receivable		$11,793,800
Less:		
Discount on notes receivable	$8,093,800	
Deferred gross profit	1,800,000	9,893,800
		$ 1,900,000

When the first annual payment of $471,752 is collected, the following entry would be made:

1984			
Dec. 31	Cash	471,752	
	Discount on Notes Receivable	444,000	
	Notes Receivable		471,752
	Deferred Gross Profit on Real Estate Sales		444,000

The unrecovered cost would be $1,428,248 ($1,900,000 − $471,752). This agrees with the balance to be reported on the balance sheet as follows:

Notes receivable		$11,322,048
Less:		
Discount on notes receivable	$7,649,800	
Deferred gross profit	2,244,000	9,893,800
		$ 1,428,248

Note that the deferred gross profit account includes both gross profit and interest revenue that will not be recognized until the cost is recovered.

At the end of 1987, the difference between the receivable and the two offset accounts would be $12,992. The 1988 collection would result in a cost recovery of $12,992 and a recognition of $458,760 revenue. In each of the remaining collection years, the total cash receipt will be recognized as revenue.

The selection of a revenue recognition method has a great impact on revenue and income, especially in the first year of a sales contract. The following summary shows how income would vary on the real estate sale of Carbon Industries Inc. depending on which revenue recognition method is used.

Revenue Recognition Method	Income for 1984
Full Accrual	$2,244,000[1]
Installment Sales	591,488[2]
Cost Recovery	-0-

Computations:
[1]$1,800,000 gross profit + $444,000 interest revenue = $2,244,000
[2]$147,488 gross profit + $444,000 interest revenue = $591,488

In subsequent years, only interest revenue is recognized as revenue under the full accrual method, but interest revenue plus a portion of the payment on the principal is recognized under the installment sales method. After four years, all the cash collected is recognized as revenue under the cost recovery method. The graph on the following page illustrates how revenue for the real estate sale would be recognized over the twenty-five years assuming all payments were made as scheduled.

Cash Method

If the probability of recovering product or service costs is remote, the cash method of accounting could be used. Seldom would this method be

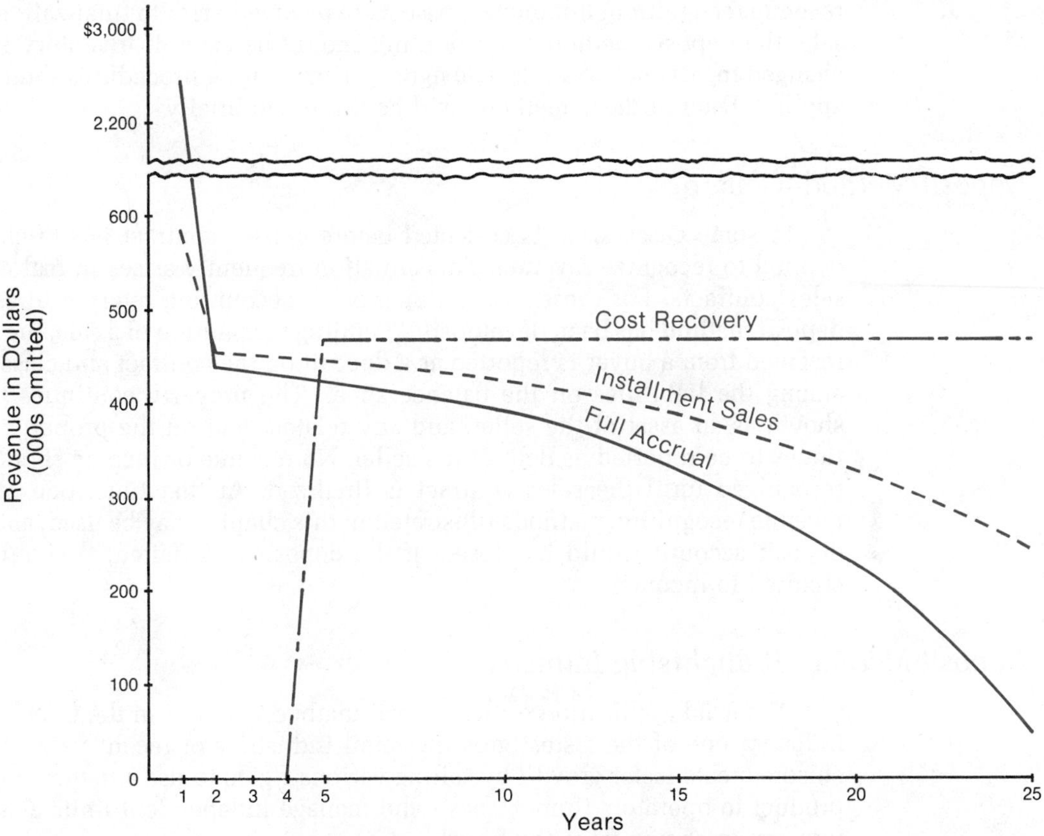

Comparison of Revenue Recognition Methods

applicable for sales of merchandise or real estate because the right of repossession would leave considerable value to the seller. However, the cash method might be appropriate for service contracts with high initial costs and considerable uncertainty as to the ultimate collection of the contract price. Under this method, all costs are charged to expense as incurred, and revenue is recognized as collections are made. This extreme method of revenue and expense recognition would be appropriate only when the potential losses on a contract cannot be estimated with any degree of certainty.

METHODS OF ACCOUNTING BEFORE REVENUE RECOGNITION

In addition to the revenue recognition methods discussed in this chapter, some sales arrangements involve an exchange of either goods or monetary assets such as cash and notes receivable prior to the point where the earnings process has been completed sufficiently to recognize revenue. Under these circumstances, special accounting procedures must be applied pending the finalization of the sale and subsequent application of one of the methods of revenue recognition. If monetary assets are received prior to finalization of a sale, the deposit method of accounting should be used. If inventory is exchanged in advance of a sale, consignment accounting procedures should be applied. Each of these methods will be discussed briefly.

Deposit Method–General

In some cases, cash is collected before a sales contract is sufficiently defined to recognize revenue. This situation frequently arises in real estate sales contracts. For these cases, a method of accounting referred to as the **deposit method** has been developed.[11] Pending recognition of a sale, the cash received from a buyer is reported as a deposit on the contract and classified among the liabilities on the balance sheet. The property continues to be shown as an asset of the seller, and any related debt on the property continues to be reported as debt of the seller. No revenue or income should be recognized until the sales contract is finalized. At that time, one of the revenue recognition methods illustrated in this chapter may be used, and the deposit account would be closed. If the deposit is forfeited, it should be credited to income.

Deposit Method–Franchising Industry

A special application of the deposit method is found in the franchising industry, one of the fastest growing retail industries of recent years. Franchisors create faster growth by selling various rights to use a name and/or a product to operators (franchisees) who manage independent units as separate entrepreneurs from the franchisor.

Sales of franchises usually include several different services, products, and/or plant assets including: (1) intangible rights to use a trademark or name, (2) property owned by the franchisor, (3) pre-opening services such as helping locate suitable business sites, constructing a building, and training employees, and (4) ongoing services, products, and processes as the operations are carried out. Many revenue recognition problems are present in typical franchises, however, most of them may be solved if the elements are separately identified and accounted for in the same manner as they would be if the sale were a separate transaction. The most troublesome revenue recognition problem has been the initial fee. Typically, the franchisor charges a substantial amount for the right to use the franchise name and to provide for pre-opening services. Sometimes these are payable immediately in cash, but typically they include a long-term note receivable. Frequently liberal refund provisions are included in the agreement, especially in the period prior to opening.

In the early days of franchising agreements, franchisors often reported the initial fee as revenue when the monetary assets were received. Future estimated costs were provided as offsets to the revenue. However, this treat-

[11] *Statement of Financial Accounting Standards No. 66, op. cit.*, par. 65–67.

ment often resulted in questionable front-end loading of revenue similar to that occurring in the real estate and retail land sale industries. As a result, the AICPA issued an Industry Accounting Guide in 1973 that established revenue recognition guidelines for the franchising industry.[12] The essentials of this guide were later incorporated into FASB Statement No. 45.[13] This standard specifies that no revenue be recognized prior to **substantial performance** of the services covered by the initial fee. Until that time, any monetary assets received should be offset by a deposit or deferred credit account, and any costs related to the services rendered should be deferred until revenue is recognized, except that such deferred costs shall not exceed anticipated revenue less estimated additional related costs. Once substantial performance is achieved, revenue should be recognized using the method that best reflects the probability of cash collection, i.e., accrual, installment sales, or cost recovery method. The latter two methods "shall be used to account for franchise fee revenue only in those exceptional cases when revenue is collectible over an extended period and no reasonable basis exists for estimating collectibility."[14]

To illustrate, assume that a franchisor charges new franchisees an initial fee of $25,000. Of this amount $10,000 is payable in cash when the agreement is signed, and the remainder is to be paid in four annual installments of $3,750 each. The agreement provides that the franchisor will assist in locating the site for a building, conduct a market survey to estimate potential income, supervise the construction of a building, and provide initial training to employees. Assume that the franchisee could borrow money at 10%. Thus, the present value of the four $3,750 payments would be $11,887 ($3,750 × 3.1699). The discount of $3,113 represents interest to be earned over the payment period.

If the down payment is refundable, and no services have been rendered at the time the arrangement is made, the deposit method would be used as long as collection on the note is reasonably certain. The following entry would be made to record the transaction:

Cash	10,000	
Notes Receivable	15,000	
Discount on Notes Receivable		3,113
Deposit on Franchise (or Unearned Franchise Fee)		21,887

When the initial services are determined to be substantially performed, the revenue recognition method to be used and the resulting journal entries depend on the probability of future cash collection. If the collection of the note is reasonably assured, the full accrual method would be used. Assume that substantial performance of the initial services costs $15,000. The entries to record this event using the full accrual method would be as follows:

---

[12] Committee on Franchise Accounting and Auditing, AICPA, *Industry Accounting Guide*, "Accounting for Franchise Fee Revenue" (New York: American Institute of Certified Public Accountants, 1973).

[13] *Statement of Financial Accounting Standards No. 45*, "Accounting for Franchise Fee Revenue" (Stamford: Financial Accounting Standards Board, March, 1981).

[14] *Ibid*, par 6.

Cost of Franchise Fee Revenue	15,000	
Cash		15,000
Deposit on Franchise (or Unearned Franchise Fee)	21,887	
Franchise Fee Revenue		21,887

If the collection of the note is doubtful, the installment sales method could be used. The following additional entries to those of the full accrual method would be required.

Franchise Fee Revenue	21,887	
Cost of Franchise Fee Revenue		15,000
Deferred Gross Profit on Franchise		6,887
Deferred Gross Profit on Franchise	3,147	
Realized Gross Profit on Franchise		3,147

Computation:
$6,887 ÷ $21,887 = 31.47% gross profit percentage
.3147 × $10,000 = $3,147

Consignment Sales

Another method of accounting has developed when property is exchanged without a transfer of title and without a sales contract being completed. This type of arrangement is referred to as a **consignment**. Under a consignment, the potential seller, the **consignor**, ships merchandise to another party, the **consignee**, who then acts as an *agent* for the consignor to sell the goods. Title to the merchandise continues to be held by the consignor until a sale is made, at which time title passes to the ultimate purchaser. The consignee is usually entitled to reimbursement for expenses incurred in relation to this arrangement, and is also entitled to a commission if a sale is successfully made.

Because title to the merchandise is held by the consignor, but physical possession is held by the consignee, special accounting records must be maintained by the consignor for control purposes. No revenue is recognized until a sale is made by the consignee. Upon shipment of the merchandise by the consignor, a special inventory account is established on the consignor's books to identify the consigned merchandise. Any consignment expenses paid by the consignor are added to the inventory balance as added costs. The consignee does not make an entry for receipt of the inventory in the general ledger; however, memorandum control records are usually kept. Any reimbursable expense paid by the consignee is charged to a receivable account by the consignee and added to the inventory balance by the consignor. When a sale is made, the consignor recognizes the sale as revenue according to one of the revenue recognition methods, and the consigned inventory cost is matched against revenue when it is recognized. The consignee recognizes the commission as revenue on the transaction.

To illustrate consignment accounting entries, assume that Harrison Products Inc. sends $500,000 worth of goods on consignment to Benson Industries. Shipping costs of $5,000 are paid by Harrison, and reimbursable advertising costs of $20,000 are paid by Benson Industries. By the end of the year, one half of the goods on consignment are sold for $400,000 cash. A 10% commission is earned by Benson Industries according to the terms of the consignment. The following journal entries would be made on the consignor's and consignee's books.

Transaction	Entries on Consignor's Books (Harrison Products Inc.)			Entries on Consignee's Books (Benson Industries)		
(1) Shipment of goods on consignment.	Inventory on Consignment	500,000		No entry (memorandum control record)		
	Finished Goods Inventory		500,000			
(2) Payment of expenses by consignor.	Inventory on Consignment	5,000		No entry		
	Cash		5,000			
(3) Payment of expenses by consignee.	Inventory on Consignment	20,000		Consignor Receivable.	20,000	
	Consignee Payable.		20,000	Cash		20,000
(4) Sale of merchandise.	No entry			Cash	400,000	
				Consignor Payable.		400,000
(5) Notification of sale to consignor and payment of cash due.	Commission Expense.	40,000		Consignor Payable . . .	400,000	
	Cash	340,000		Cash		340,000
	Consignee Payable . .	20,000		Commission Revenue		40,000
	Consignment Sales Revenue		400,000	Consignor Receivable		20,000
	Cost of Goods Sold . .	262,500*				
	Inventory on Consignment		262,500			
	*Computation: ½($500,000 + $25,000) = $262,500					

If the sale by Benson Industries had been on the installment basis, the installment sales entries illustrated earlier in this chapter could have been used in place of the accrual entries illustrated.

CONCLUDING COMMENTS

This chapter has explored some special problems that arise in recognizing revenue. Some industries such as franchising, construction, and real estate, have been used as illustrative of the types of problems that exist in applying the revenue recognition criteria included in currently accepted accounting standards. The importance of revenue recognition is based on the traditional revenue/expense approach to measuring income. Under this approach, revenue recognition is the key and most critical decision. Under the alternative method of income measurement, the asset/liability view, the emphasis shifts to definition of the elements such as assets and liabilities. The completion of the conceptual framework project will undoubtedly have a great impact upon the principles of revenue recognition discussed in this chapter.

QUESTIONS

1. Under what conditions is percentage-of-completion accounting recommended for construction contractors?
2. Distinguish between the cost-to-cost method and efforts-expended methods of measuring the percentage of completion.
3. Output measures of percentage of completion are sometimes used in preference to input measures. What are some examples of commonly used output measures?
4. What is the relationship between the construction in progress account and the progress billings on construction contracts account? How should these accounts be reported on the balance sheet?
5. When a measure of percentage of completion other than cost-to-cost is used, the amount of cost charged against revenue using the percentage of completion will usually be different from the costs incurred. How do some AICPA committee members recommend handling this situation so that the costs charged against revenue are equal to the costs incurred?
6. The construction in progress account is used to accumulate all costs of construction. What additional item is included in this account when percentage of completion accounting is followed?
7. The gross profit percentage reported on long-term construction contracts often varies from year to year. What is the major reason for this variation?
8. How are anticipated contract losses treated under the completed-contract and percentage-of-completion methods?
9. What input and output measures are usually applicable to the proportional performance method for long-term service contracts?
10. The proportional performance method spreads the profit over the periods in which services are being performed. What arguments could be made against this method of revenue recognition for newly formed service oriented companies?
11. Distinguish among the three different approaches to revenue recognition that await the receipt of cash. How does the treatment of costs incurred vary depending on the approach used?
12. Under what general conditions is the installment sales method of accounting preferred to the full accrual method?
13. The normal accounting entries for installment sales require keeping a separate record by year of receivables, collections on receivables, and the deferred gross profit percentage. Why are these separate records necessary?
14. Installment sales contracts generally include interest. Contrast the method of recognizing interest revenue from the method used to recognize the gross profit on the sale.
15. Under what conditions would the cash method of recognizing revenue be acceptable for reporting purposes?
16. What special recognition problems arise in accounting for franchise fees?
17. Consignment accounting is primarily a method of accounting for transfers of inventory prior to the point of revenue recognition. Describe the essential elements of this method from the standpoint of (a) the consignor and (b) the consignee.

DISCUSSION CASES

case 19-1 (Recognizing revenue on a percentage-of-completion basis) As the new controller for Atlanta Construction Company, you have been advised that your predecessor classified all revenues and expenses by project, each project being considered a separate venture. All revenues from uncompleted projects were treated as unearned revenue, and all expenses applicable to each uncompleted project were treated as "work in process" inventory. Thus, the income statement for the current year included only the revenues and expenses related to projects completed during that year. What do you think about the use of the completed-contract method by the previous controller? What alternative approach might you suggest to company management?

case 19-2 (What is the difference between completed-contract and percentage-of-completion accounting?) In accounting for long-term contracts (those taking longer than one year to complete), the two methods commonly followed are the percentage-of-completion method and the completed-contract method.

(1) Discuss how earnings on long-term contracts are recognized and computed under these two methods.
(2) Under what circumstances is it preferable to use one method over the other?
(3) Why is earnings recognition as measured by interim billings not generally accepted for long-term contracts? (AICPA adapted)

case 19-3 (Let's spread our losses too!) The Olsen Construction Company has several contracts to build sections of freeways, bridges, and dams. Because most of these contracts require more than one year to complete, the accountant, Bill Graham, has recommended use of the percentage-of-completion method to recognize revenue and income on these contracts. The president, Jeanne Ashby, isn't quite sure how it works, and indicates concern about the impact of this decision on income taxes. Ashby also inquires as to what happens when a contract results in a loss. When told by Graham that any estimated loss must be recognized when it is first identified, Ashby becomes upset: "If it is a percentage-of-completion method, and we are recognizing profits as production is finished, why shouldn't we be able to do the same for losses?" How would you as the accountant answer Ashby's concerns?

case 19-4 (When is the membership fee earned?) The National Health Studio has been operating for 5 years but is presently for sale. It has opened 50 salons in various cities in the United States. The normal pattern for a new opening is to advertise heavily and sell different types of memberships: 1-year, 5-year, and lifetime. For the initial membership fee, members may use the pool, exercise rooms, sauna, and other recreational facilities without charge. If special courses or programs are taken, additional fees are charged; however, members are granted certain priorities and the fees are less than those charged to outsiders. In addition, a minimal $10 a month dues charge is made to all members. Non-members may use the facilities; however, they must pay a substantial daily charge for the services they receive.

Your client, Vogel Inc., is considering purchasing the chain of health studios, and asks you to give your opinion on its operations. You are provided with financial statements that show a growing revenue and income pattern over the 5-year period. The balance sheet shows that the physical facilities are apparently owned rather than leased. But you are aware that health studios, like all service institutions, have some challenging revenue recognition problems. What questions would you want answered in preparing your report for Vogel?

case 19-5 (When is it income?) Reliable Advertising Agency handles advertising for clients under contracts that require the agency to develop advertising copy and layouts, and place ads in various media, charging clients a commission of 15% of the media cost as its fee. The agency makes advance billings to its clients of estimated media cost plus its 15% commission. Adjustments to these advances are usually small. Frequently both the billings and receipt of cash from these billings occur before the period in which the advertising actually appears in the media.

A conference meeting is held between officers of the agency and the new firm of CPAs recently engaged to perform annual audits. In this meeting, consideration is given to four possible points for measuring income: (1) at the time the advanced billing is made, (2) when payment is received from the client, (3) in the month when the advertising appears in the media, and (4) when the bill for advertising is received from the media, generally in the month following its appearance. The agency has been following the first method for the past several years on the basis that a definite contract exists and the income is earned when billed. When the billing is made, an entry is prepared to record the estimated receivable and liability to the media. Estimated expenses related to the contract are also recorded. Adjusting entries are later made for any differences between the estimated and actual amounts.

As a member of the CPA firm attending this meeting, how would you react to the agency's method of recognizing income? Discuss the strengths and weaknesses of each of the four methods of income recognition and indicate which one you would recommend the agency follow.

case 19-6 (When is the initial franchise fee really earned?) Southern Fried Shrimp sells franchises to independent operators throughout the southeastern part of the United States. The contract with the franchisee includes the following provisions:

(a) The franchisee is charged an initial fee of $25,000. Of this amount $5,000 is payable when the agreement is signed and a $4,000 non-interest-bearing note is payable at the end of each of the five subsequent years.
(b) All the initial franchise fee collected by Southern Fried Shrimp is to be refunded and the remaining obligation canceled if, for any reason, the franchisee fails to open the franchise.
(c) In return for the initial franchise fee, Southern Fried Shrimp agrees to: assist the franchisee in selecting the location for the business; negotiate the lease for the land; obtain financing and assist with building design; supervise construction; establish accounting and tax records; and, provide expert advice over a five-year period relating to such matters as employee and management training, quality control, and promotion.
(d) In addition to the initial franchise fee, the franchisee is required to pay to Southern Fried Shrimp a monthly fee of 2% of sales for menu planning, recipe innovations, and the privilege of purchasing ingredients from Southern Fried Shrimp at or below prevailing market prices.

Management of Southern Fried Shrimp estimates that the value of the services rendered to the franchisee at the time the contract is signed amounts to at least $5,000. All franchisees to date have opened their locations at the scheduled time and none has defaulted on any of the notes receivable.

The credit ratings of all franchisees would entitle them to borrow at the current interest rate of 10%.

Given the nature of Southern Fried Shrimp's agreement with its franchisees, when should revenue be recognized? Discuss the question of revenue recognition for both the initial franchise fee and the additional monthly fee of 2% of sales and give illustrative entries for both types of revenue. (AICPA adapted)

case 19-7 (I think they're sales!) The Rain-Soft Water Company distributes its water softeners to dealers upon their request. The contract agreement with the dealers is that they may have 90 days to sell and pay for the softeners. Until the 90-day period is over, any softeners may be returned at the dealer's expense and with no further obligation on the dealer's part. Full payment by the dealer is required after 90 days has elapsed, whether the softeners are sold or not. Past experience indicates that 75% of all softeners distributed on this basis are sold by the dealer. In June, 100 units are delivered to dealers at an average billed price of $800 each. The average cost of the softeners to Rain-Soft is $600. Based on the expected sales, Rain-Soft reports profit of $15,000 [$200 × .75(100)]. You are asked to evaluate the income statement for its compliance with GAAP. What recommendations would you make?

case 19-8 (Trading stamps and revenue recognition) Bonanza Trading Stamps Inc. was formed early this year to sell trading stamps throughout the Southwest to retailers who distribute the stamps gratuitously to their customers. Books for accumulating the stamps and catalogs illustrating the merchandise for which the stamps may be exchanged are given free to retailers for distribution to stamp recipients. Centers with inventories of merchandise premiums have been established for redemption of the stamps. Retailers may not return unused stamps to Bonanza.

The following schedule expresses Bonanza's expectations as to percentages of a normal month's activity that will be attained. For this purpose, a "normal month's activity" is defined as the level of operations expected when expansion of activities ceases or tapers off to a stable rate. The company expects that this level will be attained in the third year and that sales of stamps will average $2,000,000 per month throughout the third year.

Month	Actual Stamp Sales Percent	Merchandise Premium Purchases Percent	Stamp Redemptions Percent
6th	30%	40%	10%
12th	60	60	45
18th	80	80	70
24th	90	90	80
30th	100	100	95

Bonanza plans to adopt an annual closing date at the end of each 12 months of operation.

(1) Discuss the factors to be considered in determining when revenue should be recognized in measuring the income of a business enterprise.
(2) Discuss the accounting alternatives that should be considered by Bonanza Trading Stamps Inc. for the recognition of its revenues and related expenses.
(3) For each accounting alternative discussed in (2), give balance sheet accounts that should be used and indicate how each should be classified. (AICPA adapted)

EXERCISES

exercise 19-1 (Completed contract method)

On December 1, 1983, bids were submitted for a construction project to build a new municipal building and fire station. The lowest bid was $3,980,000 submitted by the Reed Construction Company, and they were awarded the contract. Reed uses the completed-contract method to report gross profit. The following data are given to summarize the activities on this contract for 1984 and 1985. Give the entries to record these transactions using the completed contract method.

Year	Cost Incurred	Estimated Cost to Complete	Billings on Contract	Collections of Billings
1984	$1,440,000	$2,060,000	$1,200,000	$1,080,000
1985	2,020,000	-0-	2,780,000	2,900,000

exercise 19-2 (Percentage-of-completion analysis)

Viking Construction Co. has used the cost-to-cost percentage-of-completion method of recognizing profits. Tom Viking assumed leadership of the business after the recent death of his father, Rudy. In reviewing the records, Viking finds the following information regarding a recently completed building project for which the total contract was $500,000.

	1982	1983	1984
Gross profit (loss)	$10,000	$35,000	$ (5,000)
Cost incurred to date	90,000	?	205,000

Viking wants to know how effectively the company operated during the last three years on this project and, since the information is not complete, has asked you to help by answering the following questions.

(1) How much cost was incurred in 1983?
(2) What percentage of the project was completed by the end of 1983?
(3) What was the total estimated gross profit on the project by the end of 1983?
(4) What was the estimated cost to complete the project at the end of 1983?

exercise 19-3 (Percentage of completion using architect's estimates)

Northern Builders Inc. entered into a contract to construct an office building and plaza at a contract price of $10,000,000. Income is to be reported using the percentage-of-completion method as determined by estimates made by the architect. The data below summarize the activities on the construction for the years 1984 through 1986. What entries are required to record this information, assuming the architect's estimate of the percentage completed is used to determine revenue?

Year	Cost Incurred	Estimated Cost to Complete	Percentage Complete—Architect's Estimate	Project Billings	Collections on Billings
1984	$3,200,000	$5,800,000	25%	$3,300,000	$3,100,000
1985	4,100,000	1,200,000	75	4,200,000	4,000,000
1986	1,300,000	0	100	2,500,000	2,900,000

exercise 19-4 (Reporting construction contracts)

Mac Builders Inc. is building a new home for Marianne Andrews at a contracted price of $80,000. The estimated cost at the time the contract is signed (January 2, 1984) is $69,000. At December 31, 1984, the total cost incurred is $42,000 with estimated costs to complete of $18,000. Mac has billed $45,000 on the job and has received a $40,000 payment. This is the only contract in process at year end. Prepare the sections of the balance sheet and the income statement of Mac Builders Inc. affected by these events assuming use of (a) the percentage-of-completion method and (b) the completed-contract method.

exercise 19-5 (Percentage-of-completion analysis)

Delta International Inc. recently acquired the Geneva Builders Company. Geneva has incomplete accounting records. On one particular project, only the information below is given. Because the information is incomplete, you are asked the following questions assuming the percentage-of-completion method is used and an output measure is used to estimate the percentage completed, and revenue is recorded using the costs actually incurred (Alternative B).

	1983	1984	1985
Costs incurred during year	$200,000	$250,000	?
Estimated cost to complete	450,000	190,000	–0–
Contract revenue	250,000	?	?
Gross profit on contract	?	10,000	$(20,000)
Contract price	700,000		

(1) How much gross profit should be reported in 1983?
(2) How much revenue should be reported in 1984?

(continued)

(3) How much revenue should be reported in 1985?
(4) How much cost was incurred in 1985?
(5) What are the total costs on the contract?
(6) What would the gross profit be for 1984 if the cost-to-cost percentage-of-completion method were used? Ignore the revenue amount for 1983 and gross profit amount for 1984.

exercise 19-6 (Completed-contract method)

On January 1, 1984, the Dependable Construction Company entered into a three-year contract to build a dam. The original contract price for the construction was $6,000,000 and the estimated cost was $5,200,000. The following cost data relate to the construction period.

Year	Cost Incurred in Year	Estimated Cost to Complete	Billings	Cash Collected
1984	$2,000,000	$3,700,000	$2,100,000	$1,800,000
1985	1,700,000	2,500,000	1,900,000	1,600,000
1986	2,550,000	–0–	2,000,000	2,600,000

Prepare the required journal entries for the three years of the contract, assuming Dependable uses the completed-contract method.

exercise 19-7 (Percentage-of-completion method with change orders)

The High-Rise Construction Company enters into a contract on January 1, 1984, to construct a twenty-story office building for $40,000,000. During the construction period, many change orders are made to the original contract. The following schedule summarizes these changes made in 1984.

	Cost Incurred 1984	Estimated Cost to Complete	Contract Price
Basic contract.	$8,000,000	$28,000,000	$40,000,000
Change Order #1	50,000	50,000	125,000
Change Order #2	——	50,000	–0–
Change Order #3	100,000	100,000	Still to be negotiated. At least cost.
Change Order #4	125,000	–0–	100,000

Compute the revenue, costs, and gross profit to be recognized in 1984, assuming use of the cost-to-cost method to determine the percentage completed. Round percentage to two decimal places.

exercise 19-8 (Service industry accounting)

The Stay-Fit Health Spa charges an annual membership fee of $300 for its services. For this fee, each member receives a fitness evaluation (value $76), a monthly magazine (value $24), and two-hour's use of the equipment each week. The initial direct costs to obtain the membership are estimated to be $60. The direct cost of the fitness evaluation is $40, and the monthly direct costs to provide the services are estimated to be $9 per person. In addition, the monthly indirect costs are estimated to average $4 per person. Give the journal entries to record the transactions in 1984 relative to a membership sold on July 1, 1984. The fitness evaluation is given in the first month of the membership, and the initial direct cost is to be spread over all direct costs using the proportional performance method. (Round percentage of performance to two decimal places and journal entries to nearest dollar.)

exercise 19-9 (Installment sales accounting)

Raymond Corporation had sales in 1984 of $210,000, in 1985 of $270,000, and in 1986 of $320,000. The gross profit percentage of each year, in order, is 28%, 27%, and 29%.

Past history has shown that 10% of total sales are collected in the first year, 20% in the second year, and 30% in the third year. Assuming these collections are made as projected, give the journal entries for 1984, 1985, and 1986, assuming use of the installment sales method. Ignore provisions for doubtful accounts and interest.

exercise 19-10 (Installment sales accounting—real estate)

On January 1, 1984, the Wilson Realty Company sold property carried in inventory at a cost of $25,000 for $40,000 to be paid 10% down and the balance in annual installments over a 10-year period at 12% interest. Installment payments are to be made at the end of each year.

(1) What is the equal annual payment necessary to pay for this property under the above terms. (Round to nearest dollar.)
(2) Give the entries for the first year assuming the installment sales method is used.

exercise 19-11 (Installment sales analysis)

Complete the following table:

	1983	1984	1985
Installment sales	$50,000	$80,000	(7)
Cost of installment sales	(1)	(5)	91,800
Gross profit	(2)	(6)	28,200
Gross profit percentage	(3)	25%	(8)
Cash collections:			
1983	(4)	25,000	10,000
1984		20,000	50,000
1985			40,000
Realized gross profit on installment sales	1,100	10,500	(9)

exercise 19-12 (Cost recovery method)

Owyhee Inc. is a land development company. It has acquired 1,000 acres of choice recreational property for $900 per acre, and is selling developed recreational building lots for $4,000 per acre. The improvement costs amount to $700 per acre. The land cost is carried on Owyhee's books as inventory. In the first year, Owyhee sold 20 one-acre lots, 10% down, the balance to be paid over 10 years in annual installments at an interest rate of 10%. Assume the lots are sold on January 1, 1984.

(1) Give the entries required for 1984 and 1985 if the cost recovery method is used to recognize revenue.
(2) Prove that the balance reported on the December 31, 1985 balance sheet is equal to the unrecovered cost of the land.

exercise 19-13 (Franchise accounting)

Karl's Bagels franchises its name to different people across the country. The franchise agreement requires the franchisee to make an initial payment of $8,000 on the agreement date and four annual payments of $4,000 each beginning one year from the agreement date. The initial payment is refundable until the date of opening. Interest rates are assumed to be 10%. The franchisor agrees to make market studies, find a location, train the employees, and a few other relatively minor services. The following transactions describe the relationship with Agnes Schmidt, a franchisee.

July 1, 1984—Entered into a franchise agreement.
September 1, 1984—Completed a market study at cost of $4,000.
November 15, 1984—Found suitable location. Service cost $2,000.
January 10, 1985—Completed training program for employees, cost $5,000.
January 15, 1985—Franchise outlet opened.

Give the journal entries in 1984-1985 to record these transactions, including any adjusting entries at December 31, 1984.

exercise 19-14 (Franchise accounting)

On September 1, 1984, Laker Company entered into franchise agreements with three franchisees. The agreement required an initial fee payment of $7,000 plus four $3,000 payments due every four months, the first payment due December 31, 1984. The interest rate is 12%. The initial deposit is refundable until substantial performance has been completed. The following table describes each agreement.

Franchisee	Probability of Full Collection	Services Performed by Franchisor at December 31, 1984	Total Cost Incurred to December 31, 1984
A	Likely	Substantial	$ 7,000
B	Doubtful	25%	2,000
C	Doubtful	Substantial	10,000

For each franchisee, identify the revenue recognition method that you would recommend considering the circumstances. What amount of revenue and income would be reported in 1984 for the method selected? Assume $10,000 was received from each franchisee during the year.

exercise 19-15 (Consignment accounting)

In 1984, Walters Wholesalers transferred goods to a retailer on consignment. The transaction was recorded as a sale by Walters. The goods cost $6,000 and were sold at a 30% markup. In 1985, $2,500 (cost) of the merchandise was sold by the retailer at the normal markup, and the balance of the merchandise was returned to Walters. The retailer withheld a 10% commission from payment. Prepare the journal entry in 1985 to correct the books for 1984, and prepare the correct entries relative to the consignment sale in 1985.

PROBLEMS

problem 19-1 (Construction accounting)

The W. W. Clements Construction Company obtained a construction contract to build a highway and bridge over the Mississippi River. It is estimated at the beginning of the contract that it would take three years to complete the project at an expected cost of $50,000,000. The contract price was $60,000,000. The project actually took four years, being accepted as completed late in 1984. The following information describes the status of the job at the close of production each year.

	1981	1982	1983	1984	1985
Annual costs incurred	$12,000,000	$15,000,000	$18,000,000	$10,000,000	
Estimated cost to complete	38,000,000	27,000,000	11,250,000		
Collections on contract	12,000,000	13,000,000	15,000,000	15,000,000	$5,000,000
Billings on contract .	13,000,000	15,500,000	17,000,000	14,500,000	

Instructions:

(1) What is the revenue, cost, and gross profit recognized for each of the years 1981–1985 under (a) the percentage-of-completion method, (b) the completed-contract method?
(2) Give the journal entries for each year assuming that the percentage-of-completion method is used.

problem 19-2 (Construction accounting)

Carter's Construction Company reports its income for tax purposes on a completed-contract basis and income for financial statement purposes on a percentage-of-completion basis. A record of construction activities for 1984 and 1985 follows:

		1984		1985	
	Contract Price	Cost Incurred 1984	Estimated Cost to Complete	Cost Incurred 1985	Estimated Cost to Complete
Project A	$1,450,000	$910,000	$390,000	$410,000	–0–
Project B	1,700,000	720,000	880,000	340,000	$650,000
Project C	850,000	160,000	640,000	431,500	253,500
Project D	1,000,000			280,000	520,000

General and administrative expenses for 1984 and 1985 were $50,000 for each year and are to be recorded as a period cost.

Instructions:

(1) Calculate the income for 1984 and 1985 that should be reported for financial statement purposes.
(2) Calculate the income for 1985 to be reported on a completed-contract basis.

problem 19-3 (Construction accounting)

The Milrose Construction Corporation contracted with the City of Fort Dawson to construct a dam on the Carson River at a price of $16,000,000. The Milrose Corporation expects to earn $1,360,000 on the contract. The percentage-of-completion method is to be used and the completion stage is to be determined by estimates made by the engineer. The following schedule summarizes the activities of the contract for the years 1983–85.

Year	Cost Incurred	Estimated cost to Complete	Engineer's Estimate of Completion	Billings on Contract	Collection on Billings
1983	$5,000,000	$9,640,000	31%	$5,000,000	$4,500,000*
1984	4,500,000	5,100,000	61%	6,000,000	5,400,000*
1985	5,250,000	–0–	100%	5,000,000	6,100,000

*A 10% retainer accounts for the difference between billings and collections.

Instructions:

(1) Prepare a schedule showing the revenue, costs, and the gross profit earned each year under the percentage-of-completion method, using the engineer's estimate as the measure of completion to be applied to revenues and costs.
(2) Prepare all journal entries required to reflect the contract.
(3) Prepare journal entries for 1985, assuming the completed-contract method is used.
(4) How would the journal entries in (2) differ if the actual costs incurred were used to calculate cost for the period instead of the engineer's estimate. (Alternative B.)

problem 19-4 (Construction accounting)

The Metro Construction Company commenced doing business in January 1984. Construction activities for the year 1984 are summarized as follows:

Project	Total Contract Price	Contract Expenditures to December 31, 1984	Estimated Additional Costs to Complete Contracts	Cash Collections to December 31, 1984	Billings to December 31, 1984
A	$ 310,000	$187,500	$ 12,500	$155,000	$155,000
B	415,000	195,000	255,000	210,000	249,000
C	350,000	320,000	—	300,000	350,000
D	300,000	16,500	183,500	—	4,000
	$1,375,000	$719,000	$451,000	$665,000	$758,000

The company is your client. The president has asked you to compute the amounts of revenue for the year ended December 31, 1984, that would be reported under the completed-contract method and the percentage-of-completion method of accounting for long-term contracts.

The following information is available:

(a) Each contract is with a different customer.
(b) Any work remaining to be done on the contracts is expected to be completed in 1985.
(c) The company's accounts have been maintained on the completed-contract method.

Instructions:

(1) Prepare a schedule computing the amount of revenue, cost, and gross profit (loss) by project for the year ended December 31, 1984, to be reported under (a) the percentage-of-completion method, and (b) the completed-contract method. (Round to two decimal places on percentages.)
(2) Prepare a schedule under the completed-contract method, computing the amount that would appear in the company's balance sheet at December 31, 1984, for (a) costs in excess of billings, and (b) billings in excess of costs.
(3) Prepare a schedule under the percentage-of-completion method that would appear in the company's balance sheet at December 31, 1984, for (a) costs and estimated earnings in excess of billings, and (b) billings in excess of costs and estimated earnings.

(AICPA adapted)

problem 19-5 (Construction accounting)

Helen Hatch is a contractor for the construction of large office buildings. At the beginning of 1984, three buildings were in progress. The following data describe the status of these buildings at the beginning of the year:

	Contract Price	Costs Incurred to 1/1/84	Estimated Cost To Complete 1/1/84
Building 1	$ 4,000,000	$2,070,000	$1,380,000
Building 2	9,000,000	6,318,000	1,782,000
Building 3	13,150,000	3,000,000	9,000,000

During 1984 the following costs were incurred:

Building 1—$930,000 (estimated cost to complete as of 12/31/84, $750,000)
Building 2—$1,800,000 (job completed)
Building 3—$7,400,000 (estimated cost to complete as of 12/31/84, $2,800,000)
Building 4—$800,000 (contract price, $2,500,000; estimated cost to complete as of 12/31/84, $1,200,000)

Instructions:

(1) Compute the total revenue, costs, and gross profit in 1984. Assume that Hatch uses the cost-to-cost percentage-of-completion method. (Round to the nearest two decimal places for percentage completed.)
(2) Compute the gross profit for 1984 if Hatch uses the completed-contract method.

problem 19-6 (Installment sales accounting)

Master Corporation has been using the cash method to account for income since its first year of operation in 1983. All sales are made on credit with notes receivable given by the customer. The income statements for 1983 and 1984 included the following amounts:

	1983	1984
Revenues—collection on principal	$32,000	$50,000
Revenues—interest	3,600	5,500
Cost of goods purchased*	50,140	52,020

*Includes increase in inventory of goods on hand of $5,000 in 1983 and $8,000 in 1984

The balance due on the notes at the end of each year were as follows:

	1983	1984
Notes receivable 1983	$54,000	$36,000
Notes receivable 1984		60,000
Discount on notes receivable—1983	7,167	5,579
Discount on notes receivable—1984		8,043

Instructions: Give the journal entries for 1983 and 1984 assuming the installment sales method was used rather than the cash method.

problem 19-7 (Cost recovery accounting)

After a two-year search for a buyer, Hobson Inc. sold its idle plant facility to Jackson Company for $700,000 on January 1, 1980. On this date the plant had a depreciated cost on Hobson's books of $500,000. Under the agreement, Jackson paid $100,000 cash on January 1, 1980, and signed a $600,000 note bearing interest at 10%. The note was payable in installments of $100,000, $200,000, and $300,000 on January 1, 1981, 1982, and 1983, respectively. The note was secured by a mortgage on the property sold. Hobson appropriately accounted for the sale under the cost recovery method since there was no reasonable basis for estimating the degree of collectibility of the note receivable. Jackson repaid the note with three late installment payments, which were accepted by Hobson, as follows:

Date of payment	Principal	Interest
July 1, 1981	$100,000	$90,000
December 31, 1982	200,000	75,000
February 1, 1984	300,000	32,500

Instructions: Prepare the journal entries required for the years 1980-1984 for the sale and subsequent collections. (AICPA adapted)

problem 19-8 (Consignment accounting)

Marvin Industries sells merchandise on a consignment basis to dealers. Shipping costs are chargeable to Marvin, although in some cases, the dealer pays them. The selling price of the merchandise averages 40% above cost. The dealer is paid a 15% commission on the sales price for all sales made. All dealer sales are made on a cash basis. The following consignment sales activities occurred during 1984.

Manufacturing cost of goods shipped on consignment		$160,000
Freight costs incurred:		
Paid by Marvin Industries	$15,000	
Paid by dealer	5,000	20,000
Sales price of merchandise sold by dealers		154,000
Payments made by dealers after deducting commission and freight costs		114,000

Instructions:

(1) Prepare summary entries on the books of the consignor for these consignment sales transactions.
(2) Prepare summary entries on the books of the dealer consignee assuming there is only one dealer involved.
(3) Prepare the parts of Marvin Industries financial statements at December 31, 1984, that relate to these consignment sales.

problem 19-9 (Revenue recognition analysis)

The Box Elder Construction Company entered into a $3,000,000 contract in early 1985 to construct a multipurpose recreational facility for the City of Logan. Construction time extended over a two-year period. The table below describes the pattern of progress payments made by the City of Logan and costs incurred by Box Elder Construction by semiannual periods. Estimated costs of $2,400,000 were incurred as expected.

Period	Progress Payments for Period	Progress Cost for Period
(1) (January 1–June 30, 1985)	$ 500,000	$ 600,000
(2) (July 1–December 31, 1985)	700,000	800,000
(3) (January 1–June 30, 1986)	1,300,000	720,000
(4) (July 1–December 31, 1986)	500,000	280,000
Total	$3,000,000	$2,400,000

The Box Elder Company prepares financial statements twice each year, June 30 and December 31.

Instructions:

(1) Based on the foregoing data, compute the amount of revenue, costs, and gross profit for the four semiannual periods under each of the following methods of revenue recognition:
   (a) Percentage of completion.
   (b) Completed contract.
   (c) Installment sales (gross profit only).
   (d) Cost recovery (gross profit only).
(2) Which method do you feel best measures the performance of Box Elder on this contract?

20 ACCOUNTING FOR INCOME TAXES

CHAPTER OBJECTIVES

Describe and illustrate intraperiod income tax allocation.

Describe and illustrate interperiod income tax allocation.

Distinguish and evaluate accounting for deferred income taxes under the liability, deferred, and net-of-tax methods.

Explain the accounting treatment for carryback and carryforward of operating losses, including the interaction of deferred income taxes.

Describe alternate accounting methods for reporting investment tax credits, including the treatment of unused investment tax credits.

Describe and illustrate the disclosure of income taxes in the financial statements.

Although the first income tax was levied by the federal government during the Civil War, it was not until the Constitution was amended in 1913 by the 16th Amendment that the legality of such a tax was established. The tax rates were sufficiently low in the first years after the 16th Amendment that little attention was paid to this new tax outlay for individuals and businesses. However, as the services provided by governments have expanded, the rates have increased and the significance of income taxes on personal and business decision making has greatly expanded. With this expansion, accounting for federal and state income taxes has become an increasingly complex topic for the accounting profession.

NATURE OF INCOME TAXES

Theoretically, income taxes could be viewed as either an expense of operating a business or as a distribution of profit between the governmental unit and the owners of the business. The private enterprise philosophy of the United States has led to an acceptance of the former view; income tax is a levy placed by a government on all businesses, and thus it is a necessary expense of doing business within our society.

Although the federal income tax is the most significant income tax in most cases, state and local income taxes are also generally an important expense outlay. Many states and local governments pattern their income tax regulations after the federal government. This simplifies the preparation of income tax returns for businesses and permits more efficient tax planning. Although the emphasis in this chapter will be on the federal tax, accounting for state and local income taxes would be handled in a similar manner, with variations depending on the particular state and local laws involved.

Because income taxes affect almost every business entity, accounting for income taxes has widespread interest. The federal tax laws and regulations are complex, and specialists in income tax are usually employed to do the tax planning and tax return preparation. The purpose of this chapter is not to discuss the income tax laws specifically, except as they might have an impact upon the timing of tax payments. Most problems in accounting for income tax relate to one of the following areas:

(1) Intraperiod income tax allocation.
(2) Interperiod income tax allocation.
(3) Operating loss carrybacks and carryforwards.
(4) The investment tax credit.

Each of these areas will be discussed in this chapter.

INTRAPERIOD INCOME TAX ALLOCATION

Because income tax is related specifically to revenue and expense items, the reporting of income tax should be directly related to the items involved. If all current revenues and expenses were directly related to continuing operations, the total income tax expense for the period would be reported as a single amount and deducted from "Income from continuing operations before income tax." However, the income statement has several major divisions. These include income from continuing operations, income from discontinued operations, extraordinary items, and cumulative effects of accounting changes. Each of these items is usually included in taxable income, either as an addition or deduction. While the details of the special items are discussed in Chapter 21, the procedures for allocating total income tax expense for the period among the various components of income will be presented in this chapter. This allocation is referred to as **intraperiod tax allocation.**

To illustrate the concept of intraperiod tax allocation, assume that a firm has a $70,000 gain on the early retirement of long-term debt, which must be reported as an extraordinary item according to generally accepted accounting principles. The gain would also be reported as income for income tax purposes, and a tax would be paid. The intraperiod tax allocation principle requires that the gain and the amount of income tax related to the gain on retirement be reported together in the income statement. If the tax rate were 40%, the disclosure might be shown as follows:

Extraordinary gain from early debt retirement	$70,000	
Less income tax on gain	28,000	$42,000

An alternative method of disclosure shows the amount of tax parenthetically as follows:

Extraordinary gain (net of $28,000 income tax)	$42,000

In either case, the income tax on ordinary operations would not include the tax on the extraordinary gain.

If the special item is a loss that must be disclosed separately, such as a loss from discontinued operations, the reduction in income tax arising from the loss is applied to reduce the reported loss. Thus, if the tax rate were 40 percent and the loss on the sale of a discontinued division were $40,000, the special item might be disclosed as follows:

Loss from discontinued operations (net of $16,000 tax reduction on loss)	$24,000

When a prior period adjustment is reported as a direct adjustment to Retained Earnings, the related tax effect should be disclosed in the statement of retained earnings. To illustrate, assume that a company discovers in 1985 that depreciation for 1983 was overstated by $30,000 and the related increase in income tax is 40 percent or $12,000. The adjustment could be presented in the statement of retained earnings as follows:

Retained earnings, January 1, 1985, as previously reported	$210,000
Add:	
Prior period adjustment for overstatement of depreciation expense for 1983 (net of $12,000 increase in income tax payable)	18,000
Adjusted retained earnings, January 1, 1985	$228,000

Intraperiod Income Tax Allocation Assuming a Single Tax Rate

Income tax rates usually are graduated and increase as income increases. Several revisions have been made in the federal corporate tax rate structure in recent years. The corporate tax is currently a five-level tax, with the following rates effective for tax years beginning in 1983:

Income	Tax Rate	Income Tax
First $25,000	15%	$ 3,750
Second $25,000	18%	4,500
Third $25,000	30%	7,500
Fourth $25,000	40%	10,000
Income tax on first $100,000 of income		$25,750
Over $100,000	46%	

To simplify the following discussion, it will be assumed that the income tax rate is 40 percent and is constant over all levels of income. Discussion of intraperiod income tax allocation with graduated rates is included in the appendix to this chapter.

Assume that examination of Springer Corporation's income tax return for 1984 revealed the following information before computation of income tax:

Income from continuing operations	$225,000
Income from discontinued operations	62,000
Loss on disposal of segment of business	(100,000)
Extraordinary loss from earthquake	(50,000)
Taxable income	$137,000

Applying the 40 percent tax rate, the income tax of $54,800 ($137,000 × .40) would be allocated as follows:

Income tax on income from continuing operations ($225,000 × .40)	$90,000
Income tax on income from discontinued operations ($62,000 × .40)	24,800
Income tax reduction from loss on disposal of a business segment ($100,000 × .40)	(40,000)
Income tax reduction from extraordinary loss ($50,000 × .40)	(20,000)
Income tax payable for current year	$54,800

The journal entry to record the computations on the books would be as follows:[1]

Income Tax on Income from Continuing Operations	90,000	
Income Tax on Income from Discontinued Operations	24,800	
Income Tax Reduction from Loss on Disposal of a Business Segment		40,000
Income Tax Reduction from Extraordinary Loss		20,000
Income Tax Payable		54,800

The abbreviated income statement on page 762 demonstrates how the amount of income tax applicable to each section might be disclosed.

INTERPERIOD INCOME TAX ALLOCATION

Perhaps the most complex area involving accounting for income tax is the adjustment necessary to apply the accrual concept to income tax expense.

[1] In practice, the allocation detail is not always recorded in the accounts. When that is the case, the journal entry would be a debit to Income Tax Expense and a credit to Income Tax Payable for $54,800.

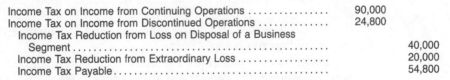

Springer Corporation Income Statement For the Year Ended December 31, 1984		
Income from continuing operations before income tax		$225,000
Income tax expense on continuing operations		90,000
Income from continuing operations		$135,000
Discontinued operations:		
Income from operation of discontinued business segment (less applicable income tax expense of $24,800)	$37,200	
Loss on disposal of business segment (less applicable income tax reduction of $40,000)	(60,000)	(22,800)
Extraordinary loss from earthquake damage (less applicable income tax reduction of $20,000)		(30,000)
Net income		$ 82,200

Because the amount of tax expense is directly related to the income earned, control of the expense is limited to tax planning that will take advantage of income tax regulations to minimize the present value of tax outlays over the life of the business. Usually, this means taking advantage of provisions to minimize the tax payment for each year.

Application of these provisions often results in taxable income that differs from the pretax income reported in the financial statements, sometimes referred to as **pretax book or accounting income.** Taxable income is defined by Congress through laws enacted and by regulations issued by the Internal Revenue Service. The objectives of Congress and the IRS are not the same as those of accounting bodies, such as the Financial Accounting Standards Board, that establish generally accepted accounting principles to determine book income. Income taxes are sometimes used to regulate the economy, to encourage additional investment, or to favor specific industries. Generally, the tax authorities are not as concerned about measuring income to determine whether a firm is better off, but are more interested in a firm's ability to pay the tax. Thus, most income is taxed when cash is received even though services are still to be rendered, and the income has not yet been recognized on the books.

Differences between tax and book or accounting income may be permanent or temporary. **Permanent differences** arise from: (1) items that are included in the computation of taxable income, but are never recognized for accounting purposes and (2) items that are recognized for accounting purposes, but are never included in the computation of taxable income. **Temporary** or **timing differences** arise from revenue and expense items that are recognized for accounting purposes in a period preceding or subsequent to the period in which they are included in the computation of taxable income. These temporary differences have created the need for **interperiod tax allocation.** This allocation and its ramifications have created some of the greatest problems in accounting for income taxes.

Permanent Differences

As the name implies, permanent differences are defined as:

> Differences between taxable income and pretax accounting income arising from transactions that, under applicable tax laws and regulations, will not be offset by corresponding differences, or "turn around" in other periods.[2]

Most permanent differences can be classified as revenues exempt from income tax or expenses not deductible in determining taxable income. Examples of nontaxable revenues include:

(1) Interest revenue on municipal bonds.
(2) Life insurance proceeds on officers' lives.
(3) 85% of dividends received from other corporations (100% of dividends from wholly owned subsidiaries).

Examples of nondeductible expenses include:

(1) Fines and expenses arising from violation of laws.
(2) Life insurance premiums paid on lives of a corporation's officers or employees if the corporation is the beneficiary.
(3) Interest on indebtedness incurred to purchase tax-exempt municipal securities.
(4) Goodwill amortization.

Expenses recognized for tax purposes but not recognized as expenses on the books are rarely encountered. An example of this type of permanent difference would be percentage depletion in excess of actual cost depletion. Although theoretically there could be revenue recognized on the tax return that is never recognized on the books, there are no common examples of such items.

Timing Differences

Most differences between pretax book income and taxable income are temporary in nature. An expense may be deducted for income tax purposes in the current year, but on the external financial statements in a subsequent year. A revenue item may be reported on the income tax return in the current year, but on the external financial statements when it is earned in a subsequent year. In order to match the tax expense with the related income, interperiod income tax allocation is necessary for timing differences. Essentially, it means that the income tax expense reported on the financial statements is the tax that would have been paid if the income on the financial statements had been used for income tax purposes. The difference between the amount reported as income tax expense and the amount currently payable is reported as a deferred charge or a deferred credit depending on the nature of its balance. When the item *reverses* in subsequent periods, the deferred balance is eliminated.

---

[2] *Opinions of the Accounting Principles Board, No. 11*, "Accounting for Income Taxes" (New York: American Institute of Certified Public Accountants, 1967), par. 13.

Timing differences may be classified into the following categories. Examples of items fitting into each category are also included.

(1) Pretax book income is less than taxable income.
  (a) Revenue is deferred for reporting purposes but is currently recognized for tax purposes.
    1. Rent revenue received in advance of period earned and deferred for reporting purposes, but taxable in period of receipt.
    2. Subscription revenue received in advance of period earned and deferred for reporting purposes, but taxable in period of receipt.
  (b) Expense is currently recognized for reporting purposes but is deferred for tax purposes.
    1. Warranty expense accrued in advance for reporting purposes but allowed for tax purposes only when costs are incurred under the warranty.
    2. Reduction in market value of current marketable securities deducted for reporting purposes in the current period, but allowed for tax purposes only when securities are sold.

(2) Pretax book income is more than taxable income.
  (a) Revenue is currently recognized for reporting purposes, but is deferred for tax purposes.
    1. Installment sales method used for tax purposes but accrual method of sales used for reporting purposes.
    2. Construction revenue recognized using the percentage-of-completion method for reporting purposes, but using the completed-contract method for tax purposes.
  (b) Expense is deferred for reporting purposes, but is currently recognized for tax purposes.
    1. Straight-line depreciation used for reporting purposes, but accelerated depreciation used for tax purposes.
    2. Intangible drilling costs for extractive industry capitalized and deferred for reporting purposes, but written off as incurred for tax purposes.

Partial vs. Comprehensive Income Tax Allocation

The principle of interperiod income tax allocation was recognized by the Committee on Accounting Procedure in Bulletin No. 43, but the Committee recognized an exception to such allocation when it could be presumed that "...particular differences between the tax return and the income statement will recur regularly over a comparatively long period of time."[3] This led to varied interpretations and alternative procedures by different companies. For example, if a company uses accelerated cost recovery system (ACRS) depreciation for equipment on the income tax return but straight-line depreciation on the books, the amount of depreciation expense for tax purposes will exceed that for reporting purposes every year as long as the company is

---

[3] *Accounting Research and Terminology Bulletins—Final Edition,* "No. 43, Restatement and Revision of Accounting Research Bulletins" (New York: American Institute of Certified Public Accountants, 1961), Ch. 10, sect. B, par. 1.

growing and adding new equipment faster than it is retiring the old equipment. This type of timing difference is defined as a **recurring timing difference** because, in total, the tax deferral will never reverse due to recurring purchases of new equipment. Some companies interpreted Bulletin No. 43 as applying to this type of item, and did not provide for interperiod income tax allocation for depreciation differences. This procedure is referred to as **partial allocation.** Other companies included these depreciation differences in their computation of interperiod income tax allocation balances. The Accounting Principles Board in Opinion No. 11 sought to extend the principle of income tax allocation, as well as to achieve uniformity in practice, by modifying the original position and concluding that "... comprehensive interperiod tax allocation is an integral part of the determination of income tax expense."[4] **Comprehensive income tax allocation** requires allocation for all timing differences whether they are expected to recur in the future or not. The Board reasoned that although the total difference between accelerated depreciation and straight-line depreciation may increase each year, depreciation on a specific asset does reverse in time, so that in the latter part of an asset's life more depreciation is charged on the books than on the income tax return.

Computation of Income Tax Expense and Income Tax Payable

To illustrate the nature of interperiod tax allocation and the effect of permanent and temporary differences on the computation of income tax, assume that for the year ending December 31, 1984, the Barg Corporation reported pretax book income of $420,000. This amount includes $20,000 of tax-exempt income and $5,000 of nondeductible expenses. Depreciation expense for tax purposes exceeds that recognized for book purposes in the current year by $30,000. Assuming a tax rate of 40 percent, the income tax expense for accounting and reporting purposes and the income tax payable in the current period would be computed and recorded as follows:

		For Accounting Purposes	For Tax Purposes
Pretax book income		$420,000	$420,000
Permanent differences:			
Nondeductible expenses	$ 5,000		
Tax-exempt income	(20,000)		
Net permanent difference		(15,000)	(15,000)
Excess of tax depreciation over book depreciation			(30,000)
Income subject to income tax		$405,000	$375,000
Income tax at 40%		$162,000	$150,000

The $12,000 difference between the tax currently payable of $150,000 and the reported tax expense of $162,000 is attributable to the timing differ-

[4] *Opinions of the Accounting Principles Board, No. 11, op. cit.*, par. 34.

ence ($30,000 × .40 = $12,000). The $12,000 would be recorded on the books by a credit to Deferred Income Taxes. Net income reported on the income statement for 1984 would be $258,000 (pretax book income of $420,000 less income tax expense of $162,000).

This simplified example is intended to illustrate the manner in which permanent and timing differences affect the computation of income tax. Interperiod tax allocation, assuming a constant tax rate over time, is discussed and illustrated in the following section. Interperiod allocation with changing tax rates is discussed in the appendix to this chapter.

Interperiod Income Tax Allocation—No Change in Rates

To illustrate the accounting for interperiod income tax allocation when income tax rates are constant at 40%, assume the following:

Year	Pretax Book Income	Excess of Accelerated Depreciation Over Straight-Line	Excess of Rent Revenue Received In Advance Over Rent Revenue Earned	Taxable Income
1984	$100,000	$15,000	$10,000	$ 95,000
1985	130,000	25,000	(6,000)	99,000
1986	175,000	(5,000)	15,000	195,000

The excess of rent revenue received in advance over rent earned causes reported book income to be lower than taxable income. The excess of accelerated depreciation over straight-line depreciation causes the opposite effect: reported book income exceeds taxable income. If the item is reversed in a particular year, reported book and taxable income are affected in the opposite direction. Different kinds of timing differences should be maintained separately for computation purposes, although they may be combined for reporting purposes.

As previously illustrated, the income tax expense for the period is computed on the reported book income adjusted for any permanent differences. The current income tax liability for the period is computed on the taxable income for the period. The difference between the computed income tax expense and the computed income tax liability is recorded as a deferred charge or a deferred credit. To illustrate, the following entries would be recorded for the years 1984–86 for the preceding example:

1984			
Dec. 31	Income Tax Expense	40,000	
	Deferred Income Tax—Rent Revenue*	4,000	
	Deferred Income Tax—Depreciation*		6,000
	Income Tax Payable		38,000

Computation:
Income tax expense: 40% × $100,000 = $40,000
Deferred income tax—rent revenue: 40% × $10,000 = $4,000
Deferred income tax—depreciation: 40% × $15,000 = $6,000
Income tax payable: 40% × $95,000 = $38,000

*These accounts may be combined and only the net effect reported as long as they are both current or both noncurrent items.

1985			
Dec. 31	Income Tax Expense	52,000	
	Deferred Income Tax—Rent Revenue		2,400
	Deferred Income Tax—Depreciation		10,000
	Income Tax Payable		39,600

Computation:
Income tax expense: 40% × $130,000 = $52,000
Deferred income tax—rent revenue: 40% × $ 6,000 = $ 2,400
Deferred income tax—depreciation: 40% × $25,000 = $10,000
Income tax payable: 40% × $99,000 = $39,600

1986			
Dec. 31	Income Tax Expense	70,000	
	Deferred Income Tax—Rent Revenue	6,000	
	Deferred Income Tax—Depreciation	2,000	
	Income Tax Payable		78,000

Computation:
Income tax expense: 40% × $175,000 = $70,000
Deferred income tax—rent revenue: 40% × $15,000 = $6,000
Deferred income tax—depreciation: 40% × $ 5,000 = $2,000
Income tax payable: 40% × $195,000 = $78,000

A comparison of reported results with and without interperiod income tax allocation is given below:

	Reported Results Without Interperiod Income Tax Allocation			Reported Results With Interperiod Income Tax Allocation		
Year	*Pretax Book Income*	*Income Tax*	*Net Income*	*Pretax Book Income*	*Income Tax*	*Net Income*
1984	$100,000	$38,000	$62,000	$100,000	$40,000	$ 60,000
1985	130,000	39,600	90,400	130,000	52,000	78,000
1986	175,000	78,000	97,000	175,000	70,000	105,000

Examination of the table shows that without interperiod income tax allocation, the income tax expense in 1985 is almost the same as for 1984 even though reported income before taxes was $30,000 higher in 1985 than in 1984. The results using interperiod income tax allocation more accurately portray the accrual concept of matching expense against revenue and disclose a significant increase in income taxes when reported income is increased.

Problem Areas in Interperiod Income Tax Allocation

Several difficult questions have arisen concerning interperiod income tax allocation as it relates to specific industries and situations. For example, the equity method of accounting for investment revenue results in book income in excess of taxable income. Income from investments is taxable only when distributed. If the distribution never occurs, the difference is really a permanent difference rather than a timing difference. The Accounting Principles Board considered this situation, and concluded that all undistributed earnings from an investment included in book income should be accounted for as timing differences and a deferred tax credit recognized.[5]

[5]*Opinions of the Accounting Principles Board, No. 24,* "Accounting for Income Taxes: Investments in Common Stock Accounted for by the Equity Method (Other than Subsidiaries and Corporate Joint Ventures)" (New York: American Institute of Certified Public Accountants, 1972), par. 7–9. Current tax regulations permit corporations to deduct an 85% dividends-received credit against dividend revenue.

Similar reasoning was used to justify treating undistributed earnings of a subsidiary to its parent as timing differences unless "sufficient evidence shows that the subsidiary has invested or will invest the undistributed earnings indefinitely or that earnings will be remitted in a tax-free liquidation."[6]

The provisions of the Internal Revenue Code permit companies such as savings and loan associations and life insurance companies to exclude from taxable income amounts determined by formulas for bad debt reserves and policyholders' surplus. In both cases, the APB concluded that the entity involved controls the decision as to whether the item would or would not reverse. Therefore, no interperiod income tax allocation is required for these items.[7]

Another question that has been extensively discussed is whether the deferred tax credit should be discounted to report the amount at the present value of the expected future payments. In Accounting Principles Board Opinion No. 10, the Board concluded that because of the uncertainty of the reversal date, deferred income tax should not be accounted for on a discounted basis.[8]

Balance Sheet Classification of Deferred Taxes

Debit balances in deferred income tax accounts are reported as deferred charges; credit balances are reported as deferred credits. The balances in the various accounts must be analyzed and classified as current or noncurrent. For reporting purposes, all current amounts are combined, and the net deferred charge or credit is presented with current assets or liabilities on the balance sheet. Likewise, all noncurrent balances are combined, and the net amount is reported. If the net noncurrent amount is a debit, it is usually reported after land, buildings, and equipment; if a credit, the amount is presented with noncurrent liabilities.

APB Opinion No. 11 states that the current or noncurrent classification of a deferred income tax charge or credit should be based on the classification of the asset or liability to which the timing difference relates.[9] For example, deferred income taxes arising from depreciation would be classified as noncurrent since the related depreciable assets are classified as noncurrent. Some timing differences, however, cannot be related to a specific asset or liability. The FASB issued Statement No. 37 to clarify the classification of deferred income taxes arising from these timing differences. The Board concluded that deferred income taxes that are not related to a specific asset or liability should be classified according to the expected reversal date of the timing difference.[10]

---

[6]*Opinions of the Accounting Principles Board, No. 23,* "Accounting for Income Taxes—Special Areas" (New York: American Institute of Certified Public Accountants, 1972), par. 12.

[7]*Ibid.*, par. 23–28.

[8]*Opinions of the Accounting Principles Board, No. 10,* "Omnibus Opinion—1966" (New York: American Institute of Certified Public Accountants, 1967), par. 6.

[9]*Opinions of the Accounting Principles Board, No. 11, op. cit.*, par. 57.

[10]*Statement of Financial Accounting Standards No. 37,* "Balance Sheet Classification of Deferred Income Taxes" (Stamford: Financial Accounting Standards Board, 1980.)

Alternative Approaches to Interperiod Income Tax Allocation

The currently followed approach to interperiod income tax allocation, discussed in the preceding sections, is referred to as the **deferred method.** The charge or credit is deferred and allocated to income tax expense of future periods. Deferred taxes are computed on the basis of current tax rates, and no adjustment is made for rate changes in subsequent years unless the deferred difference is completely reversed.

Alternatively, it has been suggested that at least two other methods might be used for interperiod income tax allocation. Under the **liability method,** credit balances are viewed as liabilities to be paid sometime in the future, and debit balances as prepaid taxes. Under this method, the amounts reported should be adjusted if the income tax rates change suggesting a different amount will actually be paid in the future.

A third method, the **net of tax method,** is really a method of disclosing the tax effects of timing differences as computed under either the deferred or liability method. Under this approach, the difference between the income tax payable and the income tax expense related to the current period book income is recorded as a direct adjustment to the amounts of the assets, liabilities, revenues, or expenses affected rather than as an adjustment to income tax expense or to a separate balance sheet account.

The deferred method is currently the only generally accepted method. However, in defining the elements of financial statements in Concepts Statement No. 3, the FASB stated that of the three methods, the deferred method is the least compatible with the recommended definitions.[11]

Evaluation of Accounting for Deferred Income Taxes

The introduction of interperiod income tax allocation into accounting has greatly complicated accounting for income taxes. Many accountants have questioned the wisdom of allocating income tax expense for timing differences that are expected to recur, such as for depreciation and installments receivable. This concern was heightened with the introduction of the Accelerated Cost Recovery System (ACRS) by Congress to replace traditional depreciation methods for tax purposes (see Chapter 11). Because most companies, large and small, will probably continue to use traditional depreciation methods for their financial statements, timing differences will become more commonplace, and almost all companies will have to make interperiod tax allocation computations.

The interplay of tax regulations as they change to stimulate and repress the economy results in changes to the rates and the tax rules that require making changes in the deferred amounts reported either immediately or at some future date when the deferred items reverse. Many foreign countries have recognized the morass of accounting rules that have accompanied deferred income tax accounting, and have rejected the comprehensive in-

---

[11] *Statement of Financial Accounting Concepts No. 3,* "Elements of Financial Statements of Business Enterprises" (Stamford: Financial Accounting Standards Board, December 1980), par. 164.

come tax allocation methods practiced in the United States and described in this chapter.

The FASB is currently studying the area of deferred income taxes for possible modification. The conceptual framework definitions and qualitative characteristics, particularly understandability and relevance, should assist the Board in its consideration of this complex topic.[12]

ACCOUNTING FOR OPERATING LOSSES

Since income tax is based on the amount of income earned, no tax is payable if a company experiences an operating loss. As an incentive to those businesses that experience alternate periods of income and losses, the income tax regulations provide a way to ease the risk of loss years. This is done through a carryback and carryforward provision that permits a company to apply an operating loss occurring in one year against income of other years. The number of years the loss can be carried backward and forward has varied over time. The tax code currently provides for a three-year carryback and a fifteen-year carryforward.

Operating Loss Carryback

A company has a choice for any given year's operating loss as to whether or not it desires to use the carryback provision. It may choose only to go forward. If it chooses to go backward, a company experiencing an operating loss for the current year first applies the loss to the income of the third previous year and an income tax refund claim is filed. If the income in the third previous year is not sufficient to use all the operating loss, the remainder is carried back two years; then one year. Operating loss carrybacks result in an entry establishing a receivable for the refund claim and reducing the operating loss for the current year reflecting the tax savings arising from recovery of the prior years' income taxes.

To illustrate, assume that the Superior Company had the following pattern of income and losses for the years 1981–1984. For simplicity, complicating factors, such as capital gains, investment credit, and timing differences are not included as part of this example.

Year	Income (Loss)	Income Tax at 40%
1981	$15,000	$6,000
1982	10,000	4,000
1983	14,000	5,600
1984	(29,000)	0

The $29,000 operating loss would be carried back to 1981 first, then to 1982, and finally, $4,000 to 1983. The income tax rate for these former years

[12]A strong case for eliminating interperiod income tax allocation is made by Paul Rosenfield and William Dent in their article, "No More Deferred Taxes," *Journal of Accountancy* (February, 1983), pp. 44–55. The article concludes that deferred taxes should be "cast out of the house of GAAP" because of the incompatability with the definitions of elements in FASB Concepts Statement No. 3.

was 40 percent. Therefore, an income tax refund claim of $11,600 would be filed for the three years ($29,000 × .40). The entry to record the income tax receivable would be as follows:

Income Tax Refund Receivable	11,600	
Refund of Income Tax from Operating Loss Carryback		11,600
Refund from applying operating loss carryback.		

The refund will be reflected on the income statement as a reduction of the operating loss as follows:

Operating loss before refundable income tax	$29,000
Refund of prior years' income tax arising from carryback of operating loss	11,600
Net loss	$17,400

The preceding example assumed there were no deferred tax credits or charges involved. Frequently a company has timing differences, and these are affected by the carryback of an operating loss. The amount of the carryback for book purposes should be based on book income rather than on the taxable income, and the difference between the amounts actually refundable and the amount computed on book income should be added or deducted from any deferred income tax amount on the balance sheet.

To illustrate this interaction, assume that the following history relates to The Strack Corporation.

Year	Reported Book Income	Taxable Income	Income Tax Expense		Cumulative Deferred Tax *Credit*
			Current	*Deferred*	
1982	$15,000	$ 5,000	$2,000	$4,000	$ 4,000
1983	15,000	5,000	2,000	4,000	8,000
1984	15,000	5,000	2,000	4,000	12,000
1985	(35,000)	(45,000)	(6,000)	(8,000)	(14,000)

For each of the first three years, the book income exceeded the taxable income by $10,000 due to timing differences, and the deferred income tax credit at a 40 percent tax rate was $4,000 each year. In year 4, or 1985, Strack Corporation had a reported operating loss for book purposes of $35,000 and a loss for tax purposes of $45,000. Again, the difference in 1985 between the operating losses was caused by timing differences. The taxable operating loss carryback of $45,000 exceeded the sum of the taxable income for the preceding three years, therefore all $6,000 paid is recoverable. The accounting operating loss of $35,000 would be applied in full to the years 1982 and 1983, and the remaining $5,000 to 1984. Based on book income, the operating loss carryback resulted in a computed recovery of $14,000 ($35,000 × .40). The $8,000 difference between the actual refund of $6,000 and the computed recovery of $14,000, based on book income, reduces the amount of deferred tax credit. The entry to record the carryback would be as follows:

Income Tax Refund Receivable	6,000	
Deferred Income Tax	8,000	
Adjustment to Net Income from Application of Operating Loss Carryback		14,000

Operating Loss Carryforward

As indicated previously, any unused operating loss may be applied against net income earned over the future fifteen years. In the example on page 770, the Superior Company had $10,000 of income left against which operating losses could be applied. Assume that in 1985, another operating loss of $40,000 was incurred. After applying $10,000 to the 1983 income, $30,000 is left to carry forward. Because the ability to earn income in the future is generally not assured, the Accounting Principles Board recommended that carryforward of operating losses be reflected in the accounts only when future earnings are assured beyond reasonable doubt. This will exist only if both of the following conditions exist, "(a) the loss results from an identifiable, isolated, and nonrecurring cause and the company either has been continuously profitable over a long period or has suffered occasional losses that were more than offset by taxable income in subsequent years, and (b) future taxable income is virtually certain to be large enough to offset the loss carryforward and will occur soon enough to provide realization during the carryforward period."[13] The Securities and Exchange Commission has given further guidelines to the virtual certainty test in its Staff Accounting Bulletin No. 8. Virtual certainty requires meeting the following conditions:

(1) The company has a strong earnings history.
(2) The loss was not caused by a general economic or industry decline.
(3) The company has reasonable alternative tax strategies available.
(4) A forecast based on reasonable assumptions indicates more than enough future income to offset the carryforward.[14]

When these requirements are met, the carryforward may be recognized in the loss period in a similar manner as was done for loss carrybacks.

When this assurance of future earnings does not exist, no entry is made in the loss period. When the carryforward benefit can be applied against subsequent income, the income tax benefit should be reported as an extraordinary gain in the year of realization.[15]

Assume a company had used up its income in carryback years, but had a $40,000 carryforward in the current year. In the subsequent year, income before taxes is $50,000, and income tax without the carryforward would have been $20,000 or 40% of $50,000. The carryforward benefit would reduce the income tax liability by $16,000, or 40% of $40,000. The following entries would be required to record the tax provision:

Income Tax Expense	20,000	
Income Tax Payable		20,000
Income tax liability assuming no carryforward.		
Income Tax Payable	16,000	
Extraordinary Gain from Use of Operating Loss Carryforward		16,000
Application of carryforward provision against current year's income tax.		

[13] *Opinions of the Accounting Principles Board, No. 11, op. cit.*, par. 47.

[14] Securities and Exchange Commission, *Staff Accounting Bulletin No. 8*, "Corrections or Changes to Bulletin No. 1—New Interpretations" (Washington, D.C.: U.S. Government Printing Office, 1976).

[15] *Opinions of the Accounting Principles Board, No. 11, op. cit.*

The income statement would reflect the carryover application as follows:

Income from continuing operations before income taxes		$50,000
Less provision for income tax:		
Income tax currently payable	$ 4,000	
Income tax reduction from carryforward of operating loss	16,000	20,000
Income from continuing operations		$30,000
Extraordinary item from reduction of income tax arising from carryforward of prior year's operating loss		16,000
Net income		$46,000

If an operating loss carryforward is not recorded because future income is not certain, an adjustment may still be required to reduce deferred income tax credits or charges by the tax effect on the amounts expected to reverse or turn around during the carryforward period. As the carryforward is actually realized, eliminated deferred credits should be reinstated at the then current tax rate. These adjustments can be very complex, especially when several timing differences and/or several operating loss years are involved.[16]

If a company has operating loss carryforwards at the time of a quasi-reorganization, any future realization of the carryforward should be added to contributed capital because the benefits are attributable to the loss periods prior to the reorganization.

The payment of deferred income tax is contingent upon earnings for the year of the reversal. If an operating loss occurs in the year of a reversal, an adjustment must be made to reduce the deferred credit and increase income for the adjustment. In addition, if there is an operating loss carryforward, an adjustment may be necessary for the expected reversal in the subsequent periods when the carryforward may be applied.

INVESTMENT TAX CREDIT

In order to encourage investment in productive facilities, the Revenue Act of 1962 permitted taxpayers to reduce their federal income tax by an **investment tax credit (ITC)** equal to a specified percentage of the cost of certain depreciable properties acquired after December 31, 1961. There have been many modifications of the original 1962 act, but the investment tax credit that began as a temporary tax provision now appears to be a permanent part of the tax structure. Because Congress continues to use the investment tax credit as a tool to stimulate the economy, the rules governing this area are continually changing. Each year's tax provisions must be carefully studied to identify any changes that have occurred.

The investment tax credit applies to property defined by the tax regulations as "Section 38 property." In general, such property includes tangible depreciable property (other than real property) having a useful life of three or more years. The credit percentage in 1983 was 10 percent of the cost of assets with an ACRS recovery period of five or more years and 6 percent of

[16] *Ibid*, par. 48.

the cost of assets qualifying as three-year recovery property. For tax purposes, a reduction in the basis of assets purchased after December 31, 1982, is required for computing depreciation and gains or losses on disposition of the property. The amount of the reduction is one-half of the credit taken. Thus, if a company acquired five-year ACRS property for $20,000 and used the 10 percent investment tax credit, the basis of the property for tax purposes would be reduced to $19,000 ($20,000 less one-half of $2,000). Alternate treatment is available if the company elects to use lower investment tax credit rates for five- and three-year ACRS assets.

The investment tax credit is applied directly against income tax otherwise due in the year the qualifying property is placed in service. However, the credit available for that year is limited by the amount of tax liability. In 1983, the credit was limited to $25,000 plus 85 percent of the income tax liability in excess of $25,000. Any unused investment tax credit can be carried back three years and forward fifteen years in the same way as described for operating losses. If a company has an investment tax credit carryforward and has additional investment credit available for the current year, the carryforward credits are applied against the current income tax first. This permits a company to more fully utilize the carryforward provision.

In order to realize the full benefit of the investment tax credit, the qualifying property must be held for a specified period called its recapture period. If the asset is disposed of before that period has passed, part of the investment tax credit is recaptured by increasing the tax liability of the current period. For three-year assets acquired after 1981, the following recapture percentages apply:

Disposed of Within	Percentage Investment Tax Credit Recapture
1st year	100%
2d year	66%
3d year	33%
Beyond	–0–

For all other qualifying assets acquired after 1981, the recapture percentages are as follows:

Disposed of Within	Percentage Investment Tax Credit Recapture
1st year	100%
2d year	80%
3d year	60%
4th year	40%
5th year	20%
Beyond	–0–

To illustrate, if a company acquires a $100,000 five-year ACRS asset and disposes of it in Year 3, 60% of the $10,000 investment tax credit, or $6,000, would be added to the tax liability of Year 3.

Leased property is subject to special rules. A lessor of new property which qualifies as "Section 38 property" may either take the investment tax credit itself or elect to let the lessee take it. A lease by itself is not considered a disposition. If the lessor retains the right to the credit, it is deducted from the fair market value of the leased asset before computing the interest rate implicit in the lease.

Accounting for the Investment Tax Credit

Accounting for the investment tax credit has been the subject of much controversy and change. Essentially, there are two methods that can be used to record the tax reduction: (1) the credit can be used to reduce the income tax expense for the year in which it is received, commonly referred to as the **flow-through method,** or (2) the credit can be deferred and reflected as a reduction of tax expense over the period during which the asset is depreciated, commonly referred to as the **deferred method.**

Flow-Through Method. Using the flow-through method, the investment tax credit is treated as a reduction of income tax expense in the year the credit is allowed. To illustrate, assume that a business acquired machinery in 1984 for $100,000, and the applicable investment tax credit rate was 10 percent. The federal income tax for 1984 is $75,000 reduced by an investment tax credit of $10,000 (10% of $100,000). The entry to record the federal income tax for 1984 would be:

Income Tax Expense	65,000	
Income Tax Payable		65,000
Recognition of income tax of $75,000 less investment tax credit of $10,000.		

Accounting for the investment tax credit was complicated by the tax provision requiring a reduction in asset basis equal to one-half the amount of investment tax credit. The FASB addressed this issue in an exposure draft and recommended that a deferred income tax credit be recognized at the time of initial recording of the investment tax credit under the flow-through method.[17] To illustrate, assume that the asset in the preceding example has a five-year useful life, and the income tax rate is 40 percent. If the FASB's proposed standard is adopted, the reduction in asset basis would be recognized as follows:

Income Tax Expense	67,000	
Deferred Income Tax		2,000*
Income Tax Payable		65,000

*Basis adjustment ($10,000 × .5) × tax rate (40%) = $2,000.

As the excess book depreciation is recognized for financial reporting purposes, the deferred tax credit will be amortized to income tax expense.

Deferred Method. Under the deferred method of accounting for the investment tax credit, the credit is viewed as a reduction of income tax expense over the life of the asset rather than in the year the credit is applied to the tax

[17]*Exposure Draft,* "Accounting for the Reduction in the Tax Basis of an Asset Caused by the Investment Tax Credit" (Stamford: Financial Accounting Standards Board, October 26, 1982).

liability. Using the information in the previous example, the entry to record income tax in 1984 under the deferred method would be:

Income Tax Expense	75,000	
Deferred Investment Tax Credit		10,000
Income Tax Payable		65,000

The following entry would be made each year to amortize the investment tax credit over the five-year life of the asset.

Deferred Investment Tax Credit	2,000	
Income Tax Expense		2,000

Investment Tax Credit Carryback and Carryforward. If in the preceding example the new machinery had cost $1,150,000, the investment tax credit would have been $115,000. However, only $67,500 of the credit could be applied against the $75,000 income tax liability because of the $25,000, 85% limitation. The remaining $47,500 would be available for carryback and carryforward treatment. Assume the business had the following income tax liability for the preceding three years:

Year	Income Tax Paid
1981	$10,000
1982	$ 5,000
1983	$30,000

Applying the limitation to each year, the investment tax credit carryback would result in the following tax refund:

1981	$10,000	
1982	5,000	
1983	29,250	($25,000 + 85% of $5,000)
Total refund	$44,250	

The remaining $3,250 ($47,500 − $44,250) would be available as a carryforward.

The entry in 1984 to record the refund receivable from the investment tax credit carryback would depend on whether the flow-through or deferred method were being used.

Flow-through method:

Income Tax Refund Receivable	44,250	
Adjustment of Prior Year's Income Tax Arising from Carryback of Investment Tax Credit*		44,250

*The first $7,500 could alternatively be used to reduce the 1984 income tax expense of $7,500 ($75,000 − $67,500 tax credit used for 1984). The balance could then be credited to this special revenue account.

Deferred method:

Income Tax Refund Receivable	44,250	
Deferred Investment Tax Credit		44,250
Deferred Investment Tax Credit	8,850	
Income Tax Expense		8,850
Amortization of deferred investment tax credit over 5 years.		

Carryforwards of investment tax credits, frequently referred to as **unused investment tax credits,** are not to be recognized as assets even if the realization of them is assured because of future income projections.[18] When they are recognized, the credit may be used to reduce income tax expense of the period, or it may be reported as a separate revenue item. Investment tax credit carryforwards are not required to be recognized as extraordinary items as are operating loss carryforwards.

To illustrate the carryforward, if in 1985 the company in the preceding example had income tax payable of $30,000 before applying the investment tax credit carryforward, the $3,250 carryforward would be recorded as follows under the two common recording methods:

Flow-through method:

Income Tax Expense	26,750	
Income Tax Payable		26,750
Tax liability, $30,000 – $3,250 = $26,750		

Deferred method:

Income Tax Expense	30,000	
Deferred Investment Tax Credit		3,250
Income Tax Payable		26,750

The existence of deferred income tax charges or credits can greatly complicate carryforward computations. Because of the complexities of these relationships, further discussion of this area is considered beyond the scope of this text.

Evaluation of Accounting Treatment of Investment Tax Credit

The Accounting Principles Board favored the deferred method and approved it in Opinion No. 2. Lack of support for this view among many prominent accountants led to the issuance in 1964 of Opinion No. 4 in which the Board accepted both methods, although still stating a preference for the deferred method. In 1968, a further attempt was made by the Accounting Principles Board to restore the deferred method as a single uniform method. Again, differences of opinion resulted in failure to adopt the original conclusions. In 1971, the Board once again made serious effort to restore the deferred method. However, they had to postpone such effort as a result of congressional action permitting the taxpayer to choose the method to be used in recognizing the benefit arising from the credit.

Good theoretical arguments can be presented for either of the methods. Those who advocate using the deferred method argue that the cost of the asset is effectively reduced by the investment credit, and the tax benefit should be spread over the acquired asset's useful life. This point of view is strengthened by the current tax requirement that a company must hold the asset for a specified period of time or return part of the allowed

---

[18] *Opinions of the Accounting Principles Board, No. 2,* "Accounting for the Investment Credit" (New York: American Institute of Certified Public Accountants, 1962) par. 21.

credit. Those who advocate using the flow-through method argue that the tax credit is in reality a tax reduction in the current period. They argue that tax regulations establish the tax liability each year, and that amount is the proper expense to match against current revenues. This latter treatment affects current income more and is favored by political leaders when the investment tax credit is being used to stimulate a sluggish economy.

It is unfortunate that this issue has become such a political item. It is an example of an area where there seems to be no justification for having two methods. It is difficult to see how different economic circumstances among companies would justify dual treatment. Uniformity in treatment of the investment tax credit is definitely preferable to the alternatives presently available under generally accepted accounting principles.

DISCLOSURE OF INCOME TAXES

As explained in the preceding sections, balance sheet accounts relating to income taxes are of two general types.

(1) Deferred charges and deferred credits relating to timing differences.
(2) Refunds of past taxes or offsets to future taxes from recognition of carrybacks and carryforwards of operating losses or investment credits.

The net amount of these balance sheet accounts should be separated between current and noncurrent categories. The deferred charge or deferred credit should be classified in the same way as are the accounts to which they relate. A deferred item is related to an asset or liability if reduction of the asset or liability causes the timing difference to reverse. Thus, if installment receivables are classified as a current asset, the deferred credit related to these receivables should be classified as a current item. Similarly, if an estimated provision for warranties is classified as a current liability, the deferred charge relating to this liability should also be classified as a current item. If deferred items are not related to an asset or liability, they should be classified according to the expected reversal date of the timing difference.[19]

The refund receivable from an operating loss or investment credit carryback should be classified according to the criteria presented in Chapter 5, i.e., current if collection is expected within one year or one operating cycle, whichever is longer; otherwise, noncurrent.

Income tax expense should be separated between tax on income before extraordinary or irregular items and the income tax related to these special items. The income tax expense on the income statement should clearly identify tax currently payable, the tax effects of timing differences, and the tax effect of operating losses. Normally, this information is contained in a note to the financial statements. In addition, the SEC requires a reconciliation of the differences between the statutory income tax rate and the effective rate

[19] *Statements of Financial Accounting Standards No. 37, op. cit.,* par. 4.

actually paid by the company. Frequently, there is a considerable difference between the two because of such items as permanent differences, investment credit and operating loss carrybacks and carryforwards, etc.

The following additional disclosure relating to income taxes is also required.

(1) Amount of any operating loss carryforward not recognized in the loss period, or any unused investment tax credit, together with expiration dates.
(2) Significant differences not already disclosed between pretax book income and taxable income.

An example of income tax disclosure is included in Note Twelve to the General Mills statements. This note separates the tax expense between federal taxes and the other taxes paid by the company to state, local, and foreign governments. It also discloses the effect of timing differences and identifies the principal causes of the differences. Finally, a reconciliation of the statutory rate and the actual rate paid is provided.

APPENDIX

INTRAPERIOD INCOME TAX ALLOCATION WITH GRADUATED RATES

Intraperiod income tax allocation was illustrated in the chapter assuming a single tax rate applied to all levels of income. As indicated earlier, however, U. S. corporate income tax rates are graduated and increase as income increases. If income before and after special items considered separately and in the aggregate exceeds the last rate break of $100,000, the tax applicable to the special items would simply be 46%, the highest rate. The lower tax rates are applied to the first $100,000 of income from continuing operations. If excluding the special items considered separately causes income to cross over the breaks, and if more than one special item exists, an allocation must be made between the items at a weighted average rate. If the special items are all gains or all losses, the allocation can be made by computing the tax effect of each special item considered separately, and then allocating the aggregate tax effect of the special items in proportion to the individual tax effects.[20]

To illustrate, assume the Martinez Company had pretax book income of $50,000 as follows:

---

[20]If some of the special items are gains and some are losses, a different allocation method is required. Although the FASB has not specifically described how such an allocation should be made, one method suggested for making it is described in an article by Kiger,, Wilcox and Williams, "Intraperiod Income Tax Allocation with Differential Rates," *Accounting Review* (July, 1977), pp. 716–720.

Income from continuing operations	$110,000
Loss on disposal of a business segment	(20,000)
Extraordinary loss	(40,000)
Pretax book income	$ 50,000

Applying the 1983 tax rates presented on page 761, the income tax expense is calculated as follows:

1st $25,000 @ 15%	$3,750
2nd $25,000 @ 18%	4,500
Tax on $50,000	$8,250

The aggregate income tax effect of the two special items would be computed as follows:

Income tax on $110,000 income from continuing operations:		
Income tax on first $100,000 of income	$25,750	
Income tax on incremental $10,000 @ 46%	4,600	$30,350
Less income tax on $50,000 income after special items		8,250
Aggregate income tax effect of special items		$22,100

The income tax effect of each special item considered separately as an adjustment to taxable income would be computed as follows:

Loss on disposal of a business segment, $20,000:	
Income tax on $70,000 income after adding back to pretax book income ($50,000) the $20,000 loss on disposal of business segment [$8,250 + .30($20,000)]	$14,250
Income tax expense on $50,000 taxable income	8,250
Income tax effect of loss on disposal of a business segment considered separately	$ 6,000
Extraordinary loss, $40,000:	
Income tax on $90,000 income after adding back to pretax book income ($50,000) the $40,000 extraordinary loss [$8,250 + $7,500 + .40($15,000)]	$21,750
Income tax on $50,000 taxable income	8,250
Income tax effect of extraordinary loss considered separately	$13,500

The total impact of the two items considered separately is $19,500 ($6,000 + $13,500), or $2,600 less than the aggregate income tax effect ($22,100 − $19,500). Therefore, the income tax allocation for reporting purposes must be made on a weighted average basis as follows:

Income tax allocation for loss on disposal of a business segment ($6,000 ÷ $19,500) × $22,100	$ 6,800
Income tax allocation for extraordinary loss ($13,500 ÷ $19,500) × $22,100	15,300
	$22,100

The journal entry to record the income tax expense for the year, assuming there are no timing differences, would be as follows:

Income Tax on Income from Continuing Operations	30,350	
Income Tax Reduction from Loss on Disposal of a Business Segment		6,800
Income Tax Reduction from Extraordinary Loss		15,300
Income Tax Payable		8,250

Sometimes the income tax rate for the different items may not be the same because of the income tax regulations. For example, items qualifying as capital gain items may be taxed at rates differing from the rate for income from normal operations. The capital gain rate should be used in making intraperiod income tax allocations for these items.

INTERPERIOD INCOME TAX ALLOCATION WITH CHANGE IN RATES

If income tax rates change over time, the change in rates must be accounted for in some manner, either currently or in the future. Under the currently accepted deferred method of interperiod tax allocation, the current income tax rate is used to determine the deferred charge or credit. No adjustment is made when tax rates change unless the item reverses itself as discussed later.

For each kind of timing difference under the deferred tax method, a company may choose to compute income tax expense on either an individual basis or for groups of transactions. Under the individual basis, any change in rates would be reflected as a gain or loss when the item is reversed. More commonly, similar timing differences are grouped. If similar timing differences are grouped, and if the income tax rate changes over time, income tax allocation under the group method may be accounted for by either the gross change or net change method. Under the **gross change method,** new timing differences arising in the current period are accrued at the current income tax rates and reversals of prior period timing differences are removed from the deferred accounts at the income tax rate reflected in the accounts at the beginning of the current period. This may be done using either a weighted average rate, or a specified rate based on a fifo flow. The gain or loss on the rate change is reflected in the current period. Under the **net change method,** the current income tax rate is applied to the net change in timing differences for the current period, and no gain or loss on rate change is reported currently. No more deferred tax can be amortized than was provided for a particular type of timing difference. Thus, until an item almost completely reverses, an adjustment for the change in rates may not be required. Once one of these methods is adopted, it should be consistently applied. If a change is made, it is subject to the principles of reporting accounting changes discussed in Chapter 21.

The following example illustrates the difference between the gross change and net change methods. Assume in the example on page 766 that the income tax rate in 1985 changed from 40% to 45%. Also assume the $25,000 depreciation was a net figure composed of equipment whose depreciation using the accelerated depreciation method exceeded the depreciation using the straight-line method by $60,000, and equipment whose depreciation had reversed and whose straight-line depreciation exceeded depreciation on the accelerated depreciation method by $35,000. The net excess of rent revenue earned over rent revenue received was composed of $30,000 rent revenue received in advance and $36,000 rent revenue earned during the period and received in the previous period.

Under the net change method, all the computations would be made using the 45% rate. No adjustment would be made currently for the change in rates, and none would ever be made unless the deferred income tax account was reduced to zero. The entry for 1985 would be as follows:

Income Tax Expense	58,500	
Deferred Income Tax—Rent Revenue		2,700
Deferred Income Tax—Depreciation		11,250
Income Tax Payable		44,550

Computation:
Income tax expense: 45% × $130,000 = $58,500
Deferred income tax—rent revenue: 45% × $6,000 = $2,700
Deferred income tax—depreciation: 45% × $25,000 = $11,250
Income tax payable: 45% × $99,000 = $44,550

Under the gross change method, new or originating balances would be added at the 45% rate; reversals would be deducted at the 1984 rate since only one prior year was involved. Weighted average or fifo may be used when multiple years exist. Thus, the computation for 1985 under the gross change method would be as follows:

Rent revenue timing differences:	
Originating in 1985 ($30,000 × .45)	$13,500
Reversing in 1985 ($36,000 × .40)	14,400
Net change in 1985	$ (900)
Depreciation timing differences:	
Originating in 1985 ($60,000 × .45)	$27,000
Reversing in 1985 ($35,000 × .40)	14,000
Net change in 1985	$13,000

The entry for 1985 would be as follows:

Income Tax Expense	58,450	
Deferred Income Tax—Rent Revenue		900
Deferred Income Tax—Depreciation		13,000
Income Tax Payable		44,550

Computation:
Income tax payable: $99,000 × .45 = $44,550

The debit to income tax, $58,450, is the net effect of the tax on current taxable income as adjusted by the effect of the change in rates. It can be compared to the $58,500 debited to income tax under the net method. The effect of the tax rate change, $50 in this example, could be reported separately; however, it is generally netted against income tax expense because of the immateriality of the rate change adjustment.

Because of its simplicity, the net change method is most commonly followed in practice, although both methods are currently acceptable.

INTERPERIOD INCOME TAX ALLOCATION WITH GRADUATED TAX RATES

The discussion of timing differences in the chapter assumed a single tax rate applied to all income items. This is referred to as the "short-cut" approach in the literature. As indicated earlier, the present federal income tax rates vary over the first $100,000 of income. In addition, special credits and other rate adjustments may cause the actual rate to differ from the normal published rates. When this occurs in practice, the total deferred credit or deferred charge is the difference between the tax expense computed at the actual rates without the timing differences and the tax expense computed with the timing difference included. If more than one timing difference exists and the timing differences cause income to cross over the differential rate levels, an allocation procedure similar to that used for intraperiod rates would be required. This method of allocation is known as the "with and without method." Because of the complexities that can be involved when a company has several timing differences and several different rate structures, only the short-cut approach is illustrated for interperiod income tax allocation.

QUESTIONS

1. What is meant by intraperiod income tax allocation?

2. Describe the entries that would be made in recognizing the income tax for the period in each of the following cases:

(a) There are earnings from ordinary operations and an extraordinary loss that is less than such earnings.

(b) There are earnings from ordinary operations and a credit to Retained Earnings for a correction of an error. An amended income tax return has been filed.

(c) There is a loss from ordinary operations, an extraordinary gain that is greater than the loss, and a debit for a correction of an error recorded directly to Retained Earnings. A claim for an income tax refund has been filed.

3. Accounting methods used by a company to determine income for reporting purposes frequently differ from those used to determine taxable income. What is the justification for these differences?

4. Distinguish between a timing difference and a permanent difference between taxable income and book income.

5. In accounting for timing differences between book and taxable income, what entries are made when (a) pretax book income is less than taxable income, and (b) pretax book income is more than taxable income? (c) What timing differences are most commonly found?

6. Under what circumstances will a Deferred Income Tax credit balance be reduced to zero? Why do most companies report an increasing balance in this account?

7. For each of the following situations, indicate whether or not interperiod income tax allocation would be required. Justify your answers.

(a) Undistributed earnings from investment accounted for under the equity method.
(b) Income tax refund from previous year.
(c) Bad debt reserve for a savings and loan association.
(d) Fine because of a violation of equal opportunity law.
(e) Depreciation using the ACRS method for tax purposes and straight-line on the books.
(f) Undistributed earnings from subsidiary to parent.
(g) Interest on municipal bonds.

8. How should deferred income taxes be classified and reported on the balance sheet?

9. How would the balance sheet account for deferred income tax differ if a company used the liability concept of interperiod income tax allocation as opposed to the deferred concept?

10. In applying the operating loss carryback and carryforward provisions, what order of application must be followed?

11. How are balances in a deferred income tax account affected by operating loss carrybacks and carryforwards?

12. What type of property is eligible for investment tax credit benefits?

13. What is meant by investment tax credit recapture?

14. Two methods of accounting are available for reporting investment tax credits. What are they, and how does the accounting differ between them?

15. What is an unused investment tax credit? What benefit, if any, is it to a company?

***16.** How is income tax allocated among the various classifications in the financial statements when tax rates are graduated?

***17.** The net change method of accounting for interperiod income tax allocation under the deferred concept is more generally followed than the gross change method. Since both were recognized as acceptable methods by the Accounting Principles Board, why has this preference developed?

*Questions to Appendix material.

DISCUSSION CASES

case 20-1 (What are deferred income taxes?) Sawyer Inc. is a new corporation that has just completed a highly successful first year of operation. Sawyer is a privately held corporation, but its president, Thomas B. Sawyer, has indicated that if the company continues to do as well for the next four or five years, it will go public. By all indications, the company should continue to be highly profitable on both a short-term and long-term basis.

The controller of the new company, Rebecca Hanley, plans on using the ACRS method of depreciating Sawyer's assets and using the installment sales method of recognizing income for tax purposes. For financial statement presentation, straight-line depreciation will be used and all sales will be fully recognized in the year of sale. There are no other differences between book and taxable income.

Sawyer has hired your firm to prepare its financial statements. You are now preparing the income statement. The controller wants to show, as "Income tax expense," the amount of the tax liability actually due. "After all," Hanley reasons, "that's the amount we'll actually pay, and in light of our plans for continued expansion, it's highly unlikely that the timing differences will ever reverse."

Draft a memo to the controller outlining your reaction to the plan. Give reasons in support of your decision.

case 20-2 (Should health of the economy govern GAAP?) Perhaps no issue has created more controversy and discussion in the accounting profession, business, and government than the investment tax credit. The government's involvement has been an intriguing one. The purpose of the investment tax credit has been to stimulate investment in new business property and thus promote a steady growth in the Gross National Product and avoid severe recession or depression. In order to have the most significant impact possible on a company's income, legislative officials who enacted the investment tax credit legislation indicated a preference for the flow-through method of accounting. Many people in the business community agree with this approach because of its favorable impact on reported income. Accounting theorists, on the other hand, argue that the deferred method of accounting for the credit is preferable because it reflects more clearly the economic reality of the credit. Evaluate these two positions. What role, if any, should public policy and the impact of accounting principles on the economy have upon the establishment of GAAP?

EXERCISES

exercise 20-1 (Intraperiod income tax allocation)

In 1984, the Berry Co. reported taxable operating income of $130,000 and a fully taxable extraordinary gain of $50,000. Assume an income tax rate for 1984 of 40% on all items. (1) Give the entry to record the income tax for 1984. (2) Assuming there was a fully deductible extraordinary loss of $50,000 rather than an extraordinary gain, give the entry to record the income tax for 1984.

exercise 20-2 (Intraperiod income tax allocation)

The Theobold Corporation reported the following income items before tax for the year 1984.

Income from continuing operations before income tax	$175,000
Loss from operations of a discontinued business segment	15,000
Gain from disposal of a business segment	20,000
Extraordinary gain on retirement of debt	100,000

The income tax rate is 40% on all items. Prepare the portion of the income statement beginning with "Income from continuing operations before income tax" for the year ended December 31, 1984, after applying proper intraperiod income tax allocation procedures.

exercise 20-3 (Identification of permanent and timing differences)

Indicate whether each of the following items is a timing difference or a permanent difference. For each timing difference, indicate whether it is a deferred credit or a deferred charge.

(a) Tax depreciation in excess of book depreciation, $200,000.
(b) Excess of income on installment sales over income reportable for tax purposes, $230,000.
(c) Premium payment for insurance policy on life of president, $50,000.
(d) Earnings of foreign subsidiary received in the current year but reported in a previous year, $150,000.
(e) Amortization of goodwill, $40,000.
(f) Rent collected in advance of period earned, $75,000.
(g) Actual expense for warranty repairs in excess of warranty provision for year, $50,000.
(h) Interest revenue received on municipal bonds, $20,000.

exercise 20-4 (Interperiod income tax allocation)

Using the information given in Exercise 3, and assuming a pretax book income of $1,680,000 and an income tax rate of 40%, calculate taxable income and give the entry to record income tax for the year. Your entry may "net" the various deferred income tax accounts into one account.

exercise 20-5 (Interperiod income tax allocation)

Billus Manufacturing Corporation reports taxable income of $645,000 on its income tax return for the year ended December 31, 1984. Timing differences between pretax book income and taxable income for the year are:

Book depreciation in excess of tax depreciation	$125,000
Accrual for product liability claims in excess of actual claims	105,000
Reported installment sales income in excess of taxable installment sales income	265,000

Assuming an income tax rate of 40%, compute the book income tax expense, deferred income tax, and income tax payable. Give the necessary journal entry to record these amounts. Use one deferred income tax account.

exercise 20-6 (Interperiod income tax allocation)

The Ritzert Co. shows pretax book income and taxable income for 1983 and 1984 as follows:

	Pretax Book Income	Taxable Income
1983	$140,600	$212,000
1984	$257,000	240,200

The differences arose because the company, organized on April 1, 1983, wrote off against revenue of that year organization costs totaling $84,000. For federal income tax purposes, however, the organization costs can be written off ratably over a period of not less than 60 months. For income tax purposes, then, the company deducted 9/60 of the costs in 1983 and 12/60 of the costs in 1984. Income tax is to be calculated at 40% of taxable income.

Give the entries that would be made on the books of the company at the end of 1983 and 1984 to recognize the income tax liability and to provide for a proper allocation of income tax in view of the differences in book and income tax reporting.

exercise 20-7 (Interperiod income tax allocation)

The Thunder Bay Mining Company reported pretax book income of $945,000 for the calendar year 1984. Included in the "Other income" section of the income statement was $100,000 of interest revenue from municipal bonds held by the company. The income statement also included depreciation expense of $450,000 for a machine that cost $4,000,000. The income tax return reported $800,000 as ACRS depreciation on the machine.

Prepare the journal entry necessary to record income tax for the year, assuming an income tax rate of 40%.

exercise 20-8 (Operating loss carryback)

The following historical financial data are available for the Rivira Manufacturing Company.

Year	Income	Tax Rate	Tax Paid
1981	$10,000	52%	$ 5,200
1982	25,000	48%	12,000
1983	35,000	44%	15,400

In 1984, the Rivira Company suffered a $75,000 net operating loss due to an economic recession. The company elects to use the carryback provision in the tax law.

(1) Using the information given, calculate the refund due arising from the loss carryback and the amount of the loss available to carryforward to future periods. Assume a 1984 tax rate of 40%. Also, assume that no adjustments need to be made to prior years' net income for purposes of the loss carryback and that there is no guarantee that future periods will be profitable.
(2) Give the entry necessary to record the refund due and the loss reduction.
(3) Using the answer from (1), prepare the bottom portion of the income statement reflecting the effect of the loss carryback on the 1984 statement.

exercise 20-9 (Investment tax credit)

Damons Plumbing Company purchased a new machine on January 1, 1983, for $200,000. The machine had a ten-year life and was depreciated by the straight-line method. Assuming a 10% investment tax credit, give the entries to record the recognition of tax for the first two years under (a) the flow-through method (assuming recognition of basis adjustment is not required) and (b) the deferred method. (Income tax before the credit in 1983 and 1984 was $265,000 and $157,000 respectively.)

exercise 20-10 (Investment tax credit)

The Dela Torre Corporation purchased a stamping press for $125,000 on January 1, 1984. The press has an estimated useful life of ten years and no salvage value. The corporation uses the straight-line method of depreciation. Assuming an income tax liability for the current year of $65,000 before the credit, give the entries to record income tax for 1984 using (a) the flow-through method and (b) the deferred method.

exercise 20-11 (Investment tax credit limitation)

The Medicine Hat Company was formed on April 1, 1984. It purchased the following equipment on the dates indicated:

Date Purchased	Equipment	Cost	Est. Useful Life	Date Placed in Service
April 30, 1984	Hat Former	$200,000	10 years	May 10, 1984
Aug. 1, 1984	Stitcher #1	$150,000	5 years	Aug. 15, 1984
Nov. 1, 1984	Boxer	$100,000	3 years	Nov. 7, 1984
Dec. 1, 1984	Stitcher #2	$150,000	5 years	Jan. 3, 1985

The investment tax credit rate was 10% for assets with recovery periods of 5 years or more and 6% for 3-year property. What is the total investment tax credit that Medicine Hat may claim for its tax year ending December 31, 1984, assuming the tax liability before the credit was $40,000?

exercise 20-12 (Investment tax credit recapture)

The Avery Corporation purchased a machine on April 30, 1981. The machine cost $24,000 and had an estimated useful life of ten years. The corporation discontinued the operations in which the machine was used, effective June 1, 1984. The machine was taken out of service at that time and sold shortly thereafter. Avery Corporation took the full amount of the investment tax credit in the year of the purchase. What amount of the credit must now be recaptured?

exercise 20-13 (Investment tax credit carryback and carryforward)

The Wabash Corporation's income tax liability for the year ended December 31, 1984, was $30,000. Investment tax credit available was $40,000. The income tax liability for the corporation for the past three years was: 1981—$4,000; 1982—$10,000; 1983—$20,000. Give the entries necessary to record the carryback of the investment tax credit. What is the amount of investment tax credit available for a carryforward to 1985?

*exercise 20-14 (Intraperiod income tax allocation—graduated rates)

Westport Company reported taxable income of $60,000 in 1984. Included in income were the following items:

Extraordinary loss	$40,000
Loss from discontinued operations	$20,000

The income tax rate for all items has five levels: 15% on the first $25,000 of income, 18% on the next $25,000 of income, 30% on the next $25,000 of income, 40% on the next $25,000 of income, and 46% on all income over $100,000. Based on these data, compute the income tax that would be allocated to income from continuing operations, the extraordinary loss, and the loss from discontinued operations, and make the required journal entries.

*exercise 20-15 (Intraperiod income tax allocation—graduated tax rates)

The Easthaven Manufacturing Company reported income from operations of $50,000, an extraordinary gain of $20,000, and a gain on disposal of a business segment of $30,000. The income tax rates are the same as those listed in Exercise 20-14. Based on these data, compute the intraperiod income tax allocation and give the proper journal entries to record the allocation.

*exercise 20-16 (Interperiod income tax allocation—gross and net methods)

The following historical information of the Kenora Corporation shows timing differences for the past three years along with their effects on deferred income tax.

Year	Timing Difference	Tax Rate	Deferred Income Tax (Credits)
1981	$ 4,000	48%	$1,920
1982	7,000	46%	3,220
1983	8,000	44%	3,520
	$19,000		$8,660

Pretax book income for 1984 was $95,000. The only timing difference for 1984 was broken down as follows:

*Exercises to Appendix material.

Originating timing differences—tax depreciation in excess of book depreciation—$16,000
Reversing timing differences—book depreciation in excess of tax depreciation—$7,000

The tax rate for 1984 is 40%.

(1) Using the gross change method, determine how much would be added to the deferred income tax liability and how much would be removed from it in 1984. Show the computation using both the fifo and the average rate methods.
(2) Using the net change method, determine the net change in the deferred income tax account for the 1984 transactions.

*exercise 20-17 (Interperiod income tax allocation—gross and net methods)

Nipigon Manufacturing Company's financial records disclosed the following historical information:

Year	Warranty Expense Accrual in Excess of Actual Expenditures	Tax Depreciation in Excess of Book Depreciation	Tax Rate	Deferred Tax
1981	$ 75,000	$150,000	48%	$ 36,000
1982	(25,000)	225,000	46%	115,000
1983	50,000	350,000	44%	132,000
	$100,000	$725,000		$283,000

In 1984, the pretax book income was $1,825,000. The timing differences for 1984 were as follows:

Originating timing differences:

Tax depreciation in excess of book depreciation	$600,000
Warranty expense accrued	65,000

Reversing timing differences:

Book depreciation in excess of tax depreciation	$200,000
Actual warranty expense	50,000

Using the 1984 tax rate of 40%, determine how much would be added to deferred income taxes:

(a) Under the gross change method, using both the fifo and the average rate methods, and,
(b) Under the net change method.

*Exercise to Appendix material.

PROBLEMS

problem 20-1 (Intraperiod income tax allocation)

Lethbridge Lithographing Inc. reported taxable income for the fiscal year ended October 31, 1984, of $775,000. Ordinary income tax rates were 40%. Included in the $775,000 was a gain of $95,000 properly classified as extraordinary. The gain was taxed at 25%. Also included in taxable income was a loss from the disposal of a business segment of $100,000. The loss was deductible from ordinary income. The annual audit disclosed a $75,000 overstatement in income of the previous year. An amended income tax return will be filed. The income tax rate on the refund will be 40%.

Instructions:

(1) Prepare journal entries to record the income tax liability, including proper intraperiod income tax allocation.
(2) Prepare the income statement for the fiscal year ending October 31, 1984, beginning with income from continuing operations before income tax.

problem 20-2 (Interperiod income tax allocation)

The Marathon Corporation accrued certain revenue on its books in 1982 and 1983 of $7,800 and $6,000 respectively, but such revenue was not subject to income tax until 1984. Pretax book income and taxable income for the three-year period are as follows:

	Pretax Book Income	Taxable Income
1982	$21,600	$13,800
1983	20,400	14,400
1984	14,400	28,200

Assume the income tax rate is 40% in each year.

Instructions: Give the entries that would be made at the end of each year to recognize the income tax liability and to provide for a proper allocation of income tax in view of the differences between pretax book income and taxable income.

problem 20-3 (Interperiod income tax allocation)

Income data of the Denny Company for the first five years of its operations are summarized below:

	1980	1981	1982	1983	1984
Sales	$1,000,000	$1,040,000	$1,120,000	$1,120,000	$1,200,000
Cost of goods sold	600,000	624,000	656,000	672,000	720,000
Gross profit on sales	$ 400,000	$ 416,000	$ 464,000	$ 448,000	$ 480,000
Operating expenses	160,000	168,000	184,000	176,000	192,000
Income before income tax	$ 240,000	$ 248,000	$ 280,000	$ 272,000	$ 288,000

Cost of goods sold includes depreciation on buildings and equipment items calculated by the straight-line method. However, for income tax purposes, the company employed the accelerated depreciation methods providing for higher charges in the early years of asset life and correspondingly lower charges in the later years. Depreciation charges on the books as compared with charges recognized for income tax purposes during the five-year period were as follows:

	1980	1981	1982	1983	1984
Depreciation per books	$132,000	$136,000	$136,000	$140,000	$140,000
Accelerated depreciation per tax return	216,000	180,800	144,000	124,000	100,000

All of the revenue of the company is taxable; all of the expenses are deductible for income tax purposes. Income tax rates in each year were 40%.

Instructions:

(1) Give the entries that would be made by the company for the years 1980 through 1984 to record the accrual of income tax if income is debited with income tax allocable to such income.
(2) Prepare comparative income statements for the Denny Company for the five-year period assuming the use of interperiod income tax allocation procedures.
(3) Prepare comparative income statements for the Denny Company for the five-year period assuming the interperiod income tax allocation procedures were not used and charges for income tax were recognized at the amounts actually becoming payable each year.

problem 20-4 **(Interperiod income tax allocation)**

The Brandon Corporation has taxable income of $2,035,000 for the year ended December 31, 1984. The controller is unfamiliar with the treatment of timing and permanent differences in reconciling taxable income to book income, and has requested your assistance. You are given the following list of differences.

Book depreciation in excess of tax depreciation	$300,000
Proceeds from life insurance policy upon death of officer	192,000
Unremitted earnings of foreign subsidiary, reported as income on the books. Remittance highly unlikely	140,000

Instructions: Using the above information:

(1) Compute pretax book income.
(2) Assuming an income tax rate of 40%, give the journal entry to record the income tax for the year.
(3) Prepare a partial income statement beginning with "Income from continuing operations before income tax."

problem 20-5 **(Interperiod income tax allocation)**

The Selkirk Manufacturing Company prepared the following reconciliation between taxable and book income for 1984:

Income per tax return	$3,300,000
Add excess depreciation taken on the tax return as compared with books	240,000
	$3,540,000
Less: Extraordinary gain on early extinguishment of debt	(180,000)
Estimated expenses of future warranties not allowable for tax purposes until expenses are actually incurred	(120,000)
Advance rent revenue taxable in period of receipt	(60,000)
Book income before income tax and extraordinary items	$3,180,000

A prior period adjustment of $3,000 for the correction of an error was debited directly against Retained Earnings. An income tax refund claim has been filed for this adjustment. Ordinary income tax rates apply.

Instructions:

(1) Assuming an ordinary income tax rate of 40%, prepare required journal entries to record the income tax liability at December 31, 1984.
(2) Prepare the income statement for 1984 beginning with "Income from continuing operations before income tax."

problem 20-6 **(Operating loss carryback and carryforward)**

The following data were taken from the financial statements of the Minot Company:

Year	Taxable and Book Income	Tax Rate	Income Tax Paid
1980	$ 8,000	40%	$3,200
1981	12,000	40%	4,800
1982	13,600	44%	5,984
1983	10,400	48%	4,992
1984	(40,000)	44%	0

The company elects to use the carryback provision in the tax law.

Instructions:

(1) Calculate the income tax refund due as a result of the 1984 operating loss.
(2) What is the amount, if any, of the operating loss carryforward?

(continued)

(3) (a) Assume the loss for 1984 was $28,000. Calculate the refund due and prepare the journal entry to record the claim for income tax refund.
(b) Assume in addition to (a) there was another loss in 1985 of $16,000. How much could be carried back and how much would be carried forward?

problem 20-7 (Operating loss carryback and carryforward)

The following financial history shows the income and losses for Eweson Corporation for the ten-year period 1975–1984.

Year	Income (Loss)	Tax Rate	Tax Paid
1975	$ 7,500	48%	$ 3,600
1976	9,000	48%	4,320
1977	10,500	44%	4,620
1978	(22,500)	44%	–0–
1979	6,000	44%	2,640
1980	(18,000)	46%	–0–
1981	15,000	46%	?
1982	30,000	40%	12,000
1983	(52,500)	40%	–0–
1984	60,000	40%	?

Assume that no adjustments to taxable income are necessary for purposes of the net operating loss carryback and the company elects to use the carryback provisions of the tax code. (Assume income tax provisions in effect for all years were as described in the text.)

Instructions:

(1) For each of the loss years, calculate the income tax refund due from the loss carryback and the amount of the carryforward (if any).
(2) For 1981 and 1984, calculate the amount of income tax paid, showing the benefit of the loss carryforward.
(3) For 1984, give the entry to record the income tax liability.
(4) For 1984, prepare the income statement beginning with "Income from continuing operations before income tax."

problem 20-8 (Operating loss carryback)

The Roylance Company had the following history of book and taxable income for the years 1981–1985. A 40% income tax rate is paid on all income.

Year	Pretax Book Income	Taxable Income	Income Tax Current	Expense Deferred	Cumulative Deferred Tax Credit
1981	$150,000	$120,000	$48,000	$12,000	$12,000
1982	120,000	100,000	40,000	8,000	20,000
1983	125,000	135,000	54,000	(4,000)	16,000
1984	(250,000)	(300,000)			
1985	(100,000)	(120,000)			

Instructions:

(1) Based on the above data, compute the amount of income tax refunds available in 1984 and 1985 for taxes paid 1981–1983. Assume the operating losses are 100% available to offset taxable and book income.
(2) Prepare the journal entries required at December 31, 1984 and 1985 to record the refund receivable and any necessary adjustment to the deferred tax account.

problem 20-9 (Investment tax credit)

On January 1, 1983, Home Grown Health Food Co. purchased a machine and the patent on the machine from Dean Equipment Co. for $900,000. An independent appraisal disclosed that the fair market value of the machine was $750,000 while the value of the patent was $250,000 on the date of acquisition. (Assume a 10 year life for the machine and a 15 year life for the patent. Taxes before a 10% investment credit in 1983 and 1984 are $755,000 and $1,450,000 respectively.)

Instructions: Give the entries to record the acquisition of the machine and patent, the recognition of tax for 1983 and 1984, and any amortization of deferred investment tax credits under both (1) the flow-through method (assuming recognition of basis adjustment is not required) and (2) the deferred method.

problem 20-10 (Investment tax credit)

The Plowman Foundry is a large manufacturer of home gardening and farming implements. Its net taxable income for the year ended December 31, 1984 was $400,000. The tax rate was 40%.

Plowman made the following investments in plant assets in 1984:

Item	Date Purchased	Cost	Estimated Useful Life	Date Placed in Service
Forge	2/23/84	$400,000	10 years	2/25/84
Welder	3/5/84	150,000	3 years	3/5/84
Metal Stamper #1	4/12/84	750,000	10 years	4/25/84
Storage Building	6/15/84	250,000	15 years	7/22/84
Delivery Trucks	8/14/84	300,000	3 years	8/21/84
Metal Stamper #2	11/2/84	730,000	10 years	11/26/84
Lathe	12/20/84	150,000	5 years	1/5/85

Plowman took advantage of the investment tax credit provisions which were as described on page 774 of the text.

Plowman was begun in 1981. It paid income tax since the year of its inception as follows:

Year	Tax Paid
1981	$12,500
1982	27,000
1983	30,000

Instructions:

(1) Using the above information, give the entries necessary to record the following:
  (a) The income tax liability for 1984, under the
    i) flow-through method of recording the investment tax credit (assuming recognition of basis adjustment is not required).
    ii) deferred method of recording the investment tax credit.
  (b) The amount of the refund of prior years' taxes due to the carryback of the investment tax credit.
  (c) The amount of the carryforward available.

(2) Assuming Plowman's 1985 taxable income was $500,000 (40% rate), and Plowman made no new purchases of Section 38 property in 1985, compute its income tax liability for 1985.

problem 20-11 (Comprehensive income tax problem)

The Mikis Company has supplied you with information regarding its 1984 income tax expense for financial statement reporting as follows:

(a) The provision for current income taxes (exclusive of investment tax credits) was $600,000 for the year ended December 31, 1984. Mikis made estimated tax payments of $550,000 during 1984.

(b) Investment tax credits of $100,000 arising from plant assets put into service in 1984 were taken for income tax reporting in 1984. Mikis defers investment tax credits and amortizes them to income over the productive life of the related assets for financial statement reporting. Unamortized deferred investment tax credits amounted to $400,000 at December 31, 1984, and $375,000 at December 31, 1983.

(c) Mikis generally depreciates plant assets using the straight-line method for financial statement reporting and the ACRS method for income tax reporting. During 1984, depreciation on plant assets amounted to $900,000 for financial statement reporting and $950,000 for income tax reporting. Commitments for the purchase of plant assets amounted to $450,000 at December 31, 1984. Such plant assets will be subject to an investment tax credit of 10%.
(d) For financial statement reporting, Mikis has accrued estimated losses from product warranty contracts prior to their occurrence. For income tax reporting, no deduction is taken until payments are made. At December 31, 1983, accrued estimated losses of $200,000 were included in the liability section of Mikis' balance sheet. Based on the latest available information, Mikis estimates that this figure should be 30% higher at December 31, 1984. Payments of $250,000 were made in 1984.
(e) In 1979, Mikis acquired another company for cash. Goodwill resulting from this transaction was $800,000 and is being amortized over a forty-year period for financial statement reporting. The amortization is not deductible for income tax reporting.
(f) Mikis has a wholly-owned foreign subsidiary. In 1984, this subsidiary had income before United States and foreign income taxes of $175,000 and a provision for taxes in its own country of $70,000. No earnings were remitted to Mikis in 1984. For United States income tax reporting, Mikis will receive a tax credit for $70,000 when these earnings are remitted. Mikis provides taxes on the unremitted earnings of this subsidiary for financial statement reporting.
(g) Premiums paid on officers' life insurance amounted to $80,000 in 1984. These premiums are not deductible for income tax reporting.
(h) Assume that the United States income tax rate was 48%.

Instructions:

(1) What amounts should be shown for (a) provision for current income taxes; (b) provision for deferred income taxes; and (c) investment tax credits recognized in Mikis' income statement for the year ended December 31, 1984? Show supporting computations in good form.
(2) Identify any information in the fact situation which was not used to determine the answer to (1) above and explain why this information was not used. (AICPA adapted)

*problem 20-12 (Intraperiod income tax allocation with graduated rates)

Industrial Computers reported the following in its income statement for the year ended December 31, 1984:

Income from continuing operations	$135,000
Extraordinary loss	45,000
Loss from discontinued operations	15,000
Loss from disposal of business segment	20,000
Gain from life insurance policy settlement upon death of President	45,000

The income tax rate is broken down into five tiers as follows:

1st	$25,000 of taxable income	15%
2d	$25,000 of taxable income	18%
3d	$25,000 of taxable income	30%
4th	$25,000 of taxable income	40%

Taxable income in excess of $100,000 is taxed at a flat rate of 46%.

Instructions: The controller of Industrial Computers has requested you, as the assistant controller, to prepare the intraperiod allocation necessary so that the tax impact of each item is properly reflected, and to prepare the necessary journal entries.

*problem 20-13 (Interperiod income tax allocation; gross and net methods)

You have been asked by the Spray-On Corp. to review their books and to indicate what effect income tax allocation procedures will have on their statements. The following reconciliations of book and taxable income are made available to you.

*Problems to Appendix material.

	1982	1983	1984
Reported book income before tax	$180,000	$270,000	$360,000
Add: Expense not deductible for tax purposes		90,000	
Excess of book depreciation over tax depreciation			30,000
Deferred revenue taxable in period of collection	48,000	42,000	24,000
	$228,000	$402,000	$414,000
Less: Excess of reported book income on installment sales over taxable income	(36,000)	(54,000)	(48,000)
Excess of tax depreciation over book depreciation	(36,000)	(12,000)	
Taxable income	$156,000	$336,000	$366,000

Instructions:

(1) Assume tax rates are 40% on taxable income for all years. For each of the three years prepare journal entries to record the income tax liability. Use separate deferred accounts for each type of timing difference.
(2) Assume the rate changed in 1984 to 44%. Prepare the journal entry to record the income tax liability for that year if the net change method is used.

*problem 20-14 (Interperiod income tax allocation; gross and net methods)

The books of Carlen Company for the year ended December 31, 1984, showed a pretax book income of $225,000. In computing the year's taxable income for federal income tax purposes, the following timing differences were taken into account:

(a) Originating timing differences:
   (1) Tax depreciation in excess of book depreciation, $18,000.
   (2) Installment sales income recognized in excess of income reported for tax purposes, $7,500.
(b) Reversing timing differences:
   (1) Book depreciation in excess of tax depreciation, $12,000.
   (2) Installment sales income reportable for tax purposes in excess of income recognized on the books, $10,500.

The income tax rate was reduced on January 1, 1984, from 44% to 40%. Prior to that date it was 44%, which was the rate in effect when the Carlen Company was organized.

Instructions:

(1) Using the net change method, calculate: (a) income tax payable, (b) the change in the deferred income tax account, and (c) income tax debit to operating income.
(2) Calculate each of the above items using the gross change method.

*Problem to Appendix material.

21 NONOPERATING INCOME COMPONENTS AND SUPPLEMENTAL DISCLOSURES

CHAPTER OBJECTIVES

Identify the major nonoperating components of income.

Discuss the reporting problems associated with discontinued operations, extraordinary items, and accounting changes.

Provide a comprehensive illustration of reporting income components.

Discuss interim reporting, segment reporting, forecasts, and related party disclosures.

The importance of measuring and reporting business income was established in Chapter 4. Information on past earnings as a measure of overall managerial performance and as an indicator of future earnings potential is useful to investors, creditors, and others. To be most beneficial, the major components of income should be clearly identified. As explained in Chapter 4, appropriate distinctions should be made between the results of ongoing central activities and the results of peripheral and incidental transactions or events that are unusual or unrelated to the normal operations of a particular business. Operating revenues and expenses result from the ongoing central activities; other revenues and expenses as well as gains and losses may result from peripheral and incidental transactions or events. All these income components are included in income from continuing operations.

A further distinction should be made between income from continuing operations and the nonoperating components of income, sometimes called **below-the-line items.** These items include all material income components listed separately after income from continuing operations. In Chapter 4, the income statement was discussed primarily from the perspective of operating income. In this chapter, the additional income components and supplementary disclosures associated with reporting income are explained.

NONOPERATING COMPONENTS OF INCOME

The main categories of nonoperating components of income are: (1) discontinued operations, (2) extraordinary items, and (3) accounting changes. As shown below, each of these items is reported as a separate component of income after income from continuing operations. The amounts are reported net of tax, as discussed in Chapter 20. Each of these categories is explained in the sections that follow.

Major Income Components

Ongoing Central Activities	Operating revenues	$XXX
	Operating expenses	XXX
	Operating income	**$XXX**
Peripheral and Incidental Transactions or Events	Other revenues and expenses	XXX
	Gains and losses	XXX
	Income from continuing operations before taxes	**$XXX**
	Income taxes	XXX
	Income from continuing operations	**$XXX**
	Below-the-line items:	
Nonoperating Income Components	Discontinued operations (net of tax)	XXX
	Extraordinary items (net of tax)	XXX
	Cumulative effect of change in accounting principle (net of tax)	XXX
	Net income	**$XXX**

Discontinued Operations

Occasionally, the management of a company will decide to discontinue or sell part of the business. The segment of the company to be disposed of may be a product line, a division, or a subsidiary company. Management may decide to dispose of the segment because it is unprofitable, it is too isolated geographically, it does not fit into future company plans, or any number of other reasons. Regardless of the reason, the discontinuance of a substantial portion of company operations is a significant event. Therefore, information about **discontinued operations** should be presented explicitly to readers of financial statements.

In APB Opinion No. 30, the Board indicated that the results of operating a business segment that has been or is expected to be discontinued should be reported as a separate component of income after income from continuing operations but before extraordinary items and the cumulative effect of accounting changes. The Board further concluded "that any gain or loss from disposal of a segment of a business . . . should be reported in conjunction with the related results of discontinued operations and not as an extraordinary item."[1]

[1] *Opinions of the Accounting Principles Board, No. 30,* "Reporting The Results of Operations" (New York: American Institute of Certified Public Accountants, 1973), par. 8.

Note that there are two aspects of the disclosure requirements for discontinued operations: (1) separate disclosure of the current year income or loss from operating the discontinued segment, and (2) disclosure of the gain or loss on the actual disposal of the business segment. To illustrate, assume the WhitCo Manufacturing Co. decides to discontinue its home furnishing division. During 1984, company income from continuing operations was $750,000, but the home furnishing division lost $40,000. The division was sold at the end of the year at a loss of $70,000. Assuming a tax rate of 40%, the partial income statement for WhitCo for 1984 should disclose the following:

Income from continuing operations		$750,000
Discontinued operations (Note X):		
Loss from operations of discontinued business segment (net of $16,000 tax reduction on loss)	$24,000	
Loss on disposal of business segment (net of $28,000 tax reduction on loss)	42,000	66,000
Net income		$684,000

Sometimes a company will decide to dispose of a business segment on a particular date, the plan date, but will have a phase-out period between that date and the disposal date, the date of sale when the gain or loss on disposal is recognized. If such circumstances exist, the gain or loss on disposal should be offset by the income or loss from operations during the phase-out period. For example, assume in the previous example that WhitCo adopted a plan to dispose of its home furnishing division on January 1, 1984. Assume further that WhitCo sold its division on July 1, 1984, at a $100,000 gain. Due to the 6-month phase-out period, the loss from operating the division during this period would be offset against the gain on disposal, all net of tax. The gain or loss from operating the discontinued segment for the prior period would also be reported, assuming comparative statements were presented.

In accounting for discontinued operations, the disposal of a business segment should be distinguished from the disposal of assets that do not represent a major segment of the business. To qualify as a business segment, the particular assets and related activities must be clearly distinguishable from the other assets, operating results, and general activities of the company, both physically and operationally, as well as for financial reporting purposes. For example, the disposal of assets incidental to the normal evolution of the entity's business would not qualify as a disposal of a business segment. Neither would the disposal of part but not all of a line of business qualify as a disposal of a business segment, nor the shifting of the production or marketing functions from one location to another, the phasing out of a product line or loss of service, or other changes caused by technological advancements.[2] Any gain or loss from the disposal of assets not qualifying as a business segment should be reported as a part of continuing operations, not as a below-the-line item.

[2] *Ibid.*, par. 13.

The reporting of discontinued operations can become complex. Only a summary of the guidelines provided by APB Opinion No. 30 is covered here. Application of the guidelines requires judgment. The goal should be to report information that will assist external users in assessing future cash flows by clearly distinguishing normal, recurring earnings patterns from those activities that are irregular yet significant in assessing the total company results of operations.

Extraordinary Items

Extraordinary items, another category of below-the-line items, were briefly introduced in Chapter 4. The Accounting Principles Board recognized that the distinction between ordinary operating items and extraordinary items will require the use of judgment by an accountant. To assist accountants in making the distinction, the Board established certain criteria that must be met before an item should be classified as extraordinary. In Accounting Principles Board Opinion No. 30, the APB provided more definitive criteria for extraordinary items and clarified and modified to some extent the existing criteria originally established in APB Opinion No. 9.

Extraordinary items, according to APB Opinion No. 30, are events and transactions that are both **unusual** in nature and **infrequent** in occurrence. Thus, to qualify as extraordinary, an item must "possess a high degree of abnormality and be of a type clearly unrelated to, or only incidentally related to, the ordinary and typical activities of the entity . . . [and] be of a type that would not reasonably be expected to recur in the foreseeable future."[3] In addition, the item must be **material** in amount.

The overall effect of APB Opinion No. 30 is to severely restrict the items that should be classified as extraordinary. The Board offers certain examples of gains and losses that should *not* be reported as extraordinary items. They include: (1) the write-down or write-off of receivables, inventories, equipment leased to others, or intangible assets; (2) the gains or losses from exchanges or translation of foreign currencies, including those relating to major devaluations and revaluations; (3) the gains or losses on disposal of a segment of a business; (4) other gains or losses from sale or abandonment of property, plant, or equipment used in the business; (5) the effects of a strike; (6) the adjustment of accruals on long-term contracts.

On the other hand, according to the FASB, at least one item—a gain or loss from extinguishment of debt—is to be reported as an extraordinary item regardless of the criteria stated in APB Opinion 30.[4] This was discussed earlier in Chapter 14.

The reporting of extraordinary items should be rare due to the restrictive criteria of APB Opinion No. 30. However, when an extraordinary item is identified as such, it should be reported as a separate item below income

---

[3] *Ibid.*, par. 20.

[4] *Statement of Financial Accounting Standards No. 4.* "Reporting Gains and Losses from Extinguishment of Debt" (Stamford: Financial Accounting Standards Board, 1975).

from continuing operations. Generally, it should be shown after the information reporting the results of discontinued operations but before net income. Extraordinary items should always be shown net of tax, and, as will be explained in Chapter 22, should have a related earnings per share figure disclosed. The comprehensive illustration on page 808 shows a proper reporting format.

Items that are either unusual in nature or that occur infrequently, but do not meet both criteria, should not be classified as extraordinary items. These items may be included in other categories comprising operating income or, if material, separately disclosed as an other revenue or expense item or in the gains and losses section prior to income from continuing operations. Examples of these items include damage settlements, strike-related costs, obsolete inventory write-downs, and fire losses.

Accounting Changes

As has been pointed out, a major objective of published financial statements is to provide users with information to help them predict, compare, and evaluate future earning power and cash flows to the reporting entity. When a reporting entity adjusts its past estimates of revenues earned or costs incurred, changes its accounting principles from one method to another, changes its nature as a reporting entity, or corrects past errors, it becomes more difficult for a user to predict the future from past historical statements. Is it better to record these changes and error corrections as adjustments of the prior periods' statements and thus increase their comparability with the current and future statements, or should the changes and error corrections affect only the current and future years?

At least four alternative procedures have been suggested as solutions for reporting accounting changes and correction of errors.

(1) Restate the financial statements presented for prior periods to reflect the effect of the change or correction. Adjust the beginning Retained Earnings balance for the current period for the cumulative effect of the change or correction.

(2) Report the cumulative effect of the change or correction in the current year
  (a) as a special item in the income statement.
  (b) as a direct entry to Retained Earnings.
  Make no adjustment to statements presented for prior periods.

(3) Report the cumulative effect in the current year as in (2a), but also present limited pro forma information for all prior periods included in the financial statements reporting "what might have been" if the change or correction had been made in the prior years.

(4) Make the change effective only for current and future periods with no catch-up adjustment. Correct errors only if they still affect the statements.

Each of these alternative methods for reporting an accounting change or correcting an error has been used by companies in the past, and arguments can be made for the various approaches. For example, some accountants argue that accounting principles should be applied consistently for all reported periods. Therefore, if a new accounting principle is used in the current period, the financial statements presented for prior periods should be restated so that the results shown for all reported periods are based on the same accounting principles. Other accountants contend that restating financial statements may dilute public confidence in those statements. Principles applied in earlier periods were presumably appropriate at that time and should be considered final. The only exceptions would be for changes in a reporting entity or for corrections of errors. In addition, restating financial statements is costly, requires considerable effort, and is sometimes impossible due to lack of data.

Because of the diversity of practice and the resulting difficulty in user understandability of the financial statements, the Accounting Principles Board issued Opinion No. 20 to bring increased uniformity to reporting practice.[5] Only two-thirds of the Board approved the opinion, the minimum required. This indicates the degree of divergence in views concerning this matter. Evidence of compromise exists in the final opinion, as the Board attempted to reflect both its desire to increase comparability of financial statements and to improve user confidence in published financial statements.

The Accounting Principles Board defined three types of accounting changes: (1) change in an accounting estimate; (2) change in an accounting principle; and (3) change in the reporting entity. In addition, the Board made recommendations for reporting a correction of a past error, although they did not classify error corrections as accounting changes.

The proper accounting for a change in estimate has already been discussed in Chapter 4 and throughout the text in areas where changes of estimates are common. By way of review, all changes in estimates should be reflected either in the current period or in the current and future periods. No retroactive adjustment or pro forma statements are to be prepared for a change in estimate. These adjustments are considered to be part of the normal accounting process and not changes of past periods.

In Chapter 18 it was noted that errors should be corrected as soon as they are discovered. If discovered in the current period, corrections should be made through adjustments to the current accounts. If errors are discovered in subsequent years and are material in amount, they must be corrected as prior period adjustments directly to Retained Earnings. Such adjustments occur infrequently.

Changes in accounting principles and a change in the reporting entity present additional problems as discussed in the following sections.

Change in Accounting Principles.[6] As indicated in previous chapters, companies may select among several alternative accounting principles to account for a business transaction. For example, a company may depreciate

[5] *Opinions of the Accounting Principles Board, No. 20,* "Accounting Changes" (New York: American Institute of Certified Public Accountants, 1971).

[6] The classification "change in accounting principle" includes changes in methods used to account for transactions. No attempt was made by the Accounting Principles Board in Opinion No. 20 to distinguish between a principle and a method.

its buildings and equipment using the straight-line depreciation method, the double-declining-balance method, the sum-of-the-years-digits method, or any other consistent and rational allocation procedure. Long-term construction contracts may be accounted for by the percentage-of-completion or the completed-contract method. The investment tax credit may be accounted for by the flow-through method or the deferred method. These alternative methods are often equally available to a given company but in most instances criteria for selection among the methods is inadequate. As a result, companies have found it rather easy to justify changing from one method to another.

Changes in accounting principles frequently have a significant impact on financial statements. In recent years, some large corporations have increased reported earnings by millions of dollars solely as a result of changing the accounting principles or methods employed. Readers of financial statements need to be aware of the impact of these changes on reported earnings.

Current Recognition of Cumulative Effect. The APB concluded that, in general, companies should not change their accounting principles from one period to the next. "Consistent use of accounting principles from one period to another enhances the utility of financial statements to users by facilitating analysis and understanding of comparative accounting data."[7] However, a company may change its accounting principles if it can justify a change because of a new pronouncement by the authoritative accounting standard-setting body, or because of a change in its economic circumstances. Just what constitutes an acceptable change in economic circumstances is not clear. However, it presumably could include a change in the competitive structure of an industry, a significant change in the rate of inflation in the economy, a change resulting from government restrictions due to economic or political crisis, and so forth.

In general, the effect of a change from one accepted accounting principle to another is reflected by reporting the cumulative effect of the change in the income statement in the period of the change. This cumulative adjustment is shown as a separate item on the income statement after extraordinary items and before net income. The financial statements for all prior periods reported for comparative purposes with the current year financial statements are presented as previously reported. However, to enhance trend analysis, pro forma income information is also required wherever possible to reflect the income before extraordinary items and net income that would have been reported if the new accounting principle had been in effect for the respective prior years. The pro forma information should include not only the direct effects of the change in method, but also the indirect effect of any nondiscretionary adjustment that would have been necessary if the new principle had been in effect for the prior periods. The indirect adjustments include items such as bonuses, profit sharing, or royalty agreements based on income. Related tax effects should be recognized for both direct and indirect adjustments. Pro forma earnings per share figures should also be reported.

---

[7] *Opinions of the Accounting Principles Board, No. 20, op. cit.*, par. 15.

The **cumulative effect of a change in accounting principle** must usually be adjusted for the effect of interperiod tax allocation. The change is often from a method that was used for both tax and reporting purposes to a different method for reporting purposes. Retroactive changes in methods for tax purposes are generally not permitted. Thus, the current income tax payable is usually not affected by the change; however, an adjustment is usually necessary to the deferred income tax account. For example, if a company has been using an accelerated method of depreciation for both reporting and tax purposes but changes to the straight-line method for reporting purposes, the tax effect should be reflected as a reduction in the cumulative change account and as a credit to Deferred Income Tax. If the change for reporting purposes is to a method used for tax purposes, the books and the tax return would be in agreement after the change; and previously recorded amounts in Deferred Income Tax would be reversed. An exception to the above situations arises when the change is made from lifo inventory to another method. This is because the income tax regulations require consistency between the books and the tax return whenever lifo inventory is involved. Thus, a change on the books must also be made on the tax return. Any additional tax arising from the change must be paid, although the income tax regulations provide for some spreading of the liability over several future years.

To illustrate the general treatment of a change in accounting principle, assume Hardware Company elected in 1984 to change from an accelerated method of depreciation used for both reporting and tax purposes to the straight-line method to bring its reporting practice in agreement with the majority of its competitors. The income tax rate is 40%, and the company pays a 20% management bonus on operating income before tax. The following information was gathered reflecting the impact of the change on net income.

		Effect of Change	
Year	*Excess of Accelerated Depreciation Over Straight-Line Depreciation*	*Direct Effect Less Tax (40% Tax Rate)*	*Direct and Indirect Effect After 20% Management Bonus, Pro Forma Data*
Prior to 1979	$ 80,000	$ 48,000 [.60($80,000)]*	$ 38,400 {.60[$80,000 − .20($80,000)]}
1979	25,000	15,000 [.60($25,000)]	12,000 {.60[$25,000 − .20($25,000)]}
1980	30,000	18,000 [.60($30,000)]	14,400 {.60[$30,000 − .20($30,000)]}
1981	28,000	16,800 [.60($28,000)]	13,440 {.60[$28,000 − .20($28,000)]}
1982	22,000	13,200 [.60($22,000)]	10,560 {.60[$22,000 − .20($22,000)]}
1983	25,000	15,000 [.60($25,000)]	12,000 {.60[$25,000 − .20($25,000)]}
	$210,000	$126,000	$100,800

*The direct effect could be computed as $80,000 − .40($80,000), or simply as the complement of the tax rate .60($80,000). The complement computation is used in this illustration.

The net income for prior years as originally reported was:

1979	$350,000	1982	$450,000
1980	400,000	1983	500,000
1981	410,000		

The partial income statement for 1984, the year of the change, would report the $126,000 after-tax, direct effect as a separate item after any extraordinary items as follows:

Income from continuing operations	$560,000
Extraordinary gain on refunding of long-term debt (less applicable income tax of $60,000)	90,000
Cumulative effect on prior years of changing from accelerated depreciation to the straight-line method (less applicable income tax of $84,000)	126,000
Net income	$776,000

In addition to the above disclosure, pro forma income information would be disclosed by adding both direct and indirect effects to the net income as originally reported. These pro forma income amounts would be included on the face of the income statements reported.

	Pro Forma Income Data				
	1983	1982	1981	1980	1979
Net income as previously reported	$500,000	$450,000	$410,000	$400,000	$350,000
Effect of change in principle—direct and indirect	12,000	10,560	13,440	14,400	12,000
Pro forma net income	$512,000	$460,560	$423,440	$414,400	$362,000

Revised earnings per share figures would also be computed and disclosed reflecting the revised net income amounts. It is recognized that in rare instances, past records are inadequate to prepare the pro forma statements for individual years. This fact should be disclosed when applicable. For example, a change to the lifo method of inventory valuation is usually made effective with the beginning inventory in the year of change rather than with some prior year because of the difficulty in identifying prior year layers or dollar value pools. Thus, the beginning inventory in the year of change is the same as the previous inventory valued at cost, and this becomes the base lifo layer. No cumulative effect adjustment is required.

Restatement of Prior Periods. The APB generally favored the reporting procedures described in the preceding section. However, the Board identified three specific changes in accounting principle and one general condition change as being of such a nature that the "advantages of retroactive treatment in prior period reports outweigh the disadvantages."[8] These special exceptions are:

(1) Change from lifo method of inventory pricing to another method.
(2) Change in the method of accounting for long-term construction contracts.
(3) Change to or from the "full cost" method of accounting used in the extractive industries.
(4) Changes made at the time of an initial distribution of company stock.[9]

[8] *Ibid.*, par. 27.

[9] This exception is available only once for a company, and may be used whenever a company first issues financial statements for (a) obtaining additional equity capital from investors, (b) effecting business combinations, or (c) registering securities, *Ibid.*, par. 29.

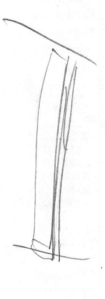

In these cases, the APB required the cumulative effect of the change to be recorded directly as an adjustment to the beginning Retained Earnings balance and all prior income statement data reported for comparative purposes to be adjusted to reflect the new principle. No justification was given by the Board for selecting these items for special treatment; however, these items usually would be material and data would generally be available to adjust the prior years' statements.

To illustrate the exceptions, assume that the Weiss Company compiles the following information concerning its change in 1984 from the completed-contract method of valuing long-term construction contracts to the percentage-of-completion method. The assumed tax rate is 40%.

Year	Net Income—Completed-Contract Method	Net Income—Percentage-of-Completion Method
1979	$ 20,000	$ 45,000
1980	60,000	70,000
1981	80,000	75,000
1982	75,000	110,000
1983	90,000	85,000
Total at beginning of 1984	$325,000	$385,000

The retained earnings statement for 1984 would reflect the effect of the change on prior years as follows:

Weiss Company
Retained Earnings Statement
For Year Ended December 31, 1984

Retained earnings, January 1, 1984, as previously reported	$ 900,000
Add adjustment for the cumulative effect on prior years of applying retroactively the percentage-of-completion method of accounting for long-term construction contracts as opposed to the completed-contract method (less applicable income tax of $40,000)	60,000
January 1, 1984, balance, as adjusted	$ 960,000
Add net income per income statement	660,000
	$1,620,000
Deduct dividends declared	400,000
Retained earnings, December 31, 1984	$1,220,000

All prior period income statements presented for comparative purposes would be adjusted to the amounts that would have been reported using the new principle. If the prior statements could not be adjusted because of inadequate data, this fact should be disclosed and the cumulative impact would be reported only on the retained earnings statement. No pro forma information is required for these exceptions because the prior periods' statements are changed directly; however, full disclosure of the effect of the change should be made for all periods presented. The earnings per share data would be recomputed taking into consideration any impact the new income amount would have on the computations.

If comparative retained earnings statements are prepared for 1983 and 1984, the cumulative adjustment to beginning retained earnings for each reported year would reflect only those years prior to that particular year. Thus, in the example, the 1983 beginning retained earnings balance would be adjusted by $65,000, the difference in net income under the two methods for the years 1979-1982 ($300,000 – $235,000).

If a change in accounting principle is caused by a new pronouncement of an authoritative accounting body, the cumulative effect may be reported retroactively or currently, depending on the instructions contained in the pronouncement. Even though APB Opinion No. 20 supports current recognition of the cumulative effect in most cases, many FASB Statements require retroactive restatement.

If an asset is affected by both a change in principle and a change in estimate during the same period, APB Opinion No. 20 requires that the change be treated as a change in estimate rather than a change in principle.[10] For example, if a company changes its depreciation method at the same time it recognizes a change in estimated asset life, this would involve both a change in method and a change in estimate. According to APB Opinion No. 20, such circumstances would be treated as a change in estimate.

Change in Reporting Entity. Companies sometimes change their nature or report their operations in such a way that the financial statements are in effect those of a different reporting entity. These changes include: (a) presenting consolidated or combined statements in place of statements of individual companies; (b) changing specific subsidiaries comprising the group of companies for which consolidated statements are presented; (c) changing the companies included in combined financial statements; and (d) a business combination accounted for as a pooling of interest.[11]

Because of the basic objective of preparing statements that assist in predicting future cash flows, the APB recommended that financial statements be adjusted retroactively to disclose what the statements would have looked like if the current entity had been in existence in the prior years. Of course, this requirement assumes that the companies acting as a unit would have made the same decisions as they did while acting alone. While this assumption is probably invalid, the retroactive adjustment will probably come closer to providing useful information for trend analysis than would statements clearly noncomparable because of the different components of the entity.

In the period of the change, the financial statements should describe the nature and reason for the change. They should also clearly show the effect of the change on income from continuing operations, net income, and the related earnings per share amounts for all periods presented. Subsequent years' statements do not need to repeat the disclosure.[12]

[10] *Opinions of the Accounting Principles Board, No. 20, op. cit.*, par. 32.
[11] *Ibid.*, par. 12.
[12] *Ibid.*, par. 35.

Summary of Accounting Changes and Correction of Errors. The following summary presents the appropriate accounting procedures applicable to each of the four main categories covered in APB Opinion No. 20. Naturally, accountants must apply these guidelines with judgment and should seek to provide the most relevant and reliable information possible.

Summary of Procedures for Reporting Accounting Changes and Corrections of Errors

Category	*Accounting Procedures*
I. Change in estimate	1. Adjust only current period results or current and future periods. 2. No separate, cumulative adjustment or restated financial statements. 3. No pro forma disclosure needed.
II. Change in accounting principle	
a. Current recognition of cumulative effect	1. Adjust for cumulative effect, i.e., a "catch-up" adjustment in current period as special item in income statement. 2. No restated financial statements. 3. Pro forma data required showing income and EPS information for all periods presented.
b. Restatement of prior periods	1. Direct cumulative adjustment to beginning Retained Earnings balance. 2. Restate financial statements to reflect new principle for comparative purposes. 3. No pro forma information required because prior period statements are changed directly.
III. Change in reporting entity	1. Restate financial statements as though new entity had been in existence for all periods presented.
IV. Error correction	1. If detected in period error occurred, correct accounts through normal accounting cycle adjustments. 2. If detected in a subsequent period, adjust for effect of material errors by prior period adjustments directly to Retained Earnings.

Comprehensive Illustration

To summarize the reporting of income, a comprehensive illustration for the Tillson Company is presented on the following page. The sections shown relate to the operating income components and the nonoperating components or below-the-line items discussed in this chapter and Chapter 4. It is unlikely that all the elements illustrated would be present in any one year for a company. They are shown here for completeness and illustrative purposes. The earnings per share amounts are also presented for the same reasons even though the EPS computations are not covered in detail until Chapter 22.

Tillson Company
Income Statement
For Year Ended December 31, 1984

Sales			$1,000,000
Cost of goods sold			600,000
Gross profit on sales			$ 400,000
Operating expenses:			
Selling expenses		$120,000	
General and administrative expenses		191,000	311,000
Operating income			$ 89,000
Other revenues and expenses:			
Interest revenue	$ 6,000		
Dividend revenue	4,000	$ 10,000	
Less interest expense		5,000	5,000
Gain on sale of investment			6,000
Income from continuing operations before income taxes			$ 100,000
Income taxes (Note X)			40,000
Income from continuing operations			$ 60,000
Discontinued operations:			
Income from operations of discontinued division (less applicable income tax of $8,360)		$ 12,540	
Gain on disposal of division (less applicable income tax of $5,820)		8,730	21,270
Extraordinary gain (less applicable income tax of $1,200)			1,800
Cumulative effect on prior years of a change in accounting principle (less applicable income tax of $2,480)			3,720
Net income			$ 86,790
Earnings per common share (50,000 shares outstanding):			
Income from continuing operations			$1.20
Income from discontinued operations			.43
Extraordinary gain			.04
Cumulative effect of change in accounting principle			.07
Net income			$1.74

INCOME-RELATED SUPPLEMENTAL DISCLOSURES

So far this chapter has emphasized the reporting of nonoperating income components. In addition to these items, there are several income-related disclosures that may assist readers of financial statements in assessing a company's operating results. The remaining sections of the chapter cover four topics: (1) interim reporting, (2) segment reporting, (3) forecasting, and (4) related party disclosures.

Interim Reporting

Statements showing financial position and operating results for intervals of less than a year are referred to as **interim financial statements.** Interim reports are considered essential in providing investors and others with more timely information as to the position and progress of an enterprise. This information is most useful in comparative form because of the relationship it shows to data for similar reporting intervals and to data in the annual report.

Notwithstanding the need for interim reports, there are significant difficulties associated with them. One problem is caused by the seasonal factors of certain businesses. For example, in some companies, revenues fluctuate widely among interim periods; in other businesses, significant fixed costs are incurred during a single period but are to benefit several periods. Not only must costs be allocated to appropriate periods of benefit, but they must be matched against the realized revenues for the interim period to determine a reasonable income measurement.

In preparing interim reports, adjustments for accrued items, generally required only at year end, have to be considered at the end of each interim period. Because of the additional time and extra costs involved to develop complete information, many estimates of expenses are made for interim reports. The increased number of estimates adds an element of subjectivity to these reports.

Another problem is that extraordinary items or the disposal of a business segment will have a greater impact on an interim period's earnings than on the results of operations for an entire year. In analyzing interim financial statements, special attention should be given to these and similar considerations.

Partially because of some of the above problems and partially because of differing views as to the objective of interim reports, there has been a variety of practices in presenting interim financial information. Two prominent viewpoints exist. One viewpoint is that each reporting interval is to be recognized as a separate accounting period. Thus, the results of operations for each interim period are determined in essentially the same manner as for the annual accounting period. Under this approach, the same judgments, estimations, accruals, and deferrals are recognized at the end of each interim period as for the annual period.

The other viewpoint, and the one accepted by the APB in Opinion No. 28, is that the interim period is an integral part of the annual period.[13] Essentially, the revenues and expenses for the total period are allocated among interim periods on some reasonable basis, e.g., time, sales volume, or productive activity.

Under the **integral part of annual period concept,** the same general accounting principles and reporting practices employed for annual reports are to be utilized for interim statements, except modifications may be required so the interim results will better relate to the total results of operations for the annual period. As an example of the type of modification that may be required, assume a company uses the lifo method of inventory valuation and encounters a situation where liquidation of the base period inventory occurs at an interim date but the inventory is expected to be replaced by

[13] *Opinions of the Accounting Principles Board, No. 28*, "Interim Financial Reporting" (New York: American Institute of Certified Public Accountants, 1973), par. 9.

the end of the annual period. Under these circumstances, the inventory reported at the interim date should not reflect the lifo liquidation, and the cost of goods sold for the interim period should include the expected cost of replacing the liquidated lifo base.[14]

Another example of a required modification deals with a change in accounting principle during an interim period. In general, these changes should follow the provisions of APB Opinion No. 20.[15] However, the FASB has concluded in Statement No. 3 that for any cumulative effect-type change, other than a change to lifo, if the change is made "in other than the first interim period of an enterprise's fiscal year, the cumulative effect of the change on retained earnings at the beginning of that year shall be included in the determination of net income of the first interim period of the year of change."[16]

Applying generally accepted accounting practices to interim financial statements can become complex. This is an area that is developing to meet the perceived needs of users. For example, the SEC has adopted rules requiring increased disclosure of interim financial information. Interpretations of old standards and the development of new standards will assist in presenting interim financial data that should help investors and others in analyzing and interpreting the financial picture and operating results of a company.

Segment Reporting

Many companies are large and complex organizations, usually engaging in a variety of activities. Sometimes these activities bear little relationship to each other. For example, a company might manufacture airplane engines, operate a real estate business, and manage a professional hockey team. Such companies are referred to as **conglomerates** or as **diversified companies.** The normal activities of other companies are more closely related, and they are sometimes called **unitary companies.**

When a company is diversified, the different segments of the company often operate in distinct and separate markets, involve different management teams, and experience different growth patterns, profit potentials, and degrees of risk. In effect, the segments of the company behave almost like, and in some cases are, separate companies within an overall corporate umbrella. Yet, if only total company information is presented for a highly diversified company, the differing degrees of risk, profitability, and growth potential for major segments of the company cannot be analyzed.

Recognizing this problem, the accounting profession has taken steps to require supplemental disclosures of selected information for **segments of diversified companies.** In Statement No. 14 the FASB requires companies presenting financial statements to include information about operations in different industries, foreign operations and export sales, and major cus-

---

[14]*Ibid.*, par. 14.

[15]*Opinions of the Accounting Principles Board, No. 20, op. cit.*

[16]*Statement of Financial Accounting Standards No. 3*, "Reporting Accounting Changes in Interim Financial Statements" (Stamford: Financial Accounting Standards Board, 1974), par. 4.

tomers.[17] Information to be reported includes revenues, operating profit, and identifiable assets for each significant industry segment of a company. Essentially, a segment is considered significant if its sales, profit, or assets are 10 percent or more of the respective total company amounts. A practical limit of 10 segments is suggested, and at least 75 percent of total company sales must be accounted for. The segment profit data may be reported in the audited financial statements, notes to the financial statements, or in a separate schedule considered an integral part of the statements. Other provisions of Statement No. 14 require disclosure of revenues from major customers and provide guidelines for determining a company's foreign operations and export sales. Normally, the above requirements do not apply to interim financial reports, nor to financial statements that are presented in another enterprise's financial report.[18]

Reporting by lines of business presents several problems. For example, how does one determine which *business segments* should be reported upon? Certainly not all companies are organized in the same manner, even if they are engaged in similar business activities. Reporting on a particular division or profit-center in one company may not be comparable to another company. Another problem relates to *transfer pricing*. Not all companies use the same method of pricing goods or services that are "sold" among the different divisions or units of a company. This could lead to distorted segment profit data. Another related problem is the *allocation of common costs* among segments of a company. Certain costs, such as general and administrative expenses, are very difficult to assign to particular segments of a company on anything other than an arbitrary basis. This, again, could lead to misleading information.

In spite of these difficulties, the accounting profession has concluded that segment reporting is necessary to assist readers of financial statements in analyzing and understanding an enterprise's past performance and future prospects. The disclosures made by General Mills in Appendix B provide an example of segment reporting by a diversified company.

Forecasts

As noted throughout the book, financial reporting has traditionally been based on historical costs and has reported past transactions. Financial analysts and others have suggested for years that disclosure of future earnings **forecasts**, that is, predictions about corporate expectations, would be useful information. Prior to 1974 the SEC would not allow forecasted earnings in registration statements. However, the Commission has reversed that long-standing policy and now allows publication of forecasts, provided they meet guidelines established by the SEC. The AICPA has also given its support to

[17] *Statement of Financial Accounting Standards No. 14*, "Financial Reporting for Segments of a Business Enterprise" (Stamford: Financial Accounting Standards Board, 1976).

[18] *Statement of Financial Accounting Standards No. 24*, "Reporting Segment Information in Financial Statements That Are Presented in Another Enterprise's Financial Report" (Stamford: Financial Accounting Standards Board, 1978).

the disclosure of financial forecasts, suggesting that appropriate care be exercised in providing the best information available and that assumptions be clearly stated and supported with adequate documentation.

The arguments *for* presenting forecasted supplemental information include:

(1) Investors are trying to predict the future. Financial forecasts would provide relevant information for such investment decisions.
(2) Forecasts are available to some individuals currently (key executives, selected analysts, etc.). Disclosing forecasts publicly would provide all investors access to the information.
(3) Disclosing forecasts publicly, under specified guidelines, would likely improve the reliability of forecasts.
(4) Management has long found it beneficial to make forecasts of future earnings and to compare forecasted and actual results. Investors should receive the benefits of similar information.

There are also seemingly valid arguments *against* presenting financial forecasts as a part of financial statements.

(1) Forecasts are affected by many variables, many of which are not controllable by the company. Accordingly, there is no assurance that forecasted results will be achieved.
(2) Forecasts are subjective and may be misunderstood by those unfamiliar with the assumptions upon which forecasts are made.
(3) There may be serious economic and legal implications if forecasts are not met. Therefore, companies may seek to meet short-run forecasted results rather than take actions in the long-run best interest of the shareholders.
(4) Required disclosure of forecasts may produce competitive disadvantages, especially with respect to foreign companies not required to disclose the same information.

So far the arguments against publicly disclosing forecasted earnings have prevailed, at least to the extent that neither the FASB nor the SEC currently *requires* forecasts. However, some U. S. companies are beginning to disclose forecasted earnings on a voluntary basis. One such company is Days Inns of America. Selected disclosures from their 1981 Annual Report are presented on pages 814 and 815. Forecasts are commonly reported in Great Britain, but it is significant to note that there are no class action suits in Great Britain. Therefore, the threat of legal liability is greatly reduced.

Related Party Disclosures

The FASB identified several important qualitative characteristics of information in Concepts Statement No. 2. One of these qualities is completeness. In issuing *Statement of Financial Accounting Standards No. 57*, the Board has concluded that financial statements may lack completeness and therefore reliability unless certain disclosures are made concerning related party transactions.[19]

---

[19]*Statement of Financial Accounting Standards No. 57*, "Related Party Disclosures" (Stamford: Financial Accounting Standards Board, March 1982).

Transactions between related parties are common. Examples include transactions between a parent company and its subsidiaries, subsidiaries of a common parent, an enterprise and the trusts it manages for the benefit of employees, and an enterprise and its principal owners and affiliates.[20] These related parties may enter into selling, purchasing, lending, borrowing, or various service transactions. Sometimes these transactions are not even given accounting recognition, as in the case where an entity may receive services from a related party without charge and where the entity does not record the receipt of the services.

Given the nature of related party transactions, they often significantly affect reported income, future cash flows, and other accounting measurements. As an example, consider the case of a manufacturer of small boats in California that was the sole supplier for a retail sail and motorboat distributing company in Hawaii. More than half of the manufacturer's output was sold in slightly unfinished form to the Hawaiian distributor at a price substantially below that charged to others for the product when completely finished. The stock of the manufacturing company was widely held, but the Hawaiian company was totally owned by six people, all of whom were officers of the manufacturing company. Without information concerning these related party transactions, external users would not be able to assess the amounts and timing of future cash flows nor would they understand why the return on stockholders' equity for the manufacturing company was averaging only five percent while the distributing company's return was almost fifty percent.

Because material related party transactions can have a significant impact on the financial statements of an entity, the FASB requires the following disclosures:

(1) The nature of the relationship(s) involved
(2) A description of the transactions, including transactions to which no amounts or nominal amounts were ascribed, for each of the periods for which income statements are presented, and such other information deemed necessary to an understanding of the effects of the transactions on the financial statements
(3) The dollar amounts of transactions for each of the periods for which income statements are presented and the effects of any change in the method of establishing the terms from that used in the preceding period
(4) Amounts due from or to related parties as of the date of each balance sheet presented and, if not otherwise apparent, the terms and manner of settlement.[21]

Excluded from the above disclosure requirements are compensation arrangements, expense allowances, and other similar items that occur regularly in the normal course of business. Also excluded are transactions that are eliminated in the preparation of consolidated or combined financial statements.

---

[20] *Ibid.*, par. 1.
[21] *Ibid*, par. 2.

Days Inns of America, Inc.

COMPARISON OF ACTUAL TO FORECASTED INCOME AND STOCKHOLDERS' EQUITY

For the year ended September 30, 1981	Actual	Forecasted	Variance
Net revenue:			
Lodging	$105,369,000	$105,452,000	($ 83,000)
Food, gasoline and novelties	66,677,000	65,544,000	1,133,000
Franchise fees	7,098,000	6,622,000	476,000
Rental income	1,350,000	1,594,000	(244,000)
Other income	4,143,000	4,269,000	(126,000)
Gains on sales of properties	4,216,000	74,000	4,142,000
	188,853,000	183,555,000	5,298,000
Cost and expenses:			
Cost of food, gasoline and novelties	44,732,000	43,953,000	779,000
Selling, general, administrative and operating expenses	98,039,000	93,037,000	5,002,000
Rental expense	5,350,000	5,307,000	43,000
Depreciation and amortization	12,602,000	13,867,000	(1,265,000)
Interest expense, net of interest income	13,057,000	14,485,000	(1,428,000)
	173,780,000	170,649,000	3,131,000
Income before provision for income taxes	15,073,000	12,906,000	2,167,000
Provision for income taxes	5,572,000	4,939,000	633,000
	9,501,000	7,967,000	1,534,000
Minority interest	793,000	901,000	(108,000)
Net income	$ 8,708,000	$ 7,066,000	$1,642,000
Stockholders' equity	$ 25,214,000	$ 23,565,000	$1,649,000
Occupancy	68.9%	69.1%	(.2)%
Average room rate	$24.09	$24.07	$.02
Number of company motel openings	11	12	(1)
Number of franchise motel openings	7	6	1
Number of motels disfranchised	3	0	3
Total rooms in chain at year end (operating and under construction)	45,726	45,200	526

COMMENTS ON FORECASTED RESULTS OF OPERATIONS 1982-1986

Policy on Forecasting

Since the Company began making earnings forecasts in 1977, there has been extensive dialogue on the subject in the business community. It is in the interest of the readers of the Company's financial statements to have insight into Management's perspective of the Company's business outlook. While historical results are readily available and amply discussed in financial reports, the probability for continuation, or for changes, in these trends is a most influential factor in reaching investment decisions.

It is important to understand what is meant by a "forecast". The forecast issued each year is the best appraisal of the Company's anticipated results. This appraisal is based on Management's interpretation of the overall business climate and willingness to support new projects and take risks, as well as the perception of operations personnel.

This financial forecast is based upon Management's assumptions concerning future events and circumstances. The assumptions discussed herein are those which Management believes are significant to the forecast or are key factors upon which the financial results of the Company depend. Some assumptions inevitably will not materialize and unanticipated events and circumstances may occur subsequent to September 30, 1981. Therefore, the actual results achieved during the forecast periods will vary from the forecasts, and the variations may be material.

Days Inns of America, Inc. will pursue an aggressive program during the next five years. The forecasts include the development of sixty properties emphasizing metropolitan locations near suburban shopping centers, office parks, commercial areas, airports, historical areas and civic centers. Both existing and new properties will experience inflationary increases in revenues and expenses. It is also expected that volume increases will occur in room occupancy and food, gasoline and novelty sales.

Assumptions Made by Management in Preparation of These Forecasts

Lodging revenues are based upon (a) an average occupancy of 70.1% in 1982 increasing to 72.4% in 1986, (b) an average room rate of $28.00 in 1982 increasing approximately 8% each year through 1986, and (c) the addition of eight to sixteen properties each year from 1982 through 1986. It is estimated that a variance from the projected occupancy of 1%, with no variance in the average room rate, would result in a change in net income of approximately 8%, and that a variance in the average room rate of 1%, with no variance in occupancy, would result in a change in net income of approximately 7%.

Food, gasoline and novelty revenues, forecasted on the basis of revenue per rented room, will increase moderately (10% per year), while the cost of goods sold will remain constant at 33%, 92% and 70%, respectively.

Initial franchise fees are forecasted at an average of $25,000 for each new opening, plus charges for conversions of other motels, ownership transfers and site inspections. Recurring franchise fees are forecasted using (a) an increase in total available rooms for motel openings, net of disfranchised properties, (b) an occupancy rate approximating company operated units and (c) an average room rate slightly lower than company operated units.

Rental and other income includes revenue from leased motels, based on agreements in effect as of September 30, 1981, membership fees and conventions related to September Days Club, commissions and miscellaneous income. No attempt has been made to forecast the impact of property disposals.

For the five-year period, selling, general, administrative and operating expenses are forecasted to increase approximately 100%. Inflation will impact various costs from 5%-10% annually and the operating costs of new properties will account for the remaining increase.

Effective October 1, 1981, substantially all lease agreements are required to be capitalized in accordance with Financial Accounting Standard No. 13—Accounting for Leases (FAS 13). Accordingly, the forecasts reflect capitalization of such leases in effect as of September 30, 1981. Capitalization of the leases will result in decreases in net income of $343,000, $234,000 and $107,000 in 1982 through 1984, respectively, and increases in net income of $8,000 and $158,000 in 1985 and 1986, respectively. The cumulative effect of the capitalization results in a decrease of $2,585,000 in stockholders' equity at September 30, 1981.

Estimates of depreciation are based on estimated lives for various classes of assets using the straight-line method of depreciation. Increases in expense are due to the addition of new properties and replacements and improvements at existing properties. Expenditures for 1982 through 1986

Days Inns of America, Inc.

CONSOLIDATED STATEMENTS OF FORECASTED INCOME AND STOCKHOLDERS' EQUITY

For the years ending September 30,	1982	1983	1984	1985	1986
Net revenue:					
Lodging	$131,327,000	$162,718,000	$194,426,000	$231,611,000	$275,217,000
Food, gasoline and novelties	76,385,000	93,301,000	110,738,000	132,681,000	159,823,000
Franchise fees	7,302,000	7,282,000	8,195,000	9,480,000	11,099,000
Rental income	2,229,000	2,300,000	2,356,000	2,434,000	2,500,000
Other income	3,517,000	4,482,000	5,101,000	6,153,000	7,021,000
	220,760,000	270,083,000	320,816,000	382,359,000	455,660,000
Costs and expenses:					
Cost of food, gasoline and novelties	50,044,000	60,124,000	70,369,000	82,917,000	98,260,000
Selling, general, administrative and operating expenses	109,628,000	132,416,000	156,348,000	185,423,000	221,991,000
Depreciation and amortization	16,627,000	19,536,000	22,296,000	25,347,000	29,070,000
Interest expense, net of interest income	23,932,000	34,482,000	42,933,000	53,039,000	64,538,000
	200,231,000	246,558,000	291,946,000	346,726,000	413,859,000
Income before provision for income taxes	20,529,000	23,525,000	28,870,000	35,633,000	41,801,000
Provision for income taxes	7,028,000	9,410,000	11,548,000	14,253,000	16,720,000
Net income	$ 13,501,000	$ 14,115,000	$ 17,322,000	$ 21,380,000	$ 25,081,000
Stockholders' equity	$ 42,594,000	$ 56,709,000	$ 74,031,000	$ 95,411,000	$120,492,000
Occupancy	70.1%	70.5%	71.0%	71.7%	72.4%
Average room rate	$28.00	$30.00	$32.50	$34.50	$36.75
Number of company motel openings	8	10	12	14	16
Number of franchise motel openings	5	5	5	5	5
Number of motels disfranchised	13	13	5	5	5
Total rooms in chain at year end (operating and under construction)	45,400	46,500	48,600	51,400	54,200

are forecasted at $425,000,000 for new properties and $32,000,000 for existing properties.

Interest expense is based on loans in effect at September 30, 1981, plus assumed financing at 16% per annum on the new properties. All other interest is based on a constant level of debt. Interest income is projected to increase due to higher cash reserves.

Provisions for income taxes are calculated using the applicable tax rates, less investment tax credits from qualifying capital expenditures and tax loss and investment tax credit carryforwards available in 1982.

Forecasted stockholders' equity assumes that the only changes arise from operations, capitalization of the lease agreements in accordance with FAS 13 in 1982, the purchase of the minority interests in subsidiary companies during 1982 (see Note 11 to Consolidated Financial Statements) and $351,000 in declared dividends payable in 1982. No attempt has been made to forecast dividends for 1983 through 1986.

The accounting policies used in the forecasts are consistent with those applied in the financial statements for 1981 except for the capitalization of the leases effective October 1, 1981. The above forecasts should be read in conjunction with the consolidated financial statements and accompanying notes for the years ended September 30, 1981 and 1980.

REPORT OF INDEPENDENT ACCOUNTANTS

To the Board of Directors
and Stockholders of
Days Inns of Amercia, Inc.

The Statements of Forecasted Income and Stockholders' Equity of Days Inns of America, Inc., for each of the five years ending September 30, 1986, including the assumptions made by Management in preparation of these forecasts, are Management's estimate of the most probable results of operations for the forecast periods. Accordingly, the forecasts reflect Management's judgment based on present circumstances of the most likely set of conditions and its most likely course of action.

We have made a review of such financial forecasts in accordance with applicable guidelines of the American Institute of Certified Public Accountants for a review of a financial forecast. Our review included procedures to evaluate the assumptions made by Management in the preparation and presentation of the forecasts. We have no responsibility to update the report for events and circumstances occurring after the date of this report. The summarized historical financial information presented with the forecasts for comparative purposes is taken from the financial statements of the Company for the year ended September 30, 1981, which we examined and reported on under this same date.

Based on our review, we believe that the accompanying financial forecasts are presented in conformity with applicable guidelines established by the American Institute of Certified Public Accountants for presentation of a financial forecast. We believe that the underlying assumptions provide a reasonable basis for Management's forecasts. However, some assumptions inevitably will not materialize and unanticipated events and circumstances may occur; therefore, the actual results achieved during the forecast periods will vary from the forecasts, and the variations may be material.

Price Waterhouse

Atlanta, Georgia
December 29, 1981

In prescribing disclosures for related party transactions, the FASB believes users will have more complete information and will be better able to assess current and future cash flows and to compare enterprise results of operations and financial position with those of prior periods and with those of other enterprises. Such information may make a difference in a user's decision and, therefore, is considered relevant information that should be reported.

Concluding Comment

Investors are demanding more information upon which to base decisions. Supplemental disclosures, such as interim and segment reports, forecasts of future earnings, and related party disclosures provide additional relevant information for external users. However, the presentation of such information is not without a cost. Users must be willing to pay for additional information as well as recognize appropriate uses and inherent limitations of the data. Such questions as legal liability, auditor involvement and responsibility, and optimum timing and manner of presentation have not yet been resolved.

QUESTIONS

1. Explain the distinctions between the major components of income: (a) operating income, (b) income from continuing operations, and (c) net income. Why are these distinctions important?

2. What are the major categories of nonoperating components of income?

3. The Pop-Up Company has decided to sell its lid manufacturing division even though the division is expected to show a small profit this year. The division's assets will be sold at a loss of $10,000 to another company. What information (if any) should Pop-Up disclose in its financial reports with respect to this division?

4. Which of the following would *not* normally qualify as an extraordinary item?

(a) The write-down or write-off of receivables.
(b) Major devaluation of foreign currency.
(c) Loss on sale of plant and equipment.
(d) Gain from early extinguishment of debt.
(e) Loss due to extensive flood damage to asphalt company in Las Vegas, Nevada.
(f) Loss due to extensive earthquake damage to furniture company in Los Angeles, California.
(g) Farming loss due to unusually heavy spring rains in the Northwest.

5. Explain briefly the difference in treatments of (a) a change in an accounting principle, and (b) a change in an accounting estimate.

6. Why does the adoption of new and different accounting principles require justification, whereas the continuation of a principle already applied requires no such justification?

7. When should the effects of a change in accounting principle be shown as a cumulative effect on current net income? (Give examples.)

8. When should the effects of a change in accounting principle be shown as a restatement of prior periods? (Give examples.)

9. Describe the effect on current net income, beginning retained earnings, deferred income tax, individual asset accounts, and contra-asset accounts when:

(a) Depreciation is converted from the straight-line method to an accelerated method.
(b) Depreciation is converted from an accelerated method to the straight-line method.
(c) Income on construction contracts that had been reported on a completed-projects basis is now reported on the percentage-of-completion basis.
(d) The valuation of inventories is changed from a fifo to a lifo basis. Records do not permit retroactive change in methods.
(e) It is determined that the warranty expenses for sales in prior years should have been 5% instead of 4%.
(f) The valuation of inventories is changed from a lifo to a fifo basis.
(g) Your accounts receivable clerk reads that a major customer has declared bankruptcy.
(h) Your patent lawyer informs you that your rival has perfected and patented a new invention making your product obsolete.
(i) Your accountant requires different reporting due to a new FASB statement.

10. Distinguish between the two primary viewpoints concerning the preparation of interim financial statements.

11. Why must investors be careful in interpreting interim reports?

12. Why has the accounting profession chosen to require supplemental disclosures for diversified companies?

13. What information is required by FASB Statement No. 14 concerning segment reporting?

14. What are the major arguments *for* and *against* requiring forecasts as supplemental information?

15. What disclosures are required for related party transactions? Why are these disclosures recommended by the FASB?

DISCUSSION CASES

case 21-1 (Reporting discontinued operations) As reported in a January 12, 1983, *Wall Street Journal* article, ASARCO Inc. charged $11 million against fourth quarter earnings to cover expenses of closing three plants and withdrawing from the solar-energy collector business. ASARCO, a metals company, has experienced curtailed operations due to the economic recession and low metals prices. Management decided to liquidate its interest in solar-energy collectors since it has not made a profit in that business segment since 1975. According to generally accepted accounting, what disclosures are required based on management's decision to liquidate part of the business? Where will the information be reported and in what manner? Why are investors interested in such disclosures?

case 21-2 (Finding the right company product mix) In analyzing the current economic situation, you become convinced that investing in a finance company might be quite profitable. You have been told that Household Finance Corporation might be a good possibility. You have also been told that many finance companies are highly diversified. What difference would that make to your investment decision? Would investing in Household Finance fit your objective?

EXERCISES

exercise 21-1 (Change in estimate and in accounting method)

Clinton Manufacturing purchased a machine on January 1, 1980, for $50,000. At that time, it was determined that the machine had an estimated useful life of 20 years and an estimated residual value of $5,000. The company used the double-declining-balance method of depreciation. On January 1, 1984, the company decided to change its depreciation method from double-declining-balance to straight-line. The machine's remaining useful life was estimated to be six years with a residual value of $2,000.

(1) Give the entry required to record Clinton's depreciation expense for 1984.
(2) Give the entry, if any, to record the effect of the change in depreciation methods.

exercise 21-2 (Reporting items on financial statements)

How would you report each of the following items on the financial statements?

(a) Plant shut-down and start-up costs due to a strike.
(b) Loss on sale of the fertilizer production division of a lawn supplies manufacturer.
(c) Material penalties arising from early payment of a mortgage.
(d) Gain resulting from changing asset balances to adjust for the effect of excessive depreciation charged in error in prior years.
(e) Loss resulting from excessive accrual in prior years of estimated revenues from long-term contracts.
(f) Costs incurred to purchase a valuable patent.
(g) Net income from the discontinued dune buggy operations of a custom car designer.
(h) Costs of rearranging plant machinery into a more efficient order.
(i) Error made in capitalizing advertising expense during the prior year.
(j) Gain on sale of land to the government.
(k) Loss from destruction of crops by a hail storm.
(l) Purchase and retirement of bonds outstanding at a price in excess of book value.
(m) Additional depreciation resulting from a change in the estimated useful life of an asset.
(n) Gain on sale of long-term investments.
(o) Loss from spring flooding.
(p) Sale of obsolete inventory at less than book value.
(q) Additional federal income tax assessment for prior years.
(r) Loss resulting from the sale of a portion of a line of business.
(s) Costs associated with moving an American business to Japan.
(t) Loss resulting from a patent that was recently determined to be worthless.

exercise 21-3 (Reporting special income items)

New Cosmetics Inc. shows a retained earnings balance on January 1, 1984, of $460,000. For 1984, the income from continuing operations was $150,000 before income tax. Following is a list of special items:

Income from operations of a discontinued cosmetics division.	$18,000
Loss on the sale of the cosmetics division.	50,000
Gain on extinguishment of long-term debt.	25,000
Correction of sales understatement in 1982.	28,000
Omission of depreciation charges of prior years (A claim has been filed for an income tax refund of $8,000)	20,000

Income tax paid during 1984 was $40,400, which consisted of the tax on continuing operations, plus $8,000 resulting from operations of the discontinued cosmetics division and $12,000 from the gain from extinguishment of debt, less a $24,600 tax reduction for loss on the sale of the cosmetics division. Dividends of $30,000 were declared by the company during the year (50,000 shares of common stock are outstanding). Prepare the income statement for New Cosmetics Inc. beginning with "Income from continuing operations before income tax." Include an accompanying retained earnings statement.

exercise 21-4 (Extraordinary losses)

You have been asked to review the December 31, 1984 financial statements of Starback Company. The company has reported extraordinary losses totaling $926,000. Upon further investigation, you found that the $926,000 in losses was composed of the following items:

(a) Obsolete inventories recorded at $120,000 were written off.
(b) Loss on the translation of foreign currency received from foreign subsidiaries amounted to $65,000.
(c) Loss of $69,000 resulting from the abandonment of equipment which was no longer needed in the business.
(d) During 1984, buildings and equipment with a book value of $509,000 were destroyed when a dormant volcano suddenly erupted. Geologists believe that it is extremely unlikely that the volcano will be active again.
(e) During the winter of 1984, Starback's factories were shut down for several days due to unusually severe weather conditions. The costs resulting from this shutdown totaled $163,000.

Ignoring income taxes, what amount of extraordinary losses should Starback have reported for the year ended December 31, 1984? How should this be reported in the financial statements?

exercise 21-5 (Change in accounting principle)

The Jiffy Build Construction Company has used the completed-contract method of accounting since it began operations in 1981. In 1984, management decided, for justifiable reasons, to adopt the percentage-of-completion method.

The company had prepared the following statement reporting income for the years 1981-1983.

	1981	1982	1983
Total sales price of completed contracts	0	$1,000,000	$800,000
Less cost of completed contracts plus anticipated loss on contract in process	0	825,000	560,000
Income from operations	0	$ 175,000	$240,000
Extraordinary loss			35,000
Income before taxes	0	$ 175,000	$205,000

Analysis of the accounting records disclosed the following income by projects was earned for the years 1981-1983 using the percentage-of-completion method of inventory valuation:

	1981	1982	1983
Project A	$125,000	$ 50,000	0
Project B	90,000	180,000	$20,000
Project C	0	20,000	80,000
Project D	0	0	(50,000)

Give the journal entry required in 1984 to reflect the change in inventory methods. Use a 40% income tax rate.

exercise 21-6 (Change in accounting principle)

Taylor Manufacturing Company decides to change from an accelerated depreciation method it has used for both reporting and tax purposes to the straight-line method for reporting purposes. From the following information, prepare the income statement for 1984. Assume a 40% tax rate.

Year	Net Income As Reported	Excess of Accelerated Depreciation Over Straight-Line Depreciation	Direct Effect Less Tax (40%)
Prior to 1981		$12,500	$ 7,500
1981	$62,500	6,250	3,750
1982	54,500	7,500	4,500
1983	78,000	11,250	6,750
		$37,500	$22,500

In 1984, net sales were $190,000; cost of goods sold, $92,500; selling expenses, $47,500, and general and administrative expenses, $14,000. In addition, Taylor had a tax deductible extraordinary loss of $22,500. Assume the fiscal year ends on December 31.

exercise 21-7 (Change in accounting principle involving lifo)

Assume the change in net income as shown in Exercise 6 is the result of a change from the lifo method of inventory pricing to another method. During 1984, dividends of $17,500 were announced and distributed. Based on this information, prepare the retained earnings statement for 1984. The December 31, 1983 retained earnings balance as reported was $260,000.

exercise 21-8 (Change in estimate)

The Wicker Corporation purchased a patent on January 2, 1979, for $405,000. The original life of the patent was estimated to be 15 years. However, in December of 1984, the controller of Wicker received information proving conclusively that the product protected by the Wicker patent would be obsolete within two years. Accordingly, the company decided to write off the unamortized portion of the patent cost over three years beginning in 1984. How would the change in estimate be reflected in the accounts for 1984 and subsequent years?

exercise 21-9 (Interim income statements)

The income statement for the year ended December 31, 1984, of Essex Technology Inc. appears below. Using the yearly income statement and the supplemental information, reconstruct the third-quarter interim income statement for Essex.

Essex Technology Inc.
Income Statement
For Year Ended December 31, 1984

Sales	$900,000
Cost of goods sold	560,000
Gross profit on sales	$340,000
Operating expenses	96,000
Operating income	$244,000
Gain on sale of equipment	28,000
Income from continuing operations before income taxes	$272,000
Income taxes	108,800
Income from continuing operations	$163,200
Extraordinary loss (less applicable income tax reduction of $40,000)	(60,000)
Net income	$103,200

Supplemental information:

(a) Assume a 40% tax rate.

(continued)

(b) Third-quarter sales were 20% of total sales.
(c) For interim reporting purposes, a gross profit rate of 38% can be justified.
(d) Variable operating expenses are allocated in the same proportion as sales. Fixed operating expenses are allocated based on the expiration of time. Of the total operating expenses, $60,000 relate to variable expenses.
(e) The equipment was sold June 1, 1984.
(f) The extraordinary loss occurred September 1, 1984.

exercise 21-10 (Reporting segment information)

Lutz Industries operates in five different industries. From the information given below, determine which segments should be classified as reportable segments according to FASB Statement No. 14. Provide justification for your answer.

Lutz Industries
Information About Company Operations in Different Industries
For Year Ended December 31, 1984
(In Millions of Dollars)

	Industry 1	Industry 2	Industry 3	Industry 4	Industry 5	Total
Revenues	$ 577	$ 84	$ 93	$117	$ 96	$ 967
Operating profit	66	11	9	10	10	106
Identifiable assets	2,124	298	328	314	353	3,417

exercise 21-11 (Income statement preparation)

The following is a condensed trial balance of Bryson Inc. at December 31, 1984 (000's omitted).

Current Assets	1,675	
Current Liabilities		860
Investments	120	
Land	500	
Plant and Intangibles (net of accumulated depreciation of $1,020)	2,480	
Invested Capital (50,000 shares, par $15, issued and outstanding during the year)		750
Long-Term Debt		2,000
Retained Earnings		705
Sales		1,800
Gain on Sale of Investments		20
Dividends Received		15
Gain on Disposal of a Division (less applicable income tax of $20)		70
Gain on Early Retirement of Debt (less applicable income tax of $40)		90
Cumulative Effect of a Change in Accounting Principle (less applicable income tax of $80)		145
Cost of Goods Sold	1,100	
Operating Expenses	200	
Income Tax Expense	180	
Interest Expense	75	
Dividends Paid	100	
Loss from Operations of Discontinued Division (less applicable income tax of $10)	25	
	6,455	6,455

(continued)

Following generally accepted accounting practice and using a multiple-step format, prepare a formal income statement for Bryson Inc. for the year ended December 31, 1984. Include earnings per share information for each significant component of income.

PROBLEMS

problem 21-1 (Change in accounting principle)

In 1984, Hutchison Shippers changed their method of depreciating equipment from an accelerated depreciation method, used for both reporting and tax purposes, to the straight-line method. The following information shows the effect of this change on the amount of depreciation to be shown on the income statement.

Year	Net Income as Reported	Excess of Accelerated Depreciation Over Straight-Line Depreciation
Prior to 1980		$40,000
1980	$200,000	15,000
1981	182,500	13,000
1982	190,000	14,000
1983	210,000	17,000
		$99,000

Assume the company has a tax rate of 40%. Employees have been given a 20% cash bonus on operating income during these years.

Instructions:

(1) Compute the effect of the change in accounting principle on income as follows: (a) the direct effect less the tax effect; (b) the direct and indirect effects.

(2) Prepare (a) a partial income statement for 1984 if income before extraordinary items was $225,000 and an extraordinary loss of $36,000 before tax was incurred, and (b) pro forma income data for the years 1980–1983.

problem 21-2 (Change in accounting principle)

In 1984, McClure Research Inc. decided to change from the straight-line method of amortizing capitalized leases to the declining-balance method, which had been used on the tax return. The following information shows the effect of this change on the amount of amortization to be shown on the income statement.

Year	Net Income As Reported	Excess of Accelerated Amortization Over Straight-Line Amortization
Prior to 1979		$27,000
1979	$387,000	9,000
1980	442,500	12,000
1981	487,500	14,000
1982	465,000	16,000
1983	600,000	18,000
		$96,000

Assume the company has a tax rate of 40%. Management personnel have been given a bonus of 20% of operating income to purchase stock during these years.

Instructions:

(1) Compute the effect of the change in accounting principle on income as follows: (a) the direct effect less the tax effect; (b) the direct and indirect effects.

(2) Prepare: (a) a partial income statement for 1984 if income after tax before extraordinary items was $637,500 and an extraordinary gain of $150,000 before tax was received, and (b) pro forma income data for the years 1979–1983.

problem 21-3 (Change in accounting principle – lifo to fifo)

On January 1, 1984, RX Drug Stores Inc. decided to change from the lifo method of inventory pricing to the fifo method. The reported income for the four years RX Drug Stores had been in business was as follows:

1980	$250,000	1982	$310,000
1981	260,000	1983	330,000

Analysis of the inventory records disclosed that the following inventories were on hand at the end of each year as valued under both the lifo and fifo methods.

	Lifo Method	Fifo Method
January 1, 1980	0	0
December 31, 1980	$228,000	$256,000
December 31, 1981	240,000	238,000
December 31, 1982	270,000	302,000
December 31, 1983	288,000	352,000

The income tax rate is 40%.

Instructions:

(1) Compute the restated net income for the years 1980–1983.

(2) Prepare the retained earnings statement for RX Drug Stores Inc. for 1984 if the 1983 ending balance had been previously reported at $600,000, 1984 net income using the fifo method is $360,000, and dividends of $200,000 were paid during 1984.

problem 21-4 (Accounting changes)

Pentek Distributors has released the following condensed financial statements for 1982 and 1983 and has prepared the following proposed statements for 1984.

Pentek Distributors
Comparative Balance Sheet
December 31

Assets	1984	1983	1982
Current assets	$249,000	$219,000	$165,000
Land	60,000	45,000	30,000
Equipment	150,000	150,000	150,000
Accumulated depreciation—equipment	(45,000)	(30,000)	(15,000)
Total assets	$414,000	$384,000	$330,000
Liabilities and Stockholders' Equity			
Current liabilities	$177,000	$177,000	$147,000
Common stock	60,000	60,000	60,000
Retained earnings	177,000	147,000	123,000
Total liabilities and stockholders' equity	$414,000	$384,000	$330,000

Pentek Distributors
Comparative Income Statement
For Years Ended December 31

	1984	1983	1982
Sales	$315,000	$300,000	$255,000
Cost of goods sold	$240,000	$225,000	$189,000
Other expenses except depreciation	30,000	36,000	33,000
Depreciation expense—equipment	15,000	15,000	15,000
Total costs	$285,000	$276,000	$237,000
Net income	$ 30,000	$ 24,000	$ 18,000

Pentek Distributors acquired the equipment for $150,000 on January 1, 1982, and began depreciating the equipment over a 10-year estimated useful life with no salvage value, using the straight-line method of depreciation. The double-declining-balance method of depreciation, under the same assumptions, would have required the following depreciation expense:

1982	20% × $150,000 = $30,000
1983	20% × $120,000 = $24,000
1984	20% × $ 96,000 = $19,200

Instructions: In comparative format, prepare a balance sheet and a combined statement of income and retained earnings for 1984, giving effect to the following changes. Ignore any income tax effect. Pentek Distributors has 10,000 shares of common stock outstanding. The following situations are independent of each other.

(1) For justifiable reasons, Pentek Distributors changed to the double-declining-balance method of depreciation in 1984. The effect of the change should be included in the net income of the period in which the change was made.
(2) During 1984, Pentek Distributors found the equipment was fast becoming obsolete and decided to change the estimated useful life from 10 years to 5 years. The books for 1984 had not yet been closed.
(3) During 1984, Pentek Distributors found additional equipment, also acquired on January 1, 1982, costing $24,000, had been recorded in the land account and had not been depreciated. This error should be corrected using straight-line depreciation over a 10-year period.

problem 21-5 (Reporting segment data)

Abcom Industries operates in several different industries, some of which are appropriately regarded as reportable segments. Total sales for Abcom are $12,000,000 and total common costs are $6,000,000 for 1984. Abcom allocates common costs based on the ratio of a segment's sales to total sales, which is considered an appropriate method of allocation. Additional information regarding the different segments is contained in the following schedule:

	Segment 1	Segment 2	Segment 3	Segment 4	Other Segments
Contribution to total sales	23%	8%	31%	28%	10%
Identifiable assets as percent of total company assets	36%	9%	32%	8%	15%
Traceable costs	$800,000	$350,000	$1,200,000	$1,000,000	$650,000

Instructions: Prepare a schedule from which operating profit is derived for Abcom Industries which conforms to the reporting criteria set forth in FASB Statement No. 14.

problem 21-6 (Reporting accounting changes)

Listed below are three independent, unrelated sets of facts concerning accounting changes.

case 1. The Pendleton Company determined that the amortization rate on its patents is unacceptably low due to current advances in technology. The company decided at the beginning of 1984, the current year, to increase the amortization rate on all existing patents from 10 percent to 20 percent. Patents purchased on January 1, 1979, for $2,400,000 had a book value of $1,200,000 on January 1, 1984.

case 2. McArthur Enterprises decided on January 1, 1984, to change its depreciation method on manufacturing equipment from an accelerated method to the straight-line method. The straight-line method is to be used for new acquisitions as well as for previously acquired equipment. It has been determined that the excess of accelerated depreciation over straight-line depreciation for the years 1981 through 1983 totals $634,000.

case 3. On December 31, 1983, Warwick Inc. owned 27% of the Bentley Company, at which time Warwick reported its investment using the equity method. During 1984, Warwick has increased its ownership in Bentley by 24%. Accordingly, Warwick is planning to prepare consolidated financial statements for Warwick and Bentley for the year ended December 31, 1984.

Instructions: For each of the situations described:

(1) Explain the type of accounting change.
(2) Explain how the accounting change should be reported under current generally accepted accounting principles, and provide, where applicable, the journal entries to effect the accounting change. (Ignore the effect of income taxes.)
(3) Explain the effect of the change on the statement of financial position and earnings statement.

(AICPA adapted)

problem 21-7 (Disposal of business segment)

The following condensed statement of income of Markham Manufacturing is presented for the two years ended December 31, 1984 and 1983:

	1984	1983
Net sales	$2,500,000	$2,400,000
Cost of sales	1,550,000	1,500,000
Gross profit	$ 950,000	$ 900,000
Operating expenses	550,000	600,000
Operating income	$ 400,000	$ 300,000
Gain on sale of division	300,000	—
Income before income taxes	$ 700,000	$ 300,000
Provision for income taxes	280,000	120,000
Net income	$ 420,000	$ 180,000

On January 1, 1984, Markham entered into an agreement to sell for $800,000 the assets and product line of one of its separate operating divisions. The sale was consummated on December 31, 1984, and resulted in a pretax gain of $300,000. This division's contribution to Markham's reported operating income before income taxes for each year was as follows:

1984	$160,000 loss
1983	$125,000 loss

Assume an income tax rate of 40%.

Instructions: Prepare a revised comparative statement of income for Markham Manufacturing for the two years ended December 31, 1984 and 1983, beginning with income from continuing operations before income taxes. (AICPA adapted)

problem 21-8 (Income statement preparation)

Global Enterprises is a highly diversified company which operates in four separate industries—communications, computers, trucking, and petroleum exploration.

Financial data for the two years ended December 31, 1984 and 1983, are presented below:

	Net Sales	
	1984	1983
Trucking	$ 7,000,000	$ 6,000,000
Computers	4,000,000	2,540,000
Communications	3,160,000	2,800,000
Petroleum exploration	1,840,000	2,660,000
	$16,000,000	$14,000,000

	Cost of Sales	
	1984	1983
Trucking	$ 4,800,000	$ 3,600,000
Computers	2,200,000	1,400,000
Communications	1,000,000	1,800,000
Petroleum exploration	1,600,000	2,000,000
	$ 9,600,000	$ 8,800,000

	Operating Expenses	
	1984	1983
Trucking	$ 1,100,000	$ 550,000
Computers	600,000	250,000
Communications	400,000	300,000
Petroleum exploration	1,300,000	1,500,000
	$ 3,400,000	$ 2,600,000

On January 1, 1984, Global adopted a plan to sell the assets and product line of the Petroleum Exploration Division and expected to realize a gain on the disposal. On August 31, 1984, the division's assets and product line were sold for $4,200,000 cash, resulting in a gain of $1,280,000 (exclusive of operations during the phase-out period).

The company's Communications Division had three manufacturing plants that produced a variety of communication equipment. In March 1984, the company sold one of these plants and realized a gain of $260,000. After the sale, the operations at the plant that was sold were transferred to the remaining two plants that the company continued to operate.

In July 1984, the main dock of the Trucking Division, located in Texas near the Gulf of Mexico, was severely damaged by a violent hurricane. The resulting loss of $840,000 is not included in the financial data given above. Historical records indicate that this particular area of Texas normally is hit by one or more hurricanes every five to six years, causing extensive damage to property.

For the two years ended December 31, 1984 and 1983, the company had interest revenue earned on investments of $140,000 and $80,000 respectively.

Assume an income tax rate of 40% for both years.

Instructions: Prepare in proper form a comparative statement of income of Global Enterprises for the two years ended December 31, 1984, and December 31, 1983. (AICPA adapted)

problem 21-9 (Income statement preparation)

The following is an adjusted trial balance for Woodbine Circle Corporation at December 31, 1984:

Cash	500,000	
Accounts Receivable (net)	1,500,000	
Inventory	2,500,000	
Property, Plant, and Equipment	15,100,000	
Accumulated Depreciation		4,900,000
Accounts Payable		1,400,000
Income Taxes Payable		100,000
Notes Payable		1,000,000
Common Stock, $1 par		1,100,000
Additional Paid-In Capital		6,100,000
Retained Earnings, January 1, 1984		3,000,000
Sales–Regular		10,000,000
Sales–AL Division		2,000,000
Interest on Municipal Bonds		100,000
Cost of Sales–Regular	6,200,000	
Cost of Sales–AL Division	900,000	
Administrative Expenses–Regular	2,000,000	
Administrative Expenses–AL Division	300,000	
Interest Expense–Regular	210,000	
Interest Expense–AL Division	140,000	
Loss on Disposal of AL Division	250,000	
Gain on Repurchase of Bonds Payable		300,000
Income Tax Expense	400,000	
	30,000,000	30,000,000

Other financial data for the year ended December 31, 1984, follow:

(a) The company had charged $400,000 to income tax expense. This included $300,000 which had been paid and $100,000 accrued. The total amount does not properly reflect current or deferred income tax expense or intraperiod income tax allocation for income statement purposes. The income per tax return was $2,150,000. The applicable tax rate is 40%. Depreciation for book purposes was $600,000 and for tax purposes was $750,000. Interest on municipal bonds was $100,000.

(b) On September 30, 1984, Woodbine sold its Auto Leasing (AL) Division for $4,000,000. Book value of this business segment was $4,250,000 at that date. For financial statement purposes, this sale was considered as discontinued operations of a segment of a business. Since there was no phase-out period, the measurement date was September 30, 1984.

(c) On June 30, 1984, Woodbine repurchased $1,000,000, carrying value, of its long-term bonds for $700,000. All other liabilities mature in 1985.

(d) Common stock, par value $1 per share, was traded on the New York Stock Exchange. The weighted average number of shares outstanding for 1984 was 1,000,000.

Instructions: Using a multiple-step format, prepare a formal income statement for Woodbine for the year ended December 31, 1984. Prepare appropriate supporting schedules. Major income components should be properly separated. All income taxes should be appropriately shown. (AICPA adapted)

22 EARNINGS PER SHARE

CHAPTER OBJECTIVES

Describe the evolution of requirements for earnings per share disclosure.

Distinguish between simple and complex capital structures.

Describe and illustrate the computation of primary earnings per share for complex capital structures.

Describe and illustrate the computation of fully diluted earnings per share for complex capital structures.

Illustrate methods of disclosing earnings per share information in financial statements.

The term **earnings per share** generally refers to the amount earned during a given period on each share of common stock outstanding. It is a useful measurement for comparing earnings of different entities and for comparing earnings of a single entity over time when changes occur in the capital structure. As a successful company grows, net income will naturally increase. But an investor is interested in determining if net income is growing relative to the size of the company's capital structure. Investors use earnings per share figures to evaluate the results of operations of a business in order to make investment decisions. For example, by dividing the earnings per share figure into the market price per share, a **price-earnings ratio** may be computed and compared among different companies. Thus, if Company A earns $3 per share on stock with a $21 per share market price, and Company B earns $6 per share on stock with a $54 per share market value, an investor can state that Company A stock is selling at seven times earnings and Company B stock is selling at nine times earnings. Other things being equal between these two companies, Company A's stock would be the better buy since its market price is lower in relation to earnings than is Company B's price.

Investors, however, may be more interested in dividends than in earnings. This information may be communicated to them by using earnings per share data to compute a **dividend payout percentage** or **payout rate.** This rate is computed by dividing earnings per share into dividends per share. Thus, if Company A in the previous example pays a dividend of $2 per share, and Company B pays $3 per share, the payout percentage would be 66⅔ percent for Company A and 50 percent for Company B.

Earnings per share data receive wide recognition in the annual reports issued by companies, in the press, and in financial reporting publications. This measurement is frequently regarded as an important determinant of the market price of common stock.

EVOLUTION OF REQUIREMENTS FOR EARNINGS PER SHARE DISCLOSURE

Earnings per share figures were historically computed and used primarily by financial analysts. Sometimes the computation was disclosed in the unaudited section of the annual report along with a message from the company's president. However, because this measurement was not audited, figures used to develop earnings per share were often different from those attested to by the auditor. The situation became more complex when some companies and analysts began computing earnings per share not only on the basis of common shares actually outstanding, but also on the basis of what shares would be outstanding if certain convertible securities were converted and if certain stock options were exercised. Usually, the conversion or exercise terms were very favorable to the holders of these securities, and earnings per share would decline if common stock were issued upon conversion or exercise. This result, a reduced earnings per share, is referred to as a **dilution of earnings.** In some cases, however, the exercise of options or conversion of securities might result in an increased earnings per share. This result is referred to as an **antidilution of earnings.** Securities that would lead to dilution are referred to as **dilutive securities,** and those that would lead to antidilution are referred to as **antidilutive securities.** Rational investors would not convert or exercise antidilutive securities because they could do better by purchasing common stock in the market place.

These forward-looking computations of earnings per share attempted to provide information as to what future earnings per share *might* be assuming conversions and exercises took place. Because these "as if" conditions were based on assumptions, they could be computed in several ways. Recognizing the diversity of reporting practices, the Accounting Principles Board became involved in establishing guidelines for the computation and disclosure of earnings per share figures. The result was the issuance in 1969 of APB Opinion No. 15, "Earnings per Share," which concluded:

> The Board believes that the significance attached by investors and others to earnings per share data, together with the importance of evaluating the data in conjunction with the financial statements, requires that such data be presented prominently in the financial statements. The Board has therefore concluded that earnings per share or net loss per share data should be shown on the face of the income statement. The extent of the data to be presented and the captions used will vary with the complexity of the company's capital structure. . . .[1]

For the first few years after Opinion No. 15 was issued, all business entities were required to include earnings per share data in their income statements. However, in 1978, the FASB issued Statement No. 21, which eliminated this requirement for nonpublic entities. A nonpublic company is defined as any enterprise other than "one (a) whose debt or equity securities trade in a public market on a foreign or domestic stock exchange or in the over-the-counter market, or (b) that is required to file financial statements with the Securities and Exchange Commission."[2]

In the process of establishing rules for computing earnings per share, the Accounting Principles Board felt it necessary to be very specific about how future-oriented "as if" figures were to be computed. Many interpretations and amendments were issued with the intent to clarify the computations for a variety of securities and under varied circumstances. In some areas the rules became arbitrary and complex, and the resulting earnings per share computations have received much criticism as to their usefulness. Indeed, for companies with complex capital structures, the **historical** or **simple earnings per share** figure based on actual shares of common stock outstanding may not even be reported. In its place the APB substituted two earnings per share amounts: (1) **primary earnings per share** based on the assumed conversion or exercise of certain securities identified as common stock equivalents and (2) **fully diluted earnings per share** based on the assumed conversion of all convertible securities or exercise of all stock options that would reduce or dilute primary earnings per share.

Although over fifteen years have passed since APB Opinion No. 15 was issued, there has been little evidence to support the usefulness of these forward-type earnings per share figures. Shortly after APB Opinion No. 15 was issued, in fact, the Canadian Institute of Chartered Accountants reviewed what the APB had done, and concluded that only a historical earnings per share and a fully diluted earnings per share had potential value. They rejected the attempt to define an intermediary figure that was intended to measure the probability of conversion or exercise.[3] A United States survey of investors in 1980 indicated that various return on investment figures are becoming more popular than earnings per share as a measure of profitability.[4]

---

[1] *Opinions of the Accounting Principles Board, No. 15,* "Earnings per Share" (New York: American Institute of Certified Public Accountants, 1969), par. 12.

[2] *Statement of Financial Accounting Standards No. 21,* "Suspension of the Reporting of Earnings Per Share and Segment Information by Nonpublic Enterprises" (Stamford: Financial Accounting Standards Board, 1978), par. 13.

[3] *CICA Handbook, Section 3500,* "Earnings per Share" (Toronto: The Canadian Institute of Chartered Accountants, February 1970).

[4] As reported by a Lou Harris survey for the Financial Accounting Foundation in the Alexander Grant Newsletter, July 1980.

Of those corporate, government, and accounting executives surveyed, 66 percent listed return on investment as highly important, while only 49 percent listed earnings per share as highly important. A majority of 3 to 1 felt that return on investment was a better or more desirable measure of corporate performance than earnings per share. However, because earnings per share figures are presently required for all public companies, accountants must understand how they are computed and the rationale for the computations. Only the basic recommendations can be presented here. When Opinion No. 15 fails to state the specific procedures to be followed under special circumstances, the accountant must exercise judgment in developing supportable presentations within the recommended framework.

SIMPLE AND COMPLEX CAPITAL STRUCTURES

The capital structure of a company may be classified as simple or complex. If a company has only common stock outstanding and there are no convertible securities, stock options, warrants, or other rights outstanding, it is classified as a company with a **simple capital structure.** Earnings per share is computed by dividing the net income for the period by the weighted average number of common shares outstanding for the period. If net income includes below-the-line items as discussed in Chapter 21, a separate earnings per share figure is required for each major component of income, as well as for net income. No future-oriented "as if" conditions need to be considered.

Even if convertible securities, stock options, warrants or other rights do exist, the company structure may be classified as simple if there is no potential material dilution to earnings per share from the conversion or exercise of these items. Potential earnings per share dilution exists if the earnings per share would decrease or the loss per share would increase as a result of the conversion of securities or exercise of stock options, warrants, or other rights based on the conditions existing at the financial statement date. The Accounting Principles Board defined **material dilution** as being a decrease of three percent or more in the earnings per share. If a company's capital structure does not qualify as simple, it is classified as a **complex capital structure,** and the two figures identified previously—primary and fully diluted earnings per share—are required.

The Simple Capital Structure—Computational Guidelines

The earnings per share computation presents no problem when only common stock has been issued and the number of shares outstanding has remained the same for the entire period. The numerator is the net income (loss), and the denominator is the number of shares outstanding for the entire period. Frequently, however, either the numerator, the denominator, or both must be adjusted because of the following conditions:

(1) When common shares have been issued or have been reacquired by a company during a period, the resources available to the company have

changed and this change should affect earnings. Under these circumstances, a weighted average for shares outstanding should be computed.

The weighted average number of shares may be computed by determining month-shares of outstanding stock and dividing by 12 to obtain the weighted average for the year. For example, if a company has 10,000 shares outstanding at the beginning of the year, issues 5,000 more shares on May 1, and retires 2,000 shares on November 1, the weighted average number of shares would be computed as illustrated below.

		Month-Shares
Jan 1 to May 1	10,000 × 4 months	40,000
May 1 to Nov. 1	15,000 × 6 months	90,000
Nov. 1 to Dec. 31	13,000 × 2 months	26,000
Total month-shares		156,000
Weighted average number of shares: 156,000 ÷ 12		13,000

The same answer can be obtained by applying a weight to each period equivalent to the portion of the year since the last change in shares outstanding, as follows:

Jan. 1 to May 1	10,000 × 4/12 year	3,333
May 1 to Nov. 1	15,000 × 6/12 year	7,500
Nov. 1 to Dec. 31	13,000 × 2/12 year	2,167
Weighted average number of shares		13,000

(2) When the number of common shares outstanding has changed during a period as a result of a stock dividend, a stock split, or a reverse split, a retroactive recognition of this change must be made in arriving at the amount of earnings per share. To illustrate, assume that in the preceding example a two-for-one stock split occurred on November 1 before the retirement of the 2,000 shares of stock. The computation of the weighted average number of shares would be changed as follows:

Jan. 1 to May 1—10,000 × 200% (two-for-one stock split) × 4/12 year	6,667
May 1 to Nov. 1—15,000 × 200% (two-for-one stock split) × 6/12 year	15,000
Nov. 1 to Dec. 31—28,000* × 2/12 year	4,667
Weighted average number of shares	26,334

*30,000 outstanding − 2,000 retired = 28,000 shares

In reporting comparative data, recognition of the stock dividend or split in the common stock of all prior periods included in the statements is necessary. Only with the retroactive recognition of changes in the number of shares can earnings per share presentations for prior periods be stated on a basis comparable with the earnings per share presentation for the current period. Similar retroactive adjustments must be made even if a stock dividend or stock split occurs after the end of the period but before the financial statements are prepared; disclosure of this situation should be made in a note to the financial statements.

(3) When a capital structure includes nonconvertible preferred stock, dividends on preferred stock should be deducted from net income and also from income before extraordinary or other special items, when such items appear on the income statement, in arriving at the earnings related to common shares. If preferred dividends are not cumulative, only the dividends declared on preferred stock during the period are deducted. If preferred dividends are cumulative, the full amount of dividends on preferred stock for the period, whether declared or not, should be deducted from income before extraordinary or other special items in arriving at the earnings or loss balance related to the common stock. If there is a loss for the period, preferred dividends for the period, including any undeclared dividends on cumulative preferred stock, are added to the loss in arriving at the full loss related to the common stock.

To illustrate the computation of earnings per share at December 31, 1984, for a company with a simple capital structure for a comparative two-year period, assume the following data:

Summary of changes in capital balances:

	8% Cumulative Preferred Stock $100 Par		Common Stock No Par		Retained Earnings
	Shares	*Amount*	*Shares*	*Amount*	
December 31, 1982 balances	10,000	$1,000,000	200,000	$1,000,000	$4,000,000
June 30, 1983 issuance of 100,000 shares of common stock			100,000	600,000	
June 30, 1983 dividend on preferred stock, 8%					(80,000)
June 30, 1983 dividend on common stock, 30¢					(90,000)
December 31, 1983 net income for year, including extraordinary gain of $75,000					380,000
December 31, 1983 balances	10,000	$1,000,000	300,000	$1,600,000	$4,210,000
May 1, 1984 50% stock dividend on common stock			150,000	800,000	(800,000)
June 30, 1984 dividend on preferred stock, 8%					(80,000)
December 31, 1984 net loss for year					(55,000)
	10,000	$1,000,000	450,000	$2,400,000	$3,275,000

Because comparative statements are desired, the denominator of weighted shares outstanding must be adjusted for the 50% stock dividend issued in 1984 as follows:

1983: January 1–June 30	—200,000 × 150% (50% stock dividend in 1984) × 6/12 year	150,000	
July 1–December 31	—200,000 + 100,000 (issuance of stock in 1983) × 150% (50% stock dividend in 1984) × 6/12 year	225,000	375,000
1984: January 1–December 31	—300,000 × 150% (50% stock dividend in 1984) × 12/12 year		450,000

The numerator of the earnings per share in this example must be separated between income from continuing operations and net income. In addition, the preferred dividends must be deducted from both income figures. Since the preferred stock is cumulative, the eight percent dividend would be deducted even if it had not been declared. The numerator for each year would be computed as follows:

1983:	Net income	$380,000
	Less extraordinary gain	75,000
	Income from continuing operations	$305,000
	Less preferred dividends	80,000
	Income from continuing operations identified with common stock	$225,000
1984:	Net loss	$ 55,000
	Less preferred dividends	80,000
	Loss identified with common stock	$135,000

The earnings per share amounts can now be computed as follows:

1983:	Earnings per common share from continuing operations ($225,000 ÷ 375,000)	$.60
	Extraordinary gain ($75,000 ÷ 375,000)	.20
	Net income per share ($300,000 ÷ 375,000)	$.80
1984:	Loss per share ($135,000 ÷ 450,000)	$.30

It would be inappropriate to report earnings per share on preferred stock in view of the limited dividend rights of such stock. In the case of preferred stock, however, it may be informative to indicate the number of times or the extent to which the dividend per share requirements were met. Such information should be designated as *earnings coverage on preferred stock* and in the foregoing example would be computed as follows:

1983: Earnings coverage on preferred stock from net income: $380,000 ÷ $80,000 (cumulative preferred requirements) = 4.75 times.*
1984: Because there was a loss in 1984, no earnings coverage on preferred stock can be computed.

*Earnings coverage on preferred stock from continuing operations, $305,000 ÷ $80,000 = 3.81 times.

The Complex Capital Structure — Computational Guidelines

As discussed earlier, complex capital structures call for a dual presentation of earnings per share data on the face of the income statement: (1) primary earnings per share — a presentation based on the number of common shares outstanding plus the shares represented by common stock equivalents that have a dilutive effect on earnings per share; (2) fully diluted earnings per share — a second presentation based on the assumption that all of the contingent issuances of shares of common stock that would individually reduce earnings per share had taken place.

Computation of dual earnings per share requires application of the procedures for the simple structure previously described as well as special analyses and additional computations described in the following sections. The first section describes the computation of primary earnings per share; the second section describes the computation of fully diluted earnings per share.

PRIMARY EARNINGS PER SHARE

The computation of primary earnings per share requires an identification of those securities qualifying as common stock equivalents. A **common stock equivalent** is a security that is in substance equivalent to common stock due to its terms or the circumstances under which it was issued.[5] Holders of these securities can expect to participate in the appreciation of the value of common stock resulting primarily from present and potential earnings of the issuing company. A security identified as a common stock equivalent enters into the computation of primary earnings per share only if its effects on earnings are dilutive. Once a security is recognized as a common stock equivalent, the Accounting Principles Board indicated that it retains this status. However, depending on its dilutive effect, it could enter into the computation of primary earnings per share in one period and not in another. Common stock equivalents are composed of the securities described in the following paragraphs.

Stock Options and Warrants

Stock options, warrants, and similar arrangements may provide no cash yield, but have value because they offer rights for the acquisition of common shares at specified prices for an extended period. By definition of the APB, these items are *always* regarded as common stock equivalents. However, they are included in the computation of earnings per share only if they are dilutive. If the price for which stock can be acquired is lower than the current market price, the options, warrants and rights would probably be exercised and their effect would be dilutive. If the exercise price is higher than the current market price, no exercise would take place; thus, there is no potential dilution from these securities. The Board stated that no assumption of exercise is necessary unless the market price has been in excess of the exercise price for substantially all of three consecutive months ending with the last month to which earnings per share data relate.[6]

If it is assumed that exercise of options, warrants, or other rights takes place as of the beginning of the year or at the date they are issued, whichever comes later, additional cash resources would have been available for the company's use. In order to compute primary earnings per share when these types of arrangements exist, either net income must be increased to take into consideration the additional revenue such additional resources would produce, or the cash must be assumed to be used for some nonrevenue producing purpose. The latter approach was selected by the APB, and they have recommended it be assumed that the cash proceeds from the exercise of the options be used to purchase common stock on the market (treasury stock) at the average market price for the period involved. It is further assumed that

[5] *Opinions of the Accounting Principles Board No. 15, op. cit.,* Appendix D.
[6] *Ibid.,* par. 36. "Substantially all" has been defined as 11 of the 13 weeks.

the shares of treasury stock are issued to those exercising their rights, and the remaining shares required to be issued will be additional shares to be added to the actual number of shares outstanding to compute primary earnings per share. This method is known as the **treasury stock method**. To illustrate, assume employees have outstanding stock options to acquire 5,000 shares of common stock at $40. The current market price is $50, so exercise may be assumed and it will be dilutive. The proceeds from the issuance of the stock to the employees would be $200,000 (5,000 × $40). Assuming the average market price for the period was also $50, these proceeds would purchase 4,000 shares of treasury stock ($200,000 ÷ $50). If it is assumed that these 4,000 shares are issued to the employees, an additional 1,000 shares would have to be issued and the number of shares of stock for computation of primary earnings per share would be increased by 1,000 shares. The interpretations of Opinion No. 15 refer to these shares as **incremental shares**.[7]

To illustrate the use of the treasury stock method for computing common stock equivalent shares, assume the following:

Summary of relevant information:		
Net income for the year (primary earnings)		$92,800
Common shares outstanding (no change during year)		100,000
Options outstanding to purchase equivalent shares		20,000
Exercise price per share on options		$ 6
Average market price for common shares		$10
Earnings per share without common stock equivalents:		
Actual net income for the year		$92,800
Actual number of shares outstanding		100,000
Earnings per share		$.93
Application of proceeds from assumed exercise of options outstanding to purchase treasury stock:		
Proceeds from assumed exercise of options outstanding, 20,000 × $6		$120,000
Number of outstanding shares assumed to be repurchased with proceeds from options, $120,000 ÷ $10		12,000
Number of shares to be used in computing primary earnings per share:		
Actual number of shares outstanding		100,000
Additional shares issued:		
On assumed exercise of options	20,000	
Less assumed repurchase of shares from proceeds of options	12,000	8,000
Total		108,000
Primary earnings per share, $92,800 ÷ 108,000		$.86

The dilution exceeds three percent (93¢ as compared to 86¢), so the common stock equivalent would be used in computing primary earnings per share.

If the number of common shares of stock involved in exercising options, warrants and other rights is large, the market price of the shares may not be

[7] *Accounting Interpretations of APB Opinion No. 15, Interpretation 51,* "Computing Earnings Per Share" (New York: American Institute of Certified Public Accountants, 1970).

a reliable figure because any attempt to purchase a large block of stock would drive the stock price upward. The Accounting Principles Board recognized this possibility, and declared the treasury stock method inappropriate for proceeds in excess of those required to purchase 20 percent of the outstanding shares. Proceeds beyond that required to purchase 20 percent of the common stock are assumed to be applied first to reduce any short-term or long-term borrowings and any remaining proceeds are assumed to be invested in U.S. Government securities or commercial paper with appropriate recognition of any income tax effect.

To illustrate the computation of primary earnings per share under these circumstances, assume the data that follow:

Summary of relevant information:		
Net income for the year		$4,000,000
Common shares outstanding (no change during year)		3,000,000
8% First-mortgage bonds outstanding		$5,000,000
Options outstanding to purchase equivalent shares		1,000,000
Limitation on assumed repurchase of shares, 3,000,000 × 20%		600,000
Exercise price per share on options		$15
Market value per common share (average)		$20
Income tax rate		40%
Earnings per share without common stock equivalents:		
Actual net income for the year		$4,000,000
Actual number of shares outstanding		3,000,000
Earnings per share		$1.33
Application of proceeds from assumed exercise of options outstanding:		
Proceeds from assumed exercise of options outstanding, 1,000,000 × $15		$15,000,000
Maximum applied toward repurchase of outstanding shares, 600,000 × $20		12,000,000
Balance of proceeds applied to retirement of 8% first-mortgage bonds		$ 3,000,000
Net income to be used in computing primary earnings per share:		
Actual net income		$4,000,000
Add interest on 8% first-mortgage bonds assumed retired, net of income tax:		
Interest, $3,000,000 × 8%	$240,000	
Less income tax ($240,000 × 40%)	96,000	144,000
Total		$4,144,000
Number of shares to be used in computing primary earnings per share:		
Actual number of shares outstanding		3,000,000
Additional shares issued:		
On assumed exercise of options	1,000,000	
Less assumed repurchase of outstanding shares from proceeds of options	600,000	400,000
Total		3,400,000
Primary earnings per share $4,144,000 ÷ 3,400,000		$1.22

The dilution again exceeds three percent ($1.33 as compared to $1.22), and the common stock equivalent options would be included.

Contingent Shares

Shares whose issuance depends merely on the passage of time or shares held in escrow pending the satisfaction of conditions unrelated to earnings or market values, are recognized as common stock equivalents. If additional shares are issuable for little or no consideration after the satisfaction of certain conditions, they should be considered as outstanding when the conditions are met.

Convertible Securities

A convertible security, whether bonds or preferred stock, that at the time of its issuance has terms indicating the purchaser is placing a premium on the conversion feature is recognized as a common stock equivalent. The Accounting Principles Board indicated that if the cash yield of the convertible security at the time of its issuance is significantly less than a comparable security without the conversion options, it is a common stock equivalent. Cash yield as used in Opinion No. 15 is the cash to be received annually expressed as a percentage of the market value of the security at the specified date. For example, a $1,000 bond paying interest at nine percent and selling for 90 would have a cash yield of ten percent ($90/$900 = 10%). To make the determination both simple and objective, the APB, after considering a number of alternatives, concluded that a convertible security should be recognized as a common stock equivalent if it had a cash yield based on its market price of less than 66⅔ percent of the bank prime interest rate for short-term loans at the time of its issuance. Because the bank prime interest rate began to fluctuate widely in the late 1970s and early 1980s, the FASB changed the base measure for convertible securities issued after February 28, 1982, to the average Aa corporate bond yield.[8] This designation is widely used in the financial community and refers to bonds of equal quality to those rated Aa by either Moody's or Standard and Poor's investment services. The identification of a convertible security as a common stock equivalent is made at the time of its issuance, and it retains this identity as long as it remains outstanding, regardless of changes in the interest rate.

For example, assume at December 31, 1984, the Aa corporate bond yield is 11 percent. A $1,000, twenty-year, convertible bond with a stated interest rate of 7 percent is sold at 109 providing a cash yield of 6.42 percent ($70/$1,090). Since the yield is less than ⅔ of the Aa corporate bond yield of 11 percent, or 7⅓ percent, the bond is recognized as a common stock equivalent. The bond will retain this classification even though future bond interest rates fall and the cash yield exceeds the ⅔ ratio.

In order to compute primary earnings per share when convertible securities exist, adjustments must be made both to net income and to the number of shares of common stock outstanding. These adjustments must reflect what these amounts would have been if the conversion had taken place at the beginning of the current year or at the date of issuance of the convertible

[8] *Statement of Financial Accounting Standards No. 55*, "Determining Whether a Convertible Security Is a Common Stock Equivalent" (Stamford: Financial Accounting Standards Board, 1982).

securities, whichever comes later. If the securities are *bonds*, net income is adjusted by adding back the interest expense, net of tax, to net income; the number of shares of common stock outstanding is increased by the number of shares that would have been issued on conversion.[9] Any amortization of initial premium or discount is included in the interest expense added back. If the convertible securities are *shares of preferred stock*, no reduction is made from net income for preferred dividends, as is done with the computation of earnings per share in a simple capital structure; the number of shares of common stock outstanding is increased by the number of shares that would have been issued upon conversion. If the convertible securities were issued during the year, adjustments would be made for only the portion of the year since the issuance date. In order to test for material dilution, it is necessary to compute earnings per share without common stock equivalents as well as primary earnings per share including common stock equivalents. As indicated earlier, if primary earnings per share exceed earnings per share without common stock equivalents, the common stock equivalents are anti-dilutive. If the primary earnings per share is less than earnings per share without a specific common stock equivalent, the common stock equivalent is dilutive. The three percent test determines if the total dilution is material.

The following examples illustrate the computation of primary earnings per share when convertible securities qualifying as common stock equivalents exist.

Summary of relevant information:	
8% convertible bonds issued at par	$500,000
Net income for the year	$ 83,000
Common shares outstanding (no change during year)	100,000
Conversion terms of convertible bonds	80 shares for each $1,000 bond
Assumed tax rate	40%

Earnings per share without common stock equivalents:	
Actual net income	$ 83,000
Actual number of shares outstanding	100,000
Earnings per share	$.83

Primary earnings per share including common stock equivalents:		
Actual net income		$ 83,000
Add interest on convertible bonds, net of tax:		
Interest, $500,000 at 8%	$40,000	
Less income tax at 40%	16,000	24,000
Adjusted net income		$107,000
Actual number of shares outstanding		100,000
Additional shares issued upon assumed conversion of bonds, 500 × 80.		40,000
Adjusted number of shares		140,000
Primary earnings per share, $107,000 ÷ 140,000		$.76

[9]In addition to adjustments for interest, adjustments to net income for nondiscretionary or indirect items would have to be made in many situations. These items would include profit-sharing bonuses and other payments whose amount is determined by the net income reported. For simplicity, no indirect effects are illustrated in this chapter. See Chapter 21 for impact of such effects on accounting changes.

In this example, material dilution has occurred because primary earnings per share (76¢) is less than 80.51¢ [83¢ − .03(83¢)], the earnings per share without common stock equivalents reduced by three percent. Therefore, primary earnings per share would be reported.

If the convertible bonds had been issued on March 31 of the current year, the adjustment would be made to reflect only the period subsequent to the issuance date, or ¾ of a year.

Primary earnings per share including common stock equivalents (¾ year):		
Actual net income		$ 83,000
Add interest on convertible bonds, net of tax:		
Interest, $500,000 at 8% for ¾ year	$30,000	
Less income tax at 40%	12,000	18,000
Adjusted net income		$101,000
Actual number of shares outstanding		100,000
Additional shares issued upon assumed conversion of bonds, 500 × 80 × ¾		30,000
Adjusted number of shares		130,000
Primary earnings per share, $101,000 ÷ 130,000		$.78

If the 8% convertible bonds had been 8% convertible preferred stock, and if the stock qualified as a common stock equivalent and was issued in a prior year, the computations would be as illustrated below.

Earnings per share without common stock equivalents:	
Net income, without the deduction for interest on bonds (as computed on page 839)	$107,000
Less preferred dividends	40,000
Net income identified with common stock	$ 67,000
Actual number of shares outstanding	100,000
Earnings per share	$.67

Primary earnings per share including common stock equivalents:	
Net income assuming no interest on bonds	$107,000
Actual number of shares outstanding	100,000
Additional shares issued upon assumed conversion of preferred stock, 500 × 80.	40,000
Adjusted number of shares	140,000
Primary earnings per share, $107,000 ÷ 140,000	$.76

In this latter case, the assumed conversion of preferred stock is antidilutive (67¢ as compared to 76¢). Thus, the preferred stock conversion would not be assumed in computing earnings per share of common stock.

It is possible to determine if a convertible security is antidilutive without actually computing primary or fully diluted earnings per share assuming conversion. If a company has net income rather than losses, the antidilutive test is performed by computing what the convertible security is costing the existing common stockholders per assumed converted share, and comparing that rate with the earnings per common share assuming no conversion. If the cost rate on the convertible security exceeds the earnings per share assuming no conversion, the convertible security is antidilutive. If the cost rate is lower, it is dilutive. To illustrate, the after-tax interest on bonds in the previous example was $24,000. Conversion would have given the bondholders 40,000 shares. The cost rate to the existing common stockholders is 60¢ ($24,000 ÷ 40,000), which is lower than 83¢ earnings per common share, and thus the convertible bonds are dilutive. However, in the example dealing with preferred stock, the cost to the existing common stockholders for the preferred dividends is $40,000, with no tax deduction, and the cost rate to the existing common stockholders is $1.00 ($40,000 ÷ 40,000). This rate is higher than 67¢ earnings per common share, and the preferred stock conversion is thus antidilutive. If a company has net losses, no antidilution test is necessary since inclusion of stock options and convertible securities would decrease the loss per share and thus be antidilutive. If a company has an operating loss but a positive net income because of favorable below-the-line items, or vice versa, the dilutive effect must be computed for both income figures. If inclusion of stock options or convertible securities results in dilution of either income figure, they are included in both figures. The test for dilution should be made in most cases before computing either primary or fully diluted earnings per share.

Multiple Potentially Dilutive Securities

When several potentially dilutive securities exist, the combination of securities and options, warrants and other rights that produce the lowest primary earnings per share should be determined and reported. This lowest figure is found by computing earnings per share for all possible combinations of potentially dilutive securities that are not antidilutive, and identifying the lowest figure. The use of computers assists greatly in testing for the lowest combination figure.

FULLY DILUTED EARNINGS PER SHARE

In calculating fully diluted earnings in the dual presentation of earnings per share, it is necessary to consider not only all common stock equivalents, but all other contingent issuances with a dilutive effect even though they do not qualify as common stock equivalents. For example, fully diluted earnings per share would include convertible securities whose cash yield equaled or exceeded 66⅔ percent of the Aa corporate bond yield at the issuance date and that were dilutive. As with common stock equivalents, all such issuances are assumed to have taken place at the beginning of the period or at the time the convertible security was issued, if later. The maximum potential dilution of current earnings per share on a prospective basis is thus determined.

When primary earnings are diluted as a result of the inclusion of outstanding options and warrants, a modification in the application of the treasury stock method may be necessary for purposes of calculating the fully diluted earnings per share. To reflect maximum potential dilution, the market price of the common stock at the close of the period is used in computing the number of shares assumed to be reacquired if the ending market price is higher than the average price that had been used in computing primary earnings per share.

As indicated earlier, computations of fully diluted earnings should exclude those antidilutive securities whose subsequent conversion, exercise, or other contingent issuance would increase the earnings per share amount or decrease the loss per share amount.

To continue with the earlier example on page 837 and illustrate the computation of fully diluted earnings, assume that the following convertible security did not qualify as a common stock equivalent and had been outstanding during the year, and that the year-end market price of common stock was $23.

7½% Convertible bonds outstanding, issued at face value	$5,000,000
Conversion terms of convertible bonds	60 shares for each $1,000 bond

Test for dilution of 7½% convertible bonds:

$$\frac{\text{Interest net of tax}}{\text{Additional shares of stock if converted}} = \frac{(\$5{,}000{,}000 \times .075).60^*}{60 \times 5{,}000} = \$.75 \text{ per share}$$

*.60 is the complement of the tax rate, or 1 − .40.

Since $.75 is less than $1.22 primary earnings per share (see page 837), the 7½% convertible bonds are dilutive and should be used in computing fully diluted earnings per share.

Application of proceeds from assumed exercise of options outstanding:	
Proceeds from assumed exercise of options outstanding, 1,000,000 × $15	$15,000,000
Maximum applied toward repurchase of outstanding shares, 600,000 × $23 (year-end market price)	13,800,000
Balance of proceeds applied to retirement of 8% first-mortgage bonds	$ 1,200,000

Net income to be used in computing fully diluted earnings per share:		
Actual net income		$4,000,000
Add: Interest on 8% first-mortgage bonds assumed retired, net of income tax:		
Interest, $1,200,000 × 8%	$ 96,000	
Less income tax ($96,000 × 40%)	38,400	57,600
Interest on 7½% convertible bonds assumed converted, net of income tax:		
Interest, $5,000,000 × 7½%	$375,000	
Less income tax ($375,000 × 40%)	150,000	225,000
Total		$ 4,282,600

Number of shares to be used in computing fully diluted earnings per share:	
Number of shares used in computing earnings per share (as computed earlier)	3,400,000
Additional shares assumed issued on conversion of convertible bonds, 5,000 × 60	300,000
Total	3,700,000
Fully diluted earnings per share $4,282,600 ÷ 3,700,000	$1.16

Primary and fully diluted earnings in the example would be reported on the income statement as shown below. This presentation would be accompanied by notes explaining the nature of the calculations.

Primary earnings per share	$1.22
Fully diluted earnings per share	1.16

Even if conversion or exercise actually takes place during the period, adjustment is made to reflect what the impact on earnings per share would have been if the conversion or exercise would have taken place at the beginning of the period or issuance date whichever comes later. This adjustment is required for all securities actually converted during the period, whether dilutive or not. When options or warrants are exercised, the adjustment for the period before exercise for primary earnings per share uses the average market price of the pre-exercise period; the adjustment for fully diluted earnings per share uses the market price at exercise date.

To illustrate, assume in the example on page 837 that options for only 500,000 shares were outstanding. The options were actually exercised on October 1 of the current year when the market price was $20. Proceeds from exercise of the options were $7,500,000 (500,000 shares × $15 exercise price), and all proceeds were used to retire common shares. The average market price from January 1 to October 1 was $18.[10] The computation of the weighted average number of shares to be used in computing primary and fully diluted earnings per share would be as follows:

Weighted average number of shares for primary earnings per share:		
Actual number of shares outstanding for full year		3,000,000
Additional shares issued on October 1:		
On exercise of options	500,000	
Less repurchase of shares with proceeds, $7,500,000 ÷ $20	375,000	
Incremental shares issued	125,000	
Weighted average of incremental shares issued, 125,000 × ¼		31,250
Additional shares if options had been exercised on January 1:		
On exercise of options	500,000	
Less repurchase of shares with proceeds, $7,500,000 ÷ $18	416,667	
Incremental shares issued	83,333	
Weighted average of incremental shares assumed to be issued, 83,333 × ¾		62,500
Weighted average number of shares for primary earnings per share		3,093,750

[10]Since the average market price ($18) exceeded the exercise price ($15), the adjustment is dilutive.

Weighted average number of shares for fully diluted earnings per share:		
Actual number of shares outstanding for full year		3,000,000
Additional shares issued on October 1:		
On exercise of options	500,000	
Less repurchase of shares with proceeds, $7,500,000 ÷ $20	375,000	
Incremental shares issued	125,000	
Weighted average of incremental shares issued, 125,000 × ¼		31,250
Additional shares if options had been exercised on January 1:		
On exercise of options	500,000	
Less repurchase of shares with proceeds, $7,500,000 ÷ $20	375,000	
Incremental shares issued	125,000	
Weighted average of incremental shares assumed to be issued, 125,000 × ¾		93,750
Weighted average number of shares for fully diluted earnings per share		3,125,000

FINANCIAL STATEMENT PRESENTATION

When earnings of a period include extraordinary items, income or loss from discontinued operations, or a cumulative effect of a change in accounting principle, earnings per share amounts should be presented for amounts before these special items and for each of these significant items and for net income, both on a primary share basis and on a fully diluted basis.

A schedule or note should be provided for a dual presentation explaining the bases upon which both primary and fully diluted earnings are calculated. Those issues included as common stock equivalents in arriving at primary earnings per share, as well as those issues included in the computation of fully diluted earnings per share, should be identified. All the assumptions made and the resulting adjustments required in developing the earnings per share data should be indicated. Additional disclosures should be made of the number of shares of common stock issued upon conversion, exercise, or satisfaction of required conditions for at least the most recent annual fiscal period. For an example of disclosure, see General Mills' statements, Appendix B.

A common stock equivalent or other dilutive security may dilute one of the several per share amounts required to be disclosed on the face of the income statement, while increasing another amount. In such a case, the common stock equivalent or other dilutive securities should be recognized for all computations even though they have an antidilutive effect on one or more of the per share amounts.[11]

Earnings per share data should be presented for all periods covered by the income statement. If potential dilution exists in any of the periods presented, the dual presentation of primary and fully diluted earnings per share should be made for all periods presented.[12] Whenever net income of

[11] *Opinions of the Accounting Principles Board, No. 15, op. cit.*, par. 30.
[12] *Ibid.*, par. 17.

prior periods has been restated as a result of a prior period adjustment, the earnings per share for these prior periods should be restated and the effect of the restatements disclosed in the year of restatement.[13]

It is important that great care be exercised in interpreting earnings per share data regardless of the degree of refinement applied in the development of the data. These values are the products of the principles and practices employed in the accounting process and are subject to the same limitations as found in the net income measurement reported on the income statement.

QUESTIONS

1. Earnings per share computations have received increased prominence on the income statement. How would an investor use such information in making investment decisions?
2. Why are earnings per share figures computed on the basis of common stock transactions that have not yet happened rather than on the basis of strictly historical common stock data?
3. What is meant by "dilution of earnings per share"?
4. What is an antidilutive security? Why are such securities generally excluded from the computation of earnings per share?
5. What distinguishes a simple from a complex capital structure?
6. A dual presentation of earnings per share is required only if the introduction of dilutive securities is material. How does the profession define materiality in this case?
7. What constitutes a common stock equivalent for calculating primary earnings per share?
8. Why are earnings per share figures adjusted retroactively for stock dividends, stock splits, and reverse stock splits?
9. (a) Under what conditions are stock options and warrants recognized as common stock equivalents? (b) Under what conditions is a convertible security recognized as a common stock equivalent?
10. What is the treasury stock method of accounting for outstanding stock options and warrants in computing primary earnings?
11. What modification to the treasury stock method is required if the number of shares obtainable from the exercise of outstanding options and warrants exceeds 20% of the number of shares outstanding?
12. Compare the concept of primary earnings per share with the concept of fully diluted earnings per share.
13. How are convertible securities converted during the period accounted for in computing fully diluted earnings per share?
14. How is the treasury stock method for stock options and warrants modified in computing fully diluted earnings per share as compared with computing primary earnings per share?
15. In case convertible debentures are not considered as common stock equivalents, explain how they are handled for purposes of earnings per share computations.
16. What limitations should be recognized in using earnings per share data?

[13] *Ibid.*, par. 18.

DISCUSSION CASES

case 22-1 (How does a complex capital structure affect EPS?) Runyon Construction Company has gradually grown in size since its inception in 1919. The third generation of Runyons who now manage the enterprise are considering selling a large block of stock to raise capital for new equipment purchases and to help finance several big projects. The Runyons are concerned about how the earnings per share information should be presented on the income statement and have many questions concerning the nature of EPS.

(1) Discuss the EPS presentation that would be required if Runyon Construction has (a) a simple capital structure; (b) a complex capital structure. What factors determine whether a capital structure is simple or complex?

(2) Are primary earnings per share for a complex structure with common stock equivalents the same as earnings per share for a simple structure? Discuss why APB Opinion No. 15 does not provide for a simple earnings per share for a complex capital structure.

(3) Assume Runyon Company has a complex capital structure. Discuss the effect, if any, of each of the following transactions on the computation of earnings per share:

(a) The firm acquires some of its outstanding common stock to hold as treasury stock.
(b) The firm pays a dividend of 50¢ per common stock share.
(c) The firm declares a dividend of 75¢ per share on cumulative preferred stock.
(d) A 3-for-1 common stock split occurs during the year.
(e) Retained earnings are appropriated for a disputed construction contract that may be litigated.

case 22-2 (Are we in trouble or not?) Wilson Yacht Company has just completed its determination of earnings per share for the year. As a result of issuing convertible securities during the year, the capital structure of Wilson is now defined as being complex. The primary earnings per share for this year is $2.90, but the fully diluted earnings per share is only $2.50, both figures down from the prior year's $3.25 simple earnings per share figure.

Roland Lewis and Donna Korth, two stockholders, have received their financial statements from Wilson, and are discussing the earnings per share figures over lunch. The following dialogue ensues:

Lewis: I guess Wilson must be having trouble. I see their earnings per share is down significantly.

Korth: Maybe so, but this year there are two figures where before there was only one.

Lewis: Something to do with the convertible bonds and preferred stock they issued during the year making it a complex capital structure. But both of the earnings per share figures are lower than the single figure the year before.

Korth: That's true. But income for the current year is higher than last year. I'm confused.

Enlighten the stockholders.

case 22-3 (When should common stock equivalency be determined?) Sue Davis and Mark Bradshaw are discussing the concept of common stock equivalents for convertible securities as defined by APB Opinion No. 15. Davis believes the status of a convertible security should be determined (using the cash yield test) not only at the time of issuance but from time to time thereafter because convertible securities are designed to react to changes in the earnings or earnings potential just as does common stock. Furthermore, although many convertible securities are issued under market and yield conditions that do not emphasize their common stock characteristics, both the issuer and the holder recognize the possibility of these characteristics becoming more significant as the value of the underlying common stock increases. But limiting determination of the common stock equivalent status to "at issuance only" disregards these factors.

Bradshaw believes that for practical simplicity, common stock equivalent status should be determined only by the conditions that exist at time of issuance and that fully diluted earnings per share adequately disclose the potential dilution that may exist.

You are asked to give a third opinion. Which argument is more valid?

EXERCISES

exercise 22-1 (Weighted average number of shares)

Compute the weighted average number of shares outstanding for Monson Tool Company, which has a simple capital structure, assuming the following transactions in common stock occurred during 1984:

Date	Transactions in Common Stock	Number of Shares $10 Par Value
January 1, 1984	Shares outstanding	32,000
February 1, 1984	Issued for cash	6,400
April 1, 1984	Acquisition of treasury stock	(6,000)
July 1, 1984	Resold part of treasury stock shares	2,800
September 1, 1984	50% stock dividend	50% of shares outstanding
December 1, 1984	Issued in exchange for property	12,800

exercise 22-2 (Weighted average number of shares)

Transactions involving the common stock account of the Kelly Gas Company during the two-year period, 1984 and 1985, were as shown below:

1984	
January 1	Balance 250,000 shares of $10 par common stock.
April 2	$2,500,000 of convertible bonds were converted with 25 shares issued for each $1,000 bond.
July 1	A 5% stock dividend was declared.
October 1	Option to purchase 6,125 shares for $20 a share was exercised.
1985	
April 1	A 2-for-1 stock split was declared.
October 1	150,000 shares were sold for $25 a share.

From the information given, compute the comparative number of weighted average shares outstanding for 1984 and 1985 to be used for earnings per share computations at the end of 1985. Assume that conversion of bonds and exercise of options at January 1, 1984, would not have resulted in material dilution, and there are no other convertible securities or options outstanding. Thus, only a simple earnings per share is required.

exercise 22-3 (Earnings per share—simple capital structure)

At December 31, 1984, the Meyers Corporation had 50,000 shares of common stock issued and outstanding, 40,000 of which had been issued and outstanding throughout the year and 10,000 of which had been issued on October 1, 1984. Operating income before income taxes for the year ended December 31, 1984, was $468,800. In 1984, a dividend of $32,000 was paid on 40,000 shares of 8% cumulative preferred stock, $10 par.

On April 1, 1985, 15,000 additional shares were issued. Total income before income taxes for 1985 was $477,000, which included an extraordinary gain before income taxes of $37,000. Assuming a 40% tax rate, what is Meyer's earnings per common share for 1984 and for 1985, rounded to the nearest cent? Show computations in good form.

exercise 22-4 (Earnings per share—simple capital structure)

The income statement for the Hampster Co. for the year ended December 31, 1984, reported the following:

Income from continuing operations before income tax	$330,000
Income tax	132,000
Income from continuing operations	$198,000
Extraordinary gain (net of tax)	90,000
Net income	$288,000

Compute earnings per share amounts for 1984 under each of the following assumptions:

(a) The company has only one class of common stock with 150,000 shares outstanding.
(b) The company has shares outstanding as follows: preferred 6% stock, $50 par, cumulative, 20,000 shares; common, $25 par, 150,000 shares. Only the current year's preferred dividends are unpaid.
(c) Same as (b) except Hampster Co. *also* has preferred 7% stock, $40 par, noncumulative, 10,000 shares. Only $14,000 in dividends on the noncumulative preferred have been declared.

exercise 22-5 (Common stock equivalents)

Which of the following securities would qualify as common stock equivalents? If a common stock equivalent, would it be used in computing primary earnings per share? Give reasons supporting each answer.

(a) Employee stock options to purchase 1,000 shares of common stock at $40 are outstanding. The market price of the common stock has been in excess of $45 for the past three months.
(b) Warrants to purchase 2,000 shares at $30 are issued. The current market price is $25.
(c) 8% convertible bonds are sold: sales price, 120. The Aa corporate bond yield is 11½%.
(d) Preferred stock, 7½%, convertible, is sold at par. The Aa corporate bond yield is 10%.
(e) An agreement is made with management to issue 2,000 shares of common stock in two years at a price equal to 75% of the market price at that date.

exercise 22-6 (Primary earnings per share—convertible bonds)

On January 2, 1985, Baker Co. issued at par $10,000 of 7% bonds convertible in total into 1,000 shares of Baker's common stock. These bonds are common stock equivalents for purposes of computing earnings per share. No bonds were converted during 1985.

Throughout 1985, Baker had 1,000 shares of common stock outstanding. Baker's 1985 net income was $1,000. Baker's tax rate is 40%.

No other potentially dilutive securities other than the convertible bonds were outstanding during 1985. For 1985, compute Baker's primary earnings per share.

exercise 22-7 (Dilutive securities)

The Wayne Corporation has earnings per common share of $1.51 for the period ended December 31, 1984. For each of the following examples, decide whether the convertible security would be dilutive or antidilutive in computing primary earnings per share.

Consider each example individually. All are common stock equivalents. The tax rate is 40%.

(a) 8½% debentures, $1,000,000 face value, are convertible into common stock at the rate of 40 shares for each $1,000 bond.
(b) $4 preferred stock is convertible into common stock at the rate of 2 shares of common for 1 share of preferred. There are 50,000 shares of preferred stock outstanding.
(c) Options to purchase 200,000 shares of common stock are outstanding. The exercise price is $25 per share. Current market price is $20 per share.
(d) $500,000 of 8% debentures are convertible at the rate of 20 shares of common stock per each $1,000 bond.
(e) Preferred 6% stock, $100 par, 5,000 shares outstanding, convertible into 5 shares of common stock for each 1 share of preferred.

exercise 22-8 (Number of shares—complex capital structure)

On January 1, 1985, Terry Corporation had 41,000 shares of outstanding common stock which did not change during 1985. In 1984 Terry Corporation granted options to certain executives to purchase 9,000 shares of its common stock at $7 each. The market price of common was $10.50 per share on December 31, 1985, and averaged $9 per share during the year. Compute the number of shares to be used in computing primary and fully diluted earnings per share for 1985.

exercise 22-9 (Primary earnings per share—convertible bonds)

The Ortiz Manufacturing Company reports long-term liabilities and stockholders' equity balances at December 31, 1984, as follows:

Convertible 6% bonds (sold at par)	$ 300,000
Common stock, $25 par, 90,000 shares issued and outstanding	2,250,000

Additional information is determined as follows:

Conversion terms of bonds	100 shares for each $1,000 bond
Income before extraordinary gain—1984	$150,000
Extraordinary gain (net of tax)	40,000
Net income—1984	$190,000

What are the primary earnings per share for the company for 1984, assuming that the income tax rate is 40% and the Aa corporate bond yield at the date the bonds were sold was 9½%? No changes occurred in the above debt and equity balances during 1984.

exercise 22-10 (Earnings per share—complex capital structure)

Information relating to the capital structure of the Star Corporation at December 31, 1983 and 1984, is as follows:

	Outstanding
Common stock	90,000 shares
Convertible preferred stock (issued in 1982)	10,000 shares
9% convertible bonds (issued in 1983)	$1,000,000

Star Corporation paid dividends of $2.50 per share on its preferred stock. The preferred stock is convertible into 20,000 shares of common stock and is considered a common stock equivalent. The 9% convertible bonds are convertible into 30,000 shares of common stock, but are *not* considered to be common stock equivalents. The net income for the year ended December 31, 1984, is $485,000. Assume that the income tax rate is 40%. Compute (1) simple earnings per share, (2) primary earnings per share, and (3) fully diluted earnings per share for the year ended December 31, 1984.

exercise 22-11 (Earnings per share—complex capital structure)

Options to purchase 4,000 common shares at $5 per share are outstanding. All these options were outstanding during the entire year and are presently exercisable or will become exercisable within four years. The average market price of the company's common stock during the year was $20 and the price of the stock at the end of the year was $25. Compute the common stock equivalent incremental shares that would be used in arriving at (1) primary earnings per share, and (2) fully diluted earnings per share. (Assume less than 20% of outstanding stock is reacquired.)

exercise 22-12 (Earnings per share—complex capital structure)

At December 31, 1984, the books of Wyatt Corporation include the following balances:

Long-term liabilities:	
Bonds payable, 8%, each $1,000 bond is convertible into 50 shares of common stock. Bonds sold at par and were issued November 3, 1983 ...	$ 500,000
Stockholders' equity:	
Preferred stock, 7%, par $50, cumulative, nonconvertible, 10,000 shares outstanding ...	500,000
Contributed capital in excess of par, preferred stock ...	300,000
Common stock, par $10, authorized 300,000 shares; 178,500 shares outstanding ...	1,785,000
Contributed capital in excess of par, common stock ...	450,000
Retained earnings ...	432,000

The records of Wyatt reveal the following additional information:

(a) 150,000 shares of common stock were outstanding January 1, 1984.
(b) 20,000 shares of common stock were sold for cash on April 30, 1984.
(c) Issued 5% stock dividend on July 2, 1984.
(d) Aa corporate bond yield was 12% when bonds were issued.
(e) Operating income before extraordinary items (after tax) was $538,000.
(f) Extraordinary loss (net of tax), $16,000.
(g) Average income tax rate, 40%.

(1) How should the earnings per share data be presented? Why is this a complex capital structure? (2) Compute the required earnings per share amounts.

exercise 22-13 (Earnings and loss per share—complex capital structure)

During all of 1984, Athens Inc. had outstanding 100,000 shares of common stock and 5,000 shares of $7 preferred stock. Each share of the preferred stock, which is classified as a common stock equivalent, is convertible into 3 shares of common stock. For 1984, Athens had $230,000 income from operations and $575,000 extraordinary losses; no dividends were paid or declared.

Compute the earnings (loss) per share for income (loss) before extraordinary items and for net income (loss) assuming:

(a) The preferred stock is noncumulative.
(b) The preferred stock is cumulative.

exercise 22-14 (Earnings per share—multiple choice)

Select the best answer for each of the following:

(1) In computing earnings per share, the equivalent number of shares of convertible preferred stock are added as an adjustment to the denominator (number of shares outstanding). If the preferred stock is preferred as to dividends, which amount should then be added as an adjustment to the numerator (net earnings)?

(a) Annual preferred dividend.
(b) Annual preferred dividend × (one − the income tax rate).
(c) Annual preferred dividend × the income tax rate.
(d) Annual preferred dividend ÷ the income tax rate.

(2) Which of the following statements *best* describes the effect of cash yield at issuance of convertible securities on calculating earnings per share (EPS)?

(a) If less than two thirds of the then current Aa corporate bond yield, these securities are used to calculate primary EPS but *not* fully diluted EPS.
(b) If less than two thirds of the then current Aa corporate bond yield, these securities are used to calculate fully diluted EPS but *not* primary EPS.
(c) If greater than two thirds of the then current Aa corporate bond yield, these securities are used to calculate primary EPS and fully diluted EPS.
(d) If greater than two thirds of the then current Aa corporate bond yield, these securities are used to calculate fully diluted EPS but *not* primary EPS.

(3) In a primary earnings per share computation, the treasury stock method is used for options and warrants to reflect assumed reacquisition of common stock at the average market price during the period. If the exercise price of the options or warrants exceeds the average market price, the computation would:

(a) Fairly present primary earnings per share on a prospective basis.
(b) Fairly present the maximum potential dilution of primary earnings per share on a prospective basis.
(c) Reflect the excess of the number of shares assumed issued over the number of shares assumed reacquired as the potential dilution of earnings per share.
(d) Be antidilutive.

(4) What is the inherent justification underlying the concept of common stock equivalents in an earnings per share computation?

(a) Form over substance.
(b) Substance over form.
(c) Form and substance considered equally.
(d) Substance over form or form over substance depending on the circumstances.

(5) Dilutive common stock equivalents must be used in the computation of:

(a) Fully diluted earnings per share only.
(b) Primary earnings per share only.
(c) Fully diluted and primary earnings per share.
(d) Other potentially dilutive securities only. (AICPA adapted)

exercise 22-15 (Weighted average number of shares)

Assume the following transactions affected owners' equity for Reiser Inc. during 1984.

February	1	10,000 shares of common stock were sold in the market.
April	1	Purchased 5,000 shares of common stock to be held as treasury stock. Paid cash dividends of 50¢ per share.
May	1	Split common stock 3-for-1.
July	1	35,000 shares of common stock sold.
October	1	A 5% stock dividend was issued.
December	31	Paid a cash dividend of 75¢ per share. The total amount paid for dividends on December 31 was $511,875.

Given the above information, compute the weighted average number of shares to be used in computing earnings per share for 1984. Because no beginning share figures are available, you must work backwards from December 31, 1984, to compute shares outstanding.

exercise 22-16 (Earnings per share—policy issues)

On January 1, 1984, Franson Company had 1,000,000 shares of common stock and 100,000 shares of $8 cumulative preferred stock issued and outstanding.

On January 1, 1985, Franson Company retired 50,000 shares of the preferred stock with excess cash and additional funds provided from the sale of a subsidiary.

At the beginning of 1986, the company borrowed $5,000,000 at 10% and used the proceeds to retire 200,000 shares of common stock. Operating income, before interest and income taxes (income tax rate is 40%), is as follows:

	1986	1985	1984
Operating income	$6,500,000	$7,000,000	$7,500,000

Compute the earnings per share for each of the three years. How did Franson Company maintain earnings per share when operating income was declining?

PROBLEMS

problem 22-1 (Weighted average number of shares)

Dan's Wholesale Products Inc. had 50,000 shares of common stock outstanding at the end of 1982. During 1983 and 1984, the transactions shown below took place.

1983		
March	31	Sold 10,000 shares at $27.
April	26	Paid cash dividend of 50¢ per share.
July	31	Paid cash dividend of 25¢ per share, and 5% stock dividend.
October	26	Paid cash dividend of 50¢ per share.
1984		
February	28	Purchased 5,000 shares of treasury stock.
March	1	Paid cash dividend of 50¢ per share.
April	30	Issued 3-for-1 stock split.
November	1	Sold 6,000 shares of treasury stock.
November	3	Paid cash dividend of 50¢ per share.
December	20	Declared cash dividend of 25¢ per share.

Dan's Wholesale Products Inc. has a simple capital structure.

Instructions: Compute the weighted average number of shares for 1983 and 1984 to be used in the earnings per share computation at the end of 1984.

problem 22-2 (Earnings per share—simple capital structure)

The following 1984 condensed financial statements for the Brooks Corporation were prepared by the accounting department:

Brooks Corporation
Income Statement
For Year Ended December 31, 1984

Sales		$10,000,000
Cost of goods sold		8,000,000
Gross profit on sales		$ 2,000,000
Expenses:		
Selling expense	$452,000	
Administrative expense	500,000	
Interest expense	48,000	1,000,000
Income from continuing operations before income taxes		$ 1,000,000
Income taxes		450,000
Income from continuing operations		$ 550,000
Extraordinary gain, net of tax		45,000
Net income		$ 595,000

Brooks Corporation
Balance Sheet
December 31, 1984

Assets	$3,500,000
Current liabilities	$1,000,000
8% Bonds, due December 31, 1991	600,000
Stockholders' equity:	
Common stock, $5 par, 250,000 shares authorized, issued and outstanding	1,250,000
Additional paid-in capital	400,000
Retained earnings	250,000
	$3,500,000

Instructions: Compute the earnings per share under each of the following separate assumptions (the company has a simple capital structure):

(1) No change in the capital structure occurred in 1984.
(2) On December 31, 1983, there were 150,000 shares outstanding. On April 1, 1984, 80,000 shares were sold at par and on October 1, 1984, 20,000 shares were sold at par.
(3) On December 31, 1983, there were 187,500 shares outstanding. On July 1, 1984, the company issued a 33⅓% stock dividend.

problem 22-3 (Earnings per share—simple capital structure)

Uncle Ernie's Yogurt Co. reported the comparative balances given below in the stockholders' equity section of its 1985 balance sheet.

	December 31, 1985	December 31, 1984	December 31, 1983
Preferred stock	$ 65,000	$ 55,000	$ 40,000
Premium on preferred stock	10,000	7,000	4,000
Common stock	450,000	440,000	350,000
Premium on common stock	81,000	75,000	40,000
Paid-in capital from sale of treasury stock at more than cost	4,000	1,000	1,000
Retained earnings	442,200	357,050	320,000
Total stockholders' equity	$1,052,200	$935,050	$755,000

In addition, the following transactions involving the stockholders' equity were recorded during 1984 and 1985:

1984

April	2	Sold 5,000 shares of $10 par value common stock for $13 per share.
June	30	Sold 300 shares of $50 par value preferred stock for $60 per share.
August	1	Issued a 10% stock dividend on common stock. The market price at the time of the sale was $14.
September	1	Declared cash dividends of 9% on preferred stock; $1 on common stock.
December	31	Income from continuing operations for the year was $149,500. In addition, the company had an extraordinary loss of $7,500 net of tax savings.

1985

January	31	Sold 1,000 shares of common stock for $16.
May	1	Sold 200 shares of preferred stock for $65.
June	1	Split common stock 2-for-1.
September	1	Purchased 600 shares of common stock for $8 to be held as treasury stock.
October	1	Declared a cash dividend on 9% preferred stock; 50¢ on common stock.
November	1	Sold 600 shares of treasury stock at $13 per share.
December	31	Net income of 1985 included an extraordinary gain net of tax of $4,000.

Uncle Ernie's Yogurt Co. has a simple capital structure.

Instructions: Compute the earnings per share amounts for 1984 and 1985 to be shown on the 1985 income statement.

problem 22-4 (Earnings per share—complex capital structure)

The capital structure of the Martinez Company as of December 31, 1983, follows:

$6 Preferred stock, $50 par, 10,000 shares issued and outstanding	$ 500,000
Premium on preferred stock	50,000
Common stock, $10 par, 200,000 shares issued and outstanding	2,000,000
Premium on common stock	250,000
Retained earnings	725,000

On April 1, 1984, the company issued 30,000 stock options to select executives, creditors, and others, allowing for the purchase of common stock for $20 a share. The market price for the stock at this date was $15. The price of the common stock rose steadily during the year and closed at $60. The average market price for the year was $40. The dividend on preferred stock was paid in 1984.

There were no other capital transactions during the year. Net income for 1984 was $400,000.

Instructions: Using the information given, compute the earnings per share data required to comply with generally accepted accounting principles.

problem 22-5 (Earnings per share—complex capital structure)

The following is an extract from the balance sheet of Jimbolee Enterprises for the year ended December 31, 1983:

9% Convertible debentures	$10,000,000
Common stock, $10 par, 1,000,000 shares issued and outstanding	$10,000,000
Retained earnings	6,750,000
Total stockholders' equity	$16,750,000

The terms of conversion state that for each $1,000 bond tendered, the corporation will transfer to the creditor 40 shares of common stock.

On June 30, 1984, the complete issue of convertible debentures was converted into common stock.

Net income for 1984 was $2,350,000. The income tax rate was 40%.

No common stock was issued or repurchased during the year, other than that issued in the conversion.

Instructions: Compute the primary earnings per share for Jimbolee Enterprises for the year ended December 31, 1984.

problem 22-6 (Earnings per share—complex capital structure)

The Aurora Hardware Co. provides the following data at December 31, 1985:

Operating revenue	$950,000
Operating expenses	$450,000
Income tax rate	40%
Common stock outstanding during the entire year	25,000 shares

On January 1, 1985, there were options outstanding to purchase 10,000 shares of common stock at $20 per share. During 1985, the average price per share was $25 but at December 31, 1985, the market price had risen to $30 per share. The balance sheet reports $200,000 of 8% nonconvertible bonds at December 31, 1985. (Interest expense is included in operating expenses.)

Instructions: Compute for 1985:

(1) Primary earnings per share.
(2) Fully diluted earnings per share.

problem 22-7 (Earnings per share—complex capital structure)

Data for the Allison Powder Company at the end of 1984 are listed below. All bonds are convertible as indicated and were issued at their face amounts.

Description of Bonds	Amount	Date Issued	Aa Corporate Bond Yield on Date Issued	Conversion Terms
10-year, 6% Convertible bonds	$ 500,000	1/1/78	9½%	80 shares of common for each $1,000 bond
20-year, 7% Convertible bonds	1,000,000	1/1/79	8½%	40 shares of common for each $1,000 bond
25-year, 9½% Convertible bonds	800,000	6/30/84	14¼%	100 shares of common for each $1,000 bond

Common shares outstanding at December 31, 1983	600,000
Net income for 1984	$1,525,000
Income tax rate	40%

Instructions:

(1) Compute primary earnings per share for 1984, assuming that no additional shares of common stock were issued during the year.
(2) Compute fully diluted earnings per share for 1984, assuming that no additional shares of common stock were issued during the year.
(3) Compute both primary and fully diluted earnings per share assuming that the 20-year bonds were converted on July 1, 1984, and that net income for the year was $1,546,000 (reflects reduction in interest due to bond conversion).

problem 22-8 (Earnings per share—complex capital structure)

At December 31, 1983, the Leon White Company had 400,000 shares of common stock outstanding. White sold 100,000 shares on October 1, 1984. Net income for 1984 was $2,565,000; the income tax rate was 40%. In addition, White had the following debt and equity securities on its books at December 31, 1983.

(a) 20,000 shares of $100 par 10% cumulative preferred stock. Aa corporate bond yield was 11% at time of sale. Stock was sold at 102.
(b) 30,000 shares of 8% convertible cumulative preferred stock, par $100, sold at 110 when Aa corporate bond yield was 11%. Each share of preferred stock is convertible into two shares of common.
(c) $2,000,000 face value of 8% bonds sold at par when Aa corporate bond yield was 10%.
(d) $3,000,000 face value of 6% convertible bonds sold at par when Aa corporate bond yield was 8%. Each $1,000 bond is convertible into 20 shares of common.

Also, options to purchase 10,000 shares were issued May 1, 1984. Option price was $30 per share; market value at date of option was $29; market value at end of year, $40; average market value May 1 to December 31, 1984, $35.

Instructions:

For the year ended December 31, 1981:
(1) Compute simple earnings per share.
(2) Compute primary earnings per share.
(3) Compute fully-diluted earnings per share.

problem 22-9 (Earnings per share—complex capital structure)

The "Stockholders' equity" section of Lowe Company's balance sheet as of December 31, 1984, contains the following:

$1 cumulative preferred stock, $25 par, convertible, 1,600,000 shares authorized, 1,400,000 shares issued, 750,000 converted to common, 650,000 shares outstanding; involuntary liquidation value, $30 a share, aggregating $19,500,000	$16,250,000
Common stock, $.25 par, 15,000,000 shares authorized, 8,800,000 shares issued and outstanding	2,200,000
Additional paid-in capital	32,750,000
Retained earnings	40,595,000
Total stockholders' equity	$91,795,000

On April 1, 1984, Lowe Company acquired the business and assets and assumed the liabilities of Diane Corporation in a transaction accounted for as a pooling of interests. (Pooling of interest accounting adjusts statements retroactively as if the new entity had existed for all reported periods.) For each of Diane Corporation's 2,400,000 shares of $1 par value common stock outstanding, the owner received one share of common stock of the Lowe Company.

Included in the liabilities of Lowe Company are 8½% convertible subordinated debentures issued at their face value of $20,000,000 in 1983. The debentures are due in 2000 and until then are convertible into the common stock of Lowe Company at the rate of five shares of common stock for each $100 debenture. To date none of these have been converted.

On April 2, 1984, Lowe Company issued 1,400,000 shares of convertible preferred stock at $40 per share. Quarterly dividends to December 31, 1984, have been paid on these shares. The preferred stock is convertible into common stock at the rate of two shares of common for each share of preferred. On October 1, 1984, 150,000 shares and on November 1, 1984, 600,000 shares of the preferred stock were converted into common stock.

During July 1983, Lowe Company granted options to its officers and key employees to purchase 500,000 shares of the company's common stock at a price of $20 a share. The options do not become exercisable until 1985.

During 1984 dividend payments and average market prices of the Lowe common stock were as follows:

	Dividend per Share	Average Market Price per Share
First quarter	$.10	$20
Second quarter	.15	25
Third quarter	.10	30
Fourth quarter	.15	25
Average for the year		25

The December 31, 1984, closing price of the common stock was $25 a share.

Assume that the Aa corporate bond yield was 12% throughout 1983 and 1984. Lowe Company's consolidated net income for the year ended December 31, 1984, was $9,200,000. The provision for income tax was computed at a rate of 40%.

Instructions:

(1) Prepare a schedule that shows the evaluation of the common stock equivalency status of the (a) convertible debentures, (b) convertible preferred stock, and (c) employee stock options.
(2) Compute simple earnings per share and test any common stock equivalents for dilution.
(3) Compute primary earnings per share.
(4) Compute fully diluted earnings per share. (AICPA adapted)

problem 22-10 (Earnings per share—complex capital structure)

The controller of Lafayette Corporation has requested assistance in determining income, primary earnings per share and fully diluted earnings per share for presentation in the company's income statement for the year ended September 30, 1984. As currently calculated, the company's net income is $400,000 for fiscal year 1983–1984. The controller has indicated that the income figure might be adjusted for the following transactions that were recorded by charges or credits directly to Retained Earnings (the amounts are net of applicable income tax):

(a) The sum of $375,000, applicable to a breached 1976 contract, was received as a result of a lawsuit. Prior to the award, legal counsel was uncertain about the outcome of the suit.
(b) A gain of $300,000 was realized on the sale of a subsidiary.
(c) A gain of $80,000 was realized on the sale of treasury stock.
(d) A special inventory write-off of $150,000 was made, of which $125,000 applied to goods manufactured prior to October 1, 1983.

Your working papers disclose the following opening balances and transactions in the company's capital stock accounts during the year:

(e) Common stock (at October 1, 1983, stated value $10, authorized 300,000 shares; effective December 1, 1983, stated value $5, authorized 600,000 shares):
  Balance, October 1, 1983—issued and outstanding 60,000 shares.
  December 1, 1983—60,000 shares issued in a 2-for-1 stock split.
  December 1, 1983—280,000 shares (stated value $5) issued at $39 per share.
(f) Treasury stock common:
  March 1, 1984—purchased 40,000 shares at $38 per share.
  April 1, 1984—sold 40,000 shares at $40 per share.
(g) Stock purchase warrants, Series A (initially, each warrant was exchangeable with $60 for one common share; effective December 1, 1983, each warrant became exchangeable for two common shares at $30 per share):
  October 1, 1983—25,000 warrants issued at $6 each.
(h) Stock purchase warrants, Series B (each warrant is exchangeable with $60 for one common share):
  April 1, 1984—20,000 warrants authorized and issued at $10 each.
(i) First-mortgage bonds, 10%, due 1988 (nonconvertible; priced to yield 8% when issued):
  Balance, October 1, 1983—authorized, issued and outstanding—the face value of $1,400,000.
(j) Convertible debentures, 7%, due 1992 (initially each $1,000 bond was convertible at any time until maturity into 18 common shares; effective December 1, 1983, the conversion rate became 36 shares for each bond):
  October 1, 1983—authorized and issued at their face value (no premium or discount) of $2,400,000.

The following table shows market prices for the company's securities and the assumed Aa corporate bond yield during 1983–1984.

	Price (or Rate) at			Average for Year Ended
	October 1, 1983	April 1, 1984	September 30, 1984	September 30, 1984
Common stock	75	55	45	50
First-mortgage bonds	88½	87	86	87
Convertible debentures	100	120	119	115
Series A Warrants	6	22	19½	15
Series B Warrants	—	10	9	9½
Aa corporate bond yield	8%	7¾%	7½%	7¾%

*Adjusted for stock split.

Instructions:

(1) Prepare a schedule computing net income as it should be presented in the company's income statement for the year ended September 30, 1984.

(2) Assuming net income for the year was $540,000 and that there were no extraordinary items, prepare a schedule computing (a) the primary earnings per share, and (b) the fully diluted earnings per share that should be presented in the company's income statement for the year ended September 30, 1984. A supporting schedule computing the number of shares to be used in these computations should also be prepared. (Because of the relative stability of the market price for its common shares, the annual average market price may be used where appropriate in your calculations. Assume an income tax rate of 40%.)

(AICPA adapted)

23 STATEMENT OF CHANGES IN FINANCIAL POSITION

CHAPTER OBJECTIVES

Identify the objectives and limitations of the funds statement.

Explain the "all financial resources" concept of funds.

Describe the steps to be followed in preparing a funds statement.

Illustrate the preparation of a funds statement on a working capital basis and on a cash basis.

As noted in Chapters 4 and 5, the primary financial statements for a business unit consist of statements reporting the results of operations, the financial position, and the changes in financial position. The financial status of a business at a given time is reported on the balance sheet. The income for a given period is reported on the income statement and on the statement of changes in financial position—the funds statement. The income statement summarizes the revenues and expenses for the period and accounts for the major changes in retained earnings in successive periods. When there are further transactions that must be recognized in explaining the change in owners' equity, these would be reported in a separate statement accompanying the income statement. The funds statement, on the other hand, offers a summary not only of the operations of a business but also of any significant financing and investing activities for the period. Thus, it accounts for all the changes in financial position as reported on successive balance sheets.

The funds statement has undergone several years of development in becoming one of the primary financial statements. In 1961 Accounting Research Study No. 2, sponsored by the AICPA, recommended that a funds statement be prepared and included with the income statement and balance sheet in annual reports to shareholders.[1] Two years later APB Opinion No. 3 was issued to provide guidelines for the preparation of the funds statement.[2] Even though Opinion No. 3 did not require a funds statement, most businesses sensed the value of the funds statement and included it in their annual reports. Thus, it was somewhat anticlimatic when the APB issued Opinion No. 19 in 1971 officially requiring that a funds statement be included as one of the three primary financial statements in annual reports to shareholders and be covered by the auditor's opinion.[3]

During this developmental period, the funds statement was referred to by a variety of titles including: *the statement of sources and uses of funds, the source and application of funds statement,* and *the statement of resources provided and applied.* In reporting funds flow, it is possible to adopt a funds concept that provides for limited recognition of financial changes or a funds concept broadened to cover all financial changes. However, the Accounting Principles Board in Opinion No. 19 recommended that the broadened concept of funds be adopted, and, in applying this concept that the funds statement be called the **statement of changes in financial position.** To simplify reference to the statement, the term "funds statement" is used in this chapter.

OBJECTIVES AND LIMITATIONS OF FUNDS STATEMENT

As indicated in Chapter 5, the funds statement provides a summary of the sources from which funds became available during a period and the purposes to which funds were applied. Essentially, there are only two main sources of funds: (1) those provided internally from the operations of a business and (2) those provided from external sources through borrowing or the sale of stock. However, it is generally useful to show the amount of funds generated from the normal, ongoing operations of a business as distinct from those funds provided from unusual or irregular operations. Similarly, it is helpful to highlight those sources generated from long-term debt financing as a separate component from equity financing. The main uses of funds are for working capital purposes, purchasing plant and equipment, paying dividends, retiring debt, and acquiring stock. These primary inflows and outflows were illustrated in the diagram on page 145.

The funds statement is based on data taken from comparative balance sheets and the income statement. However, it is not intended to be a duplicate of or a substitute for those statements. Instead, the funds statement is intended to help investors, creditors, and other external users better understand the financing and investing activities of a company for a period of time. Thus, the funds statement highlights important relationships and helps

---

[1]Perry Mason, *Accounting Research Study No. 2,* "'Cash Flow' Analysis and the Funds Statement" (New York: American Institute of Certified Public Accountants, 1961).

[2]*Opinions of the Accounting Principles Board, No. 3,* "The Statement of Source and Application of Funds" (New York: American Institute of Certified Public Accountants, 1963).

[3]*Opinions of the Accounting Principles Board, No. 19,* "Reporting Changes in Financial Position" (New York: American Institute of Certified Public Accountants, 1971).

answer questions such as: What was the total amount of funds used during the period? Where did they come from? How much was generated from normal operations that can be expected to continue in the future? What amount of funds came from long-term debt that will have to be repaid in the future? Does the amount of dividends paid seem reasonable in light of other fund outlays and the total funds available? These questions and others require answers if the readers of financial statements are to be fully informed and in the best position to evaluate the operations of a company and its management.

Notwithstanding its popular acceptance and potential usefulness, there are some accountants who feel the funds statement has some serious limitations.[4] One problem is that the term *funds* has not been specifically defined. The most common definitions are working capital and cash, but there are a variety of other possible definitions.

A more basic problem to some individuals is the confusion over the objectives of the statement. They argue that the objectives, as stated in Opinion No. 19, are unclear and that a single statement cannot do all that is expected of it. To solve this problem, they contend, requires more specific objectives and perhaps several different statements, each meeting a particular objective. For example, a statement of cash receipts and payments might better show the debt-paying ability of a company; a statement of financing activities might be presented to show the extent and nature of debt and equity financing; and a statement of investing activities showing the long-term investments of a company could highlight changes in noncurrent assets such as plant and equipment. Supporters of the funds statement feel that it already provides the information mentioned above in a single, concise statement.

Even if one were to agree with the criticisms of the funds statement, until the FASB clarifies or modifies the reporting requirements, the preparation of a statement of changes in financial position is required by generally accepted accounting principles. Therefore, the remainder of the chapter examines the complexities of funds statement analysis and preparation.

THE "ALL FINANCIAL RESOURCES" CONCEPT OF FUNDS

As explained in Chapter 5, funds may be defined in a variety of ways, and the definition used will determine the type of funds statement prepared. The two most common definitions of funds are working capital and cash. However, if these definitions were to be applied literally, a number of transactions involving highly significant information relative to financing and investing activities would be omitted from the funds statement and thus might not be considered by the user. For example, debt and equity securities may be issued in exchange for land and buildings; long-term investments may be exchanged for machinery and equipment; shares of stock may be issued in payment of long-term debt; properties may be received as gifts.

[4]See, for example, Loyd C. Heath, "Let's Scrap the 'Funds' Statement," *The Journal of Accountancy*, October 1978, pp. 94–103.

Transactions such as these carry significant implications in analyzing the change in financial position even though they are not factors in reconciling the change in funds defined either as working capital or cash. This suggests that in order to make the funds statement more useful, the funds interpretation should be broadened to recognize transactions such as those mentioned. The broadened view, for example, would recognize the issuance of capital stock for a plant asset as funds provided by the issuance of stock offset by funds applied to the acquisition of the asset. This treatment assumes that the transfer of an item in an exchange effectively provides a company with working capital or cash, which is immediately applied to the acquisition of property, the liquidation of debt, or the retirement of capital stock. Because sources and applications from such transactions are equal in amount, the remaining items reported on the funds statement will serve to reconcile the change in funds for the period. This broadened interpretation of funds, often referred to as the **all financial resources concept,** is required by generally accepted accounting principles, and is assumed throughout this text.[5]

It is important to recognize that the all financial resources concept can be applied on either a cash or working capital basis, as illustrated later in the chapter. Historically, a majority of companies have adopted the working capital format. More recently, however, both the FASB and the Financial Executives Institute have recommended the adoption of the cash flow concept for funds statement presentation. This is consistent with one of the FASB's primary reporting objectives—to assist users in assessing the amounts, timing, and uncertainty of future cash flows. An informal survey of recent annual reports indicates that a number of companies have followed this recommendation and are now reporting their funds statements on a cash or modified cash basis. Since many companies still report on a working capital basis, that format is also illustrated in the chapter. The authors favor the cash flow concept and believe that the trend will continue toward cash flow funds statement presentation.

PREPARATION OF FUNDS STATEMENT

Regardless of how funds are defined, the funds statement is prepared from comparative balance sheets supplemented by operating income data from the income statement and by other explanatory data concerning individual account balance changes. The preparation of a funds statement calls for three specific steps:

(1) Select a definition to be used for "funds."
(2) Compute the total net change in funds by analyzing the fund accounts as listed on the comparative balance sheets. This amount should be the same balancing figure as that determined in step (3).
(3) Analyze the changes in each nonfund account on the comparative balance sheets in conjunction with the other explanatory data available in order to

[5] *Opinions of the Accounting Principles Board, No. 19, op. cit.*, pars. 6 and 8.

classify the changes as sources or applications of funds. The resulting net increase or decrease arising from such changes should be the same amount as that computed in step (2). Through this analysis, the formal funds statement can be prepared. As explained earlier, application of the all financial resources concept may require certain transactions to be shown as both a source and an offsetting application of funds.

To illustrate the process of analyzing accounts and preparing a funds statement, a simple example will be considered. The working capital definition of funds is illustrated first, followed by the cash basis. For both illustrations, assume that a funds statement is to be prepared from the balance sheets and additional information for the Singleton Company as given below. To emphasize the nature of the account analysis required in preparing a funds statement, it is assumed that no other information is available. In practice, however, the data for preparing a funds statement can be taken directly from the accounting records.

Singleton Company
Comparative Balance Sheet
December 31, 1984 and 1983

Assets	1984	1983
Cash	$ 8,200	$ 4,000
Receivables (net)	18,000	15,000
Inventory	17,000	20,000
Equipment	20,000	14,000
Accumulated depreciation	(7,200)	(6,000)
	$56,000	$47,000
Liabilities and Stockholders' Equity		
Accounts payable	$10,000	$ 8,000
Long-term notes payable	10,000	5,000
Capital stock	25,000	25,000
Retained earnings	11,000	9,000
	$56,000	$47,000

Net income for the year as reported on the income statement was $9,000. Equipment that cost $3,000 and had a book value of $200 was sold during the year for $700.

Funds Defined as Working Capital

The first step in preparing a funds statement is to define the concept of funds to be used. In this case, it is working capital. The second step is to compute the net change in working capital. A schedule of changes in working capital, such as that shown on page 864, accomplishes this step and provides useful information that should be disclosed to the reader along with the formal statement of changes in financial position. This supporting schedule is important because it highlights changes within the working capital pool.

For example, a significant increase in receivables and inventory may indicate a serious marketing problem.

Schedule of Changes in Working Capital

Working Capital Items	December 31, 1984	December 31, 1983	Working Capital Increase (Decrease)
Current assets:			
Cash	$ 8,200	$ 4,000	$ 4,200
Receivables (net)	18,000	15,000	3,000
Inventory	17,000	20,000	(3,000)
	$43,200	$39,000	$ 4,200
Current liabilities:			
Accounts payable	$10,000	$ 8,000	$(2,000)
Working capital	$33,200	$31,000	$ 2,200

As shown in the schedule, the Singleton Company has experienced a net increase in working capital of $2,200 for the period. The objective of the funds statement is to explain why that change occurred. A funds statement can be prepared by analyzing all nonfund accounts (step 3) to see what financing and investing transactions took place and what effect they had on the sources and applications of funds. In this example, there are five nonfund accounts: Equipment, Accumulated Depreciation, Long-Term Notes Payable, Capital Stock, and Retained Earnings. To assist in the analysis of accounts, it is often helpful to use T accounts, especially for certain accounts such as Retained Earnings where the net change in the account balance does not clearly show the total picture of the inflows and outflows of funds.

To illustrate, the December 31, 1983 balance in Retained Earnings for the Singleton Company was $9,000. It has increased $2,000 during the period. Since net income was $9,000 for the year, there must have been a $7,000 reduction in Retained Earnings. The probable explanation for the $7,000 decrease is a declaration of dividends. The following T account illustrates the situation.

Retained Earnings

Dividends	7,000	Beginning balance	9,000
		Net income	9,000
		Ending balance	11,000

Based on this analysis, the $9,000 of net income would be shown, prior to any adjustments, as a major source of funds (working capital) and the $7,000 of dividends as a major use of funds. These items would appear on the partially completed funds statement as shown below.

Working capital was provided by:	
Operations:	
Net income	$9,000
Working capital was applied to:	
Dividends	7,000

Usually, the net income figure from the income statement must be adjusted to determine working capital from operations. In the example, Singleton Company's net income of $9,000 must be adjusted for two items. First, the $500 gain from the sale of equipment (selling price of $700 less book value of $200) must be subtracted from net income. Since it is the proceeds from the sale of equipment, $700 in this illustration, that provide working capital, this should be shown as a separate item on the funds statement. Therefore, since the gain on the sale is included in both the proceeds ($700) and the net income ($9,000), it must be subtracted to avoid being counted twice. This adjustment to eliminate the gain on the sale and to recognize separately the increase in working capital from the total proceeds of the sale is illustrated in the partially completed funds statement as follows:

Working capital was provided by:		
Operations:		
Net income	$9,000	
Less gain on sale of equipment	(500)	$8,500
Sale of equipment		700
Working capital was applied to:		
Dividends		$7,000

The procedure described and illustrated above highlights the amount of working capital generated by normal, recurring operations. It also recognizes funds provided from other activities such as the sale of assets, which may not occur with regularity. A similar approach would be followed in reporting any gains or losses from the disposal of a business segment or from an extraordinary item.

The second adjustment to net income is for depreciation. The entries for depreciation, amortization, and similar items have no effect on funds, whether defined as working capital or cash. However, they are valid expenses and have been deducted from revenues in arriving at net income. Therefore, such nonfund items must be added back to arrive at funds provided by operations.

The amount of depreciation expense for the period can be determined from the income statement. However, because of the limited information provided in this example, an analysis of Accumulated Depreciation and the related equipment account is necessary. The following T accounts facilitate the analysis.

Equipment

Beginning balance	14,000	Sale of equipment	3,000
Purchase of equipment	9,000		
Ending balance	20,000		

Accumulated Depreciation

Sale of equipment	2,800	Beginning balance	6,000
		Depreciation expense	4,000
		Ending balance	7,200

When information is missing, assumptions must be made as to the logical reasons for increases or decreases in accounts. The $4,000 increase in Accumulated Depreciation presumably represents the amount of depreciation expense for the period. Because depreciation is a nonfund item, this amount must be added back to net income as an adjustment to derive the funds from operations figure. Similarly, the T-account analysis shows an increase in the equipment account of $9,000. The logical assumption is that additional equipment has been purchased, and this should be reflected on the funds statement as an application of funds. Now two more entries can be added to the developing funds statement:

Working capital was provided by:		
Operations:		
Net income	$9,000	
Add depreciation expense	4,000	
Less gain on sale of equipment	(500)	$12,500
Sale of equipment		700
Working capital was applied to:		
Dividends		$ 7,000
Purchase of equipment		9,000

At this point, all nonfund accounts have been analyzed and explained except for the Singleton Company's long-term notes and capital stock. There has been no change in the capital stock account, but the long-term notes payable balance has increased $5,000. Apparently, the Singleton Company borrowed an additional $5,000, which should be shown as a source of funds on the funds statement. Given this is the only change that occurred, it is probably not necessary to use a T account to see the relationship. Since there are no other nonfund accounts to be analyzed, the funds statement can now be completed as follows:

Singleton Company
Statement of Changes in Financial Position—Working Capital Basis
For Year Ended December 31, 1984

Working capital was provided by:		
Operations:		
Net income	$ 9,000	
Add depreciation expense	4,000	
Less gain on sale of equipment	(500)	
Working capital provided by operations	$12,500	
Sale of equipment	700	
Borrowing on long-term notes	5,000	$18,200
Working capital was applied to:		
Dividends	$ 7,000	
Purchase of equipment	9,000	16,000
Increase in working capital*		$ 2,200

*See top of next page.

*Schedule of Changes in Working Capital

Working Capital Items	December 31, 1984	December 31, 1983	Working Capital Increase (Decrease)
Current assets:			
Cash	$ 8,200	$ 4,000	$ 4,200
Receivables (net)	18,000	15,000	3,000
Inventory	17,000	20,000	(3,000)
	$43,200	$39,000	$ 4,200
Current liabilities:			
Accounts payable	$10,000	$ 8,000	$(2,000)
Working capital	$33,200	$31,000	$ 2,200

The funds statement for the Singleton Company indicates that funds of $12,500 were provided by normal operations, another $700 from selling equipment, and $5,000 from borrowing on long-term notes. Funds of $16,000 were applied to the payment of dividends and to the purchase of equipment. The difference, $2,200, was an increase in funds (working capital).

As illustrated, the funds statement reports working capital inflow and outflow and the change in working capital for the period. The supporting schedule reports the individual changes within the working capital pool, summarizing and reconciling the individual changes with the total net change in working capital reported in the funds statement.

Funds Defined as Cash

The preparation of a cash basis funds statement follows the same three basic steps used in preparing a working capital funds statement. First, funds are defined as cash. Normally, cash is used in the same sense as that employed for cash recognized as a current asset—cash on hand and unrestricted deposits in banks. The second step is to compute the net change in cash, which is the difference between beginning and ending balances. The Singleton Company's December 31, 1984 cash balance shows a $4,200 increase over its December 31, 1983 cash balance (see page 864).

Step 3 requires the analysis of all nonfund account changes in terms of their effects on the flow of cash. Since cash is the only account included in the cash definition of funds, all balance sheet accounts (including working capital accounts), except cash, constitute the nonfund accounts. The changes in these accounts will have to be analyzed in order to determine the effect on the sources and applications of cash. The cash basis funds statement might be developed by simply classifying and summarizing cash receipts and disbursements as reported in the cash account. However, the funds statement is prepared to point out the broad categories of sources and uses of cash, and such items as cash collected from customers, cash paid for merchandise, and cash paid for expenses are generally better disclosed in a "cash provided by operations" category.

In analyzing the nonfund (noncash) working capital accounts, changes in current assets and current liabilities are recognized by adjustments to net income in arriving at cash provided by operations. All increases in current assets other than cash and decreases in current liabilities are deducted from net income; all decreases in current assets other than cash and increases in current liabilities are added to net income. An exception to this adjusting process has to do with accounting for changes in marketable securities, which are recognized separately as a source or an application of cash, since marketable securities transactions do not affect cash from operations unless the entity is a financing institution.

In addition to the current asset and current liability adjustments, the net income figure is further adjusted by those items that have no effect on cash but represent valid expenses, revenues, gains, or losses already included in net income. For example, as is the case with the working capital statement, net income must be adjusted for depreciation, amortization, and gains and losses on disposal of business assets. In this regard, many adjustments are the same as those required for a working capital funds statement. Other adjustments are required in order to convert the accrual net income measurement to the amount of cash provided by operations, a category on the funds statement that should be disclosed separately.

T accounts for the nonfund working capital accounts are presented below:

Receivables (net)

Beginning balance	15,000		
Net increase	3,000		
Ending balance	18,000		

Inventory

Beginning balance	20,000	Net decrease	3,000
Ending balance	17,000		

Accounts Payable

		Beginning balance	8,000
		Net increase	2,000
		Ending balance	10,000

The $3,000 increase in receivables requires that net income be decreased by the same amount, since cash receipts for goods and services sold were less than the revenue recognized in arriving at net income. The $3,000 decrease in inventory is added to net income since purchases were less than the charge made against revenue for cost of sales in arriving at net income. The $2,000 increase in accounts payable requires an addition to net income since the cash disbursements for goods and services purchased were less than the charges made for these items in arriving at net income. These adjustments along with the reported net income figure for the year would appear on the partially completed cash funds statement as shown below:

Cash was provided by:		
Operations:		
Net income		$9,000
Items to be added to net income:		
Decrease in inventories	$3,000	
Increase in accounts payable	2,000	5,000
Items to be deducted from net income:		
Increase in receivables	$3,000	

Now that all the noncash working capital accounts have been analyzed, attention should be directed toward the other nonfund accounts by following the same reasoning that was used in preparing the working capital funds statement. The adjustments for nonfund items such as depreciation and amortization are the same for cash as for working capital. Thus, the completed cash basis funds statement would appear as follows:

Singleton Company
Statement of Changes in Financial Position—Cash Basis
For Year Ended December 31, 1984

Cash was provided by:			
Operations:			
Net income		$ 9,000	
Items to be added to net income:			
Decrease in inventories	$3,000		
Increase in accounts payable	2,000		
Depreciation expense	4,000	9,000	
		$18,000	
Items to be deducted from net income:			
Increase in receivables	$3,000		
Gain on sale of equipment	500	3,500	
Cash provided by operations		$14,500	
Sale of equipment		700	
Borrowing on long-term notes		5,000	$20,200
Cash was applied to:			
Dividends		$ 7,000	
Purchase of equipment		9,000	16,000
Increase in cash			$ 4,200

The cash basis funds statement highlights the inflows and outflows of cash. Singleton Company generated $14,500 cash from its operations and an additional $5,700 by selling equipment and by borrowing on long-term notes. Cash was used to pay dividends, to purchase additional equipment, and to increase the cash account balance.

As noted earlier, the cash-flow approach to the analysis of financial operations has received increased attention in recent years. The statement is readily interpreted by the reader, and it can be a highly useful tool for the forecasting and planning of cash flow.

Analysis of Account Changes in Developing Funds Data

As indicated earlier, analysis of account changes is required when preparing funds statements from comparative balance sheet data supplemented by additional information. Examples in the preceding sections were relatively simple. Ordinarily, however, more complex circumstances are encountered and it is not possible to rely on the net change in an account balance for a full explanation of the effect of that item on a company's funds flow. To illustrate, assume that comparative balance sheets report a $50,000 increase in bonds payable. Without further investigation, this might be interpreted as a source of funds of $50,000. However, reference to the liability account may disclose that bonds of $100,000 were retired during the period while new bonds of $150,000 were issued. A further analysis of the transactions affecting the liability account may reveal that a call premium of $2,000 was paid on bonds retired and a discount of $7,500 was identified with the new issue. The funds statement, then, should report that funds were provided by the new issue of $142,500 and that funds were applied to retirement of the old issue of $102,000.

The use of a work sheet, such as that illustrated on page 874, facilitates the analysis of account changes. In employing a work sheet, a pair of adjustments columns is used to explain the changes in account balances in terms of the actual amount of funds provided and applied by such changes.

The adjustments required in developing funds data may be classified under three headings:

(1) *Adjustments to explain account changes not representing fund sources or applications.* Certain account changes may carry no funds-flow implications. For example, fully depreciated assets may have been applied against accumulated depreciation balances. Errors of prior periods may have been discovered requiring changes in beginning property and owners' equity balances. Stock dividends may have been issued and retained earnings transferred to paid-in capital accounts. The foregoing items result in changes in account balances but these changes should be disregarded in reporting the flow of funds. When a work sheet is prepared, the adjustments made to explain such account changes do not affect the amount of funds provided or applied.

(2) *Adjustments to report the individual fund sources and applications when several transactions are summarized in a single account.* The change in the balance of an account may result from funds provided by several different sources or applied to several different purposes, or from a combination of funds provided and applied. For example, the change in land, buildings, and equipment balance may reflect funds applied to the construction of buildings and also to the purchase of equipment. The change in the bonds payable balance may reflect both funds applied to the retirement of an old bond issue and funds provided by a new issue. The change in the capital stock balance may reflect both funds provided by the issue of shares and funds applied to the reacquisition and retirement of shares. When a work sheet is prepared, adjustments are made to report separately the different fund sources and applications.

(3) *Adjustments to report individual fund sources and applications when such information is reported in two or more accounts.* The amount of

funds provided or applied as a result of a single transaction may be reflected in two or more accounts. For example, certain investments may have been sold for more than cost; the gain reported in net income and the decrease in the investment account must be combined in arriving at the actual amount provided by the sale. Bonds may have been issued at a discount; the increase in the discount account balance must be applied against the increase in the bond account in arriving at the actual amount provided by the issue. Stock may have been retired at a premium; the decreases in the paid-in capital and retained earnings account balances must be combined in arriving at the actual amount applied to the retirement. When a work sheet is prepared, adjustments are made to combine related changes.

Retained Earnings is an example of an account that may be affected by all three types of adjustments. To illustrate, assume that a retained earnings account shows an increase for a year of $10,000. Inspection of the account discloses the following:

Account **Retained Earnings**

Date		Item	Debit	Credit	Balance	
					Debit	Credit
Jan.	1	Balance				200,000
Mar.	1	Appropriation for bond sinking fund................	20,000			180,000
July	10	Cash dividends	30,000			150,000
Dec.	31	Net income for the year....		60,000		210,000

Retained earnings was reduced by the appropriation for bond sinking fund. Although both retained earnings and the appropriated retained earnings balance show changes of $20,000, the changes do not affect funds. The decrease in retained earnings is explained by the increase in the appropriation for bond sinking fund; the account changes are thus explained and receive no recognition in the funds statement. Cash dividends of $30,000 are reported separately as funds applied. This leaves $60,000, the net income for the year, in the retained earnings account to be reported as funds provided by operations.

Remaining pages of this chapter illustrate the nature of the analysis required as well as the procedures employed in developing a more complex funds statement. A work sheet is used to facilitate the analysis of accounts. The working capital definition of funds is illustrated first, followed by a cash basis statement.

COMPREHENSIVE ILLUSTRATION OF A FUNDS STATEMENT ON A WORKING CAPITAL BASIS

Assume for Svendsen Inc. the comparative balance sheet shown on page 872 and the following additional information.

Svendsen Inc.
Comparative Balance Sheet
December 31, 1984 and 1983

	1984			1983		
Assets						
Current assets:						
Cash in banks and on hand		$ 59,300			$ 65,000	
Accounts receivable (net)		60,000			70,500	
Inventories		75,000			76,500	
Prepaid operating expenses		16,500	$210,800		12,000	$224,000
Long-term investments (at cost)			10,000			106,000
Land, buildings, and equipment:						
Land		$183,500			$ 75,000	
Buildings	$290,000			$225,000		
Less accumulated depreciation	122,600	167,400		155,000	70,000	
Machinery and equipment	$132,000			$120,000		
Less accumulated depreciation	36,300	95,700	446,600	43,500	76,500	221,500
Patents			35,000			40,000
Total assets			$702,400			$591,500
Liabilities						
Current liabilities:						
Income tax payable		$ 10,000			$ 9,500	
Accounts payable		65,000			81,200	
Salaries payable		5,000			1,500	
Dividends payable		4,400	$ 84,400			$ 92,200
Bonds payable		$ 60,000				
Less discount on bonds payable		2,700	57,300			
Deferred income tax			21,000			15,000
Total liabilities			$162,700			$107,200
Stockholders' Equity						
Common stock		$390,000			$250,000	
Retained earnings		149,700	539,700		234,300	484,300
Total liabilities and stockholders' equity			$702,400			$591,500

Changes in retained earnings during the year were as follows:

Balance, December 31, 1983		$234,300
Add net income		44,000
		$278,300
Deduct:		
Cash dividends	$ 25,100	
40% stock dividend on common stock	100,000	
Prior period adjustment resulting from understatement of depreciation on equipment	3,500	128,600
Balance, December 31, 1984		$149,700

The income statement for 1984 summarizes operations as follows:

Income from continuing operations	$36,000
Add extraordinary gain on involuntary conversion of building	8,000
Net income	$44,000

A building costing $40,000 with a book value of $2,000 was completely destroyed in an extraordinary disaster. The insurance company paid $10,000 cash; a new building was then constructed at a cost of $105,000.

Long-term investments, cost $96,000, were sold for $102,500.

Land was acquired for $108,500, the seller accepting in payment $40,000 of common stock and cash of $68,500.

New machinery was purchased for $12,000 cash. Additional machinery and equipment were overhauled, extending the useful life at a cost of $26,000, the cost being debited to the accumulated depreciation account.

The amortization of patent cost and depreciation expense on buildings and equipment were recorded as follows:

Buildings	$ 5,600
Machinery and equipment	15,300
Patents	5,000
Total	$25,900

Ten-year bonds of $60,000 were issued at a discount of $3,000 at the beginning of the year; discount amortization for the year was $300.

The company recognizes depreciation for tax purposes by the ACRS method, and for accounting purposes by the straight-line method. This depreciation timing difference caused the income tax payable on 1984 taxable income to be $6,000 less than the income tax expense based on income per books.

In preparing a funds statement for Svendsen Inc., the first step is to define funds as working capital. The second step is to determine the change in fund balances, in this case the working capital account balances. A schedule of changes in working capital for Svendsen Inc. follows:

	December 31		Working Capital Increase (Decrease)
	1983	*1984*	
Current assets:			
Cash in banks and on hand	$ 59,300	$ 65,000	$ (5,700)
Accounts receivable (net)	60,000	70,500	(10,500)
Inventories	75,000	76,500	(1,500)
Prepaid operating expenses	16,500	12,000	4,500
Total	$210,800	$224,000	$(13,200)
Current liabilities:			
Income tax payable	$ 10,000	$ 9,500	$ (500)
Accounts payable	65,000	81,200	16,200
Salaries payable	5,000	1,500	(3,500)
Dividends payable	4,400	0	(4,400)
Total	$ 84,400	$ 92,200	$ 7,800
Working capital	$126,400	$131,800	$ (5,400)

All nonfund accounts may now be analyzed using the work sheet illustrated on page 874. The funds statement is taken directly from the work sheet and is illustrated on page 878.

Svendsen Inc.
Work Sheet for Statement of Changes in Financial Position — Working Capital Basis
For Year Ended December 31, 1984

	Items	Balance Dec. 31, 1983	Adjustments Debit	Adjustments Credit	Balance Dec. 31, 1984	
1	Debits					1
2	Working capital	131,800		(p) 5,400	126,400	2
3	Long-term investments	106,000		(g) 96,000	10,000	3
4	Land	75,000	(h) 108,500		183,500	4
5	Buildings	225,000	(f) 105,000	(e) 40,000	290,000	5
6	Machinery and equipment	120,000	(j) 12,000		132,000	6
7	Patents	40,000		(l) 5,000	35,000	7
8	Discount on bonds payable		(m) 3,000	(n) 300	2,700	8
9	Total	697,800			779,600	9
10	Credits					10
11	Accumulated depr. — buildings	155,000	(e) 38,000	(l) 5,600	122,600	11
12	Accumulated depr. — mach. and equip.	43,500	(k) 26,000	(d) 3,500		12
13				(l) 15,300	36,300	13
14	Bonds payable			(m) 60,000	60,000	14
15	Deferred income tax	15,000		(o) 6,000	21,000	15
16	Common stock	250,000		(c) 100,000		16
17				(i) 40,000	390,000	17
18	Retained earnings	234,300	(b) 25,100	(a) 44,000		18
19			(c) 100,000			19
20			(d) 3,500		149,700	20
21	Total	697,800	421,100	421,100	779,600	21
22	Working capital was provided by:					22
23	Operations:					23
24	Income from continuing operations		(a) 36,000			24
25	Add items not requiring working					25
26	capital:					26
27	Amortization of patents		(l) 5,000			27
28	Depreciation expense		(l) 20,900			28
29	Amortization of bond discount		(n) 300			29
30	Increase in deferred income tax		(o) 6,000			30
31	Deduct item not providing working					31
32	capital:					32
33	Gain on sale of investments			(g) 6,500		33
34	Involuntary conversion of building		(a) 8,000			34
35			(e) 2,000			35
36	Sale of long-term investments		(g) 102,500			36
37	Issuance of common stock in part					37
38	payment of land		(i) 40,000			38
39	Issuance of bonds at discount		(m) 57,000			39
40	Working capital was applied to:					40
41	Dividends			(b) 25,100		41
42	Construct building			(f) 105,000		42
43	Purchase land ($40,000 paid by					43
44	issuance of common stock)			(h) 108,500		44
45	Purchase machinery and equipment			(j) 12,000		45
46	Overhaul machinery and equipment			(k) 26,000		46
47	Decrease in working capital		(p) 5,400			47
48	Total		283,100	283,100		48

It should be noted that the work sheet contains a summary working capital fund account and all the nonfund accounts, in this instance non-working capital accounts. These are the accounts that must be analyzed to determine the sources, uses, and net change in the fund balance already determined and shown on page 873 in the schedule of changes in working capital. The format of the work sheet is straightforward. The first column contains the beginning balances, then there are two columns for analysis of transactions to arrive at the ending balances in the fourth column. The side headings added after the account titles are those to be used in preparing the formal funds statement.

In preparing work sheets, accumulated depreciation balances, instead of being reported as credit balances in the debit section, may be more conveniently listed with liability and owners' equity balances in the credit section. Similarly, contra liability accounts and contra owners' equity balances may be separately recognized and more conveniently listed with assets in the debit section.

In developing a work sheet, it will normally prove most convenient to begin with an analysis of the change in retained earnings (see items (a) through (d) on the work sheet). In the process, the income from ordinary operations and from other income components should be separately reported (item (a)). After the change in Retained Earnings has been accounted for, the remaining nonfund accounts should be reviewed in conjunction with the income statement and supplementary information to determine what additional adjustments are required. Operating income and any other income components should be adjusted (items (e), (g), (l), (n), and (o)) to determine the actual amount of funds provided from each separately identified source; or, in the case of a loss, the amount of funds applied. Adjustments must also be made to determine all other sources and applications of funds (items (f), (h), (j), and (k)) and to reflect significant financing and investing activities that have no effect on funds (item (i)).

Explanations for individual adjustments recorded on the work sheet for Svendsen Inc. follow. The letter preceding each explanation corresponds with that used on the work sheet.

(a) Net income included in the ending retained earnings balance is composed of income from continuing operations and an extraordinary gain. The operating income must be adjusted to arrive at the total funds provided by operations; the extraordinary item requires separate recognition as a source of funds and will also be adjusted to arrive at the full amount of funds provided. Net income, then, is analyzed and is reported by an adjustment on the work sheet as follows:

Funds Provided by Income from Continuing Operations.......	36,000	
Funds Provided by Involuntary Conversion of Building........	8,000	
Retained Earnings		44,000

"Income from continuing operations" is reported on a separate line as a primary element of working capital from operations. Since a number of adjustments may be required in arriving at the actual amount of funds provided by operations, adequate space should be allowed after this line for these adjustments. Adequate space should also be allowed after each unusual or extraordinary item for adjustments necessary to show the actual amount of funds provided or applied. Additional items requiring recognition are listed subsequently.

(b) The cash dividends reported in retained earnings are reported separately as an application of funds by the following entry:

Retained Earnings	25,100	
Funds Applied to Dividends		25,100

(c) The transfer of retained earnings to capital stock as a result of a common stock dividend has no funds significance and the changes in the account balances are reconciled by the following adjustment:

Retained Earnings	100,000	
Common Stock		100,000

(d) The recognition that depreciation had been understated on equipment in prior periods is recorded by a debit to retained earnings and a credit to accumulated depreciation—machinery and equipment. The correction of earnings of prior periods has no funds significance, and the changes in the account balances may be reconciled as follows:

Retained Earnings	3,500	
Accumulated Depreciation—Machinery and Equipment		3,500

(e) The destruction of the building and the subsequent insurance reimbursement produced an extraordinary gain of $8,000. This gain was recorded as "Funds Provided by Involuntary Conversion of Building," in entry (a), as the result of the earlier recognition of the individual component of net income. Since the effect of the destruction was to provide funds of $10,000, the proceeds from the insurance company, the funds of $8,000 recognized in entry (a) may now be adjusted to show the true amount of funds provided by relating the required adjustment to the appropriate asset accounts:

Accumulated Depreciation—Buildings	38,000	
Funds Provided by Involuntary Conversion of Building	2,000	
Buildings		40,000

(f) The buildings account was increased by the cost of constructing a new building, $105,000. The cost of the new building is reported separately as an application of funds by the following entry:

Buildings	105,000	
Funds Applied to Construction of Building		105,000

(g) The sale of long-term investments was recorded by a credit to the asset account at cost $96,000, and a credit to a gain on sale of investment. At the end of the period, the gain account was closed into retained earnings as part of income from continuing operations. Since the effect of the sale was to provide funds of $102,500, this is reported on a separate line. The investments account balance is reduced and funds provided by operations are decreased by the amount of the gain. The following entry is made:

Funds Provided by Sale of Long-Term Investments	102,500	
Long-Term Investments		96,000
Income from Continuing Operations—Gain on Sale of Investments		6,500

(h) and (i) Land was acquired at a price of $108,500; payment was made in common stock valued at $40,000 and cash of $68,500. The analysis on the work sheet is as follows: (h) the increase in the land balance, $108,500, is reported separately as an application of funds; (i) the increase in the common stock balance, $40,000, is reported separately as a source of funds applied to the purchase of land. The entries are:

Land	108,500	
Funds Applied to Purchase Land		108,500
Funds Provided by Issuance of Common Stock in Part Payment of Land	40,000	
Common Stock		40,000

Although the issuance of common stock for land has no effect on funds, it is a significant transaction that should be disclosed under the all financial resources concept.

(j) and (k) Machinery of $12,000 was acquired during the year. Payment was made in cash and is reported as funds applied to purchase machinery; the cost of overhauling other machinery and equipment also represents the application of funds and is reported separately. The cost was debited to the accumulated depreciation account. The entries are:

Machinery and Equipment	12,000	
Funds Applied to Purchase Machinery and Equipment		12,000
Accumulated Depreciation—Machinery and Equipment	26,000	
Funds Applied to Overhaul Machinery and Equipment		26,000

(l) The changes in the patents account and in the accumulated depreciation accounts result from the recognition of amortization of the patents and depreciation on the plant assets. Funds provided by operations are increased by the charges against earnings not involving current funds outflow by the following adjustment:

Income from Continuing Operations—Amortization of Patents	5,000	
Income from Continuing Operations—Depreciation Expense	20,900	
Patents		5,000
Accumulated Depreciation—Buildings		5,600
Accumulated Depreciation—Machinery and Equipment		15,300

(m) and (n) During the year, bonds were issued at a discount. The result of this transaction was to credit Bonds Payable for $60,000 and debit Discount on Bonds Payable for $3,000. The funds provided by the bond issuance of $57,000 are recognized by entry (m). Subsequently, the bond discount was amortized by reducing the bond discount account. This decrease in the discount account is explained by increasing funds provided by operations by the amount of the charge against earnings not involving the use of funds—entry (n). The entries are as follows:

Discount on Bonds Payable	3,000	
Funds Provided by Issuance of Bonds	57,000	
Bonds Payable		60,000

Income from Continuing Operations—Amortization of Bond Discount	300	
Discount on Bonds Payable		300

(o) The depreciation timing difference was recognized by a debit to Income Tax Expense and credits to Income Tax Payable and Deferred Income Tax. The timing difference for 1984 is $6,000 and is shown on the work sheet by an increase in Deferred Income Tax and an increase in funds provided by operations. The extra $6,000 debit to Income Tax Expense is thus added back to income from operations because the extra charge against earnings did not involve current funds outflow. The following entry is made:

Income from Continuing Operations—Increase in Deferred Income Tax	6,000	
Deferred Income Tax		6,000

(p) The change in working capital is explained by the following entry:

Decrease in Working Capital	5,400	
Working Capital		5,400

This entry explains the net change occurring in all working capital accounts and brings the work sheet into balance.

A funds statement for Svendsen Inc. may be prepared from the work sheet as follows:

Svendsen Inc.
Statement of Changes in Financial Position—Working Capital Basis
For Year Ended December 31, 1984

Working capital was provided by:			
Operations:			
Income from continuing operations		$ 36,000	
Add items not requiring working capital:			
Amortization of patents	$ 5,000		
Depreciation expense	20,900		
Amortization of bond discount	300		
Increase in deferred income tax	6,000		
	$32,200		
Deduct item not providing working capital:			
Gain on sale of investments	6,500	25,700	
Working capital provided by continuing operations		$ 61,700	
Involuntary conversion of building		10,000	
Sale of long-term investments		102,500	
Issuance of common stock in part payment of land (total cost of land, $108,500)		40,000	
Issuance of bonds at a discount		57,000	$271,200
Working capital was applied to:			
Dividends		$ 25,100	
Construct building		105,000	
Purchase land (cash paid, $68,500; common stock issued, $40,000)		108,500	
Purchase machinery and equipment		12,000	
Overhaul machinery and equipment		26,000	276,600
Decrease in working capital			$ 5,400*

*See Schedule of Changes in Working Capital, page 873.

The funds statement should begin with a summary of the funds related to normal operations. Income or loss from continuing operations is listed, and those items reflected in this balance not requiring funds are added back while those items not providing funds are subtracted. The adjusted balance, representing funds provided by or applied to operations, is followed by any other items not related to normal financial transactions, but representing direct sources or applications of funds from operations. Remaining sources and applications of funds are then listed in their respective sections to arrive at the net fund change for the period.

The statements of General Mills, Inc., reproduced in Appendix B, provide an additional example of a funds statement. Many variations in statement format are found in practice. Frequently, in published financial statements, much of the detail is omitted, e.g., a single amount may be shown for land, building and equipment additions, and a number of individual items may be combined and presented as "Other sources" or "Other uses."

Some persons object to the presentation of funds provided by operations in the form just illustrated. This form, they maintain, implies that the depreciation of assets generates funds. Actually, it is revenues that provide funds but the income from operations balance fails to report the full amount provided because of items such as depreciation. This objection is overcome by separately listing the individual revenues and expenses but excluding items and amounts not involving current fund inflows or outflows.

Special Problems

The analysis required in developing a working capital funds statement may be simple or complex. In each instance where a noncurrent asset, a noncurrent liability, or an owners' equity account balance has changed, the question should be asked: Does this indicate a change in working capital? Frequently the answer to this question is obvious, but in some cases careful analysis is required. The following items suggest special analysis that may be required.

(1) In the previous example, charges for depreciation on the tax return exceeded those on the books. This resulted in an increase in the deferred income tax account. When charges for depreciation on the books later exceed those on the tax return, or when an asset with a related deferred tax liability is retired early, the deferred tax account will be decreased by a debit to Deferred Income Tax and a credit to Income Tax Expense. This decrease in Income Tax Expense does not increase the amount of funds provided by operations nor does the decrease in Deferred Income Tax indicate that funds have been applied; therefore, the decrease in Deferred Income Tax must be recorded and funds provided by operations must be decreased by the reduction in income tax expense that did not involve current funds inflow.

(2) Assume that retained earnings are reduced upon the declaration of a cash dividend payable in the following period. Declaration of the dividend has increased current liabilities and, thus, reduced working capital. Subsequent payment of the dividend will have no effect upon the amount of working capital, simply reducing both cash and the current liability. Declaration of a dividend, then, should be reported as funds applied. The reduction in work-

ing capital is confirmed in the summary of net change in working capital.

(3) Assume that a long-term obligation becomes payable within a year, and requires change to the current classification. This change calls for a recognition of funds applied. The change in classification has resulted in a shrinkage of working capital; subsequent payment will have no effect on the amount of working capital. The reduction in the long-term liability can be reported as "Funds applied to long-term obligations, maturing currently." The change in working capital balances will confirm the reduction in working capital.

(4) In previous examples, prepaid expenses were classified as current assets and therefore treated as working capital items in the analysis of the change in working capital. Prepaid expenses are sometimes listed under a separate heading or reported with noncurrent assets. This treatment calls for the special analysis of the prepaid expenses just as for other items classified as noncurrent, since their exclusion from the current group makes them part of the explanation for the change that took place in the current classification.

COMPREHENSIVE ILLUSTRATION OF A FUNDS STATEMENT ON A CASH BASIS

In the appendix to Chapter 2, the emphasis was on incomplete records and in going from a cash basis to financial statements on an accrual basis. When preparing a funds statement on a cash basis, the reverse analysis is required. That is, one must work from financial information on an accrual basis to the cash inflows and outflows provided and applied during the period. To illustrate, if sales for the period were $80,000 as reported on the income statement and the beginning and ending accounts receivable balances were $25,000 and $20,000 respectively, the cash provided from sales would be $85,000. The beginning accounts receivable balance would have been recorded as sales during the previous period, but collected in the current period; thus, the beginning balance should be added to the $80,000 sales figure. The ending balance is included in the $80,000 amount, but will not be collected until future periods; it should be subtracted. Therefore, the net decrease in accounts receivable should be added to the reported sales figure of $80,000 to arrive at the total cash provided from sales activity during the period.

If Svendsen Inc. wishes to prepare a funds statement on a cash basis, a work sheet might be prepared as illustrated below and on page 881. Adjustments are the same as those described on pages 875–878 but are supple-

Svendsen Inc.
Work Sheet for Statement of Changes in Financial Position—Cash Basis
For Year Ended December 31, 1984

	Items	Balance Dec. 31 1983	Adjustments Debit		Adjustments Credit		Balance Dec. 31 1984	
1	Debits							1
2	Cash in banks and on hand	65,000			(v)	5,700	59,300	2
3	Accounts receivable (net)	70,500			(p)	10,500	60,000	3
4	Inventories	76,500			(q)	1,500	75,000	4
5	Prepaid operating expenses	12,000	(r)	4,500			16,500	5

Work Sheet (continued)

Long-term investments	106,000			(g)	96,000	10,000
Land	75,000	(h)	108,500			183,500
Buildings	225,000	(f)	105,000	(e)	40,000	290,000
Machinery and equipment	120,000	(j)	12,000			132,000
Patents	40,000			(l)	5,000	35,000
Discount on bonds payable		(m)	3,000	(n)	300	2,700
Total	790,000					864,000
Credits						
Accumulated depr.—buildings	155,000	(e)	38,000	(l)	5,600	122,600
Accumulated depr.—mach. and equip.	43,500	(k)	26,000	(d)	3,500	
				(l)	15,300	36,300
Income tax payable	9,500			(s)	500	10,000
Accounts payable	81,200	(t)	16,200			65,000
Salaries payable	1,500			(u)	3,500	5,000
Dividends payable				(b)	4,400	4,400
Bonds payable				(m)	60,000	60,000
Deferred income tax	15,000			(o)	6,000	21,000
Common stock	250,000			(c)	100,000	
				(i)	40,000	390,000
Retained earnings	234,300	(b)	25,100	(a)	44,000	
		(c)	100,000			
		(d)	3,500			149,700
Total	790,000		441,800		441,800	864,000
Cash was provided by:						
Operations:						
Income before extraordinary items		(a)	36,000			
Items to be added to operating income:						
Amortization of patents		(l)	5,000			
Depreciaton expense		(l)	20,900			
Amortization of bond discount		(n)	300			
Increase in deferred income tax		(o)	6,000			
Decrease in accounts receivable (net)		(p)	10,500			
Decrease in inventories		(q)	1,500			
Increase in income tax payable		(s)	500			
Increase in salaries payable		(u)	3,500			
Items to be deducted from operating income:						
Gain on sale of investment				(g)	6,500	
Increase in prepaid operating expenses				(r)	4,500	
Decrease in accounts payable				(t)	16,200	
Involuntary conversion of building		(a)	8,000			
		(e)	2,000			
Sale of long-term investments		(g)	102,500			
Issuance of common stock in part payment of land		(i)	40,000			
Issuance of bonds at discount		(m)	57,000			
Cash was applied to:						
Pay dividends				(b)	20,700	
Construct building				(f)	105,000	
Purchase land (cash paid, $68,500; common stock issued, $40,000)				(h)	108,500	
Purchase machinery and equipment				(j)	12,000	
Overhaul machinery and equipment				(k)	26,000	
Decrease in cash		(v)	5,700			
Total			299,400		299,400	

mented by adjustments to show operations and also dividends in terms of cash. Income from operations as previously adjusted is further adjusted for the changes in working capital items other than cash. The entry for cash dividends (b) is adjusted for the change in the dividends payable balance in arriving at the cash applied to dividends during the period. In the illustration, the entry (b) would be a debit to Retained Earnings, $25,100; a credit to Dividends Payable, $4,400; and a credit to Cash $20,700. Entry (v) serves the same purpose as entry (p) on page 878. The net change in cash is explained and the work sheet is brought into balance by this entry. A statement of changes in financial position employing the cash concept for funds appears below.

Svendsen Inc.
Statement of Changes in Financial Position—Cash Basis
For Year Ended December 31, 1984

Cash was provided by:			
Operations:			
Income from continuing operations		$ 36,000	
Items to be added to operating income:			
Amortization of patents	$ 5,000		
Depreciation expense	20,900		
Amortization of bond discount	300		
Increase in deferred income tax	6,000		
Decrease in accounts receivable (net)	10,500		
Decrease in inventories	1,500		
Increase in income tax payable	500		
Increase in salaries payable	3,500	48,200	
		$ 84,200	
Items to be deducted from operating income:			
Gain on sale of investments	$ 6,500		
Increase in prepaid operating expenses	4,500		
Decrease in accounts payable	16,200	27,200	
Cash provided by operations		$ 57,000	
Involuntary conversion of building		10,000	
Sale of long-term investments		102,500	
Issuance of common stock in part payment of land (total cost of land, $108,500)		40,000	
Issuance of bonds at a discount		57,000	$266,500
Cash was applied to:			
Pay dividends		$ 20,700	
Construct building		105,000	
Purchase land (cash paid, $68,500; common stock issued, $40,000)		108,500	
Purchase machinery and equipment		12,000	
Overhaul machinery and equipment		26,000	272,200
Decrease in cash			$ 5,700

The work sheet and the statement report the net amount of cash provided by operations, $57,000. When a full explanation of the cash provided by operations is desired, this can be shown by applying adjustments to the individual revenue and expense items rather than to the net income balance. The operations section of the work sheet will require expansion in developing this detail, as illustrated on the following page. Adjustment (a), instead of reporting the results of operations as summarized on the income statement, lists the individual revenue and expense items. The adjustments required in developing the cash flow from operations are then applied to the individual revenue and expense balances.

Item	Adjustments Debit	Adjustments Credit
Cash was provided by:		
Operations:		
Sales	(a) 753,800	
Add decrease in accounts receivable	(p) 10,500	
Cost of goods sold		(a) 550,000
Add decrease in accounts payable		(t) 16,200
Deduct:		
Depreciation of building, machinery, and equipment, amortization of patents	(l) 25,900	
Decrease in inventories	(q) 1,500	
Selling and general expenses		(a) 146,400
Add increase in prepaid operating expenses		(r) 4,500
Deduct increase in salaries payable	(u) 3,500	
Other expense—interest expense		(a) 3,900
Deduct bond discount amortization	(n) 300	
Income tax expense		(a) 24,000
Deduct:		
Increase in income tax payable	(s) 500	
Increase in deferred income tax	(o) 6,000	
Gain on sale of long-term investments	(a) 6,500	
To cancel gain		(g) 6,500

Cash provided by operations, as summarized above, may be presented on the statement as follows:

Cash was provided by:		
Operations:		
Receipts—Sales		$764,300
Payments—Cost of goods sold	$538,800	
Selling and general expenses	147,400	
Interest expense	3,600	
Income tax	17,500	707,300
Cash provided by operations		$ 57,000

Special Observations

Alternate methods may be used for the presentation of exchanges interpreted as both financing and investing activities. For example, the Svendsen Inc. acquisition of land for $68,500 cash and $40,000 of common stock may be presented as follows:

Purchase of land	$108,500	
Less common stock issued in part payment	40,000	$68,500

The difference represents the *net* amount of funds and would be shown in the application section. The financing and investing aspects of the transaction are related and the net effect on funds is reported. On the other hand, it may be maintained that the issuance of stock should be reported as funds provided and the acquisition of land at the full acquisition price as funds applied. This raises the totals for funds provided and applied but does not affect the increase or decrease in funds reported for the period. This is the approach used in the chapter illustrations and is consistent with APB Opinion No. 19.

The Accounting Principles Board in Opinion No. 19 recognized that the form, terminology, and content of the funds statement will not be the same for every company in meeting its objectives under different circumstances. Although recognizing the need for flexibility, the APB indicated that there is still a need for certain guides in the preparation of the statement and in its interpretation. At a minimum, disclosures should include the following:[6]

(1) The amount of working capital or cash provided from operations;
(2) The net changes in each element of working capital, either in the statement or a related tabulation;
(3) Outlays for purchase of noncurrent assets;
(4) Proceeds from sale of noncurrent assets not normally sold in the normal course of business;
(5) Issuance, assumption, or redemption of long-term debt;
(6) Issuance, redemption, or purchase of capital stock;
(7) Conversion of long-term debt or preferred stock;
(8) Dividends in cash or in kind, but not stock dividends or stock split-ups.

The final recommendation of the board was that isolated statistics of working capital or cash provided from operations, especially per-share computations, should not be presented in annual reports to shareholders. The attempt has been made in this chapter to apply the above guidelines in funds-flow presentations.

The funds statement is now recognized as a primary statement, one that must be audited and one that is considered essential for fully reporting the activities of a business unit. Even though not officially required for external reporting until APB Opinion No. 19 was issued in 1971, the funds statement has a long history of use. Many companies prepared the statement for management purposes long before actually presenting this information to external users. It is fortunate that this important statement is now readily available for all users of financial information. It is also significant that efforts to improve the content and format are continuing.

APPENDIX

T ACCOUNT APPROACH TO PREPARING A FUNDS STATEMENT

This appendix illustrates a T account approach to preparing a funds statement. As shown, this approach produces the same results as the columnar work sheet illustrated in the chapter; only the format is different. To highlight the similarities in the two approaches, the comprehensive working

[6]*Ibid.*, pars. 12–14.

capital illustration for Svendsen Inc. (pages 871–878) will also be used for the T account illustration.

With the T account approach, a special Sources and Uses of Funds T account is established. This account is used to summarize all significant financing and investing activities during the period and provides the basis for preparing the formal statement of changes in financial position. Also, when the working capital concept is applied, a T account that summarizes all changes in current assets and current liabilities is used. This account shows the net change in working capital during the period, which is the balancing figure in the funds statement. If a cash concept is used instead of a working capital concept, individual T accounts are established for cash and all other current accounts. The change in the cash account becomes the balancing figure in a cash flow funds statement.

In addition to the Sources and Uses of Funds T account and the Working Capital T account (when using the working capital concept), a T account is established for each other account on the balance sheet. During the process of analysis, the change in each account is explained as a source or use of funds. In following the illustration, it may be helpful to refer to the detailed explanations for individual adjustments described on pages 875–878 of the text. Once the changes in all accounts have been reconciled and the Sources and Uses of Funds T account balanced, the formal funds statement can be prepared as illustrated on page 878 of the chapter.

Sources and Uses of Funds

Operations:			
(a)	36,000	(b)	25,100
(g)	(6,500)	(f)	105,000
(l)	5,000	(h)	108,500
(l)	20,900	(j)	12,000
(n)	300	(k)	26,000
(o)	6,000		
Working capital from operations	61,700		
(a)	8,000		
(e)	2,000		
(g)	102,500		
(i)	40,000		
(m)	57,000		
(p)	5,400		
	276,600		276,600

Working Capital

Beginning Bal.	131,800	(p)	5,400
Ending Bal.	126,400		

Land

Beginning Bal.	75,000		
(h)	108,500		
Ending Bal.	183,500		

Long-Term Investments

Beginning Bal.	106,000	(g)	96,000
Ending Bal.	10,000		

Buildings

Beginning Bal.	225,000	(e)	40,000
(f)	105,000		
Ending Bal.	290,000		

Accumulated Depreciation—Buildings

(e)	38,000	Beginning Bal.	155,000
		(l)	5,600
		Ending Bal.	122,600

Machinery and Equipment

Beginning Bal.	120,000		
(j)	12,000		
Ending Bal.	132,000		

Accumulated Depreciation—Machinery and Equipment

(k)	26,000	Beginning Bal.	43,500
		(d)	3,500
		(l)	15,300
		Ending Bal.	36,300

Patents

Beginning Bal.	40,000	(l)	5,000
Ending Bal.	35,000		

Bonds Payable

		Beginning Bal.	-0-
		(m)	60,000
		Ending Bal.	60,000

Discount on Bonds Payable

Beginning Bal.	-0-		
(m)	3,000	(n)	300
Ending Bal.	2,700		

Deferred Income Tax

		Beginning Bal.	15,000
		(o)	6,000
		Ending Bal.	21,000

Common Stock

		Beginning Bal.	250,000
		(c)	100,000
		(i)	40,000
		Ending Bal.	390,000

Retained Earnings

(b)	25,100	Beginning Bal.	234,300
(c)	100,000	(a)	44,000
(d)	3,500		
		Ending Bal.	149,700

QUESTIONS

1. Describe the statement of changes in financial position. What information does it offer that is not provided by the income statement? What information does it offer that is not provided by comparative balance sheets?

2. What is the "all financial resources" concept of funds? Why is use of this concept required by generally accepted accounting principles?

3. What are the major categories of funds flows for a business entity?

4. Why must all "nonfund" account balances be analyzed in preparing a funds statement?

5. In presenting a funds statement on a working capital basis, why is it important to also include a supporting schedule showing the changes in working capital?

6. Name a source of funds originating from a transaction involving (a) noncurrent assets, (b) noncurrent liabilities, (c) capital stock, (d) retained earnings. Name an application of funds identified with each group.

7. What three classes of adjustments are usually necessary in preparing the statement of changes in financial position?

8. (a) Why is it important to disclose separately the amount of working capital or cash provided from normal operations? (b) To compute "funds from operations" what adjustments are applied to the operating income figure when the funds statement is prepared on a working capital basis? (c) To compute "funds from operations" what adjustments are applied to operating income when the funds statement is prepared on a cash basis?

9. Brookshire Delivery Service had its worst year in 1984, operations resulting in a substantial loss. Nevertheless, without the sale of property items, borrowing, or the issue of additional stock, the company's working capital increased significantly. What possible explanation can you suggest for this increase?

10. Indicate how each of the following would be reported on a funds statement assuming that funds are regarded as working capital.

(a) Land and buildings are acquired for cash equal to 40% of the purchase price and a long-term mortgage note for the balance.
(b) Fully depreciated machinery is written off.
(c) Long-term notes are due within the year and their classification is changed to current.
(d) Capital stock is issued in exchange for land.

11. What alternatives exist to using work sheets in developing funds statements?

12. What uses might each of the following find for a cash-flow statement?

(a) Manager of a small laundry.
(b) Stockholder interested in regular dividends.
(c) Bank granting short-term loans.
(d) Officer of a labor union.

13. Should a funds statement be audited by public accountants? Give your conclusion and reasons for your conclusion.

DISCUSSION CASES

case 23–1 (Is depreciation a source of funds?) Todd Knight and Joe Brackner are roommates in college. Knight is an accounting major while Brackner is a finance major. Both have recently studied the "funds statement" in their classes. Brackner's finance professor stated that depreciation is a major source of funds for some companies. Knight's accounting professor indicated in class that depreciation cannot be a source of funds because no funds are involved.

Knight and Brackner wonder which professor is correct. Explain the positions taken by both professors and indicate which viewpoint you support and why.

case 23–2 (The most useful concept of funds) At a recent luncheon, DeLance Jones, Lauretta Squires, and Merlin Hawkins, all CPAs, were discussing the funds statement. Jones favors a cash-flow funds statement based on the premise that cash flows are what interest most investors and creditors. Squires prefers a working capital funds statement because it is commonly understood by many financial statement readers. Hawkins feels strongly that the all financial resources concept should be used in preparing a funds statement. Should these three concepts of funds be considered as alternatives? Which concept do you prefer and why?

EXERCISES

exercise 23–1 (Sources and uses of funds)

State how each of the following items will be reflected on the statement of changes in financial position if funds are defined as (1) working capital, and (2) cash.

(a) Marketable securities were purchased for $5,000.
(b) At the beginning of the year, equipment, book value $2,000, was traded for dissimilar equipment costing $3,500; a trade-in value of $700 was allowed on the old equipment, the balance of the purchase price to be paid in 12 monthly installments.
(c) Buildings were acquired for $187,500, the company paying $50,000 cash and signing a 12% mortgage note payable in 5 years for the balance.
(d) Uncollectible accounts of $225 were written off against the allowance for doubtful accounts.
(e) Cash of $62,500 was paid on the purchase of business assets consisting of: merchandise, $22,500; furniture and fixtures, $7,500; land and buildings, $23,750; and goodwill, $8,750.
(f) A cash dividend of $1,250 was declared in the current period, payable at the beginning of the next period.
(g) An adjustment was made increasing Deferred Income Tax by $5,000.
(h) Accounts payable shows a decrease for the period of $3,750.

exercise 23–2 (Sources and uses of working capital)

The accountant for Alpine Hobby Stores prepared the following selected information for the year ending December 31, 1984.

	December 31, 1984	December 31, 1983
Equipment	$22,000	$20,000
Accumulated depreciation	9,000	8,000
Long-term debt	12,000	17,000
Common stock	16,000	11,500

A piece of equipment with a book value of $10,500 was sold for $11,000. The original cost of the equipment was $12,000.

What is the amount of working capital provided or applied for each of the items listed above?

exercise 23–3 (Working capital provided by operations)

Compute the working capital provided by operations from the following selected information:

Sales	$2,400,000
Cost of sales	1,400,000
Income tax expense	280,000
Depreciation expense	400,000
Amortization of bond discount	1,000
Amortization of bond premium	1,500
Gain on sale of land held for investment	35,000
Net income	350,000
Increase in deferred income tax	30,000
Amortization of patents	2,000
Loss on sale of equipment	3,500
Proceeds from sale of land	150,000
Issuance of bonds at a discount	490,000

exercise 23-4 (Sources and uses of working capital)

Determine the major sources and uses of working capital for Racket Club Inc. during 1984.

Net income	$425,000
Depreciation expense	110,000
Amortization of patents	100,000
Amortization of bond premium	5,000
Investment in Jensen Co. stock	125,000
Purchase of equipment	385,000
Issuance of long-term notes in satisfaction of trade accounts payable	80,000
Issuance of common stock to purchase production plant	300,000

exercise 23-5 (Work sheet adjustments)

Give the adjustments, in journal entry form, needed for a work sheet for a statement of changes in financial position upon analyzing the following account:

Account **Retained Earnings**

Date		Item	Debit	Credit	Balance	
					Debit	Credit
1984						
Jan.	1	Balance				532,000
Mar.	20	Correction for error in inventory at end of 1983		10,500		542,500
June	1	Stock dividend	140,000			402,500
Aug.	5	Discount on sale of treasury stock, par $150,000 for $132,500	17,500			385,000
Dec.	5	Cash dividends	35,000			350,000
	31	Appropriation for loss contingencies	70,000			280,000
	31	Net income		52,500		332,500

exercise 23-6 (Working capital basis funds statement)

From the following comparative balance sheet of Worldwide Enterprises and the additional information, prepare a statement of changes in financial position on a working capital basis for the year ended December 31, 1985.

	December 31, 1985	December 31, 1984
Assets		
Cash	$ 8,500	$10,000
Accounts receivable	9,250	7,500
Inventories	5,780	13,100
Prepaid expenses	4,015	2,300
Machinery and equipment	50,100	57,600
Accumulated depreciation	(14,700)	(15,300)
Long-term investments	30,000	23,000
Total assets	$92,945	$98,200
Liabilities and Owners' Equity		
Accounts payable	$ 9,200	$12,300
Short-term notes payable	2,445	3,000
Salaries payable	2,300	1,150
Bonds payable	17,000	22,000
Common stock	22,000	24,750
Retained earnings	40,000	35,000
Total liabilities and equity	$92,945	$98,200

(continued)

(a) Sold equipment during 1985 for $6,000; original cost of equipment, $12,000; accumulated depreciation totaled $5,600 on date of sale.
(b) Net income for 1985 was $11,000.

exercise 23-7 (Funds statements—working capital and cash basis)

The Easy-Grow Seed Co. prepared for 1984 and 1983 the following balance sheet data:

	December 31	
	1984	1983
Cash	$ 349,500	$ 255,000
Marketable securities	69,000	420,000
Accounts receivable (net)	360,000	345,000
Merchandise inventory	750,000	654,000
Prepaid insurance	4,500	6,000
Buildings and equipment	5,515,500	4,350,000
Accumulated depreciation—buildings and equipment	(2,235,000)	(1,995,000)
Total	$4,813,500	$4,035,000
Accounts payable	$ 613,500	$ 945,000
Salaries payable	75,000	105,000
Notes payable—bank (current)	150,000	600,000
Mortgage payable	1,500,000	0
Capital stock, $5 par	2,400,000	2,400,000
Retained earnings (deficit)	75,000	(15,000)
Total	$4,813,500	$4,035,000

Cash needed to purchase new equipment and to improve the company's working capital position was raised by selling marketable securities costing $351,000 for $360,000 and by issuing a mortgage. Equipment costing $75,000 with a book value of $15,000 was sold for $18,000; the gain on sale was included in net income. The company paid cash dividends of $90,000 during the year and reported earnings of $180,000 for 1984. There were no entries in the retained earnings account other than to record the dividend and the net income for the year. Marketable securities are carried at cost which is lower than market.

Prepare funds statements without use of a work sheet:

(a) On a working capital basis.
(b) On a cash basis.

exercise 23-8 (Cash provided by operations)

Net income for Boman Industrial Supply for 1984 was $670,000. Compute the cash provided by operations, given the following information.

(a) Machinery costing $60,000 with a book value of $20,000 was stolen. The insurance company reimbursed Boman for $15,000, and new equipment was purchased for $85,000.
(b) Two delivery trucks were traded in for two new vans that are considered dissimilar from the trucks. Cost of the old trucks was $18,000 each and the corresponding accumulated depreciation was $13,000 each. Cash of $19,000 was paid for each new van and $6,000 was allowed on each trade-in. Market value of the new vans was $25,000 each.
(c) Boman used accelerated depreciation for income tax purposes and straight-line depreciation for book purposes. This resulted in an increase in Deferred Income Taxes of $27,000.
(d) Book depreciation for the year was $220,000.

exercise 23-9 (Adjustments to all financial resources concept)

Beck Refining Corporation showed the following statement of changes in financial position for the year ended March 31, 1985.

Beck Refining Corporation
Statement of Changes in Financial Position—Working Capital Basis
For The Year Ended March 31, 1985

Sources:		
Operations:		
Net Income		$1,500,000
Items added to net income:		
Depreciation	$1,000,000	
Amortization of patents	500,000	1,500,000
Working capital provided by operations		$3,000,000
Sale of equipment at book value		300,000
Exchange of long-term investment for inventory		200,000
		$3,500,000
Uses:		
Dividends	$ 200,000	
Purchase of equipment	1,800,000	
Purchase of office equipment	1,000,000	3,000,000
Increase in working capital		$ 500,000

Beck did not use the all financial resources concept in preparing this statement. Considering the following additional information, prepare a statement of changes in financial position on a working capital basis using the all financial resources concept.

(a) A building and land were purchased for $2,000,000, payment being made in the form of Beck common stock valued at $2,000,000.
(b) Beck exchanged $400,000 of U. S. Government securities with Sysco Inc. receiving machinery valued at $400,000 in return. The investment was considered long-term.

exercise 23-10 (Reporting sources and uses of working capital)

Determine how each of the following would be reported on a statement of changes in financial position—working capital basis.

(a) New equipment with a fair market value of $27,500 was acquired on August 1 with an issuance of common stock.
(b) Inventory showed a decrease of $7,200 during the period.
(c) Stock dividends were paid during the year. The fair market value of the dividends was $10,000.
(d) A machine with an original cost of $21,000 and a book value of $7,100 was sold for $5,900.
(e) A long-term investment in Timo Co. bonds was exchanged during the year for a long-term investment in Emo Co. common stock. The fair market value and the cost of each of the exchanged securities was $16,300.

exercise 23-11 (Cash provided by operations—revenue and expense detail)

A summary of revenues and expenses for Kelly's Hardware Company for 1984 follows:

Sales	$6,000,000
Cost of goods manufactured and sold	2,800,000
Gross profit	$3,200,000
Selling, general, and administrative expenses	2,000,000
Income before income tax	$1,200,000
Income tax	520,000
Net income	$ 680,000

Net changes in working capital items for 1984 were as follows:

	Debit	Credit
Cash	$104,000	
Trade accounts receivable (net)	400,000	
Inventories		$ 60,000
Prepaid expenses (selling and general)	10,000	
Accrued expenses (75% of increase related to manufacturing activities and 25% to general operating activities)		32,000
Income tax payable		48,000
Trade accounts payable		140,000

Depreciation on plant and equipment for the year totaled $600,000; 70% was related to manufacturing activities and 30% to general and administrative activities.

Prepare a summary of cash provided by operations for the year showing revenues and expenses in detail.

exercise 23-12 (Cash basis funds statement)

A comparative balance for United Energy Co. and a funds statement on a working capital basis are presented below. The schedule of working capital changes appears on page 893. From the information provided prepare a cash basis funds statement for 1984.

United Energy Co.
Comparative Balance Sheet
December 31, 1984 and 1983

Assets	1984	1983
Cash	$ 50,000	$ 65,000
Accounts receivable	170,000	143,000
Inventory	200,000	210,000
Prepaid items	60,000	40,000
Total current assets	$ 480,000	$458,000
Land, building and equipment (net)	690,000	510,000
Total assets	$1,170,000	$968,000
Liabilities and Equity		
Accounts payable	$ 145,000	$155,000
Cash dividends payable	70,000	50,000
Total current liabilities	$ 215,000	$205,000
Bonds payable	300,000	200,000
Total liabilities	$ 515,000	$405,000
Stockholders' equity	655,000	563,000
Total liabilities and equity	$1,170,000	$968,000

United Energy Co.
Statement of Changes in Financial Position—Working Capital Basis
For Year Ended December 31, 1984

Working capital was provided by:		
Net income	$162,000	
Add item not requiring working capital:		
Depreciation	20,000	
Working capital provided by operations	$182,000	
Issuance of bonds payable	100,000	$282,000
Working capital was applied to:		
Dividends	$ 70,000	
Purchase of Equipment	200,000	270,000
Increase in working capital		$ 12,000

	December 31, 1984	December 31, 1983	Working Capital Increase (Decrease)
Current assets:			
Cash	$ 50,000	$ 65,000	(15,000)
Accounts receivable	170,000	143,000	27,000
Inventory	200,000	210,000	(10,000)
Prepaid items	60,000	40,000	20,000
Current liabilities:			
Accounts payable	145,000	155,000	10,000
Cash dividends payable	70,000	50,000	(20,000)
Increase in working capital			$12,000

exercise 23-13 (Work sheet adjustments)

From the following information, give the necessary adjustments in journal entry form to explain the changes in accounts listed in preparing a work sheet for a statement of changes in financial position for 1984.

	December 31, 1984	December 31, 1983
Land	$ 50,000	$ 80,000
Buildings	200,000	200,000
Accumulated depreciation—buildings	137,000	125,000
Machinery	78,000	90,000
Accumulated depreciation—machinery	31,000	32,000
Delivery equipment	30,000	50,000
Accumulated depreciation—delivery equipment	13,000	25,000
Tools	28,000	24,000
Patents	7,000	9,000
Goodwill	0	80,000
Discount on bonds payable	0	12,000
Bonds payable	0	1,000,000
Capital stock	700,000	500,000
Treasury stock	44,000	0
Retained earnings appropriated for bond retirement fund	0	200,000
Retained earnings	359,000	360,000

Account **Retained Earnings**

Date		Item	Debit	Credit	Balance Debit	Balance Credit
1984 Jan.	1	Balance				360,000
		Stock dividend	200,000			160,000
		Retained earnings appropriated for bond retirement fund		200,000		360,000
		Premium on purchase of treasury stock, par $44,000	16,000			344,000
		Cash dividends	20,000			324,000
Dec.	31	Net income		35,000		359,000

The income statement reports depreciation of buildings, $12,000; depreciation of machinery, $8,000; depreciation of delivery equipment, $4,000; tools amortization, $8,000; patents amortization, $2,000; and bond discount amortization, $2,000. The following additional information was taken from the income statement and accounting records:

Operating income		$ 80,000
Gains:		
Gain on sale of land, cost $30,000	$170,000	
Gain on sale of delivery equipment, cost $20,000, book value $4,000	10,000	180,000
		$260,000
Losses:		
Loss on scrapping machinery, cost $12,000, on which accumulated depreciation of $9,000 had been recognized	$ 3,000	
Goodwill written off	80,000	83,000
Income from continuing operations before income tax		$177,000
Income tax		72,000
Income from continuing operations		$105,000
Extraordinary loss on bond retirement (unamortized discount, $10,000, and call premium, $60,000)		70,000
Net income		$ 35,000

PROBLEMS

problem 23-1 (Schedule of changes in working capital and funds statement)

The following is a comparative balance sheet for the Blinton Shoe Company:

Blinton Shoe Company
Comparative Balance Sheet
December 31, 1985 and 1984

Assets	1985	1984
Cash	$ 350,000	$ 265,000
Accounts receivable (net)	275,000	237,000
Inventory	535,000	326,000
Interest receivable	140,000	25,250
Prepaid expenses	80,000	85,000
Land	171,000	215,000
Building and equipment (net)	1,033,000	995,000
Investments	459,000	673,250
Patents (net)	57,000	63,500
Total assets	$3,100,000	$2,885,000
Liabilities and Stockholders' Equity		
Accounts payable	$ 565,000	$ 313,000
Income tax payable	148,000	155,000
Salaries and wages payable	207,000	57,250
Mortgage bonds (long-term)	305,000	378,000
Bonds payable (long-term)	63,000	51,000
Common stock	1,012,000	1,154,750
Retained earnings	800,000	776,000
Total liabilities and stockholders' equity	$3,100,000	$2,885,000

Additional information:

(a) Net income for the year was $62,000.
(b) Land with a book value of $44,000 was exchanged for a building of similar value (no gain or loss).
(c) No new patents were issued during the year.
(d) Common stock was issued in exchange for equipment that had a fair market value of $21,500 (no gain or loss).
(e) A machine with a book value of $3,700 was sold for $5,100.

Instructions: Prepare a schedule of changes in working capital and a statement of changes in financial position on a working capital basis for the year ended December 31, 1985.

problem 23-2 (Funds statements—working capital and cash basis)

Comparative balance sheet data for the firm of Baker and Lewis are given below.

	December 31 1984	December 31 1983
Cash	$ 13,500	$ 9,750
Accounts receivable	22,000	25,500
Inventory	112,500	75,000
Prepaid expenses	3,000	4,250
Furniture and fixtures	64,500	40,000
Accumulated depreciation	(33,875)	(25,125)
Total	$181,625	$129,375
Accrued expenses	$ 6,500	$ 4,750
Accounts payable	19,125	24,875
Long-term note	17,500	-0-
Charles Lewis, capital	51,375	48,875
John Baker, capital	87,125	50,875
Total	$181,625	$129,375

Income from operations for the year was $37,500 and this was transferred in equal amounts to the partners' capital accounts. Further changes in the capital accounts arose from additional investments and withdrawals by the partners. The change in the furniture and fixtures account arose from a purchase of additional furniture; part of the purchase price was paid in cash and a long-term note was issued for the balance.

Instructions: Prepare the following (work sheets are not required):

(1) A statement of changes in financial position applying the working capital concept of funds.
(2) A statement of changes in financial position applying the cash concept of funds.

problem 23-3 (Funds statements—working capital and cash basis)

Comparative balance sheet data for Thalman Inc. follow:

	December 31 1984	December 31 1983
Cash	$ 45,000	$ 80,000
Accounts receivable	120,000	100,000
Inventory	150,000	125,000
Prepaid expenses	25,000	20,000
Land, buildings, and equipment	320,000	190,000
Accumulated depreciation	(90,000)	(70,000)
	$570,000	$445,000
Accrued expenses	$ 15,000	$ 10,000
Accounts payable	105,000	85,000
Bonds payable	40,000	100,000
Capital stock, at par	250,000	200,000
Additional paid-in capital	50,000	20,000
Retained earnings	110,000	30,000
	$570,000	$445,000

Land and buildings were acquired in exchange for capital stock; the assets were recorded at $80,000, their appraised value. Equipment was acquired for $50,000 cash. Net income for the year transferred to retained earnings was $110,000; cash dividends accounted for the remaining change in retained earnings.

Instructions: Prepare the following (work sheets are not required):

(1) A statement of changes in financial position applying the working capital concept of funds.
(2) A statement of changes in financial position applying the cash concept of funds.

problem 23-4 (Funds statements—working capital and cash basis)

Empire Bicycle Co. reported net income of $6,160 for 1984 but has been showing an overdraft in its bank account in recent months. The manager has contracted you as the auditor for an explanation. The information below was given to you for examination.

Empire Bicycle Company
Comparative Balance Sheet
December 31, 1984 and 1983

	1984			1983		
Assets						
Current assets:						
Cash		$ (960)			$ 4,780	
Accounts receivable		4,000			1,000	
Inventory		2,350			750	
Prepaid insurance		70			195	
Total current assets			$ 5,460			$ 6,725
Land, buildings, and equipment:						
Land		$12,500			$12,500	
Buildings	$25,000			$25,000		
Less accumulated depreciation	15,000	10,000		14,000	11,000	
Equipment	$37,250			$30,850		
Less accumulated depreciation	22,500	14,750		18,400	12,450	
Total land, buildings, and equipment			37,250			35,950
Total assets			$42,710			$42,675
Liabilities and Stockholders' Equity						
Current liabilities:						
Accounts payable		$ 4,250			$ 3,500	
Taxes payable		1,400			2,350	
Wages payable		750			1,675	
Notes payable—current portion		1,500			3,500	
Total current liabilities			$ 7,900			$11,025
Long-term liabilities:						
Notes payable			10,500			11,500
Capital stock		$17,500			$15,000	
Retained earnings		6,810			5,150	
Total stockholders' equity			24,310			20,150
Total liabilities and stockholders' equity			$42,710			$42,675

You also determine the following:

(a) Equipment was sold for $1,500, its cost was $2,500 and its book value was $500. The gain was reported as Other Revenue.
(b) Cash dividends of $4,500 were paid.

Instructions: Prepare the following (work sheets are not required):

(1) A statement of changes in financial position applying the working capital concept of funds.
(2) A statement of changes in financial position applying the cash concept of funds.

problem 23-5 (Working capital funds statement)

Lowlands Dairy Products presented the following comparative information:

	1984	1983
Cash	$174,000	$150,000
Accounts receivable	95,000	80,000
Inventory (lower of cost or market)	160,000	175,000
Land, buildings, and equipment (net)	315,000	350,000
Current liabilities	(210,000)	(215,000)
Bonds payable	0	(200,000)
Bond premium	0	(6,000)
Common stock, $50 par	(450,000)	(250,000)
Additional paid-in capital	(35,000)	(15,000)
Retained earnings	(49,000)	(69,000)

Account **Retained Earnings**

Date		Item	Debit	Credit	Balance	
					Debit	Credit
1984 Jan.	1	Balance				69,000
		Cash dividends paid during the year	10,000			59,000
		Net loss (including $15,000 loss on bond conversion)	10,000			49,000

Buildings, with a book value of $80,000, were sold for $130,000 cash. Part of the proceeds were used to purchase land for $60,000. Depreciation recorded for the year was $15,000. The bonds payable were converted to common stock on December 31, 1984, after the annual bond premium amortization of $1,000 had been recorded. The conversion privilege provided for exchange of a $1,000 bond for 20 shares of stock. Market value of the stock on December 31, 1984, was $55 per share.

Instructions: Prepare a funds statement applying the working capital concept of funds. (A work sheet is not required.)

problem 23-6 (Work sheet and working capital funds statement)

The following data were taken from the records of Alpine Enterprises.

Balance Sheet
December 31

	1984		1983	
Current assets		$185,200		$148,300
Land, buildings, and equipment	$100,500		$96,000	
Less accumulated depreciation	34,000	66,500	30,000	66,000
Investments in stocks and bonds		32,000		35,000
Goodwill		0		25,000
Total assets		$283,700		$274,300
Current liabilities		$ 58,800		$ 43,300
Bonds payable		0		50,000
Discount on bonds payable		0		(1,250)
Preferred stock, $100 par		0		50,000
Common stock, $10 par		165,000		105,000
Additional paid-in capital		40,000		0
Retained earnings		19,900		27,250
Total liabilities and stockholders' equity		$283,700		$274,300

Account **Retained Earnings**

Date		Item	Debit	Credit	Balance	
					Debit	Credit
1984						
Jan.	1	Balance				27,250
		Premium on retirement of preferred stock	1,000			26,250
		Cash dividends	17,500			8,750
		Net income		11,150		19,900

Income statement data for the year ended December 31, 1984, summarized operations as follows:

Income before extraordinary items	$14,650
Extraordinary loss on retirement of bonds	3,500
Net income	$11,150

Fully depreciated equipment, original cost $10,500, was traded in on similar new equipment with a list price of $16,500; $1,500 was allowed by the vendor on the trade-in. No gain or loss was recognized on the trade-in. One hundred shares of Byler Co. preferred stock, cost $20,000, held as a long-term investment, were sold at a loss of $2,500 at the beginning of the year. Additional changes in the investments account resulted from the purchase of Carbon Co. bonds. The company issued common stock in April, and part of the proceeds was used to retire preferred stock at 102 shortly thereafter. On July 1, the company called in its bonds outstanding, paying a premium of 5% on the call. Discount amortization on the bonds to the date of call was $250. Depreciation for the year on buildings and equipment was $14,500. Goodwill was judged worthless and was written off.

Instructions: Prepare a work sheet and a statement of changes in financial position applying the working capital concept of funds.

problem 23-7 (Work sheet and funds statements—working capital and cash basis)

The following information was assembled for Pacific Pipeline Inc.

Balance Sheet
December 31

	1984		1983	
Cash (overdraft in 1983)		$ 38,625		$ (5,625)
Accounts receivable		82,000		95,500
Inventories		73,250		50,000
Long-term investments		12,000		27,000
Land, buildings, and equipment	$130,000		$95,000	
Less accumulated depreciation	21,500	108,500	20,000	75,000
Patents		0		35,000
Total assets		$314,375		$276,875
Accounts payable		$ 55,875		$ 49,375
Bonds payable		50,000		20,000
Premium on bonds payable		2,375		0
Preferred stock, $100 par		0		50,000
Common stock, $10 par		160,000		100,000
Premium on common stock		24,000		0
Retained earnings		22,125		57,500
Total liabilities and stockholders' equity		$314,375		$276,875

Account **Retained Earnings**

Date		Item	Debit	Credit	Balance	
					Debit	Credit
1984						
Jan.	1	Balance				57,500
Oct.	15	Cash dividends	25,000			32,500
Dec.	12	Premium on retirement of preferred stock	5,000			27,500
Dec.	31	Net loss	5,375			22,125

Income statement data for the year ended December 31, 1984, summarized operations as follows:

Loss before extraordinary items	$4,375
Extraordinary loss on retirement of bonds	1,000
Net loss	$5,375

Equipment, cost $15,000, book value $3,000, was scrapped, salvage of $900 being recovered on the disposal. Additional equipment, cost $50,000, was acquired during the year. Long-term investments, cost $15,000, were sold for $18,250; 7% bonds, face value $20,000, were called in at 105, and new 10-year, 5% bonds of $50,000 were issued at 105 on July 1. Preferred stock was retired at a cost of $110 while 6,000 shares of common stock were issued at $14. Depreciation on buildings and equipment for the year was $13,500. Patents, costing $35,000, were written off.

Instructions:

(1) Prepare a work sheet and a statement of changes in financial position applying the working capital concept of funds.
(2) Prepare a statement of changes in financial position applying the cash concept of funds.

problem 23-8 (Work sheet and comprehensive cash basis funds statement)

The Bernard Company prepared the following comparative balance sheet and combined statement of income and retained earnings.

Bernard Company
Income and Retained Earnings Statement
For Year Ended December 31, 1984

Income before extraordinary items		$319,000
Extraordinary loss on equipment (net of income tax credit of $80,000)		140,000
Net income		$179,000
Unadjusted retained earnings, January 1, 1984	$623,000	
Deduct: Prior period adjustment—correction of inventory overstatement, net of income tax refund of $18,000	20,000	
Adjusted retained earnings, January 1, 1984		603,000
Deduct: Dividends declared	$ 50,000	
10% stock dividend	120,000	(170,000)
Retained earnings, December 31, 1984		$612,000

An analysis of the accounts reveals the following:

(a) The tax refund from correction of inventory overstatement was received in cash during 1984.
(b) The usual annual cash dividend of $50,000 was declared on December 15, 1984, and paid on January 31, 1985.

Bernard Company
Comparative Balance Sheet
December 31

	1984		1983	
Assets				
Current assets:				
Cash		$ 320,000		$ 154,000
Marketable securities (cost)	$ 90,000		$160,000	
Less allowance for decline in value of marketable securities	8,000		10,000	
Marketable securities (market)		82,000		150,000
Accounts receivable (net)		640,000		520,000
Inventories (lower of cost or market)		540,000		670,000
Prepaid expenses		6,000		8,000
Total current assets		$1,588,000		$1,502,000
Land, buildings, and equipment:				
Land		$ 50,000		$ 50,000
Buildings	$825,000		$800,000	
Less accumulated depreciation—buildings	215,000	610,000	225,000	575,000
Machinery and equipment	$425,000		$380,000	
Less accumulated depreciation—machinery and equipment	75,000	350,000	120,000	260,000
Total land, buildings, and equipment		$1,010,000		$ 885,000
Investment in Tow Company (equity)		$ 970,000		$ 800,000
Goodwill		55,000		60,000
		$1,025,000		$ 860,000
Total assets		$3,623,000		$3,247,000
Liabilities				
Current liabilities:				
Accounts payable		$ 464,000		$ 407,000
Mortgage payable in 6 months		20,000		0
Income tax payable		115,000		150,000
Accrued payables		80,000		75,000
Dividends payable		50,000		50,000
Estimated liability under service contracts (current)		65,000		60,000
Long-term liabilities:				
Mortgage payable		180,000		0
Debenture bonds payable	$500,000		$500,000	
Plus unamortized premium	5,500	505,500	6,000	506,000
Long-term liability under service contracts		287,500		242,000
Other long-term liabilities:				
Deferred income tax		124,000		134,000
Total liabilities		$1,891,000		$1,624,000
Stockholders' Equity				
Common stock, $10 par	$880,000		$800,000	
Additional paid-in capital	240,000		200,000	
Retained earnings	612,000	1,732,000	623,000	1,623,000
Total liabilities and stockholders' equity		$3,623,000		$3,247,000

(c) The 10% stock dividend was declared when Bernard Company stock was selling for $15 per share.

(d) Equipment costing $300,000 with a book value of $220,000 was destroyed in an extraordinary disaster. The deferred income tax related to the difference between tax and book depreciation taken on the equipment was $35,000. This reduced the book income tax credit on the loss from $80,000 to an actual tax credit of $45,000. New equipment was purchased with cash raised by selling marketable securities, cost $150,000, for $145,000 and by taking out the mortgage for the balance due. The mortgage is due in 10 annual installments of $20,000.

(e) The allowance account for the decline in value of marketable securities was adjusted at year-end by a credit to the income account, Recovery of Recognized Decline in Value of Current Marketable Securities.
(f) The ending inventory was written down by $50,000 to properly value the inventory at the lower of cost or market.
(g) Tow Company, in which Bernard Company holds a 35% interest, paid dividends of $600,000 and reported earnings of $800,000 during 1984. Bernard Company made an additional investment in Tow Company on December 31, 1984.
(h) A warehouse costing $200,000, with a book value of $150,000 was destroyed by fire. The insurance proceeds were $210,000 cash. There was no tax on the gain of the old warehouse as a new warehouse costing $225,000 was built during the same year.
(i) Depreciation and amortization for 1984 were as follows:

Buildings	$40,000
Machinery and equipment	35,000
Goodwill	5,000
Premium on bonds payable	500

Instructions: Prepare a work sheet and a statement of changes in financial position applying the cash concept of funds.

problem 23-9 (Working capital funds statement)

The Benson Company has prepared its financial statements for the year ended December 31, 1983, and for the three months ended March 31, 1984. You have been asked to prepare a statement of changes in financial position on a working capital basis for the three months ended March 31, 1984. The company's balance sheet data at December 31, 1983, and March 31, 1984, and its income statement data for the three months ended March 31, 1984, follow. You have previously satisfied yourself as to the correctness of the amounts presented. The balance sheet data are as follows:

	March 31, 1984	December 31, 1983
Cash	$ 87,400	$ 25,300
Marketable securities	7,300	16,500
Accounts receivable (net)	49,320	24,320
Inventory	48,590	31,090
Total current assets	$192,610	$ 97,210
Land	18,700	40,000
Buildings	250,000	250,000
Equipment	81,500	0
Accumulated depreciation	(16,250)	(15,000)
Investment in 30% owned company	67,100	61,220
Other assets	15,100	15,100
Total	$608,760	$448,530
Accounts payable	$ 17,330	$ 21,220
Dividends payable	8,000	0
Income tax payable	34,616	0
Total current liabilities	$ 59,946	$ 21,220
Other liabilities	186,000	186,000
Bonds payable	115,000	50,000
Discount on bonds payable	(2,150)	(2,300)
Deferred income tax	846	510
Preferred stock	0	30,000
Common stock	110,000	80,000
Dividends declared	(8,000)	0
Retained earnings	147,118	83,100
Total	$608,760	$448,530

Income statement data for the three months ended March 31, 1984, are as follows:

Sales	$242,807
Gain on sale of marketable securities	2,400
Equity in earnings of 30% owned company	5,880
Gain on condemnation of land (capital gains)	10,700
	$261,787
Cost of goods sold	$138,407
General and administrative expenses	22,010
Depreciation	1,250
Interest expense	1,150
Income tax	34,952
	$197,769
Net income	$ 64,018

Your discussion with the company's controller and a review of the financial records revealed the following information:

(a) On January 8, 1984, the company sold marketable securities for cash.
(b) The company's preferred stock is convertible into common stock at a rate of one share of preferred for two shares of common. The preferred stock and common stock have par values of $2 and $1 respectively.
(c) On January 17, 1984, three acres of land were extraordinarily condemned. An award of $32,000 in cash was received on March 22, 1984. Purchase of additional land as a replacement is not contemplated by the company.
(d) On March 25, 1984, the company purchased equipment for cash.
(e) On March 29, 1984, bonds payable were issued by the company at par for cash.
(f) The company's tax rate is 40% for regular income and 20% for capital gains.

Instructions: Prepare in good form a statement of changes in financial position on a working capital basis for the Benson Company for the three months ended March 31, 1984. (AICPA adapted)

problem 23-10 (Comprehensive working capital funds statement)

The following schedule showing net changes in balance sheet accounts at December 31, 1984, compared to December 31, 1983, was prepared from the records of the Sodium Company. The statement of changes in financial position for the year ended December 31, 1984 has not yet been prepared.

	Increase (Decrease)
Assets	
Cash	$ 50,000
Accounts receivable (net)	76,000
Inventories	37,000
Prepaid expenses	1,000
Property, plant, and equipment (net)	64,000
Total assets	$228,000
Liabilities	
Accounts payable	$ (55,500)
Notes payable—current	(15,000)
Accrued expenses	33,000
Bonds payable	(28,000)
Less unamortized bond discount	1,200
Total liabilities	$ (64,300)
Stockholders' Equity	
Common stock, $10 par	$500,000
Paid-in capital in excess of par value	200,000
Retained earnings	(437,700)
Appropriation of retained earnings for possible future inventory price decline	30,000
Total stockholders' equity	$292,300
Total liabilities and stockholders' equity	$228,000

Additional information includes:

(a) The net income for the year ended December 31, 1984, was $172,300. There were no extraordinary items.
(b) During the year ended December 31, 1984, uncollectible accounts receivable of $26,400 were written off by a debit to Allowance for Doubtful Accounts.
(c) A comparison of Property, Plant, and Equipment as of the end of each year follows:

	December 31 1984	December 31 1983	Increase (Decrease)
Property, plant, and equipment	$570,500	$510,000	$60,500
Less accumulated depreciation	224,500	228,000	(3,500)
Property, plant, and equipment (net)	$346,000	$282,000	$64,000

During 1984, machinery was purchased at a cost of $45,000. In addition, machinery that was acquired in 1977 at a cost of $48,000 was sold for $3,600. At the date of sale, the machinery had an undepreciated cost of $4,200. The remaining increase in Property, Plant, and Equipment resulted from the acquisition of a tract of land for a new plant site.
(d) The bonds payable mature at the rate of $28,000 every year.
(e) In January 1984, the company issued an additional 10,000 shares of its common stock at $14 per share upon the exercise of outstanding stock options held by key employees. In May 1984, the company declared and issued a 5% stock dividend on its outstanding stock. During the year, a cash dividend was paid on the common stock. On December 31, 1984, there were 840,000 shares of common stock outstanding.
(f) The appropriation of retained earnings for possible future inventory price declines was provided by a debit to Retained Earnings, in anticipation of an expected future drop in the market related to goods in inventory.

Instructions:

(1) Prepare a statement of changes in financial position for the year ended December 31, 1984, based on the information presented. The statement should be prepared using a working capital format.
(2) Prepare a schedule of changes in working capital for the year 1984. (AICPA adapted)

problem 23-11 (Analysis of cash flows and cash basis funds statement)

The following schedule shows the account balances of the Sun Ray Corporation at the beginning and end of the fiscal year ended October 31, 1984.

Debits	October 31, 1984	November 1, 1983	Increase (Decrease)
Cash	$ 226,000	$ 50,000	$176,000
Accounts Receivable	148,000	100,000	48,000
Inventories	291,000	300,000	(9,000)
Prepaid Insurance	2,500	2,000	500
Long-Term Investments (at cost)	10,000	40,000	(30,000)
Sinking Fund	90,000	80,000	10,000
Land and Building	195,000	195,000	
Equipment	215,000	90,000	125,000
Discount on Bonds Payable	8,500	9,000	(500)
Treasury Stock (at cost)	5,000	10,000	(5,000)
Cost of Goods Sold	539,000		
Selling and General Expenses	287,000		
Income Tax	35,000		
Loss on Sale of Equipment	1,000		
Total debits	$2,053,000	$876,000	

Debits	October 31, 1984	November 1, 1983	Increase (Decrease)
Allowance for Doubtful Accounts	$ 8,000	$ 5,000	$ 3,000
Accumulated Depreciation—Building	26,250	22,500	3,750
Accumulated Depreciation—Equipment	39,750	27,500	12,250
Accounts Payable	55,000	60,000	(5,000)
Notes Payable—current	70,000	20,000	50,000
Miscellaneous Expenses Payable	18,000	15,000	3,000
Taxes Payable	35,000	10,000	25,000
Unearned Revenue	1,000	9,000	(8,000)
Notes Payable—Long-Term	40,000	60,000	(20,000)
Bonds Payable—Long-Term	250,000	250,000	
Common Stock	300,000	200,000	100,000
Retained Earnings Appropriated for Sinking Fund	90,000	80,000	10,000
Unappropriated Retained Earnings	94,000	112,000	(18,000)
Paid-In Capital in Excess of Par Value	116,000	5,000	111,000
Sales	898,000		
Gain on Sale of Investments	12,000		
Total credits	$2,053,000	$876,000	

The following information was also available:

(a) All purchases and sales were on account.
(b) The sinking fund will be used to retire the long-term bonds.
(c) Equipment with an original cost of $15,000 was sold for $7,000.
(d) Selling and general expenses include the following expenses:

Building depreciation	$ 3,750
Equipment depreciation	19,250
Doubtful accounts expense	4,000
Interest expense	18,000

(e) A six-months note payable for $50,000 was issued toward the purchase of new equipment.
(f) The long-term note payable requires the payment of $20,000 per year plus interest until paid.
(g) Treasury stock was sold for $1,000 more than its cost.
(h) All dividends were paid by cash.

Instructions:

(1) Prepare schedules computing: (a) collections of accounts receivable: (b) payments of accounts payable.
(2) Prepare a statement of changes in financial position applying the cash concept of funds. Supporting computations should be in good form. (AICPA adapted)

24 REPORTING THE IMPACT OF CHANGING PRICES

CHAPTER OBJECTIVES

Discuss the underlying need and the alternatives for reporting the effects of changing prices on business enterprises.

Explain the basic concepts and procedures involved in constant dollar and current cost accounting.

Identify and illustrate the reporting requirements of FASB Statement No. 33.

FASB Statement No. 33, "Financial Reporting and Changing Prices," is one of the most important and complex pronouncements issued to date by the Financial Accounting Standards Board. In this chapter the major concepts related to reporting price changes are discussed from a conceptual viewpoint and illustrated with simple examples. For many students this will provide sufficient detail and adequate exposure to this important topic. Others will need to study carefully Appendix 1 at the end of this chapter, which provides an example of comprehensive restatement under each of three approaches to reporting the impact of changing prices on business enterprises: historical cost/constant dollar; current cost/nominal dollar; and current cost/constant dollar. In addition, Appendix 1 contrasts the results of these approaches to the currently accepted method of historical cost/nominal dollar accounting and to the requirements of FASB Statement No. 33. A second appendix to this chapter illustrates the use of current values in personal financial statements.

Traditionally, financial statements have reflected transactions in terms of the number of dollars exchanged. These statements are often referred to as **historical cost/nominal dollar** or simply **historical cost** statements, meaning statements reporting unadjusted original dollar amounts. The primary reason for reporting original dollar amounts is objectivity. Historical costs generally are based on arm's-length transactions and are considered to measure appropriate exchange values at a transaction date.

With the steady increase in prices over the past several years (see the price index below), there has been a growing awareness of the limitations of historical cost statements. Fluctuations in the general purchasing power of the dollar and significantly increased replacement costs of certain assets make it difficult to interpret the dollar amounts reported in conventional statements. Furthermore, there is growing concern that a substantial part of American industry is in a state of self-liquidation, i.e., distributing more than its real income in the form of taxes and dividends. A study of 1979 annual reports of 215 companies revealed that income from continuing operations declined 40% when adjusted for inflation and that the effective tax rate of these companies increased from 39% to 53%, which is in excess of the 46% maximum corporate tax rate imposed by the Internal Revenue Code.[1] Thus, many companies are currently paying dividends and taxes out of contributed capital rather than earnings.

Consumer Price Index for All Urban Consumers (CPI-U)
(1967 = 100)

Selected Years	*Average for Year*
1920	60.0
1930	50.0
1940	42.0
1950	72.1
1960	88.7
1965	94.5
1967*	100.0
1970	116.3
1971	121.3
1972	125.3
1973	133.1
1974	147.7
1975	161.2
1976	170.5
1977	181.5
1978	195.4
1979	217.4
1980	246.8
1981	272.4
1982	289.1

**Currently the base year*

Source: U. S. Department of Labor, Bureau of Labor Statistics

---

[1] *Alexander Grant & Company Client Newsletter*, July 1980.

The validity of analytical data provided by historical cost statements has been challenged and has caused the FASB to require disclosure by most large companies of supplemental financial data reflecting price changes. The purposes of this chapter are to discuss the issues involved and to illustrate the procedures for reporting the impact of changing prices.

THE NEED FOR REPORTING THE EFFECTS OF CHANGING PRICES ON BUSINESS ENTERPRISES

As discussed in Chapter 3, the overall objective of financial reporting is to provide investors, creditors, and others with information that will assist them in making sound economic decisions. Specifically, external users need to assess the amounts, timing, and uncertainty of future cash flows. They also need to analyze the economic resources of an enterprise in a manner that provides direct and indirect evidence of cash flow potential. In fulfilling these objectives, preparers of financial statements have the responsibility to provide information that will help users evaluate the impact of changing prices on their companies.

With the effects of price changes disclosed, users of financial reports will be able to assess more realistically: (1) future cash flows, (2) enterprise performance, and (3) the erosion of operating capability and general purchasing power of enterprise capital. After careful consideration of these factors, the FASB has concluded that certain enterprises should report information about the effects of price changes on enterprise activity.[2]

General and Specific Price Changes

Two kinds of price changes have been identified. The first deals with changes in the general price level for all commodities and services. As mentioned in earlier chapters, in periods of rising prices this concept is referred to as **inflation**. The second kind of price change relates to changes in prices of particular items. Prices for individual items may fluctuate up or down and by differing magnitudes; the average of all specific price changes determines the change in the general price level. With respect to terminology, accounting for the first kind of price change is referred to as **constant dollar accounting** or general price-level adjusted accounting. Accounting for the second kind of price change is referred to as **current cost accounting** or current value accounting. This distinction is important in order to understand the reporting alternatives identified in the next section.

Reporting Alternatives

The major financial reporting alternatives, including the currently used historical cost/nominal dollar basis, may be classified as follows.

---

[2]*Statement of Financial Accounting Standards No. 33,* "Financial Reporting and Changing Prices" (Stamford: Financial Accounting Standards Board, September 1979), pars. 3 and 10.

	Historical Cost Valuation	Current Cost Valuation
Nominal Dollar Measurement	HC/ND Historical Cost/ Nominal Dollar	CC/ND Current Cost/ Nominal Dollar
Constant Dollar Measurement	HC/CD Historical Cost/ Constant Dollar	CC/CD Current Cost/ Constant Dollar

The two distinct aspects of changing prices are highlighted by the matrix: the change in the unit of measurement (nominal and constant dollars) and the change in basis of valuation (historical and current costs). These distinctions are important since the accounting for and the effects on the financial statements are significantly different.

The first cell reflects financial statements that are currently reported in terms of nominal dollars using historical cost valuation. The dollar measurement is not adjusted for changes in the general price level, and the valuation basis represents the historical exchange prices of transactions, not current costs or values of the items reported. This is contrasted to the cell labeled HC/CD. Reporting on this basis maintains historical cost valuation but measures the items in terms of constant dollars. This means that the original or nominal dollars are adjusted to constant dollars—dollars of equivalent purchasing power. Sometimes constant dollars are referred to as **general purchasing power dollars** because they represent quantities of goods or services that can be purchased given a general price level. This concept is explained in greater detail later in this chapter.

The cell identified as CC/ND does not adjust the dollar measurement; it reports nominal dollars. However, it changes the valuation basis from historical costs to current costs. This basis of reporting reflects changes in specific prices but does not account for changes in the general price level. The term **current cost** is used throughout this chapter in a general sense to mean the current value of an asset. It includes the FASB's technical definition—current replacement cost adjusted for the value of any operating advantages or disadvantages of the specific asset[3]—as well as other measures of current cost: reproduction cost, sales value, net realizable value, and net present value of expected cash flows. Current costs and current values are used interchangeably.

The cell identified as CC/CD combines current cost valuation with constant dollar measurement. Reporting on this basis reflects both specific price changes and general purchasing power changes.

In summary, reporting on the traditional basis (represented by HC/ND) does not reflect the impact of general price changes or specific price changes until assets are sold or otherwise disposed of. Reporting on the HC/CD basis

[3] *Ibid.*, par. 99.

considers general purchasing power changes but not specific price changes. The CC/ND basis is just the opposite. It reports the impact of specific price changes because of its current cost valuation but does not reflect changes in the general purchasing power of the dollar. Only by reporting on a CC/CD basis are both types of price changes accounted for.

The extent and manner of reporting the impact of changing prices is also an issue. One possibility is to choose one of the three nontraditional cells and require preparation of primary financial statements on the basis selected. Another alternative is to continue reporting the primary financial statements on the historical cost/nominal dollar basis, but to provide supplemental information adjusted to constant dollars and/or reflecting current costs. If the latter alternative were chosen, a remaining question is whether to restate all items or only selected items.

Historical Perspective: Reporting the Impact of Changing Prices

The issues involved and the proposed alternatives for reporting the effects of changing prices are not new. In the 1920s and 1930s Henry Sweeney and others advocated constant dollar accounting under the names of "stabilized" or price-level accounting.[4] However, only in recent years has the inflation rate accelerated in the United States at a rate high enough to encourage official action by accounting standard-setting bodies.

In 1963, the AICPA published Accounting Research Study No. 6, "Reporting the Financial Effects of Price-Level Changes." This study recommended that supplementary data be presented showing comprehensive restatement of all elements of financial statements using a general price index.[5] Later, in 1969, the APB issued Statement No. 3, which again recognized the potential benefits of general price-level adjusted information and suggested supplemental disclosure of such data.[6]

At the end of 1974, the FASB issued an exposure draft entitled "Financial Reporting in Units of General Purchasing Power." This proposed statement would have required constant dollar accounting, although still as supplemental information.[7] However, before the FASB adopted a final statement, the SEC issued ASR No. 190, which required many companies to disclose current replacement costs of selected assets.[8] Because this conflicted with the FASB's constant dollar exposure draft, the Board withdrew its proposal.

In 1979, after careful evaluation, the FASB decided to experiment with alternative ways of reporting the impact of changing prices by issuing State-

---

[4]See, for example, Henry W. Sweeney, *Stabilized Accounting,* (New York: Harper & Brothers, 1936).

[5]*Accounting Research Study No. 6,* "Reporting the Financial Effects of Price-Level Changes" (New York: American Institute of Certified Public Accountants, 1963).

[6]*Statement of the Accounting Principles Board, No. 3,* "Financial Statements Restated for General Price-Level Change" (New York: American Institute of Certified Public Accountants, 1969).

[7]*FASB Exposure Draft,* "Financial Reporting in Units of General Purchasing Power" (Stamford: Financial Accounting Standards Board, 1974).

[8]Securities and Exchange Commission, *Accounting Series Release No. 190,* "Disclosure of Certain Replacement Cost Data" (Washington: U. S. Government Printing Office, 1976).

ment No. 33, "Financial Reporting and Changing Prices."[9] This statement requires certain companies to disclose supplemental information for selected items on *both* a constant dollar and a current cost basis but is flexible in the manner in which the requirements may be met. Subsequently, the SEC modified its requirements, as established in ASR No. 190, to comply with the more comprehensive FASB Statement No. 33. Thus, accounting practice for most large companies today requires elements of both constant dollar and current cost accounting.

The FASB is now beginning to evaluate the results of its experiment. Several research studies have been commissioned, and a major conference was held in January, 1983, to discuss various aspects of Statement No. 33. During the next few years, the FASB will consider all available evidence and will make a decision on which reporting alternative or combination of alternatives will be acceptable for reporting the impact of changing prices. Until that decision is made, accounting students need to be familiar with Statement No. 33, including the concepts of constant dollar accounting and current cost accounting.

CONSTANT DOLLAR ACCOUNTING

Recording transactions in terms of the number of nominal dollars exchanged ignores the fact that the dollar is *not* a stable monetary unit. As a unit of measurement, the dollar has significance only in reference to a particular price level. Thus, nominal dollar measurements represent diverse amounts of purchasing power. Unless statements are adjusted, readers are likely to regard dollars in terms of current general purchasing power rather than the general purchasing power at the time the dollars were exchanged. The objective of constant dollar accounting is to convert all dollar measurements into **equivalent purchasing power units** so that a company's position and progress may be viewed in proper perspective.

To illustrate, it would not seem proper to add 100 U. S. dollars to 100 British pounds. It would seem necessary to first convert one of the figures to its exchange equivalent before adding, subtracting, or comparing amounts. Similarly, the number of dollars spent years ago for land or buildings should be converted into current equivalent purchasing power units to arrive at meaningful asset totals. This conversion of nominal dollar amounts to equivalent purchasing power units is the essence of constant dollar accounting. Historical costs, the original exchange values, are maintained as the valuation basis, but are adjusted for changes in the general price level. The basis of measurement changes from nominal dollar amounts to constant dollar amounts or equivalent purchasing power units. The conversion is accomplished using a general price index.

---

[9]*Statement of Financial Accounting Standards No. 33, op. cit.* Also see, "FASB Statement No. 33 'The Great Experiment' " by Robert W. Berliner and Dale L. Gerboth, *Journal of Accountancy,* May 1980, pp. 48–54.

Price Indexes

The value or purchasing power of a monetary unit is inversely related to the price of goods or services for which it can be exchanged. Over a period of time, the prices of specific goods or services will move up or down depending on the relative scarcity and desirability of the goods or services. It would be possible to adjust for specific items, but those price changes may be different than changes in the general price level.

The general price level cannot be measured in absolute terms, but relative changes from period to period and the direction of change can be determined. To measure changes in the general price level, a sample of commodities and services is selected and the current prices of these items are compared with their prices during a base period. The prices during the base period are assigned a value of 100, and the prices of all other periods are expressed as percentages of this amount. The resulting series of numbers is called a **price index.**

Price indexes are valuable aids in measuring inflation or deflation. However, these measurements do have limitations. In the first place, all price indexes are based on samples. Since all prices do not fluctuate in the same degree or direction, the selection of commodities to be included in the sample affects the computed amounts. In addition, improvements in products affect the general level of prices, but such qualitative changes are difficult to measure.

Although there is no perfect way to measure the changing value of the dollar, indexes have been developed that provide reasonable estimates of changes in the dollar's general purchasing power. Among these are the Consumer Price Index and the Wholesale Price Index, both provided by the Bureau of Labor Statistics, and the GNP (Gross National Product) Implicit Price Deflator provided by the Department of Commerce.

Each of these indexes exhibits a similar pattern of price-level change, but reports different values. This is because each index is based on a different sample. The index required by FASB Statement No. 33 is the Consumer Price Index for all Urban Consumers (CPI-U), which is published monthly.

Mechanics of Constant Dollar Restatement

Constant dollar accounting requires that nominal dollar amounts be restated to equivalent purchasing power units, i.e., constant dollars, usually for the current period. The general formula for restatement is:

$$\text{Nominal dollar amount} \times \frac{\text{Price index converting } \textit{to}}{\text{Price index converting } \textit{from}} = \text{Constant dollar amount}$$

To illustrate the conversion process, assume that a company issued capital stock worth $50,000 in exchange for inventory valued at $50,000. Further assume that the current end-of-year price index is 105 and that the exchange took place when the general price index was 100. The company holds inventory during the year without engaging in any other activities. A conventional balance sheet prepared at the end of the year will show both inventory and invested capital at their nominal amounts, \$50,000. In preparing a constant-dollar balance sheet at the end of the year, however, inventory and capital stock will be reported as follows:

(1) Inventory needs to be restated for the change in the general price level since its acquisition. Inventory, with a nominal acquisition cost of \$50,000, is expressed in constant dollars as $\$50,000 \times \frac{\text{Index converting to (105)}}{\text{Index converting from (100)}}$, or \$52,500.

(2) Capital stock also requires restatement so that it expresses the stockholders' investment in terms of the current general price level. The capital stock balance is expressed in constant dollars at $\$50,000 \times \frac{\text{Index converting to (105)}}{\text{Index converting from (100)}}$, or \$52,500.

Conversion ratios may be used that express the relationship of one index to another. Thus, in the example cited, $\frac{105}{100}$ may be stated as a conversion ratio of 1.05.

In the example presented, the price index converted "to" was the end-of-year index. Alternatively, an average index for the current year could have been used. If such an approach were taken, the conversion factor would have been $\frac{102.5}{100}$ rather than $\frac{105}{100}$. Another approach would be to restate all amounts in terms of the price level of an earlier period, e.g., the year of purchase of an item or a base year. Then events occurring during the current year would be restated in terms of constant dollars of the earlier period selected. Nominal dollars can be restated to constant dollars of any period by modifying the indexes used for the conversion factor.

If current-year constant dollars are used to prepare comparative summaries, all past year data, including monetary assets and liabilities (defined in the next section), must be "rolled forward" to the current year. In this manner, data presented for several years will all be stated in terms of the same purchasing power units. To illustrate, assume that land was purchased in 1978 for \$100,000. Assume further that the general price level was 150 when the land was purchased, 200 at the end of 1983, and 215 at the end of 1984. In reporting the land on the balance sheet at the end of 1983, the land would be reported in current end-of-year constant dollars as follows:

$$\text{Land} \left(\$100{,}000 \times \frac{200}{150}\right) = \$133{,}333$$

However, in reporting comparative amounts at the end of 1984 in current end-of-year constant dollars, the 1983 amount would have to be rolled forward as follows:

$$\text{Land} \left(\$133{,}333 \times \frac{215}{200}\right) = \$143{,}333$$

Alternatively, the 1984 amount could be computed directly as follows:

$$\$100,000 \times \frac{215}{150} = \$143,333$$

Thus, the comparative balance sheet for December 31, 1984, would show the following:

	1983	1984
Land	$143,333	$143,333

This correctly shows no increase in the land account during 1983 and 1984 when amounts are all stated in terms of the same constant dollars. For comparative balance sheet purposes at the end of 1985, the $143,333 would again have to be rolled forward to reflect 1985 dollars.

As indicated earlier, all items may be reported in terms of constant dollars of an earlier base year. This would eliminate the need for a roll-forward adjustment because all items would be stated in terms of a base year's constant dollars. Even though restating amounts to current-year constant dollars requires a roll-forward procedure, it provides information that relates to the current general price level as opposed to some earlier price level. Current price levels are usually more understandable and relevant for decision-making purposes.

To illustrate the application of constant dollar accounting to the balance sheet, consider a simple example—Mecham Auto Supply. All amounts are restated to current end-of-year constant dollars. Assume that the beginning-of-year index was 220; the end-of-year index was 260. The ending inventory was all purchased when the index was 225; the land was bought when the index was 125; all capital stock was issued when the index was 110.

Mecham Auto Supply
Balance Sheet
December 31, 1984
(Constant Dollar Basis)

Assets	HC/ND Amounts	Conversion Factor	HC/CD Amounts
Cash	$22,000		$22,000
Accounts receivable	14,000		14,000
Inventory	9,000	260/225	10,400
Land	20,000	260/125	41,600
Total assets	$65,000		$88,000
Liabilities and Stockholders' Equity			
Accounts payable	$ 4,000		$ 4,000
Mortgage payable	15,000		15,000
Capital stock	22,000	260/110	52,000
Retained earnings	24,000		17,000*
Total liabilities and stockholders' equity	$65,000		$88,000

*$88,000 − ($4,000 + $15,000 + $52,000)

Note that conversion is not made for cash, receivables, and payables. As explained fully in the next section, these *monetary items* are fixed in amount regardless of changes in the price level, except when rolling forward past year data for comparative statements. It also should be observed that Retained Earnings cannot be converted directly, since it represents a composite of many different price levels.

An illustration of comprehensive restatement for this and other reporting alternatives is presented in Appendix 1 to this chapter. But even this simple example shows the possible significant impact of changing price levels on a balance sheet.

Effects of General Price-Level Changes on Monetary Items

In recognizing the effects of general price-level changes, it is necessary to distinguish between monetary items and nonmonetary items. **Monetary items** are assets, liabilities, and equities whose balances are fixed in terms of numbers of dollars regardless of changes in the general price level. All items not representing a right to receive or an obligation to pay a fixed sum are **nonmonetary items.**

Monetary assets include cash and items such as accounts and notes receivable, loans to employees, cash surrender value of life insurance, and certain marketable securities, such as bonds, that are expected to be held to maturity and redeemed at a fixed number of dollars. Regardless of changes in the general price level, these balances are fixed and provide for the recovery of neither more nor less than the stated amounts. Monetary liabilities include such items as accounts and notes payable, cash dividends payable, and fixed payments for accruals under pension plans. Regardless of changes in the price level, these balances are fixed and call for the payment of neither more nor less than the stated amounts. Nonconvertible preferred stock is a monetary equity item while common stock is a nonmonetary item. (For a more extensive classification of monetary and nonmonetary items, see Appendix D of FASB Statement No. 33.) In periods of changing prices, **purchasing power gains or losses** result from holding monetary items. These gains or losses are not disclosed in conventional reporting.

For example, assume that a person placed $1,000 cash under the mattress for "safekeeping" when the price index was 100. If the price index were to rise to 110 a year later, the individual would have suffered a purchasing-power loss because it would require $1,100 to purchase the same amount of goods that $1,000 would have bought a year ago. On the other hand, a debt of $1,000 payable a year later, again assuming an increase in the price index to 110 from 100, would result in a purchasing power gain. The equivalent purchasing power would be $1,100 yet the debt can be settled for the fixed amount of $1,000.

Nonmonetary assets include such items as inventories and supplies; land, buildings, and equipment; and intangible assets. These items are nonmonetary because with changes in the general price level, the nominal dollar amounts at which they are reported on the conventional financial statements will differ from the resources they actually represent. On the other hand, nonmonetary liabilities generally include such items as obligations to furnish goods or services, advances on sales contracts, and warranties on goods sold. These items are nonmonetary because with changes in the general price level, the dollar demands they actually make will differ from the dollar amounts reported on conventional financial statements.

The difference between a company's monetary assets and its monetary liabilities and equities is referred to as its **net monetary position.** With the number of dollars relating to monetary items remaining fixed, and reflecting current dollars regardless of the change in the price level, purchasing power gains and losses arise as prices change. In any given period, the gain or loss from holding monetary assets is offset by the loss or gain from maintaining monetary liabilities and equities. The net gain or loss for a period, then, depends on whether a company's position in net monetary items is positive—monetary assets exceeding monetary liabilities and equities—or negative—monetary liabilities and equities exceeding monetary assets. Gains and losses are associated with a company's net monetary position as follows:

	Rising Prices	Declining Prices
Positive Net Monetary Position	Loss	Gain
Negative Net Monetary Position	Gain	Loss

Constant dollar accounting requires that purchasing power gains and losses be determined. The steps to be followed in determining these gains and losses are explained and illustrated using the financial information for Mecham Auto Supply on page 913 and the following additional information.

Sales for the year were $90,000, purchases were $60,000, and other expenses were $24,000. These revenues and expenses were incurred evenly throughout the year.

The net monetary positions as of January 1, 1984, and December 31, 1984, are as follows:

	January 1, 1984	*December 31, 1984*
Cash	$19,000	$22,000
Accounts receivable	11,000	14,000
Accounts payable	(3,000)	(4,000)
Mortgage payable	(16,000)	(15,000)
Net monetary position	$11,000	$17,000

The purchasing power gain or loss is calculated as follows assuming conversion to end-of-year constant dollars:

(1) The company's net monetary position at the beginning of the period is restated to end-of-year constant dollars. Mecham Auto Supply's net monetary position as of January 1, 1984, is $11,000. This amount can be restated to

end-of-year dollars by multiplying it by the ratio of the year-end price index to the index at the beginning of the year: $\$11{,}000 \times \frac{260}{220} = \$13{,}000$.

(2) Transactions involving monetary items during the year are expressed in terms of year-end constant dollars and are added to or subtracted from the beginning net monetary position. For Mecham Auto Supply, monetary items were increased by sales and decreased by purchases and other expenses. Because these items were incurred evenly during the year, the ratio of the year-end price index to the average index for 1984 can be used to restate them to end-of-year dollars.

	HC/ND	*Conversion Factor*	*HC/CD*
Sales	$90,000	260/240	$97,500
Purchases	(60,000)	260/240	(65,000)
Other expenses	(24,000)	260/240	(26,000)
Increase in net monetary position	$ 6,000	260/240	$ 6,500

If no gain or loss in purchasing power had occurred during the year, the ending net monetary position would be $19,500 computed as follows:

	HC/CD
Net monetary position, January 1, 1984	$13,000
Increase in net monetary position	6,500
Net monetary position, December 31, 1984	$19,500

(3) The actual net monetary position at the end of the year is compared with the results from Step 2. If the actual net monetary position is less than the amount computed in Step 2, the company has sustained a loss in purchasing power. If it is greater, the company has experienced a gain. Mecham Auto Supply's actual net monetary position at the end of 1984 is $17,000. Since this amount is less than the $19,500 computed above, the company has sustained a $2,500 purchasing power loss. The foregoing calculations can be summarized in the following schedule:

Mecham Auto Supply
Schedule of Purchasing Power Loss
For the Year Ended December 31, 1984

	HC/ND	*Conversion Factor*	*HC/CD*
Net monetary position, January 1, 1984	$11,000	260/220	$13,000
Increase in net monetary position	6,000	260/240	6,500
			$19,500
Net monetary position, December 31, 1984	$17,000		17,000
Purchasing power loss			$ 2,500

This schedule shows several things. First, the beginning net monetary position plus the net increase (or less the net decrease) will always equal the ending net monetary position, all stated in nominal dollars. This amount can be computed directly from the balance sheet data. Second, the $19,500 represents the amount that the ending monetary position should be in terms of current end-of-year purchasing power units (constant dollars) if no gain or loss had occurred. However, the actual net monetary position is $17,000 because monetary items are fixed in amount. The result is a purchasing power loss of $2,500, the difference between what the monetary position would be if purchasing power had been maintained and the actual amount. On a constant dollar income statement, the purchasing power gain or loss is added to or subtracted from the constant dollar operating income and becomes a part of the ending retained earnings balance, as illustrated in Appendix 1.

As indicated earlier, the objective of constant dollar accounting is to convert all nominal dollar amounts to dollars of equivalent purchasing power. Thus, nominal dollars may be converted to constant dollars of a prior period or to average dollars for the current year. The latter approach is frequently encountered in practice and is illustrated in the following schedule for Mecham Auto Supply.

Mecham Auto Supply
Schedule of Purchasing Power Loss
For the Year Ended December 31, 1984

	HC/ND	*Conversion Factor*	*HC/CD*
Net monetary position, January 1, 1984..........	$11,000	240/220	$12,000
Increase in net monetary position................	6,000		6,000
			$18,000
Net monetary position, December 31, 1984	$17,000	240/260	15,692
Purchasing power loss			$ 2,308

When average-for-the-year constant dollars are used to determine purchasing power gain or loss, both beginning and ending amounts must be restated in terms of the average price index. No restatement was required for the ending balance in the previous example since this amount reflected end-of-year dollars. When using an average current-year index, the net increase or decrease in monetary position is not converted since revenues and expenses are assumed to occur evenly throughout the period; therefore, these amounts already reflect average price levels for the year. The purchasing power loss of $2,308 differs from the $2,500 loss in the previous example because it reflects a different price level. The $2,308 can be restated to end-of-year dollars as follows: $2,308 × 260/240 = $2,500.

Arguments For and Against Constant Dollar Accounting

Proponents of constant dollar accounting maintain that meaningful comparisons of accounting data are not possible unless the measuring units are comparable. They argue that the purchasing power of the dollar is not stable, fluctuating with changes in the general price level. Constant dollar accounting corrects this deficiency by measuring transactions in terms of equivalent purchasing power units, thus giving proper recognition to changes in the general price level. Those in favor of constant dollar accounting also point out that recognition of purchasing power gains and losses highlights the impact of inflation with respect to monetary assets, liabilities, and equities. They conclude that constant dollar information is relevant to decision makers and can be provided on a reliable basis without undue cost.

Those opposed to constant dollar accounting note that changes in specific prices of goods are not considered. Constant dollar accounting reflects only changes in the general price level. It ignores many underlying reasons for specific price changes—for example, those due to improvements in quality and specialized industry circumstances. In addition, the general price index used may not be relevant to particular industries. Constant dollar opponents also point out that price indexes are based on statistical averages and have many weaknesses. They question the reliability of the data, especially if used indiscriminately. Many accountants also question whether the benefits exceed the costs of providing constant dollar data. They fear companies will incur substantial costs, only to have users of the data be confused by or uninterested in the information.

CURRENT COST ACCOUNTING

The objective of **current cost accounting** is different from constant dollar accounting. Constant dollar accounting seeks to use comparable measuring units to reflect equivalent purchasing power for a specified general price level. Current cost accounting attempts to measure the current values of assets, liabilities, and equities. The current values may be measured in nominal dollars or in constant dollars, but they are intended to represent the current exchange prices of goods or services, not historical costs.

Current cost accounting measures changes in specific prices rather than changes in the general price level. While the general price level may have increased an average 12 percent during the past year, the current values of land may be up 22 percent, inventories may be up only 8 percent, and certain types of equipment, perhaps due to technological advancements, may have even decreased in value.

Concept of Well-Offness

From an income measurement perspective, current cost accounting is based on a concept of *well-offness*. This concept is attributed to an economist, J. R. Hicks, and maintains that operating gross profit, often called economic income, is the amount a firm can spend during a period and be as well-off at the end of the period as at the beginning. Operationalized, economic income (loss) is the difference between the sales price of an item and the cost to replace that item. Alternatively, it may be viewed as the change in net assets during a period measured on a current value basis. For example, if an entity's net assets, in terms of current costs, equaled $250,000 at the beginning of a period, and $300,000 at the end of the period, given no additional investments or withdrawals and holding the general price level constant, economic income would be $50,000.

Current costs may be defined in several ways. Among the most common are: (1) input prices, i.e., replacement costs; (2) exit prices, i.e., sales values; (3) net realizable values, i.e., expected sales prices less costs to complete and sell; and (4) economic values, i.e., present values of future cash flows. These distinctions are technical refinements in implementing the general approach of reflecting current values in financial statements.

Different circumstances may require different approaches to presenting current cost information. For example, the current cost of inventory or plant assets is generally thought of as the cost to replace or reproduce those assets at the balance sheet date. However, assets such as timber can be replaced only over a long period of time; minerals and oil and gas reserves may not be renewable at all. In these circumstances, economic values probably offer better representations of current costs than do replacement costs. This again points out the need for accountants to use judgment, within the guidelines established by the profession, in applying accounting principles.

Holding Gains or Losses

Current cost accounting not only emphasizes economic income but also makes it possible to isolate any gains or losses resulting from holding assets. Traditionally, accountants have recognized income at the point of sale, measuring the difference between the sales price and the historical cost of the item sold. Under current cost accounting, changes in asset values during a period would be recognized whether the assets were sold or not. The recognition of **holding gains or losses** is therefore an essential ingredient of current cost accounting.

Two types of gains and losses from holding assets need to be accounted for. **Realized holding gains and losses** indicate the differences between the current costs and the historical costs of assets sold or used during a period. **Unrealized holding gains and losses** are increases (or decreases) in the current values of assets held during a period but not sold or used. For example, in the earlier illustration assume that the land of Mecham Auto Supply had a current value of $60,000 at the end of 1984. On a December 31, 1984, current cost balance sheet, the land would be reported at its current value of $60,000 rather than its historical cost of $20,000 or its end-of-year constant dollar value of $41,600, thus disclosing a $40,000 unrealized holding gain.

To further illustrate the concept of holding gains or losses, assume that Current Cost Company made a sale of $100,000. The cost of goods sold was $65,000, and the cost to replace the inventory sold was $80,000. The total gross profit recognized under historical cost accounting is $35,000 (sales price minus historical cost of inventory sold). However, the $35,000 includes an operating gross profit of $20,000 (sales price minus current cost of inventory sold) and an inventory holding gain of $15,000. The realized holding gain of $15,000 represents the difference between the historical cost and the replacement cost of the inventory sold. This may be illustrated as follows:

Sales	$100,000	
		$20,000 Operating gross profit
Current cost of inventory	80,000	
		15,000 Realized holding gain
Cost of goods sold	65,000	
Total gross profit		$35,000

If, in the example, Current Cost Company had additional inventory that was not sold but that had a change in value, it would have an unrealized holding gain or loss. Assume inventory that was not sold cost $50,000 and had a replacement cost of $75,000. There would be a $25,000 unrealized holding gain on the inventory.

To show how these concepts would be applied over time, assume $10,000 of inventory was purchased by a company at the beginning of Year 1. At the end of Year 1 no inventory had been sold but its current cost was $12,000. At the end of Year 2, the inventory was sold for $18,000 and was replaced at a cost of $15,000. A comparison of the historical cost and current cost approaches over time is shown in the following illustration. For simplicity, assume that the only expense is cost of goods sold.

	Historical Cost			Current Cost		
	Year 1	*Year 2*	*Total*	*Year 1*	*Year 2*	*Total*
Sales revenue	–0–	$18,000	$18,000	–0–	$18,000	$18,000
Cost of goods sold	–0–	10,000	10,000	–0–	15,000	15,000
Operating income	–0–	$ 8,000	$ 8,000	–0–	$ 3,000	$ 3,000
Holding gain (loss)	–0–	–0–	–0–	$2,000	3,000	5,000
Net income	–0–	$ 8,000	$ 8,000	$2,000	$ 6,000	$ 8,000

Note that total income recognized is the same under either method. Under current cost accounting, however, changes in the prices of inventory are recognized as they occur. The $2,000 increase in the value of the inventory during Year 1 was an unrealized holding gain, since the inventory had not been sold.

In Year 2, the difference between the current cost of the inventory and its historical cost, $5,000, is a realized holding gain. Note that this realized holding gain includes the $2,000 unrealized holding gain recognized in Year 1 as well as $3,000 realized in Year 2. There is no unrealized holding gain on the inventory in Year 2, since the ending inventory was acquired at the end of Year 2.

Current cost net income in this example consists of operating income and holding gains, both realized and unrealized. The total net income would be reflected in retained earnings and would offset changes in net asset values shown on the balance sheet. Some accountants argue, however, that holding gains and losses should be reported as a special account in the owners' equity section of the balance sheet and should not be included in the determination of net income. Another position is that only realized holding gains and losses should be reported as income, and unrealized gains or losses should be reported in an owners' equity account.

Mechanics of Current Cost Accounting

The major problem in current cost accounting is determining appropriate current values. There are two recommended approaches: (1) **Indexing** through internally or externally developed specific price indexes for the class of goods or services being measured, and (2) **direct pricing** from current invoice prices, vendors' price lists, or standard manufacturing costs that reflect current costs. If indexing is used, restatement is mechanically the same as for constant dollar accounting. The difference is that specific price indexes are used rather than a general price index. The direct pricing approach assigns current values, determined by analysis and estimate, to particular assets.

Arguments for and Against Current Cost Accounting

Many accountants were not in favor of the replacement cost reporting requirements of ASR 190. Some are opposed to FASB Statement No. 33, being especially critical of its complexity and the confusion it might cause. However, proponents of current cost accounting argue that historical cost financial statements, even if adjusted for general price-level changes, do not adequately reflect the economic circumstances of a business. The balance sheet is deficient because only historical costs are presented, and these measurements do not reflect the current financial picture of an enterprise. The income statement is deficient because charges against revenues are based on historical costs that may differ from current costs. Also, increases in net asset values are not recognized at the time of a change in asset value but must await realization at time of sale. Under current cost accounting, assets are reported at their current values, thus more closely reflecting the actual financial position of a business. Expenses are based on the expiration of current costs of assets utilized, thus providing a more meaningful income measure, and changes in values of assets held are recognized as they occur.

Opponents of current cost accounting argue that determining current values is too subjective. For example, the current cost of a particular item may not be readily available and may have to be determined by appraisal or estimation. It may be difficult or impossible to even find an identical replacement item to consider its replacement cost. If an identical asset is not used, a subjective adjustment for differences in the quality of a similar but not identical item would have to be made.

Another disadvantage is the increased subjectivity of the income measurement if changes in current values are recognized as income prior to transactions that confirm arm's-length exchange values.

Additional arguments against current cost accounting include the lack of understanding of current cost financial statements; the question of whether the benefits are worth the extra costs involved; and the uncertainty of whether financial statement users will be better served by current cost accounting.

CURRENT COST/CONSTANT DOLLAR ACCOUNTING

A number of accountants argue against both constant dollar and current cost accounting, pointing out that each approach solves only one of the problems of accounting for changing prices. Constant dollar accounting adjusts for general price changes; current cost accounting recognizes the impact of specific price changes. Current cost/constant dollar accounting combines both approaches and reflects current cost valuation on a constant dollar basis. Such an approach recognizes that adjustments for specific and general price changes are neither mutually exclusive nor competing alternatives. Conceptually, this is the best reporting alternative if the objective is to give full effect to the impact of changing prices on business enterprises. Its primary disadvantage, in addition to the shortcomings ascribed to the other approaches considered separately, is its complexity.

To a limited degree, accountants are beginning to experiment with the current cost/constant dollar approach by disclosing changes in the specific prices (current costs) of selected items, net of the impact of inflation (the change in general price level). Again referring to the Mecham Auto Supply example, on a December 31, 1984, current cost/constant dollar balance sheet, the land would be reported at its current cost stated in end-of-year constant dollars of $60,000. Note that this is the same amount as reported under the current cost/nominal dollar approach. For the $60,000 to be a current cost it would have to be a year-end amount. Conversion would be required, however, if average-year or base-year dollars were used.

In the example, the $60,000 current cost/constant dollar land amount is $40,000 higher than the $20,000 reported under the historical cost/nominal dollar approach. As explained earlier, this is an unrealized holding gain. However, only part of the $40,000 total unrealized holding gain is real; a portion of it is an inflationary component or fictitious holding gain due to changes in the general purchasing power of the dollar. This concept can be illustrated by the following diagram.

Replacement cost (current cost)	$60,000		
		$18,400	Real component of unrealized holding gain
Historical cost/constant dollars	41,600		
		21,600	Inflation component of unrealized holding gain
Historical cost/nominal dollars	20,000		
		$40,000	Total unrealized holding gain

However, it should be noted that in presenting comprehensive financial statements on a current cost/constant dollar basis, the inflationary component is not reported separately. The constant dollar adjustment is made for all nonmonetary items, and only the real component of unrealized holding gains is shown as a separate item. In the Mecham Auto Supply example, only the $18,400 holding gain on the land would be disclosed.

This example shows the impact of both general and specific price changes on only one item. It is indeed a complex problem to determine and report such information for all items on a balance sheet as well as to trace the impact of real and inflationary and realized and unrealized holding gains and losses through the income and retained earnings statements. Because of these complexities, the FASB does not require comprehensive restatement. The next sections summarize the current FASB requirements and illustrate the required disclosures.

FASB STATEMENT NO. 33 REPORTING REQUIREMENTS

FASB Statement No. 33 was published in September 1979. The statement is a part of the measurement phase of the Board's Conceptual Framework and has been called the most significant FASB statement issued to date. The statement requires large public companies to disclose supplemental accounting data in annual reports to shareholders showing the effects of price changes on enterprise activity. The main points of Statement No. 33 are summarized in the following pages. It should be noted that the FASB has tried to simplify its requirements by allowing various short cuts and a variety of disclosure alternatives, all designed to help provide experience and lead to a common solution to this important reporting issue.

Statement No. 33 applies to public companies that, at the beginning of the year, have *either* total assets of more than $1 billion (net of accumulated depreciation) *or* inventories and gross properties totaling more than $125 million (before accumulated depreciation). Properties include land, buildings, equipment, capitalized leasehold interests, and natural resources, but exclude goodwill and other intangible assets. Nonpublic companies and public enterprises not meeting the size tests are encouraged, but not required, to present the information called for by Statement No. 33.

FASB Statement No. 33 does not change the standards of financial accounting and reporting with respect to the primary financial statements. It requires three types of supplemental disclosures: (1) information relating to the latest fiscal year, (2) information for the most recent five years, and (3) narrative information. The information must be included in any published annual report that contains the primary financial statements but is not required to be included with interim financial reports. The information may be presented in statement format, schedules, or as supplementary notes to the financial statements. The minimum disclosure requirements are as follows:

(1) For the **current year**, the supplemental information presented must disclose income from continuing operations on both a constant dollar basis *and* a current cost basis. The purchasing power gain or loss on net monetary items also must be disclosed in a supplemental schedule or note. The purchasing power gain or loss is *not* to be included in income from continuing

operations but is to be shown as a separate item. In addition to the above disclosures, companies also must report the current costs of inventory and property, plant, and equipment at the end of the year. Any increases or decreases in the current costs of these items, net of inflation, must be shown. These holding gains or losses, are *not* to be included in income from continuing operations.

(2) For its **five most recent fiscal years,** a company must report:[10]
   (a) Net sales and other operating revenues, stated in constant dollars.
   (b) Income from continuing operations on both a constant dollar basis *and* current cost basis.
   (c) Income per common share from continuing operations on both a constant dollar basis *and* current cost basis.
   (d) Net assets at fiscal year-end on both a constant dollar basis *and* current cost basis. (Net assets are defined as inventory and property, plant, and equipment unless comprehensive restatement is made.)
   (e) Net increases or decreases in the current cost amounts of inventory and property, plant, and equipment, net of inflation.
   (f) Purchasing power gain or loss on net monetary items.
   (g) Cash dividends per common share.
   (h) Market price per common share at fiscal year-end.

   In disclosing the five-year comparative data, companies may use the average CPI-U for the current year or the base-year index (1967 = 100). If the current-year average is used, the prior year amounts will have to be "rolled forward" each year to present comparable amounts in units of equivalent purchasing power. Also, the average level of the CPI-U must be disclosed for each of the five years. However, if the base-year index is used for the five-year summary, the current year data, being stated in terms of average current-year dollars, will have to be "rolled back" to the base year to be comparable with the other data in the summary.

(3) In addition to these data, management is required to provide notes to the statements and narrative information explaining the bases of computations, the accounting principles employed, and the significance of the supplementary information with respect to the specific circumstances of the company.

As an illustration of how one company meets the disclosure requirements of FASB Statement No. 33, see Note Eighteen of the financial statements in Appendix B. In the note, General Mills explains the purpose of presenting inflation-adjusted data; provides supplementary income statement and balance sheet data on both a constant dollar and current cost basis; discloses selected information as required by FASB No. 33 for its five most recent fiscal years; and explains briefly the significance and limitations of the information presented. As a matter of interest, for the period ending May 30, 1982, General Mills' net earnings were $226 million as reported using unadjusted historical costs, $151 million using the constant dollar method, and $149 million using current costs. The effective tax rate changed from 44.6 percent based on income as reported on the traditional income statement to approximately 55 percent using either the constant dollar or the current cost method.

---

[10] *Ibid.*, par. 35.

Applying FASB Statement No. 33 Constant Dollar Requirements

Statement No. 33 does not require comprehensive constant dollar restatement of all nonmonetary items. It allows such restatement, but only requires constant dollar disclosures for inventory and property, plant, and equipment items and also for cost of goods sold and depreciation in reporting income from continuing operations. In addition, Statement No. 33 requires disclosures of the gain or loss on net monetary items due to general price-level changes.

Income from Continuing Operations. Statement No. 33 requires that only cost of goods sold and depreciation expense be adjusted to constant dollars in reporting income from continuing operations. The most difficult part in computing cost of goods sold and depreciation expense on a constant dollar basis is in determining when inventory and depreciable assets were acquired. This is referred to as "aging." Once the assets are aged, the process becomes mechanical, following the formula described earlier.

Conceptually, each item of inventory or depreciable asset should be adjusted for the impact of inflation since its acquisition. It is not difficult to age a single asset, but the problem becomes quite complex when many assets, which often are quite dissimilar, must be aged. Because of the magnitude of the problem, Statement No. 33 allows reasonable approximations and grouping of assets. For example, in aging inventory a turnover rate may be computed and an assumption made that the ending inventory was purchased or manufactured during the month (or quarter) indicated by that turnover rate. If the turnover rate is six times a year, it can be assumed that the ending inventory was purchased during the last two months of the year if the company values its inventory at fifo. Of course, major purchases of inventories or assets should be handled separately. An example follows, using arbitrary numbers and assumptions. The symbol C$ stands for constant dollars. In the example, the amounts are adjusted to the *average* current year index. The FASB requires the use of an average current year index unless a company elects to make comprehensive restatement; then either the average current year index or the end-of-year index may be used. Use of an average index simplifies restating certain items, which is presumably why the FASB selected that approach for noncomprehensive restatement.

Cost of goods sold		$450,000
Ending inventory, December 31, 1984	$52,000	
Major item purchased on September 1, 1984	14,500	$ 37,500
Turnover rate ($450,000 ÷ $37,500)		12 times
Constant dollar inventory, December 31, 1984:		
$\$37{,}500 \times \dfrac{258 \text{ (Average 1984)}}{265 \text{ (December 1984)*}}$		C$36,509
$\$14{,}500 \times \dfrac{258 \text{ (Average 1984)}}{260 \text{ (September 1984)}}$		14,388
		C$50,897

*Conversion factor for last month based on assumption that ending inventory purchased during last month due to inventory turnover rate.

To adjust lifo inventories, it is necessary to age and convert each lifo layer. An example is illustrated below:

	HC/ND Amounts	*Conversion Factor*	*HC/CD Amounts*
Inventory, January 1, 1984:			
1975	$30,000	258 (Average 1984) / 125 (Average 1975)	C$ 61,920
1979	15,000	258 (Average 1984) / 170 (Average 1979)	22,765
1983	10,000	258 (Average 1984) / 240 (Average 1983)	10,750
	$55,000		C$ 95,435
1984 addition	5,000	258 (Average 1984)* / 258 (Average 1984)	5,000
Inventory, December 31, 1984. . .	$60,000		C$100,435

*Assumed purchased when index at average for the year.

A similar process is required to restate property, plant, and equipment items. Again reasonable assumptions and groupings of assets may be used. The restatement of these items is necessary to report net assets on a constant dollar basis in the five year supplementary summary and the impact of depreciation, depletion, and amortization on income from continuing operations. Once the age of the assets to be adjusted is determined, the conversion process is identical to that illustrated for inventory. The following schedule is reproduced from Appendix E of FASB Statement No. 33 to illustrate the conversion process.

Historical Cost of Property, Plant, and Equipment in Average 1980 Dollars

Date of Acquisition	(1) Historical Cost/ Nominal Dollars (000s)	(2) Conversion Factor	(3) (1) × (2) Historical Cost/ Constant Dollars (000s)	(4) Percent Depreciated	(5) (3) × (4) Accumulated Depreciation (000s)	(6) (3) − (5) Net
1973	$ 50,000	× 220.9 (Avg. 1980) / 133.1 (Avg. 1973) =	C$ 82,983	80	C$66,386	
1974	5,000	× 220.9 (Avg. 1980) / 147.7 (Avg. 1974) =	7,478	70	5,235	
1975	5,000	× 220.9 (Avg. 1980) / 161.2 (Avg. 1975) =	6,852	60	4,111	
1976	5,000	× 220.9 (Avg. 1980) / 170.5 (Avg. 1976) =	6,478	50	3,239	
1977	5,000	× 220.9 (Avg. 1980) / 181.5 (Avg. 1977) =	6,085	40	2,434	
1978	5,000	× 220.9 (Avg. 1980) / 195.4 (Avg. 1978) =	5,652	30	1,696	
1979	10,000	× 220.9 (Avg. 1980) / 205.0 (Avg. 1979) =	10,776	20	2,155	
1980	15,000	× 220.9 (Avg. 1980) / 220.9 (Avg. 1980) =	15,000	10	1,500	
	$100,000		C$141,304		C$86,756	C$54,548

Purchasing Power Gains and Losses. The second item required by Statement No. 33 with respect to constant dollar accounting is disclosure of the purchasing power gain or loss during the period. As explained earlier, this gain or loss results from holding monetary items in periods of changing prices. The steps to be followed in computing the purchasing power gain or loss were illustrated earlier in this chapter. As noted previously, the gain or loss is computed in terms of the average-for-the-year index unless comprehensive restatement is elected.

Recoverable Amounts. It should be noted that Statement No. 33 requires that both constant dollar and current cost measures be reported at the **net recoverable amount** when that amount is less than the constant dollar or current cost amounts. However, this adjustment is not required unless the net recoverable amount is materially and permanently less than the other measures. For inventories, the recoverable amount is the net realizable value defined as... "the amount of cash, or its equivalent, expected to be derived from sale of an asset net of costs required to be incurred as a result of the sale."[11] For property, plant and equipment, the recoverable amount is net realizable value if the asset is about to be sold. If the asset will not be sold, the recoverable amount is the net present value of future cash flows expected to be derived from future use and disposition of the asset discounted at a reasonable rate given the attendant risks.[12] Recoverable amounts, if used, replace the historical cost/constant dollar amounts and/or current costs in the calculations and supplemental disclosures.

Applying FASB No. 33 Current Cost Requirements

FASB No. 33 requires affected companies to disclose income from continuing operations after adjusting cost of goods sold and depreciation, depletion, and amortization for current costs. In addition, the net change in the current costs of inventories and property, plant, and equipment must be disclosed both before and after the impact of general price-level changes. This, in effect, discloses the holding gains or losses due to specific changes in prices and the impact of general price-level changes. In meeting these requirements, the major difficulty is determining the appropriate current costs of affected assets. No single source for current cost information is prescribed. Instead, experimentation is encouraged, but the bases of current costs must be reasonable and well-documented.

The steps necessary to meet the required current cost disclosures of FASB No. 33 are:

(1) Determine the current cost amounts of inventory and property, plant, and equipment items.
(2) Apply the "recoverable amount test" to the current cost amounts and select the lower amount.

---

[11]*Ibid.*, p. 63
[12]*Ibid.*

(3) Calculate cost of goods sold, depreciation, depletion, and amortization based on the results of Step 2.
(4) Determine the change in current costs of inventory and property, plant, and equipment in terms of nominal amounts as well as constant dollars.

If an indexing method is used for Step 1, the process will be the same as illustrated earlier for constant dollar accounting. It is important to select an index that correlates closely with the price changes of the items included in the index and the items being adjusted. If an indexing method is not used, the amounts in Step 1 will have to be determined by direct pricing, appraisal, or estimation.

If a company determines that there is no significant difference between income from continuing operations on a constant dollar basis and on a current cost basis, the supplemental current cost information is not required. If omitted, however, the reasons for omission must be explained in a note to the supplementary disclosures.

FASB STATEMENT NO. 33 DISCLOSURES ILLUSTRATED

The supplemental disclosures required by Statement No. 33 may be shown in "reconciliation format" or in "statement format." Examples of these formats are presented as follows. The statement format, which ties to the figures reported in the primary financial statements, might be less confusing to readers.

Statement of Income from Continuing Operations Adjusted for Changing Prices
For the Year Ended December 31, 1980
(In thousands of average 1980 dollars)

Income from continuing operations, as reported in the income statement		$ 9,000
Adjustments to restate costs for the effect of general inflation:		
Cost of goods sold	$(7,384)	
Depreciation and amortization expense	(4,130)	(11,514)
Loss from continuing operations adjusted for general inflation		$ (2,514)
Adjustments to reflect the difference between general inflation and changes in specific prices (current costs):		
Cost of goods sold	$(1,024)	
Depreciation and amortization expense	(5,370)	(6,394)
Loss from continuing operations adjusted for changes in specific prices		$ (8,908)
Gain from decline in purchasing power of net amounts owed		$ 7,729
Increase in specific prices (current cost) of inventories and property, plant, and equipment held during the year*		$ 24,608
Effect of increase in general price level		18,959
Excess of increase in specific prices over increase in the general price level		$ 5,649

Reconciliation Format

Statement of Income from Continuing Operations Adjusted for Changing Prices
For the Year Ended December 31, 1980
(In thousands of dollars)

	As Reported in the Primary Statements	Adjusted for General Inflation	Adjusted for Changes in Specific Prices (Current Costs)
Net sales and other operating revenues	$253,000	$253,000	$253,000
Cost of goods sold	$197,000	$204,384	$205,408
Depreciation and amortization expense	10,000	14,130	19,500
Other operating expense	20,835	20,835	20,835
Interest expense	7,165	7,165	7,165
Provision for income tax	9,000	9,000	9,000
	$244,000	$255,514	$261,908
Income (loss) from continuing operations	$ 9,000	$ (2,514)	$ (8,908)
Gain from decline in purchasing power of net amounts owed		$ 7,729	$ 7,729
Increase in specific prices (current cost) of inventories and property, plant, and equipment held during the year*			$ 24,608
Effect of increase in general price level			18,959
Excess of increase in specific prices over increase in the general price level			$ 5,649

Statement Format

*At December 31, 1980, current cost of inventory was $65,700 and current cost of property, plant, and equipment, net of accumulated depreciation was $85,100.

Source: FASB Statement No. 33, pp. 32–33.

Five-year comparative data might be presented as shown in the example at the top of page 930. These examples are only illustrations, as the FASB has not specified an exact format to be used.

PROSPECTS FOR THE FUTURE

In some respects the FASB has taken a middle-of-the-road approach in dealing with changing prices. They have not yet determined which approach is better—constant dollar or current cost accounting—and therefore are experimenting with both. They require disclosure of only selected items—essentially inventories and depreciable assets—instead of comprehensive restatement. The required disclosures will reflect much of the impact of general and specific price changes but will not show the total impact as comprehensive restatement would (see Appendix 1 to this chapter). On the other hand, there are significant problems with total restatement, and such an approach might be even more confusing to statement users.

Inflation and other economic environmental factors have already caused several countries to adopt accounting practices that reflect price changes. The Financial Accounting Standards Board has now taken a first step to make financial reporting in the United States more useful to statement users by

Five-Year Comparison of Selected
Supplementary Financial Data Adjusted for Effects of Changing Prices
(In thousands of average 1980 dollars)

	Years Ended December 31,				
	1976	1977	1978	1979	1980
Net sales and other operating revenues	$265,000	$235,000	$240,000	$237,063	$253,000
Historical cost information adjusted for general inflation:					
Income (loss) from continuing operations				(2,761)	(2,514)
Income (loss) from continuing operations per common share				$ (1.91)	$ (1.68)
Net assets at year-end				55,518	57,733
Current cost information:					
Income (loss) from continuing operations				(4,125)	(8,908)
Income (loss) from continuing operations per common share				$ (2.75)	$ (5.94)
Excess of increase in specific prices over increase in the general price level				2,292	5,649
Net assets at year-end				79,996	81,466
Gain from decline in purchasing power of net amounts owed				7,027	7,729
Cash dividends declared per common share	$ 2.59	$ 2.43	$ 2.26	$ 2.16	$ 2.00
Market price per common share at year-end	$ 32	$ 31	$ 43	$ 39	$ 35
Average consumer price index	170.5	181.5	195.4	205.0	220.9

Source: FASB Statement No. 33, p. 34.

reflecting the impact of changing prices. Continued developments in this area of financial reporting are expected over the next several years.

APPENDIX 1

COMPREHENSIVE RESTATEMENT: REPORTING ALTERNATIVES ILLUSTRATED AND CONTRASTED

The purpose of this appendix is to illustrate comprehensive restatement of financial statements on the historical cost/constant dollar, current cost/nominal dollar, and current cost/constant dollar bases. As mentioned in the chapter, FASB Statement No. 33 does not require comprehensive restatement, but companies may use such restatement to satisfy the requirements of Statement No. 33. Throughout this appendix, the financial data for Lindsay Corporation will be used. This company began operations on January 1, 1984. The following results of operations and year-end financial position for 1984 for Lindsay Corporation are shown using five reporting alternatives. An explanation of how the numbers were derived is provided in the sections that follow.

Lindsay Corporation
Statement of Income and Retained Earnings
For Year Ended December 31, 1984

	Historical Cost (HC/ND)	Historical Cost/Constant Dollar (HC/CD) (End-of-Year)	Current Cost/ Nominal Dollar (CC/ND)	Current Cost/Constant Dollar (CC/CD) (End-of-Year)	FASB 33 Requirements: Constant Dollar (Average-Year)	FASB 33 Requirements: Current Cost
Sales	$300,000	$305,882	$300,000	$305,882	$300,000	$300,000
Cost of goods sold	190,000	194,847	230,000	234,510	191,100	230,000
Gross profit on sales	$110,000	$111,035	$ 70,000	$ 71,372	$108,900	$ 70,000
Expenses:						
Depreciation	$ 5,000	$ 5,200	$ 6,750	$ 6,882	$ 5,100	$ 6,750
Other expenses	90,000	91,765	90,000	91,765	90,000	90,000
Total expenses	$ 95,000	$ 96,965	$ 96,750	$ 98,647	$ 95,100	$ 96,750
Income (loss) from continuing operations	$ 15,000	$ 14,070	$ (26,750)	$ (27,275)	$ 13,800	$ (26,750)
Holding gains			163,250	158,370		
Purchasing power gain (loss) on net monetary items		(595)		(595)	(584)	
Net income	$ 15,000	$ 13,475	$136,500	$130,500		
Retained earnings, 1/1/84	–0–	–0–	–0–	–0–		
	$ 15,000	$ 13,475	$136,500	$130,500		
Dividends	5,000	5,000	5,000	5,000		
Retained earnings, 12/31/84	$ 10,000	$ 8,475	$131,500	$125,500		
Specific increase (decrease) in inventories and land, buildings, and equipment (net of inflation based on average-year constant dollars)						$155,325

Lindsay Corporation
Balance Sheet
December 31, 1984

	Historical Cost (HC/ND)	Historical Cost/Constant Dollar (HC/CD)	Current Cost/Nominal Dollar (CC/ND)	Current Cost/Constant Dollar (CC/CD)	FASB 33 Requirements
Assets					
Cash	$ 30,000	$ 30,000	$ 30,000	$ 30,000	
Accounts receivable	40,000	40,000	40,000	40,000	
Inventory	65,000	66,275	90,000	90,000	$ 90,000
Land	35,000	36,400	100,000	100,000	100,000
Buildings (net)	45,000	46,800	76,500	76,500	76,500
Total assets	$215,000	$219,475	$336,500	$336,500	
Liabilities and Stockholders' Equity					
Accounts payable	$ 25,000	$ 25,000	$ 25,000	$ 25,000	
Mortgage payable	30,000	30,000	30,000	30,000	
Total liabilities	$ 55,000	$ 55,000	$ 55,000	$ 55,000	
Capital stock	$150,000	$156,000	$150,000	$156,000	
Retained earnings	10,000	8,475	131,500	125,500	
Total stockholders' equity	$160,000	$164,475	$281,500	$281,500	
Total liabilities and stockholders' equity	$215,000	$219,475	$336,500	$336,500	

HISTORICAL COST/CONSTANT DOLLAR COMPREHENSIVE RESTATEMENT

The following assumptions are made in restating Lindsay Corporation's financial statements on a comprehensive basis to reflect general price-level changes.

(1) Price indexes were:

January 1, 1984	200
December 31, 1984	208

The price level rose evenly throughout the year. The average index for 1984 was 204.

(2) Sales and purchases were made evenly and expenses were incurred evenly throughout the year.

(3) Inventories are valued at cost using the first-in, first-out method. The beginning inventory was acquired at the beginning of 1984. For simplicity, it is assumed that the entire ending inventory was acquired when the price index was 204.

(4) Dividends were declared and paid at the end of the year.

(5) Land and buildings were acquired on January 1, 1984. The buildings have a 10-year useful life and are depreciated at $5,000 per year.

A historical cost/nominal dollar statement of income and retained earnings and a balance sheet for Lindsay Corporation are presented below and on the following page (income taxes are ignored).

Lindsay Corporation
Statement of Income and Retained Earnings
For the Year Ended December 31, 1984
(Historical Cost/Nominal Dollar Basis)

Sales		$300,000
Cost of goods sold:		
Beginning inventory	$ 55,000	
Purchases	200,000	
Goods available for sale	$255,000	
Ending inventory	65,000	
Cost of goods sold		190,000
Gross profit on sales		$110,000
Expenses:		
Depreciation	$ 5,000	
Other expenses	90,000	95,000
Net income		$ 15,000
Retained earnings, January 1, 1984		—
		$ 15,000
Dividends		5,000
Retained earnings, December 31, 1984		$ 10,000

Lindsay Corporation
Comparative Balance Sheet
As of January 1, 1984 and December 31, 1984
(Historical Cost/Nominal Dollar Basis)

Assets	January 1, 1984	December 31, 1984
Cash	$ 60,000	$ 30,000
Accounts receivable	—	40,000
Inventory	55,000	65,000
Land	35,000	35,000
Buildings (net)	50,000	45,000
Total assets	$200,000	$215,000
Liabilities and stockholders' equity		
Accounts payable	$ 20,000	$ 25,000
Mortgage payable	30,000	30,000
Total liabilities	$ 50,000	$ 55,000
Capital stock	$150,000	$150,000
Retained earnings	—	10,000
Total stockholders' equity	$150,000	$160,000
Total liabilities and stockholders' equity	$200,000	$215,000

Historical Cost/Constant Dollar Statement of Income and Retained Earnings

A statement of income and retained earnings for 1984, restated to end-of-year constant dollars, and a schedule reporting the purchasing power loss are presented below and on the following page.

Lindsay Corporation
Statement of Income and Retained Earnings
For the Year Ended December 31, 1984
(Historical Cost/Constant Dollar Basis)

	HC/ND	Conversion Factor	HC/CD
Sales	$300,000	208/204	$305,882
Cost of goods sold:			
Beginning inventory	$ 55,000	208/200	$ 57,200
Purchases	200,000	208/204	203,922
Goods available for sale	$255,000		$261,122
Ending inventory	65,000	208/204	66,275
Cost of goods sold	$190,000		$194,847
Gross profit on sales	$110,000		$111,035
Expenses:			
Depreciation	$ 5,000	208/200	$ 5,200
Other expenses	90,000	208/204	91,765
Total expenses	$ 95,000		$ 96,965
Income from continuing operations	$ 15,000		$ 14,070
Purchasing power loss (see schedule)	—		595
Net income	$ 15,000		$ 13,475
Retained earnings, January 1, 1984	–0–		–0–
	$ 15,000		$ 13,475
Dividends	5,000		5,000
Retained earnings, December 31, 1984	$ 10,000		$ 8,475

Lindsay Corporation
Schedule of Purchasing Power Loss
For the Year Ended December 31, 1984

		HC/ND	Conversion Factor	HC/CD
Net monetary position, January 1, 1984:				
Monetary assets (cash)	$60,000			
Monetary liabilities (accounts payable and mortgage payable)	50,000	$ 10,000	208/200	$ 10,400
Increase in net monetary position:				
Sales		300,000	208/204	305,882
		$310,000		$316,282
Decrease in net monetary position:				
Purchases		$200,000	208/204	$203,922
Other expenses		90,000	208/204	91,765
Dividends		5,000		5,000
		$295,000		$300,687
				$ 15,595
Net monetary position, December 31, 1984:				
Monetary assets (cash and accounts receivable)	$70,000			
Monetary liabilities (accounts payable and mortgage payable)	55,000	$ 15,000		15,000
Purchasing power loss				$ 595

In preparing a historical cost/constant dollar income statement, the following items should be noted.

Sales. Since sales were made evenly throughout the year, the sales balance reflects the average price index for the year. To restate the sales balance to end-of-year dollars, it is multiplied by the ratio of the year-end price index to the average index.

$$\text{Sales: } \$300{,}000 \times \frac{208}{204} = \$305{,}882$$

Cost of Goods Sold. Lindsay Corporation reports its inventory on the first-in, first-out basis. To restate cost of goods sold to end-of-year dollars, the following adjustments must be made:

(1) The beginning inventory balance reports purchases made when the business was organized, and reflects the price level at the beginning of the year. To restate the beginning inventory to end-of-year dollars, it is multiplied by the ratio of the year-end index to the index at the beginning of the year.

$$\text{Beginning inventory: } \$55{,}000 \times \frac{208}{200} = \$57{,}200$$

(2) Purchases were made evenly throughout the year. To restate the purchases balance to end-of-the-year dollars, it is multiplied by the ratio of the year-end price index to the average index.

$$\text{Purchases: } \$200{,}000 \times \frac{208}{204} = \$203{,}922$$

(3) The ending inventory was acquired when the price index was 204, the average index for the year. To restate the ending inventory balance to year-end dollars, it is multiplied by the ratio of the year-end index to the average index.

$$\text{Ending inventory: } \$65{,}000 \times \frac{208}{204} = \$66{,}275$$

Depreciation. Since depreciation expense represents the allocation of the cost of depreciable assets to operations, the adjustment for depreciation expense must be consistent with the adjustment applicable to the related assets. To restate buildings to year-end dollars, the balance in the buildings account is multiplied by the ratio of the year-end price index to the price index at the time the assets were acquired. Thus, depreciation expense for buildings is multiplied by the same ratio to be restated to year-end dollars. In the case of Lindsay Corporation, the buildings were acquired when the price index was 200. The depreciation expense is restated to year-end constant dollars as follows:

$$\text{Depreciation: } \$5{,}000 \times \frac{208}{200} = \$5{,}200$$

Other Expenses. The other expenses were incurred evenly throughout the year. To restate the total of other expenses to year-end dollars, it is multiplied by the ratio of the year-end price index to the average index for the year.

$$\text{Other expenses: } \$90{,}000 \times \frac{208}{204} = \$91{,}765$$

Purchasing Power Gain or Loss. The statement of income and retained earnings is supported by a schedule reporting the gain or loss from holding monetary items in a period of changing prices. As shown in the schedule, the net monetary position for Lindsay Corporation at the end of the year would have been $15,595 if the company had not experienced a gain or loss in purchasing power. Since the net monetary position is actually only $15,000, a loss in purchasing power of $595 was sustained by the company.

Dividends. Since dividends were declared and paid at the end of the year, the dividends balance reflects end-of-year dollars and does not have to be converted.

Historical Cost/Constant Dollar Balance Sheet

A balance sheet for Lindsay Corporation as of December 31, 1984, restated to end-of-year constant dollars, appears below.

Lindsay Corporation
Balance Sheet
December 31, 1984
(Historical Cost/Constant Dollar Basis)

Assets	HC/ND	Conversion Factor	HC/CD
Cash	$ 30,000		$ 30,000
Accounts receivable	40,000		40,000
Inventory	65,000	208/204	66,275
Land	35,000	208/200	36,400
Buildings (net)	45,000	208/200	46,800
Total assets	$215,000		$219,475
Liabilities and stockholders' equity			
Accounts payable	$ 25,000		$ 25,000
Mortgage payable	30,000		30,000
Total liabilities	$ 55,000		$ 55,000
Capital stock	$150,000	208/200	$156,000
Retained Earnings	10,000		8,475*
Total stockholders' equity	$160,000		$164,475
Total liabilities and stockholders' equity	$215,000		$219,475

*See the Statement of Income and Retained Earnings on page 933.

In preparing a historical cost/constant dollar balance sheet, monetary assets and liabilities do not require restatement and are reported without change.[13] The restatement of ending inventory was explained and illustrated on page 935 in conjunction with cost of goods sold. The following additional items should be noted.

Land and Buildings. The land and buildings accounts reflect the price level at the time the assets were acquired. To restate land and buildings to end-of-year dollars, they are multiplied by the ratio of the year-end price index to the price index at the time of acquisition.

$$\text{Land:} \quad \$35{,}000 \times \frac{208}{200} = \$36{,}400$$

$$\text{Buildings (net):} \quad \$45{,}000 \times \frac{208}{200} = \$46{,}800$$

[13] If comparative statements were being prepared at the end of 1985, the 1984 monetary items would be adjusted (rolled forward) to reflect 1985 purchasing power units.

Capital Stock. The capital stock account reports the dollars received by the firm when it issued its stock. To restate the capital stock balance to year-end dollars, it is multiplied by the ratio of the year-end price index to the price index at the time the stock was issued.

$$\text{Capital stock: } \$150{,}000 \times \frac{208}{200} = \$156{,}000$$

Retained Earnings. No single conversion factor is appropriate for retained earnings. The year-end retained earnings on the balance sheet is the same amount that appears as the ending retained earnings balance on the statement of income and retained earnings. If the procedures and assumptions used to develop the historical cost/constant dollar balance sheet and statement of income and retained earnings are consistent, the retained earnings amount computed on the statement of income and retained earnings should bring the balance sheet into balance. If the balance sheet does not balance, the errors or inconsistencies must be found and corrected.

CURRENT COST/NOMINAL DOLLAR COMPREHENSIVE RESTATEMENT

To illustrate comprehensive restatement on a current cost/nominal dollar basis, consider again the historical cost/nominal dollar financial statements of Lindsay Corporation presented on page 932 and 933 and the following additional information.

(1) The cost of goods sold, based on the average current costs of units sold during the year, is $230,000.
(2) Current costs at the end of 1984 are:

Inventory	$ 90,000
Land	100,000
Buildings (before depreciation)	85,000

Current Cost/Nominal Dollar Statement of Income and Retained Earnings

A current cost/nominal dollar income statement generally reports two major sources of income:

(1) Current cost income (loss) from operations
(2) Holding gains (losses)

Current cost operating income is the difference between revenues and the current costs of expenses. Holding gains (losses) result from increases (decreases) in current costs of inventory and property, plant, and equipment. Total holding gains include both realized and unrealized holding gains.

The following illustration is a current cost/nominal dollar statement of income and retained earnings for Lindsay Corporation for the year ended December 31, 1984.

Lindsay Corporation Statement of Income and Retained Earnings For the Year Ended December 31, 1984 (Current Cost/Nominal Dollar Basis)		
Sales		$300,000
Cost of goods sold		230,000
Gross profit on sales		$ 70,000
Less expenses:		
Depreciation	$ 6,750	
Other expenses	90,000	96,750
Loss from operations		$(26,750)
Holding gains:		
Increase in current cost of inventories	$65,000	
Increase in current cost of land and buildings	98,250	163,250
Current cost net income		$136,500
Retained earnings, January 1, 1984		–0–
		$136,500
Dividends		5,000
Retained earnings, December 31, 1984		$131,500

In preparing a current cost/nominal dollar income statement, the following items should be noted.

Sales. Since sales revenue is stated at current sales prices during the period, it reflects current values and is not restated.

Sales	$300,000

Cost of Goods Sold. The current cost of goods sold given on page 937 is the result of adjusting the historical cost of the goods sold to their current costs as of the dates they were sold.

Cost of goods sold (current cost)	$230,000

Depreciation Expense. Current costs of depreciable assets must be used to compute depreciation expense. If depreciation is incurred evenly throughout the year, the depreciation expense can be calculated from the average current costs of the depreciable assets.

Lindsay Corporation's buildings had current values before depreciation of $50,000 and $85,000 at the beginning and the end of 1984, respectively. The 1984 current cost/nominal dollar depreciation expense can be calculated as follows:

$$\text{Average current cost of buildings: } \frac{\$50{,}000 + \$85{,}000}{2} = \$67{,}500$$

$$\text{Depreciation expense: } \frac{\$67{,}500}{\text{10-year useful life}} = \$6{,}750$$

Other Expenses. Other expenses are usually reported at their current costs when paid, and do not need to be restated on a current cost/nominal dollar income statement. Thus, the other expenses on the current cost/nominal dollar income statement are the same as on the historical cost/nominal dollar income statement.

Other expenses	$90,000

Holding Gains and Losses. The holding gain on inventory is made up of two parts: the realized holding gain on the difference between historical cost of goods sold and current cost of goods sold, and the unrealized holding gain on the difference between the historical cost of the ending inventory and the current cost of the ending inventory. For the Lindsay Corporation, the holding gains would be computed as follows:

	HC/ND	CC/ND	Holding Gain	
Cost of goods sold	$190,000	$230,000	$40,000	(Realized)
Inventory, December 31, 1984	65,000	90,000	25,000	(Unrealized)
Total holding gain			$65,000	

The holding gain on land is an unrealized gain, while the holding gain on buildings is composed of a realized component and an unrealized component. The realized holding gain on buildings is the difference between historical cost depreciation and current cost depreciation. This difference is a realized holding gain, because a portion of the increase in value has been charged against revenue on the current cost income statement. The unrealized holding gain on buildings is the difference between historical cost net book value and current cost net book value. For the Lindsay Corporation, the holding gains on land and buildings would be computed as follows:

	HC/ND	CC/ND	Holding Gain	
Land, December 31, 1984	$35,000	$100,000	$65,000	(Unrealized)
Buildings (net) December 31, 1984	45,000	76,500	31,500	(Unrealized)
Depreciation expense, 1984	5,000	6,750	1,750	(Realized)
Total holding gain			$98,250	

Alternatively, the unrealized portion of the holding gain on the buildings could be computed as follows:

	December 31, 1984		
	HC/ND	*CC/ND*	*Increase (Decrease)*
Buildings (gross)	$50,000	$85,000	$35,000
Accumulated depreciation	(5,000)	(8,500)	(3,500)
Buildings (net)	$45,000	$76,500	$31,500

The difference between the current cost depreciation expense of $6,750 and the accumulated depreciation of $8,500 used to compute the current cost net book value is a **depreciation catch-up adjustment** that is reflected in a reduced unrealized holding gain for the year. If the current cost net book value had been computed using the $6,750 depreciation expense as the amount of accumulated depreciation for the first year, the holding gain would have been increased by $1,750, or to a total of $33,250. The catch-up adjustment is caused by using the current value of the building at year-end to compute accumulated depreciation but the average current value of the building for the year to compute depreciation expense. In subsequent years, a further difference between the changing current value of the building and the depreciation expense computed in earlier years would add to this catch-up adjustment.

Dividends. Since the dividends were declared and paid at the end of the year, the $5,000 dividends balance is stated at current cost and does not need to be restated.

Current Cost/Nominal Dollar Balance Sheet

A current cost/nominal dollar balance sheet for Lindsay Corporation as of December 31, 1984, is presented as follows.

Lindsay Corporation
Balance Sheet
December 31, 1984
(Current Cost/Nominal Dollar Basis)

Assets	HC/ND	CC/ND
Cash	$ 30,000	$ 30,000
Accounts receivable	40,000	40,000
Inventory	65,000	90,000
Land	35,000	100,000
Buildings (net)	45,000	76,500
Total assets	$215,000	$336,500
Liabilities and stockholders' equity		
Accounts payable	$ 25,000	$ 25,000
Mortgage payable	30,000	30,000
Total liabilities	$ 55,000	$ 55,000
Capital stock	$150,000	$150,000
Retained earnings	10,000	131,500*
Total stockholders' equity	$160,000	$281,500
Total liabilities and stockholders' equity	$215,000	$336,500

*See Statement of Income and Retained Earnings on page 938.

Since monetary assets and liabilities are reported at their face values, which are the same as their current values, they do not require restatement on a current cost/nominal dollar balance sheet. Inventory on hand at the end of the year is reported on the current cost/nominal dollar balance sheet at its year-end value of $90,000. Land and buildings are also reported at their respective year-end values: land, $100,000 and buildings (net), $76,500. Capital stock is not adjusted on a current cost/nominal dollar balance sheet since the purchasing power of the dollar is assumed constant.

Retained Earnings

The ending retained earnings balance is derived from the statement of income and retained earnings on page 938. The beginning retained earnings ($0) plus current cost net income ($136,500) minus dividends ($5,000) equals the ending balance ($131,500). The $121,500 difference between the $131,500 current cost amount and the $10,000 historical cost amount is the unrealized portion of the total holding gain (inventory $25,000 + land $65,000 + buildings $31,500 = $121,500), which is recognized prior to realization on a current cost basis but usually not until the point of sale on a historical cost basis. Obviously, the ending retained earnings balance may be computed as the difference between total assets and total liabilities less capital stock [$336,500 − ($55,000 + $150,000) = $131,500].

CURRENT COST/CONSTANT DOLLAR COMPREHENSIVE RESTATEMENT

To illustrate comprehensive restatement on a current cost/constant dollar basis, consider again the financial statements of the Lindsay Corporation.

Historical cost/constant dollar financial statements account for purchasing power gains and losses on net monetary items but do not take into account holding gains and losses. Current cost/nominal dollar financial statements account for holding gains and losses but do not account for purchasing power gains and losses. Current cost/constant dollar financial statements take into account both types of gains and losses. All amounts are stated on current cost/constant dollar statements at their current costs in end-of-year constant dollars.

Current Cost/Constant Dollar Statement of Income and Retained Earnings

A current cost/constant dollar (end-of-year dollars) statement of income and retained earnings for Lindsay Corporation for the year ended December 31, 1984, is presented at the top of the next page.

In preparing a current cost/constant dollar statement of income and retained earnings, the following items should be noted.

Operating Revenues and Expenses. On the current cost/nominal dollar income statement, sales revenue, cost of goods sold, depreciation expense, and other expenses reflect average current values for the year assuming an

Lindsay Corporation
Statement of Income and Retained Earnings
For Year Ended December 31, 1984
(Current Cost/Constant Dollar Basis)

Sales		$305,882
Cost of goods sold		234,510
Gross profit on sales		$ 71,372
Less expenses:		
Depreciation	$ 6,882	
Other expenses	91,765	98,647
Loss from operations		$(27,275)
Holding gains:		
Increase in current cost of inventories	$63,388	
Increase in current cost of land and buildings	94,982	158,370
		$131,095
Purchasing power loss on net monetary items		(595)
Current cost/constant dollar net income		$130,500
Retained earnings, January 1, 1984		-0-
		$130,500
Dividends		5,000
Retained earnings, December 31, 1984		$125,500

even flow of activities during the year. Each of these amounts can be restated to end-of-year constant dollars by multiplying the current cost/nominal dollar amount by the ratio of the year-end price index to the average price index.

Sales: $\$300,000 \times \frac{208}{204} = \$305,882$

Cost of goods sold: $\$230,000 \times \frac{208}{204} = \$234,510$

Depreciation expense: $\$\ 6,750^{*} \times \frac{208}{204} = \$\ 6,882$

Other expenses: $\$\ 90,000 \times \frac{208}{204} = \$\ 91,765$

*Assumed to be in average 1984 dollars

Holding Gains (Losses). On a current cost/constant dollar income statement, holding gains (losses) are reported net of the impact of general price-level changes. The increase in current values of inventories for Lindsay Corporation, adjusted to eliminate the inflation component can be computed as follows:

	HC/CD	CC/CD	Holding Gain	
Cost of goods sold	$194,847	$234,510	$39,663	(Realized)
Inventory, December 31, 1984	66,275	90,000	23,725	(Unrealized)
Total holding gain			$63,388	

The increase in the value of the ending inventory, $23,725, is an unrealized holding gain. The $39,663 increase in the value of the cost of goods sold is a realized holding gain.

The holding gain on land and buildings, net of the effect of changes in the general price level, can be computed as follows:

	HC/CD	CC/CD	Holding Gain	
Land, December 31, 1984	$36,400	$100,000	$63,600	(Unrealized)
Buildings (net), December 31, 1984	46,800	76,500	29,700	(Unrealized)
Depreciation expense	5,200	6,882	1,682	(Realized)
Total holding gain			$94,982	

The appreciation in the value of the land, $63,600, is an unrealized holding gain. The increase in the value of the buildings, $29,700, is also an unrealized holding gain. The difference between the current cost/constant dollar and historical cost/constant dollar depreciation expenses, $1,682, is a realized holding gain.

Purchasing Power Gain or Loss. The purchasing power gain or loss on net monetary items computed on a current cost/constant dollar basis is the same as the purchasing power gain or loss computed on a historical cost/constant dollar basis, since net monetary items are always stated at their current values.

Dividends. Since dividends are already stated at their year-end current value of $5,000, they do not require restatement on the current cost/constant dollar financial statements.

Current Cost/Constant Dollar Balance Sheet

A current cost/constant dollar balance sheet for the Lindsay Corporation as of December 31, 1984, is presented at the top of the next page.

All amounts on the current cost/constant dollar balance sheet are the same as those on the current cost/nominal dollar balance sheet except capital stock and retained earnings.

Capital Stock. Since capital stock account balance represents the dollars received by the firm when the stock was first issued, the capital stock balance must be restated to year-end dollars. This is done by multiplying the balance by the ratio of the year-end price index to the price index at the time the stock was issued.

$$\text{Capital stock: } \$150{,}000 \times \frac{208}{200} = \$156{,}000$$

Retained Earnings. The ending retained earnings balance is explained by the statement of income and retained earnings on page 942. The beginning balance plus net income on a current cost/constant dollar basis less divi-

Lindsay Corporation
Balance Sheet
December 31, 1984
(Current Cost/Constant Dollar Basis)

Assets	HC/ND	CC/CD
Cash	$ 30,000	$ 30,000
Accounts receivable	40,000	40,000
Inventory	65,000	90,000
Land	35,000	100,000
Buildings (net)	45,000	76,500
Total assets	$215,000	$336,500
Liabilities and stockholders' equity		
Accounts payable	$ 25,000	$ 25,000
Mortgage payable	30,000	30,000
Total liabilities	$ 55,000	$ 55,000
Capital stock	$150,000	$156,000
Retained earnings	10,000	125,000*
Total stockholders' equity	$160,000	$281,500
Total liabilities and stockholders' equity	$215,000	$336,500

*See Statement of Income and Retained Earnings on page 942.

dends equals the ending balance of $125,500. Since both a different valuation basis (current costs) and measuring unit (constant dollars) are used under this approach, the ending retained earnings balance is affected by the purchasing power gain or loss for monetary items and by the adjustments to operating income (loss) and to realized and unrealized holding gains (losses).

FASB STATEMENT NO. 33 REPORTING REQUIREMENTS

As mentioned in the chapter, FASB Statement No. 33 requires that the primary financial statements be reported on a historical cost/nominal dollar basis. However, certain large companies are required to present the supplemental information with respect to the effects of price changes. Comprehensive restatement as illustrated in this appendix is permitted, but not required. The minimum disclosure requirements for the current year are listed below. These will be illustrated for Lindsay Corporation and compared with the results of comprehensive restatement. As discussed in the chapter, additional disclosures are required by Statement No. 33 for the five most recent years.

(1) Income from continuing operations on a constant dollar basis (using the average price index for the year).
(2) Income from continuing operations on a current cost basis.
(3) The purchasing power gain or loss on net monetary items.
(4) Current costs of inventory and property, plant, and equipment at the end of the year.

(5) Increases or decreases in current costs of inventory and property, plant, and equipment, net of inflation.

Income from Continuing Operations—Constant Dollar Basis

The restatement of historical cost/nominal dollar operating income to average year constant dollars, as required by FASB Statement No. 33 for partial restatement, is illustrated below.

Sales. Since sales were made evenly throughout the year, the sales revenue of $300,000 is already stated in terms of the average price index and requires no restatement.

Cost of Goods Sold. The beginning inventory is restated to the average price index for the year by multiplying it by the ratio of the average price index for the year to the price index at the beginning of the year.

$$\text{Beginning inventory: } \$55{,}000 \times \frac{204}{200} = \$56{,}100$$

Since purchases were made evenly throughout the year, the $200,000 balance in the purchases account reflects the average price index for the year and does not require restatement.

The ending inventory was acquired when the price index was 204, the average for the year. Thus, the $65,000 ending inventory balance does not require restatement.

With the beginning inventory restated to reflect the average price index, cost of goods sold may be computed as follows:

	HC/CD (Average-Year Dollars)
Beginning inventory	$ 56,100
Purchases	200,000
Goods available for sale	$256,100
Ending inventory	65,000
Cost of goods sold	$191,100

Depreciation Expense. The buildings were purchased when the price index was 200. The depreciation expense is restated to average-year dollars by multiplying it by the ratio of the average price index to the index at the time the buildings were acquired.

$$\text{Depreciation expense: } \$5{,}000 \times \frac{204}{200} = \$5{,}100$$

Other Expenses. Since the other expenses of $90,000 were incurred evenly throughout the year the account balance reflects the average price index and does not require restatement.

Income from continuing operations on a historical cost/constant dollar basis using average-year constant dollars, as required by FASB Statement No. 33, is shown below. Note that the FASB approach simplifies partial restatement by using the average-year constant dollars so that many items do not require adjustment.

		HC/CD (Average-Year Dollars)
Sales		$300,000
Cost of goods sold		191,100
Gross profit on sales		$108,900
Less expenses:		
Depreciation	$ 5,100	
Other expenses	90,000	95,100
Income from continuing operations		$ 13,800

Income from Continuing Operations—Current Cost Basis

The income from continuing operations on a current cost basis as required by FASB Statement No. 33 is the same information that was previously computed in the discussion of the current cost/nominal dollar income statement in this appendix. This information for Lindsay Corporation is as follows:

		CC/ND
Sales		$ 300,000
Cost of goods sold		230,000
Gross profit on sales		$ 70,000
Less expenses:		
Depreciation	$ 6,750	
Other expenses	90,000	96,750
Loss from continuing operations		$ (26,750)

Purchasing Power Gain or Loss on Net Monetary Items

A computation of the purchasing power loss on net monetary items for Lindsay Corporation for the year ended December 31, 1984, is presented at the top of page 947.

In the computation, the net monetary position as of the beginning of the year was restated to average-year dollars by multiplying it by the ratio of the 1984 average price index to the index at the beginning of the year. This amount was increased by the sales for the year and was decreased by the purchases, other expenses, and dividends (restated to reflect the average price index for the year). This resulted in $15,296, the net monetary position at the end of the year if Lindsay Corporation had maintained its purchasing power. Since the actual net monetary position at the end of the year was $14,712 (restated to average-year dollars), the company has sustained a $584 ($15,296 − $14,712) purchasing power loss during the year.

Lindsay Corporation
Schedule of Purchasing Power Loss
For the Year Ended December 31, 1984
(Average-Year Dollars)

		HC/ND	Conversion Factor	HC/CD
Net monetary position January 1, 1984:				
Monetary assets (cash)	$60,000			
Monetary liabilities (accounts payable and mortgage payable)	50,000	$ 10,000	204/200	$ 10,200
Increase in net monetary position:				
Sales		300,000		300,000
		$310,000		$310,200
Decreases in net monetary position:				
Purchases		$200,000		$200,000
Other expenses		90,000		90,000
Dividends		5,000	204/208	4,904
		$295,000		$294,904
Net monetary position, December 31, 1984:				$ 15,296
Monetary assets (cash and accounts receivable)	$70,000			
Monetary liabilities (accounts payable and mortgage payable)	55,000	$ 15,000	204/208	14,712
Purchasing power loss				$ 584

The purchasing power loss on net monetary items, in accordance with FASB Statement No. 33 would not be added to operating income but reported as a separate disclosure.

Current Costs of Inventory and Property, Plant, and Equipment at Year-End

The current costs of inventory and property, plant, and equipment required to be disclosed by FASB Statement No. 33 are the same amounts as reported on the current cost/nominal dollar balance sheet. These current costs for Lindsay Corporation as of December 31, 1984, are as follows:

Inventory	$ 90,000
Land	100,000
Buildings (net)	76,500

Increases or Decreases in Current Costs of Inventory and Property, Plant, and Equipment, Net of Inflation

The increases or decreases in the current costs of inventory and property, plant, and equipment that are required to be disclosed by FASB Statement No. 33 are the same as the holding gains computed on a current cost/constant dollar income statement, except that the amounts are computed using average-year price indexes rather than year-end price indexes.

To make these computations for the Lindsay Corporation, historical cost/nominal dollar values for inventory, buildings, and land must be restated to reflect the 1984 average price index.

	HC/ND	*Conversion Factor*	*HC/CD (Average-Year Dollars)*
Inventory, December 31, 1984	$65,000		$65,000
Buildings, December 31, 1984	45,000	204/200	45,900
Land, December 31, 1984	35,000	204/200	35,700

In the above calculations, each asset balance was multiplied by the ratio of the average-year price index to the price index at the time the asset was acquired. The next step is to restate the current cost/nominal dollar asset value to the average price index.

	CC/ND	*Conversion Factor*	*CC/CD (Average-Year Dollars)*
Inventory, December 31, 1984	$ 90,000	204/208	$88,269
Buildings, December 31, 1984	76,500	204/208	75,029
Land, December 31, 1984	100,000	204/208	98,077

In the above calculations, each asset value was multiplied by the ratio of the average-year price index to the price index at the time the current asset value was determined. These calculations may be used together with other calculations made in this section of the appendix, to compute the total holding gain, net of inflation.

	HC/CD (Average-Year Dollars)	*CC/CD (Average-Year Dollars)*	*Difference*
Inventory, December 31, 1984	$ 65,000	$ 88,269	$ 23,269
Cost of goods sold	191,100	230,000	38,900
Buildings (net, December 31, 1984	45,900	75,029	29,129
Depreciation expense	5,100	6,750	1,650
Land, December 31, 1984	35,700	98,077	62,377
Holding gain, net of inflation			$155,325

The disclosure of the increases in the current costs of inventory, property, plant, and equipment required by FASB Statement No. 33 is as follows.

Increase in current costs of inventory, buildings, and land, net of inflation	$155,325

Note that in this example the relative impact of inflation is small when compared to changes in the specific prices.

Increase in specific prices (total current cost holding gains, page 938)	$163,250
Less increase in specific prices, net of inflation (FASB approach—average-year dollars)	155,325
Effect of increase in general price level (inflation component)	$ 7,925

The reader may again wish to refer back to page 931 where tables summarize the information presented in this appendix and contrast the amounts that would be reported under the alternatives discussed and according to the assumptions made, e.g., end-of-year dollars versus average-year dollars.

APPENDIX 2

CURRENT VALUES IN PERSONAL FINANCIAL STATEMENTS

Effective June 30, 1983, the accounting measurement basis for personal financial statements was changed from historical costs to current values. Unlike the supplementary status of current values in corporate statements as prescribed by FASB Statement No. 33, the AICPA prescribed that current values should replace historical costs in the basic financial statements of individuals. Because the Financial Accounting Standards Board did not choose to extend its jurisdiction to personal financial reporting, the Accounting Standards Division of the AICPA carefully studied the issues surrounding this area, and on October 1, 1982 issued Statement of Position 82-1 that contained their conclusions.[14]

The following reasons were given for the adoption of current values as a substitute for historical costs:

> The primary focus of personal financial statements is a person's assets and liabilities, and the primary users of personal financial statements normally consider estimated current value information to be more relevant for their decisions than historical cost information. Lenders require estimated current value information to assess collateral, and most personal loan applications require estimated current value information. Estimated current values are required for estate, gift, and income tax planning, and estimated current value information about assets is often required in federal and state filings of candidates for public office.
>
> The Accounting Standards Division therefore believes personal financial statements should present assets at their estimated current values and liabilities at their estimated current amounts at the date of the financial statements.[15]

Because this is the first authoritative source that has required the use of current values in the basic financial statements, it is useful for accountants to review the methods recommended for establishing current values and current amounts for specific assets and liabilities. Such a review may provide insight into the type of valuation that might be required if current values ever replace historical costs on corporate financial statements.

---

[14]Accounting Standards Division, AICPA, *Statement of Position 82-1,* "Accounting and Financial Reporting for Personal Financial Statements" (New York: American Institute of Certified Public Accountants, October 1, 1982).

[15]*Ibid.*, par. 3, 4.

General Guidelines

Both assets and liabilities are to be based on estimated current amounts. The estimated current value of an asset in personal financial statements "is the amount at which the item could be exchanged between a buyer and seller, each of whom is well informed and willing, and neither of whom is compelled to buy or sell."[16] Recent transactions involving similar assets and liabilities in similar circumstances ordinarily provide good bases for establishing these values. Other methods provided for in the SOP include capitalization of past or prospective earnings, the use of liquidation values, adjustment of historical cost based on changes in specific price indexes, use of appraisals, or the use of discounted amounts of projected cash receipts and payments. Whichever method is used for arriving at current values, it should be used consistently from year to year.

Guidelines for Specific Assets

(1) Receivables. Generally, receivables should be presented at the discounted amounts of cash expected to be collected. The discount rate should be determined from interest rates at the financial statement date.

(2) Marketable securities. Securities should be valued at closing prices on securities exchanges if stock is traded on the exchange. If over the counter, the mean of bid and ask prices should be used. If there are large block holdings, adjustment to market may be necessary.

(3) Options. Options should be valued at published prices if available. If such prices are unavailable, current values should be determined based on the value of assets subject to option.

(4) Life insurance. Investment in insurance policies should be valued at policy cash surrender value less any outstanding loans.

(5) Investment in closely held businesses. There is no one method of valuing these assets. Examples of methods that could be used include using a multiple of earnings, liquidation values, reproduction values, appraisals, present value of projected cash receipts and payments, buy-sell agreements, and specific adjustments to book values.

(6) Real estate and leaseholds. These long-term assets may be valued at sale price of similar property under similar circumstances. If no sales have recently occurred, discounted cash receipts and payments, appraisals, or assessed valuations may be helpful.

(7) Intangible assets. These assets should be valued at the present value of projected cash receipts and payments. In some cases, the cost of a purchased intangible may be the best indicator of market.

(8) Nonforteitable future rights. If the amounts are fixed or determinable, are not contingent on a particular event, and do not require future performance of services, these rights should be valued at discounted present value. Examples of these rights include guaranteed minimum portion of

[16] *Ibid.*, par. 12.

pensions, deferred compensation contracts, beneficial interest in trusts, and fixed amount of alimony.

(9) Payables and other liabilities. Liabilities should be discounted at the rate implicit in the contract or rate at which the debt could currently be discharged if lower.

Income Tax Deferral

The use of current values results in timing differences between income as reported on the financial statements and income being taxed. This difference will occur unless the income tax laws are altered to permit use of current values for income tax reporting. The final document of the AICPA did not label this credit as a liability but suggested it be reported between the liabilities and net worth. The tax difference is computed as if current value is recognized on the tax return and includes consideration of such tax provisions as recapture and carryover.

Financial Statement Disclosures

The Accounting Standards Division recognized that personal financial statements will be considerably different from those issued previously. Therefore, SOP 82-1 recommends that a clear explanation of how current values were determined be included. There is no mandatory list; however, disclosure should probably include:

(1) A clear indication of the individuals covered by the statement.
(2) The methods used to evaluate current amounts.
(3) Information about closely held businesses.
(4) Estimated lives for intangibles.
(5) Nonforfeitable rights that do not meet criteria for inclusion as assets.
(6) Method of computing estimated tax and unused operating and capital loss carryforwards.[17]

Auditor's Responsibility for Personal Financial Statements

It is intended that personal financial statements be subject to either compilation, review, or audit, and that eventually auditors will give some measure of credibility to the current values. This is a new area of responsibility, and the profession is exercising caution in adopting a standard of audit guidelines. An exposure draft of a proposed guide was issued in late 1982.

Summary

It is interesting that the first significant movement toward current values is occurring in the area of personal financial statements rather than in statements of business enterprises. Further research and experimentation are

[17] *Ibid.*, par. 31-34.

needed; however, the standard is clear that current values must be used wherever possible if personal financial statements are to be in accordance with GAAP. An illustrative set of personal financial statements is contained in Appendix A of SOP 82-1.

QUESTIONS

1. What has caused the increased interest in reporting financial statements adjusted for price changes?

2. Why have accountants traditionally preferred to report historical costs rather than current costs in conventional statements?

3. (1) Identify three alternatives to historical cost/nominal dollar financial statements. (2) Compare the concept of reporting current costs in financial statements with the concept of restating original dollar costs for general price-level changes.

4. How are general price indexes computed?

5. (1) Distinguish between monetary assets and nonmonetary assets. (2) Which of the following are monetary assets?

(a) Cash
(b) Investment in common stock
(c) Investment in bonds
(d) Merchandise on hand
(e) Prepaid expenses
(f) Buildings
(g) Patents
(h) Sinking fund—uninvested cash
(i) Sinking fund—investments in real estate
(j) Deferred developmental costs

6. Assume a company holds property or maintains the obligations listed below during a year in which there is an increase in the general price level. State in each case whether the real position of the company at the end of the year is better, worse, or unchanged.

(a) Cash
(b) Cash surrender value of life insurance
(c) Land
(d) Unearned subscription revenue
(e) Accounts receivable
(f) Notes payable
(g) Merchandise on hand
(h) Long-term warranties on sales

7. Indicate whether a company sustains a gain or loss in purchasing power under each condition described below.

(a) A company maintains an excess of monetary assets over monetary liabilities during a period of general price-level increase.
(b) A company maintains an excess of monetary liabilities over monetary assets during a period of general price-level increase.
(c) A company maintains an excess of monetary assets over monetary liabilities during a period of general price-level decrease.
(d) A company maintains an excess of monetary liabilities over monetary assets during a period of general price-level decrease.

8. The FASB defines current cost as current replacement cost adjusted for the value of any operating advantages or disadvantages of a specific asset. Identify several alternative ways in which current costs may be defined.

9. Distinguish between realized and unrealized holding gains and losses and between the real and inflationary components of total holding gains and losses.
10. Some have suggested that accounting for the impact of changing prices should be limited to restatement of land, buildings, equipment, and related depreciation charges in terms of current purchasing power. Would you defend or reject such a proposal? Give your reasons.
11. Describe the restatement of inventories for general price-level changes when inventories are reported (a) on a first-in, first-out basis; (b) on a last-in, first-out basis.
12. The most time-consuming step in the restatement of accounts to report general price-level changes is the aging of the depreciable property and the corresponding restatement of the periodic depreciation. What is meant by aging as used here? Do you agree with this statement?
13. Of what signficance is the "net recoverable amount" in complying with FASB Statement No. 33 disclosure requirements?
14. What are the advantages of current cost financial statements as compared to historical cost financial statements?
15. Distinguish between the current cost/constant dollar approach and the current cost/nominal dollar approach to financial reporting.
16. Presto Company purchased land for $150,000 in 1983 when the price index was 150. At the end of 1984 when the price index was 175, the land had a fair market value of $180,000. How would the land be reported on the balance sheet under each of the following approaches?
(a) Historical cost/nominal dollar
(b) Historical cost/constant dollar
(c) Current cost/nominal dollar
(d) Current cost/constant dollar
***17.** In analyzing sales as reported under the various alternatives for Lindsay Corporation (page 931), what assumption would produce the same number ($300,000) for all columns?
***18.** Why is a "catch-up adjustment" often needed in computing the unrealized holding gain or loss on depreciable assets in conjunction with the accumulated depreciation on those assets?

*Questions to Appendix 1 material.

DISCUSSION CASES

case 24-1 (What is the effective tax rate?) As the financial vice-president of Carter Corporation, you have recently read the following statement in a financial journal— "Corporations are being taxed in excess of the maximum tax rate provided by the Internal Revenue Code." You decide to examine your own company's situation with respect to this statement. The following data are obtained.

Carter Corporation
Income Statement
For the Year Ended December 31, 1984

Sales	$1,000,000
Cost of goods sold	500,000
Gross profit	$ 500,000
Operating expenses	200,000
Income from operations before income taxes	$ 300,000

The cost of goods sold on a current cost basis is $650,000.

Assume the Internal Revenue code imposes a tax on corporate income at the following rates:

Taxable Income	Tax Rate
First $25,000	15%
Second $25,000	18
Third $25,000..............................	30
Fourth $25,000	40
In excess of $100,000	46

Assuming there are no permanent or timing differences between pretax and taxable income, what is Carter's effective tax rate (income tax expense divided by pretax income)? Does the statement referred to earlier seem accurate with respect to Carter Corporation? Explain.

case 24-2 (Which reporting alternative is best?) At a recent executive committee meeting, the officers of Tenox Corporation entered into a lively discussion concerning changing prices in the economy and financial reporting. Carl Smith, the controller, argued that the FASB is smart to experiment with reporting alternatives in Statement No. 33 since something must be done to reflect price changes. The economic analyst, Stephanie Davis, argued strongly for a current cost approach. Davis had little good to say about "irrelevant" historical costs, even if adjusted to constant dollars. Howard Jones, the marketing V. P., on the other hand, felt comfortable with historical cost data. Jones understands that approach and has confidence in the objectivity of the numbers reported. As president of the company, what position do you take?

case 24-3 (What does the inflation footnote really say?) (FASB Statement No. 33 requires certain companies to include supplementary information using current costs and constant dollars. General Mills, Inc., whose financial statements are reproduced in Appendix B of the text, is one of the companies required to include this information. This case deals with the supplementary information included in Note Eighteen: Accounting for Inflation.)

Lisa Oveson and Tom Jensen, accounting students, were assigned to analyze the financial statements for General Mills, Inc. They had studied the issues of accounting for inflation and the recommendations of the FASB. However, they were having difficulty understanding the relationship between some of the numbers in the footnote and the material presented in their text book. They have come to you as their accounting instructor with the following questions. Prepare a response to each question showing clearly any computations.

(1) What assumptions caused the reported "Sales" to remain the same in all three income statements? ($5,312 million)
(2) What was the 1982 amount of (a) operating gross profit, (b) real component of realized holding gain, (c) inflation component of realized holding gains and (d) total operating gross profit plus realized holding gains.
(3) What was the cumulative amount of unrealized holding gain, (a) real component, (b) inflation component, and (c) total unrealized holding gain as indicated on the 1982 balance sheet.
(4) What was the amount of the purchasing power gain or loss for 1982?
(5) Did General Mills inadvertently pay dividends in excess of its operating income?
(6) How does information about purchasing power gains and losses affect a user's ability to predict future cash flows?

***case 24-4 (How do I value items for my personal financial statements?)** Angus Belliston, your client, has come into the office to discuss the possibility of having

*Case to Appendix 2 material.

personal financial statements prepared as of December 31, 1984, to assist him in obtaining a large bank loan. He would prefer having these statements reflect current value information as he believes it is more relevant to his banker than historical cost. In order to obtain some idea of the difficulties that may be encountered in estimating the current value of your client's assets, you have asked him to prepare a brief list. Several items on the list present potential valuation problems.

(a) One item posing valuation problems is the option to purchase 8,000 shares of Westco Inc., a closely held corporation. Belliston owns 30 percent of the company. The total number of shares issued and outstanding is 80,000. The company's net book value is $2 million. After-tax earnings for the past three years have averaged $150,000 annually. The options are freely exercisable at a price of $2 per share.
(b) Belliston owns a residence that cost $460,000 to build three years ago. The land cost $120,000 when purchased 5 years ago. A fire insurance policy is carried on the residence for $550,000, a value recommended by the insurance company as sufficient to cover replacement cost. Construction indexes for the current year are 1.15 of the index three years ago. Current land values in the area are 50% higher than they were five years ago.
(c) During the conversation, Belliston informs you that he has pledged $100,000 to the local Boy Scouts Council Camp improvement fund. He wants to know if this obligation needs to be recorded in his personal financial statements since, for tax reasons, he does not plan to make the donation until December, 1985.
(d) Belliston owes $200,000 on a mortgage taken on the residence. The interest rate on the note is 9%. Current mortgage rates for homes of this age are 12%. An approach to the holder of the mortgage indicates the loan could be settled for $190,000 in order to permit the lender to "get out from under" the lower rate note.
(e) The mention of taxes prompts an additional question from your client. Will the market values assigned to assets be reduced to reflect the income tax that would have to be paid if the recorded market estimates were realized through sale? If so, how will it be done?

How does SOP 82-1 issued by the AICPA suggest that these items be resolved?

EXERCISES

exercise 24-1 (Classification of monetary and nonmonetary items)

Classify the following accounts as either monetary or nonmonetary.

Assets

Current assets:
- Cash
- Marketable securities (stocks)
- Receivables (net of allowance)
- Inventories
- Prepaid rent
- Discount on notes payable
- Deferred income tax expense

Long-term investments:
- Affiliated companies, at cost
- Cash surrender value of life insurance
- Bond sinking fund
- Investment in bonds

Land, buildings, and equipment:
- Land
- Buildings
- Equipment

Intangible assets:
- Patents
- Goodwill

Advances paid on purchase contracts

Liabilities and Stockholders' Equity

Current liabilities:
- Accounts and notes payable
- Dividends payable
- Refundable deposits on returnable containers
- Advances on sales contracts

Long-term liabilities:
- Bonds payable
- Premium on bonds payable

Stockholders' equity:
- Preferred stock (at fixed liquidation price)
- Common stock
- Retained earnings

exercise 24-2 (Computing purchasing power gains or losses)

In each case below, compute the purchasing power gain or loss assuming that assets are held and liabilities are maintained during a period in which the general price level rises by 8%.

(a)	Cash	$ 50,000
	Accounts receivable	20,000
(b)	Cash	100,000
	Accounts payable	25,000
	Long-term payables	55,000
(c)	Cash	25,000
	Land	50,000
	Accounts payable	25,000
(d)	Cash	25,000
	Land and buildings	100,000
	Mortgage note payable	40,000

exercise 24-3 (Adjusting expenses to constant dollars)

Assuming prices rise evenly by 9% during a year, compute the amount of expenses stated in terms of year-end constant dollars in each of the following independent cases:

(a) Expenses of $500,000 were paid at the beginning of the year for services received during the first half of the year.
(b) Expenses of $125,000 were paid at the end of each quarter for services received during the quarter.
(c) Expenses of $125,000 were paid at the beginning of each quarter for services received during the quarter.
(d) Expenses of $500,000 were paid at the end of the year for services received during the year.
(e) Expenses of $500,000 were paid evenly throughout the year for services received during the year.

In terms of year-end constant dollars, when is the best time to pay for services received in periods of rising prices?

exercise 24-4 (Constant dollar adjustment of equipment and depreciation)

Captain Ben's Seafood will prepare for the first time historical cost/constant dollar statements as of June 30, 1984. In connection with the restatement, an analysis of the equipment and related accumulated depreciation account was made before the 1984 adjustments for depreciation:

Year Acquired	Cost	Accumulated Depreciation June 30, 1983	Estimated Useful Life
1978	$100,000	$ 73,786	10 years
1980	250,000	147,600	10 years
1982	300,000	74,667	15 years
1983	50,000	33,333	3 years
1984	130,000	—	5 years

The double-declining balance method of depreciation is used with a full year's depreciation taken in the year of acquisition and none taken in the year of retirement. Adjust the equipment and related accumulated depreciation accounts to constant dollars as of June 30, 1984. Round to the nearest dollar. Assume the June 30 general price index rose as follows:

June 30	June 30 Index
1978	100
1979	105
1980	110
1981	120
1982	130
1983	135
1984	145

exercise 24-5 (Constant dollar restatement of income and retained earnings statement)

A comparative income statement for the Trenton Company for the first two years of operations appears below.

	Results of Operations			
	First Year		Second Year	
Sales		$750,000		$900,000
Cost of goods sold:				
Beginning inventory	—		$300,000	
Purchases	$750,000		500,000	
Goods available for sale	$750,000		$800,000	
Ending inventory	300,000	450,000	400,000	400,000
Gross profit on sales		$300,000		$500,000
Operating expenses:				
Depreciation	$ 30,000		$ 30,000	
Other	240,000	270,000	350,000	380,000
Net income		$ 30,000		$120,000
Dividends		15,000		30,000
Increase in retained earnings		$ 15,000		$ 90,000

Prepare a comparative income and retained earnings statement expressing items in constant dollars at the end of the second year, considering the following data:

(a) Prices rose evenly and index numbers expressing the general price-level changes were:

Beginning of first year	100
End of first year	110
End of second year	140

(b) Sales and purchases were made and expenses were incurred evenly each year.
(c) Inventories were reported at cost using first-in, first-out pricing; average indexes for the year are applicable in restating inventories.
(d) Depreciation relates to equipment acquired at the beginning of the first year.
(e) Dividends were paid at the middle of each year.
(f) Assume no purchasing power gain or loss in either year.

exercise 24-6 (Constant dollar restatement of balance sheet)

Comparative balance sheet data for Fortune Industries Inc., since its formation, appear on page 958. The general price level during the two-year period went up steadily; index numbers expressing the general price-level changes are listed following the balance sheet. Restate the comparative balance sheet data in terms of constant dollars at the end of the second year.

	End of First Year	End of Second Year
Cash	$ 75,000	$ 62,500
Receivables	50,000	70,000
Land, buildings, and equipment (net)*	130,000	115,000
	$255,000	$247,500
Payables	$ 67,500	$ 45,000
Capital stock	160,000	160,000
Retained earnings	27,500	42,500
	$255,000	$247,500

*Acquired at the beginning of the first year.

	Price Index
At the beginning of the business	112
At the end of the first year	125
At the end of the second year	140

exercise 24-7 (Comprehensive constant dollar restatement of income statement)

The income statement for Blaylock Oil Company is given below. Using the income statement, together with the additional data provided, prepare an income statement restated in terms of end-of-year constant dollars accompanied by a schedule summarizing the purchasing power gain or loss for the year.

Blaylock Oil Company
Income Statement
For Year Ended December 31, 19––

Sales		$990,000
Cost of goods sold:		
Beginning inventory	$ 150,000	
Purchases	900,000	
Goods available for sale	$1,050,000	
Ending inventory	450,000	600,000
Gross profit on sales		$390,000
Operating expenses		270,000
Income before income tax		$120,000
Income tax		60,000
Net income		$ 60,000

The general price level rose evenly from 140 to 160 in the preceding year and from 160 to 200 in the current year. Sales and purchases were made evenly and expenses were incurred evenly during the year. The average index is regarded as applicable in restating inventories. All the company's assets and liabilities, both at the beginning and at the end of the period, were classified as current and, except for inventories, monetary. Current assets were $600,000 and current liabilities were $200,000 at the beginning of the year.

exercise 24-8 (Adjustment to average-year constant dollars)

The historical cost/constant dollar income statement of the Hogan Corporation shows a purchasing power loss of $1,800 based on end-of-year constant dollars. Price indexes were as follows:

Beginning of year	220
Average	230
End of year	240

Calculate the purchasing power loss in average-year dollars as required by FASB Statement No. 33.

exercise 24-9 (Income components under current cost accounting)

On September 1, 1984, Backman's Toy Store purchased 800 dolls at $2.50 per doll. As of December 31, 1984, Backman's had sold three fourths of the dolls at $6 per doll, and the doll manufacturer was selling to retailers at $3 per doll. With respect to the doll venture, how much should Backman's Toy Store recognize as (a) operating gross profit, (b) realized holding gain, and (c) unrealized holding gain under the current cost method of accounting?

exercise 24-10 (Calculating depreciation on a current cost basis)

Rizzo Corporation purchased equipment costing $50,000 at the beginning of 1983. The company uses straight-line depreciation. This piece of equipment has a five-year life with no salvage value.

Based on the following information, compute the average current cost depreciation on the equipment for the years 1984 and 1985. (Ignore recoverable amounts and round to nearest dollar.)

Year	Specific Price Index (End-of-Year)
1982	150
1983	160
1984	180
1985	200

exercise 24-11 (Current cost/constant dollar balance sheet)

The current cost/nominal dollar balance sheet for the Fox Corporation at December 31, 1984, follows.

Fox Corporation
Balance Sheet
December 31, 1984
(Current Cost/Nominal Dollar Basis)

Assets		Liabilities and Stockholders' Equity	
Cash	$ 10,000	Accounts payable	$ 20,000
Accounts receivable	15,000	Interest payable	10,000
Inventory	30,000	Total liabilities	$ 30,000
Equipment (net)	50,000	Capital stock	$ 80,000
Land	45,000	Retained earnings	40,000
		Total stockholders' equity	$120,000
Total assets	$150,000	Total liabilities and stockholders' equity	$150,000

The equipment and land were purchased at year end. The inventory is valued at year-end current prices.

The capital stock was issued when the consumer price index was 240. The consumer price index at December 31, 1984, was 270.

Prepare a current cost/constant dollar balance sheet for the Fox Corporation at December 31, 1984, stated in end-of-year constant dollars.

exercise 24-12 (Recoverable amounts)

Thistle Inc. began business last year. It sells boats and uses specific identification in valuing its inventory. The financial statements are prepared according to GAAP on a historical cost/nominal dollar basis. However, as supplemental information, management wishes to disclose the current cost of goods sold and ending inventory. The following data are available:

	Historical Cost/Nominal Dollar
Beginning inventory	$ 80,000
Purchases	205,000
Goods available for sale	$285,000
Ending inventory	111,200
Cost of goods sold	$173,800

The ending inventory consists of 10 units. A survey of the suppliers for Thistle shows the average current replacement of each inventory unit is $14,500. It is expected that these boats can each be sold for $22,000, provided that 10% is spent on advertising and related costs.

Based on these data, what impact, if any, would the recoverable amount of inventory have on the supplemental information?

*exercise 24-13 (Computation of holding gains or losses and current cost income statement)

The historical cost/nominal dollar income statement for the Mayall Corporation for the first year of operations ended June 30, 1984, is presented below in partially complete form. Historical cost/constant dollar and current cost/constant dollar values for selected items are also presented. Determine the realized and unrealized holding gains or losses, net of inflation, and prepare the income statement using the current cost/constant dollar basis.

Mayall Corporation
Income Statement
For the Year Ended June 30, 1984
Historical Cost/Nominal Dollar Basis

Sales	$1,700,000
Cost of goods sold	800,000
Gross profit	$ 900,000
Depreciation expense	100,000
Other expenses	400,000
Income from continuing operations	$ 400,000

Mayall Corporation
Historical Cost/Constant Dollar and Current Cost/Constant Dollar Values
for Selected Items

	HC/CD	CC/CD
Inventory June 30, 1984	$600,000	$720,000
Inventory July 1, 1983	750,000	750,000
Cost of goods sold	840,000	870,000
Purchases	800,000	800,000
Equipment (net) June 30, 1984	350,000	450,000
Equipment (net) July 1, 1983	400,000	400,000
Depreciation expense	150,000	200,000
Land June 30, 1984	350,000	400,000
Land July 1, 1983	200,000	200,000
Other expenses	430,000	430,000

Purchasing power loss on net monetary items, $50,000.

*Exercise to Appendix 1 material.

*exercise 24-14 (The inflation component of realized holding gains)

Singleton Company reports the following selected information for its first year of operation.

	Historical Costs	Current Costs
Sales	$1,450,000	$1,450,000
Cost of goods sold	870,000	950,000
Gross profit	580,000	536,500

Assume sales and cost of goods sold are incurred evenly. During the past year, the general price level rose from 100 to 110, or an average of 5 percent. Based on the information provided and adjusting to end-of-year prices, determine:

(1) The amount of operating gross profit (economic profit).
(2) The real component of the realized holding gain.
(3) Recognizing that the inflation component of the holding gain is not reported separately under current cost/constant dollar accounting, compute the amount of the inflation component implied by the data.

*Exercise to Appendix 1 material.

PROBLEMS

problem 24-1 (Constant dollar adjustment for cost of goods sold and depreciation)

The following information was taken from the books of the Fix-It Hardware Store during its first two years of operations:

	Useful Life	1983	1984
Beginning inventory		$150,000	$200,000
Purchases		550,000	500,000
Ending inventory		200,000	160,000
Building (acquired 1/1/83)	25 years	400,000	—
Office equipment (acquired 7/1/83)	12 years	30,000	—
Machinery (acquired 10/1/83)	8 years	16,000	—
Price index (1/1)		190	202
Price index (12/31)		202	214

Instructions:

(1) Calculate the cost of goods sold for 1983 and 1984 in terms of respective year-end dollars assuming a lifo inventory cost flow with average costs used for any increments. Assume the 1983 beginning inventory was purchased on January 1, 1983. Round to the nearest dollar amount.
(2) Restate depreciable assets and accumulated depreciation (straight-line, ignore salvage values) reporting the depreciation for 1983 and 1984 in terms of 1983 and 1984 year-end dollars respectively.

problem 24-2 (Restatement of balance sheet to constant dollars)

The Werner Co. began operations in 1953. At the end of 1984 it was decided to furnish stockholders with a balance sheet restated in terms of constant 1984 dollars as a supplement to the conventional financial statements. This is the first time such a statement was prepared. The balance sheet prepared in conventional form at the end of 1984 follows.

Werner Co.
Balance Sheet
December 31, 1984

Cash	$ 187,600	Accounts payable	$ 379,900
Accounts receivable	342,400	Mortgage note payable	450,000
Inventory	742,300	Bonds payable	1,250,000
Land	1,720,000	Capital stock	1,000,000
Building	2,115,000	Premium on capital stock	200,000
Less accumulated depreciation	(705,000)	Retained earnings	1,122,400
Total assets	$4,402,300	Total liabilities and stockholders' equity	$4,402,300

All the stock was issued in 1953. Land was purchased subject to a mortgage note of $1,000,000 at the time the company was formed. The present building is being depreciated on a straight-line basis with a 30-year life and no salvage value. The bonds were issued in 1963. The company uses the first-in, first-out method in pricing inventories.

Instructions: Prepare a balance sheet for the Werner Co. restated in terms of 1984 constant dollars. Use the indexes below in making adjustments; assume the index for each year is regarded as representative of the price level for the entire year.

Year	Price Index	Year	Price Index
1953	54.9	1981	160.1
1963	70.7	1982	168.0
1973	93.0	1983	178.6
1975	100.0	1984	185.2
1980	146.5		

problem 24-3 (Restatement of income statement to constant dollars)

The income statement prepared at the end of the year for the Photo-Graphics Corporation follows:

Photo-Graphics Corporation
Income Statement
For Year Ended December 31, 1984

Sales		$350,000
Less sales discount		15,000
Net sales		$335,000
Cost of goods sold:		
Inventory, January 1	$125,000	
Purchases	180,000	
Goods available for sale	$305,000	
Inventory, December 31	120,000	
Cost of goods sold		185,000
Gross profit on sales		$150,000
Operating expenses:		
Depreciation	$ 21,250	
Other operating expenses	50,000	
Total operating expenses		71,250
Income before income tax		$ 78,750
Income tax		31,300
Net income		$ 47,450

The following additional data are available:

(a) The price index rose evenly throughout the year from 120 on January 1 to 130 on December 31.

(b) Sales were made evenly throughout the year; expenses were incurred evenly throughout the year.
(c) The inventory was valued at cost using first-in, first-out pricing; average indexes for the year are used in restating inventories. The beginning inventory was acquired in the preceding period when the average index was 122.
(d) The depreciation charge related to the following items:

	Asset Cost	Index at Date of Acquisition	Depreciation Rate
Building	$75,000	95	3 %
Equipment	80,000	95	12½%
Equipment	20,000	98	12½%
Equipment*	39,000	120	16⅔%

*Acquired at the beginning of the current year.

(e) Semiannual dividends of $7,500 were declared and paid at the end of June and at the end of December.
(f) The balance sheet position for the company changed during the year as follows:

	January 1	December 31
Current assets	$180,000	$174,700
Building and equipment (net)	120,000	137,750
	$300,000	$312,450
Current liabilities	$ 55,000	$ 35,000
Capital stock	200,000	200,000
Retained earnings	45,000	77,450
	$300,000	$312,450

Instructions: Prepare an income statement in which items are stated in end-of-year dollars accompanied by a schedule summarizing the purchasing power gain or loss for 1984.

problem 24-4 (Comprehensive restatement of financial statements to constant dollars)

Financial statements are prepared for the Carver Co. at the end of each year in nominal dollars and are also measured in constant dollars. Balance sheet data summarized in nominal dollars and in constant dollars at the end of 1983 are given below.

	Nominal Dollars		Constant Dollars (Reporting Purchasing Power at End of Year)	
Assets:				
Cash		$ 23,000		$ 23,000
Accounts receivable		70,000		70,000
Inventory		105,000		106,500
Buildings and equipment	$120,000		$153,600	
Less accumulated depreciation	48,000	72,000	61,440	92,160
Land		50,000		64,000
Total assets		$320,000		$355,660
Liabilities:				
Accounts payable		$ 48,000		$ 48,000
Long-term liabilities		40,000		40,000
Total liabilities		$ 88,000		$ 88,000
Stockholders' equity:				
Capital stock		$150,000		$192,000
Retained earnings		82,000		75,660
Total stockholders' equity		$232,000		$267,660
Total liabilities and stockholders' equity		$320,000		$355,660

Data from statements measured in nominal dollars at the end of 1984 are given below:

Balance Sheet

Assets	
Cash	$ 83,840
Accounts receivable	72,500
Inventory	125,000
Buildings and equipment	120,000
Accumulated depreciation	(56,000)
Land	50,000
	$395,340

Liabilities and Stockholders' Equity	
Accounts payable	$ 37,000
Long-term liabilities	40,000
Capital stock	150,000
Retained earnings	168,340
	$395,340

Income Statement

Sales	$1,100,000
Cost of goods sold	600,000
Gross profit on sales	$ 500,000
Operating expenses	308,000
Income before income tax	$ 192,000
Income tax	85,660
Net income	$ 106,340
Dividends	20,000
Increase in retained earnings	$ 86,340

The following additional data are available at the end of 1984:

(a) Price indexes were as follows for the year:

January 1	150
December 31	153

The price level rose steadily during the year.

(b) Sales and purchases were made evenly, and expenses were incurred evenly throughout the year.

(c) The first-in, first-out method was used to compute inventory cost; average indexes for the year are used in restating inventories.

(d) All the land, buildings, and equipment were acquired when the company was formed.

(e) Dividends were declared and paid at the end of the year.

Instructions: Prepare in terms of end-of-year constant dollars: (1) an income and retained earnings statement accompanied by a schedule summarizing the purchasing power gain or loss for 1984; (2) a balance sheet as of December 31, 1984.

*problem 24-5 (Comparison of constant dollar and current cost income statements)

Operations of the Harris Corporation for 1984, the first year after its organization are summarized on the following statements:

Income Statement

Sales		$1,200,000
Cost of goods sold:		
Beginning inventory	$200,000	
Purchases	700,000	
Merchandise available for sale	$900,000	
Ending inventory	50,000	850,000
Gross profit on sales		$ 350,000
Expenses (including depreciation)		290,000
Net income		$ 60,000
Dividends		50,000
Increase in retained earnings		$ 10,000

*Problem to Appendix 1 material.

Comparative Balance Sheet

	Beginning of Business	End of Year
Assets		
Cash	$140,000	$312,500
Accounts receivable	—	150,000
Inventory	200,000	50,000
Land	60,000	60,000
Buildings (net)	250,000	237,500
Total assets	$650,000	$810,000
Liabilities		
Accounts payable	—	$150,000
Mortgage note payable	$150,000	150,000
Total liabilities	$150,000	$300,000
Stockholders' Equity		
Capital stock	$500,000	$500,000
Retained earnings	—	10,000
Total stockholders' equity	$500,000	$510,000
Total liabilities and stockholders' equity	$650,000	$810,000

Certain stockholders of the company request additional data that will enable them to judge the economic progress of the company during this period, and it is decided to prepare constant dollar statements for each year expressing the purchasing power of the dollar at the end of each year in addition to current cost statements. The data and assumptions to be applied in the preparation of such statements follow:

(a) Price indexes were:

Beginning of first year (at company formation)	115
End of first year	125

The price level rose evenly throughout each year.

(b) Sales, purchases, and expenses were made or incurred evenly throughout each year.
(c) The first-in, first-out method was used in calculating inventory cost; average indexes for the year are used in restating inventories.
(d) Dividends were declared and paid in the middle of the year.
(e) Buildings were depreciated at the rate of 5%.
(f) Current cost data:

Cost of goods sold	$950,000
Inventory—year-end price	75,000
Building, before depreciation—year-end price	300,000
Land—year-end price	85,000

Instructions:

(1) Prepare, in terms of end-of-year constant dollars, a historical cost income and retained earnings statement accompanied by a schedule summarizing the purchasing power gain or loss, and a balance sheet for the first year.
(2) Prepare, in nominal and constant dollars, a combined current cost income and retained earnings statement and the accompanying balance sheet. Use year-end constant dollars.

problem 24-6 (Analysis of EPS & ROI in terms of constant dollars)

To obtain a more realistic appraisal of her investment, Sharon Abbott, your client, has asked you to adjust certain financial data on the Global Company for general price-level changes. On January 1, 1982, Abbott invested $50,000 in the Global Company in return for 10,000 shares of common stock. Immediately after her investment, the trial balance data appeared as follows:

Cash and Receivables	65,200	
Merchandise Inventory	4,000	
Building	50,000	
Accumulated Depreciation—Building		8,000
Equipment	36,000	
Accumulated Depreciation—Equipment		7,200
Land	10,000	
Current Liabilities		50,000
Capital Stock, $5 par		100,000
	165,200	165,200

Balances in certain selected accounts as of December 31 of each of the next three years were as follows:

	1982	1983	1984
Sales	$39,650	$39,000	$42,350
Inventory	4,500	5,600	5,347
Purchases	14,475	16,350	18,150
Operating expenses (excluding depreciation)	10,050	9,050	9,075

Assume the 1982 price level as the base year and all changes in the price level take place at the beginning of each year. Further assume the 1983 price level is 10% above the 1982 price level and the 1984 price level is 10% above the 1983 level.

The building was constructed in 1978 at a cost of $50,000 with an estimated life of 25 years. The price level at that time was 80% of the 1982 price level.

The equipment was purchased in 1980 at a cost of $36,000 with an estimated life of ten years. The price level at that time was 90% of the 1982 price level.

The lifo method of inventory valuation is used. The original inventory was acquired in the same year the building was constructed and was maintained at a constant $4,000 until 1982. In 1982 a gradual buildup of the inventory was begun in anticipation of an increase in the volume of business.

Abbott considers the return on her investment as the dividend she actually receives. In 1982 and also in 1984 the Global Company paid cash dividends in the amount of $4,000.

On July 1, 1983, there was a reverse stock split-up of the company's stock in the ratio of one-for-ten.

Instructions:

(1) Compute the 1984 earnings per share of common stock in terms of 1982 dollars.
(2) Compute the percentage return on the investment for 1982 and 1984 in terms of 1982 dollars.

(AICPA adapted)

*problem 24-7 (Comparison of four reporting alternatives)

Inventory information for the Charlotte Company is presented below.

	Historical Cost/ Nominal Dollar	Current Cost/ Nominal Dollar
Beginning inventory	$ 60,000	—
Purchases	240,000	—
Ending inventory	75,000	90,000

The Charlotte Company uses the fifo inventory method.

The beginning inventory was purchased when the price index was 100. The ending inventory was purchased when the index was 120. Purchases and sales were made

*Problem to Appendix 1 material.

evenly throughout the year. The current value of the goods sold was $270,000 based on average current costs.

General price indexes were as follows:

Beginning of year	100
Average index	120
End of year	140

Instructions: Compute the cost of goods sold and ending inventory under each of the following accounting methods.

(a) Historical cost/nominal dollar
(b) Historical cost/end-of-year constant dollar
(c) Current cost/nominal dollar
(d) Current cost/end-of-year constant dollar

*problem 24-8 (Reporting constant dollar information under FASB Statement No. 33)

The historical cost income statement for the Hawkeye Company is presented below.

Hawkeye Company
Income Statement
For the Year Ended December 31, 1984

Sales		$180,000
Cost of goods sold:		
Beginning inventory	$ 20,000	
Purchases	140,000	
Goods available for sale	$160,000	
Ending inventory	50,000	
Cost of goods sold		110,000
Gross profit		$ 70,000
Operating expenses:		
Depreciation expense	$ 10,000	
Other expenses	20,000	30,000
Net income		$ 40,000

The following additional information is provided:

(a) Sales, purchases, and other expenses were incurred evenly over the year.
(b) The beginning inventory was purchased when the price index was 180. Assume the ending inventory was acquired when the price index was 220.
(c) Price indexes were as follows:

Beginning of year	200
Average for year	220
End of year	240

(d) The equipment on which the depreciation expense is computed was purchased when the price index was 110.

Instructions: Prepare a statement showing income from continuing operations in average-year constant dollars as required by FASB Statement No. 33.

problem 24-9 (Converting nominal dollar financial data to constant dollars)

Skadden Inc., a retailer, was organized during 1980. Skadden's management has decided to supplement its December 31, 1983 nominal dollar financial statements with

*Problem to Appendix 1 material.

constant dollar financial statements. The following general ledger trial balance (nominal dollars) and additional information have been furnished:

Skadden Inc.
Trial Balance
December 31, 1983

Cash and Receivables (net)	540,000	
Marketable Securities (common stock)	400,000	
Inventory	440,000	
Equipment	650,000	
Accumulated Depreciation—Equipment		164,000
Accounts Payable		300,000
9% First-Mortgage Bonds, due 2001		500,000
Common Stock, $10 par		1,000,000
Retained Earnings, December 31, 1982	46,000	
Sales		1,900,000
Cost of Goods Sold	1,508,000	
Depreciation	65,000	
Other Operating Expenses and Interest	215,000	
	3,864,000	3,864,000

(a) Monetary assets (cash and receivables) exceeded monetary liabilities (accounts payable and bonds payable) by $445,000 at December 31, 1982. The amounts of monetary items are fixed in terms of numbers of dollars regardless of changes in specific prices or in the general price level.
(b) Purchases ($1,840,000 in 1983) and sales are made uniformly throughout the year.
(c) Depreciation is computed on a straight-line basis with a full year's depreciation being taken in the year of acquisition and none in the year of retirement. The depreciation rate is 10%, and no salvage value is anticipated. Acquisitions and retirements have been made fairly evenly over each year, and the retirements in 1983 consisted of assets purchased during 1981 that were scrapped. An analysis of the equipment account reveals the following:

Year	Beginning Balance	Additions	Retirements	Ending Balance
1981	—	$550,000	—	$550,000
1982	$550,000	10,000	—	560,000
1983	560,000	150,000	$60,000	650,000

(d) The bonds were issued in 1981 and the marketable securities were purchased fairly evenly over 1983. Other operating expenses and interest are assumed to be incurred evenly throughout the year.
(e) Assume that price indexes were as follows:

Annual Averages	Index	Conversion Factors (1983 4th Qtr. = 1.000)
1980	141.4	1.259
1981	146.1	1.218
1982	154.3	1.153
1983	170.2	1.046
Quarterly Averages		
1982 4th	158.9	1.120
1983 1st	163.6	1.088
2d	167.3	1.064
3d	172.1	1.034
4th	178.0	1.000

Instructions:

(1) Prepare a schedule to convert the equipment account balance at December 31, 1983, from nominal dollars to fourth quarter, 1983 dollars.

(2) Prepare a schedule to analyze in nominal dollars the accumulated depreciation account for equipment for the year 1983.

(3) Prepare a schedule to analyze in constant dollars the accumulated depreciation account for equipment for the year 1983.

(4) Prepare a schedule to compute Skadden Inc.'s purchasing power gain or loss on its net holdings of monetary assets for 1983 (ignore income tax implications). The schedule should give consideration to appropriate items on or related to the balance sheet and the income statement. (AICPA adapted)

25 FINANCIAL STATEMENT ANALYSIS

CHAPTER OBJECTIVES

Describe the objectives of financial statement analysis.

Explain the major techniques used in analyzing financial statements.

Identify key company characteristics and related measurements.

Accounting provides information to assist various individuals in making economic decisions. A significant amount of information relevant to this purpose is presented in the primary financial statements of companies. Additional useful information is provided by reporting data in other than the financial statements. However, as explained in Chapter 3, financial data are only part of the total information needed by decision makers. Nonfinancial data may also be relevant. Thus, the total information spectrum is broader than just financial reporting. It encompasses financial statements, financial reporting by means other than the financial statements, and additional nonfinancial information.

The Financial Accounting Standards Board has restricted its focus to general-purpose external financial reporting by business enterprises. This chapter concentrates on analysis of information in the primary financial statements. Notes are an integral part of financial statements. Significant accounting policies and other information included in notes to financial statements should be considered carefully in performing an analysis and in evaluating results. Supplementary information should also be considered in interpreting financial statement data.

OBJECTIVES OF FINANCIAL STATEMENT ANALYSIS

Nearly all businesses prepare financial statements of some type; the form and complexity of the statements vary according to the needs of those who prepare and use them. The owner of a small business might simply list the firm's cash receipts and disbursements and prepare an income tax return. On the other hand, a large corporation's accounting staff spends considerable time in preparing the company's complex financial statements.

Whatever their form, financial statements provide information about a business and its operations to interested users. For example, questions may be raised by external users concerning matters such as a company's sales, net income, and trends for these items; the amount of working capital and changes in working capital; the relationship of income to sales, and of income to investments. Identifying these relationships requires analysis of data reported on the income statement, the balance sheet, and the statement of changes in financial position. Internal management is also concerned with analyzing the general-purpose financial statements, but requires additional special information in setting policies and making decisions. Questions may arise on matters such as the performance of various company divisions, the income from sales of individual products, and whether to make or buy product parts and equipment. These questions can be answered by establishing internal information systems to provide the necessary data. Thus, in analyzing financial data, the nature of analysis and the information needed depend on the requirements of users and the issues involved.

The analyses of financial data described in this chapter are directed primarily to the information needs of external users who must generally rely on the financial reports issued by a company. Many groups are interested in the data found in financial statements, including:

(1) Owners—sole proprietor, partners, or stockholders.
(2) Management, including board of directors.
(3) Creditors.
(4) Government—local, state, and federal (including regulatory, taxing, and statistical units).
(5) Prospective owners and prospective creditors.
(6) Stock exchanges, investment bankers, and stockbrokers.
(7) Trade associations.
(8) Employees of a business and their labor unions.
(9) The general public.

Questions raised by these groups can generally be answered by analyses that develop comparisons and measure relationships between components of financial statements. The analyses will form a basis for decisions made by the user.

Analysis is generally directed toward evaluating four aspects of a business: (1) liquidity, (2) stability, (3) profitability, and (4) growth potential.

To remain solvent, a business must be able to pay its liabilities as they mature. Financial statements are analyzed to determine whether a business is currently liquid and whether it could retain its liquidity in a period of adversity. The analysis includes studies of the relationship of current assets to current liabilities, the size and nature of creditor and ownership interests, the protection afforded creditors and owners through sound asset values, and the amounts and trends of net income.

Stability is measured by the ability of a business to make interest and principal payments on outstanding debt and to pay regular dividends to its stockholders. In judging stability, data concerning operations and financial position are studied. For example, there must be a regular demand for the goods or services sold, and the margin on sales must be sufficient to cover operating expenses, interest, and dividends. There should be a satisfactory turnover of assets, and all business resources should be productively employed.

Profitability is measured by the ability of a business to maintain a satisfactory dividend policy while at the same time steadily increasing ownership equity. The nature and amount of income, as well as its regularity and trend, are significant factors affecting profitability.

The growth potential of a company is also of primary importance. This element, along with profitability, directly affects future cash flows, derived from increased income and/or appreciation in stock values. Growth potential is measured by the expansion and growth into new markets, the rate of growth in existing markets, the rate of growth in earnings per share, and the amount of expenditures for research and development.

An analysis must serve the needs of those for whom it is made. For example, owners are interested in a company's ability to obtain additional capital for current needs and possible expansion. Creditors are interested not only in the position of a business as a going concern but also in its position should it be forced to liquidate.

ANALYTICAL PROCEDURES

Analytical procedures fall into two main categories: (1) comparisons and measurements based on financial data for two or more periods, and (2) comparisons and measurements based on financial data of only the current fiscal period. The first category includes comparative statements, ratios and trends for data on successive statements, and analyses of changes in the balance sheet, income statement, and statement of changes in financial position. The second category includes determining current balance sheet and income statement relationships and analyzing earnings and earning power. A review of financial data usually requires both types of analysis.

The analytical procedures commonly employed may be identified as: comparative statements, index-number trend series, common-size statements, and analysis of financial statement components. These techniques are described and illustrated in the following sections. It should be emphasized that the analyses illustrated herein are simply guides to the evaluation of financial data. Sound conclusions can be reached only through intelligent use and interpretation of such data. The Wycat Corporation is used as an example throughout the chapter.

Comparative Statements

Financial data become more meaningful when compared with similar data for preceding periods. Statements reflecting financial data for two or more periods are called **comparative statements.** Annual data can be compared with similar data for prior years. Monthly or quarterly data can be compared with similar data for previous months or quarters or with similar data for the same months or quarters of previous years.

Comparative data allow statement users to analyze trends in a company, thus enhancing the usefulness of information for decision making. The Accounting Principles Board stated that comparisons between financial statements are most informative and useful under the following conditions:

(1) The presentations are in good form; that is, the arrangement within the statements is identical.
(2) The content of the statements is identical; that is, the same items from the underlying accounting records are classified under the same captions.
(3) Accounting principles are not changed or, if they are changed, the financial effects of the changes are disclosed.
(4) Changes in circumstances or in the nature of the underlying transactions are disclosed.[1]

To the extent that the above criteria are not met, comparisons may be misleading. Consistent practices and procedures and reporting periods of equal and regular lengths are also important, especially when comparisons are made for a single enterprise.

Comparative financial statements may be even more useful to investors and others when the reporting format highlights absolute changes in dollar amounts as well as relative percentage changes. Statement users will benefit by considering both amounts as they make their analyses. For example, an investor may decide that any change in a financial statement amount of ten percent or more should be investigated further. A ten percent change in an amount of $1,000, however, is not as significant as a five percent change in an amount of $100,000. When absolute or relative amounts appear out of line, conclusions, favorable or unfavorable, are not justified until investigation has disclosed reasons for the changes.

---

[1] *Statements of the Accounting Principles Board, No. 4*, "Basic Concepts and Accounting Principles Underlying Financial Statements of Business Enterprises" (New York: American Institute of Certified Public Accountants, 1970), par. 95–99.

The development of data measuring changes taking place over a number of periods is known as **horizontal analysis.** Using the Wycat Corporation's income statement as an example, and a reporting format that discloses both dollar and percentage changes, horizontal analysis is illustrated below.

Wycat Corporation
Comparative Income Statement
For Years Ended December 31

				Increase(Decrease)			
				1983–1984		1982–1983	
	1984	1983	1982	Amount	Percent	Amount	Percent
Gross sales	$1,500,000	$1,750,000	$1,000,000	$(250,000)	(14%)	$750,000	75%
Sales returns	75,000	100,000	50,000	(25,000)	(25%)	50,000	100%
Net sales	$1,425,000	$1,650,000	$ 950,000	$(225,000)	(14%)	$700,000	74%
Cost of goods sold	1,000,000	1,200,000	630,000	(200,000)	(17%)	570,000	90%
Gross profit on sales	$ 425,000	$ 450,000	$ 320,000	$ (25,000)	(6%)	$130,000	41%
Selling expense	$ 280,000	$ 300,000	$ 240,000	$ (20,000)	(7%)	$ 60,000	25%
General expense	100,000	110,000	100,000	(10,000)	(9%)	10,000	10%
Total operating expenses	$ 380,000	$ 410,000	$ 340,000	$ (30,000)	(7%)	$ 70,000	21%
Operating income (loss)	$ 45,000	$ 40,000	$ (20,000)	$ 5,000	13%	$ 60,000	—
Other revenue items	85,000	75,000	50,000	10,000	13%	25,000	50%
	$ 130,000	$ 115,000	$ 30,000	$ 15,000	13%	$ 85,000	283%
Other expense items	30,000	30,000	10,000	—	—	20,000	200%
Income before income tax	$ 100,000	$ 85,000	$ 20,000	$ 15,000	18%	$ 65,000	325%
Income tax	30,000	25,000	5,000	5,000	20%	20,000	400%
Net income	$ 70,000	$ 60,000	$ 15,000	$ 10,000	17%	$ 45,000	300%

Index-Number Trend Series

When comparative financial statements present information for more than two or three years, they become cumbersome and potentially confusing. A technique used to overcome this problem is referred to as an **index-number trend series.**

To compute index numbers, the statement preparer must first choose a base year. This may be the earliest year presented or some other year considered particularly appropriate. Next, the base year amounts are all expressed as 100 percent. The amounts for all other years are then stated as a percentage of the base year amounts. Index numbers can only be computed when amounts are positive. The set of percentages for several years may thus be interpreted as trend values or as a series of index numbers relating to a particular item. For example, Wycat Corporation had gross sales of $1,000,000 in 1982, $1,750,000 in 1983, and $1,500,000 in 1984. These amounts, expressed in an index-number trend series with 1982 as the base year, would be 100, 175, and 150, respectively.

The index-number trend series technique is a type of horizontal analysis. It can give statement users a long-range view of a firm's financial position, earnings, and sources and uses of funds. The user needs to recognize, however, that long-range trend series are particularly sensitive to inflation.

Data expressed in terms of a base year are frequently useful for comparisons with similar data provided by business or industry sources or government agencies. When information used for making comparisons does not employ the same base period, it will have to be restated. Restatement of a base year calls for the expressing of each value as a percentage of the value for the base-year period.

To illustrate, assume the net sales data for the Wycat Corporation for 1982–1984 are to be compared with a sales index for its particular industry. The industry sales indexes are as follows:

	1984	1983	1982
(1975 − 1977 = 100)	146	157	124

Recognizing 1982 as the base year, industry sales are restated as follows:

1982	100
1983 (157 ÷ 124)	127
1984 (146 ÷ 124)	118

Industry sales and net sales for the Wycat Corporation can now be expressed in comparative form as follows:

	1984	1983	1982
Industry sales index	118	127	100
Wycat Corporation sales index*	150	174	100

*From comparative income statement on page 974.

Common-Size Financial Statements

Horizontal analysis measures changes over a number of accounting periods. Statement users also need data that express relationships within a single period, which is known as **vertical analysis.** Preparation of **common-size financial statements** is a widely used vertical analysis technique. The common-size relationships may be stated in terms of percentages or in terms of ratios. Common-size statements may be prepared for the same business as of different dates or periods, or for two or more business units as of the same date or for the same period.

Common-size financial statements are useful in analyzing the internal structure of a financial statement. For example, a common-size balance sheet expresses each amount as a percentage of total assets. A common-size income statement usually shows each revenue or expense item as a percentage of net sales. As an illustration, a comparative balance sheet for Wycat Corporation with each item expressed in both dollar amounts and percentages is shown on page 976. Other types of common-size financial statements, e.g., a common-size retained earnings statement or statement of changes in financial position, may be prepared. When a supporting schedule shows the

Wycat Corporation Comparative Balance Sheet December 31						
	1984		1983		1982	
	Amount	Percent	Amount	Percent	Amount	Percent
Assets						
Current assets	$ 855,000	38%	$ 955,500	40%	$ 673,500	38%
Long-term investments	500,000	22	400,000	17	250,000	14
Land, buildings, and equipment (net)	775,000	34	875,000	37	675,000	38
Intangible assets	100,000	4	100,000	4	100,000	6
Other assets	48,000	2	60,500	2	61,500	4
Total assets	$2,278,000	100%	$2,391,000	100%	$1,760,000	100%
Liabilities						
Current liabilities	$ 410,000	18%	$ 546,000	23%	$ 130,000	7%
Long-term liabilities—10% bonds	400,000	18	400,000	17	300,000	17
Total liabilities	$ 810,000	36%	$ 946,000	40%	$ 430,000	24%
Stockholders' Equity						
Preferred 6% stock	$ 350,000	15%	$ 350,000	15%	$ 250,000	14%
Common stock	750,000	33	750,000	31	750,000	43
Additional paid-in capital	100,000	4	100,000	4	100,000	6
Retained earnings	268,000	12	245,000	10	230,000	13
Total stockholders' equity	$1,468,000	64%	$1,445,000	60%	$1,330,000	76%
Total liabilities and stockholders' equity	$2,278,000	100%	$2,391,000	100%	$1,760,000	100%

detail for a group total, individual items may be expressed as percentages of either the base figure or the group total.

In preparing common-size statements for two companies, it is important that the financial data for each company reflect comparable price levels. Furthermore, the financial data should be developed using comparable accounting methods, classification procedures, and valuation bases. Comparisons should be limited to companies engaged in similar activities. When the financial policies of two companies are different, these differences should be recognized in evaluating comparative reports. For example, one company may lease its properties while the other may purchase such items; one company may finance its operations using long-term borrowing while the other may rely primarily on funds supplied by stockholders and by earnings. Operating results for two companies under these circumstances cannot be wholly comparable.

All this suggests that comparisons between different companies should be evaluated with care, and should be made with a full understanding of the inherent limitations. Reference was made earlier to the criteria that the Accounting Principles Board identified if comparisons are to be meaningful. Comparability between enterprises is more difficult to obtain than comparability within a single enterprise. Ideally, differences in companies' financial reports should arise from basic differences in the companies themselves or from the nature of their transactions and not from differences in accounting practices and procedures.

Other Analytical Procedures

In addition to the financial statement analysis procedures described in the preceding sections, various measures may be developed with respect to specific components of financial statements. Some measurements are of general interest, while others have special significance to particular groups. Creditors, for example, are concerned with the ability of a company to pay its current obligations and seek information about the relationship of current assets to current liabilities. Stockholders are concerned with dividends and seek information relating to earnings that will form the basis for dividends. Managements are concerned with the activity of the merchandise stock and seek information relating to the number of times goods have turned over during the period. All users are vitally interested in profitability and wish to be informed about the relationship of income to both liabilities and owners' equity.

The computation of percentages, ratios, turnovers, and other measures of financial position and operating results for a period is a form of vertical analysis. Comparison with the same measures for other periods is a form of horizontal analysis. The measures described and illustrated in the following sections should not be considered all-inclusive; other measures may be useful to various groups, depending on their particular needs. It should be emphasized again that sound conclusions cannot be reached from an individual measurement. But this information, together with adequate investigation and study, may lead to a satisfactory evaluation of financial data.

Liquidity Analysis

Generally, the first concern of a financial analyst is a firm's liquidity. Will the firm be able to meet its current obligations? If a firm cannot meet its obligations in the short run, it may not have a chance to be profitable or to experience growth in the long run. The two most commonly used measures of liquidity are the current ratio and the acid-test ratio.

Current Ratio. The comparison of current assets with current liabilities is regarded as a fundamental measurement of a company's liquidity. Known as the **current ratio** or **working capital ratio,** this measurement is computed by dividing total current assets by total current liabilities.

The current ratio is a measure of the ability to meet current obligations. Since it measures liquidity, care must be taken to determine that proper items have been included in the current asset and current liability categories. A ratio of current assets to current liabilities of less than 2 to 1 for a trading or manufacturing unit has frequently been considered unsatisfactory. However, because liquidity needs are different for different industries and companies, any such arbitrary measure should not be viewed as meaningful or appropriate in all cases. A comfortable margin of current assets over current liabilities suggests that a company will be able to meet maturing obligations even in the event of unfavorable business conditions or losses on such assets as marketable securities, receivables, and inventories.

For the Wycat Corporation, current ratios for 1984 and 1983 are developed as follows:[2]

	1984	1983
Current assets	$855,000	$955,500
Current liabilities	$410,000	$546,000
Current ratio	2.1:1	1.8:1

A current ratio of 2.1 to 1 means that Wycat could liquidate its total current liabilities 2.1 times using only its current assets.

Ratio calculations are sometimes carried out to two or more decimal places; however, ratios do not need to be carried beyond one place unless some particularly significant interpretative value is afforded by the more refined measurement.

It is possible to overemphasize the importance of a high current ratio. Assume a company is normally able to carry on its operations with current assets of $200,000 and current liabilities of $100,000. If the company has current assets of $500,000 and current liabilities remain at $100,000, its current ratio has increased from 2:1 to 5:1. The company now has considerably more working capital than it requires. It should also be observed that certain unfavorable conditions may be accompanied by an improving ratio. For example, a company's cash balance may rise due to a slowdown in business and the postponement of advertising and research programs or building and equipment repairs and replacements. At the same time, slower customer collections may result in rising trade receivables, and reduced sales volume may result in rising inventories.

Acid-Test Ratio. A test of a company's immediate liquidity is made by comparing the sum of cash, marketable securities, notes receivable, and accounts receivable, commonly referred to as **quick assets,** with current liabilities. The total quick assets divided by current liabilities gives the **acid-test ratio** or **quick ratio.** Considerable time may be required to convert raw materials, goods in process, and finished goods into receivables and then into cash. A company with a satisfactory current ratio may be in a relatively poor liquidity position when inventories comprise most of the total current assets. This is revealed by the acid-test ratio. In developing the ratio, the receivables and securities included in the total quick assets should be examined closely. In some cases these items may actually be less liquid than inventories.

Usually, a ratio of quick assets to current liabilities of at least 1 to 1 is considered desirable. Again, however, special conditions of the particular business must be evaluated. Questions such as the following should be considered: What is the composition of the quick assets? What special requirements are made by current activities upon these assets? How soon are current payables due?

---

[2]Comparative data for more than two years are generally required in evaluating financial trends. Analyses for only two years are given in the examples in this chapter, since these are sufficient to illustrate the analytical procedures involved.

Acid-test ratios for Wycat Corporation are computed as follows:

	1984	1983
Quick assets:		
Cash	$ 60,000	$100,500
Marketable securities	150,000	150,000
Receivables (net)	420,000	375,000
Total quick assets	$630,000	$625,500
Total current liabilities	$410,000	$546,000
Acid-test ratio	1.5:1	1.1:1

Other Measures of Liquidity. Other ratios may help to analyze a company's liquidity. For example, it may be useful to show the relationship of total current assets to total assets, and of individual current assets, such as receivables and inventories, to total current assets. In the case of liabilities, it may be useful to show the relationship of total current liabilities to total liabilities, and of individual current liabilities to total current liabilities.

The foregoing comparisons may provide information concerning the relative liquidity of total assets and the maturity of total obligations as well as the structure of working capital and shifts within the working capital group. The latter data are significant, since all items within the current classification are not equally current.

Activity Analysis

There are special tests that may be applied to measure how efficiently a firm is utilizing its assets. Several of these measures also relate to liquidity because they involve significant working capital elements, such as receivables, inventories, and accounts payable.

Accounts Receivable Turnover. The amount of receivables usually bears a close relationship to the volume of credit sales. The receivable position and approximate collection time may be evaluated by computing the **accounts receivable turnover.** This rate is determined by dividing net credit sales (or total net sales if credit sales are unknown) by the average trade notes and accounts receivable outstanding. In developing an average receivables amount, monthly balances should be used if available.

Assume in the case of Wycat Corporation that all sales are made on credit, that receivables arise only from sales, and that receivable totals for only the beginning and the end of the year are available. Receivable turnover rates are computed as follows:

	1984	1983
Net credit sales	$1,425,000	$1,650,000
Net receivables:		
Beginning of year	$ 375,000	$ 333,500
End of year	$ 420,000	$ 375,000
Average receivables	$ 397,500	$ 354,250
Receivables turnover for year	3.6	4.7

Number of Days' Sales in Receivables. Average receivables are sometimes expressed in terms of the **number of days' sales in receivables,** which shows the average time required to collect receivables. Assume for convenience that there are 360 days per year. Annual sales divided by 360 equals average daily sales. Average receivables divided by average daily sales then gives the number of days' sales in average receivables. This procedure for Wycat Corporation is illustrated below.

	1984	1983
Average receivables	$ 397,500	$ 354,250
Net credit sales	$1,425,000	$1,650,000
Average daily credit sales (net credit sales ÷ 360)	$ 3,958	$ 4,583
Number of days' sales in average receivables (average receivables ÷ average daily credit sales)	100	77

This same measurement can be obtained by dividing the number of days in the year by the receivable turnover. The same number of days for each year should be used in developing comparisons. Computations are generally based on the calendar year, consisting of 365 days, often rounded to 360 days, or a business year consisting of 300 days (365 days less Sundays and holidays). The calendar year basis, rounded to 360 days, is used here.

In some cases, instead of developing the number of days' sales in average receivables, it may be more useful to report the number of days' credit sales in receivables at the end of the period. This information would be significant in evaluating current position, and particularly the receivable position as of a given date. This information for Wycat Corporation is presented below:

	1984	1983
Receivables at end of year	$420,000	$375,000
Average daily credit sales	$ 3,958	$ 4,583
Number of days' sales in receivables at end of year	106	82

What constitutes a reasonable number of days in receivables varies with individual businesses. For example, if merchandise is sold on terms of net 60 days, 40 days' sales in receivables would be reasonable; but if terms are net 30 days, a receivable balance equal to 40 days' sales would indicate slow collections.

Sales activity just before the close of a period should be considered when interpreting accounts receivable measurements. If sales are unusually light or heavy just before the end of the fiscal period, this affects total receivables as well as the related measurements. When such unevenness prevails, it may be better to analyze accounts receivable according to their due dates, as was illustrated in Chapter 7.

The problem of minimizing accounts receivable without losing desirable business is important. Receivables often do not earn interest revenue, and the cost of carrying them must be covered by the profit margin. The longer accounts are carried, the smaller will be the percentage return realized on invested capital. In addition, heavier bookkeeping and collection charges and increased bad debts must be considered.

To attract business, credit is frequently granted for relatively long periods. The cost of granting long-term credit should be considered. Assume that a business has average daily credit sales of $5,000 and average accounts receivable of $250,000, which represents 50 days' credit sales. If collections and the credit period can be improved so that accounts receivable represent only 30 days' sales, then accounts receivable will be reduced to $150,000. Assuming a total cost of 10 percent to carry and service the accounts, the $100,000 decrease would yield annual savings of $10,000.

Inventory Turnover. The amount of inventory carried frequently relates closely to sales volume. The inventory position and the appropriateness of its size may be evaluated by computing the **inventory turnover.** The inventory turnover is computed by dividing cost of goods sold by average inventory. Whenever possible, monthly figures should be used to develop the average inventory balance.

Assume that for Wycat Corporation the inventory balances for only the beginning and the end of the year are available. Inventory turnover rates are computed as follows:

	1984	1983
Cost of goods sold	$1,000,000	$1,200,000
Inventory:		
Beginning of year	$ 330,000	$ 125,000
End of year	$ 225,000	$ 330,000
Average inventory	$ 277,500	$ 227,500
Inventory turnover for year	3.6	5.3

Number of Days' Sales in Inventories. Average inventories are sometimes expressed as the **number of days' sales in inventories.** Information is thus afforded concerning the average time it takes to turn over the inventory. The number of days' sales in inventories is calculated by dividing average inventory by average daily cost of goods sold. The number of days' sales can also be obtained by dividing the number of days in the year by the inventory turnover rate. The latter procedure for Wycat Corporation is illustrated below:

	1984	1983
Inventory turnover for year	3.6	5.3
Number of days' sales in average inventory (assuming a year of 360 days)	100	68

As was the case with receivables, instead of developing the number of days' sales in average inventories, it may be more useful to report the number of days' sales in ending inventories. The latter measurement is determined by dividing ending inventory by average daily cost of goods sold. This information is helpful in evaluating the current asset position and particularly the inventory position as of a given date.

A company with departmental classifications for inventories will find it desirable to support the company's inventory measurements with individual department measurements, since there may be considerable variation among departments. A manufacturing company may compute separate turnover rates for finished goods, goods in process, and raw materials. The finished goods turnover is computed by dividing cost of goods sold by average finished goods inventory. Goods in process turnover is computed by dividing cost of goods manufactured by average goods in process inventory. Raw materials turnover is computed by dividing the cost of raw materials used by average raw materials inventory.

The same valuation methods must be employed for inventories in successive periods if the inventory measurements are to be comparable. Maximum accuracy is possible if information relating to inventories and amount of goods sold is available in terms of physical units rather than dollar costs.

The effect of seasonal factors on the size of year-end inventories should be considered in inventory analyses. Inventories may be abnormally high or low at the end of a period. Many companies adopt a fiscal year ending when operations are at their lowest point. This is called a *natural business year.* Inventories will normally be lowest at the end of such a period, so that the organization can take inventory and complete year-end closing most conveniently. Under these circumstances, monthly inventory balances should be used to arrive at a representative average inventory figure. When a periodic inventory system is employed, monthly inventories may be estimated using the gross profit method as explained in Chapter 9.

With an increased inventory turnover, the investment necessary for a given volume of business is smaller, and consequently the return on invested capital is higher. This conclusion assumes an enterprise can acquire goods in smaller quantities sufficiently often at no price disadvantage. If merchandise must be bought in very large quantities in order to get favorable prices, then the savings on quantity purchases must be weighed against the additional investment, increased costs of storage, and other carrying charges.

The financial advantage of an increased turnover rate may be illustrated as follows. Assuming cost of goods sold of $1,000,000 and average inventory at cost of $250,000, inventory turnover is 4 times. Assume, further, that through careful buying the same business volume can be maintained with turnover of 5 times, or an average inventory of only $200,000. If interest on money invested in inventory is 10 percent, the savings on the $50,000 will be $5,000 annually. The above does not include advantages of decreased merchandise spoilage and obsolescence, savings in storage cost, taxes, and insurance, and reduction in risk of losses from price declines.

Inventory investments and turnover rates vary among different businesses. The facts of each business must be judged in terms of its financial structure and operations. Each business must plan an inventory policy that will avoid the extremes of a dangerously low stock, which may impair sales, and an overstocking of goods involving a heavy capital investment and risks of spoilage and obsolescence, price declines, and difficulties in meeting purchase obligations.

Total Asset Turnover. A measure of the overall efficiency of asset utilization is the ratio of net sales to total assets, sometimes called the **asset turnover rate.** This ratio is calculated by dividing net sales by total assets. The resulting figure indicates the contribution made by total assets to sales. With comparative data, judgments can be made concerning the relative effectiveness of asset utilization. A ratio increase may suggest more efficient asset utilization, although a point may be reached where there is a strain on assets and a company is unable to achieve its full sales potential. An increase in total assets accompanied by a ratio decrease may suggest overinvestment in assets or inefficient utilization.

In developing the asset turnover rate, long-term investments should be excluded from total assets when they make no contribution to sales. On the other hand, a valuation for leased property should be added to total assets to permit comparability between companies owning their properties and those that lease them. If monthly figures for assets are available, they may be used in developing a representative average for total assets employed. Often the year-end asset total is used for the computation. When sales can be expressed in terms of units sold, ratios of sales units to total assets offer more reliable interpretations than sales dollars, since unit sales are not affected by price changes.

Assume that for Wycat Corporation only asset totals for the beginning and end of the year are available, and that sales cannot be expressed in terms of units. Ratios of net sales to total assets are computed as follows:

	1984	1983
Net sales	$1,425,000	$1,650,000
Total assets (excluding long-term investments):		
Beginning of year	$1,991,000	$1,510,000
End of year	$1,778,000	$1,991,000
Average total assets	$1,884,500	$1,750,500
Ratio of net sales to average total assets	0.8:1	0.9:1

Other Measures of Activity. Turnover analysis, as illustrated for receivables, inventories, and total assets, can also be applied to other assets or groups of assets. For example, current asset turnover is calculated by dividing net sales by average current assets. This figure may be viewed as the number of times current assets are replenished, or as the number of sales dollars generated per dollar of current assets. Increases in turnover rates generally indicate more efficient utilization of assets.

Similar procedures may also be used to analyze specific liabilities. An accounts payable turnover, for example, may be computed by dividing purchases by average payables; the number of days' purchases in accounts payable may be computed by dividing accounts payable by average daily purchases. Assuming that all purchases are made on credit, that all accounts payable arise from purchases, and that accounts payable totals are available only for the beginning and end of the year, the accounts payable turnover and the number of days' purchases in accounts payable for Wycat Corporation are computed as follows:

	1984	1983
Net purchases	$895,000	$1,405,000
Net accounts payable:		
Beginning of year	$546,000	$ 130,000
End of year	$410,000	$ 546,000
Average accounts payable	$478,000	$ 338,000
Accounts payable turnover for year	1.9	4.2

	1984	1983
Average payables	$478,000	$ 338,000
Net purchases	$895,000	$1,405,000
Average daily purchases (net purchases ÷ 360)	$ 2,486	$ 3,903
Number of days' purchases in accounts payable	192	87

Analysis of liabilities in terms of due dates may assist management in cash planning. Useful relationships may also be obtained by comparing specific assets or liabilities with other assets or liabilities, or with asset or liability totals. For example, data concerning the relationship of cash to accounts payable or of cash to total liabilities may be useful.

Profitability Analysis

Profitability analysis provides evidence concerning the earnings potential of a company and how effectively a firm is being managed. Since the reason most firms exist is to earn profits, the profitability ratios are among the most significant financial ratios. The adequacy of earnings may be measured in terms of (1) the rate earned on sales, (2) the rate earned on total assets, (3) the rate earned on stockholders' equity, and (4) the availability of earnings to common stockholders. Thus, the most popular profitability measurements are profit margin on sales, return on investment ratios, and earnings per share.

Profit Margin on Sales. The ratio of income to sales determines the **profit margin on sales.** This measurement represents the profit percentage per dollar of sales. The percentage is computed by dividing net income by net sales for a period. For Wycat Corporation, the profit margin on sales is:

	1984	1983
Net income	$ 70,000	$ 60,000
Net sales	$1,425,000	$1,650,000
Profit margin rate	4.9%	3.6%

This means that for 1984, Wycat generated almost five cents of profit per dollar of sales revenue. Because net income is used in the computation, any extraordinary or irregular items may distort the profit margin rate with respect to normal operating activities. Adjustments may be needed in the analysis to account for such items.

Rate Earned on Total Assets. Overall asset productivity may be expressed as the **rate earned on total assets,** also referred to as the **return on investment**

(ROI) or the **asset productivity rate.** The rate is computed by dividing net income by the total assets used to produce net income. This rate measures the efficiency in using resources to generate net income. If total assets by months are available, they should be used to develop an average for the year. Frequently, however, the assets at the beginning of the year or the assets at the end of the year are used. In some cases it may be desirable to use net income from operations by excluding revenue from investments, such as interest, dividends, and rents, or from gains or losses resulting from nonoperating transactions. When this is the case, total assets should be reduced by the investments or other assets. Sometimes comparisons are developed for the rate of operating income to total assets or the rate of pretax income to total assets, so that results are not affected by financial management items or by changes in income tax rates.

Rates earned on total assets for Wycat Corporation are determined as follows:

	1984	1983
Net income	$ 70,000	$ 60,000
Total assets:		
Beginning of year	$2,391,000	$1,760,000
End of year	$2,278,000	$2,391,000
Average total assets	$2,334,500	$2,075,500
Rate earned on average total assets	3.0%	2.9%

Rate Earned on Stockholders' Equity. Net income may be expressed as the **rate earned on stockholders' equity** by dividing net income by stockholders' equity. In developing this rate, it is preferable to calculate the average stockholders' equity for a year from monthly data, particularly when significant changes have occurred during the year, such as the sale of additional stock, retirement of stock, and accumulation of earnings. Sometimes the beginning or the ending stockholders' equity is used.

For Wycat Corporation, rates earned on stockholders' equity are as follows:

	1984	1983
Net income	$ 70,000	$ 60,000
Stockholders' equity:		
Beginning of year	$1,445,000	$1,330,000
End of year	$1,468,000	$1,445,000
Average stockholders' equity	$1,456,500	$1,387,500
Rate earned on average stockholders' equity	4.8%	4.3%

As a company's liabilities increase in relationship to stockholders' equity, the spread between the rate earned on stockholders' equity and the rate earned on total assets rises. The rate earned on stockholders' equity is important to investors who must reconcile the risk of debt financing with the potentially greater profitability. The implications of debt and equity financing are further discussed on pages 970 and 971.

Rate Earned on Common Stockholders' Equity. As a refinement to the rate earned on total stockholders' equity, earnings may be measured in terms of the residual common stockholders' equity. The **rate earned on common stockholders' equity** is computed by dividing net income after preferred dividend requirements by common stockholders' equity. The average equity for common stockholders should be determined, although the rate is frequently based on beginning or ending common equity.

In the case of Wycat Corporation, preferred dividend requirements are 6%. The rate earned on common stockholders' equity, then, is calculated as follows:

	1984	1983
Net income	$ 70,000	$ 60,000
Less dividend requirements on preferred stock	21,000	21,000
Net income related to common stockholders' equity	$ 49,000	$ 39,000
Common stockholders' equity:		
Beginning of year	$1,095,000	$1,080,000
End of year	$1,118,000	$1,095,000
Average common stockholders' equity	$1,106,500	$1,087,500
Rate earned on average common stockholders' equity	4.4%	3.6%

Earnings per Share. Earnings per share calculations were described in detail in Chapter 22. Recall that the Accounting Principles Board in Opinion No. 15 indicated that earnings per share data were of such importance to investors and others that such data should be presented prominently on the income statement. In computing earnings per share on common stock, earnings are first reduced by the prior dividend right of preferred stock. Computations are made in terms of the weighted average number of common shares outstanding for each period presented. Adjustments are required when a corporation's capital structure includes potentially dilutive securities. If the total potential dilution is material, both primary earnings per share and fully diluted earnings per share must be disclosed. When net income includes below-the-line items, earnings per share should be reported for each major component of income as well as for net income.

For Wycat Corporation, there are no potentially dilutive securities. Earnings per share on common stock is calculated as follows:

	1984	1983
Net income	$70,000	$60,000
Less dividend requirements on preferred stock	21,000	21,000
Income related to common stockholders' equity	$49,000	$39,000
Number of shares of common stock outstanding	75,000	75,000
Earnings per share on common stock	$ .65	$ .52

Dividends per Share. In addition to earnings per share, many companies report **dividends per share** in the financial statements. This amount is computed simply by dividing cash dividends for the year by the number of shares of common stock outstanding. When a significant number of common shares have been issued or retired during a period, an average should be computed; otherwise, the number of common shares outstanding at the end of the period is normally used. For Wycat Corporation, the number of shares of common stock outstanding has remained constant for the past three years. Therefore, the dividends per share are $.35 for 1984 and $.32 for 1983.

Yield on Common Stock. Dividends per share may be used to compute a rate of return on the market value of common stock. Such a rate, referred to as the **yield on common stock,** is found by dividing the annual dividends per common share by the latest market price per common share. For Wycat Corporation the yield on the common stock is computed as follows:

	1984	1983
Dividends for year per common share	$ .35	$ .32
Market value per common share at end of year	$10.00	$ 6.50
Yield on common stock	3.5%	4.9%

Price-Earnings Ratio. The market price of common stock may be expressed as a multiple of earnings to evaluate the attractiveness of common stock as an investment. This measurement is referred to as the **price-earnings ratio** and is computed by dividing the market price per share of stock by the annual earnings per share. Instead of using the average market value of shares for the period covered by earnings, the latest market value is normally used. The lower the price-earnings ratio, the more attractive the investment. Assuming market values per common share of Wycat Corporation stock at the end of 1984 of $10 and at the end of 1983 of $6.50, price-earnings ratios would be computed as follows:

	1984	1983
Market value per common share at end of year	$10.00	$ 6.50
Earnings per share (calculated on page 986)	$ .65	$ .52
Price-earnings ratio	15.4	12.5

As an alternative to the above, earnings per share can be presented as a percentage of the market price of the stock.

Capital Structure Analysis

The composition of a company's capital structure has significant implications for stockholders, creditors, and potential investors and creditors. First, a company's creditors look to stockholders' equity as a margin of safety. To the extent that creditors supply the funds used in a business, they, rather than investors, bear the risks of the business. Second, when funds are obtained by borrowing, the stockholders retain control of a business; when funds are obtained by issuing additional stock, the existing shareholders must share the ownership rights with new investors. Third, as long as the return on investment of borrowed funds exceeds the cost of the debt (interest), the use of debt financing is advantageous. If, however, the return is less than the cost of borrowing, the use of debt is unfavorable. Fourth, there is a legal obligation to pay the interest on borrowed funds and to repay the principal. Dividends, however, are paid at the discretion of the board, and there is no obligation to return contributed capital to investors. Interest payments, unlike dividends, are deductible for tax purposes.

As stockholders' equity increases in relation to total liabilities, the margin of protection to the creditors also increases. From the stockholders' point of view, such an increase makes the organization less vulnerable to declines in business and an inability to meet obligations, and also serves to minimize the cost of carrying debt.

However, it is often advantageous to supplement funds invested by stockholders with borrowed capital. The effects of debt financing can be illustrated as follows. Assume that a company with 10,000 shares of stock outstanding is able to borrow $1,000,000 at 10% interest. The company estimates that pretax earnings will be $80,000 if it operates without the borrowed capital. Income tax is estimated at 40% of earnings. The summary below reports the effects upon net income and earnings per share, assuming a return on borrowed capital of (1) 20%, and (2) 8%.

	Results of Operations Without Borrowed Capital	Results of Operations If Borrowed Capital Earns 20%	Results of Operations If Borrowed Capital Earns 8%
Operating income	$ 80,000	$280,000	$160,000
Interest expense		100,000	100,000
Income before income tax	$ 80,000	$180,000	$ 60,000
Income tax at 40%	32,000	72,000	24,000
Net income	$ 48,000	$108,000	$ 36,000
Number of shares outstanding	10,000	10,000	10,000
Earnings per share	$4.80	$10.80	$3.60

The use of borrowed funds is known as **trading on the equity** or **applying leverage.** A company that relies heavily on debt financing is said to be "highly leveraged." Common leverage measurements include the equity to debt ratio, times interest earned, and fixed charge coverage.

Ratio of Stockholders' Equity to Total Liabilities. Stockholders' and creditors' equities may be expressed in terms of total assets or in terms of each other. For example, stockholders may have a 60 percent interest in total assets and creditors a 40 percent interest. This can be expressed as an **equity to debt ratio** of 1.5 to 1.

For Wycat Corporation, the relationships of stockholders' equity to total liabilities are calculated as follows:

	1984	1983
Stockholders' equity	$1,468,000	$1,445,000
Total liabilities	$ 810,000	$ 946,000
Ratio of stockholders' equity to total liabilities	1.8:1	1.5:1

In analyzing the relationship of stockholders' equity to total liabilities, particular note should be made of lease arrangements. Both property rights provided under the leases and the accompanying liabilities should be considered in evaluating the equities and changes in equities from period to period.

Often the reciprocal of the equity to debt ratio is used. The **debt to equity ratio** is computed by dividing total liabilities by total stockholders' equity. This shows the reciprocal relationship to that just described. It is still a measure of the amount of leverage used by a company. Investors generally prefer a higher debt to equity ratio while creditors favor a lower ratio.

Number of Times Interest Earned. A measure of the debt position of a company in relation to its earnings ability is the **number of times interest is earned.** The calculation is made by dividing income before any charges for interest or income tax by the interest requirements for the period. The resulting figure reflects the company's ability to meet interest payments and the degree of safety afforded the creditors. The number of times interest was earned by Wycat Corporation follows:

	1984	1983
Income before income tax	$100,000	$ 85,000
Add bond interest (10% of $400,000)	40,000	40,000
Amount available in meeting bond interest requirements	$140,000	$125,000
Number of times bond interest requirements were earned	3.5	3.1

Pretax income was used above since income tax applies only after interest is deducted, and it is pretax income that protects creditors. However, the calculation is frequently based on net income since it is consistent with other measures employing net income, and offers a more conservative approach in measuring ability to meet interest requirements. For Wycat Corporation, net income was $70,000 for 1984 and $60,000 for 1983. These amounts would be increased by interest requirements net of tax for each year and then divided by the bond interest expense to derive times interest earned.

A computation similar to times interest earned, but more inclusive, is the **fixed charge coverage.** Fixed charges include such obligations as interest on bonds and notes, lease obligations, and any other recurring financial commitments. The number of times fixed charges are covered is calculated by adding the fixed charges to pretax income and then dividing the total by the fixed charges.

Book Value per Share. Stockholders' equity can be measured by calculating the book value per share as discussed in Chapter 18. When there is only one class of stock outstanding, book value per share is calculated by dividing total stockholders' equity by the number of shares outstanding. When more than one class of stock is outstanding, total stockholders' equity must be allocated to the classes.

Summary of Analytical Measures

Financial ratios, percentages, and other measures are useful tools for analyzing financial statements. They enable statement users to make meaningful judgments about an enterprise's financial condition and operating results. These measures, like financial statements, are more meaningful when compared with similar data for more than one period and with industry averages or other available data. A summary of the major analytical measures discussed in this chapter is presented below and on the following page.

Summary of Major Analytical Measures

	Liquidity Analysis	
(1) Current ratio	$\frac{\text{Current assets}}{\text{Current liabilities}}$	Measures ability to pay short-term debts.
(2) Acid-test ratio	$\frac{\text{Quick assets}}{\text{Current liabilities}}$	Measures immediate ability to pay short-term debts.
	Activity Analysis	
(3) Accounts receivable turnover	$\frac{\text{Net credit sales}}{\text{Average accounts receivable}}$	Measures receivable position and approximate average collection time.
(4) Number of days' sales in receivables	$\frac{\text{Average accounts receivable}}{\text{Average daily credit sales}}$	Measures receivable position and approximate average collection time.
(5) Inventory turnover	$\frac{\text{Cost of goods sold}}{\text{Average inventory}}$	Measures appropriateness of inventory levels in terms of time required to sell or "turn over" goods.
(6) Number of days' sales in inventories	$\frac{\text{Average inventory}}{\text{Average daily cost of goods sold}}$	Measures appropriateness of inventory levels in terms of time required to sell or "turn over" goods.
(7) Total asset turnover	$\frac{\text{Net sales}}{\text{Average total assets}}$	Measures effectiveness of asset utilization.
	Profitability Analysis	
(8) Profit margin on sales	$\frac{\text{Net income}}{\text{Net sales}}$	Measures profit percentage per dollar of sales.
(9) Rate earned on total assets	$\frac{\text{Net income}}{\text{Average total assets}}$	Measures overall asset productivity.
(10) Rate earned on stockholders' equity	$\frac{\text{Net income}}{\text{Average stockholders' equity}}$	Measures rate of return on average stockholders' equity.

(11) Rate earned on common stockholders' equity	(Net income — preferred dividend requirements) / (Average common stockholders' equity)	Measures rate of return on average common stockholders' equity.
(12) Earnings per share	(Net income — preferred dividend requirements) / (Average number of shares of common stock outstanding)	Measures net income per share of common stock.
(13) Dividends per share	(Dividends on common stock) / (Average number of shares of common stock outstanding)	Measures dividends per share of common stock.
(14) Yield on common stock	(Dividends per share of common stock) / (Market value per share of common stock)	Measures rate of cash return to stockholders.
(15) Price-earnings ratio	(Market price per share of common stock) / (Earnings per share of common stock)	Measures attractiveness of stock as an investment.
	Capital Structure Analysis	
(16) Equity to debit ratio	(Stockholders' equity) / (Total liabilities)	Measures use of debt to finance operations.
(17) Times interest earned	(Income before taxes and interest expense) / (Interest expense)	Measures ability to meet interest payments.

INTERPRETATION OF ANALYSES

The analyses discussed in this chapter are designed to help an analyst arrive at certain conclusions with regard to a business. As previously stated, these are merely guides to intelligent interpretation of financial data.

All ratios and measurements need not be used, but only those that will actually assist in arriving at informed conclusions with respect to questions raised. The measurements developed need to be interpreted in terms of the circumstances of a particular enterprise, the conditions of the particular industry in which the enterprise operates, and the general business and economic environment. If measurements are to be of maximum value, they need to be compared with similar data developed for the particular enterprise for past periods, with standard measurements for the industry as a whole, and with pertinent data relating to general business conditions and price fluctuations affecting the individual enterprise. Only through intelligent use and integration of the foregoing sources of data can financial weaknesses and strengths be identified and reliable opinions be developed concerning business structure, operations, and growth.

QUESTIONS

1. What groups may be interested in a company's financial statements?
2. What types of questions requiring financial statement analysis might be raised by external users, such as investors and creditors, as contrasted to internal management?
3. What are the factors that one would look for in judging a company's (a) liquidity, (b) stability, (c) profitability, (d) growth potential?
4. Why are comparative financial statements considered more meaningful than statements prepared for a single period? What conditions increase the usefulness of comparative statements?
5. Distinguish between horizontal and vertical analysis. What special purpose does each serve?
6. What information is provided by analysis of comparative changes in financial position that is not available from analysis of comparative balance sheets and income statements?
7. What is meant by a *common-size* statement? What are its advantages?
8. Mention some factors that may limit the comparability of financial statements of two companies in the same industry.
9. What factors may be responsible for a change in a company's net income from one year to the next?
10. The Black Co. develops the following measurements for 1984 as compared with the year 1983. What additional information would you require before arriving at favorable or unfavorable conclusions for each item?

(a) Net income has increased $70,000.
(b) Sales returns and allowances have increased by $25,000.
(c) The gross profit rate has increased by 5%.
(d) Purchase discounts have increased by $5,000.
(e) Working capital has increased by $85,000.
(f) Accounts receivable have increased by $150,000.
(g) Inventories have decreased by $100,000.
(h) Retained earnings have decreased by $300,000.

11. Define working capital and appraise its significance.
12. Distinguish between the current ratio and the acid-test ratio.
13. Balance sheets for the Rich Corporation and the Poor Corporation each show a working capital total of $500,000. Does this indicate that the short-term liquidity of the two corporations is approximately the same? Explain.
14. (a) How is the accounts receivable turnover computed? (b) How is the number of days' purchases in accounts payable computed?
15. (a) How is the merchandise inventory turnover computed? (b) What precautions are necessary in arriving at the basis for the turnover calculation? (c) How would you interpret a rising inventory turnover rate?
16. The ratio of stockholders' equity to total liabilities offers information about the long-term liquidity of a business. Explain.
17. Indicate how each of the following measurements is calculated and appraise its significance:

(a) The number of times bond interest requirements were earned.
(b) The number of times preferred dividend requirements were earned.
(c) The rate of earnings on the common stockholders' equity.
(d) The earnings per share on common stock.
(e) The price-earnings ratio on common stock.
(f) The dividends per share on common stock.
(g) The yield on common stock.

DISCUSSION CASES

case 25-1 (How should we finance our expansion?) The Hansen Co. is considering expanding its operations. The company's balance sheet at December 31, 1984, is presented below.

Hansen Co.
Balance Sheet
December 31, 1984

Assets		Liabilities		
Cash	$ 33,500	Accounts payable	$ 30,000	
Accounts receivable	38,500	Bonds payable	110,000	
Inventory	42,000	Total liabilities		$140,000
Land	80,000			
Buildings and equipment (net)	46,000	Stockholders' Equity		
		Preferred stock, 8% cumulative, par $100	$ 30,000	
		Common stock, par $25	40,000	
		Retained earnings	30,000	
		Total stockholders' equity		100,000
Total assets	$240,000	Total liabilities and stockholders' equity		$240,000

Each $1,000 bond is convertible at the option of the bondholder to 40 shares of common stock. The bonds carry an interest rate of 12%, and are callable at 100. The company's 1984 income before taxes was $82,500 and was $50,000 after taxes. The preferred stock is callable at par. The common stock has a market price of $60 per share.

The company's management has identified several alternatives to raise the $100,000:

(1) Issue additional bonds.
(2) Call in the convertible bonds to force conversion and then issue additional bonds.
(3) Issue additional 8% cumulative preferred stock.
(4) Issue additional common stock.

Evaluate the company's leverage position and discuss the advantages and disadvantages of each alternative.

case 25-2 (Evaluating alternative investments) Sibyl Sanders is considering investing $10,000 and wishes to know which of two companies offers the better alternative.

The Green Company earned $42,000 last year on average total assets (net of interest and taxes) of $280,000, and average stockholders' equity of $210,000. The company's shares are selling on the market at $100 per share; 6,300 shares of common stock are outstanding.

The Brown Company earned $16,250 last year on average total assets (net of interest and taxes) of $125,000 and average stockholders' equity of $100,000. The company's common shares are selling on the market at $78 per share; 2,500 shares are outstanding.

Which stock should Sanders buy?

case 25-3 (Analyzing earnings) Angus Bighorn owns two businesses: a grocery store and a retail department store. The investment in land, buildings, and equipment is approximately the same in either business.

Grocery Store		Department Store	
Net sales	$1,050,000	Net sales	$670,000
Cost of goods sold	1,000,000	Cost of goods sold	600,000
Average inventory	50,000	Average inventory	200,000
Operating expenses	39,500	Operating expenses	36,500

Which business earns more income? Which business earns a higher return on its investment in inventory? Which business would you consider more profitable?

case 25-4 (Should the FASB set standards for financial ratios?) Financial ratios can be computed using many different formulas. In a 1982 article in the *CPA Journal*, the author recommends that the FASB become involved in identifying common formulas and ratios that would be included in all financial statements. What are the advantages in pursuing such a recommendation? What are the difficulties?

EXERCISES

exercise 25-1 (Index numbers)

Sales for the Higgins Company for a five-year period and an industry sales index for this period are listed below. Convert both series into indexes employing 1980 as the base year.

	1984	1983	1982	1981	1980
Sales of Higgins Company (in thousands of dollars)	$8,400	$9,030	$8,710	$8,850	$8,530
Industry sales index (1970 − 1974 = 100)	190	212	210	170	158

exercise 25-2 (Comparative cost of goods sold schedule)

Cost of goods sold data for The Tri-Arc Co. are presented below:

	1984	1983
Inventory, January 1	$ 40,000	$ 25,000
Purchases	100,000	90,000
Goods available for sale	$140,000	$115,000
Less inventory, December 31	35,000	40,000
Cost of goods sold	$105,000	$ 75,000

Prepare a comparative schedule of cost of goods sold showing dollar and percentage changes.

exercise 25-3 (Vertical analysis)

The financial position of the Anderson Co. at the end of 1984 and 1983 is as follows:

	1984	1983
Assets		
Current assets	$ 40,000	$ 42,000
Long-term investments	15,000	14,000
Land, buildings, and equipment (net)	50,000	55,000
Intangible assets	10,000	10,000
Other assets	5,000	6,000
Total assets	$120,000	$127,000

	1984	1983
Liabilities		
Current liabilities	$ 15,000	$ 20,000
Long-term liabilities	38,000	42,000
Total liabilities	$ 53,000	$ 62,000
Stockholders' Equity		
Preferred 6% stock	$ 10,000	$ 9,000
Common stock	39,000	39,000
Additional paid-in capital	5,000	5,000
Retained earnings	13,000	12,000
Total stockholders' equity	$ 67,000	$ 65,000
Total liabilities and stockholders' equity	$120,000	$127,000

Prepare a comparative balance sheet offering a percentage analysis of component items in terms of total assets and total liabilities and stockholders' equity for each year.

exercise 25-4 (Liquidity ratios)

The following data are taken from the comparative balance sheet prepared for the Morton Company:

	1984	1983
Cash	$ 20,000	$ 10,000
Marketable securities (net)	9,000	35,000
Trade receivables (net)	43,000	30,000
Inventories	65,000	50,000
Prepaid expenses	3,000	2,000
Land, buildings, and equipment (net)	79,000	75,000
Intangible assets	10,000	15,000
Other assets	7,000	8,000
	$236,000	$225,000
Current liabilities	$ 80,000	$ 60,000

(1) From the data given, compute for 1984 and for 1983: (a) the working capital, (b) the current ratio, (c) the acid-test ratio, (d) the ratio of current assets to total assets, (e) the ratio of cash to current liabilities.
(2) Evaluate each of the above changes.

exercise 25-5 (Analysis of inventory position)

Income statements for the Andrus Sales Co. show the following:

	1984	1983	1982
Sales	$105,000	$100,000	$ 75,000
Cost of goods sold:			
Beginning inventory	$ 30,000	$ 25,000	$ 5,000
Purchases	95,000	80,000	85,000
	$125,000	$105,000	$ 90,000
Ending inventory	50,000	30,000	25,000
	$ 75,000	$ 75,000	$ 65,000
Gross profit on sales	$ 30,000	$ 25,000	$ 10,000

Give whatever measurements may be developed in analyzing the inventory position at the end of each year. What conclusions would you make concerning the inventory trend?

exercise 25-6 (Inventory turnover)

The following data are taken from the Thomas Corporation records for the years ending December 31, 1984, 1983, and 1982.

	1984	1983	1982
Finished goods inventory	$ 60,000	$ 40,000	$ 30,000
Goods in process inventory	60,000	65,000	60,000
Raw materials inventory	60,000	40,000	35,000
Sales	400,000	340,000	300,000
Cost of goods sold	225,000	230,000	210,000
Cost of goods manufactured	260,000	250,000	200,000
Raw materials used in production	150,000	130,000	120,000

Compute turnover rates for 1984 and for 1983 for (a) finished goods, (b) goods in process, and (c) raw materials.

exercise 25-7 (Analysis of accounts payable)

The total purchases of goods by The Fast Sell Company during 1984 were $360,000. All purchases were on a 2/10, n/30 basis. The average balance in the vouchers payable account was $33,000. Was the company prompt, slow, or average in paying for goods? How many days' average purchases were there in accounts payable, assuming a 360-day year?

exercise 25-8 (Analysis of capital structure)

The Burlington Corporation estimates that pretax earnings for the year ended December 31, 1984, will be $70,000 if it operates without borrowed capital. Income tax is 40% of earnings. There are 15,000 shares of common stock outstanding for the entire year. Assuming that the company is able to borrow $800,000 at 12% interest, show the effects on net income if borrowed capital earns (1) 20%, and (2) 10%.

exercise 25-9 (Profitability analysis)

The balance sheets for the Smith Corp. showed long-term liabilities and stockholders' equity balances at the end of each year as given below:

	1984	1983	1982
8% Bonds payable	$ 600,000	$600,000	$600,000
Preferred 6% stock, $100 par	600,000	400,000	400,000
Common stock, $25 par	1,200,000	900,000	900,000
Additional paid-in capital	150,000	100,000	100,000
Retained earnings	300,000	100,000	50,000

Net income after income tax was: 1984, $110,000; 1983, $80,000. Using the foregoing data, compute for each year:

(a) The rate of earnings on average total stockholders' equity.
(b) The number of times bond interest requirements were earned (income after tax).
(c) The number of times preferred dividend requirements were earned.
(d) The rate earned on average common stockholders' equity.
(e) The earnings per share on common stock.

exercise 25-10 (Inventory turnover)

The controller of the Pratt Manufacturing Co. wishes to analyze the activity of the finished goods, goods in process, and raw materials inventories. Using the followng information, compute the inventory turnovers.

Finished goods inventory, 12/31/83	$112,500
Finished goods inventory, 12/31/84	237,500
Goods in process inventory, 12/31/83	211,000
Goods in process inventory, 12/31/84	239,000
Raw materials inventory, 12/31/83	125,000
Raw materials inventory, 12/31/84	175,000
Cost of goods sold, 1984	245,000
Cost of goods manufactured, 1984	337,500
Cost of materials used, 1984	225,000

exercise 25-11 (Return on stockholders' equity)

Donna Clark wishes to know which of two companies will yield the greater rate of return on an investment in common stock. Financial information for 1984 for the Lopez Company and the Baker Company is presented below:

	Lopez Co.	Baker Co.
Net income	$ 140,000	$ 120,000
Preferred stock (7%)	600,000	600,000
Common stockholders' equity:		
January 1, 1984	1,450,000	1,100,000
December 31, 1984	1,350,000	980,000

Determine which company earned the greater return on common stockholders' equity in 1984.

exercise 25-12 (Analysis of financial data)

For each of the following numbered items, you are to select the letter items that indicate its effects on the corporation's statements. Indicate your choice by giving the letters identifying the effects that you select. If there is no appropriate response among the effects listed, leave the item blank. If more than one effect is applicable to a particular item, be sure to list *all* applicable letters. (Assume the state statutes do not permit declaration of nonliquidating dividends except from earnings.)

Item

(1) Declaration of a cash dividend due in one month on preferred stock.
(2) Declaration and payment of an ordinary stock dividend.
(3) Receipt of a cash dividend, not previously recorded, on stock of another corporation.
(4) Passing of a dividend on preferred stock.
(5) Receipt of preferred shares as a dividend on stock held as a temporary investment. This was not a regularly recurring dividend.
(6) Payment of dividend mentioned in (1).
(7) Issue of new common shares in a 5-for-1 stock split.

Effect

A. Reduces working capital.
B. Increases working capital.
C. Reduces current ratio.
D. Increases current ratio.
E. Reduces the dollar amount of total capital stock.
F. Increases the dollar amount of total capital stock.
G. Reduces total retained earnings.
H. Increases total retained earnings.
I. Reduces equity per share of common stock.
J. Reduces equity of each common stockholder.

(AICPA adapted)

exercise 25-13 (Analysis of financial data)

The December 31, 1984 balance sheet of Ratio Inc. is presented on the next page. These are the only accounts in Ratio's balance sheet. Amounts indicated by a question mark (?) can be calculated from the additional information given.

Assets		Liabilities and Stockholders' Equity	
Cash	$ 25,000	Accounts payable (trade)	$?
Accounts receivable (net)	?	Income taxes payable (current)	25,000
Inventory	?	Long-term debt	?
Property, plant, and equipment (net)	294,000	Common stock	300,000
		Retained earnings	?
	$432,000		$?

Additional information:

Current ratio (at year end)	1.5 to 1
Total liabilities divided by total stockholders' equity	.8
Inventory turnover based on sales and ending inventory	15 times
Inventory turnover based on cost of goods sold and ending inventory	10.5 times
Gross margin for 1984	$315,000

(1) What was Ratio's December 31, 1984 balance in trade accounts payable?
(a) $67,000. (b) $92,000. (c) $182,000. (d) $207,000.
(2) What was Ratio's December 31, 1984 balance in retained earnings?
(a) $60,000 deficit. (b) $60,000. (c) $132,000 deficit. (d) $132,000.
(3) What was Ratio's December 31, 1984 balance in the inventory account?
(a) $21,000. (b) $30,000. (c) $70,000. (d) $135,000.

(AICPA adapted)

PROBLEMS

problem 25-1 (Comparative statements)

Operations for the Huish Company for 1984 and 1983 are summarized below:

	1984	1983
Sales	$500,000	$450,000
Sales returns	20,000	10,000
Net sales	$480,000	$440,000
Cost of goods sold	350,000	240,000
Gross profit on sales	$130,000	$200,000
Selling and general expenses	100,000	120,000
Operating income	$ 30,000	$ 80,000
Other expenses	35,000	30,000
Income (loss) before income tax	$ (5,000)	$ 50,000
Income tax		22,500
Net income (loss)	$ (5,000)	$ 27,500

Instructions:

(1) Prepare a comparative income statement showing dollar changes and percentage changes for 1984 as compared with 1983.
(2) Prepare a comparative income statement offering a percentage analysis of component revenue and expense items of net sales for each year.

problem 25-2 (Comparative and common-size statements)

The financial position of Westgate Corp. at the end of 1984 and at the end of 1983 is summarized as follows:

Assets	1984	1983
Current assets:		
Cash	$ 70,000	$ 90,000
Marketable securities	90,000	100,000
Notes and accounts receivable, less allowance	400,000	300,000
Finished goods	400,000	350,000
Goods in process	200,000	160,000
Raw materials	350,000	300,000
Miscellaneous prepaid items	40,000	60,000
Total current assets	$1,550,000	$1,360,000
Long-term investments:		
Bond redemption fund	$ 400,000	$ 300,000
Investment in properties not in current use	250,000	250,000
Total long-term investments	$ 650,000	$ 550,000
Land, buildings, and equipment at cost, less accumulated depreciation	$ 920,000	$1,000,000
Intangible assets	$ 60,000	$ 70,000
Other assets:		
Unamortized bond issue costs	$ 34,000	$ 40,000
Machinery rearrangement costs	16,000	20,000
Total other assets	$ 50,000	$ 60,000
Total assets	$3,230,000	$3,040,000
Liabilities		
Current liabilities:		
Notes and accounts payable	$ 250,000	$ 240,000
Income tax payable	80,000	50,000
Payrolls, interest, and tax payable	50,000	40,000
Dividends payable	10,000	15,000
Miscellaneous payables	10,000	15,000
Total current liabilities	$ 400,000	$ 360,000
Long-term liabilities—8%, 10-year first-mortgage bonds	300,000	350,000
Estimated employee pensions payable	110,000	150,000
Deferred revenues	20,000	30,000
Total liabilities	$ 830,000	$ 890,000
Stockholders' Equity		
Contributed capital:		
Preferred 6% stock, $25 par	$ 400,000	$ 400,000
No-par common stock, $10 stated value	600,000	600,000
Additional paid-in capital	700,000	700,000
Total contributed capital	$1,700,000	$1,700,000
Retained earnings:		
Appropriated	$ 350,000	$ 300,000
Unappropriated	350,000	150,000
Total retained earnings	$ 700,000	$ 450,000
Total stockholders' equity	$2,400,000	$2,150,000
Total liabilities and stockholders' equity	$3,230,000	$3,040,000

Instructions:

(1) Prepare a comparative balance sheet showing dollar changes and changes in terms of ratios for 1984 as compared with 1983.

(2) Prepare a common-size balance sheet comparing financial structure ratios for 1984 with those for 1983.

problem 25-3 (Common-size statements)

Balance sheet data for the Pen Company and the Ink Company are as follows:

	Pen Company	Ink Company
Assets		
Current assets	$ 51,000	$ 24,000
Long-term investments	5,000	28,000
Land, buildings, and equipment (net)	48,000	52,000
Intangible assets	6,000	10,000
Other assets	5,000	6,000
Total assets	$115,000	$120,000
Liabilities		
Current liabilities	$ 15,000	$ 18,000
Long-term liabilities	25,000	30,000
Deferred revenues	5,000	7,000
Total liabilities	$ 45,000	$ 55,000
Stockholders' Equity		
Preferred stock	$ 5,000	$ 10,000
Common stock	30,000	20,000
Additional paid-in capital	25,000	18,500
Retained earnings	10,000	16,500
Total stockholders' equity	$ 70,000	$ 65,000
Total liabilities and stockholders' equity	$115,000	$120,000

Instructions:

(1) Prepare a common-size statement comparing balance sheet data for the year.
(2) What analytical conclusions can be drawn from this comparative common-size statement?

problem 25-4 (Index numbers)

Sales for Elton Mfg. Co. and its chief competitor, the Polk Company, and the sales index for the industry, are given below:

	1984	1983	1982	1981	1980
Sales of Elton Mfg. Co. (in thousands of dollars)	$7,000	$7,280	$7,735	$8,450	$8,385
Sales of Polk Company (in thousands of dollars)	$9,700	$9,690	$9,975	$9,785	$9,880
Industry sales index (1974 = 100)	140	154	161	147	133

Instructions:

(1) Convert the three series to index numbers using 1980 as the base year.
(2) Prepare a short report for the management of Elton Mfg. Co. summarizing your findings.

problem 25-5 (Computation of various ratios)

The balance sheet data for the Passanela Corp. on December 31, 1984, are as follows:

Assets		Liabilities and Stockholders' Equity	
Cash	$ 100,000	Notes and accounts payable	$ 130,000
Marketable securities	25,000	Income tax payable	40,000
Notes and accounts receivable (net)	175,000	Wages and interest payable	10,000
Inventories	600,000	Dividends payable	25,000
Prepaid expenses	15,000	Bonds payable	450,000
Bond redemption fund (securities of other companies)	400,000	Deferred revenues	30,000
Land, buildings, and equipment (net)	780,000	Common stock, $20 par	1,200,000
Intangible assets	420,000	Preferred 6% stock, $20 par (noncumulative, liquidating value at par)	200,000
Unamortized bond issue costs	20,000	Retained earnings appropriated for plant expansion	200,000
		Retained earnings	250,000
	$2,535,000		$2,535,000

Instructions: From the balance sheet data, compute the following:

(1) The amount of working capital.

(

(

(

(

...nds payable.

problem 25-6 (Li...

The following are co... for the three-year period 1982-1984.

Income Statement Data

	1984	1983	1982
Net sales	$1,200,000	$ 900,000	$1,100,000
Cost of goods sold	760,000	600,000	650,000
Gross profit on sales	$ 440,000	$ 300,000	$ 450,000
Selling, general, and other expenses	350,000	280,000	290,000
Operating income	$ 90,000	$ 20,000	$ 160,000
Income tax	40,500	9,000	72,000
Net income	$ 49,500	$ 11,000	$ 88,000
Dividends paid	35,000	30,000	30,000
Net increase (decrease) in retained earnings	$ 14,500	$ (19,000)	$ 58,000

Balance Sheet Data

Assets	1984	1983	1982
Cash	$ 60,000	$ 40,000	$ 75,000
Trade notes and accounts receivable (net)	300,000	320,000	300,000
Inventory (at cost)	380,000	420,000	350,000
Prepaid expenses	30,000	10,000	40,000
Land, buildings, and equipment (net)	760,000	600,000	690,000
Intangible assets	100,000	100,000	125,000
Other assets	70,000	10,000	20,000
	$1,700,000	$1,500,000	$1,600,000
Liabilities and Stockholders' Equity			
Trade notes and accounts payable	$ 120,000	$ 180,000	$ 170,000
Wages, interest, dividends payable	25,000	25,000	25,000
Income tax payable	39,500	10,000	80,000
Miscellaneous current liabilities	10,000	4,000	10,000
8% bonds payable	300,000	300,000	300,000
Deferred revenues	10,000	10,000	25,000
Preferred 6% stock, cumulative, $100 par and liquidating value	200,000	200,000	200,000
No-par common stock, $10 stated value	500,000	400,000	400,000
Additional paid-in capital	310,000	200,000	200,000
Retained earnings—appropriated	80,000	60,000	60,000
Retained earnings—unappropriated	105,500	111,000	130,000
	$1,700,000	$1,500,000	$1,600,000

Instructions:

(1) From the foregoing data, calculate comparative measurements for 1984 and 1983 as follows:
  (a) The amount of working capital.
  (b) The current ratio.
  (c) The acid-test ratio.
  (d) The trade receivables turnover rate for the year (all sales are on a credit basis).
  (e) The average days' sales in trade receivables at the end of the year (assume a 360-day year and all sales on a credit basis).
  (f) The trade payables turnover rate for the year.
  (g) The average days' purchases in trade payables at the end of the year.
  (h) The inventory turnover rate.
  (i) The number of days' sales in the inventory at the end of the year.
  (j) The ratio of stockholders' equity to total liabilities.
  (k) The ratio of land, buildings, and equipment to bonds payable.
  (l) The ratio of stockholders' equity to land, buildings, and equipment.
  (m) The book value per share of preferred stock (no dividends in arrears).
  (n) The book value per share of common stock.

(2) Based on the measurements made in (1), evaluate the liquidity position of Draper Inc. at the end of 1984 as compared with the end of 1983.

problem 25-7 (Profitability analysis)

Use the comparative data for Draper Inc. as given in Problem 25-6.

Instructions:

(1) Compute comparative measurements for 1984 and 1983 as follows:
  (a) The ratio of net sales to average total assets.
  (b) The ratio of net sales to average land, buildings, and equipment.
  (c) The rate earned on net sales.
  (d) The gross profit rate on net sales.
  (e) The rate earned on average total assets.
  (f) The rate earned on average stockholders' equity.
  (g) The number of times bond interest requirements were earned (before income tax).
  (h) The number of times preferred dividend requirements were earned.
  (i) The rate earned on average common stockholders' equity.
  (j) The earnings per share on common stock.

(2) Based on the measurements made in (1), evaluate the profitability of Draper Inc. for 1984 as compared with 1983.

problem 25-8 (Analysis of inventory, receivables, and payables)

Inventory and receivable balances and also gross profit data for The Busy Baker Co. appear below:

	1984	1983	1982
Balance sheet data:			
Inventory, December 31	$100,000	$ 90,000	$ 80,000
Accounts receivable, December 31	60,000	40,000	20,000
Accounts payable, December 31	70,000	60,000	45,000
Net purchases	140,000	100,000	80,000
Income statement data:			
Net sales	$290,000	$270,000	$250,000
Cost of goods sold	210,000	200,000	180,000
Gross profit on sales	$ 80,000	$ 70,000	$ 70,000

Instructions: Assuming a 300-day business year and all sales on a credit basis, compute the following measurements for 1984 and 1983.

(1) The receivables turnover rate.

(2) The average days' sales in receivables at the end of the year.
(3) The inventory turnover rate.
(4) The number of days' sales in inventory at the end of the year.
(5) The accounts payable turnover rate.
(6) The number of days' purchases in accounts payable at the end of the year.

problem 25-9 (Book value per share)

Stockholders' equities for the Strickling Corporation at the end of 1984 and 1983 were:

	1984	1983
Preferred 6% stock, $50 par and liquidating value	$100,000	$100,000
Common stock, $10 par	300,000	200,000
Additional paid-in capital	500,000	350,000
Retained earnings	90,000	150,000

Instructions: Compute the book value per share of both preferred stock and common stock at the end of 1984 and at the end of 1983, assuming the conditions stated in each case below. (Assume dividends may legally be paid from additional paid-in capital.)

(1) Preferred is cumulative; dividend requirements on preferred stock have been met annually.
(2) Preferred is cumulative; the last dividend on preferred stock was paid for the year 1981.

problem 25-10 (Comprehensive analysis of financial data)

The following are partially condensed financial statements.

Medal Company
Balance Sheet
December 31, 1984

Assets	
Cash	$ 63,000
Trade receivables, less estimated uncollectibles of $12,000	238,000
Inventories	170,000
Prepaid expenses	7,000
Land, buildings, and equipment, cost less $182,000 charged to operations	390,000
Other assets	13,000
	$881,000
Liabilities and Stockholders' Equity	
Accounts and notes payable—trade	$ 98,000
Accrued liabilities payable	17,000
Income tax payable	18,000
First-mortgage, 7% bonds, due in 1991	150,000
$7 Preferred stock—no par value (entitled to $110 per share in liquidation); authorized 1,000 shares; in treasury 400 shares; outstanding 600 shares	108,000
Common stock—no par; authorized 100,000 shares, issued and outstanding 10,000 shares stated at a nominal value of $10 per share	100,000
Paid-in capital from sale of common stock at more than stated value	242,000
Retained earnings appropriated for plant expansion	50,000
Retained earnings appropriated for cost of treasury stock	47,000
Retained earnings	98,000
Cost of 400 shares of treasury stock	(47,000)
	$881,000

Notes: (1) Working capital—December 31, 1983, was $205,000. (2) Trade receivables—December 31, 1983, were $220,000 gross, $206,000 net. (3) Dividends for 1984 have been declared and paid. (4) There has been no change in amount of bonds outstanding during 1984.

Medal Company
Income Statement
For the Year Ended December 31, 1984

	Cash	Credit	Total
Gross sales	$116,000	$876,000	$992,000
Less: Sales discount	$ 3,000	$ 12,000	$ 15,000
Sales returns and allowances	1,000	6,000	7,000
	$ 4,000	$ 18,000	$ 22,000
Net sales	$112,000	$858,000	$970,000

Cost of goods sold:		
Inventory of finished goods, January 1	$ 92,000	
Cost of goods manufactured	680,000	
Inventory of finished goods, December 31	(100,000)	672,000
Gross profit on sales		$298,000
Selling expenses	$173,000	
General expenses	70,000	243,000
Income from operations		$ 55,000
Other additions and deductions (net)		3,000
Income before income tax		$ 58,000
Income tax (estimated)		18,000
Net income		$ 40,000

Instructions: For each item listed below select the best answer from the approximate answers. Indicate your choice by giving the appropriate letter for each. Give the calculations in support of each choice.

Items To Be Computed	Approximate Answers				
	(a)	(b)	(c)	(d)	(e)
(1) Acid test ratio	3.2:1	2.3:1	2.9:1	2.4:1	3.07:1
(2) Average number of days' charge sales uncollected	86	94	103	100	105
(3) Average finished goods turnover	7	10.1	10.3	9.7	6.7
(4) Number of times bond interest was earned (before tax)	4.81	6.83	6.52	10.3	5.92
(5) Number of times preferred dividend was earned	5.71	8.3	13.8	9.52	8.52
(6) Earnings per share of common stock	$4.00	$3.30	$3.58	$ 5.10	$5.38
(7) Book value per share of common stock	$33.80	$35.00	$49.80	$48.80	$53.20
(8) Current ratio	3.6:1	1:2.7	2.7:1	4.2:1	1:3.6

(AICPA adapted)

problem 25-11 (Financial statement analysis)

Growth Corporation's management is concerned over the corporation's current financial position and return on investment. They request your assistance in analyzing their financial statements and furnish the following information:

Schedule of Working Capital—December 31, 1984

Current liabilities		$223,050
Less current assets:		
Cash	$ 5,973	
Accounts receivable (net)	70,952	
Inventory	113,125	190,050
Working capital deficit		$ 33,000

Growth Corporation
Income Statement
For Year Ended December 31, 1984

Sales (90,500 units)	$760,200
Cost of goods sold	452,500
Gross profit	$307,700
Selling and general expenses, including depreciation of $22,980	155,660
Income before income tax	$152,040
Income tax	68,418
Net income	$ 83,622

Assets other than current assets consist of land, buildings, and equipment with a book value of $352,950 on December 31, 1984.

Sales of 100,000 units are forecasted for 1985. Within this relevant range of activity, costs are estimated as follows (excluding income tax):

	Fixed Costs	Variable Costs per Unit
Cost of goods sold		$4.90
Selling and general expenses, including depreciation of $15,450	$129,720	1.10
Total	$129,720	$6.00

The income tax rate is expected to be 40%. Past experience indicates that current assets vary in direct proportion to sales.

Instructions:

(1) Assuming Growth Corporation operates 300 days per year, compute the following (show your computations):
  (a) Number of days' sales uncollected.
  (b) Inventory turnover.
  (c) Number of days' operations to cover the working capital deficit.
  (d) Return on total assets as a product of asset turnover and the net income ratio (sometimes called profit margin).

(2) Management feels that in 1985 the market will support a sales price of $8.30 at a sales volume of 100,000 units. Compute the rate of return on book value of total assets after income tax assuming management's expectations are realized.

(AICPA adapted)

problem 25-12 (Comprehensive financial statement analysis)

Financial analysis is often applied to test the reasonableness of the relationships among current financial data against those of prior financial data. Given prior financial relationships and a few key amounts, a CPA could prepare estimates of current financial data to test the reasonableness of data furnished by a client. All Seasons Sales Corporation has in recent years maintained the following relationships among the data on its financial statements.

Gross profit on net sales	40%
Net profit rate on net sales	10%
Rate of selling expenses to net sales	20%
Accounts receivable turnover	8 per year
Inventory turnover	6 per year
Acid-test ratio	2 to 1
Current ratio	3 to 1
Quick-asset composition: 8% cash, 32% marketable securities, 60% accounts receivable	
Asset turnover	2 per year

Ratio of total assets to intangible assets	20 to 1
Ratio of accumulated depreciation to cost of fixed assets	1 to 3
Ratio of accounts receivable to accounts payable	1.5 to 1
Ratio of working capital to stockholders' equity	1 to 1.6
Ratio of total liabilities to stockholders' equity	1 to 2

The corporation had a net income of $120,000 for 1984, which resulted in earnings of $5.20 per share of common stock. Additional information includes the following:

(a) Capital stock authorized, issued (all in 1976), and outstanding: Common, $10 per share par value, issued at 10% premium; 6% Preferred, $100 per share par value, issued at a 10% premium.
(b) Market value per share of common at December 31, 1984, $78.
(c) Preferred dividends paid in 1984, $3,000.
(d) Number of times interest earned in 1984, 21.
(e) The amounts of the following were the same at December 31, 1984 as at January 1, 1984. Inventory, accounts receivable, 8% bonds payable—due 1986, and total stockholders' equity.
(f) All purchases and sales were "on account."

Instructions:

(1) Prepare in good form: (a) the condensed balance sheet, and (b) the condensed income statement for the year ending December 31, 1984, presenting the amounts you would expect to appear on All Seasons' financial statements (ignoring income tax). Major captions appearing on All Seasons' balance sheet are: Current assets, Fixed assets, Intangible assets, Current liabilities, Long-term liabilities, and Stockholders' equity. In addition to the accounts divulged in the problem, you should include accounts for prepaid expenses, miscellaneous expenses payable, and administrative expenses. Supporting computations should be in good form.
(2) Compute the following for 1984 (show your computations):
   (a) Rate of return on stockholders' equity.
   (b) Price-earnings ratio for common stock.
   (c) Dividends paid per share of common stock.
   (d) Dividends paid per share of preferred stock.
   (e) Yield on common stock.

(AICPA adapted)

Appendix A

FUTURE AND PRESENT VALUE: CONCEPTS AND APPLICATIONS

Conceptual knowledge of future and present value techniques is becoming increasingly important for accountants. To review these concepts, this appendix provides (1) a brief explanation of the basic concepts and applications of interest; and, (2) illustrations of business problems utilizing future and present value tables.

INTEREST DEFINED

Money, like other commodities, is a scarce resource, and a payment for its use is generally required. This payment (cost) for the use of money is **interest**. For example, if $100 is borrowed, whether from an individual, a business, or a bank, and $110 is paid back, $10 interest has been paid for the use of the $100. Thus, interest represents the excess cash paid or received over the amount of cash borrowed or loaned.

Generally interest is specified in terms of a percentage rate for a period of time, usually a year. For example, interest at 8% means the annual cost of borrowing an amount of money, called the **principal**, is equal to 8% of that amount. If $100 is borrowed at 8% annual interest, the total to be repaid is $108—the amount of the principal, $100, and the interest for a year, $8 ($100 × .08 × 1). Interest on a $1,000 note for 6 months at 8% is $40 ($1,000 × .08 × 6/12). Thus, the formula for computing **simple interest** is $i = p \times r \times t$, where:

i = Amount of simple interest
p = Principal amount
r = Interest rate (per period)
t = Time (number of periods)

The formula just presented relates to simple interest. Many transactions involve **compound interest.** This means that the amount of interest earned for a certain period is added to the principal for the next period. Interest for the subsequent period is computed on the new amount, which includes both principal and accumulated interest. As an example, assume $100 is deposited in a bank and left for two years at 6% annual interest. At the end of the first year, the $100 has earned $6 interest ($100 × .06 × 1). At the end of the second year, $6 has been earned for the first year, plus another $6.36 interest (6% on the $106 balance at the beginning of the second year). Thus, the total interest earned is $12.36 rather than $12 because of the compounding effect. The table below, based on the foregoing example, illustrates the computation of simple and compound interest for four years. Formulas relative to common compound interest situations are provided in the next section of this appendix.

	Simple Interest			Compound Interest		
Year	*Computation*	*Interest*	*Total*	*Computation*	*Interest*	*Total*
1	($100 × .06)	$6	106	($100.00 × .06)	$6.00	$106.00
2	(100 × .06)	6	112	(106.00 × .06)	6.36	112.36
3	(100 × .06)	6	118	(112.36 × .06)	6.74	119.10
4	(100 × .06)	6	124	(119.10 × .06)	7.15	126.25

Because of the compounding effect of interest, an adjustment of the stated annual rate of interest to its effective rate and for the appropriate number of interest periods often must be made. To illustrate, 6% annual interest for 10 years compounded semiannually would be converted to 3% for 20 periods; 12% for 6 years compounded quarterly would convert to 3% for 24 periods.

FUTURE AND PRESENT VALUE COMPUTATIONS

Since money earns interest, $100 received today is more valuable than $100 received one year from today. Future and present value analysis is a method of comparing the value of money received or expected to be received at different time periods.

Analyses requiring alternative computations in terms of present dollars relative to future dollars may be viewed from one of two perspectives, the future or the present. If a future time frame is chosen, all cash flows must be **accumulated** to that future point. In this instance, the effect of interest is to increase the amounts or values over time. Examples of questions that might be answered by future value computations include:

How much will $500 deposited today at 6% annual interest amount to in 20 years?

How long would it take to accumulate a $10,000 down payment on a home if one saved $100 a month and received 5% per year on those savings?

What rate of return on an investment must be received for money to double in 20 years?

If, on the other hand, the present is chosen as the point in time at which to evaluate alternatives, all cash flows must be **discounted** to the present. In this instance, the discounting effect reduces the amounts or values. Assuming a certain rate of interest, examples of questions using the present value approach include:

How much should be accepted today for an apartment house in lieu of rental income for the next 10 years?

How much is $5,000 due in 5 years worth today?

What lump-sum amount should be paid today for a series of equal payments of $100 a month, beginning now, for the next 5 years?

The future value and present value situations are essentially reciprocal relationships, and both are based on the concept of interest. Thus, if interest can be earned at 6% per year, the future worth of $100 one year from now is $106. Conversely, assuming the same rate of interest, the present value of a $106 payment due in one year is $100.

There are four common future and present value situations, each with a corresponding formula. Two of the situations deal with one-time, lump-sum payments or receipts[1] (either future or present values), and the other two involve annuities (either future or present values). An **annuity** consists of a series of equal payments over a specified number of periods.

Without going into the derivation of the formulas, these four situations are as follows:

(1) **Future Value of a Lump-Sum Payment:** $FV = P(1 + i)^n$

This may also be referred to as $FV = P(FVF_{\overline{n}|i})$ or simply FV = P(Table I value), where:

- FV = Future value
- P = Principal amount to be accumulated
- i = Interest rate per period
- n = Number of periods
- $FVF_{\overline{n}|i}$ = Future value factor for a particular interest rate and for a certain number of periods from Table I

(2) **Present Value of a Lump-Sum Payment:** $PV = A\left[\frac{1}{(1 + i)^n}\right]$

This may also be referred to as $PV = A(PVF_{\overline{n}|i})$ or simply PV = A(Table II value), where:

- PV = Present value
- A = Accumulated amount to be discounted
- i = Interest rate per period
- n = Number of periods
- $PVF_{\overline{n}|i}$ = Present value factor for a particular interest rate and for a certain number of periods from Table II

(3) **Future Value of an Annuity:** $FV_n = R\left[\frac{(1 + i)^n - 1}{i}\right]$

This may also be referred to as $FV_n = R(FVAF_{\overline{n}|i})$ or simply FV_n = R(Table III value), where:

- FV_n = Future value of an annuity
- R = Annuity payment or periodic rent to be accumulated
- i = Interest rate per period
- n = Number of periods
- $FVAF_{\overline{n}|i}$ = Future value annuity factor for a particular interest rate and for a certain number of periods from Table III

---

[1]Hereafter in this appendix, the terms *payments* and *receipts* will be used interchangeably. A payment by one party in a transaction becomes a receipt to the other party and vice versa. The term *rent* is used to designate either a receipt or a payment.

(4) Present Value of an Annuity: $PV_n = R\left[\frac{1 - \frac{1}{(1+i)^n}}{i}\right]$

This may also be referred to as $PV_n = R(PVAF_{\overline{n|}i})$ or simply $PV_n = R(\text{Table IV value})$, where:

PV_n = Present value of an annuity
R = Annuity payment or periodic rent to be discounted
i = Interest rate per period
n = Number of periods
$PVAF_{\overline{n|}i}$ = Present value annuity factor for a particular interest rate and for a certain number of periods from Table IV

Because using the formulas may be time-consuming, tables have been developed for each of the four situations. Such tables are provided at the end of this appendix. Each table is based on computing the value of $1 for various interest rates and periods of time. Future and present value computations can be made by multiplying the appropriate table value factor for $1 by the lump-sum or annuity payment (rent) involved in the problem. To illustrate, consider the question described earlier: How much will $500 deposited today at 6% annual interest amount to in 20 years? This is an example of the first situation, the future value of a lump-sum payment, and involves Table I. The table value for $n = 20$ and $i = 6\%$ is 3.2071. This value times $500, the principal amount to be accumulated, is approximately $1,604. Thus, the future value of $500 deposited now, accumulating at 6% per year for 20 years, is about $1,604.

The following examples demonstrate the application of future and present value tables in solving business problems. At least one example is provided for each of the four situations just described. Note that business problems sometimes require solving for the number of periods, the interest rate,[2] or the rental payment instead of the future or present value amounts. In each of the formulas there are four variables. If information is given about any three of the variables, the fourth (unknown value) can be determined.

Problem 1:

John Marsh loans Ann Brown $5,000 to purchase a car. Marsh accepts a note due in 4 years with interest at 8% compounded semiannually. After 1 year, Marsh needs cash and sells the note to Terry McKay who discounts the note at 12% compounded quarterly. How much cash did Marsh receive from McKay?

Solution to Problem 1:

This problem involves a lump-sum payment to be accumulated 4 years into the future at one interest rate, then discounted back 3 years at a different interest rate.

In many present and future value problems, a time line is helpful in visualizing the problem:

---

[2]When the interest rate is not known, it is properly called the *implicit rate of interest,* that is, the rate of interest implied by the terms of a contract or situation. (See Problems 7 and 9 in this appendix.)

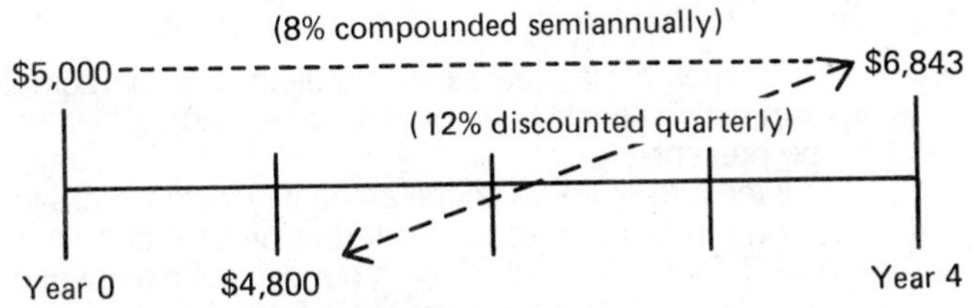

First, the $5,000 must be accumulated for 4 years at 8% compounded semiannually. Table I is used, and the applicable formula is:

$FV = P(FVF_{\overline{n}|i})$ where: FV = The future value of the lump sum
P = $5,000
n = 8 periods (4 years × 2)
i = 4% effective interest rate per period (8% ÷ 2)

$FV = \$5,000\ (\text{Table } I_{\overline{8}|4\%})$
$FV = \$5,000\ (1.3686)$
$FV = \$6,843$

In 4 years, the holder of the note will receive $6,843. After Marsh sells the note, it will be worth $6,843 to McKay in 3 years. The opportunity cost of money to McKay is apparently 12% compounded quarterly. Therefore, the $6,843 must be discounted back 3 years at 12% to find the amount McKay is willing to pay Marsh.

Table II is used, and the applicable formula is:

$PV = A(PFV_{\overline{n}|i})$ where: PV = The value of the future sum discounted back three years
A = $6,843
n = 12 periods (3 years × 4 quarters)
i = 3% effective interest rate per period (12% ÷ 4 quarters)

$PV = \$6,843\ (\text{Table } II_{\overline{12}|3\%})$
$PV = \$6,843\ (.7014)$
$PV = \$4,800$

McKay will pay approximately $4,800. Thus, Marsh is willing to give up $2,043 ($6,843 − $4,800) in order to receive cash at the end of 1 year.

Problem 2:

Miller Sporting Goods Co. is considering an investment that will require $1,250,000 capital investment and that will provide the following expected net receipts:

Year	Estimated Net Receipts
1	$195,000
2	457,000
3	593,000
4	421,000
5	95,000
6	5,000

Miller will make the investment only if the rate of return is greater than 10%. Will Miller make the investment?

Solution to Problem 2:

A series of unequal future receipts must be compared with a present lump-sum investment. For such a comparison to be made, all future cash flows must be discounted to the present.

If the rate of return on the amount invested is greater than 10%, then the total of all yearly net receipts discounted to the present at 10% will be greater than the amount invested. Since the receipts are unequal, each amount must be discounted individually. Table II is used, and the applicable formula is:

$PV = A(PVF_{\overline{n}|i})$ where:

(1) Year = n	(2) A (Net Receipts)	(3) Table $II_{\overline{n}|10\%}$	(2) × (3) = (4) PV (Discounted Amount)
1	$195,000	.9091	$ 177,275
2	457,000	.8264	377,665
3	593,000	.7513	445,521
4	421,000	.6830	287,543
5	95,000	.6209	58,986
6	5,000	.5645	2,823
	Total		$1,349,813

The total discounted receipts are greater than the investment; thus, the rate of return is more than 10%. Therefore, other things being equal, Miller will invest.

Problem 3:

Brothwell Inc. owes an installment debt of $1,000 per quarter for 5 years. The creditor has indicated a willingness to accept an equivalent lump-sum payment at the end of the contract period instead of the series of payments. If money is worth 8% compounded quarterly and the first four payments have been made, what is the equivalent lump-sum payment?

Solution to Problem 3:

The equivalent lump-sum payment can be found by accumulating the quarterly $1,000 payments to the end of the contract period. Table III is used, and the applicable formula is:

$FV_n = R(FVAF_{\overline{n}|i})$ where: FV_n = The unknown equivalent lump-sum payment

R = $1,000 quarterly installment to be accumulated

n = 16 periods [(5 years × 4 quarters) − 4 quarters already paid]

i = 2% effective compound rate (8% ÷ 4 quarters)

FV_n = $1,000 (Table $III_{\overline{16}|2\%}$)
FV_n = $1,000(18.6393)
FV_n = $18,639

$18,639 paid at the end of the 5 years is equivalent to the remaining 16 payments.

Problem 4:

Neil Robinson, proprietor of Robinson Appliance, received two offers for his last deluxe-model refrigerator. Jane Butler will pay $650 in cash. Ed McBride will pay $700 consisting of a down payment of $100 and 12 monthly

payments of $50. If the installment interest rate is 24% compounded monthly, which offer should Robinson accept?

Solution to Problem 4:

In order to compare the two alternative methods of payments, all cash flows must be accumulated or discounted to one point in time. As illustrated by the time line, the present is selected as the point of comparison.

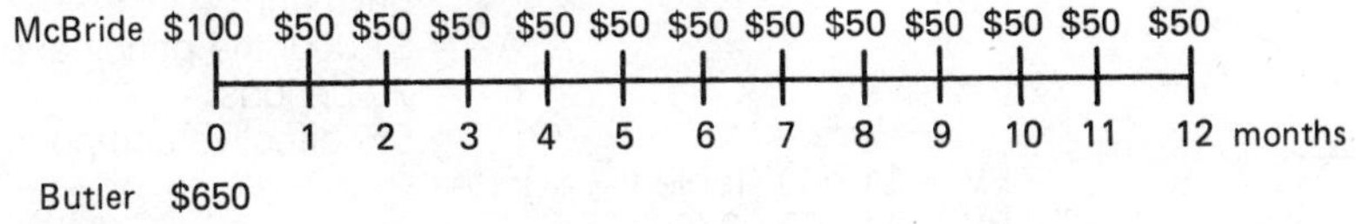

Butler's offer is $650 today. The present value of $650 today is $650.

McBride's offer consists of an annuity of 12 payments, plus $100 paid today, which is not part of the annuity. The annuity may be discounted to the present by using Table IV and the applicable formula:

$PV_n = R(PVAF_{\overline{n|}i})$ where: PV_n = Unknown present value of 12 payments
R = $50 monthly payment to be discounted
n = 12 periods (1 year × 12 months)
i = 2% effective compound rate (24% ÷ 12 periods per year)

PV_n = $50 (Table $IV_{\overline{12|}2\%}$)
PV_n = $50 (10.5753)
PV_n = $529

Present value of McBride's payments	$529
Present value of McBride's $100 down payment	100
Total present value of McBride's offer	$629

Therefore, Butler's offer of $650 cash is more desirable than McBride's offer.

Problem 5:

The Angelo Company is investigating the purchase of a block of bonds. Each $1,000 bond has a stated interest rate of 12% paid semiannually and is due in 10 years. The prevailing market rate for comparable bonds is 10%, also paid semiannually. How much should Angelo Company pay for each bond?

Solution to Problem 5:

This problem involves finding the present value of the cash flows resulting from the purchase of a bond. A bond pays both a series of equal interest payments and the principal amount when the bond matures. To ascertain the fair market price of a bond, both the series of interest payments and the future payment of the principal must be discounted to the present at the going market rate of 10% compounded semiannually.

First the series of interest payments is discounted to the present using Table IV and the applicable formula:

$PV_n = R(PVAF_{\overline{n|}i})$ where: PV_n = Unknown present value
R = $60 semiannual interest payment ($1,000 × .12 × ½ year)
n = 20 periods (10 years × 2 periods per year)
i = 5% effective compound rate (10% ÷ 2 periods per year)

$PV_n = \$60 \ (\text{Table IV}_{\overline{20|}5\%})$
$PV_n = \$60 \ (12.4622)$
$PV_n = \$748$

Second, the future payment of principal is discounted to the present using Table II and the applicable formula:

$PV = A(PVF_{\overline{n|}i})$ where: PV = Unknown present value of the principal payment
A = \$1,000, the principal payment
n = 20 periods
i = 5% effective compound rate

$PV = \$1{,}000 \ (\text{Table II}_{\overline{20|}5\%})$
$PV = \$1{,}000 \ (.3769)$
$PV = \$377$

Therefore, the price Angelo Company should pay for each bond is \$748 + \$377, or \$1,125.

INTERPOLATION

A difficulty in using future and present value tables arises when the exact factor does not appear in the table. One solution is to use the formula. **Interpolation** is another, often more practical, solution. Interpolation assumes the change between two values is linear. Although such an assumption is not correct, the margin of error is often insigificant, especially if the table value ranges are not too wide.

For example, determine the table value for the present value of \$1 due in 9 periods at 4½%. The appropriate factor does not appear in Table II. However, the two closest values are $\text{Table II}_{\overline{9|}4\%} = .7026$ and $\text{Table II}_{\overline{9|}5\%} = .6446$. Interpolation relates the unknown value to the change in the known values. This relationship may be shown as a proportion:

y (from 4½% to 5%)
4% 4½% 5%
Y (from 4% to 5%)

x (from ? to .6446)
.7026 ? .6446
X (from .7026 to .6446)

$$\frac{y}{Y} = \frac{x}{X}$$

$$\frac{5 - 4\frac{1}{2}}{5 - 4} = \frac{x}{.7026 - .6446}$$

$$\frac{\frac{1}{2}}{1} = \frac{x}{.0580}$$

$$x = .0290$$

The .0290 is the difference between the value for 5% and the value for 4½%. Therefore, the value needed is .0290 + .6446 = .6736. Using the mathematical formula for Table II

$$\left\{PV = A\left[\frac{1}{(1 + i)^n}\right]\right\},$$

the present value of \$1 at 4½% interest for 9 periods is .6729

$$\left\{PV = 1\left[\frac{1}{(1 + .045)^9}\right]\right\}.$$

The difference (.6736 − .6729 = .0007) is insignificant for most business purposes.

Interpolation is useful in finding a particular unknown table value that lies between two given values. This procedure is also used in approximating the number of periods or unknown interest rates when the table value is known. The following problems illustrate the determination of these two variables.

Problem 6:

Joan Novella leaves $600,000 to a university for a new building on the condition that construction will not begin until the bequest, invested at 5% per year, amounts to $1,500,000. How long before construction may begin?

Solution to Problem 6:

This problem involves finding the time (number of periods) required for a lump-sum payment to accumulate to a specified future amount. Table I is used and the applicable formula is:

$$FV = P(FVF_{\overline{n}|i})$$

where: FV = $1,500,000
P = $600,000
n = Unknown number of periods
i = 5% effective interest rate per year

$$\$1{,}500{,}000 = \$600{,}000\ (\text{Table } I_{\overline{n}|5\%})$$

$$\frac{\$1{,}500{,}000}{\$\ 600{,}000} = \text{Table } I_{\overline{n}|5\%}$$

$$2.5 = \text{Table } I_{\overline{n}|5\%}$$

Referring to Table I, reading down the i = 5% column:

n		Table Factor
18	=	2.4066
19	=	2.5270

Interpolating:

y: 2.5000 to 2.5270
2.4066 2.5000 2.5270
Y: 2.4066 to 2.5270

x: ? to 19
18 ? 19
X: 18 to 19

$$\frac{y}{Y} = \frac{x}{X}$$

$$\frac{2.5270 - 2.5000}{2.5270 - 2.4066} = \frac{x}{19 - 18}$$

$$\frac{.0270}{.1204} = \frac{x}{1}$$

$$x = .2243$$

The .2243 is the difference between the number of periods at table factor 2.5270 and the number of periods at table factor 2.5000. Therefore, the number of periods needed is 19.0000 − .2243 = 18.7757. In other words, about 18¾ periods (in this case, years) are required for $600,000 to amount to $1,500,000 at 5% annual interest.

Problem 7:

The Newports have entered into an automobile lease-purchase arrangement. The fair market value of the leased automobile is $5,814, and the contract calls for quarterly payments of $570 due at the end of each quarter for 3 years. What is the implicit rate of interest on the lease arrangement?

Solution to Problem 7:

The implicit interest rate must be computed for the present value of an annuity. The present value is the fair market value of the automobile, and the payment is the lease payment. Table IV is used, and the appropriate formula is given below.

$PV_n = R(PVAF_{\overline{n}|i})$ where: PV_n = \$5,814
R = \$570
n = 12 (3 years × 4 payments per year)
i = The unknown quarterly interest rate

$$\$5{,}814 = \$570\ (\text{Table IV}_{\overline{12}|i})$$

$$\frac{\$5{,}814}{\$570} = \text{Table IV}_{\overline{12}|i}$$

$$10.20 = \text{Table IV}_{\overline{12}|i}$$

Reading across the n = 12 row of Table IV:

i		Table Factor
2%	=	10.5753
3%	=	9.9540

Interpolating:

10.5753 10.200 9.9540 (y = 10.200 to 9.9540; Y = 10.5753 to 9.9540)

2.0 ? 3.0 (x = ? to 3.0; X = 2.0 to 3.0)

$$\frac{y}{Y} = \frac{x}{X}$$

$$\frac{10.2000 - 9.9540}{10.5753 - 9.9540} = \frac{x}{3.0 - 2.0}$$

$$\frac{.2460}{.6213} = \frac{x}{1.0}$$

$$x = .3959$$

The .3959 is the difference between the interest rate at the table factor 9.9540 and the interest rate at the table factor 10.2000. Therefore, the quarterly implicit interest rate is 3.0000 − .3959 = 2.6041%; and the annual implicit interest rate is 10.4164% (2.6041% × 4).

ORDINARY ANNUITY AND ANNUITY DUE

Annuities are of two types: ordinary annuities (annuities in arrears) and annuities due (annuities in advance). The periodic rents or payments for an **ordinary annuity** are made at the *end* of each period, and the last payment coincides with the end of the annuity term. The periodic rents or payments for an **annuity due** are made at the *beginning* of each period, and one period of the annuity term remains after the last payment. These differences are illustrated at the top of page 1017.

Most future and present value tables are computed for ordinary annuities; however, with slight adjustment, these same tables may be used in solving annuity due problems. To illustrate the conversion of an ordinary annuity table value to an annuity due value, consider the future amount

Ordinary Annuity for 3 Years

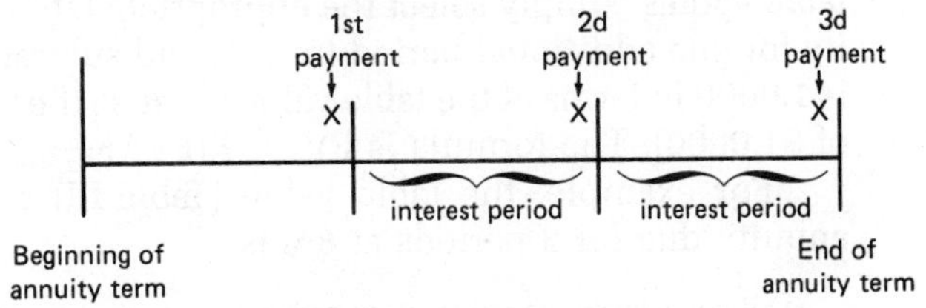

Annuity Due for 3 Years

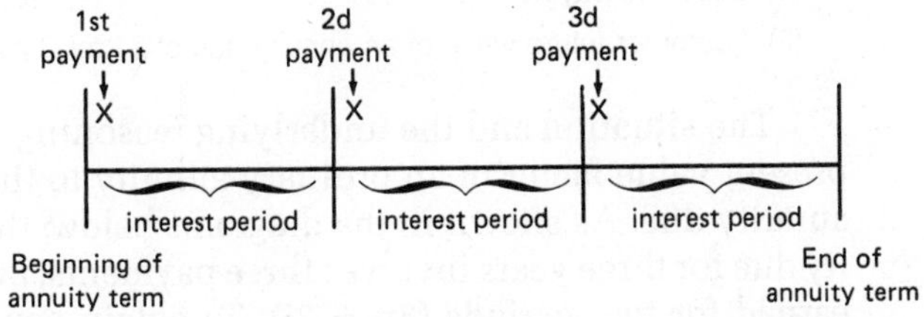

of an ordinary annuity for three years (see the diagram at the top of this page). This situation involves three payments (3p); but because the first payment is made at the end of the first period, interest is earned for only two periods (2i), or in total, 3p + 2i. On the other hand, the future amount of an annuity due for three years (the diagram above) involves three payments as well as interest for three periods because the first payment is made at the beginning of the first period (3p + 3i).

As shown below, an ordinary annuity involving four payments would earn interest for three periods (4p + 3i); thus, if the fourth payment were deducted, the value would be comparable to an annuity due of 3 periods [i.e., (4p + 3i) − 1p = 3p + 3i].

Ordinary Annuity for 4 Years

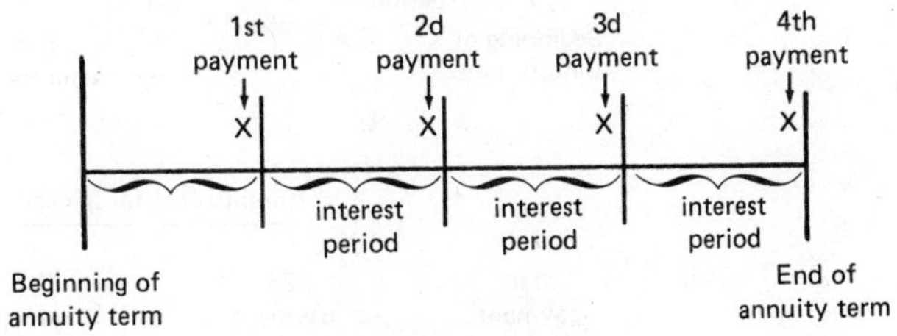

Annuity Due for 3 Years

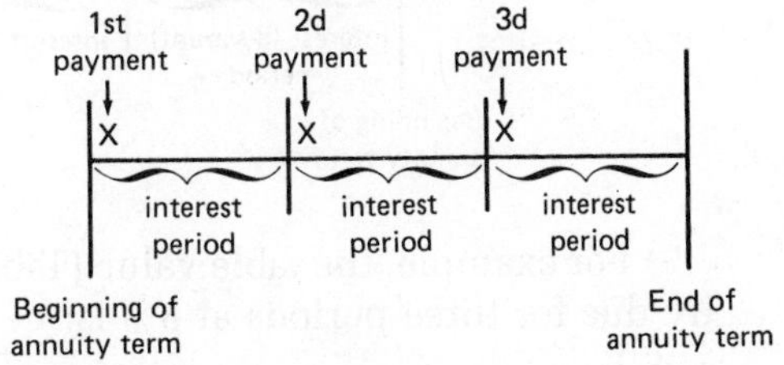

Therefore, to find the future value of an annuity due using ordinary annuity table values, simply select the appropriate table value for an ordinary annuity for one additional period (n + 1) and subtract the extra payment (which is 1.0000 in terms of the table value because the tables are computed for rents of $1.0000). The formula is $FV_n = R(FVAF_{\overline{n+1}|i} - 1)$.

For example, the table value (Table III) for the future amount of an annuity due for 3 periods at 8% is:

(1) Factor for future value of an ordinary annuity of $1 for 4 periods (n + 1) at 8%	4.5061
(2) Less one payment	1.0000
(3) Factor for future value of an annuity due of $1 for 3 periods at 8%	3.5061

The situation and the underlying reasoning are reversed in converting a present value factor of an ordinary annuity to the present value factor of an annuity due. As shown in the diagrams below, the present value of an annuity due for three years involves three payments; but interest (discount) is only earned for two periods (3p + 2i). To obtain comparable interest (discount) periods, an ordinary annuity for two years is required (2p + 2i). However, one additional payment must be added to make the situations equivalent; i.e., (2p + 2i) + 1p = 3p + 2i. Consequently, to convert the present value of an ordinary annuity to the present value of an annuity due, select the table factor for one less period (n − 1) and then add one payment (+1.0000). The formula is $PV_n = R(PVAF_{\overline{n-1}|i} + 1)$.

Ordinary Annuity for 2 Years

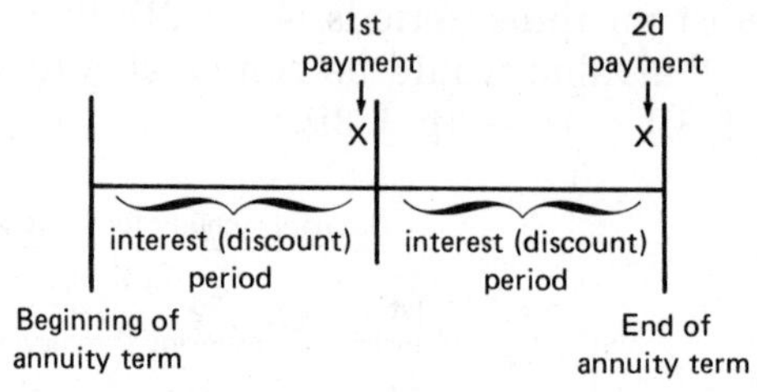

Annuity Due for 3 Years

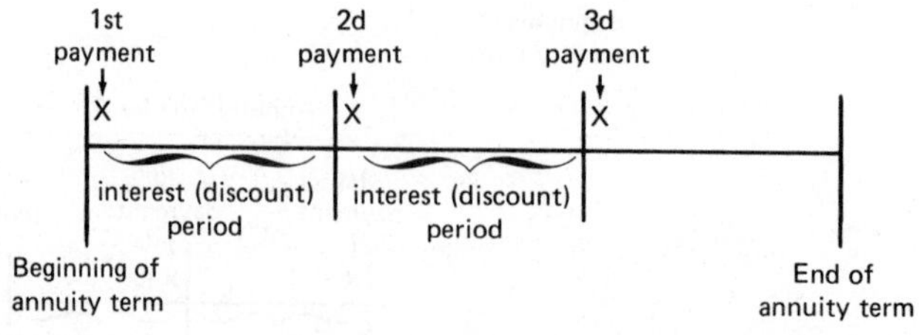

For example, the table value (Table IV) for the present value of an annuity due for three periods at 8% is:

(1) Factor for present value of an ordinary annuity of $1 for two periods (n − 1) at 8%	1.7833
(2) Plus one payment	1.0000
(3) Factor for present value of an annuity due of $1 for 3 periods at 8%	2.7833

The following problems illustrate the application of converting from ordinary annuity table values to annuity due table values.

Problem 8:

The Sampson Corporation desires to accumulate funds to retire a $200,000 bond issue at the end of 15 years. Funds set aside for this purpose can be invested to yield 6%. What annual payment starting immediately would provide the needed funds?

Solution to Problem 8:

Annuity payments of an unknown amount are to be accumulated toward a specific dollar amount at a known interest rate. Therefore, Table III is used. Because the first payment is to be made immediately, all payments will fall due at the beginning of each period and an annuity due is used. The appropriate formula is:

$$FV_n = R(FVAF_{\overline{n+1}|i} - 1)$$

where: FV_n = $200,000
R = Unknown annual payment
n = 15 periods
i = 6% annual interest

$$\$200{,}000 = R\,(\text{Table III}_{\overline{16}|6\%} - 1)$$
$$\$200{,}000 = R(24.6725)$$
$$\frac{\$200{,}000}{24.6725} = R$$
$$\$8{,}106 = R$$

Sampson Corporation must deposit $8,106 annually, starting immediately, to accumulate $200,000 in 15 years at 6% annual interest.

Problem 9:

Brigham Corporation has completed lease-purchase negotiations. The fair market value of the leased equipment is $45,897. The lease contract specifies semiannual payments of $3,775 for 10 years beginning immediately. At the end of the lease, Brigham Corporation may purchase the equipment for a nominal amount. What is the implicit annual rate of interest on the lease purchase?

Solution to Problem 9:

The implicit interest rate must be computed for the present value of an annuity due. The present value is the fair market value of the equipment, and the payment is the lease payment. Table IV is used, and the applicable formula is:

$$PV_n = R(PVAF_{\overline{n-1}|i} + 1)$$

where: PV_n = $45,897
R = $3,775
n = 20 periods (10 years × 2 payments per year)
i = The unknown semiannual interest rate

$$\$45{,}897 = \$3{,}775\,(\text{Table IV}_{\overline{19}|i} + 1)$$

$$\frac{\$45{,}897}{\$3{,}775} = 12.1581 = \text{Table IV}_{\overline{19}|i} + 1$$

$$11.1581 = \text{Table IV}_{\overline{19}|i}$$

Examination of Table IV for 19 periods and a factor of 11.1581 shows Table $\text{IV}_{\overline{19}|6\%} = 11.1581$. Therefore, $i = 6\%$. The implicit annual interest rate is twice the semi-annual rate, or $2 \times 6\% = 12\%$.

Problem 10:

Three years remain on the lease of Nyland Food Service Inc.'s building. The lease is noncancelable and requires payments of $5,000 on March 1 and September 1. During February, Nyland located a new store building and asked the lessor of the old store to accept $25,000 now in full payment of the old lease. The building is very old and will not be used again. If the value of money to the lessor is 16% compounded semiannually, should Nyland's offer be accepted?

Solution to Problem 10:

The lessor must compare the $25,000 now to the value of the six remaining lease payments. The lease payments must be discounted to the present for proper comparison. Because the next payment is due now, the lease payments are an annuity due. Table IV is adjusted to find the appropriate value. The formula is:

$$PV_n = R(\text{PVAF}_{\overline{n-1}|i} + 1)$$

where: PV_n = Unknown present value of lease payments
R = $5,000 per period (6 months)
n = 6 periods (3 years × 2 periods per year)
i = 8% (16% ÷ 2 periods per year)

$$PV_n = \$5{,}000\,(\text{Table IV}_{\overline{5}|8\%} + 1)$$
$$PV_n = \$5{,}000(3.9927 + 1)$$
$$PV_n = \$24{,}964$$

The offer of $25,000 now is greater than $24,964, the present value of the remaining lease payments. Therefore, the lessor should accept the offer.

EXERCISES

1. John Foley borrowed $500 from a credit union at 8% simple interest. The loan is to be repaid in 6 months. How much will Foley have to pay to settle this obligation? How much of this payment will be interest? If Foley were to borrow the $500 from The Commercial Bank at 12% compounded quarterly, how much interest would he have to pay?

2. Indicate the rate per period and the number of periods for each of the following:

(a) 10% per annum, for 3 years, compounded annually.
(b) 10% per annum, for 3 years, compounded semiannually.
(c) 10% per annum, for 3 years, compounded quarterly.
(d) 10% per annum, for 3 years, compounded monthly.

3. What is the future amount for each of the following independent situations?

(a) The amount of $1,000 for 4 years at 8% compounded annually.
(b) The amount of $1,000 for 4 years at 8% compounded quarterly.
(c) The amount of $500 for 1 year at 24% compounded monthly.

4. What is the present value for each of the following independent situations?

(a) The present value of $1,000 due in 5 years at 10% compounded annually.
(b) The present value of $1,000 due in 5 years at 10% compounded semiannually.
(c) The present value of $25,000 due in 10 years at 8% compounded quarterly.

5. For each of the following, compute the future amount of an ordinary annuity (also known as an annuity in arrears).

(a) 12 payments of $100 at 6%.
(b) 8 payments of $500 at 10%.
(c) 19 payments of $125 at 12%.

6. What are the future amounts in Exercise 5 if the annuities are annuities due (also known as annuities in advance)?

7. For each of the following, compute the present value of an ordinary annuity.

(a) $1,000 for 10 years at 8%.
(b) $350 for 7 years at 5%.
(c) $250 for 20 years at 10%.

8. What are the present values in Exercise 7 if the annuities are annuities due?

9. Tim Baxter has $2,000 to invest. One alternative will yield 10% per year for 4 years. A second alternative is to deposit the $2,000 in a bank that will pay 8% per year, compounded quarterly. Which alternative should Baxter select?

10. RaNae Allen wishes to have $6,000 to buy a car at the end of 5 years. How much must be invested today to accomplish this purpose if the interest rate on the investment is 6%?

11. The Nielsens plan to save $1,500 each year to apply as a down payment on a home. If their first deposit is made on January 1, 1985, and their last deposit is made on January 1, 1989, how much will the Nielsens have for their down payment by January 1, 1989? Assume an interest rate of 8%.

12. If Mike Knudsen invests $800 on July 1 of each year from 1982 to 1992, inclusive, how much will have accumulated on July 1, 1993, if the interest rate is 12%?

13. Professor Andersen has $55,000 accumulated in a retirement fund and plans to invest that amount in an annuity on September 1, 1986, when she retires. Assume that Andersen purchases an annuity of 20 annual payments, the first to be made on September 1, 1987, with an 8% rate of interest. What will be the amount of the yearly payments?

14. Jill Doakes borrowed $4,000 on a note due on August 1, 1983. On that date Doakes was unable to pay the obligation but was able to arrange for Western Loan Company to pay the holder of the note the $4,000. Doakes agreed to pay Western Loan Company a series of 5 equal annual payments beginning on August 1, 1983. Each payment is in part a payment on the unpaid principal and in part a payment of interest at 12% per annum. What is the amount of Doakes payment?

15. An accounting student bought an inexpensive computer for $250 to assist in homework assignments. The student bought the computer on time, agreeing to pay $23.64 at the end of each month for 12 months. What annual interest rate did the student pay?

16. A new freezer may be purchased for $375 cash or for 8 monthly payments of $51.75 each. If you choose to buy the freezer over time, what approximate annual interest rate will you be paying?

17. The Johnsons are trying to accumulate $5,000 to buy some mountain property. They are able to deposit $1,200 a year into their savings account which earns 6% per year. In how many years can the Johnsons expect to buy their property?

18. K agrees to lease from L certain property for 10 years at the following annual rentals, payable in advance:

Years 1 and 2	$1,000 per annum
Years 3 to 6	$2,000 per annum
Years 7 to 10	$2,500 per annum

What single immediate sum will pay all of these rents if they are discounted at 6%? Prove by setting up a table showing the reduction of the leasehold.

19. Comment on the following statement issued by the president of a large corporation: "The directors have accepted a bid of $103.75 for $10,000,000, 20-year, first mortgage, 9½% bonds, thus securing $10,375,000 new capital. They gave serious consideration to a competing offer of par for 9% bonds. Although this would have meant an interest saving, the receipt of $375,000 additional capital at this time is of great advantage and offsets the interest saving under the lower coupon rate."

20. ABC Company is offered two alternative methods of purchasing a piece of equipment: (1) $20,000 cash or (2) $10,000 down plus $1,900 per year due at the end of each year for 6 years. Should the buyer accept the cash or the time-interest installment if money is worth 10% per annum?

21. An existing building is under consideration as an investment. Estimates of expected annual cash receipts for the next 20 years are $8,000 per year. Cash outlays will be $2,000 per year. (Assume cash flows at the end of the year.)

(a) How much is the building worth to the buyer if 10% per annum is an appropriate rate of return?

(b) If $30,000 is borrowed to finance purchase of the building and is to be repaid annually by means of 10 year-end payments at 6% interest, what will the annual payments be?

22. (a) Determine the price of a 5-year, $10,000, 9% bond, with semiannual coupons, bought to yield 12%. (b) What is the price if the above bond bears interest at 12% and is bought to yield 11%?

TABLE I

Amount of $1 Due in *n* Periods

$$FV = P(1 + i)^n = P(FVF_{\overline{n}|i})$$

n	2%	3%	4%	5%	6%	8%	10%	12%	16%	20%
1	1.0200	1.0300	1.0400	1.0500	1.0600	1.0800	1.1000	1.1200	1.1600	1.2000
2	1.0404	1.0609	1.0816	1.1025	1.1236	1.1664	1.2100	1.2544	1.3456	1.4400
3	1.0612	1.0927	1.1249	1.1576	1.1910	1.2597	1.3310	1.4049	1.5609	1.7280
4	1.0824	1.1255	1.1699	1.2155	1.2625	1.3605	1.4641	1.5735	1.8106	2.0736
5	1.1041	1.1593	1.2167	1.2763	1.3382	1.4693	1.6105	1.7623	2.1003	2.4883
6	1.1262	1.1941	1.2653	1.3401	1.4185	1.5869	1.7716	1.9738	2.4364	2.9860
7	1.1487	1.2299	1.3159	1.4071	1.5036	1.7138	1.9487	2.2107	2.8262	3.5832
8	1.1717	1.2668	1.3686	1.4775	1.5938	1.8509	2.1436	2.4760	3.2784	4.2998
9	1.1951	1.3048	1.4233	1.5513	1.6895	1.9990	2.3579	2.7731	3.8030	5.1598
10	1.2190	1.3439	1.4802	1.6289	1.7908	2.1589	2.5937	3.1058	4.4114	6.1917
11	1.2434	1.3842	1.5395	1.7103	1.8983	2.3316	2.8531	3.4785	5.1173	7.4301
12	1.2682	1.4258	1.6010	1.7959	2.0122	2.5182	3.1384	3.8960	5.9360	8.9161
13	1.2936	1.4685	1.6651	1.8856	2.1329	2.7196	3.4523	4.3635	6.8858	10.6993
14	1.3195	1.5126	1.7317	1.9799	2.2609	2.9372	3.7975	4.8871	7.9875	12.8392
15	1.3459	1.5580	1.8009	2.0789	2.3966	3.1722	4.1772	5.4736	9.2655	15.4070
16	1.3728	1.6047	1.8730	2.1829	2.5404	3.4259	4.5950	6.1304	10.7480	18.4884
17	1.4002	1.6528	1.9479	2.2920	2.6928	3.7000	5.0545	6.8660	12.4677	22.1861
18	1.4282	1.7024	2.0258	2.4066	2.8543	3.9960	5.5599	7.6900	14.4625	26.6233
19	1.4568	1.7535	2.1068	2.5270	3.0256	4.3157	6.1159	8.6128	16.7765	31.9480
20	1.4859	1.8061	2.1911	2.6533	3.2071	4.6610	6.7275	9.6463	19.4608	38.3376
25	1.6406	2.0938	2.6658	3.3864	4.2919	6.8485	10.8347	17.0001	40.8742	95.3962
30	1.8114	2.4273	3.2434	4.3219	5.7435	10.0627	17.4994	29.9599	85.8499	237.3763
40	2.2080	3.2620	4.8010	7.0400	10.2857	21.7245	45.2593	93.0509	378.7212	1469.7716
50	2.6916	4.3839	7.1067	11.4674	18.4202	46.9016	117.3909	289.0022	1670.7038	9100.4382

TABLE II

Present Value of $1 Due in *n* Periods

$$PV = A\left[\frac{1}{(1+i)^n}\right] = A(PVF_{\overline{n}|i})$$

n	2%	3%	4%	5%	6%	8%	10%	12%	16%	20%
1	0.9804	0.9709	0.9615	0.9524	0.9434	0.9259	0.9091	0.8929	0.8621	0.8333
2	0.9612	0.9426	0.9246	0.9070	0.8900	0.8573	0.8264	0.7972	0.7432	0.6944
3	0.9423	0.9151	0.8890	0.8638	0.8396	0.7938	0.7513	0.7118	0.6407	0.5787
4	0.9238	0.8885	0.8548	0.8227	0.7921	0.7350	0.6830	0.6355	0.5523	0.4823
5	0.9057	0.8626	0.8219	0.7835	0.7473	0.6806	0.6209	0.5674	0.4761	0.4019
6	0.8880	0.8375	0.7903	0.7462	0.7050	0.6302	0.5645	0.5066	0.4104	0.3349
7	0.8706	0.8131	0.7599	0.7107	0.6651	0.5835	0.5132	0.4523	0.3538	0.2791
8	0.8535	0.7894	0.7307	0.6768	0.6274	0.5403	0.4665	0.4039	0.3050	0.2326
9	0.8368	0.7664	0.7026	0.6446	0.5919	0.5002	0.4241	0.3606	0.2630	0.1938
10	0.8203	0.7441	0.6756	0.6139	0.5584	0.4632	0.3855	0.3220	0.2267	0.1615
11	0.8043	0.7224	0.6496	0.5847	0.5268	0.4289	0.3505	0.2875	0.1954	0.1346
12	0.7885	0.7014	0.6246	0.5568	0.4970	0.3971	0.3186	0.2567	0.1685	0.1122
13	0.7730	0.6810	0.6006	0.5303	0.4688	0.3677	0.2897	0.2292	0.1452	0.0935
14	0.7579	0.6611	0.5775	0.5051	0.4423	0.3405	0.2633	0.2046	0.1252	0.0779
15	0.7430	0.6419	0.5553	0.4810	0.4173	0.3152	0.2394	0.1827	0.1079	0.0649
16	0.7284	0.6232	0.5339	0.4581	0.3936	0.2919	0.2176	0.1631	0.0930	0.0541
17	0.7142	0.6050	0.5134	0.4363	0.3714	0.2703	0.1978	0.1456	0.0802	0.0451
18	0.7002	0.5874	0.4936	0.4155	0.3503	0.2502	0.1799	0.1300	0.0691	0.0376
19	0.6864	0.5703	0.4746	0.3957	0.3305	0.2317	0.1635	0.1161	0.0596	0.0313
20	0.6730	0.5537	0.4564	0.3769	0.3118	0.2145	0.1486	0.1037	0.0514	0.0261
25	0.6095	0.4776	0.3751	0.2953	0.2330	0.1460	0.0923	0.0588	0.0245	0.0105
30	0.5521	0.4120	0.3083	0.2314	0.1741	0.0994	0.0573	0.0334	0.0116	0.0042
40	0.4529	0.3066	0.2083	0.1420	0.0972	0.0460	0.0221	0.0107	0.0026	0.0007
50	0.3715	0.2281	0.1407	0.0872	0.0543	0.0213	0.0085	0.0035	0.0006	0.0001

TABLE III

Amount of an Annuity of $1 per Period

$$FV_n = R\left[\frac{(1+i)^n - 1}{i}\right] = R(FVAF_{\overline{n}|i})$$

n	2%	3%	4%	5%	6%	8%	10%	12%	16%	20%
1	1.0000	1.0000	1.0000	1.0000	1.0000	1.0000	1.0000	1.0000	1.0000	1.0000
2	2.0200	2.0300	2.0400	2.0500	2.0600	2.0800	2.1000	2.1200	2.1600	2.2000
3	3.0604	3.0909	3.1216	3.1525	3.1836	3.2464	3.3100	3.3744	3.5056	3.6400
4	4.1216	4.1836	4.2465	4.3101	4.3746	4.5061	4.6410	4.7793	5.0665	5.3680
5	5.2040	5.3091	5.4163	5.5256	5.6371	5.8666	6.1051	6.3528	6.8771	7.4416
6	6.3081	6.4684	6.6330	6.8019	6.9753	7.3359	7.7156	8.1152	8.9775	9.9299
7	7.4343	7.6625	7.8983	8.1420	8.3938	8.9228	9.4872	10.0890	11.4139	12.9159
8	8.5830	8.8923	9.2142	9.5491	9.8975	10.6366	11.4359	12.2997	14.2401	16.4991
9	9.7546	10.1591	10.5828	11.0266	11.4913	12.4876	13.5795	14.7757	17.5185	20.7989
10	10.9497	11.4639	12.0061	12.5779	13.1808	14.4866	15.9374	17.5487	21.3215	25.9587
11	12.1687	12.8078	13.4864	14.2068	14.9716	16.6455	18.5312	20.6546	25.7329	32.1504
12	13.4121	14.1920	15.0258	15.9171	16.8699	18.9771	21.3843	24.1331	30.8502	39.5805
13	14.6803	15.6178	16.6268	17.7130	18.8821	21.4953	24.5227	28.0291	36.7862	48.4966
14	15.9739	17.0863	18.2919	19.5986	21.0151	24.2149	27.9750	32.3926	43.6720	59.1959
15	17.2934	18.5989	20.0236	21.5786	23.2760	27.1521	31.7725	37.2797	51.6595	72.0351
16	18.6393	20.1569	21.8245	23.6575	25.6725	30.3243	35.9497	42.7533	60.9250	87.4421
17	20.0121	21.7616	23.6975	25.8404	28.2129	33.7502	40.5447	48.8837	71.6730	105.9306
18	21.4123	23.4144	25.6454	28.1324	30.9057	37.4502	45.5992	55.7497	84.1407	128.1167
19	22.8406	25.1169	27.6712	30.5390	33.7600	41.4463	51.1591	63.4397	98.6032	154.7400
20	24.2974	26.8704	29.7781	33.0660	36.7856	45.7620	57.2750	72.0524	115.3797	186.6880
25	32.0303	36.4593	41.6459	47.7271	54.8645	73.1059	98.3471	133.3339	249.2140	471.9811
30	40.5681	47.5754	56.0849	66.4388	79.0582	113.2832	164.4940	241.3327	530.3117	1181.8816
40	60.4020	75.4013	95.0255	120.7998	154.7620	259.0565	442.5926	767.0914	2360.7572	7343.8578
50	84.5794	112.7969	152.6671	209.3480	290.3359	573.7702	1163.9085	2400.0182	10435.6488	45497.1908

TABLE IV

Present Value of an Annuity of $1 per Period

$$PV_n = R\left[\frac{1 - \frac{1}{(1+i)^n}}{i}\right] = P(PVAF_{\overline{n}|i})$$

n	2%	3%	4%	5%	6%	8%	10%	12%	16%	20%
1	0.9804	0.9709	0.9615	0.9524	0.9434	0.9259	0.9091	0.8929	0.8621	0.8333
2	1.9416	1.9135	1.8861	1.8594	1.8334	1.7833	1.7355	1.6901	1.6052	1.5278
3	2.8839	2.8286	2.7751	2.7232	2.6730	2.5771	2.4869	2.4018	2.2459	2.1065
4	3.8077	3.7171	3.6299	3.5460	3.4651	3.3121	3.1699	3.0373	2.7982	2.5887
5	4.7135	4.5797	4.4518	4.3295	4.2124	3.9927	3.7908	3.6048	3.2743	2.9906
6	5.6014	5.4172	5.2421	5.0757	4.9173	4.6229	4.3553	4.1114	3.6847	3.3255
7	6.4720	6.2303	6.0021	5.7864	5.5824	5.2064	4.8684	4.5638	4.0386	3.6046
8	7.3255	7.0197	6.7327	6.4632	6.2098	5.7466	5.3349	4.9676	4.3436	3.8372
9	8.1622	7.7861	7.4353	7.1078	6.8017	6.2469	5.7590	5.3282	4.6065	4.0310
10	8.9826	8.5302	8.1109	7.7217	7.3601	6.7101	6.1446	5.6502	4.8332	4.1925
11	9.7868	9.2526	8.7605	8.3064	7.8869	7.1390	6.4951	5.9377	5.0286	4.3271
12	10.5753	9.9540	9.3851	8.8633	8.3838	7.5361	6.8137	6.1944	5.1971	4.4392
13	11.3484	10.6350	9.9856	9.3936	8.8527	7.9038	7.1034	6.4235	5.3423	4.5327
14	12.1062	11.2961	10.5631	9.8986	9.2950	8.2442	7.3667	6.6282	5.4675	4.6106
15	12.8493	11.9379	11.1184	10.3797	9.7122	8.5595	7.6061	6.8109	5.5755	4.6755
16	13.5777	12.5611	11.6523	10.8378	10.1059	8.8514	7.8237	6.9740	5.6685	4.7296
17	14.2919	13.1661	12.1657	11.2741	10.4773	9.1216	8.0216	7.1196	5.7487	4.7746
18	14.9920	13.7535	12.6593	11.6896	10.8276	9.3719	8.2014	7.2497	5.8178	4.8122
19	15.6785	14.3238	13.1339	12.0853	11.1581	9.6036	8.3649	7.3658	5.8775	4.8435
20	16.3514	14.8775	13.5903	12.4622	11.4699	9.8181	8.5136	7.4694	5.9288	4.8696
25	19.5235	17.4131	15.6221	14.0939	12.7834	10.6748	9.0770	7.8431	6.0971	4.9476
30	22.3965	19.6004	17.2920	15.3725	13.7648	11.2578	9.4269	8.0552	6.1772	4.9789
40	27.3555	23.1148	19.7928	17.1591	15.0463	11.9246	9.7791	8.2438	6.2335	4.9966
50	31.4236	25.7298	21.4822	18.2559	15.7619	12.2335	9.9148	8.3045	6.2463	4.9995

Appendix B

ILLUSTRATIVE FINANCIAL STATEMENTS

Consolidated Statements of Income

General Mills, Inc., and Subsidiaries

	Fiscal Year Ended		
(Amounts in Millions, Except Per Share Data)	**May 30, 1982 (52 Weeks)**	May 31, 1981 (53 Weeks)	May 25, 1980 (52 Weeks)
Sales	**$5,312.1**	$4,852.4	$4,170.3
Costs and Expenses:			
Cost of sales, exclusive of items below	**3,081.6**	2,936.9	2,578.5
Selling, general and administrative expenses	**1,635.5**	1,384.0	1,145.5
Depreciation and amortization expenses	**113.2**	99.5	81.1
Interest expense	**75.1**	57.6	48.6
Total Costs and Expenses	**4,905.4**	4,478.0	3,853.7
Earnings before Income Taxes	**406.7**	374.4	316.6
Income Taxes	**(181.2)**	(177.8)	(146.6)
Net Earnings	**$ 225.5**	$ 196.6	$ 170.0
Earnings per Common Share and Common Share Equivalent	**$ 4.46**	$ 3.90	$ 3.37
Average Number of Common Shares and Common Share Equivalents	**50.6**	50.4	50.5

Consolidated Statements of Retained Earnings

	Fiscal Year Ended		
(Amounts in Millions, Except Per Share Data)	**May 30, 1982 (52 Weeks)**	May 31, 1981 (53 Weeks)	May 25, 1980 (52 Weeks)
Retained Earnings at Beginning of Year, restated for vacation accrual	**$ 942.0**	$ 817.7	$ 712.1
Add net earnings	**225.5**	196.6	170.0
Deduct dividends on common stock of $1.64 per share in 1982, $1.44 per share in 1981, and $1.28 per share in 1980	**(82.3)**	(72.3)	(64.4)
Retained Earnings at End of Year	**$1,085.2**	$ 942.0	$ 817.7

See accompanying notes to consolidated financial statements.

Consolidated Balance Sheets

General Mills, Inc., and Subsidiaries

Assets

(In Millions)	May 30, 1982	May 31, 1981
Current Assets:		
Cash and short-term investments	$ 33.4	$ 39.1
Receivables, less allowance for doubtful accounts of $16.0 in 1982 and $12.6 in 1981	408.6	391.4
Inventories	660.6	611.4
Investment in tax leases	124.9	—
Prepaid expenses	31.5	34.0
Total Current Assets	1,259.0	1,075.9
Land, Buildings and Equipment, at cost:		
Land	105.4	82.8
Buildings	560.5	494.1
Equipment	762.2	677.2
Construction in progress	124.0	114.5
	1,552.1	1,368.6
Less accumulated depreciation	(498.0)	(448.0)
Net Land, Buildings and Equipment	1,054.1	920.6
Other Assets:		
Goodwill and other intangible assets	198.0	201.5
Investments and miscellaneous assets	190.6	103.3
Total Other Assets	388.6	304.8
Total Assets	$2,701.7	$2,301.3

Liabilities and Stockholders' Equity

	May 30, 1982	May 31, 1981
Current Liabilities:		
Accounts payable	$ 333.1	$ 322.8
Current portion of long-term debt	20.0	17.7
Notes payable	409.2	155.5
Accrued taxes	68.9	84.7
Accrued payroll	96.7	84.4
Other current liabilities	120.4	91.0
Total Current Liabilities	1,048.3	756.1
Long-Term Debt	331.9	348.6
Deferred Income Taxes	46.0	38.2
Other Liabilities and Deferred Credits	43.3	26.4
Total Liabilities	1,469.5	1,169.3
Stockholders' Equity:		
Common stock	206.6	196.6
Retained earnings	1,085.2	942.0
Less common stock in treasury, at cost	(19.5)	(6.6)
Cumulative foreign currency adjustment	(40.1)	—
Total Stockholders' Equity	1,232.2	1,132.0
Total Liabilities and Stockholders' Equity	$2,701.7	$2,301.3

See accompanying notes to consolidated financial statements.

Consolidated Statements of Changes in Financial Position

General Mills, Inc., and Subsidiaries

(In Millions)	May 30, 1982 (52 Weeks)	May 31, 1981 (53 Weeks)	May 25, 1980 (52 Weeks)
	Fiscal Year Ended		
Funds Provided from (Used for) Operations:			
Net earnings	**$225.5**	$196.6	$170.0
Depreciation and amortization	**113.2**	99.5	81.1
Deferred income taxes	**12.2**	16.7	2.6
Provision for losses on dispositions	**33.8**	—	—
Other	**(17.4)**	5.0	9.0
Working capital provided from operations	**367.3**	317.8	262.7
Changes in working capital affecting operations:			
(Increase) in receivables	**(42.8)**	(10.3)	(60.8)
(Increase) in inventories	**(77.0)**	(38.5)	(41.3)
(Increase) in prepaid expenses	**(1.9)**	(2.9)	(5.4)
Increase (decrease) in accrued taxes	**(14.2)**	(2.0)	22.2
Increase in accounts payable and other current liabilities	**48.8**	79.1	15.9
Cash Provided from Operations	**280.2**	343.2	193.3
Funds Provided from (Used for) Investment Activities:			
Purchase of land, buildings and equipment	**(287.3)**	(246.6)	(196.5)
Purchase price of businesses acquired, net of cash received	**(9.3)**	(81.0)	(3.1)
Cash provided from disposal of land, buildings and equipment	**12.5**	11.5	11.2
Proceeds from completed dispositions	**24.8**	11.9	—
Decrease in net non-cash assets caused by changes in foreign currency rates	**37.7**	—	—
(Decrease) in stockholders' equity due to changes in foreign currency rates	**(40.1)**	—	—
Other	**(32.0)**	(4.7)	(26.0)
Net Cash Used for Investment Activities	**(293.7)**	(308.9)	(214.4)
Funds Used for Dividends	**(82.3)**	(72.3)	(64.4)
Funds Provided from (Used for) Financing Activities:			
Issuance of long-term debt	**69.1**	37.0	24.7
Common stock issued	**19.6**	23.0	2.7
Increase in notes payable	**263.1**	64.6	39.2
Reduction of long-term debt	**(62.7)**	(64.0)	(35.2)
Purchase of treasury stock	**(22.5)**	(22.6)	(3.8)
Investment in tax leases	**(236.5)**	—	—
Income tax cash flows from tax leases	**60.0**	—	—
Net Cash Provided from Financing Activities	**90.1**	38.0	27.6
Net (Decrease) in Cash and Short-Term Investments	**(5.7)**	—	(57.9)
Cash and Short-Term Investments at Beginning of Year	**39.1**	39.1	97.0
Cash and Short-Term Investments at End of Year	**$ 33.4**	$ 39.1	$ 39.1

See accompanying notes to consolidated financial statements.

Notes to Consolidated Financial Statements

General Mills, Inc., and Subsidiaries

Note One: Summary of Significant Accounting Policies

A. Principles of Consolidation

The consolidated financial statements include the following domestic and foreign operations:
(1) parent company and 100% owned subsidiaries; (2) majority-owned subsidiaries; and (3) General Mills' investment in and share of net earnings or losses of 20-50% owned companies.

The fiscal years of foreign operations generally end in April.

Certain 1981 and 1980 amounts have been reclassified to conform to 1982's presentation.

B. Land, Buildings, Equipment and Depreciation

Buildings and equipment are depreciated over estimated useful lives ranging from 3-50 years primarily using the straight line method. Accelerated depreciation methods are generally used for income tax purposes.

When an item is sold or retired, the accounts are relieved of cost and the related accumulated depreciation. Gains and losses on assets sold or retired are credited or charged to earnings.

C. Capitalization of Construction Interest

The company capitalizes interest costs related to certain construction projects. This capitalization decreased interest expense by $7.8 million and $6.0 million in fiscal years 1982 and 1981, respectively. No interest costs were capitalized prior to fiscal year 1981.

D. Inventories

Certain domestic inventories are valued at the lower of cost (determined by the LIFO method) or market. Other inventories are generally stated at the lower of cost (determined by the FIFO method) or market.

E. Amortization of Intangibles

Goodwill represents the difference between purchase prices of acquired companies and the related values of net assets acquired and accounted for by the purchase method of accounting. Any goodwill acquired after October, 1970, is amortized on a straight-line basis over not more than 40 years.

The costs of patents, copyrights and other intangible assets are amortized evenly over their estimated useful lives by charges against earnings. Most of these costs were incurred through purchases of businesses.

Annually, the Audit Committee of the Board of Directors reviews goodwill and other intangibles. At its meeting on May 24, 1982, the Board of Directors confirmed that the remaining amounts of these assets have continuing value.

F. Vacation Accrual

In fiscal 1982, General Mills, Inc. implemented Statement No. 43 of the Financial Accounting Standards Board, Accounting for Compensated Absences, which requires accrual of all vacation pay as earned instead of expensing when paid.

The accounting change has been applied retroactively and retained earnings at May 31, 1981 and May 25, 1980 have been reduced by $13.4 million. The effect of the change on net earnings and the related per share amounts for the year ended May 30, 1982 was not material. Net earnings and related per share amounts for the years ended May 31, 1981 and May 25, 1980 have not been restated because the effect of this change was not material.

G. Research and Development

All expenditures for research and development are charged against earnings in the year incurred. The charges for fiscal 1982, 1981 and 1980 were $53.8 million, $45.4 million and $44.4 million, respectively.

H. Income Taxes

Income taxes include deferred income taxes which result from timing differences between earnings for financial reporting and tax purposes. Investment tax credits are reflected as reductions of income taxes in the year eligible purchases are placed in service.

I. Earnings Per Share

Earnings per common share and common share equivalent is determined by dividing net earnings by the weighted average number of common shares and common share equivalents outstanding during the year. The common share equivalents consist of: (1) common stock which may be issuable upon exercise of outstanding stock options

(377,753 in 1982, 91,389 in 1981, and 5,509 in 1980); (2) shares which may be issuable under incentive compensation plans (50,232 in 1982 and 63,205 in 1981); (3) shares reserved for issuance to former owners of certain acquired companies, expected to be earned through profit performance contracts (129,009 in 1980); and (4) shares reserved for deferred stock payments to satisfy terms under which certain companies were acquired (18,546 in 1982).

Note Two: Foreign Currency Translation

The company changed its method of accounting for foreign currency translation in fiscal 1982 by adopting Statement No. 52 of the Financial Accounting Standards Board. Implementation of this new standard increased net earnings over earnings computed under the previous standard by $9.5 million (19 cents per share) for fiscal year 1982. Prior years have not been restated.

Statement No. 52 generally requires that foreign currency assets and liabilities be translated using the exchange rates in effect at the balance sheet date. Results of operations are translated using the average exchange rates prevailing throughout the period. The effects of exchange rate fluctuations on translating foreign currency assets and liabilities into U.S. dollars are accumulated as part of the cumulative foreign currency adjustment in stockholders' equity. Gains and losses from foreign currency transactions are generally included in net earnings for the period.

A reconciliation of the cumulative foreign currency adjustment (in millions) follows:

Opening adjustment from translation of June 1, 1981 balance sheet	$ 11.1
Adjustments during 1982, net of applicable income taxes of $5.1 million	29.0
Balance at May 30, 1982	$ 40.1

Foreign currency gains and losses included in net earnings are immaterial for fiscal years 1982, 1981 and 1980.

Note Three: Acquisitions

Following are the cash and common stock costs of acquisitions and increased ownership in partially-owned companies, and additional payments under performance earnings agreements:

(Dollars in Millions)	Fiscal Year **1982**	1981	1980
Acquisitions and increased ownership in partially-owned companies:			
Cash	**$.9**	$62.9	$1.2
Shares	**248,275**	680,562	34,232
Performance earnings payments:			
Shares	**—**	92,807	62,083

Sales, costs and earnings of acquired businesses are included in results of operations from the dates of acquisition. Consolidated sales and earnings would have been affected by immaterial amounts had the acquisitions been made at the beginning of the fiscal year.

Note Four: Inventories

The components of year-end inventories are as follows:

(In Millions)	**May 30, 1982**	May 31, 1981
Raw materials, work in process, finished goods and supplies:		
Valued at LIFO	**$220.1**	$188.7
Valued primarily at FIFO	**440.5**	422.7
Total inventories	**$660.6**	$611.4

If the FIFO method of inventory accounting had been used in place of LIFO, inventories would have been $75.5 million and $73.7 million higher than reported at May 30, 1982 and May 31, 1981, respectively.

Note Five: Investments in Tax Leases

At May 30, 1982, the company had $176.5 million of net investments in tax lease transactions. These transactions represent purchases of certain income tax items from other companies under the Economic Recovery Tax Act. $124.9 million of this investment will be recovered through income tax cash flows during fiscal 1983 and is classified as a current asset. The remaining investment is included in investments and miscellaneous assets and will be recovered in fiscal 1984.

These transactions had no effect on net earnings or the effective income tax rate in 1982.

Notes to Consolidated Financial Statements (continued)

General Mills, Inc., and Subsidiaries

Note Six: Short-Term Borrowings

The components of notes payable are as follows:

(In Millions)	May 30, 1982	May 31, 1981
Banks	**$ 85.0**	$ 71.6
U.S. commercial paper	**321.3**	83.6
Miscellaneous	**2.9**	.3
Total	**$409.2**	$155.5

To ensure the availability of funds during the year, the company maintained bank credit lines sufficient to cover its outstanding commercial paper. At May 30, 1982, the company had $345.0 million of such domestic lines available. These lines are on a fee-paid basis. As of May 30, 1982, foreign subsidiaries had $62.9 million of unused credit lines. The amount of the credit lines and the cost thereof are generally negotiated each year.

Note Seven: Long-Term Debt

(In Millions)	May 30, 1982	May 31, 1981
9⅜% sinking fund debentures, due March 1, 2009	**$113.3**	$125.0
8% sinking fund debentures, due February 15, 1999	**55.5**	79.2
8⅞% sinking fund debentures, due October 15, 1995	**52.7**	61.8
Bank loans at prime rate to prime rate plus ½% (not to exceed 12¾%), due in equal installments on May 1, 1983 and May 1, 1984	**16.7**	25.0
Zero coupon notes, yield 13⅝%, $102.5 due June 30, 1991	**28.5**	—
Other	**85.2**	75.3
	351.9	366.3
Less amounts due within one year	**(20.0)**	(17.7)
Total long-term debt	**$331.9**	$348.6

In fiscal 1982, the company refinanced $36 million principal amount of sinking fund debentures through the placement of zero coupon notes and satisfied $14.5 million principal amount of sinking fund debentures through the deposit of U.S. and prime-rated obligations in an irrevocable trust. These transactions increased fiscal 1982 net earnings by $8.2 million ($.16 per share). In fiscal 1981, a refinancing of notes with a face value of $30 million increased net earnings by $3.3 million ($.07 per share).

The sinking fund and principal payments due on long-term debt are (in millions) $20.0, $19.8, $7.9, $9.7 and $12.1 in fiscal years ending 1983, 1984, 1985, 1986 and 1987, respectively.

Note Eight: Changes in Capital Stock

(Dollars in Millions)	$0.75 Par Value Common Stock (70,000,000 Shares Authorized)			
	Issued		In Treasury	
	Shares	Amount	Shares	Amount
Balance at May 27, 1979	50,417,636	$194.7	158,810	$ 4.0
Stock option and profit sharing plans	4,661	.4	(21,220)	(.4)
Shares issued for acquisitions	96,315	1.9	—	—
Shares repurchased on open market	—	—	150,822	3.8
Balance at May 25, 1980	50,518,612	197.0	288,412	7.4
Stock option and profit sharing plans	48,594	1.2	(21,571)	(.5)
Shares issued for acquisitions	—	(1.6)	(773,369)	(22.9)
Shares repurchased on open market	—	—	724,840	22.6
Balance at May 31, 1981	**50,567,206**	**196.6**	**218,312**	**6.6**
Stock option and profit sharing plans	**293,319**	**9.4**	**(31,674)**	**(.9)**
Shares issued for acquisitions	—	**.6**	**(248,275)**	**(8.4)**
Shares issued—other	—	—	**(9,232)**	**(.3)**
Shares repurchased on open market	—	—	**645,895**	**22.5**
Balance at May 30, 1982	**50,860,525**	**$206.6**	**575,026**	**$19.5**

Cumulative preferred stock of 5,000,000 shares, without par value, is authorized but unissued.

The Board of Directors has authorized management to repurchase from time to time common stock for its treasury, provided that the number in the treasury shall not exceed 750,000 shares.

Shares of common stock are potentially issuable for the following purposes:

	Number of Shares as of May 30, 1982
Stock options outstanding	**1,533,877**
Stock options available for grant	**949,600**
Performance payments for acquired companies	**27,400**
Incentive plans	**62,361**

Note Nine: Stock Options

Options for a total of 949,600 shares are available for grant to officers and key employees under the company's 1980 stock option plan, under which grants may be made until October 1, 1984. The options may be granted subject to approval of the Compensation Committee of the Board of Directors, at a price of not less than 100% of the fair market value on the date the option is granted.

Options now outstanding include some granted under 1970 and 1975 option plans which have expired and under which no further options may be granted. The 1970 and 1975 plans both provide for expiration of options within ten years after date of grant.

The 1975 plan permitted the discretionary granting of stock appreciation rights (SAR's) in tandem with some options granted to certain individuals. Upon exercise of an SAR, the option for a corresponding number of shares of stock is cancelled and the holder receives in cash or stock an amount equal to the appreciation between the option price and the market value of the stock on the date of exercise. This amount may not exceed the option price. On May 30, 1982, there were 221,660 SAR's outstanding. The weighted average option price of the related stock options was $29.02.

The 1980 plan permits the discretionary granting of performance units corresponding to stock options granted. The value of performance units will be determined by growth in earnings per share measured against preset goals over three-year performance periods. After a performance period, holders may elect to receive the value of performance units as an alternative to exercising corresponding stock options. On May 30, 1982, there were 590,500 performance units outstanding.

Information on stock options is shown in the following table:

	Shares	Average Option Price Per Share
Granted:		
1982	**205,500**	**$34.50**
1981	453,500	26.25
1980	15,500	24.00
Exercised:		
1982	**293,319**	**27.25**
1981	48,594	25.01
1980	4,661	19.74
Expired:		
1982	**62,953**	**28.25**
1981	385,458	30.57
1980	82,300	28.90
Outstanding at year-end:		
1982	**1,533,877**	**28.38**
1981	1,684,649	27.43
1980	1,665,201	28.41
Exercisable at year-end:		
1982	**1,047,869**	**27.78**
1981	1,165,582	27.97
1980	1,395,301	28.72

Note Ten: Employees' Retirement Plans

The company and many of its subsidiaries have retirement plans covering most employees. Company contributions to these plans, which are expensed and funded on a current basis, were $39.5 million in 1982, $34.2 million in 1981, and $30.3 million in 1980.

Most plans provide for retirement benefits based on employees' length of service and earnings (defined benefit plans). Company contributions to such plans are determined by independent actuaries. The following table contains aggregated information about

Notes to Consolidated Financial Statements (continued)

General Mills, Inc., and Subsidiaries

defined benefit plans, determined as of January 1, 1982 and January 1, 1981 for the principal plans.

(In Millions)	1982	1981
Net plan assets available for benefits	**$323**	$307
Actuarial present value of accumulated benefits:		
Vested	**$269**	$262
Non-Vested	**23**	24
Total	**$292**	$286

Actuarial present values of accumulated benefits were determined using discount rates established by the Pension Benefit Guaranty Corporation (PBGC) for valuing plan benefits. The PBGC rates ranged from 4% to 10.5% for 1982 and 4% to 9.5% for 1981, with the latter of each range being the principal rate.

Some employees participate in various multi-employer defined benefit plans. Net assets available for benefits and actuarial present values of accumulated benefits associated with company employees participating in such plans are not determinable.

A few plans provide for benefits based on accumulated contributions and investment income (defined contribution plans). Such plans had net assets of $92.2 million in 1982.

Note Eleven: Profit-Sharing Plans

General Mills has profit-sharing plans to provide incentives to key individuals who have the greatest opportunity to contribute to current earnings and successful future operations.

These plans were approved by the Board of Directors upon recommendation of the Compensation Committee. The awards under these plans depend on profit performance in relation to pre-established goals. The plans are administered by the Compensation Committee, which consists of Directors who are not members of General Mills' management. Profit-sharing expense, including performance unit accruals, was $10.0 million in 1982, $8.6 million in 1981 and $4.8 million in 1980.

Note Twelve: Income Taxes

The components of earnings before income taxes and the income taxes thereon are:

(In Millions)	Fiscal Year 1982	1981	1980
Earnings before income taxes:			
U.S.	**$356.8**	$344.8	$293.8
Outside U.S.	**49.9**	29.6	22.8
Total earnings before income taxes	**$406.7**	$374.4	$316.6
Income taxes:			
Current:			
Federal taxes	**$136.7**	$136.2	$126.7
U.S. investment tax credit	**(13.9)**	(10.5)	(9.5)
State and local taxes	**22.1**	19.8	15.2
Foreign taxes	**24.1**	15.6	11.6
Total current income taxes	**169.0**	161.1	144.0
Deferred income taxes	**12.2**	16.7	2.6
Total income taxes	**$181.2**	$177.8	$146.6

Total current income tax expense for fiscal 1982 reflects the amount attributable to the company's operations and has not been affected by tax leases. Actual current taxes payable on fiscal 1982 operations will be reduced by the effect of cash flows from tax leases in the amount of approximately $130 million, $60 million of which reduced payments made in fiscal 1982. These cash flows result from the company's payments of $236 million to other companies for investments in tax leases, which are described in Note 5.

Deferred income taxes result from timing differences in the recognition of revenue and expense for tax and financial statement purposes. The tax effects of these differences are as follows:

(In Millions)	Fiscal Year		
	1982	1981	1980
Installment sales	**$ 13.3**	$ 13.4	
Depreciation	**9.8**	5.9	$ 4.5
Interest	**8.3**	2.8	—
Provision for losses on dispositions	**(9.7)**	—	—
Other	**(9.5)**	(5.4)	(1.9)
Total deferred income taxes	**$ 12.2**	$ 16.7	$ 2.6

The following table reconciles the U.S. statutory income tax rate with the effective income tax rate:

	Fiscal Year		
	1982	1981	1980
U.S. statutory rate	**46.0%**	46.0%	46.0%
Investment tax credit	**(3.4)**	(2.8)	(3.0)
State and local income taxes, net of Federal tax benefits	**2.9**	2.9	2.6
Other	**(.9)**	1.4	.7
Effective income tax rate	**44.6%**	47.5%	46.3%

Unremitted earnings of foreign operations amounting to $83.1 million are expected by management to be permanently reinvested. Accordingly, no provision has been made for additional foreign or U.S. taxes which would be payable if such earnings were to be remitted to the parent company as dividends.

Note Thirteen: Leases

An analysis of rent expense by property leased, follows:

(In Millions)	Fiscal Year		
	1982	1981	1980
Retail and restaurant space	**$20.3**	$14.8	$13.4
Office space	**8.5**	7.4	6.6
Computers	**7.7**	7.2	6.7
Warehousing	**7.9**	6.6	5.1
Transportation and all other	**15.9**	12.9	8.4
Total rent expense	**$60.3**	$48.9	$40.2

Some leases require payment of property taxes, insurance and maintenance costs in addition to the rent payments. Contingent and escalation rent in excess of minimum rent payments totaled approximately $3.2 million in fiscal 1982, $3.2 million in fiscal 1981 and $2.9 million in fiscal 1980. Sublease income netted in rent expense was insignificant.

Noncancelable future lease commitments (in millions) are $37.4 in 1983, $31.4 in 1984, $28.8 in 1985, $28.4 in 1986, $22.8 in 1987, and $85.2 after 1987, or a cumulative total of $234.0. Of this total, restaurant and retail leases account for 79%.

Note Fourteen: Dispositions

The company has committed itself to a plan to dispose of certain assets that do not fit well with the company's ongoing strategy. Selling, general and administrative expenses include a $33.8 million pre-tax loss in connection with this program. Operations involved represented less than 2.5% of the 1982 sales and operationally had an insignificant impact on 1982 earnings.

Note Fifteen: Litigation and Claims

In management's opinion, there are no claims or litigation pending at May 30, 1982, the outcome of which could have a significant effect on the consolidated financial position of General Mills, Inc. and its subsidiaries.

The litigation with the Federal Trade Commission (FTC), which alleged an illegal monopoly in the ready-to-eat cereal business, was dismissed by an FTC administrative law judge on September 1, 1981. On January 15, 1982, the Commission decided not to hear further appeal in the matter and made a final dismissal of the case.

Notes to Consolidated Financial Statements (continued)

General Mills, Inc., and Subsidiaries

Note Sixteen: Segment Information (a) (b)

(In Millions)	Consumer Foods	Restaurants	Toys	Fashion	Specialty Retailing and Other	Unallocated Corporate Items (c)	Consolidated Total
Sales							
1982	**$2,707.4**	**$839.4**	**$654.8**	**$657.3**	**$453.2**		**$5,312.1**
1981	2,514.6	704.0	674.3	580.5	379.0		4,852.4
1980	2,218.8	525.7	647.0	422.5	356.3		4,170.3
1979	2,062.4	436.3	583.9	360.4	302.0		3,745.0
Operating Profits							
1982	**268.6**	**79.2**	**79.2**	**101.7**	**5.5**	**$(127.5)**	**406.7**
1981	217.7	75.3	70.6	87.5	13.2	(89.9)	374.4
1980	210.5	52.7	60.1	43.7	26.4	(76.8)	316.6
1979	193.2	41.5	55.7	20.3	19.7	(66.5)	263.9
Identifiable Assets							
1982	**918.4**	**495.6**	**403.6**	**361.1**	**259.9**	**263.1**	**2,701.7**
1981	841.1	379.0	401.8	323.9	239.3	116.2	2,301.3
1980	761.1	269.1	441.2	231.2	181.6	128.2	2,012.4
1979	686.5	217.3	367.9	241.2	154.7	167.6	1,835.2
Capital Expenditures							
1982	**96.2**	**122.4**	**30.6**	**13.4**	**21.8**	**2.9**	**287.3**
1981	95.7	85.1	28.6	14.4	19.2	3.6	246.6
1980	80.6	49.8	34.7	5.2	19.3	6.9	196.5
1979	68.9	31.0	25.8	9.8	13.1	5.5	154.1
Depreciation Expense							
1982	**46.6**	**24.4**	**20.7**	**6.0**	**7.7**	**1.6**	**107.0**
1981	40.6	19.7	22.9	5.0	5.2	1.7	95.1
1980	33.6	14.3	19.2	3.9	4.1	2.8	77.9
1979	31.9	11.9	18.8	3.7	3.2	1.0	70.5

(In Millions)	U.S.A.	Other Western Hemisphere	Europe	Other	Unallocated Corporate Items (c)	Consolidated Total
Sales						
1982	**$4,783.1**	**$248.7**	**$259.1**	**$21.2**		**$5,312.1**
1981	4,300.6	223.3	307.9	20.6		4,852.4
1980	3,649.2	191.9	308.5	20.7		4,170.3
1979	3,187.5	161.8	377.8	17.9		3,745.0
Operating Profits						
1982	**482.9**	**41.3**	**7.4**	**2.6**	**$(127.5)**	**406.7**
1981	422.3	31.6	7.0	3.4	(89.9)	374.4
1980	366.5	20.4	3.9	2.6	(76.8)	316.6
1979	298.3	16.6	14.2(d)	1.3	(66.5)	263.9
Identifiable Assets						
1982	**2,147.9**	**120.8**	**157.6**	**12.3**	**263.1**	**2,701.7**
1981	1,876.2	124.3	176.0	8.6	116.2	2,301.3
1980	1,561.1	118.9	189.6	14.6	128.2	2,012.4
1979	1,384.2	97.6	172.6	13.2	167.6	1,835.2

(a) Variations between the data shown in these tables and similar amounts published in preceding reports are due principally to restatements and minor adjustments in the classification of certain items.

(b) Both inter-segment sales and export sales are immaterial.

(c) Corporate expenses include interest expense, profit sharing and general corporate expenses, and in 1982, provision for estimated losses on pending dispositions. Corporate assets consist mainly of cash and short-term investments, investment in tax leases and other miscellaneous investments.

(d) Includes a $4.4 million gain on the sale of Smiths U.K.

Note Seventeen: Quarterly Data (unaudited)

Summarized quarterly data for fiscal 1982 and 1981 follows:

(In Millions, except per share and market price amounts)	Three Months Ended			
	Aug.	Nov.	Feb.	May
Fiscal 1982:				
Sales	**$1,345.1**	**$1,494.6**	**$1,233.8**	**$1,238.6**
Gross profit (a) (b)	**560.9**	**640.4**	**510.7**	**518.5**
Net earnings (b)	**68.0**	**80.4**	**42.4**	**34.7**
Net earnings per share (b)	**1.34**	**1.60**	**.84**	**.68**
Dividends per share	**.41**	**.41**	**.41**	**.41**
Market price of common stock:				
High	**39½**	**38½**	**38⅜**	**42⅛**
Low	**32⅝**	**32⅞**	**32⅞**	**36⅜**
Fiscal 1981:				
Sales	$1,089.0	$1,394.9	$1,104.9	$1,263.6
Gross profit (a)	443.3	566.8	435.0	470.4
Net earnings	44.2	84.2	31.2	37.0
Net earnings per share	.88	1.67	.62	.73
Dividends per share	.33	.37	.37	.37
Market price of common stock:				
High	30⅝	29½	29⅞	35¾
Low	25¾	23½	23⅜	27⅛

(a) Before charges for depreciation.

(b) Amounts restated to reflect change in accounting for foreign currency translation in accordance with Statement No. 52 of the Financial Accounting Standards Board. The restatement increased first quarter net earnings by $3.4 million ($.07 per share), second quarter by $3.4 million ($.07 per share), and decreased third quarter by $1.1 million ($.02 per share).

LIFO inventory adjustments reduced earnings per share by $.02 in 1982 and $.13 in 1981. However, third and fourth quarter gains from LIFO amounted to $.04 and $.05 per share in 1982 and $.07 per share in the fourth quarter of 1981. These gains resulted from lower than expected year-end costs and quantities, plus other factors difficult to forecast during the year.

Fourth quarter fiscal 1982 net earnings include a $17.6 million ($.35 per share) provision for loss on dispositions of certain assets.

Note Eighteen: Accounting for Inflation (unaudited)

During the last decade, an increased rate of inflation became a significant factor in both the U.S. and world economies. Traditional accounting procedures are based on the "historical cost" method, where generally each individual transaction is recorded at its original cash value, and is not subsequently adjusted to a different value.

In periods of continuing rapid inflation, use of traditional accounting may cause two major concerns: (1) prior years' financial statements lose some comparability to the current year's; and (2) recent financial statements may not be a meaningful guide for tomorrow's requirements.

In September 1979, experimental accounting procedures were prescribed by the Financial Accounting Standards Board. They required that limited amounts of accounting data (prepared according to traditional procedures) be adjusted for inflation by two different methods: (1) the constant dollar method; and (2) the current cost method.

Notes to Consolidated Financial Statements (continued)

General Mills, Inc., and Subsidiaries

Constant Dollar

The constant dollar method of adjustment restates traditional, historical cost accounting results in an effort to express each year's results in dollars of similar purchasing power. Selected past years' data are changed in proportion to the change in the U.S. Urban Consumer Price Index since the time the data were first recorded at historical cost.

Current Cost

The current cost method of adjustment revalues selected past years' cost data by an estimate of what each item would cost at the current time. General Mills used a combination of specific indices, current price lists and appraisals to estimate current cost amounts.

Statement of Income, Adjusted for Inflation

The experimental regulations prescribe that constant dollar and current cost calculations include most income statement items at historical costs. Only fixed asset depreciation and cost of sales are modified for the effects of inflation. Earnings from continuing operations as adjusted for inflation under these regulations for General Mills' fiscal year ended May 30, 1982 are shown below:

(In Millions)		Adjusted for Inflation	
	Income Statement as Reported	Constant Dollar Method	Current Cost Method
Sales	$5,312	$5,312	$5,312
Cost of sales (excluding depreciation)	3,082	3,109	3,115
Depreciation	107	155	151
All other expenses	1,716	1,716	1,716
Earnings before income taxes	407	332	330
Income taxes	181	181	181
Net earnings	$ 226	$ 151	$ 149
Effective income tax rate	44.6%	54.5%	54.8%

Effects of Holding Assets and Liabilities

General Mills maintains a net liability position with its "monetary" assets and liabilities (items that have a fixed amount of cash receivable or payable). In the same sense that a homeowner "benefits" in a time of inflation by repaying his home mortgage loan with "cheaper" dollars, General Mills had an unrealized fiscal 1982 "gain" of approximately $49 million on its average net liability position.

General Mills estimates that the inflation-adjusted amounts of its May 30, 1982 inventories and fixed assets are as follows:

(In Millions)		Adjusted to basis of:	
	Historical Cost	Constant Dollar*	Current Cost
Inventories	$ 661	$ 808	$ 756
Fixed assets	1,054	1,533	1,650
Total	$1,715	$2,341	$2,406

*Expressed in average fiscal 1982 dollars.

Some of the above information, plus additional statistics, are summarized in the following five-year table. All constant dollar information is expressed in average fiscal 1982 dollars. Current cost information is expressed in current costs of each year, inflated to average fiscal 1982 dollars. Several items for fiscal 1978 and 1979 are neither required nor practicable to compute. Accordingly, no amounts are reported for these items.

(In Millions, Except Per Share Data)	1982	1981	Fiscal Year 1980	1979	1978
Sales					
Historical cost	**$5,312**	$4,852	$4,170	$3,745	$3,243
Constant dollars	**5,312**	5,284	5,095	5,161	4,878
Net earnings from continuing operations					
Historical cost	**226**	197	170	147	129
Constant dollars (a)	**151**	135	131		
Current cost (a)	**149**	159	158		
Earnings per share from continuing operations					
Historical cost	**4.46**	3.90	3.37	2.92	2.58
Constant dollars (a)	**2.98**	2.68	2.59		
Current cost (a)	**2.94**	3.16	3.11		
Net assets at year end					
Historical cost	**1,232**	1,132	1,008	916	815
Constant dollars (a)	**1,858**	1,752	1,693		
Current cost (a)	**1,923**	1,896	1,869		
Market price per share at year end					
Historical cost	**39.88**	34.62	27.88	26.13	29.88
Constant dollars	**39.13**	36.00	32.12	34.20	43.33
Dividends per share					
Historical cost	**1.64**	1.44	1.28	1.12	.97
Constant dollars	**1.64**	1.57	1.57	1.54	1.46
Unrealized "gains" from decline in purchasing power of average net amounts owed (a)	**49**	73	87		
Increases in current cost of fixed assets (land, buildings and equipment) and inventories:					
Pro forma increase, due to general inflation as measured by the U.S. Urban Consumer Price Index (a)	**$ 131**	212	266		
Compare to: estimated actual increases in specific prices of assets held by General Mills (a)	**$ 174**	173	180		
Difference: excess (deficiency) of pro forma general inflationary increase, over estimated actual specific increase (a)	**$ (43)**	39	86		
Average consumer price index for fiscal year (1967 = 100)	**280.3**	257.5	229.6	203.5	186.5

(a) Neither required nor available for years prior to 1980.

Management Comments

Inflation accounting advocates claim inflation adjusted data (1) provides better displays of real growth, (2) gives improved insight into future cash needs, and (3) promotes the concept that profit has not been earned until current cost (or purchasing power) has been recovered. The adjusted data also highlights the heavy tax burden imposed by government because tax rates are not adjusted for inflation.

General Mills cautions that the value of inflation accounting is still unproven and that the inflation-adjusted data should be used only to indicate general trends rather than as a precise measurement. Management questions the worth of using these data for operational decisions because:

1. The U.S. Urban Consumer Price Index is not a reliable measure of specific costs incurred by General Mills.

2. Current costs cannot be used automatically to forecast actual replacements of assets due to uncertain timings, technological changes, financings, and other considerations.

3. Different assumptions and estimating procedures among companies may affect the comparability of the current cost data.

General Mills attempts to combat the effects of inflation through its planning and its operating philosophy and practices.

Ten Year Financial Summary— Before Restatements (as reported)

General Mills, Inc., and Subsidiaries

Amounts in Millions, Except Per Share Data	May 30, 1982	May 31, 1981	May 25, 1980
Operating Results			
Sales	**$5,312.1**	$4,852.4	$4,170.3
Costs and expenses:			
Cost of sales, exclusive of items below	**$3,081.6**	2,936.9	2,578.5
Selling, general and administrative	**$1,635.5**	1,384.0	1,145.5
Depreciation and amortization	**$ 113.2**	99.5	81.1
Interest	**$ 75.1**	57.6	48.6
Pre-tax earnings	**$ 406.7**	374.4	316.6
Net earnings	**$ 225.5**	196.6	170.0
Net earnings as a percent of sales	**4.2%**	4.1%	4.1%
Return on average equity	**19.1%**	18.2% (c)	17.6% (c)
Per common share (a)			
Net earnings	**$ 4.46**	3.90	3.37
Dividends	**$ 1.64**	1.44	1.28
Taxes: income, payroll, property, etc.	**$ 5.88**	5.59	4.66
Weighted average number of common shares (b)	**50.6**	50.4	50.5
Financial Position			
Total assets	**$2,701.7**	2,301.3	2,012.4
Land, buildings and equipment, net	**$1,054.1**	920.6	747.5
Working capital at year-end	**$ 210.7**	337.3(c)	416.3(c)
Long-term debt, excluding current portion	**$ 331.9**	348.6	377.5
Stockholders' equity	**$1,232.2**	1,145.4(c)	1,020.7(c)
Stockholders' equity per share	**$ 24.50**	22.75(c)	20.32(c)
Other Statistics			
Working capital provided from operations	**$ 367.3**	317.8	262.7
Total dividends—common and preferred stock	**$ 82.3**	72.3	64.4
Gross expenditures for land, buildings and equipment	**$ 287.3**	246.6	196.5
Research and development	**$ 53.8**	45.4	44.4
Advertising media expenditures	**$ 284.9**	222.0	213.1
Wages, salaries and employee benefits	**$1,028.4**	907.0	781.2
Number of employees at year-end	**75,893**	71,225	66,032
Accumulated year-end LIFO inventory reduction	**$ 75.5**	73.7	60.3
Market price range—common stock (a)	**42⅛-32⅝**	35¼-23¾	28¼-19

(a) Years prior to fiscal 1976 have been adjusted for the two-for-one stock split in October of 1975.

(b) Includes common share equivalents.

(c) Amounts not restated for vacation accrual as described in note 1F.

(d) Before discontinued operations.

(e) In fiscal 1975, the company changed from the FIFO to the LIFO method of accounting for selected inventories.

May 27, 1979	May 28, 1978	May 29, 1977	May 30, 1976	May 25, 1975	May 26, 1974	May 27, 1973
$3,745.0	$3,243.0	$2,909.4	$2,645.0	$2,308.9	$2,000.1	$1,593.2
2,347.7	2,026.1	1,797.5	1,663.9	1,537.7	1,288.8	1,010.7
1,021.3	883.8	807.9	704.5	546.3	495.4	395.6
73.3	58.6	48.1	46.7	41.8	36.3	34.7
38.8	29.3	26.7	29.4	36.2	28.5	18.3
263.9	245.2(d)	229.2	200.5	146.9	151.1	133.9
147.0	135.8	117.0	100.5	76.2	75.1	65.6
3.9%	4.2%	4.0%	3.8%	3.3%	3.8%	4.1%
17.0%	17.6%	17.1%	16.7%	14.6%	16.5%	16.6%
2.92	2.72	2.36	2.04	1.59	1.59	1.40
1.12	.97	.79	.66	.58½	.53	.50
3.99	3.71	3.43	3.02	2.35	2.36	2.07
50.4	49.9	49.6	49.2	47.8	47.3	46.9
1,835.2	1,612.7	1,447.3	1,328.2	1,205.6	1,116.9	906.1
643.7	587.0	540.1	471.5	441.0	379.4	328.7
441.6	285.1	298.2	295.1	276.8	268.1	179.0
384.8	259.9	276.1	281.8	304.9	298.2	213.1
916.2	815.1	724.9	640.2	560.5	483.4	425.4
18.23	16.38	14.60	12.98	11.50	10.26	10.00
237.5	197.9	174.2	153.2	124.2	116.2	111.5
56.1	48.2	39.1	32.4	27.8	24.4	23.0
154.1	140.5	117.1	94.4	99.8	92.2	56.6
37.3	30.5	29.9	25.7	22.9	21.6	19.0
188.9	170.5	145.6	111.4	70.5	71.5	74.2
717.1	622.0	541.2	479.4	402.7	343.7	296.8
64,229	66,574	61,797	51,778	47,969	46,398	40,651
46.5	29.3	18.7	12.5	15.9	(e)	(e)
34⅛-24	31½-26¼	35⅜-26½	34⅛-23⅜	27¾-14⅛	33¼-23¼	33¾-24¼

Report of Management Responsibilities

The management of General Mills, Inc., includes corporate executives, operating managers, controllers and other personnel working full-time on company business. Such management is responsible for the fairness and accuracy of the company's financial statements. The statements have been prepared in accordance with generally accepted accounting principles, using management's best estimates and judgments where appropriate. The financial information elsewhere in this report is consistent with the statements.

Management has established a system of internal control which it believes provides reasonable assurance that in all material respects assets are maintained and accounted for in accordance with management's authorizations, and transactions are recorded accurately on the company's books.

The company's internal audit program is designed for constant evaluation of the adequacy and effectiveness of the internal controls. Audits measure adherence to established policies and procedures. The company's formally stated and communicated policies demand high ethical standards of employees.

The Audit Committee of the Board of Directors is composed solely of outside directors. The committee meets periodically with management, internal auditors and independent public accountants to review the work of each and to satisfy itself that the respective parties are properly discharging their responsibilities. Independent public accountants, internal auditors and the controller have full and free access to the Audit Committee at any time.

Peat, Marwick, Mitchell & Co., independent certified public accountants, are retained to examine the financial statements. Their opinion follows.

H. B. Atwater, Jr.

H. B. Atwater, Jr.
Chairman of the Board of
Directors and
Chief Executive Officer

Mark H. Willes

Mark H. Willes
Executive Vice President and
Chief Financial Officer

Accountants' Report

The Stockholders and the
Board of Directors of
General Mills, Inc.:

We have examined the consolidated balance sheets of General Mills, Inc. and subsidiaries as of May 30, 1982 and May 31, 1981 and the related consolidated statements of income, retained earnings and changes in financial position for each of the years in the three-year period ended May 30, 1982. Our examinations were made in accordance with generally accepted auditing standards and, accordingly, included such tests of the accounting records and such other auditing procedures as we considered necessary in the circumstances.

In our opinion, the aforementioned consolidated financial statements present fairly the financial position of General Mills, Inc. and subsidiaries at May 30, 1982 and May 31, 1981 and the results of their operations and the changes in their financial position for each of the years in the three-year period ended May 30, 1982, in conformity with generally accepted accounting principles consistently applied during the period except for the change in 1982, with which we concur, in the method of accounting for foreign currency translation as described in note 2 to the consolidated financial statements.

Peat, Marwick, Mitchell & Co.

Minneapolis, Minnesota
July 23, 1982

Appendix C

INDEX OF REFERENCES TO APB AND FASB PRONOUNCEMENTS

The following list of pronouncements by the Accounting Principles Board and the Financial Accounting Standards Board (as of August 31, 1983) is provided to give students an overview of the standards issued since 1962 and to reference these standards to the relevant chapters in this book. Earlier pronouncements by the Committee on Accounting Procedure of the AICPA have been largely superseded or amended. In those cases where no change has been made by subsequent standard-setting bodies, the earlier pronouncements are still accepted as official.

ACCOUNTING PRINCIPLES BOARD OPINIONS

Date issued	Opinion Number	Title	Chapters to Which References Most Applicable
November, 1962	1	*New Depreciation Guidelines and Rules*	11
December, 1962	2	*Accounting for the "Investment Credit"; addendum to Opinion No. 2 — Accounting Principles for Regulated Industries*	20
October, 1963	3	*The Statement of Source and Application of Funds*	23
March, 1964	4	*Accounting for the "Investment Credit"*	20
September, 1964	5	*Reporting of Leases in Financial Statements of Lessee*	15
October, 1965	6	*Status of Accounting in Research Bulletins*	7, 17
May, 1966	7	*Accounting for Leases in Financial Statements of Lessors*	15
November, 1966	8	*Accounting for the Cost of Pension Plans*	16
December, 1966	9	*Reporting the Results of Operations*	4
December, 1966	10	*Omnibus Opinion — 1966*	20
December, 1967	11	*Accounting for Income Taxes*	20
December, 1967	12	*Omnibus Opinion — 1967*	11

APB OPINIONS (concluded)

Date Issued	Opinion Number	Title	Chapters to Which References Most Applicable
March, 1969	13	*Amending Paragraph 6 of ABP Opinion No. 9, Application to Commercial Banks*	N/A
March, 1969	14	*Accounting for Convertible Debt and Debt Issued with Stock Purchase Warrants*	14, 17
May, 1969	15	*Earnings per Share*	22
August, 1970	16	*Business Combinations*	N/A
August, 1970	17	*Intangible Assets*	10, 11
March, 1971	18	*The Equity Method of Accounting for Investments in Common Stock*	12
March, 1971	19	*Reporting Changes in Financial Position*	23
July, 1971	20	*Accounting Changes*	21
August, 1971	21	*Interest on Receivables and Payables*	6, 13
April, 1972	22	*Disclosure of Accounting Policies*	5
April, 1972	23	*Accounting for Income Taxes — Special Areas*	20
April, 1972	24	*Accounting for Income Taxes — Investments in Common Stock Accounted for by the Equity Method (Other than Subsidiaries and Corporate Joint Ventures)*	20
October, 1972	25	*Accounting for Stock Issued to Employees*	17, 22
October, 1972	26	*Early Extinguishment of Debt*	14
November, 1972	27	*Accounting for Lease Transactions by Manufacturer or Dealer Lessors*	15
May, 1973	28	*Interim Financial Reporting*	21
May, 1973	29	*Accounting for Nonmonetary Transactions*	10, 12, 14
June, 1973	30	*Reporting the Results of Operations*	21
June, 1973	31	*Disclosure of Lease Commitments by Lessees*	15

ACCOUNTING PRINCIPLES BOARD STATEMENTS

Date Issued	Statement Number	Title	Chapters to Which References Most Applicable
April, 1962	1	*Statement by the Accounting Principles Board* (on Accounting Research Studies Nos. 1 and 3)	3
September, 1967	2	*Disclosure of Supplemental Financial Information by Diversified Companies*	21
June, 1969	3	*Financial Statements Restated for General Price-Level Changes*	24
October, 1970	4	*Basic Concepts and Accounting Principles Underlying Financial Statements of Business Enterprises*	3

FINANCIAL ACCOUNTING STANDARDS BOARD STATEMENTS OF FINANCIAL ACCOUNTING STANDARDS

Date Issued	Statement Number	Title	Chapters to Which References Most Applicable
December, 1973	1	*Disclosure of Foreign Currency Translation Information*	N/A
October, 1974	2	*Accounting for Research and Development Costs*	10
December, 1974	3	*Reporting Accounting Changes in Interim Financial Statements*	21
March, 1975	4	*Reporting Gains and Losses from Extinguishment of Debt*	14, 21
March, 1975	5	*Accounting for Contingencies*	13
May, 1975	6	*Classification of Short-Term Obligations Expected to be Refinanced*	14
June, 1975	7	*Accounting and Reporting by Development Stage Enterprises*	10
October, 1975	8	*Accounting for the Translation of Foreign Currency Transactions and Foreign Currency Financial Statements*	N/A
October, 1975	9	*Accounting for Income Taxes — Oil and Gas Producing Companies*	N/A
October, 1975	10	*Extension of "Grandfather" Provisions for Business Combinations*	N/A
December, 1975	11	*Accounting for Contingencies — Transition Method*	13
December, 1975	12	*Accounting for Certain Marketable Securities*	6, 12
November, 1976	13	*Accounting for Leases*	15
December, 1976	14	*Financial Reporting for Segments of a Business Enterprise*	21
June, 1977	15	*Accounting by Debtors and Creditors for Troubled Debt Restructurings*	14
June, 1977	16	*Prior Period Adjustments*	18
November, 1977	17	*Accounting for Leases — Initial Direct Costs*	15
November, 1977	18	*Financial Reporting for Segments of a Business Enterprise — Interim Financial Statements*	21
December, 1977	19	*Financial Accounting and Reporting by Oil and Gas Producing Companies*	N/A
December, 1977	20	*Accounting for Forward Exchange Contracts*	N/A
April, 1978	21	*Suspension of the Reporting of Earnings per Share and Segment Information by Nonpublic Enterprises*	21, 22
June, 1978	22	*Changes in the Provisions of Lease Agreements Resulting from Refundings of Tax-Exempt Debt*	15
August, 1978	23	*Inception of the Lease*	15

FASB STATEMENTS (continued)

Date Issued	Statement Number	Title	Chapters to Which References Most Applicable
December, 1978	24	*Reporting Segment Information in Financial Statements That Are Presented in Another Enterprise's Financial Report*	21
February, 1979	25	*Suspension of Certain Accounting Requirements for Oil and Gas Producing Companies*	N/A
April, 1979	26	*Profit Recognition on Sales-Type Leases of Real Estate*	15
May, 1979	27	*Classification of Renewals or Extensions of Existing Sales-Type or Direct Financing Leases*	15
May, 1979	28	*Accounting for Sales with Leasebacks*	15
June, 1979	29	*Determining Contingent Rentals*	15
August, 1979	30	*Disclosure of Information About Major Customers*	21
September, 1979	31	*Accounting for Tax Benefits Related to U.K. Tax Legislation Concerning Stock Relief*	N/A
September, 1979	32	*Specialized Accounting and Reporting Principles and Practices in AICPA Statements of Position and Guides on Accounting and Auditing Matters*	19
September, 1979	33	*Financial Reporting and Changing Prices*	24
October, 1979	34	*Capitalization of Interest Cost*	10
March, 1980	35	*Accounting and Reporting by Defined Benefit Pension Plans*	16
May, 1980	36	*Disclosure of Pension Information*	16
July, 1980	37	*Balance Sheet Classification of Deferred Income Taxes*	20
September, 1980	38	*Accounting for Preacquisition Contingencies of Purchased Enterprises*	N/A
October, 1980	39	*Financial Reporting and Changing Prices: Specialized Assets—Mining and Oil and Gas*	24
November, 1980	40	*Financial Reporting and Changing Prices: Specialized Assets—Timberlands and Growing Timber*	24
November, 1980	41	*Financial Reporting and Changing Prices: Specialized Assets—Income-Producing Real Estate*	24
November, 1980	42	*Determining Materiality for Capitalization of Interest Cost*	10
November, 1980	43	*Accounting for Compensated Absences*	13
December, 1980	44	*Accounting for Intangible Assets of Motor Carriers*	N/A
March, 1981	45	*Accounting for Franchise Fee Revenue*	19
March, 1981	46	*Financial Reporting and Changing Prices: Motion Picture Films*	24

FASB STATEMENTS (continued)

Date Issued	Statement Number	Title	Chapters to Which References Most Applicable
March, 1981	47	*Disclosure of Long-Term Obligations*	14
June, 1981	48	*Revenue Recognition When Right of Return Exists*	19
June, 1981	49	*Accounting for Product Financing Arrangements*	N/A
November, 1981	50	*Financial Reporting in the Record and Music Industry*	N/A
November, 1981	51	*Financial Reporting by Cable Television Companies*	N/A
December, 1981	52	*Foreign Currency Translation*	N/A
December, 1981	53	*Financial Reporting by Producers and Distributors of Motion Picture Films*	N/A
January, 1982	54	*Financial Reporting and Changing Prices: Investment Companies*	24
February, 1982	55	*Determining Whether a Convertible Security Is a Common Stock Equivalent*	22
February, 1982	56	*Designation of AICPA Guide and Statement of Position (SOP) 81-1 on Contractor Accounting and SOP 81-2 Concerning Hospital-Related Organizations as Preferable for Purposes of Applying APB Opinion 20*	19
March, 1982	57	*Related Party Disclosures*	21
April, 1982	58	*Capitalization of Interest Cost in Financial Statements that Include Investments Accounted for by the Equity Method*	N/A
April, 1982	59	*Deferral of the Effective Date of Certain Accounting Requirements for Pension Plans of State and Local Governmental Units*	N/A
June, 1982	60	*Accounting and Reporting by Insurance Enterprises*	N/A
June, 1982	61	*Accounting for Title Plant*	N/A
June, 1982	62	*Capitalization of Interest Cost in Situations Involving Certain Tax-Exempt Borrowings and Certain Gifts and Grants*	N/A
June, 1982	63	*Financial Reporting by Broadcasters*	N/A
September, 1982	64	*Extinguishments of Debt Made to Satisfy Sinking-Fund Requirements*	14
September, 1982	65	*Accounting for Certain Mortgage Banking Activities*	N/A
October, 1982	66	*Accounting for Sales of Real Estate*	19
October, 1982	67	*Accounting for Costs and Initial Rental Operations of Real Estate Projects*	N/A
October, 1982	68	*Research and Development Arrangements*	10
November, 1982	69	*Disclosures About Oil and Gas Producing Activities*	10

FASB STATEMENTS (concluded)

Date Issued	Statement Number	Title	Chapters to Which References Most Applicable
December, 1982	70	*Financial Reporting and Changing Prices: Foreign Currency Translation*	24
December, 1982	71	*Accounting for the Effects of Certain Types of Regulation*	N/A
February, 1983	72	*Accounting for Certain Acquisitions of Banking or Thrift Institutions*	N/A
August, 1983	73	*Reporting a Change in Accounting for Railroad Track Structures*	N/A
August, 1983	74	*Accounting for Special Termination Benefits Paid to Employees*	16

FINANCIAL ACCOUNTING STANDARDS BOARD STATEMENTS OF FINANCIAL ACCOUNTING CONCEPTS

Date Issued	Statement Number	Title	Chapters to Which References Most Applicable
November, 1978	1	*Objectives of Financial Reporting by Business Enterprises*	3
May, 1980	2	*Qualitative Characteristics of Accounting Information*	3
December, 1980	3	*Elements of Financial Statements of Business Enterprises*	3
December, 1980	4	*Objectives of Financial Reporting by Nonbusiness Organizations*	N/A

SELECTED FASB EXPOSURE DRAFTS AND DISCUSSION MEMORANDUM

Exposure Drafts

Date Issued	Title	Chapters to Which References Most Applicable
November, 1981	*Reporting Income, Cash Flows, and Financial Position of Business Enterprises*	3, 4
July, 1982	*Classification of Obligations that are Callable by the Creditor*	13
August, 1982	*Reporting by Transferors for Transfers of Receivables with Recourse*	7
October, 1982	*Accounting for the Reduction in the Tax Basis of an Asset Caused by the Investment Tax Credit*	20
July, 1983	*Extinguishment of Debt*	14

Preliminary View

Date Issued	Title	Chapters to Which References Most Applicable
November, 1982	*Employers' Accounting for Pensions and Other Postemployment Benefits*	16

Discussion Memorandum

Date Issued	Title	Chapters to Which References Most Applicable
April, 1983	*Employers' Accounting for Pensions and Other Postemployment Benefits*	16

INDEX

A

D

E